THE OXFORD

Essential
Desk Reference

*Oxford Titles Available
from Berkley Books*

THE OXFORD AMERICAN DESK DICTIONARY AND THESAURUS, 2ND EDITION
THE OXFORD ESSENTIAL DESK REFERENCE
THE OXFORD ESSENTIAL GUIDE TO PEOPLE & PLACES OF THE BIBLE
THE OXFORD ESSENTIAL DICTIONARY OF THE U.S. MILITARY
THE OXFORD ESSENTIAL DICTIONARY OF DIFFICULT WORDS
THE OXFORD DICTIONARY OF AMERICAN USAGE AND STYLE
THE OXFORD ESSENTIAL DICTIONARY
THE OXFORD ESSENTIAL GUIDE FOR PUZZLE SOLVERS
THE OXFORD ESSENTIAL GUIDE TO THE U.S. GOVERNMENT
THE OXFORD ESSENTIAL GUIDE TO WRITING
THE OXFORD ESSENTIAL QUOTATIONS DICTIONARY
THE OXFORD ESSENTIAL SPELLING DICTIONARY
THE OXFORD ESSENTIAL THESAURUS
THE OXFORD FRENCH DICTIONARY
THE OXFORD GERMAN DICTIONARY
THE OXFORD GREEK DICTIONARY
THE OXFORD ITALIAN DICTIONARY
THE OXFORD RUSSIAN DICTIONARY
THE OXFORD NEW SPANISH DICTIONARY

THE OXFORD

Essential
Desk Reference

BERKLEY BOOKS, NEW YORK

THE OXFORD ESSENTIAL DESK REFERENCE

A Berkley Book / published by arrangement with
Oxford University Press, Inc.

PRINTING HISTORY
Berkley edition / July 2001

All rights reserved.
Copyright © 2001 by Oxford University Press, Inc.
Project manager: Mary Kay Linge
Design: Mary Neal Meador
Illustrations: Gary Tong

Oxford is a trademark of Oxford University Press, Inc.

All rights reserved. No part of this publication may be reproduced, stored in a retrieval system, or transmitted, in any form or by any means, electronic, mechanical, photocopying, recording, or otherwise without the prior written consent of Oxford University Press, Inc.
For information address: Oxford University Press, Inc.,
198 Madison Avenue, New York, New York 10016.

The Penguin Putnam Inc. World Wide Web site address is
www.penguinputnam.com

ISBN: 0-425-18071-9

BERKLEY®
Berkley Books are published by
The Berkley Publishing Group, a division of Penguin Putnam Inc.,
375 Hudson Street, New York, New York 10014.
BERKLEY and the "B" design are trademarks
belonging to Penguin Putnam Inc.

PRINTED IN THE UNITED STATES OF AMERICA

10 9 8 7 6 5 4 3 2

Contents

Contents (cont.)

THE SCIENCES

Contents *(cont.)*

CONTENTS: *The Sciences*

Contents *(cont.)*

ARTS AND LEISURE

Contents *(cont.)*

Sports and Games *(cont.)*

PRIZES AND AWARDS

WORK AND HOME

Business and Labor   675

Contents *(cont.)*

How to Use This Book

Do you need to know the location of the 512 telephone area code? What is the difference between vitamin A and vitamin B12? How do hurricanes get their names? *The Oxford Essential Desk Reference* can help you find the answers to these questions—and thousands of others—in seconds.

The *Oxford Essential Desk Reference* is intended to be the quickest way to find facts on a wide variety of subjects. The book is arranged thematically in broad sections such as The World, The United States, and The Sciences, which proceed generally from global to personal; the section on The Sciences is followed by Arts and Leisure, Prizes and Awards, and Work and Home.

There are many ways to use the *Desk Reference*. Perhaps the most enjoyable is simply to browse its pages in any category that interests you. "Inventors and Discoverers," in The Sciences, is a fascinating list of scientific geniuses, explorers, and creative minds who have changed the way we live; or count the number of Booker Prize–winning authors you have read, in the Prizes and Awards section.

Fast facts: the index. The easiest way to find a specific fact quickly is to look up the subject in the index. While some organizations' or individuals' names can be found in the index, you will sometimes be more successful looking up a slightly broader category. For instance, you are unlikely to find the Boston Bruins in the index, but you can find out what years they won the Stanley Cup if you look under "Stanley Cup" or "ice hockey." Likewise, if you want to know the dates of carnival week in Brazil, look under "holidays (U.S. and global)," not under "carnival."

The big picture: the table of contents. While the index is a tool for looking up specific facts, the table of contents will tell you the range of information available in the *Desk Reference* on any subject of interest. If you simply wanted to know the population of China, you would look up "China, population" in the index. But if you are interested in China in general, scan the World section of the table of contents. You will see that this section offers a list of "UN Members." Is China a member? There is an atlas. What countries border China? In China's listing under "Nations" you can find not only the population, but a breakdown of religions, ethnicities, and languages in China, the highest and lowest points in its geography, and the Chinese currency. Finally, "World History" offers "Dynasties of China." The table of contents is a tool for the curious mind.

Websites and other sources for further information. After each section or list in the book, the ⊙ symbol indicates the sources of the information in that section as well as related references of special interest, whether books, government documents, or websites. Websites are correct at the time of publication but if you encounter a problem with one of them, search for the name of the website's host institution (as listed in the *Desk Reference*) using a standard search engine. With more than 300 source lists throughout the book, the *Desk Reference* is an excellent starting point for further research.

WORLD: *International Organizations and Alliances*
United Nations Members

Member	Date of Admission	Member	Date of Admission
Afghanistan	Nov. 19, 1946	Denmark	Oct. 24, 1945
Albania	Dec. 14, 1955	Djibouti	Sep. 20, 1977
Algeria	Oct. 8, 1962	Dominica	Dec. 18, 1978
Andorra	July 28, 1993	Dominican Republic	Oct. 24, 1945
Angola	Dec. 1, 1976	Ecuador	Dec. 21, 1945
Antigua and Barbuda	Nov. 11, 1981	Egypt	Oct. 24, 1945
Argentina	Oct. 24, 1945	El Salvador	Oct. 24, 1945
Armenia	Mar. 2, 1992	Equatorial Guinea	Nov. 12, 1968
Australia	Nov. 1, 1945	Eritrea	May 28, 1993
Austria	Dec. 14, 1955	Estonia	Sep. 17, 1991
Azerbaijan	Mar. 9, 1992	Ethiopia	Nov. 13, 1945
Bahamas	Sep. 18, 1973	Fiji	Oct. 13, 1970
Bahrain	Sep. 21, 1971	Finland	Dec. 14, 1955
Bangladesh	Sep. 17, 1974	France	Oct. 24, 1945
Barbados	Dec. 9, 1966	Gabon	Sep. 20, 1960
Belarus	Oct. 24, 1945	Gambia	Sep. 21, 1965
Belgium	Dec. 27, 1945	Georgia	July 31, 1992
Belize	Sep. 25, 1981	Germany	Sep. 18, 1973
Benin	Sep. 20, 1960	Ghana	Mar. 8, 1957
Bhutan	Sep. 21, 1971	Greece	Oct. 25, 1945
Bolivia	Nov. 14, 1945	Grenada	Sep. 17, 1974
Bosnia and		Guatemala	Nov. 21, 1945
Herzegovina	May 22, 1992	Guinea	Dec. 12, 1958
Botswana	Oct. 17, 1966	Guinea-Bissau	Sep. 17, 1974
Brazil	Oct. 24, 1945	Guyana	Sep. 20, 1966
Brunei Darussalam	Sep. 21, 1984	Haiti	Oct. 24, 1945
Bulgaria	Dec. 14, 1955	Honduras	Dec. 17, 1945
Burkina Faso	Sep. 20, 1960	Hungary	Dec. 14, 1955
Burundi	Sep. 18, 1962	Iceland	Nov. 19, 1946
Cambodia	Dec. 14, 1955	India	Oct. 30, 1945
Cameroon	Sep. 20, 1960	Indonesia	Sep. 28, 1950
Canada	Nov. 9, 1945	Iran, Islamic	
Cape Verde	Sep. 16, 1975	Republic of	Oct. 24, 1945
Central African		Iraq	Dec. 21, 1945
Republic	Sep. 20, 1960	Ireland	Dec. 14, 1955
Chad	Sep. 20, 1960	Israel	May 11, 1949
Chile	Oct. 24, 1945	Italy	Dec. 14, 1955
China	Oct. 24, 1945	Jamaica	Sep. 18, 1962
Colombia	Nov. 5, 1945	Japan	Dec. 18, 1956
Comoros	Nov. 12, 1975	Jordan	Dec. 14, 1955
Congo	Sep. 20, 1960	Kazakhstan	Mar. 2, 1992
Costa Rica	Nov. 2, 1945	Kenya	Dec. 16, 1963
Côte d'Ivoire	Sep. 20, 1960	Kiribati	Sep. 14, 1999
Croatia	May 22, 1992	Kuwait	May 14, 1963
Cuba	Oct. 24, 1945	Kyrgyzstan	Mar. 2, 1992
Cyprus	Sep. 20, 1960	Lao People's	
Czech Republic	Jan. 19, 1993	Democratic Republic	Dec. 14, 1955
Democratic People's		Latvia	Sep. 17, 1991
Republic of Korea	Sep. 17, 1991	Lebanon	Oct. 24, 1945
Democratic Republic		Lesotho	Oct. 17, 1966
of the Congo	Sep. 20, 1960	Liberia	Nov. 2, 1945

Member	Date of Admission	Member	Date of Admission
Libyan Arab Jamahiriya	Dec. 14, 1955	Samoa	Dec. 15, 1976
Liechtenstein	Sep. 18, 1990	San Marino	Mar. 2, 1992
Lithuania	Sep. 17, 1991	São Tomé and Príncipe	Sep. 16, 1975
Luxembourg	Oct. 24, 1945	Saudi Arabia	Oct. 24, 1945
Madagascar	Sep. 20, 1960	Senegal	Sep. 28, 1960
Malawi	Dec. 1, 1964	Seychelles	Sep. 21, 1976
Malaysia	Sep. 17, 1957	Sierra Leone	Sep. 27, 1961
Maldives	Sep. 21, 1965	Singapore	Sep. 21, 1965
Mali	Sep. 28, 1960	Slovakia	Jan. 19, 1993
Malta	Dec. 1, 1964	Slovenia	May 22, 1992
Marshall Islands	Sep. 17, 1991	Solomon Islands	Sep. 19, 1978
Mauritania	Oct. 7, 1961	Somalia	Sep. 20, 1960
Mauritius	Apr. 24, 1968	South Africa	Nov. 7, 1945
Mexico	Nov. 7, 1945	Spain	Dec. 14, 1955
Micronesia,		Sri Lanka	Dec. 14, 1955
Federated States of	Sep. 17, 1991	Sudan	Nov. 12, 1956
Monaco	May 28, 1993	Suriname	Dec. 4, 1975
Mongolia	Oct. 27, 1961	Swaziland	Sep. 24, 1968
Morocco	Nov. 12, 1956	Sweden	Nov. 19, 1946
Mozambique	Sep. 16, 1975	Syrian Arab Republic	Oct. 24, 1945
Myanmar	Apr. 19, 1948	Tajikistan	Mar. 2, 1992
Namibia	Apr. 23, 1990	Thailand	Dec. 16, 1946
Nauru	Sep. 14, 1999	The former Yugoslav	
Nepal	Dec. 14, 1955	Republic of	
Netherlands	Dec. 10, 1945	Macedonia	Apr. 8, 1993
New Zealand	Oct. 24, 1945	Tonga	Sep. 14, 1999
Nicaragua	Oct. 24, 1945	Togo	Sep. 20, 1960
Niger	Sep. 20, 1960	Trinidad and Tobago	Sep. 18, 1962
Nigeria	Oct. 7, 1960	Tunisia	Nov. 12, 1956
Norway	Nov. 27, 1945	Turkey	Oct. 24, 1945
Oman	Oct. 7, 1971	Turkmenistan	Mar. 2, 1992
Pakistan	Sep. 30, 1947	Uganda	Oct. 25, 1962
Palau	Dec. 15, 1994	Ukraine	Oct. 24, 1945
Panama	Nov. 13, 1945	United Arab Emirates	Dec. 9, 1971
Papua New Guinea	Oct. 10, 1975	United Kingdom of	
Paraguay	Oct. 24, 1945	Great Britain and	
Peru	Oct. 31, 1945	Northern Ireland	Oct. 24, 1945
Philippines	Oct. 24, 1945	United Republic of	
Poland	Oct. 24, 1945	Tanzania	Dec. 14, 1961
Portugal	Dec. 14, 1955	United States of	
Qatar	Sep. 21, 1971	America	Oct. 24, 1945
Republic of Korea	Sep. 17, 1991	Uruguay	Dec. 18, 1945
Republic of Moldova	Mar. 2, 1992	Uzbekistan	Mar. 2, 1992
Romania	Dec. 14, 1955	Vanuatu	Sep. 15, 1981
Russian Federation	Oct. 24, 1945	Venezuela	Nov. 15, 1945
Rwanda	Sep. 18, 1962	Vietnam	Sep. 20, 1977
Saint Kitts and Nevis	Sep. 23, 1983	Yemen	Sep. 30, 1947
Saint Lucia	Sep. 18, 1979	Yugoslavia	Oct. 24, 1945
Saint Vincent and the		Zambia	Dec. 1, 1964
Grenadines	Sep. 16, 1980	Zimbabwe	Aug. 25, 1980

⊙ United Nations. "United Nations Member States," www.un.org/Overview/
  unmember.html

UN Permanent Observer Missions

States

Holy See   Switzerland

Non-Governmental Organizations

Asian-African Legal Consultative
  Committee
Caribbean Community
Commonwealth Secretariat
European Community
International Committee of the Red
  Cross
International Federation of Red Cross
  and Red Crescent
International Organization of La
  Francophonie
International Organization for
  Migration

International Seabed Authority
International Tribunal for the Law of
  the Sea
International Union for the
  Conservation of Nature and Natural
  Resources
League of Arab States
Organization of African Unity
Organization of the Islamic
  Conference
Palestine
Sovereign Military Order of Malta

⊙ United Nations. "Permanent Missions to the United Nations," www.un.org/
  Overview/missions.htm#nperm

Principal Organs of the United Nations

Organ: General Assembly
Members: all members of the United Nations
Function: serves as a forum for members to launch initiatives on international
  questions of peace, economic progress, and human rights; initiates studies;
  makes recommendations; develops and codifies international law; promotes
  human rights and other economic, social, cultural, and educational programs

Organ: Economic and Social Council
Members: 54 members, elected for 3-year terms
Function: promotes higher standards of living, full employment, and conditions
  of economic and social progress and development; solutions to international
  economic, social, health, and related problems; international cultural and educational cooperation; universal respect for, and observance of, human rights
  and fundamental freedoms for all

Organ: International Court of Justice
Members: 15 judges, elected for 9-year terms; may not include more than one
  judge of any nationality
Function: settles in accordance with international law legal disputes submitted to
  it by member countries and gives advice on legal questions

Organ Security Council
Members: 5 permanent members (China, France, Russian Federation, United Kingdom, United States) and 10 elected for 2-year terms; presidency rotates monthly
Function: maintains international peace and security; investigates disputes and recommends solutions; calls on members to take non-aggressive action in cases of
  threats to peace; takes military action when necessary; recommends admission
  of new members; exercises UN trusteeship functions; recommends appointment of the secretary-general and elects judges of the International Court

Organ: Trusteeship Council
Members: 5 permanent members; suspended 11/1/94 after Palau, last UN trust
  territory, gained independence

Principal Organs of the United Nations *(cont.)*

Functions: examines and discusses reports from administering authority on political, economic, social and educational advancement of peoples of trust territories and examines petitions from and undertakes special missions to trust territories

Organ: Secretariat

Members: more than 8,600 employees, headed by the Secretary-General

Functions: carries out the day-to-day work of the United Nations, servicing the other principal organs and administering their programs and policies worldwide

⊙ United Nations. "About the United Nations," www.un.org/aboutun/

United Nations Secretaries-General

Name	Country	Term of Office
Trygve Lie	Norway	1946–1952
Dag Hammarskjöld	Sweden	1953–1961
U Thant	Myanmar	1961–1971
Kurt Waldheim	Austria	1972–1981
Javier Perez de Cuellar	Peru	1982–1991
Boutros Boutros-Ghali	Egypt	1992–1996
Kofi Annan	Ghana	1997–

⊙ United Nations. "UN Secretaries-General," www.un.org/Overview/SG/index.html

International Organizations and Groups

African Development Bank (AfDB)
Established: 4 August 1963
Aim: to promote economic and social development
Regional members (53): Algeria, Angola, Benin, Botswana, Burkina Faso, Burundi, Cameroon, Cape Verde, Central African Republic, Chad, Comoros, Democratic Republic of the Congo, Republic of the Congo, Côte d'Ivoire, Djibouti, Egypt, Equatorial Guinea, Eritrea, Ethiopia, Gabon, Gambia, Ghana, Guinea, Guinea-Bissau, Kenya, Lesotho, Liberia, Libya, Madagascar, Malawi, Mali, Mauritania, Mauritius, Morocco, Mozambique, Namibia, Niger, Nigeria, Rwanda, São Tomé and Príncipe, Senegal, Seychelles, Sierra Leone, Somalia, South Africa, Sudan, Swaziland, Tanzania, Togo, Tunisia, Uganda, Zambia, Zimbabwe
Nonregional members (25): Argentina, Austria, Belgium, Brazil, Canada, China, Denmark, Finland, France, Germany, India, Italy, Japan, South Korea, Kuwait, Netherlands, Norway, Portugal, Saudi Arabia, Spain, Sweden, Switzerland, U.A.E., U.K., U.S.

Andean Community of Nations (CAN)
Established: 26 May 1969
Aim: to promote harmonious development through economic integration
Members (5): Bolivia, Colombia, Ecuador, Peru, Venezuela

Arab Bank for Economic Development in Africa (ABEDA)
Established: 18 February 1974 (effective 16 September 1974)
Aim: to promote economic development
Members (18): Algeria, Bahrain, Egypt, Iraq, Jordan, Kuwait, Lebanon, Libya, Mauritania, Morocco, Oman, Qatar, Saudi Arabia, Sudan, Syria, Tunisia, U.A.E., Palestine Liberation Organization

Arab League (AL)
Established: 22 March 1945

Aim: to promote economic, social, political, and military cooperation

Members (22): Algeria, Bahrain, Comoros, Djibouti, Egypt, Iraq, Jordan, Kuwait, Lebanon, Libya, Mauritania, Morocco, Oman, Qatar, Saudi Arabia, Somalia, Sudan, Syria, Tunisia, U.A.E., Yemen, Palestine Liberation Organization

Asia Pacific Economic Cooperation (APEC)

Established: 7 November 1989

Aim: to promote trade and investment in the Pacific basin

Members (19): Australia, Brunei, Canada, Chile, China, Hong Kong, Indonesia, Japan, South Korea, Malaysia, Mexico, N.Z., Papua New Guinea, Philippines, Singapore, Taiwan, Thailand, U.S., Vietnam

Association of Southeast Asian Nations (ASEAN)

Established: 9 August 1967

Aim: to encourage regional economic, social, and cultural cooperation among the non-Communist countries of Southeast Asia

Members (9): Brunei, Burma, Indonesia, Laos, Malaysia, Philippines, Singapore, Thailand, Vietnam

Australia Group

Established: 1984

Aim: to consult on and coordinate export controls related to chemical and biological weapons

Members (30): Australia, Argentina, Austria, Belgium, Canada, Czech Republic, Denmark, Finland, France, Germany, Greece, Hungary, Iceland, Ireland, Italy, Japan, Luxembourg, Netherlands, New Zealand, Norway, Poland, Portugal, Romania, Slovak Republic, South Korea, Spain, Sweden, Switzerland, U.K., U.S.

Observer: European Union

Big Seven

Established: 1975

Aim: to discuss and coordinate major economic policies

Members (7): Canada, France, Germany, Italy, Japan, U.K., U.S.

Commonwealth (Commonwealth of Nations)

Established: 31 December 1931

Aim: to foster multinational cooperation and assistance, as a voluntary association that evolved from the British Empire

Members (52): Antigua and Barbuda, Australia, The Bahamas, Bangladesh, Barbados, Belize, Botswana, Brunei, Cameroon, Canada, Cyprus, Dominica, Fiji, Gambia, Ghana, Grenada, Guyana, India, Jamaica, Kenya, Kiribati, Lesotho, Malawi, Malaysia, Maldives, Malta, Mauritius, Mozambique, Namibia, N.Z., Nigeria (suspended), Pakistan, Papua New Guinea, Saint Kitts and Nevis, Saint Lucia, Saint Vincent and the Grenadines, Samoa, Seychelles, Sierra Leone, Singapore, Solomon Islands, South Africa, Sri Lanka, Swaziland, Tanzania, Tonga, Trinidad and Tobago, Uganda, U.K., Vanuatu, Zambia, Zimbabwe

Special members (2): Nauru, Tuvalu

Commonwealth of Independent States (CIS)

Established: 8 December 1991 (effective 21 December 1991)

Aim: to coordinate intercommonwealth relations and to provide a mechanism for the orderly dissolution of the USSR

Members (12): Armenia, Azerbaijan, Belarus, Georgia, Kazakhstan, Kyrgyzstan, Moldova, Russia, Tajikistan, Turkmenistan, Ukraine, Uzbekistan

European Monetary Union (EMU)

Proposed 7 February 1992 (full implementation 1 July 2002)

Aim: to promote a single market by creating a single currency, the euro

Members (11): Austria, Beligum, Finland, France, Germany, Ireland, Italy, Luxembourg, Netherlands, Portugal, Spain

International Organizations and Groups *(cont.)*

European Union (EU)
Established: 7 February 1992 (effective 1 November 1993)

Aim: to coordinate policy among members in economics, building on the European Economic Community's efforts to establish a common market; defense, within the concept of a Common Foreign and Security Policy (CFSP); and justice and home affairs, including immigration, drugs, terrorism, and labor

Members (15): Austria, Belgium, Denmark, Finland, France, Germany, Greece, Ireland, Italy, Luxembourg, Netherlands, Portugal, Spain, Sweden, U.K.

Membership applicants (12): Albania, Bulgaria, Cyprus, Czech Republic, Estonia, Hungary, Latvia, Lithuania, Malta, Poland, Romania, Slovakia

International Atomic Energy Agency (IAEA)
Established: 26 October 1956 (effective 29 July 1957)
Aim: to promote peaceful uses of atomic energy
Members: 127 nations

International Bank for Reconstruction and Development (IBRD or World Bank)
Established: 22 July 1944 (effective 27 December 1945)
Aim: to provide economic development loans as a UN specialized agency
Members: 181 nations

International Committee of the Red Cross (ICRC)
Established: 1863
Aim: to provide humanitarian aid in wartime
Members: 25 individual Swiss nationals

International Court of Justice (ICJ)
Established: 26 June 1945 (effective 24 October 1945)
Aim: primary judicial organ of the United Nations
Members: 15 judges elected by the UN General Assembly and Security Council to represent all principal legal systems

International Labor Organization (ILO)
Established: 11 April 1919 (affiliated with the UN 14 December 1946)
Aim: to deal with world labor issues as a UN specialized agency
Members: 174 nations

International Monetary Fund (IMF)
Established: 22 July 1944 (effective 27 December 1945)
Aim: to promote world monetary stability and economic development as a UN specialized agency
Members: 182 nations

International Organization for Standardization (ISO)
Established: February 1947
Aim: to promote the development of international standards with a view to facilitating international exchange of goods and services and to developing cooperation in the sphere of intellectual, scientific, technological, and economic activity
Members: 85 national standards organizations

North Atlantic Treaty Organization (NATO)
Established: 17 September 1949
Aim: to promote mutual defense and cooperation
Members (19): Belgium, Canada, Czech Republic, Denmark, France, Germany, Greece, Hungary, Iceland, Italy, Luxembourg, Netherlands, Norway, Poland, Portugal, Spain, Turkey, U.K., U.S.

Organization for Economic Cooperation and Development (OECD)
Established: 14 December 1960 (effective 30 September 1961)

Aim: to promote economic cooperation and development

Members (29): Australia, Austria, Belgium, Canada, Czech Republic, Denmark, Finland, France, Germany, Greece, Hungary, Iceland, Ireland, Italy, Japan, Luxembourg, Mexico, Netherlands, N.Z., Norway, Poland, Portugal, South Korea, Spain, Sweden, Switzerland, Turkey, U.K., U.S.

Organization of African Unity (OAU)

Established: 25 May 1963

Aim: to promote unity and cooperation among African states

Members (53): Algeria, Angola, Benin, Botswana, Burkina Faso, Burundi, Cameroon, Cape Verde, Central African Republic, Chad, Comoros, Democratic Republic of the Congo, Republic of the Congo, Côte d'Ivoire, Djibouti, Egypt, Equatorial Guinea, Eritrea, Ethiopia, Gabon, Gambia, Ghana, Guinea, Guinea-Bissau, Kenya, Lesotho, Liberia, Libya, Madagascar, Malawi, Mali, Mauritania, Mauritius, Mozambique, Namibia, Niger, Nigeria, Rwanda, Sahrawi Arab Democratic Republic, São Tomé and Príncipe, Senegal, Seychelles, Sierra Leone, Somalia, South Africa, Sudan, Swaziland, Tanzania, Togo, Tunisia, Uganda, Zambia, Zimbabwe

Organization of American States (OAS)

Established: 30 April 1948 (effective 13 December 1951)

Aim: to promote regional peace and security as well as economic and social development

Members (35): Antigua and Barbuda, Argentina, The Bahamas, Barbados, Belize, Bolivia, Brazil, Canada, Chile, Colombia, Costa Rica, Cuba (excluded from formal participation since 1962), Dominica, Dominican Republic, Ecuador, El Salvador, Grenada, Guatemala, Guyana, Haiti, Honduras, Jamaica, Mexico, Nicaragua, Panama, Paraguay, Peru, Saint Kitts and Nevis, Saint Lucia, Saint Vincent and the Grenadines, Suriname, Trinidad and Tobago, U.S., Uruguay, Venezuela

Observers (40): Algeria, Angola, Austria, Belgium, Bosnia and Herzegovina, Croatia, Cyprus, Czech Republic, Egypt, Equatorial Guinea, EU, Finland, France, Germany, Greece, Holy See, Hungary, India, Israel, Italy, Japan, Kazakhstan, Latvia, Lebanon, Morocco, Netherlands, Pakistan, Poland, Portugal, Romania, Russia, Saudi Arabia, South Korea, Spain, Sri Lanka, Sweden, Switzerland, Tunisia, Ukraine, U.K.

Organization of Petroleum Exporting Countries (OPEC)

Established: 14 September 1960

Aim: to coordinate petroleum policies

Members (11): Algeria, Indonesia, Iran, Iraq, Kuwait, Libya, Nigeria, Qatar, Saudi Arabia, U.A.E., Venezuela

World Health Organization (WHO)

Established: 22 July 1946 (effective 7 April 1948)

Aim: to deal with health matters worldwide as a UN specialized agency

Members: 191 nations

World Trade Organization (WTO)

Established: 15 April 1994 (effective 1 January 1995)

Aim: to provide a means to resolve trade conflicts between members and to carry on negotiations with the goal of further lowering and/or eliminating tariffs and other trade barriers

Members: 134 nations

⊙ www.cia.gov/cia/publications/factbook/appc.html
   Central Intelligence Agency (CIA). *The World Factbook* 1999. Washington, D.C.: Central Intelligence Agency, 1999.
   McFarlane, Theresa. *Encyclopedia of Associations: International Organizations.* 33rd ed. 2 vols. Detroit: Gale Research, 1998.

WORLD: *Geography*
Global Statistics

Circumference:
Equatorial: 24,902 mi. (40,067 km.)
Polar: 24,860 mi. (40,000 km.)
Diameter:
Equatorial: 7926 mi. (12,753 km.)
Polar: 7899 mi. (12,709 km.)
Surface area:
Total surface area: 196,939,000 sq. mi. (510,072,520 sq. km.)
Land area: 57,506,000 sq. mi. (148,940,689 sq. km.)
Water surface: 139,433,000 sq. mi. (361,131,831 sq. km.)
Note: 70.8% of the world's surface is water, 29.2% is land
Coastline: 221,208 mi. (356,000 km.)
Greatest ocean depth: Mariana Trench, 35,839 ft. (10,924 m.) in the Pacific Ocean
Elevation extremes: lowest point: Dead Sea –1339 ft. (–408 m.); *highest point:* Mount Everest 29,028 ft. (8,848 m.)
Land use:
arable land: 10%
permanent crops: 1%
meadows and pastures: 26%
forests and woodland: 32%
other: 31%
Irrigated land: 958,016 sq. mi. (2,481,250 sq. km)
Population:
6,080,671,215 (July 2000)
Population growth rate: 1.3% (2000 est.)
Birth rate: 22 births/1,000 population (2000 est.)
Sex ratio: (2000 est.)
   at birth: 1.05 male(s)/female
   under 15 years: 1.05 male(s)/female
   15–64 years: 1.02 male(s)/female
   65 years and over: 0.78 male(s)/female

Infant mortality rate: 54 deaths/1,000 live births (2000 est.)
Life expectancy at birth: (2000 est.)
   total population: 64 years
   male: 62 years
   female: 65 years
Total fertility rate: 2.8 children born/woman (2000 est.)
Literacy rate (% of those age 15 and over who can read and write, 1999 est.):
   Combined: 79.4%
   Male: 85.2%
   Female: 73.6%
Economy:
GDP (GWP: gross world product): purchasing power parity— USD$40.7 trillion (1999 est.)
GDP (real growth rate): 3% (1999 est.)
GDP (per capita): purchasing power parity—USD$6800 (1999 est.)
Inflation rate (consumer price index): all countries 25%; developed countries 1% to 3% typically; developing countries range from 5% to 60% (1999 est.)
Labor force:
total: 2.24 billion (1992 est.)
Unemployment rate: 30% combined unemployment and underemployment in many non-industrialized countries; developed countries typically 4–12% unemployment (1999 est.)
Railways:
total: 746, 476 mi. (1,201,337 km.) (1997 est.)
Merchant marine:
total: 27,825 ships (Jan. 1999)
Military expenditures
(percent of GDP): roughly 2% of gross world product (1998 est.)

⊙ www.cia.gov/cia/publications/factbook/geos/xx.html
   Central Intelligence Agency, *The World Factbook, 1998.* Washington, D.C.: CIA Printing and Photography Group, 1999.
   Brunner, Borgna, ed. *Time Almanac 2000.* Boston: Information Please, 1999.

Continents

Continent	Africa	Antarctica	Asia	Europe	North America	Oceania	South America
Population*	805,243,217	0	3,688,072,099	728,981,999	480,545,248	30,794,760	346,504,360
Percent of world population**	13%	0	61%	12%	8%	1%	6%
Pop. density	27	0	118.9	31.9	22.5	3.7	19.8
Pop. growth rate	2.27	0	1.33	0.00	1.14	1.35	1.25
Life expectancy at birth	50.8	0	66	74.1	73.7	73.2	67.7
Area, sq. mi. (sq. km.)	11,507,729 (29,805,048)	3,355,209 (8,690,000)	11,979,613 (31,027,230)	8,813,096 (22,825,942)	8,260,131 (21,393,762)	3,254,321 (8,428,702)	6,765,387 (17,522,371)

*all figures as of July 2000

**percentages may not add to 100 due to rounding

†Oceania includes American Samoa, Australia, Cook Islands, Fiji, French Polynesia, Guam, Kiribati, Marshall Islands, Federated States of Micronesia, Nauru, New Caledonia, New Zealand, Northern Mariana Islands, Palau, Papua New Guinea, Samoa, Solomon Islands, Tonga, Tuvalu, Vanuatu, and Wallis and Futuna.

© U.S. Census Bureau. "International Data Base (IDB)," www.census.gov/ipc/www/idbnew.html

World Population: Future Estimates

Year	Estimated World Population	Estimated Average Annual Growth Rate (%)	Average Annual Population Increase
2000	6,080,141,683	1.26	77,258,877
2005	6,460,553,564	1.14	73,759,794
2010	6,823,634,553	1.03	70,770,206
2015	7,175,675,066	.97	69,613,925
2020	7,518,010,600	.88	66,371,114
2025	7,840,660,355	.78	61,682,010
2030	8,140,344,240	.70	57,189,977
2035	8,416,742,278	.62	52,278,271
2040	8,668,391,454	.55	47,462,555
2045	8,897,075,495	.48	43,234,092

⊙ U.S. Census Bureau. "Total Midyear Population for the World: 1950–2050," www.census.gov/ipc/www/worldpop.html

World Population: Historical Estimates

Year	Population Estimates in millions (lower to upper)*	Year	Population Estimates in millions (lower to upper)*
−10000	1 to 10	1300	360 to 432
−5000	5 to 20	1400	350 to 374
−4000	7	1500	425 to 540
−3000	14	1600	545 to 579
−2000	27	1650	470 to 545
−1000	50	1700	600 to 679
−500	100	1750	629 to 961
−400	162	1800	813 to 1,125
−200	150 to 231	1850	1,128 to 1,402
1	170 to 400	1900	1,550 to 1,762
200	190 to 256	1910	1,750
400	190 to 206	1920	1,860
500	190 to 206	1930	2,070
600	200 to 206	1940	2,300
700	207 to 210	1950	2,556
800	220 to 224	1960	3,039
900	226 to 240	1970	3,706
1000	254 to 345	1980	4,453
1100	301 to 320	1990	5,283
1200	360 to 450	2000	6,080
1250	400 to 416		

*Single figures indicate no variation in estimates.

⊙ U.S. Census Bureau. "Historical Estimates of World Population," www.census.gov/ipc.www.worldhis.html

Largest Islands

Island	National Sovereignty	Area sq. mi. (sq. km.)
Greenland	Denmark	839,900 (1,175,600)
New Guinea	Papua New Guinea, Indonesia	309,000 (800,000)
Borneo	Indonesia, Malaysia, Brunei	283,400 (734,000)
Madagascar	Madagascar	226,658 (587,040)
Baffin	Canada	195,928 (507,451)
Sumatra	Indonesia	167,600 (434,000)
Honshu	Japan	87,805 (227,414)
Great Britain	Great Britain	88,795 (229,978)
Victoria	Canada	81,930 (212,199)
Ellesmere	Canada	75,767 (192,236)
Celebes (Sulawesi)	Indonesia	73,057 (189,216)
South Island	New Zealand	58,676 (151,971)
Java	Indonesia	48,900 (126,602)
North Island	New Zealand	44,204 (114,489)
Cuba	Cuba	42,800 (110,851)
Newfoundland	Canada	42,031 (108,860)
Luzon	Philippines	40,420 (104,688)
Iceland	Iceland	39,699 (103,000)
Mindanao	Philippines	36,537 (94,630)
Ireland	Ireland, U.K.	32,589 (84,406)
Hokkaido	Japan	30,144 (78,073)
Sakhalin	Russia	29,500 (76,400)
Hispaniola	Haiti, Dominican Republic	29,418 (76,192)
Banks	Canada	27,038 (70,028)
Tasmania	Australia	26,383 (68,332)

⊙ Wright, John W., ed. *The New York Times Almanac, Millennium Edition*. New York: Penguin, 1999.

Largest Deserts

Desert	Location	Area sq. mi. (sq. km.)
Sahara	North Africa	3,320,000 (8,600,000)
Gobi (Shamo)	Mongolia, China	500,000 (1,294,994)
Libyan	Libya, Egypt, Sudan	450,000 (1,165,495)
Rub' al-Khali	Saudi Arabia	200,000 (517,998)
Great Basin	United States	189,000 (489,500)
Chihuahuan	Mexico	175,000 (450,000)
Great Sandy	Australia	150,000 (388,498)
Great Victoria	Australia	150,000 (388,498)
Atacama	Chile	140,000 (362,598)
Takla Makan	China	140,000 (362,598)
Kalahari	South Africa	120,000 (310,798)
Sonoran	Arizona, California, Mexico	120,000 (310,800)
Kara Kum	Turkmenistan	115,000 (297,849)
Kavir	Iran	100,000 (258,999)
Kyzyl Kum	Uzbekistan and Kazakhstan	100,000 (258,999)
Nubian	North Africa	100,000 (258,999)
Syrian (Al-Hamad)	Iraq, Jordan, Saudi Arabia, Syria	100,000 (258,999)
Thar (Indian)	Pakistan-India	100,000 (258,999)
Namib	Namibia	52,000 (134,679)
Mojave	California	25,000 (64,750)

⊙ Allan, Tony, and Andrew Warren, eds. *Deserts: The Encroaching Wilderness*. New York: Oxford University Press, 1993.

Highest Mountains

Mountain Peak	Range	Country	Elevation ft. (m.)
Everest	Himalayas	Nepal, Tibet	29,028 (8,848)
K2 (Godwin Austen)	Karakoram	Pakistan, China	28,250 (8,611)
Kanchenjunga	Himalayas	India, Nepal	28,169 (8,586)
Lhotse I	Himalayas	Nepal, Tibet	27,940 (8,516)
Makalu I	Himalayas	Nepal, Tibet	27,766 (8,463)
Cho Oyu	Himalayas	Nepal, Tibet	26,906 (8,201)
Dhaulagiri	Himalayas	Nepal	26,795 (8,167)
Manaslu I	Himalayas	Nepal	26,781 (8,163)
Nanga Parbat	Himalayas	Pakistan	26,660 (8,125)
Annapurna	Himalayas	Nepal	26,545 (8,091)
Gasherbrum I	Karakoram	Pakistan, China	26,470 (8,068)
Broad Peak	Karakoram	Pakistan, China	26,400 (8,047)
Gosainthan (Shishma Pangma)	Himalayas	Tibet	26,397 (8,046)
Gasherbrum II	Karakoram	Pakistan, China	26,360 (8,035)
Annapurna II	Himalayas	Nepal	26,041 (7,937)
Gyachung Kang	Himalayas	Nepal	25,910 (7,897)
Disteghil Sar	Karakoram	Pakistan	25,858 (7,882)
Himalchuli	Himalayas	Nepal	25,801 (7,864)
Nuptse	Himalayas	Nepal	25,726 (7,841)
Nanda Devi	Himalayas	India	25,663 (7,824)
Masherbrum	Karakoram	Kashmir	25,660 (7,821)
Rakaposhi	Karakoram	Pakistan	25,551 (7,788)
Kanjut Sar	Karakoram	Pakistan	25,461 (7,761)
Kamet	Himalayas	India, Tibet	25,446 (7,756)
Namcha Barwa	Himalayas	Tibet	25,445 (7,756)
Gurla Mandhata	Himalayas	Tibet	25,355 (7,728)
Ulugh Muztagh	Kunlun	Tibet	25,340 (7,723)
Kungur	Muztagh Ata	China	25,325 (7,719)
Tirich Mir	Hindu Kush	Pakistan	25,230 (7,690)
Saser Kangri	Karakoram	India	25,172 (7,672)
Makalu II	Himalayas	Nepal	25,120 (7,657)
Minya Konka (Gongga Shan)	Daxue Shan	China	24,900 (7,590)
Kula Kangri	Himalayas	Bhutan	24,783 (7,554)
Chang-tzu	Himalayas	Tibet	24,780 (7,553)
Muztagh Ata	Muztagh Ata	China	24,757 (7,546)
Skyang Kangri	Himalayas	Kashmir	24,750 (7,544)
Ismail Samani Peak (formerly Communism Peak)	Pamirs	Tajikistan	24,590 (7,495)
Jongsong Peak	Himalayas	Nepal	24,472 (7,459)
Pobeda Peak	Tien Shan	Kyrgyzstan	24,406 (7,439)
Sia Kangri	Himalayas	Kashmir	24,350 (7,422)
Haramosh Peak	Karakoram	Pakistan	24,270 (7,397)
Istoro Nal	Hindu Kush	Pakistan	24,240 (7,388)
Tent Peak	Himalayas	Nepal	24,165 (7,365)
Chomo Lhari	Himalayas	Tibet, Bhutan	24,040 (7,327)
Chamlang	Himalayas	Nepal	24,012 (7,319)

Kabru	Himalayas	Nepal	24,002 (7,316)
Alung Gangri	Himalayas	Tibet	24,000 (7,315)
Baltoro Kangri	Himalayas	Kashmir	23,990 (7,312)
Muztagh Ata (K-5)	Kunlun	China	23,890 (7,282)
Mana	Himalayas	India	23,860 (7,237)
Baruntse	Himalayas	Nepal	23,688 (7,220)
Nepal Peak	Himalayas	Nepal	23,500 (7,163)
Amne Machin	Kunlun	China	23,490 (7,160)
Gauri Sankar	Himalayas	Nepal, Tibet	23,440 (7,145)
Badrinath	Himalayas	India	23,420 (7,138)
Nunkun	Himalayas	Kashmir	23,410 (7,135)
Lenin Peak	Pamirs	Tajikistan, Kyrgyzstan	23,405 (7,134)
Pyramid	Himalayas	Nepal	23,400 (7,132)
Api	Himalayas	Nepal	23,399 (7,132)
Pauhunri	Himalayas	India, China	23,385 (7,128)
Trisul	Himalayas	India	23,360 (7,120)
Korzhenevski Peak	Pamirs	Tajikistan	23,310 (7,105)
Kangto	Himalayas	Tibet	23,260 (7,090)
Nyainqentanglha	Nyainqentanglha Shan	China	23,255 (7,088)
Trisuli	Himalayas	India	23,210 (7,074)
Dunagiri	Himalayas	India	23,184 (7,066)
Revolution Peak	Pamirs	Tajikistan	22,880 (6,974)
Aconcagua	Andes	Argentina	22,834 (6,960)
Ojos del Salado	Andes	Argentina, Chile	22,664 (6,908)
Bonete	Andes	Argentina, Chile	22,546 (6,872)
Tupungato	Andes	Argentina, Chile	22,310 (6,800)
Moscow Peak	Pamirs	Tajikistan	22,260 (6,785)
Pissis	Andes	Argentina	22,241 (6,779)
Mercedario	Andes	Argentina, Chile	22,211 (6,770)
Huascarán	Andes	Peru	22,205 (6,768)
Llullaillaco	Andes	Argentina, Chile	22,057 (6,723)
El Libertador	Andes	Argentina	22,047 (6,720)
Cachi	Andes	Argentina	22,047 (6,720)
Kailas	Himalayas	Tibet	22,027 (6,714)
Incahuasi	Andes	Argentina, Chile	21,720 (6,620)
Yerupaja	Andes	Peru	21,709 (6,617)
Kurumda	Pamirs	Tajikistan	21,686 (6,610)
Galan	Andes	Argentina	21,654 (6,600)
El Muerto	Andes	Argentina, Chile	21,463 (6,542)
Sajama	Andes	Bolivia	21,391 (6,520)
Nacimiento	Andes	Argentina	21,302 (6,493)
Illampu	Andes	Bolivia	21,276 (6,485)
Illimani	Andes	Bolivia	21,201 (6,462)
Coropuna	Andes	Peru	21,083 (6,426)
Laudo	Andes	Argentina	20,997 (6,400)
Ancohuma	Andes	Bolivia	20,958 (6,388)
Cuzco (Ausangate)	Andes	Peru	20,945 (6,384)
Toro	Andes	Argentina, Chile	20,932 (6,380)
Tres Cruces	Andes	Argentina, Chile	20,853 (6,356)
Huandoy	Andes	Peru	20,852 (6,356)
Parinacota	Andes	Bolivia, Chile	20,768 (6,330)

Highest Mountains *(cont.)*

Mountain Peak	Range	Country	Elevation ft. (m.)
Tortolas	Andes	Argentina, Chile	20,745 (6,323)
Chimborazo	Andes	Ecuador	20,702 (6,310)
Ampato	Andes	Peru	20,702 (6,310)
El Condor	Andes	Argentina	20,669 (6,300)
Salcantay	Andes	Peru	20,574 (6,271)
Huancarhuas	Andes	Peru	20,531 (6,258)
Famatina	Andes	Argentina	20,505 (6,250)
Pumasillo	Andes	Peru	20,492 (6,246)
Solo	Andes	Argentina	20,492 (6,246)
Polleras	Andes	Argentina	20,456 (6,235)
Pular	Andes	Chile	20,423 (6,225)
Chañi	Andes	Argentina	20,341 (6,200)
McKinley (Denali)	Alaska	Alaska	20,320 (6,194)
Aucanquilcha	Andes	Chile	20,295 (6,186)
Juncal	Andes	Argentina, Chile	20,276 (6,180)
Negro	Andes	Argentina	20,184 (6,152)
Quela	Andes	Argentina	20,128 (6,135)
Condoriri	Andes	Bolivia	20,095 (6,125)
Palermo	Andes	Argentina	20,079 (6,120)
Solimana	Andes	Peru	20,068 (6,117)
San Juan	Andes	Argentina, Chile	20,049 (6,111)
Sierra Nevada	Andes	Argentina	20,023 (6,103)
Antofalla	Andes	Argentina	20,013 (6,100)
Marmolejo	Andes	Argentina, Chile	20,013 (6,100)

⊙ Wright, John W., ed. *The New York Times Almanac, Millennium Edition.* New York: Penguin, 1999.

Largest Lakes

Name	Location	Area sq. mi. (sq. km.)	Maximum Depth ft. (m.)
Caspian Sea	Azerbaijan, Russia, Kazakhstan, Turkmenistan, Iran	143,550 (371,800)	3,363 (1,025)
Superior	U.S., Canada	31,800 (82,362)	1,333 (406)
Victoria	Tanzania, Uganda	26,820 (68,000)	279 (85)
Aral Sea	Kazakhstan, Uzbekistan	24,904 (64,500)	220 (67)
Huron	U.S., Canada	23,000 (59,570)	750 (227)
Michigan	U.S.	22,400 (58,000)	923 (281)
Tanganyika	Tanzania, Congo	12,350 (31,986)	4,800 (1,463)
Baikal	Russia	12,160 (31,494)	5,315 (1,620)
Great Bear	Canada	12,028 (31,152)	1,356 (413)
Nyasa	Malawi, Mozambique, Tanzania	11,150 (28,878)	2,280 (695)
Great Slave	Canada	11,030 (28,568)	2,015 (614)
Erie	U.S., Canada	9,910 (25,666)	210 (64)

Winnipeg	Canada	9,417 (24,390)	92 (28)
Ontario	U.S., Canada	7,600 (19,684)	802 (244)
Balkhash	Kazakhstan	7,115 (18,428)	87 (27)
Ladoga	Russia	6,835 (17,703)	755 (230)
Chad	Chad, Niger, Nigeria	6,300 (16,317)	36 (11)
Maracaibo	Venezuela	5,200 (13,468)	115 (35)
Eyre	Australia	3,920 (10,153)	4 (1.5)*
Onega	Russia	3,720 (9,635)	394 (120)
Titicaca	Bolivia, Peru	3,200 (8,288)	990 (301)
Nicaragua	Nicaragua	3,150 (8,158)	230 (70)
Athabaska	Canada	3,064 (7,936)	407 (124)
Reindeer	Canada	2,568 (6,651)	720 (219)
Rudolf	Kenya	2,473 (6,405)	240 (73)
Issyk Kul	Kyrgyzstan	2,355 (6,099)	2,303 (702)
Torrens	South Australia	2,230 (5,776)	.5 (.15)*
Vänern	Sweden	2,156 (5,584)	325 (99)
Nettilling	Baffin Island, Canada	2,140 (5,543)	38 (11)
Winnipegosis	Canada	2,075 (5,374)	38 (11)
Lake Albert	Uganda, Democratic Republic of the Congo	2,075 (5,374)	168 (51)
Kariba	Uganda	2,050 (5,309)	390 (119)
Nipigon	Canada	1,872 (4,848)	540 (165)
Urmia	Iran	1,815 (4,701)	49 (15)
Manitoba	Canada	1,800 (4,662)	92 (28)

*Depth varies dramatically with rainfall in wet season

⊙ United States Department of Commerce, National Oceanic and Atmospheric Administration, *Principal Rivers and Lakes of the World*, 1982.
Wright, John W., ed. *The New York Times Almanac 2000*. New York: Penguin Reference, 1999.

Longest Rivers

River	Continent	Length mi.(km.)
Nile	Africa	4,145 (6,669)
Amazon	South America	3,860 (7,148)
Mississippi-Missouri	North America	3,740 (6,018)
Yangtze (Chang Jiang)	Asia	3,720 (5,985)
Yenisei-Angara	Asia	3,650 (5,873)
Amur	Asia	3,590 (5,776)
Ob	Asia	3,360 (5,406)
Río de la Plata-Paraná	South America	3,030 (4,875)
Yellow (Huang He)	Asia	2,903 (4,671)
Congo (Zaire)	Africa	2,900 (4,666)
Lena	Asia	2,730 (4,393)
Mackenzie	North America	2,635 (4,240)
Niger	Africa	2,600 (4,183)
Mekong	Asia	2,600 (4,183)

Longest Rivers *(cont.)*

River	Continent	Length mi.(km.)
Murray-Darling	Australia	2,330 (3,749)
Volga	Europe	2,290 (3,685)
Madeira	South America	2,013 (3,239)
São Francisco	South America	1,988 (3,199)
Yukon	North America	1,979 (3,665)
Rio Grande	North America	1,885 (3,491)
Purus	South America	1,860 (2,993)
Indus	Asia	1,800 (2,896)
Danube	Europe	1,776 (2,858)
Brahmaputra (Tsangpo)	Asia	1,770 (2,848)
Salween (Saluen, Chiama Ngu Chu)	Asia	1,750 (2,816)
Tocantins-Para	South America	1,710 (2,751)
Zambezi	Africa	1,700 (2,735)
Paraguay	South America	1,610 (2,590)
Saskatchewan	North America	1,600 (2,574)
Amu Darya	Asia	1,578 (2,539)
Ural	Europe	1,575 (2,534)
Ganges	Asia	1,560 (2,510)
Euphrates	Asia	1,510 (2,430)
Colorado	North America	1,450 (2,333)
Arkansas	North America	1,450 (2,333)
Dnieper	Europe	1,420 (2,285)
Kasai	Africa	1,338 (2,153)
Orange	Africa	1,300 (2,092)
Irrawaddy	Asia	1,300 (2,092)
Kolyma	Asia	1,300 (2,092)
Orinoco	South America	1,280 (2,060)
Columbia	North America	1,243 (2,000)
Don	Europe	1,224 (1,969)
Dniester	Europe	875 (1,408)
Rhine	Europe	820 (1,319)
Brazos	North America	800 (1,287)
Saint Lawrence	North America	800 (1,287) *
Vistula	Europe	663 (1,067)
Loire	Europe	625 (1,006)
Tagus	Europe	625 (1,006)

*not including waterway provided by the Great Lakes

⊙ *The World Almanac and Book of Facts, 2000: Millennium Collector's Edition.* Mahwah, N.J.: World Almanac Books, 1999.

Ocean	Area (in millions) sq. mi. (sq. km.)	Coastline mi. (km.)	Maximum Depth ft. (m.)	Location of Maximum Depth	Marginal Seas
Pacific	69.35 (179.68)	84,246 (135,663)	35,839 (10,924)	Mariana Trench	Bali, Bellingshausen, Bering, Coral, Flores, Java, Philippine, Ross, Savu, Sea of Japan, Sea of Okhotsk, South China, Tasman, Timor
Atlantic	35.65 (92.37)	69,468 (111,866)	28,231 (8,605)	Puerto Rico Trench	Baltic, Black, Caribbean, Mediterranean, North, Norwegian, Scotia, Weddell
Indian	28.53 (73.91)	41,312 (66,526)	23,812 (7,258)	Java Trench	Arabian, Bass Strait, Bay of Bengal
Arctic	5.44 (14.09)	28,186 (45,389)	17,881 (5,450)	Eurasia Basin	Barents, Beaufort, Chukchi, East Siberian, Greenland, Hudson Bay, Kara, Laptev

© Central Intelligence Agency. *The World Factbook, 1998.* Washington, D.C.: CIA Printing and Photography Group, 1999.

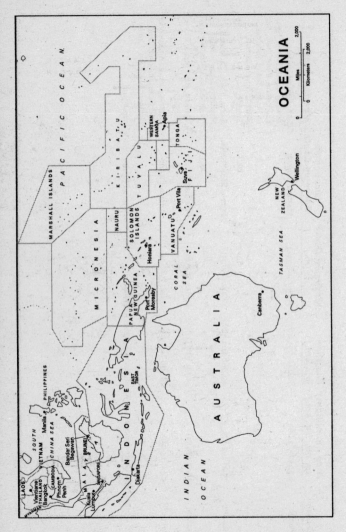

OCEANIA

SOUTH AMERICA

CARIBBEAN SEA

SAINT VINCENT AND THE GRENADINES

SAINT LUCIA

GRENADA

BARBADOS

Port of Spain

TRINIDAD AND TOBAGO

Caracas

Panama

PANAMA

VENEZUELA

ATLANTIC OCEAN

Georgetown

Paramaribo

GUYANA

French Guiana

Bogotá

SURINAME

COLOMBIA

Quito

ECUADOR

P E R U

B R A Z I L

Lima

La Paz

Brasília

B O L I V I A

PACIFIC OCEAN

PARAGUAY

Asunción

A R G E N T I N A

C H I L E

URUGUAY

Santiago

Buenos Aires

Montevideo

Miles 1,000

Kilometers 1,000

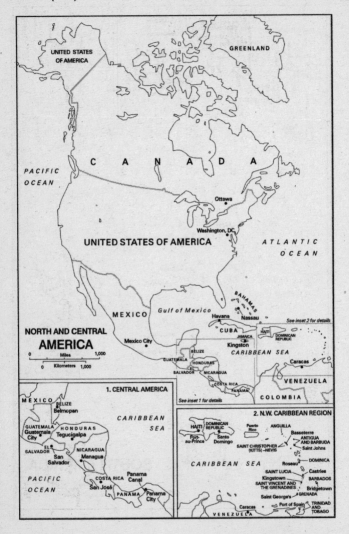

NORTH AND CENTRAL
AMERICA

0 — Miles — 1,000
0 — Kilometers — 1,000

1. CENTRAL AMERICA

2. N.W. CARIBBEAN REGION

See inset 2 for details

See inset 1 for details

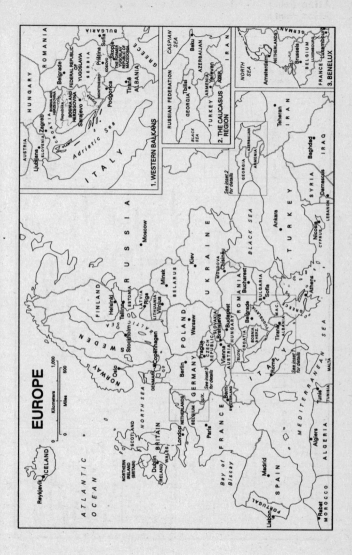

EUROPE

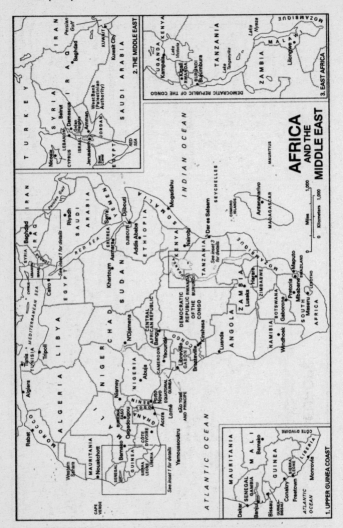

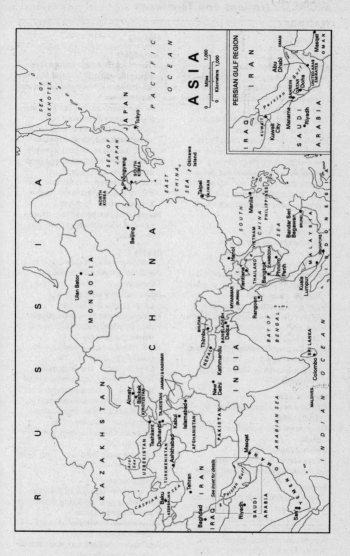

ASIA

Miles 1,000
Kilometers 1,000

PERSIAN GULF REGION

WORLD: *Nations and Territories*

Nations

Afghanistan

Geography

Location: Southern Asia

Area: 250,000 sq. mi.; 647,500 sq. km. (slightly smaller than Texas)

Climate: arid to semiarid; cold winters and hot summers

Terrain: mostly rugged mountains; plains in north and southwest

Elevation: lowest point: Amu Darya 846 ft. (258 m.); highest point: Nowshak 24,557 ft. (7,485 m.)

Natural resources: natural gas, petroleum, coal, copper, talc, barites, sulfur, lead, zinc, iron ore, salt, precious and semiprecious stones

People

Population: 25,824,882

Population growth rate: 4.21%

Infant mortality rate: 143.63 deaths/1,000 live births

Life expectancy at birth: total population: 46.83 years; male: 47.35 years; female: 46.29 years

Major ethnic groups: Pashtun 38%, Tajik 25%, Uzbek 6%, Hazara 19%

Major religions: Sunni Muslim 84%, Shi'a Muslim 15%

Major languages: Pashtu 35%, Afghan Persian (Dari) 50%, Turkic languages (primarily Uzbek and Turkmen) 11%

Government

Official name: Islamic Emirate of Afghanistan

Government type: transitional government

National capital: Kabul

Independence: August 19, 1919

Legal system: Shari'a (Islamic law)

Economy

Industries: small-scale production of textiles, soap, furniture, shoes, fertilizer, and cement; handwoven carpets; natural gas, oil, coal, copper

Agricultural products: wheat, fruits, nuts, karakul pelts; wool, mutton

Currency: 1 afghani (AF) = 100 puls

Albania

Geography

Location: Southeastern Europe, bordering the Adriatic Sea and Ionian Sea, between Greece and Serbia and Montenegro

Area: 11,100 sq. mi. (28,750 sq. km.); slightly larger than Maryland

Climate: mild temperate; cool, cloudy, wet winters; hot, clear, dry summers; interior is cooler and wetter

Terrain: mostly mountains and hills; small plains along coast

Elevation: lowest point: Adriatic Sea 0 ft. (0 m.); highest point: Maja e Korabit 1,063 ft. (2,753 m.)

Natural resources: petroleum, natural gas, coal, chromium, copper, timber, nickel

People

Population: 3,364,571 (July 1999 est.)

Population growth rate: 1.05% (July 1999 est.)

Infant mortality rate: 42.9 deaths/1,000 live births

Life expectancy at birth: total population: 67 years; male: 65.92 years; female: 72.33 years

Major ethnic groups: Albanian 95%, Greeks 3%, other 2% (Vlachs, Gypsies, Serbs, and Bulgarians). NOTE: in 1989, otner estimates of the Greek population ranged from 1% (official Albanian statistics) to 12% (from a Greek organization)

Major religions: Muslim 70%, Albanian Orthodox 20%, Roman Catholic 10%

Major languages: Albanian (Tosk is the official dialect), Greek

Government

Official name: Republic of Albania

Government type: emerging democracy

National capital: Tirana

Independence: November 28, 1912 (from Ottoman Empire)

Legal system: has not accepted compulsory ICJ jurisdiction

Economy

Industries: food processing, textiles and clothing; lumber, oil, cement, chemicals, mining, basic metals, hydropower

Agricultural products: wide range of temperate-zone crops and livestock

Currency: 1 lek (L) = 100 qintars

Algeria

Geography

Location: Northern Africa, bordering the Mediterranean Sea, between Morocco and Tunisia

Area: 919,590 sq. mi. (2,381,740 sq. km.); slightly less than 3.5 times the size of Texas

Climate: arid to semiarid; mild, wet winters with hot, dry summers along coast; drier with cold winters and hot summers on high plateau; sirocco is a hot, dust/sand-laden wind especially common in summer

Terrain: mostly high plateau and desert; some mountains; narrow, discontinuous coastal plain

Elevation: lowest point: Chott Melrhir −131 ft. (−40 m.); highest point: Tahat 9,852 ft. (3,003 m.)

Natural resources: petroleum, natural gas, iron ore, phosphates, uranium, lead, zinc

People

Population: 31,133,486 (July 1999 est.)

Population growth rate: 2.1%

Infant mortality rate: 43.82 deaths/1,000 live births

Life expectancy at birth: total population: 69.24 years; male: 68.07 years; female: 70.46 years

Major ethnic groups: Arab-Berber 99%, European less than 1%

Major religions: Sunni Muslim (state religion) 99%, Christian and Jewish 1%

Major languages: Arabic (official), French, Berber dialects

Government

Official name: Democratic and Popular Republic of Algeria

Government type: republic

National capital: Algiers

Independence: July 5, 1962 (from France)

Legal system: socialist, based on French and Islamic law; judicial review of legislative acts in ad hoc Constitutional Council composed of various public officials, including several Supreme Court justices; has not accepted compulsory ICJ jurisdiction

Economy

Industries: petroleum, light industries, natural gas, mining, electrical, petrochemical, food processing

Agricultural products: wheat, barley, oats, grapes, olives, citrus, fruits; sheep, cattle

Currency: 1 Algerian dinar (DA) = 100 centimes

American Samoa

Geography

Location: Oceania, group of islands in the South Pacific Ocean, about one-half of the way from Hawaii to New Zealand

Area: 77 sq. mi. (199 sq. km.); slightly larger than Washington, D.C.

Climate: tropical marine, moderated by southeast trade winds; annual rainfall averages 124 inches; rainy season from November to April, dry season from May to October; little seasonal temperature variation

Terrain: five volcanic islands with rugged peaks and limited coastal plains, two coral atolls (Rose Island, Swains Island)

Elevation: lowest point: Pacific Ocean 0 ft. (0 m.); highest point: highest point: Lata 373 ft. (966 m.)

Natural resources: pumice, pumicite

People

Population: 63,786 (July 1999 est.)

Population growth rate: 2.64 %

Infant mortality rate: 10.19 deaths/1,000 live births

Life expectancy at birth: total population: 75.46 years; male: 71.23 years; female: 79.95 years

Nations (cont.)

Major ethnic groups: Samoan
(Polynesian) 89%, Caucasian 2%,
Tongan 4%, other 5%

Major religions: Christian
Congregationalist 50%, Roman
Catholic 20%, Protestant denomina-
tions and other 30%

Major languages: Samoan (closely
related to Hawaiian and other
Polynesian languages), English;
most people are bilingual

Government

Official name: Territory of American
Samoa

Government type: unincorporated and
unorganized territory of the U.S.;
administered by the U.S. Department of Interior, Office of
Territorial and International Affairs

National capital: Pago Pago

Independence: none (territory of the
U.S.)

Legal system: N/A

Economy

Industries: tuna canneries (largely
dependent on foreign fishing vessels), meat canning, handicrafts

Agricultural products: bananas,
coconuts, vegetables, taro, breadfruit, yams, copra, pineapples,
papayas, dairy

Currency: 1 U.S. dollar (US$) = 100
cents

Andorra

Geography

Location: Southwestern Europe,
between France and Spain

Area: 174 sq. mi. (450 sq. km.); comparative area: 2.5 times the size of
Washington, D.C.

Climate: temperate; snowy, cold winters and warm, dry summers

Terrain: rugged mountains dissected
by narrow valleys

Elevation: lowest point: Riu Valira
2,756 ft. (840 m.); highest point:
Coma Pedrosa 9,665 ft. (2,946 m.)

Natural resources: hydropower, mineral
water, timber, iron ore, lead

People

Population: 65,939 (July 1999 est.)

Population growth rate: 2.24%

Infant mortality rate: 4.0 deaths/1,000
live births

Life expectancy at birth: total population: 83.46 years; male: 80.55 years;
female: 86.55 years

Major ethnic groups: Spanish 61%,
Andorran 30%, French 6%

Major religions: Roman Catholic (predominant)

Major languages: Catalan (official),
French, Castilian

Government

Official name: Principality of Andorra

Government type: parliamentary
democracy that retains as its heads
of state a coprincipality; the two
princes are the president of France
and Spanish bishop of Seo de Urgel,
who are represented locally by officials called veguers

National capital: Andorra la Vella

Independence: 1278

Legal system: based on French and
Spanish civil codes; no judicial review of legislative acts; has not
accepted compulsory ICJ jurisdiction

Economy

Industries: tourism (particularly
skiing), sheep, timber, tobacco,
banking

Agricultural products: small quantities
of tobacco, rye, wheat, barley, oats,
vegetables; sheep raising

Currency: 1 French franc (F) = 100
centimes; 1 peseta (Pta) = 100 centimos; the French and Spanish cur-
rencies are used

Angola

Geography

Location: Southern Africa, bordering
the South Atlantic Ocean, between
Namibia and Zaire

Area: 481,351 sq. mi. (1,246,700 sq.
km.);comparative area: slightly less
than twice the size of Texas

Climate: semiarid in south and along coast to Luanda; north has cool, dry season (May to October) and hot, rainy season (November to April)
Terrain: narrow coastal plain rises abruptly to vast interior plateau
Elevation: lowest point: Atlantic Ocean 0 ft. (0 m.); highest point: Moro de Moco 8,596 ft. (2,620 m.)
Natural resources: petroleum, diamonds, iron ore, phosphates, copper, feldspar, gold, bauxite, uranium

People
Population: 11,177,537 (July 1999 est.)
Population growth rate: 2.84%
Infant mortality rate: 129.19 deaths/1,000 live births
Life expectancy at birth: total population: 48.93 years; male: 46.08 years; female: 50.82 years
Major ethnic groups: Ovimbundu 37%, Kimbundu 25%, Bakongo 13%, mestico (mixed European and Native African) 2%, European 1%, other 22%
Major religions: indigenous beliefs 47%, Roman Catholic 38%, Protestant 15%
Major languages: Portuguese (official), Bantu and other African languages

Government
Official name: Republic of Angola
Government type: transitional government nominally a multiparty democracy with a strong presidential system
National capital: Luanda
Independence: November 11, 1975 (from Portugal)
Legal system: based on Portuguese civil law system and customary law; recently modified to accommodate political pluralism and increased use of free markets

Economy
Industries: petroleum; diamonds, iron ore, phosphates, feldspar, bauxite, uranium, and gold; fish processing; food processing; brewing; tobacco; sugar; textiles; cement; basic metal products

Agricultural products: bananas, sugarcane, coffee, sisal, corn, cotton, manioc (tapioca), tobacco, vegetables, plantains; livestock; forest products; fish
Currency: 1 new kwanza (NKz) = 100 lwei

Anguilla

Geography
Location: Caribbean, island in the Caribbean Sea, east of Puerto Rico
Area: 35 sq. mi. (91 sq. km.); about half the size of Washington, D.C.
Climate: tropical; moderated by northeast trade winds
Terrain: flat and low-lying island of coral and limestone
Elevation: lowest point: Caribbean Sea 0 ft. (0 m.); highest point: Crocus Hill 213 ft. (65 m.)
Natural resources: salt, fish, lobster

People
Population: 11,510 (July 1999 est.)
Population growth rate: 3.16%
Infant mortality rate: 18.72 deaths/1,000 live births
Life expectancy at birth: total population: 77.71 years; male: 74.72 years; female: 80.78 years
Major ethnic group: black African
Major religions: Anglican 40%, Methodist 33%, Seventh-Day Adventist 7%, Baptist 5%, Roman Catholic 3%, other 12%
Major language: English (official)

Government
Official name: Anguilla
Government type: dependent territory of the U.K.
National capital: The Valley
Independence: none (dependent territory of the U.K.)
Legal system: based on English common law

Economy
Industries: tourism, boat building, offshore financial services
Agricultural products: pigeon peas, corn, sweet potatoes; sheep, goats,

Nations *(cont.)*

pigs, cattle, poultry; fishing (including lobster)
Currency: 1 East Caribbean dollar (EC$) = 100 cents

Antigua and Barbuda

Geography

Location: Caribbean, islands between the Caribbean Sea and the North Atlantic Ocean, east-southeast of Puerto Rico
Area: 170 sq. mi. (440 sq. km.) comparative area: 2.5 times the size of Washington, D.C.
Climate: tropical marine; little seasonal temperature variation
Terrain: mostly low-lying limestone and coral islands with some higher volcanic areas
Elevation: lowest point: Caribbean Sea 0 ft. (0 m.); highest point: Boggy Peak 1,319 ft. (402 m.)
Natural resources: negligible; pleasant climate fosters tourism

People

Population: 64,246 (July 1999 est.)
Population growth rate: 0.36%
Infant mortality rate: 20.69 deaths/1,000 live births
Life expectancy at birth: total population: 71.46 years; male: 69.06 years; female: 73.98 years
Major ethnic groups: black, British, Portuguese, Lebanese, Syrian
Major religions: Anglican (predominant), other Protestant sects, some Roman Catholic
Major languages: English (official), local dialects

Government

Official name: Antigua and Barbuda
Government type: parliamentary democracy
National capital: Saint John's
Independence: November 1, 1981 (from U.K.)
Legal system: based on English common law

Economy

Industries: tourism, construction, light manufacturing (clothing, alcohol, household appliances)
Agricultural products: cotton, fruits, vegetables, bananas, coconuts, cucumbers, mangoes, sugarcane; livestock
Currency: 1 East Caribbean dollar (EC$) = 100 cents

Argentina

Geography

Location: Southern South America, bordering the South Atlantic Ocean, between Chile and Uruguay
Area: 1,068,296 sq. mi. (2,766,890 sq. km.); slightly less than three-tenths the size of the U.S.
Climate: mostly temperate; arid in southeast; subantarctic in southwest
Terrain: rich plains of the Pampas in northern half, flat to rolling plateau of Patagonia in south, rugged Andes along western border
Elevation: lowest point: Salinas Chicas −131 ft. (−40 m.); highest point: Cerro Aconcagua 22,841 ft. (6,962 m.)
Natural resources: fertile plains of the pampas, lead, zinc, tin, copper, iron ore, manganese, petroleum, uranium

People

Population: 36,737,664 (July 1999 est.)
Population growth rate: 1.29%
Infant mortality rate: 18.41 deaths/ 1,000 live births
Life expectancy at birth: total population: 74.76 years; male: 71.13 years; female: 78.56 years
Major ethnic groups: white 85%, mestizo, Indian, or other nonwhite groups 15%
Major religions: nominally Roman Catholic 90% (less than 20% practicing), Protestant 2%, Jewish 2%, other 6%
Major languages: Spanish (official), English, Italian, German, French

Government

Official name: Argentine Republic
Government type: republic
National capital: Buenos Aires

Independence: July 9, 1816 (from Spain)

Legal system: mixture of US and West European legal systems, has not accepted compulsory IJC jurisdiction

Economy

Industries: food processing, motor vehicles, consumer durables, textiles, chemicals and petrochemicals, printing, metallurgy, steel

Agricultural products: wheat, corn, sorghum, soybeans, sugar beets; livestock

Currency: 1 nuevo peso argentino = 100 centavos

Armenia

Geography

Location: Southwestern Asia, east of Turkey

Area: 11,506 sq. mi. (29,800 sq. km.); slightly larger than Maryland

Climate: highland continental, hot summers, cold winters

Terrain: high Armenian Plateau with mountains; little forest land; fast flowing rivers; good soil in Aras River valley

Elevation: lowest point: Debed River 1,312 ft. (400 m.); highest point: Aragats Lerr 13,435 ft. (4,095 m.)

Natural resources: small deposits of gold, copper, molybdenum, zinc, alumina

People

Population: 3,409,234 (July 1999 est.)

Population growth rate: -0.38%

Infant mortality rate: 41.12 deaths/ 1,000 live births

Life expectancy at birth: total population: 66.56 years; male: 62.21 years; female: 71.13 years

Major ethnic groups: Armenian 93%, Azeri 3%, Russian 2%

Major religions: Armenian Orthodox 94%

Major languages: Armenian 96%, Russian 2%,

Government

Official name: Republic of Armenia

Government type: republic

National capital: Yerevan

Independence: May 28, 1918 (First Armenian Republic); September 23, 1991 (from Soviet Union)

Legal system: based on civil law system

Economy

Industries: much of industry is shut down; metal-cutting machine tools, forging-pressing machines, electric motors, tires, knitted wear, hosiery, shoes, silk fabric, washing machines, chemicals, trucks, watches, instruments, microelectronics

Agricultural products: fruit (especially grapes), vegetables; vineyards near Yerevan are famous for brandy and other liqueurs; minor livestock sector

Currency: 1 dram = 100 luma (introduced new currency in November 1993)

Aruba

Geography

Location: Caribbean, island in the Caribbean Sea, north of Venezuela

Area: 75 sq. mi. (193 sq. km.); slightly larger than Washington, D.C.

Climate: tropical marine; little seasonal temperature variation

Terrain: flat with a few hills; scant vegetation

Elevation: lowest point: Caribbean Sea 0 ft. (0 m.); highest point: Mount Jamanota 617 ft. (188 m.)

Natural resources: negligible

People

Population: 68,675 (July 1999 est.)

Population growth rate: 0.55%

Infant mortality rate: 7.84 deaths/ 1,000 live births

Life expectancy at birth: total population: 77.04 years; male: 73.33 years; female: 80.94 years

Major ethnic groups: mixed European/ Caribbean Indian 80%

Major religions: Roman Catholic 82%, Protestant 8%, Hindu, Muslim, Confucian, Jewish

Major languages: Dutch (official), Papiamento (a Spanish, Portuguese, Dutch, English dialect), English (widely spoken), Spanish

Nations *(cont.)*

Government
Official name: Aruba
Government type: part of the Dutch realm; full autonomy in internal affairs obtained in 1986 upon separation from the Netherlands Antilles
National capital: Oranjestad
Independence: none (part of the Dutch realm; in 1990, Aruba requested and received from the Netherlands cancellation of the agreement to automatically give independence to the island in 1996)
Legal system: based on Dutch civil law system, with some English common law influence

Economy
Industries: tourism, transshipment facilities, oil refining
Agricultural products: aloes; livestock; fishing
Currency: 1 Aruban florin (Af.) = 100 cents

Australia

Geography
Location: Oceania, continent between the Indian Ocean and the South Pacific Ocean
Area: 2,967,893 sq. mi. (7,686,850 sq. km.) slightly smaller than the U.S.
Climate: generally arid to semiarid; temperate in south and east; tropical in north
Terrain: mostly low plateau with deserts; fertile plain in southeast
Elevation: lowest point: Lake Eyre −49 ft. (−15 m.); highest point: Mount Kosciusko 7,313 ft. (2,229 m.)
Natural resources: bauxite, coal, iron ore, copper, tin, silver, uranium, nickel, tungsten, mineral sands, lead, zinc, diamonds, natural gas, petroleum

People
Population: 18,783,551 (July 1999 est.)
Population growth rate: 0.99%

Infant mortality rate: 5.11 deaths/1,000 live births
Life expectancy at birth: total population: 80.14 years; male: 77.22 years; female: 83.23 years
Major ethnic groups: Caucasian 92%, Asian 4%, aboriginal and other 1%
Major religions: Anglican 26.1%, Roman Catholic 26%, other Christian 24.3%
Major languages: English, native languages

Government
Official name: Commonwealth of Australia
Government type: federal parliamentary state
National capital: Canberra
Independence: January 1, 1901 (federation of U.K. colonies)
Legal system: based on English common law

Economy
Industries: mining, industrial and transportation equipment, food processing, chemicals, steel
Agricultural products: wheat, barley, sugarcane, fruits; cattle, sheep, poultry
Currency: 1 Australian dollar ($A) = 100 cents

Austria

Geography
Location: Central Europe, north of Italy
Area: 32,374 sq. mi. (83,850 sq. km.); slightly smaller than Maine
Climate: temperate; continental, cloudy; cold winters with frequent rain in lowlands and snow in mountains; cool summers with occasional showers
Terrain: in the west and south mostly mountains (Alps); along the eastern and northern margins mostly flat or gently sloping
Elevation: lowest point: Neusiedler See 377 ft. (115 m.); highest point: Grossglockner 12,457 ft. (3,797 m.)

Natural resources: iron ore, oil, timber, magnesite, lead, coal, lignite, copper, hydropower

People

Population: 8,139,299 (July 1999 est.)

Population growth rate: 0.09%

Infant mortality rate: 5.1 deaths/1,000 live births

Life expectancy at birth: total population: 77.48 years; male: 74.31 years; female: 80.82 years

Major ethnic groups: German 99.4%, Croatian 0.3%, Slovene 0.2%, other 0.1%

Major religions: Roman Catholic 85%, Protestant 6%, other 9%

Major languages: German

Government

Official name: Republic of Austria

Government type: federal republic

National capital: Vienna

Independence: November 12, 1918 (from Austro-Hungarian Empire)

Legal system: civil law system with Roman law origin; judicial review of legislative acts by the Constitutional Court; separate administrative and civil/penal supreme courts

Economy

Industries: food, iron and steel, machines, textiles, chemicals, electrical, paper and pulp, tourism, mining, motor vehicles

Agricultural products: grains, fruit, potatoes, sugar beets; cattle, pigs, poultry; sawn wood

Currency: 1 Austrian schilling (S) = 100 groschen

Azerbaijan

Geography

Location: Southwestern Asia, bordering the Caspian Sea, between Iran and Russia

Area: 33,436 sq. mi. (86,600 sq. km.); slightly larger than Maine

Climate: dry, semiarid steppe

Terrain: large, flat Kur-Araz Lowland (much of it below sea level) with Great Caucasus Mountains to the north, Qarabag (Karabakh) Upland in west; Baku lies on Abseron (Apsheron) Peninsula that juts into the Caspian Sea

Elevation: lowest point: Caspian Sea −92 ft. (−28 m.); highest point: Bazarduzu Dagi 14,714 ft. (4,485 m.)

Natural resources: petroleum, natural gas, iron ore, nonferrous metals, alumina

People

Population: 7,908,224 (July 1999 est.)

Population growth rate: 0.63%

Infant mortality rate: 82.52 deaths/ 1,000 live births

Life expectancy at birth: total population: 63.08 years; male: 58.76 years; female: 67.63 years

Major ethnic groups: Azeri 90%, Dagestani Peoples 3.2%, Russian 2.5%, Armenian 2.3%

Major religions: Muslim 93.4%, Russian Orthodox 2.5%, Armenian Orthodox 2.3%, other 1.8%

Major languages: Azeri 89%, Russian 3%, Armenian 2%, other 6%

Government

Official name: Azerbaijani Republic

Government type: republic

National capital: Baku (Baki)

Independence: August 30, 1991 (from Soviet Union)

Legal system: based on civil law system

Economy

Industries: petroleum and natural gas, petroleum products, oilfield equipment; steel, iron ore, cement; chemicals and petrochemicals; textiles

Agricultural products: cotton, grain, rice, grapes, fruit, vegetables, tea, tobacco; cattle, pigs, sheep, goats

Currency: 1 manat = 100 gopik

Bahamas, The

Geography

Location: 24 15 N, 76 00 W; Caribbean, chain of islands in the North Atlantic Ocean, southeast of Florida

Area: 5,382 sq. mi. (13,940 sq. km.) slightly larger than Connecticut

Climate: tropical marine; moderated by warm waters of Gulf Stream

Terrain: long, flat coral formations with some low rounded hills

Elevation: lowest point: Atlantic Ocean 0 ft. (0 m.); highest point: Mount Alvernia 207 ft. (63 m.)

Natural resources: salt, aragonite, timber

People

Population: 283,705 (July 1999 est.)

Population growth rate: 1.36%

Infant mortality rate: 18.38 deaths/1,000 live births

Life expectancy at birth: total population: 74.25 years; male: 70.94 years; female: 77.64 years

Major ethnic groups: black 85%, white 15%

Major religions: Baptist 32%, Anglican 20%, Roman Catholic 19%, Methodist 6%, Church of God 6%, other Protestant 12%

Major languages: English, Creole (among Haitian immigrants)

Government

Official name: Commonwealth of The Bahamas

Government type: commonwealth

National capital: Nassau

Independence: July 10, 1973 (from U.K.)

Legal system: based on English common law

Economy

Industries: tourism, banking, cement, oil refining and transshipment, salt production, rum, aragonite, pharmaceuticals, spiral-welded steel pipe

Agricultural products: citrus, vegetables; poultry

Currency: 1 Bahamian dollar (B$) = 100 cents

Bahrain

Geography

Location: Middle East, archipelago in the Persian Gulf, east of Saudi Arabia

Area: 239 sq. mi. (620 sq. km.); 3.5 times the size of Washington, D.C.

Climate: arid; mild, pleasant winters; very hot, humid summers

Terrain: mostly low desert plain rising gently to low central escarpment

Elevaton: lowest point: Persian Gulf 0 ft. (0 m.); highest point: Jabal ad Dukhan 400 ft. (122 m.)

Natural resources: oil, associated and nonassociated natural gas, fish

People

Population: 629,090 (July 1999 est.)

Population growth rate: 2.27%

Infant mortality rate: 14.81 deaths/1,000 live births

Life expectancy at birth: total population: 75.32 years; male: 72.25 years; female: 77.96 years

Major ethnic groups: Bahraini 63%, Asian 13%, other Arab 10%, Iranian 8%

Major religions: Shi'a Muslim 75%, Sunni Muslim 25%

Major languages: Arabic, English, Farsi, Urdu

Government

Official name: State of Bahrain

Government type: traditional monarchy

National capital: Manama

Independence: August 15, 1971 (from U.K.)

Legal system: based on Islamic law and English common law

Economy

Industries: petroleum processing and refining, aluminum smelting, offshore banking, ship repairing

Agricultural products: fruit, vegetables; poultry, dairy products; shrimp, fish

Currency: 1 Bahraini dinar (BD) = 1,000 fils

Bangladesh

Geography

Location: Southern Asia, bordering the Bay of Bengal, between Burma and India

Area: 55,598 sq. mi. (144,000 sq. km.); slightly smaller than Wisconsin

Climate: tropical; cool, dry winter (October to March); hot, humid summer (March to June); cool, rainy monsoon (June to October)

Terrain: mostly flat alluvial plain; hilly in southeast

Elevation: lowest point: Indian Ocean 0 ft. (0 m.); highest point: Keodradong 4,035 ft. (1,230m.)

Natural resources: natural gas, arable land, timber

People

Population: 127,117,967 (July 1999 est.)

Population growth rate: 1.59%

Infant mortality rate: 69.68 deaths/1,000 live births

Life expectancy at birth: total population: 60.6 years; male: 60.73 years; female: 60.46 years

Major ethnic groups: Bengali 98%, Biharis 250,000, tribals less than 1 million

Major religions: Muslim 83%, Hindu 16%, other 1.2%

Major languages: Bangla (official), English

Government

Official name: People's Republic of Bangladesh

Government type: republic

National capital: Dhaka

Independence: December 16, 1971 (from Pakistan)

Legal system: based on English common law

Economy

Industries: jute manufacturing, cotton textiles, food processing, steel, fertilizer

Agricultural products: jute, rice, wheat, tea, sugarcane, potatoes; beef, milk, poultry

Currency: 1 taka (Tk) = 100 poiska

Barbados

Geography

Location: Caribbean, island between the Caribbean Sea and the North Atlantic Ocean, northeast of Venezuela

Area: 166 sq. mi. (430 sq. km.); 2.5 times the size of Washington, D.C.

Climate: tropical; rainy season (June to October)

Terrain: relatively flat; rises gently to central highland region

Elevation: lowest point: Atlantic Ocean 0 ft. (0 m.); highest point: Mount Hillaby 1,102 ft. (336 m.)

Natural resources: petroleum, fish, natural gas

People

Population: 259,191 (July 1999 est.)

Population growth rate: 0.04%

Infant mortality rate: 16.74 deaths/1,000 live births

Life expectancy at birth: total population: 74.98 years; male: 72.22 years; female: 77.81 years

Major ethnic groups: African 80%, European 4%, other 16%

Major religions: Protestant 67% (Anglican 40%, Pentecostal 8%, Methodist 7%, other 12%), Roman Catholic 4%, none 17%,

Major languages: English

Government

Official name: Barbados

Government type: parliamentary democracy

National capital: Bridgetown

Independence: November 30, 1966 (from U.K.)

Legal system: English common law; no judicial review of legislative acts

Economy

Industries: tourism, sugar, light manufacturing, component assembly for export

Agricultural products: sugarcane, vegetables, cotton

Currency: 1 Barbadian dollar (Bds$) = 100 cents

Belarus

Geography

Location: Eastern Europe, east of Poland

Area: 80,154 sq. mi. (207,600 sq. km.); slightly smaller than Kansas

Nations *(cont.)*

Climate: cold winters, cool and moist summers; transitional between continental and maritime

Terrain: generally flat and contains much marshland

Elevation: lowest point: Nyoman River 295 ft. (90 m.); highest point: Dzyarzhynskaya Hara 1,135 ft. (346 m.)

Natural resources: forests, peat deposits, small quantities of oil and natural gas

People

Population: 10,401,784 (July 1999 est.)

Population growth rate: -0.09%

Infant mortality rate: 14.39 deaths/ 1,000 live births

Life expectancy at birth: total population: 68.13 years; male: 62.04 years; female: 74.52 years

Major ethnic groups: Byelorussian 77.9%, Russian 13.2%, Polish 4.1%, Ukrainian 2.9%, other 1.9%

Major religions: Eastern Orthodox 60%, other (including Roman Catholic and Muslim) 40%

Major languages: Byelorussian, Russian

Government

Official name: Republic of Belarus

Government type: republic

National capital: Minsk

Independence: August 25, 1991 (from Soviet Union)

Legal system: based on civil law system

Economy

Industries: tractors, metal-cutting machine tools, off-highway dump trucks up to 110-metric-ton load capacity, wheel-type earth movers for construction and mining, eight-wheel-drive, high-flotation trucks, equipment for animal husbandry and livestock feeding, motorcycles, television sets, chemical fibers, fertilizer, linen fabric, wool fabric, radios, refrigerators, other consumer goods

Agricultural products: grain, potatoes, vegetables; meat, milk

Currency: Belarusian rubel (BR)

Belgium

Geography

Location: Western Europe, bordering the North Sea, between France and the Netherlands

Area: 11,780 sq. mi. (30,510 sq. km.); slightly larger than Maryland

Land boundaries: total: 1,385 km.

Climate: temperate; mild winters, cool summers; rainy, humid, cloudy

Terrain: flat coastal plains in northwest, central rolling hills, rugged mountains of Ardennes Forest in southeast

Elevation: lowest point: North Sea 0 ft. (0 m.); highest point: Signal de Botrange 2,277 ft. (694 m.)

Natural resources: coal, natural gas

People

Population: 10,182,034 (July 1999 est.)

Population growth rate: 0.06%

Infant mortality rate: 6.17 deaths/1,000 live births

Life expectancy at birth: total population: 77.53 years; male: 74.31 years; female: 80.9 years

Major ethnic groups: Fleming 55%, Walloon 33%

Major religions: Roman Catholic 75%, Protestant or other 25%

Major languages: Dutch 56%, French 32%, German 1%, legally bilingual 11%

Government

Official name: Kingdom of Belgium

Government type: constitutional monarchy

National capital: Brussels

Independence: October 4, 1830 (from the Netherlands)

Legal system: civil law system influenced by English constitutional theory; judicial review of legislative acts

Economy

Industries: engineering and metal

products, motor vehicle assembly, processed food and beverages, chemicals, basic metals, textiles, glass, petroleum, coal

Agricultural products: sugar beets, fresh vegetables, fruits, grain, tobacco; beef, veal, pork, milk

Currency: 1 Belgian franc (BF) = 100 centimes

Belize

Geography

Location: Central America, bordering the Caribbean Sea, between Guatemala and Mexico

Area: 8,865 sq. mi. (22,960 sq. km.) slightly larger than Massachusetts

Climate: tropical; hot and humid; rainy season (May to February)

Terrain: flat, swampy coastal plain; low mountains in south

Elevation: lowest point: Caribbean Sea 0 ft. (0 m.); highest point: Victoria Peak 3,806 ft. (1,160 m.)

Natural resources: arable land potential, timber, fish

People

Population: 235,789 (July 1999 est.)

Population growth rate: 2.42%

Infant mortality rate: 31.57 deaths/ 1,000 live births

Life expectancy at birth: total population: 69.2 years; male: 67.23 years; female: 71.26 years

Major ethnic groups: mestizo 44%, Creole 30%, Maya 11%, Garifuna 7%

Major religions: Roman Catholic 62%, Protestant 30%

Major languages: English (official), Spanish, Mayan, Garifuna (Carib)

Government

Official name: Belize

Government type: parliamentary democracy

National capital: Belmopan

Independence: September 21, 1981 (from U.K.)

Legal system: English law

Economy

Industries: garment production, food processing, tourism, construction

Agricultural products: bananas, coca, citrus, sugarcane; lumber; fish, cultured shrimp

Currency: 1 Belizean dollar (Bz$) = 100 cents

Benin

Geography

Location: Western Africa, bordering the North Atlantic Ocean, between Nigeria and Togo

Area: 43,483 sq. mi. (112,620 sq. km.); slightly smaller than Pennsylvania

Climate: tropical; hot, humid in south; semiarid in north

Terrain: mostly flat to undulating plain; some hills and low mountains

Elevation: lowest point: Atlantic Ocean 0 ft. (0 m.); highest point: Mount Tanekas 2,103 ft. (641 m.)

Natural resources: small offshore oil deposits, limestone, marble, timber

People

Population: 6,305,567 (July 1999 est.)

Population growth rate: 3.32%

Infant mortality rate: 97.76 deaths/ 1,000 live births

Life expectancy at birth: total population: 54.08 years; male: 51.98 years; female: 56.24 years

Major ethnic groups: African 99% (42 ethnic groups, most important being Fon, Adja, Yoruba, Bariba)

Major religions: indigenous beliefs 70%, Muslim 15%, Christian 15%

Major languages: French (official), Fon and Yoruba (most common vernaculars in south), tribal languages (at least six major ones in north)

Government

Official name: Republic of Benin

Government type: republic under multiparty democratic rule dropped Marxism-Leninism December 1989; democratic reforms adopted February 1990; transition to multiparty system completed April 4, 1991

National capital: Porto-Novo

Independence: August 1, 1960 (from France)

Nations *(cont.)*

Legal system: based on French civil law and customary law, has not accepted compulsory IJC jurisdiction

Economy

Industries: textiles, cigarettes; beverages, food; construction materials, petroleum

Agricultural products: corn, sorghum, cassava (tapioca), yams, beans, rice, cotton, palm oil, peanuts; poultry, livestock

Currency: 1 Communauté Financière Africaine franc (CFAF) = 100 centimes

Bermuda

Geography

Location: North America, group of islands in the North Atlantic Ocean, east of North Carolina (U.S.)

Area: 19 sq. mi. (50 sq. km.); about 0.3 times the size of Washington, D.C.

Climate: subtropical; mild, humid; gales, strong winds common in winter

Terrain: low hills separated by fertile depressions

Elevation: lowest point: Atlantic Ocean (0 m.); highest point: Town Hill 249 ft. (76 m.)

Natural resources: limestone, pleasant climate fostering tourism

People

Population: 62,472 (July 1999 est.)

Population growth rate: 0.72%

Infant mortality rate: 13.16 deaths/ 1,000 live births

Life expectancy at birth: total population: 76.97 years; male: 75.19 years; female: 78.83 years

Major ethnic groups: black 61%, white and other 39%

Major religions: Anglican 37%, Roman Catholic 14%, African Methodist Episcopal (Zion) 10%, Methodist 6%, Seventh-Day Adventist 5%, other 28%

Major language: English

Government

Official name: Bermuda

Government type: dependent territory of the U.K.

National capital: Hamilton

Independence: none (dependent territory of the U.K.)

Legal system: English law

Economy

Industries: tourism, finance, structural concrete products, paints, pharmaceuticals, ship repairing

Agricultural products: bananas, vegetables, citrus, flowers; dairy products

Currency: 1 Bermudian dollar (Bd$) = 100 cents

Bhutan

Geography

Location: Southern Asia, between China and India

Area: 18,147 sq. mi. (47,000 sq. km.); slightly more than half the size of Indiana

Climate: varies; tropical in southern plains; cool winters and hot summers in central valleys; severe winters and cool summers in Himalayas

Terrain: mostly mountainous with some fertile valleys and savanna

Elevation: lowest point: Dangme Chu 318 ft. (97 m.); highest point: Khula Kangri I 24,780 ft. (7,553 m.)

Natural resources: timber, hydropower, gypsum, calcium carbide

People

Population: 1,951,965 (July 1999 estimate, other estimates range as low as 600,000)

Population growth rate: 2.25%

Infant mortality rate: 109.33 deaths/ 1,000 live births

Life expectancy at birth: total population: 52.75 years; male: 53.19 years; female: 52.29 years

Major ethnic groups: Bhote 50%, ethnic Nepalese 35%, indigenous or migrant tribes 15%

Major religions: Lamaistic Buddhism 75%, Indian- and Nepalese-influenced Hinduism 25%

Major languages: Dzongkha (official), Bhotes speak various Tibetan dialects, Nepalese speak various Nepalese dialects

Government

Official name: Kingdom of Bhutan

Government type: monarchy; special treaty relationship with India

National capital: Thimphu

Independence: August 8, 1949 (from India)

Legal system: based on Indian law and English common law

Economy

Industries: cement, wood products, processed fruits, alcoholic beverages, calcium carbide

Agricultural products: rice, corn, root crops, citrus, foodgrains; dairy products, eggs

Currency: 1 ngultrum (Nu) = 100 chetrum; note—Indian currency is also legal tender

Bolivia

Geography

Location: Central South America, southwest of Brazil

Area: 424,162 sq. mi. (1,098,580 sq. km.) slightly less than three times the size of Montana

Climate: varies with altitude; humid and tropical to cold and semiarid

Terrain: rugged Andes Mountains with a highland plateau (Altiplano), hills, lowland plains of the Amazon Basin

Elevation: lowest point: Rio Paraguay 295 ft. (90 m.); highest point: Nevado Sajama 6,542 m.

Natural resources: tin, natural gas, petroleum, zinc, tungsten, antimony, silver, iron, lead, gold, timber

People

Population: 7,982,850 (July 1999 est.)

Population growth rate: 1.96%

Infant mortality rate: 62.02 deaths/ 1,000 live births

Life expectancy at birth: total population: 61.43 years; male: 58.51 years; female: 64.51 years

Major ethnic groups: Quechua 30%, Aymara 25%, mestizo (mixed European and Indian ancestry) 25%–30%, European 5%–15%

Major religions: Roman Catholic 95%, Protestant (Evangelical Methodist)

Major languages: Spanish (official), Quechua (official), Aymara (official)

Government

Official name: Republic of Bolivia

Government type: republic

National capital: La Paz (seat of government); Sucre (legal capital and seat of judiciary)

Independence: August 6, 1825 (from Spain)

Legal system: based on Spanish law and Napoleonic Code

Economy

Industries: mining, smelting, petroleum, food and beverages, tobacco, handicrafts, clothing

Agricultural products: coffee, coca, cotton, corn, sugarcane, rice, potatoes; timber

Currency: 1 boliviano ($B) = 100 centavos

Bosnia and Herzegovina

Geography

Location: Southeastern Europe, bordering the Adriatic Sea and Croatia

Area: 19,781 sq. mi. (51,233 sq. km.); comparative area: slightly smaller than West Virginia

Climate: hot summers and cold winters; areas of high elevation have short, cool summers and long, severe winters; mild, rainy winters along coast

Terrain: mountains and valleys

Elevation: lowest point: Adriatic Sea 0 ft. (0 m.); highest point: Maglic 7,828 ft. (2,386 m.)

Natural resources: coal, iron, bauxite, manganese, forests, copper, chromium, lead, zinc

Nations *(cont.)*

People

Population: 3,482,495 (July 1999 est.)
  Note—all data dealing with population is subject to considerable error because of the dislocations caused by military action and ethnic cleansing
Population growth rate: 3.2%
Infant mortality rate: 43.2 deaths/1,000 live births
Life expectancy at birth: total population: 66.98 years; male: 62.55 years; female: 71.71 years
Major ethnic groups: Serb 40%, Muslim 38%, Croat 22% (est.-Croats claim they now make up only 17% of the total population)
Major religions: Muslim 40%, Orthodox 31%, Catholic 15%, Protestant 4%, other 10%
Major languages: Serbo-Croatian 99%

Government

Official name: Bosnia and Herzegovina
Government type: emerging democracy
National capital: Sarajevo
Independence: April 1992 (from Yugoslavia)
Legal system: based on civil law system

Economy

Industries: steel, coal, iron ore, lead, zinc, manganese, bauxite, vehicle assembly, textiles, tobacco products, wooden furniture, tank and aircraft assembly, domestic appliances, oil refining
Agricultural products: wheat, corn, fruits, vegetables; livestock
Currency: 1 convertible marka (KM) = 100 convertible pfenniga

Botswana

Geography

Location: Southern Africa, north of South Africa
Area: 231,803 sq. mi. (600,370 sq. km.); slightly smaller than Texas
Climate: semiarid; warm winters and hot summers
Terrain: predominately flat to gently rolling tableland; Kalahari Desert in southwest
Elevation: lowest point: junction of the Limpopo and Shashe Rivers 1,683 ft. (513 m.); highest point: Tsodilo Hill 4,885 ft. (1,489 m.)
Natural resources: diamonds, copper, nickel, salt, soda ash, potash, coal, iron ore, silver

People

Population: 1,464,167 (July 1999 est.)
Population growth rate: 1.05%
Infant mortality rate: 59.08 deaths/1,000 live births
Life expectancy at birth: total population: 39.89 years; male: 39.42 years; female: 40.37 years
Major ethnic groups: Batswana 95%, Kalanga, Basarwa, and Kgalagadi 4%, white 1%
Major religions: indigenous beliefs 50%, Christian 50%
Major languages: English (official), Setswana

Government

Official name: Republic of Botswana
Government type: parliamentary republic
National capital: Gaborone
Independence: September 30, 1966 (from U.K.)
Legal system: based on Roman-Dutch law and local customary law; judicial review limited to matters of interpretation

Economy

Industries: diamonds, copper, nickel, coal, salt, soda ash, potash; livestock processing
Agricultural products: sorghum, maize, millet, pulses, groundnuts (peanuts), beans, cowpeas, sunflower seed; livestock
Currency: 1 pula (P) = 100 thebe

Brazil

Geography

Location: Eastern South America, bordering the Atlantic Ocean

Area: 3,286,470 sq. mi. (8,511,965 sq. km.); slightly smaller than the U.S.
Climate: mostly tropical, but temperate in south
Terrain: mostly flat to rolling lowlands in north; some plains, hills, mountains, and narrow coastal belt
Elevation: lowest point: Atlantic Ocean 0 ft. (0 m.); highest point: Pico da Neblina 9,888 ft. (3,014 m.)
Natural resources: bauxite, gold, iron ore, manganese, nickel, phosphates, platinum, tin, uranium, petroleum, hydropower, timber

People
Population: 171,853,126 (July 1999 est.)
Population growth rate: 1.16%
Infant mortality rate: 35.37 deaths/ 1,000 live births
Life expectancy at birth: total population: 64.06 years; male: 59.35 years; female: 69.01 years
Major ethnic groups: white (includes Portuguese, German, Italian, Spanish, Polish) 55%, mixed white and African 38%, African 6%
Major religions: Roman Catholic (nominal) 70%
Major languages: Portuguese (official), Spanish, English, French

Government
Official name: Federative Republic of Brazil
Government type: federal republic
National capital: Brasilia
Independence: September 7, 1822 (from Portugal)
Legal system: based on Roman codes

Economy
Industries: textiles, shoes, chemicals, cement, lumber, iron ore, tin, steel, aircraft, motor vehicles and parts, other machinery and equipment
Agricultural products: coffee, soybeans, wheat, rice, corn, sugarcane, cocoa, citrus; beef
Currency: 1 real (R$) = 100 centavos

Brunei

Geography
Location: Southeastern Asia, bordering the South China Sea and Malaysia
Area: 2,228 sq. mi. (5,770 sq. km.); slightly larger than Delaware
Climate: tropical; hot, humid, rainy
Terrain: flat coastal plain rises to mountains in east; hilly lowland in west
Elevation: lowest point: South China Sea 0 ft. (0 m.); highest point: Bukit Pagon 6,069 ft. (1,850 m.)
Natural resources: petroleum, natural gas, timber

People
Population: 322,982 (July 1999 est.)
Population growth rate: 2.38%
Infant mortality rate: 22.83 deaths/ 1,000 live births
Life expectancy at birth: total population: 71.84 years; male: 70.35 years; female: 73.42 years
Major ethnic groups: Malay 64%, Chinese 20%, other 16%
Major religions: Muslim (official) 63%, Buddhism 14%, Christian 8%, indigenous beliefs and other 15%
Major languages: Malay (official), English, Chinese

Government
Official name: Negara Brunei Darussalam
Government type: constitutional sultanate
National capital: Bandar Seri Begawan
Independence: January 1, 1984 (from U.K.)
Legal system: based on Islamic law

Economy
Industries: petroleum, petroleum refining, liquefied natural gas, construction
Agricultural products: rice, cassava (tapioca), bananas; water buffalo, pigs
Currency: 1 Bruneian dollar (B$) = 100 cents

Bulgaria

Geography
Location: Southeastern Europe, bordering the Black Sea, between Romania and Turkey

Nations (cont.)

Area: 42,822 sq. mi. (110,910 sq. km.); slightly larger than Tennessee
Climate: temperate; cold, damp winters; hot, dry summers
Terrain: mostly mountains with lowlands in north and southeast
Elevation: lowest point: Black Sea 0 ft. (0 m.); highest point: Musala 9,596 ft. (2,925 m.)
Natural resources: bauxite, copper, lead, zinc, coal, timber, arable land

People

Population: 8,194,772 (July 1999 est.)
Population growth rate: –0.52%
Infant mortality rate: 12.37 deaths/1,000 live births
Life expectancy at birth: total population: 72.27 years; male: 68.72 years; female: 76.03 years
Major ethnic groups: Bulgarian 85.3%, Turk 8.5%, Gypsy 2.6%, Macedonian 2.5%
Major religions: Bulgarian Orthodox 85%, Muslim 13%
Major languages: Bulgarian, secondary languages closely correspond to ethnic breakdown

Government

Official name: Republic of Bulgaria
Government type: emerging democracy
National capital: Sofia
Independence: September 22, 1908 (from Ottoman Empire)
Legal system: based on civil law system with Soviet law influence; accepts compulsory IJC jurisdiction

Economy

Industries: machine building and metal working, food processing, chemicals, textiles, construction materials, ferrous and nonferrous metals
Agricultural products: grain, oilseed, vegetables, fruits, tobacco; livestock
Currency: 1 lev (Lv) = 100 stotinki

Burkina Faso

Geography

Location: Western Africa, north of Ghana

Area: 105,869 sq. mi. (274,200 sq. km.); slightly larger than Colorado
Climate: tropical; warm, dry winters; hot, wet summers
Terrain: mostly flat to dissected, undulating plains; hills in west and southeast
Elevation: lowest point: Black Volta River 656 ft. (200 m.); highest point: Tena Kourou 2,457 ft. (749 m.)
Natural resources: manganese, limestone, marble; small deposits of gold, antimony, copper, nickel, bauxite, lead, phosphates, zinc, silver

People

Population: 11,575,898 (July 1999 est.)
Population growth rate: 2.7%
Infant mortality rate: 107.19 deaths/1,000 live births
Life expectancy at birth: total population: 45.89 years; male: 44.97 years; female: 46.84 years
Major ethnic groups: Mossi about 24%, Gurunsi, Senufo, Lobi, Bobo, Mande, Fulani
Major religions: indigenous beliefs 40%, Muslim 50%, Christian 10%
Major languages: French (official), tribal languages belonging to Sudanic family, spoken by 90% of the population

Government

Official name: Burkina Faso
Government type: parliamentary
National capital: Ouagadougou
Independence: August 5, 1960 (from France)
Legal system: based on French civil law system and customary law

Economy

Industries: cotton lint, beverages, agricultural processing, soap, cigarettes, textiles, gold
Agricultural products: peanuts, shea nuts, sesame, cotton, sorghum, millet, corn, rice; livestock
Currency: 1 Communauté Financière Africaine franc (CFAF) = 100 centimes

Burma

Geography

Location: Southeastern Asia, bordering the Andaman Sea and the Bay of Bengal, between Bangladesh and Thailand

Area: 261,969 sq. mi. (678,500 sq. km.); slightly smaller than Texas

Climate: tropical monsoon; cloudy, rainy, hot, humid summers (southwest monsoon, June to September); less cloudy, scant rainfall, mild temperatures, lower humidity during winter (northeast monsoon, December to April)

Terrain: central lowlands ringed by steep, rugged highlands

Elevation: lowest point: Andaman Sea 0 ft. (0 m.); highest point: Hkakabo Razi 19,294 ft. (5,881 m.)

Natural resources: petroleum, timber, tin, antimony, zinc, copper, tungsten, lead, coal, some marble, limestone, precious stones, natural gas

People

Population: 48,081,302 (July 1999 est.)

Population growth rate: 1.61%

Infant mortality rate: 76.25 deaths/ 1,000 live births

Life expectancy at birth: total population: 54.74 years; male: 53.24 years; female: 56.32 years

Major ethnic groups: Burman 68%, Shan 9%, Karen 7%, Rakhine 4%, Chinese 3%, Mon 2%

Major religions: Buddhist 89%, Christian 4%

Major languages: Burmese, minority ethnic groups have their own languages

Government

Official name: Union of Burma (regime refers to Burma as Myanmar)

Government type: military regime

National capital: Rangoon (regime refers to the capital as Yangon)

Independence: January 4, 1948 (from U.K.)

Legal system: NA, does not accept compulsory IJC jurisdiction

Economy

Industries: agricultural processing; textiles and footwear; wood and wood products; petroleum refining; copper, tin, tungsten, iron; construction materials; pharmaceuticals; fertilizer

Agricultural products: paddy rice, corn, oilseed, sugarcane, pulses; hardwood

Currency: 1 kyat (K) = 100 pyas

Burundi

Geography

Location: Central Africa, east of Zaire

Area: 10,745 sq. mi. (27,830 sq. km.); slightly larger than Maryland

Climate: temperate; warm; occasional frost in uplands; dry season from June to September

Terrain: hilly and mountainous, dropping to a plateau in east, some plains

Elevation: lowest point: Lake Tanganyika 2,533 ft. (772 m.) highest point: Mount Heha 9,055 ft. (2,760 m.)

Natural resources: nickel, uranium, rare earth oxides, peat, cobalt, copper, platinum (not yet exploited), vanadium

People

Population: 5,735,937 (July 1999 est.)

Population growth rate: 3.54%

Infant mortality rate: 99.36 deaths/ 1,000 live births

Life expectancy at birth: total population: 45.44 years; male: 43.54 years; female: 47.41 years

Major ethnic groups: Africans: Hutu (Bantu) 85%, Tutsi (Hamitic) 14%, Twa (Pygmy)

Major religions: Christian 67% (Roman Catholic 62%, Protestant 5%), indigenous beliefs 32%

Major languages: Kirundi (official), French (official), Swahili (along Lake Tanganyika and in the Bujumbura area)

Government

Official name: Republic of Burundi

Government type: republic

National capital: Bujumbura

Nations *(cont.)*

Independence: July 1, 1962 (from UN trusteeship under Belgian administration)

Legal system: based on German and Belgian civil codes and customary law

Economy
Industries: light consumer goods such as blankets, shoes, soap; assembly of imported components; public works construction; food processing

Agricultural products: coffee, cotton, tea, corn, sorghum, sweet potatoes, bananas, manioc; meat, milk, hides

Currency: 1 Burundi franc (FBu) = 100 centimes

Cambodia

Geography
Location: Southeastern Asia, bordering the Gulf of Thailand, between Thailand and Vietnam

Area: 69,900 sq. mi. (181,040 sq. km.); slightly smaller than Oklahoma

Climate: tropical; rainy, monsoon season (May to November); dry season (December to April); little seasonal temperature variation

Terrain: mostly low, flat plains; mountains in southwest and north

Elevation: lowest point: Gulf of Thailand 0 ft. (0 m.); highest point: Phnum Aoral 5938 ft. (1,810 m.)

Natural resources: timber, gemstones, some iron ore, manganese, phosphates, hydropower potential

People
Population: 11,626,520 (July 1999 est.)

Population growth rate: 2.49%

Infant mortality rate: 105.06 deaths/ 1,000 live births

Life expectancy at birth: total population: 48.24 years; male: 46.81 years; female: 49.75 years

Major ethnic groups: Khmer 90%, Vietnamese 5%

Major religions: Theravada Buddhism 95%

Major languages: Khmer (official), French

Government
Official name: Kingdom of Cambodia

Government type: multiparty liberal democracy under a constitutional monarchy established in September 1993

National capital: Phnom Penh

Independence: November 9, 1949 (from France)

Legal system: currently being defined

Economy
Industries: rice milling, fishing, wood and wood products, rubber, cement, gem mining

Agricultural products: rice, rubber, corn, vegetables

Currency: 1 new riel (CR) = 100 sen

Cameroon

Geography
Location: Western Africa, bordering the North Atlantic Ocean, between Equatorial Guinea and Nigeria

Area: 183,567 sq. mi. (475,440 sq. km.); slightly larger than California

Climate: varies with terrain, from tropical along coast to semiarid and hot in north

Terrain: diverse, with coastal plain in southwest, dissected plateau in center, mountains in west, plains in north

Elevation: lowest point: Atlantic Ocean 0 ft. (0 m.); highest point: Fako 13,434 ft. (4,095 m.)

Natural resources: petroleum, bauxite, iron ore, timber, hydropower potential

People
Population: 15,456,092 (July 1992 est.)

Population growth rate: 2.79%

Infant mortality rate: 75.69 deaths/ 1,000 live births

Life expectancy at birth: total population: 51.32 years; male: 49.75 years; female: 52.94 years

Major ethnic groups: Cameroon Highlanders 31%, Equatorial Bantu 19%, Kirdi 11%, Fulani 10%, Northwestern Bantu 8%, Eastern Nigritic 7%, other African 13%

Major religions: indigenous beliefs
51%, Christian 33%, Muslim 16%

Major languages: 24 major African language groups, English (official),
French (official)

Government

Official name: Republic of Cameroon

Government type: unitary republic;
multiparty presidential regime
(opposition parties legalized 1990)

National capital: Yaounde

Independence: January 1, 1960 (from
UN trusteeship under French
administration)

Legal system: based on French civil law
system, with common law influence

Economy

Industries: petroleum production and
refining, food processing, light consumer goods, textiles, lumber

Agricultural products: coffee, cocoa, cotton, rubber, bananas, oilseed, grains,
root starches; livestock; timber

Currency: 1 Communauté Financière
Africaine franc (CFAF) = 100 centimes

Canada

Geography

Location: Northern North America,
bordering the North Atlantic Ocean
and North Pacific Ocean, north of
the conterminous U.S.

Area: 3,851,788 sq. mi. (9,976,140 sq.
km.); slightly larger than U.S.

Climate: varies from temperate in
south to subarctic and arctic in north

Terrain: mostly plains with mountains
in west and lowlands in southeast

Elevation: lowest point: Atlantic Ocean
0 ft. (0 m.); highest point: Mount
Logan 19,520 ft. (5,950 m.)

Natural resources: nickel, zinc, copper,
gold, lead, molybdenum, potash, silver, fish, timber, wildlife, coal,
petroleum, natural gas

People

Population: 31,006,347 (July 1999 est.)

Population growth rate: 1.06%

Infant mortality rate: 5.47 deaths/1,000
live births (1996 est.)

Life expectancy at birth: total population: 79.37 years; male: 76.12 years;
female: 82.79 years

Major ethnic groups: British Isles origin 40%, French origin 27%, other
European 20%, indigenous Indian
and Eskimo 1.5%, other (mostly
Asian) 11.5%

Major religions: Roman Catholic 45%,
United Church 12%, Anglican 8%,
other 35%

Major languages: English (official),
French (official)

Government

Official name: Canada

Government type: confederation with
parliamentary democracy

National capital: Ottawa

Independence: July 1, 1867 (from U.K.)

Legal system: based on English common law, except in Quebec, where
civil law system based on French
law prevails

Economy

Industries: processed and unprocessed
minerals, food products, wood and
paper products, transportation
equipment, chemicals, fish products, petroleum and natural gas

Agricultural products: wheat, barley,
oilseed, tobacco, fruits, vegetables;
dairy products; forest products;
commercial fisheries provide annual
catch of 1.5 million metric tons, of
which 75% is exported

Currency: 1 Canadian dollar (Can$) =
100 cents

Cape Verde

Geography

Location: Western Africa, group of
Islands in the North Atlantic Ocean,
west of Senegal

Area: 1,556 sq. mi. (4,030 sq. km.);
slightly larger than Rhode Island

Climate: temperate; warm, dry summer; precipitation meager and very
erratic

Terrain: steep, rugged, rocky, volcanic

Elevation: lowest point: Atlantic Ocean
0 ft. (0 m.); highest point: Mt. Fogo
9,281 ft. (2,829 m.)

Nations *(cont.)*

Natural resources: salt, basalt rock, pozzolana, limestone, kaolin, fish

People

Population: 405,748 (July 1999 est.)

Population growth rate: 1.44%

Infant mortality rate: 45.5 deaths/1,000 live births

Life expectancy at birth: total population: 70.96 years; male: 67.66 years; female: 74.36 years

Major ethnic groups: Creole (mulatto) 71%, African 28%, European 1%

Major religions: Roman Catholicism fused with indigenous beliefs

Major languages: Portuguese, Crioulo, a blend of Portuguese and West African words

Government

Official name: Republic of Cape Verde

Government type: republic

National capital: Praia

Independence: July 5, 1975 (from Portugal)

Legal system: derived from the legal system of Portugal

Economy

Industries: fish processing, salt mining, garments, ship repair, food and beverages

Agricultural products: bananas, corn, beans, sweet potatoes, sugarcane, coffee, peanuts; fish

Currency: 1 Cape Verdean escudo (CVEsc) = 100 centavos

Cayman Islands

Geography

Location: Caribbean, island group in Caribbean Sea, nearly one-half of the way from Cuba to Honduras

Area: 100 sq. mi. (260 sq. km.) 1.5 times the size of Washington, D.C.

Climate: tropical marine; warm, rainy summers (May to October) and cool, relatively dry winters (November to April)

Terrain: low-lying limestone base surrounded by coral reefs

Elevation: lowest point: Caribbean Sea

0 ft. (0 m.); highest point: The Bluff 141 ft. (43 m.)

Natural resources: fish, climate and beaches that foster tourism

People

Population: 39,335 (July 1999 est.)

Population growth rate: 4.19%

Infant mortality rate: 8.4 deaths/1,000 live births

Life expectancy at birth: total population: 77.1 years; male: 75.37 years; female: 78.81 years

Major ethnic groups: mixed 40%, white 20%, black 20%, expatriates of various ethnic groups 20%

Major religions: United Church, Anglican, Baptist, Roman Catholic, Church of God, other Protestant denominations

Major languages: English

Government

Official name: Cayman Islands

Government type: dependent territory of the U.K.

National capital: George Town

Independence: none (dependent territory of the U.K.)

Legal system: British common law and local statutes

Economy

Industries: tourism, banking, insurance and finance, construction, construction materials, furniture

Agricultural products: vegetables, fruit; livestock; turtle farming

Currency: 1 Caymanian dollar (CI$) = 100 cents

Central African Republic

Geography

Location: Central Africa, north of Zaire

Area: 240,533 sq. mi. (622,980 sq. km.); slightly smaller than Texas

Climate: tropical; hot, dry winters; mild to hot, wet summers

Terrain: vast, flat to rolling, monotonous plateau; scattered hills in northeast and southwest

Elevation: lowest point: Oubangui River 1099 ft. (335 m.); highest

point: Mount Gaou 4659 ft.
(1,420 m.)
Natural resources: diamonds, uranium,
timber, gold, oil

People
Population: 3,444,951 (July 1999 est.)
Population growth rate: 2.04%
Infant mortality rate: 103.42 deaths/
1,000 live births
Life expectancy at birth: total popula-
tion: 47.19 years; male: 45.35 years;
female: 49.09 years
Major ethnic groups: Baya 34%, Banda
27%, Sara 10%, Mandjia 21%,
Mboum 4%, M'Baka 4%
Major religions: indigenous beliefs
24%, Protestant 25%, Roman
Catholic 25%, Muslim 15%
Major languages: French (official),
Sangho (lingua franca and national
language), Arabic, Hunsa, Swahili

Government
Official name: Central African Republic
Government type: republic
National capital: Bangui
Independence: August 13, 1960 (from
France)
Legal system: based on French law

Economy
Industries: diamond mining, sawmills,
breweries, textiles, footwear, assembly of bicycles and motorcycles
Agricultural products: cotton, coffee,
tobacco, manioc (tapioca), yams,
millet, corn, bananas; timber
Currency: 1 Communauté Financière
Africaine franc (CFAF) = 100 centimes

Chad
Geography
Location: Central Africa, south of
Libya
Area: 495,752 sq. mi. (1,284,000 sq.
km.); slightly more than three times
the size of California
Climate: tropical in south, desert in
north
Terrain: broad, arid plains in center,
desert in north, mountains in north-
west, lowlands in south

Elevation: lowest point: Djourab
Depression 574 ft. (175 m.); highest
point: Emi Koussi 11,204 ft.
(3,415 m.)
Natural resources: petroleum (unexploited but exploration under way),
uranium, natron, kaolin, fish (Lake
Chad)

People
Population: 7,557,436 (July 1999
est.)
Population growth rate: 2.65%
Infant mortality rate: 115.27 deaths/
1,000 live births
Life expectancy at birth: total popula-
tion: 48.56 years; male: 46.13 years;
female: 51.09 years
Major ethnic groups: Muslims (Arabs,
Toubou, Hadjerai, Fulbe, Kotoko,
Kanembou, Baguirmi, Boulala,
Zaghawa, and Maba); South: non-
Muslims (Sara, Ngambaye, Mbaye,
Goulaye, Moundang, Moussei,
Massa)
Major religions: Muslim 50%,
Christian 25%, indigenous beliefs
(mostly animism) 25%
Major languages: French (official),
Arabic (official), Sara and Sango (in
south), more than 100 different lan-
guages and dialects

Government
Official name: Republic of Chad
Government type: republic
National capital: N'Djamena
Independence: August 11, 1960 (from
France)
Legal system: based on French civil law
system and Chadian customary law,
does not accept compulsory IJC
jurisdiction

Economy
Industries: cotton textiles, meat packing, beer brewing, natron (sodium
carbonate), soap, cigarettes, construction materials
Agricultural products: cotton, sorghum,
millet, peanuts, rice, potatoes, manioc (tapioca); cattle, sheep, goats,
camels

Nations (cont.)

Currency: 1 Communauté Financière
Africaine franc (CFAF) = 100 centimes

Chile

Geography
Location: Southern South America,
bordering the South Atlantic Ocean
and South Pacific Ocean, between
Argentina and Peru
Area: 292,258 sq. mi. (756,950 sq.
km.) slightly smaller than twice the
size of Montana
Climate: temperate; desert in north;
cool and damp in south
Terrain: low coastal mountains; fertile
central valley; rugged Andes in east
Elevation: lowest point: Pacific Ocean
0 ft. (0 m.); highest point: Cerro
Aconcagua 22,841 ft. (6,962 m.)
Natural resources: copper, timber, iron
ore, nitrates, precious metals,
molybdenum

People
Population: 14,973,843 (July 1999 est.)
Population growth rate: 1.23%
Infant mortality rate: 10.02 deaths/
1,000 live births
Life expectancy at birth: total popula-
tion: 75.46 years; male: 72.33 years;
female: 78.75 years
Major ethnic groups: European and
European-Indian 95%, Indian 3%
Major religions: Roman Catholic 89%,
Protestant 11%
Major languages: Spanish

Government
Official name: Republic of Chile
Government type: republic
National capital: Santiago
Independence: September 18, 1810
(from Spain)
Legal system: based on Code of 1857
derived from Spanish law and subsequent codes influenced by French
and Austrian law; judicial review of
legislative acts in the Supreme Court

Economy
Industries: copper, other minerals, foodstuffs, fish processing, iron and steel,
wood and wood products, transport
equipment, cement, textiles
Agricultural products: wheat, corn,
grapes, beans, sugar beets, potatoes,
fruit; beef, poultry, wool; timber; fish
Currency: 1 Chilean peso (Ch$) = 100
centavos

China

Geography
Location: Eastern Asia, bordering the
East China Sea, Korea Bay, Yellow
Sea, and South China Sea, between
North Korea and Vietnam
Area: 3,705,386 sq. mi. (9,596,960
sq. km.); slightly larger than the
U.S.
Climate: extremely diverse; tropical in
south to subarctic in north
Terrain: mostly mountains, high
plateaus, deserts in west; plains,
deltas, and hills in east
Elevation: lowest point: Turpan Pendi
−505 ft. (−154 m.); highest point:
Mount Everest 29,028 ft. (8,848 m.)
Natural resources: coal, iron ore, petroleum, mercury, tin, tungsten, antimony, manganese, molybdenum,
vanadium, magnetite, aluminum,
lead, zinc, uranium, hydropower
potential

People
Population: 1,246,871,951 (July 1999
est.)
Population growth rate: 0.77%
Infant mortality rate: 43.31 deaths/
1,000 live births
Life expectancy at birth: total popula-
tion: 69.92 years; male: 68.57 years;
female: 71.48 years
Major ethnic groups: Han Chinese
91.9%, Zhuang, Uygur, Hui, Yi,
Tibetan, Miao, Manchu, Mongol,
Buyi, Korean, and other nationali-
ties 8.1%
Major religions: Daoism (Taoism),
Buddhism, Muslim 2%–3%
Major languages: Standard Chinese or
Mandarin (Putonghua, based on the
Beijing dialect), Yue (Cantonese),
Wu (Shanghaiese), Minbei (Fu-

zhou), Minnan (Hokkien-Taiwanese), Xiang, Gan, Hakka dialects

Government

Official name: People's Republic of China

Government type: Communist state

National capital: Beijing

Independence: 221 BC (unification under the Qin or Ch'in Dynasty 221 BC; Qing or Ch'ing Dynasty replaced by the Republic on February 12, 1912; People's Republic established October 1, 1949)

Legal system: a complex amalgam of custom and statute, largely criminal law; rudimentary civil code in effect since 1 January 1987; continuing efforts are being made to improve civil, administrative, criminal, and commercial law

Economy

Industries: iron and steel, coal, machine building, armaments, textiles and apparel, petroleum, cement, chemical fertilizers, consumer durables, food processing, autos, consumer electronics, telecommunications

Agricultural products: rice, potatoes, sorghum, peanuts, tea, millet, barley, cotton, other fibers, oilseed; pork and other livestock products; fish

Currency: 1 yuan (•) = 10 jiao

Christmas Island

Geography

Location: Southeastern Asia, island in the Indian Ocean, south of Indonesia

Area: 52 sq. mi. (135 sq. km.); about 0.7 times the size of Washington, D.C.

Climate: tropical; heat and humidity moderated by trade winds

Terrain: steep cliffs along coast rise abruptly to central plateau

Elevation: extremes: lowest point: Indian Ocean 0 ft. (0 m.); highest point: Murray Hill 1,184 ft. (361 m.)

Natural resources: phosphate

People

Population: 2,373 (July 1999 est.)

Population growth rate: 7.77%

Major ethnic groups: Chinese 61%, Malay 25%, European 11%

Major religions: Buddhist 55%, Christian 15%, Muslim 10%, other 20%

Major languages: English

Government

Official name: Territory of Christmas Island

National capital: The Settlement

Independence: none (territory of Australia)

Legal system: under the authority of the governor general of Australia and Australian law

Economy

Industries: tourism, phosphate extraction (near depletion)

Currency: 1 Australian dollar ($A) = 100 cents

Colombia

Geography

Location: Northern South America, bordering the Caribbean Sea, between Panama and Venezuela, and bordering the North Pacific Ocean, between Ecuador and Panama

Area: 439,733 sq. mi. (1,138,910 sq. km.); slightly less than three times the size of Montana

Climate: tropical along coast and eastern plains; cooler in highlands

Terrain: flat coastal lowlands, central highlands, high Andes Mountains, eastern lowland plains

Elevation: lowest point: Pacific Ocean 0 ft. (0 m.); highest point: Nevado del Huila 18,865 ft. (5,750 m.)

Natural resources: petroleum, natural gas, coal, iron ore, nickel, gold, copper, emeralds

People

Population: 39,309,422 (July 1999 est.)

Population growth rate: 1.85%

Infant mortality rate: 24.3 deaths/ 1,000 live births

Life expectancy at birth: total population: 70.48 years; male: 66.54 years; female: 74.54 years

Nations *(cont.)*

Major ethnic groups: mestizo 58%, white 20%, mulatto 14%, black 4%, mixed black-Indian 3%, Indian 1%
Major religions: Roman Catholic 95%
Major languages: Spanish

Government
Official name: Republic of Colombia
Government type: republic; executive branch dominates government structure
National capital: Bogota
Independence: July 20, 1810 (from Spain)
Legal system: based on Spanish law; a new criminal code modeled after U.S. procedures was enacted in 1992–93; judicial review of executive and legislative acts

Economy
Industries: textiles, food processing, oil, clothing and footwear, beverages, chemicals, cement; gold, coal, emeralds
Agricultural products: coffee, cut flowers, bananas, rice, tobacco, corn, sugarcane, cocoa beans, oilseed, vegetables; forest products; shrimp farming
Currency: 1 Colombian peso (Col$) = 100 centavos

Comoros

Geography
Location: Southern Africa, group of islands in the Mozambique Channel, about two-thirds of the way between northern Madagascar and northern Mozambique
Area: 838 sq. mi. (2,170 sq. km.); slightly more than 12 times the size of Washington, D.C.
Climate: tropical marine; rainy season (November to May)
Terrain: volcanic islands, interiors vary from steep mountains to low hills
Elevation: lowest point: Indian Ocean 0 ft. (0 m.); highest point: Mount Kartala 7,743 ft. (2,360 m.)
Natural resources: negligible

People
Population: 562,723 (July 1999 est.)
Population growth rate: 3.11%
Infant mortality rate: 81.63 deaths/1,000 live births
Life expectancy at birth: total population: 60.85 years; male: 58.39 years; female: 63.38 years
Major ethnic groups: Antalote, Cafre, Makoa, Oimatsaha, Sakalava
Major religions: Sunni Muslim 86%, Roman Catholic 14%
Major languages: Arabic (official), French (official), Comoran (a blend of Swahili and Arabic)

Government
Official name: Federal Islamic Republic of the Comoros
Government type: independent republic
National capital: Moroni
Independence: July 6, 1975 (from France)
Legal system: French and Muslim law in a new consolidated code

Economy
Industries: tourism, perfume distillation, textiles, furniture, jewelry, construction materials, soft drinks
Agricultural products: vanilla, cloves, perfume essences, copra, coconuts, bananas, cassava (tapioca)
Currency: 1 Comoran franc (CF) = 100 centimes

Congo, Democratic Republic of the

Geography
Location: Central Africa, northeast of Angola
Area: 905,568 sq. mi. (2,345,410 sq. km.); slightly less than one-fourth the size of U.S.
Climate: tropical; hot and humid in equatorial river basin; cooler and drier in southern highlands; cooler and wetter in eastern highlands; north of Equator—wet season April to October, dry season December to February; south of Equator—wet

season November to March, dry season April to October

Terrain: vast central basin is a low-lying plateau; mountains in east

Elevation: extremes: lowest point: Atlantic Ocean 0 m. (0 ft.); highest point: Margherita Peak (Mount Stanley) 5,110 m. (16,765 ft.)

Natural resources: cobalt, copper, cadmium, petroleum, industrial and gem diamonds, gold, silver, zinc, manganese, tin, germanium, uranium, radium, bauxite, iron ore, coal, hydropower potential, timber

People

Population: 50,481,305 (July 1999 est.)

Population growth rate: 2.96%

Infant mortality rate: 99.45 deaths/1,000 live births

Life expectancy at birth: total population: 49.44 years; male: 47.28 years; female: 51.67 years

Major ethnic groups: over 200 African ethnic groups of which the majority are Bantu; the four largest tribes— Mongo, Luba, Kongo (all Bantu), and the Mangbetu-Azande (Hamitic) make up about 45% of the population

Major religions: Roman Catholic 50%, Protestant 20%, Kimbanguist 10%, Muslim 10%, other syncretic sects and traditional beliefs 10%

Major languages: French (official), Lingala (a lingua franca trade language); Kingwana (a dialect of Kiswahili or Swahili), Kikongo, Tshiluba

Government

Official name: Democratic Republic of the Congo (formerly Zaire)

Government type: dictatorship; presumably undergoing a transition to representative government

Independence: June 30, 1960 (from Belgium)

Legal system: based on Belgian civil law system and tribal law, has not accepted compulsory IJC jurisdiction

Economy

Industries: mining, mineral processing, consumer products (including textiles, footwear, cigarettes, processed foods and beverages), cement, diamonds

Agricultural products: coffee, sugar, palm oil, rubber, tea, quinine, cassava (tapioca), palm oil, bananas, root crops, corn, fruits; wood products

Currency: 1 zaire (Z) = 100 makuta

Congo, Republic of the

Geography

Location: Western Africa, bordering the South Atlantic Ocean, between Angola and Gabon

Area: 132,046 sq. mi. (342,000 sq. km.); slightly smaller than Montana

Climate: tropical; rainy season (March to June); dry season (June to October); constantly high temperatures and humidity

Terrain: coastal plain, southern basin, central plateau, northern basin

Elevation: lowest point: Atlantic Ocean 0 ft. (0 m.); highest point: Mount Berongou 2,963 ft. (903 m.)

Natural resources: petroleum, timber, potash, lead, zinc, uranium, copper, phosphates, natural gas

People

Population: 2,716,814 (July 1999 est.)

Population growth rate: 2.16%

Infant mortality rate: 100.58 deaths/1,000 live births

Life expectancy at birth: total population: 47.14 years; male: 45.42 years; female: 48.92 years

Major ethnic groups: Kongo 48%, Sangha 20%, M'Bochi 12%, Teke 17%, Europeans

Major religions: Christian 50%, Animist 48%, Muslim 2%

Major languages: French (official), Lingala and Monokutuba (lingua franca trade languages)

Government

Country name: Republic of the Congo

Government type: republic

National capital: Brazzaville

Independence: August 15, 1960 (from France)

Legal system: based on French civil law system and customary law

Nations (cont.)

Economy

Industries: petroleum extraction, cement kilning, lumbering, brewing, sugar milling, palm oil, soap, cigarette making

Agricultural products: cassava (tapioca) accounts for 90% of food output, sugar, rice, corn, peanuts, vegetables, coffee, cocoa; forest products

Currency: 1 Communauté Financière Africaine franc (CFAF) = 100 centimes

Cook Islands

Geography

Location: Oceania, group of islands in the South Pacific Ocean, about one-half of the way from Hawaii to New Zealand

Area: 93 sq. mi. (240 sq. km.); slightly more than one times the size of Washington, D.C.

Climate: tropical; moderated by trade winds

Terrain: low coral atolls in north; volcanic, hilly islands in south

Elevation: lowest point: Pacific Ocean 0 ft. (0 m.); highest point: Te Manga 2,139 ft. (652 m.)

Natural resources: negligible

People

Population: 20,200 (July 1999 est.)

Population growth rate: 1.04%

Infant mortality rate: 24.7 deaths/ 1,000 live births

Life expectancy at birth: total population: 71.14 years; male: 69.2 years; female: 73.1 years

Major ethnic groups: Polynesian (full blood) 81.3%, Polynesian and European 7.7%, Polynesian and non-European 7.7%, European 2.4%

Major religions: Christianity

Major languages: English (official), Maori

Government

Official name: Cook Islands

Government type: self-governing parliamentary government in free association with New Zealand; Cook Islands is fully responsible for internal affairs; New Zealand retains responsibility for external affairs, in consultation with the Cook Islands

National capital: Avarua

Independence: none (became self-governing in free association with New Zealand on August 4, 1965 and has the right at any time to move to full independence by unilateral action)

Economy

Industries: fruit processing, tourism

Agricultural products: copra, citrus, pineapples, tomatoes, bananas, yams, taro

Currency: 1 New Zealand dollar (NZ$) = 100 cents

Costa Rica

Geography

Location: Central America, bordering both the Caribbean Sea and the North Pacific Ocean, between Nicaragua and Panama

Area: 19,730 sq. mi. (51,100 sq. km.); slightly smaller than West Virginia

Climate: tropical; dry season (December to April); rainy season (May to November)

Terrain: coastal plains separated by rugged mountains

Elevation: lowest point: Pacific Ocean 0 ft. (0 m.); highest point: Cerro Chirripo 12,500 ft. (3,810 m.)

Natural resources: hydropower potential

People

Population: 3,674,490 (July 1999 est.)

Population growth rate: 1.89%

Infant mortality rate: 12.89 deaths/ 1,000 live births

Life expectancy at birth: total population: 76.04 years; male: 73.6 years; female: 78.61 years

Major ethnic groups: white (including mestizo) 96%, black 2%

Major religions: Roman Catholic 95%

Major languages: Spanish (official), English spoken around Puerto Limon

Government

Official name: Republic of Costa Rica

Government type: democratic republic

National capital: San Jose

Independence: September 15, 1821 (from Spain)

Legal system: based on Spanish civil law system; judicial review of legislative acts in the Supreme Court

Economy

Industries: food processing, textiles and clothing, construction materials, fertilizer, plastic products

Agricultural products: coffee, bananas, sugar, corn, rice, beans, potatoes; beef; timber (depletion of forest resources has resulted in declining timber output)

Currency: 1 Costa Rican colon (C) = 100 centimos

Côte d'Ivoire

Geography

Location: Western Africa, bordering the North Atlantic Ocean, between Ghana and Liberia

Area: 124,502 sq. mi. (322,460 sq. km.); slightly larger than New Mexico

Climate: tropical along coast, semiarid in far north; three seasons—warm and dry (November to March), hot and dry (March to May), hot and wet (June to October)

Terrain: mostly flat to undulating plains; mountains in northwest

Elevation: lowest point: Atlantic Ocean 0 ft. (0 m.); highest point: Mont Nimba 5,748 ft. (1,752 m.)

Natural resources: petroleum, diamonds, manganese, iron ore, cobalt, bauxite, copper

People

Population: 15,818,068 (July 1999 est.)

Population growth rate: 2.35%

Infant mortality rate: 94.17 deaths/1,000 live births

Life expectancy at birth: total population: 46.05 years; male: 44.48 years; female: 47.67 years

Major ethnic groups: Baoule 23%, Bete 18%, Senoufou 15%, Malinke 11%, Agni,

Major religions: indigenous 25%, Muslim 60%, Christian 12%

Major languages: French (official), 60 native dialects with Dioula the most widely spoken

Government

Official name: Republic of Côte d'Ivoire

Government type: republic; multiparty presidential regime established 1960

National capital: Yamoussoukro

Independence: August 7, 1960 (from France)

Legal system: based on French civil law system and customary law; judicial review in the Constitutional Chamber of the Supreme Court; has not accepted compulsory IJC jurisdiction

Economy

Industries: foodstuffs, beverages; wood products, oil refining, automobile assembly, textiles, fertilizer, construction materials, electricity

Agricultural products: coffee, cocoa beans, bananas, palm kernels, corn, rice, manioc, sweet potatoes, sugar; cotton, rubber; timber

Currency: 1 Communauté Financière Africaine franc (CFAF) = 100 centimes

Croatia

Geography

Location: Southeastern Europe, bordering the Adriatic Sea, between Bosnia and Herzegovina and Slovenia

Area: 21,829 sq. mi. (56,538 sq. km.); slightly smaller than West Virginia

Climate: Mediterranean and continental; continental climate predominant with hot summers and cold winters; mild winters, dry summers along coast

Terrain: geographically diverse; flat plains along Hungarian border, low mountains and highlands near Adriatic coast, coastline, and islands

Nations *(cont.)*

Elevation: lowest point: Adriatic Sea 0 ft. (0 m.); highest point: Dinara 6,004 ft. (1,830 m.)

Natural resources: oil, some coal, bauxite, low-grade iron ore, calcium, natural asphalt, silica, mica, clays, salt

People

Population: 4,676,865 (July 1999 est.)

Population growth rate: 0.1%

Infant mortality rate: 7.84 deaths/1,000 live births

Life expectancy at birth: total population: 74 years; male: 70.69 years; female: 77.52 years

Major ethnic groups: Croat 78%, Serb 12%

Major religions: Catholic 76.5%, Orthodox 11.1%

Major languages: Serbo-Croatian 96%

Government

Official name: Republic of Croatia

Government type: parliamentary democracy

National capital: Zagreb

Independence: June 25, 1991 (from Yugoslavia)

Legal system: based on civil law system

Economy

Industries: chemicals and plastics, machine tools, fabricated metal, electronics, pig iron and rolled steel products, aluminum, paper, wood products, construction materials, textiles, shipbuilding, petroleum and petroleum refining, food and beverages

Agricultural products: wheat, corn, sugar beets, sunflower seed, alfalfa, clover, olives, citrus, grapes, vegetables; livestock breeding, dairy farming

Currency: 1 Croatian kuna (HRK) = 100 paras

Cuba

Geography

Location: Caribbean, island between the Caribbean Sea and the North Atlantic Ocean, south of Florida

Area: 42,803 sq. mi. (110,860 sq. km.); slightly smaller than Pennsylvania

Climate: tropical; moderated by trade winds; dry season (November to April); rainy season (May to October)

Terrain: mostly flat to rolling plains with rugged hills and mountains in the southeast

Elevation: lowest point: Caribbean Sea 0 ft. (0 m.); highest point: Pico Turquino 6,578 ft. (2,005 m.)

Natural resources: cobalt, nickel, iron ore, copper, manganese, salt, timber, silica, petroleum

People

Population: 11,096,395 (July 1999 est.)

Population growth rate: 0.44%

Infant mortality rate: 7.81 deaths/1,000 live births

Life expectancy at birth: total population: 75.78 years; male: 73.41 years; female: 78.3 years

Major ethnic groups: mulatto 51%, white 37%, black 11%

Major religions: nominally Roman Catholic 85% prior to Castro assuming power

Major languages: Spanish

Government

Official name: Republic of Cuba

Government type: Communist state

National capital: Havana

Independence: May 20, 1902 (from Spain, December 10, 1898; administered by the U.S. from 1898 to 1902)

Legal system: based on Spanish and American law, with large elements of Communist legal theory; does not accept compulsory ICJ jurisdiction

Economy

Industries: sugar, petroleum, food, tobacco, textiles, chemicals, paper and wood products, metals (particularly nickel), cement, fertilizers, consumer goods, agricultural machinery

Agricultural products: sugarcane, tobacco, citrus, coffee, rice, potatoes and other tubers, beans; livestock

Currency: 1 Cuban peso (Cu$) = 100 centavos

Cyprus

Geography

Location: Middle East, island in the Mediterranean Sea, south of Turkey

Area: 3,571 sq. mi. (9,250 sq. km.); about 0.7 times the size of Connecticut

Climate: temperate; Mediterranean with hot, dry summers and cool, wet winters

Terrain: central plain with mountains to north and south; scattered but significant plains along southern coast

Elevation: lowest point: Mediterranean Sea 0 ft. (0 m.); highest point: Olympus 6,404 ft. (1,952 m.)

Natural resources: copper, pyrites, asbestos, gypsum, timber, salt, marble, clay earth pigment

People

Population: 754,064 (July 1999 est.)

Population growth rate: 0.67%

Infant mortality rate: 7.68 deaths/1,000 live births

Life expectancy at birth: total population: 77.1 years; male: 74.91 years; female: 79.39 years

Major ethnic groups: total: Greek 78% (99.5% of the Greeks live in the Greek area), Turkish 18% (98.7% of the Turks live in the Turkish area)

Major religions: Greek Orthodox 78%, Muslim 18%

Major languages: Greek, Turkish, English

Government

Official name: Republic of Cyprus

Government type: republic

National capital: Nicosia; note: the Turkish area's capital is Lefkosa (Nicosia)

Independence: August 16, 1960 (from U.K.)

Legal system: based on common law, with civil law modifications

Economy

Industries: food, beverages, textiles, chemicals, metal products, tourism, wood products

Agricultural products: potatoes, vegetables, barley, grapes, olives, citrus, vegetables

Currency: 1 Cypriot pound (£C) = 100 cents; 1 Turkish lira (TL) = 100 kurus

Czech Republic

Geography

Location: Central Europe, southeast of Germany

Area: 30,387 sq. mi. (78,703 sq. km.); slightly smaller than South Carolina

Climate: temperate; cool summers; cold, cloudy, humid winters

Terrain: Bohemia in the west consists of rolling plains, hills, and plateaus surrounded by low mountains; Moravia in the east consists of very hilly country

Elevation: lowest point: Elbe River 377 ft. (115 m.); highest point: Snezka 5,256 ft. (1,602 m.)

Natural resources: hard coal, soft coal, kaolin, clay, graphite

People

Population: 10,280,513 (July 1999 est.)

Population growth rate: -0.01%

Infant mortality rate: 6.67 deaths/1,000 live births

Life expectancy at birth: total population: 74.35 years; male: 71.01 years; female: 77.88 years

Major ethnic groups: Czech 94.4%, Slovak 3%

Major religions: atheist 39.8%, Roman Catholic 39.2%, Protestant 4.6%, Orthodox 3%

Major languages: Czech, Slovak

Government

Official name: Czech Republic

Government type: parliamentary democracy

National capital: Prague

Independence: January 1, 1993 (from Czechoslovakia)

Legal system: civil law system based on Austro-Hungarian codes

Nations *(cont.)*

Economy
Industries: fuels, ferrous metallurgy, machinery and equipment, coal, motor vehicles, glass, armaments
Agricultural products: grains, potatoes, sugar beets, hops, fruit; pigs, cattle, poultry; forest products
Currency: 1 koruna (Kc) = 100 haleru

Denmark

Geography
Location: Northern Europe, bordering the Baltic Sea and the North Sea, on a peninsula north of Germany
Area: 16,629 sq. mi. (43,070 sq. km.); slightly more than twice the size of Massachusetts
Climate: temperate; humid and overcast; mild, windy winters and cool summers
Terrain: low and flat to gently rolling plains
Elevation: lowest point: Lammefjord −23 ft. (−7 m.); highest point: Ejer Bavnehoj 568 ft. (173 m.)
Natural resources: petroleum, natural gas, fish, salt, limestone

People
Population: 5,356,845 (July 1999 est.)
Population growth rate: 0.38%
Infant mortality rate: 5.11 deaths/1,000 live births
Life expectancy at birth: total population: 76.51 years; male: 73.83 years; female: 79.33 years
Major ethnic groups: Scandinavian, Eskimo, Faroese, German
Major religions: Evangelical Lutheran 91%
Major languages: Danish, Faroese, Greenlandic (an Eskimo dialect)

Government
Official name: Kingdom of Denmark
Government type: constitutional monarchy
National capital: Copenhagen
Independence: 10th century first organized as a unified state; in 1849 became a constitutional monarchy

Legal system: civil law system; judicial review of legislative acts

Economy
Industries: food processing, machinery and equipment, textiles and clothing, chemical products, electronics, construction, furniture, and other wood products, shipbuilding
Agricultural products: grain, potatoes, rape, sugar beets; meat, dairy products; fish
Currency: 1 Danish krone (DKr) = 100 oere

Djibouti

Geography
Location: Eastern Africa, bordering the Gulf of Aden and the Red Sea, between Eritrea and Somalia
Area: 8,494 sq. mi. (22,000 sq. km.); slightly larger than Massachusetts
Climate: desert; torrid, dry
Terrain: coastal plain and plateau separated by central mountains
Elevation: lowest point: Asal −509 ft. (−155 m.); highest point: Mousa Alli 6,653 ft. (2,028 m.)
Natural resources: geothermal areas

People
Population: 447,439 (July 1999 est.)
Population growth rate: 1.5%
Infant mortality rate: 100.24 deaths/ 1,000 live births
Life expectancy at birth: total population: 50.54 years; male: 49.48 years; female: 53.67 years
Major ethnic groups: Somali 60%, Afar 35%
Major religions: Muslim 94%, Christian 6%
Major languages: French (official), Arabic (official), Somali, Afar

Government
Official name: Republic of Djibouti
Government type: republic
National capital: Djibouti
Independence: June 27, 1977 (from France)

Legal system: based on French civil law system, traditional practices, and Islamic law

Economy
Industries: limited to a few small-scale enterprises, such as dairy products and mineral-water bottling
Agricultural products: fruits, vegetables; goats, sheep, camels
Currency: 1 Djiboutian franc (DF) = 100 centimes

Dominica

Geography
Location: Caribbean, island between the Caribbean Sea and the North Atlantic Ocean, about one-half of the way from Puerto Rico to Trinidad and Tobago
Area: 290 sq. mi. (750 sq. km.); more than four times the size of Washington, D.C.
Climate: tropical; moderated by northeast trade winds; heavy rainfall
Terrain: rugged mountains of volcanic origin
Elevation: lowest point: Caribbean Sea 0 ft. (0 m.); highest point: Morne Diablatins 4,747 ft. (1,447 m.)
Natural resources: timber

People
Population: 64,881 (July 1999 est.)
Population growth rate: −1.41%
Infant mortality rate: 8.75 deaths/1,000 live births
Life expectancy at birth: total population: 78.01 years; male: 75.15 years; female: 81.01 years
Major ethnic groups: black, Carib Indians
Major religions: Roman Catholic 77%, Protestant 15%
Major languages: English (official), French patois

Government
Official name: Commonwealth of Dominica
Government type: parliamentary democracy
National capital: Roseau

Independence: November 3, 1978 (from U.K.)
Legal system: based on English common law

Economy
Industries: soap, coconut oil, tourism, copra, furniture, cement blocks, shoes
Agricultural products: bananas, citrus, mangoes, root crops, coconuts; forestry and fisheries potential not exploited
Currency: 1 East Caribbean dollar (EC$) = 100 cents

Dominican Republic

Geography
Location: Caribbean, eastern two-thirds of the island of Hispaniola, between the Caribbean Sea and the North Atlantic Ocean, east of Haiti
Area: 18,815 sq. mi. (48,730 sq. km.); slightly more than twice the size of New Hampshire
Climate: tropical maritime; little seasonal temperature variation; seasonal variation in rainfall
Terrain: rugged highlands and mountains with fertile valleys interspersed
Elevation; lowest point: Lago Enriquillo −151 ft. (−46 m.); highest point: Pico Duarte 10,417 ft. (3,175 m.)
Natural resources: nickel, bauxite, gold, silver

People
Population: 8,129,734 (July 1999 est.)
Population growth rate: 1.62%
Infant mortality rate: 42.52 deaths/1,000 live births
Life expectancy at birth: total population: 70.07 years; male: 67.86 years; female: 72.4 years
Major ethnic groups: white 16%, black 11%, mixed 73%
Major religions: Roman Catholic 95%
Major languages: Spanish

Government
Official name: Dominican Republic
Government type: republic
National capital: Santo Domingo

Nations *(cont.)*

Independence: February 27, 1844 (from Haiti)

Legal system: based on French civil codes

Economy

Industries: tourism, sugar processing, ferronickel and gold mining, textiles, cement, tobacco

Agricultural products: sugarcane, coffee, cotton, cocoa, tobacco, rice, beans, potatoes, corn, bananas; cattle, pigs, dairy products, meat, eggs

Currency: 1 Dominican peso (RD$) = 100 centavos

Ecuador

Geography

Location: Western South America, bordering the Pacific Ocean at the Equator, between Colombia and Peru

Area (including Galapagos Islands): 109,483 sq. mi. (283,560 sq. km.); slightly smaller than Nevada

Climate: tropical along coast becoming cooler inland

Terrain: coastal plain, inter-Andean central highlands (sierra), and flat to rolling eastern jungle

Elevation: lowest point: Pacific Ocean 0 ft. (0 m.); highest point: Chimborazo 20,561 ft. (6,267 m.)

Natural resources: petroleum, fish, timber

People

Population: 12,562,496 (July 1999 est.)

Population growth rate: 1.78%

Infant mortality rate: 30.69 deaths/ 1,000 live births

Life expectancy at birth: total population: 72.16 years; male: 69.54 years; female: 74.9 years

Major ethnic groups: mestizo (mixed Indian and Spanish) 55%, Indian 25%, Spanish 10%, black 10%

Major religions: Roman Catholic 95%

Major languages: Spanish (official), Indian languages (especially Quechua)

Government

Official name: Republic of Ecuador

Government type: republic

National capital: Quito

Independence: May 24, 1822 (from Spain)

Legal system: based on civil law system, has not accepted compulsory ICJ jurisdiction

Economy

Industries: petroleum, food processing, textiles, metal work, paper products, wood products, chemicals, plastics, fishing, lumber

Agricultural products: bananas, coffee, cocoa, rice, potatoes, manioc, plantains, sugarcane; cattle, sheep, pigs, beef, pork, dairy products; balsa wood; fish, shrimp

Currency: 1 sucre (S/) = 100 centavos

Egypt

Geography

Location: Northern Africa, bordering the Mediterranean Sea, between Libya and the Gaza Strip

Area: 386,660 sq. mi. (1,001,450 sq. km.); slightly more than three times the size of New Mexico

Climate: desert; hot, dry summers with moderate winters

Terrain: vast desert plateau interrupted by Nile valley and delta

Elevation: lowest point: Qattara Depression −436 ft. (−133 m.); highest point: Mount Catherine 8,625 ft. (2,629 m.)

Natural resources: petroleum, natural gas, iron ore, phosphates, manganese, limestone, gypsum, talc, asbestos, lead, zinc

People

Population: 67,273,906 (July 1999 est.)

Population growth rate: 1.28%

Infant mortality rate: 67.46 deaths/ 1,000 live births

Life expectancy at birth: total population: 62.39 years; male: 60.39 years; female: 64.49 years

Major ethnic groups: Eastern Hamitic stock (Egyptians, Bedouins, and

Berbers) 99%, Greek, Nubian,
Armenian

Major religions: Muslim (mostly Sunni)
94%, Coptic Christian and other 6%

Major languages: Arabic (official),
English and French widely understood by educated classes

Government

Official name: Arab Republic of Egypt

Government type: republic

National capital: Cairo

Independence: February 28, 1922 (from
U.K.)

Legal system: based on English common law, Islamic law, and
Napoleonic codes

Economy

Industries: textiles, food processing,
tourism, chemicals, petroleum, construction, cement, metals

Agricultural products: cotton, rice, corn,
wheat, beans, fruits, vegetables; cattle, water buffalo, sheep, goats;
annual fish catch about 140,000
metric tons

Currency: 1 Egyptian pound (£E) = 100
piasters

El Salvador

Geography

Location: Central America, bordering
the North Pacific Ocean, between
Guatemala and Honduras

Area: 8,124 sq. mi. (21,040 sq. km.);
slightly smaller than Massachusetts

Climate: tropical; rainy season (May to
October); dry season (November to
April)

Terrain: mostly mountains with narrow coastal belt and central plateau

Elevation: lowest point: Pacific Ocean
0 ft. (0 m.); highest point: Cerro El
Pital 8,957 ft. (2,730 m.)

Natural resources: hydropower, geothermal power, petroleum

People

Population: 5,839,079 (July 1999
est.)

Population growth rate: 1.53%

Infant mortality rate: 28.38 deaths/
1,000 live births

Life expectancy at birth: total population: 70.02 years; male: 66.7 years;
female: 73.5 years

Major ethnic groups: mestizo 94%,
Amerindian 5%

Major religions: Roman Catholic 75%
and Protestant

Major languages: Spanish, Nahua
(among some Amerindians)

Government

Official name: Republic of El Salvador

Government type: republic

National capital: San Salvador

Independence: September 15, 1821
(from Spain)

Legal system: based on civil and Roman
law, with traces of common law

Economy

Industries: food processing, beverages,
petroleum, chemicals, fertilizer, textiles, furniture, light metals

Agricultural products: coffee, sugarcane,
corn, rice, beans, oilseed, cotton, sorghum; beef, dairy products; shrimp

Currency: 1 Salvadoran colon (C) = 100
centavos

Equatorial Guinea

Geography

Location: Western Africa, bordering
the Bight of Biafra, between
Cameroon and Gabon

Area: 10,830 sq. mi. (28,050 sq. km.);
slightly smaller than Maryland

Climate: tropical; always hot, humid

Terrain: coastal plains rise to interior
hills; islands are volcanic

Elevation: lowest point: Atlantic Ocean
0 ft. (0 m.); highest point: Mount
Malabo 9,869 ft. (3,008 m.)

Natural resources: timber, petroleum,
small unexploited deposits of gold,
manganese, uranium

People

Population: 465,746 (July 1999 est.)

Population growth rate: 2.55%

Infant mortality rate: 91.18 deaths/
1,000 live births

Life expectancy at birth: total population: 54.39 years; male: 52.03 years;
female: 56.83 years

Nations *(cont.)*

Major ethnic groups: Bioko (primarily Bubi, some Fernandinos), Rio Muni (primarily Fang)

Major religions: nominally Christian and predominantly Roman Catholic, pagan practices

Major languages: Spanish (official), French (official), pidgin English, Fang, Bubi, Ibo

Government

Official name: Republic of Equatorial Guinea

Government type: republic in transition to multiparty democracy

National capital: Malabo

Independence: October 12, 1968 (from Spain)

Legal system: partly based on Spanish civil law and tribal custom

Economy

Industries: fishing, sawmilling

Agricultural products: coffee, cocoa, rice, yams, cassava (tapioca), bananas, palm oil nuts, manioc; livestock; timber

Currency: 1 Communauté Financière Africaine franc (CFAF) = 100 centimes

Eritrea

Geography

Location: Eastern Africa, bordering the Red Sea, between Djibouti and Sudan

Area: 46,842 sq. mi. (121,320 sq. km.); slightly larger than Pennsylvania

Climate: hot, dry desert strip along Red Sea coast; cooler and wetter in the central highlands (up to 61 cm of rainfall annually); semiarid in western hills and lowlands; rainfall heaviest during June-September except on coastal desert

Terrain: dominated by extension of Ethiopian north-south trending highlands, descending on the east to a coastal desert plain, on the northwest to hilly terrain and on the southwest to flat-to-rolling plains

Elevation: lowest point: Kobar Sink –246 ft. (–75 m.); highest point: Soira 9,885 ft. (3,013 m.)

Natural resources: gold, potash, zinc, copper, salt, probably oil and natural gas (petroleum geologists are prospecting for it), fish

People

Population: 3,984,723 (July 1999 est.)

Population growth rate: 3.88%

Infant mortality rate: 76.84 deaths/ 1,000 live births

Life expectancy at birth: total population: 55.74 years; male: 53.61 years; female: 57.95 years

Major ethnic groups: ethnic Tigrinya 50%, Tigre and Kunama 40%, Afar 4%, Saho (Red Sea coast dwellers) 3%

Major religions: Muslim, Coptic Christian, Roman Catholic, Protestant

Major languages: Afar, Amharic, Arabic, Tigre and Kunama, Tigrinya

Government

Official name: State of Eritrea

Government type: transitional government

National capital: Asmara (formerly Asmera)

Independence: May 27, 1993 (from Ethiopia; formerly the Eritrea Autonomous Region)

Economy

Industries: food processing, beverages, clothing and textiles

Agricultural products: sorghum, lentils, vegetables, maize, cotton, tobacco, coffee, sisal (for making rope); livestock (including goats); fish

Currency: 1 nafka = 100 cents

Estonia

Geography

Location: Eastern Europe, bordering the Baltic Sea and Gulf of Finland, between Latvia and Russia

Area: 17,462 sq. mi. (45,226 sq. km.); slightly smaller than New Hampshire and Vermont combined
Climate: maritime, wet, moderate winters, cool summers
Terrain: marshy, lowlands
Elevation: lowest point: Baltic Sea 0 ft. (0 m.); highest point: Suur Munamagi 1,043 ft. (318 m.)
Natural resources: shale oil (kukersite), peat, phosphorite, amber, cambrian blue clay

People

Population: 1,408,523 (July 1999 est.)
Population growth rate: −0.82%
Infant mortality rate: 13.83 deaths/1,000 live births
Life expectancy at birth: total population: 68.65 years; male: 62.61 years; female: 75 years
Major ethnic groups: Estonian 64.2%, Russian 28.7
Major religions: Evangelical Lutheran, Russian Orthodox, Estonian Orthodox,
Major languages: Estonian (official), Russian, Ukrainian

Government

Official name: Republic of Estonia
Government type: parliamentary democracy
National capital: Tallinn
Independence: September 6, 1991 (from Soviet Union)
Legal system: based on civil law system; no judicial review of legislative acts

Economy

Industries: oil shale, shipbuilding, phosphates, electric motors, excavators, cement, furniture, clothing, textiles, paper, shoes, apparel
Agricultural products: potatoes, fruits, vegetables; livestock and dairy products; fish
Currency: 1 Estonian kroon (EEK) = 100 cents

Ethiopia

Geography

Location: Eastern Africa, west of Somalia
Area: 435,184 sq. mi. (1,127,127 sq. km.); slightly less than twice the size of Texas
Climate: tropical monsoon with wide topographic-induced variation
Terrain: high plateau with central mountain range divided by Great Rift Valley
Elevation: lowest point: Denakil −410 ft. (−125 m.); highest point: Ras Dashen Terara 15,157 ft. (4,620 m.)
Natural resources: small reserves of gold, platinum, copper, potash, natural gas

People

Population: 58,680,383 (July 1999 est.)
Population growth rate: 2.16%
Infant mortality rate: 124.57 deaths/1,000 live births
Life expectancy at birth: total population: 40.46 years; male: 39.22 years; female: 41.73 years
Major ethnic groups: Oromo 40%, Amhara and Tigrean 32%, Sidamo 9%, Shankella 6%, Somali 6%, Afar 4%, Gurage 2%
Major religions: Muslim 45–50%, Ethiopian Orthodox 35–40%, animist 12%
Major languages: Amharic (official), Tigrinya, Orominga, Guaraginga, Somali, Arabic

Government

Official name: Federal Democratic Republic of Ethiopia
Government type: federal republic
National capital: Addis Ababa
Independence: oldest independent country in Africa and one of the oldest in the world—at least 2,000 years
Legal system: (currently transitional)

Economy

Industries: food processing, beverages, textiles, chemicals, metals processing, cement
Agricultural products: cereals, pulses, coffee, oilseed, sugarcane, potatoes, other vegetables; hides, cattle, sheep, goats
Currency: 1 birr (Br) = 100 cents

Nations *(cont.)*

Falkland Islands; (Islas Malvinas)

Geography

Location: Southern South America, islands in the South Atlantic Ocean, east of southern Argentina

Area: 4,700 sq. mi. (12,173 sq. km.); slightly smaller than Connecticut

Climate: cold marine; strong westerly winds, cloudy, humid; rain occurs on more than half of days in year; occasional snow all year, except in January and February, but does not accumulate

Terrain: rocky, hilly, mountainous with some boggy, undulating plains

Elevation: lowest point: Atlantic Ocean 0 ft. (0 m.); highest point: Mount Usborne 2,313 ft. (705 m.)

Natural resources: fish, wildlife

People

Population: 2,758 (July 1999 est.)

Population growth rate: 2.43%

Major ethnic groups: British

Major religions: primarily Anglican

Major languages: English

Government

Official name: Colony of the Falkland Islands

National capital: Stanley

Independence: none (dependent territory of the U.K., also claimed by Argentina)

Legal system: English common law

Economy

Industries: wool and fish processing; sale of stamps and coins

Agricultural products: fodder and vegetable crops; sheep farming, small dairy herds

Currency: 1 Falkland pound (£F) = 100 pence

Faroe Islands

Geography

Location: Northern Europe, island group between the Norwegian Sea and the north Atlantic Ocean, about one-half of the way from Iceland to Norway

Area: 540 sq. mi. (1,399 sq. km.); eight times the size of Washington, D.C.

Climate: mild winters, cool summers; usually overcast; foggy, windy

Terrain: rugged, rocky, some low peaks; cliffs along most of coast

Elevation: lowest point: Atlantic Ocean 0 ft. (0 m.); highest point: Slaettaratindur 2,894 ft. (882 m.)

Natural resources: fish, whales

People

Population: 41,059 (July 1999 est.)

Population growth rate: –2.03%

Infant mortality rate: 10.26 deaths/ 1,000 live births

Life expectancy at birth: total population: 78.56 years; male: 75.66 years; female: 81.58 years

Major ethnic groups: Scandinavian

Major religions: Evangelical Lutheran

Major languages: Faroese (derived from Old Norse), Danish

Government

Official name: Faroe Islands

National capital: Torshavn

Independence: none (part of the Kingdom of Denmark; self-governing overseas administrative division of Denmark)

Legal system: Danish

Economy

Industries: fishing, shipbuilding, construction, handicrafts

Agricultural products: milk, potatoes, vegetables; sheep; salmon farming; fish

Currency: 1 Danish krone (DKr) = 100 oere

Fiji

Geography

Location: Oceania, island group in the South Pacific Ocean, about two-thirds of the way from Hawaii to New Zealand

Area: 7,054 sq. mi. (18,270 sq. km.); slightly smaller than New Jersey

Climate: tropical marine; only slight seasonal temperature variation

Terrain: mostly mountains of volcanic origin

Elevation: lowest point: Pacific Ocean 0 ft. (0 m.); highest point: Tomanivi 4,344 ft. (1,324 m.)

Natural resources: timber, fish, gold, copper, offshore oil potential

People

Population: 812,918 (July 1999 est.)

Population growth rate: 1.28%

Infant mortality rate: 16.3 deaths/1,000 live births

Life expectancy at birth: total population: 66.59 years; male: 64.19 years; female: 69.11 years

Major ethnic groups: Fijian 49%, Indian 46%

Major religions: Christian 52% , Hindu 38%

Major languages: English (official), Fijian, Hindustani

Government

Official name: Republic of the Fiji Islands

Government type: republic; note: military coup leader Maj. Gen. Sitiveni Rabuka formally declared Fiji a republic on October 6, 1987

National capital: Suva

Independence: October 10, 1970 (from U.K.)

Legal system: based on British system

Economy

Industries: sugar, tourism, copra, gold, silver, clothing, lumber, small cottage industries

Agricultural products: sugarcane, coconuts, cassava (tapioca), rice, sweet potatoes, bananas; cattle, pigs, horses, goats; fish

Currency: 1 Fijian dollar (F$) = 100 cents

Finland

Geography

Location: Northern Europe, bordering the Baltic Sea, Gulf of Bothnia, and Gulf of Finland, between Sweden and Russia

Area: 130,127 sq. mi. (337,030 sq. km.); slightly smaller than Montana

Climate: cold temperate; potentially sub-arctic, but comparatively mild because of moderating influence of the North Atlantic Current, Baltic Sea, and more than 60,000 lakes

Terrain: mostly low, flat to rolling plains interspersed with lakes and low hills

Elevation: lowest point: Baltic Sea 0 ft. (0 m.); highest point: Haltiatunturi 4,357 ft. (1,328 m.)

Natural resources: timber, copper, zinc, iron ore, silver

People

Population: 5,158,372 (July 1999 est.)

Population growth rate: 0.15%

Infant mortality rate: 3.82 deaths/ 1,000 live births

Life expectancy at birth: total population: 77.32 years; male: 73.81 years; female: 80.98 years

Major ethnic groups: Finn 93%, Swede 6%, Lapp 0.11%, Gypsy 0.12%, Tatar 0.02%

Major religions: Evangelical Lutheran 89%, Greek Orthodox 1%, none 9%, other 1%

Major languages: Finnish 93.5% (official), Swedish 6.3% (official), small Lapp and Russian-speaking minorities

Government

Official name: Republic of Finland

Government type: republic

National capital: Helsinki

Independence: December 6, 1917 (from Russia)

Legal system: civil law system based on Swedish law; Supreme Court may request legislation interpreting or modifying laws

Economy

Industries: metal products, shipbuilding, pulp and paper, copper refining, foodstuffs, chemicals, textiles, clothing

Agricultural products: cereals, sugar beets, potatoes; dairy cattle; fish

Nations *(cont.)*

Currency: 1 markka (FMk) or Finmark = 100 pennia

France

Geography

Location: Western Europe, bordering the Bay of Biscay and English Channel, between Belgium and Spain southeast of the U.K.; bordering the Mediterranean Sea, between Italy and Spain

Area: 211,208 sq. mi. (547,030 sq. km.); slightly less than twice the size of Colorado

Climate: generally cool winters and mild summers, but mild winters and hot summers along the Mediterranean

Terrain: mostly flat plains or gently rolling hills in north and west; remainder is mountainous, especially Pyrenees in south, Alps in east

Elevation: lowest point: Rhone River delta –7 ft. (–2 m.); highest point: Mont Blanc 15,771 ft. (4,807 m.)

Natural resources: coal, iron ore, bauxite, fish, timber, zinc, potash

People

Population: 58,978,172 (July 1999 est.)

Population growth rate: 0.27%

Infant mortality rate: 5.62 deaths/ 1,000 live births

Life expectancy at birth: total population: 78.63 years; male: 74.76 years; female: 82.71 years

Major ethnic groups: Celtic and Latin with Teutonic, Slavic, North African, Indochinese, Basque minorities

Major religions: Roman Catholic 90%, Protestant 2%, Jewish 1%

Major languages: French 100%, rapidly declining regional dialects and languages (Provencal, Breton, Alsatian, Corsican, Catalan, Basque, Flemish)

Government

Official name: French Republic

Government type: republic

National capital: Paris

Independence: 486 (unified by Clovis)

Legal system: civil law system with indigenous concepts; review of administrative but not legislative acts

Economy

Industries: steel, machinery, chemicals, automobiles, metallurgy, aircraft, electronics, mining, textiles, food processing, tourism

Agricultural products: wheat, cereals, sugar beets, potatoes, wine grapes; beef, dairy products; fish

Currency: 1 French franc (F) = 100 centimes

French Guiana

Geography

Location: Northern South America, bordering the North Atlantic Ocean, between Brazil and Suriname

Area: 35,135 sq. mi. (91,000 sq. km.); slightly smaller than Indiana

Climate: tropical; hot, humid; little seasonal temperature variation

Terrain: low-lying coastal plains rising to hills and small mountains

Elevation: lowest point: Atlantic Ocean 0 ft. (0 m.); highest point: Bellevue de l'Inini 2,792 ft. (851 m.)

Natural resources: bauxite, timber, gold (widely scattered), cinnabar, kaolin, fish

People

Population: 167,982 (July 1999 est.)

Population growth rate: 3.19%

Infant mortality rate: 12.93 deaths/ 1,000 live births

Life expectancy at birth: total population: 76.61 years; male: 73.41 years; female: 79.97 years

Major ethnic groups: black or mulatto 66%, white 12%, East Indian, Chinese, Amerindian 12%

Major religions: Roman Catholic

Major languages: French

Government

Official name: Department of Guiana

National capital: Cayenne

Independence: none (overseas department of France)

Legal system: French legal system

Economy

Industries: construction, shrimp processing, forestry products, rum, gold mining

Agricultural products: rice, corn, manioc, cocoa, vegetables, bananas, sugar; cattle, pigs, poultry

Currency: 1 French franc (F) = 100 centimes

French Polynesia

Geography

Location: Oceania, archipelago in the South Pacific Ocean, about one-half of the way from South America to Australia

Area: 1,609 sq. mi. (4,167 sq. km.); slightly less than one-third the size of Connecticut

Climate: tropical, but moderate

Terrain: mixture of rugged high islands and low islands with reefs

Elevation: lowest point: Pacific Ocean 0 ft. (0 m.); highest point: Mount Orohena 7,352 ft. (2,241 m.)

Natural resources: timber, fish, cobalt

People

Population: 242,073 (July 1999 est.)

Population growth rate: 1.72%

Infant mortality rate: 13.59 deaths/1,000 live births

Life expectancy at birth: total population: 72.33 years; male: 69.93 years; female: 74.85 years

Major ethnic groups: Polynesian 78%, Chinese 12%, local French 6%, metropolitan French 4%

Major religions: Protestant 54%, Roman Catholic 30%

Major languages: French (official), Tahitian (official)

Government

Official name: Territory of French Polynesia

National capital: Papeete

Independence: none (overseas territory of France)

Legal system: based on French system

Economy

Industries: tourism, pearls, agricultural processing, handicrafts

Agricultural products: coconuts, vanilla, vegetables, fruits; poultry, beef, dairy products

Currency: 1 Communauté Financière Africaine franc (CFAF) = 100 centimes

Gabon

Geography

Location: Western Africa, bordering the Atlantic Ocean at the Equator, between Republic of the Congo and Equatorial Guinea

Area: 103,347 sq. mi. (267,670 sq. km.); slightly smaller than Colorado

Climate: tropical; always hot, humid

Terrain: narrow coastal plain; hilly interior; savanna in east and south

Elevation: lowest point: Atlantic Ocean 0 ft. (0 m.); highest point: Mont Iboundji 5,167 ft. (1,575 m.)

Natural resources: petroleum, manganese, uranium, gold, timber, iron ore

People

Population: 1,225,853 (July 1999 est.)

Population growth rate: 1.48%

Infant mortality rate: 83.1 deaths/1,000 live births

Life expectancy at birth: total population: 56.98 years; male: 53.98 years; female: 60.08 years

Major ethnic groups: Bantu tribes including four major tribal groupings (Fang, Eshira, Bapounou, Bateke), other Africans and Europeans 154,000, including 6,000 French and 11,000 persons of dual nationality

Major religions: Christian 55%–75%, Muslim less than 1%, animist

Major languages: French (official), Fang, Myene, Bateke, Bapounou/ Eschira, Bandjabi

Government

Official name: Gabonese Republic

Government type: republic; multiparty presidential regime (opposition parties legalized 1990)

National capital: Libreville

Independence: August 17, 1960 (from France)

Nations (cont.)

Legal system: based on French civil law system and customary law; judicial review of legislative acts in Constitutional Chamber of the Supreme Court; compulsory ICJ jurisdiction not accepted

Economy

Industries: food and beverage; textile; lumbering and plywood; cement; petroleum extraction and refining; manganese, uranium, and gold mining; chemicals; ship repair

Agricultural products: cocoa, coffee, sugar, palm oil; rubber; okoume (a tropical softwood); cattle; small fishing operations

Currency: 1 Communauté Financière Africaine franc (CFAF) = 100 centimes

Gambia, The

Geography

Location: Western Africa, bordering the North Atlantic Ocean and Senegal

Area: 4,363 sq. mi. (11,300 sq. km.); slightly less than twice the size of Delaware

Climate: tropical; hot, rainy season (June to November); cooler, dry season (November to May)

Terrain: flood plain of the Gambia River flanked by some low hills

Elevation: lowest point: Atlantic Ocean 0 ft. (0 m.); highest point: unnamed location 174 ft. (53 m.)

Natural resources: fish

People

Population: 1,336,320 (July 1999 est.)

Population growth rate: 3.35%

Infant mortality rate: 75.33 deaths/ 1,000 live births

Life expectancy at birth: total population: 54.39 years; male: 52.02 years; female: 56.83 years

Major ethnic groups: African 99% (Mandinka 42%, Fula 18%, Wolof 16%, Jola 10%, Serahuli 9%)

Major religions: Muslim 90%, Christian 9%

Major languages: English (official), Mandinka, Wolof, Fula, other indigenous vernaculars

Government

Official name: Republic of The Gambia

Government type: republic under multiparty democratic rule

National capital: Banjul

Independence: February 18, 1965 (from U.K.)

Legal system: based on a composite of English common law, Koranic law, and customary law

Economy

Industries: processing peanuts, fish, and hides; tourism; beverages; agricultural machinery assembly, woodworking, metalworking; clothing

Agricultural products: peanuts, millet, sorghum, rice, corn, cassava (tapioca), palm kernels; cattle, sheep, goats; forest and fishing resources not fully exploited

Currency: 1 dalasi (D) = 100 butut

Gaza Strip

Geography

Location: Middle East, bordering the Mediterranean Sea, between Egypt and Israel

Area: 139 sq. mi. (360 sq. km.); slightly more than twice the size of Washington, D.C.

Climate: temperate, mild winters, dry and warm to hot summers

Terrain: flat to rolling, sand- and dune-covered coastal plain

Elevation: lowest point: Mediterranean Sea 0 ft. (0 m.); highest point: Abu 'Awdah (Joz Abu 'Auda) 344 ft. (105 m.)

Natural resources: negligible

People

Population: 1,112,654 (July 1999 est.)
Note: there are approximately 6,000 Israeli settlers in the Gaza Strip (August 1998 est.)

Population growth rate: 4.44%

Infant mortality rate: 22.92 deaths/ 1,000 live births

Life expectancy at birth: total population: 73.44 years; male: 72.01 years; female: 74.95 years
Major ethnic groups: Palestinian Arab
Major religions: Muslim (predominantly Sunni) 98.7%
Major languages: Arabic, Hebrew

Government

Government note: Under the Israeli-PLO Declaration of Principles on Interim Self-Government Arrangements ("the DOP"), Israel agreed to transfer certain powers and responsibilities to the Palestinian Authority, which includes a Palestinian Legislative Council elected in January 1996, as part of interim self-governing arrangements in the West Bank and Gaza Strip.
Official name: Gaza Strip

Economy

Industries: generally small family businesses that produce textiles, soap, olive-wood carvings, and mother-of-pearl souvenirs; the Israelis have established some small-scale modern industries in an industrial center
Agricultural products: olives, citrus, other fruits, vegetables; beef, dairy products
Currency: 1 new Israeli shekel (NIS) = 100 new agorot

Georgia

Geography

Location: Southwestern Asia, bordering the Black Sea, between Turkey and Russia
Area: 26,911 sq. mi. (69,700 sq. km.); slightly smaller than South Carolina
Climate: warm and pleasant; Mediterranean-like on Black Sea coast
Terrain: largely mountainous with Great Caucasus Mountains in the north and Lesser Caucasus Mountains in the south; Kolkhida Lowland opens to the Black Sea in the west; Mtkvari River Basin in the east; good soils in river valley flood plains, foothills of Kolkhida Lowland

Elevation: lowest point: Black Sea 0 ft. (0 m.); highest point: Mt'a Mqinvartsveri (Gora Kazbek) 16,561 ft. (5,048 m.)
Natural resources: forests, hydropower, manganese deposits, iron ore, copper, minor coal and oil deposits; coastal climate and soils allow for important tea and citrus growth

People

Population: 5,066,499 (July 1999 est.)
Population growth rate: –0.74%
Infant mortality rate: 52.01 deaths/1,000 live births
Life expectancy at birth: total population: 64.63 years; male: 61.13 years; female: 68.32 years
Major ethnic groups: Georgian 70.1%, Armenian 8.1%, Russian 6.3%, Azeri 5.7%, Ossetian 3%, Abkhaz 1.8%
Major religions: Christian Orthodox 75% (Georgian Orthodox 65%, Russian Orthodox 10%), Muslim 11%, Armenian Apostolic 8%
Major languages: Armenian 7%, Azeri 6%, Georgian 71% (official), Russian 9%

Government

Official name: Georgia
Government type: republic
National capital: T'bilisi
Independence: April 9, 1991 (from Soviet Union)
Legal system: based on civil law system

Economy

Industries: steel, aircraft, machine tools, foundry equipment, electric locomotives, tower cranes, electric welding equipment, machinery for food preparation and meat packing, electric motors, process control equipment, trucks, tractors, textiles, shoes, chemicals, wood products, wine
Agricultural products: citrus, grapes, tea, vegetables, potatoes; small livestock sector
Currency: lari introduced September 1995 replacing the coupon

Nations *(cont.)*

Germany

Geography

Location: Central Europe, bordering the Baltic Sea and the North Sea, between the Netherlands and Poland, south of Denmark

Area: 137,803 sq. ft. (356,910 sq. km.); slightly smaller than Montana

Climate: temperate and marine; cool, cloudy, wet winters and summers; occasional warm, tropical foehn wind; high relative humidity

Terrain: lowlands in north, uplands in center, Bavarian Alps in south

Elevation: lowest point: Freepsum Lake –7 ft. (–2 m.); highest point: Zugspitze 9,718 ft. (2,962 m.)

Natural resources: iron ore, coal, potash, timber, lignite, uranium, copper, natural gas, salt, nickel

People

Population: 82,087,361 (July 1999 est.)

Population growth rate: 0.01%

Infant mortality rate: 5.14 deaths/1,000 live births

Life expectancy at birth: total population: 77.17 years; male: 74.01 years; female: 80.5 years

Major ethnic groups: German 91.5%, Turkish 2.4%

Major religions: Protestant 38%, Roman Catholic 34%

Major languages: German

Government

Official name: Federal Republic of Germany

Government type: federal republic

National capital: Berlin

Independence: January 18, 1871 (German Empire unification); unification of West Germany and East Germany took place October 3, 1990

Legal system: civil law system with indigenous concepts; judicial review of legislative acts in the Federal Constitutional Court

Economy

Industries: among world's largest and most technologically advanced producers of iron, steel, coal, cement, chemicals, machinery, vehicles, machine tools, electronics, food and beverages; eastern: metal fabrication, chemicals, brown coal, shipbuilding, machine building, food and beverages, textiles, petroleum refining

Agricultural products: western: potatoes, wheat, barley, sugar beets, fruit, cabbage; cattle, pigs, poultry; eastern: wheat, rye, barley, potatoes, sugar beets, fruit; pork, beef, chicken, milk, hides

Currency: 1 deutsche mark (DM) = 100 pfennige

Ghana

Geography

Location: Western Africa, bordering the Gulf of Guinea, between Côte d'Ivoire and Togo

Area: 92,100 sq. mi. (238,540 sq. km.); slightly smaller than Oregon

Climate: tropical; warm and comparatively dry along southeast coast; hot and humid in southwest; hot and dry in north

Terrain: mostly low plains with dissected plateau in south-central area

Elevation: lowest point: Atlantic Ocean 0 ft. (0 m.); highest point: Mount Afadjato 2,887 ft. (880 m.)

Natural resources: gold, timber, industrial diamonds, bauxite, manganese, fish, rubber

People

Population: 18,887,626 (July 1999 est.)

Population growth rate: 2.05%

Infant mortality rate: 76.15 deaths/1,000 live births

Life expectancy at birth: total population: 57.14 years; male: 53.08 years; female: 59.27 years

Major ethnic groups: black African 99.8% (major tribes: Akan 44%, Moshi-Dagomba 16%, Ewe 13%, Ga 8%)

Major religions: indigenous beliefs 38%, Muslim 30%, Christian 24%

Major languages: English (official),
African languages (including Akan,
Moshi-Dagomba, Ewe, and Ga)

Government

Official name: Republic of Ghana
Government type: constitutional
democracy
National capital: Accra
Independence: March 6, 1957 (from
U.K.)
Legal system: based on English com-
mon law and customary law

Economy

Industries: mining, lumbering, light
manufacturing, aluminum smelting, food processing
Agricultural products: cocoa, rice, coffee, cassava (tapioca), peanuts, corn,
shea nuts, bananas; timber
Currency: 1 new cedi (C) = 100 pesewas

Gibraltar

Geography

Location: Southwestern Europe, bor-
dering the Strait of Gibraltar, which
links the Mediterranean Sea and the
North Atlantic Ocean, on the south-
ern coast of Spain
Area: 3 sq. mi. (6.5 sq. km.); about 11
times the size of The Mall in
Washington, D.C.
Climate: Mediterranean with mild
winters and warm summers
Terrain: a narrow coastal lowland bor-
ders the Rock of Gibraltar
Elevation: lowest point: Mediterranean
Sea 0 ft. (0 m.); highest point: Rock
of Gibraltar 1,398 ft. (426 m.)
Natural resources: negligible

People

Population: 29,165 (July 1999 est.)
Population growth rate: 0.39%
Infant mortality rate: 6.47 deaths/
1,000 live births
Life expectancy at birth: total popula-
tion: 78.37 years; male: 75.1 years;
female: 81.81 years
Major ethnic groups: Italian, English,
Maltese, Portuguese, Spanish
Major religions: Roman Catholic 74%,
Protestant 11%

Major languages: English (used in
schools and for official purposes),
Spanish

Government

Official name: Gibraltar
National capital: Gibraltar
Independence: none (dependent terri-
tory of the U.K.)
Legal system: English law

Economy

Industries: tourism, banking and
finance, ship-building and repairing; support two large U.K. naval
and air bases; tobacco, mineral
waters, beer, canned fish
Agricultural products: none
Currency: 1 Gibraltar pound (£G) =
100 pence

Greece

Geography

Location: Southern Europe, bordering
the Aegean Sea, Ionian Sea, and the
Mediterranean Sea, between
Albania and Turkey
Area: 50,942 sq. mi. (131,940 sq. km.);
slightly smaller than Alabama
Climate: temperate; mild, wet winters;
hot, dry summers
Terrain: mostly mountains with
ranges extending into sea as penin-
sulas or chains of islands
Elevation: : lowest point:
Mediterranean Sea 0 ft. (0 m.);
highest point: Mount Olympus
9,570 ft. (2,917 m.)
Natural resources: bauxite, lignite, magnesite, petroleum, marble

People

Population: 10,707,135 (July 1999
est.)
Population growth rate: 0.41%
Infant mortality rate: 7.13 deaths/1,000
live births
Life expectancy at birth: total popula-
tion: 78.43 years; male: 75.87 years;
female: 81.18 years
Major ethnic groups: Greek 98%,
other 2%
Major religions: Greek Orthodox 98%,
Muslim 1.3%, other 0.7%

Nations *(cont.)*

Major languages: Greek (official),
English, French

Government

Official name: Hellenic Republic
Government type: parliamentary repub-
lic
National capital: Athens
Independence: 1829 (from the Ottoman
Empire)
Legal system: based on codified Roman
law; judiciary divided into civil,
criminal, and administrative courts

Economy

Industries: tourism; food and tobacco
processing, textiles; chemicals,
metal products; mining, petroleum
Agricultural products: wheat, corn, barley, sugar beets, olives, tomatoes,
wine, tobacco, potatoes; meat, dairy
products
Currency: 1 drachma (Dr) = 100 lepta

Greenland

Geography

Location: Northern North America,
island between the Arctic Ocean and
the North Atlantic Ocean, northeast
of Canada
Area: 839,999 sq. mi. (2,175,600 sq.
km.) slightly more than three times
the size of Texas
Climate: arctic to subarctic; cool summers, cold winters
Terrain: flat to gradually sloping icecap
covers all but a narrow, mountainous, barren, rocky coast
Elevation: lowest point: Atlantic Ocean
0 ft. (0 m.); highest point:
Gunnbjorn 12,139 ft. (3,700 m.)
Natural resources: zinc, lead, iron ore,
coal, molybdenum, gold, platinum,
uranium, fish, seals, whales

People

Population: 59,827 (July 1999 est.)
Population growth rate: 0.84%
Infant mortality rate: 20.06 deaths/
1,000 live births
Life expectancy at birth: total population: 70.01 years; male: 65.98 years;
female: 74.24 years

Major ethnic groups: Greenlander 87%
(Eskimos and Greenland-born
whites), Danish and others 13%
Major religions: Evangelical Lutheran
Major languages: Eskimo dialects,
Danish, Greenlandic (an Inuit
dialect)

Government

Official name: Greenland
National capital: Nuuk (Godthab)
Independence: none (part of the
Kingdom of Denmark; self-
governing overseas administrative
division of Denmark since 1979)
Legal system: Danish

Economy

Industries: fish processing (mainly
shrimp), handicrafts, furs, small
shipyards
Agricultural products: forage crops,
small garden vegetables; sheep, fish
Currency: 1 Danish krone (DKr) = 100
oere

Grenada

Geography

Location: Caribbean, island between
the Caribbean Sea and Atlantic
Ocean, north of Trinidad and
Tobago
Area: 131 sq. mi. (340 sq. km.); twice
the size of Washington, D.C.
Climate: tropical; tempered by north-
east trade winds
Terrain: volcanic in origin with central
mountains
Elevation: lowest point: Caribbean
Sea 0 ft. (0 m.); highest point:
Mount Saint Catherine 2,756 ft.
(840 m.)
Natural resources: timber, tropical fruit,
deepwater harbors

People

Population: 97,008 (July 1999 est.)
Population growth rate: 0.87%
Infant mortality rate: 11.13 deaths/
1,000 live births
Life expectancy at birth: total population: 71.6 years; male: 68.97 years;
female: 74.29 years

Major ethnic groups: black
Major religions: Roman Catholic 53%, Anglican 13.8%, other Protestant sects 33.2%
Major languages: English (official), French patois

Government
Official name: Grenada
Government type: parliamentary democracy
National capital: Saint George's
Independence: February 7, 1974 (from U.K.)
Legal system: based on English common law

Economy
Industries: food and beverages, textiles, light assembly operations, tourism, construction
Agricultural products: bananas, cocoa, nutmeg, mace, citrus, avocados, root crops, sugarcane, corn, vegetables
Currency: 1 East Caribbean dollar (EC$) = 100 cents

Guadeloupe

Geography
Location: Caribbean, islands in the eastern Caribbean Sea, southeast of Puerto Rico
Area: 687 sq. mi. (1,780 sq. km.); 10 times the size of Washington, D.C.
Climate: subtropical tempered by trade winds; moderately high humidity
Terrain: Basse-Terre is volcanic in origin with interior mountains; Grande-Terre is low limestone formation; most of the seven other islands are volcanic in origin
Elevation: lowest point: Caribbean Sea 0 ft. (0 m.); highest point: Soufriere 4,813 ft. (1,467 m.)
Natural resources: cultivable land, beaches and climate that foster tourism

People
Population: 420,943 (July 1999 est.)
Population growth rate: 1.06%
Infant mortality rate: 8.54 deaths/ 1,000 live births

Life expectancy at birth: total population: 78.01 years; male: 74.98 years; female: 81.18 years
Major ethnic groups: black or mulatto 90%, white 5%
Major religions: Roman Catholic 95%, Hindu and pagan African 4%
Major languages: French (official) 99%, Creole patois

Government
Official name: Department of Guadeloupe
National capital: Basse-Terre
Independence: none (overseas department of France)
Legal system: French legal system

Economy
Industries: construction, cement, rum, sugar, tourism
Agricultural products: bananas, sugarcane, tropical fruits and vegetables; cattle, pigs, goats
Currency: 1 French franc (F) = 100 centimes

Guam

Geography
Location: Oceania, island in the North Pacific Ocean, about three-quarters of the way from Hawaii to the Philippines
Area: 209 sq. mi. (541.3 sq. km.); three times the size of Washington, D.C.
Climate: tropical marine; generally warm and humid, moderated by northeast trade winds; dry season from January to June, rainy season from July to December; little seasonal temperature variation
Terrain: volcanic origin, surrounded by coral reefs; relatively flat coralline limestone plateau (source of most fresh water) with steep coastal cliffs and narrow coastal plains in north, low-rising hills in center, mountains in south
Elevation: lowest point: Pacific Ocean 0 ft. (0 m.); highest point: Mount Lamlam 1,332 ft. (406 m.)
Natural resources: fishing (largely undeveloped), tourism

Nations *(cont.)*

People

Population: 151,716 (July 1999 est.)

Population growth rate: 1.67%

Infant mortality rate: 7.81 deaths/1,000 live births

Life expectancy at birth: total population: 77.78 years; male: 74.6 years; female: 81.31 years

Major ethnic groups: Chamorro 47%, Filipino 25%, white 10%, Chinese, Japanese, Korean, and other 18%

Major religions: Roman Catholic 98%, other 2%

Major languages: English, Chamorro, Japanese

Government

Official name: Territory of Guam

National capital: Hagatna (Agana)

Independence: none (territory of the U.S.)

Legal system: modeled on U.S.; U.S. federal laws apply

Economy

Industries: U.S. military, tourism, construction, transshipment services, concrete products, printing and publishing, food processing, textiles

Agricultural products: fruits, copra, vegetables; eggs, pork, poultry, beef

Currency: 1 U.S. dollar (US$) = 100 cents

Guatemala

Geography

Location: Central America, bordering the Caribbean Sea, between Honduras and Belize and bordering the North Pacific Ocean, between El Salvador and Mexico

Area: 42,042 sq. mi. (108,890 sq. km.); slightly smaller than Tennessee

Climate: tropical; hot, humid in lowlands; cooler in highlands

Terrain: mostly mountains with narrow coastal plains and rolling limestone plateau (Peten)

Elevation: lowest point: Pacific Ocean 0 ft. (0 m.); highest point: Volcan Tajumulco 13,815 ft. (4,211 m.)

Natural resources: petroleum, nickel, rare woods, fish, chicle

People

Population: 12,335,580 (July 1999 est.)

Population growth rate: 2.68%

Infant mortality rate: 46.15 deaths/ 1,000 live births

Life expectancy at birth: total population: 66.45 years; male: 63.78 years; female: 69.24 years

Major ethnic groups: Mestizo (mixed Amerindian-Spanish—in local Spanish called Ladino) 56%, Amerindian or predominantly Amerindian 44%

Major religions: Roman Catholic, Protestant, traditional Mayan

Major languages: Spanish 60%, Amerindian languages 40% (23 Amerindian languages, including Quiche, Cakchiquel, Kekchi)

Government

Official name: Republic of Guatemala

Government type: republic

National capital: Guatemala

Independence: September 15, 1821 (from Spain)

Legal system: civil law system; judicial review of legislative acts

Economy

Industries: sugar, textiles and clothing, furniture, chemicals, petroleum, metals, rubber, tourism

Agricultural products: sugarcane, corn, bananas, coffee, beans, cardamom; cattle, sheep, pigs, chickens

Currency: 1 quetzal (Q) = 100 centavos

Guernsey

Geography

Location: Western Europe, islands in the English Channel, northwest of France

Area: 75 sq. mi. (194 sq. km.); slightly larger than Washington, D.C.

Climate: temperate with mild winters and cool summers; about 50% of days are overcast

Terrain: mostly level with low hills in southwest

Elevation: lowest point: Atlantic Ocean
0 ft. (0 m.); highest point: unnamed
location on Sark 374 ft. (114 m.)
Natural resources: cropland

People
Population: 65,386 (July 1999 est.)
Population growth rate: 1.27%
Infant mortality rate: 8.42 deaths/
1,000 live births
Life expectancy at birth: total popula-
tion: 78.72 years; male: 75.78 years;
female: 81.77 years
Major ethnic groups: U.K. and Norman-
French descent
Major religions: Anglican, Roman
Catholic, Presbyterian, Baptist,
Congregational, Methodist
Major languages: English, French,
Norman-French dialect spoken in
country districts

Government
Official name: Bailiwick of Guernsey
National capital: Saint Peter Port
Independence: none (British crown
dependency)
Legal system: English law and local
statute; justice is administered by
the Royal Court

Economy
Industries: tourism, banking
Agricultural products: tomatoes, green-
house flowers, sweet peppers, egg-
plant, other vegetables, fruit;
Guernsey cattle
Currency: 1 Guernsey (£G) pound =
100 pence

Guinea

Geography
Location: Western Africa, bordering
the North Atlantic Ocean, between
Guinea-Bissau and Sierra Leone
Area: 94,927 sq. mi. (245,860
sq. km.); slightly smaller than
Oregon
Climate: generally hot and humid;
monsoonal-type rainy season (June
to November) with southwesterly
winds; dry season (December to
May) with northeasterly harmattan
winds

Terrain: generally flat coastal plain,
hilly to mountainous interior
Elevation: lowest point: Atlantic Ocean
0 ft. (0 m.); highest point: Mont
Nimba 5,748 ft. (1,752 m.)
Natural resources: bauxite, iron ore,
diamonds, gold, uranium,
hydropower, fish

People
Population: 7,538,953 (July 1999
est.)
Population growth rate: 0.82%
Infant mortality rate: 126.32 deaths/
1,000 live births
Life expectancy at birth: total popula-
tion: 46.5 years; male: 44.02 years;
female: 49.06 years
Major ethnic groups: Peuhl 40%,
Malinke 30%, Soussou 20%,
smaller tribes 10%
Major religions: Muslim 85%,
Christian 8%, indigenous beliefs
7%
Major languages: French (official), each
tribe has its own language

Government
Official name: Republic of Guinea
Government type: republic
National capital: Conakry
Independence: October 2, 1958 (from
France)
Legal system: based on French civil law
system, customary law, and decree;
legal codes currently being revised

Economy
Industries: bauxite, gold, diamonds;
alumina refining; light manufacturing and agricultural processing
industries
Agricultural products: rice, coffee,
pineapples, palm kernels, cassava
(tapioca), bananas, sweet potatoes;
cattle, sheep, goats; timber
Currency: 1 Guinean franc (FG) = 100
centimes

Guinea-Bissau

Geography
Location: Western Africa, bordering
the North Atlantic Ocean, between
Guinea and Senegal

Nations (cont.)

Area: 13,946 sq. mi. (36,120 sq. km.); slightly less than three times the size of Connecticut

Climate: tropical; generally hot and humid; monsoonal-type rainy season (June to November) with south-westerly winds; dry season (December to May) with northeasterly harmattan winds

Terrain: mostly low coastal plain rising to savanna in east

Elevation: lowest point: Atlantic Ocean 0 ft. (0 m.); highest point: unnamed location in the northeast corner of the country 984 ft. (300 m.)

Natural resources: fish, timber, phosphates, bauxite, unexploited deposits of petroleum

People

Population: 1,234,555 (July 1999 est.)

Population growth rate: 2.31%

Infant mortality rate: 109.5 deaths/ 1,000 live births

Life expectancy at birth: total population: 49.57 years; male: 47.91 years; female: 51.28 years

Major ethnic groups: African 99% (Balanta 30%, Fula 20%, Manjaca 14%, Mandinga 13%, Papel 7%)

Major religions: indigenous beliefs 50%, Muslim 45%, Christian 5%

Major languages: Portuguese (official), Crioulo, African languages

Government

Official name: Republic of Guinea-Bissau

Government type: republic, multiparty since mid-1991

National capital: Bissau

Independence: September 24, 1973 (unilaterally declared by Guinea-Bissau); September 10, 1974 (recognized by Portugal)

Economy

Industries: agricultural products processing, beer, soft drinks

Agricultural products: rice, corn, beans, cassava (tapioca), cashew nuts, peanuts, palm kernels, cotton; fish-

ing and forest potential not fully exploited

Currency: 1 Communauté Financière Africaine franc (CFAF) = 100 centimes

Guyana

Geography

Location: Northern South America, bordering the North Atlantic Ocean, between Suriname and Venezuela

Area: 83,000 sq. mi. (214,970 sq. km.); slightly smaller than Idaho

Climate: tropical; hot, humid, moderated by northeast trade winds; two rainy seasons (May to mid-August, mid-November to mid-January)

Terrain: mostly rolling highlands; low coastal plain; savanna in south

Elevation: lowest point: Atlantic Ocean 0 ft. (0 m.); highest point: Mount Roraima 9,301 ft. (2,835 m.)

Natural resources: bauxite, gold, diamonds, hardwood timber, shrimp, fish

People

Population: 705,156 (July 1999 est.)

Population growth rate: -0.32%

Infant mortality rate: 48.64 deaths/ 1,000 live births

Life expectancy at birth: total population: 61.82 years; male: 59.15 years; female: 64.61 years

Major ethnic groups: East Indian 49%, black 32%, mixed 12%, Amerindian 6%

Major religions: Christian 57%, Hindu 33%, Muslim 9%

Major languages: English, Amerindian dialects

Government

Official name: Co-operative Republic of Guyana

Government type: republic

National capital: Georgetown

Independence: May 26, 1966 (from U.K.)

Legal system: based on English common law with certain admixtures of Roman-Dutch law

Economy

Industries: bauxite, sugar, rice milling, timber, fishing (shrimp), textiles, gold mining

Agricultural products: sugar, rice, wheat, vegetable oils; beef, pork, poultry, dairy products; development potential exists for fishing and forestry

Currency: 1 Guyanese dollar (G$) = 100 cents

Haiti

Geography

Location: Caribbean, western one-third of the island of Hispaniola, between the Caribbean Sea and the North Atlantic Ocean, west of the Dominican Republic

Area: 10,714 sq. mi. (27,750 sq. km.); slightly smaller than Maryland

Climate: tropical; semiarid where mountains in east cut off trade winds

Terrain: mostly rough and mountainous

Elevation: lowest point: Caribbean Sea 0 ft. (0 m.); highest point: Chaine de la Selle 8,793 ft. (2,680 m.)

Natural resources: none

People

Population: 6,884,264 (July 1999 est.)

Population growth rate: 1.53%

Infant mortality rate: 97.64 deaths/ 1,000 live births

Life expectancy at birth: total population: 51.65 years; male: 49.53 years; female: 53.88 years

Major ethnic groups: black 95%, mulatto plus white 5%

Major religions: Roman Catholic 80%, Protestant 16%; note: roughly one-half of the population also practices Voodoo

Major languages: French (official) 20%, Creole

Government

Official name: Republic of Haiti

Government type: republic

National capital: Port-au-Prince

Independence: January 1, 1804 (from France)

Legal system: based on Roman civil law system

Economy

Industries: sugar refining, flour milling, textiles, cement, tourism, light assembly industries based on imported parts

Agricultural products: coffee, mangoes, sugarcane, rice, corn, sorghum; wood

Currency: 1 gourde (G) = 100 centimes

Holy See (Vatican City)

Geography

Location: Southern Europe, an enclave of Rome (Italy)

Area: 0.2 sq. mi. (0.44 sq. km.); about 0.7 times the size of The Mall in Washington, D.C.

Climate: temperate; mild, rainy winters (September to mid-May) with hot, dry summers (May to September)

Terrain: low hills

Elevation: lowest point: unnamed location 62 ft. (19 m.); highest point: unnamed location 246 ft. (75 m.)

Natural resources: none

People

Population: 860 (July 1999 est.)

Population growth rate: 1.15%

Major ethnic groups: Italians, Swiss

Major religions: Roman Catholic

Major languages: Italian, Latin, various other languages

Government

Official name: The Holy See (State of the Vatican City)

Government type: monarchical-sacerdotal state

National capital: Vatican City

Independence: February 11, 1929 (from Italy)

Economy

Industries: printing and production of a small amount of mosaics and staff uniforms; worldwide banking and financial activities

Nations *(cont.)*

Currency: 1 Vatican lira (VLit) = 100 centesimi

Honduras

Geography

Location: Central America, bordering the Caribbean Sea, between Guatemala and Nicaragua and bordering the North Pacific Ocean, between El Salvador and Nicaragua

Area: 43,278 sq. mi. (112,090 sq. km.); slightly larger than Tennessee

Climate: subtropical in lowlands, temperate in mountains

Terrain: mostly mountains in interior, narrow coastal plains

Elevation: lowest point: Caribbean Sea 0 ft. (0 m.); highest point: Cerro Las Minas 9,416 ft. (2,870 m.)

Natural resources: timber, gold, silver, copper, lead, zinc, iron ore, antimony, coal, fish

People

Population: 5,997,327 (July 1999 est.)

Population growth rate: 2.24%

Infant mortality rate: 40.84 deaths/ 1,000 live births

Life expectancy at birth: total population: 64.68 years; male: 63.16 years; female: 66.27 years

Major ethnic groups: mestizo (mixed Amerindian and European) 90%, Amerindian 7%, black 2%, white 1%

Major religions: Roman Catholic 97%, Protestant minority

Major languages: Spanish, Amerindian dialects

Government

Official name: Republic of Honduras

Government type: republic

National capital: Tegucigalpa

Independence: September 15, 1821 (from Spain)

Legal system: rooted in Roman and Spanish civil law; some influence of English common law

Economy

Industries: sugar, coffee, textiles, clothing, wood products

Agricultural products: bananas, coffee, citrus; beef; timber; shrimp

Currency: 1 lempira (L) = 100 centavos

Hong Kong

Geography

Location: Eastern Asia, bordering the South China Sea and China

Area: 422 sq. mi. (1,092 sq. km.); six times the size of Washington, D.C.

Climate: tropical monsoon; cool and humid in winter, hot and rainy from spring through summer, warm and sunny in fall

Terrain: hilly to mountainous with steep slopes; lowlands in north

Elevation: lowest point: South China Sea 0 ft. (0 m.); highest point: Tai Mo Shan 3,143 ft. (958 m.)

Natural resources: outstanding deepwater harbor, feldspar

People

Population: 6,847,125 (July 1999 est.)

Population growth rate: 2.24%

Infant mortality rate: 5.2 deaths/1,000 live births

Life expectancy at birth: total population: 78.91 years; male: 76.15 years; female: 81.85 years

Major ethnic groups: Chinese 95%, other 5%

Major religions: eclectic mixture of local religions 90%, Christian 10%

Major languages: Chinese (Cantonese), English

Government

Official name: Hong Kong Special Administrative Region

National capital: Victoria

Independence: none (special administrative region of China)

Legal system: based on English common law

Economy

Industries: textiles, clothing, tourism, electronics, plastics, toys, watches, clocks

Agricultural products: fresh vegetables; poultry

Currency: 1 Hong Kong dollar (HK$) = 100 cents

Hungary

Geography
Location: Central Europe, northwest of Romania

Area: 35,919 sq. mi. (93,030 sq. km.); slightly smaller than Indiana

Climate: temperate; cold, cloudy, humid winters; warm summers

Terrain: mostly flat to rolling plains; hills and low mountains on the Slovakian border

Elevation: lowest point: Tisza River 256 ft. (78 m.); highest point: Kekes 3,327 ft. (1,014 m.)

Natural resources: bauxite, coal, natural gas, fertile soils

People
Population: 10,186,372 (July 1999 est.)

Population growth rate: -0.2%

Infant mortality rate: 9.46 deaths/1,000 live births

Life expectancy at birth: total population: 71.18 years; male: 66.85 years; female: 75.74 years

Major ethnic groups: Hungarian 89.9%, Gypsy 4%, German 2.6%, Serb 2%, Slovak 0.8%, Romanian 0.7%

Major religions: Roman Catholic 67.5%, Calvinist 20%, Lutheran 5%, atheist and other 7.5%

Major languages: Hungarian 98.2%, other 1.8%

Government
Official name: Republic of Hungary

Government type: republic

National capital: Budapest

Independence: 1001 (unification by King Stephen I)

Legal system: in process of revision, moving toward rule of law based on Western model

Economy
Industries: mining, metallurgy, construction materials, processed foods, textiles, chemicals (especially pharmaceuticals), motor vehicles

Agricultural products: wheat, corn, sunflower seed, potatoes, sugar beets; pigs, cattle, poultry, dairy products

Currency: 1 forint (Ft) = 100 filler

Iceland

Geography
Location: Northern Europe, island between the Greenland Sea and the North Atlantic Ocean, northwest of the U.K.

Area: 39,768 sq. mi. (103,000 sq. km.); slightly smaller than Kentucky

Climate: temperate; moderated by North Atlantic Current; mild, windy winters; damp, cool summers

Terrain: mostly plateau interspersed with mountain peaks, ice fields; coast deeply indented by bays and fiords

Elevation: lowest point: Atlantic Ocean 0 ft. (0 m.); highest point; Hvannadalshnukur 6,952 ft. (2,119 m.)

Natural resources: fish, hydropower, geothermal power, diatomite

People
Population: 272,512 (July 1999 est.)

Population growth rate: 0.57%

Infant mortality rate: 5.22 deaths/1,000 live births

Life expectancy at birth: total population: 78.96 years; male: 76.85 years; female: 81.19 years

Major ethnic groups: homogeneous mixture of descendants of Norwegians and Celts

Major religions: Evangelical Lutheran 96%, other Protestant and Roman Catholic 3%

Major languages: Icelandic

Government
Official name: Republic of Iceland

Government type: constitutional republic

National capital: Reykjavik

Independence: June 17, 1944 (from Denmark)

Legal system: civil law system based on Danish law, does not accept compulsory ICJ jurisdiction

Nations (cont.)

Economy

Industries: fish processing; aluminum smelting, ferrosilicon production, geothermal power; tourism

Agricultural products: potatoes, turnips; cattle, sheep; fish

Currency: 1 Icelandic krona (IKr) = 100 aurar

India

Geography

Location: Southern Asia, bordering the Arabian Sea and the Bay of Bengal, between Burma and Pakistan

Area: 1,269,338 sq. mi. (3,287,590 sq. km.); slightly more than one-third the size of the U.S.

Climate: varies from tropical monsoon in south to temperate in north

Terrain: upland plain (Deccan Plateau) in south, flat to rolling plain along the Ganges, deserts in west, Himalayas in north

Elevation: lowest point: Indian Ocean 0 ft. (0 m.); highest point: Kanchenjunga 28,208 ft. (8,598 m.)

Natural resources: coal (fourth-largest reserves in the world), iron ore, manganese, mica, bauxite, titanium ore, chromite, natural gas, diamonds, petroleum, limestone

People

Population: 1,000,848,550 (July 1999 est.)

Population growth rate: 1.68%

Infant mortality rate: 60.81 deaths/ 1,000 live births

Life expectancy at birth: total population: 63.4 years; male: 62.54 years; female: 64.29 years

Major ethnic groups: Indo-Aryan 72%, Dravidian 25%, Mongoloid

Major religions: Hindu 80%, Muslim 14%, Christian 2.4%, Sikh 2%

Major languages: English enjoys associate status but is the most important language for national, political, and commercial communication, Hindi is the national language and primary tongue of 30% of the people, Bengali (official), Telugu (official), Marathi (official), Tamil (official), Urdu (official), Gujarati (official), Malayalam (official), Kannada (official), Oriya (official), Punjabi (official), Assamese (official), Kashmiri (official), Sindhi (official), Sanskrit (official), Hindustani a popular variant of Hindu/ Urdu, is spoken widely throughout northern India. (Note: 24 languages each spoken by a million or more persons; numerous other languages and dialects, for the most part mutually unintelligible)

Government

Official name: Republic of India

Government type: federal republic

National capital: New Delhi

Independence: August 15, 1947 (from U.K.)

Legal system: based on English common law; limited judicial review of legislative acts

Economy

Industries: textiles, chemicals, food processing, steel, transportation equipment, cement, mining, petroleum, machinery

Agricultural products: rice, wheat, oilseed, cotton, jute, tea, sugarcane, potatoes; cattle, water buffalo, sheep, goats, poultry; fish

Currency: 1 Indian rupee (Re) = 100 paise

Indonesia

Geography

Location: Southeastern Asia, archipelago between the Indian Ocean and the Pacific Ocean

Area: 741,096 sq. mi. (1,919,440 sq. km.); slightly less than three times the size of Texas

Climate: tropical; hot, humid; more moderate in highlands

Terrain: mostly coastal lowlands; larger islands have interior mountains

Elevation: lowest point: Indian Ocean
0 ft. (0 m.); highest point: Puncak
Jaya 16,502 ft. (5,030 m.)
Natural resources: petroleum, tin,
natural gas, nickel, timber, bauxite,
copper, fertile soils, coal, gold,
silver

People
Population: 216,108,345 (July 1999
est.)
Population growth rate: 1.46%
Infant mortality rate: 57.3 deaths/1,000
live births
Life expectancy at birth: total popula-
tion: 62.92 years; male: 60.67
years; female: 65.29 years
Major ethnic groups: Javanese 45%,
Sundanese 14%, Madurese 7.5%,
coastal Malays 7.5%, other 26%
Major religions: Muslim 87%,
Protestant 6%, Roman Catholic
3%
Major languages: Bahasa Indonesia
(official, modified form of Malay),
English, Dutch, local dialects, the
most widely spoken of which is
Javanese

Government
Official name: Republic of Indonesia
Government type: republic
National capital: Jakarta
Independence: August 17, 1945 (proclaimed independence; on
December 27, 1949, Indonesia
became legally independent from
the Netherlands)
Legal system: based on Roman-Dutch
law, substantially modified by indigenous concepts and by new criminal
procedures code, has not accepted
compulsory ICJ jurisdiction

Economy
Industries: petroleum and natural gas,
textiles, mining, cement, chemical
fertilizers, plywood, food, rubber;
tourism
Agricultural products: rice, cassava
(tapioca), peanuts, rubber, cocoa,
coffee, palm oil, copra, other tropical
products; poultry, beef, pork, eggs

Currency: Indonesian rupiah (Rp)

Iran

Geography
Location: Middle East, bordering the
Gulf of Oman, the Persian Gulf,
and the Caspian Sea, between Iraq
and Pakistan
Area: 636,293 sq. mi. (1,648,000
sq. km.); slightly larger than Alaska
Climate: mostly arid or semiarid, subtropical along Caspian coast
Terrain: rugged, mountainous rim;
high, central basin with deserts,
mountains; small, discontinuous
plains along both coasts
Elevation: lowest point: Caspian Sea
–92 ft. (–28 m.); highest point:
Qolleh-ye Damavand 18,605 ft.
(5,671 m.)
Natural resources: petroleum, natural
gas, coal, chromium, copper, iron
ore, lead, manganese, zinc, sulfur

People
Population: 65,179,752 (July 1999
est.)
Population growth rate: 1.07%
Infant mortality rate: 29.73 deaths/
1,000 live births
Life expectancy at birth: total popula-
tion: 69.76 years; male: 68.43 years;
female: 71.16 years
Major ethnic groups: Persian 51%,
Azerbaijani 24%, Gilaki and
Mazandarani 8%, Kurd 7%, Arab
3%, Lur 2%, Baloch 2%, Turkmen
2%
Major religions: Shi'a Muslim 89%,
Sunni Muslim 10%
Major languages: Persian and Persian
dialects 58%, Turkic and Turkic
dialects 26%, Kurdish 9%

Government
Official name: Islamic Republic of
Iran
Government type: theocratic republic
National capital: Tehran
Independence: April 1, 1979 (Islamic
Republic of Iran proclaimed)
Legal system: the Constitution codifies
Islamic principles of government

Nations *(cont.)*

Economy

Industries: petroleum, petrochemicals, textiles, cement and other construction materials, food processing (particularly sugar refining and vegetable oil production), metal fabricating, armaments

Agricultural products: wheat, rice, other grains, sugar beets, fruits, nuts, cotton; dairy products, wool; caviar

Currency: 10 Iranian rials (IR) = 1 toman (Note: domestic figures are generally given in terms of the toman)

Iraq

Geography

Location: Middle East, bordering the Persian Gulf, between Iran and Kuwait

Area: 168,753 sq. mi. (437,072 sq. km.); slightly more than twice the size of Idaho

Climate: mostly desert; mild to cool winters with dry, hot, cloudless summers; northern mountainous regions along Iranian and Turkish borders experience cold winters with occasionally heavy snows that melt in early spring, sometimes causing extensive flooding in central and southern Iraq

Terrain: mostly broad plains; reedy marshes along Iranian border in south with large flooded areas; mountains along borders with Iran and Turkey

Elevation: lowest point: Persian Gulf 0 ft. (0 m.); highest point Gundah Zhur 11,837 ft. (3,608 m.)

Natural resources: petroleum, natural gas, phosphates, sulfur

People

Population: 22,427,150 (July 1999 est.)

Population growth rate: 3.19%

Infant mortality rate: 62.41 deaths/ 1,000 live births

Life expectancy at birth: total population: 66.52 years; male: 65.54 years; female: 67.56 years

Major ethnic groups: Arab 75%–80%, Kurdish 15%–20%,

Major religions: Muslim 97% (Shi'a 60%–65%, Sunni 32%–37%)

Major languages: Arabic, Kurdish (official in Kurdish regions), Assyrian, Armenian

Government

Official name: Republic of Iraq

Government type: republic

National capital: Baghdad

Independence: October 3, 1932 (from League of Nations mandate under British administration)

Legal system: based on Islamic law in special religious courts, civil law system elsewhere; has not accepted compulsory ICJ jurisdiction

Economy

Industries: petroleum, chemicals, textiles, construction materials, food processing

Agricultural products: wheat, barley, rice, vegetables, dates, other fruit, cotton; cattle, sheep

Currency: 1 Iraqi dinar (ID) = 1,000 fils

Ireland

Geography

Location: Western Europe, occupying five-sixths of the island of Ireland in the North Atlantic Ocean, west of Great Britain

Area: 27,135 sq. mi. (70,280 sq. km.); slightly larger than West Virginia

Climate: temperate maritime; modified by North Atlantic Current; mild winters, cool summers; consistently humid; overcast about half the time

Terrain: mostly level to rolling interior plain surrounded by rugged hills and low mountains; sea cliffs on west coast

Elevation: lowest point: Atlantic Ocean 0 ft. (0 m.); highest point: Carrauntoohill 3,415 ft. (1,041 m.)

Natural resources: zinc, lead, natural gas, barite, copper, gypsum, limestone, dolomite, peat, silver

People
Population: 3,632,944 (July 1999 est.)
Population growth rate: 0.38%
Infant mortality rate: 5.94 deaths/ 1,000 live births
Life expectancy at birth: total population: 76.39 years; male: 73.64 years; female: 79.32 years
Major ethnic groups: Celtic, English
Major religions: Roman Catholic 93%, Anglican 3%, none 1%, unknown 2%, other 1%
Major languages: Irish (Gaelic), spoken mainly in areas located along the western seaboard, English is the language generally used

Government
Official name: Ireland
Government type: republic
National capital: Dublin
Independence: December 6, 1921 (from U.K.)
Legal system: based on English common law, substantially modified by indigenous concepts; judicial review of legislative acts in Supreme Court; has not accepted compulsory ICJ jurisdiction

Economy
Industries: food products, brewing, textiles, clothing, chemicals, pharmaceuticals, machinery, transportation equipment, glass and crystal
Agricultural products: turnips, barley, potatoes, sugar beets, wheat; meat and dairy products
Currency: 1 Irish pound (£Ir) = 100 pence

Israel

Geography
Location: Middle East, bordering the Mediterranean Sea, between Egypt and Lebanon
Area: 8,019 sq. mi. (20,770 sq. km.); slightly smaller than New Jersey
Climate: temperate; hot and dry in southern and eastern desert areas
Terrain: Negev desert in the south; low coastal plain; central mountains; Jordan Rift Valley
Elevation: lowest point: Dead Sea −1,339 ft. (−408 m.); highest point: Har Meron 3,963 ft. (1,208 m.)
Natural resources: copper, phosphates, bromide, potash, clay, sand, sulfur, asphalt, manganese, small amounts of natural gas and crude oil

People
Population: 5,749,760 (July 1999 est.) [Note: this figure includes about 166,000 Israeli settlers in the West bank, about 19,000 in the Israeli-occupied Golan Heights, 6,000 in the Gaza Strip, and about 176,000 in East Jerusalem (August 1998 est.)]
Population growth rate: 1.81%
Infant mortality rate: 7.78 deaths/ 1,000 live births
Life expectancy at birth: total population: 78.61 years; male: 76.71 years; female: 80.61 years
Major ethnic groups: Jewish 82%, non-Jewish 18% (mostly Arab)
Major religions: Judaism 82%, Islam 14%
Major languages: Hebrew (official), Arabic used officially for Arab minority

Government
Official name: State of Israel
Government type: republic
National capital: Jerusalem
Note: Israel proclaimed Jerusalem as its capital in 1950, but the U.S., like nearly all other countries, maintains its Embassy in Tel Aviv
Independence: May 14, 1948 (from League of Nations mandate under British administration)
Legal system: mixture of English common law, British Mandate regulations, and, in personal matters, Jewish, Christian, and Muslim legal systems; has not, since 1985, accepted compulsory ICJ jurisdiction

Nations *(cont.)*

Economy

Industries: food processing, diamond cutting and polishing, textiles and apparel, metal products, military equipment, transport equipment, electrical equipment, potash mining, high-technology electronics, tourism

Agricultural products: citrus and other fruits, vegetables, cotton; beef, poultry, dairy products

Currency: 1 new Israeli shekel (NIS) = 100 new agorot

Italy

Geography

Location: Southern Europe, a peninsula extending into the central Mediterranean Sea, northeast of Tunisia

Area: 116,305 sq. mi. (301,230 sq. km.); slightly larger than Arizona

Climate: predominantly Mediterranean; Alpine in far north; hot, dry in south

Terrain: mostly rugged and mountainous; some plains, coastal lowlands

Elevation: lowest point: Mediterranean Sea 0 ft. (0 m.); highest point: Mont Blanc 15,771 ft. (4,807 m.)

Natural resources: mercury, potash, marble, sulfur, dwindling natural gas and crude oil reserves, fish, coal

People

Population: 56,735,130 (July 1999 est.)

Population growth rate: -0.08%

Infant mortality rate: 6.3 deaths/1,000 live births

Life expectancy at birth: total population: 75.51 years; male: 75.4 years; female: 81.82 years

Major ethnic groups: Italian (includes small clusters of German-, French-, and Slovene-Italians in the north and Albanian-Italians and Greek-Italians in the south)

Major religions: Roman Catholic 98%

Major languages: Italian, German, French, Slovene

Government

Official name: Italian Republic

Government type: republic

National capital: Rome

Independence: March 17, 1861 (Kingdom of Italy proclaimed)

Legal system: based on civil law system, with ecclesiastical law influence; appeals treated as trials de novo

Economy

Industries: tourism, machinery, iron and steel, chemicals, food processing, textiles, motor vehicles, clothing, footwear, ceramics

Agricultural products: fruits, vegetables, grapes, potatoes, sugar beets, soybeans, grain, olives; meat and dairy products; fish

Currency: 1 Italian lira (Lit) = 100 centesimi

Jamaica

Geography

Location: Caribbean, island in the Caribbean Sea, south of Cuba

Area: 4,243 sq. mi. (10,990 sq. km.); slightly smaller than Connecticut

Climate: tropical; hot, humid; temperate interior

Terrain: mostly mountains with narrow, discontinuous coastal plain

Elevation: lowest point: Caribbean Sea 0 ft. (0 m.); highest point: Blue Mountain Peak 7,401 ft. (2,256 m.)

Natural resources: bauxite, gypsum, limestone

People

Population: 2,652,443 (July 1999 est.)

Population growth rate: 0.64%

Infant mortality rate: 13.93 deaths/1,000 live births

Life expectancy at birth: total population: 75.62 years; male: 73.22 years; female: 78.13 years

Major ethnic groups: black 90.4%, East Indian 1.3%, white 0.2%, Chinese 0.2%, mixed 7.3%

Major religions: Protestant 61.3%, Roman Catholic 4%, other, including some spiritual cults 34.7%

Major languages: English, Creole

Government
Official name: Jamaica
Government type: parliamentary democracy
National capital: Kingston
Independence: August 6, 1962 (from U.K.)
Legal system: based on English common law

Economy
Industries: tourism, bauxite, textiles, food processing, light manufactures
Agricultural products: sugarcane, bananas, coffee, citrus, potatoes, vegetables; poultry, goats, milk
Currency: 1 Jamaican dollar (J$) = 100 cents

Japan

Geography
Location: Eastern Asia, island chain between the North Pacific Ocean and the Sea of Japan, east of the Korean Peninsula
Area: 145,882 sq. mi. (377,835 sq. km.); slightly smaller than California
Climate: varies from tropical in south to cool temperate in north
Terrain: mostly rugged and mountainous
Elevation: lowest point: Hachiro-gata –13 ft. (–4 m.); highest point: Fujiyama 12,388 ft. (3,776 m.)
Natural resources: negligible mineral resources, fish

People
Population: 126,182,077 (July 1999 est.)
Population growth rate: 0.2%
Infant mortality rate: 4.07 deaths/ 1,000 live births
Life expectancy at birth: total population: 80.11 years; male: 77.02 years; female: 83.35 years
Major ethnic groups: Japanese 99.4%, other 0.6% (mostly Korean)
Major religions: observe both Shinto and Buddhist 84%, other 16%
Major languages: Japanese

Government
Official name: Japan
Government type: constitutional monarchy
National capital: Tokyo
Independence: 660 BC (traditional founding by Emperor Jimmu)
Legal system: modeled after European civil law system with English-American influence; judicial review of legislative acts in the Supreme Court

Economy
Industries: among world's largest and technologically advanced producers of steel and nonferrous metallurgy, heavy electrical equipment, construction and mining equipment, motor vehicles and parts, electronic and telecommunication equipment, machine tools, automated production systems, locomotives and railroad rolling stock, ships, chemicals; textiles, processed foods
Agricultural products: rice, sugar beets, vegetables, fruit; pork, poultry, dairy products, eggs; fish
Currency: Yen (¥)

Jersey

Geography
Location: Western Europe, island in the English Channel, northwest of France
Area: 45 sq. mi. (116 sq. km.); about 0.7 times the size of Washington, D.C.
Climate: temperate; mild winters and cool summers
Terrain: gently rolling plain with low, rugged hills along north coast
Elevation: lowest point: Atlantic Ocean 0 ft. (0 m.); highest point: unnamed location 469 ft. (143 m.)
Natural resources: agricultural land

People
Population: 89,721 (July 1999 est.)
Population growth rate: 0.63%
Infant mortality rate: 2.76 deaths/ 1,000 live births
Life expectancy at birth: total population: 78.83 years; male: 76.08 years; female: 81.87 years

Nations *(cont.)*

Major ethnic groups: U.K. and Norman-French descent
Major religions: Anglican, Roman Catholic, Baptist, Congregational New Church, Methodist, Presbyterian
Major languages: English (official), French (official), Norman-French dialect spoken in country districts

Government
Official name: Bailiwick of Jersey
National capital: Saint Helier
Independence: none (British crown dependency)
Legal system: English law and local statute

Economy
Industries: tourism, banking and finance, dairy
Agricultural products: potatoes, cauliflowers, tomatoes; meat, dairy products
Currency: 1 Jersey pound (£J) = 100 pence

Jordan

Geography
Location: Middle East, northwest of Saudi Arabia
Area: 34,445 sq. mi. (89,213 sq. km.); slightly smaller than Indiana
Climate: mostly arid desert; rainy season in west (November to April)
Terrain: mostly desert plateau in east, highland area in west; Great Rift Valley separates East and West Banks of the Jordan River
Elevation: lowest point: Dead Sea −1,339 ft. (−408 m.); highest point: Jabal Ram 5,755 ft. (1,754 m.)
Natural resources: phosphates, potash, shale oil

People
Population: 4,561,147 (July 1999 est.)
Population growth rate: 3.05%
Infant mortality rate: 32.7 deaths/1,000 live births
Life expectancy at birth: total population: 73.06 years; male: 71.15 years; female: 75.08 years

Major ethnic groups: Arab 98%
Major religions: Sunni Muslim 96%, Christian 4%
Major languages: Arabic (official)

Government
Official name: Hashemite Kingdom of Jordan
Government type: constitutional monarchy
National capital: Amman
Independence: May 25, 1946 (from League of Nations mandate under British administration)
Legal system: based on Islamic law and French codes; judicial review of legislative acts in a specially provided High Tribunal; has not accepted compulsory ICJ jurisdiction

Economy
Industries: phosphate mining, petroleum refining, cement, potash, light manufacturing
Agricultural products: wheat, barley, citrus, tomatoes, melons, olives; sheep, goats, poultry
Currency: 1 Jordanian dinar (JD) = 1,000 fils

Kazakhstan

Geography
Location: Central Asia, northwest of China
Area: 1,049,150 sq. mi. (2,717,300 sq. km.) slightly less than four times the size of Texas
Climate: continental, cold winters and hot summers, arid and semiarid
Terrain: extends from the Volga to the Altai Mountains and from the plains in western Siberia to oasis and desert in Central Asia
Elevation: lowest point: Vpadina Kaundy −433 ft.(−132 m.); highest point: Zhengis Shingy (Pik Khan-Tengri) 22,949 ft. (6,995 m.)
Natural resources: major deposits of petroleum, natural gas, coal, iron ore, manganese, chrome ore, nickel, cobalt, copper, molybdenum, lead, zinc, bauxite, gold, uranium

People

Population: 16,824,825 (July 1999 est.)

Population growth rate: -0.09%

Infant mortality rate: 58.82 deaths/ 1,000 live births

Life expectancy at birth: total population: 63.39 years; male: 57.92 years; female: 69.13 years

Major ethnic groups: Kazakh (Qazaq) 46%, Russian 34.7%, Ukrainian 4.9%, German 3.1%, Uzbek 2.3%, Tatar 1.9%

Major religions: Muslim 47%, Russian Orthodox 44%, Protestant 2%

Major languages: Kazakh (Qazaq) official language spoken by over 40% of population, Russian official language spoken by two-thirds of population and used in everyday business

Government

Official name: Republic of Kazakhstan

Government type: republic

National capital: Astana (Akmola)

Note: the government has recently moved from Almaty to Astana

Independence: December 16, 1991 (from the Soviet Union)

Legal system: based on civil law system

Economy

Industries: oil, coal, iron ore, manganese, chromite, lead, zinc, copper, titanium, bauxite, gold, silver, phosphates, sulfur, iron and steel, nonferrous metal, tractors and other agricultural machinery, electric motors, construction materials; much of industrial capacity is shut down and/or is in need of repair

Agricultural products: grain, mostly spring wheat, cotton; wool, meat

Currency: 1 Kazakhstani tenge = 100 tiyn

Kenya

Geography

Location: Eastern Africa, bordering the Indian Ocean, between Somalia and Tanzania

Area: 224,961 sq. mi. (582,650 sq. km.); slightly more than twice the size of Nevada

Climate: varies from tropical along coast to arid in interior

Terrain: low plains rise to central highlands bisected by Great Rift Valley; fertile plateau in west

Elevation: lowest point: Indian Ocean 0 ft. (0 m.); highest point: Mount Kenya 17,057 ft. (5,199 m.)

Natural resources: gold, limestone, soda ash, salt barytes, rubies, fluorspar, garnets, wildlife

People

Population: 28,808,658 (July 1999 est.)

Population growth rate: 1.59%

Infant mortality rate: 59.07 deaths/ 1,000 live births

Life expectancy at birth: total population: 47.02 years; male: 46.56 years; female: 47.49 years

Major ethnic groups: Kikuyu 22%, Luhya 14%, Luo 13%, Kalenjin 12%, Kamba 11%, Kisii 6%, Meru 6%, other African 15%

Major religions: Protestant (including Anglican) 38%, Roman Catholic 28%, indigenous beliefs 26%, Muslim 6%

Major languages: English (official), Swahili (official), numerous indigenous languages

Government

Official name: Republic of Kenya

Government type: republic

National capital: Nairobi

Independence: December 12, 1963 (from U.K.)

Legal system: based on English common law, tribal law, and Islamic law; judicial review in High Court

Economy

Industries: small-scale consumer goods (plastic, furniture, batteries, textiles, soap, cigarettes, flour), processing agricultural products; oil refining, cement; tourism

Agricultural products: coffee, tea, corn, wheat, sugarcane, fruit, vegetables; dairy products, beef, pork, poultry, eggs

Currency: 1 Kenyan shilling (KSh) = 100 cents

Nations *(cont.)*

Kiribati

Geography

Location: Oceania, group of islands in the Pacific Ocean, straddling the equator, about one-half of the way from Hawaii to Australia

Area: 277 sq. mi. (717 sq. km.); four times the size of Washington, D.C.

Climate: tropical; marine, hot and humid, moderated by trade winds

Terrain: mostly low-lying coral atolls surrounded by extensive reefs

Elevation: lowest point: Pacific Ocean 0 ft. (0 m.); highest point: unnamed location on Banaba 266 ft. (81 m.)

Natural resources: phosphate (production discontinued in 1979)

People

Population: 85,501 (July 1999 est.)

Population growth rate: 1.78%

Infant mortality rate: 48.22 deaths/1,000 live births

Life expectancy at birth: total population: 62.88 years; male: 61.02 years; female: 64.98 years

Major ethnic groups: Micronesian

Major religions: Roman Catholic 53%, Protestant (Congregational) 41%, Seventh-Day Adventist, Baha'i, Church of God, Mormon 6%

Major languages: English (official), Gilbertese

Government

Official name: Republic of Kiribati

Government type: republic

National capital: Tarawa

Independence: July 12, 1979 (from U.K.)

Economy

Industries: fishing, handicrafts

Agricultural products: copra, taro, breadfruit, sweet potatoes, vegetables; fish

Currency: 1 Australian dollar ($A) = 100 cents

Korea, North

Geography

Location: Eastern Asia, northern half of the Korean Peninsula bordering the Korea Bay and the Sea of Japan, between China and South Korea

Area: 46,540 sq. mi. (120,540 sq. km.); slightly smaller than Mississippi

Climate: temperate with rainfall concentrated in summer

Terrain: mostly hills and mountains separated by deep, narrow valleys; coastal plains wide in west, discontinuous in east

Elevation: extremes: lowest point: Sea of Japan 0 ft. (0 m.); highest point: Paektu-san 9,003 ft. (2,744 m.)

Natural resources: coal, lead, tungsten, zinc, graphite, magnesite, iron ore, copper, gold, pyrites, salt, fluorspar, hydropower

People

Population: 21,386,109 (July 1999 est.)

Population growth rate: 1.45%

Infant mortality rate: 25.52 deaths/1,000 live births

Life expectancy at birth: total population: 70.07 years; male: 67.41 years; female: 72.86 years

Major ethnic groups: racially homogenous; there is a small Chinese community and a few ethnic Japanese

Major religions: Buddhism and Confucianism, some Christianity and syncretic Chondogyo

Major languages: Korean

Government

Official name: Democratic People's Republic of Korea; Note: the North Koreans generally use the term "Choson" to refer to their country

Government type: Communist state; one-man dictatorship

National capital: P'yongyang

Independence: September 9, 1948 Democratic People's Republic of Korea

Legal system: based on German civil law system with Japanese influences and Communist legal theory; no judicial review of legislative acts; has not accepted compulsory ICJ jurisdiction

Economy

Industries: military products; machine building, electric power, chemicals; mining (coal, iron ore, magnesite, graphite, copper, zinc, lead, and precious metals), metallurgy; textiles, food processing

Agricultural products: rice, corn, potatoes, soybeans, pulses; cattle, pigs, pork, eggs

Currency: 1 North Korean won (Wn) = 100 chon

Korea, South

Geography

Location: Eastern Asia, southern half of the Korean Peninsula bordering the Sea of Japan and the Yellow Sea

Area: 38,023 sq. mi. (98,480 sq. km.); slightly larger than Indiana

Climate: temperate, with rainfall heavier in summer than winter

Terrain: mostly hills and mountains; wide coastal plains in west and south

Elevation: lowest point: Sea of Japan 0 ft. (0 m.); highest point: Halla-san 6,398 ft. (1,950 m.)

Natural resources: coal, tungsten, graphite, molybdenum, lead, hydropower

People

Population: 46,884,800 (July 1999 est.)

Population growth rate: 1%

Infant mortality rate: 7.57 deaths/1,000 live births

Life expectancy at birth: total population: 74.3 years; male: 70.75 years; female: 78.32 years

Major ethnic groups: racially homogenous; there is a small (≈ 20,000) Chinese community

Major religions: Christianity 49%, Buddhism 47%, Confucianism 3%, pervasive folk religion (shamanism), Chondogyo (Religion of the Heavenly Way)

Major languages: Korean

Government

Official name: Republic of Korea

Government type: republic

National capital: Seoul

Independence: August 15, 1945; note-date of liberation from Japanese colonial rule

Legal system: combines elements of continental European civil law systems, Anglo-American law, and Chinese classical thought

Economy

Industries: electronics, automobile production, chemicals, shipbuilding, steel, textiles, clothing, footwear, food processing

Agricultural products: rice, root crops, barley, vegetables, fruit; cattle, pigs, chickens, milk, eggs; fish catch of 2.9 million metric tons, seventh largest in world

Currency: 1 South Korean won (W) = 100 chun (theoretical)

Kuwait

Geography

Location: Middle East, bordering the Persian Gulf, between Iraq and Saudi Arabia

Area: 6,880 sq. mi. (17,820 sq. km.) slightly smaller than New Jersey

Climate: dry desert; intensely hot summers; short, cool winters

Terrain: flat to slightly undulating desert plain

Elevation: lowest point: Persian Gulf 0 ft. (0 m.); highest point: unnamed location 1,004 ft. (306 m.)

Natural resources: petroleum, fish, shrimp, natural gas

People

Population: 1,991,115 (Note: includes 1,220,935 non-nationals)

Population growth rate: 3.88% (Note: this rate reflects the continued post-Gulf crisis return of expatriates)

Infant mortality rate: 10.26 deaths/1,000 live births

Life expectancy at birth: total population: 77.15 years; male: 75.11 years; female: 79.3 years

Major ethnic groups: Kuwaiti 45%, other Arab 35%, South Asian 9%, Iranian 4%

Major religions: Muslim 85% (Sunni 45%, Shi'a 40%), Christian, Hindu, Parsi

Nations *(cont.)*

Major languages: Arabic (official)

Government

Official name: State of Kuwait
Government type: nominal constitutional monarchy
National capital: Kuwait
Independence: June 19, 1961 (from U.K.)
Legal system: civil law system with Islamic law significant in personal matters

Economy

Industries: petroleum, petrochemicals, desalination, food processing, construction materials, salt, construction
Agricultural products: practically no crops; extensive fishing in territorial waters
Currency: 1 Kuwaiti dinar (KD) = 1,000 fils

Kyrgyzstan

Geography

Location: Central Asia, west of China
Area: 76,641 sq. mi. (198,500 sq. km.); slightly smaller than South Dakota
Climate: dry continental to polar in high Tien Shan; subtropical in southwest (Fergana Valley); temperate in northern foothill zone
Terrain: peaks of Tien Shan and associated valleys and basins encompass entire nation
Elevation: lowest point: Kara-Darya 433 ft. (132 m.); highest point: Jengish Chokusu (Pik Pobedy) 24,406 ft. (7,439 m.)
Natural resources: abundant hydroelectric potential; significant deposits of gold and rare earth metals; locally exploitable coal, oil, and natural gas; other deposits of nepheline, mercury, bismuth, lead, and zinc

People

Population: 4,546,055 (July 1999 est.)
Population growth rate: 0.68%
Infant mortality rate: 75.92 deaths/ 1,000 live births

Life expectancy at birth: total population: 63.57 years; male: 59.25 years; female: 68.1 years
Major ethnic groups: Kirghiz 52.4%, Russian 18%, Uzbek 12.9%, Ukrainian 2.5%, German 2.4%
Major religions: Muslim 75%, Russian Orthodox 20%
Major languages: Kirghiz (Kyrgyz)-official language, Russian-official language

Government

Official name: Kyrgyz Republic
Government type: republic
National capital: Bishkek
Independence: August 31, 1991 (from Soviet Union)
Legal system: based on civil law system

Economy

Industries: small machinery, textiles, food processing, cement, shoes, sawn logs, refrigerators, furniture, electric motors, gold, rare earth metals
Agricultural products: wool, tobacco, cotton, potatoes, vegetables, grapes, fruits and berries; sheep, goats, cattle
Currency: 1 Kyrgyzstani som (KGS) = 100 tyiyn

Laos

Geography

Location: Southeastern Asia, northeast of Thailand, west of Vietnam
Area: 91,428 sq. mi. (236,800 sq. km.); slightly larger than Utah
Climate: tropical monsoon; rainy season (May to November); dry season (December to April)
Terrain: mostly rugged mountains; some plains and plateaus
Elevation: lowest point: Mekong River 230 ft. (70 m.); highest point: Phou Bia 9,242 ft. (2,817 m.)
Natural resources: timber, hydropower, gypsum, tin, gold, gemstones

People

Population: 5,407,453 (July 1999 est.)

Population growth rate: 2.74%

Infant mortality rate: 89.32 deaths/ 1,000 live births

Life expectancy at birth: total population: 54.21 years; male: 52.63 years; female: 55.87 years

Major ethnic groups: Lao Loum (lowland) 68%, Lao Theung (upland) 22%, Lao Soung (highland) including the Hmong ("Meo") and the Yao (Mien) 9%

Major religions: Buddhist 60%, animist and other 40%

Major languages: Lao (official), French, English, and various ethnic languages

Government

Official name: Lao People's Democratic Republic

Government type: Communist state

National capital: Vientiane

Independence: July 19, 1949 (from France)

Legal system: based on traditional customs, French legal norms and procedures, and Socialist practice

Economy

Industries: tin and gypsum mining, timber, electric power, agricultural processing, construction, garments

Agricultural products: sweet potatoes, vegetables, corn, coffee, sugarcane, cotton; water buffalo, pigs, cattle, poultry; tobacco

Currency: 1 new kip (NK) = 100 at

Latvia

Geography

Location: Eastern Europe, bordering the Baltic Sea, between Estonia and Lithuania

Area: 24,749 sq. mi. (64,100 sq. km.); slightly larger than West Virginia

Climate: maritime; wet, moderate winters

Terrain: low plain

Elevation: lowest point: Baltic Sea 0 ft. (0 m.); highest point: Gaizinkalns 1,024 ft. (312 m.)

Natural resources: minimal; amber, peat, limestone, dolomite

People

Population: 2,353,874 (July 1999 est.)

Population growth rate: −1.25%

Infant mortality rate: 17.19 deaths/ 1,000 live births

Life expectancy at birth: total population: 67.3 years; male: 61.24 years; female: 73.66 years

Major ethnic groups: Latvian 56.5%, Russian 30.4%, Byelorussian 4.3%, Ukrainian 2.8%, Polish 2.6%

Major religions: Lutheran, Roman Catholic, Russian Orthodox

Major languages: Lettish (official), Lithuanian, Russian

Government

Official name: Republic of Latvia

Government type: parliamentary democracy

National capital: Riga

Independence: September 6, 1991 (from Soviet Union)

Legal system: based on civil law system

Economy

Industries: buses, vans, street and railroad cars, synthetic fibers, agricultural machinery, fertilizers, washing machines, radios, electronics, pharmaceuticals, processed foods, textiles; dependent on imports for energy, raw materials, and intermediate products

Agricultural products: grain, sugar beets, potatoes, vegetables; meat, milk, eggs; fish

Currency: 1 Latvian lat (LVL) = 100 santims; introduced March 1993

Lebanon

Geography

Location: Middle East, bordering the Mediterranean Sea, between Israel and Syria

Area: 4,015 sq. mi. (10,400 sq. km.); about 0.7 times the size of Connecticut

Climate: Mediterranean; mild to cool, wet winters with hot, dry summers; Lebanon mountains experience heavy winter snows

Nations *(cont.)*

Terrain: narrow coastal plain; Al Biqa' (Bekaa Valley) separates Lebanon and Anti-Lebanon Mountains

Elevation: lowest point: Mediterranean Sea 0 ft. (0 m.); highest point: Jabal al Makmal 10,128 ft. (3,087 m.)

Natural resources: limestone, iron ore, salt, water-surplus state in a water-deficit region

People

Population: 3,562,699 (July 1999 est.)

Population growth rate: 1.61%

Infant mortality rate: 30.53 deaths/1,000 live births

Life expectancy at birth: total population: 70.93 years; male: 68.34 years; female: 73.66 years

Major ethnic groups: Arab 95%, Armenian 4%

Major religions: Islam 70%, Christian 30%

Major languages: Arabic (official), French

Government

Official name: Lebanese Republic

Government type: republic

National capital: Beirut

Independence: November 22, 1943 (from League of Nations mandate under French administration)

Legal system: mixture of Ottoman law, canon law, Napoleonic code, and civil law; no judicial review of legislative acts; has not accepted compulsory ICJ jurisdiction

Economy

Industries: banking; food processing; jewelry; cement; textiles; mineral and chemical products; wood and furniture products; oil refining; metal fabricating

Agricultural products: citrus, vegetables, potatoes, olives, tobacco, hemp (hashish); sheep, goats

Currency: 1 Lebanese pound (£L) = 100 piasters

Lesotho

Geography

Location: Southern Africa, an enclave of South Africa

Area: 11,718 sq. mi. (30,350 sq. km.); slightly smaller than Maryland

Climate: temperate; cool to cold, dry winters; hot, wet summers

Terrain: mostly highland with plateaus, hills, and mountains

Elevation: lowest point: junction of the Orange and Makhaleng Rivers 4,593 ft. (1,400 m.); highest point: Mount Thabana Ntlenyana 11,424 ft. (3,482 m.)

Natural resources: water, agricultural and grazing land, some diamonds and other minerals

People

Population: 2,128,950 (July 1999 est.)

Population growth rate: 1.8%

Infant mortality rate: 77.58 deaths/1,000 live births

Life expectancy at birth: total population: 52.99 years; male: 51.37 years; female: 54.65 years

Major ethnic groups: Sotho 99.7%

Major religions: Christian 80%, indigenous beliefs

Major languages: Sesotho (southern Sotho), English (official), Zulu, Xhosa

Government

Official name: Kingdom of Lesotho

Government type: parliamentary constitutional monarchy

National capital: Maseru

Independence: October 4, 1966 (from U.K.)

Legal system: based on English common law and Roman-Dutch law; judicial review of legislative acts in High Court and Court of Appeal; has not accepted compulsory ICJ jurisdiction

Economy

Industries: food, beverages, textiles, handicrafts; construction; tourism

Agricultural products: corn, wheat, pulses, sorghum, barley; livestock
Currency: 1 loti (L) = 100 lisente

Liberia

Geography
Location: Western Africa, bordering the North Atlantic Ocean, between Cote d'Ivoire and Sierra Leone
Area: 43,000 sq. mi. (111,370 sq. km.); slightly larger than Tennessee
Climate: tropical; hot, humid; dry winters with hot days and cool to cold nights; wet, cloudy summers with frequent heavy showers
Terrain: mostly flat to rolling coastal plains rising to rolling plateau and low mountains in northeast
Elevation: lowest point: Atlantic Ocean 0 ft. (0 m.); highest point: Mount Wuteve 4,528 ft. (1,380 m.)
Natural resources: iron ore, timber, diamonds, gold

People
Population: 2,923,725 (July 199 est.)
Population growth rate: 5.76%
Infant mortality rate: 100.63 deaths/1,000 live births
Life expectancy at birth: total population: 59.88 years; male: 57.2 years; female: 62.64 years
Major ethnic groups: indigenous African tribes 95% (including Kpelle, Bassa, Gio, Kru, Grebo, Mano, Krahn, Gola, Gbandi, Loma, Kissi, Vai, and Bella), Americo-Liberians 2.5% (descendants of immigrants from the U.S. who had been slaves)
Major religions: traditional 70%, Muslim 20%, Christian 10%
Major languages: English 20% (official), about 20 tribal languages

Government
Official name: Republic of Liberia
Government type: republic
National capital: Monrovia
Independence: July 26, 1847
Legal system: dual system of statutory law based on Anglo-American common law for the modern sector and customary law based on unwritten tribal practices for indigenous sector

Economy
Industries: rubber processing, food processing, construction materials, furniture, palm oil processing, iron ore, diamonds
Agricultural products: rubber, coffee, cocoa, rice, cassava (tapioca), palm oil, sugarcane, bananas; sheep, goats; timber
Currency: 1 Liberian dollar (L$) = 100 cents

Libya

Geography
Location: Northern Africa, bordering the Mediterranean Sea, between Egypt and Tunisia
Area: 679,358 sq. mi. (1,759,540 sq. km.); slightly larger than Alaska
Climate: Mediterranean along coast; dry, extreme desert interior
Terrain: mostly barren, flat to undulating plains, plateaus, depressions
Elevation: lowest point: Sabkhat Ghuzayyil −154 ft. (−47 m.); highest point: Bikku Bitti 7,438 ft. (2,267 m.)
Natural resources: petroleum, natural gas, gypsum

People
Population: 4,992,838 (July 1999 est.)
Population growth rate: 2.4%
Infant mortality rate: 28.15 deaths/1,000 live births
Life expectancy at birth: total population: 75.73 years; male: 73.81 years; female: 77.74 years
Major ethnic groups: Berber and Arab 97%
Major religions: Sunni Muslim 97%
Major languages: Arabic, Italian

Government
Official name: Socialist People's Libyan Arab Jamahiriya
Government type: Jamahiriya (a state of the masses) in theory, governed by the populace through local councils; in fact, a military dictatorship
National capital: Tripoli

Independence: December 24, 1951
(from Italy)
Legal system: based on Italian civil law
system and Islamic law; separate
religious courts; no constitutional
provision for judicial review of legislative acts; has not accepted compulsory ICJ jurisdiction

Economy

Industries: petroleum, food processing,
textiles, handicrafts, cement
Agricultural products: wheat, barley,
olives, dates, citrus, vegetables,
peanuts; meat, eggs
Currency: 1 Libyan dinar (LD) = 1,000
dirhams

Liechtenstein

Geography

Location: Central Europe, between
Austria and Switzerland
Area: 62 sq. mi. (160 sq. km.); about
0.9 times the size of Washington,
D.C.
Climate: continental; cold, cloudy win-
ters with frequent snow or rain; cool
to moderately warm, cloudy, humid
summers
Terrain: mostly mountainous (Alps)
with Rhine Valley in western third
Elevation: lowest point: Ruggeller Riet
1,411 ft. (430 m.); highest point:
Grauspitz 8,527 ft. (2,599 m.)
Natural resources: hydroelectric poten-
tial

People

Population: 32,057 (July 199 est.)
Population growth rate: 1.08%
Infant mortality rate: 5.23 deaths/1,000
live births
Life expectancy at birth: total popula-
tion: 78.11 years; male: 75.64 years;
female: 80.69 years
Major ethnic groups: Alemannic
87.5%, Italian, Turkish, and other
12.5%
Major religions: Roman Catholic 80%,
Protestant 7.4%
Major languages: German (official),
Alemannic dialect

Government

Official name: Principality of
Liechtenstein
Government type: hereditary constitu-
tional monarchy
National capital: Vaduz
Independence: January 23, 1719
(Imperial Principality of
Liechtenstein established)
Legal system: local civil and penal codes

Economy

Industries: electronics, metal manufacturing, textiles, ceramics, pharmaceuticals, food products, precision
instruments, tourism
Agricultural products: wheat, barley,
maize, potatoes; livestock, dairy
products
Currency: 1 Swiss franc, franken, or
franco (SwF) = 100 centimes

Lithuania

Geography

Location: Eastern Europe, bordering
the Baltic Sea, between Latvia and
Russia
Area: 25,174 sq. mi. (65,200 sq. km.);
slightly larger than West Virginia
Climate: transitional, between mar-
itime and continental; wet, moder-
ate winters and summers
Terrain: lowland, many scattered small
lakes, fertile soil
Elevation: lowest point: Baltic Sea 0 ft.
(0 m.); highest point: Juozapines/
Kalnas 958 ft. (292 m.)
Natural resources: peat

People

Population: 3,584,966 (July 1999 est.)
Population growth rate: -0.4%
Infant mortality rate: 14.71 deaths/
1,000 live births
Life expectancy at birth: total popula-
tion: 68.96 years; male: 62.91 years;
female: 75.31 years
Major ethnic groups: Lithuanian
80.6%, Russian 8.7%, Polish 7%,
Byelorussian 1.6%
Major religions: primarily Roman
Catholic, others include Lutheran,

Russian Orthodox, Protestant, evangelical Christian Baptist, Islam, Judaism

Major languages: Lithuanian (official), Polish, Russian

Government

Official name: Republic of Lithuania

Government type: parliamentary democracy

National capital: Vilnius

Independence: September 6, 1991 (from Soviet Union)

Legal system: based on civil law system; no judicial review of legislative acts

Economy

Industries: metal-cutting machine tools, electric motors, television sets, refrigerators and freezers, petroleum refining, shipbuilding (small ships), furniture making, textiles, food processing, fertilizers, agricultural machinery, optical equipment, electronic components, computers, amber

Agricultural products: grain, potatoes, sugar beets, vegetables; meat, milk, eggs; fish; flax fiber

Currency: 1 Lithuanian litas = 100 centas

Luxembourg

Geography

Location: Western Europe, between France and Germany

Area: 998 sq. mi. (2,586 sq. km.); slightly smaller than Rhode Island

Climate: modified continental with mild winters, cool summers

Terrain: mostly gently rolling uplands with broad, shallow valleys; uplands to slightly mountainous in the north; steep slope down to Moselle floodplain in the southeast

Elevation: lowest point: Moselle River 436 ft. (133 m.); highest point: Burgplatz 1,834 ft. (559 m.)

Natural resources: iron ore (no longer exploited)

People

Population: 429,080 (July 1999 est.)

Population growth rate: 0.88%

Infant mortality rate: 4.99 deaths/ 1,000 live births

Life expectancy at birth: total population: 77.65 years; male: 74.58 years; female: 80.83 years

Major ethnic groups: Celtic base (with French and German blend), Portuguese, Italian, and European (guest and worker residents)

Major religions: Roman Catholic 97%, Protestant and Jewish 3%

Major languages: Luxembourgian, German, French, English

Government

Official name: Grand Duchy of Luxembourg

Government type: constitutional monarchy

National capital: Luxembourg

Independence: 1839 (from the Netherlands)

Legal system: based on civil law system

Economy

Industries: banking, iron and steel, food processing, chemicals, metal products, engineering, tires, glass, aluminum

Agricultural products: barley, oats, potatoes, wheat, fruits, wine grapes; livestock products

Currency: 1 Luxembourg franc (LuxF) = 100 centimes

Macau

Geography

Location: Eastern Asia, bordering the South China Sea and China

Area: 8 sq. mi. (21 sq. km.); about 0.1 times the size of Washington, D.C.

Climate: subtropical; marine with cool winters, warm summers

Terrain: generally flat

Elevation: lowest point: South China Sea 0 ft. (0 m.); highest point: Coloane Alto 571 ft. (174 m.)

Natural resources: negilible

People

Population: 437,312 (July 1999 est.)

Population growth rate: 1.86%

Infant mortality rate: 4.23 deaths/ 1,000 live births

Nations *(cont.)*

Life expectancy at birth: total population: 81.88 years; male: 78.79 years; female: 85.13 years
Major ethnic groups: Chinese 95%, Portuguese 3%
Major religions: Buddhist 50%, Roman Catholic 15%, other 35%
Major languages: Portuguese, Chinese (Cantonese)

Government
Official name: Macau Special Administrative Region
National capital: Macau
Independence: none (special administrative region of China)
Legal system: Portuguese civil law system

Economy
Industries: clothing, textiles, toys, electronics, footwear, tourism
Agricultural products: rice, vegetables
Currency: 1 pataca (P) = 100 avos

Macedonia, The Former Yugoslav Republic of

Geography
Location: Southeastern Europe, north of Greece
Area: 9,781 sq. mi. (25,333 sq. km.); slightly larger than Vermont
Climate: hot, dry summers and autumns and relatively cold winters with heavy snowfall
Terrain: mountainous territory covered with deep basins and valleys; there are three large lakes, each divided by a frontier line; country bisected by the Vardar River
Elevation: lowest point: Vardar River 164 ft. (50 m.); highest point: Korab 9,032 ft. (2,753 m.)
Natural resources: chromium, lead, zinc, manganese, tungsten, nickel, low-grade iron ore, asbestos, sulfur, timber

People
Population: 2,022,604 (July 1999 est.)
Population growth rate: 0.64%
Infant mortality rate: 18.68 deaths/1,000 live births

Life expectancy at birth: total population: 73.05 years; male: 70.93 years; female: 75.34 years
Major ethnic groups: Macedonian 65%, Albanian 22%, Turkish 4%, Serb 2%, Gypsies 3%
Major religions: Eastern Orthodox 67%, Muslim 30%
Major languages: Macedonian 70%, Albanian 21%, Turkish 3%, Serbo-Croatian 3%

Government
Official name: The Former Yugoslav Republic of Macedonia
Government type: emerging democracy
National capital: Skopje
Independence: September 17, 1991 (from Yugoslavia)
Legal system: based on civil law system; judicial review of legislative acts

Economy
Industries: coal, metallic chromium, lead, zinc, ferronickel, textiles, wood products, tobacco
Agricultural products: rice, tobacco, wheat, corn, millet, cotton, sesame, mulberry leaves, citrus, vegetables; beef, pork, poultry, mutton
Currency: 1 Macedonian denar (MKD) = 100 deni

Madagascar

Geography
Location: Southern Africa, island in the Indian Ocean, east of Mozambique
Area: 226,656 sq. mi. (587,040 sq. km.); slightly less than twice the size of Arizona
Climate: tropical along coast, temperate inland, arid in south
Terrain: narrow coastal plain, high plateau and mountains in center
Elevation: lowest point: Indian Ocean 0 ft. (0 m.); highest point: Maromokotro 9,436 ft. (2,876 m.)
Natural resources: graphite, chromite, coal, bauxite, salt, quartz, tar sands, semiprecious stones, mica, fish

People

Population: 14,873,387 (July 1999 est.)

Population growth rate: 2.8%

Infant mortality rate: 89.1 deaths/ 1,000 live births

Life expectancy at birth: total population: 53.24 years; male: 52.01 years; female: 54.51 years

Major ethnic groups: Malayo-Indonesian (Merina and related Betsileo), Cotiers (mixed African, Malayo-Indonesian, and Arab ancestry), French, Indian, Creole, Comoran

Major religions: indigenous beliefs 52%, Christian 41%, Muslim 7%

Major languages: French (official), Malagasy (official)

Government

Official name: Republic of Madagascar

Government type: republic

National capital: Antananarivo

Independence: June 26, 1960 (from France)

Legal system: based on French civil law system and traditional Malagasy law

Economy

Industries: meat processing, soap, breweries, tanneries, sugar, textiles, glassware, cement, automobile assembly plant, paper, petroleum, tourism

Agricultural products: coffee, vanilla, sugarcane, cloves, cocoa, rice, cassava (tapioca), beans, bananas, peanuts; livestock products

Currency: 1 Malagasy franc (FMG) = 100 centimes

Malawi

Geography

Location: Southern Africa, east of Zambia

Area: 45,745 sq. mi. (118,480 sq. km.); slightly smaller than Pennsylvania

Climate: tropical; rainy season (November to May); dry season (May to November)

Terrain: narrow elongated plateau with rolling plains, rounded hills, some mountains

Elevation: lowest point: junction of the Shire River and international boundary with Mozambique 121 ft. (37 m.); highest point: Mount Mlanje Sapitwa 9,849 ft. (3,002 m.)

Natural resources: limestone, unexploited deposits of uranium, coal, and bauxite

People

Population: 10,000,416 (July 1999 est.)

Population growth rate: 1.57%

Infant mortality rate: 132.14 deaths/ 1,000 live births

Life expectancy at birth: total population: 36.3 years; male: 36.49 years; female: 36.2 years

Major ethnic groups: Chewa, Nyanja, Tumbuko, Yao, Lomwe, Sena, Tonga, Ngoni, Ngonde, Asian, European

Major religions: Protestant 55%, Roman Catholic 20%, Muslim 20%, traditional indigenous beliefs

Major languages: English (official), Chichewa (official), other languages important regionally

Government

Official name: Republic of Malawi

Government type: multiparty democracy

National capital: Lilongwe

Independence: July 6, 1964 (from U.K.)

Legal system: based on English common law and customary law; judicial review of legislative acts in the Supreme Court of Appeal; has not accepted compulsory ICJ jurisdiction

Economy

Industries: tea, tobacco, sugar, sawmill products, cement, consumer goods

Agricultural products: tobacco, sugarcane, cotton, tea, corn, potatoes, cassava (tapioca), sorghum, pulses; cattle, goats

Currency: 1 Malawian kwacha (MK) = 100 tambala

Nations (cont.)

Malaysia

Geography

Location: Southeastern Asia, peninsula and northern one-third of the island of Borneo, bordering Indonesia and the South China Sea, south of Vietnam

Area: 127,316 sq. mi. (329,750 sq. km.); slightly larger than New Mexico

Climate: tropical; annual southwest (April to October) and northeast (October to February) monsoons

Terrain: coastal plains rising to hills and mountains

Elevation: lowest point: Indian Ocean 0 ft. (0 m.); highest point: Mount Kinabalu 13,451 ft. (4,100 m.)

Natural resources: tin, petroleum, timber, copper, iron ore, natural gas, bauxite

People

Population: 21,376,066 (July 1999 est.)

Population growth rate: 2.08%

Infant mortality rate: 21.68 deaths/1,000 live births

Life expectancy at birth: total population: 70.67 years; male: 67.62 years; female: 73.9 years

Major ethnic groups: Malay and other indigenous 58%, Chinese 26%, Indian 7%

Major religions: Muslim 38%, Christian 17%; Sarawak-tribal religion 35%, Buddhist and Confucianist 24%, Muslim 20%, Christian 16%,

Major languages: Peninsular Malaysia-Malay (official), English, Chinese dialects, numerous tribal languages

Government

Official name: Malaysia

Government type: constitutional monarchy

National capital: Kuala Lumpur

Independence: August 31, 1957 (from U.K.)

Legal system: based on English common law; judicial review of legislative acts in the Supreme Court at request of supreme head of the federation; has not accepted compulsory ICJ jurisdiction

Economy

Industries: Peninsular Malaysia—rubber and oil palm processing and manufacturing, light manufacturing industry, electronics, tin mining and smelting, logging and processing timber; Sabah—logging, petroleum production; Sarawak—agriculture processing, petroleum production and refining, logging

Agricultural products: Peninsular Malaysia—natural rubber, palm oil, rice; Sabah—subsistence crops, rubber, timber, coconut, rice; Sarawak—rubber, pepper; timber

Currency: 1 ringgit (M$) = 100 sen

Maldives

Geography

Location: Southern Asia, group of atolls in the Indian Ocean, south-southwest of India

Area: 116 sq. mi. (300 sq. km.); about 1.7 times the size of Washington, D.C.

Climate: tropical; hot, humid; dry, northeast monsoon (November to March); rainy, southwest monsoon (June to August)

Terrain: flat, with white sandy beaches

Elevation: lowest point: Indian Ocean 0 ft. (0 m.); highest point: unnamed location on Wilingili 79 ft. (24 m.)

Natural resources: fish

People

Population: 300,220 (July 1999 est.)

Population growth rate: 3.37%

Infant mortality rate: 38.14 deaths/1,000 live births

Life expectancy at birth: total population: 68.29 years; male: 66.53 years; female: 70.15 years

Major ethnic groups: Sinhalese, Dravidian, Arab, African

Major religions: Sunni Muslim

Major languages: Maldivian Divehi (dialect of Sinhala, script derived from Arabic), English spoken by most government officials

Government
Official name: Republic of Maldives
Government type: republic
National capital: Male (Maale)
Independence: July 26, 1965 (from U.K.)
Legal system: based on Islamic law with admixtures of English common law primarily in commercial matters; has not accepted compulsory ICJ jurisdiction

Economy
Industries: fish processing, tourism, shipping, boat building, coconut processing, garments, woven mats, rope, handicrafts, coral and sand mining
Agricultural products: coconuts, corn, sweet potatoes; fishing
Currency: 1 rufiyaa (Rf) = 100 laari

Mali

Geography
Location: Western Africa, southwest of Algeria
Area: 478,764 sq. mi. (1,240,000 sq. km.); slightly less than twice the size of Texas
Climate: subtropical to arid; hot and dry February to June; rainy, humid, and mild June to November; cool and dry November to February
Terrain: mostly flat to rolling northern plains covered by sand; savanna in south, rugged hills in northeast
Elevation: lowest point: Senegal River 75 ft. (23 m.); highest point: Hombori Tondo 3,789 ft. (1,155 m.)
Natural resources: gold, phosphates, kaolin, salt, limestone, uranium, bauxite, iron ore, manganese, tin, and copper deposits are known but not exploited

People
Population: 10,429,124 (July 1999 est.)
Population growth rate: 3.01%
Infant mortality rate: 119.44 deaths/ 1,000 live births

Life expectancy at birth: total population: 47.5 years; male: 46.09 years; female: 48.96 years
Major ethnic groups: Mande 50% (Bambara, Malinke, Sarakole), Peul 17%, Voltaic 12%, Songhai 6%, Tuareg and Moor 10%
Major religions: Muslim 90%, indigenous beliefs 9%
Major languages: French (official), Bambara 80%, numerous African languages

Government
Official name: Republic of Mali
Government type: republic
National capital: Bamako
Independence: September 22, 1960 (from France)
Legal system: based on French civil law system and customary law; judicial review of legislative acts in Constitutional Court; has not accepted compulsory ICJ jurisdiction

Economy
Industries: minor local consumer goods production and food processing; construction; phosphate and gold mining
Agricultural products: cotton, millet, rice, corn, vegetables, peanuts; cattle, sheep, goats
Currency: 1 Communauté Financière Africaine franc (CFAF) = 100 céntimes

Malta

Geography
Location: Southern Europe, islands in the Mediterranean Sea, south of Sicily (Italy)
Area: 124 sq. mi. (320 sq. km.); slightly less than twice the size of Washington, D.C.
Climate: Mediterranean with mild, rainy winters and hot, dry summers
Terrain: mostly low, rocky, flat to dissected plains; many coastal cliffs
Elevation: lowest point: Mediterranean Sea 0 ft. (0 m.); highest point: Dingli Cliffs 804 ft. (245 m.)
Natural resources: limestone, salt

Nations (cont.)

People

Population: 381,603 (July 1999 est.)
Population growth rate: 0.49%
Infant mortality rate: 7.42 deaths/ 1,000 live births
Life expectancy at birth: total population: 77.76 years; male: 75.43 years; female: 80.23 years
Major ethnic groups: Maltese (descendants of ancient Carthaginians and Phoenicians, with strong elements of Italian and other Mediterranean stock)
Major religions: Roman Catholic 98%
Major languages: Maltese (official), English (official)

Government

Official name: Republic of Malta
Government type: parliamentary democracy
National capital: Valletta
Independence: September 21, 1964 (from U.K.)
Legal system: based on English common law and Roman civil law

Economy

Industries: tourism; electronics, ship building and repair, construction; food and beverages, textiles, footwear, clothing, tobacco
Agricultural products: potatoes, cauliflower, grapes, wheat, barley, tomatoes, citrus, cut flowers, green peppers; pork, milk, poultry, eggs
Currency: 1 Maltese lira (LM) = 100 cents

Man, Isle of

Geography

Location: Western Europe, island in the Irish Sea, between Great Britain and Ireland
Area: 227 sq. mi. (588 sq. km.); slightly more than three times the size of Washington, D.C.
Climate: cool summers and mild winters; humid; overcast about half the time
Terrain: hills in north and south bisected by central valley

Elevation: lowest point: Irish Sea 0 ft. (0 m.); highest point: Snaefell 2,034 ft. (620 m.)
Natural resources: lead, iron ore

People

Population: 75,686 (July 1999 est.)
Population growth rate: 0.71%
Infant mortality rate: 2.45 deaths/ 1,000 live births
Life expectancy at birth: total population: 77.79 years; male: 74.28 years; female: 81.47 years
Major ethnic groups: Manx (Norse-Celtic descent), Briton
Major religions: Anglican, Roman Catholic, Methodist, Baptist, Presbyterian, Society of Friends
Major languages: English, Manx Gaelic

Government

Official name: Isle of Man
National capital: Douglas
Independence: none (British crown dependency)
Legal system: English law and local statute

Economy

Industries: financial services, light manufacturing, tourism
Agricultural products: cereals, vegetables; cattle, sheep, pigs, poultry
Currency: 1 Manx pound (£M) = 100 pence

Marshall Islands

Geography

Location: Oceania, group of atolls and reefs in the North Pacific Ocean, about one-half of the way from Hawaii to Papua New Guinea
Area: 70.0 sq. mi. (181.3 sq. km.); about the size of Washington, D.C.
Climate: wet season from May to November; hot and humid; islands border typhoon belt
Terrain: low coral limestone and sand islands
Elevation: lowest point: Pacific Ocean 0 ft. (0 m.); highest point: unnamed location on Likiep 33 ft. (10 m.)

Natural resources: phosphate deposits, marine products, deep seabed minerals

People
Population: 65,507 (July 1999 est.)
Population growth rate: 3.86%
Infant mortality rate: 43.38 deaths/ 1,000 live births
Life expectancy at birth: total population: 64.81 years; male: 63.21 years; female: 66.5 years
Major ethnic groups: Micronesian
Major religions: Christian (mostly Protestant)
Major languages: English (universally spoken and is the official language), two major Marshallese dialects from the Malayo-Polynesian family, Japanese

Government
Official name: Republic of the Marshall Islands
Government type: constitutional government in free association with the U.S.; the Compact of Free Association entered into force October 21, 1986
National capital: Majuro
Independence: October 21, 1986 (from the U.S.-administered UN trusteeship)
Legal system: based on adapted Trust Territory laws, acts of the legislature, municipal, common, and customary laws

Economy
Industries: copra, fish, tourism, craft items from shell, wood, and pearls, offshore banking (embryonic)
Agricultural products: coconuts, cacao, taro, breadfruit, fruits; pigs, chickens
Currency: 1 U.S. dollar (US$) = 100 cents

Martinique

Geography
Location: Caribbean, island in the Caribbean Sea, north of Trinidad and Tobago
Area: 425 sq. mi. (1,100 sq. km.); slightly more than six times the size of Washington, D.C.
Climate: tropical; moderated by trade winds; rainy season (June to October); vulnerable to devastating cyclones ((hurricanes) every eight year on average; average temperature 63.1 degrees F (17.3 degrees C); humid
Terrain: mountainous with indented coastline; dormant volcano
Elevation: lowest point: Caribbean Sea 0 ft. (0 m.); highest point: Montagne Pelee 4,583 ft. (1,397 m.)
Natural resources: coastal scenery and beaches, cultivable land

People
Population: 411,539 (July 1999 est.)
Population growth rate: 1.03%
Infant mortality rate: 6.76 deaths/ 1,000 live births
Life expectancy at birth: total population: 79.27 years; male: 76.47 years; female: 82.13 years
Major ethnic groups: African and African-white-Indian mixture 90%, white 5%, East Indian, Lebanese, Chinese less than 5%
Major religions: Roman Catholic 95%, Hindu and pagan African 5%
Major languages: French, Creole patois

Government
Official name: Department of Martinique
National capital: Fort-de-France
Independence: none (overseas department of France)
Legal system: French legal system

Economy
Industries: construction, rum, cement, oil refining, sugar, tourism
Agricultural products: pineapples, avocados, bananas, flowers, vegetables, sugarcane for rum
Currency: 1 French franc (F) = 100 centimes

Nations *(cont.)*

Mauritania

Geography

Location: Northern Africa, bordering the North Atlantic Ocean, between Senegal and Western Sahara

Area: 397,953 sq. mi. (1,030,700 sq. km.); slightly larger than three times the size of New Mexico

Climate: desert; constantly hot, dry, dusty

Terrain: mostly barren, flat plains of the Sahara; some central hills

Elevation: lowest point: Sebkha de Ndrhamcha –10 ft. (–3 m.); highest point: Kediet Ijill 2,986 ft. (910 m.)

Natural resources: iron ore, gypsum, fish, copper, phosphate

People

Population: 2,581,738 (July 1999 est.)

Population growth rate: 2.99%

Infant mortality rate: 76.46 deaths/ 1,000 live births

Life expectancy at birth: total population: 50.48 years; male: 47.39 years; female: 53.65 years

Major ethnic groups: mixed Maur/black 40%, Maur 30%, black 30%

Major religions: Muslim 100%

Major languages: Hasaniya Arabic (official), Pular, Soninke, Wolof (official), French

Government

Official name: Islamic Republic of Mauritania

Government type: republic

National capital: Nouakchott

Independence: November 28, 1960 (from France)

Legal system: three-tier system: Islamic (Shari'a) courts, special courts, and state security courts (in the process of being eliminated)

Economy

Industries: fish processing, mining of iron ore and gypsum

Agricultural products: dates, millet, sorghum, root crops; cattle, sheep; fish products

Currency: 1 ouguiya (UM) = 5 khoums

Mauritius

Geography

Location: Southern Africa, island in the Indian Ocean, east of Madagascar

Area: 718 sq. mi. (1,860 sq. km.); almost 11 times the size of Washington, D.C.

Climate: tropical, modified by southeast trade winds; warm, dry winter (May to November); hot, wet, humid summer (November to May)

Terrain: small coastal plain rising to discontinuous mountains encircling central plateau

Elevation: lowest point: Indian Ocean 0 ft. (0 m.); highest point: Piton de la Petite Riviere Noire 2,717 ft. (828 m.)

Natural resources: arable land, fish

People

Population: 1,182,212 (July 1999 est.)

Population growth rate: 1.18%

Infant mortality rate: 16.2 deaths/ 1,000 live births

Life expectancy at birth: total population: 71.09 years; male: 67.21 years; female: 74.96 years

Major ethnic groups: Indo-Mauritian 68%, Creole 27%, Sino-Mauritian 3%, Franco-Mauritian 2%

Major religions: Hindu 52%, Christian 28.3% (Roman Catholic 26%, Protestant 2.3%), Muslim 16.6%

Major languages: English (official), Creole, French, Hindi, Urdu, Hakka, Bojpoori

Government

Official name: Republic of Mauritius

Government type: parliamentary democracy

National capital: Port Louis

Independence: March 12, 1968 (from U.K.)

Legal system: based on French civil law system with elements of English common law in certain areas

Economy

Industries: food processing (largely

sugar milling), textiles, apparel, chemicals, metal products, transport equipment, nonelectrical machinery, tourism

Agricultural products: sugarcane, tea, corn, potatoes, bananas, pulses; cattle, goats; fish

Currency: 1 Mauritian rupee (MauR) = 100 cents

Mayotte

Geography

Location: Southern Africa, island in the Mozambique Channel, about one-half of the way from northern Madagascar to northern Mozambique

Area: 145 sq. mi. (375 sq. km.); slightly more than twice the size of Washington, D.C.

Climate: tropical; marine; hot, humid, rainy season during northeastern monsoon (November to May); dry season is cooler (May to November)

Terrain: generally undulating, with deep ravines and ancient volcanic peaks

Elevation: lowest point: Indian Ocean 0 ft. (0 m.); highest point: Benara 2,165 ft. (660 m.)

Natural resources: negligible

People

Population: 149,336 (July 1999 est.)

Population growth rate: 5%

Infant mortality rate: 69.06 deaths/ 1,000 live births

Life expectancy at birth: total population: 60.02 years; male: 57.61 years; female: 62.15 years

Major religions: Muslim 99%, Christian (mostly Roman Catholic)

Major languages: Mahorian (a Swahili dialect), French

Government

Official name: Territorial Collectivity of Mayotte

National capital: Mamoutzou

Independence: none (territorial collectivity of France)

Legal system: French law

Economy

Industries: newly created lobster and shrimp industry

Agricultural products: vanilla, ylang-ylang (perfume essence), coffee, copra

Currency: 1 French franc (F) = 100 centimes

Mexico

Geography

Location: North America, bordering the Caribbean Sea and the Gulf of Mexico, between Belize and the U.S. and bordering the North Pacific Ocean, between Guatemala and the U.S.

Area: 761,602 sq. mi. (1,972,550 sq. km.); slightly less than three times the size of Texas

Climate: varies from tropical to desert

Terrain: high, rugged mountains, low coastal plains, high plateaus, and desert

Elevation: lowest point: Laguna Salada −33 ft. (−10 m.); highest point: Volcan Pico de Orizaba 18,701 ft. (5,700 m.)

Natural resources: petroleum, silver, copper, gold, lead, zinc, natural gas, timber

People

Population: 100,294,036 (July 1999 est.)

Population growth rate: 1.73%

Infant mortality rate: 24.62 deaths/ 1,000 live births

Life expectancy at birth: total population: 72 years; male: 68.98 years; female: 75.17 years

Major ethnic groups: mestizo (Amerindian-Spanish) 60%, Amerindian or predominantly Amerindian 30%, white 9%

Major religions: nominally Roman Catholic 89%, Protestant 6%

Major languages: Spanish, various Mayan, Nahuatl, and other regional indigenous languages

Government

Official name: United Mexican States

Nations *(cont.)*

Government type: federal republic operating under a centralized government

National capital: Mexico

Independence: September 16, 1810 (from Spain)

Legal system: mixture of U.S. constitutional theory and civil law system; judicial review of legislative acts

Economy

Industries: food and beverages, tobacco, chemicals, iron and steel, petroleum, mining, textiles, clothing, motor vehicles, consumer durables, tourism

Agricultural products: corn, wheat, soybeans, rice, beans, cotton, coffee, fruit, tomatoes; beef, poultry, dairy products; wood products

Currency: 1 New Mexican peso (Mex$) = 100 centavos

Micronesia, Federated States of

Geography

Location: Oceania, island group in the North Pacific Ocean, about three-quarters of the way from Hawaii to Indonesia

Area: 271 sq. mi. (702 sq. km.); four times the size of Washington, D.C.

Climate: tropical; heavy year-round rainfall, especially in the eastern islands; located on southern edge of the typhoon belt with occasionally severe damage

Terrain: islands vary geologically from high mountainous islands to low, coral atolls; volcanic outcroppings on Pohnpei, Kosrae, and Truk

Elevation: lowest point: Pacific Ocean 0 ft. (0 m.); highest point: Totolom 2,595 ft. (791 m.)

Natural resources: forests, marine products, deep-seabed minerals

People

Population: 131,500 (July 1999 est.)

Population growth rate: 3.3%

Infant mortality rate: 33.99 deaths/ 1,000 live births

Life expectancy at birth: total population: 68.48 years; male: 66.52 years; female: 70.48 years

Major ethnic groups: nine ethnic Micronesian and Polynesian groups

Major religions: Roman Catholic 50%, Protestant 47%

Major languages: English (official and common language), Trukese, Pohnpeian, Yapese, Kosrean

Government

Official name: Federated States of Micronesia

Government type: constitutional government in free association with the U.S.; the Compact of Free Association entered into force November 3, 1986

National capital: Palikir

Independence: November 3, 1986 (from the U.S.-administered UN Trusteeship)

Legal system: based on adapted Trust Territory laws, acts of the legislature, municipal, common, and customary laws

Economy

Industries: tourism, construction, fish processing, craft items from shell, wood, and pearls

Agricultural products: black pepper, tropical fruits and vegetables, coconuts, cassava (tapioca), sweet potatoes; pigs, chickens

Currency: 1 U.S. dollar (US$) = 100 cents

Moldova

Geography

Location: Eastern Europe, northeast of Romania

Area: 13,012 sq. mi. (33,700 sq. km.); slightly more than twice the size of Hawaii

Climate: moderate winters, warm summers

Terrain: rolling steppe, gradual slope south to Black Sea

Elevation: lowest point: Nistru River 7 ft. (2 m.); highest point: Mount Balaneshty 1,411 ft. (430 m.)
Natural resources: lignite, phosphorites, gypsum

People

Population: 4,460,838 (July 1999 est.)
Population growth rate: 0.1%
Infant mortality rate: 43.52 deaths/ 1,000 live births
Life expectancy at birth: total population: 64.39 years; male: 59.76 years; female: 69.24 years
Major ethnic groups: Moldavian/ Romanian 64.5%, Ukrainian 13.8%, Russian 13%, Gagauz 3.5%, Bulgarian 2%, Jewish 1.5%
Major religions: Eastern Orthodox 98.5%, Jewish 1.5%
Major languages: Moldovan (official, virtually the same as the Romanian language), Russian, Gagauz (a Turkish dialect)

Government

Official name: Republic of Moldova
Government type: republic
National capital: Chisinau
Independence: August 27, 1991 (from Soviet Union)
Legal system: based on civil law system; Constitutional Court reviews legality of legislative acts and governmental decisions of resolution

Economy

Industries: food processing, agricultural machinery, foundry equipment, refrigerators and freezers, washing machines, hosiery, sugar, vegetable oil, shoes, textiles
Agricultural products: vegetables, fruits, wine, grain, sugar beets, sunflower seed, tobacco; meat, milk
Currency: Moldovan leu (MLD)

Monaco

Geography

Location: Western Europe, bordering the Mediterranean Sea, on the southern coast of France, near the border with Italy

Area: 0.8 sq. mi. (1.95 sq. km.); about three times the size of The Mall in Washington, D.C.
Climate: Mediterranean with mild, wet winters and hot, dry summers
Terrain: hilly, rugged, rocky
Elevation: extremes: lowestt point: Mediterranean Sea 0 ft. (0 m.); highest point: Mont Agel 459 ft. (140 m.)
Natural resources: none

People

Population: 32,149 (July 1999 est.)
Population growth rate: 0.31%
Infant mortality rate: 6.47 deaths/ 1,000 live births
Life expectancy at birth: total population: 78.58 years; male: 75 years; female: 82.35 years
Major ethnic groups: French 47%, Monegasque 16%, Italian 16%
Major religions: Roman Catholic 95%
Major languages: French (official), English, Italian, Monegasque

Government

Official name: Principality of Monaco
Government type: constitutional monarchy
National capital: Monaco
Independence: 1419 (rule by the House of Grimaldi)
Legal system: based on French law; has not accepted compulsory ICJ jurisdiction

Economy

Industries: negligible
Agricultural products: none
Currency: 1 French franc (F) = 100 centimes

Mongolia

Geography

Location: Northern Asia, between China and Russia
Area: 604,247 sq. mi. (1,565,000 sq. km.); slightly smaller than Alaska
Climate: desert; continental (large daily and seasonal temperature ranges)

Nations *(cont.)*

Terrain: vast semidesert and desert plains; mountains in west and southwest; Gobi Desert in southeast

Elevation: lowest point: Hoh Nuur 1,699 ft. (518 m.); highest point: Tavan Bogd Uul 14,350 ft. (4,374 m.)

Natural resources: oil, coal, copper, molybdenum, tungsten, phosphates, tin, nickel, zinc, wolfram, fluorspar, gold

People

Population: 2,617,379 (July 1999 est.)

Population growth rate: 1.45%

Infant mortality rate: 64.63 deaths/ 1,000 live births

Life expectancy at birth: total population: 61.81 years; male: 59.71 years; female: 64.02 years

Major ethnic groups: Mongol 90%, Kazakh 4%, Chinese 2%, Russian 2%

Major religions: predominantly Tibetan Buddhist, Muslim 4%

Major languages: Khalkha Mongol 90%, Turkic, Russian, Chinese

Government

Official name: Mongolia

Government type: republic

National capital: Ulaanbaatar

Independence: March 13, 1921 (from China)

Legal system: blend of Russian, Chinese, and Turkish systems of law; no constitutional provision for judicial review of legislative acts; has not accepted compulsory ICJ jurisdiction

Economy

Industries: copper, construction materials, mining (particularly coal); food and beverage, processing of animal products

Agricultural products: wheat, barley, potatoes, forage crops; sheep, goats, cattle, camels, horses

Currency: 1 tughrik (Tug) = 100 mongos

Montserrat

Geography

Location: Caribbean, island in the Caribbean Sea, southeast of Puerto Rico

Area: 39 sq. mi. (100 sq. km.); about 0.6 times the size of Washington, D.C.

Climate: tropical; little daily or seasonal temperature variation

Terrain: volcanic islands, mostly mountainous, with small coastal lowland

Elevation: lowest point: Caribbean Sea 0 ft. (0 m.); highest point: Chances Peak 2,999 ft. (914 m.)

Natural resources: negligible

People

Population: 112,853 (July 1999 est.) Note—demographic figures include an estimated 8,000 refugees who fled the island following the resumption of volcanic activity in July 1995

Population growth rate: 0.21%

Infant mortality rate: 12 deaths/1,000 live births

Life expectancy at birth: total population: 75.56 years; male: 73.79 years; female: 77.37 years

Major ethnic groups: black, white

Major religions: Anglican, Methodist, Roman Catholic, Pentecostal, Seventh-Day Adventist

Major languages: English

Government

Official name: Montserrat

National capital: Plymouth (abandoned in 1997 due to volcanic activity)

Independence: none (dependent territory of the U.K.)

Legal system: English common law and statute law

Economy

Industries: tourism, rum, textiles, electronic appliances

Agricultural products: cabbages, carrots, cucumbers, tomatoes, onions, peppers; livestock products

Currency: 1 East Caribbean dollar
(EC$) = 100 cents

Morocco

Geography

Location: Northern Africa, bordering
the North Atlantic Ocean and the
Mediterranean Sea, between Algeria
and Western Sahara

Area: 172,413 sq. mi. (446,550 sq.
km.); slightly larger than California

Climate: Mediterranean, becoming
more extreme in the interior

Terrain: northern coast and interior
are mountainous with large areas of
bordering plateaus, intermontane
valleys, and rich coastal plains

Elevation: lowest point: Sebkha Tah
–180 ft. (–55 m.); highest point:
Jebel Toubkal 13,665 ft. (4,165 m.)

Natural resources: phosphates, iron
ore, manganese, lead, zinc, fish, salt

People

Population: 29,661,636 (July 1999
est.)

Population growth rate: 1.84%

Infant mortality rate: 50.96 deaths/
1,000 live births

Life expectancy at birth: total population: 68.87 years; male: 66.85 years;
female: 70.99 years

Major ethnic groups: Arab-Berber
99.1%, Jewish 0.2%, other 0.7%

Major religions: Muslim 98.7%,
Christian 1.1%, Jewish 0.2%

Major languages: Arabic (official),
Berber dialects, French (often the
language of business, government,
and diplomacy)

Government

Official name: Kingdom of Morocco

Government type: constitutional
monarchy

National capital: Rabat

Independence: March 2, 1956 (from
France)

Legal system: based on Islamic law and
French and Spanish civil law system; judicial review of legislative
acts in Constitutional Chamber of
Supreme Court

Economy

Industries: phosphate rock mining and
processing, food processing, leather
goods, textiles, construction,
tourism

Agricultural products: barley, wheat, citrus, wine, vegetables, olives; livestock

Currency: 1 Moroccan dirham (DH) =
100 centimes

Mozambique

Geography

Location: Southern Africa, bordering
the Mozambique Channel, between
South Africa and Tanzania

Area: 309,494 sq. mi. (801,590 sq.
km.); slightly less than twice the
size of California

Climate: tropical to subtropical

Terrain: mostly coastal lowlands,
uplands in center, high plateaus in
northwest, mountains in west

Elevation: lowest point: Indian Ocean
0 ft. (0 m.); highest point: Monte
Binga 7,992 ft. (2,436 m.)

Natural resources: coal, titanium, natural gas

People

Population: 19,124,335 (July 1999
est.)

Population growth rate: 2.54%

Infant mortality rate: 117.56 deaths/
1,000 live births

Life expectancy at birth: total population: 45.89 years; male: 44.73 years;
female: 47.09 years

Major ethnic groups: indigenous tribal
groups 99.66% (Shangaan,
Chokwe, Manyika, Sena, Makua,
and others)

Major religions: indigenous beliefs
50%, Christian 30%, Muslim 20%

Major languages: Portuguese (official),
indigenous dialects

Government

Official name: Republic of
Mozambique

Government type: republic

National capital: Maputo

Independence: June 25, 1975 (from
Portugal)

Nations *(cont.)*

Legal system: based on Portuguese civil law system and customary law

Economy

Industries: food, beverages, chemicals (fertilizer, soap, paints), petroleum products, textiles, cement, glass, asbestos, tobacco

Agricultural products: cotton, cashew nuts, sugarcane, tea, cassava (tapioca), corn, rice, tropical fruits; beef, poultry

Currency: 1 metical (Mt) = 100 centavos

Namibia

Geography

Location: Southern Africa, bordering the South Atlantic Ocean, between Angola and South Africa

Area: 318,694 sq. mi. (825,418 sq. km.); slightly more than half the size of Alaska

Climate: desert; hot, dry; rainfall sparse and erratic

Terrain: mostly high plateau; Namib Desert along coast; Kalahari Desert in east

Elevation: lowest point: Atlantic Ocean 0 ft. (0 m.); highest point: Konigstein 8,550 ft. (2,606 m.)

Natural resources: diamonds, copper, uranium, gold, lead, tin, lithium, cadmium, zinc, salt, vanadium, natural gas, fish; suspected deposits of oil, natural gas, coal, iron ore

People

Population: 1,648,270 (July 1999 est.)

Population growth rate: 1.57%

Infant mortality rate: 66.94 deaths/1,000 live births

Life expectancy at birth: total population: 41.26 years; male: 41.64 years; female: 40.87 years

Major ethnic groups: black 86%, white 6.6%, mixed 7.4% (Note—about 50% of the population belong to the Ovambo tribe and 9% to the Kavangos tribe); other ethnic groups are: Herero 7%, Damara 7%, Nama 5%, Caprivian 4%, Bushmen 3%, Baster 2%, Tswana 0.5%

Major religions: Christian 80% to 90% (Lutheran 50% at least, other Christian denominations 30%), native religions 10% to 20%

Major languages: English 7% (official), Afrikaans common language of most of the population and about 60% of the white population, German 32%, indigenous languages: Oshivambo, Herero, Nama

Government

Official name: Republic of Namibia

Government type: republic

National capital: Windhoek

Independence: March 21, 1990 (from South African mandate)

Legal system: based on Roman-Dutch law and 1990 constitution

Economy

Industries: meat packing, fish processing, dairy products; mining (diamond, lead, zinc, tin, silver, tungsten, uranium, copper)

Agricultural products: millet, sorghum, peanuts; livestock; fish

Currency: 1 Namibian dollar (N$) = 100 cents

Nauru

Geography

Location: Oceania, island in the South Pacific Ocean, south of the Marshall Islands

Area: 8 sq. mi. (21 sq. km.); about 0.1 times the size of Washington, D.C.

Climate: tropical; monsoonal; rainy season (November to February)

Terrain: sandy beach rises to fertile ring around raised coral reefs with phosphate plateau in center

Elevation: lowest point: Pacific Ocean 0 ft. (0 m.); highest point: unnamed location along plateau rim 200 ft. (61 m.)

Natural resources: phosphates

People

Population: 10,605 (July 1999 est.)

Population growth rate: 0%

Major ethnic groups: Nauruan 58%, other Pacific Islander 26%, Chinese 8%, European 8%

Major religions: Christian (two-thirds Protestant, one-third Roman Catholic)

Major languages: Nauruan (official, a distinct Pacific Island language), English widely understood, spoken, and used for most government and commercial purposes

Government

Official name: Republic of Nauru

Government type: republic

National capital: no official capital; government offices in Yaren District

Independence: January 31, 1968 (from the Australia-, New Zealand-, and U.K.-administered UN trusteeship)

Legal system: acts of the Nauru Parliament and British common law

Economy

Industries: phosphate mining, financial services, coconut products

Agricultural products: coconuts predominate

Currency: 1 Australian dollar ($A) = 100 cents

Nepal

Geography

Location: Southern Asia, between China and India

Area: 54,363 sq. mi. (140,800 sq. km.); slightly larger than Arkansas

Climate: varies from cool summers and severe winters in north to subtropical summers and mild winters in south

Terrain: Terai or flat river plain of the Ganges in south, central hill region, rugged Himalayas in north

Elevation: lowest point: Kanchan Kalan 230 ft. (70 m.); highest point: Mount Everest 29,028 ft. (8,848 m.)

Natural resources: quartz, water, timber, hydropower potential, scenic beauty, small deposits of lignite, copper, cobalt, iron ore

People

Population: 24,302,653 (July 1999 est.)

Population growth rate: 2.51%

Infant mortality rate: 73.58 deaths/1,000 live births

Life expectancy at birth: total population: 58.42 years; male: 58.47 years; female: 58.36 years

Major ethnic groups: Newars, Indians, Tibetans, Gurungs, Magars, Tamangs, Bhotias, Rais, Limbus, Sherpas

Major religions: Hindu 90%, Buddhist 5%, Muslim 3%

Major languages: Nepali (official), 20 other languages divided into numerous dialects

Government

Official name: Kingdom of Nepal

Government type: parliamentary democracy as of May 12, 1991

National capital: Kathmandu

Independence: 1768 (unified by Prithvi Narayan Shah)

Legal system: based on Hindu legal concepts and English common law

Economy

Industries: tourism, carpet, textiles; small rice, jute, sugar, and oilseed mills; cigarette; cement and brick production

Agricultural products: rice, corn, wheat, sugarcane, root crops; milk, water buffalo meat

Currency: 1 Nepalese rupee (NR) = 100 paisa

Netherlands

Geography

Location: Western Europe, bordering the North Sea, between Belgium and Germany

Area: 16,033 sq. mi. (41,526 sq. km.); slightly less than twice the size of New Jersey

Climate: temperate; marine; cool summers and mild winters

Terrain: mostly coastal lowland and reclaimed land (polders); some hills in southeast

Elevation: lowest point: Prins Alexanderpolder −23 ft. (−7 m.); highest point: Vaalserberg 1,053 ft. (321 m.)

Nations *(cont.)*

Natural resources: natural gas, petroleum, fertile soil

People

Population: 15,807,641 (July 1999 est.)
Population growth rate: 0.47%
Infant mortality rate: 5.11 deaths/1,000 live births
Life expectancy at birth: total population: 78.15 years; male: 75.28 years; female: 81.17 years
Major ethnic groups: Dutch 96%, Moroccans, Turks
Major religions: Roman Catholic 34%, Protestant 25%, Muslim 3%
Major languages: Dutch

Government

Official name: Kingdom of the Netherlands
Government type: constitutional monarchy
National capital: Amsterdam; The Hague is the seat of government
Independence: 1579 (from Spain)
Legal system: civil law system incorporating French penal theory; constitution does not permit judicial review of acts of the States General

Economy

Industries: agroindustries, metal and engineering products, electrical machinery and equipment, chemicals, petroleum, fishing, construction, microelectronics
Agricultural products: grains, potatoes, sugar beets, fruits, vegetables; livestock
Currency: 1 Netherlands guilder, gulden, or florin (f.) = 100 cents

Netherlands Antilles

Geography

Location: Caribbean, two island groups in the Caribbean Sea—one includes Curacao and Bonaire north of Venezuela and the other is east of the Virgin Islands
Area: 371 sq. mi. (960 sq. km.); more than five times the size of Washington, D.C.

Climate: tropical; ameliorated by northeast trade winds
Terrain: generally hilly, volcanic interiors
Elevation: lowest point: Caribbean Sea 0 ft. (0 m.); highest point: Mount Scenery 2,828 ft. (862 m.)
Natural resources: phosphates (Curacao only), salt (Bonaire only)

People

Population: 207,827 (July 1999 est.)
Population growth rate: 1.01%
Infant mortality rate: 12.59 deaths/1,000 live births
Life expectancy at birth: total population: 74.25 years; male: 72.19 years; female: 76.41 years
Major ethnic groups: mixed black 85%, Carib Amerindian, white, East Asian
Major religions: Roman Catholic, Protestant, Jewish, Seventh-Day Adventist
Major languages: Dutch (official), Papiamento, a Spanish-Portuguese-Dutch-English dialect predominates, English widely spoken, Spanish

Government

Official name: Netherlands Antilles
Government type: parliamentary
National capital: Willemstad
Independence: none (part of the Kingdom of the Netherlands)
Legal system: based on Dutch civil law system, with some English common law influence

Economy

Industries: tourism (Curacao, Sint Maarten, and Bonaire), petroleum refining (Curacao), petroleum transshipment facilities (Curacao and Bonaire), light manufacturing (Curacao)
Agricultural products: aloes, sorghum, peanuts, vegetables, tropical fruit
Currency: 1 Netherlands Antillean guilder, gulden, or florin (NAf.) = 100 cents

New Caledonia

Geography

Location: Oceania, islands in the South Pacific Ocean, east of Australia

Area: 7,359 sq. mi. (19,060 sq. km.); slightly smaller than New Jersey

Climate: tropical; modified by south-east trade winds; hot, humid

Terrain: coastal plains with interior mountains

Elevation: lowest point: Pacific Ocean 0 ft. (0 m.); highest point: Mont Panie 5,341 ft. (1,628 m.)

Natural resources: nickel, chrome, iron, cobalt, manganese, silver, gold, lead, copper

People

Population: 197,361 (July 1999 est.)

Population growth rate: 1.59%

Infant mortality rate: 12.15 deaths/1,000 live births

Life expectancy at birth: total population: 75.35 years; male: 72.1 years; female: 78.77 years

Major ethnic groups: Melanesian 42.5%, European 37.1%, Wallisian 8.4%, Polynesian 3.8%, Indonesian 3.6%, Vietnamese 1.6%

Major religions: Roman Catholic 60%, Protestant 30%

Major languages: French, 28 Melanesian-Polynesian dialects

Government

Official name: Territory of New Caledonia and Dependencies

National capital: Noumea

Independence: none (overseas territory of France)

Legal system: the 1988 Matignon Accords grant substantial autonomy to the islands; formerly under French law

Economy

Industries: nickel mining and smelting

Agricultural products: vegetables; beef, other livestock products

Currency: 1 CFP franc (CFPF) = 100 centimes

New Zealand

Geography

Location: Oceania, islands in the South Pacific Ocean, southeast of Australia

Area: 103,737 sq. mi. (268,680 sq. km.); about the size of Colorado

Climate: temperate with sharp regional contrasts

Terrain: predominately mountainous with some large coastal plains

Elevation: lowest point: Pacific Ocean 0 ft. (0 m.); highest point: Mount Cook 12,349 ft. (3,764 m.)

Natural resources: natural gas, iron ore, sand, coal, timber, hydropower, gold, limestone

People

Population: 3,662,265 (July 1999 est.)

Population growth rate: 1.04%

Infant mortality rate: 6.22 deaths/1,000 live births

Life expectancy at birth: total population: 78.82 years; male: 74.55 years; female: 81.27 years

Major ethnic groups: New Zealand European 74.5%, Maori 9.7%, other European 4.6%, Pacific Islander 3.8%, Asian and others 7.4%

Major religions: Anglican 24%, Presbyterian 18%, Roman Catholic 15%, Methodist 5%, Baptist 2%, other Protestant 3%

Major languages: English (official), Maori

Government

Official name: New Zealand

Government type: parliamentary democracy

National capital: Wellington

Independence: September 26, 1907 (from U.K.)

Legal system: based on English law, with special land legislation and land courts for Maoris

Economy

Industries: food processing, wood and paper products, textiles, machinery, transportation equipment, banking and insurance, tourism, mining

Nations (cont.)

Agricultural products: wheat, barley,
potatoes, pulses, fruits, vegetables;
wool, meat, dairy products; fish
Currency: 1 New Zealand dollar (NZ$)
= 100 cents

Nicaragua

Geography
Location: Central America, bordering
both the Caribbean Sea and the
North Pacific Ocean, between Costa
Rica and Honduras
Area: 49,998 sq. mi. (129,494 sq.
km.); slightly smaller than New
York State
Climate: tropical in lowlands, cooler in
highlands
Terrain: extensive Atlantic coastal
plains rising to central interior
mountains; narrow Pacific coastal
plain interrupted by volcanoes
Elevation: lowest point: Pacific Ocean
0 ft. (0 m.); highest point: Mogoton
7,999 ft. (2,438 m.)
Natural resources: gold, silver, copper,
tungsten, lead, zinc, timber, fish

People
Population: 4,717,132 (July 1999 est.)
Population growth rate: 2.84%
Infant mortality rate: 40.47 deaths/
1,000 live births
Life expectancy at birth: total popula-
tion: 67.08 years; male: 64.7 years;
female: 69.56 years
Major ethnic groups: mestizo (mixed
Amerindian and white) 69%, white
17%, black 9%, Amerindian 5%
Major religions: Roman Catholic 95%,
Protestant 5%
Major languages: Spanish (official),
English- and Amerindian-speaking
minorities on Atlantic coast

Government
Official name: Republic of Nicaragua
Government type: republic
National capital: Managua
Independence: September 15, 1821
(from Spain)
Legal system: civil law system; Supreme
Court may review administrative acts

Economy
Industries: food processing, chemicals,
metal products, textiles, clothing,
petroleum refining and distribution,
beverages, footwear
Agricultural products: coffee, bananas,
sugarcane, cotton, rice, corn, cassava (tapioca), citrus, beans; beef,
veal, pork, poultry, dairy products
Currency: 1 gold cordoba (C$) = 100
centavos

Niger

Geography
Location: Western Africa, southeast of
Algeria
Area: 489,189 sq. mi. (1,267,000 sq.
km.); slightly less than twice the
size of Texas
Climate: desert; mostly hot, dry, dusty;
tropical in extreme south
Terrain: predominately desert plains
and sand dunes; flat to rolling
plains in south; hills in north
Elevation: lowest point: Niger River
656 ft. (200 m.); highest point:
Mont Greboun 6,378 ft. (1,944 m.)
Natural resources: uranium, coal, iron
ore, tin, phosphates, gold, petroleum

People
Population: 9,962,242 (July 1999 est.)
Population growth rate: 2.95%
Infant mortality rate: 112.79 deaths/
1,000 live births
Life expectancy at birth: total popula-
tion: 41.96 years; male: 42.22 years;
female: 41.7 years
Major ethnic groups: Hausa 56%,
Djerma 22%, Fula 8.5%, Tuareg
8%, Beri Beri (Kanouri) 4.3%, Arab,
Toubou, and Gourmantche 1.2%
Major religions: Muslim 80%, remain-
der indigenous beliefs and
Christians
Major languages: French (official),
Hausa, Djerma

Government
Official name: Republic of Niger
Government type: republic
National capital: Niamey

Independence: August 3, 1960 (from France)

Legal system: based on French civil law system and customary law

Economy

Industries: cement, brick, textiles, food processing, chemicals, slaughterhouses, and a few other small light industries; uranium mining

Agricultural products: cowpeas, cotton, peanuts, millet, sorghum, cassava (tapioca), rice; cattle, sheep, goats, camels, donkeys, horses, poultry

Currency: 1 Communauté Financière Africaine franc (CFAF) = 100 centimes

Nigeria

Geography

Location: Western Africa, bordering the Gulf of Guinea, between Benin and Cameroon

Area: 356,668 sq. mi. (923,770 sq. km.); slightly more than twice the size of California

Climate: varies; equatorial in south, tropical in center, arid in north

Terrain: southern lowlands merge into central hills and plateaus; mountains in southeast, plains in north

Elevation: lowest point: Atlantic Ocean 0 ft. (0 m.); highest point: Chappal Waddi 7,936 ft. (2,419 m.)

Natural resources: petroleum, tin, columbite, iron ore, coal, limestone, lead, zinc, natural gas

People

Population: 113,828,587 (July 1999 est.)

Population growth rate: 2.92%

Infant mortality rate: 69.46 deaths/ 1,000 live births

Life expectancy at birth: total population: 53.3 years; male: 52.55 years; female: 54.06 years

Major ethnic groups: Hausa, Fulani, Yoruba, Ibo, Kanuri, Ibibio, Tiv, Ijaw

Major religions: Muslim 50%, Christian 40%, indigenous beliefs 10%

Major languages: English (official), Hausa, Yoruba, Ibo, Fulani

Government

Official name: Federal Republic of Nigeria

Government type: military government

National capital: Abuja

Independence: October 1, 1960 (from U.K.)

Legal system: based on English common law, Islamic law, and tribal law

Economy

Industries: crude oil, coal, tin, columbite, palm oil, peanuts, cotton, rubber, wood, hides and skins, textiles, cement and other construction materials, food products, footwear, chemicals, fertilizer, printing, ceramics, steel

Agricultural products: cocoa, peanuts, palm oil, corn, rice, sorghum, millet, cassava (tapioca), yams, rubber; cattle, sheep, goats, pigs; fishing and forest resources extensively exploited

Currency: 1 naira (N) = 100 kobo

Niue

Geography

Location: Oceania, island in the South Pacific Ocean, east of Tonga

Area: 100 sq. mi. (260 sq. km.); 1.5 times the size of Washington, D.C.

Climate: tropical; modified by southeast trade winds

Terrain: steep limestone cliffs along coast, central plateau

Elevation: lowest point: Pacific Ocean 0 ft. (0 m.); highest point: unnamed location near Mutalau settlement 223 ft. (68 m.)

Natural resources: fish, arable land

People

Population: 2,103 (July 1999 est.)

Population growth rate: 0.5%

Major ethnic groups: Polynesian

Major religions: Ekalesia Niue (Niuean Church) 75%-a Protestant church closely related to the London Missionary Society, Latter-Day Saints 10%, other 15%

Major languages: Polynesian closely related to Tongan and Samoan, English

Nations (cont.)

Government
Official name: Niue

Government type: self-governing parliamentary democracy

National capital: Alofi

Independence: on October 19, 1974, Niue became a self-governing parliamentary government in free association with New Zealand

Legal system: English common law

Economy
Industries: tourism, handicrafts, food processing

Agricultural products: coconuts, passion fruit, honey, limes, taro, yams, cassava (tapioca), sweet potatoes; pigs, poultry, beef cattle

Currency: 1 New Zealand dollar (NZ$) = 100 cents

Norfolk Island

Geography
Location: Oceania, island in the South Pacific Ocean, east of Australia

Area: 13 sq. mi. (34.6 sq. km.); about 0.2 times the size of Washington, D.C.

Climate: subtropical, mild, little seasonal temperature variation

Terrain: volcanic formation with mostly rolling plains

Elevation: lowest point: Pacific Ocean 0 ft. (0 m.); highest point: Mount Bates 1,047 ft. (319 m.)

Natural resources: fish

People
Population: 1,905 (July 1999 est.)

Population growth rate: -0.71%

Major ethnic groups: descendants of the Bounty mutineers, Australian, New Zealander, Polynesians

Major religions: Anglican 39%, Roman Catholic 11.7%, Uniting Church in Australia 16.4%, Seventh-Day Adventist 4.4%

Major languages: English (official), Norfolk (a mixture of 18th century English and ancient Tahitian)

Government
Official name: Territory of Norfolk Island

National capital: Kingston (administrative center); Burnt Pine (commercial center)

Independence: none (territory of Australia)

Legal system: based on the laws of Australia, local ordinances and acts; English common law applies in matters not covered by either Australian or Norfolk Island law

Economy
Industries: tourism

Agricultural products: Norfolk Island pine seed, Kentia palm seed, cereals, vegetables, fruit; cattle, poultry

Currency: 1 Australian dollar ($A) = 100 cents

Northern Mariana Islands

Geography
Location: Oceania, islands in the North Pacific Ocean, about three-quarters of the way from Hawaii to the Philippines

Area: 184 sq. mi. (477 sq. km.); 2.5 times the size of Washington, D.C.

Climate: tropical marine; moderated by northeast trade winds, little seasonal temperature variation; dry season December to June, rainy season July to October

Terrain: southern islands are limestone with level terraces and fringing coral reefs; northern islands are volcanic

Elevation: lowest point: Pacific Ocean 0 ft. (0 m.); highest point: unnamed location on Agrihan 3,166 ft. (965 m.)

Natural resources: arable land, fish

People
Population: 69,398

Population growth rate: 3.99%

Infant mortality rate: 6.8 deaths/1,000 live births

Life expectancy at birth: total population: 75.36 years; male: 72.19 years; female: 78.72 years

Major ethnic groups: Chamorro, Carolinians and other Micronesians, Caucasian, Japanese, Chinese, Korean

Major religions: Christian (Roman Catholic majority, although traditional beliefs and taboos may still be found)

Major languages: English, Chamorro, Carolinian; Note—86% of population speaks a language other than English at home

Government

Official name: Commonwealth of the Northern Mariana Islands

Government type: commonwealth; self-governing with locally elected governor, lieutenant governor, and legislature

National capital: Saipan

Independence: none (commonwealth in political union with the U.S.)

Legal system: based on U.S. system except for customs, wages, immigration laws, and taxation

Economy

Industries: tourism, construction, garments, handicrafts

Agricultural products: coconuts, fruits, vegetables; cattle

Currency: 1 U.S. dollar (US$) = 100 cents

Norway

Geography

Location: Northern Europe, bordering the North Sea and the North Atlantic Ocean, west of Sweden

Area: 125,181 sq. mi. (324,220 sq. km.); slightly larger than New Mexico

Climate: temperate along coast, modified by North Atlantic Current; colder interior; rainy year-round on west coast

Terrain: glaciated; mostly high plateaus and rugged mountains broken by fertile valleys; small, scattered plains; coastline deeply indented by fjords; arctic tundra in north

Elevation: lowest point: Norwegian Sea 0 ft. (0 m.); highest point: Glittertinden 8,110 ft. (2,472 m.)

Natural resources: petroleum, copper, natural gas, pyrites, nickel, iron ore, zinc, lead, fish, timber, hydropower

People

Population: 4,438,547 (July 1999 est.)

Population growth rate: 0.4%

Infant mortality rate: 4.96 deaths/1,000 live births

Life expectancy at birth: total population: 78.36 years; male: 75.55 years; female: 81.35 years

Major ethnic groups: Germanic (Nordic, Alpine, Baltic), Lapps (Sami) 20,000

Major religions: Evangelical Lutheran 87.8% (state church), other Protestant and Roman Catholic 3.8%, none 3.2%, unknown 5.2%

Major languages: Norwegian (official); Note—small Lapp- and Finnish-speaking minorities

Government

Official name: Kingdom of Norway

Government type: constitutional monarchy

National capital: Oslo

Independence: October 26, 1905 (from Sweden)

Legal system: mixture of customary law, civil law system, and common law traditions; Supreme Court renders advisory opinions to legislature when asked

Economy

Industries: petroleum and gas, food processing, shipbuilding, pulp and paper products, metals, chemicals, timber, mining, textiles, fishing

Agricultural products: oats, other grains; beef, milk (livestock output exceeds value of crops); fish

Currency: 1 Norwegian krone (NKr) = 100 oere

Oman

Geography

Location: Middle East, bordering the Arabian Sea, Gulf of Oman, and Persian Gulf, between Yemen and United Arab Emirates

Nations *(cont.)*

Area: 82,031 sq. mi. (212,460 sq. km.);
slightly smaller than Kansas

Climate: dry desert; hot, humid along
coast; hot, dry interior; strong southwest summer monsoon (May to
September) in far south

Terrain: vast central desert plain, rugged mountains in north and south

Elevation: lowest point: Arabian Sea 0
ft. (0 m.); highest point: Jabal ash
Sham 9,777 ft. (2,980 m.)

Natural resources: petroleum, copper,
asbestos, some marble, limestone,
chromium, gypsum, natural gas

People

Population: 2,446,645 (July 1999 est.)

Population growth rate: 3.45%

Infant mortality rate: 25.55 deaths/
1,000 live births

Life expectancy at birth: total population: 71.3 years; male: 69.31 years;
female: 73.39 years

Major ethnic groups: Arab, Baluchi,
South Asian (Indian, Pakistani, Sri
Lankan, Bangladeshi), African

Major religions: Ibadhi Muslim 75%,
Sunni Muslim, Shi'a Muslim, Hindu

Major languages: Arabic (official),
English, Baluchi, Urdu, Indian
dialects

Government

Official name: Sultanate of Oman

Government type: monarchy

National capital: Muscat

Independence: 1650 (expulsion of the
Portuguese)

Legal system: based on English common law and Islamic law; ultimate
appeal to the sultan; has not accepted compulsory ICJ jurisdiction

Economy

Industries: crude oil production and.
refining, natural gas production,
construction, cement, copper

Agricultural products: dates, limes,
bananas, alfalfa, vegetables; camels,
cattle; fish

Currency: 1 Omani rial (RO) = 1,000
baiza

Pakistan

Geography

Location: Southern Asia, bordering the
Arabian Sea, between India on the
east and Iran and Afghanistan on
the west and China in the north

Area: 310,401 sq. mi. (803,940 sq.
km.); slightly less than twice the
size of California

Climate: mostly hot, dry desert; temperate in northwest; arctic in north

Terrain: flat Indus plain in east;
mountains in north and northwest;
Balochistan plateau in west

Elevation: lowest point: Indian Ocean
0 ft. (0 m.); highest point: K2
(Mt. Godwin-Austen) 28,251 ft.
(8,611 m.)

Natural resources: land, extensive natural gas reserves, limited petroleum,
poor quality coal, iron ore, copper,
salt, limestone

People

Population: 138,123,359 (July 1999
est.)

Population growth rate: 2.18%

Infant mortality rate: 91.86 deaths/
1,000 live births

Life expectancy at birth: total population: 59.38 years; male: 58.49 years;
female: 60.3 years

Major ethnic groups: Punjabi, Sindhi,
Pashtun (Pathan), Baloch, Muhajir

Major religions: Muslim 97% (Sunni
77%, Shi'a 20%)

Major languages: Punjabi 48%, Sindhi
12%, Siraiki (a Punjabi variant) 10%,
Pashtu 8%, Urdu (official) 8%,
Balochi 3%, Hindko 2%, Brahui 1%,
English (official and lingua franca of
Pakistani elite and most govern-
ment ministries)

Government

Official name: Islamic Republic of
Pakistan

Government type: federal republic

National capital: Islamabad

Independence: August 14, 1947 (from
U.K.)

Legal system: based on English common law with provisions to accommodate Pakistan's status as an Islamic state

Economy
Industries: textiles, food processing, beverages, construction materials, clothing, paper products, shrimp
Agricultural products: cotton, wheat, rice, sugarcane, fruits, vegetables; milk, beef, mutton, eggs
Currency: 1 Pakistani rupee (PRe) = 100 paisa

Palau

Geography
Location: Oceania, group of islands in the North Pacific Ocean, southeast of the Philippines
Area: 177 sq. mi. (458 sq. km.); slightly more than 2.5 times the size of Washington, D.C.
Climate: wet season May to November; hot and humid
Terrain: varying geologically from the high, mountainous main island of Babelthuap to low, coral islands usually fringed by large barrier reefs
Elevation: lowest point: Pacific Ocean 0 ft. (0 m.); highest point: Mount Ngerchelchauus 794 ft. (242 m.)
Natural resources: forests, minerals (especially gold), marine products, deep-seabed minerals

People
Population: 18,467 (July 1999 est.)
Population growth rate: 1.94%
Infant mortality rate: 18.5 deaths/1,000 live births
Life expectancy at birth: total population: 67.75 years; male: 64.69 years; female: 70.98 years
Major ethnic groups: Palauans are a composite of Polynesian, Malayan, and Melanesian races
Major religions: Christian, Modekngei religion (one-third of the population observes this religion which is indigenous to Palau)
Major languages: English (official in all of Palau's 16 states), Sonsorolese (official in the state of Sonsoral), Angaur and Japanese (in the state of Anguar), Tobi (in the state of Tobi), Palauan (in the other 13 states)

Government
Official name: Republic of Palau
Government type: constitutional government in free association with the U.S.; the Compact of Free Association entered into force 1 October 1994
National capital: Koror (Note: a new capital is being built about 20 km. northeast in eastern Babelthuap)
Independence: October 1, 1994 (from the U.S.-administered UN Trusteeship)
Legal system: based on Trust Territory laws, acts of the legislature, municipal, common, and customary laws

Economy
Industries: tourism, craft items (from shell, wood, pearls), some commercial fishing and some commercial fishing
Agricultural products: coconuts, copra, cassava (tapioca), sweet potatoes
Currency: 1 U.S. dollar (US$) = 100 cents

Panama

Geography
Location: Central America, bordering both the Caribbean Sea and the North Pacific Ocean, between Colombia and Costa Rica
Area: 30,193 sq. mi. (78,200 sq. km.); slightly smaller than South Carolina
Climate: tropical; hot, humid, cloudy; prolonged rainy season (May to January), short dry season (January to May)
Terrain: interior mostly steep, rugged mountains and dissected, upland plains; coastal areas largely plains and rolling hills
Elevation: lowest point: Pacific Ocean 0 ft. (0 m.); highest point: Volcan de Chiriqui 11,401 ft. (3,475 m.)
Natural resources: copper, mahogany forests, shrimp

People
Population: 2,778,526 (July 1999 est.)

Nations *(cont.)*

Population growth rate: 1.53%
Infant mortality rate: 23.35 deaths/
1,000 live births
Life expectancy at birth: total popula-
tion: 74.66 years; male: 71.91 years;
female: 77.51 years
Major ethnic groups: mestizo (mixed
Amerindian and white) 70%,
Amerindian and mixed (West
Indian) 14%, white 10%,
Amerindian 6%
Major religions: Roman Catholic 85%,
Protestant 15%
Major languages: Spanish (official),
English 14%

Government

Official name: Republic of Panama
Government type: constitutional repub-
lic
National capital: Panama
Independence: November 3, 1903 (from
Colombia; became independent
from Spain November 28 , 1821)
Legal system: based on civil law system;
judicial review of legislative acts in
the Supreme Court of Justice

Economy

Industries: construction, petroleum
refining, brewing, cement and other
construction materials, sugar
milling
Agricultural products: bananas, rice,
corn, coffee, sugarcane, vegetables;
livestock; fishing (shrimp)
Currency: 1 balboa (B) = 100 centesi-
mos

Papua New Guinea

Geography

Location: Southeastern Asia, group of
islands including the eastern half of
the island of New Guinea between
the Coral Sea and the South Pacific
Ocean, east of Indonesia
Area: 178,703 sq. mi. (462,840 sq.
km.); slightly larger than California
Climate: tropical; northwest monsoon
(December to March), southeast
monsoon (May to October); slight
seasonal temperature variation

Terrain: mostly mountains with
coastal lowlands and rolling foothills
Elevation: lowest point: Pacific Ocean
0 ft. (0 m.); highest point: Mount
Wilhelm 14,793 ft. (4,509 m.)
Natural resources: gold, copper, silver,
natural gas, timber, oil, fisheries

People

Population: 4,705,126 (July 1999 est.)
Population growth rate: 2.26%
Infant mortality rate: 55.58 deaths/
1,000 live births
Life expectancy at birth: total popula-
tion: 58.47 years; male: 57.58 years;
female: 59.4 years
Major ethnic groups: Melanesian,
Papuan, Negrito, Micronesian,
Polynesian
Major religions: Roman Catholic 22%,
Lutheran 16%, Presbyterian/
Methodist/London Missionary
Society 8%, Anglican 5%,
Evangelical Alliance 4%, Seventh-
Day Adventist 1%, other Protestant
sects 10%, indigenous beliefs 34%
Major languages: English spoken by
1%–2%, pidgin English widespread,
Motu spoken in Papua region;
Note— 715 indigenous languages

Government

Official name: Independent State of
Papua New Guinea
Government type: parliamentary
democracy
National capital: Port Moresby
Independence: September 16, 1975
(from the Australian-administered
UN trusteeship)
Legal system: based on English com-
mon law

Economy

Industries: copra crushing, palm oil
processing, plywood production,
wood chip production; mining of
gold, silver, and copper; crude oil
production; construction, tourism
Agricultural products: coffee, cocoa,
coconuts, palm kernels, tea, rubber,
sweet potatoes, fruit, vegetables;
poultry, pork

Currency: 1 kina (K) = 100 toea

Paraguay

Geography

Location: Central South America, northeast of Argentina

Area: 157,046 sq. mi. (406,750 sq. km.); slightly smaller than California

Climate: subtropical; substantial rainfall in the eastern portions, becoming semiarid in the far west

Terrain: grassy plains and wooded hills east of Rio Paraguay; Gran Chaco region west of Rio Paraguay mostly low, marshy plain near the river, and dry forest and thorny scrub elsewhere

Elevation: lowest point: junction of Rio Paraguay and Rio Parana 151 ft. (46 m.); highest point: Cerro San Rafael 2,789 ft. (850 m.)

Natural resources: hydropower, timber, iron ore, manganese, limestone

People

Population: 5,434,095 (July 1999 est.)

Population growth rate: 2.65%

Infant mortality rate: 36.35 deaths/ 1,000 live births

Life expectancy at birth: total population: 72.43 years; male: 70.47 years; female: 74.49 years

Major ethnic groups: mestizo (mixed Spanish and Amerindian) 95%, white plus Amerindian 5%

Major religions: Roman Catholic 90%, Mennonite and other Protestant denominations

Major languages: Spanish (official), Guarani

Government

Official name: Republic of Paraguay

Government type: republic

National capital: Asuncion

Independence: May 14, 1811 (from Spain)

Legal system: based on Argentine codes, Roman law, and French codes; judicial review of legislative acts in Supreme Court of Justice

Economy

Industries: meat packing, oilseed crushing, milling, brewing, textiles, other light consumer goods, cement, construction

Agricultural products: cotton, sugarcane, soybeans, corn, wheat, tobacco, cassava (tapioca), fruits, vegetables; beef, pork, eggs, milk; timber

Currency: 1 guarani (G) = 100 centimos

Peru

Geography

Location: Western South America, bordering the South Pacific Ocean, between Chile and Ecuador

Area: 496,223 sq. mi. (1,285,220 sq. km.); slightly smaller than Alaska

Climate: varies from tropical in east to dry desert in west

Terrain: western coastal plain (costa), high and rugged Andes in center (sierra), eastern lowland jungle of Amazon Basin (selva)

Elevation: lowest point: Pacific Ocean 0 ft. (0 m.); highest point: Nevado Huascaran 22,204 ft. (6,768 m.)

Natural resources: copper, silver, gold, petroleum, timber, fish, iron ore, coal, phosphate, potash

People

Population: 26,624,582 (July 1999 est.)

Population growth rate: 1.93%

Infant mortality rate: 38.97 deaths/ 1,000 live births

Life expectancy at birth: total population: 70.38 years; male: 68.08 years; female: 72.78 years

Major ethnic groups: Amerindian 45%, mestizo (mixed Amerindian and white) 37%, white 15%

Major religions: Roman Catholic

Major languages: Spanish (official), Quechua (official), Aymara

Government

Official name: Republic of Peru

Government type: republic

National capital: Lima

Independence: July 28, 1821 (from Spain)

Nations *(cont.)*

Legal system: based on civil law system; has not accepted compulsory ICJ jurisdiction

Economy

Industries: mining of metals, petroleum, fishing, textiles, clothing, food processing, cement, auto assembly, steel, shipbuilding, metal fabrication

Agricultural products: coffee, cotton, sugarcane, rice, wheat, potatoes, plantains, coca; poultry, red meats, dairy products, wool; fish

Currency: 1 nuevo sol (S/.) = 100 centimos

Philippines

Geography

Location: Southeastern Asia, archipelago between the Philippine Sea and the South China Sea, east of Vietnam

Area: 115,830 sq. mi. (300,000 sq. km.); slightly larger than Arizona

Climate: tropical marine; northeast monsoon (November to April); southwest monsoon (May to October)

Terrain: mostly mountains with narrow to extensive coastal lowlands

Elevation: lowest point: Philippine Sea 0 ft. (0 m.); highest point: Mount Apo 9,691 ft. (2,954 m.)

Natural resources: timber, petroleum, nickel, cobalt

People

Population: 79,345,812 (July 1999 est.)

Population growth rate: 2.04%

Infant mortality rate: 33.89 deaths/1,000 live births

Life expectancy at birth: total population: 66.58 years; male: 63.79 years; female: 69.5 years

Major ethnic groups: Christian Malay 91.5%, Muslim Malay 4%, Chinese 1.5%

Major religions: Roman Catholic 83%, Protestant 9%, Muslim 5%

Major languages: Pilipino (official, based on Tagalog), English (official)

Government

Official name: Republic of the Philippines

Government type: republic

National capital: Manila

Independence: July 4, 1946 (from U.S.)

Legal system: based on Spanish and Anglo-American law

Economy

Industries: textiles, pharmaceuticals, chemicals, wood products, food processing, electronics assembly, petroleum refining, fishing

Agricultural products: rice, coconuts, corn, sugarcane, bananas, pineapples, mangoes; pork, eggs, beef; fish catch of 2 million metric tons annually

Currency: 1 Philippine peso (P) = 100 centavos

Pitcairn Islands

Geography

Location: Oceania, islands in the South Pacific Ocean, about one-half of the way from Peru to New Zealand

Area: 18 sq. mi. (47 sq. km.); about 0.3 times the size of Washington, D.C.

Climate: tropical, hot, humid, modified by southeast trade winds; rainy season (November to March)

Terrain: rugged volcanic formation; rocky coastline with cliffs

Elevation: lowest point: Pacific Ocean 0 ft. (0 m.); highest point: Pawala Valley Ridge 1,138 ft. (347 m.)

Natural resources: miro trees (used for handicrafts), fish; Note—manganese, iron, copper, gold, silver, and zinc have been discovered offshore

People

Population: 49 (July 1999 est.)

Population growth rate: –2.04%

Major ethnic groups: descendants of the Bounty mutineers and their Tahitian wives

Major religions: Seventh-Day Adventist 100%

Major languages: English (official), Tahitian/English dialect

Government

Official name: Pitcairn, Henderson, Ducie, and Oeno Islands
National capital: Adamstown
Independence: none (dependent territory of the U.K.)
Legal system: local island by-laws

Economy

Industries: postage stamps, handicrafts
Agricultural products: wide variety of fruits and vegetables
Currency: 1 New Zealand dollar (NZ$) = 100 cents

Poland

Geography

Location: Central Europe, east of Germany
Area: 120,727 sq. mi. (312,683 sq. km.); slightly smaller than New Mexico
Climate: temperate with cold, cloudy, moderately severe winters with frequent precipitation; mild summers with frequent showers and thundershowers
Terrain: mostly flat plain; mountains along southern border
Elevation: lowest point: Raczki Elblaskie –6 ft. (–2 m.); highest point: Rysy 8,199 ft. (2,499 m.)
Natural resources: coal, sulfur, copper, natural gas, silver, lead, salt

People

Population: 38,608,929 (July 1999 est.)
Population growth rate: 0.05%
Infant mortality rate: 12.76 deaths/ 1,000 live births
Life expectancy at birth: total population: 73.06 years; male: 68.93 years; female: 77.41 years
Major ethnic groups: Polish 97.6%, German 1.3%
Major religions: Roman Catholic 95%
Major languages: Polish

Government

Official name: Republic of Poland
Government type: democratic state
National capital: Warsaw
Independence: November 11, 1918 (independent republic proclaimed)

Legal system: mixture of Continental (Napoleonic) civil law and holdover communist legal theory; changes being gradually introduced as part of broader democratization process; limited judicial review of legislative acts although under the new constitution, the Constitutional Tribunal ruling will become final as of October 1999; court decisions can be appealed to the European Court of Justice in Strasbourg

Economy

Industries: machine building, iron and steel, coal mining, chemicals, shipbuilding, food processing, glass, beverages, textiles
Agricultural products: potatoes, milk, cheese, fruits, vegetables, wheat; poultry and eggs; pork, beef
Currency: 1 zloty (Zl) = 100 groszy

Portugal

Geography

Location: Southwestern Europe, bordering the North Atlantic Ocean, west of Spain
Area: 35,672 sq. mi. (92,391 sq. km.); slightly smaller than Indiana
Climate: maritime temperate; cool and rainy in north, warmer and drier in south
Terrain: mountainous north of the Tagus, rolling plains in south
Elevation: lowest point: Atlantic Ocean 0 ft. (0 m.); highest point: Ponta do Pico in Azores 7,713 ft. (2,351 m.)
Natural resources: fish, forests (cork), tungsten, iron ore, uranium ore, marble

People

Population: 9,918,040 (July 1999 est.)
Population growth rate: -0.13%
Infant mortality rate: 6.73 deaths/ 1,000 live births
Life expectancy at birth: total population: 75.88 years; male: 72.51 years; female: 79.46 years

Major ethnic groups: homogeneous
Mediterranean stock in mainland,
Azores, Madeira Islands; citizens
of black African descent who im-
migrated to mainland during decol-
onization number less than
100,000

Major religions: Roman Catholic 97%,
Protestant denominations 1%,
other 2%

Major languages: Portuguese

Government

Official name: Portuguese Republic

Government type: parliamentary
democracy

National capital: Lisbon

Independence: 1140 (independent
republic proclaimed October 5,
1910)

Legal system: civil law system; the
Constitutional Tribunal reviews the
constitutionality of legislation

Economy

Industries: textiles and footwear; wood
pulp, paper, and cork; metalworking; oil refining; chemicals; fish canning; wine; tourism

Agricultural products: grain, potatoes,
olives, grapes; sheep, cattle, goats,
poultry, meat, dairy products

Currency: 1 Portuguese escudo (Esc) =
100 centavos

Puerto Rico

Geography

Location: Caribbean, island between
the Caribbean Sea and the North
Atlantic Ocean, east of the
Dominican Republic

Area: 3,515 sq. mi. (9,104 sq. km.);
slightly less than three times the
size of Rhode Island

Climate: tropical marine, mild; little
seasonal temperature variation

Terrain: mostly mountains with
coastal plain belt in north; mountains precipitous to sea on west
coast; sandy beaches along most
coastal areas

Elevation: lowest point: Caribbean Sea
0 ft. (0 m.); highest point: Cerro de
Punta 4,390 ft. (1,338 m.)

Natural resources: some copper and
nickel; potential for onshore and offshore oil

People

Population: 3,887,652 (July 1999 est.)

Population growth rate: 0.59%

Infant mortality rate: 10.79 deaths/
1,000 live births

Life expectancy at birth: total population: 75.06 years; male: 70.95 years;
female: 79.41 years

Major ethnic groups: Hispanic

Major religions: Roman Catholic 85%,
Protestant denominations and
other 15%

Major languages: Spanish, English

Government

Official name: Commonwealth of
Puerto Rico

Government type: commonwealth

National capital: San Juan

Independence: none (commonwealth
associated with the U.S.)

Legal system: based on Spanish civil
code

Economy

Industries: pharmaceuticals, electronics, apparel, food products; tourism

Agricultural products: livestock products, chickens; sugarcane, coffee,
pineapples, plantains, bananas

Currency: 1 U.S. dollar (US$) = 100
cents

Qatar

Geography

Location: Middle East, peninsula bordering the Persian Gulf and Saudi
Arabia

Area: 4,416 sq. mi. (11,437 sq. km.);
slightly smaller than Connecticut

Climate: desert; hot, dry; humid and
sultry in summer

Terrain: mostly flat and barren desert
covered with loose sand and gravel

Elevation: lowest point: Persian Gulf
0 ft. (0 m.); highest point: Qurayn
Aba al Bawl 338 ft. (103 m.)

Natural resources: petroleum, natural gas, fish

People

Population: 723,542 (July 1999 est.) Note—includes 516,508 non-nationals)
Population growth rate: 3.62%
Infant mortality rate: 17.25 deaths/1,000 live births
Life expectancy at birth: total population: 74.23 years; male: 71.7 years; female: 76.89 years
Major ethnic groups: Arab 40%, Pakistani 18%, Indian 18%, Iranian 10%, other 14%
Major religions: Muslim 95%
Major languages: Arabic (official), English commonly used as a second language

Government

Official name: State of Qatar
Government type: traditional monarchy
National capital: Doha
Independence: September 3, 1971 (from U.K.)
Legal system: discretionary system of law controlled by the amir, although civil codes are being implemented; Islamic law is significant in personal matters

Economy

Industries: crude oil production and refining, fertilizers, petrochemicals, steel reinforcing bars, cement
Agricultural products: fruits, vegetables; poultry, dairy products, beef; fish
Currency: 1 Qatari riyal (QR) = 100 dirhams

Reunion

Geography

Location: Southern Africa, island in the Indian Ocean, east of Madagascar
Area: 969 sq. mi. (2,510 sq. km.); slightly smaller than Rhode Island
Climate: tropical, but temperature moderates with elevation; cool and dry from May to November, hot and rainy from November to April
Terrain: mostly rugged and mountainous; fertile lowlands along coast

Elevation: extremes: lowest point: Indian Ocean 0 ft. (0 m.); highest point: Piton des Neiges 10,069 ft. (3,069 m.)
Natural resources: fish, arable land

People

Population: 717,723 (July 1999 est.)
Population growth rate: 1.75%
Infant mortality rate: 6.9 deaths/1,000 live births
Life expectancy at birth: total population: 75.73 years; male: 72.69 years; female: 78.93 years
Major ethnic groups: French, African, Malagasy, Chinese, Pakistani, Indian
Major religions: Roman Catholic 94%, Hindu, Islam, Buddhist
Major languages: French (official), Creole widely used

Government

Official name: Department of Reunion
National capital: Saint-Denis
Independence: none (overseas department of France)
Legal system: French law

Economy

Industries: sugar, rum, cigarettes, handicraft items, flower oil extraction
Agricultural products: sugarcane, vanilla, tobacco, tropical fruits, vegetables, corn
Currency: 1 French franc (F) = 100 centimes

Romania

Geography

Location: Southeastern Europe, bordering the Black Sea, between Bulgaria and Ukraine
Area: 91,699 sq. mi. (237,500 sq. km.); slightly smaller than Oregon
Climate: temperate; cold, cloudy winters with frequent snow and fog; sunny summers with frequent showers and thunderstorms
Terrain: central Transylvanian Basin is separated from the Plain of Moldavia on the east by the Carpathian Mountains and separated from the Walachian Plain on the south by the Transylvanian Alps

Nations *(cont.)*

Elevation: lowest point: Black Sea 0 ft. (0 m.); highest point: Moldoveanu 8,346 ft. (2,544 m.)

Natural resources: petroleum (reserves declining), timber, natural gas, coal, iron ore, salt

People

Population: 22,334,312 (July 1999 est.)

Population growth rate: -0.23%

Infant mortality rate: 18.12 deaths/ 1,000 live births

Life expectancy at birth: total population: 70.83 years; male: 67.05 years; female: 74.81 years

Major ethnic groups: Romanian 89.1%, Hungarian 8.9%, Ukrainian, Serb, Croat, Russian, Turk, Gypsy 1.6%, and German 0.4%

Major religions: Romanian Orthodox 70%, Roman Catholic 6%, Protestant 6%

Major languages: Romanian, Hungarian, German

Government

Official name: Romania

Government type: republic

National capital: Bucharest

Independence: 1881 (from Turkey; republic proclaimed December 30, 1947)

Legal system: based on the Constitution of France's Fifth Republic

Economy

Industries: mining, timber, construction materials, metallurgy, chemicals, machine building, food processing, petroleum production and refining

Agricultural products: wheat, corn, sugar beets, sunflower seed, potatoes, grapes; milk, eggs, meat

Currency: 1 leu (L) = 100 bani

Russia

Geography

Location: Northern Asia (that part west of the Urals is sometimes included with Europe), bordering the Arctic Ocean, between Europe and the North Pacific Ocean

Area: 6,592,735 sq. mi. (17,075,200 sq. km.); slightly less than 1.8 times the size of the U.S.

Climate: ranges from steppes in the south through humid continental in much of European Russia; subarctic in Siberia to tundra climate in the polar north; winters vary from cool along Black Sea coast to frigid in Siberia; summers vary from warm in the steppes to cool along Arctic coast

Terrain: broad plain with low hills west of Urals; vast coniferous forest and tundra in Siberia; uplands and mountains along southern border regions

Elevation: lowest point: Caspian Sea –92 ft. (–8 m.); highest point: Mount El'brus 18,481 ft. (5,633 m.)

Natural resources: wide natural resource base including major deposits of oil, natural gas, coal, and many strategic minerals, timber note: formidable obstacles of climate, terrain, and distance hinder exploitation of natural resources

People

Population: 146,393,569 (July 1999 est.)

Population growth rate: –0.33%

Infant mortality rate: 23 deaths/1,000 live births

Life expectancy at birth: total population: 65.12 years; male: 58.83 years; female: 71.72 years

Major ethnic groups: Russian 81.5%, Tatar 3.8%, Ukrainian 3%

Major religions: Russian Orthodox, Muslim

Major languages: Russian, other

Government

Official name: Russian Federation

Government type: federation

National capital: Moscow

Independence: August 24, 1991 (from Soviet Union)

Legal system: based on civil law system; judicial review of legislative acts

Economy

Industries: complete range of mining and extractive industries producing coal, oil, gas, chemicals, and metals; all forms of machine building from rolling mills to high-performance aircraft and space vehicles; shipbuilding; road and rail transportation equipment; communications equipment; agricultural machinery, tractors, and construction equipment; electric power generating and transmitting equipment; medical and scientific instruments; consumer durables, textiles, foodstuffs, handicrafts

Agricultural products: grain, sugar beets, sunflower seed, vegetables, fruits; meat, milk

Currency: 1 ruble (R) = 100 kopeks

Rwanda

Geography

Location: Central Africa, east of Democratic Republic of the Congo

Area: 10,170 sq. mi. (26,340 sq. km.); slightly smaller than Maryland

Climate: temperate; two rainy seasons (February to April, November to January); mild in mountains with frost and snow possible

Terrain: mostly grassy uplands and hills; relief is mountainous with altitude declining from west to east

Elevation: lowest point: Rusizi River 3,117 ft. (950 m.); highest point: Volcan Karisimbi 14,826 ft. (4,519 m.)

Natural resources: gold, cassiterite (tin ore), wolframite (tungsten ore), natural gas, hydropower

People

Population: 8,154,933 (July 1999 est.)

Population growth rate: 2.43%

Infant mortality rate: 112.86 deaths/1,000 live births

Life expectancy at birth: total population: 41.31 years; male: 40.84 years; female: 41.8 years

Major ethnic groups: Hutu 80%, Tutsi 19%, Twa (Pygmoid) 1%

Major religions: Roman Catholic 65%, Protestant 9%, Muslim 1%, indigenous beliefs and other 25%

Major languages: Kinyarwanda (official) universal Bantu vernacular, French (official), English (official), Kiswahili (Swahili) used in commercial centers

Government

Official name: Rwandese Republic

Government type: republic; presidential, multiparty system

National capital: Kigali

Independence: July 1, 1962 (from Belgium-administered UN trusteeship)

Legal system: based on German and Belgian civil law systems and customary law; judicial review of legislative acts in the Supreme Court; has not accepted compulsory ICJ jurisdiction

Economy

Industries: mining of cassiterite (tin ore) and wolframite (tungsten ore), tin, cement, processing of agricultural products, small-scale beverage production, soap, furniture, shoes, plastic goods, textiles, cigarettes

Agricultural products: coffee, tea, pyrethrum (insecticide made from chrysanthemums), bananas, beans, sorghum, potatoes; livestock

Currency: 1 Rwandan franc (RF) = 100 centimes

Saint Helena

Geography

Location: islands in the South Atlantic Ocean, about mid-way between South America and Africa

Area: 158 sq. mi. (410 sq. km.); slightly more than two times the size of Washington, D.C.

Climate: Saint Helena—tropical; marine; mild, tempered by trade winds; Tristan da Cunha—temperate; marine, mild, tempered by trade winds (tends to be cooler than Saint Helena)

Nations *(cont.)*

Terrain: Saint Helena—rugged, volcanic; small scattered plateaus and plains

Elevation: lowest point: Atlantic Ocean 0 ft. (0 m.); highest point: Queen Mary's Peak 6,758 ft. (2,060 m.)

Natural resources: fish

People

Population: 7,145 (July 1999 est.)

Population growth rate: 0.74%

Infant mortality rate: 28.98 deaths/1,000 live births

Life expectancy at birth: total population: 75.88 years; male: 72.78 years; female: 79.13 years

Major ethnic groups: African descent, white

Major religions: Anglican (majority), Baptist, Seventh-Day Adventist, Roman Catholic

Major languages: English

Government

Official name: Saint Helena

National capital: Jamestown

Independence: none (dependent territory of the U.K.)

Economy

Industries: crafts (furniture, lacework, fancy woodwork), fishing

Agricultural products: maize, potatoes, vegetables; timber production being developed; fishing, including crawfishing on Tristan da Cunha

Currency: 1 Saint Helenian pound (£S) = 100 pence

Saint Kitts and Nevis

Geography

Location: Caribbean, islands in the Caribbean Sea, about one-third of the way from Puerto Rico to Trinidad and Tobago

Area: 104 sq. mi. (269 sq. km.); 1.5 times the size of Washington, D.C.

Climate: subtropical tempered by constant sea breezes; little seasonal temperature variation; rainy season (May to November)

Terrain: volcanic with mountainous interiors

Elevation: lowest point: Caribbean Sea 0 ft. (0 m.); highest point: Mount Liamuiga 3,793 ft. (1,156 m.)

Natural resources: negligible

People

Population: 42,838 (July 1999 est.)

Population growth rate: 1.34%

Infant mortality rate: 17.39 deaths/1,000 live births

Life expectancy at birth: total population: 67.94 years; male: 64.87 years; female: 71.21 years

Major ethnic groups: black

Major religions: Anglican, other Protestant sects, Roman Catholic

Major languages: English

Government

Official name: Federation of Saint Kitts and Nevis

Government type: constitutional monarchy

National capital: Basseterre

Independence: September 19, 1983 (from U.K.)

Legal system: based on English common law

Economy

Industries: sugar processing, tourism, cotton, salt, copra, clothing, footwear, beverages

Agricultural products: sugarcane, rice, yams, vegetables, bananas; fishing potential not fully exploited

Currency: 1 East Caribbean dollar (EC$) = 100 cents

Saint Lucia

Geography

Location: Caribbean, island between the Caribbean Sea and North Atlantic Ocean, north of Trinidad and Tobago

Area: 239 sq. mi. (620 sq. km.); 3.5 times the size of Washington, D.C.

Climate: tropical, moderated by northeast trade winds; dry season from January to April, rainy season from May to August

Terrain: volcanic and mountainous with some broad, fertile valleys

Elevation: extremes: lowest point: Caribbean Sea 0 ft. (0 m.); highest point: Mount Gimie 3,117 ft. (950 m.)

Natural resources: forests, sandy beaches, minerals (pumice), mineral springs, geothermal potential

People

Population: 154,020 (July 1999 est.)

Population growth rate: 1.09%

Infant mortality rate: 16.55 deaths/ 1,000 live births

Life expectancy at birth: total population: 71.81 years; male: 68.14 years; female: 75.74 years

Major ethnic groups: black 90%, mixed 6%, East Indian 3%, white 1%

Major religions: Roman Catholic 90%, Protestant 7%, Anglican 3%

Major languages: English (official), French patois

Government

Official name: Saint Lucia

Government type: parliamentary democracy

National capital: Castries

Independence: February 22, 1979 (from U.K.)

Legal system: based on English common law

Economy

Industries: clothing, assembly of electronic components, beverages, corrugated cardboard boxes, tourism, lime processing, coconut processing

Agricultural products: bananas, coconuts, vegetables, citrus, root crops, cocoa

Currency: 1 East Caribbean dollar (EC$) = 100 cents

Saint Pierre and Miquelon

Geography

Location: Northern North America, islands in the North Atlantic Ocean, south of Newfoundland (Canada)

Area: 93 sq. mi. (242 sq. km.); 1.5 times the size of Washington, D.C.

Climate: cold and wet, with much mist and fog; spring and autumn are windy

Terrain: mostly barren rock

Elevation: extremes: lowest point: Atlantic Ocean 0 ft. (0 m.); highest point: Morne de la Grande Montagne 787 ft. (240 m.)

Natural resources: fish, deepwater ports

People

Population: 6,966 (July 1999 est.)

Population growth rate: 0.75%

Infant mortality rate: 8.12 deaths/1,000 live births

Life expectancy at birth: total population: 77.13 years; male: 75.58 years; female: 79 years

Major ethnic groups: Basques and Bretons (French fishermen)

Major religions: Roman Catholic 99%

Major languages: French

Government

Official name: Territorial Collectivity of Saint Pierre and

National capital: Saint-Pierre

Independence: none (territorial collectivity of France; has been under French control since 1763)

Legal system: French law with special adaptations for local conditions, such as housing and taxation

Economy

Industries: fish processing and supply base for fishing fleets; tourism

Agricultural products: vegetables; cattle, sheep, pigs; fish

Currency: 1 French franc (F) = 100 centimes

Saint Vincent and the Grenadines

Geography

Location: Caribbean, islands in the Caribbean Sea, north of Trinidad and Tobago

Area: 131 sq. mi. (340 sq. km.); twice the size of Washington, D.C.

Climate: tropical; little seasonal temperature variation; rainy season (May to November)

Terrain: volcanic, mountainous

Nations (cont.)

Elevation: lowest point: Caribbean Sea 0 ft. (0 m.); highest point: Soufriere 4,049 ft. (1,234 m.)

Natural resources: negligible

People

Population: 120,519 (July 1999 est.)

Population growth rate: 0.57%

Infant mortality rate: 15.16 deaths/ 1,000 live births

Life expectancy at birth: total population: 73.8 years; male: 72.29 years; female: 75.36 years

Major ethnic groups: black, white, East Indian, Carib Amerindian

Major religions: Anglican, Methodist, Roman Catholic, Seventh-Day Adventist

Major languages: English, French patois

Government

Official name: Saint Vincent and the Grenadines

Government type: constitutional monarchy

National capital: Kingstown

Independence: 27, October 1979 (from U.K.)

Legal system: based on English common law

Economy

Industries: food processing, cement, furniture, clothing, starch

Agricultural products: bananas, coconuts, sweet potatoes, spices; small numbers of cattle, sheep, pigs, goats; small fish catch used locally

Currency: 1 East Caribbean dollar (EC$) = 100 cents

Samoa

Geography

Location: Oceania, group of islands in the South Pacific Ocean, about one-half of the way from Hawaii to New Zealand

Area: 1,104 sq. mi. (2,860 sq. km.); slightly smaller than Rhode Island

Climate: tropical; rainy season (October to March), dry season (May to October)

Terrain: narrow coastal plain with volcanic, rocky, rugged mountains in interior

Elevation: lowest point: Pacific Ocean 0 ft. (0 m.); highest point: Mauga Silisili 6,092 ft. (1,857 m.)

Natural resources: hardwood forests, fish

People

Population: 229,979 (July 1999 est.)

Population growth rate: 2.3%

Infant mortality rate: 30.5 deaths/1,000 live births

Life expectancy at birth: total population: 69.82 years; male: 67.43 years; female: 72.33 years

Major ethnic groups: Samoan 92.6%, Euronesians 7% (persons of European and Polynesian blood)

Major religions: Christian 99.7%

Major languages: Samoan (Polynesian), English

Government

Official name: Independent State of Samoa

Government type: constitutional monarchy under native chief

National capital: Apia

Independence: January 1, 1962 (from New Zealand-administered UN trusteeship)

Legal system: based on English common law and local customs; judicial review of legislative acts with respect to fundamental rights of the citizen

Economy

Industries: timber, tourism, food processing, fishing

Agricultural products: coconuts, bananas, taro, yams

Currency: 1 tala (WS$) = 100 sene

San Marino

Geography

Location: Southern Europe, an enclave in central Italy

Area: 23 sq. mi. (60 sq. km.); about 0.3 times the size of Washington, D.C.

Climate: Mediterranean; mild to cool winters; warm, sunny summers
Terrain: rugged mountains
Elevation: lowest point: Fiume Ausa 180 ft. (55 m.); highest point: Monte Titano 2,457 ft. (749 m.)
Natural resources: building stone

People
Population: 25,061 (July 1999 est.)
Population growth rate: 0.64%
Infant mortality rate: 5.39 deaths/1,000 live births
Life expectancy at birth: total population: 81.47 years; male: 77.59 years; female: 85.35 years
Major ethnic groups: Sammarinese, Italian
Major religions: Roman Catholic
Major languages: Italian

Government
Official name: Republic of San Marino
Government type: republic
National capital: San Marino
Independence: 301 AD (by tradition)
Legal system: based on civil law system with Italian law influences

Economy
Industries: tourism, textiles, electronics, ceramics, cement, wine
Agricultural products: wheat, grapes, maize, olives; cattle, pigs, horses, meat, cheese, hides
Currency: 1 Italian lire (Lit) = 100 centesimi; note-also mints its own coins

São Tomé and Príncipe

Geography
Location: Western Africa, island in the Gulf of Guinea, straddling the Equator, west of Gabon
Area: 371 sq. mi. (960 sq. km.); more than five times the size of Washington, D.C.
Climate: tropical; hot, humid; one rainy season (October to May)
Terrain: volcanic, mountainous
Elevation: extremes: lowest point: Atlantic Ocean 0 ft. (0 m.); highest point: Pico de São Tomé 6,640 ft. (2,024 m.)

Natural resources: fish

People
Population: 154,878 (July 1999 est.)
Population growth rate: 3.14%
Infant mortality rate: 52.93 deaths/1,000 live births
Life expectancy at birth: total population: 64.71 years; male: 63.18 years; female: 66.28 years
Major ethnic groups: mestiço, angolares (descendants of Angolan slaves), forros (descendants of freed slaves), servicais (contract laborers from Angola, Mozambique, and Cape Verde), tongas (children of servicais born on the islands), Europeans (primarily Portuguese)
Major religions: Roman Catholic, Evangelical Protestant, Seventh-Day Adventist
Major languages: Portuguese (official)

Government
Official name: Democratic Republic of São Tomé and Príncipe
Government type: republic
National capital: São Tomé
Independence: July 12, 1975 (from Portugal)
Legal system: based on Portuguese legal system and customary law

Economy
Industries: light construction, textiles, soap, beer; fish processing; timber
Agricultural products: cocoa, coconuts, palm kernels, copra, cinnamon, pepper, coffee, bananas, papaya, beans; poultry; fish
Currency: 1 dobra (Db) = 100 centimos

Saudi Arabia

Geography
Location: Middle East, bordering the Persian Gulf and the Red Sea, north of Yemen
Area: 756,981 sq. mi. (1,960,582 sq. km.); slightly more than one-fifth the size of the U.S.
Climate: harsh, dry desert with great extremes of temperature
Terrain: mostly uninhabited, sandy desert

Nations *(cont.)*

Elevation: lowest point: Persian Gulf
0 ft. (0 m.); highest point: Jabal
Sawda' 10,279 ft. (3,133 m.)
Natural resources: petroleum, natural
gas, iron ore, gold, copper

People

Population: 21,504,613 (July 1999 est.)
(Note: includes 5,244,058 non-
nationals)
Population growth rate: 3.39%
Infant mortality rate: 38.8 deaths/
1,000 live births
Life expectancy at birth: total popula-
tion: 70.55 years; male: 68.67 years;
female: 72.53 years
Major ethnic groups: Arab 90%, Afro-
Asian 10%
Major religions: Muslim 100%
Major languages: Arabic

Government

Official name: Kingdom of Saudi
Arabia
Government type: monarchy
National capital: Riyadh
Independence: September 23, 1932
(unification)
Legal system: based on Islamic law,
several secular codes have been
introduced; commercial disputes
handled by special committees; has
not accepted compulsory ICJ jurisdiction

Economy

Industries: crude oil production, petroleum refining, basic petrochemicals,
cement, two small steel-rolling mills,
construction, fertilizer, plastics
Agricultural products: wheat, barley,
tomatoes, melons, dates, citrus;
mutton, chickens, eggs, milk
Currency: 1 Saudi riyal (SR) = 100
halalah

Senegal

Geography

Location: Western Africa, bordering
the North Atlantic Ocean, between
Guinea-Bissau and Mauritania
Area: 75,749 sq. mi. (196,190 sq. km.);
slightly smaller than South Dakota

Climate: tropical; hot, humid; rainy
season (May to November) has
strong southeast winds; dry season
(December to April) dominated by
hot, dry, harmattan wind
Terrain: generally low, rolling plains
rising to foothills in southeast
Elevation: lowest point: Atlantic Ocean
0 ft. (0 m.); highest point: unnamed
location in the Futa Jaldon foothills
1,906 ft. (581 m.)
Natural resources: fish, phosphates,
iron ore

People

Population: 10,051,930 (July 1999 est.)
Population growth rate: 3.32%
Infant mortality rate: 59.81 deaths/
1,000 live births
Life expectancy at birth: total popula-
tion: 57.83 years; male: 54.95 years;
female: 60.78 years
Major ethnic groups: Wolof 36%,
Fulani 17%, Serer 17%, Toucouleur
9%, Diola 9%, Mandingo 9%,
European and Lebanese 1%
Major religions: Muslim 92%, indige-
nous beliefs 6%, Christian 2%
(mostly Roman Catholic)
Major languages: French (official),
Wolof, Pulaar, Diola, Mandingo

Government

Official name: Republic of Senegal
Government type: republic under multiparty democratic rule
National capital: Dakar
Independence: April 4, 1960 from
France; complete independence was
achieved upon dissolution of federation with Mali on August 20, 1960
(The Gambia and Senegal signed an
agreement on December 12, 1981
that called for the creation of a loose
confederation to be known as
Senegambia, but the agreement was
dissolved on September 30, 1989)
Legal system: based on French civil law
system; judicial review of legislative
acts in Constitutional Court; the
Council of State audits the government's accounting office

Economy

Industries: agricultural and fish processing, phosphate mining, fertilizer production, petroleum refining, construction materials

Agricultural products: peanuts, millet, corn, sorghum, rice, cotton, tomatoes, green vegetables; cattle, poultry, pigs; fish

Currency: 1 Communauté Financière Africaine franc (CFAF) = 100 centimes

Serbia and Montenegro

Geography

Location: Southeastern Europe, bordering the Adriatic Sea, between Albania and Bosnia and Herzegovina

Area: 39,517 sq. mi. (102,350 sq. km.); slightly smaller than Kentucky (Serbia is slightly larger than Maine; Montenegro is slightly smaller than Connecticut)

Climate: in the north, continental climate (cold winter and hot, humid summers with well distributed rainfall); central portion, continental and Mediterranean climate; to the south, Adriatic climate along the coast, hot, dry summers and autumns and relatively cold winters with heavy snowfall inland

Terrain: extremely varied; to the north, rich fertile plains; to the east, limestone ranges and basins; to the southeast, ancient mountains and hills; to the southwest, extremely high shoreline with no islands off the coast

Elevation: lowest point: Adriatic Sea 0 ft. (0 m.); highest point: Daravica 8,714 ft. (2,656 m.)

Natural resources: oil, gas, coal, antimony, copper, lead, zinc, nickel, gold, pyrite, chrome

People

Population: 11,206,847 (Montenegro 680,369; Serbia 10,526,478) (July 1999 est.)

Population growth rate: Montenegro 0.07%; Serbia 0.02%

Infant mortality rate: Montenegro 10.99 deaths/1,000 live births; Serbia 16.49 deaths/1,000 live births

Life expectancy at birth: total population: Montenegro 76.32 years; Serbia 73.45 years; male: Montenegro 72.87 years; Serbia 71.03 years; female: Montenegro 80.07 years; Serbia 76.05 years

Major ethnic groups: Serbs 63%, Albanians 14%, Montenegrins 6%, Hungarians 4%, other 13%

Major religions: Orthodox 65%, Muslim 19%, Roman Catholic 4%, Protestant 1%, other 11%

Major languages: Serbo-Croatian 95%, Albanian 5%

Government

Official name: Serbia and Montenegro (Note: Serbia and Montenegro has proclaimed itself the "Federal Republic of Yugoslavia," but the U.S. view is that the Socialist Federal Republic of Yugoslavia [SFRY] has dissolved and that none of the successor republics represents its continuation.)

Government type: republic

National capital: Belgrade (Serbia), Podgorica (Montenegro)

Independence: April 11, 1992 (Federal Republic of Yugoslavia formed as self-proclaimed successor to the Socialist Federal Republic of Yugoslavia-SFRY)

Legal system: based on civil law system

Economy

Industries: machine building (aircraft, trucks, and automobiles; tanks and weapons; electrical equipment; agricultural machinery); metallurgy (steel, aluminum, copper, lead, zinc, chromium, antimony, bismuth, cadmium); mining (coal, bauxite, non-ferrous ore, iron ore, limestone); consumer goods (textiles, footwear, foodstuffs, appliances); electronics, petroleum products, chemicals, and pharmaceuticals

Agricultural products: cereals, fruits, vegetables, tobacco, olives; cattle, sheep, goats

Nations *(cont.)*

Currency: 1 Yugoslav new dinar (YD) = 100 paras

Seychelles

Geography
Location: Eastern Africa, group of islands in the Indian Ocean, northeast of Madagascar

Area: 176 sq. mi. (455 sq. km.); 2.5 times the size of Washington, D.C.

Climate: tropical marine; humid; cooler season during southeast monsoon (late May to September); warmer season during northwest monsoon (March to May)

Terrain: Mahe Group is granitic, narrow coastal strip, rocky, hilly; others are coral, flat, elevated reefs

Elevation: extremes: lowest point: Indian Ocean 0 ft. (0 m.); highest point: Morne Seychellois 2,969 ft. (905 m.)

Natural resources: fish, copra, cinnamon trees

People
Population: 79,164 (July 1999 est.)

Population growth rate: 0.65%

Infant mortality rate: 16.65 deaths/1,000 live births

Life expectancy at birth: total population: 70.95 years; male: 66.61 years; female: 75.42 years

Major ethnic groups: Seychellois (mixture of Asians, Africans, Europeans)

Major religions: Roman Catholic 90%, Anglican 8%

Major languages: English (official), French (official), Creole

Government
Official name: Republic of Seychelles

Government type: republic

National capital: Victoria

Independence: June 29, 1976 (from U.K.)

Legal system: based on English common law, French civil law, and customary law

Economy
Industries: fishing; tourism; processing of coconuts and vanilla, coir (coconut fiber) rope, boat building, printing, furniture; beverages

Agricultural products: coconuts, cinnamon, vanilla, sweet potatoes, cassava (tapioca), bananas; broiler chickens; tuna fishing (expansion under way)

Currency: 1 Seychelles rupee (SRe) = 100 cents

Sierra Leone

Geography
Location: Western Africa, bordering the North Atlantic Ocean, between Guinea and Liberia

Area: 27,699 sq. mi. (71,740 sq. km.); slightly smaller than South Carolina

Climate: tropical; hot, humid; summer rainy season (May to December); winter dry season (December to April)

Terrain: coastal belt of mangrove swamps, wooded hill country, upland plateau, mountains in east

Elevation: lowest point: Atlantic Ocean 0 ft. (0 m.); highest point: Loma Mansa (Bintimani) 6,391 ft. (1,948 m.)

Natural resources: diamonds, titanium ore, bauxite, iron ore, gold, chromite

People
Population: 5,296,651 (July 1999 est.)

Population growth rate: 4.34%

Infant mortality rate: 126.23 deaths/1,000 live births

Life expectancy at birth: total population: 49.13 years; male: 46.07 years; female: 52.27 years

Major ethnic groups: 20 native African tribes 90% (Temne 30%, Mende 30%, other 30%), Creole 10% (descendents of freed Jamaican slaves who were settled in the Freetown area in the late-eighteenth century), refugees from Liberia's recent civil war, small numbers of Europeans, Lebanese, Pakistanis and Indians

Major religions: Muslim 60%, indigenous beliefs 30%, Christian 10%

Major languages: English (official, regular use limited to literate minority),
Mende (principal vernacular in the
south), Temne (principal vernacular
in the north), Krio (English-based
Creole, spoken by the descendents
of freed Jamaican slaves who were
settled in the Freetown area, a lingua franca and a first language for
10% of the population but understood by 95%)

Government
Official name: Republic of Sierra Leone
Government type: constitutional
democracy
National capital: Freetown
Independence: April 27, 1961 (from
U.K.)
Legal system: based on English law and
customary laws indigenous to local
tribes; has not accepted compulsory
ICJ jurisdiction

Economy
Industries: mining (diamonds); small-
scale manufacturing (beverages, textiles, cigarettes, footwear);
petroleum refining
Agricultural products: rice, coffee,
cocoa, palm kernels, palm oil, peanuts; poultry, cattle, sheep, pigs; fish
Currency: 1 leone (Le) = 100 cents

Singapore

Geography
Location: Southeastern Asia, islands
between Malaysia and Indonesia
Area: 250 sq. mi. (647.5 sq. km.);
slightly more than 3.5 times the size
of Washington, D.C.
Climate: tropical; hot, humid, rainy;
no pronounced rainy or dry seasons;
thunderstorms occur on 40% of all
days (67% of days in April)
Terrain: lowland; gently undulating
central plateau contains water catch-
ment area and nature preserve
Elevation: lowest point: Singapore
Strait 0 ft. (0 m.); highest point:
Bukit Timah 166 (m166 m.)
Natural resources: fish, deepwater
ports

People
Population: 3,531,600 (July 1999 est.)
Population growth rate: 1.15%
Infant mortality rate: 3.84 deaths/
1,000 live births
Life expectancy at birth: total popula-
tion: 78.84 years; male: 75.79 years;
female: 82.14 years
Major ethnic groups: Chinese 76.4%,
Malay 14.9%, Indian 6.4%
Major religions: Buddhist (Chinese),
Muslim (Malays), Christian, Hindu,
Sikh, Taoist, Confucianist
Major languages: Chinese (official),
Malay (official and national), Tamil
(official), English (official)

Government
Official name: Republic of Singapore
Government type: republic within
Commonwealth
National capital: Singapore
Independence: August 9, 1965 (from
Malaysia)
Legal system: based on English com-
mon law

Economy
Industries: electronics, financial services, oil drilling equipment, petroleum refining, rubber processing
and rubber products, processed food
and beverages, ship repair, entrepot
trade, biotechnology
Agricultural products: rubber, copra,
fruit, vegetables; poultry
Currency: 1 Singapore dollar (S$) =
100 cents

Slovakia

Geography
Location: Central Europe, south of
Poland
Area: 18,859 sq. mi. (48,845 sq. km.);
about twice the size of New
Hampshire
Climate: temperate; cool summers;
cold, cloudy, humid winters
Terrain: rugged mountains in the cen-
tral and northern part and lowlands
in the south
Elevation: lowest point: Bodrok River
308 ft. (94 m.); highest point:
Gerlachovka 8,711 ft. (2,655 m.)

Nations *(cont.)*

Natural resources: brown coal and lignite; small amounts of iron ore, copper and manganese ore; salt

People

Population: 5,396,193 (July 1999 est.)
Population growth rate: 0.04%
Infant mortality rate: 9.48 deaths/1,000 live births
Life expectancy at birth: total population: 73.46 years; male: 69.71 years; female: 77.4 years
Major ethnic groups: Slovak 85.7%, Hungarian 10.7%, Gypsy 1.5% (the 1992 census figures underreport the Gypsy/Romany community, which could reach 500,000 or more), Czech 1%
Major religions: Roman Catholic 60.3%, atheist 9.7%, Protestant 8.4%, Orthodox 4.1%
Major languages: Slovak (official), Hungarian

Government

Official name: Slovak Republic
Government type: parliamentary democracy
National capital: Bratislava
Independence: January 1, 1993 (from Czechoslovakia)
Legal system: civil law system based on Austro-Hungarian codes; legal code modified to comply with the obligations of Organization on Security and Cooperation in Europe (OSCE) and to expunge Marxist-Leninist legal theory

Economy

Industries: metal and metal products; food and beverages; electricity, gas, coke, oil, and nuclear fuel; chemicals and manmade fibers; machinery; paper and printing; earthenware and ceramics; transport vehicles; textiles; electrical and optical apparatus; rubber products
Agricultural products: grains, potatoes, sugar beets, hops, fruit; hogs, cattle, poultry; forest products
Currency: 1 koruna (Sk) = 100 halierov

Slovenia

Geography

Location: Southeastern Europe, eastern Alps bordering the Adriatic Sea, between Austria and Croatia
Area: 7,821 sq. mi. (20,256 sq. km.); slightly smaller than New Jersey
Climate: Mediterranean climate on the coast, continental climate with mild to hot summers and cold winters in the plateaus and valleys to the east
Terrain: a short coastal strip on the Adriatic, an alpine mountain region adjacent to Italy, mixed mountain and valleys with numerous rivers to the east
Elevation: lowest point: Adriatic Sea 0 ft. (0 m.); highest point: Triglav 9,396 ft. (2,864 m.)
Natural resources: lignite coal, lead, zinc, mercury, uranium, silver

People

Population: 1,970,570 (July 1999 est.)
Population growth rate: −0.04%
Infant mortality rate: 5.28 deaths/1,000 live births
Life expectancy at birth: total population: 75.36 years; male: 71.71 years; female: 79.21 years
Major ethnic groups: Slovene 91%, Croat 3%, Serb 2%, Muslim 1%
Major religions: Roman Catholic 70.8% (including 2% Uniate), Lutheran 1%, Muslim 1%, atheist 4.3%
Major languages: Slovenian 91%, Serbo-Croatian 6%

Government

Official name: Republic of Slovenia
Government type: parliamentary democratic republic
National capital: Ljubljana
Independence: June 25, 1991 (from Yugoslavia)
Legal system: based on civil law system

Economy

Industries: ferrous metallurgy and rolling mill products, aluminum reduction and rolled products, lead and zinc smelting, electronics

(including military electronics),
trucks, electric power equipment,
wood products, textiles, chemicals,
machine tools
Agricultural products: potatoes, hops,
wheat, sugar beets, corn, grapes; cattle, sheep, poultry
Currency: 1 tolar (SlT) = 100 stotins

Solomon Islands

Geography
Location: Oceania, group of islands in
the South Pacific Ocean, east of
Papua New Guinea
Area: 10,985 sq. mi. (28,450 sq. km.);
slightly smaller than Maryland
Climate: tropical monsoon; few ex-
tremes of temperature and weather
Terrain: mostly rugged mountains
with some low coral atolls
Elevation: lowest point: Pacific
Ocean 0 ft. (0 m.); highest point:
Mount Makarakomburu 8,028 ft.
(2,447 m.)
Natural resources: fish, forests, gold,
bauxite, phosphates, lead, zinc,
nickel

People
Population: 455,429 (July 1999 est.)
Population growth rate: 3.18%
Infant mortality rate: 23 deaths/1,000
live births
Life expectancy at birth: total popula-
tion: 72.09 years; male: 69.55 years;
female: 74.75 years
Major ethnic groups: Melanesian 93%,
Polynesian 4%, Micronesian 1.5%
Major religions: Anglican 34%, Roman
Catholic 19%, Baptist 17%, United
(Methodist/Presbyterian) 11%,
Seventh-Day Adventist 10%, other
Protestant 5%, traditional beliefs 4%
Major languages: Melanesian pidgin in
much of the country, English spo-
ken by 1% of population; Note—120
indigenous languages

Government
Official name: Solomon Islands
Government type: parliamentary
democracy
National capital: Honiara

Independence: July 7, 1978 (from U.K.)
Legal system: English common law

Economy
Industries: copra, fish (tuna)
Agricultural products: cocoa, beans,
coconuts, palm kernels, rice, pota-
toes, vegetables, fruit; cattle, pigs;
timber; fish
Currency: 1 Solomon Islands dollar
(SI$) = 100 cents

Somalia

Geography
Location: Eastern Africa, bordering the
Gulf of Aden and the Indian Ocean,
east of Ethiopia
Area: 246,201 sq. mi. (637,660 sq.
km.); slightly smaller than Texas
Climate: principally desert; December
to February—northeast monsoon,
moderate temperatures in north and
very hot in south; May to October—
southwest monsoon, torrid in the
north and hot in the south, irregular
rainfall, hot and humid periods
(tangambili) between monsoons
Terrain: mostly flat to undulating
plateau rising to hills in north
Elevation: lowest point: Indian Ocean
0 ft. (0 m.); highest point: Shimbiris
8,038 ft. (2,450)m.
Natural resources: uranium and largely
unexploited reserves of iron ore, tin,
gypsum, bauxite, copper, salt

People
Population: 7,140,643 (July 1999 est.)
Population growth rate: 4.13%
Infant mortality rate: 125.77 deaths/
1,000 live births
Life expectancy at birth: total popula-
tion: 46.23 years; male: 44.66 years;
female: 47.85 years
Major ethnic groups: Somali 85%,
Bantu, Arabs 30,000
Major religions: Sunni Muslim
Major languages: Somali (official),
Arabic, Italian

Government
Official name: Somalia
Government type: none
National capital: Mogadishu

Nations (cont.)

Independence: July 1, 1960 (from a merger of British Somaliland, which became independent from the U.K. on June 26, 1960, and Italian Somaliland, which became independent from the Italian-administered UN trusteeship on July 1, 1960, to form the Somali Republic)

Economy
Industries: a few small industries, including sugar refining, textiles, petroleum refining (mostly shut down)
Agricultural products: bananas, sorghum, corn, sugarcane, mangoes, sesame seeds, beans; cattle, sheep, goats; fishing potential largely unexploited
Currency: 1 Somali shilling (So. Sh.) = 100 cents

South Africa

Geography
Location: Southern Africa, at the southern tip of the continent of Africa
Area: 471,008 sq. mi. (1,219,912 sq. km.); slightly less than twice the size of Texas
Climate: mostly semiarid; subtropical along east coast; sunny days, cool nights
Terrain: vast interior plateau rimmed by rugged hills and narrow coastal plain
Elevation: lowest point: Atlantic Ocean 0 ft. (0 m.); highest point: Njesuthi 11,181 ft. (3,408 m.)
Natural resources: gold, chromium, antimony, coal, iron ore, manganese, nickel, phosphates, tin, uranium, gem diamonds, platinum, copper, vanadium, salt, natural gas

People
Population: 43,426,386 (July 1999 est.)
Population growth rate: 1.32%
Infant mortality rate: 51.99 deaths/1,000 live births
Life expectancy at birth: total population: 54.76 years; male: 52.68 years; female: 56.9 years

Major ethnic groups: black 75.2%, white 13.6%, Colored 8.6%, Indian 2.6%
Major religions: Christian 68% (includes most whites and Coloreds, about 60% of blacks and about 40% of Indians), Muslim 2%, Hindu 1.5% (60% of Indians), traditional and animistic 28.5%
Major languages: 11 official languages, including Afrikaans, English, Ndebele, Pedi, Sotho, Swazi, Tsonga, Tswana, Venda, Xhosa, Zulu

Government
Official name: Republic of South Africa
Government type: republic
National capital: Pretoria (administrative); Cape Town (legislative); Bloemfontein (judicial)
Independence: May 31, 1910 (from U.K.)
Legal system: based on Roman-Dutch law and English common law

Economy
Industries: mining (world's largest producer of platinum, gold, chromium), automobile assembly, metalworking, machinery, textile, iron and steel, chemical, fertilizer, foodstuffs
Agricultural products: corn, wheat, sugarcane, fruits, vegetables, beef, poultry, mutton, wool, dairy products
Currency: 1 rand (R) = 100 cents

Spain

Geography
Location: Southwestern Europe, bordering the Bay of Biscay, Mediterranean Sea, North Atlantic Ocean, and Pyrenees Mountains, southwest of France
Area: 194,884 sq. mi. (504,750 sq. km.); slightly more than twice the size of Oregon
Climate: temperate; clear, hot summers in interior, more moderate and cloudy along coast; cloudy, cold winters in interior, partly cloudy and cool along coast

Terrain: large, flat to dissected plateau surrounded by rugged hills; Pyrenees in north

Elevation: lowest point: Atlantic Ocean 0 ft. (0 m.); highest point: Pico de Teide on Canary Islands 12,198 ft. (3,718 m.)

Natural resources: coal, lignite, iron ore, uranium, mercury, pyrites, fluorspar, gypsum, zinc, lead, tungsten, copper, kaolin, potash, hydropower

People

Population: 39,167,744 (July 1999 est.)

Population growth rate: 0.1%

Infant mortality rate: 6.41 deaths/1,000 live births

Life expectancy at birth: total population: 77.71 years; male: 73.97 years; female: 81.71 years

Major ethnic groups: composite of Mediterranean and Nordic types

Major religions: Roman Catholic 99%

Major languages: Castilian Spanish 74%, Catalan 17%, Galician 7%, Basque 2%

Government

Official name: Kingdom of Spain

Government type: parliamentary monarchy

National capital: Madrid

Independence: 1492 (expulsion of the Moors and unification)

Legal system: civil law system, with regional applications

Economy

Industries: textiles and apparel (including footwear), food and beverages, metals and metal manufactures, chemicals, shipbuilding, automobiles, machine tools, tourism

Agricultural products: grain, vegetables, olives, wine grapes, sugar beets, citrus; beef, pork, poultry, dairy products; fish

Currency: 1 peseta (Pta) = 100 centimos

Sri Lanka

Geography

Location: Southern Asia, island in the Indian Ocean, south of India

Area: 25,332 sq. mi. (65,610 sq. km.); slightly larger than West Virginia

Climate: tropical monsoon; northeast monsoon (December to March); southwest monsoon (June to October)

Terrain: mostly low, flat to rolling plain; mountains in south-central interior

Elevation: lowest point: Indian Ocean 0 ft. (0 m.); highest point: Pidurutalagala 8,281 ft. (2,524 m.)

Natural resources: limestone, graphite, mineral sands, gems, phosphates, clay

People

Population: 19,144,875 (July 1999 est.)

Population growth rate: 1.1%

Infant mortality rate: 16.12 deaths/1,000 live births

Life expectancy at birth: total population: 72.67 years; male: 69.89 years; female: 75.59 years

Major ethnic groups: Sinhalese 74%, Tamil 18%, Moor 7%, Burgher, Malay, and Vedda 1%

Major religions: Buddhist 69%, Hindu 15%, Christian 8%, Muslim 8%

Major languages: Sinhala (official and national language) 74%, Tamil (national language) 18%; Note—English is commonly used in government and is spoken by about 10% of the population

Government

Official name: Democratic Socialist Republic of Sri Lanka

Government type: republic

National capital: Colombo

Independence: February 4, 1948 (from U.K.)

Legal system: a highly complex mixture of English common law, Roman-Dutch, Muslim, Sinhalese, and customary law

Economy

Industries: processing of rubber, tea, coconuts, and other agricultural commodities; clothing, cement, petroleum refining, textiles, tobacco

Nations *(cont.)*

Agricultural products: rice, sugarcane, grains, pulses, oilseed, roots, spices, tea, rubber, coconuts; milk, eggs, hides, meat

Currency: 1 Sri Lankan rupee (SLRe) = 100 cents

Sudan

Geography

Location: Northern Africa, bordering the Red Sea, between Egypt and Eritrea

Area: 967,493 sq. mi. (2,505,810 sq. km.); slightly more than one-quarter the size of the U.S.

Climate: tropical in south; arid desert in north; rainy season (April to October)

Terrain: generally flat, featureless plain; mountains in east and west

Elevation: lowest point: Red Sea o ft. (o m.); highest point: Kinyeti 10,456 ft. (3,187 m.)

Natural resources: petroleum; small reserves of iron ore, copper, chromium ore, zinc, tungsten, mica, silver, gold

People

Population: 34,475,690 (July 1999 est.)

Population growth rate: 2.71%

Infant mortality rate: 72.94 deaths/ 1,000 live births

Life expectancy at birth: total population: 56.4 years; male: 55.41 years; female: 57.44 years

Major ethnic groups: black 52%, Arab 39%, Beja 6%

Major religions: Sunni Muslim 70% (in north), indigenous beliefs 25%, Christian 5% (mostly in south and Khartoum)

Major languages: Arabic (official), Nubian, Ta Bedawie, diverse dialects of Nilotic, Nilo-Hamitic, Sudanic languages

Government

Official name: Republic of the Sudan

Government type: transitional—previously ruling military junta; presidential and National Assembly elections held in March 1996; new constitution drafted by Presidential Committee, went before public in national referendum in May-June 1998

National capital: Khartoum

Independence: January 1, 1956 (from Egypt and U.K.)

Legal system: based on English common law and Islamic law; as of January 20, 1991, the now defunct Revolutionary Command Council imposed Islamic law in the northern states; Islamic law applies to all residents of the northern states regardless of their religion; some separate religious courts

Economy

Industries: cotton ginning, textiles, cement, edible oils, sugar, soap distilling, shoes, petroleum refining

Agricultural products: cotton, groundnuts, sorghum, millet, wheat, gum arabic, sesame; sheep

Currency: 1 Sudanese pound (£Sd) = 100 piastres

Suriname

Geography

Location: Northern South America, bordering the North Atlantic Ocean, between French Guiana and Guyana

Area: 63,039 sq. mi. (163,270 sq. km.); slightly larger than Georgia

Climate: tropical; moderated by trade winds

Terrain: mostly rolling hills; narrow coastal plain with swamps

Elevation: lowest point: unnamed location in the coastal plain −6 ft. (−2 m.); highest point: Wilhelmina Gebergte 4,219 ft. (1,286 m.)

Natural resources: timber, hydropower potential, fish, kaolin, shrimp, bauxite, gold, and small amounts of nickel, copper, platinum, iron ore

People

Population: 431,156 (July 1999 est.)

Population growth rate: 0.71%

Infant mortality rate: 26.52 deaths/
1,000 live births
Life expectancy at birth: total population: 70.89 years; male: 68.32 years;
female: 73.59 years
Major ethnic groups: Hindustani (also
known locally as "East Indians")
37%, Creole (mixed white and black)
31%, Javanese 15.3%, "Maroons"
(their African ancestors were
brought to the country in the 17th
and 18th centuries as slaves and
escaped to the interior) 10.3%,
Amerindian 2.6%, Chinese 1.7%,
white 1%
Major religions: Hindu 27.4%,
Muslim 19.6%, Roman Catholic
22.8%, Protestant 25.2% (predominantly Moravian), indigenous
beliefs 5%
Major languages: Dutch (official),
English (widely spoken), Sranang
Tongo (Surinamese, sometimes
called Taki-Taki, is native language
of Creoles and much of the younger
population and is lingua franca
among others), Hindustani (a
dialect of Hindi), Javanese

Government

Official name: Republic of Suriname
Government type: republic
National capital: Paramaribo
Independence: November 25, 1975
(from Netherlands)
Legal system: based on Dutch legal
system incorporating French penal
theory

Economy

Industries: bauxite and gold mining,
alumina and aluminum production, lumbering, food processing,
fishing
Agricultural products: paddy rice,
bananas, palm kernels, coconuts,
plantains, peanuts; beef, chicken;
forest products and shrimp of
increasing importance
Currency: 1 Surinamese guilder,
gulden, or florin (Sf.) = 100 cents

Svalbard

Geography

Location: Northern Europe, islands
between the Arctic Ocean, Barents
Sea, Greenland Sea, and Norwegian
Sea, north of Norway
Area: 23,957 sq. mi. (62,049 sq. km.);
slightly smaller than West Virginia
Climate: arctic, tempered by warm
North Atlantic Current; cool summers, cold winters; North Atlantic
Current flows along west and north
coasts of Spitsbergen, keeping water
open and navigable most of the year
Terrain: wild, rugged mountains;
much of high land ice covered; west
coast clear of ice about one-half of
the year; fjords along west and
north coasts
Elevation: lowest point: Arctic Ocean
0 ft. (0 m.); highest point: Newton-
toppen 5,633 ft. (1,717 m.)
Natural resources: coal, copper, iron
ore, phosphate, zinc, wildlife, fish

People

Population: 2,503 (July 1999 est.)
Population growth rate: −3.55%
Major ethnic groups: Russian and
Ukrainian 62%, Norwegian 38%
Major languages: Russian, Norwegian

Government

Official name: Svalbard (sometimes
referred to as Spitzbergen)
National capital: Longyearbyen
Independence: none (territory of
Norway)

Economy

Industries: Coal mining.
Agricultural products: none
Currency: 1 Norwegian krone (NKr) =
100 oere

Swaziland

Geography

Location: Southern Africa, between
Mozambique and South Africa
Area: 6,703 sq. mi. (17,360 sq. km.);
slightly smaller than New Jersey
Climate: varies from tropical to near
temperate

Nations *(cont.)*

Terrain: mostly mountains and hills; some moderately sloping plains

Elevation: lowest point: Great Usutu River 69 ft. (21 m.); highest point: Emlembe 6,109 ft. (1,862 m.)

Natural resources: asbestos, coal, clay, cassiterite, hydropower, forests, small gold and diamond deposits, quarry stone, and talc

People

Population: 985,335 (July 1999 est.)

Population growth rate: 1.91%

Infant mortality rate: 101.87 deaths/ 1,000 live births

Life expectancy at birth: total population: 38.11 years; male: 36.86 years; female: 39.4 years

Major ethnic groups: African 97%, European 3%

Major religions: Christian 60%, indigenous beliefs 40%

Major languages: English (official, government business conducted in English), siSwati (official)

Government

Official name: Kingdom of Swaziland

Government type: monarchy; independent member of Commonwealth

National capital: Mbabane (administrative); Lobamba (legislative)

Independence: September 6, 1968 (from U.K.)

Legal system: based on South African Roman-Dutch law in statutory courts and Swazi traditional law and custom in traditional courts; has not accepted compulsory ICJ jurisdiction

Economy

Industries: mining (coal and asbestos), wood pulp, sugar, soft drink concentrates

Agricultural products: sugarcane, cotton, maize, tobacco, rice, citrus, pineapples, corn, sorghum, peanuts; cattle, goats, sheep

Currency: 1 lilangeni (E) = 100 cents

Sweden

Geography

Location: Northern Europe, bordering the Baltic Sea, Gulf of Bothnia, Kattegat, and Skagerrak, between Finland and Norway

Area: 173,731 sq. mi. (449,964 sq. km.); slightly larger than California

Climate: temperate in south with cold, cloudy winters and cool, partly cloudy summers; subarctic in north

Terrain: mostly flat or gently rolling lowlands; mountains in west

Elevation: lowest point: Baltic Sea 0 ft. (0 m.); highest point: Kebnekaise 6,926 ft. (2,111 m.)

Natural resources: zinc, iron ore, lead, copper, silver, timber, uranium, hydropower potential

People

Population: 8,911,296 (July 1999 est.)

Population growth rate: 0.29%

Infant mortality rate: 3.91 deaths/1,000 live births

Life expectancy at birth: total population: 79.29 years; male: 76.61 years; female: 82.11 years

Major ethnic groups: white, Lapp (Sami), foreign-born or first-generation immigrants 12% (Finns, Yugoslavs, Danes, Norwegians, Greeks, Turks)

Major religions: Evangelical Lutheran 94%, Roman Catholic 1.5%, Pentecostal 1%

Major languages: Swedish (Note: small Lapp- and Finnish-speaking minorities exist)

Government

Official name: Kingdom of Sweden

Government type: constitutional monarchy

National capital: Stockholm

Independence: June 6, 1523, Gustav Vasa was elected king; June 6, 1809, a constitutional monarchy was established

Legal system: civil law system influenced by customary law

Economy

Industries: iron and steel, precision
equipment (bearings, radio and telephone parts, armaments), wood
pulp and paper products, processed
foods, motor vehicles

Agricultural products: grains, sugar
beets, potatoes; meat, milk

Currency: 1 Swedish krona (SKr) = 100
oere

Switzerland

Geography

Location: Central Europe, east of
France, north of Italy

Area: 15,942 sq. mi. (41,290 sq. km.);
slightly less than twice the size of
New Jersey

Climate: temperate, but varies with
altitude; cold, cloudy, rainy/snowy
winters; cool to warm, cloudy,
humid summers with occasional
showers

Terrain: mostly mountains (Alps in
south, Jura in northwest) with a central plateau of rolling hills, plains,
and large lakes

Elevation: lowest point: Lake Maggiore
640 ft. (195 m.); highest point:
Dufourspitze 15,203 ft. (4,634 m.)

Natural resources: hydropower potential, timber, salt

People

Population: 7,275,467 (July 1999
est.)

Population growth rate: 0.2%

Infant mortality rate: 4.87 deaths/
1,000 live births

Life expectancy at birth: total population: 78.99 years; male: 75.83 years;
female: 82.32 years

Major ethnic groups: German 65%,
French 18%, Italian 10%, Romansch
1%, other 6% (Note: Swiss
nationals are German 74%, French
20%, Italian 4%, Romansch 1%)

Major religions: Roman Catholic
46.1%, Protestant 40%

Major languages: German 63.7%,
French 19.2%, Italian 7.6%,
Romansch 0.6%

Government

Official name: Swiss Confederation

Government type: federal republic

National capital: Bern

Independence: August 1, 1291

Legal system: civil law system influenced by customary law; judicial
review of legislative acts, except with
respect to federal decrees of general
obligatory character

Economy

Industries: machinery, chemicals,
watches, textiles, precision instruments

Agricultural products: grains, fruits,
vegetables; meat, eggs

Currency: 1 Swiss franc, franken, or
franco (SFR) = 100 centimes, rap-
pen, or centesimi

Syria

Geography

Location: Middle East, bordering the
Mediterranean Sea, between
Lebanon and Turkey

Area: 71,498 sq. mi. (185,180 sq. km.);
slightly larger than North Dakota

Climate: mostly desert; hot, dry, sunny
summers (June to August) and
mild, rainy winters (December to
February) along coast; cold weather
with snow or sleet periodically hit-
ting Damascus

Terrain: primarily semiarid and desert
plateau; narrow coastal plain; mountains in west

Elevation: lowest point: unnamed location near Lake Tiberias –656 ft.
(–200 m.); highest point: Mount
Hermon 9,232 ft. (2,814 m.)

Natural resources: petroleum, phosphates, chrome and manganese
ores, asphalt, iron ore, rock salt,
marble, gypsum

People

Population: 17,213,871 (July 1999 est.)

Population growth rate: 3.15%

Infant mortality rate: 36.42 deaths/
1,000 live births

Life expectancy at birth: total population: 68.09 years; male: 66.75 years;
female: 69.48 years

Nations (cont.)

Major ethnic groups: Arab 90.3%,
Kurds, Armenians

Major religions: Sunni Muslim 74%,
Alawite, Druze, and other Muslim
sects 16%, Christian (various
sects) 10%

Major languages: Arabic (official);
Kurdish, Armenian, Aramaic,
Circassian widely understood

Government

Official name: Syrian Arab Republic

Government type: republic under military regime since March 1963

National capital: Damascus

Independence: April 17,1946 (from
League of Nations mandate under
French administration)

Legal system: based on Islamic law and
civil law system; special religious
courts

Economy

Industries: petroleum, textiles, food
processing, beverages, tobacco,
phosphate rock mining

Agricultural products: wheat, barley,
cotton, lentils, chickpeas; beef,
lamb, eggs, poultry, milk

Currency: 1 Syrian pound (£S) = 100
piastres

Taiwan

Geography

Location: Eastern Asia, islands bordering the East China Sea, Philippine
Sea, South China Sea, and Taiwan
Strait, north of the Philippines, off
the southeastern coast of China

Area: 13,892 sq. mi. (35,980 sq. km.);
slightly smaller than Maryland and
Delaware combined

Climate: tropical; marine; rainy season
during southwest monsoon (June to
August); cloudiness is persistent
and extensive all year

Terrain: eastern two-thirds mostly
rugged mountains; flat to gently
rolling plains in west

Elevation: lowest point: South China
Sea 0 ft. (0 m.); highest point: Yu
Shan 13,113 ft. (3,997 m.)

Natural resources: small deposits of
coal, natural gas, limestone, marble,
and asbestos

People

Population: 22,113,250 (July 1999 est.)

Population growth rate: 0.94%

Infant mortality rate: 6.34
deaths/1,000 live births

Life expectancy at birth: total population: 76.82 years; male: 73.82 years;
female: 80.05 years

Major ethnic groups: Taiwanese
(including Hakka) 84%, mainland
Chinese 14%, aborigine 2%

Major religions: mixture of Buddhist,
Confucian, and Taoist 93%,
Christian 4.5%

Major languages: Mandarin Chinese
(official), Taiwanese (Min), Hakka
dialects

Government

Official name: Taiwan

Government type: multiparty democratic regime headed by popularly
elected president

National capital: Taipei

Independence: constitution adopted
January 1, 1947 (status in relation to
China still in dispute)

Legal system: based on civil law system

Economy

Industries: electronics, petroleum
refining, chemicals, textiles, iron
and steel, machinery, cement, food
processing

Agricultural products: rice, corn, vegetables, fruit, tea; pigs, poultry, beef,
milk; fish

Currency: 1 New Taiwan dollar (NT$)
= 100 cents

Tajikistan

Geography

Location: Central Asia, west of China

Area: 88,722 sq. mi. (143,100 sq. km.);
slightly smaller than Wisconsin

Climate: mid-latitude continental, hot
summers, mild winters; semiarid to
polar in Pamir Mountains

Terrain: Pamirs and Alay Mountains dominate landscape; western Fergana Valley in north, Kofarnihon and Vakhsh Valleys in southwest

Elevation: lowest point: Syrdariya 984 ft. (300 m.); highest point: Qullai Kommunizm 24,590 ft. (7,495 m.)

Natural resources: significant hydropower potential, some petroleum, uranium, mercury, brown coal, lead, zinc, antimony, tungsten

People

Population: 6,102,854 (July 1999 est.)

Population growth rate: 1.3%

Infant mortality rate: 112.14 deaths/1,000 live births

Life expectancy at birth: total population: 64.48 years; male: 61.35 years; female: 67.77 years

Major ethnic groups: Tajik 64.9%, Uzbek 25%, Russian 3.5% (declining because of emigration)

Major religions: Sunni Muslim 80%, Shi'a Muslim 5%

Major languages: Tajik (official), Russian widely used in government and business

Government

Official name: Republic of Tajikistan

Government type: republic

National capital: Dushanbe

Independence: September 9, 1991 (from Soviet Union)

Legal system: based on civil law system; no judicial review of legislative acts

Economy

Industries: aluminum, zinc, lead, chemicals and fertilizers, cement, vegetable oil, metal-cutting machine tools, refrigerators and freezers

Agricultural products: cotton, grain, fruits, grapes, vegetables; cattle, sheep, goats

Currency: Tajikistani ruble (TJR) = 100 tanga

Tanzania

Geography

Location: Eastern Africa, bordering the Indian Ocean, between Kenya and Mozambique

Area: 364,899 sq. mi.(945,090 sq. km.), slightly larger than twice the size of California

Climate: varies from tropical along coast to temperate in highlands

Terrain: plains along coast; central plateau; highlands in north, south

Elevation: lowest point: Indian Ocean 0 ft. (0 m.); highest point: Kilimanjaro 19,340 ft. (5,895 m.)

Natural resources: hydropower potential, tin, phosphates, iron ore, coal, diamonds, gemstones, gold, natural gas, nickel

People

Population: 31,270,820 (July 1999 est.)

Population growth rate: 2.14%

Infant mortality rate: 96.94 deaths/1,000 live births

Life expectancy at birth: total population: 46.37 years; male: 44.22 years; female: 48.59 years

Major ethnic groups: mainland-native African 99% (95% Bantu from more than 130 tribes), other 1% (Asian, European, Arab). Zanzibar: Arab, native African, mixed Arab-native African

Major religions: Christian 45%, Muslim 35%, indigenous beliefs 20%. Zanzibar: more than 99% Muslim

Major languages: Kiswahili or Swahili (official), Kiunguju (name for Swahili in Zanzibar), English (official, primary language of commerce, administration, and higher education), Arabic (widely spoken in Zanzibar), many local languages

Government

Official name: United Republic of Tanzania

Government type: republic

National capital: Dar es Salaam (some government offices have been transferred to Dodoma, which is planned as the new national capital; the National Assembly now meets there on regular basis)

Nations (cont.)

Independence: April 26, 1964;
  Tanganyika became independent
  December 9, 1961 (from U.K.-
  administered UN trusteeship);
  Zanzibar became independent
  December 19, 1963 (from U.K.);
  Tanganyika united with Zanzibar
  April 26, 1964 to form the United
  Republic of Tanganyika and
  Zanzibar; renamed United Republic
  of Tanzania October 29, 1964
Legal system: based on English com-
  mon law; judicial review of legisla-
  tive acts limited to matters of
  interpretation

Economy
Industries: primarily agricultural processing (sugar, beer, cigarettes, sisal
  twine), diamond and gold mining,
  oil refining, shoes, cement, textiles,
  wood products, fertilizer, salt
Agricultural products: coffee, sisal, tea,
  cotton, pyrethrum (insecticide made
  from chrysanthemums), cashews,
  tobacco, cloves (Zanzibar), corn,
  wheat, cassava (tapioca), bananas,
  fruits, vegetables; cattle, sheep,
  goats
Currency: 1 Tanzanian shilling (TSh) =
  100 cents

Thailand

Geography
Location: Southeastern Asia, border-
  ing the Andaman Sea and the Gulf
  of Thailand, southeast of Burma
Area: 198,455 sq. mi. (514,000 sq.
  km.); slightly more than twice the
  size of Wyoming
Climate: tropical; rainy, warm, cloudy
  southwest monsoon (mid-May to
  September); dry, cool northeast
  monsoon (November to mid-
  March); southern isthmus always
  hot and humid
Terrain: central plain; Khorat Plateau
  in the east; mountains elsewhere
Elevation: lowest point: Gulf of
  Thailand 0 ft. (0 m.); highest point:
  Doi Inthanon 8,451 ft. (2,576 m.)

Natural resources: tin, rubber, natural
  gas, tungsten, tantalum, timber,
  lead, fish, gypsum, lignite, fluorite

People
Population: 60,609,046 (July 1999
  est.)
Population growth rate: 0.93%
Infant mortality rate: 29.54 deaths/
  1,000 live births
Life expectancy at birth: total popula-
  tion: 69.21 years; male: 65.58 years;
  female: 72.01 years
Major ethnic groups: Thai 75%,
  Chinese 14%
Major religions: Buddhism 95%,
  Muslim 3.8%
Major languages: Thai, English (sec-
  ondary language of the elite), ethnic
  and regional dialects

Government
Official name: Kingdom of Thailand
Government type: constitutional
  monarchy
National capital: Bangkok
Independence: 1238 (traditional founding date; never colonized)
Legal system: based on civil law system,
  with influences of common law; has
  not accepted compulsory ICJ jurisdiction

Economy
Industries: tourism; textiles and garments, agricultural processing, beverages, tobacco, cement, light
  manufacturing, such as jewelry;
  electric appliances and components,
  computers and parts, integrated
  circuits, furniture, plastics; world's
  second-largest tungsten producer
  and third-largest tin producer
Agricultural products: rice, cassava
  (tapioca), rubber, corn, sugarcane,
  coconuts, soybeans
Currency: 1 baht (B) = 100 satang

Togo

Geography
Location: Western Africa, bordering
  the Bight of Benin, between Benin
  and Ghana

Area: 21,927 sq. mi. (56,790 sq. km.); slightly smaller than West Virginia

Climate: tropical; hot, humid in south; semiarid in north

Terrain: gently rolling savanna in north; central hills; southern plateau; low coastal plain with extensive lagoons and marshes

Elevation: lowest point: Atlantic Ocean 0 ft. (0 m.); highest point: Pic Agou 3,235 ft. (986 m.)

Natural resources: phosphates, limestone, marble

People

Population: 5,081,413 (July 1999 est.)

Population growth rate: 3.51%

Infant mortality rate: 77.55 deaths/ 1,000 live births

Life expectancy at birth: total population: 59.25 years; male: 56.93 years; female: 61.64 years

Major ethnic groups: native African 99% (37 tribes; largest and most important are Ewe, Mina, and Kabre)

Major religions: indigenous beliefs 70%, Christian 20%, Muslim 10%

Major languages: French (official and the language of commerce), Ewe and Mina (the two major African languages in the south), Kabye (sometimes spelled Kabiye) and Dagomba (the two major African languages in the north)

Government

Official name: Togolese Republic

Government type: republic under transition to multiparty democratic rule

National capital: Lome

Independence: April 27, 1960 (from French-administered UN trusteeship)

Legal system: French-based court system

Economy

Industries: phosphate mining, agricultural processing, cement; handicrafts, textiles, beverages

Agricultural products: coffee, cocoa, cotton, yams, cassava (tapioca), corn, beans, rice, millet, sorghum; meat; fish

Currency: 1 Communauté Financière Africaine franc (CFAF) = 100 centimes

Tonga

Geography

Location: Oceania, archipelago in the South Pacific Ocean, about two-thirds of the way from Hawaii to New Zealand

Area: 289 sq. mi. (748 sq. km.); four times the size of Washington, D.C.

Climate: tropical; modified by trade winds; warm season (December to May), cool season (May to December)

Terrain: most islands have limestone base formed from uplifted coral formation; others have limestone overlying volcanic base

Elevation: lowest point: Pacific Ocean 0 ft. (0 m.); highest point: unnamed location on Kao Island 3,389 ft. (1,033 m.)

Natural resources: fish, fertile soil

People

Population: 109,082 (July 1999 est.)

Population growth rate: 0.8%

Infant mortality rate: 37.93 deaths/ 1,000 live births

Life expectancy at birth: total population: 69.78 years; male: 67.73 years; female: 72.22 years

Major ethnic groups: Polynesian, Europeans about 300

Major religions: Christian

Major languages: Tongan, English

Government

Official name: Kingdom of Tonga

Government type: hereditary constitutional monarchy

National capital: Nuku'alofa

Independence: June 4, 1970 (emancipation from U.K. protectorate)

Legal system: based on English law

Economy

Industries: tourism, fishing

Agricultural products: coconuts, copra, bananas, vanilla beans, cocoa, coffee, ginger, black pepper; fish

Currency: 1 pa'anga (T$) = 100 seniti

Nations *(cont.)*

Trinidad and Tobago

Geography
Location: Caribbean, islands between the Caribbean Sea and the Atlantic Ocean, northeast of Venezuela

Area: 1,981 sq. mi. (5,130 sq. km.); slightly smaller than Delaware

Climate: tropical; rainy season (June to December)

Terrain: mostly plains with some hills and low mountains

Elevation: lowest point: Caribbean Sea 0 ft. (0 m.); highest point: El Cerro del Aripo 3,084 ft. (940 m.)

Natural resources: petroleum, natural gas, asphalt

People
Population: 1,102,096 (July 1999 est.)

Population growth rate: −1.35%

Infant mortality rate: 18.56 deaths/ 1,000 live births

Life expectancy at birth: total population: 70.66 years; male: 68.19 years; female: 73.19 years

Major ethnic groups: black 40%, East Indian (a local term-primarily immigrants from northern India) 40.3%, mixed 14%, white 1%, Chinese 1%

Major religions: Roman Catholic 32.2%, Hindu 24.3%, Anglican 14.4%, other Protestant 14%, Muslim 6%

Major languages: English (official), Hindi, French, Spanish

Government
Official name: Republic of Trinidad and Tobago

Government type: parliamentary democracy

National capital: Port-of-Spain

Independence: August 31, 1962 (from U.K.)

Legal system: based on English common law; judicial review of legislative acts in the Supreme Court

Economy
Industries: petroleum, chemicals, tourism, food processing, cement, beverage, cotton textiles

Agricultural products: cocoa, sugarcane, rice, citrus, coffee, vegetables; poultry

Currency: 1 Trinidad and Tobago dollar (TT$) = 100 cents

Tunisia

Geography
Location: Northern Africa, bordering the Mediterranean Sea, between Algeria and Libya

Area: 63,170 sq. mi. (163,610) sq. km.; slightly larger than Georgia

Climate: temperate in north with mild, rainy winters and hot, dry summers; desert in south

Terrain: mountains in north; hot, dry central plain; semiarid south merges into the Sahara

Elevation: lowest point: Shatt al Gharsah −56 ft. (−17 m.); highest point: Jabal ash Shanabi 5,066 ft. (1,544 m.)

Natural resources: petroleum, phosphates, iron ore, lead, zinc, salt

People
Population: 9,513,603 (July 1999 est.)

Population growth rate: 1.39%

Infant mortality rate: 31.38 deaths/ 1,000 live births

Life expectancy at birth: total population: 73.35 years; male: 71.95 years; female: 74.86 years

Major ethnic groups: Arab 98%, European 1%

Major religions: Muslim 98%, Christian 1%

Major languages: Arabic (official and one of the languages of commerce), French (commerce)

Government
Official name: Republic of Tunisia

Government type: republic

National capital: Tunis

Independence: March 20, 1956 (from France)

Legal system: based on French civil law system and Islamic law; some judicial review of legislative acts in the Supreme Court in joint session

Economy

Industries: petroleum, mining (particularly phosphate and iron ore), tourism, textiles, footwear, food, beverages

Agricultural products: olives, dates, oranges, almonds, grain, sugar beets, grapes; poultry, beef, dairy products

Currency: 1 Tunisian dinar (TD) = 1,000 millimes

Turkey

Geography

Location: southwestern Asia (that part west of the Bosporus is sometimes included with Europe), bordering the Black Sea, between Bulgaria and Georgia, and bordering the Aegean Sea and the Mediterranean Sea, between Greece and Syria

Area: 301,382 sq. mi. (780,580 sq. km.); slightly larger than Texas

Climate: temperate; hot, dry summers with mild, wet winters; harsher in interior

Terrain: mostly mountains; narrow coastal plain; high central plateau (Anatolia)

Elevation: extremes: lowest point: Mediterranean Sea 0 ft. (0 m.); highest point: Mount Ararat 16,949 ft. (5,166 m.)

Natural resources: antimony, coal, chromium, mercury, copper, borate, sulfur, iron ore

People

Population: 65,599,206 (July 1999 est.)

Population growth rate: 1.57%

Infant mortality rate: 35.81 deaths/ 1,000 live births

Life expectancy at birth: total population: 73.29 years; male: 70.81 years; female: 75.88 years

Major ethnic groups: Turkish 80%, Kurdish 20%

Major religions: Muslim 99.8% (mostly Sunni)

Major languages: Turkish (official), Kurdish, Arabic

Government

Official name: Republic of Turkey

Government type: republican parliamentary democracy

National capital: Ankara

Independence: October 29, 1923 (successor state to the Ottoman Empire)

Legal system: derived from various European continental legal systems

Economy

Industries: textiles, food processing, mining (coal, chromite, copper, boron), steel, petroleum, construction, lumber, paper

Agricultural products: tobacco, cotton, grain, olives, sugar beets, pulses, citrus; livestock

Currency: Turkish lira (TL)

Turkmenistan

Geography

Location: Central Asia, bordering the Caspian Sea, between Iran and Kazakhstan

Area: 188,455 sq. mi. (488,100 sq. km.); slightly larger than California

Climate: subtropical desert

Terrain: flat-to-rolling sandy desert with dunes rising to mountains in the south; low mountains along border with Iran; borders Caspian Sea in west

Elevation: lowest point: Sarygamysh Koli –361 ft. (–110 m.); highest point: Ayrybaba 10,298 ft. (3,139 m.)

Natural resources: petroleum, natural gas, coal, sulfur, salt

People

Population: 4,366,383 (July 1999 est.)

Population growth rate: 1.58%

Infant mortality rate: 73.1 deaths/1,000 live births

Life expectancy at birth: total population: 61.11 years; male: 57.48 years; female: 64.91 years

Major ethnic groups: Turkmen 77%, Uzbek 9.2%, Russian 6.7%, Kazakh 2%

Major religions: Muslim 89%, Eastern Orthodox 9%

Major languages: Turkmen 72%, Russian 12%, Uzbek 9%

Nations (cont.)

Government

Official name: Turkmenistan
Government type: republic
National capital: Ashgabat
Independence: October 27,1991 (from the Soviet Union)
Legal system: based on civil law system

Economy

Industries: natural gas, oil, petroleum products, textiles, food processing
Agricultural products: cotton, grain; livestock
Currency: 1 Tukmen manat (TMM) = 100 tenesi

Turks and Caicos Islands

Geography

Location: Caribbean, two island groups in the North Atlantic Ocean, southeast of The Bahamas
Area: 166 sq. mi. (430 sq. km.); 2.5 times the size of Washington, D.C.
Climate: tropical; marine; moderated by trade winds; sunny and relatively dry
Terrain: low, flat limestone; extensive marshes and mangrove swamps
Elevation: lowest point: Caribbean Sea 0 ft. (0 m.); highest point: Blue Hills 161 ft. (49 m.)
Natural resources: spiny lobster, conch

People

Population: 16,863 (July 1999 est.)
Population growth rate: 3.65%
Infant mortality rate: 21.11 deaths/ 1,000 live births
Life expectancy at birth: total population: 72.35 years; male: 70.4 years; female: 74.4 years
Major ethnic groups: black
Major religions: Baptist 41.2%, Methodist 18.9%, Anglican 18.3%, Seventh-Day Adventist 1.7%
Major languages: English (official)

Government

Official name: Turks and Caicos Islands
National capital: Grand Turk
Independence: none (dependent territory of the U.K.)

Legal system: based on laws of England and Wales with a small number adopted from Jamaica and The Bahamas

Economy

Industries: tourism, offshore financial services
Agricultural products: corn, beans, cassava, citrus fruits; fish
Currency: 1 U.S dollar (US$) = 100 cents

Tuvalu

Geography

Location: Oceania, island group consisting of nine coral atolls in the South Pacific Ocean, about one-half of the way from Hawaii to Australia
Area: 10 sq. mi. (26 sq. km.); 0.1 times the size of Washington, D.C.
Climate: tropical; moderated by easterly trade winds (March to November); westerly gales and heavy rain (November to March)
Terrain: very low-lying and narrow coral atolls
Elevation: lowest point: Pacific Ocean 0 ft. (0 m.); highest point: unnamed location 16 ft. (5 m.)
Natural resources: fish

People

Population: 10,588 (July 1999 est.)
Population growth rate: 1.34%
Infant mortality rate: 25.53 deaths/ 1,000 live births
Life expectancy at birth: total population: 64.15 years; male: 63.01 years; female: 65.34 years
Major ethnic groups: Polynesian 96%
Major religions: Church of Tuvalu (Congregationalist) 97%, Seventh-Day Adventist 1.4%, Baha'i 1%
Major languages: Tuvaluan, English

Government

Official name: Tuvalu
Government type: constitutional monarchy with a parliamentary democracy; began debating republic status in 1992
National capital: Funafuti

Independence: October 1, 1978 (from U.K.)

Economy
Industries: fishing, tourism, copra
Agricultural products: coconuts; fish
Currency: 1 Tuvaluan dollar ($T) or 1 Australian dollar ($A) = 100 cents

Uganda

Geography
Location: Eastern Africa, west of Kenya
Area: 91,135 sq. mi. (236,040 sq. km.); slightly smaller than Oregon
Climate: tropical; generally rainy with two dry seasons (December to February, June to August); semiarid in northeast
Terrain: mostly plateau with rim of mountains
Elevation: lowest point: Lake Albert 2,037 ft. (621 m.); highest point: Margherita (Mount Stanley) 16,765 ft. (5,110 m.)
Natural resources: copper, cobalt, limestone, salt

People
Population: 22,804,973 (July 1999 est.)
Population growth rate: 2.83%
Infant mortality rate: 90.68 deaths/ 1,000 live births
Life expectancy at birth: total population: 43.06 years; male: 42.2 years; female: 43.94 years
Major ethnic groups: Baganda 17%, Karamojong 12%, Basogo 8%, Iteso 8%, Langi 6%, Rwanda 6%, Bagisu 5%, Acholi 4%, Lugbara 4%, Bunyoro 3%, Batobo 3%
Major religions: Roman Catholic 33%, Protestant 33%, Muslim 16%, indigenous beliefs 18%
Major languages: English (official national language, taught in grade schools, used in courts of law and by most newspapers and some radio broadcasts), Ganda or Luganda (most widely used of the Niger-Congo languages, preferred for native language publications and may be taught in school), other Niger-Congo languages, Nilo-Saharan languages, Swahili, Arabic

Government
Official name: Republic of Uganda
Government type: republic
National capital: Kampala
Independence: October 9, 1962 (from U.K.)
Legal system: in 1995, the government restored the legal system to one based on English common law and customary law and reinstituted a normal judicial system

Economy
Industries: sugar, brewing, tobacco, cotton textiles, cement
Agricultural products: coffee, tea, cotton, tobacco, cassava (tapioca), potatoes, corn, millet, pulses; beef, goat meat, milk, poultry
Currency: 1 Ugandan shilling (USh) = 100 cents

Ukraine

Geography
Location: Eastern Europe, bordering the Black Sea, between Poland and Russia
Area: 233,089 sq. mi. (603,700 sq. km.); slightly smaller than Texas
Climate: temperate continental; Mediterranean only on the southern Crimean coast; precipitation disproportionately distributed, highest in west and north, lesser in east and southeast; winters vary from cool along the Black Sea to cold farther inland; summers are warm across the greater part of the country, hot in the south
Terrain: most of Ukraine consists of fertile plains (steppes) and plateaus, mountains being found only in the west (the Carpathians), and in the Crimean Peninsula in the extreme south
Elevation: lowest point: Black Sea 0 ft. (0 m.); highest point: Hora Hoverla 6,762 ft. (2,061 m.)
Natural resources: iron ore, coal, manganese, natural gas, oil, salt, sulfur, graphite, titanium, magnesium, kaolin, nickel, mercury, timber

People

Population: 49,811,174 (July 1999 est.)

Population growth rate: –0.62%

Infant mortality rate: 21.73 deaths/
1,000 live births

Life expectancy at birth: total population: 65.91 years; male: 60.23 years;
female: 71.87 years

Major ethnic groups: Ukrainian 73%,
Russian 22%, Jewish 1%

Major religions: Ukrainian Orthodox-
Moscow Patriarchate, Ukrainian
Orthodox-Kiev Patriarchate,
Ukrainian Autocephalous Orthodox,
Ukrainian Catholic (Uniate),
Protestant, Jewish

Major languages: Ukrainian, Russian,
Romanian, Polish, Hungarian

Government

Official name: Ukraine

Government type: republic

National capital: Kiev

Independence: December 1, 1991 (from
Soviet Union)

Legal system: based on civil law system;
judicial review of legislative acts

Economy

Industries: coal, electric power, ferrous
and nonferrous metals, machinery
and transport equipment, chemicals, food-processing (especially
sugar)

Agricultural products: grain, sugar
beets, sunflower seeds, vegetables;
meat, milk

Currency: 1 hryvnia = 100,000 karbo-
vantsi

United Arab Emirates

Geography

Location: Middle East, bordering the
Gulf of Oman and the Persian Gulf,
between Oman and Saudi Arabia

Area: 32,000 sq. mi. (82,880 sq. km.);
slightly smaller than Maine

Climate: desert; cooler in eastern
mountains

Terrain: flat, barren coastal plain merg-
ing into rolling sand dunes of vast
desert wasteland; mountains in east

Elevation: lowest point: Persian Gulf
0 ft. (0 m.); highest point: Jabal
Yibir 5,010 ft. (1,527 m.)

Natural resources: petroleum, natural
gas

People

Population: 2,344,402 (July 1999 est.)

Population growth rate: 1.78%

Infant mortality rate: 14.1 deaths/1,000
live births

Life expectancy at birth: total population: 75.24 years; male: 73.83 years;
female: 76.72 years

Major ethnic groups: Emiri 19%, other
Arab and Iranian 23%, South Asian
50%, other expatriates (includes
Westerners and East Asians) 8%

Major religions: Muslim 96% (Shi'a
16%), Christian, Hindu

Major languages: Arabic (official),
Persian, English, Hindi, Urdu

Government

Official name: United Arab Emirates

Government type: federation with spec-
ified powers delegated to the U.A.E.
federal government and other powers reserved to member emirates

National capital: Abu Dhabi

Independence: December 2, 1971 (from
U.K.)

Legal system: federal court system
introduced in 1971; all emirates
except Dubayy (Dubai) and Ra's al
Khaymah have joined the federal
system; all emirates have secular
and Islamic law for civil, criminal,
and high courts

Economy

Industries: petroleum, fishing, petrochemicals, construction materials,
some boat building, handicrafts,
pearling

Agricultural products: dates, vegetables,
watermelons; poultry, eggs, dairy
products; fish

Currency: 1 Emirian dirham (Dh) =
100 fils

United Kingdom

Geography

Location: Western Europe, islands including the northern one-sixth of the island of Ireland between the North Atlantic Ocean and the North Sea, northwest of France

Area: 244,820 sq. mi. (244,820 sq. km.); slightly smaller than Oregon

Climate: temperate; moderated by prevailing southwest winds over the North Atlantic Current; more than one-half of the days are overcast

Terrain: mostly rugged hills and low mountains; level to rolling plains in east and southeast

Elevation: lowest point: Fenland −13 ft. (−4 m.); highest point: Ben Nevis 4,406 ft. (1,343 m.)

Natural resources: coal, petroleum, natural gas, tin, limestone, iron ore, salt, clay, chalk, gypsum, lead, silica

People

Population: 59,113,439 (July 1999 est.)

Population growth rate: 0.24%

Infant mortality rate: 5.78 deaths/1,000 live births

Life expectancy at birth: total population: 77.37 years; male: 74.73 years; female: 80.15 years

Major ethnic groups: English 81.5%, Scottish 9.6%, Irish 2.4%, Welsh 1.9%, Ulster 1.8%,

Major religions: Anglican 27 million, Roman Catholic 9 million, Muslim 1 million, Presbyterian 800,000, Methodist 760,000, Sikh 400,000, Hindu 350,000, Jewish 300,000

Major languages: English, Welsh (about 26% of the population of Wales), Scottish form of Gaelic (about 60,000 in Scotland)

Government

Official name: United Kingdom of Great Britain and Northern Ireland

Government type: constitutional monarchy

National capital: London

Independence: England has existed as a unified entity since the 10th century; the union between England and Wales was enacted under the Statute of Rhuddlan in 1284; in the Act of Union of 1707, England and Scotland agreed to permanent union as Great Britain; the legislative union of Great Britain and Ireland was implemented in 1801 adopting the name the United Kingdom of Great Britain and Ireland; the Anglo-Irish treaty of 1921 formalized a partition of Ireland; six northern Irish counties remained part of the United Kingdom as Northern Ireland and the current name of the country, the United Kingdom of Great Britain and Northern Ireland, was adopted in 1927

Legal system: common law tradition with early Roman and modern continental influences; no judicial review of Acts of Parliament

Economy

Industries: production machinery including machine tools, electric power equipment, automation equipment, railroad equipment, shipbuilding, aircraft, motor vehicles and parts, electronics and communications equipment, metals, chemicals, coal, petroleum, paper and paper products, food processing, textiles, clothing, and other consumer goods

Agricultural products: cereals, oilseed, potatoes, vegetables; cattle, sheep, poultry; fish

Currency: 1 British pound (£) = 100 pence

United States

Geography

Location: North America, bordering both the North Atlantic Ocean and the North Pacific Ocean, between Canada and Mexico

Area: 3,717,792 sq. mi. (9,629,091 sq. km.); about one-half the size of Russia

Climate: mostly temperate, but tropical in Hawaii and Florida and arctic in Alaska, semiarid in the great plains west of the Mississippi River

Nations *(cont.)*

and arid in the Great Basin of the southwest; low winter temperatures in the northwest are ameliorated occasionally in January and February by warm chinook winds from the eastern slopes of the Rocky Mountains

Terrain: vast central plain, mountains in west, hills and low mountains in east; rugged mountains and broad river valleys in Alaska; rugged, volcanic topography in Hawaii

Elevation: lowest point: Death Valley −282 ft. (−86 m.); highest point: Mount McKinley 20,321 ft. (6,194 m.)

Natural resources: coal, copper, lead, molybdenum, phosphates, uranium, bauxite, gold, iron, mercury, nickel, potash, silver, tungsten, zinc, petroleum, natural gas, timber

People

Population: 272,639,608 (July 1999 est.)

Population growth rate: 0.85%

Infant mortality rate: 6.33 deaths/1,000 live births

Life expectancy at birth: total population: 76.23 years; male: 72.95 years; female: 79.67 years

Major ethnic groups: white 83.4%, black 12.4%, Asian 3.3%, Amerindian 0.8%

Major religions: Protestant 56%, Roman Catholic 28%, Jewish 2%, other 4%, none 10%

Major languages: English, Spanish (spoken by a sizable minority)

Government

Official name: United States of America

Government type: federal republic; strong democratic tradition

National capital: Washington, D.C.

Independence: July 4, 1776 (from England)

Legal system: based on English common law; judicial review of legislative acts

Economy

Industries: leading industrial power in the world, highly diversified and technologically advanced; petroleum, steel, motor vehicles, aerospace, telecommunications, chemicals, electronics, food processing, consumer goods, lumber, mining

Agricultural products: wheat, other grains, corn, fruits, vegetables, cotton; beef, pork, poultry, dairy products; forest products; fish

Currency: 1 U.S. dollar (US$) = 100 cents

Uruguay

Geography

Location: Southern South America, bordering the South Atlantic Ocean, between Argentina and Brazil

Area: 68,039 sq. mi. (176,220 sq. km.); slightly smaller than Washington State

Climate: warm temperate; freezing temperatures almost unknown

Terrain: mostly rolling plains and low hills; fertile coastal lowland

Elevation: extremes: lowest point: Atlantic Ocean 0 ft. (0 m.); highest point: Cerro Catedral 1,686 ft. (514 m.)

Natural resources: fertile soil, hydropower, minor minerals, fisheries

People

Population: 3,308,523 (July 1999 est.)

Population growth rate: 0.73%

Infant mortality rate: 13.49 deaths/ 1,000 live births

Life expectancy at birth: total population: 75.83 years; male: 72.69 years; female: 79.15 years

Major ethnic groups: white 88%, mestizo 8%, black 4%, Amerindian, practically nonexistent

Major religions: Roman Catholic 66% (less than one-half of the adult population attends church regularly), Protestant 2%, Jewish 2%

Major languages: Spanish, Portunol, or Brazilero (Portuguese-Spanish mix)

Government
Official name: Oriental Republic of Uruguay
Government type: republic
National capital: Montevideo
Independence: August 25, 1825 (from Brazil)
Legal system: based on Spanish civil law system

Economy
Industries: meat processing, wool and hides, sugar, textiles, footwear, leather apparel, tires, cement, petroleum refining, wine
Agricultural products: wheat, rice, corn, sorghum; livestock; fishing
Currency: 1 Uruguayan peso ($Ur) = 100 centesimos

Uzbekistan

Geography
Location: Central Asia, north of Afghanistan
Area: 172,741 sq. mi. (447,400 sq. km.); slightly larger than California
Climate: mostly mid-latitude desert; long, hot summers; mild winters; semiarid grassland in east
Terrain: mostly flat-to-rolling sandy desert with dunes; broad, flat intensely irrigated river valleys along course of Amu Darya, Sirdaryo, and Zarafshon; Fergana Valley in east surrounded by mountainous Tajikistan and Kyrgyzstan; shrinking Aral Sea in west
Elevation: lowest point: Sariqarnish Kuli –39 ft. (–12 m.); highest point: Adelunga Toghi 14,111 ft. (4,301 m.)
Natural resources: natural gas, petroleum, coal, gold, uranium, silver, copper, lead and zinc, tungsten, molybdenum

People
Population: 24,102,473 (July 1999 est.)
Population growth rate: 1.32%
Infant mortality rate: 71.85 deaths/1,000 live births
Life expectancy at birth: total population: 63.91 years; male: 60.29 years; female: 67.71 years

Major ethnic groups: Uzbek 80%, Russian 5.5%, Tajik 5%, Kazakh 3%, Karakalpak 2.5%, Tatar 1.5%
Major religions: Muslim 88% (mostly Sunnis), Eastern Orthodox 9%
Major languages: Uzbek 74.3%, Russian 14.2%, Tajik 4.4%

Government
Official name: Republic of Uzbekistan
Government type: republic; effectively authoritarian presidential rule, with little power outside the executive branch and executive power concentrated in the presidency
National capital: Tashkent (Toshkent)
Independence: August 31, 1991 (from Soviet Union)
Legal system: evolution of Soviet civil law; still lacks independent judicial system

Economy
Industries: textiles, food processing, machine building, metallurgy, natural gas
Agricultural products: cotton, vegetables, fruits, grain; livestock
Currency: 1 Som = 100 tiyin

Vanuatu

Geography
Location: Oceania, group of islands in the South Pacific Ocean, about three-quarters of the way from Hawaii to Australia
Area: 5,699 sq. mi. (14,760 sq. km.); slightly larger than Connecticut
Climate: tropical; moderated by southeast trade winds
Terrain: mostly mountains of volcanic origin; narrow coastal plains
Elevation: lowest point: Pacific Ocean 0 ft. (0 m.); highest point: Mount Tabwemasana 6,158 ft. (1,877 m.)
Natural resources: manganese, hardwood forests, fish

People
Population: 189,036 (July 1999 est.)
Population growth rate: 2.02%
Infant mortality rate: 59.58 deaths/1,000 live births

Nations (cont.)

Life expectancy at birth: total population: 61.44 years; male: 59.41 years; female: 63.57 years
Major ethnic groups: indigenous Melanesian 94%, French 4%, Vietnamese, Chinese, Pacific Islanders
Major religions: Presbyterian 36.7%, Anglican 15%, Catholic 15%, indigenous beliefs 7.6%, Seventh-Day Adventist 6.2%, Church of Christ 3.8%
Major languages: English (official), French (official), pidgin (known as Bislama or Bichelama)

Government
Official name: Republic of Vanuatu
Government type: republic
National capital: Port-Vila
Independence: July 30, 1980 (from France and U.K.)
Legal system: unified system being created from former dual French and British systems

Economy
Industries: food and fish freezing, wood processing, meat canning
Agricultural products: copra, coconuts, cocoa, coffee, taro, yams, coconuts, fruits, vegetables; fish, beef
Currency: 1 vatu (VT) = 100 centimes

Venezuela

Geography
Location: Northern South America, bordering the Caribbean Sea and the North Atlantic Ocean, between Colombia and Guyana
Area: 352,143 sq. mi. (912,050 sq. km.); slightly more than twice the size of California
Climate: tropical; hot, humid; more moderate in highlands
Terrain: Andes Mountains and Maracaibo Lowlands in northwest; central plains (llanos); Guiana Highlands in southeast
Elevation: lowest point: Caribbean Sea 0 ft. (0 m.); highest point: Pico Bolívar (La Columna) 16,427 ft. (5,007 m.)

Natural resources: petroleum, natural gas, iron ore, gold, bauxite, other minerals, hydropower, diamonds

People
Population: 23,203,466 (July 1999 est.)
Population growth rate: 1.71%
Infant mortality rate: 26.51 deaths/ 1,000 live births
Life expectancy at birth: total population: 72.95 years; male: 69.97 years; female: 76.16 years
Major ethnic groups: mestizo 67%, white 21%, black 10%, Amerindian 2%
Major religions: nominally Roman Catholic 96%, Protestant 2%
Major languages: Spanish (official), native dialects spoken by about 200,000 Amerindians in the remote interior

Government
Official name: Republic of Venezuela
Government type: republic
National capital: Caracas
Independence: July 5, 1811 (from Spain)
Legal system: based on Napoleonic code; judicial review of legislative acts in Cassation Court only

Economy
Industries: petroleum, iron ore mining, construction materials, food processing, textiles, steel, aluminum, motor vehicle assembly
Agricultural products: corn, sorghum, sugarcane, rice, bananas, vegetables, coffee; beef, pork, milk, eggs; fish
Currency: 1 bolívar (Bs) = 100 céntimos

Vietnam

Geography
Location: Southeastern Asia, bordering the Gulf of Thailand, Gulf of Tonkin, and South China Sea, alongside China, Laos, and Cambodia
Area: 127,243 sq. mi. (329,560 sq. km.); slightly larger than New Mexico
Climate: tropical in south; monsoonal in north with hot, rainy season

(mid-May to mid-September) and warm, dry season (mid-October to mid-March)

Terrain: low, flat delta in south and north; central highlands; hilly, mountainous in far north and northwest

Elevation: lowest point: South China Sea 0 ft. (0 m.); highest point: Ngoc Linh 10,312 ft. (3,143 m.)

Natural resources: phosphates, coal, manganese, bauxite, chromate, offshore oil and gas deposits, forests

People

Population: 77,311,210 (July 1999 est.)

Population growth rate: 1.37%

Infant mortality rate: 38.84 deaths/ 1,000 live births

Life expectancy at birth: total population: 68.1 years; male: 65.71 years; female: 70.64 years

Major ethnic groups: Vietnamese 85–90%, Chinese 3%, Muong, Tai, Meo, Khmer, Man, Cham

Major religions: Buddhist, Taoist, Roman Catholic, indigenous beliefs, Islam, Protestant, Cao Dai, Hoa Hao

Major languages: Vietnamese (official), Chinese, English, French, Khmer, tribal languages (Mon-Khmer and Malayo-Polynesian)

Government

Official name: Socialist Republic of Vietnam

Government type: Communist state

National capital: Hanoi

Independence: September 2, 1945 (from France)

Legal system: based on communist legal theory and French civil law system

Economy

Industries: food processing, garments, shoes, machine building, mining, cement, chemical fertilizer, glass, tires, oil

Agricultural products: paddy rice, corn, potatoes, rubber, soybeans, coffee, tea, bananas; poultry, pigs; fish

Currency: 1 new dong (D) = 100 xu

Virgin Islands, British

Geography

Location: Caribbean, between the Caribbean Sea and the North Atlantic Ocean, east of Puerto Rico

Area: 58 sq. mi. (150 sq. km.) comparative area: about 0.9 times the size of Washington, D.C.

Climate: subtropical; humid; temperatures moderated by trade winds

Terrain: coral islands relatively flat; volcanic islands steep, hilly

Elevation: lowest point: Caribbean Sea 0 ft. (0 m.); highest point: Mount Sage 1709 ft. (521 m.)

Natural resources: negligible

People

Population: 19,156 (July 1999 est.)

Population growth rate: 1.19%

Infant mortality rate: 10.07 deaths/ 1,000 live births

Life expectancy at birth: total population: 77.74 years; male: 74.04 years; female: 81.67 years

Major ethnic groups: black 90%, white, Asian

Major religions: Protestant 86%, Roman Catholic 6%

Major languages: English (official)

Government

Official name: British Virgin Islands

Government type: dependent territory of the U.K.

National capital: Road Town

Independence: none (dependent territory of the U.K.)

Legal system: English law

Economy

Industries: tourism, light industry, construction, rum, concrete block, offshore financial center

Agricultural products: fruits, vegetables; livestock, poultry; fish

Currency: 1 U.S. dollar (US$) = 100 cents

Virgin Islands, U.S.

Geography

Location: Caribbean, islands between the Caribbean Sea and the North Atlantic Ocean, east of Puerto Rico

Area: 136 sq. mi. (352 sq. km.); twice
the size of Washington, D.C.

Climate: subtropical, tempered by easterly trade winds, relatively low
humidity, little seasonal temperature variation; rainy season May to
November

Terrain: mostly hilly to rugged and
mountainous with little level land

Elevation: lowest point: Caribbean Sea
0 ft. (0 m.); highest point: Crown
Mountain 1,555 ft. (474 m.)

Natural resources: sun, sand, sea, surf

People

Population: 119,827 (July 1999 est.)

Population growth rate: 1.19%

Infant mortality rate: 10.07 deaths/
1,000 live births

Life expectancy at birth: total population: 77.74 years; male: 74.04 years;
female: 81.67 years

Major ethnic groups: black 80%, white
15%

Major religions: Baptist 42%, Roman
Catholic 34%, Episcopalian 17%

Major languages: English (official),
Spanish, Creole

Government

Official name: Virgin Islands of the
United States

National capital: Charlotte Amalie

Legal system: based on U.S. laws

Economy

Industries: tourism, petroleum refining, watch assembly, rum distilling,
construction, pharmaceuticals, textiles, electronics

Agricultural products: truck garden
products, fruit, vegetables, sorghum;
Senepol cattle

Currency: 1 U.S. dollar (US$) = 100
cents

Wallis and Futuna

Geography

Location: Oceania, islands in the South
Pacific Ocean, about two-thirds of
the way from Hawaii to New
Zealand

Area: 106 sq. mi. (274 sq. km.); 1.5
times the size of Washington, D.C.

Climate: tropical; hot, rainy season
(November to April); cool, dry season (May to October); rains
2,500–3,000 mm per year (80%
humidity); average temperature
79.9 degrees F (26.6 degrees C)

Terrain: volcanic origin; low hills

Elevation: lowest point: Pacific Ocean
0 ft. (0 m.); highest point: Mount
Singavi 2,510 ft. (765 m.)

Natural resources: negligible

People

Population: 15,129 (July 1999 est.)

Population growth rate: 1.04%

Major ethnic groups: Polynesian

Major religions: Roman Catholic 100%

Major languages: French, Wallisian
(indigenous Polynesian language)

Government

Official name: Territory of the Wallis
and Futuna Islands

Dependency status: overseas territory
of France

National capital: Mata-Utu (on Ile
Uvea)

Independence: none (overseas territory
of France)

Legal system: French legal system

Economy

Industries: copra, handicrafts, fishing,
lumber

Agricultural products: breadfruit, yams,
taro, bananas; pigs, goats

Currency: 1 CFP franc (CFPF) = 100
centimes

West Bank

Geography

Location: Middle East, west of Jordan

Area: 2,263 sq. mi. (5,860) sq. km.;
slightly smaller than Delaware

Climate: temperate, temperature and
precipitation vary with altitude,
warm to hot summers, cool to mild
winters

Terrain: mostly rugged dissected
upland, some vegetation in west,
but barren in east

Elevation: lowest point: Dead Sea
−1339 ft. (−408 m.); highest point:
Tall Asur 3,353 ft. (1,022 m.)
Natural resources: negligible

People
Population: 1,611,109; Note—in addition, there are 155,000 Israeli settlers in the West Bank and 164,000
in East Jerusalem (July 1999 est.)
Population growth rate: 3.14%
Infant mortality rate: 25.22 deaths/
1,000 live births
Life expectancy at birth: total population: 72.83 years; male: 70.96 years;
female: 74.79 years
Major ethnic groups: Palestinian Arab
and other 83%, Jewish 17%
Major religions: Muslim 75% (predominantly Sunni), Jewish 17%,
Christian and other 8%
Major languages: Arabic, Hebrew (spoken by Israeli settlers and many
Palestinians), English (widely understood)

Government
Official name: West Bank
Status: Former territory of Jordan now
occupied by Israel; negotiations
between Israel and the Palestinians
are being conducted
National capital: none

Economy
Industries: generally small family businesses that produce cement, textiles,
soap, olive-wood carvings, and
mother-of-pearl souvenirs; the
Israelis have established some small-
scale, modern industries in the set-
tlements and industrial centers
Agricultural products: olives, citrus and
other fruits, vegetables; beef, dairy
products
Currency: 1 new Israeli shekel (NIS) =
100 new agorot; 1 Jordanian dinar
(JD) = 1,000 fils

Western Sahara

Geography
Location: Northern Africa, bordering
the North Atlantic Ocean, between
Mauritania and Morocco

Area: 102,703 sq. mi. (266,000 sq.
km.); about the size of Colorado
Climate: hot, dry desert; rain is rare;
cold offshore air currents produce fog
and heavy dew
Terrain: mostly low, flat desert with
large areas of rocky or sandy surfaces rising to small mountains in
south and northeast
Elevation: lowest point: Sebjet Tah
−180 ft. (−55 m.); highest point:
unnamed location 1,519 ft.
(463 m.)
Natural resources: phosphates, iron ore

People
Population: 239,333 (July 1999 est.)
Population growth rate: 2.34%
Infant mortality rate: 139.67 deaths/
1,000 live births
Life expectancy at birth: total popula-
tion: 49.1 years; male: 47.98 years;
female: 50.57 years
Major ethnic groups: Arab, Berber
Major religions: Muslim
Major languages: Hassaniya Arabic,
Moroccan Arabic

Government
Official name: Western Sahara
Government type: legal status of
territory and question of sovereignty
unresolved; territory contested by
Morocco and Polisario Front (Popu-
lar Front for the Liberation of the
Saguia el Hamra and Rio de Oro)
National capital: none

Economy
Industries: phosphate mining, handicrafts
Agricultural products: fruits and vegetables (grown in the few oases);
camels, sheep, goats (kept by the
nomads)
Currency: 1 Moroccan dirham (DH) =
100 centimes

Yemen

Geography
Location: Middle East, bordering the
Arabian Sea, Gulf of Aden, and Red
Sea, between Oman and Saudi
Arabia

Nations *(cont.)*

Area: 203,849 sq. mi. (527,970 sq. km.); slightly larger than twice the size of Wyoming

Climate: mostly desert; hot and humid along west coast; temperate in western mountains affected by seasonal monsoon; extraordinarily hot, dry, harsh desert in east

Terrain: narrow coastal plain backed by flat-topped hills and rugged mountains; dissected upland desert plains in center slope into the desert interior of the Arabian Peninsula

Elevation: lowest point: Arabian Sea o ft. (o m.); highest point: Jabal an Nabi Shu'ayb 12,336 ft. (3,760 m.)

Natural resources: petroleum, fish, rock salt, marble, small deposits of coal, gold, lead, nickel, and copper, fertile soil in west

People

Population: 16,942,230 (July 1999 est.)

Population growth rate: 3.34%

Infant mortality rate: 69.82 deaths/1,000 live births

Life expectancy at birth: total population: 59.98 years; male: 58.17 years; female: 61.88 years

Major ethnic groups: predominantly Arab; Afro-Arab concentrations in western coastal locations; South Asians in southern regions; small European communities in major metropolitan areas

Major religions: Muslim including Shaf'i (Sunni) and Zaydi (Shi'a), small numbers of Jewish, Christian, and Hindu

Major languages: Arabic

Government

Official name: Republic of Yemen

Government type: republic

National capital: Sanaa

Independence: May 22, 1990 Republic of Yemen was established with the merger of the Yemen Arab Republic (Yemen [Sanaa] or North Yemen) and the Marxist-dominated People's Democratic Republic of Yemen (Yemen [Aden] or South Yemen)

Legal system: based on Islamic law, Turkish law, English common law, and local tribal customary law

Economy

Industries: crude oil production and petroleum refining; small-scale production of cotton textiles and leather goods; food processing; handicrafts; small aluminum products factory; cement

Agricultural products: grain, fruits, vegetables, qat (mildly narcotic shrub), coffee, cotton; dairy products, poultry, meat; fish

Currency: Yemeni rial (YRl) (new currency)

Zambia

Geography

Location: Southern Africa, east of Angola

Area: 290,583 sq. mi. (752,610 sq. km.); slightly larger than Texas

Climate: tropical; modified by altitude; rainy season (October to April)

Terrain: mostly high plateau with some hills and mountains

Elevation: lowest point: Zambezi river 1,079 ft. (329 m.); highest point: in Mafinga Hills 7,549 ft. (2,301 m.)

Natural resources: copper, cobalt, zinc, lead, coal, emeralds, gold, silver, uranium, hydropower potential

People

Population: 9,663,535 (July 1999 est.)

Population growth rate: 2.12%

Infant mortality rate: 91.85 deaths/1,000 live births

Life expectancy at birth: total population: 36.96 years; male: 36.72 years; female: 37.21 years

Major ethnic groups: African 98.7%, European 1.1%

Major religions: Christian 50–75%, Muslim and Hindu 24–49%, indigenous beliefs 1%

Major languages: English (official), major vernaculars—Bemba, Kaonda, Lozi, Lunda, Luvale, Nyanja, Tonga, and about 70 other indigenous languages

Government

Official name: Republic of Zambia

Government type: republic

National capital: Lusaka

Independence: October 24, 1964 (from U.K.)

Legal system: based on English common law and customary law; judicial review of legislative acts in an ad hoc constitutional council

Economy

Industries: copper mining and processing, construction, foodstuffs, beverages, chemicals, textiles, fertilizer

Agricultural products: corn, sorghum, rice, peanuts, sunflower seed, tobacco, cotton, sugarcane, cassava (tapioca); cattle, goats, pigs, poultry, beef, pork, poultry, milk, eggs, hides

Currency: 1 Zambian kwacha (ZK) = 100 ngwee

Zimbabwe

Geography

Location: Southern Africa, northeast of Botswana

Area: 150,803 sq. mi. (390,580 sq. km.); slightly larger than Montana

Climate: tropical; moderated by altitude; rainy season (November to March)

Terrain: mostly high plateau with higher central plateau (high veld); mountains in east

Elevation: lowest point: junction of the Lundi and Savi rivers 531 ft. (162 m.); highest point: Inyangani 8,504 ft. (2,592 m.)

Natural resources: coal, chromium ore, asbestos, gold, nickel, copper, iron ore, vanadium, lithium, tin, platinum group metals

People

Population: 11,163,160 (July 1999 est.)

Population growth rate: 1.02%

Infant mortality rate: 61.21 deaths/ 1,000 live births

Life expectancy at birth: total population: 38.86 years; male: 38.77 years; female: 38.94 years

Major ethnic groups: African 98% (Shona 71%, Ndebele 16%, other 11%), white 1%, mixed and Asian 1%

Major religions: syncretic (part Christian, part indigenous beliefs) 50%, Christian 25%, indigenous beliefs 24%, Muslim

Major languages: English (official), Shona, Sindebele (sometimes called Ndebele), numerous but minor tribal dialects

Government

Official name: Republic of Zimbabwe

Government type: parliamentary democracy

National capital: Harare

Independence: April 18, 1980 (from U.K.)

Legal system: mixture of Roman-Dutch and English common law

Economy

Industries: mining (coal, clay, numerous metallic and nonmetallic ores), copper, steel, nickel, tin, wood products, cement, chemicals, fertilizer, clothing and footwear, foodstuffs, beverages

Agricultural products: corn, cotton, tobacco, wheat, coffee, sugarcane, peanuts; cattle, sheep, goats, pigs

Currency: 1 Zimbabwean dollar (Z$) = 100 cents

⊙ Central Intelligence Agency. "The World Fact Book 1999," www.cia.gov/cia/publications/factbok/index.html

Nations and Territories: Population

Rank	Nation/Territory	Population	Rank	Nation/Territory	Population
1	China	1,261,832,482	45	Romania	22,411,121
2	India	1,014,003,817	46	Taiwan	22,191,087
3	United States	275,562,673	47	Saudi Arabia	22,023,506
4	Indonesia	224,784,210	48	Malaysia	21,793,293
5	Brazil	172,860,370	49	Korea, Democratic People's Republic of	21,687,550
6	Russia	146,001,176			
7	Pakistan	141,553,775			
8	Bangladesh	129,194,224			
9	Japan	126,549,976	50	Ghana	19,533,560
10	Nigeria	123,337,822	51	Australia	19,164,620
11	Mexico	100,349,766	52	Sri Lanka	19,238,757
12	Germany	82,797,408	53	Mozambique	19,104,696
13	Philippines	81,159,644	54	Yemen	17,479,206
14	Vietnam	78,773,873	55	Kazakhstan	16,733,227
15	Egypt	68,359,979	56	Syria	16,305,659
16	Turkey	65,666,677	57	Côte d'Ivoire	15,980,950
17	Iran	65,619,636	58	Netherlands	15,892,237
18	Ethiopia	64,227,452	59	Madagascar	15,506,472
19	Thailand	61,230,874	60	Cameroon	15,421,937
20	United Kingdom	59,508,382	61	Chile	15,153,797
21	France	59,329,691	62	Ecuador	12,920,092
22	Italy	57,634,327	63	Guatemala	12,639,939
23	Congo, Democratic Republic of the	51,964,999	64	Cambodia	12,212,306
			65	Burkina Faso	11,946,065
			66	Zimbabwe	11,342,521
24	Ukraine	49,153,027	67	Cuba	11,141,997
25	Korea, Republic of	47,470,969	68	Mali	10,685,948
			69	Greece	10,601,527
26	South Africa	43,421,021	70	Malawi	10,385,849
27	Burma	41,734,853	71	Belarus	10,366,719
28	Spain	39,996,671	72	Czech Republic	10,272,179
29	Colombia	39,685,655	73	Belgium	10,241,506
30	Argentina	36,955,182	74	Angola	10,145,267
31	Poland	38,646,023	75	Hungary	10,138,844
32	Tanzania	35,306,126	76	Niger	10,075,511
33	Sudan	35,079,814	77	Portugal	10,048,232
34	Canada	31,278,097	78	Senegal	9,987,494
35	Algeria	31,193,917	79	Serbia	9,981,929
36	Kenya	30,339,770	80	Tunisia	9,593,402
37	Morocco	30,122,350	81	Zambia	9,582,418
38	Peru	27,012,899	82	Sweden	8,873,052
39	Afghanistan	25,888,797	83	Chad	8,424,504
40	Uzbekistan	24,755,519	84	Bolivia	8,152,620
41	Nepal	24,702,119	85	Austria	8,131,111
42	Venezuela	23,542,649	86	Dominican Republic	8,442,533
43	Uganda	23,317,560	87	Bulgaria	7,796,694
44	Iraq	22,675,617	88	Azerbaijan	7,748,163

89	Guinea	7,466,200	137	Mongolia	2,616,383
90	Switzerland	7,276,372	138	Oman	2,533,389
92	Rwanda	7,229,129	139	Latvia	2,404,926
93	Somalia	7,253,137	140	United Arab	
94	Hong Kong			Emirates	2,369,153
	S.A.R.	7,115,620	141	Lesotho	2,143,141
95	Haiti	6,867,995	142	Macedonia,	
96	Tajikistan	6,440,732		The Former	
97	Benin	6,395,919		Yugo. Rep. of	2,041,467
98	Honduras	6,249,598	143	West Bank	2,020,298
99	El Salvador	6,122,515	144	Bhutan	2,005,222
100	Burundi	6,054,714	145	Kuwait	1,973,572
101	Israel	5,842,454	146	Slovenia	1,927,593
102	Paraguay	5,585,282	147	Namibia	1,771,327
103	Laos	5,497,459	148	Botswana	1,574,470
104	Slovakia	5,407,956	149	Estonia	1,431,471
105	Denmark	5,336,394	150	Gambia, The	1,367,124
106	Sierra Leone	5,232,624	151	Guinea-Bissau	1,285,715
107	Finland	5,167,486	152	Gabon	1,208,436
108	Libya	5,115,450	153	Mauritius	1,179,368
109	Togo	5,081,502	154	Trinidad and	
110	Georgia	5,019,538		Tobago	1,175,523
111	Jordan	4,998,564	155	Gaza Strip	1,132,063
112	Papua		156	Swaziland	1,083,289
	New Guinea	4,926,984	157	Fiji	832,494
113	Nicaragua	4,812,591	158	Cyprus	758,363
114	Kyrgyzstan	4,685,230	159	Qatar	744,483
115	Turkmenistan	4,518,268	160	Reunion	720,934
116	Norway	4,481,162	161	Guyana	697,286
117	Moldova	4,430,654	162	Montenegro	680,158
118	Croatia	4,282,216	163	Bahrain	634,137
119	Singapore	4,151,720	164	Comoros	578,400
120	Eritrea	4,135,933	165	Equatorial Guinea	474,214
121	Puerto Rico	3,915,798	166	Solomon Islands	466,194
122	Bosnia and		167	Djibouti	451,442
	Herzegovina	3,835,777	168	Macau	445,594
123	New Zealand	3,819,762	169	Luxembourg	437,389
124	Ireland	3,797,257	170	Suriname	431,303
125	Costa Rica	3,710,558	171	Guadeloupe	426,493
126	Lithuania	3,620,756	172	Martinique	414,516
127	Lebanon	3,578,036	173	Cape Verde	401,343
128	Central African		174	Malta	391,670
	Republic	3,512,751	175	Brunei	336,376
129	Albania	3,490,435	176	Maldives	301,475
130	Armenia	3,344,336	177	Bahamas, The	294,982
131	Uruguay	3,334,074	178	Iceland	276,365
132	Liberia	3,164,156	179	Barbados	274,059
133	Panama	2,808,268	180	Belize	249,183
134	Congo,		181	French Polynesia	249,110
	Republic of the	2,830,961	182	Western Sahara	244,943
135	Mauritania	2,667,859	183	Netherlands Antilles	210,134
136	Jamaica	2,652,689	184	New Caledonia	201,816

Nations and Territories: Population *(cont.)*

Rank	Nation/ Territory	Population	Rank	Nation/ Territory	Population
185	Vanuatu	189,618	207	American Samoa	65,446
186	Samoa	179,466	208	Guernsey	64,080
187	French Guiana	172,605	209	Bermuda	63,033
188	São Tomé and Príncipe	159,883	210	Greenland	56,309
			211	Faroe Islands	45,296
189	Mayotte	155,911	212	Saint Kitts and Nevis	38,819
190	Guam	154,623	213	Cayman Islands	34,736
191	Saint Lucia	156,260	214	Liechtenstein	32,204
192	Micronesia, Federated States of	133,144	215	Monaco	31,693
			216	Gibraltar	27,578
193	Virgin Islands	120,917	217	San Marino	26,937
194	Saint Vincent and the Grenadines	115,461	218	Cook Islands	20,407
			219	Virgin Islands, British	20,353
195	Tonga	102,321	220	Palau	18,766
196	Kiribati	91,985	221	Turks and Caicos Islands	17,502
197	Grenada	89,312			
198	Jersey	88,915	222	Wallis and Futuna	15,283
199	Seychelles	79,326	223	Nauru	11,845
200	Isle of Man	73,112	224	Anguilla	11,797
201	Northern Mariana Islands	71,912	225	Tuvalu	10,383
			226	Saint Helena	7,212
202	Dominica	71,540	227	Saint Pierre and Miquelon	6,896
203	Aruba	69,539			
204	Marshall Islands	68,126	228	Montserrat	6,409
205	Andorra	66,824	229	Falkland Islands	2,805
206	Antigua and Barbuda	66,464	230	Norfolk Island	2,179

⊙ United States Bureau of the Census. "IDB Data Access," www.census.gov/ipc/ www.idbacc.html

United Nations Population Information Network. "U.N Population Division Department of Economic and Social Affairs," www.undp.org/popin

Urban Areas: Population Over 2 Million (in millions as of 1996)

Rank	Urban Area	Country	Pop.	Rank	Urban Area	Country	Pop.
1	Tokyo	Japan	27.2	12	Lagos	Nigeria	10.9
2	Mexico City	Mexico	16.9	13	Osaka	Japan	10.6
3	São Paulo	Brazil	16.8	14	Delhi	India	10.3
4	New York	United States	16.4	15	Rio de Janeiro	Brazil	10.3
5	Bombay	India	15.7	16	Karachi	Pakistan	10.1
6	Shanghai	China	13.7	17	Cairo	Egypt	9.9
7	Los Angeles	United States	12.6	18	Metro Manila	Philippines	9.6
8	Calcutta	India	12.1	19	Tianjin	China	9.6
9	Buenos Aires	Argentina	11.9	20	Paris	France	9.6
10	Seoul	South Korea	11.8	21	Moscow	Russia	9.3
11	Beijing	China	11.4	22	Dhaka	Bangladesh	9.0
				23	Jakarta	Indonesia	8.8

24	Istanbul	Turkey	8.2
25	London	United Kingdom	7.6
26	Teheran	Iran	6.9
27	Chicago	United States	6.9
28	Lima	Peru	6.8
29	Bangkok	Thailand	6.7
30	Essen	Germany	6.5
31	Bogota	Columbia	6.2
32	Madras	India	6.1
33	Hong Kong	China	5.9
34	Hyderabad	India	5.7
35	Shenyang	China	5.2
36	Lahore	Pakistan	5.2
37	Saint Petersburg	Russia	5.1
38	Santiago	Chile	5.0
39	Bangalore	India	5.0
40	Harbin	China	4.7
41	Guangzhou	China	4.6
42	Hangzhou	China	4.6
43	Chengdu	China	4.5
44	Changchun	China	4.4
45	Baghdad	Iraq	4.4
46	Toronto	Canada	4.4
47	Kinshasa	Democratic Republic of the Congo	4.4
48	Wuhan	China	4.3
49	Philadelphia	United States	4.3
50	Milan	Italy	4.2
51	Pusan	South Korea	4.1
52	Madrid	Spain	4.1
53	Yangon	Myanmar	4.0
54	San Francisco	United States	3.9
55	Belo Horizonte	Brazil	3.9
56	Algiers	Algeria	3.8
57	Ahmedabad	India	3.8
58	Washington, D.C.	United States	3.7
59	Detroit	United States	3.7
60	Jinan	China	3.7
61	Dallas	United States	3.7
62	Alexandria	Egypt	3.7
63	Frankfurt	Germany	3.6
64	Sydney	Australia	3.6
65	Ho Chi Min	Vietnam	3.6
66	Chongqing	China	3.6
67	Guadalajara	Mexico	3.5
68	Katowice	Poland	3.4
69	Porto Alegre	Brazil	3.4
70	Medellin	Colombia	3.4
71	Singapore	Singapore	3.4
72	Qingdao	China	3.4
73	Montreal	Canada	3.3

74	Berlin	Germany	3.3
75	Santo Domingo	Dominican Republic	3.3
76	Nagoya	Japan	3.3
77	Houston	United States	3.2
78	Casablanca	Morocco	3.2
79	Recife	Brazil	3.1
80	Melbourne	Australia	3.1
81	Athens	Greece	3.1
82	Dusseldorf	Germany	3.1
83	Monterrey	Mexico	3.1
84	Pune	India	3.1
85	Nanjing	China	3.0
86	Xian	China	3.0
87	Caracas	Venezuela	3.0
88	Cologne	Germany	3.0
89	Naples	Italy	3.0
90	Bandung	Indonesia	3.0
91	Ankara	Turkey	2.9
92	Abidjan	Côte d'Ivoire	2.9
93	Salvador	Brazil	2.9
94	Handan	China	2.9
95	Boston	United States	2.9
96	Kiev	Ukraine	2.8
97	Barcelona	Spain	2.8
98	Cape Town	South Africa	2.8
99	San Diego	United States	2.8
100	Kitakyushu	Japan	2.8
101	Riyadh	Saudi Arabia	2.8
102	Fortaleza	Brazil	2.7
103	Taipei	China	2.7
104	Dalian	China	2.7
105	Rome	Italy	2.7
106	Hamburg	Germany	2.6
107	Stuttgart	Germany	2.6
108	Chittagong	Bangladesh	2.6
109	Addis Ababa	Ethiopia	2.6
110	Pyongyang	North Korea	2.5
111	Atlanta	United States	2.5
112	Taegu	South Korea	2.5
113	Inch'on	South Korea	2.4
114	Phoenix	United States	2.4
115	Maputo	Mozambique	2.4
116	Khartoum	Sudan	2.3
117	Tashkent	Uzbekistan	2.3
118	Guatemala City	Guatemala	2.3
119	Curitiba	Brazil	2.3
120	Surabaja	Indonesia	2.3
121	Kanpur	India	2.3
122	Birmingham	United Kingdom	2.3
123	Minneapolis	United States	2.3
124	Munich	Germany	2.3
125	Manchester	United Kingdom	2.2

Urban Areas: Population Over 2 Million *(cont.)*

Rank	Urban Area	Country	Pop.	Rank	Urban Area	Country	Pop.
126	Havana	Cuba	2.2	137	Mashhad	Iran	2.1
127	Warsaw	Poland	2.2	138	Vienna	Austria	2.1
128	Johannesburg	South Africa	2.2	139	Esfahan	Iran	2.1
129	Luanda	Angola	2.2	140	Zhengzhou	China	2.0
130	Lucknow	India	2.2	141	Saint Louis	United States	2.0
131	Kabul	Afghanistan	2.2	142	Budapest	Hungary	2.0
132	Taiyuan	China	2.1	143	Tel-Aviv-Yafo	Israel	2.0
133	Izmir	Turkey	2.1	144	Guiyang	China	2.0
134	Miami	United States	2.1	145	Surat	India	2.0
135	Bucharest	Romania	2.1	146	Baltimore	United States	2.0
136	Damascus	Syria	2.1	147	Seattle	United States	2.0

⊙ United Nations Population Division. www.un.org/esa/population/unpop.htm
United Nations Population Division. "United Nations Population Division
Population Information Network," www.undp.org/popin

WORLD: *History*

Chronology

c. 6000 BC	Farming begins in Tigris-Euphrates and Nile River Valleys
c. 4000 BC	Farming begins in Yellow River Valley
c. 3500 BC	Sumerian city-states emerge
3300 BC	Rulers divide Nile Valley into Upper and Lower Egypt by this time
c. 3100 BC	Egypt unified into single kingdom
c. 2800	Indus River Valley civilization begins
2180 BC	Egypt's Middle Kingdom established
c. 2000 BC	Stonehenge built in England
c. 1760 BC	Hammurabi rules in Babylon
c. 1700 BC	Hebrew monotheism emerges
c. 1650 BC	Minoan civilization, based on Crete, expands
c. 1600 BC	Shang dynasty introduces writing in China
c. 1500 BC	Olmecs settle in Mexico.
c. 1450 BC	Earthquake destroys Minoan civilization
1299 BC	Egyptian pharoah Ramses I fights Hittites at Kadesh
c. 1250 BC	Moses leads Jews from Egypt to promised land of Palestine
c. 1200 BC	Trojan War
1122 BC	Zhou dynasty established in China
1000 BC	David begins reign as king of the Jews, defeats Philistines before his death in 961
c. 814 BC	Carthage founded by Phoenicians
776 BC	1st Olympic Games are staged at Olympia, Greece
753 BC	Traditional founding date of Rome
725 BC	Kushite kingdom of Nubia conquers Egypt
c. 600 BC	Zoroaster announces Zoroastrianism, a religion emphasizing spirits of good and evil
c. 545 BC	Cyrus the Great solidifies power and founds Persian Empire
509 BC	Rome forces out Etruscan kings, Roman Republic founded
492 BC	Persian Wars, a 40-year series of Persian military expeditions against the Greeks, begin

431 BC	Athens and Sparta oppose each other in Peloponnesian War
405 BC	Peloponnesian War concludes with Athens' defeat at Aegospotami
371 BC	Thebes and Athens defeat Sparta
336 BC	Alexander the Great of Macedon conquers Greece
333 BC	Alexander defeats Darius at Issus
323 BC	Alexander dies; in less than 20 years his empire has been divided several times
241 BC	Rome defeats Carthage in 1st Punic War
218 BC	Hannibal leads Cathaginian forces across the Alps in 2nd Punic War
214 BC	Earliest version of the Great Wall amalgamated in China
201 BC	Roman general Scipio defeats Hannibal at Zama, ending 2nd Punic War
146 BC	3rd Punic War ends with destruction of Carthage, which becomes Roman province
136 BC	China's Emperor Wudi makes Confucianism the basis of government administration
c. 60 BC	China's Han dynasty extends control to central Asia
44 BC	Julius Caesar assassinated in Roman Senate by opponents of his dictatorship
27 BC	Augustus Caesar becomes emperor
c. 4 BC	Jesus born in Bethlehem, Palestine
c. 50 AD	Buddhist monks reach China
70	Jews revolt; Romans destroy temple in Jerusalem, end of Hebrew state
79	Roman city of Pompeii buried in volcanic ash from Vesuvius eruption
c. 100	Paper invented in China
265	China reunited under Western Jin dynasty, ending Three Kingdoms period
285	Emperor Diocletian divides Roman Empire into Eastern and Western realms
c. 300	Axum (Ethiopia) adopts Christianity
313	Eastern Roman Emperor Constantine grants freedom to all religions; Christians gain major influence by 330
410	Visigoths, led by Alaric, sack Rome
452	Attila the Hun's invasion of Gaul stopped
476	Western Roman Empire begins to decline
486	Clovis defeats Romans in Gaul and establishes Merovingian dynasty
534	Byzantine Emperor Justinian conquers North Africa and Italy (554)
550	Northern India's Gupta dynasty falls
551	Buddhism introduced into Japan
589	Sui dynasty reunifies China
618	Tang dynasty founded in China
622	Mohammed flees from Mecca to Medina in episode known as the Hejira
632	Death of Mohammed leads to struggle over succession; Islam divided
638	Umayyad dynasty founded in Jerusalem
652	Koran completed in final form
688	Islam's Dome of the Rock begun in Jerusalem
710	Nara era begins in Japan
711	Moorish invasion of Spain starts
732	Charles Martel halts Muslim invasion of France
750	Al Mansur establishes Abbasid caliphate
774	Charlemagne conquers Italy, beginning major expansion of his empire
800	Charlemagne crowned Holy Roman Emperor in Rome
843	Treaty of Verdun divides Charlemagne's empire into three parts

Chronology *(cont.)*

865	Byzantine (Eastern Orthodox) and Roman Catholic forms of Christianity separate
955	Otto I, Holy Roman Emperor since 936, defeats Magyars at Lechfeld
960	Northern Song dynasty established in China
987	Quetzalcoatl, ruler of Mexico's Toltecs, abdicates
c. 1000	Viking invasions of Europe peak; Leif Ericson sails to North America; Norse colony set up in Newfoundland
1031	Umayyad dynasty falls in Spain
1055	Muslims driven from Portugal by Ferdinand of Castile
1066	William of Normandy becomes king of England after defeating King Harold at Battle of Hastings
1071	Ottoman Empire established
1096	1st Crusade begins; crusaders take Jerusalem from Arabs
c. 1100	Cambodia's Khmer empire achieves height of power
1204	4th Crusade takes Constatinople and founds Latin Empire of the East
1206	Genghis Khan begins reign as Mongol leader, assembling vast empire before his death in 1227
1215	England's King John is pressured to sign Magna Carta, curbing royal power
1234	Mongols absorb China's Chin Empire
1244	Turks capture Jerusalem; 7th Crusade (1248-50) is unable to retake city
1260	Kublai Khan becomes leader of the Mongols, establishes Yuan dynasty in China (1280)
1270	Louis IX of France dies in Tunis leading the 9th Crusade
1271	Marco Polo begins expedition to China
1273	1st Mongol invasion of Japan fails
1325	Aztec capital of Tenochtitlan established in Mexico
1327	England's King Edward II deposed and killed
1337	Hundred Years' War between England and France begins over claims to England's throne
1348	Black Death begins to ravage Europe
1368	Rebellion against Mongol rule leads to founding of Ming dynasty in China
1378	Papacy splits, Great Schism results in popes installed at Rome and Avignon, France
1391	Tamerlane extends his power into Central Asia with defeat of Mongols' Golden Horde
1399	England's Richard II deposed; Henry IV ascends the throne
1421	Beijing becomes capital of China's Ming dynasty
1431	French heroine Joan of Arc burned at the stake
1434	Medici family begins 60-year control of Florence
1453	Fall of Constantinople to Ottomans ends Byzantine Empire
1472	Russia's Ivan the Great takes the title of tsar
1479	Spain's Ferdinand and Isabella unite their kingdoms of Aragon and Castile
1482	Agreement with the papacy permits Spain to put the church and Inquisition under royal control
1488	Explorer Bartolomeu Diaz sails around Africa's Cape of Good Hope
1492	Christopher Columbus reaches the New World (Hispaniola); Spain captures Granada, completing reconquest of Spain from Moors

1498	Vasco da Gama lands in India after sailing around Cape of Good Hope
1500	Portugal claims Brazil
1517	Martin Luther writes 95 theses
1519	Hernan Cortes begins conquest of the Aztecs in Mexico; Ferdinand Magellan starts voyage that circumnavigates the world
c. 1519	Nanak establishes Sikhism as a religion
1520	Luther, excommunicated in 1520, addresses the Diet of Worms
1540	Jesuit order founded by Ignatius de Loyola
1541	Puritan theocracy founded by John Calvin at Geneva, Switzerland
1546	Catholic Counter Reformation, supported by Holy Roman Emperor Charles V, opposes German Protestant princes
1563	Church of England (Anglican Church) established
1580	Philip II unites Spain and Portugal
1587	Japan expels Portuguese missionaries
1588	England defeats the Spanish Armada
1598	France's Henry IV grants Protestant Huguenots equal rights with Catholics in Edict of Nantes
1603	Tokugawa (Edo) period begins in Japan
1618	Thirty Years War starts in Europe
1619	*Mayflower* lands Pilgrims on Cape Cod, Massachusetts
1642	English Civil War starts
1648	Peace of Westphalia ends Thirty Years War; Fronde uprisings try unsuccessfully to challenge royal power in France
1649	Charles I of England executed; Oliver Cromwell governs England through Commonwealth
1660	England restores monarchy with Charles II as king
1661	France's Louis XIV begins ruling in his own right
1673	Jacques Marquette and Louis Joliet explore Mississippi River for France
1676	King Philip's War ends with defeat of Indians after decimating New England
1685	Louis XIV revokes Edict of Nantes, resulting in Huguenot emigration from France
1687	Austro-Hungarian forces defeat Turks at Mohacs, halting Turks expansion into Europe
1688	In Glorious Revolution, England deposes Catholic-supporting James II and replaces him with his Protestant daughter Mary
1713	Treaty of Utrecht, ending War of the Spanish Succession, keeps France and Spain separate
1725	Peter the Great of Russia dies
1726	Spiritual movement called the Great Awakening begins in American colonies
1741	Russia's Vitus Bering explores Alaska
1754	French and Indian War begins in North America, with Britain and France vying for control of the continent
1756	Seven Years War starts in Europe
1763	Britain's supremacy over France in North American and India confirmed by Treaty of Paris
1764	Stamp Act inspires protests in American colonies
1765	Egypt declares independence from Ottoman Empire
1768	James Cook begins exploration of Australia
1770	Boston Massacre increases American resentment of British
1773	Boston Tea Party protests British tax on tea in American colonies

Chronology (cont.)

1774	1st Continental Congress meets
1775	Battle of Lexington and Concord opens Revolutionary War
1776	American independence declared; Declaration of Independence signed
1783	Treaty of Paris formalizes American independence. Russia occupies Crimea
1788	U.S. Constitution ratified
1789	French Revolution begins
1792	France becomes a republic; Louis XVI executed in 1793
1793	Eli Whitney invents cotton gin, immensely speeding cotton production
1798	Britain's Admiral Nelson defeats French at Battle of the Nile
1804	Napoleon takes the title of emperor
1807	British abolish slave trade
1811	Venezuela and Paraguay gain independence from Spain
1812	United States and Britain begin War of 1812. Napoleon invades Russia, resulting in huge losses
1814	Napoleon forced to abdicate and goes into exile. Washington, D.C. burned by British
1815	Napoleon returns to power but is defeated at Battle of Waterloo and exiled again. War of 1812 ends with American victory over British at Battle of New Orleans
1818	U.S.-Canadian border agreed upon
1819	Missouri Compromise establishes line between free and slave states
1820	Mexico and Peru gain independence from Spain
1821	Brazil becomes independent of Portugal
1822	Through Monroe Doctrine, United States warns European powers to stay out of colonial affairs in the Americas
1830	French depose Charles X, replacing him with Louis Philippe
1831	Nat Turner's Rebellion, a U.S. slave uprising, results in about 60 white and 100 slave deaths
1836	Americans annihilated at Alamo during Texas Rebellion
1837	Queen Victoria ascends British throne
1839	Opium Wars start in China
1845	Potato Famine beings in Ireland, resulting in starvation and widespread emigration
1849	California gold rush follows discovery of gold at Sutter's Mill in 1848
1850	Compromise of 1850 attempts to resolve U.S. slavery questions
1852	Napoleon III takes power in France as emperor
1856	Crimean War ends
1858	Last of Indian Mutinies are suppressed by British in India
1861	Civil War begins with Confederate shelling of Ft. Sumter
1865	Civil War ends with Confederate surrender at Appomattox; Lincoln assassinated
1866	Prussia defeats Austria in Austro-Prussian War
1867	British North America Act forms Dominion of Canada. Shogunate abolished in Japan; Emperor Meiji ascends throne
1869	Suez Canal opens
1870	Empire falls after Prussia's defeat of France in Franco-Prussian War
1876	Battle of the Little Bighorn. Alexander Graham Bell patents telephone
1878	Thomas Edison patents his light bulb
1881	Germany signs alliance with Russia and Austria

1884	Treaty of Berlin states the rights of European powers in Africa
1885	Canadian-Pacific Railway completed
1894	Dreyfus Affair surfaces in France
1895	After military victories, Japan wins concessions from China
1898	Spanish-American War results in U.S. territorial gains
1899	Boxer Rebellion in China brings foreign intervention
1902	Boer War ends in southern Africa
1903	Wilbur and Orville Wright make 1st airplane flight
1904	Revolution in Russia brings few reforms
1906	San Francisco earthquake and fire destroy much of the city
1908	Henry Ford markets 1st Model T
1910	Union of South Africa formed
1911	Mexican dictator Porfirio Diaz overthrown. Sun Yat-sen establishes republic in China
1914	World War I begins after Austrian Archduke Ferdinand is assassinated. Panama Canal opens
1917	Russian Revolution overthrows tsar
1918	World War I ends with defeat of Germany
1919	Treaty of Versailles. League of Nations is established
1923	Modernization of Turkey begins under Kemal Ataturk
1927	Charles Lindbergh makes 1st non-stop solo flight across Atlantic Ocean
1928	Chiang Kai-shek becomes president of China
1929	Stock market crash on Wall St. leads to business depression
1931	Japan occupies Manchuria
1933	Adolf Hitler and Nazis come to power in Germany. Franklin Roosevelt inaugurates New Deal programs in United States
1935	Italy invades Ethiopia. Nuremberg Laws deprive Jews of all citizenship rights in Germany
1937	Japan starts war against China
1938	Germany annexes Austria
1939	World War II starts with Germany's invasion of Poland
1940	Germany overruns France
1941	Japanese bombing of Pearl Harbor brings United States into World War II
1944	Normandy invasion initiates final phase of war against Germany
1945	Germany surrenders; United States drops two atomic bombs on Japan to end war in Pacific; United Nations founded
1947	Marshall Plan devised to rebuild post-war Europe. India gains independence from Britain
1948	Israel becomes independent. Berlin Airlift carries supplies to blockaded city
1949	Mao Zedong and communists set up People's Republic of China. North Atlantic Treaty Organization (NATO) established
1950	Korean War opens as North Korea invades South Korea
1954	Egypt declared a republic with Nasser as prime minister
1955	Warsaw Pact of Soviet Union and its satellites formed to oppose NATO. Vietnam divided into North and South by Geneva Conference
1956	Soviet troops intervene in Hungary to crush nationalist uprising. Egypt nationalizes Suez Canal, triggering war with Britain, France, and Israel
1957	Treaty of Rome establishes European Common Market
1958	Russians build Berlin Wall. U.S.-supported Bay of Pigs invasion fails in Cuba
1962	Soviets back down during Cuban Missile Crisis

Chronology (cont.)

1963   U.S. President Kennedy is assassinated and is succeeded by Lyndon Johnson

1964   Gulf of Tonkin Resolution authorizes U.S. action in Vietnam

1967   Israel defeats Arab coalition in Six Day War

1968   China's Cultural Revolution comes to an end. Martin Luther King assassinated

1969   American astronauts walk on the moon

1973   Arab forces oppose Israel in Yom Kippur War. Last U.S. troops leave Vietnam. Military coup in Chile

1974   U.S. President Nixon resigns in wake of Watergate scandal

1975   Communist regimes take power in Vietnam and Cambodia

1978   Leaders of Egypt and Israel meet at Camp David. Spain returns to constitutional monarchy

1979   Soviet Union invades Afghanistan

1982   Britain defeats Argentina in Falklands War

1986   Soviet Union starts reforms of glasnost and perestroika

1987   Iran-Contra Affair tarnishes Reagan administration

1988   Long Iran-Iraq war halted by truce. Soviets withdraw from Afghanistan

1989   Communist governments fall in Soviet Union and Eastern Europe. United States invades Panama to topple General Noriega's government. China kills pro-democracy demonstrators in Beijing's Tiananmen Square

1990   Iraq invades Kuwait, provoking international opposition. Germany reunifies. Yugoslavia's republics begin to declare independence. Maastricht Treaty proposes European monetary union

1991   Iraq defeated by U.S.-led international force. Most former Soviet republics reassemble in looser Commonwealth of Independent States

1992   South Africa decides to end white-minority rule. Brutal civil wars continue in former Yugoslavia

1993   North American Free Trade Agreement (NAFTA) signed. South Africa moves toward a multi-racial society. Israel and Palestinians sign peace agreement

1994   Nelson Mandela elected as South Africa's 1st black president. Civil war breaks out in Rwanda. Russia faces internal unrest

1995   Israeli prime minister Itzhak Rabin is assassinated

1996   Bosnia, Croatia, and Serbia reach agreement on peace

1997   Hong Kong comes under Chinese rule, ending British control. Rebellion in Zaire results in toppling of long-time leader Mobutu Sese Seko; nation takes new name as Democratic Republic of Congo

1998   Irish factions agree on basic framework for peace. Serbian province of Kosovo is the scene of massacres of ethnic Albanians

1999   U.S. President Clinton acquitted during impeachment trial. Conflict between Russians and Chechnyans escalates

2000   United Nations report on AIDS released; disease has killed 19 million people worldwide, another 34 million infected with AIDS virus, HIV

⊙ *Atlas of World History*. Chicago: Rand McNally, 1995.

Beeching, Cyril Leslie. *A Dictionary of Dates*, 2d ed. New York: Oxford University Press, 1997.

McKay, John P., Bennett Hill, John Buckler, and Patricia Buckley Ebrey. *A History of World Societies*, 2 vols. Boston: Houghton Mifflin, 2000.

Dynasties of China

Dynasty	Dates	Dynasty	Dates
Qin	221–207 BC	Western Wei	535–557
Western Han	207 BC–AD 9	Northern Chou	557–581
Xin	9–25	Sui	581–618
Eastern Han	25–220	Tang	618–907
The Three Kingdoms		**The Five Dynasties**	
Wei	220–266	Later Liang	907–923
Shu Han	221–263	Later Tang	923–937
Wu	222–280	Later Jin	937–947
Western Jin	266–316	Later Han	947–951
Southern Dynasties		Later Zhou	951–960
Eastern Jin	317–420	**The Border Empires**	
Liu Sung	420–479	Liao	907–1125
Southern Ch'i	479–502	Chin	1115–1234
Liang	502–557	Northern Song	960–1127
Ch'en	557–589	Southern Song	1127–1279
Northern Dynasties		Yuan	1206–1368
Northern Wei	386–535	Ming	1368–1644
Eastern Wei	534–550	Qing	1644–1912
Northern Ch'i	550–577		

⊙ Ebrey, Patricia Buckley, ed. *Chinese Civilization: A Sourcebook*, 2d ed. New York: Free Press/Macmillan, 1993.

Paludan, Ann. *Chronicle of the Chinese Emperors: The Reign-By-Reign Record of the Rulers of Imperial China*. New York: Thames and Hudson, 1998.

Pei, Ming L., ed. "China the Beautiful," www.chinapage.org/history1.html

Monarchs of England and Britain

House	Monarch	Reign	House	Monarch	Reign
Wessex (West Saxon)			**Danish**		
	Egbert	802–839		Canute (Cnut)	1016–1035
	Ethelwulf	839–856		Harold I	1035–1040
	Ethelbald	856–860		Hardecanute	1040–1042
	Ethelbert	860–866	**West Saxon (restored)**		
	Ethelred I	866–871		Edward II	
	Alfred the Great	871–899		(the Confessor)	1042–1066
	Edward the Elder	899–924		Harold II	1066
	Athelstan	925–939	**Normandy**		
	Edmund I	939–946		William I	
	Edred	946–955		(the Conqueror)	1066–1087
	Edwy	955–957		William II	1087–1100
	Edgar	959–975		Henry I	1100–1135
	Edward			Stephen	1135–1154
	the Martyr	975–978	**Plantagenet (Anjou)**		
	Ethelred II (the			Henry II	1154–1189
	Unready)	978–1016		Richard I (the	
	Edmund II			Lion-heart)	1189–1199
	(Ironside)	1016		John	1199–1216
				Harold I	1035–1040
				Henry III	1216–1272
				Edward I	1272–1307

Monarchs of England and Britain *(cont.)*

House	Monarch	Reign	House	Monarch	Reign
	Edward II	1307–1327	**Protectorate**		
	Edward III	1327–1377		Oliver Cromwell	1653–1658
	Richard II	1377–1399		Richard Cromwell	1658–1660
Lancaster			**Stuart**		
	Henry IV	1399–1413		Charles II	1660–1685
	Henry V	1413–1422		James II	1685–1688
	Henry VI	1422–1461		interregnum	1688–1689
York				William III and	
	Edward IV	1461–1483		Mary II	1689–1694
	Edward V	1483		Anne	1702–1714
	Richard III	1483–1485	**Hanover**		
Tudor				George I	1714–1727
	Henry VII	1485–1509		George II	1727–1760
	Henry VIII	1509–1547		George III	1760–1820
	Edward VI	1547–1553		George IV	1820–1830
	Jane (Lady Jane			William IV	1830–1837
	Grey)	1553	**Saxe-Coburg-Gotha**		
	Mary I	1553–1558		Victoria	1837–1901
	Elizabeth I	1558–1603		Edward VII	1901–1910
Stuart			**Windsor**		
	James I	1603–1625		George V	1910–1936
	Charles I	1625–1649		Edward VIII	1936
Commonwealth				George VI	1936–1952
	Long Parliament	1649–1660		Elizabeth II	1952–

⊙ Davies, Norman. *The Isles: A History.* New York: Oxford University Press, 2000.
Fraser, Antonia. *The Lives of the Kings and Queens of England*, rev. ed. Berkeley: University of California Press, 1998.
Morgan, Kenneth O. *The Oxford Illustrated History of Britain.* Oxford: Oxford University Press, 1984.

Kings and Emperors of France

House	Monarch	Reign	House	Monarch	Reign
Carolingian			**Carolingian**		
	Pepin (the Short)	751–768		Charles III	
	Carloman	768–771		(the Simple)	893–923
	Charles		**Robertian**		
	(Charlemagne)	768–814		Robert I	922–923
	Louis I (the Pious)	814–840		Rudolf	923–936
	Charles II		**Carolingian**		
	(the Bald)	840–877		Louis IV	936–954
	Louis II (the			Lothair	954–986
	Stammerer)	877–879		Louis V	986–987
	Louis III	879–882	**Capetian**		
	Carloman	879–884		Hugh Capet	987–996
	Charles III (the Fat)	885–888		Robert II	996–1031
Robertian				Hugh	1017–1025
	Eudes	888–898		Henry I	1031–1060
				Philip I	1060–1108

Louis VI (the Fat)	1108–1137	Henry II	1547–1559
Philip	1129–1131	Francis II	1559–1560
Louis VII	1137–1180	Charles IX	1560–1574
Philip II	1180–1223	Henry III	1574–1589
Louis VIII	1223–1226	**Bourbon**	
Louis IX (St.)	1226–1270	Henry IV	1589–1610
Philip III	1270–1285	Louis XIII	1610–1643
Philip IV		Louis XIV	1643–1715
(the Fair)	1285–1314	Louis XV	1715–1774
Louis X		Louis XVI	1774–1792
(the Stubborn)	1314–1316	Louis XVII	1793–1795
John I	1316	**First Republic**	
Philip V (the Tall)	1316–1322	National	
Charles IV		Convention	1792–1795
(the Fair)	1322–1328	Directory	1795–1799
Valois		Consulate	1799–1804
Philip VI	1328–1350	**Bonaparte**	
John II		Napoleon I	1804–1814
(the Good)	1350–1364	Napoleon I	1815
Charles V		Napoleon II	1815
(the Wise)	1364–1380	**Bourbon**	
Charles VI		Louis XVIII	1814–1824
(the Mad)	1380–1422	Charles X	1824–1830
Charles VII		**Orléans**	
(the Victorious)	1422–1461	Louis Philippe I	1830–1848
Louis XI	1461–1498	**Second Republic**	
Charles VIII	1483–1498	Louis Napoleon	
Orléans		Bonaparte	1848–1852
Louis XII	1498–1515	**Bonaparte**	
Angoulême		Napoleon III	1852–1870
Francis I	1515–1547		

⊙ James, E. *The Franks*. New York: Basil Blackwell, 1988.
  McKitterick, R. *The Frankish Kingdoms and the Early Carolingians, 751–987*. New York: Longman, 1983.
  Price, R. *A Concise History of France*. Cambridge: Cambridge University Press, 1993.

Dynasties of Japan

Dynasty	*Dates*	*Dynasty*	*Dates*
Yamato	40 BC–AD 70	Northern Court	1331–1392
Asuka	552–710	Muromachi	1392–1573
Nara	710–784	Tokugawa	1600–1868
Early Heian	794–857	Kamakura Shogunate	1185–1195
Late Heian or Fujiwara	858–1185	Hojo Regency	1203–1333
Kamakura	1185–1336	Ashikaga Shogunate	1338–1358
Southern Court	1336–1392	Tokugawa Shogunate	1603–1868

⊙ Collcott, M., M. Jansen, and I. Kumakura, *Cultural Atlas of Japan*. New York: Facts on File, 1988.
  Morton, W. Scott. *Japan: Its History and Culture*, 3d ed. New York: McGraw-Hill, 1994.

Holy Roman Emperors

House	Monarch	Reign	House	Monarch	Reign
Carolingian				[William of Holland	1247–1256]
	Charles (Charlemagne)	800–814		Conrad IV	1250–1254
	Louis I (the Pious)	814–840		[Richard of Cornwall	1257–1272]
	Lothair I	840–855	**Habsburg**		
	Louis II	855–875		Rudolf I	1273–1291
	Charles II (the Bald)	875–877	**Nassau**		
	Charles III (the Fat)	881–887		Adolf	1292–1298
	Arnulf of Carinthia	887–899	**Habsburg**		
	Louis III (the Child)	900–911		Albert I of Austria	1298–1308
Franconia			**Luxemburg**		
	Conrad I	911–918		Henry VII	1308–1313
Saxony			**Wittelsbach**		
	Henry I (the Fowler)	919–936		Louis IV of Bavaria	1314–1347
	Otto I (the Great)	936–973		[Frederick of Austria	1314–1330]
	Otto II	973–983	**Luxemburg**		
	Otto III	983–1002		Charles IV	1346–1378
	St. Henry II	1002–1024		[Günther of Schwarzburg	1349]
Salian				Wenceslas	1378–1400
	Conrad II	1024–1039	**Wittelsbach**		
	Henry III	1039–1056		Rupert of the Palatinate	1400–1410
	Henry IV	1056–1105	**Luxemburg**		
	[Rudolf of Swabia	1077–1080]		Sigismund	1410–1437
	[Herman of Salm	1081–1088]		[Jobst of Moravia	1410–1411]
	Conrad	1087–1098	**Habsburg**		
	Henry V	1105–1125		Albert II of Austria	1438–1439
Suplinburg				Frederick III	1440–1493
	Lothair II of Saxony	1125–1137		Maximilian I	1493–1558
Hohenstaufen				Charles V	1519–1558
	Conrad III	1138–1152		Ferdinand I	1558–1564
	Henry	1147–1150		Maximilian II	1564–1576
	Fredrick I (Barbarosa)	1152–1190		Rudolf II	1576–1612
	Henry VI	1190–1197		Matthias	1612–1619
	Philip of Swabia	1198–1208		Ferdinand II	1619–1637
Welf				Ferdinand III	1637–1657
	Otto IV	1198–1218		Leopold I	1658–1705
Hohenstaufen				Joseph I	1705–1711
	Fredrick II	1212–1250		Charles VI	1711–1740
	Henry	1220–1235	**Wittelsbach**		
	[Henry Raspe of Thuringia	1246–1247]		Charles VII of Bavaria	1742–1745

Habsburg-Lorraine		Joseph II	1765–1790
Francis I of		Leopold II	1790–1792
Lorraine	1745–1765	Francis II	1792–1806

⊙ Bartlett, R. *The Making of Europe: Conquest, Colonization, and Cultural Change, 950–1350.* Princeton, N.J.: Princeton University Press, 1993.

Scott, H., ed. *The European Nobilities in the Seventeenth and Eighteenth Centuries.* New York: Addison-Wesley, 1995.

Roman Emperors from Augustus to Constantine

Dynasty Emperor	Reign	Dynasty Emperor	Reign
Julio-Claudians		**The Soldier-Emperors**	
Augustus	27 BC–AD 14	Maximinus	
Tiberius	AD 14–37	the Thracian	235–238
Gaius (Caligula)	37–41	Gordian I and	
Claudius	41–54	Gordian II	238
Nero	54–68	Balbinus and	
Galba	68–69	Pupienus	
Otho	69	Maximus	238
Vitellius	69	Gordian III	238–244
Flavians		Philip I the Arab	244–249
Vespasian	69–79	Philip II	247–249
Titus	79–81	Decius	249–251
Domitian	81–96	Trebonianus Gallus	251–253
Antonines		Aemilian	253
Nerva	96–98	Valerian	253–260
Trajan	97–117	Gallienus	253–268
Hadrian	117–138	Claudius II	
Antoninus Pius	138–161	Gothicus	268–270
Marcus		Aurelian	270–275
Aurelius	161–180	Tacitus	275–276
Lucius Verus		Florian	276
(co-emperor)	161–169	Probus	276–282
Commodus	180–192	Carus	282–283
Pertinax	193	Carinus	283–285
Didius Julianus	193	Numerian	283–284
Severi		**Diocletian and the Tetrarchy**	
Septimius		Diocletian	284–305
Severus	193–211	Maximian	286–305
Caracalla	211–217	Constantius	292–306
Macrinus	217–218	Galerius	293–311
Elagabalus	218–222	Licinius	311–323
Severus		**Dynasty of Constantine**	
Alexander	222–235	Constantine	306–337

⊙ Louisiana State University. "List of Roman Emperors to AD 235," http://skross.hist.lsu.edu/emperors.htm

Oxford University Press. *Oxford Illustrated Encyclopedia: Index and Ready Reference.* New York: Oxford University Press, 1993.

University of Illinois at Urbana-Champaign. "The Roman Achievement," www.classics.uiuc.edu/RomanCiv/Overheads/Emperors.htm

Czars and Czarinas of Russia

House	Monarch	Reign
Rurik		
	Daniel	1263–1303
	Yurii	1303–1325
	Ivan I (Kalita)	1325–1340
	Simeon (the Proud)	1340–1353
	Ivan II (the Gentle)	1353–1359
Grand Princes of Moscow-Vladimir		
	Dimitri Donskoi	1359–1389
	Basil I	1389–1425
	Basil II (the Blind)	1425–1462
	Ivan III (the Great)	1462–1505
	Ivan the Younger	1471–1490
	Basil III	1505–1533
Czars of Russia		
	Ivan IV (the Terrible)	1533–1584
	Theodore I	1584–1598
Godunov		
	Boris Godunov	1598–1605
	Theodore II	1605
	Dimitri	1605–1606

House	Monarch	Reign
Shuiskii		
	Basil IV Shuiskii	1606–1610
Romanov		
	Michael Romanov	1613–1645
	Alexis	1645–1676
	Theodore III	1676–1682
	Ivan V	1682–1696
	Peter I (the Great)	1682–1725
	Catherine I	1725–1727
	Peter II	1727–1730
	Anne	1730–1740
	Ivan VI	1740–1741
	Elizabeth	1741–1762
Holstein-Gottorp-Romanov		
	Peter III	1762
	Catherine II (the Great)	1762–1796
	Paul I	1796–1801
	Alexander I	1801–1825
	Nicholas I	1825–1855
	Alexander II	1855–1881
	Alexander III	1881–1894
	Nicholas II	1894–1917

⊙ Dukes, Paul. *A History of Russia: Medieval, Modern, Contemporary c. 882–1996*, 3d ed. Durham, N.C.: Duke University Press, 1998.

Lawrence, John. *A History of Russia: A Brilliant Chronicle of Russian History from Its Ancient Beginnings to the Present Day*, 7th ed., rev. New York: Meridian, 1993.

Rulers of Spain

House	Monarch	Reign
House of Habsburg		
	Charles I	1516–1556
	Philip II	1556–1598
	Philip III	1598–1621
	Philip IV	1621–1665
	Charles II	1665–1700
House of Bourbon		
	Philip V	1700–1724
	Louis I	1724
	Philip V (second reign)	1724–1746
	Ferdinand VI	1746–1759
	Charles III	1759–1788

House	Monarch	Reign
	Charles IV	1788–1808
	Ferdinand VII	1808
House of Bonaparte		
	Joseph Napoleon	1808–1813
House of Bourbon		
	Ferdinand VII (second reign)	1813–1833
	Isabel II	1833–1868
Provisional Government:		
		1868–1870

House of Savoy		Second Republic	
Amadeus I	1870–1873		1931–1939
First Republic		Spanish State	
	1873–1874	(Francisco	
House of Bourbon		Franco)	1939–1975
Alfonso XII	1874–1885	House of Bourbon	
Alfonso XIII	1886–1931	Juan Carlos I	1975–

⊙ Oxford University Press. *Oxford Illustrated Encyclopedia: Index and Ready Reference.*
New York: Oxford University Press, 1993.
Wetterau, Bruce. *World History.* New York: Henry Holt, 1994.

WORLD: *Religion*

Major World Religions

Religion	Approximate Number of Adherents	Religion	Approximate Number of Adherents
Christianity	2,000,000,000	Spiritism	14,000,000
Islam	1,200,000,000	Babi and Baha'i	6,000,000
Hinduism	880,000,000	Jainism	4,000,000
Buddhism	350,000,000	Shinto	4,000,000
Chinese traditional religion (including Confucianism and Taoism)	200,000,000	Cao Dai	3,000,000
		Tenrikyo	2,400,000
		Neo-Paganism	1,000,000
Primal (or tribal) indigenous religion (including animism, shamanism, and paganism)	190,000,000	Unitarian Universalism	800,000
		Scientology	750,000
		Rastafarianism	700,000
		Zoroastrianism	150,000
Yoruba	20,000,000	Nonreligion (including secularism, atheism, and agnosticism)	900,000,000
Juche	19,000,000		
Sikhism	18,000,000		
Judaism	16,000,000		

⊙ Adherents.com. "List of World's Major Religions,"
www.adherents.com/Religions_By_Adherents.html
Bach, Marcus. *Major Religions of the World.* Marina Del Rey, Calif.: DeVorss, 1984.

Major U.S. Religions and Their Principal Denominations

Religion and Denomination	Approximate Number of Adherents	Religion and Denomination	Approximate Number of Adherents
Christianity		Lutheran	9,000,000
Protestant	105,500,000	Presbyterian	5,000,000
Baptist	34,000,000	Pentecostal	3,200,000
Methodist	14,000,000	Episcopalian	3,000,000

Major U.S. Religions *(cont.)*

Religion and Denomination	Approximate Number of Adherents	Religion and Denomination	Approximate Number of Adherents
Mormon (Latter-Day Saints)	3,000,000	Conservative	1,600,000
		Reform	900,000
United Church of Christ	1,700,000	Orthodox	700,000
Church of Christ	1,600,000	Islam	1,000,000
Jehovah's Witnesses	1,300,000	Black Muslim	460,000
Mennonites	180,000		
Society of Friends (Quakers)	140,000	Unitarian Universalism	500,000
Amish Mennonites	50,000	Buddhism	400,000
Anglican Orthodox (Church of England)	6,000	Hinduism	230,000
Christianity		Baha'i	64,000
Roman Catholic	50,000,000	Native American traditional religion	50,000
Judaism	3,200,000	Scientology	45,000

⊙ Adherents.com. "List of World's Major Religions,"
   www.adherents.com/Religions_By_Adherents.html
   Bach, Marcus. *Major Religions of the World*. Marina Del Rey, Calif.: DeVorss, 1984.

Major Religious Holidays and Festivals

Religion	Holiday/Festival	Date*
Baha'i	Ayyam-i-Ha (Days of Ha)	February 25–March 1
	Feast of Ridvan	April 21–May 2
	Declaration of the Bab	May 23
	Ascension of Baha'u'llah	May 29
	Martyrdom of the Bab	July 9
	Birth of the Bab	October 20
	Birth of Baha'u'llah	November 12
	Ascension of Abdu'l-Baha	November 28
Buddhism	Magha Puja (Full Moon Day)	full moon of March or April*
	Songkran (Pi Mai)	April 12–14
	Vesak (Buddha Day)	full moon of May or June*
	Obon (Festival of the Dead)	July 13–15 or August 13–15 (regional)
	Loi Krathong	full moon of November*
Christianity (in U.S.)	Feast of the Epiphany	January 6
	Candlemas	February 2
	Shrove Tuesday	day before Ash Wednesday*
	Ash Wednesday (1st day of Lent)	between February 4 and March 10*
	Palm Sunday	Sunday before Easter*

(*movable date on Gregorian calendar)

	Maundy Thursday	day before Good Friday*
	Good Friday	Friday before Easter*
	Easter Sunday	between March 22 and April 25*
	Pentecost	seventh Sunday after Easter*
	All Saints' Day	November 1
	Christmas	December 25
Confucianism	Qing Ming (Ching Ming) Festival	106 days after winter solstice (April)*
	Chongmyo Taeje	first Sunday in May*
	Birth of Confucius	September 28
Hinduism	Vasant Panchami	waxing moon of January or February*
	Holi	waxing moon of February or March*
	Ram Navami (birth of Rama)	waxing moon of March or April*
	Naag Panchami	waxing moon of July or August*
	Janmashtami (birth of Krishna)	new moon of August or September*
	Ganesh Chathurthi	waxing moon of August or September*
	Durga Puja	waxing moon of September or October*
	Dhan Teras	2 days before Dewali*
	Dewali (Festival of Lights)	waning moon of October or November*
	Pongal	3 days in December and/or January*
	Kumbh Mela (Pitcher Fair)	once every 12 years*
Islam	Nawruz (New Year)	first day of 1st lunar month (usu. March 21)*
	Ashura	first 10 days of 1st lunar month*
	Data Ganj Baksh Death Festival	18th and 19th days of 2nd lunar month*
	Mawlid al-Nabi (birth of Prophet)	12th day of 3rd lunar month*
	Ramadan	all days of 9th lunar month (late autumn)*
	'Id al-Fitr (end of Ramadan fast)	first day of 10th lunar month*
	Hajj (Pilgrimage to Mecca)	8th–13th days of 12th lunar month*
	'Id al-Adha (Feast of Sacrifice)	10th–12th days of 12th lunar month*
Jainism	Mahavir Jayanti	waxing moon of March or April*
	Paryushana	8–10 days in August and/or September*
Judaism	Rosh Hashanah (New Year)	2 days in September and/or October*

Major Religious Holidays and Festivals *(cont.)*

Religion	Holiday/Festival	Date*
Judaism *(cont.)*	Yom Kippur (Day of Atonement)	between September 15 and October 13*
	Sukkot (Feast of Booths)	8–9 days in September and/or October*
	Shemini Atzeret	8th day of Sukkot*
	Simhat Torah	first 2 days following Sukkot*
	Hanukkah (Chanukah)	8 days in November and/or December*
	Purim	between February 25 and March 25*
	Passover	7–8 days in March and/or April*
	Shavuot	50th day after Passover*
Rastafarianism	Haile Selassie's Coronation Day	around November 15*
Shinto	Hari-Kuyo (Broken Needles)	February 8 (or December 8)
	Rice-Planting Festival at Osaka	June 14
	Bettara-Ichi (Pickle Market)	October 19
	Tori-no-Ichi (Eagle Market)	various days in November*
	Shichi-Go-San	November 15
Sikhism	Hola Mohalla	the day after the Hindu Holi festival*
	Vaisakh	first day of month of Vaisakha (April or May)*
	Guru Parab	full moon of October or November*
Taoism	Tam Kung Festival	8th day of 4th lunar month (usu. May)*
	Birth of Lu Pan	13th day of 6th lunar month (usu. July)*
	Festival of Hungry Ghosts	full moon of July or August*
	Festival of the Nine Imperial Gods	9 days in September and/or October*
Yoruba	Awoojoh (thanksgiving feast)	observed at any time of year
Zoroastrianism	Farvardegan Days	March 11–20 (or 10 days in July or August)
	Jamshed Navaroz (New Year)	March 21
	Khordad Sal	March 21 (or July 13 or August 15)
	Zarthastno Diso	April 30 (or May 29 or June 1)

⊙ Hartford Seminary Library. "Religious Holidays," www.library.hartsem.edu/guides/holidays/htm

Henderson, Helene, and Sue Ellen Thompson. *Holidays, Festivals, and Celebrations of the World Dictionary, Second Edition.* Detroit, Mich.: Omnigraphics, 1997.

Books of the Bible

Hebrew Bible (Old Testament)

Genesis	Ezra	Daniel
Exodus	Nehemiah	Hosea
Leviticus	Esther	Joel
Numbers	Job	Amos
Deuteronomy	Psalms	Obadiah
Joshua	Proverbs	Jonah
Judges	Ecclesiastes	Micah
Ruth	Song of Songs	Nahum
1 Samuel	(Song of Solomon)	Habakkuk
2 Samuel	Isaiah	Zephaniah
1 Kings	Jeremiah	Haggai
2 Kings	Lamentations	Zechariah
1 Chronicles	Ezekiel	Malachi
2 Chronicles		

New Testament

Matthew	Ephesians	Hebrews
Mark	Philippians	James
Luke	Colossians	1 Peter
John	1 Thessalonians	2 Peter
Acts	2 Thessalonians	1 John
Romans	1 Timothy	2 John
1 Corinthians	2 Timothy	3 John
2 Corinthians	Titus	Jude
Galatians	Philemon	Revelation

⊙ American Bible Society. www.americanbible.org/
New Revised Standard Version Bible with Apocrypha. New York: Oxford University Press, 1991.

Other Books of The Bible

Hebrew Bible Apocrypha

Of the numerous apocryphal works associated with the Old Testament, the most familiar are those that comprise the body of books known (primarily by Protestants) as the Apocrypha ("Hidden Books"). Protestants have rejected the authority of these works since the Reformation of the 16th century, but often include them as a separate section of the Bible. Roman Catholics and Greek Orthodox Christians embrace the holiness of a number of these books (usually 12 to 16 of them), which, when so considered, are called the Deuterocanonical Books ("Second-Level Books"). In addition, there are the works known collectively as the Pseudepigrapha ("False Writings"). These books, although associated with the Hebrew Bible, are regarded as strictly noncanonical.

Note: Because there is no universal agreement on which books belong to the Apocrypha, which books are recognized as authoritative, or even by which titles the books properly go, any classification of the apocryphal works is subject to dispute.

The Apocrypha (incorporating the Deuterocanonical Books)

1 Esdras
2 Esdras
1 Maccabees
2 Maccabees
3 Maccabees
Tobit
Judith
Ecclesiasticus (Sirach)

Wisdom of Solomon
1 Baruch (with Epistle of Jeremiah)
Prayer of Manasseh
Additions to Book of Daniel
Song of the Three Holy Children

Prayer of Azariah
Susanna
Bel and the Dragon
Additions to Book of Esther
Psalm 151

The Pseudepigrapha (selected works)

Jubilees
Letter of Aristeas
Books of Adam and Eve
Martyrdom of Isaiah
1 Enoch
2 Enoch

Testament of the Twelve Patriarchs
Sybilline Oracles
Assumption of Moses
2 Baruch

3 Baruch
4 Esdras
Psalms of Solomon
4 Maccabees (Story of Ahiqar)

New Testament Apocrypha

The extracanonical Christian writings associated with the New Testament are typically classified in accordance with the four major genres of New Testament literature: gospels, acts, epistles (letters), and apocalypses. Lacking a widely accepted definitive list of contents, this body of works includes the following books:

Gospels

Protoevangelium of James
Infancy Gospel of Thomas
Gospel of Peter

Gospel of Nicodemus
Gospel of the Nazoreans
Gospel of the Ebionites
Gospel of the Hebrews

Gospel of the Egyptians
Gospel of Thomas
Gospel of Philip
Gospel of Mary

Acts

Acts of John
Acts of Peter
Acts of Paul
Acts of Andrew
Acts of Thomas

Acts of Andrew and Matthias
Acts of Philip
Acts of Thaddaeus
Acts of Peter and Paul

Acts of Peter and Andrew
Martyrdom of Matthew
Slavonic Act of Peter
Acts of Peter and the Twelve Apostles

Epistles

3 Corinthians (Letter of Paul)
Epistle to the Laodiceans
Letters of Paul and Seneca

Didache (Teachings of the Twelve Apostles)
Letters of Jesus and Abgar
Epistle of Barnabas
Epistle to Diognetus

Letter of Lentulus
Letters of Ignatius
Letters of Clement to the Corinthians
Epistle of Titus

Apocalypses

Apocalypse of Peter
Coptic Apocalypse of Peter
Apocalypse of Paul
1 Apocalypse of James

2 Apocalypse of James
Apocryphon of John
Sophia of Jesus Christ
Letter of Peter to Philip

Apocalypse of Mary
Apocalypse of Bartholomew
Apocalypse of Thomas

⊙ Christian Classics Ethereal Library at Calvin College. "World Wide Study Bible," www.ccel.org/wwsb/
New Revised Standard Version Bible with Apocrypha. New York: Oxford University Press, 1991.

Roman Catholic Popes

Note: Where indicated, "antipope" identifies an individual whose election to the papacy has been contested, and therefore declared noncanonical.

Pope	Reign	Pope	Reign
St. Peter	c.32– c.64	St. Caius (Gaius)	283–296
St. Linus	c.66– c.78	St. Marcellinus	296–304
St. Anacletus (Cletus)	c.79– c.91	St. Marcellus I	306–308
St. Clement I	c.91– c.101	St. Eusebius	c.310
St. Evaristus	c.100– c.109	St. Miltiades	
St. Alexander I	c.109– c.116	(Melchiades)	311–314
St. Sixtus I (Xystus I)	c.116– c.125	St. Sylvester I	
St. Telesphorus	c.125– c.136	(St. Silvester I)	314–335
St. Hyginus	c.138– c.142	St. Mark	336
St. Pius I	c.142– c.155	St. Julius I	337–352
St. Anicetus	c.155– c.166	Liberius	352–366
St. Soter	c.166– c.174	St. Felix II	355–365
St. Eleutherius			*antipope*
(Eleutherus)	c.174–189	St. Damasus I	366–384
St. Victor I	189–198	Ursinus	366–367
St. Zephyrinus	199–217		*antipope*
St. Callistus I		St. Siricius	384–399
(Calixtus I)	217–222	St. Anastasius I	399–401
St. Hippolytus	217–235	St. Innocent I	401–417
	antipope	St. Zosimus	417–418
St. Urban I	222–230	Eulalius	418–419
St. Pontain	230–235		*antipope*
St. Anterus	235–236	St. Boniface I	418–422
St. Fabian	236–250	St. Celestine I	422–432
St. Cornelius	251–253	St. Sixtus III	
Novatian	251–258	(Xystus III)	432–440
	antipope	St. Leo I (the Great)	440–461
St. Lucius I	253–254	St. Hilarus (Hilary)	461–468
St. Stephen I	254–257	St. Simplicius	468–483
St. Sixtus II		St. Felix III (or II)	483–492
(St. Xystus II)	257–258	St. Gelasius I	492–496
St. Dionysius	260–268	Anastasius II	496–498
St. Felix I	269–274	St. Symmachus	498–514
St. Eutychian	275–283		

Pope	Reign	Pope	Reign
Lawrence	498–499; 501–506 *antipope*	St. Zacharius (St. Zachary)	741–752
		Stephen (II)	752 *(died before consecration)*
St. Hormisdas	514–523		
St. John I	523–526	Stephen II (or III)	752–757
St. Felix IV (or III)	526–530	St. Paul I	757–767
Dioscorus	530 *antipope (or pope)*	Constantine	767–768 *antipope*
Boniface II	530–532	Philip	768 *antipope*
John II	533–535	Stephen III (or IV)	768–772
St. Agapitus I (Agapetus I)	535–536	Adrian I (Hadrian I)	772–795
St. Silverius	536–537	St. Leo III	795–816
Vigilius	537–555	Stephen IV (or V)	816–817
Pelagius I	556–561	St. Paschal I	817–824
John III	561–574	Eugene II	824–827
Benedict I	575–579	Valentine	827
Pelagius II	579–590	Gregory IV	827–844
St. Gregory I (the Great)	590–604	John	844 *antipope*
Sabinian	604–606	Sergius II	844–847
Boniface III	607	St. Leo IV	847–855
St. Boniface IV	608–615	Benedict III	855–858
St. Deusdedit (Adeodatus I)	615–618	Anastasius Bibliothecarius	855 *antipope*
Boniface V	619–625	St. Nicholas I (the Great)	858–867
Honorius I	625–638	Adrian II (Hadrian II)	867–872
Severinus	640	John VIII	872–882
John IV	640–642	Marinus I	882–884
Theodore I	642–649	St. Adrian III (St. Hadrian III)	884–885
St. Martin I	649–653	Stephen V (or VI)	885–891
St. Eugene I	654–657	Formosus	891–896
St. Vitalian	657–672	Boniface VI	896
Adeodatus II	672–676	Stephen VI (or VII)	896–897
Donus	676–678	Romanus	897
St. Agatho	678–681	Theodore II	897
St. Leo II	682–683	John IX	898–900
St. Benedict II	684–685	Benedict IV	900–903
John V	685–686	Leo V	903
Conon	686–687	Christopher	903–904 *antipope*
Theodore	687 *antipope*		
Paschal	687 *antipope*	Sergius III	904–911
St. Sergius I	687–701	Anastasius III	911–913
John VI	701–705	Lando	913–914
John VII	705–707	John X	914–928
Sisinnius	708	Leo VI	928
Constantine	708–715	Stephen VII (or VIII)	928–931
St. Gregory II	715–731	John XI	931–935
St. Gregory III	731–741	Leo VII	936–939

Stephen VIII (or (IX)	939–942	Sylvester IV	
Marinus II	942–946	(Silvester IV)	1105–1111
Agapitus II			*antipope*
(Agapetus II)	946–955	Gelasius II	1118–1119
John XII	955–964	Gregory (VIII)	1118–1121
Leo VIII	963–965		*antipope*
Benedict V	964	Callistus II (Calixtus II)	1119–1124
John XIII	965–972	Honorius II	1124–1130
Benedict VI	973–974	Celestine (II)	1124 *antipope*
Boniface VII	974 *antipope*	Innocent II	1130–1143
Benedict VII	974–983	Anacletus II	1130–1138
John XIV	983–984		*antipope*
Boniface VII	984–985	Victor IV*	1138 *antipope*
	antipope	Celestine II	1143–1144
John XV	985–996	Lucius II	1144–1145
Gregory V	996–999	Blessed Eugene III	1145–1153
John XVI	997–998	Anastasius IV	1153–1154
	antipope	Adrian IV (Hadrian IV)	1154–1159
Sylvester II		Alexander III	1159–1181
(Silvester II)	999–1003	Victor IV (*not the same*)	1159–1164
John XVII	1003		*antipope*
John XVIII	1003–1009	Paschal III	1164–1168
Sergius IV	1009–1012		*antipope*
Benedict VIII	1012–1024	Calistus III	
Gregory (VI)	1012 *antipope*	(Calixtus III)	1168–1178
John XIX	1024–1032		*antipope*
Benedict IX	1032–1044	Innocent (III)	1179–1180
Sylvester III			*antipope*
(Silvester III)	1045	Lucius III	1181–1185
Benedict IX	1045	Urban I!I	1185–1187
Gregory VI	1045–1046	Gregory VIII	1187
Clement II	1046–1047	Clement III	1187–1191
Benedict IX	1047–1048	Celestine III	1191–1198
Damasus II	1048	Innocent III	1198–1216
St. Leo IX	1049–1054	Honorius III	1216–1227
Victor II	1055–1057	Gregory IX	1227–1241
Stephen IX (or X)	1057–1058	Celestine IV	1241
Benedict X	1058–1059	Innocent IV	1243–1254
	antipope	Alexander IV	1254–1261
Nicholas II	1058–1061	Urban IV	1261–1264
Alexander II	1061–1073	Clement IV	1265–1268
Honorius (II)	1061–1064	Blessed Gregory X	1271–1276
	antipope	Blessed Innocent V	1276
St. Gregory VII	1073–1085	Adrian V (Hadrian V)	1276
Clement III (Guibert)	1080;	John XXI	1276–1277
	1084–1100	Nicholas III	1277–1280
	antipope	Martin IV	1281–1285
Blessed Victor III	1086–1087	Honorius IV	1285–1287
Blessed Urban II	1088–1099	Nicholas IV	1288–1292
Paschal II	1099–1118	St. Celestine V	1294
Theoderic	1100–1101	Boniface VIII	1294–1303
	antipope	Blessed Benedict XI	1303–1304
Albert (Adalbert)	1101 *antipope*	Clement V	1305–1314

Roman Catholic Popes *(cont.)*

Pope	Reign	Pope	Reign
John XXII	1316–1334	Marcellus II	1555
Nicholas (V)	1328–1330 *antipope*	Paul IV	1555–1559
		Pius IV	1559–1565
Benedict XII	1334–1342	St. Pius V	1566–1572
Clement VI	1342–1352	Gregory XIII	1572–1585
Innocent VI	1352–1362	Sixtus V	1585–1590
Blessed Urban V	1362–1370	Urban VII	1590
Gregory XI	1370–1378	Gregory XIV	1590–1591
Urban VI	1378–1389	Innocent IX	1591
Clement (VII)	1378–1394 *antipope*	Clement VIII	1592–1605
		Leo XI	1605
Boniface IX	1389–1404	Paul V	1605–1621
Benedict (XIII)	1394–1417 *antipope*	Gregory XV	1621–1623
		Urban VIII	1623–1644
Innocent VII	1404–1406	Innocent X	1644–1655
Gregory XII	1406–1415	Alexander VII	1655–1667
Alexander V	1409–1415 *antipope*	Clement IX	1667–1669
		Clement X	1670–1676
John (XXIII)	1410–1429 *antipope*	Blessed Innocent XI	1676–1689
		Alexander VIII	1689–1691
Martin V	1417–1431	Innocent XII	1691–1700
Clement (VIII)	1423–1429 *antipope*	Clement XI	1700–1721
		Innocent XIII	1721–1724
Benedict (XIV)	1425–c.1430 *antipope*	Benedict XIII	1724–1730
		Clement XII	1730–1740
Eugene IV	1431–1447	Benedict XIV	1740–1758
Felix V	1439–1449 *antipope*	Clement XIII	1758–1769
		Clement XIV	1769–1774
Nicholas V	1447–1455	Pius VI	1775–1799
Callistus III (Calixtus III)	1455–1458	Pius VII	1800–1823
		Leo XII	1823–1829
Pius II	1458–1464	Pius VIII	1829–1830
Paul II	1464–1471	Gregory XVI	1831–1846
Sixtus IV	1471–1484	Pius IX	1846–1878
Innocent VIII	1484–1492	Leo XIII	1878–1903
Alexander VI	1492–1503	St. Pius X	1903–1914
Pius III	1503	Benedict XV	1914–1922
Julius II	1503–1513	Pius XI	1922–1939
Leo X	1513–1521	Pius XII	1939–1958
Adrian VI (Hadrian VI)	1522–1523	John XXIII	1958–1963
Clement VII	1523–1534	Paul VI	1963–1978
Paul III	1534–1549	John Paul I	1978
Julius III	1550–1555	John Paul II	1978–

⊙ Kelly, J. N. D. *The Oxford Dictionary of Popes.* New York: Oxford University Press, 1989.

New Advent. "Catholic Encyclopedia: The List of Popes," www.newadvent.org/cathen/12272b.htm

Roman Catholic Patron Saints

Note: Any one group may claim the patronage of several saints. What follows is a selection of those saints who are typically associated with the groups listed, along with the traditionally observed date of each saint's Memorial/Feast Day.

Patron of	Saint	Day
Abandoned Children	Jerome Emiliani	Feb. 8
Accountants	Matthew	Sep. 21
Actors	Genesius	Aug. 25
Advertisers	Bernadine of Siena	May 20
Air Travelers	Joseph of Cupertino	Sep. 18
Altar Servers	John Berchmans	Nov. 26
Anesthetists	Rene Goupil	Oct.19
Animals	Francis of Assisi	Oct. 4
Archaeologists	Damasus I	Dec. 11
Archers	Sebastian	Jan. 20
Architects	Barbara	Dec. 4
Armies	Maurice	Sep. 22
Art & Artists	Catherine of Bologna	Mar. 9
Astronauts	Joseph of Cupertino	Sep. 18
Astronomers	Dominic	Aug. 8
Athletes	Sebastian	Jan. 20
Authors	Francis de Sales	Jan. 24
Babies	Nicholas of Tolentino	Sep. 10
Bakers	Elizabeth of Hungary	Nov. 17
Bankers	Matthew	Sep. 21
Barbers	Martin de Porres	Nov. 3
Basket Makers	Anthony the Abbot	Jan. 17
Beekeepers	Ambrose	Dec. 7
Beggars	Giles	Sep. 1
Birds	Gall	Oct.16
Blacksmiths	Dunstan	May 19
Blind	Raphael the Archangel	Sep. 29
Bookbinders	Celestine V	May 19
Bookkeepers	Matthew	Sep. 21
Booksellers	John of God	Mar. 8
Boys	Dominic Savio	Mar. 9
Brewers	Augustine of Hippo	Aug. 28
Bricklayers	Stephen	Dec. 26
Brides	Nicholas of Myra	Dec. 6
Broadcasters	Gabriel the Archangel	Sep. 29
Builders	Vincent Ferrer	Apr. 5
Businessmen	Homobonus	Nov. 13
Businesswomen	Margaret of Clitherow	Mar. 26
Butchers	Adrian of Nicomedia	Sep. 8
Cab Drivers	Fiacre	Sep. 1
Cancer Victims	Peregrine Laziosi	May 1
Candle Makers	Ambrose	Dec. 7
Carpenters	Joseph	Mar. 19/May 1
Cattle Breeders	Mark the Evangelist	Apr. 25
Chaplains	John of Capistrano	Oct. 23
Charities	Vincent de Paul	Sep. 27

Roman Catholic Patron Saints *(cont.)*

Patron of	Saint	Day
Childbirth	Gerard Majella	Oct. 16
Children	Nicholas of Myra	Dec. 6
Childless Women	Anne (Mother of Mary)	July 26
Choirs	Dominic Savio	Mar. 9
Church	Joseph	Mar. 19/May 1
Civil Servants	Thomas More	June 22
Clerics	Thomas a Becket	Dec. 29
Colleges	Thomas Aquinas	Jan. 28
Comedians	Vitus	June 15
Cooks	Martha	July 29
Court Clerks	Thomas More	June 22
Craftspeople	Eligius (Eloi)	Dec. 1
Criminals	Dismas	Mar. 25
Cripples	Giles	Sep. 1
Dairy Workers	Brigid of Ireland	Feb. 1
Dancers	Vitus	June 15
Deaf	Francis de Sales	Jan. 24
Dentists	Apollonia	Feb. 9
Desperate Cases	Jude	Oct. 28
Domestic Workers	Zita	Apr. 27
Doubters	Joseph	Mar. 19/May 1
Drought Relief	Herbert	Mar. 20
Dyers	Maurice	Sep. 22
Dying	Joseph	Mar. 19/May 1
Ecologists	Francis of Assisi	Oct. 4
Editors	John Bosco	Jan. 31
Education, Public	Martin de Porres	Nov. 3
Embroiderers	Clare of Assisi	Aug. 11
Emigrants	Frances Xavier Cabrini	Nov. 13
Falsely Accused	Raymond Nonnatus	Aug. 31
Farmers	Isidore the Farmer	May 15
Farm Workers	Benedict	July 11
Fathers	Joseph	Mar. 19/May 1
Firefighters	Florian	May 4
Fire Prevention	Catherine of Siena	Apr. 29
Fishermen	Andrew	Nov. 30
Florists	Therese of Lisieux	Oct. 1
Foundlings	Holy Innocents	Dec. 28
Funeral Directors	Joseph of Arimathea	Mar. 17
Gardeners	Adelard	Jan. 2
Garment Workers	Homobonus	Nov. 13
Geese	Martin of Tours	Nov. 11
Girls	Agnes of Rome	Jan. 21
Glassworkers	Luke	Oct. 18
Gravediggers	Anthony the Abbot	Jan. 17
Grocers	Michael the Archangel	Sep. 29/May 8
Hairdressers	Martin de Porres	Nov. 3
Harvest	Anthony of Padua	June 13
Health Inspectors	Raphael the Archangel	Sep. 29
Heart Patients	John of God	Mar. 8
Highways	John the Baptist	June 24

Horse Riders	Martin of Tours	Nov. 11
Horses	Hippolytus of Rome	Aug. 13
Hospitals	Camillus de Lellis	July 14
Hotelkeepers	Amand	Feb. 6
Housewives	Martha	July 29
Hunters	Hubert	Nov. 3
Immigrants	Frances Xavier Cabrini	Nov. 13
Impossible Cases	Rita Cascia	May 22
Infertile Women	Anthony of Padua	June 13
Invalids	Roch	Aug. 16
Jewelers	Eligius (Eloi)	Dec. 1
Journalists	Francis de Sales	Jan. 24
Judges & Jurists	John of Capistrano	Oct. 23
Juvenile Delinquents	Dominic Savio	Mar. 9
Laborers	Isidore the Farmer	May 15
Lacemakers	Luke	Oct. 18
Lawyers	Thomas More	June 22
Learning	Ambrose	Dec. 7
Leatherworkers	Crispin & Crispinian	Oct. 25
Lecturers	Justin	June 1
Lepers	Giles	Sep. 1
Librarians	Jerome	Sep. 30
Lighthouse Keepers	Venerius	May 4
Lost Articles	Anthony of Padua	June 13
Lovers	Valentine	Feb. 14
Maids	Zita	Apr. 27
Mariners	Nicholas of Tolentino	Sep. 10
Married Women	Monica	Aug. 27
Mentally Ill	Dymphna	May 15
Merchants	Francis of Assisi	Oct. 4
Messengers	Gabriel the Archangel	Sep. 29
Metalworkers	Eligius (Eloi)	Dec. 1
Midwives	Raymond Nonnatus	Aug. 31
Migrants	Frances Xavier Cabrini	Nov. 13
Milliners	James the Greater	July 25
Miners	Anne (Mother of Mary)	July 26
Missionary Priests	Vincent Pallotti	Jan. 22
Missions	Therese of Lisieux	Oct. 1
Motorists	Frances of Rome	Mar. 9
Mothers	Monica	Aug. 27
Mountain Climbers	Bernard of Montjoux	May 28
Munitions Workers	Erasmus (Elmo)	June 2
Musicians	Cecilia	Nov. 22
Navigators	Francis of Paola	Apr. 2
Notaries	Mark	Apr. 25
Nurses	Agatha	Feb. 5
Nursing Mothers	Basilissa	May 20
Orators	John Chrysostom	Sep. 13
Orphans	Jerome Emiliani	Feb. 8
Painters	Luke	Oct. 18
Pallbearers	Joseph of Arimathea	Mar. 17
Paratroopers	Michael the Archangel	Sep. 29
Pawnbrokers	Nicholas of Myra	Dec. 6
Pets	Anthony the Abbot	Jan. 17

Roman Catholic Patron Saints *(cont.)*

Patron of	Saint	Day
Pharmacists	Cosmas & Damian	Sep. 26
Philatelists	Gabriel the Archangel	Sep. 29
Philosophers	Catherine of Alexandria	Nov. 25
Physicians	Luke	Oct. 18
Plasterers	Bartholomew	Aug. 24
Poets	Columba	June 9
Police Officers	Michael the Archangel	Sep. 29
Poor	Anthony of Padua	June 13
Postal Workers	Gabriel the Archangel	Sep. 29
Preachers	Catherine of Alexandria	Nov. 25
Pregnant Women	Gerard Majella	Oct. 16
Priests	John Vianney	Aug. 4
Printers	Genesius	Aug. 25
Prisoners	Dismas	Mar. 25
Prison Guards	Adrian of Nicomedia	Sep. 8
Radio Workers	Gabriel the Archangel	Sep. 29
Rape Victims	Maria Goretti	July 6
Rheumatism	James the Greater	July 25
Rulers	Ferdinand III of Castile	May 30
Sailors	Erasmus (Elmo)	June 2
Scholars	Brigid of Ireland	Feb. 1
Schools	Thomas Aquinas	Jan. 28
Scientists	Albert the Great	Nov. 15
Scripture Scholars	Jerome	Sep. 30
Sculptors	Claude	Feb. 15
Secretaries	Genesius	Aug. 25
Security Guards	Matthew	Sep. 21
Senior Citizens	Anthony of Padua	June 13
Servants	Martha	July 29
Shepherds	Cuthman	Feb. 8
Shoemakers	Crispin & Crispinian	Oct. 25
Sick	John of God	Mar. 8
Silversmiths	Andronicus	Oct. 11
Skaters	Lidwina (Lydwina)	Apr. 14
Skiers	Bernard of Montjoux	May 28
Sleepwalkers	Dymphna	May 15
Snakebite Victims	Hilary of Poitiers	Jan. 13
Social Justice	Joseph	Mar. 19/May 1
Social Workers	Louise de Marillac	Mar. 15
Soldiers	Martin of Tours	Nov. 11
Souls in Purgatory	Nicholas of Tolentino	Sep. 10
Spinners	Parasceva	Oct. 14
Stenographers	Cassian	Dec. 3
Stonemasons	Stephen	Dec. 26
Storms, Safety in	Vitus	June 15
Stroke Victims	Andrew Avellino	Nov. 10
Students	Thomas Aquinas	Jan. 28
Surgeons	Cosmas & Damian	Sep. 26
Surveyors	Thomas	July 3

Swimmers	Adjutor	Apr. 30
Tailors	Homobonus	Nov. 13
Tax Collectors	Matthew	Sep. 21
Taxi Drivers	Fiacre	Sep. 1
Teachers	John Baptist de la Salle	Apr. 7
Television	Clare of Assisi	Aug. 11
Theologians	Alphonsus	Aug. 1
Throat Ailments	Blaise	Feb. 3
Toothaches	Apollonia	Feb. 9
Tradespeople	Homobonus	Nov. 13
Travelers	Raphael the Archangel	Sep. 29
Undertakers	Dismas	Mar. 25
Universities	Contardo Ferrini	Oct. 17
Unmarried Men	Benezet	Apr. 14
Unmarried Women	Nicholas of Myra	Dec. 6
Veterinarians	Eligius (Eloi)	Dec. 1
Vintners	Morand	June 3
Vocations	Alphonsus	Aug. 1
Waitpersons	Martha	July 29
Weavers	Parasceva	Oct. 14
Widows	Paula	Jan. 26
Winegrowers	Vincent of Saragossa	Jan. 22
Women in Labor	Anne (Mother of Mary)	July 26
Workers	Joseph	Mar. 19/May 1
Writers	Francis de Sales	Jan. 24
Youth	Aloysius Gonzaga	June 2

⊙ Adels, Jill Haak. *The Wisdom of the Saints: An Anthology.* New York: Oxford University Press, 1989.

Catholic Community Forum. "Patron Saints Index," www.catholic-forum.com/saints/indexsnt.htm

Catholic Online Saints. "Patron Saints," http://saints.catholic.org/patron.html

Deities of Classical Mythology

Greek

Name	Realm, Position, or Symbolism	Name	Realm, Position, or Symbolism
Adonis	god of the cycle of vegetation; personification of beautiful youth	Athena	goddess of wisdom
		Carpo	goddess of summer fruit
Aeolus	god of the winds	Chaos	personification of confusion
Amphitrite	goddess of the oceans		
Aphrodite	goddess of love and beauty	Chloris	goddess of flowers
Apollo	god of youth, music, poetry, archery, and prophecy	Cronus	ruler of the Titans, after deposing his father, Uranus
		Demeter	goddess of grains and harvest
Ares	god of war		
Artemis	goddess of the hunt and the moon	Dionysus	god of wine
		Enyo	goddess of war
Asclepius	god of medicine and healing	Eos	goddess of the dawn
		Eris	goddess of discord

Deities of Classical Mythology *(cont.)*

Name	Realm, Position, or Symbolism	Name	Realm, Position, or Symbolism
Eros	god of love	Melpomene	muse of tragedy
Fates (or Moirai)	3 goddesses of human destiny (Atropos, Clotho, Lachesis)	Polyhymnia	muse of sacred poetry
		Terpsichore	muse of dance
		Thalia	muse of comedy
Graces (or Charities)	personification of charm, grace, and beauty; 3 daughters of Zeus (Aglaia, Euphrosyne, Thalia)	Urania	muse of astronomy
		Nemesis	goddess of vengeance
		Nereids	sea nymphs
		Nereus	old sea god; father of the Nereids
Hades (or Pluto)	god of the underworld	Nike	goddess of victory
Hebe	cupbearer of the gods	Nymphs	female spirits of nature
Hecate	goddess of dark places	Nyx	goddess of night
Helios	god of the sun	Pan	god of shepherds, flocks, forests, and pastures
Hephaestus	god of fire and the forge		
Hera	queen of the goddesses; wife and sister of Zeus	Persephone	queen of the underworld; goddess of spring
Heracles	superhuman hero; performed 12 labors to win immortality	Pleiades	seven daughters of Atlas; changed into cluster of stars by Zeus
Hermaphroditus	a male-female deity, having been joined as one with the nymph Salmacis	Plutus	god of wealth
		Poseidon	god of the oceans
		Priapus	god of fertility
		Psyche	female personification of the soul
Hermes	messenger of the gods	Rhea	wife of Cronus; mother of Zeus
Hestia	goddess of the hearth		
Hygeia	goddess of health		
Hymen	god of marriage	Satyrs	gods of woodlands
Hypnos	god of sleep	Selene	goddess of the moon
Irene (or Eirene)	goddess of peace	Sirens	sea nymphs and enchantresses
Iris	goddess of the rainbow	Thanatos	god of death
Masyas	satyr flayed to death after losing flute-playing contest to Apollo	Themis	personification of order and justice; daughter of Uranus and Gaia
Metis	personification of prudence; first wife of Zeus		
		Titans	children of Uranus, who helped, then defeated, Cronus
Morpheus	god of dreams		
Muses	9 sisters; goddesses of arts/sciences:	Triton	trumpeter of the sea; son of Poseidon
Calliope	chief of the Muses	Tyche	goddess of fortune
Clio	muse of history	Uranus	god of heaven; father of the Titans
Erato	muse of erotic poetry		
Euterpe	muse of lyric poetry	Zeus	chief god of Olympus

Roman

Name	Realm, Position, or Symbolism	Name	Realm, Position, or Symbolism
Aesculapius	god of medicine and healing	Lemures	spirits of the dead
Apollo	god of youth, music, poetry, archery, and prophecy	Libitina	goddess of the underworld
		Lucina	goddess of childbirth
Aurora	goddess of the dawn	Luna	goddess of the moon
Bacchus (or Liber)	god of wine	Mars	god of war
		Mercury	messenger of the gods
Bellona	goddess of war		
Ceres	goddess of grains and harvest	Minerva	goddess of wisdom
		Mors	god of death
Coelus	god of heaven	Neptune	god of the oceans
Cupid (or Amor)	god of love	Nox	goddess of night
		Orcus (or Pluto)	god of the underworld
Diana	goddess of the hunt and the moon	Picus	god who could predict the future
Discordia	goddess of discord	Pomona	goddess of fruit trees and their fruit
Fauna	goddess of fields		
Faunus (or Inuus)	god of shepherds and flocks	Proserpina	queen of the under-world;
Flora	goddess of flowers	(Persipina)	goddess of spring
Fortuna	goddess of fortune	Psyche	female personification of the soul
Graces (or Gratiae)	personification of charm, grace, and beauty; 3 daughters of Jupiter (Aglaia, Euphrosyne, Thalia)	Salacia	goddess of the oceans
		Saturn	god of agriculture (equivalent of Greeks' Cronus)
Hercules	superhuman hero; performed 12 labors to win immortality	Sol	god of the sun
		Somnus	god of sleep
Janus	god of beginnings, especially of the year and the seasons	Silvanus (Sylvanus)	god of forests and un-cultivated land
		Tartarus	primeval god of the underworld
Juno	queen of the goddesses; wife of Jupiter	Terminus	guardian of boundaries
		Trivia	goddess of dark places
Jupiter (or Jove)	chief of all gods	Venus	goddess of love and beauty
Juturna	goddess of springs of water		
		Vesta	goddess of the hearth
Juventas	goddess of youth	Victoria	goddess of victory
Juventus	god of youth	Voluptas	goddess of pleasure
Lares and Penates	household gods who watch over homes and cities	Vulcan	god of fire and the forge

⊙ Hamilton, Edith. *Mythology*. Boston: Little, Brown, 1950.
  Morford, Mark P. O., and Robert J. Lenardon. *Classical Mythology, Sixth Edition*. New York: Oxford University Press, 1999.
  ThinkQuest. "Mythology," http://library.thinkquest.org/25535/

UNITED STATES: *Government and History*
U.S. Presidents

President	Party	Life Dates	Term	Vice President
George Washington	Federalist	1732–1799	1789–1797	John Adams
John Adams	Federalist	1735–1826	1797–1801	Thomas Jefferson
Thomas Jefferson	Democratic-Republican	1743–1826	1801–1809	Aaron Burr; George Clinton
James Madison	Democratic-Republican	1751–1836	1809–1817	George Clinton; Elbridge Gerry
James Monroe	Democratic-Republican	1758–1831	1817–1825	Daniel D. Tompkins
John Quincy Adams	Democratic-Republican	1767–1848	1825–1829	John C. Calhoun
Andrew Jackson	Democratic	1767–1845	1829–1837	John C. Calhoun; Martin Van Buren
Martin Van Buren	Democratic	1782–1862	1837–1841	Richard M. Johnson
William Henry Harrison	Whig	1773–1841	1841	John Tyler
John Tyler	Whig	1790–1862	1841–1845	
James Knox Polk	Democratic	1795–1849	1845–1849	George M. Dallas
Zachary Taylor	Whig	1784–1850	1849–1850	Millard Fillmore
Millard Fillmore	Whig	1800–1874	1850–1853	
Franklin Pierce	Democratic	1804–1869	1853–1857	William R. King
James Buchanan	Democratic	1791–1868	1857–1861	John C. Breckinridge
Abraham Lincoln	Republican	1809–1865	1861–1865	Hannibal Hamlin; Andrew Johnson
Andrew Johnson	Union	1808–1875	1865–1869	
Ulysses Simpson Grant (b. Hiram Ulysses Grant)	Republican	1822–1885	1869–1877	Schuyler Colfax; Henry Wilson
Rutherford Birchard Hayes	Republican	1822–1893	1877–1881	William A. Wheeler
James Abram Garfield	Republican	1831–1881	1881	Chester A. Arthur
Chester Alan Arthur	Republican	1829–1886	1881–1885	
Stephen Grover Cleveland	Democratic	1837–1908	1885–1889	Thomas A. Hendricks
Benjamin Harrison	Republican	1833–1901	1889–1893	Levi P. Morton
[Stephen] Grover Cleveland	Democratic	1837–1908	1893–1897	Adlai E. Stevenson
William McKinley	Republican	1843–1901	1897–1901	Garret A. Hobart; Theodore Roosevelt
Theodore Roosevelt	Republican	1858–1919	1901–1909	Charles W. Fairbanks
William Howard Taft	Republican	1857–1930	1909–1913	James S. Sherman
[Thomas] Woodrow Wilson	Democratic	1856–1924	1913–1921	Thomas R. Marshall
Warren Gamaliel Harding	Republican	1865–1923	1921–1923	Calvin Coolidge
[John] Calvin Coolidge	Republican	1872–1933	1923–1929	Charles G. Dawes
Herbert Clark Hoover	Republican	1874–1964	1929–1933	Charles Curtis
Franklin Delano Roosevelt	Democratic	1882–1945	1933–1945	John N. Garner; Henry A. Wallace; Harry S. Truman
Harry S. Truman	Democratic	1884–1972	1945–1953	Alben W. Barkley
Dwight David Eisenhower	Republican	1890–1969	1953–1961	Richard M. Nixon

John Fitzgerald Kennedy	Democratic	1917–1963	1961–1963	Lyndon B. Johnson
Lyndon Baines Johnson	Democratic	1908–1973	1963–1969	Hubert H. Humphrey
Richard Milhous Nixon	Republican	1913–1994	1969–1974	Spiro T. Agnew; Gerald R. Ford
Gerald Rudolph Ford (b. Leslie Lynch King)	Republican	1913–	1974–1977	Nelson A. Rockefeller
James Earl Carter, Jr.	Democratic	1924–	1977–1981	Walter F. Mondale
Ronald Wilson Reagan	Republican	1911–	1981–1989	George Bush
George Herbert Walker Bush	Republican	1924–	1989–1993	J. Danforth Quayle
William Jefferson Clinton (b. William Jefferson Blythe)	Democratic	1946–	1993–2001	Albert A. Gore, Jr.

⊙ The White House. "Presidents of the United States," www.whitehouse.gov/WH/glimpse/presidents/html/presidents/html
Patrick, John J. et al. *The Oxford Guide to the U.S. Government.* New York: Oxford University Press, 2001.

First Ladies of the United States

First Lady	Life Dates	President	Term	Notes
Martha Dandridge Custis Washington	1731–1802	George Washington	1789–1797	
Abigail Smith Adams	1744–1818	John Adams	1797–1801	
Martha Jefferson Randolph	1772–1836	Thomas Jefferson	1801–1809	Jefferson's elder daughter
Dolley Payne Todd Madison	1768–1849	James Madison	1809–1817	
Elizabeth Kortright Monroe	1763–1830	James Monroe	1817–1825	
Louisa Catherine Johnson Adams	1775–1852	John Quincy Adams	1825–1829	
Emily Donelson	1809–1836	Andrew Jackson	1829–1836	Jackson's niece
Sarah Yorke Jackson	1805–1887	Andrew Jackson	1836–1837	Jackson's daughter-in-law
Angelica Singleton Van Buren	1816–1878	Martin Van Buren	1838–1841	Van Buren's daughter-in-law
Anna Symmes Harrison	1775–1864	William Henry Harrison	1841	
Letitia Christian Tyler	1790–1842	John Tyler	1841–1842	
Julia Gardiner Tyler	1820–1889	John Tyler	1844–1845	
Sarah Childress Polk	1803–1891	James K. Polk	1845–1849	
Margaret Smith Taylor	1788–1852	Zachary Taylor	1849–1850	nickname: Peggy
Abigail Powers Fillmore	1798–1853	Millard Fillmore	1850–1853	
Jane Appleton Pierce	1806–1863	Franklin Pierce	1853–1857	
Harriet Rebecca Lane	1830–1903	James Buchanan	1857–1861	Buchanan's niece
Mary Ann Todd Lincoln	1818–1882	Abraham Lincoln	1861–1865	
Eliza McCardle Johnson	1810–1876	Andrew Johnson	1865–1869	
Julia Dent Grant	1826–1902	Ulysses S. Grant	1869–1877	

First Lady	Life Dates	President	Term	Notes
Lucy Webb Hayes	1831–1889	Rutherford B. Hayes	1877–1881	nickname: "Lemonade Lucy" (for White House temperance policy)
Lucretia Rudolph Garfield	1832–1918	James Garfield	1881	nickname: Crete
Mary Arthur McElroy	1836–1916	Chester Alan Arthur	1881–1885	Arthur's sister
Rose Elizabeth Cleveland	1846–1918	Grover Cleveland	1885–1886	Cleveland's sister; served until his 1886 marriage
Frances Folsom Cleveland	1864–1947	Grover Cleveland	1886–1889	nickname: Frankie
Caroline Lavinia Scott Harrison	1832–1892	Benjamin Harrison	1889–1892	nickname: Carrie
Ida Saxton McKinley	1847–1907	William McKinley	1897–1901	
Edith Kermit Carow Roosevelt	1861–1948	Theodore Roosevelt	1901–1909	nickname: Edie
Helen Herron Taft	1861–1943	William Howard Taft	1909–1913	nickname: Nellie
Ellen Axson Wilson	1860–1914	Woodrow Wilson	1913–1914	nickname: Ellie
Edith Bolling Galt Wilson	1872–1961	Woodrow Wilson	1915–1921	
Florence Kling de Wolfe Harding	1860–1924	Warren G. Harding	1921–1923	nickname: Flossie
Grace Goodhue Coolidge	1879–1957	Calvin Coolidge	1923–1929	
Lou Henry Hoover	1874–1944	Herbert Hoover	1929–1933	
Anna Eleanor Roosevelt	1884–1962	Franklin D. Roosevelt	1933–1945	
Elizabeth Virginia Wallace Truman	1885–1982	Harry S. Truman	1945–1953	nickname: Bess
Mamie Geneva Doud Eisenhower	1896–1979	Dwight D. Eisenhower	1953–1961	
Jacqueline Lee Bouvier Kennedy	1929–1994	John Fitzgerald Kennedy	1961–1963	nickname: Jackie
Claudia Alta Taylor Johnson	1912–	Lyndon B. Johnson	1963–1969	nickname: Lady Bird
Thelma Catharine Ryan Nixon	1912–93	Richard M. Nixon	1969–1974	nickname: Pat
Elizabeth Ann Bloomer Warren Ford	1918–	Gerald R. Ford	1974–1977	nickname: Betty
Eleanor Rosalynn Smith Carter	1927–	Jimmy Carter	1977–1981	
Anne Francis Robbins Davis Reagan	1921–	Ronald Reagan	1981–1989	nickname: Nancy
Barbara Pierce Bush	1925–	George Bush	1989–1993	
Hillary Diane Rodham Clinton	1947–	Bill Clinton	1993–2001	

⊙ The First Ladies Library. "The First Ladies Library," www.firstladies.org/
The White House. "The First Ladies," www.whitehouse.gov/WH/glimpse/
firstladies/html/firstladies.html.

U.S. Vice Presidents

Name	Party	Life Dates	Term	President
John Adams	Federalist	1735–1826	1789–97	George Washington
Thomas Jefferson	Democratic-Republican	1743–1826	1797–1801	John Adams
Aaron Burr	Democratic-Republican	1756–1836	1801–05	Thomas Jefferson
George Clinton	Democratic-Republican	1739–1812	1805–12	Thomas Jefferson; James Madison
Elbridge Gerry	Democratic-Republican	1744–1814	1813–14	James Madison
Daniel D. Tompkins	Democratic-Republican	1774–1825	1817–25	James Monroe
John Caldwell Calhoun	Democratic-Republican	1782–1850	1825–32	John Quincy Adams; Andrew Jackson
Martin Van Buren	Democratic	1782–1862	1833–37	Andrew Jackson
Richard Mentor Johnson	Democratic	1780–1850	1837–41	Martin Van Buren
John Tyler	Whig	1790–1862	1841	William Henry Harrison
George Miflin Dallas	Democratic	1792–1864	1845–49	James K. Polk
Millard Filmore	Whig	1800–74	1849–50	Zachary Taylor
William Rufus DeVane King	Democratic	1786–1853	1853	Franklin Pierce
John Cabel Breckinridge	Democratic	1821–75	1857–61	James Buchanan
Hannibal Hamlin	Republican	1809–91	1861–65	Abraham Lincoln
Andrew Johnson	Union	1808–75	1865	Abraham Lincoln
Schuyler Colfax	Republican	1823–85	1869–73	Ulysses S. Grant
Henry Wilson	Republican	1812–75	1873–75	Ulysses S. Grant
William Alnom Wheeler	Republican	1819–87	1877–81	Rutherford B. Hayes
Chester Alan Arthur	Republican	1829–86	1881	James Garfield
Thomas Andrews Hendricks	Democratic	1819–85	1885	[S.] Grover Cleveland
Levi Parsons Morton	Republican	1824–1920	1889–93	Benjamin Harrison
Adlai Ewing Stevenson	Democratic	1835–1914	1893–97	[S.] Grover Cleveland
Garret Augustus Hobart	Republican	1844–99	1897–99	William McKinley
Theodore Roosevelt	Republican	1858–1919	1901	William McKinley
Charles Warren Fairbanks	Republican	1852–1918	1905–09	Theodore Roosevelt
James Schoolcraft Sherman	Republican	1855–1912	1909–12	William H. Taft
Thomas Riley Marshall	Democratic	1854–1925	1913–21	[T.] Woodrow Wilson
[John] Calvin Coolidge	Republican	1872–1933	1921–23	Warren Harding
Charles Gates Davies	Republican	1865–1951	1925–29	[J.] Calvin Coolidge
Charles Curtis	Republican	1860–1936	1929–33	Herbert Hoover
John Nance Garner	Democratic	1868–1967	1933–41	Franklin D. Roosevelt
Henry A. Wallace	Democratic	1888–1965	1941–45	Franklin D. Roosevelt
Harry S. Truman	Democratic	1884–1972	1945	Franklin D. Roosevelt
Alben W. Barkley (b. Willie Alben Barkley)	Democratic	1877–1956	1949–53	Harry S. Truman

U.S. Vice Presidents *(cont.)*

Name	Party	Life Dates	Term	President
Richard Milhous Nixon	Republican	1913–94	1953–61	Dwight D. Eisenhower
Lyndon Baines Johnson	Democratic	1908–73	1961–63	John F. Kennedy
Hubert Horatio Humphrey	Democratic-Farmer Labor	1911–78	1965–69	Lyndon B. Johnson
Spiro Theodore Agnew	Republican	1918–96	1969–73	Richard M. Nixon
Gerald Randolph Ford	Republican	1913–	1973–74	Richard M. Nixon
Nelson Adlrich Rockefeller	Republican	1908–79	1974–77	Gerald R. Ford
Walter Frederick Mondale	Democratic	1928–	1977–81	James E. Carter, Jr.
George Herbert Walker Bush	Republican	1924–	1981–89	Ronald W. Reagan
James Danforth Quayle	Republican	1947–	1989–93	George H. Bush
Albert A. Gore, Jr.	Democratic	1948–	1993–00	William J. Clinton

⊙ Southwick, Leslie H. *Presidential Also-Rans and Running Mates.* Jefferson, N.C.: McFarland & Co., 1998.

Witcover, Jules. *Crapshoot: Rolling the Dice on the Vice Presidency.* New York: Crown, 1992.

Cabinet Departments

Department	Year Created	Main Agencies
Department of Agriculture (USDA)	1862	Forest Service; Natural Resources Conservation Service; Farm Service Agency; Foreign Agricultural Service; Rural Utilities Service; Rural Housing Service; Rural Business-Cooperative Service; Food and Nutrition Service; Food Safety and Inspection Service; Agricultural Research Service; Cooperative State Research, Education, and Extension Service; Economic Research Service, National Agricultural Statistics Service; Agricultural Marketing Service; Animal and Plant Health Inspection Service; Grain Inspection, Packers and Stockyards Administration; Rural Community Development
Department of Commerce (DOC)	1913	National Oceanic and Atmospheric Administration; International Trade Administration; Bureau of Export Administration; Economics and Statistics Administration; Technology Administration; Patent and Trademark Office; Minority Business Development Agency; Economic Development Administration; National Telecommunications and Information Administration; Bureau of the Census; National Institute of Standards and Technology; National Technical Information Service; Bureau of Economic Analysis

Department of Defense (DOD)	1949	Department of the Army; Department of the Navy; Department of the Air Force, Joint Chiefs of Staff; National Guard; Advanced Research Projects Agency; American Forces Information Service; American Forces Press Service; Ballistic Missile Defense Organization; Defense Contract and Audit Agency; Defense Finance and Accounting Service; Defense Information Systems Agency; Defense Intelligence Agency; Defense Logistics Agency; Defense Special Weapons Agency; Defense Technical Information Center; National Imagery and Mapping Agency; National Security Agency; On-Site Inspection Agency
Department of Education	1979	Office of Elementary and Secondary Education; Office of Post-Secondary Education; Office of Special Education and Rehabilitative Services; Office of Bilingual Education and Minority Languages Affairs; Office of Vocational and Adult Education; Office for Civil Rights; Office of Educational Research and Improvement
Department of Energy (DOE)	1977	Environment, Safety and Health; Defense Nuclear Facilities Safety Board; Office of Environmental Management; Office of Economic Impact and Diversity; Office of Worker and Community Transition; Energy Efficiency and Renewable Energy; Fossil Energy; Energy Information Administration; Office of Non-Proliferation and National Security; Office of Civilian Radioactive Waste Management; Office of Fissile Materials Disposition; Office of Energy Research; Office of Nuclear Energy, Science and Technology; Power Marketing Administrations: Southeastern, Alaska, Southwestern, Western; Bonneville
Department of Health and Human Services (HHS)	1953	Administration for Children and Families; Food and Drug Administration; Administration on Aging; Health Care and Financing Administration; Agency for Health Care Policy and Research; Centers for Disease Control and Prevention; Agency for Toxic Substances and Disease Registry; Health Resources and Services Administration; Indian Health Service, National Institutes of Health; Substance Abuse and Mental Health Services Administration; Program Support Center
Department of Housing and Urban Development (HUD)	1965	Office of Small and Disadvantaged Business Utilization; Federal Housing Enterprise Oversight; Office of Community Planning and Development; Federal Housing Finance Board; Office of Public and Indian Housing; Office of Lead Hazard Control; Government National Mortgage Association (Ginnie Mae)

Cabinet Departments (cont.)

Department	Year Created	Main Agencies
Department of the Interior (DOI)	1849	U.S. Fish and Wildlife Service; National Park Service; National Biological Service; Bureau of Indian Affairs; Bureau of Land Management; Minerals Management Service; Office of Surface Mining Reclamation and Enforcement; U.S. Geological Survey; Bureau of Reclamation
Department of Justice (DOJ)	1870	Foreign Claims Settlement Commission; Office of Information and Privacy; Community-Oriented Policing Services; Civil Division, Civil Rights Division; Criminal Division; Antitrust Division; Tax Division; Environment and Natural Resources Division; Community Relations Service; Drug Enforcement Agency; Executive Office for U.S. Attorneys; Immigration and Naturalization Service; Federal Bureau of Investigation; Federal Bureau of Prisons; U.S. Marshals Service; U.S. National Central Bureau-Interpol; Office of Justice Programs
Department of Labor (DOL)	1913	Office of Small Business Programs; Occupational Safety and Health Administration; Employment and Training Administration; Mine Safety and Health Administration; Pension and Welfare Benefits Administration; Veterans' Employment and Training Service; Employment Standards Administration; Bureau of Labor Statistics; Women's Bureau; Bureau of International Labor Affairs; Employees' Compensation Appeal Board
Department of State	1789	African Affairs; East Asian and Pacific Affairs; European and Canadian Affairs; Inter-American Affairs; Near Eastern Affairs; South Asian Affairs; International Organization Affairs; Economic and Business Affairs; Political-Military Affairs; Office of Foreign Missions; Foreign Service Institute; Consular Affairs; Diplomatic Security; Finance and Management Policy; Democracy, Human Rights and Labor; International Narcotics and Law Enforcement Affairs; Oceans and International Environmental and Scientific Affairs; Population, Refugees, and Migration
Department of Transportation (DOT)	1966	U.S. Coast Guard; Federal Aviation Administration; Federal Highway Administration; Federal Railroad Administration; National Highway Traffic Safety Administration; Federal Transit Administration; Saint Lawrence Seaway Development Corporation; Maritime Administration; Research and Special Programs Administration; Bureau of Transportation Statistics; Transportation Administrative Service Center; Surface Transportation Board

Department of the Treasury	1789	Office of the Comptroller of the Currency; Office of Thrift Supervision; Bureau of Alcohol, Tobacco and Firearms; U.S. Secret Service; Federal Law Enforcement Training Center; Internal Revenue Service; U.S. Mint; Bureau of Engraving and Printing; U.S. Customs Service; Bureau of the Public Debt
Department of Veterans Affairs	1930	Center for Minority Veterans; Center for Women Veterans; National Center for Veteran Analysis and Statistics; National Cemetery Administration; Veterans Benefits Administration; Veterans Health Administration

⊙ The White House. "The President's Cabinet," www.whitehouse.gov/WH/Cabinet/html/cabinet_links.html

Independent Federal Agencies and Commissions

Agency/Commission	Created	Mission
Advisory Council on Historic Preservation	1966	to influence federal policy, programs, and decisions as they affect historic resources in communities and on public lands nationwide
Arms Control and Disarmament Agency	1961	to strengthen the national security of the United States by formulating, advocating, negotiating, implementing, and verifying effective arms control, nonproliferation, and disarmament policies, strategies, and agreements
Central Intelligence Agency	1947	to provide accurate, evidence-based, comprehensive, and timely foreign intelligence related to national security, and to conduct counter-intelligence activities, special activities, and other functions related to foreign intelligence and national security as directed by the President
Consumer Product Safety Commission	1972	to protect the public against unreasonable risks of injuries and deaths associated with consumer products; to develop voluntary standards with industry; to issue and enforce mandatory standards; to obtain recalls of defective products; to conduct research and inform and educate consumers
Corporation for National Service	1993	to work with community organizations to provide opportunities for Americans of all ages to serve their community and country through such organizations as AmeriCorps, Learn & Serve America, and the National Senior Service Corps
Commodity Futures Trading Commission	1974	to regulate U.S. commodity futures and option markets; to protect market participants against manipulation, abusive trade practices, and fraud, and to enable markets to provide a mechanism for price discovery and a means of offsetting price risk

Independent Federal Agencies and Commissions *(cont.)*

Agency/ Commission	Created	Mission
Environmental Protection Agency	1970	to solve urgent environmental problems and to protect the public health
Farm Credit Administration	1933	to regulate and examine banks, associations, and related entities that collectively comprise the Farm Credit System, including the Federal Agricultural Mortgage Corporation
Federal Communications Commission	1934	to encourage competition in all communications markets and to protect the public interest; to develop and implement policy concerning inter-state and international communications by radio, television, wire, satellite, and cable
Federal Deposit Insurance Corporation	1933	to insure deposits of banks and saving associa-tions; to promote the safety and soundness of insured depository institutions and the U.S. finan-cial system; to maintain stability and public confi-dence in the nation's banking system; to provide financial and economic information and analyses
Federal Election Commission	1975	to govern the financing of federal elections; to disclose campaign finance information; to enforce the limits, prohibitions, and other provi-sions of the election law; to administer the public funding of presidential elections
Federal Emergency Management Agency	1979	to reduce loss of life and property and protect our nation's critical infrastructure from all types of hazards through a comprehensive, risk-based, emergency management program of mitigation, preparedness, response, and recovery
Federal Housing Finance Board	1989	to regulate the Federal Home Loan Bank and to oversee residential mortgage lending banks
Federal Trade Commission	1914	to enforce a variety of federal antitrust and con-sumer protection laws to ensure that markets function competitively; to eliminate unfair or deceptive acts or practices toward consumers
General Services Administration	1949	to provide workspace, supplies, services, and solutions, at the best value, for Federal employees
Institute of Museum and Library Services	1996	to improve museum, library, and information services; to consolidate federal programs of support for museums; to support public libraries
U.S. Merit Systems Protection Board	1978	to regulate federal merit-based system of employ-ment, principally by hearing and deciding appeals from federal employees of removals and other major personnel actions; to review significant actions and regulations of the Office of Personnel Management; to hear and decide on other types of civil service cases; and to conduct studies of the merit systems

National Aeronautics and Space Administration	1958	to plan, direct, and conduct aeronautical and space activities; to arrange for participation by the scientific community in planning scientific measurements and observations to be made through use of aeronautical and space vehicles; to provide for the widest practicable and appropriate dissemination of information concerning its activities the results thereof
National Archives and Records Administration	1985	to preserve the nation's history and to oversee the management of all federal records
National Endowment for the Arts	1965	to nurture the expression of human creativity; to support the cultivation of community spirit; to foster the recognition and appreciation of the excellence and diversity of the nation's artistic accomplishments
National Endowment for the Humanities	1965	to provide grants to individuals and organizations for research in the humanities, educational opportunities for teachers, preservation of texts and materials, translations of important works, museum exhibitions, television and radio programs, and public discussion and study
National Partnership for Reinventing Government	1993	to reinvent government to work better, cost less, and get results most important to Americans
National Science Foundation	1950	to promote the progress of science; to advance the national health, prosperity, and welfare; to secure the national defense
National Security Agency	1952	to be responsible for the centralized coordination, direction, and performance of highly specialized technical functions in support of U.S. government activities to protect U.S. information systems and produce foreign intelligence information; a separate organized agency within the Department of Defense
National Technology Transfer Center	1980	to strengthen U.S. industrial competitiveness by identifying industry's needs and matching those needs with technologies and commercialization services required to bring new products or services to market
Nuclear Regulatory Commission	1974	to ensure adequate protection of the public health and safety, the common defense and security, and the environment in the use of nuclear materials in the United States
Peace Corps	1961	to serve the cause of peace by living, working, and teaching in underdeveloped countries
President's Commission to Study Capital Budgeting	1997	to develop a report that addresses: capital budgeting practices by other governments and the private sector and their pertinence for the federal government; the appropriate definition of capital for federal budgeting; the role of depreciation in capital budgeting; and the effect of a federal

Agency/ Commission	Created	Mission
		capital budget on budgetary choices, implications for macroeconomic stability, and potential mechanisms for budgetary discipline
President's Council on Physical Fitness	1963	to foster improvements in existing programs and promote additional efforts to enhance the physical fitness of Americans; to coordinate, stimulate, and improve the functions of federal agencies with respect to physical fitness; to enlist the active support and assistance of individuals and groups in a vigorous effort to promote and improve physical fitness in the United States
President's Council on Sustainable Development	1993	to advise the president on sustainable development and to develop bold, new approaches to achieve economic, environmental, and equity goals
President's Interagency Council on Women	1995	to make sure that all the effort and good ideas of the United Nations Fourth World Conference on Women in Beijing are implemented; to implement the Platform for Action adopted at the conference; to further women's progress through outreaching and public education
Railroad Retirement Board	1934	to administer comprehensive retirement-survivor and unemployment-sickness benefit programs for U.S. railroad workers and their families; to administer certain benefit payments and railroad workers' Medicare coverage
Securities and Exchange Commission	1934	to administer federal securities laws that protect investors in securities markets that operate fairly and to ensure that investors have access to disclosure of all material information concerning publicly traded securities; to regulate firms engaged in the purchase or sale of securities, people who provide investment advice, and investment companies
Selective Service System	1940	to provide manpower to the armed forces in an emergency; to run an Alternative Service Program for men classified as conscientious objectors during a draft
Small Business Administration	1953	to provide financial, technical, and management assistance to help Americans start, run, and grow their businesses through loans, loan guarantees, and disaster loans
Smithsonian Institution	1846	to hold artifacts and specimens in trust for "the increase and diffusion of knowledge"; to act as a center for research dedicated to public education, national service, and scholarship in the arts, sciences, and history

Social Security Administration	1935	to provide for the material needs of individuals and families; to protect the aged and disabled against the expenses of illnesses that could otherwise exhaust their savings; to keep families together; to give children the opportunity to grow up in health and security
United States Advisory Commission on Public Diplomacy	1948	to assess public diplomacy policies and programs of the United States Information Agency, other U.S. foreign affairs agencies, and U.S. missions abroad
United States Agency for International Development	1961	to provide economic development and humanitarian assistance to advance U.S. economic and political interests overseas
United States Chemical Safety and Hazard Investigation Board	1990	to work in concert with industry, labor, government, and communities to help prevent chemical accidents
United States Information Agency	1948	to support U.S. foreign policy and national interests abroad; to inform foreign citizens about America and its foreign policy by conducting international educational and cultural exchanges, broadcasting, and information programs
United States International Trade Commission	1916	to provide objective trade expertise to both the legislative and executive branches of government; to determine the impact of imports on U.S. industries; to direct actions against certain unfair trade practices; to investigate and publish reports on U.S. industries and the global trends that affect them; to update and publish the Harmonized Tariff Schedule of the United States
United States Office of Government Ethics	1978	to prevent conflicts of interest on the part of government employees and to resolve them when they do occur; to foster high ethical standards for government employees and to strengthen the public's confidence that government business is conducted with impartiality and integrity
United States Postal Service	1789	to provide postal services to bind the nation together through the personal, educational, literary, and business correspondence of the people; to provide prompt, reliable, and efficient services to patrons in all areas
United States Trade and Development Agency	1981	to help U.S. companies compete for infrastructure and industrial project business opportunities in middle-income and developing countries
Voice of America	1942	to represent the United States to the people of the world via radio by broadcasting news reliably, authoritatively, and accurately in a comprehensive and objective manner and by projecting a comprehensive, well-balanced picture of American thought and institutions; part of the U.S. Information Agency

Agency/ Commission	Created	Mission
White House Fellows	1964	to provide gifted and highly motivated young Americans with some first-hand experience in the process of governing the nation and a sense of personal involvement in the leadership of society
Women's History Commission	1998	to consider how best to acknowledge and celebrate the roles and accomplishments of women in American history

⊙ The White House. "Federal Agencies and Commissions," www.whitehouse.gov/ WH/Independent_Agencies/html/independent_links.html

Lobbyist Groups

Lobbyist groups are required to register with the federal government and to report semi-annually to the government on their lobbying activities. The following table lists some of the larger lobbying groups.

Group	Mission
American Association of Retired Persons (AARP)	to inform, educate, and serve as an advocate for the important issues regarding aging Americans
American Bar Association (ABA)	to uphold the Constitution and the honor of the legal profession and to serve as a legislative and judicial advocate for uniformity in laws
American Civil Liberties Union (ACLU)	to achieve, through litigation, legislation, and education, the preservation of the Bill of Rights and individual rights
American Medical Association (AMA)	to uphold the standards of the medical profession and to promote research and education in the healthcare field
American Public Health Association (APHA)	to provide health professionals with the latest information in the field and to serve as an advocate for issues, such as funding for health programs and for pollution control, that affect personal and environmental health
Association of American Universities (AAU)	to provide an environment for the formation of national policy on academic issues and for the discussion of institutional issues
Christian Coalition	to encourage Christians, particularly those who are conservatives, to be pro-active in government through social and political action
Common Cause	to hold government accountable; to promote openness and honesty in government; to protest against corruption in government
Concord Coalition	to serve as a watchdog of the federal budget and to ensure that Social Security, Medicare, and Medicaid are secure
Family Research Council (FRC)	to promote traditional family and Judeo-Christian values

Federation of American Scientists (FAS)	to bring the scientific perspective to the legislative arena; to end the arms race and avoid the use of nuclear weapons
Greenpeace	to expose crimes against the environment and to work to find solutions
Judicial Watch	to watch over government and judicial systems and to promote political and legal reform
League of Conservation Voters	to make Congress more aware of voters' environmental concerns and to inform the public about legislators' voting records on the environment
League of Women Voters (LWV)	to encourage informed and active participation of citizens in government and to influence public policy through education and advocacy
National Association for the Advancement of Colored People (NAACP)	to ensure the political, educational, social, and economic equality of minority groups
National Education Association (NEA)	to advance the cause of public education and to make public schools as effective as possible
National Gay and Lesbian Task Force (NGLTF)	to promote the civil rights of lesbians, gays, bisexuals, and transgenders and to work for social change
National Organization for Women (NOW)	to push for social change that will achieve equality for all women
National Priorities Project	to offer citizen and community groups tools and resources to shape federal budget and policy priorities that promote social and economic justice
National Rifle Association (NRA)	to uphold the Second Amendment right to keep and bear arms; to assure that firearms are used lawfully, effectively, responsibly, and safely
Public Citizen	to work for the consumer for safer drugs and medical devices, cleaner and safer energy sources, a cleaner environment, fair trade, and a more open, democratic government
Sierra Club	to preserve America's natural resources
The Wilderness Society	to preserve wilderness and wildlife; to protect America's prime forest, parks, rivers, deserts, and shorelands; to foster an American land ethic

⊙ Hrebenar, Ronald J. *Interest Group Politics in America.* Armonk, N.Y.: M.E. Sharpe, 1997.
 Government Publishing Office. *Congress and Pressure Groups: Lobbying in a Modern Democracy.* Washington, D.C.: U.S. GPO, 1986.

Foreign Embassies in the United States

Afghanistan: Consulate of the
 Islamic State of Afghanistan
369 Lexington Avenue, 19th Floor
New York, NY 10017
(212) 972-2277

Albania: Embassy of the Republic of
 Albania
2100 S Street, NW
Washington, D.C. 20008
(202) 223-4942

Algeria: Embassy of the Democratic
and Popular Republic of Algeria
2137 Wyoming Avenue, NW
Washington, D.C. 20008
(202) 265-2800

Andorra: Embassy of Spain
2375 Pennsylvania Avenue, NW
Washington, D.C. 20037
(202) 728-2330
or
Andorran Mission to the United
Nations: 212-750-8064

Angola: Embassy of Angola
1819 L Street, NW, Suite 400
Washington, D.C. 20036
(202) 452-1042/3

Anguilla: See United Kingdom
or
U.S. Embassy, Bridgetown, Barbados
(246) 431-0225
or
U.S. Consulate, English Harbour,
Antigua
(268) 463-6531

Antigua and Barbuda: Embassy of
Antigua and Barbuda
3216 New Mexico Avenue, NW
Washington, D.C. 20016
(202) 362-5122

Argentina: Consul Section of the
Argentine Embassy
1718 Connecticut Avenue, NW
Washington, D.C. 20009
(202) 797-8826
Consulates in CA (213) 954-9155
FL (305) 373-7794
GA (404) 880-0805
IL (312) 819-2620
NY (212) 603-0400
TX (713) 871-8335

Armenia: Embassy of the Republic of
Armenia
2225 R Street NW
Washington, D.C. 20008
(202) 319-1976
or
Consulate General
50 North La Cienega Blvd.,
Suite 210
Los Angeles, CA 90211
(310) 657-6102

Australia: Embassy of Australia
1601 Massachusetts Avenue, NW
Washington, D.C. 20036
(202) 797-3000
Consulates in CA (213) 469-4300
or (415) 362-6160
MI (808) 524-5050
NY (212) 245-4000
TX (713) 629-9131

Austria: Embassy of Austria
3524 International Court, NW
Washington, D.C. 20008
(202) 895-6767
Consulates in CA (310) 444-9310
IL (312) 222-1515
NY (212) 737-6400

Azerbaijan: Embassy of the Republic
of Azerbaijan
927 15th Street, NW, Suite 700
Washington, D.C. 20035
(202) 842-0001

Azores: See Portugal

Bahamas: Embassy of the
Commonwealth of the Bahamas
2220 Massachusetts Avenue, NW
Washington, D.C. 20008
(202) 319-2660
Consulate: FL (305) 373-6295
NY (212) 421-6420

Bahrain: Embassy of the State of
Bahrain
3502 International Drive, NW
Washington, D.C. 20008
(202) 342-0741
or
Permanent Mission to the United
Nations: (212) 223-6200

Bangladesh: Embassy of the People's
Republic of Bangladesh
2201 Wisconsin Avenue, NW
Washington, D.C. 20007
(202) 342-8373

Barbados: Embassy of Barbados
2144 Wyoming Avenue, NW
Washington, D.C. 20008
(202) 939-9200
or
Consulate General:
(212) 867-8435

Belarus: Embassy of the Republic of
Belarus
1619 New Hampshire Avenue, NW
Washington, D.C. 20009
(202) 986-1606
or
Consulate General: (212) 682-5392
Belgium: Embassy of Belgium
3330 Garfield Street, NW
Washington, D.C. 20008
(202) 333-6900
Consulates in CA (213) 857-1244
GA (404) 659-2150
IL (312) 263-6624
NY (212) 586-5110
Belize: Embassy of Belize
2535 Massachusetts Avenue, NW
Washington, D.C. 20008
(202) 332-9636
Belize Mission: (212) 599-0233
Benin: Embassy of the Republic of
Benin
2737 Cathedral Avenue, NW
Washington, D.C. 10008
(202) 232-6656
Bermuda. See United Kingdom
Bhutan: Tourism Authority of
Bhutan in Bhutan
011-975-2-23251/2
Bolivia: Embassy of Bolivia (Consular
Section)
3014 Massachusetts Avenue, NW
Washington, D.C. 20008
(202) 483-4410
Consulates: FL (305) 358-3450
NY (212) 687-0530
CA (415) 495-5173
Bosnia and Herzegovina: Embassy
of the Republic of Bosnia and
Herzegovina
2109 E Street NW
Washington, D.C. 20037
(202) 833-3612
or
Consulate General: (212) 751-9015
Botswana: Embassy of the Republic
of Botswana
3400 International Drive, NW,
Suite 7M
Washington, D.C. 20008
(202) 244-4990/1
Consulates: CA (213) 626-8484
TX (713) 622-1900

Brazil: Embassy of Brazil (Consular
Section)
3009 Whitehaven Street
Washington, D.C. 20008
(202) 238-2820 or 2831
Consulates: CA (213) 651-2664 or
(415) 981-8170
FL (305) 285-6200
IL (312) 464-0244
MA (617) 542-4000
NY (212) 757-3080
PR (809) 754-7983
TX (713) 961-3063
British Virgin Islands: U.S.
Embassy, Bridgetown, Barbados
(246) 431-0225
or
U.S. Consulate, English Harbour,
Antigua
(268) 463-6531
Brunei: Embassy of the State of
Brunei Darussalam
2600 Virginia Avenue, NW,
Suite 300
Washington, D.C. 20037
(202) 342-0159
or
Brunei Permanent Mission to the
United Nations: (212) 838-1600
Bulgaria: Embassy of the Republic of
Bulgaria
1621 22nd Street, NW
Washington, D.C. 20008
(202) 387-7969
Burkina Faso: Embassy of Burkina
Faso
2340 Massachusetts Avenue, NW
Washington, D.C. 20008
(202) 332-5577
Consulates: GA (404) 378-7278
CA (213) 824-5100
LA (504) 945-3152
Burma: See Myanmar
Burundi: Embassy of the Republic of
Burundi
2233 Wisconsin Avenue, NW,
Suite 212
Washington, D.C. 20007
(202) 342-2574
or
Permanent Mission to the United
Nations: 212-687-1180

Foreign Embassies in the United States *(cont.)*

Cambodia: Royal Embassy of
Cambodia
4500 16th Street NW
Washington, D.C. 20011
(202) 726-7742
Cameroon: Embassy of the Republic
of Cameroon
2349 Massachusetts Avenue, NW
Washington, D.C. 20008
(202) 265-8790/94
Canada: Embassy of Canada
501 Pennsylvania Avenue, NW
Washington, D.C. 20001
(202) 682-1740
Consulates: CA (213) 346-2700
MI (313) 567-2085
NY (212) 596-1700 or
(716) 852-1252
WA (206) 443-1377
Cape Verde: Embassy of the
Republic of Cape Verde
3415 Massachusetts Avenue, NW
Washington, D.C. 20007
(202) 965-6820
Cayman Islands: See United
Kingdom
or
U.S. Embassy, Kingston, Jamaica
(876) 949-4850
or
U.S. Consulate, English Harbour,
Antigua
(268) 463-6531
Central African Republic: Embassy
of the Central African Republic
1618 22nd Street, NW
Washington, D.C. 20008
No operating public telephone;
communicate by mail
Chad: Embassy of the Republic of
Chad
2002 R Street, NW
Washington, D.C. 20009
(202) 462-4009
Chile: Embassy of Chile
1732 Massachusetts Avenue, NW
Washington, D.C. 20036
(202) 785-1746
Consulates: CA (310) 785-0113
or (415)982-7662

FL (305) 373-8623
IL (312) 654-8780
PA (215) 829-9520
NY (212) 980-3366
TX (713) 621-5853
PR (809) 725-6365
China: Embassy of the People's
Republic of China
2300 Connecticut Ave., NW
Washington, D.C. 20008
(202) 328-2500/2
Consulates: IL (312) 803-0098
TX (713) 524-4311
CA (213) 807-8018 or
(415) 563-4857
NY (212) 330-7409
Colombia: Embassy of Colombia
2118 Leroy Place, NW
Washington, D.C. 20008
(202) 387-8338
Consulates: CA (213) 382-1137 or
(415) 495-7191
FL (315) 448-5558
GA (404) 237-1045
IL (312) 923-1196
LA (504) 525-5580
MA (617) 536-6222
MN (612) 933-2408
MO (314) 991-3636
OH (216) 943-1200
NY (212) 949-9898
PR (809) 754-6885
TX (713) 527-8919
WV (304) 234-8561
Comoros Islands: Mission of the
Federal and Islamic Republic of
the Comoros
336 East 45th Street, 2nd Floor
New York, NY 10017
(212) 972-8010
Congo, Republic of the: Embassy of
the Republic of the Congo
4891 Colorado Avenue, NW
Washington, D.C. 20011
726-0825
or
Permanent Mission to the UN: (212)
744-7840

Congo, Democratic Republic of:
Embassy of the Democratic
Republic of Congo
1800 New Hampshire Avenue, NW
Washington, D.C. 20009
(202) 234-7690
Costa Rica: Embassy of Costa Rica
2114 S Street, NW
Washington, D.C. 20008
(202) 328-6628
Consulates: CA (415) 392-8488
GA (404) 951-7025
FL (305) 371-7485
IL (312) 263-2772
LA (504) 887-8131
NY (212) 425-2620
TX (713) 266-1527
Côte d'Ivoire: Embassy of the
Republic of Côte d'Ivoire
2424 Massachusetts Avenue, NW
Washington, D.C. 20008
(202) 797-0300
or
Consulate: (415) 391-0176
Croatia: Embassy of the Republic of
Croatia
2343 Massachusetts Avenue, NW
Washington, D.C. 20008
(202) 588-5899
Consulates: OH (216) 951-4246
NY (212) 599-3066
Cuba: Cuba Interests Section
2639 16th Street, NW
Washington, D.C. 20009
(202) 797-8509 or 8518
Curacao: See Netherlands Antilles
Cyprus: Embassy of the Republic of
Cyprus
2211 R Street, NW
Washington, D.C. 20008
(202) 462-5772
or
Consulate General
13 East 40th Street
New York, NY 10016
(212) 686-6016
Other consulates:
AR (602) 264-9701
CA (310) 397-0771 or
(510) 547-5689
GA (404) 941-3764
IN (219) 481-6897

LA (504) 388-8701
MA (617) 497-0219
MI (513) 582-1411
OH (330) 296-8191
OR (503) 248-0500
PA (215) 928-4290
TX (713) 928-2264,
VA (804) 481-3538
WA (206) 827-1700
Czech Republic: Embassy of the
Czech Republic
3900 Spring of Freedom Street, NW
Washington, D.C. 20008
(202) 274-9173
Consulates: CA (310) 473-0889
NY (212) 717-5643
Denmark: Royal Danish Embassy
3200 Whitehaven Street, NW
Washington, D.C. 20008
(202) 234-4300
Consulates: CA (310) 443-2090
IL (312) 787-8780
NY (212) 223-4545
Djibouti: Embassy of the Republic of
Djibouti
1156 15th Street, NW, Suite 515
Washington, D.C. 20005
(202) 331-0202
or
Djibouti Mission to the United
Nations: (212) 753-3163
Dominica: Embassy of the
Commonwealth of Dominica
3216 New Mexico Avenue, NW
Washington, D.C. 20015
(202) 364-6781
Dominican Republic: Embassy of
the Dominican Republic
1715 22nd Street, NW
Washington, D.C. 20008
(202) 332-6280
Consulates: CA (415) 982-5144
FL (305) 358-3220
IL (312) 486-8400
LA (504) 522-1843
MA (617) 482-8121
NY (212) 768-2480
PA (215) 923-3006
PR (787) 833-4756
TX (713) 266-0165

Ecuador: Embassy of Ecuador
2535 15th Street, NW
Washington, D.C. 20009
(202) 234-7200
Consulates: IL (312) 329-0266
TX (713) 622-1787
CA (213) 628-3014 or
(415) 957-5921
FL (305) 461-2363
NJ (201) 985-1707
LA (504) 523-3229
NY (212) 808-0170

Egypt: Embassy of the Arab Republic
of Egypt
3521 International Court, NW
Washington, D.C. 20008
(202) 895-5400
Consulates: CA (415) 346-9700
IL (312) 828-9162
NY (212) 759-7120
TX (713) 961-4915

El Salvador: Consulate General of El
Salvador
1010 16th Street, NW, 3rd Floor
Washington, D.C. 20036
(202) 331-4032
Consulates: CA (213) 383-5776
(415) 781-7924, or
(714) 542-3250)
FL (305) 371-8850
IL (312) 322-1393
LA (504) 522-4266
MA (617) 577-9111
NY (212) 889-3608
TX (713) 270-6239 or
(214) 637-1018

England: See United Kingdom

Equatorial Guinea: Embassy of the
Republic of Equatorial Guinea
1511 K Street, NW
Washington, D.C. 20005
(202) 393-0525

Eritrea: Embassy of Eritrea
1708 New Hampshire Avenue, NW
Washington, D.C. 20009
(202) 319-1991

Estonia: Embassy of Estonia
2131 Massachusetts Avenue, NW
Washington, D.C. 20008
(202) 588-0101
or

Consulate General of Estonia
630 Fifth Avenue, Suite 2415
New York, NY 10111
(212) 247-7634 or 1450

Ethiopia: Embassy of Ethiopia
2134 Kalorama Road, NW
Washington, D.C. 20008
(202) 234-2281/2

Fiji: Embassy of Fiji
2233 Wisconsin Avenue, NW, #240
Washington, D.C. 20007
(202) 337-8320

Finland: Embassy of Finland
3301 Massachusetts Avenue, NW
Washington, D.C. 20008
(202) 298-5800
Consulates: CA (310) 203-9903
NY (212) 750-4400

**Former Yugoslav Republic of
Macedonia:** Embassy of the
Former Yugoslav Republic of
Macedonia
3050 K Street, NW, Suite 210
Washington, D.C. 20007
(202) 337-3063 or
Consulate General: (212) 317-1727

France: Consulate General of France
4101 Reservoir Road, NW
Washington, D.C. 20007
(202) 944-6000
Other Consulates:
CA (310) 235-3200 or
(415) 397-4330
FL (305) 372-9798
GA (404) 522-4226
IL (312) 787-5359
LA (504) 523-5772
MA (617) 542-7374
NY (212) 606-3644
TX (713) 528-2181

French Guiana: See France

French Polynesia: See France

Gabon: Embassy of the Gabonese
Republic
2035 20th Street, NW
Washington, D.C. 20009
(202) 797-1000
or
Permanent Mission of the
Gabonese Republic to the United
Nations: (212) 686-6720

Galapagos Islands: See Ecuador

Gambia: Embassy of the Gambia
1155 15th Street, NW, Suite 1000
Washington, D.C. 20005
(202) 785-1399
or
Permanent Mission of The Gambia
to the United Nations:
(212) 949-6640

Georgia: Embassy of the Republic of
Georgia
1615 New Hampshire Avenue, NW,
Suite 300
Washington, D.C. 20009
(202) 347-3415

Germany: Embassy of the Federal
Republic of Germany
4645 Reservoir Road, NW
Washington, D.C. 20007
(202) 298-4000
Consulates: CA (415) 775-1061 or
(213) 930-2703
FL (305) 358-0290
GA (404) 659-4760
IL (312) 580-1199
MA (617) 536-4414
MI (313) 962-6526
NY (212) 308-8700
TX (713) 627-7770
WA (206) 682-4312

Ghana: Embassy of Ghana
3512 International Drive, NW
Washington, D.C. 20008
(202) 686-4520
or
Consulate General:
(212) 832-1300

Gilbert Islands: See Kiribati

Greece: Embassy of Greece
2221 Massachusetts Avenue, NW
Washington, D.C. 20008
(202) 939-5818
Consulates: CA (310) 826-5555 or
(415) 775-2102/4
GA (404) 261-3313
IL (312) 335-3915 or 17
LA (504) 523-1167
MA (617) 543-0100
NY (212) 988-5500
TX (713) 840-7522

Greenland: See Denmark

Grenada: Consulate General of
Grenada
1701 New Hampshire Ave., NW
Washington, D.C. 20009
(202) 265-2561
or
Permanent Mission of Grenada to
the United Nations:
(212) 599-0301

Guadeloupe: See France

Guatemala: Embassy of Guatemala
2220 R Street, NW
Washington, D.C. 20008-4081
(202) 745-4952
Consulates: CA (213) 365-9251 or
(415) 788-5651
FL (305) 443-4828
IL (312) 332-3170
NY (212) 686-3837
TX (713) 953-9531

Guinea: Embassy of the Republic of
Guinea
2112 Leroy Place, NW
Washington, D.C. 20008
(202) 483-9420

Guinea-Bissau: Embassy of the
Republic of Guinea-Bissau
918 16th Street, NW, Mezzanine
Suite
Washington, D.C. 20006
(202) 872-4222

Guyana: Embassy of Guyana
2490 Tracy Place, NW
Washington, D.C. 20008
(202) 265-6900/03

Haiti: Embassy of the Republic of
Haiti
2311 Massachusetts Avenue, NW
Washington, D.C. 20008
(202) 332-4090
Consulates: FL (305) 859-2003
MA (617) 266-3660
NY (212) 697-9767
PR (809) 764-1392
IL (312) 922-4004

Holy See (Vatican): Apostolic
Nunciature of the Holy See
3339 Massachusetts Avenue, NW
Washington, D.C. 20008
(202) 333-7121
or
Embassy of Italy: (202) 328-5500

Honduras: Embassy of Honduras
3007 Tilden Street, NW
Washington, D.C. 20008
(202) 966-7702
  Consulates: CA (213) 383-9244 or
    (415) 392-0076
    FL (304) 447-8927
    IL (312) 951-6382
    LA (504) 522-3118
    NY (212) 269-3611
    TX (713) 622-4572
Hong Kong: Embassy of the People's
  Republic of China
2300 Connecticut Avenue, NW
Washington, D.C. 20008
(202) 328-2500
Hungary: Embassy of the Republic of
  Hungary
3910 Shoemaker Street, NW
Washington, D.C. 20008
(202) 362-6730
  Consulates: NY (212) 752-0661
    CA (310) 473-9344
Iceland: Embassy of Iceland
1156 15th Street, NW, Suite 1200
Washington, D.C. 20005
(202) 265-6653/5
  or
  Consulate General: (212) 593-2700
India: Embassy of India
2536 Massachusetts Avenue, NW
Washington, D.C. 20008
(202) 939-9806
  Consulates: IL (312) 515-0405
    TX (713) 626-2355
    NY (212) 774-0600
    CA (415) 668-0683
Indonesia: Embassy of the Republic
  of Indonesia
2020 Massachusetts Avenue, NW
Washington, D.C. 20036
(202) 775-5200
  Consulates: CA (213) 383-5126 or
    (415) 474-9571
    IL (312-) 345-9300
    NY (212) 879-0600
    TX (713) 785-1691

Iran: Embassy of Pakistan
  Iranian Interests Section
2209 Wisconsin Avenue NW
Washington, D.C. 20007
(202) 965-4990
Iraq: Iraqi Interests Section
1801 P Street, NW
Washington, D.C. 20036
(202) 483-7500
Ireland: Embassy of Ireland
2234 Massachusetts Avenue, NW
Washington, D.C. 20008
(202) 462-3939
  Consulates: CA (415) 392-4214
    IL (312) 337-1868
    MA (617) 267-9330
    NY (212) 319-2555
Israel: Embassy of Israel
3514 International Drive, NW
Washington, D.C. 20008
(202) 364-5500
  Consulates: CA (213) 852-5500 or
    (415) 398-8885
    FL (305) 358-8111
    GA (404) 875-7851
    IL (312) 565-3300
    MA (617) 542-0041
    NY (212) 499-5300
    PA (215) 546-5556
    TX (713) 627-3780
Italy: Embassy of Italy
1601 Fuller Street, NW
Washington, D.C. 20009
(202) 328-5500
  Consulates: CA (310) 820-0622 or
    (415) 931-4924
    FL (305) 374-6322
    TX (713) 850-7520
    IL (312) 467-1550
    MA (617) 542-0483/4
    MI (313) 963-8560
    NJ (201) 643-1448
    NY (212) 737-9100
    PA (215) 592-7329
Jamaica: Embassy of Jamaica
1520 New Hampshire Avenue, NW
Washington, D.C. 20036
(202) 452-0660
  Consulates: CA (310) 559-3822 or
    (510) 266-0072
    FL (305) 374-8431

IL (312) 663-0023
NY (212) 935-9000
MA (617) 266-8604
WA (206) 872-8950
Japan: Embassy of Japan
2520 Massachusetts Avenue NW
Washington, D.C. 20008
(202) 939-6700
Consulates: AK (907) 279-8428
CA (213) 617-6700 or
(415) 777-3533
FL (305) 530-9090
GA (404) 892-2700
HI (808) 536-2226
IL (312) 280-0400
LA (504) 529-2101
MA (617) 973-9772
MI (313) 567-0120
MO (816) 471-0111
NY (212) 371-8222
OR (503) 221-1811
TX (713) 652-2977
WA (206) 682-9107
CNMI (670) 234-8764
Guam (671) 646-1290
Jordan: Embassy of the Hashemite
Kingdom of Jordan
3504 International Drive, NW
Washington, D.C. 20008
(202) 966-2664
Kazakhstan: Embassy of the
Republic of Kazakhstan
1401 16th Street, NW
Washington, D.C. 20036
(202) 232-5488
Kenya: Embassy of Kenya
2249 R. Street, NW
Washington, D.C. 20008
(202) 387-6101
or
Consulate General: (212) 486-1300
Korea, South: Embassy of the
Republic of Korea (Consular
Division)
2320 Massachusetts Avenue, NW
Washington, D.C. 20008
(202) 939-5600 or 63
Consulates: CA (213) 385-9300 or
(415) 921-2251/3

FL (305) 372-1555
GA (404) 522-1611/3
HI (808) 595-6109
IL (312) 822-9485
MA (617) 348-3660
NY (212) 752-1700
TX (713) 961-0186
WA (206) 441-1011/4
Guam (671) 472-6109
Korea, North: Permanent Represen-
tative to the Democratic Republic
of Korea to the United Nations
515 East 72nd Street, 38-F
New York, NY 10021
(212) 972-3106
Kuwait: Embassy of the State of
Kuwait
2940 Tilden Street, NW
Washington, D.C. 20008
(202) 966-0702
or
Consulate: (212) 973-4318
Kyrgyz Republic: Embassy of the
Kyrgyz Republic
1732 Wisconsin Avenue, NW
Washington, D.C. 20007
(202) 338-5141
Laos: Embassy of the Lao People's
Democratic Republic
2222 S Street, NW
Washington, D.C. 20008
(202) 332-6416
Latvia: Embassy of Latvia
4325 17th Street, NW
Washington, D.C. 20011
(202) 726-8213
Lebanon: Embassy of Lebanon
2560 28th Street, NW
Washington, D.C. 20008
(202) 939-6300
Consulates: CA (213) 467-1253
MI (313) 567-0233
NY (212) 744-7905
Lesotho: Embassy of the Kingdom of
Lesotho
2511 Massachusetts Avenue, NW
Washington, D.C. 20008
(202) 797-5533

Liberia: Embassy of the Republic of
Liberia
5201 16th Street, NW
Washington, D.C. 20011
(202) 723-0437
Consulates: CA (213) 277-7692
GA (404) 753-4754
IL (312) 643-8635
LA (504) 523-7784
MI (313) 342-3900
NY (212) 687-1025

Libya: Passport Services
U.S. Department of State
1111 19th Street, NW
Washington, D.C. 20524
Attn.: CA/PPT/PAS

Liechtenstein: Embassy of
Switzerland
2900 Cathedral Avenue, NW
Washington, D.C. 20008
(202) 745-7900

Lithuania: Embassy of Lithuania
2622 Sixteenth Street, NW
Washington, D.C. 20009
(202) 234-5860
or
Consulate General: (212) 354-7849

Luxembourg: Embassy of
Luxembourg
2200 Massachusetts Avenue, NW
Washington, D.C. 20008
(202) 265-4171
Consulates: CA (415) 788-0816
NY (212) 888-6664

Macau: Embassy of Portugal
2125 Kalorama Road, NW
Washington, D.C. 20008
(202) 328-8610

Macedonia: See Former Yugoslav
Republic of Macedonia

Madagascar: Embassy of the Demo-
cratic Republic of Madagascar
2374 Massachusetts Avenue, NW
Washington, D.C. 20008
(202) 265-5525/6
Consulates: CA 800-856-2721
PA (215) 893-3067
NY (212) 986-9411

Madeira Islands: See Portugal

Malawi: Embassy of Malawi
2408 Massachusetts Avenue, NW
Washington, D.C. 20008
(202) 797-1007
or
Mission to the United Nations: (212)
949-0180

Malaysia: Embassy of Malaysia
2401 Massachusetts Avenue, NW
Washington, D.C. 20008
(202) 328-2700
Consulates: CA (213) 892-1238
NY (212) 490-2722

Maldives: Mission to the United
Nations
(212) 599-6195

Mali: Embassy of the Republic of
Mali
2130 R Street, NW
Washington, D.C. 20008
(202) 332-2249

Malta: Embassy of Malta
2017 Connecticut Avenue, NW
Washington, D.C. 20008
(202) 462-3611/2
Consulates: CA (415) 468-4321
MI (313) 525-9777
MO (816) 833-0033
MN (612) 228-0935
NY (212) 725-2345
PA (610) 664-7475
TX (713) 428-7800 or
(214) 777-4463

Marshall Islands: Embassy of
Marshall Islands
2433 Massachusetts Avenue, NW
Washington, D.C. 20008
(202) 234-5414
or
Permanent Mission to the United
Nations: (212) 983-3040
Consulate General: (808) 545-7767

Martinique: See France

Mauritania: Embassy of the Islamic
Republic of Mauritania
2129 Leroy Place, NW
Washington, D.C. 20008
(202) 232-5700
or
Permanent Mission to the United
Nations: (212) 986-7963

Mauritius: Embassy of Mauritius
4301 Connecticut Avenue, NW,
Suite 441
Washington, D.C. 20008
244-1491/2
Consulates: GA (404) 892-8733 and
CA (818) 788-3720

Mexico: Embassy of Mexico
1911 Pennsylvania Avenue, NW
Washington, D.C. 20006
(202) 736-1000
Consulates: AZ (602) 242-7398
CA (213) 351-6800 or
(619) 231-8414
CO (303) 331-1110
FL (305) 716-4977
GA (404) 266-1913
IL (312) 855-1380
LA (504) 522-3596
NY (212) 689-0460
PR (809) 764-0258
TX (210) 227-1085
(214) 630-7231, or (713) 542-2300

Micronesia: Embassy of the
Federated States of Micronesia
1725 N Street, NW
Washington, D.C. 20038
(202) 223-4383
Consulates: HI (808) 836-4775
Guam (671) 646-9154

Moldova: Embassy of the Republic of
Moldova
2101 S Street, NW
Washington, D.C. 20008
(202) 667-1131

Monaco: See France
or
Consulate General of Monaco
565 Fifth Avenue
New York, NY 10017
(212) 759-5227
Consulates: CA (213) 655-8970
IL (312) 642-1242
LA (504) 522-5700
NY (212) 759-5227
PR (809) 721-4215

Mongolia: Embassy of Mongolia
2833 M Street, NW
Washington, D.C. 20007
(202) 333-7117
or
United Nations Mission of
Mongolia: (212) 861-9460

Montserrat: See United Kingdom
or
U.S. Embassy, Bridgetown,
Barbados
(246) 431-0225
or
U.S. Consulate, English Harbour,
Antigua
(268) 463-6531

Morocco: Embassy of the Kingdom
of Morocco
1601 21st Street, NW
Washington, D.C. 20009
(202) 462-7979/82
or
Consulate General: (212) 758-2625

Mozambique: Embassy of the
Republic of Mozambique
1990 M Street, NW, Suite 570
Washington, D.C. 20036
(202) 293-7146

Myanmar (formerly Burma):
Embassy of the Union of
Myanmar
2300 S Street, NW
Washington, D.C. 20008
(202) 332-9044/5

Namibia: Embassy of the Republic of
Namibia
1605 New Hampshire Avenue, NW
Washington, D.C. 20009
(202) 986-0540

Nauru: Consulate of the Republic of
Nauru in Guam
Ada Professional Building
Marine Drive, 1st Floor
Agana, Guam 96910
(671) 649-7106/7

Nepal: Royal Nepalese Embassy
2131 Leroy Place, NW
Washington, D.C. 20008
(202) 667-4550
or
Consulate General: (212) 370-4188

Netherlands: Embassy of the
Netherlands
4200 Linnean Avenue, NW
Washington, D.C. 20008
(202) 244-5300
Consulates: CA (310) 268-1598
IL (312) 856-0110
NY (212) 246-1429
TX (713) 622-8000

Netherlands Antilles: Embassy of
the Netherlands
4200 Linnean Avenue, NW
Washington, D.C. 20008
(202) 244-5300

New Zealand: Embassy of New
Zealand
37 Observatory Circle, NW
Washington, D.C. 20008
(202) 328-4800
or
Consulate General: (213) 477-8241

Nicaragua: Consulate of Nicaragua
1627 New Hampshire Avenue, NW
Washington, D.C. 20009
(202) 939-6531 or 6570
Consulates: CA (213) 252-1170 or
   (415) 765-6821
   FL (305) 220-6900
   LA (504) 523-1507
   NY (212) 983-1981
   TX (713) 272-9628

Niger: Embassy of the Republic of
Niger
2204 R Street, NW
Washington, D.C. 20008
(202) 483-4224

Nigeria: Embassy of the Federal
Republic of Nigeria
2201 M Street, NW
Washington, D.C. 20037
(202) 822-1500 or 1522
or
Consulate General: (212) 715-7200

Northern Ireland: See United
Kingdom

Norway: Royal Embassy of Norway
2720 34th Street, NW
Washington, D.C. 20008
(202) 333-6000
Consulates: CA (415) 986-0766/68
   MN (612) 332-3338
   NY (212) 421-7333
   TX (713) 521-2900

Oman: Embassy of the Sultanate of
Oman
2535 Belmond Road, NW
Washington, D.C. 20008
(202) 387-1980/2

Pakistan: Embassy of the Islamic
Republic of Pakistan (Consular
Section)
2315 Massachusetts Avenue, NW
Washington, D.C. 20008
(202) 939-6200
Consulates: CA (310) 441-5114
   NY (212) 879-5800

Palau: Representative Office
1150 18th Street, NW, Suite 750
Washington, D.C. 20036
(202) 452-6814

Panama: Embassy of the Republic of
Panama
2862 McGill Terrace, NW
Washington, D.C. 20008
(202) 483-1407
Consulates: CA (415) 391-4268
   FL (305) 371-7031 or
   (813) 831-6685
   LA (504) 525-3458
   NY (212) 840-2450
   PA (215) 574-2994
   TX (713) 622-4451

Papua New Guinea: Embassy of
Papua New Guinea
1615 New Hampshire Avenue, NW,
Suite 300
Washington, D.C. 20009
(202) 745-3680

Paraguay: Embassy of Paraguay
2400 Massachusetts Avenue, NW
Washington, D.C. 20008
(202) 483-6960

Peru: Consulate General of Peru
1625 Massachusetts Avenue, NW,
6th Floor
Washington, D.C. 20036
(202) 462-1084
Other Consulates:
   CA (213) 383-9896 or
   (415) 362-5185
   FL (305) 374-1407
   IL (312) 374-1407
   NY (212) 644-2850
   PR (809) 763-769
   TX (713) 781-5000

Philippines: Embassy of the
Philippines
1600 Massachusetts Avenue, NW
Washington, D.C. 20036

(202) 467-9300

Consulates: CA (213) 387-5321 or
(415) 433-6666
HI (808) 595-6316
IL (312) 332-6458
NY (212) 764-1330
Guam (671) 646-4620

Poland: Embassy of the Republic of
Poland (Consular Division)
2224 Wyoming Avenue, NW
Washington, D.C. 20009
(202) 232-4517

Consulates: IL (312) 337-8166
CA (310) 442-8500
NY (212) 889-8360

Portugal: Embassy of Portugal
2310 Tracy Place, NW
Washington, D.C. 20008
(202) 332-3007

Consulates: CA (415) 346-3400
MA (617) 536-8740 or
(508) 997-6151
NJ (201) 622-7300
NY (212) 246-4580
RI (401) 272-2003

Qatar: Embassy of the State of Qatar
4200 Wisconsin Ave, NW.
Suite 200
Washington, D.C. 20016
(202) 274-1600

Reunion: See France

Romania: Embassy of Romania
1607 23rd Street, NW
Washington, D.C. 20008
(202) 332-4847

Consulates: NY (212) 682-9120
CA (310) 444-0043

Russia: Embassy of Russia (Consular
Division)
2641 Tunlaw Road, NW
Washington, D.C. 20007
(202) 939-8907

Consulates: NY (212) 348-0926
CA (415) 928-6878
WA (206) 728-1910

Rwanda: Embassy of the Republic of
Rwanda
1714 New Hampshire Avenue, NW
Washington, D.C. 20009
(202) 232-2882

or
Permanent Mission to the
United Nations:
(212) 696-0644/45/46

Consulates: IL (708) 205-1188
CO (303) 321-2400

Saint Kitts and Nevis: Embassy of
Saint Kitts and Nevis
OECS Building
3216 New Mexico Avenue, NW
Washington, D.C. 20016
(202) 686-2636

or
Permanent Mission to the United
Nations: (212) 535-1234

Saint Lucia: Embassy of Saint Lucia
3216 New Mexico Avenue, NW
Washington, D.C. 20016
(202) 364-6792

or
Permanent Mission to the United
Nations: (212) 697-9360

Saint Martin (Saint Maarten): See
Netherlands Antilles

Saint Pierre: Embassy of France
(202) 944-6000

Saint Vincent and the Grenadines:
Embassy of Saint Vincent and the
Grenadines
3216 New Mexico Avenue, NW
Washington, D.C. 20016
(202) 364-6730

Samoa: Samoa Mission to the United
Nations
820 Second Avenue, Suite 800
New York, NY 10017

Consulates: HI (808) 677-7197

San Marino: Honorary Consulate of
the Republic of San Marino
1899 L St., NW, Suite 500
Washington, D.C. 20036
(202) 223-3517

Other Consulates: MI (313) 528-1190
NY (516) 242-2212

São Tomé and Príncipe: Permanent
Mission of São Tomé and
Príncipe to the United Nations
400 Park Avenue, 7th Floor
New York, NY 10022
(212) 317-0533

Saudi Arabia: Royal Embassy of
Saudi Arabia
601 New Hampshire Avenue, NW
Washington, D.C. 20037
(202) 333-2740
Consulates: CA (310) 479-6000
NY (212) 752-2740
TX (713) 785-5577
Scotland: See United Kingdom
Senegal: Embassy of the Republic of
Senegal
2112 Wyoming Avenue, NW
Washington, D.C. 20008
(202) 234-0540
Serbia and Montenegro: Embassy
of the Former Federal Republic of
Yugoslavia (Serbia & Montenegro)
2410 California Street, NW
Washington, D.C. 20008
(202) 462-6566
Seychelles: Permanent Mission of
the Seychelles to the United
Nations
820 Second Avenue, Suite 203
New York, NY 10017
(212) 687-9766
Sierra Leone: Embassy of Sierra
Leone
1701 19th Street, NW
Washington, D.C. 20009
(202) 939-9261
Singapore: Embassy of the Republic
of Singapore
3501 International Place, NW
Washington, D.C. 20008
(202) 537-3100
Slovak Republic: Embassy of the
Slovak Republic
2201 Wisconsin Avenue, NW,
Suite 250
Washington, D.C. 20007
(202) 965-5160, Extension 270
Slovenia: Embassy of the Republic of
Slovenia
1525 New Hampshire Avenue, NW
Washington, D.C. 20036
(202) 667-5363
or
Consulate General: (212) 370-3006
Solomon Islands: British Embassy
(202) 986-0205

or
Solomon Islands Mission to the
United Nations
800 Second Avenue, 4th Floor
New York, NY 10017
(212) 599-6192
Somalia: no embassy, consulate, or
mission in the United States
South Africa: Embassy of South
Africa
3051 Massachusetts Avenue, NW
Washington, D.C. 20008
(202) 232-4400
Consulates: CA (310) 657-9200
IL (312) 939-7929
NY (212) 213-4880
Spain: Embassy of Spain
2375 Pennsylvania Avenue, NW
Washington, D.C. 20037
(202) 452-0100 and 728-2330
Consulates: CA (415) 922-2995 or
(213) 938-0158
FL (305) 446-5511
IL (312) 782-4588
LA (504) 525-4951
MA (617) 536-2506
NY (212) 355-4080
PR (809) 758-6090
TX (713) 783-6200
Sri Lanka: Embassy of Sri Lanka
2148 Wyoming Avenue, NW
Washington, D.C. 20008
(202) 483-4025
Consulates: CA (805) 323-8975 and
(504) 362-3232
HI (808) 373-2040
NJ (201) 627-7855
NY (212) 986-7040
Sudan: Embassy of the Republic of
the Sudan
2210 Massachusetts Avenue, NW
Washington, D.C. 20008
(202) 338-8565/70
or
Consulate General: (212) 573-6033
or 6035
Suriname: Embassy of the Republic
of Suriname
4301 Connecticut Avenue, NW,
Suite 460
Washington, D.C. 20008

(202) 244-7488
or
Consulate: FL (305) 593-2163

Swaziland: Embassy of the Kingdom of Swaziland
3400 International Drive, NW, Suite 3M
Washington, D.C. 20008
(202) 362-6683

Sweden: Embassy of Sweden
1501 M Street, NW
Washington, D.C. 20005-1702
(202) 467-2600
Consulates: CA (310) 445-4008
FL (954) 467-3507
IL (312) 781-6262
NY (212) 583-2550

Switzerland: Embassy of Switzerland
2900 Cathedral Avenue, NW
Washington, D.C. 20008
(202) 745-7900
Consulates: CA (310) 575-1145 or
(415) 788-2272
GA (404) 870-2000
IL (312) 915-0061
NY (212) 758-2560
TX (713) 650-0000

Syria: Embassy of the Syrian Arab Republic
2215 Wyoming Avenue, NW
Washington, D.C. 20008
(202) 232-6313

Tahiti: See France

Taiwan: Taipei Economic and Cultural Representative Office
4201 Wisconsin Avenue, NW
Washington, D.C. 20016-2137
(202) 895-1800
Other Offices: GA (404) 872-0123,
MA (617) 737-2050
IL (312) 616-0100
Guam (671) 472-5865
HI (808) 595-6347
TX (713) 626-7445
MO (816) 531-1298
CA (213) 389-1215 or
(415) 362-7680
FL (305) 443-8917
NY (212) 486-0088
WA (206) 441-4586

Tajikistan: Embassy of Russia (Consular Division)
(202) 939-8907

Tanzania: Embassy of the United Republic of Tanzania
2139 R Street, NW
Washington, D.C. 20008
(202) 939-6125
or
Tanzanian Permanent Mission to the United Nations:
(212) 972-9160

Thailand: Royal Thai Embassy
1024 Wisconsin Avenue, NW
Washington, D.C. 20007
(202) 944-3608
Consulates: CA (213) 962-9574/77
IL (312) 236-2447
NY (212) 754-1770

Togo: Embassy of the Republic of Togo
2208 Massachusetts Avenue, NW
Washington, D.C. 20008
(202) 234-4212/3

Tonga: Consulate General of Tonga
360 Post Street, Suite 604
San Francisco, CA 94108
(415) 781-0365

Trinidad and Tobago: Embassy of the Republic of Trinidad and Tobago
1708 Massachusetts Avenue, NW
Washington, D.C. 20036
(202) 467-6490
Consulates: NY (212) 682-7272
MI (305) 374-2199

Tunisia: Embassy of Tunisia
1515 Massachusetts Avenue, NW
Washington, D.C. 20005
(202) 862-1850
Consulates: CA (415) 922-9222
NY (212) 272-6962

Turkey: Embassy of the Republic of Turkey
1714 Massachusetts Avenue, NW
Washington, D.C. 20036
(202) 659-8200
Consulates: CA (213) 937-0118
IL (312) 263-0644
NY (212) 949-0160
TX (713) 622-5849

Turkmenistan: Embassy of Turkmenistan
2207 Massachusetts Avenue, NW
Washington, D.C. 20008
(202) 588-1500

Turks and Caicos: See United
Kingdom
or
U.S. Embassy, Nassau, Bahamas
(242) 322-1181 or 328-2206
Tuvalu: See United Kingdom
Uganda: Embassy of the Republic of
Uganda
5909 16th Street, NW
Washington, D.C. 20011
(202) 726-7100/02
or
Permanent Mission to the United
Nations: (212) 949-0110
Ukraine: Embassy of Ukraine
3350 M Street, NW
Washington, D.C. 20007
(202) 333-0606 or 7507/09
Consulates: IL (312) 642-4388
NY (212) 371-5690
United Arab Emirates: Embassy of
the United Arab Emirates
1255 22nd Street, NW, Suite 700
Washington, D.C. 20037
(202) 955-7999
United Kingdom: British Embassy
(Consular Section)
19 Observatory Circle, NW
Washington, D.C. 20008
(202) 986-0205
Consulates: CA (415) 922-9222
NY (212) 272-6962
Uruguay: Embassy of Uruguay
2715 M Street, NW, 3rd Floor
Washington, D.C. 20007
(202) 331-1313
Consulates: CA (213) 394-5777
FL (305) 358-9350
LA (504) 525-8354
NY (212) 753-8191/2
Uzbekistan: Embassy of the Republic
of Uzbekistan
1746 Massachusetts Avenue, NW
Washington, D.C. 20036
(202) 293-6803
or
Uzbekistan Consulate:
(212) 754-6178 or 7403

Vanuatu: See United Kingdom
or
Vanuatu Mission to the United
Nations: (212) 593-0144
Venezuela: Embassy the Republic of
Venezuela.
1099 30th Street NW
Washington, D.C. 20007
(202) 342-2214
Consulates: CA (415) 512-8340
FL (305) 577-3834
IL (312) 236-9655
LA (504) 522-3284
MA (617) 266-9355
NY (212) 826-1660
PR (809) 766-4250/1
TX (713) 961-5141
Vietnam: Embassy of Vietnam
1233 20th Street NW, Suite 400
Washington, D.C. 20036
(202) 861-2293 or 0694
Virgin Islands, British: See United
Kingdom
Wales: See United Kingdom
Western Samoa: See Samoa
West Indies, British: See United
Kingdom
West Indies, French: See France
Yemen: Embassy of the Republic of
Yemen
2600 Virginia Avenue, NW,
Suite 705
Washington, D.C. 20037
(202) 965-4760
or
Yemen Mission to the United
Nations: (212) 355-1730
Zambia: Embassy of the Republic of
Zambia
2419 Massachusetts Avenue, NW
Washington, D.C. 20008
(202) 265-9717/19
Zimbabwe: Embassy of Zimbabwe
1608 New Hampshire Avenue, NW
Washington, D.C. 20009
(202) 332-7100

⊙ Central Intelligence Agency. "World Fact Book 2000," www.cia.gov/publications/
factbook/fields/diplomatic_representation_in_the_us.html

Congress: The House of Representatives and the Senate

"All legislative Powers herein granted shall be vested in a Congress of the United States, which shall consist of a Senate and a House of Representatives." (U.S. Constitution, 1787)

Although the first Congress in 1789 consisted of 20 senators and 59 representatives, today there are 100 senators—2 from each state—and 435 representatives. The number of representatives from each state is determined by the population of the state. There is a resident commissioner from Puerto Rico, who is elected for a 4-year term, and delegates from American Samoa, the District of Columbia, Guam, and the Virgin Islands, who are elected for two-year terms.

A representative must reside in the state from which he or she is elected, be at least 25 years old, and have been a citizen of the United States for at least seven years. A senator must reside in the state from which he or she is elected, be at least 30 years old, and have been a citizen of the United States for at least nine years.

The Senate and the House have equal responsibility for declaring war, maintaining the armed forces, assessing taxes, borrowing money, minting currency, regulating commerce, and making all laws necessary for the operation of the government. The Senate holds exclusive authority to advise and consent on treaties and nominations. In cases of impeachment, the House votes to impeach and the Senate conducts the impeachment trial.

⊙ GPO. *History of the House of Representatives.* Washington, D.C.: U.S. GPO, 1994.
   United States House of Representatives. "Historical Facts-Historical Highlights-Office of the Clerk," www.clerkweb.house.gov/histrecs/househis/index.htm
   United States Senate. "Learning about the Senate," www.senate.gov/learning

House Committees and Subcommittees

Standing Committees	*Subcommittees*
Agriculture	General Farm Commodities, Resource Conservation, and Credit; Livestock and Horticulture; Risk Management, Research, and Specialty Crops; Department Operations, Oversight, Nutrition, and Forestry
Appropriations	Agriculture, Rural Development, Food and Drug Administration, and Related Agencies; Commerce, Justice, State, and Judiciary; Defense; District of Columbia; Energy and Water Development; Foreign Operations, Export Financing, and Related Programs; Interior; Labor, Health and Human Services, and Education; Legislative; Military Construction; Transportation; Treasury, Postal Service, and General Government; VA, HUD, and Independent Agencies
Armed Services	Military Procurement; Military Research and Development; Military Readiness; Military Installations and Facilities
Budget	
Education and the Workforce	Employer-Employee Relations; Workforce Protections; Early Childhood, Youth, and Families; Oversight and Investigations
Energy and Commerce	Telecommunications, Trade, and Consumer Protection; Finance and Hazardous Materials; Health and Environment; Energy and Power; Oversight and Investigations

House Committees and Subcommittees (cont.)

Standing Committees	Subcommittees
Financial Services	Housing and Community Opportunity; Financial Institutions and Consumer Credit; Domestic and International Monetary Policy; Capital Markets, Securities, and Government Sponsored Enterprises; General Oversight
Government Reform	National Security, International Affairs, and Criminal Justice; Civil Service; Human Resources; Postal Service; Government Management, Information, and Technology; District of Columbia; National Economic Growth, Natural Resources, and Regulatory Affairs; Census
House Administration	
International Relations	International Economic Policy and Trade; Asia and the Pacific; International Operations and Human Rights; The Western Hemisphere; Africa
Judiciary	Courts and Intellectual Property; Crime; Immigration and Claims; The Constitution; Commercial and Administrative Law
Resources	National Parks and Public Lands; Fisheries, Conservation, Wildlife, and Oceans; Energy and Mineral Resources; Water and Power; Forests and Forest Health
Rules	Rules and Organization of the House; Legislative and Budget Process
Science	Basic Research; Energy and Environment; Space and Aeronautics; Technology
Small Business	Empowerment; Government Programs and Oversight; Regulatory Reform and Paperwork Reduction; Tax, Finance, and Exports; Rural Enterprises, Business Opportunities, and Special Small Business Problems
Standards of Official Conduct	
Transportation and Infrastructure	Aviation; Coast Guard and Maritime Transportation; Public Buildings and Economic Development; Railroads; Surface Transportation; Water Resources and Environment
Veterans' Affairs	Health; Benefits; Oversight and Investigations
Ways and Means	Trade; Oversight; Health; Social Security; Human Resources

Select Committees	
Permanent Select Committee on Intelligence	Human Intelligence, Analysis, and Counterintelligence; Technical and Tactical Intelligence

Select Committee on U.S. National Security and Military/Commercial Concerns with the People's Republic of China

Joint Committees

Joint Economic Committee

Joint Committee on the Library

Joint Committee on Printing

Joint Committee on Taxation

⊙ U.S. House of Representatives. "House Committee Information,"
www.clerkweb.house.gov/mbrcmtee/members/commem.htm

Speakers of the House of Representatives

Congress	Speaker	Party	State	Date Elected	President
1	Frederick A. C. Muhlenberg	—	Pennsylvania	Apr. 1, 1789	Washington
2	Jonathan Trumbull	—	Connecticut	Oct. 24, 1791	Washington
3	Frederick A. C. Muhlenberg	—	Pennsylvania	Dec. 2, 1793	Washington
4, 5	Jonathan Dayton—	—	New Jersey	Dec. 7, 1795	Washington
6	Theodore Sedgwick		Massachusetts	Dec. 2, 1799	J. Adams
7, 8, 9	Nathaniel Macon	Republican	North Carolina	Dec. 7, 1801	Jefferson
10, 11	Joseph B. Varnum	Republican	Massachusetts	Oct. 26, 1807	Jefferson
12	Henry Clay	Republican	Kentucky	Nov. 4, 1811	Madison
13	Henry Clay	Republican	Kentucky	May 24, 1813	Madison
13	Langdon Cheves	Republican	South Carolina	Jan. 19, 1814	Madison
14, 15	Henry Clay	Republican	Kentucky	Dec. 4, 1815	Madison
16	Henry Clay	Republican	Kentucky	Dec. 6, 1819	Monroe
16	John W. Taylor	Republican	New York	Nov. 15, 1820	Monroe
17	Philip P. Barbour	Republican	Virginia	Dec. 4, 1821	Monroe
18	Henry Clay	Republican	Kentucky	Dec. 1, 1823	Monroe
19	John W. Taylor	Republican	New York	Dec. 5, 1825	Monroe
20, 21,	Andrew Stevenson	Jacksonian	Virginia	Dec. 3, 1827	J. Q. Adams
22, 23	Andrew Stevenson	Jacksonian	Virginia	Dec. 2, 1833	Jackson
23	John Bell	Whig	Tennessee	June 2, 1834	Jackson
24, 25	James K. Polk	Republican	Tennessee	Dec. 7, 1835	Jackson
26	Robert M. T. Hunter	States Rights Whig	Virginia	Dec. 16, 1839	Van Buren
27	John White	Whig	Kentucky	May 31, 1841	Van Buren
28	John W. Jones	Democrat	Virginia	Dec. 4, 1843	Tyler

Speakers of the House of Representatives *(cont.)*

Congress	Speaker	Party	State	Date Elected	President
29	John W. Davis	Democrat	Indiana	Dec. 1, 1845	Tyler
30	Robert C. Winthrop	Whig	Massachusetts	Dec. 6, 1847	Polk
31	Howell Cobb	Democrat	Georgia	Dec. 22, 1849	Taylor
32, 33	Linn Boyd	Democrat	Kentucky	Dec. 1, 1851	Fillmore
34	Nathaniel P. Banks	American	Massachusetts	Feb. 2, 1856	Pierce
35	James L. Orr	Democrat	South Carolina	Dec. 7, 1857	Pierce
36	William Pennington	Republican	New Jersey	Feb. 1, 1860	Buchanan
37	Galusha A. Grow	Republican	Pennsylvania	July 4, 1861	Lincoln
38, 39	Schuyler Colfax	Republican	Indiana	Dec. 7, 1863	Lincoln
40	Schuyler Colfax	Republican	Indiana	Mar. 4, 1867	Johnson
40	Theodore M. Pomeroy	Republican	New York	Mar. 3, 1869	Grant
41, 42, 43	James G. Blaine	Republican	Maine	Mar. 4, 1869	Grant
44	Michael C. Kerr	Democrat	Indiana	Dec. 6, 1875	Grant
44	Samuel J. Randall	Democrat	Pennsylvania	Dec. 4, 1876	Grant
45, 46	Samuel J. Randall	Democrat	Pennsylvania	Oct. 15, 1877	Grant
47	J. Warren Keifer	Republican	Ohio	Dec. 5, 1881	Hayes
48, 49, 50	John G. Carlisle	Democrat	Kentucky	Dec. 3, 1883	Arthur
51	Thomas B. Reed	Republican	Maine	Dec. 2, 1889	Cleveland
52	Charles F. Crisp	Democrat	Georgia	Dec. 8, 1891	Harrison, B.
54, 55	Thomas B. Reed	Republican	Maine	Dec. 2, 1895	Cleveland
56, 57	David B. Henderson	Republican	Iowa	Dec. 4, 1899	McKinley
58, 59, 60, 61	Joseph G. Cannon	Republican	Illinois	Nov. 9, 1903	Roosevelt, T.
62, 63, 64, 65	Champ Clark	Democrat	Missouri	Apr. 4, 1911	Taft

Congress	Speaker	Party	State	Date	President
66, 67, 68	Frederick H. Gillett	Republican	Massachusetts	May 19, 1919	Wilson
69, 70, 71	Nicholas Longworth	Republican	Ohio	Dec. 7, 1925	Coolidge
72	John N. Garner	Democrat	Texas	Dec. 7, 1931	Hoover
73	Henry T. Rainey	Democrat	Illinois	Mar. 9, 1933	Hoover
74	Joseph W. Byrns	Democrat	Tennessee	Jan. 3, 1935	F. D. Roosevelt
74	William B. Bankhead	Democrat	Alabama	June 4, 1936	F. D. Roosevelt
75, 76	William B. Bankhead	Democrat	Alabama	Jan. 5, 1937	F. D. Roosevelt
77, 78, 79	Sam T. Rayburn	Democrat	Texas	Jan. 3, 1941	F. D. Roosevelt
80	Joseph W. Martin	Republican	Massachusetts	Jan. 3, 1947	Truman
81, 82	Sam T. Rayburn	Democrat	Texas	Jan. 3, 1949	Truman
83	Joseph W. Martin	Republican	Massachusetts	Jan. 3, 1953	Truman
84, 85, 86, 87	Sam T. Rayburn	Democrat	Texas	Jan. 5, 1955	Eisenhower
88, 89, 90, 91	John W. McCormack	Democrat	Massachusetts	Jan. 9, 1963	Johnson
92, 93, 94	Carl Albert	Democrat	Oklahoma	Jan. 21, 1971	Nixon
95, 96, 97, 98, 99	Thomas P. O'Neill, Jr.	Democrat	Massachusetts	Jan. 4, 1977	Ford
100	James C. Wright, Jr.	Democrat	Texas	Jan. 6, 1987	Reagan
101	James C. Wright, Jr.	Democrat	Texas	Jan. 3, 1989	Bush
101	Thomas S. Foley	Democrat	Washington	June 6, 1989	Bush
102, 103	Thomas S. Foley	Democrat	Washington	Jan. 3, 1991	Bush
104, 105	Newt Gingrich	Republican	Georgia	Jan. 4, 1995	Clinton
106	John Dennis Hastert	Republican	Illinois	Jan. 6, 1999	Clinton

☉ United States House of Representatives. "Historical Facts-Historical Highlights-Office of the Clerk," http://clerkweb.house.gov/histrecs/househis/lead.htm

House of Representatives Membership by State

(valid through the 2000 election)

State	No. of Representatives	State	No. of Representatives
Alabama	7	Nevada	2
Alaska	1	New Hampshire	2
Arizona	6	New Jersey	13
Arkansas	4	New Mexico	3
California	52	New York	31
Colorado	6	North Carolina	12
Connecticut	6	North Dakota	1
Delaware	1	Ohio	19
Florida	23	Oklahoma	6
Georgia	11	Oregon	5
Hawaii	2	Pennsylvania	21
Idaho	2	Rhode Island	2
Illinois	20	South Carolina	6
Indiana	10	South Dakota	1
Iowa	5	Tennessee	9
Kansas	4	Texas	30
Kentucky	6	Utah	3
Louisiana	7	Vermont	1
Maine	2	Virginia	11
Maryland	8	Washington	9
Massachusetts	10	West Virginia	3
Michigan	16	Wisconsin	9
Minnesota	8	Wyoming	1
Mississippi	5	District of Columbia	1
Missouri	9	Puerto Rico	1
Montana	1	U.S. Virgin Islands	1
Nebraska	3		

⊙ United States House of Representatives. "Historical Facts-Historical Highlights-Office
of the Clerk," www.clerkweb.house.gov/histrecs/househis/index.html

Wawro, Gregory. *Legislative Entrepreneurship in the U.S. House of Representatives*. Ann
Arbor: University of Michigan Press, 2000.

Women Representatives

Name	State	Party	Years of Service
Jeannette Rankin	Montana	Republican	1917–19; 1941–43
Alice Mary Robertson	Oklahoma	Republican	1921–23
Winnifred Sprague Mason Huck	Illinois	Republican	1922–23
Mae Ella Nolan	California	Republican	1923–25
Florence Prag Kahn	California	Republican	1925–37
Mary Teresa Norton	New Jersey	Democrat	1925–51
Edith Nourse Rogers	Massachusetts	Republican	1925–60
Katherine Gudger Langley	Kentucky	Republican	1927–31
Pearl Peden Oldfield	Arkansas	Democrat	1929–31
Ruth Hanna McCormick	Illinois	Republican	1929–31

Ruth Bryan Owen	Florida	Democrat	1929–33
Ruth Sears Baker Pratt	New York	Republican	1929–33
Effiegene Locke Wingo	Arkansas	Democrat	1930–33
Willa McCord Blake Eslick	Tennessee	Democrat	1932–33
Kathryn Ellen O'Loughlin (McCarthy)	Kansas	Democrat	1933–35
Virginia Ellis Jenckes	Indiana	Democrat	1933–39
Isabella Selmes Greenway	Arizona	Democrat	1933–37
Marian Williams Clarke	New York	Republican	1933–35
Caroline Love Goodwin O'Day	New York	Democrat	1935–43
Nan Wood Honeyman	Oregon	Democrat	1937–39
Elizabeth Hawley Gasque	South Carolina	Democrat	1938–39
Jessie Sumner	Illinois	Republican	1939–47
Clara Gooding McMillan	South Carolina	Democrat	1939–41
Frances Payne Bolton	Ohio	Republican	1940–69
Margaret Chase Smith	Maine	Republican	1940–49
Florence Reville Gibbs	Georgia	Democrat	1940–41
Katharine Edgar Byron	Maryland	Democrat	1941–43
Veronica Grace Boland	Pennsylvania	Democrat	1942–43
Clare Boothe Luce	Connecticut	Republican	1943–47
Winifred Claire Stanley	New York	Republican	1943–45
Willa Lybrand Fulmer	South Carolina	Democrat	1944–45
Emily Taft Douglas	Illinois	Democrat	1945–47
Helen Gahagan Douglas	California	Democrat	1945–51
Chase Going Woodhouse	Connecticut	Democrat	1945–47; 1949–51
Helen Douglas Mankin	Goergia	Democrat	1946–47
Eliza Jane Pratt	North Carolina	Democrat	1946–47
Georgia Lee Lusk	New Mexico	Democrat	1947–49
Katharine Price Collier St. George	New York	Republican	1947–65
Reva Zilpha Beck Bosone	Utah	Democrat	1949–53
Cecil Murray Harden	Indiana	Republican	1949–59
Edna Flannery Kelly	New York	Democrat	1949–69
Marguerite Stitt Church	Illinois	Republican	1951–63
Ruth Thompson	Michigan	Republican	1951–57
Maude Elizabeth Kee	West Virginia	Democrat	1951–65
Vera Daerr Buchanan	Pennsylvania	Democrat	1951–55
Gracie Bowers Pfost	Idaho	Democrat	1953–63
Leonor Kretzer Sullivan	Missouri	Democrat	1953–77
Mary Elizabeth Pruett Farrington (Delegate)	Hawaii	Republican	1954–57
Iris Faircloth Blitch	Georgia	Democrat	1955–63
Edith Starrett Green	Oregon	Democrat	1955–74
Martha Wright Griffiths	Michigan	Democrat	1955–74
Coya Gjesdal Knutson	Florida, Minnesota	Democrat	1955–59
Kathryn Elizabeth Granahan	Pennsylvania	Democrat	1956–63
Florence Price Dwyer	New Jersey	Republican	1957–73
Catherine Dean May	Washington	Republican	1959–71
Edna Oakes Simpson	Illinois	Republican	1959–61
Jessica McCullough Weis	New York	Republican	1959–63

Women Representatives *(cont.)*

Name	State	Party	Years of Service
Julia Butler Hansen	Washington	Democrat	1960–74
Catherine Dorris Norrell	Arkansas	Democrat	1961–63
Louise Goff Reece	Tennessee	Republican	1961–63
Corinne Boyd Riley	South Carolina	Democrat	1962–63
Charlotte Thompson Reid	Illinois	Republican	1963–71
Irene Bailey Baker	Tennessee	Republican	1964–65
Patsy Takemoto Mink	Hawaii	Democrat	1965–77; 1990–
Lera Millard Thomas	Texas	Democrat	1966–67
Nargaret M. Heckler	Massachusetts	Republican	1967–83
Shirley Anita Chisholm	New York	Democrat	1969–83
Bella Savitzky Abzug	New York	Democrat	1971–77
Ella Tambussi Grasso	Connecticut	Democrat	1971–75
Louise Day Hicks	Massachusetts	Democrat	1971–73
Elizabeth Bullock Andrews	Alabama	Democrat	1972–73
Yvonne Brathwaite Burke	California	Democrat	1973–79
Marjorie Sewell Holt	Maryland	Republican	1973–87
Elizabeth Holtzman	New York	Democrat	1973–81
Barbara Charline Jordan	Texas	Democrat	1973–79
Patricia Scott Schroeder	Colorado	Democrat	1973–97
Corinne Claiborne (Lindy) Boggs	Louisiana	Democrat	1973–91
Cardiss Collins	Illinois	Democrat	1973–97
Millicent Hammond Fenwick	New Jersey	Republican	1975–83
Martha Elizabeth Keys	Kansas	Democrat	1975–89
Marilyn Laird Lloyd	Tennessee	Democrat	1975–95
Helen Stevenson Meyner	New Jersey	Democrat	1975–79
Virginia Dodd Smith	Nebraska	Republican	1975–91
Gladys Noon Spellman	Maryland	Democrat	1975–81
Shirley Neil Pettis	California	Republican	1975–79
Barbara Ann Mikulski	Maryland	Democrat	1977–87
Mary Rose Oakar	Ohio	Democrat	1977–93
Beverly Barton Butcher Byron	Maryland	Democrat	1979–93
Geraldine Anne Ferraro	New York	Democrat	1979–85
Olympia Jean Snowe	Maine	Republican	1979–95
Bobbi Fiedler	California	Republican	1981–87
Lynn Morley Martin	Illinois	Republican	1981–91
Margaret Scafati Roukema	New Jersey	Republican	1981–
Claudene Schneider	Rhode Island	Republican	1981–91
Barbara Bailey Kennelly	Connecticut	Democrat	1982–99
Jean Spencer Ashbrook	Ohio	Republican	1982–83
Katie Beatrice Hall	Indiana	Democrat	1982–85
Barbara Boxer	California	Democrat	1983–93
Nancy Lee Johnson	Connecticut	Republican	1983–
Marcia Carolyn (Marcy) Kaptur	Ohio	Democrat	1983–
Barbara Farrell Vucanovich	Nevada	Republican	1983–97
Sala Burton	California	Democrat	1983–87
Helen Delich Bentley	Maryland	Republican	1985–95

Jan Meyers	Kansas	Republican	195–97
Catherine S. Long	Louisiana	Democrat	1985–87
Constance A. Morella	Maryland	Republican	1987–
Elizabeth J. Patterson	South Carolina	Democrat	1987–93
Patricia Fukuda Saiki	Hawaii	Republican	1987–91
Louise M. Slaughter	New York	Democrat	1987–
Nancy Pelosi	California	Democrat	1987–
Nita M. Lowey	New York	Democrat	1989–
Jolene Unsoeld	Washington	Democrat	1989–95
Jill Long	Indiana	Democrat	1989–95
Ileana Ros-Lehtinen	Florida	Republican	1989–
Susan Molinari	New York	Republican	1990–97
Barbara-Rose Collins	Mississippi	Democrat	1991–97
Rosa DeLauro	Connecticut	Democrat	1991–
Joan Kelly Horn	Missouri	Democrat	1991–93
Eleanor Holmes Norton (Delegate)	District of Columbia	Democrat	1991–
Maxine Waters	California	Democrat	1991–
Eva Clayton	North Carolina	Democrat	1992–
Corrine Brown	Florida	Democrat	1993–
Leslie Byrne	Virginia	Democrat	1993–95
Maria Cantwell	Washington	Democrat	1993–95
Pat Danner	Missouri	Democrat	1993–
Jennifer Dunn	Washington	Republican	1993–
Karan English	Arizona	Democrat	1993–95
Anna G. Eshoo	California	Democrat	1993–
Tillie Fowler	Florida	Republican	1993–
Elizabeth Furse	Oregon	Democrat	1993–99
Jane Harman	California	Democrat	1993–99
Eddie Bernice Johnson	Texas	Democrat	1993–
Blanche Lambert Lincoln	Arkansas	Democrat	1993–97
Carolyn B. Maloney	New York	Democrat	1993–
Marjorie Margolies-Mezvinsky	Pennsylvania	Democrat	1993–95
Cynthia McKinney	Georgia	Democrat	1993–
Carrie P. Meek	Florida	Democrat	1993–
Deborah Pryce	Ohio	Republican	1993–
Lucille Roybal-Allard	California	Democrat	1993–
Lynn Schenk	California	Democrat	1993–95
Karen Shepherd	Utah	Democrat	1993–95
Karen Thurman	Florida	Democrat	1993–
Nydia M. Velazquez	New York	Democrat	1993–
Lynn Woolsey	California	Democrat	1993
Helen Chenoweth	Idaho	Republican	1995–
Barbara Cubin	Wyoming	Republican	1995–
Sheila Jackson-Lee	Texas	Democrat	1995–
Sue Kelly	New York	Republican	1995–
Zoe Lofgren	California	Democrat	1995–
Karen McCarthy	Missouri	Democrat	1995–
Sue Myrick	North Carolina	Republican	1995–
Lynn Rivers	Mississippi	Democrat	1995–
Andrea Seastrand	California	Republican	1995–97

Women Representatives *(cont.)*

Name	State	Party	Years of Service
Linda Smith	Washington	Republican	1995–99
Enid Greene (Waldholtz)	Utah	Republican	1995–97
Juanita Millender-McDonald	California	Democrat	1997–
JoAnn Emerson	Missouri	Republican	1997–
Julia Carson	Indiana	Democrat	1997–
Donna M. Christian-Green (Delegate)	Virginia	Democrat	1997–
Diana DeGette	Colorado	Democrat	1997–
Kay Granger	Texas	Republican	1997–
Darlene Hooley	Oregon	Democrat	1997–
Carolyn Cheeks Kilpatrick	Mississippi	Democrat	1997–
Carolyn McCarthy	New York	Democrat	1997–
Anne Northup	Kentucky	Republican	1997–
Loretta Sanchez	California	Democrat	1997–
Debbie Stabenow	Mississippi	Democrat	1997–
Ellen Tauscher	California	Democrat	1997–
Mary Bono	California	Republican	1998–
Lois Capps	California	Democrat	1998–
Barbara Lee	California	Democrat	1998–
Heather Wilson	New Mexico	Republican	1998–
Janice Schakowsky	Illinois	Democrat	1998–

⊙ United States House of Representatives. "Women in Congress," http://bioguide.congress.gov/congresswomen/index.asp

Young, Lisa. *Feminists and Party Politics.* Vancouver: University of British Columbia Press, 2000.

Foerstel, Karen. *Climbing the Hill: Gender Conflict in Congress.* Wesport, Conn.: Praeger, 1996.

Senate Committees and Subcommittees

Standing Committees	Subcommittees
Agriculture, Nutrition, and Forestry	Forestry, Conservation, and Rural Revitalization; Marketing, Inspection, and Product Promotion; Production and Price Competitiveness; Research, Nutrition, and General Legislation
Appropriations	Agriculture, Rural Development, and Related Agencies; Commerce, Justice, State, and Judiciary; Defense; District of Columbia; Energy and Water Development; Interior; Labor, Health, and Human Services; Education; Legislative Branch; Military Construction; Transportation; Treasury and General Government; Va-Hud-Independent Agencies
Armed Services	Acquisitions and Technology; Airland Forces; Personnel; Readiness; Sea Power; Strategic Forces
Banking, Housing, and Urban Affairs	Financial Institutions and Regulatory Relief; Financial Services and Technology; Housing Opportunity and Community Development; International Finance; Securities

Budget	
Commerce, Science, and Transportation	Aviation; Communications; Consumer Affairs, Foreign Commerce and Tourism; Manufacturing and Competitiveness; Oceans and Fisheries; Science, Technology, and Space; Surface Transportation and Merchant Marine
Energy and Natural Resources	Energy Research, Development, Production, and Regulation; Forests and Public Land Management; Parks, Historic Preservation and Recreation; Water and Power
Environment and Public Works	Clean Air Wetlands, Private Property, and Nuclear Safety; Drinking Water, Fisheries, and Wildlife; Superfund, Waste Control, and Risk Assessment; Transportation and Infrastructure
Finance	Health Care; International Trade; Long-Term Growth, Debt, and Deficit Reduction; Social Security and Family Policy; Taxation and IRS Oversight
Foreign Relations	African Affairs; East Asian and Pacific Affairs; European Affairs; International Economic Policy, Export, and Trade Promotion; International Operations; Near Eastern and South Asian Affairs; Western Hemisphere, Peace Corps, Narcotics, and Terrorism
Governmental Affairs	International Security Proliferation and Federal Services; Oversight of Government Management, Restructuring, and the District of Columbia; Permanent Subcommittee on Investigations
Judiciary	Administration Oversight and the Courts; Antitrust, Business Rights, and Competition; Constitution, Federalism and Property Rights; Immigration; Technology, Terrorism, and Government Information; Youth Violence
Health, Education, Labor, and Pensions	Aging; Children and Families; Employment and Training; Public Health and Safety

Rules and Administration

Small Business

Veterans' Affairs

Select and Special Committees

Senate Select Committee on Intelligence

Senate Select Committee on Ethics

Senate Select Committee on Indian Affairs

Senate Special Committee on Aging

Joint Committees of Congress

Joint Economic Committee

Joint Committee on Taxation

Joint Committee on the Library of Congress

⊙ U.S. Senate. "Senate Committees," www.senage.gov/committees/index.cfm
Congressional Research Service. *The Committee System in the U.S. Congress.*
Washington, D.C.: Congressional Research Service, Library of Congress, 1994.

Senate Majority and Minority Leaders from 1920

Congress	Majority Leader	Minority Leader	President
66th 1920–21	Henry Cabot Lodge [R]	Oscar W. Underwood [D]	Wilson (D)
67th 1921–23	Henry Cabot Lodge [R]	Oscar W. Underwood [D]	Harding (R)
68th 1923–25	Henry Cabot Lodge [R]		
	Charles Curtis [R]	Joseph T. Robinson [D]	Harding (R)
			Coolidge (R)
69th 1925–27	Charles Curtis [R]	Joseph T. Robinson [D]	Coolidge (R)
70th 1927–29	Charles Curtis [R]	Joseph T. Robinson [D]	Coolidge (R)
71st 1929–31	James E. Watson [R]	Joseph T. Robinson [D]	Hoover (R)
72nd 1931–33	James E. Watson [R]	Joseph T. Robinson [D]	Hoover (R)
73rd 1933–35	Joseph T. Robinson [D]	Charles L. McNary [R]	Roosevelt (D)
74th 1935–37	Joseph T. Robinson [D]	Charles L. McNary [R]	Roosevelt (D)
75th 1937–39	Joseph T. Robinson [D]		
	Alben Barkley [D]	Charles L. McNary [R]	Roosevelt (D)
76th 1939–41	Alben Barkley [D]	Charles L. McNary [R]	Roosevelt (D)
77th 1941–43	Alben Barkley [D]	Charles L. McNary [R]	Roosevelt (D)
78th 1943–45	Alben Barkley [D]	W. H. White, Jr. [R]	Roosevelt (D)
79th 1945–47	Alben Barkley [D]	W. H. White, Jr. [R]	Roosevelt (D)
			Truman (D)
80th 1947–49	W. H. White, Jr. [R]	Alben Barkley [D]	Truman (D)
81st 1949–51	Scott W. Lucas [D]	Kenneth S. Wherry [R]	Truman (D)
82nd 1951–53	E. W. McFarland [D]	Kenneth S. Wherry [R]	
		Styles Bridges [R]	Truman (D)
83rd 1953–55	Robert A. Taft [R]		
	William F. Knowland [R]	Lyndon Johnson [D]	Eisenhower (R)
84th 1955–57	L. B. Johnson [D]	William F. Knowland [R]	Eisenhower (R)
85th 1957–59	L. B. Johnson [D]	William F. Knowland [R]	Eisenhower (R)
86th 1959–61	L. B. Johnson [D]	Everett Dirksen [R]	Eisenhower (R)
87th 1961–63	Mike Mansfield [D]	Everett Dirksen [R]	Kennedy (D)
88th 1963–65	Mike Mansfield [D]	Everett Dirksen [R]	Kennedy (D)
			Johnson (D)
89th 1965–67	Mike Mansfield [D]	Everett Dirksen [R]	Johnson (D)
90th 1967–69	Mike Mansfield [D]	Everett Dirksen {R}	Nixon (R)
91st 1969–71	Mike Mansfield [D]	Everett Dirksen [R]	
		Hugh D. Scott, Jr. [R]	Nixon (R)
92nd 1971–73	Mike Mansfield [D]	Hugh D. Scott, Jr. [R]	Nixon (R)
93rd 1973–75	Mike Mansfield [D]	Hugh D. Scott, Jr. [R]	Nixon (R)
			Ford (R)
94th 1975–77	Mike Mansfield [D]	Hugh D. Scott, Jr. [R]	Ford (R)
95th 1977–79	Robert C. Byrd [D]	Howard H. Baker, Jr. [R]	Carter (D)
96th 1979–81	Robert C. Byrd [D]	Howard H. Baker, Jr. [R]	Carter (D)
97th 1981–83	Howard H. Baker, Jr. [R]	Robert C. Byrd [D]	Reagan (R)
98th 1983–85	Howard H. Baker, Jr. [R]	Robert C. Byrd [D]	Reagan (R)
99th 1985–87	Bob Dole [R]	Robert C. Byrd [D]	Reagan (R)
100th 1987–89	Robert C. Byrd [D]	Bob Dole [R]	Reagan (R)
101st 1989–91	George J. Mitchell [D]	Bob Dole [R]	Bush (R)
102nd 1991–93	George J. Mitchell [D]	Bob Dole [R]	Bush (R)
103rd 1993–95	George J. Mitchell [D]	Bob Dole [R]	Clinton (D)

104th	1995–97	Bob Dole [R]		
		Trent Lott [R]	Thomas A. Daschle [D]	Clinton (D)
105th	1997–99	Trent Lott [R]	Thomas A. Daschle [D]	Clinton (D)
106th	1999–2001	Trent Lott [R]	Thomas A. Daschle [D]	Clinton (D)

⊙ Congressional Quarterly. *First Among Equals: Outstanding Senate Leaders of the Twentieth Century.* Washington, D.C: Congressional Quarterly, 1991.

   U.S. Congress, Senate. *Majority and Minority Leaders of the Senate.* Washington, D.C.: U.S. Congress, Senate Doc. 100-29.

   United States Senate. www.senate.gov/learning

Women Senators

Name	*State*	*Party*	*Years of Service*
Rebecca Latimer Felton	Georgia	Democrat	1922
Hattie Wyatt Caraway	Arkansas	Democrat	1931–45
Rose McConnell Long	Louisiana	Democrat	1936–37
Dixie Bibb Graves	Alabama	Democrat	1937–38
Gladys Pyle	South Dakota	Republican	1938–39
Vera Cahlahan Bushfield	South Dakota	Republican	1948
Margaret Chase-Smith	Maine	Republican	1949–73
Eva Kelley Bowring	Nebraska	Republican	1954
Maurice Brown Neuberger	Oregon	Democrat	1960–67
Elaine S. Edwards	Louisiana	Democrat	1972
Muriel Humphrey	Minnesota	Democrat	1978
Maryon Allen	Alabama	Democrat	1978
Nancy Landon Kassebaum	Kansas	Republican	1978–97
Paula Hawkins	Florida	Republican	1981–87
Barbara Mikulski	Maryland	Democrat	1987–
Jocelyn Burdick	North Dakota	Democrat	1992
Dianne Feinstein	California	Democrat	1993–
Barbara Boxer	California	Democrat	1993–
Carol Moseley-Braun	Illinois	Democrat	1993–99
Patty Murray	Washington	Democrat	1993–
Kay Bailey Hutchison	Texas	Republican	1993–
Olympia Jean Snowe	Maine	Republican	1995–
Shelia Frahm	Kansas	Republican	1996
Mary Landrieu	Louisiana	Democrat	1997–
Susan Collins	Maine	Republican	1997–
Blanche Lincoln	Arkansas	Democrat	1999–

⊙ Schenken, Suzanne O'Dea, and Ann Richards. *From Suffrage to the Senate: An Encyclopedia of American Women in Politics.* Santa Barbara, Calif.: ABC-CLIO, 1999.

   Rinehart, Sue Tolleson. *Gender Consciousness and Politics.* New York: Routledge, 1992.

   United States Senate. "Learning About the Senate," www.senate.gov/learning/stat–14.html

Presidential Election Results

Year	Candidates	Parties	Electoral Vote	Popular Vote/Notes
1789	**George Washington**	Federalist	69	Adams becomes V.P.
	John Adams	Federalist	34	
1792	**George Washington**	Federalist	132	
	John Adams	Federalist	77	
	George Clinton		50	
	Thomas Jefferson		4	
1796	**John Adams**	Federalist	71	Jefferson becomes V.P.
	Thomas Jefferson	Democratic-Republican	68	
1800	**Thomas Jefferson**	Democratic-Republican	73	House of Representatives breaks the tie:
	Aaron Burr	Democratic-Republican	73	Jefferson 10, Burr 4
	John Adams	Federalist	65	
1804	**Thomas Jefferson**	Democratic-Republican	162	
	Charles Pickney	Federalist		
1808	**James Madison**	Democratic-Republican	122	
	Charles C. Pinckney	Federalist	47	
1812	**James Madison**	Democratic-Republican	128	
	DeWitt Clinton	Federalist	89	
1816	**James Monroe**	Democratic-Republican	183	
	Rufus King	Federalist	34	
1820	**James Monroe**	Democratic-Republican	231	
	John Quincy Adams	National-Republican	1	
1824	**John Quincy Adams**	Coalition	84	Adams 108,740
	Andrew Jackson	Democratic-Republican	99	Jackson 153,544; House vote: Adams: 13, Jackson 7
1828	**Andrew Jackson**	Democrat	178	Jackson 647,286
	John Quincy Adams	National-Republican	83	Adams 508,064
1832	**Andrew Jackson**	Democrat	219	Jackson 687,502
	Henry Clay	National-Republican	49	Clay 530,189
1836	**Martin Van Buren**	Democrat	179	VanBuren 726,678
	William Henry Harrison	Whig	73	Harrison 735,651
1840	**William Henry Harrison**	Whig	234	Harrison 1,275,016
	Martin Van Buren	Democrat	60	Van Buren 1,129,102
1844	**James K. Polk**	Democrat	170	Polk 1,337,243
	Henry Clay	Whig	105	Clay 1,299,062

1848	**Zachary Taylor**	Whig	163	Taylor 1,360,099
	Lewis Cass	Democrat	127	Cass 1,220,544
1852	**Franklin Pierce**	Democrat	254	Pierce 1,601,274
	Winfield Scott	Whig	42	Scott 1,386,580
1856	**James Buchanan**	Democrat	174	Buchanan 1,838,169
	John C. Fremont	Republican	114	Fremont 1,341,264
1860	**Abraham Lincoln**	Republican	180	Lincoln 1,866,452
	John C. Breckinridge	Democrat	72	Breckinridge 847,953
1864	**Abraham Lincoln**	Republican	212	Lincoln 2,213,665
	George B. McClellan	Democrat	21	McClellan 1,805,237
1868	**Ulysses S. Grant**	Republican	214	Grant 3,012,833
	Horatio Seymour	Democrat	80	Seymour 2,703,249
1872	**Ulysses S. Grant**	Republican	286	Grant 3,597,132
	Horace Greeley	Democrat-Liberal Republican	0	Greeley 2,843,125; the House does not count 3 electoral votes for Greeley
1876	**Rutherford B. Hayes**	Republican	185	Hayes 4,036,289
	Samuel J. Tilden	Democrat	184	Tilden 4,300,590
1880	**James Garfield**	Republican	214	Garfield 4,454,416
	Winfield S. Hancock	Democrat	155	Hancock 4,444,952
1884	**Grover Cleveland**	Democrat	219	Cleveland 4,874,986
	James G. Blaine	Republican	182	Blaine 4,851,981
1888	**Benjamin Harrison**	Republican	233	Harrison 5,439,853
	Grover Cleveland	Democrat	168	Cleveland 5,540,309
1892	**Grover Cleveland**	Democrat	277	Cleveland 5,556,918
	Benjamin Harrison	Republican	145	Harrison 5,176,108
1896	**William McKinley**	Republican	271	McKinley 7,104,779
	William Jennings Bryan	Democrat-Populist	176	Bryan 6,502,925
1900	**William McKinley**	Republican	292	McKinley 7,207,923
	William Jennings Bryan	Democrat-Populist	155	Bryan 6,358,133
1904	**Theodore Roosevelt**	Republican	336	Roosevelt 7,623,486
	Alton B. Parker	Democrat	140	Parker 5,077,911
1908	**William Howard Taft**	Republican	321	Taft 7,678,908
	William Jennings Bryan	Democrat	162	Bryan 6,409,104
1912	**Woodrow Wilson**	Democrat	435	Wilson 6,293,454
	Theodore Roosevelt	Progressive	88	Roosevelt 3,484,980
	William Howard Taft	Republican	8	Taft 3,483,922
1916	**Woodrow Wilson**	Democrat	277	Wilson 9,120,606
	Charles Evans Hughes	Republican	254	Hughes 8,538,221
1920	**Warren G. Harding**	Republican	404	Harding 16,152,200
	James M. Cox	Democrat	127	Cox 9,147,353
1924	**Calvin Coolidge**	Republican	382	Coolidge 15,725,016
	John W. Davis	Democrat	136	Davis 8,386,503
1928	**Herbert Hoover**	Republican	444	Hoover 21,391,381
	Alfred E. Smith	Republican	87	Smith 15,016,443
1932	**Franklin D. Roosevelt**	Democrat	472	Roosevelt 22,821,579
	Herbert Hoover	Republican	59	Hoover 15,761,841
1936	**Franklin D. Roosevelt**	Democrat	523	Roosevelt 27,751,597
	Alfred M. Landon	Republican	8	Landon 16,679,583

Presidential Election Results *(cont.)*

Year	Candidates	Parties	Electoral Vote	Popular Vote/Notes
1940	**Franklin D. Roosevelt**	Democrat	449	Roosevelt 27,244,160
	Wendell L. Wilkie	Republican	82	Wilkie 22,305,198
1944	**Franklin D. Roosevelt**	Democrat	432	Roosevelt 25,602,504
	Thomas E. Dewey	Republican	99	Dewey 22,006,285
1948	**Harry S. Truman**	Democrat	303	Truman 24,105,695
	Thomas E. Dewey	Republican	189	Dewey 21,969,170
1952	**Dwight D. Eisenhower**	Republican	442	Eisenhower 33,778,963
	Adlai Stevenson	Democrat	89	Stevenson 27,314,992
1956	**Dwight D. Eisenhower**	Republican	457	Eisenhower 35,581,003
	Adlai Stevenson	Democrat	73	Stevenson 25,738,765
1960	**John F. Kennedy**	Democrat	303	Kennedy 34,227,096
	Richard M. Nixon	Republican	219	Nixon 34,107,646
1964	**Lyndon B. Johnson**	Democrat	486	Johnson 42,825,463
	Barry M. Goldwater	Republican	52	Goldwater 27,146,969
1968	**Richard M. Nixon**	Republican	301	Nixon 31,170,470
	Hubert H. Humphrey	Democrat	191	Humphrey 30,898,055
1972	**Richard M. Nixon**	Republican	520	Nixon 46,740,323
	George McGovern	Democrat	17	McGovern 28,901,598
1976	**Jimmy Carter**	Democrat	297	Carter 40,825,839
	Gerald R. Ford	Republican	240	Ford 39,147,770
1980	**Ronald Reagan**	Republican	538	Reagan 43,901,812
	Jimmy Carter	Democrat	49	Carter 35,483,820
1984	**Ronald Reagan**	Republican	525	Reagan 54,455,000
	Walter Mondale	Democrat	13	Mondale 37,577,000
1988	**George Bush**	Republican	426	Bush 47,946,000
	Michael S. Dukakis	Democrat	111	Dukakis 41,016,000
1992	**Bill Clinton**	Democrat	370	Clinton 44,908,254
	George Bush	Republican	168	Bush 39,102,343
	Ross Perot	Independent	0	Perot 7,866,284
1996	**Bill Clinton**	Democrat	379	Clinton 45,590,703
	Robert Dole	Republican	159	Dole 37,816,307
	Ross Perot	Independent	0	Perot 7,866,284
2000	**George W. Bush**	Republican	271	Bush 49,820,518
	Albert A. Gore, Jr.	Democrat	267	Gore 50,158,094

⊙ Schantz, Harvey L., ed. *The American Presidential Elections: Progress, Policy, and Political Change.* Albany: State University of New York, 1996.

   Campbell, James E. *The American Campaign: U.S. Presidential Campaigns and the National Vote.* College Station: Texas A&M University Press, 2000.

The Electoral College

The Electoral College was established by the Founders as a compromise between election of the president by Congress and election by popular vote. The electors are a popularly elected body chosen by the states and the District of Columbia on the Tuesday after the first Monday in November. The Electoral College consists of 538 electors. Each state's allotment of electors is equal to the number of House members to which it is entitled plus its two Senators. The District of Columbia received three electors.

In most states, each political party nominates electors, and the state's voters select them when they vote for a presidential candidate. The states prepare a list of the slate of electors for the candidate who receives the most popular votes on a Certificate of Ascertainment.

The electors meet in each state on the first Monday after the second Wednesday in December. A majority of 270 electoral votes is required to elect the president and vice president. No constitutional provision or federal law requires electors to vote in accordance with the popular vote in their state.

The electors prepare six original Certificates of Vote. Each Certificate of Vote lists all persons voted for as President and the number of electors voting for each person and separately lists all persons voted for as Vice President and the number of electors voting for each person.

If no presidential candidate wins a majority of electoral votes, the 12th Amendment to the Constitution provides for the presidential election to be decided by the House of Representatives. The House would select the president by majority vote, choosing from the three candidates who received the greatest number of electoral votes. The vote would be taken by state, with each state delegation having one vote. Similarly, the Senate would elect a vice president.

Electoral Votes Per State (as of 1990 census results)

State	Votes	State	Votes
Alabama	9	Montana	3
Alaska	3	Nebraska	5
Arizona	8	Nevada	4
Arkansas	6	New Hampshire	4
California	54	New Jersey	15
Colorado	8	New Mexico	5
Connecticut	8	New York	33
Delaware	3	North Carolina	14
District of Columbia	3	North Dakota	3
Florida	25	Ohio	21
Georgia	13	Oklahoma	8
Hawaii	4	Oregon	7
Idaho	4	Pennsylvania	23
Illinois	22	Rhode Island	4
Indiana	12	South Carolina	8
Iowa	7	South Dakota	3
Kansas	6	Tennessee	11
Kentucky	8	Texas	32
Louisiana	9	Utah	5
Maine	4	Vermont	3
Maryland	10	Virginia	13
Massachusetts	12	Washington	11
Michigan	18	West Virginia	5
Minnesota	10	Wisconsin	11
Mississippi	7	Wyoming	3
Missouri	11		

⊙ Berns, Walter, ed. *After the People Vote: A Guide to the Electoral College*. Washington, D.C.: AEI Press, 1992.

National Archives and Records Administration. "Office of the Federal Register," www.nara.gov/fedreg/elctcoll/proced.html

Major Political Parties in U.S. History

American Party (Know-Nothings): Founded during the early 1850s by nativists who wished to restrict immigration to the United States because they feared that jobs would be taken away from Americans and that Americans would be forced to pay more taxes to support the immigrants. When asked about their party, members would respond, "I know nothing." The party, split over the question of slavery, was short-lived.

Anti-Masonic Party: Founded in 1827 as a protest against Masonic principles when it was alleged that a member of the Masons was murdered because he had threatened to make the group's secret rites public. More successful at the state level, the party was eventually folded into the Whig Party.

Communist Party of the U.S.A.: Founded in 1919 by the most radical members of the Socialist Party. Supported by the Soviet Union, it advocated the overthrow of American capitalism. Although it exerted some influence on U.S. politics during the 1930s, the party was virtually powerless after the 1950s.

Democratic Party: Founded in 1793, first as the Democratic-Republican Party, by Thomas Jefferson to promote his philosophy of state and individual rights and his belief that government involved all citizens rather than a select few. By the election of 1828, the party's name had been shortened to Democratic Party. During the administration of Pres. Franklin D. Roosevelt, and because of the Great Depression of the 1930s, the party's platform was directed more toward the involvement of the federal government, especially regarding social welfare issues.

Farmer-Labor Party: Founded in 1920 to promote the interests of farmers and of labor. Not very successful on the national front, the party had a significant influence on state politics in Minnesota. By 1944, it had merged with the Democratic Party in Minnesota.

Federalist Party: Founded in 1794 in support of the U.S. Constitution, its interpretation and direction, and of a strong central government. The party's major leaders were George Washington, Alexander Hamilton, and John Adams. The party declined during the early 1800s.

Free-Soil Party: Founded in 1848 in the belief that allowing slavery in new territories would lessen the amount of land available for homesteading. The party was weakened by the Compromise of 1850 and ceased to exist after the election of 1852.

Green Party: Founded in 1984 in response to the Green Party of Germany and focusing on issues of environmentalism, social justice, and peace. The party nominated consumer activist Ralph Nader as its presidential candidate in 2000.

Greenback Party: Founded around 1875 to protest the U.S. government's plan to stop the circulation of greenbacks, paper money printed to finance the Civil War, and return to a hard-currency economy. The party later broadened its platform to include support of current labor issues but by 1884 the movement had failed.

Liberal-Republican Party: Founded in 1872 in Missouri by dissident Republicans to oppose Pres. Ulysses S. Grant's renomination. The party's presidential nominee, Horace Greeley, ran on a platform that included civil service reform. It disbanded after the 1872 elections when Grant was returned to office.

Loco-Focos or **Equal Rights Party:** Founded in 1835 by some New York Democrats who were disenchanted with the conservative politics of the controlling Tammany political machine and who advocated free banking in order to prevent bribery of officials. By 1839, Loco-Focos had returned to the Democratic fold.

Populist (People's) Party: Founded in 1892 by down-and-out farmers, who still felt the effects of an earlier depression. They advocated currency, transportation, banking, taxation, election, and civil service reforms. Although they made a significant showing in the 1892 presidential election, the party disbanded in 1896.

Progressive Party: Initially founded in 1911 by Republicans who felt that President Taft's administration was too conservative. The party was seized by Theodore Roosevelt in 1912, enabling him to run unsuccessfully for the presidency as the "Bull Moose" Party's candidate after he lost the Republican nomination. Resurrected in 1924 by Robert LaFollette, the party presented a platform of government, agriculture, and labor reform. A new Progressive Party nominated presidential candidate Henry Wallace in the 1948 election.

Reform Party: Founded in 1997 as a grassroots outgrowth of Ross Perot's presidential campaigns of 1992 and 1996 and his United We Stand, America movement. Advocating the restoration of "integrity, accountability and fiscal responsibility to government and its leadership," the party platform includes campaign reform, a balanced budget, and a new tax system.

Republican Party: Founded in 1854 in answer to the waning influence of the Whig Party and in opposition to slavery in new U.S. territories. Abraham Lincoln, the first Republican president, based his election campaign on this issue. By 1896, the Republican Party often favored conservatism as well as a lack of government involvement in business The party defended the gold standard in the late 1800s and was dubbed the "Grand Old Party" (GOP), a moniker by which it is still known today.

Socialist Party: Founded in 1898 as the Socialist Democratic Party of America. One of its founders, Eugene V. Debs, was often its presidential candidate. Opposed to U.S. entry into World War I, the Socialists, after 1920, campaigned for the abolishment of capitalism.

States' Rights Party or **Dixiecrats:** Founded in 1948 by some Democrats, among them South Carolina's governor Strom Thurmond, who were disgruntled over the civil rights section of the Democratic platform at the Democratic National Convention.

Whig Party: Founded in 1836 as an outgrowth of the National Republicans with the purpose of opposing Andrew Jackson. Led by Henry Clay and Daniel Webster, the party was successful in having two of its candidates become president—William Henry Harrison and Zachary Taylor. A split over the slavery question caused the decline of the party in the mid-1850s.

⊙ Congressional Quarterly. *Congressional Quarterly's Guide to U.S. Elections.* 3d ed. Washington, D.C.: Congressional Quarterly Inc., 1994.

Martí, José. *Political Parties and Elections in the United States: An Encyclopedia.* Philadelphia: Temple University Press, 1989.

University of Pennsylvania Library. "U.S. Political Parties and Elections," www.library.upenn.edu/vanpelt/guides/elections.html

The Declaration of Independence

When in the course of human events it becomes necessary for one people to dissolve the political bands which have connected them with another and to assume, among the powers of the earth, the separate and equal station to which the laws of nature and of nature's God entitle them, a decent respect to the opinions of mankind requires that they should declare the causes which impel them to the separation.

We hold these truths to be self-evident, that all men are created equal; that they are endowed by their Creator with certain unalienable rights; that among these are life, liberty, and the pursuit of happiness. That, to secure these rights, governments are instituted among men, deriving their just powers from the consent of the governed; that, whenever any form of government becomes destructive of these ends, it is the right of the people to alter or to abolish it, and to institute a new government, laying its foundation on such principles, and organizing its powers in such form, as to them shall seem most likely to effect their safety and happiness. Prudence, indeed, will dictate that governments long established should not be changed for light and transient causes; and, accordingly, all experience hath shown that mankind are more disposed to suffer, while evils are sufferable, than to right themselves by abolishing the forms to which they are accustomed. But when a long train of abuses and usurpations, pursuing invariably the same object, evinces a design to reduce them under absolute despotism, it is their right, it is their duty, to throw off such government and to provide new guards for their future security. Such has been the patient sufferance of these colonies, and such is now the necessity which constrains them to alter their former systems of government. The history of the present King of Great Britain is a history of repeated injuries and usurpations, all having, in direct object, the establishment of an absolute tyranny over these States. To prove this, let facts be submitted to a candid world:

He has refused his assent to laws the most wholesome and necessary for the public good.

He has forbidden his governors to pass laws of immediate and pressing importance, unless suspended in their operation till his assent should be obtained; and, when so suspended, he has utterly neglected to attend to them.

He has refused to pass other laws for the accommodation of large districts of people, unless those people would relinquish the right of representation in the legislature; a right inestimable to them and formidable to tyrants only.

He has called together legislative bodies at places unusual, uncomfortable, and distant from the depository of their public records, for the sole purpose of fatiguing them into compliance with his measures.

He has dissolved representative houses, repeatedly for opposing, with manly firmness, his invasions on the rights of the people.

He has refused, for a long time after such dissolutions, to cause others to be elected; whereby the legislative powers, incapable of annihilation, have returned to the people at large for their exercise; the state remaining, in the meantime, exposed to all the danger of invasion from without and convulsions within.

He has endeavored to prevent the population of these States; for that purpose, obstructing the laws for naturalization of foreigners, refusing to pass others to encourage their migration hither, and raising the conditions of new appropriations of lands.

He has obstructed the administration of justice by refusing his assent to laws for establishing judiciary powers.

He has made judges dependent on his will alone for the tenure of their offices and the amount and payment of their salaries.

He has erected a multitude of new offices and sent hither swarms of officers to harass our people and eat out their substance.

He has kept among us, in time of peace, standing armies, without the consent of our legislatures.

He has affected to render the military independent of, and superior to, the civil power.

He has combined with others to subject us to a jurisdiction foreign to our Constitution and unacknowledged by our laws, giving his assent to their acts of pretended legislation—For quartering large bodies of armed troops among us; For protecting them by a mock trial from punishment for any murders which they should commit on the inhabitants of these States; For cutting off our trade with all parts of the world; For imposing taxes on us without our consent; For depriving us, in many cases, of the benefit of trial by jury; For transporting us beyond seas to be tried for pretended offences; For abolishing the free system of English laws in a neighboring province, establishing therein an arbitrary government, and enlarging its boundaries, so as to render it at once an example and fit instrument for introducing the same absolute rule into these colonies; For taking away our charters, abolishing our most valuable laws, and altering, fundamentally, the powers of our governments; For suspending our own legislatures and declaring themselves invested with power to legislate for us in all cases whatsoever.

He has abdicated government here by declaring us out of his protection and waging war against us.

He has plundered our seas, ravaged our coasts, burnt our towns, and destroyed the lives of our people.

He is, at this time, transporting large armies of foreign mercenaries to complete the works of death, desolation, and tyranny already begun with circumstances of cruelty and perfidy scarcely paralleled in the most barbarous ages, and totally unworthy the head of a civilized nation.

He has constrained our fellow citizens, taken captive on the high seas, to bear arms against their country, to become the executioners of their friends and brethren, or to fall themselves by their hands.

He has excited domestic insurrections amongst us and has endeavored to bring on the inhabitants of our frontiers, the merciless Indian savages, whose known rule of warfare is an undistinguished destruction of all ages, sexes, and conditions.

In every stage of these oppressions, we have petitioned for redress in the most humble terms; our repeated petitions have been answered only by repeated injury. A prince whose character is thus marked by every act which may define a tyrant is unfit to be the ruler of a free people. Nor have we been wanting in attention to our British brethren. We have warned them, from time to time, of attempts made by their legislature to extend an unwarrantable jurisdiction over us. We have reminded them of the circumstances of our emigration and settlement here. We have appealed to their native justice and magnanimity, and we have conjured them, by the ties of our common kindred, to disavow these usurpations, which would inevitably interrupt our connections and correspondence. They, too, have been deaf to the voice of justice and consanguinity. We must, therefore, acquiesce in the necessity which denounces our separation, and hold them, as we hold the rest of mankind, enemies in war, in peace, friends.

We, therefore, the representatives of the United States of America, in general Congress assembled, appealing to the Supreme Judge of the world for the

The Declaration of Independence *(cont.)*

rectitude of our intentions, do, in the name and by the authority of the good people of these colonies, solemnly publish and declare, that these united colonies are, and of right ought to be, free and independent states: that they are absolved from all allegiance to the British Crown, and that all political connection between them and the state of Great Britain is, and ought to be, totally dissolved; and that, as free and independent states, they have full power to levy war, conclude peace, contract alliances, establish commerce, and to do all other acts and things which independent states may of right do. And, for the support of this declaration, with a firm reliance on the protection of Divine Providence, we mutually pledge to each other our lives, our fortunes, and our sacred honor.

John Hancock

New Hampshire	**Connecticut**	**Pennsylvania**	**Maryland**
Josiah Bartlett	Robert Sherman	Robert Morris	Samuel Chase
William Whipple	Samuel Huntingdon	Benjamin Rush	William Paca
Matthew Thorton	William Williams	Benjamin Franklin	Thomas Stone
	Oliver Wolcott	John Morton	Charles Carroll of Carrollton
		George Clymer	
Massachusetts Bay	**New York**	James Smith	**Virginia**
Samuel Adams	William Floyd	George Taylor	George Wythe
John Adams	Philip Livingston	James Wilson	Richard Henry Lee
Robert Treat Paine	Francis Lewis	George Ross	Thomas Jefferson
Elbridge Gerry	Lewis Morris		Benjamin Harrison
			Thomas Nelson, Jr.
Rhode Island	**New Jersey**	**Delaware**	Francis Lightfoot Lee
Stephen Hopkins	Richard Stockton	Caesar Rodney	Carter Braxton
William Ellery	John Witherspoon	George Read	
	Francis Hopkinson	Thomas McKean	
	John Hart		
North Carolina	Abraham Clark	**South Carolina**	**Georgia**
William Hooper		Edward Routledge	Button Gwinnett
Joseph Huges		Thomas Heyward, Jr.	Lyman Hall
John Penn		Arthur Middleton	George Walton

⊙ National Archives and Records Administration. "The Declaration of Independence," www.nara.gov/exhall/charters/declaration/decmain.html

Jayne, Allen. *Jefferson's Declaration of Independence: Origins, Philosophy, and Theology.* Lexington: University Press of Kentucky, 1998.

The Constitution

We the people of the United States, in order to form a more perfect union, establish justice, insure domestic tranquillity, provide for the common defense, promote the general welfare, and secure the blessings of liberty to ourselves and our posterity, do ordain and establish this Constitution for the United States of America.

Article I

Section 1.

All legislative powers herein granted shall be vested in a Congress of the United States, which shall consist of a Senate and House of Representatives.

Section 2.

1. The House of Representatives shall be composed of members chosen every second year by the people of the several States, and the electors in each State shall have the qualifications requisite for electors of the most numerous branch of the State legislature.

2. No person shall be a representative who shall not have attained to the age of twenty-five years, and been seven years a citizen of the United States, and who shall not, when elected, be an inhabitant of that State in which he shall be chosen.

3. Representatives and direct taxes shall be apportioned among the several States which may be included within this Union, according to their respective numbers, which shall be determined by adding to the whole number of free persons, including those bound to service for a term of years, and excluding Indians not taxed, three fifths of all other persons. The actual enumeration shall be made within three years after the first meeting of the Congress of the United States, and within every subsequent term of ten years, in such manner as they shall by law direct. The number of representatives shall not exceed one for every thirty thousand, but each State shall have at least one representative; and until such enumeration shall be made, the State of New Hampshire shall be entitled to choose three, Massachusetts eight, Rhode Island and Providence Plantations one, Connecticut five, New York six, New Jersey four, Pennsylvania eight, Delaware one, Maryland six, Virginia ten, North Carolina five, South Carolina five, and Georgia three.

4. When vacancies happen in the representation from any State, the executive authority thereof shall issue writs of election to fill such vacancies.

5. The House of Representatives shall choose their speaker and other officers; and shall have the sole power of impeachment.

Section 3.

1. The Senate of the United States shall be composed of two senators from each State, chosen by the legislature thereof, for six years; and each senator shall have one vote.

2. Immediately after they shall be assembled in consequence of the first election, they shall be divided as equally as may be into three classes. The seats of the senators of the first class shall be vacated at the expiration of the second year, of the second class at the expiration of the fourth year, and of the third class at the expiration of the sixth year, so that one third may be chosen every second year; and if vacancies happen by resignation, or otherwise, during the recess of the legislature of any State, the executive thereof may make temporary appointments until the next meeting of the legislature, which shall then fill such vacancies.

3. No person shall be a senator who shall not have attained to the age of thirty years, and been nine years a citizen of the United States, and who shall not, when elected, be an inhabitant of that State for which he shall be chosen.

4. The Vice President of the United States shall be President of the Senate, but shall have no vote, unless they be equally divided.

5. The Senate shall choose their other officers, and also a president pro tempore, in the absence of the Vice President, or when he shall exercise the office of the President of the United States.

6. The Senate shall have the sole power to try all impeachments. When sitting for that purpose, they shall be on oath or affirmation. When the President of the United States is tried, the chief justice shall preside: and no person shall be convicted without the concurrence of two thirds of the members present.

The Constitution *(cont.)*

7. Judgment in cases of impeachment shall not extend further than to removal from office, and disqualification to hold and enjoy any office of honor, trust or profit under the United States: but the party convicted shall nevertheless be liable and subject to indictment, trial, judgment and punishment, according to law.

Section 4.

1. The times, places, and manner of holding elections for senators and representatives, shall be prescribed in each State by the legislature thereof; but the Congress may at any time by law make or alter such regulations, except as to the places of choosing senators.

2. The Congress shall assemble at least once in every year, and such meeting shall be on the first Monday in December, unless they shall by law appoint a different day.

Section 5.

1. Each House shall be the judge of the elections, returns and qualifications of its own members, and a majority of each shall constitute a quorum to do business; but a smaller number may adjourn from day to day, and may be authorized to compel the attendance of absent members, in such manner, and under such penalties as each House may provide.

2. Each House may determine the rules of its proceedings, punish its members for disorderly behavior, and, with the concurrence of two thirds, expel a member.

3. Each House shall keep a journal of its proceedings, and from time to time publish the same, excepting such parts as may in their judgment require secrecy; and the yeas and nays of the members of either House on any question shall, at the desire of one fifth of those present, be entered on the journal.

4. Neither House, during the session of Congress, shall, without the consent of the other, adjourn for more than three days, nor to any other place than that in which the two Houses shall be sitting.

Section 6.

1. The senators and representatives shall receive a compensation for their services, to be ascertained by law, and paid out of the Treasury of the United States. They shall in all cases, except treason, felony, and breach of the peace, be privileged from arrest during their attendance at the session of their respective Houses, and in going to and returning from the same; and for any speech or debate in either House, they shall not be questioned in any other place.

2. No senator or representative shall, during the time for which he was elected, be appointed to any civil office under the authority of the United States, which shall have been created, or the emoluments whereof shall have been increased, during such time; and no person holding any office under the United States shall be a member of either House during his continuance in office.

Section 7.

1. All bills for raising revenue shall originate in the House of Representatives; but the Senate may propose or concur with amendments as on other bills.

2. Every bill which shall have passed the House of Representatives and the Senate, shall, before it become a law, be presented to the President of the United States; If he approves he shall sign it, but if not he shall return it, with his objec-

tions, to that House in which it shall have originated, who shall enter the objections at large on their journal, and proceed to reconsider it. If after such reconsideration two thirds of that House shall agree to pass the bill, it shall be sent, together with the objections, to the other House, by which it shall likewise be reconsidered, and if approved by two thirds of that House, it shall become a law. But in all such cases the votes of both Houses shall be determined by yeas and nays, and the names of the persons voting for and against the bill shall be entered on the journal of each House respectively. If any bill shall not be returned by the President within ten days (Sundays excepted) after it shall have been presented to him, the same shall be a law, in like manner as if he had signed it, unless the Congress by their adjournment prevent its return, in which case it shall not be a law.

3. Every order, resolution, or vote to which the concurrence of the Senate and the House of Representatives may be necessary (except on a question of adjournment) shall be presented to the President of the United States; and before the same shall take effect, shall be approved by him, or being disapproved by him, shall be repassed by two thirds of the Senate and House of Representatives, according to the rules and limitations prescribed in the case of a bill.

Section 8.

The Congress shall have the power

1. To lay and collect taxes, duties, imposts, and excises, to pay the debts and provide for the common defense and general welfare of the United States; but all duties, imposts, and excises shall be uniform throughout the United States;

2. To borrow money on the credit of the United States;

3. To regulate commerce with foreign nations, and among the several States, and with the Indian tribes;

4. To establish a uniform rule of naturalization, and uniform laws on the subject of bankruptcies throughout the United States;

5. To coin money, regulate the value thereof, and of foreign coin, and fix the standard of weights and measures;

6. To provide for the punishment of counterfeiting the securities and current coin of the United States;

7. To establish post offices and post roads;

8. To promote the progress of science and useful arts, by securing for limited times to authors and inventors the exclusive right to their respective writings and discoveries;

9. To constitute tribunals inferior to the Supreme Court;

10. To define and punish piracies and felonies committed on the high seas, and offenses against the law of nations;

11. To declare war, grant letters of marque and reprisal, and make rules concerning captures on land and water;

12. To raise and support armies, but no appropriation of money to that use shall be for a longer term than two years;

13. To provide and maintain a navy;

14. To make rules for the government and regulation of the land and naval forces;

15. To provide for calling forth the militia to execute the laws of the Union, suppress insurrections and repel invasions;

16. To provide for organizing, arming, and disciplining the militia, and for governing such part of them as may be employed in the service of the United States, reserving to the States respectively, the appointment of the officers,

and the authority of training the militia according to the discipline prescribed by Congress;

17. To exercise exclusive legislation in all cases whatsoever, over such district (not exceeding ten miles square) as may, by cession of particular States, and the acceptance of Congress, become the seat of the government of the United States, and to exercise like authority over all places purchased by the consent of the legislature of the State in which the same shall be, for the erection of forts, magazines, arsenals, dockyards, and other needful buildings; and

18. To make all laws which shall be necessary and proper for carrying into execution the foregoing powers, and all other powers vested by this Constitution in the government of the United States, or any department or officer thereof.

Section 9.

1. The migration or importation of such persons as any of the States now existing shall think proper to admit, shall not be prohibited by the Congress prior to the year one thousand eight hundred and eight, but a tax or duty may be imposed on such importation, not exceeding ten dollars for each person.

2. The privilege of the writ of habeas corpus shall not be suspended, unless when in cases of rebellion or invasion the public safety may require it.

3. No bill of attainder or ex post facto law shall be passed.

4. No capitation, or other direct, tax shall be laid, unless in proportion to the census or enumeration hereinbefore directed to be taken.

5. No tax or duty shall be laid on articles exported from any State.

6. No preference shall be given by any regulation of commerce or revenue to the ports of one State over those of another: nor shall vessels bound to, or from, one State be obliged to enter, clear, or pay duties in another.

7. No money shall be drawn from the treasury, but in consequence of appropriations made by law; and a regular statement and account of the receipts and expenditures of all public money shall be published from time to time.

8. No title of nobility shall be granted by the United States: and no person holding any office of profit or trust under them, shall, without the consent of the Congress, accept of any present, emolument, office, or title, of any kind whatever, from any king, prince, or foreign State.

Section 10.

1. No State shall enter into any treaty, alliance, or confederation; grant letters of marque and reprisal; coin money; emit bills of credit; make any thing but gold and silver coin a tender in payment of debts; pass any bill of attainder, ex post facto law, or law impairing the obligation of contracts, or grant any title of nobility.

2. No State shall, without the consent of the Congress, lay any imposts or duties on imports or exports, except what may be absolutely necessary for executing its inspection laws: and the net produce of all duties and imposts laid by any State on imports or exports, shall be for the use of the treasury of the United States; and all such laws shall be subject to the revision and control of the Congress.

3. No State shall, without the consent of the Congress, lay any duty of tonnage, keep troops, or ships of war in time of peace, enter into any agreement or compact with another State, or with a foreign power, or engage in war, unless actually invaded, or in such imminent danger as will not admit of delay.

Article II

Section 1.

1. The executive power shall be vested in a President of the United States of America. He shall hold his office during the term of four years, and, together with the Vice President, chosen for the same term, be elected, as follows:

2. Each State shall appoint, in such manner as the legislature thereof may direct, a number of electors, equal to the whole number of senators and representatives to which the State may be entitled in the Congress: but no senator or representative, or person holding any office of trust or profit under the United States, shall be appointed an elector.

The electors shall meet in their respective States, and vote by ballot for two persons, of whom one at least shall not be an inhabitant of the same State with themselves. And they shall make a list of all the persons voted for, and of the number of votes for each; which list they shall sign and certify, and transmit sealed to the seat of the government of the United States, directed to the president of the Senate. The president of the Senate shall, in the presence of the Senate and House of Representatives, open all the certificates, and the votes shall then be counted. The person having the greatest number of votes shall be the President, if such number be a majority of the whole number of electors appointed; and if there be more than one who have such majority, and have an equal number of votes, then the House of Representatives shall immediately choose by ballot one of them for President; and if no person have a majority, then from the five highest on the list the said House shall in like manner choose the President. But in choosing the President, the votes shall be taken by States, the representation from each State having one vote; a quorum for this purpose shall consist of a member or members from two thirds of the States, and a majority of all the States shall be necessary to a choice. In every case after the choice of the President, the person having the greatest number of votes of the electors shall be the Vice President. But if there should remain two or more who have equal votes, the Senate shall chose from them by ballot the Vice President.

3. The Congress may determine the time of choosing the electors, and the day on which they shall give their votes; which day shall be the same throughout the United States.

4. No person except a natural born citizen, or a citizen of the United States, at the time of the adoption of this Constitution, shall be eligible to the office of President; neither shall any person be eligible to the office who shall not have attained to the age of thirty-five years, and been fourteen years a resident within the United States.

5. In case of the removal of the President from office, or of his death, resignation, or inability to discharge the powers and duties of the said office, the same shall devolve on the Vice President, and the Congress may by law provide for the case of removal, death, resignation or inability, both of the President and Vice President, declaring what officer shall then act as President, and such officer shall act accordingly until the disability be removed, or a President shall be elected.

6. The President shall, at stated times, receive for his services a compensation which shall neither be increased nor diminished during the period for which he shall have been elected, and he shall not receive within that period any other emolument from the United States, or any of them.

7. Before he enter on the execution of his office, he shall take the following oath or affirmation:—"I do solemnly swear (or affirm) that I will faithfully execute the office of President of the United States, and will to the best of my ability, preserve, protect and defend the Constitution of the United States."

Section 2.

1. The President shall be commander in chief of the army and navy of the United States, and of the militia of the several States, when called into the actual service of the United States; he may require the opinion in writing, of the principal officer in each of the executive departments, upon any subject relating to the duties of their respective offices, and he shall have power to grant reprieves and pardons for offenses against the United States, except in cases of impeachment.

2. He shall have power, by and with the advice and consent of the Senate, to make treaties, provided two thirds of the senators present concur; and he shall nominate, and by and with the advice and consent of the Senate, shall appoint ambassadors, other public ministers and consuls, judges of the Supreme Court, and all other officers of the United States, whose appointments are not herein otherwise provided for, and which shall be established by law; but the Congress may by law vest the appointment of such inferior officers, as they think proper, in the President alone, in the courts of laws, or in the heads of departments.

3. The President shall have power to fill up all vacancies that may happen during the recess of the Senate, by granting commissions which shall expire at the end of their next session.

Section 3.

He shall from time to time give to the Congress information of the state of the Union, and recommend to their consideration such measures as he shall judge necessary and expedient; he may, on extraordinary occasions, convene both Houses, or either of them, and in case of disagreement between them with respect to the time of adjournment, he may adjourn them to such time as he shall think proper; he shall receive ambassadors and other public ministers; he shall take care that the laws be faithfully executed, and shall commission all the officers of the United States.

Section 4.

The President, Vice President, and all civil officers of the United States, shall be removed from office on impeachment for, and conviction of, treason, bribery, or other high crimes and misdemeanors.

Article III

Section 1.

The judicial power of the United States shall be vested in one Supreme Court, and in such inferior courts as the Congress may from time to time ordain and establish. The judges, both of the Supreme and inferior courts, shall hold their offices during good behavior, and shall, at stated times, receive for their services, a compensation, which shall not be diminished during their continuance in office.

Section 2.

1. The judicial power shall extend to all cases, in law and equity, arising under this Constitution, the laws of the United States, and treaties made, or which shall be made, under their authority;—to all cases affecting ambassadors, other public ministers and consuls;—to all cases of admiralty and maritime jurisdiction;—to controversies to which the United States shall be a party;—to controversies between two or more States;—between a State and citizens of another State;—between citizens of different States;—between citizens of the same State claiming lands under grants of different States, and between a State, or the citizens thereof, and foreign States, citizens or subjects.

2. In all cases affecting ambassadors, other public ministers and consuls, and those in which a State shall be party, the Supreme Court shall have original jurisdiction. In all the other cases before mentioned, the Supreme Court shall have appellate jurisdiction, both as to law and fact, with such exceptions, and under such regulations as the Congress shall make.

3. The trial of all crimes, except in cases of impeachment, shall be by jury; and such trial shall be held in the State where the said crimes shall have been committed; but when not committed within any State, the trial shall be at such place or places as the Congress may by law have directed.

Section 3.

1. Treason against the United States shall consist only in levying war against them, or in adhering to their enemies, giving them aid and comfort. No person shall be convicted of treason unless on the testimony of two witnesses to the same overt act, or on confession in open court.

2. The Congress shall have power to declare the punishment of treason, but no attainder of treason shall work corruption of blood, or forfeiture except during the life of the person attainted.

Article IV

Section 1.

Full faith and credit shall be given in each State to the public acts, records, and judicial proceedings of every other State. And the Congress may by general laws prescribe the manner in which such acts, records and proceedings shall be proved, and the effect thereof.

Section 2.

1. The citizens of each State shall be entitled to all privileges and immunities of citizens in the several States.

2. A person charged in any State with treason, felony, or other crime, who shall flee from justice, and be found in another State, shall on demand of the executive authority of the State from which he fled, be delivered up to be removed to the State having jurisdiction of the crime.

3. No person held to service or labor in one State under the laws thereof, escaping into another, shall, in consequence of any law or regulation therein, be discharged from such service or labor, but shall be delivered up on claim of the party to whom such service or labor may be due.

Section 3.

1. New States may be admitted by the Congress into this Union; but no new State shall be formed or erected within the jurisdiction of any other State; nor any

The Constitution (cont.)

State be formed by the junction of two or more States, or parts of States, without the consent of the legislatures of the States concerned as well as of the Congress.

2. The Congress shall have power to dispose of and make all needful rules and regulations respecting the territory or other property belonging to the United States; and nothing in this Constitution shall be so construed as to prejudice any claims of the United States, or of any particular State.

Section 4.

The United States shall guarantee to every State in this Union a republican form of government, and shall protect each of them against invasion; and on application of the legislature, or of the executive (when the legislature cannot be convened) against domestic violence.

Article V

The Congress, whenever two thirds of both Houses shall deem it necessary, shall propose amendments to this Constitution, or, on the application of the legislatures of two thirds of the several States, shall call a convention for proposing amendments, which in either case, shall be valid to all intents and purposes, as part of this Constitution, when ratified by the legislatures of three fourths of the several States, or by conventions in three fourths thereof, as the one or the other mode of ratification may be proposed by the Congress; Provided that no amendment which may be made prior to the year one thousand eight hundred and eight shall in any manner affect the first and fourth clauses in the ninth section of the first article; and that no State, without its consent, shall be deprived of its equal suffrage in the Senate.

Article VI

1. All debts contracted and engagements entered into, before the adoption of this Constitution, shall be as valid against the United States under this Constitution, as under the Confederation.

2. This Constitution, and the laws of the United States which shall be made in pursuance thereof; and all treaties made, or which shall be made, under the authority of the United States, shall be the supreme law of the land; and the judges in every State shall be bound thereby, any thing in the Constitution or laws of any State to the contrary notwithstanding.

3. The senators and representatives before mentioned, and the members of the several State legislatures, and all executive and judicial officers, both of the United States and of the several States, shall be bound by oath or affirmation to support this Constitution; but no religious test shall ever be required as a qualification to any office or public trust under the United States.

Article VII

The ratification of the conventions of nine States shall be sufficient for the establishment of this Constitution between the States so ratifying the same.

Done in Convention by the unanimous consent of the States present the seventeenth day of September in the year of our Lord one thousand seven hundred and eighty-seven, and of the independence of the United States of America the twelfth. In witness whereof we have hereunto subscribed our names.

Articles in addition to, and amendment of, the Constitution of the United States of America, proposed by Congress, and ratified by the legislatures of the several States, pursuant to the fifth article of the original Constitution.

George Washington
President and deputy from Virginia

New Hampshire	**New York**	**Massachusetts**	**New Jersey**
John Langdon	Alexander Hamilton	Nathaniel Gorman	William Livingston
Nicholas Gilman	Rufus King	David Bearley	
	William Paterson		
	Jonathan Dayton		

Connecticut	**Pennsylvania**	**Virginia**	**North Carolina**
William Samuel	Benjamin Franklin	John Blair	William Blount
Johnson	Thomas Mifflin	James Madison, Jr.	Richard Dobbs
Roger Sherman	Robert Morris		Spaight
	George Clymer	**Georgia**	Hugh Williamson
	Thomas FitzSimons	William Few	
	Jared Ingersoll	Abraham Baldwin	
	James Wilson		
	Gouverner Morris		

Delaware	**South Carolina**	**Maryland**
George Reed	John Rutledge	James McHenry
Gunning Beford, Jr.	Charles Cotesworth	Daniel of St. Thomas Jenifer
John Dickinson	Pinckney	Daniel Carroll
Richard Bassett	Charles Pinckney	
Jacob Broom	Pierce Butler	

Amendment I [First ten amendments ratified December 15, 1791]

Congress shall make no law respecting an establishment of religion, or prohibiting the free exercise thereof; or abridging the freedom of speech, or of the press; or the right of the people peaceably to assemble, and to petition the government for a redress of grievances.

Amendment II

A well regulated militia, being necessary to the security of a free State, the right of the people to keep and bear arms, shall not be infringed.

Amendment III

No soldier shall, in time of peace be quartered in any house, without the consent of the owner, nor in time of war, but in a manner to be prescribed by law.

Amendment IV

The right of the people to be secure in their persons, houses, papers, and effects, against unreasonable searches and seizures, shall not be violated, and no warrants shall issue, but upon probable cause, supported by oath or affirmation, and particularly describing the place to be searched, and the persons or things to be seized.

Amendment V

No person shall be held to answer for a capital or otherwise infamous crime, unless on a presentment or indictment of a grand jury, except in cases arising in the land or naval forces, or in the militia, when in actual service in time of war or public danger; nor shall any person be subject for the same offense to be twice put in jeopardy of life or limb; nor shall be compelled in any criminal case to be a witness against himself, nor be deprived of life, liberty, or property, without due process of law; nor shall private property be taken for public use, without just compensation.

Amendment VI

In all criminal prosecutions, the accused shall enjoy the right to a speedy and public trial, by an impartial jury of the State and district wherein the crime shall have been committed, which district shall have been previously ascertained by law, and to be informed of the nature and cause of the accusation; to be confronted with the witnesses against him; to have compulsory process for obtaining witnesses in his favor, and to have the assistance of counsel for his defense.

Amendment VII

In suits at common law, where the value in controversy shall exceed twenty dollars, the right of trial by jury shall be preserved, and no fact tried by a jury shall be otherwise reexamined in any court of the United States, than according to the rules of the common law.

Amendment VIII

Excessive bail shall not be required, nor excessive fines imposed, nor cruel and unusual punishments inflicted.

Amendment IX

The enumeration in the Constitution of certain rights shall not be construed to deny or disparage others retained by the people.

Amendment X

The powers not delegated to the United States by the Constitution, nor prohibited by it to the States, are reserved to the States respectively, or to the people.

Amendment XI [January 8, 1798]

The judicial power of the United States shall not be construed to extend to any suit in law or equity, commenced or prosecuted against one of the United States by citizens of another State, or by citizens or subjects of any foreign State.

Amendment XII [September 25, 1804]

The electors shall meet in their respective States, and vote by ballot for President and Vice President, one of whom, at least, shall not be an inhabitant of the same State with themselves; they shall name in their ballots the person voted for as President, and in distinct ballots the person voted for as Vice President, and they shall make distinct lists of all persons voted for as President and of all persons voted for as Vice President, and of the number of votes for each, which lists they shall sign and certify, and transmit sealed to the seat of the government of the United States, directed to the President of the Senate;—The President of the Senate shall, in the presence of the Senate and House of Representatives, open all the certificates and the votes shall then be counted;— The person having the greatest number of votes for President, shall be the President, if such number be a majority of the whole number of electors appointed; and if no person have such majority, then from the persons having the highest numbers not exceeding three on the list of those voted for as President, the House of Representatives shall choose immediately, by ballot, the President. But in choosing the President, the votes shall be taken by States, the representation from each State having one vote; a quorum for this purpose shall consist of a member or members from two thirds of the States, and a majority of all the States shall be necessary to a choice. And if the House of Representatives shall not choose a President whenever the right of choice shall devolve upon them, before the fourth day of March next following, then the Vice President shall act as President, as in the case of the death or other constitutional disability of the President. The person having the greatest number of votes as Vice President shall be the Vice President, if such number be a majority of the whole number of electors appointed, and if no person have a majority, then from the two highest numbers on the list, the Senate shall choose the Vice President; a quorum for the purpose shall consist of two thirds of the whole number of Senators, and a majority of the whole number shall be necessary to a choice. But no person constitutionally ineligible to the office of President shall be eligible to that of Vice President of the United States.

Amendment XIII [December 18, 1865]

Section 1.

Neither slavery nor involuntary servitude, except as a punishment for crime whereof the party shall have been duly convicted, shall exist within the United States, or any place subject to their jurisdiction.

Section 2.

Congress shall have power to enforce this article by appropriate legislation.

Amendment XIV [July 28, 1868]

Section 1.

All persons born or naturalized in the United States, and subject to the jurisdiction thereof, are citizens of the United States and of the State wherein they reside. No State shall make or enforce any law which shall abridge the privileges or immunities of citizens of the United States; nor shall any State deprive any person of life, liberty, or property, without due process of law; nor deny to any person within its jurisdiction the equal protection of the laws.

Section 2.

Representatives shall be apportioned among the several States according to their respective numbers, counting the whole number of persons in each State, excluding Indians not taxed. But when the right to vote at any election for the choice of electors for President and Vice President of the United States, representatives in Congress, the executive and judicial officers of a State, or the members of the legislature thereof, is denied to any of the male inhabitants of such State, being twenty-one years of age, and citizens of the United States, or in any way abridged, except for participating in rebellion, or other crime, the basis of representation therein shall be reduced in the proportion which the number of such male citizens shall bear to the whole number of male citizens twenty-one years of age in such State.

The Constitution *(cont.)*

Section 3.

No person shall be a senator or representative in Congress, or elector of President and Vice President, or hold any office, civil or military, under the United States, or under any State, who having previously taken an oath, as a member of Congress, or as an officer of the United States, or as a member of any State legislature, or as an executive or judicial officer of any State, to support the Constitution of the United States, shall have engaged in insurrection or rebellion against the same, or given aid or comfort to the enemies thereof. But Congress may by a vote of two thirds of each House, remove such disability.

Section 4.

The validity of the public debt of the United States, authorized by law, including debts incurred for payment of pensions and bounties for services in suppressing insurrection or rebellion; shall not be questioned. But neither the United States nor any State shall assume or pay any debt or obligation incurred in aid of insurrection or rebellion against the United States, or any claim for the loss or emancipation of any slave; but all such debts, obligations, and claims shall be held illegal and void.

Section 5.

The Congress shall have the power to enforce, by appropriate legislation, the provisions of this article.

Amendment XV [March 30, 1870]

Section 1.

The right of citizens of the United States to vote shall not be denied or abridged by the United States or by any State on account of race, color, or previous condition of servitude.

Section 2.

The Congress shall have power to enforce this article by appropriate legislation.

Amendment XVI [February 25, 1913]

The Congress shall have power to lay and collect taxes on incomes, from whatever source derived, without apportionment among the several States, and without regard to any census or enumeration.

Amendment XVII [May 31, 1913]

The Senate of the United States shall be composed of two senators from each State, elected by the people thereof, for six years; and each senator shall have one vote. The electors in each State shall have the qualifications requisite for electors of the most numerous branch of the State legislature.

When vacancies happen in the representation of any State in the Senate, the executive authority of such State shall issue writs of election to fill such vacancies: *Provided,* That the legislature of any State may empower the executive thereof to make temporary appointments until the people fill the vacancies by election as the legislature may direct.

This amendment shall not be so construed as to affect the election or term of any senator chosen before it becomes valid as part of the Constitution.

Amendment XVIII [January 29, 1919]

After one year from the ratification of this article, the manufacture, sale, or transportation of intoxicating liquors within, the importation thereof into, or the exportation thereof from the United States and all territory subject to the jurisdiction thereof for beverage purposes is thereby prohibited.

The Congress and the several States shall have concurrent power to enforce this article by appropriate legislation.

This article shall be inoperative unless it shall have been ratified as an amendment to the Constitution by the legislatures of the several States, as provided in the Constitution, within seven years from the date of the submission hereof to the States by Congress.

Amendment XIX [August 26, 1920]

The right of citizens of the United States to vote shall not be denied or abridged by the United States or by any State on account of sex.

Congress shall have the power to enforce this article by appropriate legislation.

Amendment XX [January 23, 1933]

Section 1.

The terms of the President and Vice President shall end at noon on the 20th day of January and the terms of Senators and Representatives at noon on the 3d day of January, of the years in which such terms would have ended if this article had not been ratified; and the terms of their successors shall then begin.

Section 2.

The Congress shall assemble at least once in every year, and such meeting shall begin at noon on the 3d day of January, unless they shall by law appoint a different day.

Section 3.

If, at the time fixed for the beginning of the term of President, the President-elect shall have died, the Vice President-elect shall become President. If a President shall not have been chosen before the time fixed for the beginning of his term, or if the President-elect shall have failed to qualify, then the Vice President-elect shall act as President until a President shall have qualified; and the Congress may by law provide for the case wherein neither a President-elect nor a Vice President-elect shall have qualified, declaring who shall then act as President, or the manner in which one who is to act shall be selected, and such person shall act accordingly until a President or Vice President shall have qualified.

Section 4.

The Congress may by law provide for the case of the death of any of the persons from whom the House of Representatives may choose a President whenever the right of choice shall have devolved upon them, and for the case of the death of any of the persons from whom the Senate may choose a Vice President whenever the right of choice shall have devolved upon them.

Section 5.

Sections 1 and 2 shall take effect on the 15th day of October following the ratification of this article.

The Constitution *(cont.)*

Section 6.

This article shall be inoperative unless it shall have been ratified as an amendment to the Constitution by the legislatures of three-fourths of the several States within seven years from the date of its submission.

Amendment XXI [December 5, 1933]

Section 1.

The Eighteenth Article of amendment to the Constitution of the United States is hereby repealed.

Section 2.

The transportation or importation into any State, Territory, or possession of the United States for delivery or use therein of intoxicating liquors in violation of the laws thereof, is hereby prohibited.

Section 3.

This article shall be inoperative unless it shall have been ratified as an amendment to the Constitution by conventions in the several States, as provided in the Constitution, within seven years from the date of the submission thereof to the States by the Congress.

Amendment XXII [March 1, 1951]

No person shall be elected to the office of the President more than twice, and no person who has held the office of President, or acted as President, for more than two years of a term to which some other person was elected President shall be elected to the office of the President more than once.

But this article shall not apply to any person holding the office of President when this article was proposed by the Congress, and shall not prevent any person who may be holding the office of President, or acting as President, during the term within which this article becomes operative from holding the office of President or acting as President during the remainder of such term.

This article shall be inoperative unless it shall have been ratified as an amendment to the Constitution by the legislatures of three-fourths of the several States within seven years from the date of its submission to the States by the Congress.

Amendment XXIII [March 29, 1961]

Section 1.

The District constituting the seat of Government of the United States shall appoint in such manner as the Congress may direct.

A number of electors of President and Vice President equal to the whole number of Senators and Representatives in Congress to which the District would be entitled if it were a State, but in no event more than the least populous State; they shall be in addition to those appointed by the States, but they shall be considered, for the purposes of the election of President and Vice President, to be electors appointed by a State; and they shall meet in the District and perform such duties as provided by the twelfth article of amendment.

Section 2.

The Congress shall have power to enforce this article by appropriate legislation.

Amendment XXIV [January 23, 1964]

Section 1.

The right of citizens of the United States to vote in any primary or other election for President or Vice President, for electors for President or Vice President, or for Senator or Representative in Congress, shall not be denied or abridged by the United States or any State by reason of failure to pay any poll tax or other tax.

Section 2.

The Congress shall have power to enforce this article by appropriate legislation.

Amendment XXV [February 10, 1967]

Section 1.

In case of the removal of the President from office or of his death or resignation, the Vice President shall become President.

Section 2.

Whenever there is a vacancy in the office of the Vice President, the President shall nominate a Vice President who shall take office upon confirmation by a majority of both Houses of Congress.

Section 3.

Whenever the President transmits to the President pro tempore of the Senate and the Speaker of the House of Representatives his written declaration that he is unable to discharge the powers and duties of his office, and until he transmits to them a written declaration to the contrary, such powers and duties shall be discharged by the Vice President as Acting President.

Section 4.

Whenever the Vice President and a majority of either the principal officers of the executive departments or of such other body as Congress may by law provide, transmit to the President pro tempore of the Senate and the Speaker of the House of Representatives their written declaration that the President is unable to discharge the powers and duties of his office, the Vice President shall immediately assume the powers and duties of the office as Acting President.

Thereafter, when the President transmits to the President pro tempore of the Senate and the Speaker of the House of Representatives his written declaration that no inability exists, he shall resume the powers and duties of his office unless the Vice President and a majority of either the principal officers of the executive departments or of such other body as Congress may by law provide, transmit within four days to the President pro tempore of the Senate and the Speaker of the House of Representatives their written declaration that the President is unable to discharge the powers and duties of his office. Thereupon Congress shall decide the issue, assembling within forty-eight hours for that purpose if not in session. If the Congress, within twenty-one days after receipt of the latter written declaration, or, if Congress is not in session, within twenty-one days after Congress is required to assemble, determines by two-thirds vote of both Houses that the President is unable to discharge the powers and duties of his office, the Vice President shall continue to discharge the same as Acting President; otherwise, the President shall resume the powers and duties of his office.

The Constitution (cont.)

Amendment XXVI [June 30, 1971]

Section 1.

The right of citizens of the United States who are eighteen years of age or older to vote shall not be denied or abridged by the United States or by any State on account of age.

Section 2.

The Congress shall have power to enforce this article by appropriate legislation.

Amendment XXVII [May 7, 1992]

Section 1.

No law, varying the compensation for the services of the Senators and Representatives, shall take effect, until an election of Representatives shall have intervened.

⊙ Brinkley, Alan. *American History, A Survey.* 10th ed. New York: McGraw Hill, 1999.
National Archives and Records Administration. "The Constitution of the United States," www.nara.gov/exhall/charters/constitution/conmain.html
Mayer, David N. *The Constitutional Thought of Thomas Jefferson.* Charlottesville: University Press of Virginia, 1994.

The Gettysburg Address

Four score and seven years ago our fathers brought forth on this continent, a new nation, conceived in Liberty, and dedicated to the proposition that all men are created equal.

Now we are engaged in a great civil war, testing whether that nation, or any nation so conceived and so dedicated, can long endure. We are met on a great battle-field of that war. We have come to dedicate a portion of that field, as a final resting place for those who here gave their lives that that nation might live. It is altogether fitting and proper that we should do this.

But, in a larger sense, we can not dedicate—we can not consecrate—we can not hallow—this ground. The brave men, living and dead, who struggled here, have consecrated it, far above our poor power to add or detract. The world will little note, nor long remember what we say here, but I can never forget what they did here. It is for us the living, rather, to be dedicated here to the unfinished work which they who fought here have thus far so nobly advanced. It is rather for us to be here dedicated to the great task remaining before us—that from these honored dead we take increased devotion to that cause for which they gave the last full measure of devotion—that we here highly resolve that these dead shall not have died in vain—that this nation, under God, shall have a new birth of freedom—and that government of the people, by the people, for the people, shall not perish from the earth.

⊙ Brinkley, Alan. *American History: A Survey.* 10th ed. New York: McGraw Hill, 1999.
Wills, Garry. *Lincoln at Gettysburg.* New York: Simon & Schuster, 1992.

Chronology: American History

Time Period	Event
25,000 BC	Approximate date of earliest human settlement in the Americas
c.5000 BC	Beginning of Athapaskan migration
c.3000 BC	Inupiat and Aleut migrations
2500 BC	Date of the Serpent Mound located in the Ohio Valley
1000 BC	Leif Eriksson sails to Newfoundland
C.AD 500	Height of Mayan culture (Mexico)
AD 650	Earliest evidence of bow and arrow, flint hoes, and Northern Flint corn in the Northeast
1000	Cultivation of tobacco throughout North America
1050–1250	Peak of Cahokia Culture (Illinois)
C.1200	High point of Mississippian and Anasazi cultures
1300	Athapaskans reach Southwest
1325	Aztec city Tenochititlán founded
1451	Founding of the Iroquois Confederacy
1492	Christopher Columbus reaches Caribbean
1497	John Cabot explores east coast of North America
1513	Juan Ponce de Leon lands in Florida
1519	Hernan Cortés arrives in Mexico; imprisons Aztec emperor Montezuma, who later dies in battle
1519–22	Ferdinand Magellan circumnavigates the world
1535	Jacques Cartier begins exploring the St. Lawrence River
1539–40	Expeditions of Hernando de Soto and Francisco de Coronado
1565	Spanish found St. Augustine; French Huguenot colony of Ft. Caroline in Florida is destroyed by Spanish; Spanish missions introduce Roman Catholicism to Florida
1584–87	Sir Walter Raleigh establishes colony on Roanoke Island
1586	Sir Francis Drake destroys Spanish settlements in Florida and the West Indies
1598	Juan de Onate leads Spain into New Mexico; Spanish missions are established in New Mexico
1607	Settlement of Jamestown, Virginia
1608	Samuel Champlain founds Quebec
1609	Henry Hudson discovers the Hudson River; Spanish found Santa Fe (first Spanish settlement in New Mexico); Church of England is established by law in Virginia
1612	Introduction of tobacco cultivation in Virginia
1619	First Africans are sold as slaves in Virginia
1620	Pilgrims settle Plymouth
1621	William Bradford is elected governor of the Plymouth Colony; Treaty between Plymouth and Massasoit, Wampanoag chief
1625	Puritans settle Massachusetts Bay; Jesuit missionaries arrive in New France
1650–96	Parliament enacts the Navigation Acts
1656	First Quakers arrive in Boston

Chronology: American History *(cont.)*

1661	Algonquian New Testament becomes the first Bible printed in North America
1664	English conquer New Amsterdam
1665	New Jersey colony founded
1669	South Carolina founded
1675	King Philip's War
1676	Bacon's Rebellion
1681	Settlement of Philadelphia; Exploration of the Mississippi River by Sieur de La Salle
1683	Earliest Mennonites settle in Pennsylvania
1692	Salem witch trials
1696	Introduction of rice cultivation in South Carolina
1700s	Plains Indians begin using horses
1702	St. Augustine burned by South Carolinians
1705	Virginia Slave Code established
1716	Spanish build missions in Texas
1732	Benjamin Franklin begins publication of *Poor Richard's Almanac*
1733	Molasses Act; Georgia settled
1738	George Whitefield begins preaching in the colonies
1740s	Indigo production starts in South Carolina
1740	Naturalization Act
1741	Vitus Bering explores Alaska
1745	British take Louisburg, Canada, from France
1754–63	French and Indian War
1759	John Winthrop publishes *Two Lectures on Comets*
1760s	Height of the Great Awakening
1763	Pontiac's Rebellion; Paxton Boys Massacre; Proclamation of 1763
1764	Sugar Act
1765	Stamp Act
1767	Townshend Acts
1767–68	Daniel Boone explores Kentucky; Spanish begin settling California; Boston Massacre
1773	Boston Tea Party
1774	First Continental Congress meets
1775	Daniel Boone crosses Cumberland Gap to Kentucky's bluegrass region; Battles of Lexington and Concord and Bunker Hill; George Washington named commander-in-chief of Continental Army
1776	Declaration of Independence; Washington occupies Boston; Battles of Long Island, Trenton, and Princeton; San Francisco founded; Thomas Paine publishes *Common Sense*
1777	Battle of Saratoga
1777–78	Continental Army winters over at Valley Forge
1778	British capture Savannah and Charleston
1781	Ratification of the Articles of Confederation; General Cornwallis surrenders at Yorktown
1783	Treaty of Paris; Britain recognizes U.S. independence
1784	Russians settle Aleutian Islands of Alaska

1785	Land Ordinance of 1785
1787	Shays' Rebellion; Constitutional Convention; Northwest Ordinance; first American steamboat is launched on the Delaware River by John Fitch
1789	Washington inaugurated as president; Annapolis Convention; Bill of Rights
1790	First U.S. ship reaches Hawaii; Samuel Slater opens his first mill in Rhode Island
1793	Eli Whitney invents the cotton gin
1794	Whiskey Rebellion
1795	Ratification of Jay's Treaty
1798	XYZ Affair; Alien and Sedition Acts are passed
1803	Louisiana Purchase
1804–6	Louis and Clark expedition
1806	Zebulon Pike explores the Great Plains to the Rocky Mountains
1807	Robert Fulton builds his first successful steamboat, the *Clermont*
1808	Congress bars importation of slaves
1811	Battle of Tippecanoe
1812	War of 1812
1814	Francis Scott Key writes "The Star Spangled Banner"
1815	Battle of New Orleans; Stephen Decatur's Algerian expedition
1817	Rush-Bagot Agreement with Great Britain
1818	1st Seminole War
1820	Missouri Compromise
1821	Mexico achieves independence from Spain
1823	Monroe Doctrine
1825	Baltimore and Ohio railroad begins operation; Erie Canal opens
1830	Indian Removal Act; Joseph Smith founds Mormon Church
1830s	Height of the Second Great Awakening
1831	Nat Turner's slave uprising
1835	Texas Revolt against Mexico
1836	Battles of the Alamo and San Jacinto
1843–44	John C. Fremont maps trails to Oregon and California
1844	First successful telegraph transmission
1845	U.S. annexes Texas as slave state
1846	Beginning of Mexican-American War; Wilmot Proviso; Oregon Treaty; Elias Howe invents the sewing machine
1848	Women's Rights Convention at Seneca Falls, N.Y.; treaty of Guadalupe Hidalgo ends Mexican-American War
1849	California Gold Rush
1850	Compromise of 1850; California admitted as a free state
1851	Publication of Harriet Beecher Stowe's *Uncle Tom's Cabin*
1853	Commodore Matthew Perry opens Japan to U.S. trade; Washington Territory established
1854	Kansas-Nebraska Act; Henry David Thoreau publishes *Walden*
1856	John Brown's raid; caning of Sen. Charles Sumner
1857	Dred Scott case
1858	Lincoln-Douglas debates
1860	Abraham Lincoln elected president; Pony Express established

Chronology: American History *(cont.)*

1861	Civil War begins; First Battle of Bull Run
1862	Battles of the *Monitor* and the *Merrimack*, Shiloh, Antietam, and Fredericksburg; Pacific Railway Act; Homestead Act
1863	Emancipation Proclamation; Battles of Chancellorsville, Gettysburg, and Vicksburg
1864	Sherman's march to the sea
1865	Freedmen's Bureau established; Lee surrenders at Appomattox; Lincoln assassinated
1865–66	Enactment of Black Codes in the South
1865–67	Great Sioux War
1867	Reconstruction Acts passed; U.S. purchases Alaska from Russia
1868	House of Representatives impeaches Andrew Johnson; Senate acquits him in 1871
1871	Chicago fire
1871–86	Apache Wars in New Mexico
1874	Invention of barbed wire
1876	Battle of Little Big Horn; Rutherford B. Hayes wins disputed presidential election; Alexander Graham Bell invents telephone
1879	Carlisle Indian School founded; Thomas Edison invents light bulb
1881	President Garfield assassinated; Tuskegee Institute founded
1882	Chinese Exclusion Act
1886	American Federation of Labor founded; Haymarket bombing
1887	Dawes Severalty (Allotment) Act; Interstate Commerce Act
1889	Jane Addams founds Hull House
1890	Wounded Knee Massacre; National American Women's Suffrage Association founded; Sherman Antitrust Act
1894	Pullman Strike
1896	*Plessy* v. *Ferguson* upholds "separate but equal" doctrine; William Jennings Bryan's "Cross of Gold" speech
1898	Spanish-American War; U.S. acquires overseas territories from Spain; annexes Hawaii
1901	Pres. McKinley assassinated, V.P. Theodore Roosevelt succeeds as president
1903	U.S. secures canal rights in Panama; W.E.B. Du Bois publishes *The Souls of Black Folk;* Wright brothers launch the first successful manned flight in Kittyhawk, N.C.
1905	Albert Einstein develops his theory of relativity
1907	"Gentlemen's Agreement" with Japan
1908	Henry Ford produces first Model T automobile
1909	W.E.B. Du Bois helps found National Association for the Advancement of Colored People (NAACP)
1914	World War I begins; Panama Canal opens; Clayton Anti-Trust Act
1914	Keating-Owen Act bars child-labor products from interstate commerce
1916–17	Mexican Border Campaign
1917	U.S. declares war on the Central Powers; 18th Amendment passes, prohibiting the manufacture and sale of alcoholic beverages

1918	U.S. troops fight in France; armistice ends World War I; Wilson announces his Fourteen Points; Sedition Act passed; Eugene Debs imprisoned
1919	Senate rejects the Treaty of Versailles; Red Scare and Palmer Raids begin; Chicago race riot
1919–30	Harlem Renaissance
1920	19th Amendment guarantees women's right to vote
1921	Congress establishes first immigration quotas
1921–22	Washington Armament Conference
1923	Pres. Warren Harding dies; exposure of Teapot Dome and other Harding administration scandals
1924	Congress extends citizenship to all Indians
1925	Scopes Monkey trial in Dayton, Tenn.
1927	Execution of Sacco and Vanzetti; Charles Lindbergh's solo flight from New York to Paris
1929	New York Stock Exchange crashes
1930s	Great Depression
1932	Bonus March on Washington
1933	First New Deal
1934	Indian Reorganization Act
1935	Social Security Act passed
1937	Franklin D. Roosevelt's Court Packing plan thwarted
1938	Formation of Congress of Industrial Organizations
1939	World War II begins
1940	Selective Service and Raining Act passed
1941	Japan attacks Pearl Harbor; United States enters World War II
1942	Internment of Japanese Americans; Congress of Racial Equality (CORE) established
1943	Race riots in Detroit and Los Angeles
1945	Yalta Conference; Roosevelt dies and V.P. Harry Truman becomes president; Germany surrenders; first atomic bomb detonated at Alamogordo, N.M.; U.S. drops atomic bombs on Hiroshima and Nagasaki; Japan surrenders; union membership reaches 14.8 million
1946	United Mine Workers' strike; Richard Evelyn Byrd leads an expedition to the South Pole
1947	Marshall Plan proposed; Truman Doctrine; HUAC hearings in Hollywood; Jackie Robinson becomes the first African-American major league baseball player; Taft-Hartley (Labor-Management Relations) Act
1948	Military desegregation ordered by Harry Truman
1948–49	Berlin Airlift
1949	Truman announces Fair Deal; NATO founded
1950	Korean War starts
1951	Gen. MacArthur dismissed by Pres. Truman
1952	Dwight D. Eisenhower elected president
1953	Armistice agreement in Korea
1954	Supreme Court *Brown* v. *Board of Education* desegregation decision; United States explodes first hydrogen bomb; Army-McCarthy Hearings; first atomic-powered ship, USS *Nautilus*, launched

Chronology: American History *(cont.)*

1955	Merger of AFL and CIO; Jonas Salk develops polio vaccine
1956	Montgomery, Alabama, bus boycott ends successfully
1957	Pres. Eisenhower sends the National Guard to desegregate Little Rock High School
1960	John F. Kennedy elected president; founding of the Student-Nonviolent Coordinating Committee (SNCC)
1962	Cuban Missile Crisis
1963	Pres. Kennedy assassinated; V.P. Lyndon B. Johnson succeeds
1964	Civil Rights Act; U.S. role in Vietnam expands after Gulf of Tonkin Resolution; Economic Opportunity Act
1965	Malcolm X assassinated
1966	Formation of National Organization of Women (NOW) and of Black Panthers
1968	Vietnam War protests grow; Martin Luther King, Jr. and Robert Kennedy assassinated
1969	American Neil Armstrong becomes first man to walk on the moon
1970	Shooting of Kent State student protesters against Vietnam War
1972	Pres. Nixon visits China
1973	Signing of the Vietnam cease-fire; OPEC forms; Supreme Court issues *Roe v. Wade* abortion decision; American Indian Movement occupies Wounded Knee; Watergate hearings
1974	House Judiciary Committee votes to impeach Pres. Nixon; Nixon resigns; Gerald Ford pardons Nixon
1980	Ronald Reagan elected president
1982	Equal Rights Amendment (ERA) dies
1983	U.S. leads international force to occupy Grenada to halt Communist influence
1986	Space shuttle *Challenger* explodes, killing all aboard
1987	Iran-Contra hearings
1989	United States invades Panama, overthrows regime of Gen. Noriega; tanker *Exxon Valdez* causes the largest oil spill in U.S. history in the Gulf of Alaska
1990–91	Persian Gulf War
1991	Hewlett-Packard introduces a handheld lightweight computer
1993	Congress approves North American Free Trade Agreement (NAFTA)
1997	Congress and Pres. Bill Clinton agree to balance budget
1998	House of Representatives impeaches Clinton for perjury and obstruction of justice
1999	Senate fails to convict Clinton of impeachment charges

⊙ Brinkley, Alan. *American History: A Survey.* 10th ed. New York: McGraw Hill, 1999.
Divine, Robert A., et al. *America Past and Present.* 5th ed. New York: Longman, 1998.
Goldfield, David, et al. *The American Journey: A History of the United States.* Paramus, N.J.: Prentice Hall, 1997.

UNITED STATES: *U.S. Courts and Law*

Legal Terms

Acquittal: A release, absolution, or discharge of an obligation or liability. In criminal law, the finding of not guilty

Affidavit: A voluntary, written, or printed declaration of facts, confirmed by oath of the party making it before a person with authority to administer the oath

Allegation: A statement of the issues in a written document (a pleading) which a person is prepared to prove in court

Appeal: A proceeding brought to a higher court to review a lower court's decision for the purpose of reversing a judgment or granting a new trial

Arraignment: The hearing at which the accused is brought before the court to plead to the criminal charge in the indictment

Arrest: To take into custody by legal authority

Bail: Money or other security (such as a bail bond) provided to the court to temporarily allow a person's release from jail and assure their appearance in court. "Bail" and "Bond" are often used interchangeably. (Applies mainly to state courts.)

Bail bond: An obligation signed by the accused to secure his or her presence at the trial. This obligation means that the accused may lose money by not properly appearing for the trial. Often referred to simply as "bond."

Bankruptcy: Refers to statutes and judicial proceedings involving persons or businesses that cannot pay their debts and seek the assistance of the court in getting a fresh start

Burden of proof: In the law of evidence, the necessity or duty of affirmatively proving a fact or facts in dispute on an issue raised between the parties in a lawsuit

Capital crime: A crime punishable by death

Contempt of court: Willful disobedience of a judge's command or of an official court order

Conviction: A judgment of guilt against a criminal defendant

Cross-examination: The questioning of a witness produced by the other side in order to discredit or clarify testimony

Defendant: The person defending or denying a suit

Dismissal: The termination of a lawsuit without a complete trial; denial of a motion

Double jeopardy: Putting a person on trial more than once for the same crime. It is forbidden by the 5th Amendment to the United States Constitution

Due process of law: The right of all persons to receive the guarantees and safeguards of the law and the judicial process

Equal Protection of the Law: The guarantee in the 14th Amendment to the U.S. Constitution that all persons be treated equally by the law

Exhibit: A document or other item introduced as evidence during a trial or hearing

Exonerate: Removal of a charge, responsibility, or duty

File: To place a paper in the official custody of the clerk of court/court administrator to enter into the files or records of a case

Finding: Formal conclusion by a judge or regulatory agency on issues of fact. Also, a conclusion by a jury regarding a fact

Grand Jury: A jury that receives complaints and accusations in criminal matters and issues a formal indictment if appropriate

Habeas corpus: A legal writ that causes a person to be brought before the court to discover whether the individual is lawfully detained

Legal Terms *(cont.)*

Hostile witness: A witness whose testimony is not favorable to the party who calls him or her as a witness. A hostile witness may be asked leading questions and may be cross-examined by the party who calls him or her to the stand

Impeachment: The raising of criminal charges against a public official for wrongdoing while in office

Indictment: A written accusation by a grand jury charging a person with a crime

Jurisdiction: The power or authority of a court to hear and try a case; the geographic area in which a court has power or the types of cases it has power to hear

Jury: A certain number of citizens (frequently six or twelve) selected according to law and sworn to try a question of fact or indict a person for public offense

Lawsuit: An action or proceeding in a civil court; term used for a suit or action between two private parties in a court of law

Miranda warning: Requirement that police tell a suspect in their custody that he or she has the right to remain silent and has the right to the presence and advice of a lawyer

Objection: The process by which one party takes exception to some statement or procedure

Overrule: A judge's decision not to allow an objection. Also, a decision by a higher court finding that a lower court decision was in error

Pardon: An act of grace from governing power which mitigates punishment and restores rights and privileges forfeited on account of the offense

Parole: Supervised release of a prisoner from imprisonment on certain prescribed conditions which entitle him or her to serve the remainder of his or her sentence outside the prison if all the conditions are satisfactorily complied with

Plaintiff: A person who brings an action; the party who complains or sues in a civil action

Plea: The first pleading by a criminal defendant, the defendant's declaration in open court that he or she is guilty or not guilty

Probation: An alternative to imprisonment allowing a person found guilty of an offense to stay in the community, usually under conditions and under the supervision of a probation officer

Prosecutor: A trial lawyer who represents the government in a criminal case, or the interests of the state in civil matters

Reasonable doubt: An accused person is entitled to acquittal if, in the minds of the jury, his or her guilt has not been proved beyond a "reasonable doubt;" that state of minds of jurors in which they cannot say they feel an abiding conviction as to the truth of the charge

Remand: To send a dispute back to the court where it was originally heard. Usually it is an appellate court that remands a case for proceedings in the trial court consistent with the appellate court's ruling

Restitution: Act of restoring anything to its rightful owner; the act of restoring someone to an economic position he enjoyed before he suffered a loss

Search warrant: A written order issued by a judge that directs a law enforcement officer to search a specific area for a particular piece of evidence

Sentence: The punishment ordered by a court for a defendant convicted of a crime

Settlement: An agreement between the parties disposing of a lawsuit

Summons: Instrument used to commence a civil action or special proceeding; formal notification of a defendant that a civil action or special proceeding has begun against him or her and that he or she is required to appear in court to answer the complaint

Testimony: Verbal evidence given by a witness under oath

United States Attorney: A federal district attorney appointed by the President to prosecute for all offenses committed against the United States

Verdict: The opinion of a jury, or a judge where there is no jury, on a question of fact; used by the court in formulating the final judgment

Warrant: Most commonly, a court order authorizing law enforcement officers to make an arrest or conduct a search

Witness: One who personally sees or perceives a thing; one who testifies as to what he has seen, heard, or otherwise observed

Writ: A judicial order directing a person to do something

⊙ Oran, Daniel, and Mark Tosti. Oran's Dictionary of the Law. 3d ed. Albany, N.Y.:Delmar, 1999.
   United States Judiciary. www.id.uscourts.gov/glossary.htm

Chief Justices of the United States

Name	Life Dates	Appointed by	Years Served
John Jay	1745–1829	Washington	1789–1795
John *Rutledge	1739–1800	Washington	1795
Oliver Ellsworth	1745–1807	Washington	1796–1800
John Marshall	1755–1835	J. Adams	1801–1835
Roger Brooke Taney	1777–1864	Jackson	1836–1864
Salmon Portland Chase	1808–1873	Lincoln	1864–1873
Morrison Remick Waite	1816–1888	Grant	1874–1888
Melville Weston Fuller	1833–1910	Cleveland	1888–1910
Edward Douglass *White Jr.	1845–1921	Taft	1910–1921
William Howard Taft	1857–1930	Harding	1921–1930
Charles Evans *Hughes	1862–1948	Hoover	1930–1941
Harlan Fiske *Stone	1872–1946	F. D. Roosevelt	1941–1946
Frederick Moore Vinson	1890–1953	Truman	1946–1953
Earl Warren	1891–1974	Eisenhower	1953–1969
Warren Earl Burger	1907–1995	Nixon	1969–1986
William Hubbs *Rehnquist	1924–	Reagan	1986–

*also served as Associate Justice

⊙ Choper, Jesse H, ed. Supreme Court and Its Justices. Chicago: American Bar Association, 2000.
   Brinkley, Allan. American History, A Survey. 10th ed. New York: McGraw Hill, 1999.

Associate Justices of the Supreme Court

Name	Life Dates	Appointed by	Years Served	Chief Justice(s)
Henry Baldwin	1780–1844	Jackson	1830–1844	Marshall; Taney
Philip Pendleton Barbour	1783–1841	Jackson	1836–1841	Taney
Hugo Lafayette Black	1886–1971	F. D. Roosevelt	1937–1971	Hughes; Stone; Vinson; Warren; Burger

Associate Justices of the Supreme Court (cont.)

Name	Life Dates	Appointed by	Years Served	Chief Justice(s)
Harry Andrew Blackmun	1908–1999	Nixon	1970–1994	Burger; Rehnquist
John Blair	1732–1800	Washington	1789–1796	Jay
Samuel Milford Blatchford	1820–1893	Arthur	1882–1893	Waite; Fuller
Joseph P. Bradley	1813–1892	Grant	1870–1892	Chase; Waite; Fuller
Louis Dembitz Brandeis	1856–1941	Wilson	1916–1939	White; Taft; Hughes
William Joseph Brennan, Jr.	1906–1997	Eisenhower	1956–1990	Warren; Burger; Rehnquist
David Josiah Brewer	1837–1910	Harrison	1889–1910	Fuller
Stephen Gerald Breyer	1938–	Clinton	1994–	Rehnquist
Henry Billings Brown	1836–1913	Harrison	1890–1906	Fuller
Harold Hitz Burton	1888–1964	Truman	1945–1958	Stone; Vinson; Warren
Pierce Butler	1866–1939	Harding	1922–1939	Taft; Hughes
James Francis Byrnes	1879–1972	F. D. Roosevelt	1941–1942	Stone
John Archibald Campbell	1811–1889	Pierce	1853–1861	Taney
Benjamin Nathan Cardozo	1870–1938	Hoover	1932–1938	Hughes
John Catron	1786–1865	Jackson	1837–1865	Taney; Chase
Samuel Chase	1741–1811	Washington	1796–1811	Ellsworth; Marshall
Tom Campbell Clark	1899–1977	Truman	1949–1967	Vinson; Warren
John Hessin Clarke	1857–1945	Wilson	1916–1922	White; Taft
Nathan Clifford	1803–1881	Buchanan	1858–1881	Taney; Chase; Waite
Benjamin R. Curtis	1809–1874	Fillmore	1851–1857	Taney
William Cushing	1732–1810	Washington	1789–1810	Jay; Ellsworth; Marshall
Peter Vivian Daniel	1784–1860	Van Buren	1841–1860	Taney
David Davis	1815–1886	Lincoln	1862–1877	Taney; Chase; Waite
William Rufus Day	1849–1923	T. Roosevelt	1903–1922	Fuller; White; Taft
William Orville Douglas	1898–1980	F. D. Roosevelt	1939–1975	Hughes; Stone; Vinson; Warren; Burger
Gabriel Duvall	1752–1844	Madison	1811–1835	Marshall
Stephen Johnson Field	1816–1899	Lincoln	1863–1897	Taney; Chase; Waite; Fuller
Abe Fortas	1910–1982	Johnson	1965–1969	Warren
Felix Frankfurter	1882–1965	F. D. Roosevelt	1939–1962	Hughes; Stone; Vinson; Warren
Ruth Bader Ginsburg	1933–	Clinton	1993–	Rehnquist
Arthur Joseph Goldberg	1908–1990	Kennedy	1962–1965	Warren
Horace Gray	1828–1902	Arthur	1881–1902	Waite; Fuller
Robert Cooper Grier	1794–1870	Polk	1846–1870	Taney; Chase
John Marshall Harlan	1833–1911	Hayes	1877–1911	Waite; Fuller; White

John Marshall Harlan	1899–1971	Eisenhower	1955–1971	Warren; Burger
Oliver Wendell Holmes, Jr.	1841–1935	T. Roosevelt	1902–1932	Fuller; White; Taft; Hughes
Charles Evans Hughes *	1862–1948	Taft	1910–1916	Fuller; White
Ward Hunt	1810–1886	Grant	1872–1882	Chase; Waite
James Iredell	1751–1799	Washington	1790–1799	Jay; Ellsworth
Howell Edmunds Jackson	1832–1895	Harrison	1893–1895	Fuller
Robert Houghwout Jackson	1892–1954	F. D. Roosevelt	1941–1954	Stone; Vinson; Warren
Thomas Johnson	1732–1819	Washington	1791–1793	Jay
William Johnson	1771–1834	Jefferson	1803–1834	Marshall
Anthony McLeod Kennedy	1936–	Reagan	1988–	Rehnquist
Joseph Rucker Lamar	1857–1916	Taft	1911–1916	White
Lucius Quintus Cincinnatus Lamar	1825–1893	Cleveland	1888–1893	Waite; Fuller
Henry Brockholst Livingston	1757–1823	Jefferson	1806–1823	Marshall
Horace Harmon Lurton	1844–1914	Taft	1909–1914	Fuller; White
Thurgood Marshall	1908–1993	Johnson	1967–1991	Warren; Burger; Rehnquist
Stanley Matthews	1824–1889	Garfield	1881–1889	Waite; Fuller
Joseph McKenna	1843–1926	McKinley	1898–1925	Fuller; White; Taft
John McKinley	1780–1852	Van Buren	1837–1852	Taney
John McLean	1785–1861	Jackson	1829–1861	Marshall; Taney
James Clark McReynolds	1862–1946	Wilson	1914–1941	White; Taft; Hughes
Samuel Freeman Miller	1816–1890	Lincoln	1862–1890	Taney; Chase; Waite; Fuller
Sherman Minton	1890–1965	Truman	1949–1956	Vinson; Warren
William Henry Moody	1853–1917	T. Roosevelt	1906–1910	Fuller
Alfred Moore	1755–1810	Adams	1799–1804	Ellsworth; Marshall
Frank Murphy	1890–1949	F. D. Roosevelt	1940–1949	Hughes; Stone; Vinson
Samuel Nelson	1792–1873	Tyler	1845–1872	Taney; Chase
Sandra Day O'Connor	1930–	Reagan	1981–	Burger; Rehnquist
William Paterson	1745–1806	Washington	1793–1806	Jay; Ellsworth; Marshall
Rufus Wheeler Peckham, Jr.	1838–1909	Cleveland	1895–1909	Fuller
Mahlon Pitney	1858–1924	Taft	1912–1922	White; Taft
Lewis Franklin Powell, Jr.	1907–1998	Nixon	1971–1987	Burger; Rehnquist
Stanley Forman Reed	1884–1980	F. D. Roosevelt	1938–1957	Hughes; Stone; Vinson; Warren
William Hubbs Rehnquist *	1924–	Nixon	1971–1986	Burger
Owen Josephus Roberts	1875–1955	Hoover	1930–1945	Hughes; Stone
John Rutledge *	1739–1800	Washington	1789–1791	Jay
Wiley Blout Rutledge, Jr.	1894–1949	F. D. Roosevelt	1943–1949	Stone; Vinson
Edward Terry Sanford	1865–1930	Harding	1923–1930	Taft
Antonin Scalia	1936–	Reagan	1986–	Rehnquist
George Shiras, Jr.	1832–1924	Harrison	1892–1903	Fuller
David H. Souter	1939–	Bush	1990–	Rehnquist

Associate Justices of the Supreme Court *(cont.)*

Name	Life Dates	Appointed by	Years Served	Chief Justice(s)
John Paul Stevens	1920–	Ford	1975–	Burger; Rehnquist
Potter Stewart	1915–1985	Eisenhower	1958–1981	Warren; Burger
Joseph Story	1779–1845	Madison	1811–1845	Marshall; Taney
Harlan Fiske Stone*	1872–1946	Coolidge	1925–1941	Taft; Hughes
William Strong	1808–1895	Grant	1870–1880	Chase; Waite
George Sutherland	1862–1942	Harding	1922–1938	Taft; Hughes
Noah Haynes Swayne	1804–1884	Lincoln	1862–1881	Taney; Chase; Waite
Clarence Thomas	1948–	Bush	1991–	Rehnquist
Smith Thompson	1768–1843	Monroe	1823–1843	Marshall; Taney
Thomas Todd	1765–1826	Jefferson	1807–1826	Marshall
Robert Trimble	1776–1828	J. Q. Adams	1826–1828	Marshall
Willis Van Devanter	1859–1941	Taft	1910–1937	White; Taft; Hughes
Bushrod Washington	1762–1829	Adams	1798–1829	Ellsworth; Marshall
James Moore Wayne	c.1790–1867	Jackson	1835–1867	Marshall; Taney; Chase
Byron Raymond White	1917–	Kennedy	1962–1993	Warren; Burger; Rehnquist
Edward D. White*	1845–1921	Cleveland	1894–1910	Fuller
Charles Evans Whittaker	1901–1973	Eisenhower	1957–1962	Warren
James Wilson	1742–1798	Washington	1789–1798	Jay; Ellsworth
Levi Woodbury	1789–1851	Polk	1846–1851	Taney
William Burnham Woods	1824–1887	Hayes	1880–1887	Waite

* also served as Chief Justice

⊙ Choper, Jesse H, ed. *Supreme Court and Its Justices.* Chicago: American Bar Association, 2000.

Brinkley, Allan. *American History, A Survey.* 10th ed. New York: McGraw Hill, 1999.

Landmark Supreme Court Cases

Baker v. *Carr* **(1962)** Supreme Court held that the federal courts have jurisdiction to review state apportionment cases; led to implementation of "one person, one vote" principle.

Bank of Augusta v. *Earle* **(1839)** Corporate-law case that set the stage for the emergence of national corporations by holding that an out-of-state corporation had legal status in other states.

Barron v. *Baltimore* **(1833)** Limited federal power by declaring that the first eight constitutional amendments applied only to the federal government and did not protect individual rights from actions of state governments.

Brown v. *Board of Education of Topeka* **(1954)** Found that segregated educational facilities violated the 14th Amendment's equal protection clause; overturned *Plessy* v. *Ferguson* (1896).

Charles River Bridge v. *Warren Bridge* **(1837)** Held that state legislatures could regulate private property; the dissenters stated that the rights of private property were absolute.

Cherokee Nation v. *Georgia* (1831) Held that a Native American tribe was neither a state in the Union nor a foreign nation within the meaning of the Constitution and, therefore, could not maintain an action in the federal courts. Tribes were described as "domestic dependent nations" under the sovereignty and dominion of the U.S.

Civil Rights Cases (1883) Limited the application of the 14th amendment to state action; the amendment did not prevent discrimination by private individuals or businesses, a doctrine that remained influential for 80 years.

Cruzan v. *Director, Missouri Department of Health* (1990) Established the right of a state to regulate the "right to die."

Dartmouth College v. *Woodward* (1819) Established that the contract clause of the Constitution was intended as a protection for private property; ruling was based on the validity of Dartmouth College's colonial charter.

In re Debs (1895) Upheld the federal government's right to use court injunctions to resolve conflicts with striking unions; the Court held that labor leader Eugene V. Debs' use of a strike violated the Sherman Antitrust Act by hindering inter-state commerce.

Dennis v. *U.S.* (1951) Greatly restricted freedom of speech by narrowing the defi-nition of the "clear and present danger" test.

Dred Scott v. *Sandford* (1857) Ruled that African Americans were not citizens and could not bring suit in federal court; intended to answer the question of slav-ery's legality, the opinion declared the Missouri Compromise unconstitutional and heightened tensions before the Civil War.

Edwards v. *Aguillard* (1987) Invalidated Louisiana's creation-science law as violat-ing the 1st Amendment prohibition of establishing religion.

Engel v. *Vitale* (1962) School-prayer case that struck down a New York law allow-ing a prayer on the basis that such prayer was barred by the 1st Amendment prohibition against the establishment of religion.

Fletcher v. *Peck* (1810) Held that a Georgia law violated the Constitution's contract clause; established the Court's right of judicial review over the laws of the states.

Frontiero v. *Richardson* (1973) Established that gender discrimination, like racial discrimination, was unconstitutional.

Furman v. *Georgia* (1972) Found the death penalty, when imposed without spe-cific guidelines or limits on juries' decisions, to be cruel and unusual punish-ment; *Gregg* v. *Georgia* (1976) upheld statutes that guide judge and jury when imposing the death penalty.

In re Gault (1967) Held that "due process" provisions should be applied to juve-nile courts, an extension of constitutional protections.

Gibbons v. *Ogden* (1824) Highlighted the power of the federal government over the states, holding that the Constitution's commerce clause gave the federal gov-ernment broad regulatory powers (the case upheld the federal government's right to grant a ferry-service contract in competition with a service that had been granted a monopoly by a state government).

Gideon v. *Wainwright* (1963) Expanded defendants' (including indigent defen-dants') rights to legal counsel in virtually all criminal cases in both state and federal courts, extending the principles laid out in *Powell* v. *Alabama* (1932).

Hammer v. *Dagenhart* (1918) Overturned the Keating-Owen Child Labor Act (1916), holding that child labor involved manufacturing and was therefore a state concern.

Heart of Atlanta Motel v. *U.S.* (1964) Held racial discrimination in public accom-modation to be unlawful; upheld the Civil Rights Act of 1964 barring such dis-crimination and Congressional authority to pass such laws; *Katzenbach* v. *McClung* (1964) applied the same standard to ban discrimination in restaurants.

Landmark Supreme Court Cases (cont.)

Immigration and Naturalization Service v. *Cardoza-Fonseca* (1987) Granted immigrants political asylum if a refugee had a well-founded fear of prosecution in his or her country of origin.

Immigration and Naturalization Service v. *Chadha* (1983) Barred the "legislative veto" that Congress had used to restrict executive power.

Korematsu v. *U.S.* (1944) Japanese-internment case during World War II, in which the Court upheld the right of military authorities to evacuate persons of Japanese ancestry from the West Coast; reversed by writ of error filed in 1983.

Lemon v. *Kurtzman* (1971) Ensured the First Amendment separation of church and state by promulgating a three-prong test to determine establishment: a law must have a secular legislative purpose, its primary effect must be one that neither advances nor inhibits religions, and it must not foster an excessive entanglement with religion.

Lochner v. *New York* (1905) Set the precedent for an era of judicial activism when the Court declared a state labor regulation unconstitutional.

Mapp v. *Ohio* (1961) Forced the states to apply the 4th Amendment's protection against unreasonable searches to state courts.

Marbury v. *Madison* (1803) Established the power of judicial review, the federal courts' authority to find laws unconstitutional.

Martin v. *Hunter's Lessee* (1816) Held that states do not share sovereignty equally with the federal government; the case upheld federal supremacy.

McCulloch v. *Maryland* (1819) Case involving the Bank of the United States, in which the Court held that Maryland's tax on federal banks violated the concept of the federal government's supremacy, as set forth in the Constitution's Article I, Section 8, the necessary-and-proper clause; established the principle that the federal government had implied powers.

Ex parte Merryman (1861) Confronted President Lincoln's declaration of martial law during the Civil War; the issue remained open until *Ex Parte Milligan* (1866).

Ex parte Milligan (1866) Case brought by a civilian convicted in a military court in a non-combat area during the Civil War, in which the Court ruled that Milligan should not have been tried by the military and that military courts should not try civilians outside a war zone.

Minor v. *Happersett* (1875) Denied the claim of Virginia Minor that the right to vote was guaranteed by the Constitution's 14th Amendment; woman suffrage supporters thereafter concluded that a constitutional amendment was needed to obtain the vote.

Miranda v. *Arizona* (1966) Established that suspects have to be informed of the right to remain silent and the right to counsel under the 5th Amendment.

Muller v. *Oregon* (1908) Upheld, because of women's physical differences from men, an Oregon law regulating women's work hours; indicated the Court's acceptance of protective labor legislation for women, but not for men.

National Association for the Advancement of Colored People v. *Alabama* (1958) Case in which the Court reversed the contempt conviction of the NAACP for refusing to provide membership lists on the basis of the 1st Amendment's guarantee of freedom of association and the 14th Amendment's extension of that guarantee to the states.

National Labor Relations Board v. *Jones & Laughlin Steel Corp.* (1937) Upheld the National Labor Relations Act, a piece of New Deal Legislation that guaranteed the right of workers involved in interstate commerce to organize; the ruling averted the constitutional crisis raised by President F. D. Roosevelt's court-packing plan.

New York Times v. *Sullivan* (1964) Case in which the Court established a higher standard of libel for public figures because the public's right to public debate overrode the individual's rights.

Plessy v. *Ferguson* (1896) Upheld the constitutionality of the "separate but equal" philosophy that served as the basis for racial segregation in the South for the first half of the 20th century; overturned by *Brown* v. *Board of Education of Topeka* (1954).

Powell v. *Alabama* (1932) Case in which the Court held that defendants were guaranteed a fair trial, including the right to counsel, under the due process clause of the 14th Amendment; one of the "Scottsboro Boys" cases.

Regents of the University of California v. *Bakke* (1978) Affirmative action case in which the Court held that state universities could consider race as one of several factors in selecting students for admission, but could not establish racial quotas.

Roe v. *Wade* (1973) Upheld a woman's unrestricted right to an abortion during the first three months of pregnancy, an extension of the right to sexual privacy established by *Griswold* v. *Connecticut* (1965)

Roth v. *U.S.* (1970) Declared that obscenity was unprotected by the free-speech guarantee of the First Amendment on the ground that it is "utterly without redeeming social importance."

Schenck v. *U.S.* (1919) Upheld the WWI-era Espionage Act and laid out the "clear and present danger" test to determine the limits of First Amendment protection of political speech.

Standard Oil Company of New Jersey v. *U.S.* (1911) Held that the Sherman Antitrust Act applied only when trusts "unreasonably" hindered competition; this "rule of reason" became the test for the legality of a monopoly.

Texas v. *Johnson* (1989) Defined flag burning as "symbolic" speech that was protected under the 1st Amendment; Congress then passed the Flag Protection Act, which the Court invalidated in *U.S.* v. *Eichman* (1990).

U.S. v. *Darby Lumber Co.* (1941) Interpreted the commerce powers of Congress broadly in upholding minimum-wage and maximum-hour laws, overturning *Hammer* v. *Dagenhart* (1918).

U.S. v. *Wong Kim Ark* (1898) Upheld the principle, based on the 14th Amendment, that anyone born in the United States is a citizen, overturning a California law barring citizenship to those of Chinese descent.

Webster v. *Reproductive Health Services* (1989) Case in which the Court declared constitutional a Missouri law limiting the use of public money and facilities for abortion; the decision indicated that the Court was open to revisions of *Roe* v. *Wade* (1973).

West Virginia State Board of Education v. *Barnette* (1943) Jehovah's Witness case that upheld a refusal to salute the American flag as a protected right to free expression under the 1st Amendment; overturned *Minersville School District* v. *Gobitis* (1940).

Youngstown Sheet & Tube Co. v. *Sawyer* (1952) Rejected the claim of President Truman of authority to take control of private companies for national security reasons because Congress held the authority to intervene in labor disputes and the power to seize private property.

⊙ Brinkley, Allan. *American History, A Survey*. 10th ed. New York: McGraw Hill, 1999.
  U.S. Supreme Court Reports. *The Decisions of the United States Supreme Court*. Charlottesville, Va.: U.S. Supreme Court Reports, 1997.
  Virginia Foundation for the Humanities and Public Policy. *The Bill of Rights, the Courts & Law: The Landmark Cases that have Shaped American Society*. Charlottesville, Va.: Virginia Foundation for the Humanities and Public Policy, 1999.

Structure of the Federal Courts

Supreme Court

The Supreme Court, the highest court in the federal judiciary, consists of the Chief Justice of the United States and eight associate justices. As decreed by the Constitution, the Supreme Court hears a limited number of cases, usually those that involve questions about interpretation of the Constitution or federal law.

Trial Courts

Congress established two levels of courts beneath the Supreme Court, the trial and the appellate courts. The trial courts consist of the U.S. District Courts, the Bankruptcy Courts, the U.S. Court of International Trade, and the U.S. Court of Federal Claims. There are ninety-four federal judicial districts, with at least one in each state, the District of Columbia, and Puerto Rico. The U.S. Court of International Trade addresses cases involving trade and customs issues, while the U.S. Court of Federal Claims has jurisdiction over most claims for money damages and other claims against the United States.

Appellate Courts

The appellate courts consist of twelve regional Circuit Courts of Appeals, and one U.S. Court of Appeals for the Federal Circuit. Each of the twelve appellate courts can hear cases appealed from the Federal Trial Courts. The Court of Appeals for the Federal Circuit hears appeals in special cases, such as those involving patent law and cases decided by the Court of International Trade and the Court of Federal Claims.

Other Federal Courts

Beneath the Appellate and Trial Courts are the Military Courts, the Court of Veterans Appeals, the U.S. Tax Court, and various federal administrative agencies and boards.

⊙ The U.S. Federal Judiciary. "Understanding the Federal Courts," www.uscourts.gov/about.html

Federal Judiciary Center. *The Federal Courts and What They Do.* Washington, D.C.: Federal Judiciary Center, 1997.

Federal Judiciary Center. *Understanding the Federal Courts.* Washington, D.C.: Federal Judiciary Center, 1999.

Types of Crime

The Federal Bureau of Investigation collects crime data from local law-enforcement agencies under the following definitions.

Aggravated Assault: An unlawful attack by one person upon another for the purpose of inflicting severe or aggravated bodily injury. This type of assault is usually accompanied by the use of a weapon or by means likely to produce death or great bodily harm.

Arson: Any willful or malicious burning or attempt to burn, with or without intent to defraud, a dwelling house, public building, motor vehicle or aircraft, personal property of another, etc.

Assault (simple): To knowingly or recklessly cause or attempt to cause physical harm to another, but without use of a weapon

Burglary: Unlawful entry of a structure to commit a felony or a theft

Disorderly Conduct: Any unlawful breach of the peace

Driving under the Influence: Driving or operating any vehicle while drunk or under the influence of liquor or narcotics

Drug Abuse Violations: Violations of state and local laws relating to the unlawful possession, sale, use, growing, manufacturing, and making of narcotic drugs, including opium or cocaine and their derivatives (morphine, heroin, codeine); marijuana; synthetic narcotics (Demerol, methadone); and dangerous non-narcotic drugs (barbiturates, Benzedrine)

Drunkenness: Offenses relating to drunkenness or intoxication, not including "driving under the influence"

Embezzlement: The misappropriation or misapplication of money or property entrusted to one's care, custody, or control

Forgery and Counterfeiting: Making, altering, uttering, or possessing, with intent to defraud; anything false that resembles that which is true (e.g. a document or monetary note)

Fraud: Converting or obtaining money or property by false pretense, including confidence games and the use of bad checks

Gambling: Promoting, permitting, or engaging in illegal gambling

Hate Crime: Also called bias crime, a criminal offense committed against a person, property, or society that is motivated, in whole or in part, by the offender's bias against a race, religion, ethnic/national origin group, or sexual-orientation group

Larceny-Theft: Unlawful taking of property from the possession or constructive possession of another; includes shoplifting, pocket picking, purse snatching, thefts from motor vehicles, thefts of motor vehicle parts and accessories, and bicycle thefts

Liquor Law Violations: Violations of laws or ordinances prohibiting the manufacture, sale, transporting, furnishing, or possessing of intoxicating liquor

Manslaughter by Negligence: The death of a person through another person or organization's act of gross negligence

Motor Vehicle Theft: Theft or attempted theft of a motor vehicle

Murder and Non-negligent Manslaughter: Willful (non-negligent) killing of one human being by another

Non-forcible Rape: Unlawful but unforced sexual conduct; includes the crimes of incest and statutory rape

Offenses against the Family and Children: Nonsupport, neglect, desertion, or abuse of family and children

Prostitution and Commercialized Vice: Sex offenses of a commercialized nature, such as prostitution, procuring, or transporting women for immoral purposes

Rape: Carnal knowledge of a person, forcibly and against that person's will; in non-forcible rape, the victim is incapable of giving consent because of a temporary or permanent mental or physical incapacity or because of his/her youth

Robbery: Taking or attempting to take anything of value from the care, custody, or control of a person or persons by force or threat of force or violence and/or by putting the victim in fear

Sex Offenses: Statutory rape and offenses against chastity, common decency, morals, and the like, including voyeurism, forcible sodomy, and forcible fondling

Stolen Property: Buying, Receiving, Possessing: Knowingly buying, receiving, and possessing stolen property

Vandalism: Willful or malicious destruction, injury, disfigurement, or defacement of any public or private property, real or personal, without consent of the owner or persons having custody or control

Types of Crime (cont.)

Weapons Law Violations: Violation of laws or ordinances dealing with regulatory weapons offenses, including unlawful manufacturing, selling, or possession of deadly weapons; carrying deadly weapons, concealed or openly; and furnishing deadly weapons to minors

⊙ Federal Bureau of Investigation. "Uniform Crime Reporting Handbook," www.fbi.gov/ucr/Cius_98/98crime/98cius05.pdf
  Federal Bureau of Investigation. "Uniform Crime Reports," www.fbi.gov/ucr.htm

Patents and Copyrights

The United States Patent and Trademark Office was established under Article 1, section 8 of the United States Constitution. Its main purpose is to "promote the progress of science and the useful arts by securing for limited times to inventors the exclusive right to their respective discoveries."

The office itself is part of the Department of Commerce and since 1991 it has operated as a private business, providing patents, trademarks, and patent information for fees that are used to fund day-to-day operations.

A large part of the duties of the Patent Office is the issuing of trademarks and copyrights. Copyright is a form of protection given to authors of "original works" that include literary, dramatic, musical, artistic, and other intellectual works. Copyright law allows the owner of the copyright to authorize others to reproduce the work, produce derivative works, to distribute copies of the work, perform or display the work publicly, and in the case of sound recordings to perform them publicly by means of digital audio transmission. If the owner of the copyright does not authorize any of the above activities, it is illegal for anyone to violate that authorization and produce the work. There are, however, limitations on copyright law that can allow for specific exemptions from copyright liability.

Copyright protection, unlike the indefinite protection a patent can offer, cannot extend indefinitely. In this case, a work that is created on or after January 1, 1978, is protected from the moment of creation and is given protection through the author's life and an additional 70 years after the author's death. For works created and registered before 1978, there are different rules that sustain copyright for 95 years.

Patent law is a complex procedure that categorizes different kinds of inventions into various groups. Different offices examine each application to ascertain if the product is, in fact, original. The law then protects the item and its creator(s) from fraudulent claims of ownership. A patent lawyer is well versed the laws protecting patented items.

To obtain more information or to register for copyright, the Library of Congress may be contacted by telephone (202-707-3000) or fax (202-707-2600), or regular mail:

Library of Congress
Copyright Office
Publications Section, LM-455
101 Independence Avenue, SE
Washington, D.C. 20559-6000

The United States Patent and Trademark office can be reached by telephone (800-786-9199 or 703-308-4375) or regular mail:

Commissioner for Patents and Trademarks
United States Patent and Trademark Office
Washington, D.C. 20231

⊙ Library of Congress. "U.S. Copyright Office Home Page," www.loc.gov/copyright
  United States Patent and Trademark Office. www.uspto.gov

UNITED STATES: *Military*

Branches of the Armed Forces

The Department of Defense is a Cabinet-level organization charged with deterring war and preserving America's national security. Its major branches are the Departments of the Air Force, Army, and Navy. The Marine Corps is a separate armed service within the Department of the Navy. The Coast Guard reports to the Department of the Navy in wartime; normally it is under the jurisdiction of the Department of Transportation.

Military operations are coordinated by the Joint Chiefs of Staff, the chairman of which is the principal military advisor to the president. Field operations are directed by one or more of the nine Unified Combatant Commands.

⊙ U.S. Department of Defense. "DOD at a Glance," www.defenselink.mil/pubs/almanac/

Military Branches: Structure and Strength

Conventional Force Structure Summary, FY 2001

Force	Number	Troop Strength
Army		
Active Corps	4	Active: 480,000
Divisions (Active/National Guard)	10/8	Nat'l Guard: 350,000
Active Armored Cavalry Regiments	2	Reserve: 205,000
Enhanced Separate Brigades (National Guard)	15	
Separate Brigades (National Guard)	3	
Navy		
Aircraft Carriers	12	Active: 371,300
Air Wings (Active/Reserve)	10/1	Reserve: 89,600
Amphibious Ready Groups	12	
Attack Submarines	55	
Ballistic Missile Submarines	18	
Logistics Force Ships/Support Force	59	
Mine Warfare Ships (Active/Reserve)	11/5	
Surface Combatants (Active/Reserve)	108/8	
Air Force		
Active Fighter Wings	12+	Active: 354,400
Reserve Fighter Wings	7+	Air Nat'l Guard: 160,700
Reserve Air Defense Squadrons	4	Reserve: 73,900
Bombers (Total Inventory)*	190	
Marine Corps		
Marine Expeditionary Forces	3	Active: 172,000
Divisions (Active/Reserve)	3/1	Reserve: 39,500
Air Wings (Active/Reserve)	3/1	
Force Service Support Groups (Active/Reserve)	3/1	

*Reflects intended reduction of 18 B–52 aircraft.

⊙ Annual Report of the Secretary of Defense (FY 2000). "Chapter 5," www.dtic.mil/execsec/adr2000/chap5.html
Annual Report of the Secretary of Defense (FY 2000). "Appendix C-1," www.dtic.mil.execsec/adr2000/toc.html

(As of May 31, 1999)

Pay grades are levels of compensation that have been standardized across the services. O = commissioned Officer. W = Warrant officer. E = Enlisted personnel. Some E-level pay grades encompass two ranks.

Pay Grade	Army Title	No.	Air Force Title	No.	Navy Title	No.	Marine Corps Title	No.	Total No.
O-10	General	10	General	11	Admiral	9	General	4	34
O-9	Lieutenant General	45	Lieutenant General	36	Vice Admiral	24	Lieutenant General	11	116
O-8	Major General	98	Major General	87	Rear Admiral, Upper Half	73	Major General	25	283
O-7	General	154	General	139	Rear Admiral, Lower Half; Commodore	112	General	40	445
O-6	Colonel	3,558	Colonel	3,999	Captain	3,254	Colonel	620	11,431
O-5	Lieutenant Colonel	9,091	Lieutenant Colonel	10,409	Commander	7,217	Lieutenant Colonel	1,755	28,472
O-4	Major	14,348	Major	15,859	Lieutenant Commander	10,110	Major	3,393	43,710
O-3	Captain	20,341	Captain	26,216	Lieutenant	17,136	Captain	4,848	68,541
O-2	1st Lieutenant	10,843	1st Lieutenant	7,176	Lieutenant, JG	8,006	1st Lieutenant	3,073	29,098
O-1	2nd Lieutenant	7,917	2nd Lieutenant	5,707	Ensign	6,232	2nd Lieutenant	2,430	22,286
W-5	Master Warrant Officer 5	357	Warrant Officer 5	96	Chief Warrant Officer	453			
W-4	Chief Warrant Officer 4	1,427	—		Chief Warrant Officer	415	Warrant Officer 4	265	2,107
W-3	Chief Warrant Officer 3	3,074	—		Chief Warrant Officer	498	Warrant Officer 3	452	4,024
W-2	Chief Warrant Officer 2	5,073	—		Chief Warrant Officer	756	Warrant Officer 2	692	6,521

Grade	Army		Air Force		Navy		Marine Corps		Total
W-1	Chief Warrant Officer 1	1,823	—		—		Warrant Officer 1	431	2,254
Total Officers		78,159		69,639		53,842		18,135	219,775
E-9	Sergeant Major; Command Master Sergeant	3,220	Chief Master Sergeant; 1st Sergeant	2,960	Master Chief Petty Officer	2,908	Master Gunnery Sergeant/ Sergeant Major	1,287	10,375
E-8	Master Sergeant; 1st Sergeant	10,609	Sr. Master Sergeant; 1st Sergeant	5,955	Sr. Chief Petty Officer	6,094	Master Sergeant; 1st Sergeant	3,491	26,149
E-7	Sergeant 1st Class	38,136	Master Sergeant	28,901	Chief Petty Officer	23,338	Gunnery Sergeant	8,646	99,021
E-6	Staff Sergeant	54,720	Technical Sergeant	39,396	Petty Officer 1st Class	54,572	Staff Sergeant	14,959	163,647
E-5	Sergeant	69,871	Staff Sergeant	70,925	Petty Officer 2nd Class	67,983	Sergeant	23,241	232,020
E-4	Specialist Corporal	110,021	Senior Airman; Sergeant	65,280	Petty Officer 3rd Class	63,402	Corporal	30,328	269,031
E-3	Private 1st Class	52,112	Airman 1st Class	46,274	Seaman	47,791	Lance Corporal	40,453	186,630
E-2	Private 2	33,320	Airman	16,180	Seaman Apprentice	23,976	Private 1st Class	20,378	93,854
E-1	Private	14,464	Airman Basic	10,866	Seaman Recruit	18,503	Private	9,811	53,644
Total Enlisted		386,473		286,737		308,567		152,594	1,134,371
Cadets & Midshipmen		3,125		3,840		4,096		—	11,061
Grand Total		467,757		360,216		366,505		170,729	1,365,207

☉ U.S. Department of Defense. "Active Duty Military Personnel By Rank/Grade," www.defenselink.mil/pubs/almanac/

Wars and Conflicts

Historical Conflicts: Statistics

Conflict (a)	Number Serving	Battle Deaths	Other Deaths (b)	Wounded, not Fatal (c)
Revolutionary War				
1775–83				
Total	184,000–250,000 (est.)	4,435		6,188
Army		4,044		6,004
Navy		342		114
Marines		49		70
War of 1812				
1812–15				
Total	286,730	2,260		4,505
Army		1,950		4,000
Navy		265		439
Marines		45		66
Mexican War				
1846–48				
Total	78,718	1,733	11,550	4,152
Army		1,721	11,550	4,102
Navy		1		3
Marines		11		47
Civil War				
1861–65				
Union Forces				
Total	2,213,363	140,414	224,097	281,881
Army	2,128,948	138,154	221,374	280,040
Navy		2,112	2,411	1,710
Marines	84,415	148	312	131
Confederate Forces				
Total	600,000–1,500,000 (est.)	74,524	59,297	
Spanish-American War				
1898				
Total	306,760	385	2,061	1,662
Army	280,564	369	2,061	1,594
Navy	22,875	10		47
Marines	3,321	6		21
World War I				
1917–18				
Total	4,734,991	53,402	63,114	204,002
Army (inc. Air Corps)	4,057,101	50,510	55,868	193,663
Navy	599,051	431	6,856	819
Marines	78,839	2,461	390	9,520

World War II
1941–46 (d)

Total	16,112,566	291,557	113,842	671,846
Army	11,260,000	234,874	83,400	565,861
(inc. Air Corps)				
Navy	4,183,466	36,950	25,664	37,778
Marines	669,100	19,733	4,778	68,207

Korean Conflict
1950–53

Total	5,720,000	33,651	3,262	103,284
Army	2,834,000	27,709	2,452	77,596
Navy	1,177,000	475	173	1,576
Marines	424,000	4,269	339	23,744
Air Force	1,285,000	1,198	298	368

Vietnam Conflict
1964–73

Total	8,744,000	47,378	10,799	153,303
Army	4,368,000	30,922	7,273	96,802
Navy	1,842,000	1,631	931	4,178
Marines	794,000	13,084	1,753	51,392
Air Force	1,740,000	1,741	842	931

(a) Data prior to World War I are based on incomplete records in many cases. Casualty data are confined to dead and wounded and, therefore, exclude personnel captured or missing in action who were subsequently returned to military control.

(b) For example, disease, accident, etc.

(c) Marine Corps data for World War II, the Spanish-American War, and prior wars represent the number of individuals wounded, whereas all other data in this column represent the total number (incidence) of wounds.

(d) Data are for the period December 1, 1941, through December 31, 1946, when hostilities were officially terminated by Presidential Proclamation, but few battle deaths or wounds not mortal were incurred after the Japanese acceptance of the Allied peace terms on August 14, 1945. Number serving from December 1, 1941, through August 31, 1945: Total–14,903,213; Army–10,420,000; Navy–3,883,520; and Marine Corps–599,693.

⊙ U.S. Department of Defense. "Principal Wars in Which the United States Participated, U.S. Military Personnel Serving and Casualties," http://web1.whs.osd.mil/mmid/m01/SMS223R.HTM

Recent Conflicts: Statistics

Military Operation/ Incident	Casualty Type	Army	Navy	Air Force	Marine Corps	Total
Iranian Hostage Rescue Mission *April 25, 1980*						
	Nonhostile	0	0	5	3	8

Wars and Conflicts *(cont.)*

Recent Conflicts: Statistics *(cont.)*

Military Operation/ Incident	Casualty Type	Army	Navy	Air Force	Marine Corps	Total
Lebanon Peacekeeping						
August 25, 1982–February 26, 1984						
	Hostile	3	19	0	234	256
	Nonhostile	5	2	0	2	9
	Total	8	21	0	236	265
Urgent Fury, Grenada						
1983						
	Hostile	11	4	0	3	18
	Nonhostile	1				1
	Total	12	4	0	3	19
Just Cause, Panama						
1989						
	Hostile	18	4	0	1	23
Persian Gulf War						
1990–91						
Desert Shield	Nonhostile	21	36	9	18	84
Desert Storm	Hostile	98	6	20	24	148
	Nonhostile	105	14	6	26	151
	Total	203	20	26	50	299
Desert Shield/Storm						
	Total	224	56	35	68	383
Restore Hope/UNOSOM, Somalia						
1992–94						
	Hostile	27	0	0	2	29
	Nonhostile	4	0	8	2	14
	Total	31	0	8	4	43
Uphold Democracy, Haiti						
1994–96						
	Nonhostile	3	0	0	1	4

Note: "Nonhostile" casualties are those not directly caused by enemy action.

⊙ U.S. Army. "Worldwide U.S. Active Duty Military Deaths, Selected Military Operations," http://web1.whs.osd.mil/mmid/casualty/table13.htm

Veterans' and Retirees' Organizations

American Gulf War Veterans Association
P.O. Box 85
Versailles, MO 65084
800-231-7631
www.gulfwarvets.com
webmaster@golfwarvets.com

American Legion*
Indianapolis Office
700 North Pennsylvania Street
P.O. Box 1055
Indianapolis, IN 46206
Phone: (317) 630-1200
Fax: (317) 630-1223
www.legion.org
pr@legion.org

Washington Office
1608 K Street, NW
Washington, D.C. 20006
Phone: (202) 861-2700
Fax: (202) 861-2728
www.legion.org

AMVETS*
4647 Forbes Boulevard
Lanham, MD 20706-4380
(877) 726-8387 (877-7AMVETS)
www.amvets.org

Disabled American Veterans*
P.O. Box 14301
Cincinnati, OH 45250-0301
www.dav.org

American Military Retirees Association
22 U.S. Oval, Suite 1200
Plattsburgh, NY 12903
(518) 563-9479
www.amra1973.org
infoamra1973@westelcom.com

Korean War Veterans Association
P.O. Box 10806
Arlington, VA 22210
(703) 522-9629
www.kwva.org

Military Order of the Purple Heart*
5413-B Backlick Road
Springfield, VA 22151-3960

(703) 642-5360
www.purpleheart.org
info@purpleheart.org

Military Order of the World Wars*
435 North Lee Street
Alexandria, VA 22314
(703) 683-4911
www.militaryorder.org

National Association for Black Veterans*
P.O. Box 11432
Milwaukee, WI 53211-0432
800-842-4597
www.execpc.com/~nabvets

National Association for Uniformed Services
5535 Hempstead Way
Springfield, VA 22151
(703) 750-1342
www.naus.org

National Veterans Legal Services Program, Inc.*
2001 S Street, NW, Suite 610
Washington, D.C. 20009
Phone (202) 265-8305, Ext. 105
www.nvlsp.org
nvlsp@nvlsp.org

National Veterans Organization of America
7700 Alabama Street
P.O. Box 640064
El Paso, TX 79904-0064
(915) 759-8387
www.nvo.org

The Retired Enlisted Association*
1111 S. Abilene Court
Aurora, CO 80012
800-338-9337
(303) 752-0660
www.trea.org

The Retired Officers Association (TROA)
201 N. Washington Street
Alexandria, VA 22314
800-245-TROA
www.troa.org

Veterans' and Retirees' Organizations *(cont.)*

United Armed Forces Association
P.O. Box 20672
Waco, TX 76702
888-457-7667

Veterans News and Information Service
38620 Pleasant Avenue, #B
Sandy, OR 97055-9348
www.vnis.org

Veterans of Foreign Wars of the United States*
406 West 34th Street
Kansas City, MO 64111
(816) 756-3390
www.vfw.org
info@vfw.org

Veterans Resource Network Association
P.O. Box 3011
Frazer, PA 19355-9778
877-848-VRNA (8762)
www.vrna.org

Vietnam Veterans of America*
8605 Cameron Street, Suite 400
Silver Spring, MD 20910-3710
Phone: (301) 585-4000
Fax: (301) 585-0519
www.vva.org
communications@vva.org

*These organizations have been chartered by Congress and/or recognized by the Veterans Administration to represent veterans' claims.

⊙ Veterans Administration. "Veterans Service Organizations," www.va.gov/ vso.view.asp
  Military.com. "Veteran and Retiree Organizations," http://military.com/UnReg/ Association/?aType=veterans

Service Academies

Army:
United States Military Academy
  Attn: Public Affairs Office
  Taylor Hall, Bldg. 600
  West Point, NY 10996-1788
  (914) 938-4261 www.usma.edu

Navy:
United States Naval Academy
  Attn: Public Affairs Officer
  121 Blake Road
  Annapolis, MD 21402-5000
  (410) 267-2291 www.nadn.navy.mil

Air Force:
United States Air Force Academy
  Attn: Public Affairs Officer
  2304 Cadet Drive, Suite 320

U.S. Air Force Academy, CO 80840-5016
  (719) 472-2990 www.usafa.af.mil

Coast Guard:
United States Coast Guard Academy*
  Attn: Public Affairs Officer
  15 Mohegan Avenue
  New London, CT 06320-4195
  (203) 444-8270 www.cga.edu

United States Merchant Marine Academy**
  Attn: Public Affairs Officer
  300 Steamboat Road
  Kings Point, NY 11024
  (516) 773-5000 www.usmma.edu

*The Coast Guard reports to the Department of the Navy in wartime; normally it is under the jurisdiction of the Department of Transportation.
**The Merchant Marine Academy works closely with the U.S. armed forces, but is not a Defense Department organization.

⊙ U.S. Department of Defense. "Military Service Academies," www.defenselink.mil/ faq/pis/20.html

Largest Islands

Island	Area sq. mi. (sq. km.)	Location
Kodiak Island	5,363 (13,890)	Alaska, in Gulf of Alaska
Hawaii	4,021 (10,414)	Hawaii
Prince of Wales Island	2,587 (6,700)	Alaska, Alexander Archipelago
Chichagof Island	2,062 (5,340)	Alaska, Alexander Archipelago
St. Lawrence Island	1,712 (4,434)	Alaska, in Bering Sea
Admiralty Island	1,650 (4,273)	Alaska, Alexander Archipelago
Nunivak Island	1,625 (4,209)	Alaska, in Bering Sea
Baranof Island	1,600 (4,144)	Alaska, Alexander Archipelago
Unimak	1,600 (4,144)	Alaska, Aleutian Islands
Long Island	1,401 (3,628)	New York
Revillagigedo Island	1,145 (2,965)	Alaska, Alexander Archipelago
Kupreanof Island	1,084 (2,807)	Alaska, Alexander Archipelago
Unalaska	1,064 (2,755)	Alaska, Aleutian Islands
Nelson Island	843 (2,183)	Alaska
Kuiu Island	750 (1,942)	Alaska
Maui	727 (1,883)	Hawaii
Afognak	721 (1,867)	Alaska
Umnak	675 (1,748)	Alaska, Aleutian Islands
Oahu	597 (1,546)	Hawaii
Kauai	555 (1,437)	Hawaii
Atka Island	422 (1,093)	Alaska, Aleutian Islands
Attu Island	338 (875)	Alaska, Aleutian Islands
Montague Island	315 (816)	Alaska
Adak Island	289 (748)	Alaska, Aleutian Islands
Dall Island	260 (673)	Alaska, Alexander Archipelago
Molokai	260 (673)	Hawaii
Wrangell Island	217 (562)	Alaska
Mitkof Island	213 (551)	Alaska
Isle Royale	209 (541)	Michigan, in Lake Superior
Tanaga Island	209 (541)	Alaska, Aleutian Islands
Zarembo Island	180 (466)	Alaska
Whidbey Island	172 (445)	Washington, in Puget Sound
Lanai	141 (365)	Hawaii
Drummond Island	134 (347)	Michigan, in Lake Huron
Marsh Island	117 (303)	Louisiana
Martha's Vineyard	108 (279)	Massachusetts
Mount Desert Island	106 (274)	Maine, part of Acadia National Park
Santa Cruz Island	96 (248)	California, Santa Barbara Islands
Niihau	70 (181)	Hawaii
Nantucket	57 (148)	Massachusetts
Padre Island	46 (119)	Texas
Kahoolawe	45 (117)	Hawaii
Antelope Island	39 (101)	Utah, in Great Salt Lake
Rhode Island	39 (101)	Rhode Island, in Narragansett Bay
Madeline Island	24 (62)	Wisconsin, in Lake Superior
Manhattan	23 (60)	New York

⊙ Wright, John W., ed. *The New York Times Almanac, Millennium Edition.* New York: Penguin, 1999.

North American Deserts

Desert	Type	Location	Area sq. mi. (sq. km.)	Sub-deserts
Great Basin	Cold	Nevada; parts of Idaho, Oregon, California, and Utah	189,000 (489,500)	Black Rock, Escalante, Great Sandy, Red, Sevier, Smoke Creek
Chihuahuan	Hot	Mexico; parts of southern New Mexico, southeast Arizona, and west Texas	175,000 (450,000)	Trans-Pecos
Sonoran	Hot	Southwest Arizona, southeast California, Baja Peninsula, northwest Mexico	120,000 (310,800)	Arizona Upland, Borrego, Colorado, Magdalena, Vizcaino, Yuha, Yuma
Mojave	Hot	between the Great Basin and Sonoran deserts; southern California, southern Nevada, northwest Arizona	25,000 (64,750)	Northern Mojave, Southern Mojave, Death Valley

⊙ Desert USA, "Desert Life in the American Southwest," www.desertusa.com/life.html

Highest Mountains

Mountain	Height ft. (m.)	State	Mountain	Height ft. (m.)	State
Mount McKinley	20,320 (6,193)	Alaska	Mount Hubbard	14,950 (4,556)	Alaska
Mount St. Elias	18,008 (5,488)	Alaska	Mount Bear	14,831 (4,520)	Alaska
Mount Foraker	17,400 (5,303)	Alaska	East Buttress	14,730 (4,489)	Alaska
Mount Bona	16,500 (5,029)	Alaska	Mount Hunter	14,537 (4,430)	Alaska
Mount Blackburn	16,390 (4,995)	Alaska	Browne Tower	14,530 (4,428)	Alaska
Mount Sanford	16,237 (4,949)	Alaska	Mount Alverstone	14,500 (4,419)	Alaska
Mount Vancouver	15,979 (4,870)	Alaska	Mount Whitney	14,494 (4,417)	California
South Buttress	15,885 (4,841)	Alaska	University Peak	14,470 (4,410)	Alaska
Mount Churchill	15,638 (4,766)	Alaska	Mount Elbert	14,433 (4,399)	Colorado
Mount Fairweather	15,300 (4,663)	Alaska	Mount Massive	14,421 (4,395)	Colorado

Mount Harvard	14,420 (4,395)	Colorado	Mount Wrangell	14,163 (4,316)	Alaska
Mount Rainier	14,410 (4,392)	Washington	Mount Sill	14,163 (4,316)	California
Mount Williamson	14,370 (4,380)	California	Mount Shasta	14,162 (4,316)	California
La Plata Peak	14,361 (4,377)	Colorado	El Diente Peak	14,159 (4,315)	Colorado
Blanca Peak	14,345 (4,372)	Colorado	Point Success	14,158 (4,315)	Washington
Uncompahgre Peak	14,309 (4,361)	Colorado	Maroon Peak	14,156 (4,314)	Colorado
Crestone Peak	14,294 (4,356)	Colorado	Tabeguache Mountain	14,155 (4,314)	Colorado
Mount Lincoln	14,286 (4,354)	Colorado	Mount Oxford	14,153 (4,313)	Colorado
Grays Peak	14,270 (4,349)	Colorado	Mount Sill	14,153 (4,313)	California
Mount Antero	14,269 (4,349)	Colorado	Mount Sneffels	14,150 (4,312)	Colorado
Torreys Peak	14,267 (4,348)	Colorado	Mount Democrat	14,148 (4,312)	Colorado
Castle Peak	14,265 (4,348)	Colorado	Capitol Peak	14,130 (4,306)	Colorado
Quandary Peak	14,265 (4,348)	Colorado	Liberty Cap	14,112 (4,301)	Washington
Mount Evans	14,264 (4,347)	Colorado	Pikes Peak	14,110 (4,300)	Colorado
Longs Peak	14,255 (4,345)	Colorado	Snowmass Mountain	14,092 (4,295)	Colorado
Mount Wilson	14,246 (4,342)	Colorado	Mount Russell	14,088 (4,294)	California
White Mountain	14,246 (4,342)	California	Mount Eolus	14,083 (4,292)	Colorado
North Palisade	14,242 (4,341)	California	Windom Peak	14,082 (4,292)	Colorado
Mount Cameron	14,238 (4,339)	Colorado	Mount Columbia	14,073 (4,289)	Colorado
Mount Shavano	14,229 (4,337)	Colorado	Mount Augusta	14,070 (4,288)	Alaska
Crestone Needle	14,197 (4,327)	Colorado	Missouri Mountain	14,067 (4,287)	Colorado
Mount Belford	14,197 (4,327)	Colorado	Humboldt Peak	14,064 (4,286)	Colorado
Mount Princeton	14,197 (4,327)	Colorado	Mount Bierstadt	14,060 (4,285)	Colorado
Mount Yale	14,196 (4,327)	Colorado	Sunlight Peak	14,059 (4,285)	Colorado
Mount Bross	14,172 (4,319)	Colorado	Split Mountain	14,058 (4,284)	California
Kit Carson Mountain	14,165 (4,317)	Colorado	Handies Peak	14,048 (4,281)	Colorado

Highest Mountains *(cont.)*

Mountain	Height ft. (m.)	State	Mountain	Height ft. (m.)	State
Culebra Peak	14,047 (4,281)	Colorado	Wilson Peak	14,017 (4,272)	Colorado
Mount Lindsey	14,042 (4,280)	Colorado	Wetterhorn Peak	14,015 (4,271)	Colorado
Ellingwood Point	14,042 (4,280)	Colorado	North Maroon Peak	14,014 (4,271)	Colorado
Middle Palisade	14,040 (4,279)	California	San Luis Peak	14,014 (4,271)	Colorado
Little Bear Peak	14,037 (4,278)	Colorado	Middle Palisade	14,012 (4,270)	California
Mount Sherman	14,036 (4,278)	Colorado	Mount Muir	14,012 (4,270)	California
Redcloud Peak	14,034 (4,277)	Colorado	Mount of the Holy Cross	14,005 (4,268)	Colorado
Mount Langley	14,027 (4,275)	California	Huron Peak	14,003 (4,268)	Colorado
Conundrum Peak	14,022 (4,274)	Colorado	Thunderbolt Peak	14,003 (4,268)	California
Mount Tyndall	14,019 (4,273)	California	Sunshine Peak	14,001 (4,267)	Colorado
Pyramid Peak	14,018 (4,272)	Colorado			

Other notable mountains:

Mountain	Height ft. (m.)	State	Mountain	Height ft. (m.)	State
Grand Teton	13,766 (4,195)	Wyoming	Mount Rushmore	5,600 (1,706)	South Dakota
Mount Mitchell	6,684 (2,037)	North Carolina	Mount Marcy	5,344 (1,628)	New York
Mount Washington	6,288 (1,916)	New Hampshire	Mount Katahdin	5,268 (1,605)	Maine

⊙ *The World Almanac and Book of Facts, 2000: Millennium Collector's Edition.* Mahwah, N.J.: World Almanac Books, 1999.

Largest Lakes

Lake	Area sq. mi. (sq. km.)	Location
Superior	31,800 (82,362)	Michigan; Wisconsin; Minnesota; Ontario, Canada
Huron	23,000 (59,570)	Michigan; Canada
Michigan	22,400 (58,000)	Michigan; Indiana; Illinois; Wisconsin
Erie	9,910 (25,666)	New York; Pennsylvania; Ohio; Michigan; Canada
Ontario	7,600 (19,684)	New York; Canada
Great Salt Lake	2,000 (5,180)	Utah

Lake of the Woods	1,695 (4,390)	Minnesota; Canada
Iliamna	1,033 (2,675)	Alaska
Okeechobee	730 (1,890)	Florida
Pontchartrain	630 (1,632)	Louisiana
Becharof	458 (1,186)	Alaska
Red Lake	451 (1,168)	Minnesota
St. Clair	450 (1,150)	Michigan; Canada
Champlain	430 (1,114)	New York; Vermont; Canada
Salton Sea	360 (932)	California
Mead	227 (588)	Arizona; Nevada
Winnebago	215 (557)	Wisconsin
Tahoe	192 (497)	California; Nevada
Yellowstone	137 (355)	Wyoming
Moosehead	117 (303)	Maine
Owasco	110 (284)	New York

⊙ *The World Almanac and Book of Facts, 2000: Millennium Collector's Edition.* Mahwah,
   N.J.: World Almanac Books, 1999.

Longest Rivers

River	Length mi. (km.)	Location
Mississippi	3,860 (7,148)	Minnesota-Wisconsin-Iowa-Illinois-Missouri-Kentucky-Tennessee-Arkansas-Mississippi-Louisiana
Missouri	2,466 (4,567)	Montana-North Dakota-South Dakota-Nebraska-Iowa-Missouri-Kansas-Missouri
Yukon	1,979 (3,665)	Canada-Alaska
Rio Grande	1,885 (3,491)	Colorado-New Mexico-Texas-Mexico
Arkansas	1,450 (2,685)	Colorado-Kansas-Oklahoma-Arkansas
Colorado	1,450 (2,685)	Colorado-Utah-Arizona-Nevada-California-Mexico
Columbia	1,214 (2,248)	British Columbia-Washington-Oregon
Snake	1,038 (1,922)	Wyoming-Idaho-Oregon-Washington
Red	1,018 (1,885)	New Mexico-Texas-Oklahoma-Arkansas-Louisiana
Ohio	975 (1,805)	Pennsylvania-Ohio-West Virginia-Kentucky-Indiana-Illinois
Canadian	906 (1,678)	Colorado-New Mexico-Texas-Oklahoma
Brazos	840 (1,555)	Texas
Colorado	840 (1,555)	Texas
Saint Lawrence	800 (1,287)*	Canada-New York
Kansas (Kaw)	743 (1,376)	Kansas
Green	730 (1,351)	Wyoming-Utah
Dakota (James)	710 (1,314)	North Dakota-South Dakota
Yellowstone	691 (1,279)	Wyoming-Montana
White	690 (1,277)	Arkansas
Cumberland	687 (1,272)	Kentucky-Tennessee-Kentucky
North Platte	680 (1,259)	Colorado-Wyoming-Nebraska
Tennessee	652 (1,207)	Tennessee-Alabama-Tennessee-Kentucky
Milk	625 (1,157)	Montana-Canada-Montana
Ouachita	605 (1,120)	Arkansas-Louisiana
Kuskokwim	600 (1,111)	Alaska

Longest Rivers *(cont.)*

River	Length mi. (km.)	Location
Little Missouri	560 (1,037)	Wyoming-Montana-South Dakota-North Dakota
Trinity	550 (1,018)	Texas
Smoky Hill	540 (1,000)	Colorado-Kansas
Cimarron	500 (926)	New Mexico-Kansas-Oklahoma
Gila	500 (926)	New Mexico-Arizona
Koyukuk	500 (926)	Alaska
Osage	500 (926)	Missouri
Pecos	500 (926)	New Mexico-Texas
Washita	500 (926)	Texas-Oklahoma
Pearl	490 (907)	Mississippi-Louisiana
Tanana	475 (879)	Alaska
Wabash	475 (879)	Ohio-Indiana-Illinois
Neosho (Grand)	460 (851)	Kansas-Oklahoma
Porcupine	448 (829)	Canada-Alaska
Susquehanna	444 (822)	New York-Pennsylvania-Maryland
North Canadian	440 (814)	Oklahoma
Chattahoochee	436 (807)	Georgia-Alabama-Florida
Niobrara	431 (798)	Wyoming-Nebraska
Wisconsin	430 (796)	Wisconsin
Saint Francis	425 (787)	Missouri-Arkansas
South Platte	424 (785)	Colorado-Nebraska
Republican	422 (781)	Colorado-Nebraska-Kansas
Salmon	420 (777)	Idaho
Roanoke	410 (759)	Virginia-North Carolina
Tombigbee	409 (757)	Mississippi-Alabama
Connecticut	407 (753)	New Hampshire-Vermont-Massachusetts-Connecticut
Noatak	400 (740)	Alaska
Wateree-Catawba	395 (731)	North Carolina-South Carolina
Colville	375 (694)	Alaska
Powder	375 (694)	Wyoming-Montana
Green	360 (666)	Kentucky
Sabine	360 (666)	Texas-Louisiana
San Juan	360 (666)	Colorado-New Mexico-Colorado-Utah
Red River of the North	355 (657)	Minnesota-North Dakota-Canada
San Joaquin	350 (648)	California
James	340 (629)	Virginia
Stikine	335 (620)	Canada-Alaska
Allegheny	325 (601)	Pennsylvania-New York-Pennsylvania
Licking	320 (592)	Kentucky
New	320 (592)	Virginia-West Virginia
Sacramento	320 (592)	California
Alabama	315 (583)	Alabama
Platte	310 (574)	Nebraska
Hudson	306 (566)	New York
Clark Fork	300 (555)	Montana-Idaho
Platte	300 (555)	Iowa-Missouri
Willamette	300 (555)	Oregon

Potomac	287 (531)	West Virginia-Virginia-Maryland-Washington, D.C.
Coosa	286 (529)	Alabama
Delaware	280 (518)	New York-Pennsylvania-New Jersey-Delaware
Illinois	273 (505)	Illinois
Ocmulgee	255 (472)	Georgia
Pee Dee	233 (431)	North Carolina-South Carolina
Yadkin	202 (374)	North Carolina
Santee	143 (264)	South Carolina
Altamaha	137 (253)	Georgia
Pend Oreille	100 (185)	Idaho-Washington-Canada

* not including waterway provided by the Great Lakes

⊙ *The World Almanac and Book of Facts, 2000: Millennium Collector's Edition.* Mahwah, N.J.: World Almanac Books, 1999.

UNITED STATES: *States and Cities*

Date and Order of Admittance

State	Date Admitted	Order	State	Date Admitted	Order
Alabama	Dec. 14, 1819	22	Montana	Nov. 8, 1889	41
Alaska	Jan. 3, 1959	49	Nebraska	Mar. 1, 1867	37
Arizona	Feb. 14, 1912	48	Nevada	Oct. 31, 1864	36
Arkansas	June 15, 1836	25	New Hampshire	June 21, 1788	9
California	Sep. 9, 1850	31	New Jersey	Dec. 18, 1787	3
Colorado	Aug. 1, 1876	38	New Mexico	Jan. 6, 1912	47
Connecticut	Jan. 9, 1788	5	New York	July 26, 1788	11
Delaware	Dec. 7, 1787	1	North Carolina	Nov. 21, 1789	12
Florida	Mar. 3, 1845	27	North Dakota	Nov. 2, 1889	39
Georgia	Jan. 2, 1788	4	Ohio	Mar. 1, 1803	17
Hawaii	Aug. 21, 1959	50	Oklahoma	Nov. 16, 1907	46
Idaho	July 3, 1890	43	Oregon	Feb. 14, 1859	33
Illinois	Dec. 3, 1818	21	Pennsylvania	Dec. 12, 1787	2
Indiana	Dec. 11, 1816	19	Rhode Island	May 29, 1790	13
Iowa	Dec. 28, 1846	29	South Carolina	May 23, 1788	8
Kansas	Jan. 29, 1861	34	South Dakota	Nov. 2, 1889	40
Kentucky	June 1, 1792	15	Tennessee	June 1, 1796	16
Louisiana	Apr. 30, 1812	18	Texas	Dec. 29, 1845	28
Maine	Mar. 15, 1820	23	Utah	Jan. 4, 1896	45
Maryland	Apr. 28, 1788	7	Vermont	Mar. 4, 1791	14
Massachusetts	Feb. 6, 1788	6	Virginia	June 25, 1788	10
Michigan	Jan. 26, 1837	26	Washington	Nov. 11, 1889	42
Minnesota	May 11, 1858	32	West Virginia	June 20, 1863	35
Mississippi	Dec. 10, 1817	20	Wisconsin	May 29, 1848	30
Missouri	Aug. 10, 1821	24	Wyoming	July 10, 1890	44

Capitals and Area

State	Capital	Total Area [land and water] sq. mi. (sq. km.)	Area Rank
Alabama	Montgomery	52,423 (277,317)	30
Alaska	Juneau	656,424 (1,700,130)	1
Arizona	Phoenix	114,006 (295,274)	6
Arkansas	Little Rock	53,182 (137,740)	29
California	Sacramento	163,707 (423,999)	3
Colorado	Denver	104,100 (296,618)	8
Connecticut	Hartford	5,544 (14,359)	48
Delaware	Dover	2,489 (6,446)	49
Florida	Tallahassee	65,758 (170,312)	22
Georgia	Atlanta	59,441 (153,951)	24
Hawaii	Honolulu	10,931 (28,311)	43
Idaho	Boise	83,574 (216,456)	14
Illinois	Springfield	57,918 (150,007)	25
Indiana	Indianapolis	36,420 (94,327)	38
Iowa	Des Moines	56,276 (145,754)	26
Kansas	Topeka	82,282 (213,109)	15
Kentucky	Frankfort	40,411 (104,664)	37
Louisiana	Baton Rouge	51,844 (134,275)	31
Maine	Augusta	35,387 (91,652)	39
Maryland	Annapolis	12,407 (32,134)	42
Massachusetts	Boston	10,555 (27,337)	44
Michigan	Lansing	96,810 (250,737)	11
Minnesota	St. Paul	86,943 (225,181)	12
Mississippi	Jackson	48,434 (126,739)	32
Missouri	Jefferson City	69,709 (180,546)	21
Montana	Helena	147,046 (380,847)	4
Nebraska	Lincoln	77,358 (200,356)	16
Nevada	Carson City	110,567 (286,367)	7
New Hampshire	Concord	9,351 (24,219)	46
New Jersey	Trenton	8,722 (22,590)	47
New Mexico	Santa Fe	123,598 (320,117)	5
New York	Albany	54,475 (140,090)	27
North Carolina	Raleigh	53,821 (139,396)	28
North Dakota	Bismarck	70,704 (183,122)	19
Ohio	Columbus	44,828 (116,104)	34
Oklahoma	Oklahoma City	69,903 (181,048)	20
Oregon	Salem	98,386 (254,819)	9
Pennsylvania	Harrisburg	46,058 (119,290)	33
Rhode Island	Providence	1,545 (4,001)	50
South Carolina	Columbia	32,007 (82,898)	40
South Dakota	Pierre	77,122 (199,745)	17
Tennessee	Nashville	42,146 (109,158)	36
Texas	Austin	268,601 (695,673)	2
Utah	Salt Lake City	84,904 (219,900)	13
Vermont	Montpelier	9,615 (24,903)	45
Virginia	Richmond	42,769 (110,771)	35
Washington	Olympia	71,303 (184,674)	18
West Virginia	Charleston	24,231 (62,758)	41
Wisconsin	Madison	65,503 (169,652)	23
Wyoming	Cheyenne	97,818 (253,347)	10

State Flowers, Birds, and Trees

State	Flower	Bird	Tree
Alabama	Camellia	Yellowhammer	Southern Pine
Alaska	Forget-Me-Not	Willow Ptarmigan	Sitka Spruce
Arizona	Saguaro Blossom	Cactus Wren	Paloverde
Arkansas	Apple Blossom	Mockingbird	Pine
California	Golden Poppy	California Valley Quail	California Redwood
Colorado	Rocky Mtn. Columbine	Lark Bunting	Colorado Blue Spruce
Connecticut	Mountain Laurel	American Robin	White Oak
Delaware	Peach Blossom	Blue Hen Chicken	American Holly
Florida	Orange Blossom	Mockingbird	Sabal Palm
Georgia	Cherokee Rose	Brown Thrasher	Live Oak
Hawaii	Red Hibiscus	Nene (Hawaiian Goose)	Kukui (Candlenut)
Idaho	Syringa (Mock Orange)	Mountain Bluebird	White Pine
Illinois	Native Violet	Cardinal	White Oak
Indiana	Peony	Cardinal	Tulip Poplar
Iowa	Wild Rose	Eastern Goldfinch	Oak
Kansas	Sunflower	Western Meadowlark	Cottonwood
Kentucky	Goldenrod	Cardinal	Tulip Poplar
Louisiana	Magnolia Bloom	Brown Pelican	Bald Cypress
Maine	White Pine Cone & Tassel	Chickadee	Eastern White Pine
Maryland	Black-eyed Susan	Baltimore Oriole	White Oak
Massachusetts	Mayflower	Chickadee	American Elm
Michigan	Apple Blossom	Robin	White Pine
Minnesota	Pink & White Lady's Slipper	Common Loon	Red (Norway)Pine
Mississippi	Magnolia Bloom	Mockingbird	Magnolia
Missouri	Hawthorn Blossom	Eastern Bluebird	Dogwood
Montana	Bitterroot	Western Meadowlark	Ponderosa Pine
Nebraska	Goldenrod	Western Meadowlark	Cottonwood
Nevada	Sagebrush	Mountain Bluebird	Single-leaf Piñon Pine
New Hampshire	Purple Lilac	Purple Finch	White Birch
New Jersey	Purple Violet	Eastern Goldfinch	Red Oak
New Mexico	Yucca	Roadrunner	Piñon
New York	Rose	Bluebird	Sugar Maple
North Carolina	Dogwood Blossom	Cardinal	Pine
North Dakota	Wild Prairie Rose	Western Meadowlark	American Elm
Ohio	Scarlet Carnation	Cardinal	Buckeye
Oklahoma	Mistletoe	Scissor-tailed Flycatcher	Redbud
Oregon	Oregon Grape	Western Meadowlark	Douglas Fir
Pennsylvania	Mountain Laurel	Ruffed Grouse	Hemlock
Rhode Island	Violet	Rhode Island Red Hen	Red Maple
South Carolina	Carolina Yellow Jessamine	Carolina Wren	Palmetto

State Flowers, Birds, and Trees *(cont.)*

State	Flower	Bird	Tree
South Dakota	Pasqueflower	Chinese Ring-necked Pheasant	Black Hills Spruce
Tennessee	Iris	Mockingbird	Tulip Poplar
Texas	Bluebonnet	Mockingbird	Pecan
Utah	Sego Lily	Seagull	Blue Spruce
Vermont	Red Clover	Hermit Thrush	Sugar Maple
Virginia	Dogwood Blossom	Cardinal	Dogwood
Washington	Western Rhododendron	Willow Goldfinch	Western Hemlock
West Virginia	Big Rhododendron	Cardinal	Sugar Maple
Wisconsin	Wood Violet	Robin	Sugar Maple
Wyoming	Indian Paintbrush	Meadowlark	Cottonwood

State Mottoes and Nicknames

State	Motto	Nickname
Alabama	We Dare Defend Our Rights	Yellowhammer State; Heart of Dixie
Alaska	North to the Future	The Last Frontier
Arizona	*Diat Deus* (God Enriches)	Grand Canyon State
Arkansas	*Regnat Populus* (The People Rule)	Land of Opportunity
California	Eureka (I Have Found It)	Golden State
Colorado	*Nil Sine Numine* (Nothing Without Providence)	Centennial State
Connecticut	*Qui Transtulit Sustinet* (He Who Transplanted Still Sustains)	Constitution State
Delaware	Liberty and Independence	First State; Diamond State
Florida	In God We Trust	Sunshine State
Georgia	Wisdom, Justice, and Moderation	Peach State
Hawaii	The Life of the Land Is Perpetuated in Righteousness	Aloha State
Idaho	*Esto Perpetua* (May It Endure Forever)	Gem State
Illinois	State Sovereignty—National Union	Land of Lincoln; Prairie State
Indiana	Crossroads of America	Hoosier State
Iowa	Our Liberties We Prize and Our Rights We Will Maintain	Hawkeye State
Kansas	*Ad Astra Per Aspera* (To the Stars with Difficulty)	Sunflower State
Kentucky	United We Stand, Divided We Fall	Bluegrass State
Louisiana	Union, Justice, and Confidence	Pelican State
Maine	*Dirigo* (I Direct)	Pine Tree State
Maryland	*Fatti Maschii, Parole Femine* (Manly Deeds, Womanly Words)	Old Line State; Free State

Massachusetts	*Ense Petit Placidam sub Libertate Quietem* (By the Sword We Seek Peace, But Peace Only Under Liberty)	Bay State
Michigan	*Si Quaeris Peninsulam Amoenam Circimspice* (If You Seek a Pleasant Peninsula, Look About You)	Great Lake State; Wolverine State
Minnesota	*L'etoile du Nord* (The Star of the North)	North Star State; Gopher State
Mississippi	*Virtute et Armis* (By Valor and Arms)	Magnolia State
Missouri	*Salus Populi Suprema Lex Esto* (The Welfare of the People Shall Be the Supreme Law)	Show-Me State
Montana	*Oro y Plata* (Gold and Silver)	Big Sky Country; Treasure State
Nebraska	Equality Before the Law	Cornhusker State
Nevada	All for Our Country	Silver State; Sagebrush State
New Hampshire	Live Free or Die	Granite State
New Jersey	Liberty and Prosperity	Garden State
New Mexico	*Crescit Eundo* (It Grows As It Goes)	Land of Enchantment
New York	*Excelsior* (Ever Upward)	Empire State
North Carolina	*Esse Quam Videri* (To Be Rather Than to Seem)	Tarheel State; Old North State
North Dakota	Liberty and Union, Now and Forever, One and Inseparable	Peace Garden State; Flickertail State
Ohio	With God, All Things Are Possible	Buckeye State
Oklahoma	*Labor Omnia Vincit* (Labor Conquers All Things)	Sooner State
Oregon	She Flies with Her Own Wings	Beaver State
Pennsylvania	Virtue, Liberty, and Independence	Keystone State
Rhode Island	Hope	Little Rhody; Ocean State
South Carolina	*Sum Spiro Spero* (While I Breathe, I Hope)	Palmetto State
South Dakota	Under God, the People Rule	Mount Rushmore State; Coyote State; Sunshine State
Tennessee	Agriculture and Commerce	Volunteer State
Texas	Friendship	Lone Star State
Utah	Industry	Beehive State
Vermont	Freedom and Unity	Green Mountain State
Virginia	*Sic Semper Tyrannis* (Thus Always to Tyrants)	Old Dominion
Washington	*Alki* (Bye and Bye)	Evergreen State
West Virginia	*Montani Semper Liberi* (Mountaineers Are Always Free)	Mountain State
Wisconsin	Forward	Badger State
Wyoming	Equal Rights	Equality State

State Resources, Industries, Features, and Attractions

State	Resources	Industries/Products	Noted Physical Features	Attractions
Alabama	coal; marble; salt; iron ore; natural gas; petroleum; timber	poultry and cattle; peanuts and pecans; fishing; cotton; paper and plastic products; lumber; chemicals; textiles; metals; food; clothing	Black Belt; Cumberland Plateau; Appalachian foothills; underground caves; swamplands; beaches	Huntsville Space and Rocket Center; Motorsports Hall of Fame and Museum; home of Jefferson Davis; Mobile Bay's exhibition of World War II ships and aircraft; 17th-century plantations
Alaska	oil; natural gas; fish; timber; coal; gold; silver; copper; zinc; uranium; platinum	oil; natural gas; fish and seafood processing; lumber; tourism	Mt. McKinley; Arctic Slope; glaciers	Mount McKinley; Iditarod race; glaciers; Inside Passage; Glacier Bay National Park and Preserve; Denali National Park
Arizona	copper; gold; silver	cattle; grain; tourism	mountains; Grand Canyon; Painted Desert; Sonoran Desert; Canyon Diablo	The Grand Canyon of the Colorado; Painted Desert; Petrified Forest National Park; Meteor Crater; Sedona; Hoover Dam; rodeos
Arkansas	bauxite; coal; oil; natural gas; iron ore; zinc; lead; sandstone; timber	cotton; rice; soybeans; wheat; steel; aluminum; chemicals; plastics; paper, food, and wood products; tourism	mountains; wilderness; Mississippi Delta; Ozark Plateaus	Hot Springs National Park; Ozark Mountains; Crater of Diamonds; Eureka Springs
California	timber; gold; petroleum; borax	fruits; vegetables; flowers; film; wine; computers; telecommunications; mining; tourism	mountains; Mt. Whitney; Mojave Desert; seashore; Death Valley;	Hollywood; Disneyland; Sea World; Alcatraz; San Diego Zoo; Yosemite, Sequoia, King's Canyon, Redwood, and Joshua

Colorado	gold; molybdenum; vanadium; tungsten; uranium; coal; oil; natural gas; marble; granite; sand; gravel	vegetables; cattle; pigs; chemicals; high technology equipment; heavy machinery; skiing; tourism	Yosemite National Park; redwood forests	Tree national parks; Death Valley; Golden Gate Bridge; Spanish missions; Napa Valley
			Rocky Mountains; high plains	Rocky Mountain and Mesa Verde national parks; Grand Mesa National Forest; winter sports
Connecticut	sand, gravel, stone; clay	insurance; banking; aircraft engine and helicopter manufacturing; chemicals; submarine construction; dairy and tobacco farming; gambling; tourism	seashore; Berkshire foothills	Mystic Seaport; Mystic Aquarium; Peabody Museum; American Shakespeare Festival Theater; Goodspeed Opera House; Eugene O'Neill Memorial Theater; Long Island Sound beaches; Foxwoods Resort and Casino; Mark Twain House
Delaware	sand; gravel; magnesium	soybeans; corn; poultry; dairy farming; fishing; chemicals; food, rubber, plastic, and paper products; tourism	seashore; piedmont plateau; Delmarva Peninsula	Winterthur Museum and Garden; Rehoboth Beach; fishing
Florida	phosphate; oil; natural gas; limestone; clay; sand; gravel; titanium	citrus fruits; cattle; lumber; telecommunications; aerospace; tourism	seashore; peninsula; Florida Keys; Everglades; Lake Okeechobee	Everglades National Park; Florida Keys; Kennedy Space Center; Walt Disney World; Sea World; St. Augustine; water sports; Miami Beach

State	Resources	Industries/Products	Noted Physical Features	Attractions
Georgia	clay; stone; kaolin; bauxite; coal; iron ore; barite	tobacco; peanuts; cattle; cotton; fruits; food products; textiles	Okefenokee Swamp; Blue Ridge Mountains	Andersonville Confederate Cemetery; Okefenokee Swamp; beaches; Sea Island; Savannah's historic riverfront district
Hawaii	limestone	sugarcane; fruits; flowers; coffee; tourism	seashore; volcanoes (Mauna Loa, Kilauea); islands	water sports; Pearl Harbor; volcanoes; Waikiki Beach; Diamond Head
Idaho	silver; lead; zinc; gold; tungsten; copper; timber	mining; logging; cattle; sheep; potatoes and other vegetables; technology	mountains; Hells Canyon	Hells Canyon; Craters of the Moon; Sun Valley; winter sports; Shoshone Falls
Illinois	coal; oil; lead; zinc	corn; soybeans; livestock; food products; iron; steel; clay; mining; publishing	prairies; plains	Chicago sites (Museum of Science and Industry; Sears tower); Lincoln Heritage Trail
Indiana	coal; oil; gypsum; sandstone; sand; gravel	soybeans; corn; oil refining; steel; plastics; furniture; automobile parts;	plains; dunes along Lake Michigan shores	Wyandotte Cave; Indianapolis 500; Lincoln Log Cabin Historical Site
Iowa	cement; stone; clay; coal; gypsum; limestone; sand; gravel	cattle; pigs; corn; oats; banking; insurance; farm equipment; food products; mining	Mississippi River; Missouri River watershed	Herbert Hoover Presidential Library; Effigy Mounds National Monument; Amana Colony

Kansas	oil; natural gas; coal; lead; zinc	cattle; pigs; wheat; hay; food products; aircraft	Prairies; Osage plains	Dwight D. Eisenhower Presidential Library; Fort Leavenworth; Dodge City; U.S. Cavalry Museum
Kentucky	coal; timber; natural gas; oil; crushed stone	farming; heavy machinery; transportation equipment; textiles; whiskey; horse breeding; tourism	Appalachian Mountains; Bluegrass; Western Coal Field	Kentucky Derby; Fort Knox; Mammoth Cave National Park; Cumberland Gap
Louisiana	oil; natural gas; fish; timber	oil refining; wood products; sugarcane; vegetables; cotton; food products; tourism	Mississippi Delta; Lake Pontchartrain; Gulf Coast	Mardi Gras; French Quarter of New Orleans; jazz; Louisiana Hayride
Maine	fish; timber; sand; gravel; zinc; clay; lead	blueberries; shellfish; potatoes; fishing; lumber; dairy farming; tourism	seashore; Mount Katahdin; wilderness	Acadia National Park; Bar Harbor; Freeport/L.L. Bean; cool summers; hunting; fishing
Maryland	coal; fish; timber	technical and scientific research; fishing (crab, oyster, clam); dairy; poultry, and vegetable farming; food products; tourism	Chesapeake Bay; Chincoteague Island; Assateague Island; Appalachian foothills	U.S. Naval Academy; Ocean City; Baltimore's Inner Harbor; the Preakness at Pimlico Track; Fort McHenry

State	Resources	Industries/Products	Noted Physical Features	Attractions
Massachusetts	stone; gravel; clay	technology; textiles; shoes; telecommunications; cranberries; tourism	seashore; Cape Cod; Martha's Vineyard; Nantucket Island; Berkshire Mountains	Freedom Trail; Quincy Market; Faneuil Hall; Tanglewood; John F. Kennedy Library; Cape Cod National Seashore; Provincetown; Lexington and Concord; water sports; Plymouth Rock and Plantation
Michigan	iron; copper; timber; fish	automobiles; furniture; food products; dairy farming; flowers; tourism	Great Lakes; Upper Peninsula; Lower Peninsula; Straits of Mackinac	Great Lakes; Erie Canal; Mackinac Island; Soo Canals; Dezwann Windmill and Tulip Festival; Greenfield Village; Henry Ford Museum; Kellogg's Cereal City U.S.A.
Minnesota	iron; taconite; timber	dairy farming; wheat; soybeans; corn; oats; logging; mining; technology; computers; health care and equipment; food products; paper; tourism	Great Lakes Storm Belt; Lake Superior	water sports; camping; Mayo Clinic; St. Paul Winter Carnival
Mississippi	oil; natural gas; sand; gravel; clay; salt; fish	cotton; textiles; clothing; chemicals; shipbuilding; lumber; shrimp; tourism	Black Prairie Belt; Mississippi delta; Pontotoc Ridge	John C. Stennis Space Center; Natchez Trace Parkway; Vicksburg and other Civil War sites; Gulf Islands National Seashore; antebellum homes

Missouri	lead; iron; crushed stone; fire clay; limestone; portland cement; zinc	soybeans; wheat; oats; corn; cattle; mining; aircraft and electronic equipment; paper products; food and dairy products; beer; greeting cards; automobile parts; chemicals	plains; prairies; Mississippi River; Missouri River	Branson country music theaters; Lake of the Ozark; Mark Twain Area historic sites; Harry S. Truman Library and Museum; St. Louis's Gateway Arch
Montana	coal; gold; copper; silver; oil; timber	wheat; barley; sugar beets; lumber; paper products	Rocky Mountains; Great Plains; glaciers	Rocky Mountains; Glacier and Yellowstone national parks; Badlands; hunting and fishing; Little Bighorn Battlefield National Monument and Custer National Cemetery
Nebraska	oil; natural gas; sand; gravel; limestone	corn; wheat; cattle; food products; tourism	Great Plains	Chimney Rock; Scotts Bluff National Monument
Nevada	gold; silver; copper; stone; clay; oil; gypsum; limestone; barite	gambling; food products; electronic equipment; mining; cattle; sheep; glass products; entertainment; tourism	mountains; Mojave Desert	gambling casinos (Las Vegas, Reno); Hoover Dam; Virginia City; Lake Tahoe; Great Basin National Park
New Hampshire	timber; granite	lumber; wood and paper products; livestock; dairy and fruit farming; electrical equipment; heavy machinery; precision instruments; tourism	White Mountains	autumn foliage; White Mountains attractions (The Flume; Mt. Washington; Franconia Notch); winter sports; Portsmouth; Lake Winnipesaukee

State Resources, Industries, Features, and Attractions (cont.)

State	Resources	Industries/Products	Noted Physical Features	Attractions
New Jersey	zinc; limonite; magnetite; sand; gravel	vegetables; fruit; cattle; chemicals; pharmaceuticals; printing; publishing; shipping; gambling casinos tourism	seashore; Palisades; Piedmont Plateau; Appalachian Highlands coastal plain	Beaches (127 total mi.); Cape May historic district; Delaware Water Gap; Atlantic City; Pine Barrens Wilderness Area
New Mexico	oil; natural gas; coal; uranium; copper; molybdenum; timber	cattle and sheep; grain; mining; defense installations; tourism	Rocky Mountains; Great Plains	Carlsbad Caverns National Park; White Sands National Monument; Chaco Culture National Historic Park; Palace of the Governors; Indian reservations; Acoma Pueblo
New York	timber; wollastonite; zinc; lead; aluminum; talc; salt	dairy and poultry farming; financial, information, and media services; textiles and apparel; photographic and ophthalmic supplies; glass; electrical equipment; transportation equipment; tourism	Adirondack Mountains; Appalachian Mountains; Finger Lakes; Lake Champlain; Great Lakes; Catskill Mountains	New York City sites (United Nations; Statue of Liberty); National Baseball Hall of Fame and Museum; Adirondack Mountains; Fort Ticonderoga; West Point; Seneca Falls; winter and summer sports; Franklin D. Roosevelt National Historic Site; Niagara Falls; Corning Glass Center; Lake Placid; Saranac Lake

North Carolina	corn; tobacco and tobacco products; soybeans; furniture; textiles; paper; electronics; telecommunications; tourism	timber; fish; rock	Great Smoky Mountains; Blue Ridge Mountains; Mount Mitchell; Cape Hatteras; seashore	Wright Brothers National Memorial; Blue Ridge and Great Smoky Mountains; Blue Ridge Parkway; Biltmore House and Gardens; Roanoke Island; Cape Hatteras and Cape Lookout National Seashores; Outer Banks
North Dakota	wheat; barley; oats; rye; cattle farming; mining; tourism	coal; oil; lignite; limestone; clay	Badlands; Black Hills; Great Plains; Red River Valley; Rolling Drift Prairie	Badlands; International Peace Garden; hunting; fishing; Fort Abraham Lincoln State Park and Museum; Bonanzaville
Ohio	automotive products; iron and steel; glass; tires; chemicals; mining	coal; oil; natural gas; stone; clay; salt	Lake Erie; Allegheny Plateau	Professional Football Hall of Fame; birthplaces of presidents William Henry Harrison, Ulysses S. Grant, James A. Garfield, Rutherford B. Hayes, William McKinley, Warren G. Harding; Mound City Group National Monuments
Oklahoma	cattle; sheep; hogs; cotton; wheat; peanuts; mining; milling; aircraft; machinery; metal products	oil; natural gas; coal; gypsum; pumice; bentonite; helium; stone; sand; gravel; feldspar	mountains; plains; Black Mesa; Arkansas River basin	Cowboy Hall of Fame; Ouachita National Forest; Will Rogers Memorial; Fort Sill; Cherokee Heritage Center
Oregon	fruits and vegetables; cattle; sheep; lumber; tourism	timber; mercury; nickel; uranium; stone; sand; gravel; clay; limestone; talc; fish	Coastal range of rugged mountains; Willamette River Valley	Crater Lake National Park; Hells Canyon; Bonneville Hatchery; John Day Fossil Beds National Monument

State Resources, Industries, Features, and Attractions (cont.)

State	Resources	Industries/Products	Noted Physical Features	Attractions
Pennsylvania	coal; oil; natural gas; copper; lead; zinc; nickel; cement; limestone; timber	mining; iron; steel; stone products; cattle; food products; chemicals; wood products; tourism	Lake Erie; Cumberland Valley; Pocono Mountains; Delaware Water Gap; Allegheny Mountains	Philadelphia sites (Independence Hall; Liberty Bell); Valley Forge National Historic Park; Brandywine; Pennsylvania Dutch country; Gettysburg National Military Park
Rhode Island	sand; gravel; fish	textiles; electronics; fishing; lobsters; tourism	Block Island; Narragansett Basin	Newport mansions; Block Island; Slater Mill Historic Site
South Carolina	kaolin; vermiculite; barite; sand; gravel; clay; timber	tobacco; soybeans; fruit; textiles; furniture; chemicals; paper and wood products; tourism	Blue Ridge Mountains; Whitewater Falls; coastal plain	Historic Charleston; Cypress Gardens; Myrtle Beach and other coast beaches; Hilton Head Island; Fort Sumter National Monument
South Dakota	gold; silver; lignite; oil; manganese; sand; gravel; granite	livestock; flaxseed; rye; oats; sunflower seeds; hay; wheat; sorghum; meat packing and other food products; machinery and equipment	Black Hills; Great Plains; Prairie Plains	Mount Rushmore; Badlands; Jewel Cave National Monument; Wind Cave National Park; Spirit Mound; Black Hills Passion Play
Tennessee	coal; oil; natural gas; zinc; aluminum; phosphate; marble; hydroelectric power	tobacco; cotton; music; chemicals; food products; textiles; paper products; tourism	Blue Ridge Mountains; Great Smoky Mountains; Cumberland Plateau; Mississippi Alluvial Plain	Grand Old Opry; Graceland; Great Smoky Mountains National Park; Cumberland Gap National Park; Natchez Trace Parkway; The Hermitage (Andrew Jackson's home)

	Minerals	Industries	Physical Features	Places of Interest
Texas	oil; natural gas; sulfur; helium; salt; iron; gypsum; uranium	cotton; cattle; oil refining; transportation equipment; food processing; textiles; clothing; lumber; tourism	Great Plains; Guadalupe Mountains; Big Bend, Rio Grande; coastal plains; Rocky Mountains; Great Plains Gulf of Mexico	Houston Space Center; The Alamo; Big Bend; Guadalupe Mountains National Parks; Padre Island National Seashore; San Antonio Missions National Historic Park rodeos
Utah	copper; beryllium; gold; silver; lead; uranium	cattle; steel; food products; electrical equipment; tourism	Bryce Canyon; Great Salt Lake; Great Basin; Bonneville Salt Flats; Rocky Mountains	Temple Square, Mormon Church headquarters; Bryce Canyon, Zion, Capitol Reef, Canyonlands, and Arches national parks; Flaming Gorge National Recreation Area; Dinosaur National Monument
Vermont	granite; marble; asbestos; timber	quarrying; dairy farming; lumber; machinery and tools; stone and marble products; food processing; tourism	Green Mountains	foliage; winter and summer sports; Rock of Ages Quarry
Virginia	coal; timber; kyanite; pyrites; titanium; limestone	tobacco products; government services; shipbuilding; chemicals; food products; lumber; stone products; shellfish; tourism	Blue Ridge Mountains; Piedmont Plateau; coastal plains	Colonial Williamsburg; Monticello; Mount Vernon (estate of George Washington); Civil War battlefields, including Yorktown; Jamestown; plantations; Blue Ridge Mountains (Blue Ridge Parkway); estate of Robert E. Lee; Virginia Beach

State	Resources	Industries/Products	Noted Physical Features	Attractions
Washington	timber; fish; zinc; lead; magnesium; gold; coal; sand; gravel; hydroelectric power	wheat; livestock; vegetables; flowers; fruit; fish; lumber; paper products; aircraft; fish products; transportation equipment; computer software; biotechnology; technological research; shipbuilding; tourism	Mt. Rainier; Mt. St. Helens; Cascade Mountains; Olympic Mountains; Puget Sound lowlands; Columbia basin	Seattle Center; Space Needle; Mt. Rainier, Olympic and North Cascades National Parks; Bonneville and Grand Coulee dams; rodeos
West Virginia	coal; timber; oil; natural gas; salt; barite	dairy and fruit farming; lumber; iron; steel; chemicals; glass, clay, and stone products	Allegheny Mountains	Allegheny Mountains; Seneca Rocks; Harpers Ferry National Historic Park; Mammoth Mound; White Sulphur and Berkeley Springs Mineral Water Spas
Wisconsin	iron ore; lead; zinc; copper; timber; fish	dairy products; livestock; machinery; paper; food products; automobiles; lumber; leather good; breweries; tourism	Lake Winnebago; Lake Michigan; Lake Superior	Water activities; The Wisconsin Dells; Great Lakes; Little Norway; Frank Lloyd Wright's house, Taliesin
Wyoming	oil; natural gas; coal; bentonite; trona; uranium; agate; jade	mining; petroleum, coal, and uranium processing; cattle and sheep farming; food products; hay; wheat; lumber products; wool; tourism	Rocky Mountains foothills; Great Plains; desert; Continental Divide; Black Hills; Devil's Tower; Big Horn and Great Divide Basins; desert	Devil's Tower National Monument; Yellowstone and Grand Teton National Parks; Jackson Hole Wildlife Preserve; Periodic Spring; Cheyenne Frontier Days; Buffalo Bill Historical Center; dude ranches

U.S. Territories and Possessions

American Samoa

Geography

Location: Oceania, group of islands in the South Pacific Ocean, about one-half of the way from Hawaii to New Zealand

Area: 77 mi. (199 sq. km.); slightly larger than Washington, D.C.

Climate: tropical marine, moderated by southeast trade winds; annual rainfall averages 124 inches; rainy season from November to April, dry season from May to October; little seasonal temperature variation

Terrain: five volcanic islands with rugged peaks and limited coastal plains, two coral atolls (Rose Island, Swains Island)

Elevation: lowest point: Pacific Ocean 0 ft. (0 m.); highest point: Lata 373 ft. (966 m.)

Natural resources: pumice, pumicite

People

Population: 65,446 (July 2000 est.)

Population growth rate: 2.53%

Infant mortality rate: 10.63 deaths/1,000 live births

Life expectancy at birth: total population: 75.12 years; male: 70.66 years; female: 79.84 years

Major ethnic groups: Samoan (Polynesian) 89%, Caucasian 2%, Tongan 4%, other 5%

Major religions: Christian Congregationalist 50%, Roman Catholic 20%, Protestant denominations and other 30%

Major languages: Samoan (closely related to Hawaiian and other Polynesian languages), English; Note—most people are bilingual

Government

Official name: Territory of American Samoa

Government type: unincorporated and unorganized territory of the U.S.; administered by the U.S. Department of Interior, Office of Territorial and International Affairs

National capital: Pago Pago

Economy

Industries: tuna canneries (largely dependent on foreign fishing vessels), meat canning, handicrafts

Agricultural products: bananas, coconuts, vegetables, taro, breadfruit, yams, copra, pineapples, papayas; dairy farming

Currency: 1 U.S. dollar (US$) = 100 cents

Guam

Geography

Location: Oceania, island in the North Pacific Ocean, about three-quarters of the way from Hawaii to the Philippines

Area: 209 sq. mi. (541.3 sq. km.); three times the size of Washington, D.C.

Climate: tropical marine; generally warm and humid, moderated by northeast trade winds; dry season from January to June, rainy season from July to December; little seasonal temperature variation

Terrain: volcanic origin, surrounded by coral reefs; relatively flat coralline limestone plateau (source of most fresh water) with steep coastal cliffs and narrow coastal plains in north, low-rising hills in center, mountains in south

Elevation: lowest point: Pacific Ocean 0 ft. (0 m.); highest point: Mount Lamlam 1,332 ft. (406 m.)

Natural resources: fishing (largely undeveloped), tourism

People

Population: 154,623 (July 2000 est.)

Population growth rate: 1.67%

Infant mortality rate: 6.83 deaths/1,000 live births

Life expectancy at birth: total population: 77.78 years; male: 75.51 years; female: 80.37 years

Major ethnic groups: Chamorro 47%, Filipino 25%, white 10%, Chinese, Japanese, Korean, and other 18%

Major religions: Roman Catholic 85%, other 15%

Major languages: English, Chamorro, Japanese

U.S. Territories and Possessions *(cont.)*

Government
Official name: Territory of Guam
Dependency status: organized, unincorporated territory of the U.S. with policy relations between Guam and the U.S. under the jurisdiction of the Office of Insular Affairs, U.S. Department of the Interior
National capital: Hagatna (Agana)
Legal system: modeled on U.S.; U.S. federal laws apply

Economy
Industries: U.S. military, tourism, construction, transshipment services, concrete products, printing and publishing, food processing, textiles
Agricultural products: fruits, copra, vegetables; eggs, pork, poultry, beef
Currency: 1 U.S. dollar (US$) = 100 cents

Northern Mariana Islands

Geography
Location: Oceania, islands in the North Pacific Ocean, about three-quarters of the way from Hawaii to the Philippines
Area: 184 sq. mi. (477 sq. km.); 2.5 times the size of Washington, D.C.
Climate: tropical marine; moderated by northeast trade winds; little seasonal temperature variation; dry season December to June, rainy season July to October
Terrain: southern islands are limestone with level terraces and fringing coral reefs; northern islands are volcanic
Elevation: lowest point: Pacific Ocean 0 ft. (0 m.); highest point: unnamed location on Agrihan 3,166 ft. (965 m.)
Natural resources: arable land, fish

People
Population: 71,912 (July 2000 est.)
Population growth rate: 3.75%
Infant mortality rate: 5.79 deaths/1,000 live births
Life expectancy at birth: total population: 75.54 years; male: 72.45 years; female: 78.82 years

Major ethnic groups: Chamorro, Carolinians and other Micronesians, Caucasian, Japanese, Chinese, Korean
Major religions: Christian (Roman Catholic majority, although traditional beliefs and taboos may still be found)
Major languages: English, Chamorro, Carolinian; note: 86% of population speaks a language other than English at home

Government
Official name: Commonwealth of the Northern Mariana Islands
Dependency status: commonwealth in political union with the U.S.
Government type: commonwealth; self-governing with locally elected governor, lieutenant governor, and legislature
National capital: Saipan
Legal system: based on U.S. system except for customs, wages, immigration laws, and taxation

Economy
Industries: tourism, construction, garments, handicrafts
Agricultural products: coconuts, fruits, vegetables; cattle
Currency: 1 U.S. dollar (US$) = 100 cents

Puerto Rico

Geography
Location: Caribbean, island between the Caribbean Sea and the North Atlantic Ocean, east of the Dominican Republic
Area: 3,515 sq. mi. (9,104 sq. km.); slightly less than three times the size of Rhode Island
Climate: tropical marine, mild; little seasonal temperature variation
Terrain: mostly mountains with coastal plain belt in north; mountains precipitous to sea on west coast; sandy beaches along most coastal areas
Elevation: lowest point: Caribbean Sea 0 ft. (0 m.); highest point: Cerro de Punta 4,390 ft. (1,338 m.)

Natural resources: some copper and nickel; potential for onshore and offshore oil

People

Population: 3,915,798 (July 2000 est.)
Population growth rate: 0.56%
Infant mortality rate: 9.71 deaths/1,000 live births
Life expectancy at birth: total population: 75.55 years; male: 71.05 years; female: 80.30 years
Major ethnic groups: Hispanic
Major religions: Roman Catholic 85%, Protestant denominations and other 15%
Major languages: Spanish, English

Government

Official name: Commonwealth of Puerto Rico
Dependency status: commonwealth associated with the U.S.
Government type: commonwealth
National capital: San Juan
Legal system: based on Spanish civil code

Economy

Industries: pharmaceuticals, electronics, apparel, food products; tourism
Agricultural products: livestock products, chickens; sugarcane, coffee, pineapples, plantains, bananas
Currency: 1 U.S. dollar (US$) = 100 cents

Virgin Islands

Geography

Location: Caribbean, islands between the Caribbean Sea and the North Atlantic Ocean, east of Puerto Rico
Area: 136 sq. mi. (352 sq. km.); twice the size of Washington, D.C.

Climate: subtropical, tempered by easterly trade winds, relatively low humidity, little seasonal temperature variation; rainy season May to November
Terrain: mostly hilly to rugged and mountainous with little level land
Elevation: lowest point: Caribbean Sea 0 ft. (0 m.); highest point: Crown Mountain 1,555 ft. (474 m.)
Natural resources: sun, sand, sea, surf

People

Population: 120,917 (July 2000 est.)
Population growth rate: 1.07%
Infant mortality rate: 9.64 deaths/1,000 live births
Life expectancy at birth: total population: 78.11 years; male: 74.2 years; female: 82.25 years
Major ethnic groups: black 80%, white 15%
Major religions: Baptist 42%, Roman Catholic 34%, Episcopalian 17%
Major languages: English (official), Spanish, Creole

Government

Official name: Virgin Islands of the United States
Dependency status: organized, unincorporated territory of the U.S.;
National capital: Charlotte Amalie
Legal system: based on U.S. laws

Economy

Industries: tourism, petroleum refining, watch assembly, rum distilling, construction, pharmaceuticals, textiles, electronics
Agricultural products: truck garden products, fruit, vegetables, sorghum; Senepol cattle
Currency: 1 U.S. dollar (US$) = 100 cents

The following U.S. territories are uninhabited:
Baker Island, Howland Island, Jarvis Island, Johnston Atoll, Kingman Reef, Midway Islands, Navassa Island, Palmyra Atoll, Wake Island

⊙ Central Intelligence Agency. "*The World Factbook 2000* Country Listing," www.odci.gov/publications/factbook/indexgeo.html

100 Largest Cities

Rank	City	Population (July 1, 1998, est.)	Change in Population (1990–98)	Percent Change (1990–98)
1	New York City, NY	7,420,166	+97,602	+1.3
2	Los Angeles, CA	3,597,556	+111,999	+3.2
3	Chicago, IL	2,802,079	+18,353	+.7
4	Houston, TX	1,786,691	+132,343	+8.0
5	Philadelphia, PA	1,436,287	−149,290	−9.4
6	San Diego, CA	1,220,666	+110,043	+9.9
7	Phoenix, AZ	1,198,064	+210,049	+21.3
8	San Antonio, TX	1,114,130	+137,616	+14.1
9	Dallas, TX	1,075,894	+68,276	+6.8
10	Detroit, MI	970,196	−57,778	−5.6
11	San Jose, CA	861,284	+79,060	+10.1
12	San Francisco, CA	745,774	+21,815	+3.0
13	Indianapolis, IN	741,304	+10,026	+1.4
14	Jacksonville, FL	693,630	+58,400	+9.2
15	Columbus, OH	670,234	+37,289	+5.9
16	Baltimore, MD	645,593	−90,421	−12.3
17	El Paso, TX	615,032	+99,690	+19.3
18	Memphis, TN	603,507	−15,145	−2.4
19	Milwaukee, WI	578,364	−49,724	−7.9
20	Boston, MA	555,447	−18,836	−3.3
21	Austin, TX	552,434	+80,414	+17.0
22	Seattle, WA	536,978	+20,719	+4.0
23	Washington, DC	523,124	−83,776	−13.8
24	Nashville-Davidson, TN	510,274	+21,908	+4.5
25	Charlotte, NC	504,637	+85,079	+20.3
26	Portland, OR	503,891	+17,916	+3.7
27	Denver, CO	499,055	+31,445	+6.7
28	Cleveland, OH	495,817	−9,799	−1.9
29	Fort Worth, TX	491,801	+44,182	+9.9
30	Oklahoma City, OK	472,221	+27,497	+6.2
31	New Orleans, LA	465,538	−31,400	−6.3
32	Tucson, AZ	460,466	+45,022	+10.8
33	Kansas City, MO	441,574	+6,745	+1.6
34	Virginia Beach, VA	432,380	+39,291	+10.0
35	Long Beach, CA	430,905	+1,584	+.4
36	Albuquerque, NM	419,311	+34,396	+8.9
37	Las Vegas, NV	404,288	+145,411	+56.2
38	Sacramento, CA	404,168	+34,803	+9.4
39	Atlanta, GA	403,819	+9,890	+2.5
40	Fresno, CA	398,133	+44,042	+12.4
41	Honolulu, HI	395,789	+18,730	+5.0
42	Tulsa, OK	381,393	+14,091	+3.8
43	Omaha, NE	371,291	+26,828	+7.8
44	Miami, FL	368,624	+9,976	+2.8
45	Oakland, CA	365,874	−6,368	−1.7
46	Mesa, AZ	360,076	+70,877	+24.5
47	Minneapolis, MN	351,731	−16,652	−4.5
48	Colorado Springs, CO	344,987	+64,557	+23.0
49	Pittsburgh, PA	340,520	−29,359	−7.9

50	St. Louis, MO	339,316	–57,369	–14.5
51	Cincinnati, OH	336,400	–27,714	–7.6
52	Wichita, KS	329,211	+25,194	+8.3
53	Toledo, OH	312,174	–20,769	–6.2
54	Arlington, TX	306,497	+44,780	+17.1
55	Santa Ana, CA	305,955	+12,128	+4.1
56	Buffalo, NY	300,717	–27,458	–8.4
57	Anaheim, CA	295,153	28,747	+10.8
58	Tampa, FL	289,156	+9,141	+3.3
59	Corpus Christi, TX	281,453	+24,025	+9.3
60	Newark, NJ	267,823	–7,398	–2.7
61	Riverside, CA	262,140	+35,594	+15.7
62	Raleigh, NC	259,423	+40,564	+18.5
63	St. Paul, MN	257,284	–14,951	–5.5
64	Louisville, KY	255,045	–14,510	–5.4
65	Anchorage, AK	254,982	+28,644	+12.7
66	Birmingham, AL	252,997	–12,350	–4.7
67	Aurora, CO	250,604	+28,501	+12.8
68	Lexington-Fayette, KY	241,749	+16,383	+7.3
69	Stockton, CA	240,143	+29,200	+13.8
70	St. Petersburg, FL	236,029	–4,289	–1.8
71	Jersey City, NJ	232,429	+3,912	+1.7
72	Plano, TX	219,486	+91,601	+71.6
73	Rochester, NY	216,887	–13,469	–5.8
74	Akron, OH	215,712	–7,307	–3.3
75	Norfolk, VA	215,215	–46,035	–17.6
76	Lincoln, NE	213,088	+21,116	+11.0
77	Baton Rouge, LA	211,551	–7,980	–3.6
78	Hialeah, FL	211,392	+23,384	+12.4
79	Bakersfield, CA	210,284	+34,020	+19.3
80	Madison, WI	209,306	+18,540	–9.7
81	Fremont, CA	204,298	+30,959	+17.9
82	Mobile, AL	202,181	+2,208	+1.1
83	Chesapeake, VA	199,564	+47,582	+31.3
84	Greensboro, NC	197,910	+12,785	+6.9
85	Montgomery, AL	197,014	+6,664	+3.5
86	Scottsdale, AZ	195,394	+65,295	+50.2
87	Huntington Beach, CA	195,316	+13,797	+7.6
88	Richmond, VA	194,173	–8,625	–4.3
89	Glendale, AZ	193,482	+46,412	+31.6
90	Garland, TX	193,408	+12,773	+7.1
91	Des Moines, IA	191,293	–1,896	–1.0
92	Lubbock, TX	190,974	+4,768	+2.6
93	Yonkers, NY	190,153	+2,071	+1.1
94	Jackson, MS	188,419	–13,643	–6.8
95	Shreveport, LA	188,319	–10,199	–5.1
96	Augusta, GA	187,689	+1,073	+.6
97	San Bernardino, CA	186,402	+16,366	+9.6
98	Fort Wayne, IN	185,716	–9,964	–5.1
99	Grand Rapids, MI	185,437	–3,689	–2.0
100	Glendale, CA	185,086	+5,048	+2.8

⊙ U.S. Bureau of the Census. "Population Estimates for Cities With Populations of
100,000 and Greater," www.census.gov/population/estimates/metro-city/
SC100K98-T1-DR.txt

100 Largest Metropolitan Areas

Rank	Metro Area	Population (July 1, 1998, est.)
1	New York-Northern New Jersey-Long Island, NY-NJ-CT-PA	20,126,150
2	Los Angeles-Riverside-Orange County, CA	15,781,273
3	Chicago-Gary-Kenosha, IL-IN-WI	8,809,846
4	Washington-Baltimore, DC-MD-VA-WV	7,285,206
5	San Francisco-Oakland-San Jose, CA	6,816,047
6	Philadelphia-Wilmington-Atlantic City, PA-NJ-DE-MD	5,988,348
7	Boston-Worcester-Lawrence, MA-NH-ME-CT	5,633,060
8	Detroit-Ann Arbor-Flint, MI	5,457,583
9	Dallas-Fort Worth, TX	4,802,463
10	Houston-Galveston-Brazoria, TX	4,407,579
11	Atlanta, GA	3,746,059
12	Miami-Fort Lauderdale, FL	3,655,844
13	Seattle-Tacoma-Bremerton, WA	3,424,361
14	Phoenix-Mesa, AZ	2,931,004
15	Cleveland-Akron, OH	2,911,683
16	Minneapolis-St. Paul, MN-WI	2,831,234
17	San Diego, CA	2,780,592
18	St. Louis, MO-IL	2,563,801
19	Denver-Boulder-Greeley, CO	2,365,345
20	Pittsburgh, PA	2,346,153
21	Tampa-St. Petersburg-Clearwater, FL	2,256,559
22	Portland-Salem, OR-WA	2,149,056
23	Cincinnati-Hamilton, OH-KY-IN	1,948,264
24	Kansas City, MO-KS	1,737,025
25	Sacramento-Yolo, CA	1,685,812
26	Milwaukee-Racine, WI	1,645,924
27	Norfolk-Virginia Beach-Newport News, VA-NC	1,542,143
28	San Antonio, TX	1,538,338
29	Indianapolis, IN	1,519,194
30	Orlando, FL	1,504,569
31	Columbus, OH	1,469,604
32	Charlotte-Gastonia-Rock Hill, NC-SC	1,383,080
33	Las Vegas, NV-AZ	1,321,546
34	New Orleans, LA	1,309,445
35	Salt Lake City-Ogden, UT	1,267,745
36	Greensboro–Winston-Salem–High Point, NC	1,167,629
37	Nashville, TN	1,156,225
38	Buffalo-Niagara Falls, NY	1,152,541
39	Hartford, CT	1,143,859
40	Providence-Fall River-Warwick, RI-MA	1,122,974
41	Austin-San Marcos, TX	1,105,909
42	Memphis, TN-AR-MS	1,093,427
43	Rochester, NY	1,081,883
44	Raleigh–Durham–Chapel Hill, NC	1,079,873
45	Jacksonville, FL	1,044,684
46	Oklahoma City, OK	1,038,999
47	Grand Rapids-Muskegon-Holland, MI	1,037,933
48	West Palm Beach-Boca Raton, FL	1,032,625
49	Louisville, KY-IN	999,267

50	Richmond-Petersburg, VA	957,032
51	Dayton-Springfield, OH	948,522
52	Greenville-Spartanburg-Anderson, SC	918,351
53	Birmingham, AL	908,508
54	Honolulu, HI	872,478
55	Albany-Schenectady-Troy, NY	871,604
56	Fresno, CA	870,478
57	Tucson, AZ	790,755
58	Tulsa, OK	776,906
59	Syracuse, NY	734,640
60	El Paso, TX	703,127
61	Omaha, NE-IA	693,900
62	Albuquerque, NM	678,633
63	Knoxville, TN	659,074
64	Bakersfield, CA	631,459
65	Allentown-Bethlehem-Easton, PA	616,877
66	Harrisburg-Lebanon-Carlisle, PA	616,031
67	Scranton–Wilkes-Barre–Hazelton, PA	615,491
68	Toledo, OH	609,935
69	Youngstown-Warren, OH	591,751
70	Baton Rouge, LA	575,129
71	Springfield, MA	573,727
72	Little Rock, North Little Rock, AR	556,295
73	Stockton-Lodi, CA	550,445
74	Wichita, KS	544,343
75	Sarasota-Bradenton, FL	543,082
76	Charleston-North Charleston, SC	541,159
77	Mobile, AL	532,257
78	McAllen-Edinburg-Mission, TX	522,204
79	Columbia, SC	512,316
80	Colorado Springs, CO	490,378
81	Fort Wayne, IN	481,191
82	Daytona Beach, FL	470,864
83	Melbourne-Titusville-Palm Bay, FL	466,093
84	Johnson City-Kingsport-Bristol, TN-VA	462,345
85	Augusta-Aiken, GA-SC	458,271
86	Lancaster, PA	456,414
87	Lakeland-Winter Haven, FL	452,584
88	Chattanooga, TN-GA	450,283
89	Lansing-East Lansing, MI	449,683
90	Lexington, KY	449,645
91	Kalamazoo-Battle Creek, MI	446,331
92	Des Moines, IA	436,922
93	Jackson, MS	429,614
94	Modesto, CA	426,460
95	Madison, WI	424,586
96	Spokane, WA	408,669
97	Canton-Massillon, OH	402,207
98	Saginaw-Bay City–Midland, MI	401,991
99	Pensacola, FL	399,625
100	Boise City, ID	395,953

⊙ U.S. Bureau of the Census. "Metro Area and Central City Population Estimates for July 1, 1998," www.census.gov/population/estimates/metro-city/ma98-05.txt

UNITED STATES: *Population*

Population Estimates: Current, Historical, and Projected

Current

Oct. 16, 2000 est.: 275,950,532

Historical

1790:	3,929,214	1890:	62,979,766
1800:	5,308,483	1900:	76,212,168
1810:	7,239,881	1910:	92,228,496
1820:	9,638,453	1920:	106,021,537
1830:	12,860,702	1930:	123,202,624
1840:	17,063,353	1940:	132,164,569
1850:	23,191,876	1950:	151,325,798
1860:	31,443,321	1960:	179,323,175
1870:	38,558,371	1970:	203,302,031
1880:	50,189,209	1980:	226,542,199
		1990:	248,709,873

Projected

2010:	299,862,000	2040:	377,350,000
2020:	324,927,000	2050:	403,687,000
2030:	351,070,000	2100:	570,954,000

⊙ The United States Bureau of the Census. "Annual Projections of the Total Resident Population as of July 1: Middle, Lowest, and Highest, and Zero International Migration Series, 1999–2100,"
www.census.gov/population/projections/nation/summary/np-t1.txt
———. "Historical National Population Estimates: July 1, 1900 to July 1, 1999,"
www.census.gov/population/estimates/nation/popclockest.txt
———. "Population: 1790 to 1990," www.census.gov/population/censusdata/table-16.pdf

State Population (inc. District of Columbia), 1999

State	Population (est.)	Rank	State	Population (est.)	Rank
Alabama	4,369,862	23	Illinois	12,128,370	5
Alaska	619,500	48	Indiana	5,942,901	14
Arizona	4,778,332	20	Iowa	2,869,413	30
Arkansas	2,551,373	33	Kansas	2,654,052	32
California	33,145,121	1	Kentucky	3,960,825	25
Colorado	4,056,133	24	Louisiana	4,372,035	22
Connecticut	3,282,031	29	Maine	1,253,040	39
Delaware	753,538	45	Maryland	5,171,634	19
District of Columbia	519,000	50	Massachusetts	6,175,169	13
			Michigan	9,863,775	8
Florida	15,111,244	4	Minnesota	4,775,508	21
Georgia	7,788,240	10	Mississippi	2,768,619	31
Hawaii	1,185,497	42	Missouri	5,468,338	17
Idaho	1,251,700	40	Montana	882,779	44

Nebraska	1,666,028	38	
Nevada	1,809,253	35	
New Hampshire	1,201,134	41	
New Jersey	8,143,412	9	
New Mexico	1,739,844	37	
New York	18,1196,601	3	
North Carolina	7,650,789	11	
North Dakota	633,666	47	
Ohio	11,256,654	7	
Oklahoma	3,358,044	27	
Oregon	3,316,154	28	
Pennsylvania	11,994,016	6	

Rhode Island	990,819	43
South Carolina	3,885,736	26
South Dakota	733,133	46
Tennessee	5,483,535	16
Texas	20,044,141	2
Utah	2,129,836	34
Vermont	593,740	49
Virginia	6,872,912	12
Washington	5,756,361	15
West Virginia	1,806,928	36
Wisconsin	5,250,446	18
Wyoming	479,602	51

⊙ The United States Bureau of the Census. "State Population Estimates and Demographic Components of Population Change: July 1, 1998 to July 1, 1999," www.census.gov/population/estimates/state/st-99-1.txt

Racial Percentages by State (incl. District of Columbia), 1999

State	% White (est.)	% Black (est.)	% American Indian and Alaska Native (est.)	% Asian and Pacific Islander (est.)
United States	82.5	12.7	.9	3.9
Alabama	73.0	26.1	.3	.7
Alaska	75.2	3.9	16.4	4.5
Arizona	88.7	3.7	5.5	2.1
Arkansas	82.6	16.1	.5	.7
California	79.4	7.5	.9	12.2
Colorado	92.3	4.3	.9	2.5
Connecticut	87.8	9.4	.2	2.6
Delaware	77.7	19.8	.5	2.1
District of Columbia	35.2	61.4	.3	3.1
Florida	82.3	15.4	.4	1.9
Georgia	69.0	28.7	.2	2.1
Hawaii	33.0	2.8	.6	63.6
Idaho	96.9	.6	1.3	1.2
Illinois	81.1	15.3	.2	3.4
Indiana	90.4	8.4	.3	1.0
Iowa	96.4	2.0	.3	1.3
Kansas	91.4	5.9	.9	1.8
Kentucky	91.9	7.3	.1	.7
Louisiana	65.9	32.4	.4	1.3
Maine	98.3	.5	.5	.8
Maryland	67.5	28.1	.3	4.0
Massachusetts	89.4	6.6	.2	3.8
Michigan	83.4	14.3	.6	1.7
Minnesota	92.9	3.1	1.2	2.7
Mississippi	62.4	36.5	.4	.7
Missouri	87.2	11.3	.4	1.1

Racial Percentages by State
(incl. District of Columbia), 1999 *(cont.)*

State	% White (est.)	% Black (est.)	% American Indian and Alaska Native (est.)	% Asian and Pacific Islander (est.)
Montana	92.5	.4	6.5	.6
Nebraska	93.6	4.1	.9	1.4
Nevada	85.6	7.7	1.8	4.9
New Hampshire	97.8	.8	.2	1.2
New Jersey	79.3	14.7	.3	5.8
New Mexico	86.3	2.6	9.5	1.5
New York	76.2	17.7	.4	5.6
North Carolina	75.3	22.0	1.3	1.4
North Dakota	93.7	.6	4.8	.8
Ohio	87.0	11.6	.2	1.2
Oklahoma	83.0	7.8	7.8	1.3
Oregon	93.4	1.9	1.4	3.3
Pennsylvania	88.4	9.8	.2	1.7
Rhode Island	92.1	5.1	.5	2.3
South Carolina	69.1	29.8	.2	.9
South Dakota	90.4	.7	8.2	.7
Tennessee	82.1	16.6	.2	1.0
Texas	84.3	12.3	.5	2.9
Utah	95.1	.9	1.4	2.6
Vermont	98.4	.5	.2	.8
Virginia	75.8	20.1	.3	3.8
Washington	88.7	3.5	1.8	6.0
West Virginia	96.3	3.1	.1	.5
Wisconsin	91.9	5.6	.9	1.6
Wyoming	96.0	.9	2.3	.9

⊙ The United States Bureau of the Census. "States Ranked by White Population, July 1, 1999," www.census.gov/population/estimates/state/rank/white.txt

———. "States Ranked by Black Population, July 1, 1999," www.census.gov/population/estimates/state/rank/black.txt

———. "States Ranked by American Indian and Alaska Native Population, July 1, 1999," www.census.gov/population/estimates/state/rank/aiea.txt

———. "States Ranked by Asian and Pacific Islander Population, July 1, 1999," www.census.gov/population/estimates/state/rank/api.txt

100 Most Populous Native American Tribes

Name	Population (1990)	Name	Population (1990)
Cherokee	369,035	Apache	53,330
Navajo	225,298	Iroquois	52,557
Sioux	107,321	Lumbee	50,888
Chippewa	105,988	Creek	45,872
Choctaw	86,231	Blackfoot	37,992
Pueblo	55,330	Canadian and Latin American	27,179

Chickasaw	21,522	Karok	3,077
Tohono O'odham	16,876	Laddo	2,984
Potawatomi	16,719	Yokuts	2,967
Seminole	15,564	Haliwa	2,946
Pima	15,074	Gros Ventres	2,875
Tlingit	14,417	Luiseno	2,798
Alaskan Athabaskans	14,198	Ponca	2,788
Cheyenne	11,809	Milmac	2,726
Comanche	11,437	Warm Springs	2,685
Paiute	11,369	Narragansett	2,564
Osage	10,430	Quinault	2,513
Puget Sound Salish	10,384	Passamaquoddy	2,466
Yaqui	9,838	Penobscot	2,407
Delaware	9,800	Hoopa	2,390
Shoshone	9,506	Wampanoag	2,334
Kiowa	9,460	Maidu	2,334
Crow	9,394	Shoshone Paiute	2,320
Cree	8,467	Wintu	2,319
Menominee	8,064	Salish and Kootenai	2,293
Ottawa	7,885	Diegueno	2,249
Houma	7,809	Stolkbridge	2,219
Ute	7,658	Tsimshian	2,157
Yakima	7,577	Mission Indians	2,056
Yuman	7,319	Spokane	2,042
Colville	7,057	Haida	1,936
Arapaho	6,918	Otoe-Missouria	1,762
Shawnee	6,640	Pit River	1,753
Winnebago	6,591	Siletz	1,726
Assiniboine	5,521	Algonquian	1,700
Pomo	4,898	Mono	1,697
Salish	4,830	Arikara	1,671
Sac and Fox	4,774	Shinnecock	1,670
Miami	4,580	Makah	1,661
Yurok	4,444	Colorado River	1,645
Omaha	4,363	Fort Berthold	1,643
Nez Perce	4,003	Juaneno	1,605
Eastern Tribes	3,853	Iowa	1,555
Kickapoo	3,576	Abenaki	1,549
Fort Hall	3,450	Hidatsa	1,539
Miwok	3,438	Nantikoke	1,529
Pawnee	3,387	Klallam	1,522
Chumash	3,208	Washo	1,489
Lummi	3,125	Gila River	1,484
Klamath	3,113	Quapaw	1,438

⊙ The United States Bureau of the Census. *Characteristics of American Indians by Tribe and Language* "Table 1: American Indian Population by Selected Tribes: 1990," www.census.gov/prod/3/98pubs/CP-3-7-1.PDF

United States Immigrants by Decade

Decade	Number of Immigrants	Decade	Number of Immigrants
1820–1998 (H1)	64,599,082	1911–1920	5,735,811
1821–1830	143,439	1921–1930	4,107,209
1831–1840	599,125	1931–1940	528,431
1841–1850	1,713,251	1941–1950	1,035,039
1851–1860	2,598,214	1951–1960	2,515,479
1861–1870	2,314,824	1961–1970	3,321,677
1871–1880	2,812,191	1971–1980	4,493,314
1881–1890	5,246,613	1981–1990	7,338,062
1891–1900	3,687,564	1991–1998	7,605,068
1901–1910	8,795,386		

⊙ The United States Department of Justice Immigration and Naturalization Service.
*1998 Statistical Yearbook of the Immigration and Naturalization Service: Immigrants,
Fiscal Year 1998.* "Table 1: Immigration to the U.S.: Fiscal Years: 1820–1998,"
www.ins.usdoj.gov/graphics/aboutins/statistics/imm98.pdf

United States Immigrants by Region and Country of Origin (Fiscal Year 1998)

Region	Number of Legal Immigrants	Region	Number of Legal Immigrants
Total	660,477	North America	252,996
Africa	40,660	Oceania	3,935
Asia	219,696	South America	45,394
Europe	90,793	Unknown	7,003

Country (Top 20)	Number of Legal Immigrants	Country (Top 20)	Number of Legal Immigrants
Mexico	131,575	Korea	14,268
China (People's Republic)	36,884	Haiti	13,449
		Pakistan	13,094
India	36,482	Colombia	11,836
Philippines	34,466	Russia	11,529
Dominican Republic	20,387	Canada	10,190
		Peru	10,154
Vietnam	17,649	United Kingdom	9,011
Cuba	17,375	Bangladesh	8,621
Jamaica	15,146	Poland	8,469
El Salvador	14,590	Iran	7,883

⊙ The United States Department of Justice Immigration and Naturalization Service.
*U.S. DOJ Immigration and Naturalization Service Annual Report: Legal Immigration,
Fiscal Year 1998.* "Table 2: Immigrants Admitted by Region and Selected Country
of Birth: Fiscal Years 1995–1998," www.ins.usdoj.gov/graphics/publicaffairs/
newsrels/98legal.pdf

Common Medical Tests

Name	Purpose	Procedure	Requirements	Other
Blood Pressure	To test for hypertension	Blood pressure is measured with a rubber cuff wrapped around your upper arm. The cuff is inflated to measure blood pressure.	To ensure accuracy, try to avoid caffeine, nicotine, and certain medications (such as non-steroidal anti-inflammatory drugs and cold medications) before being tested.	The American Heart Association recommends getting blood pressure checked at least every two years.
Bone Mineral Density Test	To test for osteoporosis	A scanner uses a small amount of radiation to measure bone density.	Bone density can be measured at the spine, hip, wrist, or heel. Your doctor will determine the best test for you.	
Breast Self-Exam	To screen for breast cancer	Feel for any unusual lumps, dimpling, or thickening and look for discharge from the nipple or any other abnormalities.		The American Cancer Society recommends monthly self-exams for women 20 and older. The best time to examine your breasts is about a week after your period begins, or if you have reached menopause, choose the same time to do it each month.
Clinical Breast Exam	To screen for breast cancer	The doctor palpates the breasts to check for any unusual lumps, dimpling, or thickening, and looks for discharge from the nipple or any other abnormalities.		The American Cancer Society recommends a clinical breast exam every three years for women age 20–39 and every year for women 40 and older.

Name	Purpose	Procedure	Requirements	Other
Cholesterol	To test for hyper-cholesterolemia, which poses an increased risk of coronary heart disease	The test requires a quick blood sample drawn from your finger or arm.	Avoid any medications that influence cholesterol levels prior to testing. (Ask your doctor for a list of such medications.) An overnight fast is required if testing for a full lipid profile.	According to the National Heart, Lung, and Blood Institute, adults age 20 and older should have both their total and HDL cholesterol measured at least once every five years.
Colorectal Cancer	To screen for colorectal cancer	*Sigmoidoscopy:* a soft, bendable tube the thickness of the index finger is gently inserted into the rectal opening and advanced into the rectum and the lower colon to examine their linings. *Colonoscopy:* a visual exam of the interior lining of the large intestine using a colonoscope, a flexible fiberoptic tube.	Thorough cleansing of the bowel is mandatory. Your health care provider may ask you to abstain from all solid foods 2 or 3 days before the test, ingest laxatives, or have an enema.	The American Cancer Society recommends men and women age 50 and older follow this schedule for colorectal cancer testing: sigmoidoscopy every five years, or colonoscopy every ten years, or double contrast barium enema every five to ten years.
Digital Rectal Exam	To test for colorectal cancer	The doctor inserts a gloved, lubricated finger into the rectum to feel for any type of growth or abnormality.		The American Cancer Society recommends men and women age 50 and older have a digital rectal exam with their chosen colorectal exam schedule (see above).

Dental Exam	To screen for tooth decay and gum disease	Your dentist performs a visual examination of your teeth and gums.
Eye Exam	To test general eye health, including tests for glaucoma, macular degeneration, cataracts, and diabetic retinopathy	Your ophthalmologist may have you read letters at a distance, examine your retinas with special viewing machinery, and measure your eyeball's elasticity with a puff of compressed air.	The American Academy of Ophthalmology recommends the following schedule for eye exams. Under 40: a single comprehensive exam if your vision is normal; every three to five years for African Americans and others at higher risk for glaucoma. Ages 40–64: every two to four years, even if you have no symptoms. Age 65 and older: every one to two years, even if you have no symptoms.
Fasting Plasma Glucose	To test for diabetes	A blood sample is taken after an eight-hour overnight fast.	The American Diabetes Association recommends that all adults over 45 get tested for Type II (adult onset) diabetes every three years.

Common Medical Tests (cont.)

Name	Purpose	Procedure	Requirements	Other
Fecal Occult Blood	To screen for colorectal cancer	You will collect stool samples for three days in a row before the test, or your doctor will collect a sample during a rectal exam.	Eat a high-fiber diet for 48 to 72 hours before the test. Avoid red meat, poultry, aspirin, large amounts of vitamin C, iron supplements, and certain fruits and vegetables (get a complete list from your doctor), all of which can interfere with test results. You may also need to stop certain medications for two days prior to the test.	The American Cancer Society recommends yearly testing for men and women age 50 and older.
FSH (follicle-stimulating hormone)	To screen for ovarian failure, which leads to menopause	A blood sample is taken and tested by your doctor.		
HIV Test	To screen for human immunodeficiency virus (HIV) antibodies	A blood sample is taken and tested by your doctor.		The Centers for Disease Control and Prevention (CDC) recommends HIV testing if: *You have used intravenous drugs or had a partner who did; *You have had another sexually transmitted disease; *You have had unprotected sex with anyone whose HIV status you weren't sure of; *You are pregnant or plan to conceive.

Mammogram	To screen for breast cancer and non-cancerous breast disease	A low-dose x-ray of the breast is taken and examined by your doctor.	On the day of your mammogram, do not wear any powder, cream, or deodorant on your upper body.	Most experts recommend annual mammograms for women 40 and over.
Pap Test	To screen for cervical cancer	The doctor inserts a speculum into the vagina and collects a tissue sample from the cervix. The procedure takes five to ten minutes and can be done during a pelvic exam.	For the greatest accuracy, have the test done 12 to 14 days after the first day of your period. If you douche within 24 hours before the test, or are menstruating, the results may be distorted.	The College of American Pathologists recommends that women who are sexually active or who have reached 18 years of age get annual Pap tests.
Pelvic Exam	To screen for cervical and ovarian cancers and precancerous cells	The physician performs a speculum exam to view the vagina and cervix. A bimanual is also performed to check the uterus and ovaries for any palpable mass. Pap tests are often performed during a pelvic exam.		The American Cancer Society recommends annual pelvic exams for women 18 and older, and for younger women who are sexually active.
PSA	To screen for prostate cancer with a prostate-specific antigen (PSA)	A blood sample is taken and tested by your doctor.	The sample is collected in the morning, if possible.	The American Cancer Society recommends that the PSA test be offered annually, beginning at age 50, to men who have at least a 10-year life expectancy.

Name	Purpose	Procedure	Requirements	Other
Skin Self-Exam	To screen for skin cancer	Look for any changes in moles or freckles, as well as any new spots that are asymmetrical, more than one color, the size of a pencil eraser or larger, or have uneven borders.		The American Academy of Dermatology recommends self-exams every month.
Clinical Skin Exam	To screen for skin cancer	The doctor will examine your entire body, including back, buttocks, genitals, soles of the feet, scalp, and underarms.		The American Academy of Dermatology recommends yearly skin exams by a dermatologist.
Testicular Self-Exam	To screen for testicular cancer	Look for any change in the size, shape, or consistency of the testes, as well as any hard lumps or smooth, rounded masses, which might feel like a grain of uncooked rice or a hard pea.		Testicular cancer often produces no symptoms, so many doctors recommend monthly self-exams.
Thyroid Stimulating Hormone (TSH)	To test for hypothyroidism and hyperthyroidism	A blood sample is taken and tested by your doctor.		The American College of Obstetrics and Gynecology recommends that women 65 and older get tested every three to five years.

© Merck.com. "Common Medical Tests," www.merck.com/pubs/mmanual_home/appndxs/app3.htm MSN. "The Yale University School of Medicine Patient's Guide to Medical Tests," http://content.health.msn.com/yale_books Thrive Online. "Medical Tests Not to Miss," www.thriveonline.com/health/medicaltests/index.html

Diseases: Common Types

Infectious diseases are communicable illnesses caused by pathogens that invade a host. Pathogens include bacteria, viruses, fungi, and parasites (protozoans, flatworms, and roundworms). The table lists some well-known examples in these categories.

Bacterial	Viral	Fungal	Parasites (Protozoans, Flatworms, Roundworms)
e. coli infection	common colds	athlete's foot	malaria
cholera	mumps	yeast infection	giardiasis
tetanus	measles	ringworm	schistosomiasis
gonorrhea	hepatitis		trichinosis
meningococcal diseases	herpes simplex		
ulcer	HIV		
pneumonia	yellow fever		
toxic shock syndrome	viral hemorrhagic fever		
strep throat			
urinary tract infections	West Nile encephalitis		
syphilis	chickenpox (varicella)		
salmonella	influenza		

Noninfectious diseases include malignancies (cancer) of all kinds, hereditary and congenital disorders, degenerative disorders, immunological diseases, and deficiency diseases.

Hereditary and Congenital Disorders	Degenerative Disorders	Immunological Diseases	Deficiency Diseases
hemophilia	Parkinson's disease	allergies	scurvy
sickle-cell anemia	arthritis	lupus	malnutrition
birth defects	Alzheimer's disease		osteoporosis
asthma			rickets

◉ OnHealth.com. "Disease Categories," http://onhealth.webmd.com/conditions/cond-ctr/index.asp

Thrive Online. "Index of Illnesses and Conditions," www.thriveonline.com/health/library/lookitup.ills.html

Centers for Disease Control. "Health Topics A-Z," www.cdc.gov/health/diseases.htm

Diseases: Common Symptoms

Name	Type	Symptoms
Acne vulgaris	bacterial	Blackheads (black spots the size of a pinhead); whiteheads (white spots similar to blackheads); pustules (small pus-filled lesions); cysts (larger and firm swellings) and abscesses (swollen and inflamed areas with pus) with severe acne; redness and inflammation around eruptions

Diseases: Common Symptoms *(cont.)*

Name	Type	Symptoms
AIDS (acquired immune deficiency syndrome)	viral	Initial HIV infection may produce no symptoms; fatigue; unexplained weight loss; night sweats; fever; diarrhea; recurrent respiratory and skin infections; swollen lymph glands throughout the body; genital changes; enlarged spleen; mouth sores
Alcoholism	genetic; lifestyle-related	Frequent blackouts; memory loss; delirium tremens (tremors, hallucinations, confusion, sweating, rapid heartbeat)—these occur most often with alcohol withdrawal; liver disease
Alzheimer's disease	unknown; there may be a genetic predisposition.	Forgetfulness of recent events; increasing difficulty performing intellectual tasks, such as accustomed work, balancing a checkbook or maintaining a household; personality changes, including poor impulse control and poor judgment
Asthma	environmental; may be genetic	Difficulty breathing; bluish skin; exhaustion; grunting respiration; inability to speak; mental changes, including restlessness or confusion
Bronchitis	viral	Cough that produces little or no sputum initially, but does later on; low fever (usually less than 101°F or 38.3°C); burning chest discomfort or feeling of pressure behind the breastbone; wheezing or uncomfortable breathing (sometimes)
Chickenpox (varicella)	viral	The following are usually mild in children, severe in adults: fever; abdominal pain or a general ill feeling that lasts 1 or 2 days; skin eruptions that appear almost anywhere on the body, including the scalp, penis, and inside the mouth, nose, throat, or vagina. They may be scattered over large areas, and they occur least on the arms and legs. Blisters collapse within 24 hours and form scabs. New crops of blisters erupt every 3 to 4 days; adults have additional symptoms that resemble influenza
Common cold	viral	Runny or stuffy nose. Nasal discharge is watery at first, then becomes thick and greenish yellow; sore throat; hoarseness; cough that produces little or no sputum; low fever; fatigue; watering eyes; appetite loss
Depression	genetic; lifestyle-related; environmental	Loss of interest in life; listlessness and fatigue; insomnia; excessive or disturbed sleeping; social isolation; feeling not useful or needed; appetite loss or overeating; constipation; loss of sex drive; difficulty making decisions; concentration difficulty; unexplained crying bouts;

		intense guilt feelings over minor or imaginary misdeeds; irritability; restlessness; thoughts of suicide; various pains, such as headache or chest pain, without evidence of disease
Diabetes mellitus (non–insulin dependent)	strong genetic predisposition; may be lifestyle-related	Fatigue; excess thirst; increased appetite; frequent urination; decreased resistance to infection, especially urinary-tract infections and yeast infections of the skin, mouth, or vagina
Ear infection (otitis media)	various (viral, bacterial, allergic reaction)	Irritability; earache; feeling of fullness in the ear; hearing loss; fever; discharge or leakage from the ear; diarrhea, vomiting (sometimes); pulling at the ear (small children)
Eczema	allergy	Itching (sometimes severe); small blisters with oozing; thickening and scaling from chronic inflammation
Gingivitis	lifestyle and environmental, sometimes caused by blood disorders	Gums that are swollen, tender, red, and soft around the teeth; gums that bleed easily; bad breath; fever (rarely); no pain
Glaucoma	unknown; may be genetic	Loss of peripheral vision in small areas; blurred vision on one side toward the nose
Hepatitis	viral	Flu-like symptoms, such as fever, fatigue, nausea, vomiting, diarrhea, and loss of appetite; jaundice (yellow eyes and skin) caused by a buildup of bile in the blood; dark urine from bile spilling into the urine; light, "clay-colored," or whitish stools
Herpes	viral	Usually found around the mouth, but sometimes on the genitals. The blisters are grouped together and each is surrounded by a red ring. They fill with fluid, then dry up and disappear. If the eye is infected: eye pain and redness; feeling that something is in the eye; sensitivity to light; tearing
Influenza	viral	Chills and moderate to high fever; muscle aches, including backache; cough, usually with little or no sputum; sore throat; hoarseness; runny nose; headache; fatigue
Lyme disease	viral	*Early stages:* Muscle aches and pains; fatigue and lethargy; chills and fever *Middle stages:* Stiff neck with headache; backache; nausea and vomiting; sore throat; enlargement of the spleen and lymph glands; migrating joint pain, eventually accompanied by redness and warmth; cardiac symptoms; migrating arthritis *Late stages:* Neurological disease; chronic arthritis

Diseases: Common Symptoms *(cont.)*

Name	Type	Symptoms
Osteoporosis	various causes (nutrient deficiency; genetic; lifestyle-) related	Compression fractures; deformed spinal column with humps; loss of height; fractures occurring with minor injury, especially of the hip or arm
Sinusitis	various causes, most often bacterial	Nasal congestion with green-yellow (sometimes blood-tinged) discharge; feeling of pressure inside the head; headache that is worse in the morning or when bending forward. With chronic sinusitis, the headache may occur daily for weeks at a time. Cheek pain that may resemble a toothache; post-nasal drip; cough (sometimes) that is usually non-productive; tiredness; lack of energy; disturbed sleep (sometimes); fever (sometimes); eye pain
Strep throat	bacterial	Rapid onset of throat pain; throat pain that is worse when swallowing; appetite loss; headache; fever; general ill feeling; ear pain when swallowing (sometimes); tender, swollen glands in the neck; bright-red tonsils that may have specks of pus
Ulcer (Peptic)	believed to be bacterial	Appetite and weight loss (with duodenal, may be weight gain, as person eats more to ease discomfort); recurrent vomiting; blood in the stool; anemia; a burning, boring, or gnawing feeling that lasts 30 minutes to 3 hours (often interpreted as heartburn, indigestion, or hunger).

⊙ OnHealth.com. "Disease Categories," onhealth.webmd.com/conditions/condctr/index.asp

Thrive Online. "Index of Illnesses and Conditions," www.thriveonline.com/health/library/lookitup.ills.html

Encarta.com. "Human Disease," encarta.msn.com/find/Concise.asp?z=1&pg=2&ti=761566075

First Aid

The information below provides general guidelines for some first aid techniques. The guidelines offered are not intended to replace the formal training in CPR, artificial respiration, or other first aid offered by the American Red Cross or the American Heart Association. In any serious emergency, the first step is always to call emergency medical services.

Adult CPR

Cardiopulmonary Resuscitation (CPR) involves three basic steps, defined by the American Heart Association as:

Airway (ensure a clear airway)
Breathing (restore breathing using artificial respiration)
Circulation (restore heartbeat)

1. Check for consciousness: If the victim appears to be unconscious, tap or gently shake him/her and ask if she is OK. If she does not respond, instruct someone else to call emergency medical services, or shout for help.

2. Make sure the person is on his or her back on a firm surface.

3. Open airway and check for breathing: Tilt the victim's head back by gently lifting the chin while pushing the forehead. Look, listen, and feel for the victim's breath. [fig. 1]

Fig. 1

4. If no breath, check to be sure nothing is obstructing the throat. If necessary, clear the obstruction using the method below (see Adult Choking) and again check for breathing.

5. If no breath, pinch the nostrils shut, open the mouth, and fit your mouth firmly over the victim's mouth. Give 2 full breaths. [fig. 2]

Fig. 2

6. Feel for a pulse at the side of the neck.

7. If no pulse, position yourself beside the victim's chest. Use two fingers to find the bottom of the center of the breastbone. Position the heel of your other hand above the two fingers on the breastbone; then place the heel of the second hand over the heel of the first. [fig. 3]

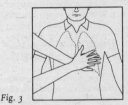

Fig. 3

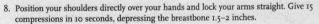

8. Position your shoulders directly over your hands and lock your arms straight. Give 15 compressions in 10 seconds, depressing the breastbone 1.5–2 inches.

9. Return to Step 5 above and administer another 2 breaths.

10. Continue alternating compressions and breathing until victim revives or help arrives.

Adult Choking

1. First ask the victim if he/she can cough or speak.*

2. If the victim cannot cough or speak, stand behind him, reach around to his front, and locate his bottom rib.

3. At the level of the bottom rib, move your hand across the abdomen until it is above the navel. Make a fist and place it in that spot with the thumb-side against the abdomen. Cover the fist with your other hand. [fig. 1]

4. Quickly pull your fist into the victim's abdomen with an upward thrust to dislodge the object obstructing his breathing.

Fig. 1

First Aid *(cont.)*

*If the victim is lying down, turn him face-up, straddle his hips, and locate the correct hand position using the method above. Place your hands one on top of the other and move so your shoulders are directly above the victim's abdomen. Give a sharp forward thrust to dislodge the object and immediately clear the object from the victim's mouth. If the victim does not begin breathing, call emergency medical services and begin artificial respiration. (See Adult CPR above)

External Bleeding

1. If bleeding is heavy, call emergency medical services.
2. Wash hands and put on sterile gloves if available.
3. Remove loose debris from wound.
4. Put a barrier such as layers of sterile dressing or clean cloth between you and the wound and press dressing firmly. If further dressing is required, do not remove first dressing but apply a fresh layer over the soaked dressing.
5. If no bones are broken, raise wound above heart level.

Insect Stings

If a person is stung:
1. Have someone stay with the person to make sure they do not have an allergic reaction.*
2. Wash the area with soap and water.
3. Remove the stinger by wiping a piece of gauze over the area or by scraping a fingernail over the area. Do not squeeze the area or use tweezers as this causes more venom to go into the skin.
4. Apply ice to reduce swelling.
5. Do not scratch the sting. This will cause the sting to swell more and increase the chance of infection.

*Allergic reactions to bee stings can be deadly. People with allergies to stings should always carry an insect sting allergy kit and wear a medical ID bracelet stating their allergy. Signs of an allergic reaction to insect stings include swelling that moves to other parts of the body, especially the face or neck; difficulty breathing; wheezing; dizziness; or a drop in blood pressure. Call for emergency medical care if any of these signs is present.

⊙ American Red Cross and Kathleen A. Handal. *The American Red Cross First Aid & Safety Handbook.* Boston: Little, Brown, 1992.
World Publishing Systems. "First Aid Online," www.wps.com.au/business/firstaid/firstaid.htm

Common Over-the-Counter Drugs and Uses

Generic Name	Brand Names	Purpose
acetaminophen	Excedrin; Tylenol	analgesic
aluminum hydroxide	Alternagel	antacid
aspirin (acetylsalicylic acid)	Bayer; Bufferin	analgesic
bisacodyl	Dulcolax	stimulant laxative
brompheniramine	Dimetane	antihistamine
caffeine	No-Doz; Vivarin	stimulant
calcium carbonate	Tums; Rolaids	antacid
chlorpheniramine		antihistamine
cimetidine	Tagamet HB	anti-ulcer
clotrimazole	Lotrimin	anti-fungal

codeine	Robitussin A-C	cough suppressant
dexbrompheniramine		antihistamine
dextromethorphan	Robitussin Pediatric Cough; Sucrets; Vicks Formula 44	cough suppressant (anti-tussive)
dimenhydrinate	Dramamine; Calm-X	motion sickness
diphenhydramine	Benadryl; Sominex; Unisom; Nytol	antihistamine; motion sickness; sleep aid
doxylamine		antihistamine; sleep aid
famotidine	Pepcid AC; Mylanta AR	anti-ulcer
guaifenesin	Robitussin	expectorant
ibuprofen	Advil; Nuprin; Motrin-IB	anti-inflammatory
ketoprofen	Orudis KT; Actron	analgesic
lidocaine	Xylocaine	anesthetic
loperamide	Immodium; Kaopectate	anti-diarrhea
magnesium salts	Phillips' Milk of Magnesia	antacid; laxative
meclizine	Dramamine II	motion sickness
miconazole nitrate	Monistat	anti-fungal
naphazoline	Clear Eyes	ophthalmic decongestant
naproxen sodium	Aleve	anti-inflammatory
oxymetazoline hydrochloride	Afrin	decongestant
phenolphthalein	Ex-Lax	stimulant laxative
phenylephrine hydrochloride	Dristan; Sinex	decongestant
pink bismuth	Pepto Bismol	anti-diarrhea; anti-emetic
polymyxin B	Neosporin	topical antibiotic
pramoxine	Anusol	anti-hemorrhoid
pseudoephedrine hydrochloride	Chlor-Trimeton; Dimetapp; Drixoral; Sudafed; Triaminic	decongestant
ranitidine	Zantac 75	anti-ulcer
simethicone	Maalox; Mylanta; Gas-X	anti-flatulent
sodium bicarbonate	Alka-Seltzer	antacid
tetrahydrozoline	Visine Allergy Relief	ophthalmic decongestant
tolnaftate	Tinactin	anti-fungal
undecylenate	Desenex	anti-fungal

⊙ Merck.com. "Over-the-Counter Drugs," www.merck.com/pubs/mmanual_home/sec2/13.htm

Eckerd.com. "Healthcare," 146.235.6.106/storefront/Healthcare/otc/table1_2.asp

National Women's Health Information Center. "Drug Interactions," www.4woman.gov/faq/drug.html

Common Prescription Drugs and Uses

Generic Name	Brand Names*	Purpose
albuterol	Proventil	orally inhaled bronchodilator
alclometasone	Alclovate	topical steroid
amlodipine	Norvasc	calcium channel blocker
amoxicillin/ clavulanic acid	Augmentin	antibiotic
ampicillin		antibiotic
ampicillin		antibiotic

Common Prescription Drugs and Uses *(cont.)*

Generic Name	Brand Names	Purpose
atenolol	Tenormin	beta-blocker
atorvastatin	Lipitor	lipid lowering agent
azithromycin	Zithromax	antibiotic
beclomethasone	Vanceril	orally inhaled steroid
benazepril	Lotensin	anti-hypertensive
budesonide	Rhinocort	nasally inhaled steroid
bupropion	Wellbutrin/Wellbutrin SR	antidepressant
captoril	Capotril	antihypertensive
carvedilol	Coreg	beta-blocker
celecoxib	Celebrex	NSAID (non-steroidal anti-inflammatory drug)
cephalexin	Keflex	antibiotic
cetirizine	Zyrtec	antihistamine
cholestipol	Cholestid	lipid lowering agent
cimetidine	Tagamet	anti-ulcer
desonide	Tridesilon	topical steroid
desoximetasone	Topicort	topical steroid
doxepin	Sinequan	antidepressant
enalapril	Vasotec	anti-hypertensive
erythromycin		antibiotic
estradiol	Estrace	estrogen replacement
estrogen conjugated	Premarin	estrogen replacement
estrogens progesterone	Premphase; Prempro	estrogen replacement
estropipate	Ogen; Ortho EST	estrogen replacement
ethinyl estradiol/ norethindrone	Ortho-Novum; Loestrin	oral contraceptive
ethinyl estradiol/ norgestimate	Ortho Tri-Cyclen	oral contraceptive
fexophenadine	Allegra	antihistamine
fluocinonide	Derma-Smoothe	topical steroid
fluoxetine	Prozac	antidepressant (SSRI)
fluticasone	Flonase; Flovent	nasally inhaled steroid
fluvoxamine	Luvox	antidepressant
hydrocortisone 2.5%		topical steroid
hydrocortisone valerate	Westcort	topical steroid
ibuprofen	Motrin	NSAID (non-steroidal anti-inflammatory drug)
insulin		diabetes treatment
labetalol	Normodyne; Trandate	alpha- and beta-blocker
lansoprazole	Prevacid	anti-ulcer
lisinopril	Zestril	anti-hypertensive
loratadine	Claritin	antihistamine
losartan	Cozaar	A2 blocker
metronidazole		antibiotic
mometasone	Nasonex	nasally inhaled steroid
nabumetone	Relafen	NSAID (non-steroidal anti-inflammatory drug)
naproxen	Naprosyn	NSAID (non-steroidal anti-inflammatory drug)

nefazodone	Serzone	antidepressant
omeprazole	Prilosec	anti-ulcer
paroxetine	Paxil	antidepressant (SSRI)
penicillin VK		antibiotic
phenelzine	Nardil	antidepressant (MAO inhibitor)
pirbuterol	Maxair	orally inhaled bronchodilator
pravastatin	Pravachol	lipid lowering agent
prioxicam	Feldene	NSAID (non-steroidal anti-inflammatory drug)
quinapril	Accupril	anti-hypertensive
ranitidine	Zantac	anti-ulcer
salmeterol	Serevent	orally inhaled bronchodilator
salsalate	Disalcid	NSAID (non-steroidal anti-inflammatory drug)
sertaline	Zoloft	antidepressant (SSRI)
sildenafil citrate	Viagra	impotence treatment
sulfamethoxazole/ trimethoprin		antibiotic
sulindac	Clinoril	NSAID (non-steroidal anti-inflammatory drug)
tetracycline		antibiotic
tranylcypromine	Parnate	antidepressant (MAO inhibitor)
triamcinolone	Azmacort	orally inhaled steroid
valsartan	Diovan	A2 blocker
venlafaxine	Effexor	antidepressant
verapamil	Calan	calcium channel blocker

*Brand names not provided for drugs generally referred to by generic name.

◉ Minnesota Council of Health Plans. "Prescription Drug Guide," www.mnhealthplans.org/prescrip_guide.html
  Thrive Online Medical Library. "Index to Prescription and Non-Prescription Drugs," www.thriveonline.com/medical/library/treatments.html

Recommended Childhood Vaccines

	Birth	2 mos.	4 mos.	6 mos.	12 mos.	15 mos.	24 mos.	4–6 yrs.	11–12 yrs.
Hepatitis B	Hep B	Hep B		Hep B					
Diphtheria, Tetanus, Pertussis		DTaP	DTaP	DTaP		DTaP		DTaP	+Td*
H. influenzae type b		Hib	Hib	Hib	Hib				
Pneumococcal†		PCV7	PCV7	PCV7	PCV7				
Polio		IPV	IPV	IPV					
Measles, Mumps, Rubella					MMR			MMR	
Varicella					Var			Var	
Hepatitis A							Hep A		

* +Td stands for tetanus and diphtheria.
†Pneumococcal vaccine was added to the recommended vaccine schedule on June 6, 2000. Ask your doctor for more information.

Initial doses of all these immunizations need to be given before children are 2 years old in order for them to be protected during their most vulnerable period.

Recommended Childhood Vaccines *(cont.)*

Recommended ages above are guidelines; acceptable ages can range from 2 to 12 months beyond the one given. Consult your doctor.

The hepatitis B, MMR, and varicella vaccines may be given at 11–12 years of age if previously recommended doses were missed or given earlier than the recommended ages.

All children and adolescents (through 18 years of age) who have not been immunized against hepatitis B may begin the series during any medical visit. Special efforts should be made to immunize children who were born in or whose parents were born in areas of the world with moderate or high endemicity of hepatitis B virus infection.

The fourth dose of diphtheria and tetanus toxoids and acellular pertussis vaccine may be administered as early as 12 months of age, provided 6 months have elapsed since the third dose and the child is unlikely to return at age 15–18 months. Tetanus and diphtheria toxoids vaccine is recommended at 11–12 years of age if at least 5 years have elapsed since the last dose of DTP, DTaP, or DT. Subsequent routine +Td boosters are recommended every 10 years.

The second dose of measles, mumps, and rubella (MMR) vaccine is recommended routinely at 4–6 years of age but may be administered during any visit, provided at least 4 weeks have elapsed since receipt of the first dose and that both doses are administered beginning at or after 12 months of age. Those who have not previously received the second dose should complete the schedule by the 11- to 12-year-old visit.

Varicella (chickenpox) vaccine is recommended at any medical visit on or after the first birthday for susceptible children (for example, those who lack a reliable history of chickenpox as judged by a health care professional and who have not been immunized). Susceptible persons 13 years of age or older should receive two doses, given at least 4 weeks apart.

⊙ OnHealth.com. "Recommended Childhood Vaccination Schedule,"
   http://onhealth.webmd.com/baby/in-depth/item/item,92164_1_1.asp
   American Academy of Pediatrics. "Recommended Childhood Immunization
   Schedule," www.aap.org/family/parents/immunize.html

Sunburn Index

Sunburn (UV) Index	Level	Description
0–2	Minimal	Minimal danger for the average person; most can stay in the sun for up to 1 hour during peak times (10am–4pm) without burning. Fair-skinned people should always protect skin with a sunscreen that has a sun protection factor (SPF) of at least 15.
3–4	Low	Low risk of harm from unprotected sun exposure. Fair-skinned people may burn in less than 20 minutes.
5–6	Moderate	Moderate risk of harm from unprotected sun exposure. Fair-skinned people may burn in less than 15 minutes.
7–9	High	High risk of harm from unprotected sun exposure. Fair-skinned people may burn in less than 10 minutes.
10+	Very High	High risk of harm from unprotected sun exposure. Fair-skinned people may burn in less than 10 minutes.

To protect yourself from the sun:
• Always use a sunscreen and lip balm with an SPF of at least 15.
• Wear sunglasses that block 99–100 percent of UV radiation.
• Seek shade.

⊙ U.S. Environmental Protection Agency. "SunWise School Program," www.epa.gov/
   sunwise1

THE SCIENCES: *Health, Nutrition, Fitness*

Life Expectancy in the United States (1997 avg.)

Life expectancy in the United States varies by gender and race. Once a person has reached age 65 the estimate is adjusted because the original estimate factors in premature deaths due to accidents and diseases.

	At Birth	**At Age 65**
All Americans	76.5	+17.7
All Males	73.6	+15.9
All Females	79.4	+19.2

⊙ Centers for Disease Control and Prevention. "National Center for Health Statistics," www.cdc.gov/nchs/fastats/lifexpec.htm

Causes of Death

Heart disease, cancer, and stroke continue to be the top three causes of death in the United States. Leading causes of death differ by age, race, and gender. The estimated causes (for all groups combined) and ranking for 1998:

Heart disease	724,859	Pneumonia and influenza	91,871
Cancer	541,532	Diabetes	64,751
Stroke	158,448	Suicide	30,575
Lung disease	112,584	Kidney disease	26,182
Accidents	97,835	Liver disease and cirrhosis	25,192

⊙ Centers for Disease Control. *National Vital Statistics Report* 48, no. 11, 1998. www.cdc.gov/nchs/fastats/deaths.htm.

Height and Weight Standards

The tables below show the desirable weight ranges, in pounds, for various heights and body-frame types for men and women between the ages of 25–59. Shoes with 1-inch heels and clothing weighing 5 lbs. for men and 3 lbs. for women are factored into the target ranges.

Height & Weight Table for Men

Height (Feet/Inches)	Small Frame	Medium Frame	Large Frame
5'2"	128–134	131–141	138–150
5'3"	130–136	133–143	140–153
5'4"	132–138	135–145	142–156
5'5"	134–140	137–148	144–160
5'6"	136–142	139–151	146–164
5'7"	138–145	142–154	149–168
5'8"	140–148	145–157	152–172
5'9"	142–151	148–160	155–176
5'10"	144–154	151–163	158–180
5'11"	146–157	154–166	161–184
6'0"	149–160	157–170	164–188
6'1"	152–164	160–174	168–192
6'2"	155–168	164–178	172–197
6'3"	158–172	167–182	176–202
6'4"	162–176	171–187	181–207

Height and Weight Standards (cont.)

Height & Weight Table for Women

Height (Feet/Inches)	Small Frame	Medium Frame	Large Frame
4'10"	102–111	109–121	118–131
4'11"	103–113	111–123	120–134
5'0"	104–115	113–126	122–137
5'1"	106–118	115–129	125–140
5'2"	108–121	118–132	128–143
5'3"	111–124	121–135	131–147
5'4"	114–127	124–138	134–151
5'5"	117–130	127–141	137–155
5'6"	120–133	130–144	140–159
5'7"	123–136	133–147	143–163
5'8"	126–139	136–150	146–167
5'9"	129–142	139–153	149–170
5'10"	132–145	142–156	152–173
5'11"	135–148	145–159	155–176
6'0"	138–151	148–162	158–179

Ⓒ Metropolitan Life Insurance Company. www.metlife.com

Food Guide Pyramid

In 1992, the U.S. Food and Drug Administration and the Department of Health and Human Services created the Food Pyramid, containing six food groups. In the pyramid, foods that should be eaten more often are placed at the base, and those that should be eaten less frequently are at the top.

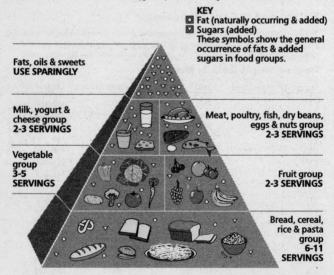

KEY
🔲 Fat (naturally occurring & added)
🔽 Sugars (added)
These symbols show the general occurrence of fats & added sugars in food groups.

Fats, oils & sweets USE SPARINGLY

Milk, yogurt & cheese group 2-3 SERVINGS

Meat, poultry, fish, dry beans, eggs & nuts group 2-3 SERVINGS

Vegetable group 3-5 SERVINGS

Fruit group 2-3 SERVINGS

Bread, cereal, rice & pasta group 6-11 SERVINGS

THE SCIENCES: *Health, Nutrition, Fitness*

Breads, cereal, rice, and pasta are at the bottom of the pyramid. The USDA recommends six to eleven servings of these foods daily. The next level recommends two to three servings of fruits and three to five servings of vegetables. The third level includes two to three servings of dairy, and two to three servings of meat or other proteins. Fats, oils, and sweets should be eaten sparingly.

What Is a Serving?

- Grains and starches: one slice bread; one ounce ready-to-eat cereal; one-half cup cooked cereal, rice, or pasta
- Vegetables: one cup raw leafy greens; three-quarters cup vegetable juice; one-half cup other chopped vegetables
- Fruits: one medium apple, banana, or orange; one melon wedge; one-half cup chopped fruits or berries; three-quarters cup fruit juice
- Dairy: one cup milk or yogurt; 1.5 ounces cheese
- Meat: two to three ounces cooked, lean meat, poultry or fish; one egg; one-half cup cooked beans; two tablespoons seeds or nuts

Recommended Daily Servings

	Children, Women, Older Adults	Teen Girls, Active Women, Most Men	Teen Boys, Active Men
Milk & Milk Products	2–4	2–4	2–4
Meat & Meat Alternatives	2	2	2
Vegetables	3	4	5
Fruits	2	3	4
Breads and Cereals	6	9	11
Total Fat, in grams*	36–53	49–73	62–93
Calories	about 1,600	about 2,200	about 2,800

*Fat should comprise 20–30% of calories consumed; 1 gram fat = 9 calories

⊙ U.S. Department of Agriculture. "Center for Nutrition Policy Promotion," www.usda.gov/cnpp/

Recommended Daily Allowances

The U.S. Department of Agriculture first developed the Recommended Daily Allowances (RDA) more than 50 years ago to provide a measure of "the levels of intake of essential nutrients that, on the basis of scientific knowledge, are judged by the Food and Nutrition Board to be adequate to meet the known nutrient needs of practically all healthy persons."

Since the RDA's inception, scientific knowledge about nutrition has changed significantly. A simple measure as defined above is no longer adequate. Contemporary nutrition concerns itself not only with preventing diseases caused by nutritional deficiency, but aims to reduce the risk of chronic diseases such as osteoporosis, cancer, and heart disease.

The USDA is in the process of revising its guidelines and will eventually replace the RDA with a new measurement standard, the Dietary Reference Intake (DRI). The DRI will comprise three levels of evaluation, including an average, a minimum, and a maximum recommended amount for each nutrient. Until the new standards are fully in place, a combination of the two will continue to be used, as reflected in the tables below.

1989 Recommended Daily Allowances (RDA)

(ages)	Children		Males			Females			Pregnant
	0–3	4–10	11–24	25–50	51+	11–24	25–50	51+	
Protein (g)	13–16	24–28	45–59	63	63	44–46	50	50	60
Vitamin A (µg)	375–400	500–700	1,000	1,000	1,000	800	800	800	800
Vitamin E (µg)	3–6	7	10	10	10	8	8	8	10
Vitamin K (µg)	5–15	20–30	45–70	80	80	45–60	65	65	65
Vitamin C (mg)	30–40	45	50–60	60	60	50–60	60	60	70
Thiamin (mg)	0.3–0.7	0.9–1.0	1.3–1.5	1.5	1.2	1.1	1.1	1.0	1.5
Riboflavin (mg)	0.4–0.8	1.1–1.2	1.5–1.8	1.7	1.4	1.3	1.3	1.2	1.6
Niacin (mg)	5–9	12–13	17–20	19	15	15	15	13	17
Vitamin B6 (mg)	0.3–1.0	1.1–1.4	1.7–2.0	2.0	2.0	1.4–1.6	1.6	1.6	2.2
Folate (µg)	25–50	75–100	150–200	200	200	150–180	180	180	400
Vitamin B12 (µg)	0.3–0.7	1.0–1.4	2.0	2.0	2.0	2.0	2.0	2.0	2.2
Iron (mg)	6–10	10	10–12	10	10	15	15	10	30
Zinc (mg)	5–10	10	15	15	15	12	12	12	15
Iodine (µg)	40–70	90–120	150	150	150	150	150	150	175
Selenium (µg)	10–20	20–30	40–70	70	70	45–55	55	55	65

1997 Dietary Reference Intake (DRI)

	Children		Males			Females			Pregnant
	0–3	4–10	11–24	25–50	51+	11–24	25–50	51+	
Vitamin D (µg)	5	5	5	5	10	5	5	10	*
Calcium (mg)	210–500	800	1,300	1,000	1,200	1,300	1,000	1,200	*
Phosphorus (mg)	100–460	500	1,250	700	700	1,250	700	700	*
Magnesium (mg)	30–80	130	240–410	400–420	420	240–360	310–320	320	+40
Fluoride (mg)	0.01–0.7	1.1	2.0–3.2	3.8	3.8	2.0–2.9	3.1	3.1	*

* values are the same as for other women of comparable age

⊙ U.S. Department of Agriculture. "Recommended Dietary Intakes," www.nal.usda.gov/fnic/dga/rda.pdf
Food and Nutrition Board, Institute of Medicine. "Frequently Asked Questions about the DRIs."
www.nas.edu/IOM/IOMhome.nsf/pages/FNB+FAQ+DRI

Vitamins and Minerals

Vitamins

Name	Organs and systems affected	Other health benefits
A (Beta Carotene)	body tissues, skin, mucous membranes, eyesight, bones, and teeth	reduces risk of lung and certain oral cancers
B1 (Thiamin)	metabolism, nervous system, muscles, heart	stabilizes appetite and aids in digestion of carbohydrates
B2 (Riboflavin)	vision, skin, nails, hair	metabolizes carbohydrates, fats, and proteins; helps form antibodies and red blood cells
B3 (Niacin)	skin, tongue, digestive system	reduces cholesterol and high blood pressure; improves circulation; metabolizes protein, sugar, and fat; prevents pellagra
B6 (Pyridoxine)	skin, central nervous system	helps break down amino acids and form antibodies; metabolizes fats and carbohydrates; helps remove excess fluid and maintain proper balance of sodium and phosphorus
B12 (Cobalamin)	nervous system and growth	assists in formation and regeneration of red blood cells; metabolizes carbohydrate, fats, and protein; aids calcium absorption
Pantothenic Acid	central nervous system, adrenal glands	aids in stress reduction, cell building, fighting infection; releases energy from carbohydrates, fats, and protein; helps body to utilize vitamins
Biotin	hair	aids in utilization of protein, folic acid, pantothenic acid, and vitamin B12
Folic Acid	formation of red blood cells	synthesizes DNA and RNA for cell growth and reproduction; aids in amino acid metabolism
Inositol	hair and formation of lecithin	assists in breakdown of fats and cholesterol reduction
Choline	liver, kidneys, gallbladder	facilitates nerve transmission, memory, fat and cholesterol control
PABA (Paraaminobenzoic Acid)	hair	aids in production of folic acid and red blood cells and in assimilation of pantothenic acid; has sun screen properties
C (Ascorbic Acid)	teeth, gums, bones, blood vessels	aids in healing wounds, resisting infection and preventing common colds and cancer; helps to synthesize collagen

Vitamins and Minerals *(cont.)*

Name	Organs and systems affected	Other health benefits
D	bones, teeth, nervous system, heart	improves absorption and utilization of calcium and phosphorus; antioxidant
E	cells, capillary walls	retards cellular aging; alleviates fatigue; prevents and dissolves blood clots; helps prevent sterility, muscular dystrophy, heart conditions; antioxidant
K	blood	assists in blood clotting

Minerals

Name	Organs and systems affected	Other health benefits
Calcium	bones and teeth	regulates heart rhythm, eases insomnia, nutrient absorption and blood clotting; maintains nerve and muscle function; lowers blood pressure and cholesterol levels; reduces risk of colon cancer
Chromium	digestive system	assists insulin in metabolizing sugar and stabilizing blood sugar levels; cleans arteries; transports amino acids; controls appetite
Copper		facilitates absorption and utilization of iron, oxidation of vitamin C and formation of elastin for muscles; helps red blood cell and bone formation
Fluorine	bones and teeth	
Iodine	thyroid gland	assists metabolism; regulates energy; burns excess fat
Iron		supports the making of hemoglobin and myoglobin; increases resistance to stress and disease; promotes good skin tone; prevents fatigue
Magnesium		helps metabolize calcium and vitamin C; regulates neuromuscular activity of heart and maintains heart rhythm; converts blood sugar to energy
Manganese		aids digestion, blood breakdown of amino acids, metabolism of vitamins B1 and E; triggers breakdown of fats and cholesterol;

		nourishes nerves and brain; enables normal skeletal development; maintains sex hormone production; antioxidant
Phosphorus	bones and teeth, kidneys, muscles, and heart	
Potassium	blood pressure, skin, heart, brain	preserves proper alkalinity of body fluids; stimulates kidneys to eliminate body wastes
Selenium	cell membranes	prevents free-radical generation; decreases risk of breast, colon, lung, and prostate cancer; preserves tissue elasticity; slows aging process; aids in treatment of dandruff; antioxidant
Zinc		synthesizes protein; heals wounds; aids in development of reproductive organs, prostate functions and male hormone activity; governs contraction of muscles; stabilizes blood and maintains body's alkaline balance; aids in normal tissue function and the digestion and metabolism of phosphorus; antioxidant

⊙ Feinstein, Alice, ed. *Prevention's Healing With Vitamins.* Emmaus, Penn.: Rodale, 1998.
  Murray, Michael T. *The Encyclopedia of Nutritional Supplements.* Rocklin, Calif.: Prima, 1996.

Diet Types

Diabetic: Ten to 20% of calories should come from protein, no more than 30% from fats, and the rest from carbohydrates. Eat frequently to stabilize blood-sugar levels.

Gout: To avoid purines, generally found in meat, poultry, fish, and shellfish, restrict to no more than seven ounces per day. An increased intake of carbohydrates is recommended.

Healthy Heart: Avoid foods high in fat, saturated fat, and cholesterol. No more than 30% of calories consumed should contain fat.

High-Calcium: To combat or halt osteoporosis, consume three to four calcium-rich foods per day, as well as calcium supplements.

High-Fiber: To treat some conditions of the intestinal tract, obtain more fiber from foods such as beans, lentils, whole-grain breads and cereals, fruits, and vegetables.

Lactose-Restricted: Avoid food that contains milk or other dairy products unless they are lactose-reduced. A lactase enzyme pill may assist in lactose toleration.

Low-Sodium: To combat hypertension, substitute herbs and low-sodium spices for table salt and avoid processed foods.

Low-Fiber: To treat some intestinal problems in order to decrease the amount of solid waste products, reduce intake of nuts, seeds, and raw fruits and vegetables.

Diet Types *(cont.)*

Reactive Hypoglycemia: Consume three regular meals and several snacks per day and severely restrict sugar intake.

Vegetarian: Meat, fish, and poultry—and sometimes dairy products—are excluded. Nutritional supplements may be necessary.

⊙ Applegate, Elizabeth. *Eat Your Way to a Healthy Heart.* Paramus, N.J.: Prentice Hall, 1999.

Colbin, Annemarie. *Food and Our Bones: The Natural Way to Prevent Osteoporosis.* New York: Plume, 1998.

International Food Information Council. "Coping with Lactose Intolerance," http://ificinfo.health.org/insight/fi1112c.htm

Food Additives

Food additives play a vital role in today's food supply. Because most Americans do not grow their own food, additives extend the shelf life of groceries, making it possible to obtain safe, wholesome, and tasty foods year-round.

Additives are used for five main reasons: to maintain product consistency, to improve or maintain nutritional value, to maintain palatability and wholesomeness, to provide leavening and control acidity/alkalinity, or to enhance flavor and color.

Some additives come from natural sources while others are man-made. Salt, baking soda, vanilla, and yeast are some of the most common. All food additives are regulated by federal authorities and various international organizations to ensure that foods are safe to eat and are accurately labeled.

Glossary of Terms

Anticaking and Free-Flow Agents prevent lumping, clustering, or caking in crystalline and finely divided powders; absorb water.

Antimicrobal Agents prevent the growth of microorganisms such as yeast, mold, and bacteria.

Antioxidants retard the oxidation of unsaturated fats and oils, colorings, and flavorings.

Bleaching or Maturing Agents are added to flour during or after milling to improve the color and baking qualities.

Chelating Agents trap trace amounts of metal atoms that would otherwise cause food to discolor or go rancid.

Colors provide or enhance the color of food.

Curing Agents impart color and flavor to foods, increase shelf stability.

Dough Conditioners modify the starch and/or protein (gluten) fractions of flour.

Drying Agents absorb moisture to maintain a "dry" environment for the food or ingredient.

Emulsifiers keep oil and water mixed together.

Enzymes are proteins that catalyze (speed up) reactions.

Firming Agents act on pectins to help them resist the softening that may accompany food processing (canning).

Flavor Enhancers accentuate the natural flavor of foods; usually used when very little of a natural ingredient is present.

Flavoring Agents add flavor or aroma or replace flavors lost in processing.

Formulation Aids help to produce the desired texture of the food.

Fumigants are used to control pests (insects, molds, etc.).

Humectants help foods to retain moisture.

Leavening Agents produce carbon dioxide (usually in baked products) to give a characteristic texture.

Lubricants are added to food-contact surfaces to prevent food from sticking.

Non-Nutritive Sweeteners provide the sweetness of sugar with less than 2% of the calories.

Nutrient Supplements provide essential nutrients for human metabolism.

Nutritive Sweeteners sweeten food, but add more than 2% of the calories of a sugar-sweetened product.

Oxidizing and Reducing Agents cause chemical changes (oxidize or reduce) to help make the product more acceptable, easier to process, or more stable.

pH Control Substances affect the acidity/alkalinity of a product or ingredient.

Processing Aids enhance the ability of a food ingredient to be processed into a desired end product.

Propellants and Aerating Agents provide force for the expulsion of a product or add "air" to a product.

Sequestrants combine with metal ions to prevent the metal from entering into unwanted reactions.

Solvents are used to separate one substance from another.

Stabilizers and Thickeners increase the viscosity of a solution to improve body, consistency, and prevent emulsions from separating.

Surface Active Agents modify the surface properties (surface tension) of liquid food ingredients to enhance characteristics such as whipping, foaming or anti-foaming, wetting, and dispersing.

Synergists interact with other food ingredients to produce an effect that is greater than the additive effect of the two ingredients alone.

Texturizers alter the viscosity and "feel" of food.

Thickening Agents absorb some of the liquid that is present in food, thereby making the food thicker.

⊙ U.S. Food and Drug Administration. "Food Additives," http://vm.cfsan.fda.gov/
  ~lrd/foodaddi.html

Food Labels

The definitions of terms on food labels are set by the U.S. Food and Drug Administration. Common terms are defined below.

Extra lean: In meat, poultry, and seafood, per serving: 5 g fat, 2 g saturated fat, and 95 mg cholesterol

Free: Must contain only trivial amounts of fat, saturated fat, cholesterol, sodium, sugars, or calories per serving. "Calorie free" means fewer than five calories; "sugar free" or "fat free" means less than 0.5 g.

Fresh: For food that is raw, has never been frozen or heated (other than blanched), and contains no preservatives

Healthy: Must be low in fat and contain limited amounts of cholesterol and sodium. A single-item food must provide at least 10% of vitamins A or C, iron, calcium, protein, or fiber and no more than 360 mg of sodium. A meal-type product must provide 10% of two or three of these vitamins or minerals or of protein or fiber and no more than 480 mg of sodium.

Lean: In meat, poultry, and seafood, per serving: 10 g fat, 4.5 g saturated fat, 95 mg cholesterol

Less: Contains 25% less of a nutrient or of calories than the reference food. For example, pretzels that have 25% less fat than potato chips could carry a "less" claim.

Food Labels (*cont.*)

Good source: Contains 10 to 19% of the Daily Value for a particular nutrient

High: Contains 20 percent or more of the Daily Value for a particular nutrient

Light: Contains one-third fewer calories or half the fat of the reference food. "Light in sodium" may be used when the sodium content has been reduced by at least 50%. Also used to describe such properties as texture and color.

Low: Must not exceed dietary guidelines for fat, saturated fat, cholesterol, sodium, or calories per serving. Low-fat: 3 g; low-saturated fat: 1 g; low-sodium: 140 mg; very low sodium: 35 mg; low-cholesterol: 20 mg (and 2 g of saturated fat); low-calorie: 40 calories.

More: Contains a nutrient that is at least 10 percent of the Daily Value more than the reference food

Not a significant source: Used when food contains less the following amounts, per serving: 5 calories from fat, 0.5 g of saturated fat, 2 mg of cholesterol, 1g of dietary fiber, 1 g of sugars, and two percent of the RDA for vitamins/ minerals

Percent fat free: Must accurately reflect the amount of fat present in 100 g of the food. If a food contains less than 0.5 g of fat per 100 g, the claim may be "100 percent fat free."

Reduced: Contains at least 25% less of a nutrient or of calories than the regular product

⊙ U.S. Food and Drug Administration. "A Food Labeling Guide," http://vm.cfsan.fda.gov/~dms/flg-toc.html

Poisoning

Children and adults can be poisoned by medicines and household products, lead, and carbon monoxide.

Protect your family by:

- Locking away dangerous substances like medicines, vitamins, beauty products, cleaning supplies, and pesticides, even if they are in child-resistant packaging.
- Keeping syrup of ipecac (which is available in drug stores) on hand in case of poisoning. Use it only after instructed to do so by a doctor or poison control center.

Emergency Action for Poisoning

If poison is inhaled, open all doors and windows and get the victim into the fresh air as quickly as possible. If the victim has stopped breathing, start artificial respiration.

If poison is on the skin, remove the victim's clothing and rinse the skin with water for at least 15 minutes and then wash the skin with soap and water and rinse again.

If poison is in the eye, rinse the eye by pouring lukewarm water into the eye for at least 15 minutes, with the victim blinking as often as possible. It is important that the eyelid not be forced open.

If poison is swallowed and the victim is awake, give water—nothing else—and call the poison center or doctor. If instructed to do so by a doctor or poison control personnel, administer syrup of ipecac.

After the emergency actions, call your area's poison control center:

Alabama

Alabama Poison Center
408-A Paul Bryant Drive
Tuscaloosa, AL 35401
800-462-0800 [AL only]; (205) 345-0600
Regional Poison Control Center
The Children's Hospital of Alabama
1600 - 7th Avenue South
Birmingham, AL 35233-1711
(205) 939-9201; (205) 939-9202;
  800-292-6678 [AL only];
  (205) 933-4050

Alaska

Anchorage Poison Control Center
3200 Providence Drive
Anchorage, AK 95519-6604
800-478-3193; (907) 261-3193

Arizona

*Arizona Poison and Drug Information
  Center*
Arizona Health Sciences Center
1501 N. Campbell Avenue, Rm. 1156
Tucson, AZ 85724
800-362-0101 [AZ only]; (520) 626-6016
Samaritan Regional Poison Center
1111 E. McDowell Road, Ancillary - 1
Phoenix, AZ 85006
(602) 253-3334; 800-362-0101 [AZ only]

Arkansas

*Arkansas Poison and Drug Information
  Center*
College of Pharmacy
University of Arkansas for Medical
  Sciences
4301 West Markham-Slot 522
Little Rock, AR 72205
800-376-4766

California

*California Poison Control System, Central
  Office*
University of California, San Francisco
School of Pharmacy, Box 1262
San Francisco, CA 94143
800-876-4766 [All of CA]

Colorado

Rocky Mountain Poison and Drug Center
8802 E. 9th Avenue
Denver, CO 80220-6800
(303) 629-1123

Connecticut

Connecticut Poison Control Center
University of Connecticut Health Center
263 Farmington Avenue
Farmington, CT 06030
800-343-2722 [CT only]; (203) 679-3056

Delaware

The Poison Control Center
3600 Sciences Center, Suite 220
Philadelphia, PA 19104-2641
(215) 386-2100; 800-722-7112

District of Columbia

National Capital Poison Center
3201 New Mexico Avenue, NW, Suite 310
Washington, DC 20016
(202) 625-3333; (202) 362-8563 [TTY]

Florida

Florida Poison Information Center
University Medical Center
University of Florida Health Science
  Center
655 West 8th Street
Jacksonville, FL 32209
(904) 549-4465; 800-282-3171 [FL only]
Florida Poison Information Center
University of Miami/Jackson Memorial
  Hospital
1611 NW 12th Avenue
Urgent Care Center Bldg., Rm. 219
Miami, FL 33136
800-282-3171 [FL only]
*The Florida Poison Information and
  Toxicology Resource Center*
Tampa General Hospital
P.O. Box 1289
Tampa, FL 33601
(813) 256-4444 [Tampa only];
  800-282-3171 [FL only]

Georgia

Georgia Poison Center
Hughes Spalding Children's Hospital
Grady Health Systems
80 Butler Street, SE
PO Box 26066
Atlanta, GA 30335-3801
800-282-5846 [GA only];
  (404) 616-9000

Hawaii

Hawaii Poison Center
1500 S. Beretania Street, Rm. 113
Honolulu, HI 96826
(808) 941-4411

Idaho

Idaho Poison Center
3092 Elder Street
Boise, ID 83720-0036
(208) 334-4570; 800-632-8000
  [ID only]

Poisoning (cont.)

Illinois

Illinois Poison Center
222 South Riverside Plaza, Suite 1900
Chicago, IL 60606
800-942-5969

Indiana

Indiana Poison Center
Methodist Hospital of Indiana
I-65 and 21st Street
P.O. Box 1367
Indianapolis, IN 46206-1367
800-382-9097 [IN only]; (317) 929-2323

Iowa

St. Luke's Poison Center
St. Luke's Regional Medical Center
2720 Stone Park Boulevard
Sioux City, IA 51104
(712) 277-2222; 800-352-2222
*Mid-Iowa Poison and Drug Information
Center*
Variety Club Poison and Drug
Information Center
Iowa Methodist Medical Center
1200 Pleasant Street
Des Moines, IA 50309
(515) 241-6254; 800-362-2327 [IA only]
Poison Control Center
The University of Iowa Hospitals and
Clinics
Pharmacy Department
200 Hawkins Drive
Iowa City, IA 52242
800-272-6477

Kansas

Mid-America Poison Control Center
University of Kansas Medical Center
3901 Rainbow Blvd., Room B-400
Kansas City, KS 66160-7231
(913) 588-6633; 800-332-6633 [KS only]

Kentucky

*Kentucky Regional Poison Center of Kosair
Children's Hospital*
Medical Towers South, Suite 572
P.O. Box 35070
Louisville, KY 40232-5070
(502) 589-8222; 800-722-5725 [KY only]

Louisiana

*Louisiana Drug and Poison Information
Center*
Northeast Louisiana University
Sugar Hall
Monroe, LA 71209-6430
800-256-9822 [LA only]; (318) 362-5393

Maine

Maine Poison Control Center
Maine Medical Center
Department of Emergency Medicine
22 Bramhall Street
Portland, ME 04102
(207) 871-2950; 800-442-6305 [ME only]

Maryland

Maryland Poison Center
University of Maryland School of
Pharmacy
20 N. Pine Street
Baltimore, MD 21201
(410) 528-7701; 800-492-2414 [MD only]

Massachusetts

Massachusetts Poison Control System
300 Longwood Avenue
Boston, MA 02115
(617) 232-2120; 800-682-9211

Michigan

Blodgett Regional Poison Center
1840 Wealthy SE
Grand Rapids, MI 49506-2968
800-POISON1; 800-356-3232 [TTY]
Poison Control Center
Children's Hospital of Michigan
Harper Professional Office Bldg.
4160 John Road, Suite 425
Detroit, MI 48201
(313) 745-5711; 800-764-7661
Marquette General Hospital
420 W. Magnetic Street
Marquette, MI 49855
(906) 225-3497; 800-562-9781

Minnesota

Hennepin Regional Poison Center
Hennepin County Medical Center
701 Park Avenue
Minneapolis, MN 55415
(612) 347-3141; (612) 337-7387 [Petline];
(612) 337-7474 [TDD]
Minnesota Regional Poison Center
8100 34th Avenue S.
P.O. Box 1309
Minneapolis, MN 55440-1309
(612) 221-2113

Mississippi

Mississippi Regional Poison Control Center
University of Mississippi Medical Center
2500 North State Street
Jackson, MS 39216-4505
(601) 354-7660

Missouri

Cardinal Glennon Children's Hospital
Regional Poison Center
1465 S. Grand Boulevard
St. Louis, MO 63104
(314) 772-5200; 800-366-8888;
    800-392-9111
Children's Mercy Hospital
2401 Gillham Road
Kansas City, MO 64108
(816) 234-3430

Montana

Rocky Mountain Poison and Drug Center
8802 E. 9th Avenue
Denver, CO 80220-6800
(303) 629-1123

Nebraska

The Poison Center
8301 Dodge Street
Omaha, NE 68114
(402) 390-5555 [Omaha]; 800-955-9119
    [NE & WY]

Nevada

Rocky Mountain Poison and Drug Center
8802 E. 9th Avenue
Denver, CO 80220-6800
(303) 629-1123;
    800-332-3073 [COLO WATTS];
    800-525-5042 [MONT WATTS];
    800-446-6179 [NEV WATTS];
    (303) 739-1127 [TTY]

New Hampshire

New Hampshire Poison Information Center
Dartmouth-Hitchcock Medical Center
One Medical Center Drive
Lebanon, NH 03756
(603) 650-8000; (603) 650-5000
    [11pm-8am]; 800-562-8236 [NH only]

New Jersey

New Jersey Poison Information and
    Education System
201 Lyons Avenue
Newark, NJ 07112
800-POISON1 [800-764-7661]

New Mexico

New Mexico Poison and Drug Information
    Center
University of New Mexico
Health Sciences Library, Room 125
Albuquerque, NM 87131-1076
(505) 843-2551; 800-432-6866 [NM only]

New York

Central New York Poison Control Center
SUNY Health Science Center
750 E. Adams Street
Syracuse, NY 13210
(315) 476-4766; 800-252-5655
Finger Lakes Regional Poison Center
University of Rochester Medical Center
601 Elmwood Avenue, Box 321,
    Rm. G-3275
Rochester, NY 14642
(716) 275-5151; 800-333-0542
Hudson Valley Regional Poison Center
Phelps Memorial Hospital Center
701 North Broadway
North Tarrytown, NY 10591
800-336-6997; (914) 366-3030
Long Island Regional Poison Control Center
Winthrop University Hospital
259 First Street
Mineola, NY 11501
(516) 542-2323
New York City Poison Control Center
NYC Department of Health
455 First Avenue, Rm. 123
New York, NY 10016
(212) 340-4494; (212) POISONS;
    (212) 689-9014 [TDD]
Western New York Regional Poison Control
    Center
Children's Hospital of Buffalo
219 Bryant Street
Buffalo, NY 14222
(716) 878-7654, also extensions 7655,
    7856, 7857

North Carolina

Carolinas Poison Center
1000 Blythe Boulevard
P.O. Box 32861
Charlotte, NC 28232-2861
(704) 355-4000; 800-84-TOXIN
    [800-848-6946]
Catawba Memorial Hospital Poison Control
    Center
Pharmacy Department
810 Fairgrove Church Road
Hickory, NC 28602
(704) 322-6649
Duke Poison Control Center
North Carolina Regional Center
Box 3007
Duke University
Durham, NC 27710
(919) 684-8111; 800-672-1697 [NC only]

Poisoning (cont.)

North Carolina (cont.)

Triad Poison Center
1200 N. Elm Street
Greensboro, NC 27401-1020
(910) 574-8105; 800-953-4001 [NC only]

North Dakota

North Dakota Poison Information Center
MeritCare Medical Center
720 4th Street North
Fargo, ND 58122
(701) 234-5575; 800-732-2200
[ND, MN, SD only]

Ohio

Akron Regional Poison Center
1 Perkins Square
Akron, OH 44308
(216) 379-8562; 800-362-9922
[OH only]; (216) 379-8446 [TTY]
Bethesda Poison Control Center
2951 Maple Avenue
Zanesville, OH 43701
(614) 454-4221
Central Ohio Poison Center
700 Children's Drive
Columbus, OH 43205-2696
(614) 228-1323; 800-682-7625;
(614) 228-2272 [TTY]; (614) 461-2012
Cincinnati Drug & Poison Information and
Regional Poison Control System
P.O. Box 670144
Cincinnati, OH 45267-0144
(513) 558-5111; 800-872-5111 [OH only];
800-253-7955 [TTY]
Greater Cleveland Poison Control Center
11100 Euclid Avenue
Cleveland, OH 44106
(216) 231-4455
Medical College of Ohio Poison and Drug
Information Center
3000 Arlington Avenue
Toledo, OH 43614
(419) 381-3897; 800-589-3897
[419 area code only]
Northeast Ohio Poison Education/
Information Center
1320 Timken Mercy Drive NW
Canton, OH 44708
800-456-8662 [OH only]

Oklahoma

Oklahoma Poison Control Center
940 N.E. 13th Street, Rm. 3N118
Oklahoma, OK 73104
(405) 271-5454; 800-522-4611
[OK only]

Oregon

Oregon Poison Center
Oregon Health Sciences University
3181 SW Sam Jackson Park Road,
CB550
Portland, OR 97201
(503) 494-8968; 800-452-7165
[OR only]

Pennsylvania

Central Pennsylvania Poison Center
University Hospital
Milton S. Hershey Medical Center
Hershey, PA 17033-0850
800-521-6110; (717) 531-6111
The Poison Control Center
3600 Sciences Center, Suite 220
Philadelphia, PA 19104-2641
(215) 386-2100
Pittsburgh Poison Center
3705 Fifth Avenue
Pittsburgh, PA 15213
(412) 681-6669; 800-722-7112

Rhode Island

Rhode Island Poison Center
593 Eddy Street
Providence, RI 02903
(401) 444-5727

South Carolina

Palmetto Poison Center
College of Pharmacy
University of South Carolina
Columbia, SC 29208
(803) 765-7359; 800-922-1117
[SC only]; (706) 724-5050;
(803) 777-1117

South Dakota

McKennan Poison Control Center
Box 5045
800 E. 21st Street
Sioux Falls, SD 57117-5045
(605) 336-3894; 800-952-0123;
800-843-0505

Tennessee

Middle Tennessee Poison Center
The Center for Clinical Toxicology
Vanderbilt University Medical Center
1161 21st Avenue South
501 Oxford House
Nashville, TN 37232-4632
(615) 936-2034 [local]; 800-288-9999
[regional]; (615) 322-0157 [TDD]

Southern Poison Center, Inc.
847 Monroe Avenue, Suite 230
Memphis, TN 38163
(901) 528-6048; 800-228-9999
[TN only]

Texas
Central Texas Poison Center
Scott & White Memorial Clinic &
  Hospital
2401 S. 31st Street
Temple, TX 76508
(817) 774-2005; 800-POISON1
  [800-764-7661] [TX only]
North Texas Poison Center
Texas Poison Center Network at
  Parkland Memorial Hospital
5201 Harry Hines Boulevard
P.O. Box 35926
Dallas, TX 75235
800-POISON1 [800-764-7661]
  [TX only]
South Texas Poison Center
7703 Floyd Curl Drive
San Antonio, TX 78284-7834
800-POISON1 [800-764-7661]
  [TX only]
Texas Poison Control Network
P.O. Box 1110, 1501 S. Coulter
Amarillo, TX 79175
800-POISON1 [800-764-7661]
  [TX only]
Texas Poison Control Network
Southeast Texas Poison Center
The University of Texas Medical Branch
301 University Avenue
Galveston, TX 77555-1175
(409)-765-1420 [Galveston];
  (713) 654-1701 [Houston];
800-POISON1 [800-764-7661]
  [TX only]
West Texas Regional Poison Center
4815 Alameda Avenue
El Paso, TX 79905
800-POISON1 [800-764-7661]
  [TX only]

Utah
Utah Poison Control Center
410 Chipeta Way, Suite 230
Salt Lake City, UT 84108
(801) 581-2151; 800-456-7707 [UT only]

Vermont
Vermont Poison Center
Fletcher Allen Health Care
111 Colchester Avenue
Burlington, VT 05401
(802) 658-3456

Virginia
Blue Ridge Poison Center
University of Virginia
Blue Ridge Hospital
Box 67
Charlottesville, VA 22901
(804) 924-5543; 800-451-1428
Virginia Poison Center
401 N. 12th Street
Virginia Commonwealth University
Richmond, VA 23298-0522
(804) 828-9123 [Richmond];
  800-552-6337 [VA only]

Washington
Washington Poison Center
155 N.E. 100th Street, Suite 400
Seattle, WA 98125
(206) 526-2121; 800-732-6985 [WA only];
  (206) 517-2394 [TDD]; (206) 517-2394
  [TDD; WA only]

West Virginia
West Virginia Poison Center
3110 MacCorkle Avenue, SE
Charleston, WV 25304
800-642-3625 [WV only]; (304) 348-4211

Wisconsin
Poison Center of Eastern Wisconsin
Children's Hospital of Wisconsin
P.O. Box 1997
Milwaukee, WI 53201
(414) 266-2222; 800-815-8855 [WI only]
University of Wisconsin Hospital Regional
  Poison Center
E5/238 CSC
600 Highland Avenue
Madison, WI 53792
(608) 262-3702; 800-815-8855 [WI only]

Wyoming
The Poison Center
8301 Dodge Street
Omaha, NE 68114
(402) 390-5555 [Omaha NE];
  800-955-9119 [NE & WY]

⊙ American Association of Poison Control Centers. www.aapcc.org/
  Kids Health. "U.S. Poison Control Centers," www.kidshealth.org/parent/
  firstaid_safe/home/poison_control_center.html
  U.S. Department of Housing and Urban Development. "Are Your Children Safe
  from Poisons?" www.hud.gov/poison.html

World Time Zones

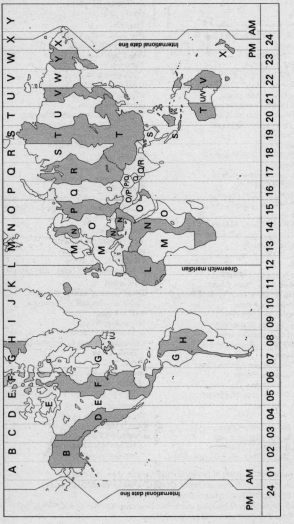

© U.S. Naval Observatory. "World Time Zone Map." http://aa.usno.navy.mil/AA/faq/docs/world_tzones.html

U.S. Times Zones by State

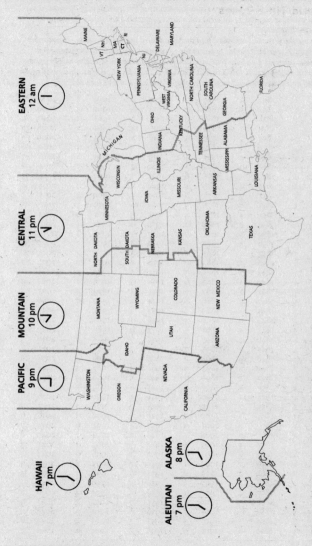

© Intrasearch.com. "Standard Time Zones for the US," www.intrasearch.com/tzone.htm World Time Zones, "USA Time Zones Map," www.worldtimezone.com/time-usa2.htm

Perpetual Calendar

A perpetual calendar lets you find the day of the week for any date in any year, past, present, or future. Since January 1 may fall on any of the seven days of the week, a perpetual calendar requires 14 different calendars to cover all possibilities, including leap and non–leap years.

To use the perpetual calendar, find the year desired in the table below. The number next to each year corresponds to one of the 14 calendars on the following pages. For example, calendar 9 (a leap year in which January 1 fell on a Monday) was in use during 1776, meaning that July 4 of that year was a Thursday. Calendar 9 was used again in 1816 and 1844 and was last used in 1996. Calendar 4 will be used in 2002.

1775	1	1821	2	1867	3	1913	4	1959	5	2005	7
1776	9	1822	3	1868	11	1914	5	1960	13	2006	1
1777	4	1823	4	1869	6	1915	6	1961	1	2007	2
1778	5	1824	12	1870	7	1916	14	1962	2	2008	10
1779	6	1825	7	1871	1	1917	2	1963	3	2009	5
1780	14	1826	1	1872	9	1918	3	1964	11	2010	6
1781	2	1827	2	1873	4	1919	4	1965	6	2011	7
1782	3	1828	10	1874	5	1920	12	1966	7	2012	8
1783	4	1829	5	1875	6	1921	7	1967	1	2013	3
1784	12	1830	6	1876	14	1922	1	1968	9	2014	4
1785	7	1831	7	1877	2	1923	2	1969	4	2015	5
1786	1	1832	8	1878	3	1924	10	1970	5	2016	13
1787	2	1833	3	1879	4	1925	5	1971	6	2017	1
1788	10	1834	4	1880	12	1926	6	1972	14	2018	2
1789	5	1835	5	1881	7	1927	7	1973	2	2019	3
1790	6	1836	13	1882	1	1928	8	1974	3	2020	11
1791	7	1837	1	1883	2	1929	3	1975	4	2021	6
1792	8	1838	2	1884	10	1930	4	1976	12	2022	7
1793	3	1839	3	1885	5	1931	5	1977	7	2023	1
1794	4	1840	11	1886	6	1932	13	1978	1	2024	9
1795	5	1841	6	1887	7	1933	1	1979	2	2025	4
1796	13	1842	7	1888	8	1934	2	1980	10	2026	5
1797	1	1843	1	1889	3	1935	3	1981	5	2027	6
1798	2	1844	9	1890	4	1936	11	1982	6	2028	14
1799	3	1845	4	1891	5	1937	6	1983	7	2029	2
1800	4	1846	5	1892	13	1938	7	1984	8	2030	3
1801	5	1847	6	1893	1	1939	1	1985	3	2031	4
1802	6	1848	14	1894	2	1940	9	1986	4	2032	12
1803	7	1849	2	1895	3	1941	4	1987	5	2033	7
1804	8	1850	3	1896	11	1942	5	1988	13	2034	1
1805	3	1851	4	1897	6	1943	6	1989	1	2035	2
1806	4	1852	12	1898	7	1944	14	1990	2	2036	10
1807	5	1853	7	1899	1	1945	2	1991	3	2037	5
1808	13	1854	1	1900	2	1946	3	1992	11	2038	6
1809	1	1855	2	1901	3	1947	4	1993	6	2039	7
1810	2	1856	10	1902	4	1948	12	1994	7	2040	8
1811	3	1857	5	1903	5	1949	7	1995	1	2041	3
1812	11	1858	6	1904	13	1950	1	1996	9	2042	4
1813	6	1859	7	1905	1	1951	2	1997	4	2043	5
1814	7	1860	8	1906	2	1952	10	1998	5	2044	13
1815	1	1861	3	1907	3	1953	5	1999	6	2045	1
1816	9	1862	4	1908	11	1954	6	2000	14	2046	2
1817	4	1863	5	1909	6	1955	7	2001	2	2047	3
1818	5	1864	13	1910	7	1956	8	2002	3	2048	11
1819	6	1865	1	1911	1	1957	3	2003	4	2049	6
1820	14	1866	2	1912	9	1958	4	2004	12	2050	7

1

January
S	M	T	W	T	F	S
1	2	3	4	5	6	7
8	9	10	11	12	13	14
15	16	17	18	19	20	21
22	23	24	25	26	27	28
29	30	31				

February
S	M	T	W	T	F	S
				1	2	3
4	5	6	7	8	9	10
11	12	13	14	15	16	17
18	19	20	21	22	23	24
25	26	27	28			

March
S	M	T	W	T	F	S
			1	2	3	4
5	6	7	8	9	10	11
12	13	14	15	16	17	18
19	20	21	22	23	24	25
26	27	28	29	30	31	

April
S	M	T	W	T	F	S
						1
2	3	4	5	6	7	8
9	10	11	12	13	14	15
16	17	18	19	20	21	22
23	24	25	26	27	28	29
30						

May
S	M	T	W	T	F	S
	1	2	3	4	5	6
7	8	9	10	11	12	13
14	15	16	17	18	19	20
21	22	23	24	25	26	27
28	29	30	31			

June
S	M	T	W	T	F	S
				1	2	3
4	5	6	7	8	9	10
11	12	13	14	15	16	17
18	19	20	21	22	23	24
25	26	27	28	29	30	

July
S	M	T	W	T	F	S
						1
2	3	4	5	6	7	8
9	10	11	12	13	14	15
16	17	18	19	20	21	22
23	24	25	26	27	28	29
30	31					

August
S	M	T	W	T	F	S
		1	2	3	4	5
6	7	8	9	10	11	12
13	14	15	16	17	18	19
20	21	22	23	24	25	26
27	28	29	30	31		

September
S	M	T	W	T	F	S
					1	2
3	4	5	6	7	8	9
10	11	12	13	14	15	16
17	18	19	20	21	22	23
24	25	26	27	28	29	30

October
S	M	T	W	T	F	S
1	2	3	4	5	6	7
8	9	10	11	12	13	14
15	16	17	18	19	20	21
22	23	24	25	26	27	28
29	30	31				

November
S	M	T	W	T	F	S
			1	2	3	4
5	6	7	8	9	10	11
12	13	14	15	16	17	18
19	20	21	22	23	24	25
26	27	28	29	30		

December
S	M	T	W	T	F	S
					1	2
3	4	5	6	7	8	9
10	11	12	13	14	15	16
17	18	19	20	21	22	23
24	25	26	27	28	29	30
31						

2

January
S	M	T	W	T	F	S
	1	2	3	4	5	6
7	8	9	10	11	12	13
14	15	16	17	18	19	20
21	22	23	24	25	26	27
28	29	30	31			

February
S	M	T	W	T	F	S
				1	2	3
4	5	6	7	8	9	10
11	12	13	14	15	16	17
18	19	20	21	22	23	24
25	26	27	28			

March
S	M	T	W	T	F	S
				1	2	3
4	5	6	7	8	9	10
11	12	13	14	15	16	17
18	19	20	21	22	23	24
25	26	27	28	29	30	31

April
S	M	T	W	T	F	S
1	2	3	4	5	6	7
8	9	10	11	12	13	14
15	16	17	18	19	20	21
22	23	24	25	26	27	28
29	30					

May
S	M	T	W	T	F	S
		1	2	3	4	5
6	7	8	9	10	11	12
13	14	15	16	17	18	19
20	21	22	23	24	25	26
27	28	29	30	31		

June
S	M	T	W	T	F	S
					1	2
3	4	5	6	7	8	9
10	11	12	13	14	15	16
17	18	19	20	21	22	23
24	25	26	27	28	29	30

July
S	M	T	W	T	F	S
1	2	3	4	5	6	7
8	9	10	11	12	13	14
15	16	17	18	19	20	21
22	23	24	25	26	27	28
29	30	31				

August
S	M	T	W	T	F	S
				1	2	3
4	5	6	7	8	9	10
11	12	13	14	15	16	17
18	19	20	21	22	23	24
25	26	27	28	29	30	31

September
S	M	T	W	T	F	S
						1
2	3	4	5	6	7	8
9	10	11	12	13	14	15
16	17	18	19	20	21	22
23	24	25	26	27	28	29
30						

October
S	M	T	W	T	F	S
	1	2	3	4	5	6
7	8	9	10	11	12	13
14	15	16	17	18	19	20
21	22	23	24	25	26	27
28	29	30	31			

November
S	M	T	W	T	F	S
				1	2	3
4	5	6	7	8	9	10
11	12	13	14	15	16	17
18	19	20	21	22	23	24
25	26	27	28	29	30	

December
S	M	T	W	T	F	S
						1
2	3	4	5	6	7	8
9	10	11	12	13	14	15
16	17	18	19	20	21	22
23	24	25	26	27	28	29
30	31					

3

January
S	M	T	W	T	F	S
		1	2	3	4	5
6	7	8	9	10	11	12
13	14	15	16	17	18	19
20	21	22	23	24	25	26
27	28	29	30	31		

February
S	M	T	W	T	F	S
					1	2
3	4	5	6	7	8	9
10	11	12	13	14	15	16
17	18	19	20	21	22	23
24	25	26	27	28		

March
S	M	T	W	T	F	S
					1	2
3	4	5	6	7	8	9
10	11	12	13	14	15	16
17	18	19	20	21	22	23
24	25	26	27	28	29	30
31						

April
S	M	T	W	T	F	S
	1	2	3	4	5	6
7	8	9	10	11	12	13
14	15	16	17	18	19	20
21	22	23	24	25	26	27
28	29	30				

May
S	M	T	W	T	F	S
			1	2	3	4
5	6	7	8	9	10	11
12	13	14	15	16	17	18
19	20	21	22	23	24	25
26	27	28	29	30	31	

June
S	M	T	W	T	F	S
						1
2	3	4	5	6	7	8
9	10	11	12	13	14	15
16	17	18	19	20	21	22
23	24	25	26	27	28	29
30						

July
S	M	T	W	T	F	S
	1	2	3	4	5	6
7	8	9	10	11	12	13
14	15	16	17	18	19	20
21	22	23	24	25	26	27
28	29	30	31			

August
S	M	T	W	T	F	S
				1	2	3
4	5	6	7	8	9	10
11	12	13	14	15	16	17
18	19	20	21	22	23	24
25	26	27	28	29	30	31

September
S	M	T	W	T	F	S
1	2	3	4	5	6	7
8	9	10	11	12	13	14
15	16	17	18	19	20	21
22	23	24	25	26	27	28
29	30					

October
S	M	T	W	T	F	S
		1	2	3	4	5
6	7	8	9	10	11	12
13	14	15	16	17	18	19
20	21	22	23	24	25	26
27	28	29	30	31		

November
S	M	T	W	T	F	S
					1	2
3	4	5	6	7	8	9
10	11	12	13	14	15	16
17	18	19	20	21	22	23
24	25	26	27	28	29	30

December
S	M	T	W	T	F	S
1	2	3	4	5	6	7
8	9	10	11	12	13	14
15	16	17	18	19	20	21
22	23	24	25	26	27	28
29	30	31				

4

January
S	M	T	W	T	F	S
			1	2	3	4
5	6	7	8	9	10	11
12	13	14	15	16	17	18
19	20	21	22	23	24	25
26	27	28	29	30	31	

February
S	M	T	W	T	F	S
						1
2	3	4	5	6	7	8
9	10	11	12	13	14	15
16	17	18	19	20	21	22
23	24	25	26	27	28	

March
S	M	T	W	T	F	S
						1
2	3	4	5	6	7	8
9	10	11	12	13	14	15
16	17	18	19	20	21	22
23	24	25	26	27	28	29
30	31					

April
S	M	T	W	T	F	S
		1	2	3	4	5
6	7	8	9	10	11	12
13	14	15	16	17	18	19
20	21	22	23	24	25	26
27	28	29	30			

May
S	M	T	W	T	F	S
				1	2	3
4	5	6	7	8	9	10
11	12	13	14	15	16	17
18	19	20	21	22	23	24
25	26	27	28	29	30	31

June
S	M	T	W	T	F	S
1	2	3	4	5	6	7
8	9	10	11	12	13	14
15	16	17	18	19	20	21
22	23	24	25	26	27	28
29	30					

July
S	M	T	W	T	F	S
		1	2	3	4	5
6	7	8	9	10	11	12
13	14	15	16	17	18	19
20	21	22	23	24	25	26
27	28	29	30	31		

August
S	M	T	W	T	F	S
					1	2
3	4	5	6	7	8	9
10	11	12	13	14	15	16
17	18	19	20	21	22	23
24	25	26	27	28	29	30
31						

September
S	M	T	W	T	F	S
	1	2	3	4	5	6
7	8	9	10	11	12	13
14	15	16	17	18	19	20
21	22	23	24	25	26	27
28	29	30				

October
S	M	T	W	T	F	S
			1	2	3	4
5	6	7	8	9	10	11
12	13	14	15	16	17	18
19	20	21	22	23	24	25
26	27	28	29	30	31	

November
S	M	T	W	T	F	S
						1
2	3	4	5	6	7	8
9	10	11	12	13	14	15
16	17	18	19	20	21	22
23	24	25	26	27	28	29
30						

December
S	M	T	W	T	F	S
	1	2	3	4	5	6
7	8	9	10	11	12	13
14	15	16	17	18	19	20
21	22	23	24	25	26	27
28	29	30	31			

5

January
S	M	T	W	T	F	S
				1	2	3
4	5	6	7	8	9	10
11	12	13	14	15	16	17
18	19	20	21	22	23	24
25	26	27	28	29	30	31

February
S	M	T	W	T	F	S
1	2	3	4	5	6	7
8	9	10	11	12	13	14
15	16	17	18	19	20	21
22	23	24	25	26	27	28

March
S	M	T	W	T	F	S
1	2	3	4	5	6	7
8	9	10	11	12	13	14
15	16	17	18	19	20	21
22	23	24	25	26	27	28
29	30	31				

April
S	M	T	W	T	F	S
			1	2	3	4
5	6	7	8	9	10	11
12	13	14	15	16	17	18
19	20	21	22	23	24	25
26	27	28	29	30		

May
S	M	T	W	T	F	S
					1	2
3	4	5	6	7	8	9
10	11	12	13	14	15	16
17	18	19	20	21	22	23
24	25	26	27	28	29	30
31						

June
S	M	T	W	T	F	S
	1	2	3	4	5	6
7	8	9	10	11	12	13
14	15	16	17	18	19	20
21	22	23	24	25	26	27
28	29	30				

July
S	M	T	W	T	F	S
			1	2	3	4
5	6	7	8	9	10	11
12	13	14	15	16	17	18
19	20	21	22	23	24	25
26	27	28	29	30	31	

August
S	M	T	W	T	F	S
						1
2	3	4	5	6	7	8
9	10	11	12	13	14	15
16	17	18	19	20	21	22
23	24	25	26	27	28	29
30	31					

September
S	M	T	W	T	F	S
		1	2	3	4	5
6	7	8	9	10	11	12
13	14	15	16	17	18	19
20	21	22	23	24	25	26
27	28	29	30			

October
S	M	T	W	T	F	S
				1	2	3
4	5	6	7	8	9	10
11	12	13	14	15	16	17
18	19	20	21	22	23	24
25	26	27	28	29	30	31

November
S	M	T	W	T	F	S
1	2	3	4	5	6	7
8	9	10	11	12	13	14
15	16	17	18	19	20	21
22	23	24	25	26	27	28
29	30					

December
S	M	T	W	T	F	S
		1	2	3	4	5
6	7	8	9	10	11	12
13	14	15	16	17	18	19
20	21	22	23	24	25	26
27	28	29	30	31		

6

January
S	M	T	W	T	F	S
					1	2
3	4	5	6	7	8	9
10	11	12	13	14	15	16
17	18	19	20	21	22	23
24	25	26	27	28	29	30
31						

February
S	M	T	W	T	F	S
	1	2	3	4	5	6
7	8	9	10	11	12	13
14	15	16	17	18	19	20
21	22	23	24	25	26	27
28						

March
S	M	T	W	T	F	S
	1	2	3	4	5	6
7	8	9	10	11	12	13
14	15	16	17	18	19	20
21	22	23	24	25	26	27
28	29	30	31			

April
S	M	T	W	T	F	S
				1	2	3
4	5	6	7	8	9	10
11	12	13	14	15	16	17
18	19	20	21	22	23	24
25	26	27	28	29	30	

May
S	M	T	W	T	F	S
						1
2	3	4	5	6	7	8
9	10	11	12	13	14	15
16	17	18	19	20	21	22
23	24	25	26	27	28	29
30	31					

June
S	M	T	W	T	F	S
	1	2	3	4	5	
6	7	8	9	10	11	12
13	14	15	16	17	18	19
20	21	22	23	24	25	26
27	28	29	30			

July
S	M	T	W	T	F	S
				1	2	3
4	5	6	7	8	9	10
11	12	13	14	15	16	17
18	19	20	21	22	23	24
25	26	27	28	29	30	31

August
S	M	T	W	T	F	S
1	2	3	4	5	6	7
8	9	10	11	12	13	14
15	16	17	18	19	20	21
22	23	24	25	26	27	28
29	30	31				

September
S	M	T	W	T	F	S
			1	2	3	4
5	6	7	8	9	10	11
12	13	14	15	16	17	18
19	20	21	22	23	24	25
26	27	28	29	30		

October
S	M	T	W	T	F	S
					1	2
3	4	5	6	7	8	9
10	11	12	13	14	15	16
17	18	19	20	21	22	23
24	25	26	27	28	29	30
31						

November
S	M	T	W	T	F	S
	1	2	3	4	5	6
7	8	9	10	11	12	13
14	15	16	17	18	19	20
21	22	23	24	25	26	27
28	29	30				

December
S	M	T	W	T	F	S
			1	2	3	4
5	6	7	8	9	10	11
12	13	14	15	16	17	18
19	20	21	22	23	24	25
26	27	28	29	30	31	

7

January
S	M	T	W	T	F	S
						1
2	3	4	5	6	7	8
9	10	11	12	13	14	15
16	17	18	19	20	21	22
23	24	25	26	27	28	29
30	31					

February
S	M	T	W	T	F	S
	1	2	3	4	5	6
7	8	9	10	11	12	13
14	15	16	17	18	19	20
21	22	23	24	25	26	27
28						

March
S	M	T	W	T	F	S
		1	2	3	4	5
6	7	8	9	10	11	12
13	14	15	16	17	18	19
20	21	22	23	24	25	26
27	28	29	30	31		

April
S	M	T	W	T	F	S
					1	2
3	4	5	6	7	8	9
10	11	12	13	14	15	16
17	18	19	20	21	22	23
24	25	26	27	28	29	30

May
S	M	T	W	T	F	S
1	2	3	4	5	6	7
8	9	10	11	12	13	14
15	16	17	18	19	20	21
22	23	24	25	26	27	28
29	30	31				

June
S	M	T	W	T	F	S
			1	2	3	4
5	6	7	8	9	10	11
12	13	14	15	16	17	18
19	20	21	22	23	24	25
26	27	28	29	30		

July
S	M	T	W	T	F	S
					1	2
3	4	5	6	7	8	9
10	11	12	13	14	15	16
17	18	19	20	21	22	23
24	25	26	27	28	29	30
31						

August
S	M	T	W	T	F	S
	1	2	3	4	5	6
7	8	9	10	11	12	13
14	15	16	17	18	19	20
21	22	23	24	25	26	27
28	29	30	31			

September
S	M	T	W	T	F	S
				1	2	3
4	5	6	7	8	9	10
11	12	13	14	15	16	17
18	19	20	21	22	23	24
25	26	27	28	29	30	

October
S	M	T	W	T	F	S
						1
2	3	4	5	6	7	8
9	10	11	12	13	14	15
16	17	18	19	20	21	22
23	24	25	26	27	28	29
30	31					

November
S	M	T	W	T	F	S
	1	2	3	4	5	
6	7	8	9	10	11	12
13	14	15	16	17	18	19
20	21	22	23	24	25	26
27	28	29	30			

December
S	M	T	W	T	F	S
				1	2	3
4	5	6	7	8	9	10
11	12	13	14	15	16	17
18	19	20	21	22	23	24
25	26	27	28	29	30	31

8

January
S	M	T	W	T	F	S
1	2	3	4	5	6	7
8	9	10	11	12	13	14
15	16	17	18	19	20	21
22	23	24	25	26	27	28
29	30	31				

February
S	M	T	W	T	F	S
			1	2	3	4
5	6	7	8	9	10	11
12	13	14	15	16	17	18
19	20	21	22	23	24	25
26	27	28	29			

March
S	M	T	W	T	F	S
				1	2	3
4	5	6	7	8	9	10
11	12	13	14	15	16	17
18	19	20	21	22	23	24
25	26	27	28	29	30	31

April
S	M	T	W	T	F	S
1	2	3	4	5	6	7
8	9	10	11	12	13	14
15	16	17	18	19	20	21
22	23	24	25	26	27	28
29	30					

May
S	M	T	W	T	F	S
	1	2	3	4	5	
6	7	8	9	10	11	12
13	14	15	16	17	18	19
20	21	22	23	24	25	26
27	28	29	30	31		

June
S	M	T	W	T	F	S
					1	2
3	4	5	6	7	8	9
10	11	12	13	14	15	16
17	18	19	20	21	22	23
24	25	26	27	28	29	30

July
S	M	T	W	T	F	S
1	2	3	4	5	6	7
8	9	10	11	12	13	14
15	16	17	18	19	20	21
22	23	24	25	26	27	28
29	30	31				

August
S	M	T	W	T	F	S
		1	2	3	4	
5	6	7	8	9	10	11
12	13	14	15	16	17	18
19	20	21	22	23	24	25
26	27	28	29	30	31	

September
S	M	T	W	T	F	S
						1
2	3	4	5	6	7	8
9	10	11	12	13	14	15
16	17	18	19	20	21	22
23	24	25	26	27	28	29
30						

October
S	M	T	W	T	F	S
	1	2	3	4	5	6
7	8	9	10	11	12	13
14	15	16	17	18	19	20
21	22	23	24	25	26	27
28	29	30	31			

November
S	M	T	W	T	F	S
				1	2	3
4	5	6	7	8	9	10
11	12	13	14	15	16	17
18	19	20	21	22	23	24
25	26	27	28	29	30	

December
S	M	T	W	T	F	S
						1
2	3	4	5	6	7	8
9	10	11	12	13	14	15
16	17	18	19	20	21	22
23	24	25	26	27	28	29
30	31					

9

January
S	M	T	W	T	F	S
	1	2	3	4	5	6
7	8	9	10	11	12	13
14	15	16	17	18	19	20
21	22	23	24	25	26	27
28	29	30	31			

February
S	M	T	W	T	F	S
				1	2	3
4	5	6	7	8	9	10
11	12	13	14	15	16	17
18	19	20	21	22	23	24
25	26	27	28	29		

March
S	M	T	W	T	F	S
					1	2
3	4	5	6	7	8	9
10	11	12	13	14	15	16
17	18	19	20	21	22	23
24	25	26	27	28	29	30
31						

April
S	M	T	W	T	F	S
	1	2	3	4	5	6
7	8	9	10	11	12	13
14	15	16	17	18	19	20
21	22	23	24	25	26	27
28	29	30				

May
S	M	T	W	T	F	S
			1	2	3	4
5	6	7	8	9	10	11
12	13	14	15	16	17	18
19	20	21	22	23	24	25
26	27	28	29	30	31	

June
S	M	T	W	T	F	S
						1
2	3	4	5	6	7	8
9	10	11	12	13	14	15
16	17	18	19	20	21	22
23	24	25	26	27	28	29
30						

July
S	M	T	W	T	F	S
	1	2	3	4	5	6
7	8	9	10	11	12	13
14	15	16	17	18	19	20
21	22	23	24	25	26	27
28	29	30	31			

August
S	M	T	W	T	F	S
				1	2	3
4	5	6	7	8	9	10
11	12	13	14	15	16	17
18	19	20	21	22	23	24
25	26	27	28	29	30	31

September
S	M	T	W	T	F	S
1	2	3	4	5	6	7
8	9	10	11	12	13	14
15	16	17	18	19	20	21
22	23	24	25	26	27	28
29	30					

October
S	M	T	W	T	F	S
		1	2	3	4	5
6	7	8	9	10	11	12
13	14	15	16	17	18	19
20	21	22	23	24	25	26
27	28	29	30	31		

November
S	M	T	W	T	F	S
					1	2
3	4	5	6	7	8	9
10	11	12	13	14	15	16
17	18	19	20	21	22	23
24	25	26	27	28	29	30

December
S	M	T	W	T	F	S
1	2	3	4	5	6	7
8	9	10	11	12	13	14
15	16	17	18	19	20	21
22	23	24	25	26	27	28
29	30	31				

10

January
S	M	T	W	T	F	S
		1	2	3	4	5
6	7	8	9	10	11	12
13	14	15	16	17	18	19
20	21	22	23	24	25	26
27	28	29	30	31		

February
S	M	T	W	T	F	S
					1	2
3	4	5	6	7	8	9
10	11	12	13	14	15	16
17	18	19	20	21	22	23
24	25	26	27	28	29	

March
S	M	T	W	T	F	S
						1
2	3	4	5	6	7	8
9	10	11	12	13	14	15
16	17	18	19	20	21	22
23	24	25	26	27	28	29
30	31					

April
S	M	T	W	T	F	S
		1	2	3	4	5
6	7	8	9	10	11	12
13	14	15	16	17	18	19
20	21	22	23	24	25	26
27	28	29	30			

May
S	M	T	W	T	F	S
				1	2	3
4	5	6	7	8	9	10
11	12	13	14	15	16	17
18	19	20	21	22	23	24
25	26	27	28	29	30	31

June
S	M	T	W	T	F	S
1	2	3	4	5	6	7
8	9	10	11	12	13	14
15	16	17	18	19	20	21
22	23	24	25	26	27	28
29	30					

July
S	M	T	W	T	F	S
		1	2	3	4	5
6	7	8	9	10	11	12
13	14	15	16	17	18	19
20	21	22	23	24	25	26
27	28	29	30	31		

August
S	M	T	W	T	F	S
					1	2
3	4	5	6	7	8	9
10	11	12	13	14	15	16
17	18	19	20	21	22	23
24	25	26	27	28	29	30
31						

September
S	M	T	W	T	F	S
	1	2	3	4	5	6
7	8	9	10	11	12	13
14	15	16	17	18	19	20
21	22	23	24	25	26	27
28	29	30				

October
S	M	T	W	T	F	S
			1	2	3	4
5	6	7	8	9	10	11
12	13	14	15	16	17	18
19	20	21	22	23	24	25
26	27	28	29	30	31	

November
S	M	T	W	T	F	S
						1
2	3	4	5	6	7	8
9	10	11	12	13	14	15
16	17	18	19	20	21	22
23	24	25	26	27	28	29
30						

December
S	M	T	W	T	F	S
	1	2	3	4	5	6
7	8	9	10	11	12	13
14	15	16	17	18	19	20
21	22	23	24	25	26	27
28	29	30	31			

11

January
S	M	T	W	T	F	S
			1	2	3	4
5	6	7	8	9	10	11
12	13	14	15	16	17	18
19	20	21	22	23	24	25
26	27	28	29	30	31	

February
S	M	T	W	T	F	S
						1
2	3	4	5	6	7	8
9	10	11	12	13	14	15
16	17	18	19	20	21	22
23	24	25	26	27	28	29

March
S	M	T	W	T	F	S
1	2	3	4	5	6	7
8	9	10	11	12	13	14
15	16	17	18	19	20	21
22	23	24	25	26	27	28
29	30	31				

April
S	M	T	W	T	F	S
			1	2	3	4
5	6	7	8	9	10	11
12	13	14	15	16	17	18
19	20	21	22	23	24	25
26	27	28	29	30		

May
S	M	T	W	T	F	S
					1	2
3	4	5	6	7	8	9
10	11	12	13	14	15	16
17	18	19	20	21	22	23
24	25	26	27	28	29	30
31						

June
S	M	T	W	T	F	S
	1	2	3	4	5	6
7	8	9	10	11	12	13
14	15	16	17	18	19	20
21	22	23	24	25	26	27
28	29	30				

July
S	M	T	W	T	F	S
			1	2	3	4
5	6	7	8	9	10	11
12	13	14	15	16	17	18
19	20	21	22	23	24	25
26	27	28	29	30	31	

August
S	M	T	W	T	F	S
						1
2	3	4	5	6	7	8
9	10	11	12	13	14	15
16	17	18	19	20	21	22
23	24	25	26	27	28	29
30	31					

September
S	M	T	W	T	F	S
		1	2	3	4	5
6	7	8	9	10	11	12
13	14	15	16	17	18	19
20	21	22	23	24	25	26
27	28	29	30			

October
S	M	T	W	T	F	S
				1	2	3
4	5	6	7	8	9	10
11	12	13	14	15	16	17
18	19	20	21	22	23	24
25	26	27	28	29	30	31

November
S	M	T	W	T	F	S
1	2	3	4	5	6	7
8	9	10	11	12	13	14
15	16	17	18	19	20	21
22	23	24	25	26	27	28
29	30					

December
S	M	T	W	T	F	S
		1	2	3	4	5
6	7	8	9	10	11	12
13	14	15	16	17	18	19
20	21	22	23	24	25	26
27	28	29	30	31		

12

January
S	M	T	W	T	F	S
				1	2	3
4	5	6	7	8	9	10
11	12	13	14	15	16	17
18	19	20	21	22	23	24
25	26	27	28	29	30	31

February
S	M	T	W	T	F	S
1	2	3	4	5	6	7
8	9	10	11	12	13	14
15	16	17	18	19	20	21
22	23	24	25	26	27	28
29						

March
S	M	T	W	T	F	S
	1	2	3	4	5	6
7	8	9	10	11	12	13
14	15	16	17	18	19	20
21	22	23	24	25	26	27
28	29	30	31			

April
S	M	T	W	T	F	S
				1	2	3
4	5	6	7	8	9	10
11	12	13	14	15	16	17
18	19	20	21	22	23	24
25	26	27	28	29	30	

May
S	M	T	W	T	F	S
						1
2	3	4	5	6	7	8
9	10	11	12	13	14	15
16	17	18	19	20	21	22
23	24	25	26	27	28	29
30	31					

June
S	M	T	W	T	F	S
		1	2	3	4	5
6	7	8	9	10	11	12
13	14	15	16	17	18	19
20	21	22	23	24	25	26
27	28	29	30			

July
S	M	T	W	T	F	S
				1	2	3
4	5	6	7	8	9	10
11	12	13	14	15	16	17
18	19	20	21	22	23	24
25	26	27	28	29	30	31

August
S	M	T	W	T	F	S
1	2	3	4	5	6	7
8	9	10	11	12	13	14
15	16	17	18	19	20	21
22	23	24	25	26	27	28
29	30	31				

September
S	M	T	W	T	F	S
			1	2	3	4
5	6	7	8	9	10	11
12	13	14	15	16	17	18
19	20	21	22	23	24	25
26	27	28	29	30		

October
S	M	T	W	T	F	S
					1	2
3	4	5	6	7	8	9
10	11	12	13	14	15	16
17	18	19	20	21	22	23
24	25	26	27	28	29	30
31						

November
S	M	T	W	T	F	S
	1	2	3	4	5	6
7	8	9	10	11	12	13
14	15	16	17	18	19	20
21	22	23	24	25	26	27
28	29	30				

December
S	M	T	W	T	F	S
			1	2	3	4
5	6	7	8	9	10	11
12	13	14	15	16	17	18
19	20	21	22	23	24	25
26	27	28	29	30	31	

13

January
S	M	T	W	T	F	S
					1	2
3	4	5	6	7	8	9
10	11	12	13	14	15	16
17	18	19	20	21	22	23
24	25	26	27	28	29	30
31						

February
S	M	T	W	T	F	S
	1	2	3	4	5	6
7	8	9	10	11	12	13
14	15	16	17	18	19	20
21	22	23	24	25	26	27
28	29					

March
S	M	T	W	T	F	S
		1	2	3	4	5
6	7	8	9	10	11	12
13	14	15	16	17	18	19
20	21	22	23	24	25	26
27	28	29	30	31		

April
S	M	T	W	T	F	S
					1	2
3	4	5	6	7	8	9
10	11	12	13	14	15	16
17	18	19	20	21	22	23
24	25	26	27	28	29	30

May
S	M	T	W	T	F	S
1	2	3	4	5	6	7
8	9	10	11	12	13	14
15	16	17	18	19	20	21
22	23	24	25	26	27	28
29	30	31				

June
S	M	T	W	T	F	S
			1	2	3	4
5	6	7	8	9	10	11
12	13	14	15	16	17	18
19	20	21	22	23	24	25
26	27	28	29	30		

July
S	M	T	W	T	F	S
					1	2
3	4	5	6	7	8	9
10	11	12	13	14	15	16
17	18	19	20	21	22	23
24	25	26	27	28	29	30
31						

August
S	M	T	W	T	F	S
	1	2	3	4	5	6
7	8	9	10	11	12	13
14	15	16	17	18	19	20
21	22	23	24	25	26	27
28	29	30	31			

September
S	M	T	W	T	F	S
				1	2	3
4	5	6	7	8	9	10
11	12	13	14	15	16	17
18	19	20	21	22	23	24
25	26	27	28	29	30	

October
S	M	T	W	T	F	S
						1
2	3	4	5	6	7	8
9	10	11	12	13	14	15
16	17	18	19	20	21	22
23	24	25	26	27	28	29
30	31					

November
S	M	T	W	T	F	S
		1	2	3	4	5
6	7	8	9	10	11	12
13	14	15	16	17	18	19
20	21	22	23	24	25	26
27	28	29	30			

December
S	M	T	W	T	F	S
				1	2	3
4	5	6	7	8	9	10
11	12	13	14	15	16	17
18	19	20	21	22	23	24
25	26	27	28	29	30	31

14

January
S	M	T	W	T	F	S
						1
2	3	4	5	6	7	8
9	10	11	12	13	14	15
16	17	18	19	20	21	22
23	24	25	26	27	28	29
30	31					

February
S	M	T	W	T	F	S
		1	2	3	4	5
6	7	8	9	10	11	12
13	14	15	16	17	18	19
20	21	22	23	24	25	26
27	28	29				

March
S	M	T	W	T	F	S
		1	2	3	4	
5	6	7	8	9	10	11
12	13	14	15	16	17	18
19	20	21	22	23	24	25
26	27	28	29	30	31	

April
S	M	T	W	T	F	S
						1
2	3	4	5	6	7	8
9	10	11	12	13	14	15
16	17	18	19	20	21	22
23	24	25	26	27	28	29
30						

May
S	M	T	W	T	F	S
	1	2	3	4	5	6
7	8	9	10	11	12	13
14	15	16	17	18	19	20
21	22	23	24	25	26	27
28	29	30	31			

June
S	M	T	W	T	F	S
				1	2	3
4	5	6	7	8	9	10
11	12	13	14	15	16	17
18	19	20	21	22	23	24
25	26	27	28	29	30	

July
S	M	T	W	T	F	S
						1
2	3	4	5	6	7	8
9	10	11	12	13	14	15
16	17	18	19	20	21	22
23	24	25	26	27	28	29
30	31					

August
S	M	T	W	T	F	S
		1	2	3	4	5
6	7	8	9	10	11	12
13	14	15	16	17	18	19
20	21	22	23	24	25	26
27	28	29	30	31		

September
S	M	T	W	T	F	S
					1	2
3	4	5	6	7	8	9
10	11	12	13	14	15	16
17	18	19	20	21	22	23
24	25	26	27	28	29	30

October
S	M	T	W	T	F	S
1	2	3	4	5	6	7
8	9	10	11	12	13	14
15	16	17	18	19	20	21
22	23	24	25	26	27	28
29	30	31				

November
S	M	T	W	T	F	S
			1	2	3	4
5	6	7	8	9	10	11
12	13	14	15	16	17	18
19	20	21	22	23	24	25
26	27	28	29	30		

December
S	M	T	W	T	F	S
					1	2
3	4	5	6	7	8	9
10	11	12	13	14	15	16
17	18	19	20	21	22	23
24	25	26	27	28	29	30
31						

National Holidays: U.S.

Holiday	Date
New Year's Day	January 1 (observed Friday or Monday if it falls on a weekend)
Martin Luther King Jr. Day	third Monday in January
President's Day	third Monday in February
Memorial Day	last Monday in May
Independence Day	July 4
Labor Day	first Monday in September
Columbus Day	second Monday in October
Veterans' Day	November 11
Thanksgiving	fourth Thursday in November
Christmas Day	December 25

⊙ United States Office of Personnel Management. "Federal Holidays,"
www.opm.gov/fedhol
Dallas Tour Planner Online. "US Holidays," www.dallascvb.com/tourplanner/
USHolidays.htm

Major Holidays in Selected Countries (excluding U.S.)

Holiday	Nation	Date
Bank Holiday	Japan, Scotland	January 2
Second Day of New Year	Russia	January 2
Bank Holiday	Japan	January 3
Coming of Age Day	Japan	second Monday in January
Republic Day	India	January 26
Australia Day	Australia	January 26 (if this holiday falls on a Saturday or Sunday, it is observed the following Monday)
Anniversary of the Constitution	Mexico	February 5
Waitangi Day	New Zealand	February 6
National Foundation Day	Japan	February 11
Defenders of the Motherland Day	Russia	February 23
Carnival Week	Brazil	five days before Ash Wednesday
Independence Movement Day	South Korea	March 1
St. Patrick's Day	Northern Ireland	March 17
Human Rights Day	South Africa	March 21
Emancipation Day	Puerto Rico	March 22
Liberation Day	Italy	April 25
ANZAC Day	Australia, New Zealand	April 25 (if this holiday falls on a Saturday or Sunday, it is observed the following Monday)
Sinai Liberation Day	Egypt	April 25
Freedom Day	South Africa	April 27
Queen's Day	Netherlands	April 30
May Day	Italy, Sweden	May 1
Labo(u)r Day	Belgium, Brazil, Canada, Egypt, France, Germany, Mexico, Philippines	May 1
Workers Day	South Africa	May 1
International Labour Day	China, Russia	May 1–2
Constitution Memorial Day	Japan	May 3
May Day Bank Holiday	U.K.	first Monday in May
Youth Day	China	May 4
Holiday for a Nation	Japan	May 4
Cinco de Mayo	Mexico	May 5
Liberation Day	Netherlands	May 5
WWII Victory Day	France	May 8
WWII Victory Day	Russia	May 9
Victoria Day	Canada	last Monday before May 25
Bank Holiday	U.K.	last Monday in May
Children's Day	China	June 1
Anniversary of the Republic	Italy	Sunday nearest June 2
Queen's Birthday	New Zealand	first Monday in June
Independence Day	Russia	June 12
Independence Day	Philippines	June 12
Evacuation Day	Egypt	June 18
Midsummer Day	Sweden	Saturday after June 19

Anniversary of the Founding of the Communist Party	China	July 1
Canada Day	Canada	July 1
Bastille Day	France	July 14
Constitution Day	South Korea	July 17
National Holiday	Belgium	July 21
Revolution Day	Egypt	July 23
Constitution Day	Puerto Rico	July 25
Summer Bank Holiday	Scotland	first Monday in August
Anniversary of the Founding of the Chinese PLA	China	August 1
Independence Day	India	August 15
Independence Day	Indonesia	August 17
Victory Day	Turkey	August 30
National Heroes Day	Philippines	August 31
Summer Bank Holiday	U.K.	last Monday in August
National Day	Vietnam	September 2
Independence Day	Brazil	September 7
Independence Day	Mexico	September 16
National Day	China	October 1–2
Mahatma Gandhi's Birthday	India	October 2
Day of German Unity	Germany	October 3
National Foundation Day	South Korea	October 3
Armed Forces Day	Egypt	October 6
Thanksgiving Day	Canada	second Monday in October
Spanish National Day	Spain	October 12
Suez Victory Day	Egypt	October 24
Republic Day	Turkey	October 29
Labour Day	New Zealand	fourth Monday in October
National Culture Day	Japan	November 3
World War I Victory Anniversary Day	Italy	Sunday nearest November 4
Day of Accord and Reconciliation	Russia	November 7
Armistice Day	France	November 11
Proclamation of the Republic	Brazil	November 15
Discovery of Puerto Rico Day	Puerto Rico	November 19
Anniversary of the Mexican Revolution	Mexico	November 20
Labor Thanksgiving Day	Japan	November 23
Day of the Constitution	Spain	December 6
Constitution Day	Russia	December 12
Independence Day	Kenya	December 12
Day of Reconciliation	South Africa	December 16
Emperor's Birthday	Japan	December 23
Victory Day	Egypt	December 23
St. Stephen's Day	Italy	December 26
Boxing Day	Australia, Canada, Germany, Netherlands, Sweden, U.K.	December 26
Bank Holiday	Japan	December 31

Holiday Festival. "National Holidays," www.holidayfestival.com/Ctr.html

☉ Tyzo.com. "World Holidays Database," www.tyzo.com/tools/holidays.html.

Earthcalendar.net. "Earth Calendar 2000," http://www.earthcalendar.net/

Zodiac Signs

♈ Aries

Dates:	Mar. 21–Apr. 19
Element:	fire
Type:	masculine
Quality:	cardinal
Symbol:	ram
Gemstone:	diamond
Metal:	iron
Color:	red
Ruled by:	Mars
Motto:	"I am"
Rules:	head

♉ Taurus

Dates:	Apr. 20–May 20
Element:	earth
Type:	feminine
Quality:	fixed
Symbol:	bull
Gemstone:	emerald
Metal:	copper
Colors:	pink or blue
Ruled by:	Venus
Motto:	"I have"
Rules:	throat

♊ Gemini

Dates:	May 21–June 20
Element:	air
Type:	masculine
Quality:	mutable
Symbols:	Castor & Pollux (twins)
Gemstone:	beryl
Metal:	mercury
Color:	orange
Ruled by:	Mercury
Motto:	"I think"
Rules:	nervous system, hands, shoulders, arms, lungs

♋ Cancer

Dates:	June 21–July 22
Element:	water
Type:	feminine
Quality:	cardinal
Symbol:	crab
Gemstone:	moonstone
Metal:	silver
Color:	silver
Ruled by:	Moon
Motto:	"I feel"
Rules:	breast, stomach

♌ Leo

Dates:	July 23–Aug. 22
Element:	fire
Type:	masculine
Quality:	fixed
Symbol:	lion
Gemstone:	ruby
Metal:	gold
Colors:	yellow or orange
Ruled by:	Sun
Motto:	"I will"
Rules:	heart, spine

♍ Virgo

Dates:	Aug. 23–Sep. 22
Element:	earth
Type:	feminine
Quality:	mutable
Symbol:	virgin
Gemstone:	agate
Metal:	nickel
Colors:	green, brown, or blue
Ruled by:	Mercury
Motto:	"I analyze"
Rules:	intestinal tract

♎ Libra

Dates:	Sep. 23–Oct. 22
Element:	air
Type:	masculine
Quality:	cardinal
Symbol:	scale of justice
Gemstone:	opal
Metal:	bronze
Colors:	pink or blue
Ruled by:	Venus
Motto:	"we balance"
Rules:	kidneys, lower back

♏ Scorpio

Dates:	Oct. 23–Nov. 21
Element:	water
Type:	feminine
Quality:	fixed
Symbols:	scorpion, eagle, or phoenix
Gemstone:	topaz
Metal:	steel
Color:	red
Ruled by:	Mars or Pluto
Motto:	"I create"
Rules:	generative system

Sagittarius

↗ **Dates:** Nov. 22–Dec. 21
Element: fire
↗ **Type:** masculine
Quality: mutable
↗ **Symbol:** centaur
Gemstone: turquoise
Metal: tin
Colors: purple or dark blue
Ruled by: Jupiter
Motto: "I perceive"
Rules: hips, thighs

≋ Aquarius

Dates: Jan. 20–Feb. 18
Element: air
Type: masculine
Quality: fixed
Symbol: water bearer
Gemstone: amethyst
Metal: aluminum
Color: bright blue
Ruled by: Uranus
Motto: "I know"
Rules: circulation, ankles

♑ Capricorn

Dates: Dec. 22–Jan. 19
Element: earth
♄ **Type:** feminine
Quality: cardinal
Symbol: goat with dolphin's tail
Gemstone: garnet
Metal: lead
Color: brown
Ruled by: Saturn
Motto: "I use"
Rules: knees, bones, skin

♓ Pisces

Dates: Feb. 19–Mar. 20
Element: water
Type: feminine
Quality: mutable
Symbol: two fish
Gemstone: aquamarine
Metal: platinum
Color: green
Ruled by: Neptune or Jupiter
Motto: "I believe"
Rules: feet

⊙ Zodiachouse.com. "The Signs," http://zodiachouse.com/signs.html
   Astrology For Beginners. "The Signs," http://astro4begin.terrashare.com/

Birthstones and Flowers

Month	Birthstone(s)	Flower(s)
January	Garnet	Carnation, Snowdrop
February	Amethyst	Violet
March	Aquamarine, Bloodstone	Daffodil, Jonquil
April	Diamond	Sweet Pea
May	Emerald	Lily of the Valley, Hawthorn
June	Pearl, Moonstone, Alexandrite	Rose
July	Ruby	Larkspur, Delphinium
August	Peridot, Sardonyx	Gladiolus
September	Sapphire	Aster
October	Opal, Tourmaline	Calendula, Marigold
November	Yellow Topaz, Citrine	Chrysanthemum
December	Blue Topaz, Turquoise, Blue Zircon, Lapis Lazuli	Narcissus, Holly

⊙ Infoplease.com. "Birthstones," www.infoplease.com/ipa/A0002118.html
   The Gift Chick.com. "Birthstone and Flower Guide," www.thegiftchick.com/
   birthstones.htm

Wedding Anniversary Gifts

Year	Gift(s)	Year	Gift(s)
1	Paper	14	Ivory
2	Cotton	15	Crystal
3	Leather	20	China
4	Linen; Fruit and Flowers	25	Silver
5	Wood	30	Pearl
6	Iron, Sugar	35	Coral, Jade
7	Wool, Copper	40	Ruby
8	Bronze, Rubber	45	Sapphire
9	Pottery, Willow	50	Gold
10	Tin, Aluminum	55	Emerald
11	Steel	60	Diamond
12	Silk	75	Diamond, Gold
13	Lace		

⊙ Infoplease.com. "Traditional Wedding Anniversary Gift List,"
www.infoplease.com/ipa/A0763772.html

THE SCIENCES: *Climate, Weather, Environment*

Meteorology Symbols

COMMON WEATHER SYMBOLS

Symbol	Meaning	Symbol	Meaning	Symbol	Meaning
L	Low pressure	Moderate snow		Freezing drizzle	
H	High pressure	Heavy snow		Rain shower	
Lxxx	Tropical depression	Light fog		Snow shower	
xxx	Tropical storm	Heavy fog		Showers of hail	
xxx	Hurricane/typhoon	Light drizzle		Drift/blowing snow	
••	Light rain	Light icing		Dust storm	
	Moderate rain	Heavy icing		Haze	
	Heavy rain	Ice pellets (sleet)		Smoke	
✳✳	Light snow	Freezing rain		Thunderstorm	

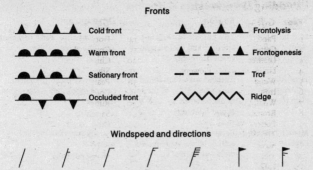

Fronts

▲▲▲ Cold front	▲ ▲ ▲ ▲ Frontolysis
●●● Warm front	▲ _ ▲ _ ▲ _ Frontogenesis
●▲●▲ Sationary front	– – – – – Trof
●▼●▼ Occluded front	∧∧∧∧∧ Ridge

Windspeed and directions

NE 2 KT   NE 6 KT   NE 10 KT   NE 15 KT   NNE 45 KT   N 50 KT   N 65 KT

⊙ National Oceanographic and Atmospheric Administration. "Key Terms and
  Symbols," www.mpc.ncep.noaa.gov/product_description/keyterm.html
  University of Wisconsin–Stout Meteorology Physics Department. "Common
  Weather Symbols," http://physics.uwstout.edu/WX/reference/symbols/
  commonsymb.htm

Climate Types

Type	*Region*	*Description*
Wet equatorial climate	Within about 12° latitude of the Equator	High temperatures around 86° F (30° C), with plentiful precipitation 59–394 inches (150–1,000 cm), heavy cloud cover, and high humidity, with very little annual temperature variation
Tropical monsoon and trade-wind littoral climates	Between 15° and 30° latitude	Small annual temperature ranges, high temperatures, and plentiful precipitation. A short dry season, usually in the "winter" season
Tropical wet-dry climate	Between 15° and 30° latitude	This climate has distinct wet and dry seasons, with most of the precipitation occurring in "summer."
Tropical and subtropical desert climate	Between 15° and 30° latitude	Arid
Tropical and subtropical steppe climate	The periphery of tropical and subtropical desert climate.	Semiarid

Climate Types (cont.)

Type	Region	Description
Mid-latitude steppe and desert climate	This climate extends to 50° latitude, and cool steppes reach nearly 60° N.	Extreme temperature variations and little precipitation
Humid subtropical climate	These climates are found on the eastern sides of the continents between 20° and 35° N and S latitude.	A relatively uniform distribution of precipitation throughout the year.
Mediterranean climate	Between about 30° and 45° latitude on the western sides of the continents	Hot, dry summers and cool, wet winters.
Marine west coast climate	Poleward of the Mediterranean climate region on the western sides of the continents, between 35° and 60° N and S latitude	Precipitation is plentiful and frequent. Few extremes of temperature.
Humid continental climate	The humid continental subgroup occupies a region between 30° and 60° N in central and eastern North America and Asia in the major zone of conflict between polar and tropical air masses.	Large seasonal temperature contrasts with hot summers and cold winters. Precipitation is plentiful throughout the year.
Continental subarctic climate	North of the humid continental climate, from about 50° to 70° N, in a broad swath extending from Alaska to Newfoundland in North America and from northern Scandinavia to Siberia in Eurasia, lie the continental subarctic climates.	These are regions dominated by the winter season, a long, bitterly cold period with short, clear days, and relatively little precipitation.
Tundra climate	Tundra climates occur between 60° and 75° of latitude, mostly along the Arctic coast of North America and Eurasia and on the coastal margins of Greenland.	Mean annual temperatures are below freezing and annual ranges are large. Summers are generally mild and days are long, but they are often cloudy. The snow cover of winter melts in the warmer season. Winters are long and cold and precipitation generally consists of dry snow.

| Snow and ice climate | This climate occurs poleward of 65° N and S latitude over the ice caps of Greenland and Antarctica and over the permanently frozen portion of the Arctic Ocean, | Winters are frigid, with mean monthly temperatures from –4°F to –85° F (–20° C to –65° C). Daily temperature variations are very small, because at such high latitudes the Sun's elevation varies little over the daylight period. Precipitation is meager in the cold, stable air with the largest amounts occurring on the coastal margins. Precipitation is usually in the form of snow and ice pellets, with strong winds, and blizzards. High winds also occur in the outer portions of the Greenland and Antarctic EF climates. |
| Highland climates | The major highland regions of the world (the Cascades, Sierra Nevada, and Rockies of North America, the Andes of South America, the Himalayas and adjacent ranges and the Tibetan Highlands [or Plateau] of Asia, the eastern highlands of Africa, and the central portions of Borneo and New Guinea) | Highland climates tend to resemble cooler, wetter versions of the climates of nearby lowlands in terms of their annual temperature ranges and seasonality of precipitation. |

⦿ Encyclopedia Britannica. "Climate," www.britannica.com/bcom/eb/article/print-able/4/0,5722,109114,00.html

Wind Chill and Heat Index

The wind chill index combines the temperature and wind speed to tell you how cold the wind makes the temperature "feel."

Air Temperature (°Fahrenheit)

Wind Speed (MPH)	35	30	25	20	15	10	5	0	–5	–10	–15	–20	–25	–30	–35
4	35	30	25	20	15	10	5	0	–5	–10	–15	–20	–25	–30	–35
5	32	27	22	16	11	6	0	–5	–10	–15	–21	–26	–31	–36	–42
10	22	16	10	3	–3	–9	–15	–22	–27	–34	–40	–46	–52	–58	–64
15	16	9	2	–5	–11	–18	–25	–31	–38	–45	–51	–58	–65	–72	–78
20	12	4	–3	–10	–17	–24	–31	–39	–46	–53	–60	–67	–74	–81	–88
25	6	1	–7	–15	–22	–29	–36	–44	–51	–59	–66	–74	–81	–88	–96
30	5	–2	–10	–18	–25	–33	–41	–49	–55	–64	–71	–79	–86	–93	–101
35	4	–4	–12	–20	–27	–35	–43	–52	–58	–67	–74	–82	–89	–97	–105
40	3	–5	–13	–21	–29	–37	–45	–53	–60	–69	–76	–84	–92	–100	–107
45	2	–6	–14	–22	–30	–38	–46	–54	–62	–70	–78	–85	–93	–102	–109

⬤ Cold   ⬤ Very Cold   ⬤ Bitter Cold   ◯ Extreme Cold

Wind Chill and Heat Index *(cont.)*

The heat index is an accurate measure of how hot it feels when the effects of humidity are added to high temperature. Heat index is shown either as a function of Temperature/Dewpoint or as a function of Temperature/Relative Humidity (RH).

Relative Humidity (Percent)

Air Temp (°F)	0	5	10	15	20	25	30	35	40	45	50	55	60	65	70	75	80	85	90	95	100
140	125																				
135	120	128																			
130	117	122	131																		
125	111	116	123	131	141																
120	107	111	116	123	130	148															
115	103	107	111	115	120	127	135	143	151												
110	99	102	105	108	112	117	123	130	137	143	151										
105	95	97	100	102	105	109	113	118	123	129	135	142	149								
100	91	93	95	97	99	101	104	107	110	115	120	126	132	139	144						
95	87	88	90	91	93	94	96	98	101	104	107	110	114	119	124	130	136				
90	83	84	85	86	87	88	90	91	93	95	96	98	100	102	106	109	113	118	122		
85	78	79	80	81	82	83	84	85	86	87	88	89	90	91	93	95	97	99	102	105	108
80	73	74	75	76	77	77	78	79	79	80	81	81	82	83	84	85	86	87	88	89	91
75	69	69	70	71	72	72	73	73	74	74	75	75	76	76	77	77	78	78	79	79	80
70	64	64	65	65	66	66	67	67	68	68	69	69	70	70	71	71	71	71	71	72	72

Air Temperature (°Fahrenheit)

⬤ Extreme Danger   ⬤ Danger   ⬤ Extreme Caution   ◯ Caution

⊙ USA Today. "Windchill," www.usatoday.com/weather/windchill.htm
National Oceanographic and Atmospheric Administration. "Heat Index Table," www.nws.noaa.gov/er/lwx/wxcalc/heatindx.htm
USA Today. "Heat Index," www.usatoday.com/weather/wheat3.htm

Clouds

Name	Height	Description	Indicates
Cirrus	High (45,000 to 16,500 feet)	Wispy and thin	Fair weather
Stratus	Low (6,500 to 0 feet)	Cover most of the sky with an even, gray color similar to a fog	Light rain
Cumulonimbus	Low (6,500 to 0 feet)	Tall, dense, shaped like a block or anvil	Violent weather, such as hail and lightning. Signal thunderstorms and can spawn tornadoes
Nimbostratus	Middle (23,000 to 6,500 feet)	Dark and low	Light rain
Cirrostratus	Troposphere	Halo	Precipitation is likely within 15 to 25 hours if winds steady from NE E to S, or sooner if winds SE to S. Other wind directions bring overcast skies.

Cumulus	Low (6,500 to o feet)	Have the appearance of floating cotton and have a lifetime of 5–40 minutes. Known for their flat bases and distinct outlines	Fair weather
Altocumulus	Middle (23,000 to 6,500 feet)	Parallel bands or rounded masses	The presence of altocumulus clouds on a warm and humid summer morning is commonly followed by thunderstorms later in the day.
Stratocumulus	Low (6,500 to o feet)	Vary in color from dark gray to light gray and may appear as rounded masses, rolls, etc., with breaks of clear sky in between	Light precipitation

⊙ Annenberg/CPB. "Weather," www.learner.org/exhibits/weather/watercycle.html
Cloud Types: Common Cloud Classifications. www.gfdl.gov/~io/WEATHER/clouds.html

Storms and Storm Warnings

These terms are used by the U.S. National Weather Service to describe potentially dangerous weather patterns and effects.

Type	Description
Tornado	A violently rotating column of air, pendant to a cumulonimbus, with circulation reaching the ground
Hurricane	A tropical cyclone with winds of 74 mph or greater that occurs especially in the western Atlantic, that is usually accompanied by rain, thunder, and lightning, and that sometimes moves into temperate latitudes
Severe Thunderstorm	A thunderstorm that produces a tornado, and/or winds of at least 50 kt (58 mph), and/or hail. Structural damage may imply the occurrence of a severe thunderstorm.
Flood	The filling with water of a normally dry area of land caused by an increased water level in a watercourse (stream, river, drainage ditch) or by the ponding of rainwater
Flash Flood	A flood that is caused by heavy or excessive rainfall in a short period of time, generally less than 6 hours. These conditions are often produced by slow-moving thunderstorms that train one behind the other or tropical systems that make landfall.
Winter Storm	Severe winter conditions, such as accumulations of heavy snow and/or ice of 4″ or more possible within the next 24 hours

⊙ National Weather Service. "Storm Warnings," http://iwin.nws.noaa.gov/iwin/nationalwarnings.html

Beaufort Wind Scale

The Beaufort wind scale is used for estimating wind speed when there is no standard instrumentation available.

Beaufort number	Wind Speed [knots]	Wind Speed [mph]	Wind Speed [m/s]	Sea Wave Height [feet]	Sea Wave Height [meters]	Description	Effects observed on sea	Effects observed on land
0	< 1	< 1	0.0–0.2	~0	~0	Calm	Sea like mirror	Calm; smoke rises vertically
1	1–3	1–3	0.3–1.5	0.25	0.1	Light air	Ripples with appearance of scales; no foam crests	Direction of wind shown by smoke drift but not by wind vanes
2	4–6	4–7	1.6–3.3	0.5–1.0	0.2–0.3	Light breeze	Small wavelets; crests of glassy appearance, not breaking	Wind felt on face; leaves rustle; vanes moved by wind
3	7–10	8–12	3.4–5.4	2.0–3.0	0.6–1.0	Gentle breeze	Large wavelets; crests begin to break; scattered whitecaps	Leaves and small twigs in constant motion; wind extends light flag
4	11–16	13–18	5.5–7.9	3.5–5.0	1.0–1.5	Moderate breeze	Small waves, becoming longer; numerous whitecaps	Raises dust and loose paper; small branches are moved
5	17–21	19–24	8.0–10.7	6.0–8.0	2 – 2.5	Fresh breeze	Moderate waves, taking longer form; many whitecaps; some spray	Small trees in leaf begin to sway; crested wavelets form on inland waters
6	22–27	25–31	10.8–13.8	9.5–13.0	3.0–4.0	Strong breeze	Larger waves forming; whitecaps everywhere; more spray	Large branches in motion; whistling heard in telegraph wires; umbrellas used with difficulty
7	28–33	32–38	13.9–17.1	13.5–19.0	4.0–5.5	Near gale	Sea heaps up; white foam from breaking waves begin to be blown in streaks	Whole trees in motion; inconvenience felt when walking against the wind

#						Sea conditions	Land conditions
8	34–40	39–46	17.2–20.7	18.0–25.0	Gale	Moderately high waves of greater length; edges of crests begin to break into spindrift; foam is blown in well-marked streaks	Breaks twigs off trees; generally impedes progress
9	41–47	47–54	20.8–24.4	23.0–32.0	Strong gale	High waves; sea begins to roll; dense streaks of foam; spray may reduce visibility	Slight structural damage occurs
10	48–55	55–63	24.5–28.4	29.0–41.0	Storm	Very high waves with overhanging crests; sea takes white appearance as foam is blown in very dense streaks; rolling is heavy and visibility reduced	Trees uprooted; considerable structural damage occurs
11	56–63	64–72	28.5–32.6	37.0–52.0	Violent storm	Exceptionally high waves; sea covered with white foam patches; visibility still more reduced	Accompanied by widespread damage
12	64 +	73 +	32.7 +	45 +	Hurricane	Air filled with foam; sea completely white with driving spray; visibility greatly reduced	Accompanied by widespread damage

⊙ National Weather Service. "Beaufort Wind Scale," www.nws.noaa.gov/er/cae/beaufort.htm

Hurricane Intensity Scale

The Saffir-Simpson scale measures hurricane intensity on the basis of observed damage and top windspeeds.

Category	Wind Speed	Effect
1	74–95 mph (64–82 kts) Minimal	No real damage to building structures. Damage primarily to unanchored mobile homes, shrubbery, and trees. Some damage to poorly constructed signs. Also, some coastal road flooding and minor pier damage.
2	96–110 mph (83–95 kts) Moderate	Some roofing material, door, and window damage of buildings. Considerable damage to shrubbery and trees with some trees blown down. Considerable damage to mobile homes, poorly constructed signs, and piers. Coastal and low-lying escape routes flood 2–4 hours before arrival of the hurricane center. Small craft in unprotected anchorages break moorings.
3	111–130 mph (96–113 kts) Extensive	Some structural damage to small residences and utility buildings with a minor amount of curtainwall failures. Damage to shrubbery and trees with foliage blown off trees and large trees blown down. Mobile homes and poorly constructed signs are destroyed. Low-lying escape routes are cut by rising water 3–5 hours before arrival of the hurricane center. Flooding near the coast destroys smaller structures with larger structures damaged by battering of floating debris. Terrain continuously lower than 5 ft. above mean sea level may be flooded inland 8 miles or more. Evacuation of low-lying residences within several blocks of the shoreline may be required.
4	131–155 mph (114–135 kts) Extreme	More extensive curtainwall failures with some complete roof structure failures on small residences. Shrubs, trees, and all signs are blown down. Complete destruction of mobile homes. Extensive damage to doors and windows. Low-lying escape routes may be cut by rising water 3–5 hours before arrival of the hurricane center. Major damage to lower floors of structures near the shore. Terrain lower than 10 ft. above sea level may be flooded, requiring massive evacuation of residential areas as far inland as 6 miles.
5	156 mph + (135 kts) Catastrophic	Complete roof failure on many residences and industrial buildings. Some complete building failures with small utility buildings blown over or away. All shrubs, trees, and signs blown down. Complete destruction of mobile homes. Severe and extensive window and door damage. Low-lying escape routes are cut by rising water 3–5 hours before arrival of the hurricane center. Major damage to lower floors of all structures located less than 15 ft. above sea level and within 500 yards of the shoreline. Massive evacuation of residential areas on low ground 5–10 miles of the shoreline may be required.

⊙ National Hurricane Center. "The Saffir-Simpson Hurricane Scale," www.nhc.noaa.gov/aboutsshs.html

Hurricanes

Following are the 25 most intense hurricanes that have struck the continental United States since 1900.

Ranking	Hurricane	Year	Category	Pressure (Millibars)	Pressure (Inches of Mercury)
1	FL (Keys)	1935	5	892	26.35
2	Camille (MS/SE LA/VA)	1969	5	909	26.84
3	Andrew (SE FL/SE LA)	1992	4	922	27.23
4	FL (Keys)/S TX	1919	4	927	27.37
5	FL (Lake Okeechobee)	1928	4	929	27.43
6	Donna (FL/Eastern U.S.)	1960	4	930	27.46
7	TX (Galveston)	1900	4	931	27.49
8	LA (Grand Isle)	1909	4	931	27.49
9	LA (New Orleans)	1915	4	931	27.49
10	Carla (N & Cent. TX)	1961	4	931	27.49
11	Hugo (SC)	1989	4	934	27.58
12	FL (Miami)/MS/AL/NW FL	1926	4	935	27.61
13	Hazel (SC/NC)	1954	4	938	27.70
14	SE FL/SE LA/MS	1947	4	940	27.76
15	N TX	1932	4	941	27.79
16	Gloria (Eastern U.S.)	1985	3	942	27.82
17	Opal (NW FL/AL)	1995	3	942	27.82
18	Audrey (SW LA/N TX)	1957	4	945	27.91
19	TX (Galveston)	1915	4	945	27.91
20	Celia (S TX)	1970	3	945	27.91
21	Allen (S TX)	1980	3	945	27.91
22	New England	1938	3	946	27.94
23	Frederic (AL/MS)	1979	3	946	27.94
24	NE U.S.	1944	3	947	27.97
25	SC/NC	1906	3	947	27.97

☉ NOAA Atlantic Oceanographic and Meteorological Laboratory. "Hurricane FAQ," www.aoml.noaa.gov/hrd/tcfaq/tcfaqE.html#E1o

Hurricane Names

Names of tropical storms are selected by a committee of the World Meteorological Association. The lists are recycled every six years. A name is retired if it becomes associated with a particularly deadly or destructive storm.

Atlantic Hurricanes

Year 2001	Year 2002	Year 2003	Year 2004	Year 2005
Allison	Arthur	Ana	Alex	Arlene
Barry	Bertha	Bill	Bonnie	Brett
Chantal	Cristobal	Claudette	Charley	Cindy
Dean	Dolly	Danny	Danielle	Dennis
Erin	Edouard	Erika	Earl	Emily
Felix	Fay	Fabian	Frances	Franklin
Gabrielle	Gustav	Grace	Gaston	Gert
Humberto	Hanna	Henri	Hermione	Harvey
Iris	Isidore	Isabel	Ivan	Irene
Jerry	Josephine	Juan	Jeanne	Jose
Karen	Kyle	Kate	Karl	Katrina
Lorenzo	Lili	Larry	Lisa	Lee
Michelle	Marco	Mindy	Matthew	Maria
Noel	Nana	Nicholas	Nicole	Nate
Olga	Omar	Odette	Otto	Ophelia
Pablo	Paloma	Peter	Paula	Philippe
Rebekah	Rene	Rose	Richard	Rita
Sebastien	Sally	Sam	Shary	Stan
Tanya	Teddy	Teresa	Tomas	Tammy
Van	Vicky	Victor	Virginie	Vince
Wendy	Wilfred	Wanda	Walter	Wilma

Eastern North Pacific Hurricanes

Year 2001	Year 2002	Year 2003	Year 2004	Year 2005
Adolph	Alma	Andres	Agatha	Adrian
Barbara	Boris	Blanca	Blas	Beatris
Cosme	Cristina	Carlos	Celia	Calvin
Dalila	Douglas	Dolores	Darby	Dora
Erick	Elida	Enrique	Estelle	Eugene
Flossie	Fausto	Felicia	Frank	Fernanda
Gil	Genevieve	Guillermo	Georgette	Greg
Henriette	Hernan	Hilda	Howard	Hilary
Israel	Iselle	Ignacio	Isis	Irwin
Juliette	Julio	Jimena	Javier	Jova
Kiko	Kenna	Kevin	Kay	Kenneth
Lorena	Lowell	Linda	Lester	Lidia
Manuel	Marie	Marty	Madeline	Max
Narda	Norbert	Nora	Newton	Norma
Octave	Odile	Olaf	Orlene	Otis
Priscilla	Polo	Patricia	Paine	Pilar
Raymond	Rachel	Rick	Roslyn	Ramon
Sonia	Simon	Sandra	Seymour	Selma
Tico	Trudy	Terry	Tina	Todd
Velma	Vance	Vivian	Virgil	Veronica
Wallis	Winnie	Waldo	Winifred	Wiley
Xina	Xavier	Xina	Xavier	Xina
York	Yolanda	York	Yolanda	York
Zelda	Zeke	Zelda	Zeke	Zelda

☉ NOAA. "Hurricane Names," www.nhc.noaa.gov/aboutnames.html

Tornado Intensity Scale

The TORRO Tornado Intensity Scale was devised in 1972 by Dr. G. Terence Meaden, of Bradford-on-Avon, Wiltshire (United Kingdom), in order to categorize windspeeds in tornadoes. The scale is directly related to—and is a natural extension of—the Beaufort Scale. The scale allows for the rating of a tornado's windspeed by various means, namely by

- *viewing the damage caused*
- *engineering analysis of the damage caused*
- *Doppler radar*
- *photogrammetric analysis*
- *direct measurement*

TORRO Intensity	Description of Tornado & Windspeeds	Description of Damage
T0	**Light Tornado** 39–54 miles/hour (17–24 meters/sec)	Loose light litter raised from ground-level in spirals. Tents, marquees seriously disturbed; most exposed tiles, slates on roofs dislodged. Twigs snapped; trail visible through crops.
T1	**Mild Tornado** 55–72 miles/hour (25–32 meters/sec)	Deckchairs, small plants, heavy litter made airborne; minor damage to sheds. More serious dislodging of tiles, slates, chimney pots. Wooden fences flattened. Slight damage to hedges and trees.
T2	**Moderate Tornado** 73–92 miles/hour (33–41 meters/sec)	Heavy mobile homes displaced, light caravans blown over, garden sheds destroyed, garage roofs torn away, much damage to tiled roofs and chimney stacks. General damage to trees, some big branches twisted or snapped off, small trees uprooted.
T3	**Strong Tornado** 93–114 miles/hour (42–51 meters/sec)	Mobile homes overturned/badly damaged; light caravans destroyed; garages, outbuildings destroyed; house roof timbers considerably exposed. Some bigger trees snapped or uprooted.
T4	**Severe Tornado** 115–136 miles/hour (52–61 meters/sec)	Mobile homes destroyed; some sheds airborne for considerable distances; entire roofs removed from some houses or prefabricated buildings; roof timbers of stronger brick or stone houses completely exposed; possible collapse of gable ends. Numerous trees uprooted or snapped.
T5	**Intense Tornado** 137–160 miles/hour (62–72 meters/sec)	Motor cars levitated; more serious building damage than T4, yet house walls usually remaining; weak/old buildings may collapse completely.
T6	**Moderately Devastating Tornado** 161–186 miles/hour (73–83 meters/sec)	Heavy motor vehicles levitated; strong houses lose entire roofs and perhaps also a wall; more of the weaker buildings collapse.

Tornado Intensity Scale *(cont.)*

TORRO Intensity	Description of Tornado & Windspeeds	Description of Damage
T7	**Strongly Devastating Tornado** 187–212 miles/hour (84–95 meters/sec)	Frame house completely demolished; some walls of stone or brick houses beaten down or collapse; steel-framed warehouse-type buildings may buckle slightly. Locomotives thrown over. Noticeable de-barking of any standing trees by flying debris.
T8	**Severely Devastating Tornado** 213–240 miles/hour (96–107 meters/sec)	Frame houses and their contents dispersed over big distances; most other stone or brick houses irreparably damaged; steel-framed buildings buckled; motor cars hurled great distances.
T9	**Intensely Devastating Tornado** 241–269 miles/hour (108–120 meters/sec)	Many steel-framed buildings badly damaged; locomotives or trains hurled some distance. Complete debarking of any standing tree-trunks.
T10	**Super Tornado** 270–299 miles/hour (121–134 meters/sec)	Entire frame houses and similar buildings lifted bodily from foundations and carried some distances. Steel-reinforced concrete buildings may be severely damaged.

Tornado intensities are grouped more generally thus:
T0, T1, T2, T3 - weak tornadoes
T4, T5, T6, T7 - strong tornadoes
T8, T9, T10 - violent tornadoes

⊙ Tornado Storm and Research Organisation. "The TORRO Tornado Intensity Scale," www.torro.org.uk/tnintens.htm

10 Deadliest Tornadoes

Most of the world's tornadoes—about 75%—occur in the United States. The following are the deadliest tornadoes ever recorded in American history.

State	Date	Dead	Injured
MO-IL-IN	Mar. 18, 1925	695	2,027
LA-MS	May 7, 1840	317	109
MO-IL	May 27, 1896	255	1,000
MS	Apr. 5, 1936	216	700
GA	Apr. 6, 1936	203	1,600
TX-OK-KS	Apr. 9, 1947	181	970
LA-MS	Apr. 24, 1908	143	770
WI	June 12, 1899	117	220
MI	June 8, 1953	115	844
TX	May 11, 1953	114	597

⊙ Disaster Relief. "Tornadoes of the Twentieth Century," www.disasterrelief.org/Disasters/000104tornadocentury/
Weather.com. "Tornadoes!," www.weather.com/weather_center/tornado/inside/about.html

Earthquake Intensity Scales

Richter Scale	Mercalli Scale	Description
0–4.3	I	Mild; not felt
0–4.3	II	Mild; felt by a few, usually those at rest
0–4.3	III	Mild; noticeable to persons indoors, especially on upper floors
4.3–4.8	IV	Moderate; felt indoors by many, a few outside; dishes, windows, and doors rattle, walls make cracking sound; sensation like truck hitting building
4.3–4.8	V	Moderate; felt by nearly everyone; broken dishes and windows
4.8–6.2	VI	Intermediate; felt by all; heavy furniture moved; plaster falls
4.8–6.2	VII	Intermediate; considerable damage to poorly built, badly designed buildings; some chimneys broken
6.2–7.3	VIII	Severe; considerable damage in ordinary substantial buildings; heavy furniture overturned
6.2–7.3	IX	Severe; considerable damage to specially designed buildings; buildings shifted off foundations
6.2–7.3	X	Severe; well-built wooden structures and masonry and frame structures destroyed; rails bent
7.3–8.9	XI	Catastrophic; most structures and bridges destroyed; rails greatly bent
7.3–8.9	XII	Catastrophic; total damage

⊙ U.S. Geologic Survey Earthquake Hazards Program. "Magnitude and Intensity," http://neic.usgs.gov/neis/general/handouts/magnitude_intensity.html

10 Strongest U.S. Earthquakes

Location	Date	Magnitude	Casualties	Damage (US$)
Prince William Sound, Alaska	Mar. 28, 1964	9.2 Mw	125	$311 million
Andreanof Islands, Alaska	Mar. 9, 1957	8.8 Mw	0	$5 million
Rat Islands, Alaska	Feb. 4, 1965	8.7 Mw	0	$10,00 from resulting flooding
East of Shumagin Islands, Alaska	Nov. 10, 1938	8.3 Mw	0	0
Lituya Bay, Alaska	July 10, 1958	8.3 Mw	3	unknown
Yakutat Bay, Alaska	Sept. 10, 1899	8.2 Mw	0	0
Near Cape Yakataga, Alaska	Sept. 4, 1899	8.2 Mw	0	0
Andreanof Islands, Alaska	May 7, 1986	8.0 Mw	0	0
New Madrid, Missouri	Feb. 7, 1812	7.9 Mw	unknown	unknown
Fort Tejon, California	Jan. 9, 1857	7.9 Mw	2	unknown

⊙ U. S. Geological Survey Earthquake Hazards Program. "Fifteen Largest Earthquakes," http://neic.usgs.gov/neis/eqlists/10maps_usa.html

10 Strongest World Earthquakes

Location	Date	Magnitude	Casualties	Damage (US$)
Chile	May 22, 1960	9.5 Mw	2,000	$550 million
Alaska	Mar. 28, 1964	9.2 Mw	125	$311 million
Russia	Nov. 4, 1952	9.0 Mw	0	$1 million in Alaska from resulting tsunami
Ecuador	Jan. 31, 1906	8.8 Mw	500–1,500	unknown
Alaska	Mar. 9, 1957	8.8 Mw	0	$5 million in Hawaii from resulting tsunami
Kuril Islands	Nov. 6, 1958	8.7 Mw	0	0
Alaska	Feb. 4, 1965	8.7 Mw	0	~$10,000 from resulting flooding
India	Aug. 8, 1950	8.6 Mw	1,526	$25 million
Chile	Nov. 11, 1922	8.5 Mw	100	$5–25 million
Indonesia	Feb. 1, 1938	8.5 Mw	unknown	unknown

⊙ U. S. Geological Survey. "Ten Largest Earthquakes in the World Since 1900," http://neis.usgs.gov/neis/eqlists/10mpas_world.html

Endangered U.S. Animals and Birds

Lead Regions

1. Far West: CA, HI, ID, NV, OR, WA
2. Southwest: AZ, NM, OK, TX
3. Midwest: IL, IN, IA, MI, MN, OH, WI
4. South: AL, AR, FL, GA, KY, LA, MS, NC, PR, SC, TN
5. East: CT, DE, ME, MD, MA, NH, NJ, NY, PA, RI, VT, VA, WV
6. West: CO, KS, MO, MT, NE, ND, UT, SD, WY
7. Alaska: AK
8. Similarity of appearance to a listed species is a regulatory designation to facilitate the enforcement and further the policy of the Endangered Species Act. It is used when a species is so closely similar to a listed species that enforcement personnel would have substantial difficulty in attempting to differentiate between the listed and unlisted species.

N. National Marine Fisheries Service has jurisdiction for the species.

Lead Region Common Name (Scientific Name)

Mammals

3	Bat, gray (Myotis grisescens)
1	Bat, Hawaiian hoary (Lasiurus cinereus semotus)
3	Bat, Indiana (Myotis sodalis)
2	Bat, lesser (=Sanborn's) long-nosed (Leptonycteris curasoae yerbabuenae)
1	Bat, little Mariana fruit (Pteropus tokudae)
1	Bat, Mariana fruit (Pteropus mariannus mariannus)
2	Bat, Mexican long-nosed (Leptonycteris nivalis)
2	Bat, Ozark big-eared (Corynorhinus [=Plecotus] townsendii ingens)

5	Bat, Virginia big-eared (Corynorhinus [=Plecotus] townsendii virginianus)
1	Caribou, woodland (Rangifer tarandus caribou)
1	Deer, Columbian white-tailed (Odocoileus virginianus leucurus)
4	Deer, key (Odocoileus virginianus clavium)
6	Ferret, black-footed (Mustela nigripes)
1	Fox, San Joaquin kit (Vulpes macrotis mutica)
2	Jaguar (Panthera onca)
2	Jaguarundi, Gulf Coast (Herpailurus [=Felis] yagouaroundi cacomitli)
2	Jaguarundi, Sinaloan (Herpailurus [=Felis] yagouaroundi tolteca)
1	Kangaroo rat, Fresno (Dipodomys nitratoides exilis)
1	Kangaroo rat, giant (Dipodomys ingens)
1	Kangaroo rat, Morro Bay (Dipodomys heermanni morroensis)
1	Kangaroo rat, Stephens' (Dipodomys stephensi [incl. D. cascus])
1	Kangaroo rat, Tipton (Dipodomys nitratoides nitratoides)
1	Kangaroo rat, San Bernardino Merriam's (Dipodomys merriami parvus)
4	Manatee, West Indian (Trichechus manatus)
1	Mountain beaver, Point Arena (Aplodontia rufa nigra)
4	Mouse, Alabama beach (Peromyscus polionotus ammobates)
4	Mouse, Anastasia Island beach (Peromyscus polionotus phasma)
4	Mouse, Choctawhatchee beach (Peromyscus polionotus allophrys)
4	Mouse, Key Largo cotton (Peromyscus gossypinus allapaticola)
1	Mouse, Pacific pocket (Perognathus longimembris pacificus)
4	Mouse, Perdido Key beach (Peromyscus polionotus trissyllepsis)
1	Mouse, salt marsh harvest (Reithrodontomys raviventris)
4	Mouse, St. Andrew beach (Peromyscus polionotus peninsularis)
2	Ocelot (Leopardus [=Felis] pardalis)
4	Panther, Florida (Puma [=Felis] concolor coryi)
2	Pronghorn, Sonoran (Antilocapra americana sonoriensis)
5	Puma, eastern (=eastern cougar) (Puma [=Felis] concolor couguar)
4	Rabbit, Lower Keys (Sylvilagus palustris hefneri)
4	Rice rat, silver (Oryzomys palustris natator)
N	Sea-lion, Steller (=northern), western pop. (Eumetopias jubatus)
N	Seal, Caribbean monk (Monachus tropicalis)
N	Seal, Hawaiian monk (Monachus schauinslandi)
1	Sheep, bighorn (Peninsular Ranges pop. in CA) (Ovis canadensis)
4	Squirrel, Carolina northern flying (Glaucomys sabrinus coloratus)
5	Squirrel, Delmarva Peninsula fox (Sciurus niger cinereus)
2	Squirrel, Mount Graham red (Tamiasciurus hudsonicus grahamensis)
5	Squirrel, Virginia northern flying (Glaucomys sabrinus fuscus)
1	Vole, Amargosa (Microtus californicus scirpensis)
4	Vole, Florida salt marsh (Microtus pennsylvanicus dukecampbelli)
2	Vole, Hualapai Mexican (Microtus mexicanus hualpaiensis)
N	Whale, blue (Balaenoptera musculus)
N	Whale, bowhead (Balaena mysticetus)
N	Whale, finback (Balaenoptera physalus)
N	Whale, humpback (Megaptera novaeangliae)
N	Whale, right (Balaena glacialis [incl. australis])
N	Whale, Sei (Balaenoptera borealis)
N	Whale, sperm (Physeter catodon [=macrocephalus])
3	Wolf, gray (Canis lupus)
4	Wolf, red (Canis rufus)
4	Woodrat, Key Largo (Neotoma floridana smalli)

Lead
Region   *Common Name (Scientific Name)*

Birds

I	`Akepa, Hawaii (honeycreeper) (Loxops coccineus coccineus)
I	`Akepa, Maui (honeycreeper) (Loxops coccineus ochraceus)
I	`Akialoa, Kauai (honeycreeper) (Hemignathus procerus)
I	`Akiapola`au (honeycreeper) (Hemignathus munroi)
4	Blackbird, yellow-shouldered (Agelaius xanthomus)
2	Bobwhite, masked (quail) (Colinus virginianus ridgwayi)
I	Broadbill, Guam (Myiagra freycineti)
I	Condor, California (Gymnogyps californianus)
I	Coot, Hawaiian (=`alae-ke`oke`o) (Fulica americana alai)
4	Crane, Mississippi sandhill (Grus canadensis pulla)
2	Crane, whooping (Grus americana)
I	Creeper, Hawaii (Oreomystis mana)
I	Creeper, Molokai (=kakawahie) (Paroreomyza flammea)
I	Creeper, Oahu (=alauwahio) (Paroreomyza maculata)
I	Crow, Hawaiian (=`alala) (Corvus hawaiiensis)
I	Crow, Mariana (Corvus kubaryi)
7	Curlew, Eskimo (Numenius borealis)
I	Duck, Hawaiian (=koloa) (Anas wyvilliana)
I	Duck, Laysan (Anas laysanensis)
I	Falcon, American peregrine (Falco peregrinus anatum)
2	Falcon, northern aplomado (Falco femoralis septentrionalis)
8	Falcon, peregrine (Falco peregrinus)
I	Finch, Laysan (honeycreeper) (Telespyza cantans)
I	Finch, Nihoa (honeycreeper) (Telespyza ultima)
2	Flycatcher, Southwestern willow (Empidonax traillii extimus)
I	Goose, Hawaiian (=nene) (Branta [=Nesochen] sandvicensis)
I	Hawk, Hawaiian (=io) (Buteo solitarius)
4	Hawk, Puerto Rican broad-winged (Buteo platypterus brunnescens)
4	Hawk, Puerto Rican sharp-shinned (Accipiter striatus venator)
I	Honeycreeper, crested (=`akohekohe) (Palmeria dolei)
I	Kingfisher, Guam Micronesian (Halcyon cinnamomina cinnamomina)
4	Kite, Everglade snail (Rostrhamus sociabilis plumbeus)
I	Mallard, Mariana (Anas oustaleti)
I	Megapode, Micronesian (=La Perouse's) (Megapodius laperouse)
I	Millerbird, Nihoa (old world warbler) (Acrocephalus familiaris kingi)
I	Moorhen (=gallinule), Hawaiian common (Gallinula chloropus sandvicensis)
I	Moorhen (=gallinule), Mariana common (Gallinula chloropus guami)
4	Nightjar, Puerto Rican (=whip-poor-will) (Caprimulgus noctitherus)
I	Nukupu`u (honeycreeper) (Hemignathus lucidus)
I	`O`o, Kauai (=`o`o `a`a) (honeyeater) (Moho braccatus)
I	`O`u (honeycreeper) (Psittirostra psittacea)
I	Palila (honeycreeper) (Loxioides bailleui)
4	Parrot, Puerto Rican (Amazona vittata)
I	Parrotbill, Maui (honeycreeper) (Pseudonestor xanthophrys)
I	Pelican, brown (Pelecanus occidentalis)
I	Petrel, Hawaiian dark-rumped (Pterodroma phaeopygia sandwichensis)

4	Pigeon, Puerto Rican plain (Columba inornata wetmorei)
3	Plover, piping (Charadrius melodus)
1	Po`ouli (honeycreeper) (Melamprosops phaeosoma)
2	Prairie-chicken, Attwater's greater (Tympanuchus cupido attwateri)
2	Pygmy-owl, cactus ferruginous (Glaucidium brasilianum cactorum)
1	Rail, California clapper (Rallus longirostris obsoletus)
1	Rail, Guam (Rallus owstoni)
1	Rail, light-footed clapper (Rallus longirostris levipes)
2	Rail, Yuma clapper (Rallus longirostris yumanensis)
1	Shrike, San Clemente loggerhead (Lanius ludovicianus mearnsi)
4	Sparrow, Cape Sable seaside (Ammodramus maritimus mirabilis)
4	Sparrow, Florida grasshopper (Ammodramus savannarum floridanus)
1	Stilt, Hawaiian (=ae`o) (Himantopus mexicanus knudseni)
4	Stork, wood (Mycteria americana)
1	Swiftlet, Mariana gray (=vanikoro) (Aerodramus vanikorensis bartschi)
1	Tern, California least (Sterna antillarum browni)
3	Tern, least (Sterna antillarum)
5	Tern, roseate (Sterna dougallii dougallii)
1	Thrush, large Kauai (Myadestes myadestinus)
1	Thrush, Molokai (=oloma`o) (Myadestes lanaiensis rutha)
1	Thrush, small Kauai (=puaiohi) (Myadestes palmeri)
2	Vireo, black-capped (Vireo atricapillus)
1	Vireo, least Bell's (Vireo bellii pusillus)
4	Warbler, Bachman's (Vermivora bachmanii)
2	Warbler, golden-cheeked (Dendroica chrysoparia)
3	Warbler, Kirtland's (Dendroica kirtlandii)
1	Warbler, nightingale reed (Acrocephalus luscinia)
1	White-eye, bridled (Zosterops conspicillatus conspicillatus)
4	Woodpecker, ivory-billed (Campephilus principalis)
4	Woodpecker, red-cockaded (Picoides borealis)

Reptiles

8	Alligator, American (Alligator mississippiensis)
4	Anole, Culebra Island giant (Anolis roosevelti)
4	Boa, Puerto Rican (Epicrates inornatus)
4	Boa, Virgin Islands tree (Epicrates monensis granti)
4	Crocodile, American (Crocodylus acutus)
4	Gecko, Monito (Sphaerodactylus micropithecus)
1	Lizard, blunt-nosed leopard (Gambelia silus)
4	Lizard, St. Croix ground (Ameiva polops)
4	Sea turtle, green (Chelonia mydas)
4	Sea turtle, hawksbill (Eretmochelys imbricata)
2	Sea turtle, Kemp's (=Atlantic) ridley (Lepidochelys kempii)
4	Sea turtle, leatherback (Dermochelys coriacea)
1	Snake, San Francisco garter (Thamnophis sirtalis tetrataenia)
4	Turtle, Alabama redbelly (Pseudemys alabamensis)
5	Turtle, Plymouth redbelly (Pseudemys rubriventris bangsi)

Amphibians

2	Salamander, Barton Springs (Eurycea sosorum)
1	Salamander, desert slender (Batrachoseps aridus)

Lead
Region Common Name (Scientific Name)

1	Salamander, Santa Cruz long-toed (Ambystoma macrodactylum croceum)
5	Salamander, Shenandoah (Plethodon shenandoah)
2	Salamander, Sonoran tiger (Ambystoma tigrinum stebbinsi)
2	Salamander, Texas blind (Typhlomolge rathbuni)
1	Toad, arroyo (Bufo microscaphus californicus)
2	Toad, Houston (Bufo houstonensis)
6	Toad, Wyoming (Bufo hemiophrys baxteri)

⊙ U.S. Fish and Wildlife Service, Division of Endangered Species. "Endangered
   Species List," www.fws.gov

Pollution

The United States Environmental Protection Agency (EPA) is the federal body responsi-
ble for regulating pollution and for protecting human health and the environment.
Learn more about the EPA at www.epa.gov.

Air

Pollutant	Health Effect	Environmental Effect
Carbon Monoxide	Reduces ability of blood to bring oxygen to body cells and tissues; cells and tissues need oxygen to work. Carbon monoxide may be particularly hazardous to people who have heart or circulatory (blood vessel) problems and people who have damaged lungs or breathing passages	
Lead	Brain and other nervous system damage; children are at special risk. Some lead-containing chemicals cause cancer in animals. Lead causes digestive and other health problems.	Lead can harm wildlife
Ground Level Ozone	Breathing problems, reduced lung function, asthma, irritates eyes, stuffy nose, reduced resistance to colds and other infections, may speed up aging of lung tissue	Ozone can damage plants and trees; smog can cause reduced visibility
Nitrogen Oxides (NOx)	Lung damage, illnesses of breathing passages and lungs (respiratory system)	Nitrogen dioxide is an ingredient of acid rain (acid aerosols), which can damage trees and lakes. Acid aerosols can reduce visibility.

Particulate Matter	Nose and throat irritation, lung damage, bronchitis, early death	Particulates are the main source of haze that reduces visibility
Sulfur Oxides (SOx)	Breathing problems, may cause permanent damage to lungs	SO_2 is an ingredient in acid rain (acid aerosols), which can damage trees and lakes. Acid aerosols can also reduce visibility.
Volatile Organic Compounds (VOCs)	In addition to ozone (smog) effects, many VOCs can cause serious health problems such as cancer and other effects.	In addition to ozone (smog) effects, some VOCs such as formaldehyde and ethylene may harm plants.

Water

Pollutant	Health Effect
Contaminated Sediment	Metals, PAHs, and organics listed above are toxic to various plants and animals, including people. These contaminants tend to biomagnify as they travel up the food chain. All have been linked to health problems in people.
Disinfection Byproducts	Acute and chronic gastrointestinal illness, cancer, liver toxicity, and reproductive and developmental disorders
Dredged Materials	Acute and chronic gastrointestinal illness, cancer, liver toxicity, and reproductive and developmental disorders
Microbial Pathogens	Acute and chronic gastrointestinal illness, cancer, liver toxicity, and reproductive and developmental disorders

Land

Pollutant	Health Effect
Arsenic	Skin damage; circulatory system problems; increased risk of cancer
Barium	Increase in blood pressure
Benzene	Anemia; decrease in blood platelets; increased risk of cancer
Cadmium	Kidney damage
Cyanide	Nerve damage or thyroid problems
Lead	Infants and children: Delays in physical or mental development. Adults: Kidney problems; high blood pressure
Mercury	Kidney damage

Pollution (cont.)

Land (cont.)

Pollutant	Health Effect
Polychlorinated Biphenyls (PCBs)	Skin changes; thymus gland problems; immune deficiencies; reproductive or nervous system difficulties; increased risk of cancer
Toluene	Nervous system, kidney, or liver problems
Trichloroethylene (TCE)	Liver problems; increased risk of cancer

⊙ United States Environmental Protection Agency. "Water Pollutants,"
   www.epa.gov/ebtpages/pwaterpollutants.html
  United States Environmental Protection Agency. "Air Pollutants,"
   www.epa.gov/ebtpages/pairpollutants.html
  United States Environmental Protection Agency. "Soil Pollutants,"
   www.epa.gov/ebtpages/psoilcontaminants.html

THE SCIENCES: *Mathematics*

Mathematical Terms

Area	the number of square units that can fit inside a figure
Circumference	distance around the circle
Composite number	a number with more than two factors
Diameter	distance across a circle, passing through its center; equals two times the radius
Factor	any number that can divide evenly into a given number; for example, 2 and 3 are factors of 6
Hypotenuse	the longest side of a right triangle
Integer	the set of whole numbers and their additive inverses
Irrational number	real numbers that cannot be expressed as the quotient of two integers
Mean	the average
Median	the middle number when the data are listed in size order
Mode	the piece of data that appears most often
Perimeter	the distance around a figure
Pi (π)	the ratio of the measure of the circumference and diameter of a circle; estimated value is 3.14
Prime Number	a number with only two factors, itself and 1
Radius	the distance from the center of circle to any point on the circle; one-half of the diameter
Rational number	a number that can be expressed as the quotient of two integers
Reciprocal	a fraction that is the result of switching a fraction's numerator and denominator; the multiplicative inverse of a fraction
Volume	the number of cubic units that can fit inside a three-dimensional figure

⊙ Heddens, James W., and William R. Speer. *Today's Mathematics*. 7th ed. New York: Macmillan, 1992.

Mathematical Symbols

Below are some of the more common symbols and expressions used in mathematics, geometry, and statistics.

+	1. plus	$\cup$	union
	2. positive (number or charge)	$\subset$	is a subset of
−	1. minus	$\Rightarrow$	implies
	2. negative (number or charge)	$\sqrt{}$	square root
±	plus or minus	$\sqrt[3]{}$	cube root
× or ·	multiplied by	x^2	x squared
÷	divided by	x^3	x cubed
=	is equal to	x^n	x to the power n
≠	is not equal to	π	pi
≈	approximately equal to	r	radius of circle
≡	is equivalent to	n!	n factorial
<	is less than	$\int$	the integral of
≤	is less than or equal to	$\angle$	angle
>	is greater than	$\llcorner$	right angle
≥	is greater than or equal to	$\triangle$	triangle
%	percent	$\parallel$	is parallel to
∞	infinity	$\perp$	is perpendicular to
∝	varies as	°	degree
:	is to, the ratio of	'	1. minute (of an arc)
∈	is an element of (a set)		2. foot, feet
∉	is not an element of (a set)	"	1. second (of an arc)
Ø	empty set		2. inch, inches
∩	intersection		

Roman Numerals

Roman Numeral	Arabic Numeral	Roman Numeral	Arabic Numeral	Roman Numeral	Arabic Numeral
I	1	XVII	17	CC	200
II	2	XVIII	18	CCL	250
III	3	XIX	19	CCC	300
IIII or IV	4	XX	20	CCCL	350
V	5	XXV	25	CD	400
VI	6	XXX	30	CDL	450
VII	7	XXXV	35	D	500
VIII	8	XL	40	DC	600
IX	9	XLV	45	DCC	700
X	10	L	50	DCCC	800
XI	11	LX	60	CM	900
XII	12	LXX	70	M	1,000
XIII	13	LXXX	80	MD	1,500
XIV	14	XC	90	MM	2,000
XV	15	C	100	MMD	2,500
XVI	16	CL	150	MMM	3,000

⊙ Roman Numerals 101. "Starting Off," www.cod.edu/people/faculty/lawrence/ romaindx.htm

Common Mathematical Procedures

Addition of fractions with like denominators	$\frac{1}{8} + \frac{6}{8} = \frac{7}{8}$	Add numerators; keep denominators
Addition of fractions with unlike denominators	$\frac{3}{4} + \frac{1}{8} = \frac{6}{8} + \frac{1}{8} = \frac{7}{8}$	Rewrite the fractions with common denominators, then add as usual
Addition of mixed numbers	$1\frac{5}{8} + 3\frac{1}{8} = 4\frac{6}{8}$	Add the whole number part, then add the fraction part
Subtraction of fractions with like denominators	$\frac{6}{8} - \frac{1}{8} = \frac{5}{8}$	Subtract the numerators and keep the denominators
Subtraction of fractions with unlike denominators	$\frac{3}{4} - \frac{3}{8} = \frac{6}{8} - \frac{3}{8} = \frac{3}{8}$	Rewrite the fractions with common denominators, then subtract as usual
Multiplying fractions	$\frac{1}{2} \times \frac{3}{4} = \frac{3}{8}$	Multiply the numerators, then multiply the denominators
Dividing fractions	$\frac{1}{7} \div \frac{1}{2} = \frac{1}{7} \times 2 = \frac{2}{7}$	Multiply the first fraction by the reciprocal of the second fraction
Proportions	$\frac{2}{10} \times \frac{1}{5}$ $2 \times 5 = 1 \times 10$ $10 = 10$	When two ratios form a proportion, then the cross products are equal
Finding the part of a whole when the percentage is known	50% of 84 is ____. $50 \div 100 = .50$ $.50 \times 84 = 42$	Divide the percentage by 100, then multiply the result by the whole
Finding the whole when the percentage is known	20% of ____ is 12. $20 \div 100 = .20$ $12 \div .20 = 60$	Divide the percentage by 100, then divide the result into the part
Finding the percentage of a number	____% of 80 is 20 $20 \div 80 = .25$ $.25 \times 100 = 25\%$	Divide the part by the whole, then multiply the result by 100
Combining like terms	$5x^2 + 4x^2 = 9x^2$ $11y^6 - 7y^6 = 4y^6$	Add or subtract the coefficients; the base and exponents remain the same

⊙ Occhiogrosso, Marilyn, et al. *Integrated Mathematics Integrated Course.* New York: Amsco, 1995.

Areas and Volumes

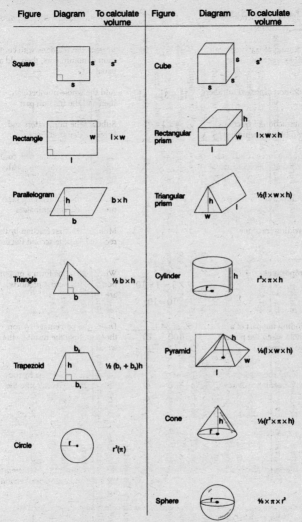

Figure	Diagram	To calculate volume	Figure	Diagram	To calculate volume
Square		s^2	Cube		s^3
Rectangle		$l \times w$	Rectangular prism		$l \times w \times h$
Parallelogram		$b \times h$	Triangular prism		$\frac{1}{2}(l \times w \times h)$
Triangle		$\frac{1}{2}b \times h$	Cylinder		$r^2 \times \pi \times h$
Trapezoid		$\frac{1}{2}(b_1 + b_2)h$	Pyramid		$\frac{1}{3}(l \times w \times h)$
Circle		$r^2(\pi)$	Cone		$\frac{1}{3}(r^2 \times \pi \times h)$
			Sphere		$\frac{4}{3} \times \pi \times r^3$

⊙ The Math Forum. "Area and Volume Formulas," http://forum.swarthmore/edu/dr.math

THE SCIENCES: *Astronomy*

The Solar System

Planets

Name	Orbits (Designation)	Distance ooo mi. / ooo km.	Radius mi. / km.	Rotate (days)	Period (days)	Discoverer	Date
Sun	—	—	431,520 / 696,000	25.4	—	Known in antiquity	
Mercury	Sun (I)	36,000 / 57,910	1,600 / 2,440	58.7	87.97	Known in antiquity	
Venus	Sun (II)	67,000 / 108,200	3,350 / 6,052	243*	224.70	Known in antiquity	
Earth	Sun (III)	93,000 / 149,600	3,960 / 6,378	0.99	365.26	Known in antiquity	
Mars	Sun (IV)	141,000 / 227,940	2,100 / 3,397	1.03	686.98	Known in antiquity	
Jupiter	Sun (V)	483,000 / 778,570	44,320 / 71,492	0.41	4,331.59	Known in antiquity	
Saturn	Sun (VI)	886,000 / 1,433,525	37,250 / 60,268	0.45	10,747	Known in antiquity	
Uranus	Sun (VII)	1,782,000 / 2,872,450	16,000 / 25,559	0.72*	30,589	Herschel	1781
Neptune	Sun (VIII)	2,793,000 / 4,495,100	15,500 / 24,764	0.67	59,800	Adams, LeVerrier, Galle, and d'Arrest	1846
Pluto	Sun (IX)	3,670,000 / 5,869,660	750 / 1,195	6.39*	90,588	Tombaugh	1930

Planetary Satellites

Planet (No. of Satellites)	Satellite Name	Distance ooo mi. / ooo km.	Radius mi. / km.	Period (days)	Discoverer	Date
Earth (1)	Moon	238 / 384	1,077 / 1,737	27.32	Known in antiquity	
Mars (2)	Phobos	6 / 9	8x7x6 / 13x11x9	0.32	Hall	1877
	Deimos	14 / 23	5x4x3 / 8x6x5	1.26	Hall	1877
Jupiter (16)	Metis	79 / 128	12 / 20	0.29	Synnott**	1979

Adrastea	80 / 129	8×6×5 / 13×10×8	0.30	Jewitt, Danielson	1979
Amalthea	112 / 181	8×14×5×42 / 13×17×3×67	0.50	Barnard	1892
Thebe	138 / 222	34×28 / 55×45	0.67	Synnott***	1979
Io	262 / 422	1,129 / 1,821	1.77	Galileo	1610
Europa	416 / 671	970 / 1,565	3.55	Galileo	1610
Ganymede	665 / 1,070	1,633 / 2,634	7.15	Galileo	1610
Callisto	1,167 / 1,883	1,490 / 2,403	16.69	Galileo	1610
Leda	6,878 / 11,094	3 / 5	238.72	Kowal	1974
Himalia	7,118 / 11,480	58 / 85	250.57	Perrine	1904
Lysithea	7,266 / 11,720	7 / 12	259.22	Nicholson	1938
Elara	7,277 / 11,737	25 / 40	259.65	Perrine	1905
Ananke	13,144 / 21,200	6 / 10	631*	Nicholson	1951
Carme	14,012 / 22,600	9 / 15	692*	Nicholson	1938
Pasiphae	14,570 / 23,500	11 / 18	735*	Melotte	1908
Sinope	14,694 / 23,700	9 / 14	758*	Nicholson	1914
Saturn (18)					
Pan	83 / 134	6 / 10	0.58	Showalter**	1990
Atlas	86 / 138	12×11×9 / 19×17×14	0.60	Terrile***	1980
Prometheus	86 / 139	40×3×21 / 74×50×34	0.61	Collins***	1980
Pandora	88 / 142	34×27×19 / 55×44×31	0.63	Collins***	1980
Epimetheus	94 / 151	43×34×34 / 69×55×55	0.69	Fountain, Larson, Reitsema, Smith***	1980
Janus	94 / 151	60×59×48 / 97×89×77	0.69	Dollfus	1966

Notes: * Retrograde motion
** Identified from photographs returned from *Voyager 2*
*** Identified from photographs returned from *Voyager 1*

Planet (No. of Satellites)	Satellite Name	Distance 000 mi. / 000 km.	Radius mi. / km.	Period (days)	Discoverer	Date
Saturn (18) (cont.)	Mimas	115 / 186	130x122x118 / 209x196x191	0.94	Herschel	1789
	Enceladus	148 / 238	159x153x152 / 256x247x245	1.37	Herschel	1789
	Tethys	183 / 295	332x327x326 / 536x528x526	1.89	Cassini	1684
	Telesto	183 / 295	9x8x5 / 15x13x8	1.89	Fountain, Larson, Reitsema, Smith***	1980
	Calypso	183 / 295	9x5x5 / 15x8x8	1.89	Pascu, Seidelman, Baum, Currie	1980
	Dione	234 / 377	347 / 560	2.74	Cassini	1684
	Helene	234 / 377	11x10x9 / 18x16x15	2.74	Laques, Lecacheux	1980
	Rhea	327 / 527	474 / 764	4.52	Cassini	1672
	Titan	758 / 1,222	1,597 / 2,575	15.95	Huygens	1655
	Hyperion	918 / 1,481	115x87x70 / 185x141x113	21.28	Bond, Lassell	1848
	Iapetus	2,208 / 3,561	445 / 718	79.33	Cassini	1671
	Phoebe	8,030 / 12,952	71x68x65 / 115x110x105	550.48*	Pickering	1898
Uranus (17)	Cordelia	31 / 50	8 / 13	0.34	Terrile**	1986
	Ophelia	33 / 54	9 / 15	0.38	Terrile**	1986
	Bianca	37 / 59	13 / 21	0.43	Voyager 2 photos	1986
	Cressida	38 / 62	19 / 31	0.46	Synnott**	1986
	Desdemona	39 / 63	17 / 27	0.47	Synnott**	1986
	Juliet	40 / 64	26 / 42	0.49	Synnott**	1986
	Portia	41 / 66	33 / 54	0.51	Synnott**	1986
	Rosalind	43 / 70	17 / 27	0.56	Synnott**	1986
	Belinda	47 / 75	20 / 33	0.62	Synnott**	1986
	Puck	53 / 86	48 / 77	0.76	Synnott**	1985

Miranda	80 / 129	149x145x144 / 240x234x233	1.41	Kuiper	1948
Ariel	118 / 191	360x358x358 / 581x578x578	2.52	Lassell	1851
Umbriel	165 / 266	363 / 585	4.14	Lassell	1851
Titania	270 / 436	489 / 789	8.71	Herschel	1787
Oberon	362 / 584	472 / 761	13.46	Herschel	1787
Caliban	4,445 / 7,169	19 / 30	579.38*	Gladman, Nicholson, Burns, Kavelaars	1997
Sycorax	7,549 / 12,175	37 / 60	1289*	Gladman, Nicholson, Burns, Kavelaars	1997
Neptune (8)					
Naiad	30 / 48	18 / 29	0.29	Terrile**	1989
Thalassa	31 / 50	25 / 40	0.31	Terrile**	1989
Despina	33 / 53	46 / 74	0.33	Synnott**	1989
Galatea	38 / 62	49 / 79	0.43	Synnott**	1989
Larissa	46 / 74	65x55x56 / 104x89x90	0.55	Reitsema, Tholen, Hubbard, Lebofsky**	1989
Proteus	73 / 118	135x129x125 / 218x208x201	1.12	Synnott**	1989
Triton	220 / 355	839 / 1,353	5.88*	Lassell	1846
Nereid	3,418 / 5,513	105 / 170	360.14	Kuiper	1949
Pluto (1)					
Charon	12 / 20	368 / 593	6.39	Christy	1978

Notes: * Retrograde motion
** Identified from photographs returned from *Voyager 2*
*** Identified from photographs returned from *Voyager 1*

© Encrenaz, Thérèse. *The Solar System*. Berlin, New York: Springer, 1995.
National Space Science Data Center. "Planetary Fact Sheet," http://nssdc.gsfc.nasa.gov/planetary/planetfact.html

Phases of the Moon

The moon is visible from Earth as a disk that reflects light from the sun. Only one hemisphere of the moon is illuminated, and as it orbits Earth the illuminated face moves in and out of view. This results in what are known as the phases of the moon. When the moon is on the far side of Earth, directly opposite the sun, the whole of its illuminated face can be seen as a circle—a full moon. As the moon circles around and the illuminated portion moves out of view, it is said to be waning; when it is between Earth and the sun and none of the illuminated face is visible, it is a new moon; and as it returns to full visibility it is said to be waxing.

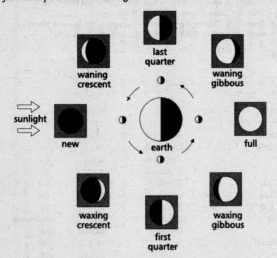

⊙ U.S. Naval Observatory. "Phases of the Moon," http://aa.usno.navy.mil/AA/data/docs/MoonPhase.html

Future Total Solar Eclipses

Date	Duration	Where Visible
June 21, 2001	4 min. 57 sec.	Southern Africa, Madagascar
Dec. 4, 2002	2 min. 4 sec.	Southern Africa, Australia
Nov. 23, 2003	1 min. 57 sec.	Antarctica
Mar. 29, 2006	4 min. 7 sec.	Africa, Turkey, Russia
Aug. 1, 2008	2 min. 27 sec.	Greenland, northern Russia, China
July 22, 2009	6 min. 39 sec.	India, Himalayan region, China
July 11, 2010	5 min. 20 sec.	South Pacific, southern Chile, Argentina
Nov. 13, 2012	4 min. 2 sec.	Northern Australia
Mar. 20, 2015	2 min. 47 sec.	North Atlantic
Mar. 9, 2016	4 min. 9 sec.	Indonesia, North Pacific
Aug. 21, 2017	2 min. 40 sec.	United States
July 2, 2019	4 min. 33 sec.	South Pacific, Chile, Argentina

Dec. 14, 2020	2 min. 10 sec.	Chile, Argentina
Dec. 4, 2021	1 min. 54 sec.	Antarctica
Apr. 8, 2024	4 min. 38 sec.	Mexico, United States, Canada
Aug. 12, 2026	2 min. 18 sec.	Greenland, Iceland, Spain
Aug. 2, 2027	6 min. 23 sec.	North Africa, Saudi Arabia
July 22, 2028	5 min. 10 sec.	Australia, New Zealand
Nov. 25, 2030	3 min. 44 sec.	Southern Africa, Australia

⊙ Espenak, Fred. "Eclipse Predictions by Fred Espenak, NASA/GSFC," http://sun-earth.gsfc.nasa.gov/eclipse/SEcat/SE2001-2100.html

Harrington, Philip S. *Eclipse! The What, Where, When, Why, and How Guide to Watching Solar and Lunar Eclipses.* New York: Wiley, 1997.

U.S. Naval Observatory. "Upcoming and Recent Eclipses of the Sun and Moon," http://riemann.usno.navy.mil/AA/data/docs/UpcomingEclipses.html

Galaxies

Name	Type	Distance[1]	Diameter
Milky Way*	Spiral	—	110
Small Magellanic Cloud (SMC)*	Irregular	18	20
Large Magellanic Cloud (LMC)*	Irregular	160	30
Ursa Minor*	Dwarf elliptical	222	7.8
Sculptor system*	Dwarf elliptical	280	7.5
Fornax system*	Dwarf elliptical	612	20
NGC 6822*	Irregular	2,150	5.5
NGC 205*	Elliptical	2,220	14
M32 / NGC 221*	Elliptical	2,220	6.8
M31 / NGC 224* (Andromeda)	Spiral	2,220	170
M33 / NGC 598* (Triangulum)	Spiral	2,720	59
Maffei I	Elliptical	3,300	unknown
M82	Irregular	10,000	23
M81 (Ursa Major group)	Spiral	10,500	100
M51 (Whirlpool)	Spiral	13,000	65
Centaurus A	Elliptical	16,000	30
M101 (Pinwheel)	Spiral	20,000	200
M83	Spiral	27,000	100
M104 (Sombrero)	Spiral	40,000	30
M87 (Virgo A)	Elliptical	50,000	40

1. Distances and diameters are given in thousands of light-years and are approximate.

M refers to the Messier Catalog number.

NGC refers to the New General Catalogue number.

* Indicates a member of the Local Group

⊙ Friedman, Herbert. *The Astronomer's Universe: Stars, Galaxies, and Cosmos.* New York: Norton, 1990.

Sandage, Allan, and John Bedke. *The Carnegie Atlas of Galaxies.* Washington, D.C.: Carnegie Institution of Washington, 1994.

Wray, James D. *A Color Atlas of Galaxies.* Cambridge: Cambridge University Press, 1988.

Stars: 10 Closest to the Sun

Rank	Star	Distance in light-years	Magnitude
1	Proxima Centauri	4.2	11.3
2	Alpha Centauri A	4.3	.33
3	Alpha Centauri B	4.3	1.70
4	Barnard's Star	5.96	9.5
5	Wolf 359	7.6	13.5
6	Lalande 21185	8.11	7.5
7	UV Ceti A	8.55	12.52
8	UV Ceti B	8.55	13.02
9	Alpha Sirius	8.7	-1.47
10	Beta Sirius	8.7	8.3

⊙ Royal Observatory Greenwich. "The 30 Closest Stars," www.rog.nmm.ac.uk/leaflets/closeststars/closeststars.html

Speer, Gordon. "Table of the Earth's Nearest Stars," www.essex1.com/people/speer/stars.html

Constellations

Constellation	Common Name(s)	When Visible*
Andromeda		autumn (Nov.)
Aquarius	Water bearer	autumn (Oct.)
Aquila	Eagle	summer (Sep.)
Ara	Altar	summer (July)
Aries	Ram	winter (Dec.)
Boötes	Herdsman	spring (June)
Cancer	Crab	spring (Mar.)
Canis major	Greater dog	winter (Feb.)
Canis minor	Lesser dog	spring (Mar.)
Capricornus	Goat	autumn (Sep.)
Cassiopeia		all year (Nov.)
Centaurus	Centaur	spring (May)
Cepheus		all year (Oct.)
Cetus	Sea monster	winter (Dec.)
Crater	Cup	spring (Apr.)
Crux	Southern cross	spring (May)
Cygnus	Swan, Northern cross	summer (Sep.)
Draco		all year (July)
Eridanus	River	winter (Dec.)
Gemini	Twins	winter (Feb.)
Hercules		summer (July)
Hydra	Sea serpent	spring (Apr.)
Leo	Lion	spring (Apr.)
Libra	Balance	summer (June)
Lynx		spring (Mar.)
Lyra	Harp	summer (Aug.)
Ophiuchus	Serpent bearer	summer (July)
Orion	Hunter	winter (Jan.)
Pegasus		autumn (Oct.)

Perseus		winter (Dec.)
Pisces	Fishes	autumn (Nov.)
Sagittarius	Archer ·	summer (Aug.)
Scorpius	Scorpion	summer (July)
Taurus	Bull	winter (Jan.)
Ursa major	Big dipper, Great bear, Plough	all year (Apr.)
Ursa minor	Little dipper, Little bear	all year (June)
Virgo	Maiden, Virgin	spring (May)

*Visibility information is for the northern hemisphere; month in parentheses is the best time for observation.

⊙ Bakich, Michael Eli. *The Cambridge Guide to the Constellations*. New York: Cambridge University Press, 1995.
  "The Constellations and Their Stars," www.astro.wisc.edu/~dolan/constellations/

Potentially Hazardous Asteroids*

Asteroids are listed in order of date of close-approach to Earth.

Asteroid Name or Designation	Earth Close-Approach Date	AU**	Asteroid Name or Designation	Earth Close-Approach Date	AU**
1998 VD35	Jan. 2, 2001	0.098	1998 SF36	June 25, 2004	0.014
1994 WR12	Jan. 17, 2001	0.135	4179 Toutatis	Sep. 29, 2004	0.010
1998 WT	Feb. 26, 2001	0.148	1999 LF6	Oct. 18, 2004	0.071
1998 SF36	Mar. 28, 2001	0.043	1998 WT24	Nov. 12, 2004	0.096
4034 1986 PA	Apr. 3, 2001	0.147	7753 1988 XB	Nov. 21, 2004	0.073
1998 HD14	Aug. 26, 2001	0.076	1998 DV9	Jan. 11, 2005	0.078
1998 WT24	Dec. 16, 2001	0.012	1998 WT	Mar. 7, 2005	0.072
3362 Khufu	Dec. 29, 2001	0.160	1992 UY4	Aug. 8, 2005	0.040
4660 Nereus	Jan. 22, 2002	0.029	1862 Apollo	Nov. 6, 2005	0.075
3361 Orpheus	Jan. 27, 2002	0.170	3361 Orpheus	Jan. 11, 2006	0.160
5604 1992 FE	June 22, 2002	0.077	1999 A010	Mar. 18, 2006	0.090
2101 Adonis	June 29, 2002	0.161	4450 Pan	Sep. 8, 2006	0.146
1998 WT	Oct. 17, 2002	0.103	7341 1991 VK	Jan. 21, 2007	0.068
1997 XF11	Oct. 31, 2002	0.064	1998 VO	May 7, 2007	0.063
3362 Khufu	Dec. 25, 2002	0.150	1862 Apollo	May 8, 2007	0.071
6489 Golevka	May 20, 2003	0.092	1999 AQ10	Oct. 1, 2007	0.138
1998 FH12	June 27, 2003	0.049	2340 Hathor	Oct. 22, 2007	0.060
1994 PM	Aug. 16, 2003	0.025	11500 1989 UR	Nov. 24, 2007	0.071
1998 VS	Sep. 11, 2003	0.158	3200 Phaethon	Dec. 10, 2007	0.121
1998 FG2	Oct. 22, 2003	0.035	4450 Pan	Feb. 19, 2008	0.041
1989 UQ	Oct. 24, 2003	0.150	6037 1988 EG	Mar. 7, 2008	0.167
1990 OS	Nov. 10, 2003	0.030	1620 Geographo	Mar. 17, 2008	0.125
1996 GT	Nov. 12, 2003	0.048	1991 DG	Aug. 2, 2008	0.175
1998 UT18	Nov. 28, 2003	0.066	1991 VH	Aug. 15, 2008	0.046
1996 JG	Nov. 30, 2003	0.142	1998 VO	Oct. 29, 2008	0.080
3362 Khufu	Dec. 20, 2003	0.195	4179 Toutatis	Nov. 9, 2008	0.050
6239 Minos	Feb. 2, 2004	0.056	1993 KH	Nov. 22, 2008	0.099
1993 KH	June 14, 2004	0.132	2000 AF6	Dec. 13, 2008	0.074

Asteroid Name or Designation	Earth Close-Approach Date	AU**			
1998 CS1	Jan. 17, 2009	0.028	2340 Hathor	Oct. 21, 2014	0.048
1999 AQ10	Feb. 18, 2009	0.012	1998 HD14	Apr. 14, 2015	0.195
144021991 DB	Mar. 15, 2009	0.113	1566 Icarus	June 16, 2015	0.054
1998 OR2	Mar. 19, 2009	0.123	1994 AW1	July 15, 2015	0.065
1996 FG3	May 6, 2009	0.156	7822 1991 CS	Sep. 4, 2015	0.160
1991 JW	May 23, 2009	0.081	1998 WT24	Dec. 11, 2015	0.028
1994 CC	June 10, 2009	0.017	7822 1991 CS	Feb. 23, 2016	0.168
8566 1996 EN	Aug. 28, 2009	0.194	1998 HD14	Apr. 9, 2016	0.155
1999 AP10	Oct. 20, 2009	0.076	1997 XF11	June 10, 2016	0.180
3361 Orpheus	Dec. 25, 2009	0.138	1998 HL3	July 6, 2016	0.195
4486 Mithra	Mar. 12, 2010	0.189	1999 AQ10	Oct. 18, 2016	0.144
6239 Minos	Aug. 10, 2010	0.099	1998 VN	Nov. 16, 2016	0.087
1989 UQ	Oct. 21, 2010	0.153	2102 Tantalus	Dec. 30, 2016	0.137
1991 JW	Nov. 28, 2010	0.095	5604 1992 FE	Feb. 24, 2017	0.034
2000 AZ93	Jan. 11, 2011	0.047	6063 Jason	May 27, 2017	0.099
1998 FH12	June 23, 2011	0.135	1998 FW4	Sep. 26, 2017	0.029
1998 SC15	Oct. 18, 2011	0.121	1989 UQ	Oct. 16, 2017	0.156
1996 FG3	Nov. 23, 2011	0.101	1989 UP	Nov. 2, 2017	0.055
1996 FG3	Nov. 23, 2011	0.101	3361 Orpheus	Nov. 25, 2017	0.061
1996 SK	Apr. 18, 2012	0.175	3200 Phaethon	Dec. 16, 2017	0.069
4183 Cuno	May 20, 2012	0.122	1999 AQ10	Jan. 29, 2018	0.139
1999 BJ8	June 16, 2012	0.177	1981 Midas	Mar. 21, 2018	0.090
1994 PM	Aug. 12, 2012	0.095	1998 WT24	Nov. 11, 2018	0.134
4581 Asclepius	Aug. 16, 2012	0.108	4953 1990 MU	Nov. 29, 2018	0.107
4769 Castalia	Aug. 28, 2012	0.114	2340 Hathor	Jan. 13, 2019	0.144
1998 QC1	Sep. 15, 2012	0.161	4581 Asclepius	Mar. 22, 2019	0.138
4179 Toutatis	Dec. 12, 2012	0.046	1998 SC15	Apr. 16, 2019	0.141
1998 WT24	Dec. 23, 2012	0.178	12538 1998 OH	May 16, 2019	0.187
4034 1986 PA	Apr. 1, 2013	0.153	5604 1992 FE	June 18, 2019	0.132
7753 1988 XB	July 10, 2013	0.118	11500 1989 UR	June 21, 2019	0.187
6037 1988 EG	Aug. 12, 2013	0.185	1620 Geographos	Aug. 31, 2019	0.137
1998 ML14	Aug. 24, 2013	0.056	1998 HL1	Oct. 25, 2019	0.042
4581 Asclepius	Aug. 25, 2013	0.119	1993 KH	Nov. 8, 2019	0.101
1998 UT18	Nov. 21, 2013	0.172	4581 Asclepius	Mar. 25, 2020	0.071
1996 RG3	Nov. 25, 2013	0.159	1991 DG	Apr. 6, 2020	0.085
3361 Orpheus	Dec. 7, 2013	0.103	1997 BQ	May 21, 2020	0.041
1995 SA	Apr. 2, 2014	0.191	8014 1990 MF	July 23, 2020	0.055

*Asteroids approaching within 0.2 Astronomical Units (18.58 million mi./30 million km.) of the Earth

**AU=Astronomical Unit (92.9 million mi./150 million km. Earth is about one AU from the Sun.)

⊙ Remo, John L, ed. *Near-Earth Objects: The United Nations International Conference.* New York: New York Academy of Sciences, 1997.

Williams, David R. "Near Earth Object Fact Sheet," http://nssdc.gsfc.nasa.gov/planetary/factsheet/neofact.html

Astronomical Units and Constants

Name	Symbol	Metric Equivalent
Astronomical unit	AU	1.496×10^{11} m
Earth mass	$M_\oplus$	5.98×10^{24} kg
Gravitational Constant	G	$(6.6726 \pm 0.0001) \times 10^{-11}$ N·m²/kg²
Light year	ly	9.463×10^{15} m
Parsec	pc	3.086×10^{16} m [3.26 ly]
Solar luminosity	$L_\odot$	3.9×10^{26} Watts
Solar mass	$M_\odot$	1.99×10^{30} kg
Solar Temperature	$T_\odot$	5.780×10^3 K

⊙ Dolan, C. "Physical Constants and Astronomical Data," www.astro.wisc.edu/
~dolan/constants.html

   NASA Astronomical Data Center. "Units and Constants," http://adc.gsfc.nasa.gov/
   adc/quick_ref/ref_units.html#astroconst

   Smith, S. "Some Non-SI Units," http://alpha.lasalle.edu/~smithsc/Astronomy/
   Units/astro_units.html

THE SCIENCES: *Chemistry*

Types of Chemistry

Organic Chemistry

Organic chemistry is the study of compounds containing carbon (known as organic molecules) and of their interactions. Because silicon is very similar to carbon, it and its compounds have also come to be included in the definition of organic chemistry.

The most common and basic of organic compounds, hydrocarbons, are made up of only carbon and hydrogen. The simplest example of a hydrocarbon is methane, which consists of one carbon atom surrounded by four hydrogen atoms. Some other elements common in organic molecules are oxygen, sulfur, chlorine, and nitrogen.

Much of the complexity and abundance of the compounds studied in organic chemistry is the result of a unique property of carbon: its atoms can bond with each other to form long chains, and can also link with each other to form circular agglomerations. This allows carbon to form myriad different molecules, which themselves can be transformed into entirely new compounds by the addition of one atom of a different atom. Thus there are millions of different organic compounds in the world. Some of the major types of organic compounds are alkanes, alkenes, alkynes, aromatic hydrocarbons, alcohols, isomers, ethers, aldehydes, ketones, carboxylic acids, and esters.

Biochemistry

Biochemistry differs from organic chemistry in that it is concerned primarily with the molecular basis of life processes. It studies the organic molecules such as lipids, proteins, and carbohydrates that make up living cells, and their interactions with other fundamental compounds in living organisms, such as vitamins and hormones. Biochemistry uses concepts and methods drawn from both the biological and the physical sciences to study the many and highly complex chemical interactions involved in the creation and maintenance of living organisms. Processes examined by biochemists include protein synthesis, hormone

Types of Chemistry *(cont.)*

production and activity, the transformation of food into energy, and the transmission of genetic information.

Acids and Bases

One of the more fundamental categorizations in chemistry is the grouping of substances into acids and bases. Acids are commonly defined as compounds that when dissolved in water release one or more hydrogen atoms as positively charged hydrogen ions. Acids share various identifying properties: they have a sour taste, corrode metals, and turn certain blue dyes (such as that used in litmus paper) red. Bases, when dissolved in water, release hydroxide ions (OH). They are bitter to the taste, slippery to the touch when in water, and turn red dyes blue. The release of hydrogen or hydroxide ions is called dissociation; the stronger an acid or base, the more completely it dissociates in water. This commonly used definition of acids and bases is known as the Arrhenius definition.

When acids and bases come into contact, they react vigorously and exchange one or more hydrogen ions. In the process, they neutralize each other and produce water and salts that have characteristics entirely different from those of both acids and bases.

The level of acidity or alkalinity (basicity), of a substance can be quantified by measuring the amount of hydrogen ions it releases or consumes when in solution. This measurement yields a scale known as the pH scale, which runs from 0 to 14, with the neutral 7 (pure water) in the center—the pH is defined as the negative log of the concentration of hydrogen ions in the solution. A pH below 7 is considered acidic, and one above 7 alkaline.

Approximate pH of Some Common Substances

Substance	Hydrogen ions*	pH
Hydrochloric acid (HCl)	1×10^{0}	0
Stomach acid	1×10^{-1}	1
Lemon juice	1×10^{-2}	2
Vinegar	1×10^{-3}	3
Root beer	1×10^{-4}	4
Unpolluted rainwater	1×10^{-5}	5
Milk	1×10^{-6}	6
Pure water	1×10^{-7}	7
Egg whites	1×10^{-8}	8
Baking soda	1×10^{-9}	9
Ammonia	1×10^{-10}	10
Drain cleaner	1×10^{-12}	12
Sodium hydroxide (NaOH)	1×10^{-13}	13

*Moles per liter

⊙ McQuarrie, Donald A., and Peter A. Rock. *General Chemistry, Third Edition.* New York: W. H. Freeman, 1991.

Stine, William, et al. *Applied Chemistry, Third Edition.* Lexington, Mass.: D.C. Heath, 1994.

Virginia Tech Chemistry Department. "A Brief Introduction to Organic Chemistry," www.chemistry.vt.edu/RVGS/ACT/notes/Organic_Intro.html

Periodic Table of Elements

1 IA	2 IIA	3 IIIB	4 IVB	5 VB	6 VIB	7 VIIB	8	9 VIIIB	10	11 IB	12 IIB	13 IIIA	14 IVA	15 VA	16 VIA	17 VIIA	18 VIIIA
1 H 1.00794																	2 He 4.00260
3 Li 6.941	4 Be 9.01218											5 B 10.811	6 C 12.011	7 N 14.00674	8 O 15.9994	9 F 18.99840	10 Ne 20.1797
11 Na 22.98977	12 Mg 24.3050											13 Al 26.98154	14 Si 28.0855	15 P 30.97376	16 S 32.066	17 Cl 35.4527	18 Ar 39.948
19 K 39.0983	20 Ca 40.078	21 Sc 44.95591	22 Ti 47.88	23 V 50.9415	24 Cr 51.9961	25 Mn 54.9380	26 Fe 55.847	27 Co 58.93320	28 Ni 58.6934	29 Cu 63.546	30 Zn 65.39	31 Ga 69.723	32 Ge 72.61	33 As 74.92159	34 Se 78.96	35 Br 79.904	36 Kr 83.80
37 Rb 85.4678	38 Sr 87.62	39 Y 88.90585	40 Zr 91.224	41 Nb 92.90638	42 Mo 95.94	43 Tc** 97.9072	44 Ru 101.07	45 Rh 102.90550	46 Pd 106.42	47 Ag 107.8682	48 Cd 112.411	49 In 114.82	50 Sn 118.710	51 Sb 121.757	52 Te 127.60	53 I 126.90447	54 Xe 131.29
55 Cs 132.90543	56 Ba 137.327	57 *La 138.9055	72 Hf 178.49	73 Ta 180.9479	74 W 183.85	75 Re 186.207	76 Os 190.2	77 Ir 192.22	78 Pt 195.08	79 Au 196.96654	80 Hg 200.59	81 Tl 204.3833	82 Pb 207.2	83 Bi 208.98037	84 Po** 208.9824	85 At** 209.9871	86 Rn** 222.0176
87 Fr** 223.0197	88 Ra** 226.0254	89 †Ac** 227.0278	104 Rf** 261.11	105 Db** 262.114	106 Sg** 263.118	107 Bh** 262.12	108 Hs** (269)	109 Mt** (266)	110 Uun** (269)	111 Uuu** (272)	112 Uub** (277)		114 Uuq** (285)		116 Uuh** (289)		118 Uuo** (293)

* Lanthanide series

58 Ce 140.115	59 Pr 140.90765	60 Nd 144.24	61 Pm** 144.9127	62 Sm 150.36	63 Eu 151.965	64 Gd 157.25	65 Tb 158.92534	66 Dy 162.50	67 Ho 164.93032	68 Er 167.26	69 Tm 168.93421	70 Yb 173.04	71 Lu 174.967

† Actinide series

90 Th** 232.0381	91 Pa** 223.0359	92 U** 238.0289	93 Np** 237.0482	94 Pu** 244.0642	95 Am** 243.0614	96 Cm** 247.0703	97 Bk** 247.0703	98 Cf** 251.0796	99 Es** 252.083	100 Fm** 257.0951	101 Md** 258.10	102 No** 259.1009	103 Lr** 262.11

Atomic number
Chemical symbol
Atomic weight

H 1.00794

** All the isotopes of this element are radioactive. With the exception of uranium and thorium, the atomic weight shown represents the relative atomic weight of the longest lived isotope. The numbers in parenthesis are the mass numbers of the longest lived isotope.

Periods

Levi, Primo. *The Periodic Table.* New York: Random House, 1996.

Stwertka, Albert, and Eve Stwertka. *A Guide to the Elements.* New York: Oxford University Press, 1999.

Wilson, Bruce. "Numbering the Columns of the Periodic Table," www.carolina.com/tips/97oct/1097d.htm

Winter, Mark. "WebElementsTM Periodic Table," www.webelements.com/

Chemical Elements

Element Name	Symbol	Number	Atomic Weight* (amu)	Discoverer	Date
Actinium	Ac	89	[227]	Debierne	1899
Aluminum	Al	13	26.98154	Oersted	1825
Americium	Am	95	[243]	Seaborg et al.	1944
Antimony	Sb	51	121.75	Known in antiquity	
Argon	Ar	18	39.948	Ramsay, Rayleigh	1894
Arsenic	As	33	74.9216	Known in antiquity	
Astatine	At	85	[210]	Corson et al.	1940
Barium	Ba	56	137.34	Davy	1808
Berkelium	Bk	97	[247]	Seaborg et al.	1949
Beryllium	Be	4	9.012182	Vacquelin	1798
Bismuth	Bi	83	208.98038	Known in antiquity	
Bohrium	Bh	107	[262]	Armbruster et al.	1981
Boron	B	5	10.811	Davy, Gay-Lussac	1808
Bromine	Br	35	79.904	Balard	1826
Cadmium	Cd	48	112.411	Stromeyer	1817
Calcium	Ca	20	40.078	Davy	1808
Californium	Cf	98	[251]	Seaborg et al.	1950
Carbon	C	6	12.0107	Known in antiquity	
Cerium	Ce	58	140.116	Hisinger, Klaproth	1803
Cesium	Cs	55	132.9054	Bunsen, Kirchoff	1860
Chlorine	Cl	17	35.4527	Scheele	1774
Chromium	Cr	24	51.9961	Vauquelin	1797
Cobalt	Co	27	58.9332	Brandt	1735
Copper	Cu	29	63.546	Known in antiquity	
Curium	Cm	96	[247]	Seaborg et al.	1944
Dubnium	Db	105	[262]	Ghiorso et al.	1970
Dysprosium	Dy	66	162.5	Boisbaudran	1886
Einsteinium	Es	99	[252]	Ghiorso et al.	1952
Erbium	Er	68	167.26	Mosander	1843
Europium	Eu	63	151.964	Demarcay	1901
Fermium	Fm	100	[257]	Ghiorso et al.	1953
Fluorine	F	9	18.998403	Moissan	1886
Francium	Fr	87	[223]	Perey	1939
Gadolinium	Gd	64	157.25	Marignac	1880
Gallium	Ga	31	69.723	Boisbaudran	1875
Germanium	Ge	32	72.61	Winkler	1886
Gold	Au	79	196.96655	Known in antiquity	
Hafnium	Hf	72	178.49	Coster, von Hevesy	1923
Hassium	Hs	108	[265]	Armbruster et al.	1984
Helium	He	2	4.0026	A Ramsay	1895
Holmium	Ho	67	164.9304	Soret, Delafontaine	1878
Hydrogen	H	1	1.00794	Cavendish	1766
Indium	In	49	114.818	Reich, Richter	1863
Iodine	I	53	126.90447	Courtois	1811
Iridium	Ir	77	192.217	Tennant	1803
Iron	Fe	26	55.847	Known in antiquity	
Krypton	Kr	36	83.8	Ramsay, Travers	1898
Lanthanum	La	57	138.9055	Mosander	1839
Lawrencium	Lr	103	[262]	Ghiorso et al.	1961
Lead	Pb	82	207.2	Known in antiquity	

Lithium	Li	3	6.941	Arfvedson	1817
Lutetium	Lu	71	174.967	Urbain	1907
Magnesium	Mg	12	24.305	Davy	1808
Manganese	Mn	25	54.938049	Gahn	1774
Meitnerium	Mt	109	[265]	Münzenberg et al.	1982
Mendelevium	Md	101	[258]	Seaborg et al.	1955
Mercury	Hg	80	200.59	Known in antiquity	
Molybdenum	Mo	42	95.94	Scheele	1778
Neodymium	Nd	60	144.24	von Welsbach	1885
Neon	Ne	10	20.1797	Ramsay, Travers	1898
Neptunium	Np	93	[237]	McMillan, Abelson	1940
Nickel	Ni	28	58.6934	Cronstedt	1751
Niobium	Nb	41	92.90638	Hatchett	1801
Nitrogen	N	7	14.00674	Rutherford	1772
Nobelium	No	102	[259]	Seaborg et al.	1958
Osmium	Os	76	190.23	Tennant	1803
Oxygen	O	8	15.9994	Priestly, Scheele	1774
Palladium	Pd	46	106.42	Wollaston	1803
Phosphorus	P	15	30.973762	Brand	1669
Platinum	Pt	78	195.078	Ulloa	1735
Plutonium	Pu	94	[244]	Seaborg et al.	1940
Polonium	Po	84	[209]	Curie	1898
Potassium	K	19	39.0983	Davy	1807
Praseodymium	Pr	59	140.90765	von Welsbach	1885
Promethium	Pm	61	[145]	Marinsky et al.	1945
Protactinium	Pa	91	231.03587	Hahn, Meitner	1918
Radium	Ra	88	[22]	P. & M. Curie	1898
Radon	Rn	86	[222]	Dorn	1900
Rhenium	Re	75	186.207	Noddack, Tacke, Berg	1925
Rhodium	Rh	45	102.9055	Wollaston	1803
Rubidium	Rb	37	85.4678	Bunsen, Kirchhoff	1861
Ruthenium	Ru	44	101.07	Klaus	1844
Rutherfordium	Rf	104	[261]	Ghiorso et al.	1969
Samarium	Sm	62	150.36	Boisbaudran	1879
Scandium	Sc	21	44.95591	Nilson	1879
Seaborgium	Sg	106	[263]	Ghiorso et al.	1974
Selenium	Se	34	78.96	Berzelius	1817
Silicon	Si	14	28.0855	Berzelius	1824
Silver	Ag	47	107.8682	Known in antiquity	
Sodium	Na	11	22.98977	Davy	1807
Strontium	Sr	38	87.62	Crawford	1790
Sulfur	S	16	32.06	Known in antiquity	
Tantalum	Ta	73	180.9479	Ekeberg	1802
Technetium	Tc	43	[97]	Perrier, Segre	1937
Tellurium	Te	52	127.6	Reichenstein	1782
Terbium	Tb	65	158.9254	Mosander	1843
Thallium	Tl	81	204.3833	Crookes	1861
Thorium	Th	90	232.0381	Berzelius	1828
Thulium	Tm	69	168.93421	Cleve	1879
Tin	Sn	50	118.69	Known in antiquity	
Titanium	Ti	22	47.90	Gregor	1791
Tungsten	W	74	183.85	F. & J. de Elhuyar	1783
Ununbium	Uub	112	[27]	Armbruster et al.	1996
Ununnilium	Uun	110	[269]	Armbruster et al.	1994
Ununhexium	Uuh	116	[289]	Ninov et al.	1999

Chemical Elements (cont.)

Element Name	Symbol	Number	Atomic Weight* (amu)	Discoverer	Date
Ununoctium	Uuo	118	[293]	Ninov et al.	1999
Ununquadium	Uuq	114	[285]	Joint Institute for Nuclear Research, Dubna (unconfirmed)	1999
Unununium	Uuu	111	[27]	Armbruster et al.	1994
Uranium	U	92	238.0289	Klaproth	1789
Vanadium	V	23	50.9415	Sefstrom	1830
Xenon	Xe	54	131.29	A Ramsay, Travers	1898
Ytterbium	Yb	70	173.04	Marignac	1878
Yttrium	Y	39	88.9059	Gadolin	1794
Zinc	Zn	30	65.38	Marggraf	1746
Zirconium	Zr	40	91.224	Klaproth	1789

* Brackets indicate mass of most stable isotope

⊙ Bentor, Yinon. "An Online, Interactive Periodic Table of the Elements," www.chemicalelements.com/index.html

Los Alamos National Laboratory, CST Division. "Elements with Their Symbol and Atomic Number," http://pearl1.lanl.gov/periodic/list1.html

Lide, David. *CRC Handbook of Chemistry and Physics*. Boca Raton, Fl.: CRC Press, 1992.

Stwertka, Albert, and Eve Stwertka. *A Guide to the Elements*. New York: Oxford University Press, 1999.

Radioisotopes

Isotopes are atoms of a chemical element whose nuclei have the same number of protons but a different number of neutrons. An element's isotopes have nearly identical chemical properties, but differ in certain observable physical properties—their spectral line emission may be different, or they may be radioactive. Radioisotopes are isotopes that decay by spontaneously emitting particles. The two most important types of decay are:

Alpha decay, the emission of a positively charged particle consisting of two protons bound to two neutrons. An alpha emission thus reduces the isotope's atomic number by two and its mass number by four.

Beta decay, the emission of a charged particle, an electron or a positron, along with a neutrino or an antineutrino. Electron emission changes a neutron into a proton; positron emission changes a proton into a neutron. Both change the isotope's atomic number but not its mass number.

By changing an isotope's atomic number, decay creates a different element. The time it takes for half of an isotope to decay into another isotope is called its half-life. The sequence of emissions results in a consistent chain of isotopes called a decay series, which ends with a stable isotope (one that does not decay). Only four decay series occur naturally.

Alpha and beta radiation (and the gamma radiation that accompanies decay) can be dangerous, but can also be harnessed for useful purposes.

⊙ Firestone, Richard B. *Table of Isotopes*. New York: Wiley, 1999.

The Regulation and Use of Radioisotopes in Today's World. Washington, D.C.: U.S. Nuclear Regulatory Commission, 1996.

Elementary Particles

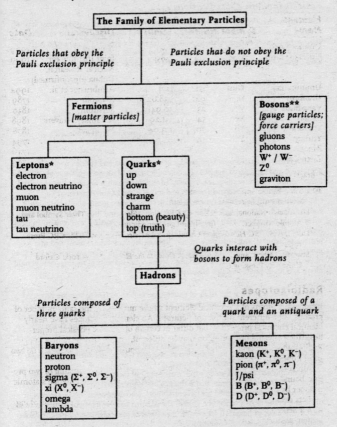

The Family of Elementary Particles

Particles that obey the Pauli exclusion principle

Particles that do not obey the Pauli exclusion principle

Fermions
[matter particles]

Bosons**
[gauge particles; force carriers]
gluons
photons
W⁺ / W⁻
Z⁰
graviton

Leptons*
electron
electron neutrino
muon
muon neutrino
tau
tau neutrino

Quarks*
up
down
strange
charm
bottom (beauty)
top (truth)

Quarks interact with bosons to form hadrons

Hadrons

Particles composed of three quarks

Particles composed of a quark and an antiquark

Baryons
neutron
proton
sigma (Σ^+, Σ^0, Σ^-)
xi (X^0, X^-)
omega
lambda

Mesons
kaon (K^+, K^0, K^-)
pion (π^+, π^0, π^-)
J/psi
B (B^+, B^0, B^-)
D (D^+, D^0, D^-)

*Each lepton and quark has an antiparticle, a particle with a number of opposite properties
**Each gauge boson carries a force that interacts with quarks to form hadrons. The gluon carries the strong nuclear force of protons and neutrons, the photon carries the electromagnetic force, the W and Z bosons carry the weak force that affects neutrinos, and the graviton carries the gravitational force.

⊙ Hughes, I. S. *Elementary Particles*. 3d ed. Cambridge: Cambridge University Press, 1991.
 Griffiths, David. *Introduction to Elementary Particles*. New York: Wiley, 1987.
 Nave, C. R. "Hyperphysics: Particle Concepts," http://hyperphysics.phy-astr.gsu.edu/hbase/particles/parcon.html

THE SCIENCES: *Biology*

Basic Taxonomic Classifications

The living world is categorized by biologists into hierarchically arranged groups, starting with the most closely related organisms (a species) and expanding outward to include organisms of more distant relatedness (e.g., a family is a group of genera, and each genus is a group of species). In descending order of size, the classifications are as follows—group names for the honeybee are given alongside as examples:

Species	*mellifera*
Genus	*Apis*
Family	Apidae (bees)
Order	Hymenoptera (wasps, ants, and bees)
Class	Insecta (all insects)
Phylum	Arthropoda (spiders, crustaceans, etc.)
Kingdom	Animalia

To refer to a specific organism, biologists use the genus and species names together, genus first and capitalized, species second and lowercased; in writing, these are always italicized. Certain conventions are followed in assigning names to categories of organisms. For example, order names usually end in "-era," and family names in "-ae." Classifications can be refined further if a main classification group shows variation within it that is great enough to merit further subdivision, but the groups being subdivided would not properly fall into the next major category. Families can contain subfamilies—the family Rosaceae contains several subfamilies, including Pomoideae (apples, pears, and loquats), and Rosoideae (roses). Species are sometimes subdivided into groups that are clearly distinct, but not differentiated enough to be separate species (one of the principal criteria for distinguishing species is the inability of matings between different species to produce viable offspring).

Genetics

Genetics is the science of the study of genes—the molecules (DNA) that are arranged like strings of beads on the chromosomes within living cells. Genetics is a fundamental branch of biology because it deals with the units of inheritance that are passed from parent to offspring during reproduction and that thus carry and develop the characteristics of a species or population.

There are many branches of genetics. Molecular genetics studies the nature and replication of DNA during the formation of eggs and sperm, and during cell division that occurs within an organism as it grows.

Developmental genetics studies the "expression" of the genes, or the process by which the DNA makes proteins that influence individual development.

Mendelian genetics, named for Gregor Mendel, who discovered important genetic principles in the late 19th century, studies the patterns of inheritance of particular traits, such as eye color or height. It focuses on the effects of particular genes by using abnormalities due to "mutation" or altered DNA.

Population genetics studies the frequencies or proportions of occurrence of genes in populations of organisms. For example, it examines how successful traits become more common as the genes that influence them spread in a population.

Quantitative genetics is related to population genetics. It studies how traits of organisms change through human-induced "artificial selection"—for example, in the breeding of farm animals and crops.

Advances in genetics are regularly featured in the news, as the techniques of biotechnology result in new strains of plants and animals. The human genome (the complete set of chromosomes containing all the DNA instructions that create an organism) is on the verge of translation, and cloning (the creation of a genetically identical individual from an adult's cell) methods are now sophisticated enough to produce healthy mammals.

Cell Biology

As its name suggests, cell biology is the science that studies the cells of organisms. This field was born when scientists discovered that the bodies of plants and animals are composed of microscopic units, named "cells." Later, as microscopes improved, it was found that the cells contain even smaller structures, now called "organelles," including such

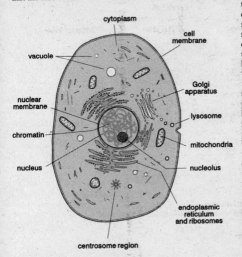

things as the mitochondria, chloroplasts, nucleus (with chromosomes), and many other smaller structures. At this stage cell biology was called "cytology."

Modern cell biology takes advantage of progress in molecular biology and biochemistry to study dynamic processes within and between cells in minute detail. For example, it is possible to study the individual molecules (polymers) that form, move, and interact as the mitotic spindles pull apart chromosomes during mitosis, or cell division.

Cell biology examines the structure and function of many different kinds of cells: nerve cells and their special properties for transmitting signals; brain cells as they function in storage of memory and integration of behavior; cells of other organs, such as the liver or kidney with their special functions of concentrating wastes or secreting hormones. Cell biologists also study the fascinating movements of animal cells during the growth of embryos, and the membranes cells have that allow chemical communication among them and with the outside world.

Microbiology

Microbiology is the study of microscopic organisms. The term derives from "microbe," a word coined in the late 19th century to refer to these life forms that are invisible to the naked eye. Microorganisms, as they are now called, form a group of very diverse organisms, ranging from viruses and bacteria to protozoans, molds, and algae, and microbiology is accordingly divided into various specialties such as bacteriology, virology, and so on.

Because microorganisms inhabit almost all the organic and inorganic realms of the Earth, they are closely involved with the life processes of many other life forms. Some microorganisms are largely responsible for the decay of dead organic matter, others are often the causes of disease, yet others inhabit the mammalian gastrointestinal tract and aid in digestion.

⊙ Berg, Paul, and Maxine Singer. *Dealing with Genes: The Language of Heredity*. Mill Valley, Calif.: University Science Books, 1992.

Campbell, Neil. *Biology, Fifth Edition*. Menlo Park, Calif.: Benjamin Cummings, 1999.

Margulis, Lynn, and Karlene V. Schwartz. *Five Kingdoms: An Illustrated Guide to the Phyla of Life on Earth, Third Edition*. New York: W. H. Freeman, 1998.

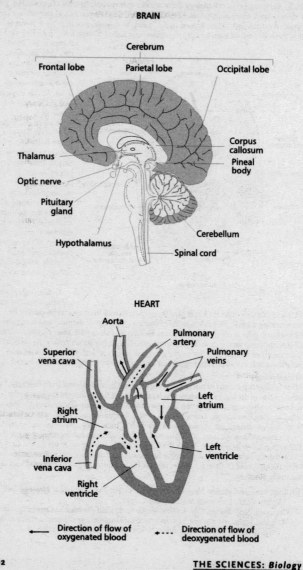

BRAIN

Cerebrum

Frontal lobe   Parietal lobe   Occipital lobe

Thalamus

Corpus callosum

Pineal body

Optic nerve

Pituitary gland

Hypothalamus

Cerebellum

Spinal cord

HEART

Aorta

Superior vena cava

Pulmonary artery

Pulmonary veins

Right atrium

Left atrium

Inferior vena cava

Left ventricle

Right ventricle

⟶ Direction of flow of oxygenated blood

⟶ Direction of flow of deoxygenated blood

REPRODUCTIVE SYSTEM

FEMALE

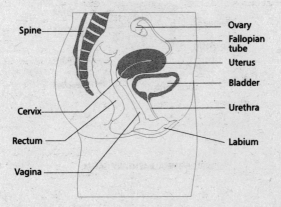

Spine — Ovary
Fallopian tube
Uterus
Bladder
Cervix — Urethra
Rectum — Labium
Vagina

MALE

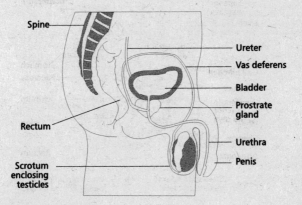

Spine — Ureter
Vas deferens
Bladder
Prostrate gland
Rectum — Urethra
Scrotum enclosing testicles — Penis

NOSE, MOUTH, AND THROAT

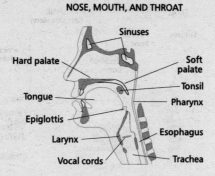

Sinuses

Hard palate

Soft palate

Tonsil

Tongue

Pharynx

Epiglottis

Larynx

Esophagus

Vocal cords

Trachea

THE ALIMENTARY CANAL

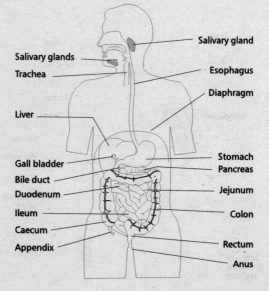

Salivary gland

Salivary glands

Esophagus

Trachea

Diaphragm

Liver

Gall bladder

Stomach

Bile duct

Pancreas

Duodenum

Jejunum

Ileum

Colon

Caecum

Appendix

Rectum

Anus

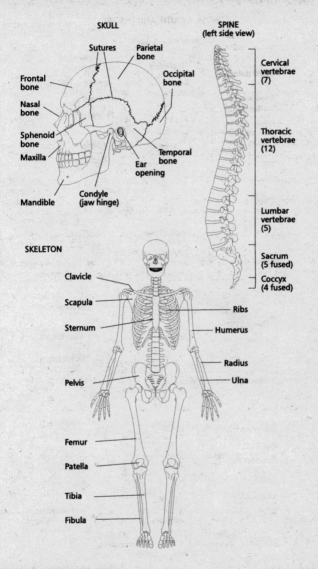

SKULL

Sutures
Parietal bone
Occipital bone
Frontal bone
Nasal bone
Sphenoid bone
Maxilla
Mandible
Condyle (jaw hinge)
Ear opening
Temporal bone

SPINE
(left side view)

Cervical vertebrae (7)
Thoracic vertebrae (12)
Lumbar vertebrae (5)
Sacrum (5 fused)
Coccyx (4 fused)

SKELETON

Clavicle
Scapula
Sternum
Pelvis
Femur
Patella
Tibia
Fibula
Ribs
Humerus
Radius
Ulna

EYE

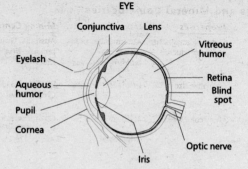

Conjunctiva

Lens

Eyelash

Vitreous humor

Aqueous humor

Retina

Blind spot

Pupil

Cornea

Optic nerve

Iris

EAR

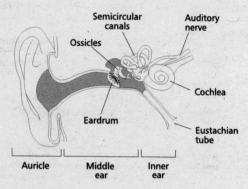

Semicircular canals

Auditory nerve

Ossicles

Cochlea

Eardrum

Eustachian tube

Auricle

Middle ear

Inner ear

TEETH

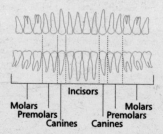

Incisors

Molars
Premolars
Canines

Molars
Premolars
Canines

Minerals and Mineral Commodities*

Mineral	Properties	Uses	Mining Centers**
Aluminum*	Light; nonmagnetic; malleable; ductile	Automobiles; product packaging; building materials	Australia, Guinea, Jamaica, Brazil, India
Asbestos	Insulator; fire resistant	Insulation; roofing	Russia, Canada, China, Brazil
Beryl	Many colors; hard	Main source of beryllium; gemstones (emerald, aquamarine)	Colombia, Brazil, Russia, South Africa, Austria
Bismuth	Expands when solidifying; diamagnetic	Electronics	Mexico, Peru, Bolivia, China
Borax	Dissolves in water	Antiseptic; water softener; detergent	Southwest United States
Boron*	Variable conductivity of electricity; transmits infrared light	Glass production; detergents; fire retardants	United States, Russia, Turkey, Argentina, Chile
Calcite	Fluorescent; main component of many kinds of rock	Agriculture; ore of calcium; chalk; base for cement; many other industrial uses	Iceland, Mexico, United States, many others
Chromite	Resistant to corrosion; hard	Ore of chromium; used in making stainless steel	South Africa, Kazakhstan, India, Turkey, Finland
Cobalt*	Brittle; hard; resistant to corrosion	Aircraft metal alloys; magnetic alloys	Zambia, Canada, Australia, Russia, Cuba
Copper	Highly conductive of electricity; malleable; ductile	Electrical wire and machinery; coins; cooking utensils	Chile, United States, Canada, Russia, Australia
Corundum	Very hard; stable; easily synthesized; many colors; insoluble in acids	Abrasives; gemstones (ruby, sapphire)	Myanmar, Sri Lanka, Tanzania, Thailand, United States

Mineral	Properties	Uses	Mining Centers**
Diamond	Hardest, best heat conductor, highest melting point, and highest refractive index of known natural materials	Jewelry; abrasives; thermal insulation; optics; electronics	South Africa, Australia, Botswana, Russia, Brazil, Canada
Fluorite	Fluorescent; many colors (but colorless when pure)	Main source of fluorine; steel manufacture; optics	England, Switzerland, Mexico, United States
Gold	Highly conductive of electricity; malleable; ductile; very stable	Jewelry and ornaments; coins; photography; dentistry	South Africa, United States, Australia, China, Russia
Graphite	Conductive of electricity; soft; smudges	Pencil leads; lubricant; electrical applications	New York, Alabama, Finland, Italy, England, Quebec
Gypsum	Flexible crystals	Primary ingredient of plaster; cement; sheetrock; decorative (alabaster); dentistry	United States, Thailand, Iran, China, Canada, others
Iodine*	Volatile at room temperature	Food supplementation; colorants; pharmaceuticals	Chile, Japan, United States, China
Iron*	Conductive of heat; corrodes easily; brittle; can be magnetized	Main ingredient of steel; building materials; automobiles; containers	China, Brazil, Australia, Russia, United States
Lead*	Heavy; malleable; soft	Batteries; paint pigments; glasswork; radioactive shielding	Australia, United States, China, Peru, Canada
Magnesium*	Light; strong; ignites when heated in air	Aluminum alloys; iron and steel production; cathodes	United States, Canada, China, Russia, Norway
Manganese*	Hard; brittle	Steel production	South Africa, China, Gabon, Brazil, Ukraine
Mercury*	Liquid at room temperature; poisonous	Thermometers; amalgams for extracting metals from ores	Kyrgyzstan, Spain, Algeria
Molybdenum*	High melting point; very hard	Iron and steel production	United States, China, Chile, Canada, Mexico

Nickel*	Hard; takes high polish; ductile; malleable	Stainless steel production; batteries	Russia, Canada, Australia, New Caledonia
Nitrogen*	Colorless; odorless; inert gas	Ammonia; fertilizers; plastics and resins production	China, United States, India, Russia
Platinum	Ductile; malleable; heavy; does not tarnish	Jewelry; catalysts; dentistry	South Africa, Russia, Canada, United States
Potash*	Alkaline	Fertilizers; soaps	Canada, Russia, Belarus, Germany, Israel
Quartz	Piezoelectric (generates electrical charge when subjected to pressure)	Electronics; optical equipment; timepieces	Brazil, Germany, Madagascar (all sources of lascas, used for synthesizing quartz crystal)
Salt	Lowers freezing point of water; enhances food flavors; preserves organic material	Highway deicing; food; water treatment	United States, China, Germany, Canada, India
Silicon*	Resistant to most acids; conductive of heat	Iron and steel production; aluminum production; semiconductors	China, United States, Norway, Russia, Brazil
Silver*	Ductile; conductive of electricity	Jewelry; tableware; photography; coins; dentistry	Mexico, Peru, United States, Australia, Canada
Sulfur	Odorless; brittle; insoluble in water	Sulfuric acid; fertilizers; petroleum refining	United States, Canada, China, Russia, Japan
Talc	Very soft; smooth and slippery; high luster; low conductivity	Ceramics; paper production; paints; roofing; cosmetics	China, United States, Japan, South Korea, India
Tin*	Malleable; crystalline structure; corrosion resistant	Containers; roofing; electrical applications	China, Indonesia, Peru, Brazil, Bolivia, Australia
Titanium*	Light and strong; corrosion resistant; burns in air	Aerospace industry; armor; sporting goods; paint (as titanium dioxide)	Japan, Russia, Kazakhstan, China, Ukraine
Tungsten*	Highest melting point of metals; corrosion resistant	Industrial cutting blades; light bulb filaments	China, Russia, Austria, North Korea, Portugal

Minerals and Mineral Commodities (cont.)

Mineral	Properties	Uses	Mining Centers**
Uraninite	Highly radioactive	Primary ore of uranium	France, Czech Republic, Germany, South Africa, Canada
Yttrium*	Lustrous; fine bits can ignite in air	Color television phosphors; fluorescent lights; laser crystals	China, Russia, India, Brazil
Zinc*	Fairly conductive of electricity; burns in air	Galvanizing of steel; brass and bronze production	China, Australia, Canada, Peru, United States
Zirconium*	Very heat and corrosion resistant; strong	Ceramics; abrasives; sandblasting	Australia, South Africa, Ukraine

*The mineral commodities included here are not minerals but are chemical elements or compounds recovered from minerals.

**Countries listed in order of production, larger to smaller

⊙ Skinner, Brian J. *Earth Resources, Third Edition.* Englewood Cliffs, N.J.: Prentice-Hall, 1986.

United States Geological Survey. "Mineral Commodity Summaries 2000," http://minerals.usgs.gov/minerals/pubs/mcs/2000/mcs2000.pdf

Geology

Layers of the Earth

The interior of the Earth has three distinct compositional layers. The thin outermost layer, called the crust, varies in thickness between averages of 5 kilometers (under the oceans) and 31 kilometers (under the continents). It is composed of various kinds of solid rock and sits atop the mantle, the Earth's middle layer. The mantle is about 2,900 kilometers thick. It is made up primarily of silicate rock at temperatures that vary between 1000°C nearest the crust and 5000°C in the deepest regions. At these temperatures, the rock has little strength and can flow very slowly (centimeters per year) like a very viscous liquid. The innermost layer, the core, has a radius of about 3,480 kilometers, and is made up primarily of iron and nickel. It has two distinct layers as well: the outer one is liq-

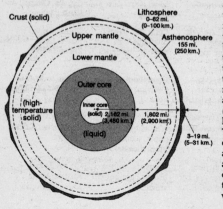

Crust (solid)

Lithosphere 0–62 mi. (0–100 km.)

Upper mantle

Asthenosphere 155 mi. (250 km.)

Lower mantle

Outer core

Inner core (solid)

(high-temperature solid)

2,162 mi. (3,480 km.)

1,802 mi. (2,900 km.)

(liquid)

3–19 mi. (5–31 km.)

uid, and the inner is a rigid mass of superhot iron that spins faster than the rest of the Earth around its axis. It is believed that whirlpool-like currents in the outer core give rise to the Earth's magnetic field.

Plate Tectonics

The Earth's outer layer is not a solid shell, but is broken up into many irregular segments known as plates, which extend through the top 100 km. of the earth's surface, known as the lithosphere. The nine largest plates are the Pacific, North American, South American, Eurasian, Indo-Australian, Antarctic, African, Nazca, and Cocos. The convection movements of the Earth's mantle appear to create local areas of circulation in the upper mantle called convection cells, which cause a boundary layer of hot, malleable rock called the asthenosphere to flow slowly. The asthenosphere carries the plates of the lithosphere along in a constant motion. These pull apart in some places, collide in others, and in some slide past each other. This movement is known as plate tectonics, and gives rise to many geological phenomena such as earthquakes (caused by sudden movement of plates past each other), mountain ranges (caused by the buckling up of one plate as another pushes under it), and mid-ocean ridges, underwater mountain ranges formed where plates pull apart and hot magma (highly heated rock) wells up from the mantle.

The movement of plate tectonics means that the continents carried on the plates have not always been arranged as we know them. Some 250 million years ago, Earth's landmasses were all joined into the supercontinent known as Pangea. In the Triassic period, about 200 million years ago, Pangea had divided into the northern mass of Laurasia and southern Gondwanaland. The component plates of these two supercontinents slowly continued to drift apart until the continents reached today's configuration. This drifting continues.

Types of Rock

There are three main types of rock: igneous, sedimentary, and metamorphic. Igneous rock is formed when molten rock (magma) rises through the crust and cools into solid form; it may cool beneath the crust's surface (intrusive) or above the surface (extrusive). Fine-grained extrusive rock such as basalt results when hot mantle rocks are brought close to the crust and a partial melting occurs. This cools too quickly for large crystals to form. Intrusive rock such as granite forms when pockets of magma cool slowly while trapped underground, giving crystals of quartz, feldspar, and other minerals a chance to grow large.

Sedimentary rock is formed when particles of rock weathered from granite and other rocky masses accumulate and eventually are compacted and cemented together into a new rocky mass. Some examples of sedimentary rock are sandstone, breccia, shale, and limestone.

When sedimentary or igneous rock is subjected to extreme pressure, high temperature, and hot water underground, its mineral constituents are changed, and it transforms into what is known as metamorphic rock. Some examples of metamorphic rock are slate, schist, marble, and gneiss.

⊙ Chernicoff, Stanley. *Essentials of Geology, Second Edition*. Boston: Houghton Mifflin, 2000.

Encyclopedia of Geology. London: Fitzroy Dearborn, 1999.

Kious, Jacqueline, and Robert I. Tilling. *This Dynamic Earth: The Story of Plate Tectonics*. Washington, D.C.: U.S. Government Printing Office, 1996. (also online at http://pubs.usgs.gov/publications/text/dynamic.html)

Layers of the Earth's Atmosphere

Layer	Altitude mi (km)*	Temp. °F (°C)	Primary Gases	Properties
Troposphere	0<->5 (0<->10)	63 <->-71 (17<->-57)	N_2 (78%), O_2 (21%), Ar (1%), CO_2 (.04%), water vapor	Temp. decreases with altitude; vertical circulation; weather and clouds
Stratosphere	5<->30 (10<->45)	-71 <> 65 (-57<->18)	Same proportions as troposphere, but at much lower densities	Temp. increases with altitude; horizontal circulation
Ozone layer	15 (25)	-71 <> 65 (-57<->18)	O_3 (10ppm—about 90% of all O_3 in atmosphere)	Absorbs ultraviolet solar radiation
Mesosphere	30<->50 (45<->95)	65 <> -225 (18<->-143)	O_2, He, H, N_2	Temp. decreases with altitude
Thermosphere	50<->400 (95<->640)	-225 <> 3,600 (-143<->2,000)	O_2, He, H, N_2	Temp. increases with altitude
Ionosphere (D, E, F layers)	55<->375 (90<->600)	-225 <> 3,600 (-143<->2,000)	O_2, He, H, N_2	Auroras, radio waves, absorbs x-rays
Exosphere	>400 (>640)	> 3,600 (>2,000)	H, He	Temp. constant

*Atmospheric layers are continuous, and the general boundaries between them can vary in altitude depending on latitude and various other factors; altitudes given are therefore approximate. The symbol <>, used for altitude and temperature, indicates "greater than, and less than" the two numbers given.

© Houghton, John T. *The Physics of Atmospheres, Second Edition*. Cambridge: Cambridge University Press, 1986.
NASA Atmospheric Chemistry Data and Resources. "Atmospheric Structure." http://daac-gsfc.nasa.gov/CAMPAIGN_DOCS/ATM_CHEM/atmospheric_structure.html
University of Oulu (Finland). "Atmosphere (Earth's)." www.oulu.fi/~spaceweb/textbook/atmosphere.html

THE SCIENCES: *Earth Science*

THE SCIENCES: Physics

Laws of Physics

Physics is the science that is concerned with the fundamental structure of matter and with the interactions among the basic forces and materials that make up the universe. The various areas of study within the vast field of physics address topics ranging from the elementary particles that make up atoms to the movements of galaxies.

Scholars have studied the phenomena of the natural world for many centuries, and in 1687 Sir Isaac Newton formulated the basic laws of motion that serve as the foundation for modern physics. (Newton was the first to publish practical formulations of the laws, but they had been observed decades earlier by Galileo.)

Newton's First Law: If a body is at rest or moving at a constant speed, it will remain at rest or moving at that speed unless it is acted upon by external forces. This is also known as the law of inertia, which is a property of all bodies with mass—the tendency of things to remain in their current state of motion.

Newton's Second Law: When force is applied to an object, the acceleration induced is directly proportional to the force, and inversely proportional to its mass. Specifically,

$$F = ma,$$

where F is the force applied to a body with mass m, inducing acceleration a. All the basic equations of dynamics can be derived from this fundamental law through calculus.

Newton's Third Law: Every action has an equal and opposite reaction. For example, just as the Earth pulls on all objects with its gravitational field, it is equally true that each object pulls up on the Earth in exactly the opposite direction with its own gravitational field.

A fourth fundamental law of physics, formulated by Newton, is the law of gravitation. This law states that bodies attract each other with forces proportional to their mass: bodies with masses m_1 and m_2, that are at distance r from one another, will exert on each other attractive forces proportional to $m_1 m_2 / r$. The proportionality is given by the gravitational constant G, which is universal. The law of gravity is expressed as $F = G\, m_1 m_2 / r^2$.

Heat

All matter in the universe has a certain amount of energy stored in it. Some of that energy is stored in the natural vibration of the component atoms. Heat is the transfer of that energy from one body to another, from the warmer (more energetic) to the colder (less energetic). Heat transfer usually means that the warmer substance decreases in temperature and the cooler one's temperature increases. It is, however, possible for materials to absorb or release heat without changing temperature: this happens in the instant at which the substance is changing from one state to another, such as when ice melts into water. The three laws of thermodynamics govern the mechanics of heat and its transfer to and from other forms of energy.

Light

Light, as the term is commonly used, is electromagnetic radiation visible to the human eye—wavelengths shorter or longer than those in the visual spectrum are not visible to us, but are also light and are known as ultraviolet (shorter) and

Physics (cont.)

infrared (longer). The fundamental unit of light is the *photon*, but depending on the properties being observed, light can behave either like a wave or like a particle. Light moves at a very high speed (its 299,792,458 meters per second in a vacuum is one of the fundamental physical constants), and it is the only form of energy that is always moving. As soon as it stops (i.e., is absorbed by matter), it ceases to be light and becomes some other form of energy, such as heat. Another, very useful, property of light is that it can carry large amounts of information, only a small amount of which can be detected and processed by the human eye and brain.

Mechanics

Mechanics is the study of the motion of bodies, and how that motion may exert forces on other bodies in a system. Newtonian (or classical) mechanics is based on Newton's three basic laws, which hold for most motion on Earth. Celestial mechanics studies the motion and interaction of moons, planets, stars, and other celestial bodies; these motions can differ somewhat from the predictions of classical mechanics, which are corrected by the theory of relativity. A third type of mechanics, quantum mechanics, examines motion at the atomic and subatomic level, a realm in which classical mechanics has limited use.

Electricity

Electricity is energy that is stored and transmitted by electrons, which by definition carry a negative charge. Many metals allow the free flow of electrons through their molecules, and we thus describe these as conductive and use them for electric motors and other applications. However, electricity may move through many media. The most striking example is lightning. Lightning results when the accumulation of highly charged electrons causes a strong electric charge differential to accumulate between clouds and the ground. When that difference is large enough, the air's resistance to the flow of electrons is overcome and the electrons flow freely from one point to another in the form of lightning.

Sound

Sound can be defined as the transfer of energy via vibrations through a solid, a fluid, or a gaseous medium. Sound moves through any given medium as a wave, which propagates at different speeds through different materials, depending on specific properties of the materials such as density and equilibrium pressure. For example, sound travels much farther and faster through steel (5,000 meters per second) and seawater (1,490 meters per second) than through air (331.29 meters per second). Some of the basic parameters of sound are velocity, frequency (pitch), and intensity.

Nuclear Physics

Nuclear physics is the study of the particles that make up the nucleus of the atom, and the forces with which they interact. These particles are bound together by very powerful nuclear forces that are about one million times stronger than forces involved in other atomic structures. The extremely high energy of these bonds requires a special branch of physics, quantum theory, for the study of nuclear behavior. One of the principal methods for studying nuclear structures is the bombardment of nuclear material with streams of particles such as protons and electrons, followed by analysis of the reactions of the nuclear particles to these collisions.

⊙ Encyclopaedia Britannica Online. "Physics," www.eb.com:180/bol/
   topic?eu=61378&sctn=1

Holton, Gerald J., and Stephen G. Brush. *Physics, the Human Adventure: From Copernicus to Einstein and Beyond.* New Brunswick, N.J.: Rutgers University Press , 2001.

Lerner, Rita G., and George L. Trigg, eds. *Encyclopedia of Physics, Second Edition.* New York: VCH, 1991.

THE SCIENCES: *Technology*

Automobiles: Chronology

1670   A steam-powered cart is built in China.

1769   Nicolas-Joseph Cugnot builds a steam-powered, three-wheeled tractor to transport artillery for the French Army.

1801   In England, Richard Trevithick builds the first steam-powered passenger vehicle.

1802   In England, a steam-powered automobile travels from Cornwall to London, a journey of over 100 miles.

1830s   London's first omnibus service transports passengers in steam-powered carriages.

1860   In France, the first one-cylinder internal-combustion engine is patented; it uses kerosene for fuel.

1864   In Australia, a two-cylinder gasoline engine is introduced.

1865   In Germany, Karl Benz builds a three-wheeled, gas-powered motor vehicle.

1876   In Germany, Nikolaus August Otto builds the first four-stroke gas engine.

1887   In Germany, Gottlieb Daimler and Wilhelm Maybech manufacture their first automobile.

1888   In Scotland, John Dunlop invents the pneumatic tire.

1890   Daimler and Maybech start the Daimler Motor Company.

1893   In the United States, brothers Charles Edgar Duryea and James Frank Duryea build their first one-cylinder, four-horsepower automobile.

1893   In the United States, engineer Henry Ford builds his first internal-combustion engine.

1894   A French company, Panhard-Levassor, begins producing automobiles using the Daimler patent; Panhard-Levassor is the first manufacturer to use gears and a clutch.

1899   In Italy, FIAT begins manufacturing cars.

1899   Electric cars make up 38 percent of American automobile market; an electric car sets a speed record of 65.79 miles per hour.

1901   The 1901 Mercedes reaches a speed of 53 miles per hour.

1902   The Locomobile is the first automobile in the United States to use a four-cylinder, water-cooled, front-mounted engine.

1902   In France, Louis Renault develops the drum brake.

1903   Henry Ford starts the Ford Motor Company and introduces its first car, the Model A.

Automobiles: Chronology *(cont.)*

1904   Approximately eight percent of roads in the United States are surfaced.

1907   Ford Motor Company's share of the American automobile market is 35 percent.

1908   Ford Motor Company introduces the Model T; it sells for $825.

1911   The electric starter replaces the hand-cranked engine starter.

1913   Approximately 80 percent of the world's automobiles are manufactured in the United States.

1914   Ford Motor Company begins using the assembly-line method of automobile production.

1915   Production of Ford's Model T exceeds 500,000; it now sells for $440.

1919   In the United States, a gasoline tax is imposed to fund highway construction.

1920   In the United States, Deusenberg develops four-wheel hydraulic brakes.

1920   More than 8 million Americans own cars.

1930s   Franklin D. Roosevelt proposes a federal interstate highway system.

1936   Mercedes introduces the first diesel-powered car.

1938   In Germany, a prototype of the Volkswagen Beetle is introduced.

1939   In the United States, air conditioning becomes available in some automobiles.

1947   In the United States, Goodyear develops the tubeless tire.

1949   The Volkswagen Beetle is introduced in the United States, prompting some American manufacturers to begin producing smaller cars.

1950s   In Germany, Mercedes-Benz develops fuel injection.

1956   In the United States, the Interstate Highway Act provides funding for approximately 43,000 miles of interstate highways.

1956   The first Japanese passenger vehicles are introduced in the United States.

1958   In the United States, aluminum car engines are developed.

1966   In England, the electronic fuel-injection system is introduced.

1970s   To reduce exhaust emissions, catalytic converters are introduced.

1970s   The energy crisis prompts more consumers to purchase fuel-efficient compact cars; Japanese imports become increasingly popular.

1980   Japan is the world's leading automobile manufacturer.

1980s   In Australia, a solar-powered vehicle travels 1,846 miles in six days.

1980s   Japanese automobile manufacturers open plants in the United States.

1999   53.2 million passenger vehicles are produced this year; approximately 16.8 million of them are sold in North America.

⊙ Microsoft® Encarta® Online Encyclopedia 2000. "Automobile," www.encarta.msn.com

The History Channel. "Automobiles," www.historychannel.com

Wetterau, Bruce. *The New York Public Library Book of Chronologies*. New York: Simon & Schuster, 1990.

Boats: Chronology

c.6000 BC   In Africa, wooden dugout boats are built.

c.5000 BC   Earliest evidence of wood-plank construction of boats

c.4500 BC	In Mesopotamia, boats are made of wood frames covered with bark or animal skins.
c.4000 BC	In China, flat bamboo rafts are built.
c.3300 BC	Early Egyptian boats have one square sail and one row of oarsmen. As Egyptians begin navigating the Mediterranean Sea, they develop long, narrow warships with two rows of oarsmen; they also develop rounder ships to transport cargo.
c.3000 BC	Earliest evidence of rudders
c.700 BC	In Greece, the trireme (a warship with three levels of oarsmen) is invented.
800s AD	In northern Europe, lapstrake boat construction is developed; in lapstrake construction, overlapping wood planks are attached to the boat frame with lashings or nails.
800s	Byzantines build carvel-planked ships; in carvel-plank construction, wood planks are nailed to the frame edge-to-edge instead of overlapping.
1200s	Most Mediterranean sailing ships now have two masts.
1300s	Italians build ships with three decks.
1400s	Chinese junks are the most sophisticated and most seaworthy ships in the world.
c.1540	The galleon, powered solely by sail, is introduced.
1783	In France, the first steam-powered paddleboat is built.
1814	The first steam-powered warship is built.
1838	The British ship *Archimedes* is the first propeller-driven steamship.
1838	The ship *Sirius* is the first large passenger ship to cross the Atlantic Ocean using only steam power; it crosses the Atlantic in 18 days.
1840s	The iron hull is developed.
1843	The *Great Britain* is the first propeller-powered ship to cross the Atlantic Ocean.
1853	The *Monumental City*, a paddle wheeler, is the first steamship to cross the Pacific Ocean, traveling from San Francisco to Sydney, Australia.
1857	The British steamship *Great Eastern* is built; constructed of iron, it weighs 18,000 tons and is 693 feet long.
1861	In the United States, the first tanker (*Elizabeth Watts*) is built; it carries oil in wooden barrels from Pennsylvania to London.
1869	The clipper ship *Cutty Sark* is introduced.
1880s	Boat builders begin using internal-combustion inboard engines.
1884	In England, Sir Charles Parsons introduces the steam turbine.
1891	The aluminum boat is introduced in Europe.
1910s	Boat builders begin using outboard motors.
1918	Alexander Graham Bell and Casey Baldwin invent the hydrofoil, which reaches a speed of 70 miles per hour; the hydrofoil has fins on its hull that create hydrodynamic pressure, allowing the boat to be lifted out of the water when in motion.
1918	In the United States, boat builders begin using plywood construction; plywood boats are either paneled or molded.
1922	The United States Navy builds its first aircraft carrier.

Boats: Chronology (cont.)

1952   The ocean liner *United States* crosses the Atlantic Ocean in 3 days, 10 hours.

1959   The first hovercraft crosses the English Channel in two hours; the hovercraft travels on a cushion of air, not coming into contact with water when in motion.

1970s   The surface-piercing propeller is introduced.

⊙ Microsoft® Encarta® Online Encyclopedia 2000. "Boats and Boatbuilding," www.encarta.msn.com

   Mount, Ellis, and Barbara A. List. *Milestones in Science and Technology*. Phoenix: Oryx, 1994.

   Wetterau, Bruce. *The New York Public Library Book of Chronologies*. New York: Simon & Schuster, 1990.

Boats: Rules of the Sea

Maritime law refers to the body of laws that govern navigation, shipping, and recreational boating. Most maritime law deals with legal issues surrounding the private shipping industry. Today's maritime law is derived from laws created by ancient Greeks, Egyptians, and Phoenicians. English admiralty courts were in place by the 14th century. Maritime law includes the following components:

Maritime liens: Covers liens against ships, cargo, or freight. In maritime law, a ship can be named as a defendant in legal cases (proceeding *in rem*), and the ship can be "arrested" and held in custody until its owner satisfies a condition, such as paying bail.

Carriage of goods: Covers the transport of cargo or passengers

Charter parties: Covers contracts between ship owners and those who charter their ships

Limitation of liability: Covers the extent to which ship owners are liable in claims against them

Collision liability: Covers responsibility for damage and losses caused by collisions

Salvage and general average: Covers possession of, and awards for the return of, salvaged property

Marine insurance: Covers insurance of ships as well as liability insurance

The **Law of the Sea** refers to the maritime issues of public international law. The **Convention on the Law of the Sea** is a United Nations agreement that establishes rules governing the use of oceans and their resources. It was signed by 119 nations on December 10, 1982.

The **Rules of the Road at Sea** refer to a set of international traffic regulations for oceans. These rules cover lights, sounds, collision avoidance, and other regulations.

⊙ United Nations. "Oceans and Law of the Sea," www.un.org/Depts/los/index.htm

   Encyclopedia Britannica. "Maritime Law," www.britannica.com/bcom/eb/article/0,5716,115491+1_108706,00.html

   Maritime Legal Resources. "Maritime Law in Detail," www.marlegal.com/law.html

Computers: Bits and Bytes

Binary Code uses two symbols, 0 and 1, to represent numbers. Binary numbering is used in computer technology because it is compact and reliable, and can easily represent two states such as "on-off," or "start-stop."

A bit is short for "binary digit." Bits are the smallest units of computer data, having a binary value of either 0 or 1. A byte consists of 8 adjacent bits. Bytes are the basic unit of information in computer storage and processing and are the smallest operable units of storage in computer technology.

Computer Data Information and Storage Units

Common Computer Storage Capacities	Number of Bytes
Nibble	one-half (four bits)
Byte	8
Kilobytes (KB)	1024
Megabytes (MB)	1,048,576
Gigabytes (GB)	about 1 billion
Terabytes (TB)	about 1 trillion

⊙ Britannica.com. "Bit," www.britannica.com/bcom/eb/article/3/
 0,5716,82463+1+80319,00.html

Britannica.com. "Byte," "Binary Number System," www.britannica.com/
 bcom/eb/article/2/0,5716,2002+1+1994,00.html

Computers: ASCII

The American Standard Code for Information Interchange (ASCII) is a code used to represent textual information, such as letters, numbers, and punctuation, as well as non-input device commands such as control characters. It is the most common code format for representing text files in computers and on the Internet and is used for information exchange between computers.

ASCII was originally developed by the American National Standards Institute. In an ASCII file, each character is represented with a 7-digit binary number, making 128 possible characters defined. Since digital computers use 8-digit binary code (bytes), ASCII code is commonly embedded in an 8-bit field, known as extended ASCII. 256 characters are defined in extended ASCII.

While different operating systems use different code for text file representation, conversion programs allow different operating systems to change from one file format to another.

Operating System Text File Codes

Operating System	Code
UNIX	ASCII
DOS	ASCII
Windows 98 and Windows 2000	ASCII
Macintosh	ASCII modified for use with Macintosh operating systems
Windows NT	Unicode
IBM	ASCII modified for use with IBM system 390 computers, known as the IBM extended character set

⊙ Britannica.com. "ASCII," www.britannica.com/bcom/eb/article/9/
 0,5716,1609+1+1602,00.html

Whatis.com. "ASCII," www.whatis.com/WhatIs_Definition_Page/
 0,4152,211600,00.html

Computers: Languages and Uses

Computer languages are used to communicate instructions to a computer. Similar to natural languages, such as English, programming languages have a vocabulary, syntax, and grammar. Computer languages differ from natural languages because they are logical and have no ambiguity. There are many types of computer languages that are used for different purposes.

Programming languages can be classified as either low-level languages or high-level languages. Low-level programming languages, or machine languages, are the most basic type of programming languages and can be understood directly by a computer. Machine languages differ depending on the manufacturer and model of computer. High-level languages are programming languages that must first be translated into a machine language before they can be understood and processed by a computer. Examples of high-level languages are C, C++, PASCAL, and FORTRAN. Assembly languages are intermediate languages that are very close to the machine language and do not have the level of linguistic sophistication exhibited by other high-level languages, but must still be translated into machine language.

Some programming languages are written to address a particular kind of computing problem or for use on a specific type of computer system. Although these languages were designed to address specific categories of computer problems, they are highly portable, meaning that they may be used to program many types of computers. Other languages, such as machine languages, are designed for use by one specific model of computer system, or even by one specific computer in certain research applications. The most commonly used programming languages are highly portable and are used to solve diverse types of computing problems. Languages like C, PASCAL, and BASIC fall into this category.

High-level languages are commonly classified as procedure-oriented, functional, object-oriented, or logic languages. The most common high-level languages today are procedure-oriented languages. Object-oriented languages, such as C++ and Java, use self-contained collections of instructions, called objects, which can be re-used in other programs.

Major Computer Programming Languages

Language	Description and Use
Machine Language	Low-level basic programming languages, expressed in binary digits, which are understood directly by a computer and are used to represent operation codes and memory addresses. Machine languages differ depending on the manufacturer and model of computer.
Assembly Language	Low-level language expressed in alphanumeric characters. Used to minimize the time it takes to run a program. Also used when some part of the computer has to be controlled directly, such as individual dots on a monitor or the flow of individual characters to a printer.
FORTRAN (FORmula TRANslation)	A high-level procedural language commonly used for scientific applications
COBOL (Common Business-Oriented Language)	A high-level procedural language commonly used for business applications
BASIC (Beginner's All-Purpose Instruction Code)	A high-level, procedural language that is easy to learn and understand
PASCAL	A high-level procedural language designed for instructional purposes in 1967 by Nicholas Wirth. Most serious programmers now use C, C++, or Java instead of PASCAL.

Smalltalk	A high-level object-oriented language developed in the early 1970s by Alan Kay at Xerox for a variety of business purposes. C++ and Java have replaced Smalltalk as the most popular object-oriented programming languages.
Visual Basic (VB)	An object-oriented language developed at Microsoft. VB is easy to learn and understand, and is used for a variety of programming purposes.
C	A high-level procedural language. It is a compiled, structured programming language used for a variety of purposes.
C++	A high-level language that is an object-oriented version of C invented by Bjarne Stroustrup in the 1980s.
JAVA	A high-level object-oriented language similar to C++ but it allows programmers to build small application modules, called "applets," for use as part of a Web page. Applets make it possible for a Web page user to interact with the page.

⊙ Britannica.com. "Computer Programming Language," www.britannica.com/bcom/
  eb/article/0/0,5716,25460+1+25054,00.html
  Microsoft® Encarta® Online Encyclopedia 2000. "Programming Language,"
  www.encarta.msn.com/find/Concise.asp?z=1&pg=2&ti=761575695.

Aviation: Chronology

Year(s)	Inventions and Aircraft Evolution	Company and/or Inventor	Statistics (Military, Commercial, Etc.)
1781	ornithopter (flapping-wing machine resembling a glider)	Karl Friedrich Meerwein (Germany)	Limited testing and documentation of first flying machine
1783	hot-air balloon	Joseph and Etienne Montgolfier (France)	First manned flight of hot-air balloon
early 1800s	hydrogen balloon		Same construction as hot-air balloon, but filled with hydrogen gas; specialized warfare vehicle for spying
early 1800s	blimp		First non-rigid structure with aerodynamic shape
early 1800s	dirigible		First rigid structure with aerodynamic shape
1852	glider	George Cayley (England)	First glider trials
1900	luftschiff (airship based on the design of the dirigible)	Count Ferdinand von Zeppelin (Germany)	First experimental flight of a luftschiff

Aviation: Chronology *(cont.)*

Year(s)	Inventions and Aircraft Evolution	Company and/or Inventor	Statistics (Military, Commercial, Etc.)
1903	aeroplane (biplane)	Wilbur and Orville Wright (USA)	First manned flight of a motorized airplane
1909	monoplane	Louis Bleriot (France)	First aerial crossing of the English Channel
1910–15	LZ-5 (luftschiff/airship)	Deutsche-Luftschiffahrts AG (Germany)	First well-financed commercial air transportation company operated the LZ-5; 1,588 flights; 34,228 passengers
1913	four-engine plane	Sikorsky	First four-engine plane
1914	twin-engine seaplane	Glenn Curtiss (USA)	First commercial airplane service in the world, flying between Tampa and St. Petersburg, Florida
during WWI	zeppelin (luftschiff/airship)	Zeppelin Company (Germany)	88 constructed for military purposes; first sustained distant aerial warfare, which included the bombing of London; 45 mph
1919	Curtiss NC-4 flying boat	Curtiss Company (USA)	First aerial crossing of the Atlantic
mid-1920s	Graf Zeppelin	Zeppelin Company (Germany)	First around-the-world air voyage; continued commercial flights into the mid-1930s
1927	Vega (radial-engined airplane with a stressed wooden skin)	Lockheed Aircraft Company / John Northrup (USA)	Model for modern commercial aircraft; 110–135 mph
1928	trimotor airplane (with strongest yet-used radial engines)	Ford (USA)	Commercial flight
1930	Monomail (all-metal airplane with retractable landing gear)	Boeing (USA)	
1933	Boeing-247 (twin-engine)	Boeing (USA)	Advanced model for modern commercial aircraft; safer than trimotors
1935	Martin M-130—The China Clipper (four-engine flying boat with a 130-foot wingspan)	Martin Company (USA)	First airmail flight between California and Manila; passengers added in 1936
1936	DC-3 (twin-engine)	Douglas Company (USA)	First airliner to operate at a profit; 21- passenger transcontinental routes; 175 mph; unrivaled master airliner for several years; used for military cargo as the C-47 in the U.S.

1940	Stratoliner	Boeing Company (USA)	First plane with an airtight cabin, capable of flying at 14,000 at 200 mph; could navigate above weather and mountains, choosing routes of shortest possible distance; used for military flights during WWII
1940	DC-4	Douglas Company (USA)	DC-3 transformed into a four-engine size; 200 mph; unpressurized cabin; main transatlantic aircraft used during WWII in the form of the US Army's C-54 troop transport
1940	Constellation	Lockheed Company (USA)	280 mph; main commercial competitor of DC-4
1945–55	multiple advances in aircraft technology		Rapid growth in air traffic calls forth advanced aircraft technology to extend routes and enlarge markets
1953	DC-7	Douglas Company (USA)	First plane to fly 3,000 miles; 300 mph
1957			Number of passengers crossing Atlantic by air was greater than by sea
1958	Boeing 707	Boeing Company (USA)	The jet engine replaces the piston engine; 550 mph
1969	Concorde	British Aircraft Corp. (U.K.) and Sud-Aviation (France)	Concorde becomes first airplane to break sound barrier
1970	Boeing 747 (jumbo jet)	Boeing Company (USA)	Becomes longest, widest plane with greatest passenger capacity (416–524), and greatest maximum take-off weight (875,000 pounds); 565 mph
1970s	Gossamer Albatross (human-powered aircraft)	Paul MacCready (USA)	First human-powered aerial crossing of the English Channel
1970s	Solar Challenger (solar-powered aircraft)	Paul MacCready (USA)	First solar-powered aerial crossing of the English Channel
1976	Concorde	British Airways and Air France	First commercial passenger flight of supersonic jet

⊙ Encyclopaedia Britannica. "History of Transportation, Aviation: the ultimate ubiquity," www.britannica.com/bcom/eb/article/2/0,5716,120012+24+110734,00.html

The Boeing Company. "Product Line Family Overview," www.boeing.com/commercial/productline/index.html.

The Unofficial Concorde Home Page. "Concorde Jet History," www.concorde-jet.com/

Type of Aircraft	Wing Span	Overall Length	Max. Takeoff Weight (000 lbs.)	Avg. Cruise Speed (mph)	Seating Cap.	Cargo Space (cu. ft.)	Use
717	93 ft. 3 in.	124 ft.	121	504	106	935	Commercial short-range, high-frequency passenger airliner
737-200	93 ft.	100 ft. 2 in.	115.5	575	95–130	875	Commercial passenger airliner
737-200C	93 ft.	100 ft. 2 in.	115.5	575	95–130	875–2,605	Commercial convertible passenger or freight airliners
737-200C Advanced	93 ft.	100 ft. 2 in.	128.1	575	95–130	875–2,635	
737-300	94 ft. 9 in.	101 ft. 9 in.	138.5	495	128–149	1,068	Commercial passenger airliners
737-400	94 ft. 9 in.	109 ft. 7 in.	138.5	495	147–168	1,373	
737-500	94 ft. 9 in.	119 ft. 7 in.	133.5	495	110–132	822	
747 Passenger	211 ft. 5 in.	231 ft. 10 in.	875	565	416–524	6,025	Commercial passenger airliners
747 Domestic	195 ft. 8 in.	231 ft. 10 in.	833	565	568	6,025	
747 Freighter	211 ft. 5 in.	231 ft. 10 in.	875	565	N/A	27,467	Commercial cargo airliner (largest in service)
747 Combi	211 ft. 5 in.	231 ft. 10 in.	875	565	410	10,422	Commercial long-range passenger and freight combination airliner
757-200	124 ft. 10 in.	155 ft. 3 in.	272.5	530	192–239	1,670	Commercial passenger airliners
757-300	124 ft. 10 in.	178 ft. 7 in.	255	530	238–289	2,370	
757-200 Freighter	124 ft. 10 in.	155 ft. 3 in.	255	530	N/A	8,430	Commercial cargo airliner

767-200	156 ft. 1 in.	159 ft. 2 in.	395	530	181–285	2,875	Commercial long-range passenger airliners
767-300	156 ft. 1 in.	180 ft. 3 in.	412	530	218–269	3,770	Commercial long-range cargo airliner
767-300 Freighter	156 ft. 1 in.	180 ft. 3 in.	412	530	N/A	16,034	
777-200	199 ft. 11 in.	209 ft. 1 in.	545	560	320–440	5,656	Commercial long-range passenger airliners
777-200ER	199 ft. 11 in.	209 ft. 1 in.	656	560	320–440	5,656	
777-300	199 ft. 11 in.	242 ft. 4 in.	660	560	386–440	7,552	
MD-11 Passenger	169 ft. 5 in.	200 ft. 8 in.	630.5	588	285–410	6,850	Commercial long-range passenger airliners
MD-11 Combi	169 ft. 5 in.	200 ft. 8 in.	630.5	588	181–285	6,850–10,440	Commercial long-range convertible and combination airliner for passengers and cargo
MD-11 Convertible	169 ft. 5 in.	200 ft. 8 in.	630.5	588	350–410	6,850–21,358	Commercial long-range cargo airliner
MD-11 Freighter	169 ft. 5 in.	200 ft. 8 in.	630.5	588	N/A	22,380	
MD-81	107 ft. 8 in.	147 ft. 8 in.	140	504	144–172	1,253	Commercial passenger airliners
MD-82	107 ft. 8 in.	147 ft. 8 in.	149.5	504	144–172	1,253	
MD-83	107 ft. 8 in.	147 ft. 8 in.	160	504	144–172	1,103	
MD-88	107 ft. 8 in.	130 ft. 4 in.	140	504	144–172	938	
MD-90-30	107 ft. 8 in.	152 ft. 6 in.	156	504	152–172	1,300	Commercial passenger airliners
MD-90-30ER	107 ft. 8 in.	152 ft. 6 in.	166	504	152–172	1,183	
DC-8	N/A	N/A	N/A	N/A	258	N/A	Commercial passenger airliner

Type of Aircraft	Wing Span	Overall Length	Max. Takeoff Weight (000 lbs.)	Avg. Cruise Speed (mph)	Seating Cap.	Cargo Space (cu. ft.)	Use
DC-9-10	89.4 ft.	104.4 ft.	90.7	561	80-90	600	Commercial passenger airliners designed for short runways and short- to medium-range routes
DC-9-21	93.3 ft.	104.4 ft.	98	557	80-90	600	
DC-9-30	93.3 ft.	119.3 ft.	110	570	80-90	895	
DC-9-40	93.3 ft.	125.6 ft.	114	561	80-90	1,019	
DC-9-50	93.3 ft.	133.5 ft.	121	558	80-90	1,034	
DC-10 Series 10	155 ft. 4 in.	182 ft. 3 in.	430	600	250-380	4,618	Commercial passenger airliners
DC-10 Series 15	155 ft. 4 in.	180 ft. 8 in.	455	600	250-380	4,618	
DC-10 Series 30	165 ft. 4 in.	180 ft. 8 in.	572	600	250-380	4,618	
DC-10 Series 40	165 ft. 4 in.	180 ft. 7 in.	555	600	250-380	4,618	
DC-10 Series 10	155 ft. 4 in.	182 ft. 3 in.	430	600	250-380	4,618	Commercial convertible all-passenger or all-cargo airliners
DC-10 Series 30	165 ft. 4 in.	180 ft. 8 in.	572	600	250-380	4,618	
DC-10 Series 40	165 ft. 4 in.	180 ft. 7 in.	555	600	250-380	4,618	
DC-10 Series 30F	165 ft. 4 in.	180 ft. 8 in.	572	600	N/A	N/A	Commercial cargo-only airliner; military variant is the U.S. Air Force KC-10 tanker/cargo aircraft

© The Boeing Company. "Product Line Family Overview," www.boeing.com/commercial/productline/index.html

Launch/ Flight Date(s)	Project/ Vehicle	Astronaut(s) Cosmonaut(s)	Country	Accomplishments and Mission Description
3/25/61	Sputnik 5	Simulated cosmonaut Ivan Ivanovich; Zvezdochka (dog)	USSR	First dog in space; first simulated person in space
4/12/61	Vostok 1	Yury A. Gagarin	USSR	First person in space; single orbit around the Earth
5/5/61	Mercury/Freedom 7	Alan B. Shepard, Jr.	U.S.	First person in space from U.S.
2/20/62	Mercury/Friendship 7	John Glenn	U.S.	First person to circle Earth; 3 orbits
6/16/63	Vostok VI	Valentina Tereshkova	USSR	First woman in space
3/18/65	Voskhod 2	Pavel I Belyayev; Alexei A. Leonov	USSR	First space walk
6/3-7/65	Gemini 4	Edward H. White II; James A. McDevitt	U.S.	First space walk by U.S.
12/4/65	Gemini 7	Frank Borman; James A. Lovell, Jr.	U.S.	Set endurance record for longest space flight of 14 days
4/23/67	Soyuz 1	V. M. Komarov	USSR	Largest; most complex spacecraft launched up to that time; cosmonaut killed in failure of parachute recovery system
7/16-24/69	Apollo/Apollo 11	Neil A. Armstrong; Edwin E. Aldrin; Michael Collins	U.S.	First astronauts to walk on the moon; Lunar Module landed on moon; took core samples and collected data
4/11-17/70	Apollo/Apollo 13	James A. Lovell, Jr.; Fred W. Haise, Jr.; John L. Sweigert, Jr.	U.S.	Near-disastrous mission: ruptured oxygen tank forced emergency return to Earth
7/26/71	Apollo 15	David R. Scott; James B. Irwin; Alfred M. Worden	U.S.	First extensive exploration of Moon's surface by crew members in a Lunar Roving Vehicle

Launch/ Flight Date(s)	Project/ Vehicle	Astronaut(s) Cosmonaut(s)	Country	Accomplishments and Mission Description
12/7–19/72	Apollo/Apollo 17	Eugene Cernan; Ronald B. Evans; Harrison H. Schmitt	U.S.	Last men to walk on the moon (so far)
5/25– 6/22/73	Skylab/Skylab II	Charles Conrad, Jr.; Paul J. Weitz; Joseph P. Kerwin	U.S.	*Skylab* is repaired after damage during initial launch; crew able to exit and reenter *Skylab* for work in space through Airlock Module; mission more than doubled the previous American space endurance record
11/16/73– 2/8/74	Skylab/Skylab IV	Gerald P. Carr; William R. Pogue; Edward G. Gibson	U.S.	Longest *Skylab* mission and U.S. space flight: over 84 days with 1,214 orbits of Earth
7/15–24/75	Apollo-Soyuz Test Project: Apollo 18, Soyuz 19	U.S.: Thomas P. Stafford; Vance D. Brand; Donald K. Slayton USSR: Alexei Leonov; Valeri Kubasov	U.S.– USSR	First joint international meeting in space; crafts remained linked for 2 days; final flight of the Apollo spacecraft
4/12/81	Space Shuttle/ Columbia	John W. Young; Robert L. Crippen	U.S.	First reusable space craft; first to use liquid- and solid-propellant rocket engines
6/18/83	Space Shuttle/ Challenger	Robert L. Crippen; Frederick H. Hauck; John M. Fabian; Sally K. Ride; Norman E. Thagard	U.S.	First U.S. female astronaut in space (Ride)
8/30/83	Space Shuttle/ Challenger	Richard H. Truly; Daniel C. Brandenstein; Dale A. Gardner; Guion S. Bluford; William E. Thornton	U.S.	First African American astronaut in space (Bluford)

Date	Vehicle	Crew	Country	Notes
1/28/86	*Space Shuttle/ Challenger*	Francis R. Scobee; Michael J. Smith; Judith A. Resnik; Ellison S. Onizuka; Ronald E. McNair; Gregory B. Jarvis; Sharon Christa McAuliffe	U.S.	Destroyed during launch with all crew aboard; first U.S. civilian astronaut in space (schoolteacher McAuliffe) aboard
3/13/86	*Soyuz to Mir*	Leonid Kizim; Vladimir Solovyev	USSR	First occupants of space station *Mir* (core of a large, permanent, multi-manned orbiting complex designed to accommodate various expansion modules for crew living quarters and research facilities)
4/24–29/90	*Space Shuttle/ Discovery*	Loren J. Shriver; Charles F. Bolden, Jr.; Steven A. Hawley; Bruce McCandless; Kathryn D. Sullivan	U.S.	Deployed Hubble Space Telescope
1/94 10/29– 11/7/98	*Mir project Space Shuttle/ Discovery*	Valery Polyakov Curtis L. Brown, Steven W. Lindsey; Stephen K. Robinson; Scott F. Parazynski; Pedro Duque; Chiaki Mukai; John Glenn	USSR U.S.	Mission length record: 438 days Glenn (77) becomes the oldest person to go into space; medical links between aging and spaceflight studied
7/25–28/99	*Space Shuttle/ Columbia*	Eileen M. Collins; Jeffrey S. Ashby; Steven A. Hawley; Catherine G. Coleman; Michel Tognini	U.S.	First female commander (Collins) of a U.S. spaceflight

© Encyclopaedia Britannica. "Space Exploration," www.britannica.com/bcom/eb/article/6/0,5716,120716+1+111026,00.html
NASA. "Astronaut Information," www.hq.nasa.gov/office/pao.History/apollo/welcome.html#chart
NASA. "Human Spaceflight Programs History," www.hq.nasa.gov/office/pao/History/humansp.html

Space Flight: 25 Major Unmanned Missions

Launch Date	Mission Name or Vehicle	Country	Mission Description
10/4/57	Sputnik 1	USSR	First satellite ever launched
1/31/58	Explorer 1	U.S.	First satellite launched by U.S.
1/4/59	Luna 1	USSR	First space craft to reach escape velocity; passed Moon and orbited Sun
10/7/59	Luna 3	USSR	First photographs of another celestial body: far side of the Moon
3/7/62	OSO: Orbiting Solar Observatory	U.S.	Satellite pointed toward the sun to record and transmit scientific data
8/27/62	Mariner 2	U.S.	Gathered temperature and atmospheric density measurements of Venus
12/7/68	OAO: Orbiting Astronomical Observatory	U.S.	Satellite equipped to map entire electromagnetic spectrum and record other astronomical data
2/24/69	Mariner 6	U.S.	Obtained photographs, atmosphere analyses, and thermal maps of Mars
8/17/70	Venera 7	USSR	Instrumented capsule dropped by parachute into Venusian atmosphere yielded useful data from surface of Venus
11/10/70	Luna 17	USSR	Automated television-equipped roving vehicle landed on the Moon
3/3/72	Pioneer 10	U.S.	First spacecraft to fly by Jupiter; returned physical data and photographs
5/14/73	Skylab	U.S.	First U.S. space station launched
11/3/73	Mariner 10	U.S.	Used Venusian gravity to increase velocity to fly by Mercury; obtained first close-up photographs of Mercury
8/20/77	Viking 1	U.S.	First landing on Mars; transmitted detailed color images of planet's landscape back to Earth; conducted in situ analyses of Martian soil and atmosphere
8/20/77	Voyager 1	U.S.	Fly-by of Jupiter in 1979 and Saturn in 1980; revealed features of their moons, magnetic fields, and ring systems

Date	Mission	Country	Description
9/5/77	*Voyager 2*	U.S.	Fly-bys of Jupiter and Saturn, and then passed Uranus in 1986; passed by Neptune's clouds in 1989, provided data and images of Neptune
9/29/77	*Salyut 6*	USSR	Second generation of Soviet space station; two docking ports; increased length of time crews could live and work on board the station, reaching a record 211 days; visited by guest cosmonauts from Communist-bloc nations, France, and India
1/83	*IRAS: Infrared Astronomy Satellite*	U.S. w/ U.K., Netherlands	Study of infrared sources beyond the limits of the solar system
2/20/86	*Mir*	USSR	Space station satellite with six docking ports; core of a large, permanent, multi-manned orbiting complex designed to accommodate various expansion modules for crew living quarters and research facilities
3/31/87	*Kvant 1 to Mir*	USSR	Astrophysics observatory module docked at Mir complex
5/4/89	*Magellan*	U.S.	Placed in orbit around Venus for scientific studies
11/89	*Kvant 2 to Mir*	USSR	Delivered equipment for producing oxygen, recycling water supplies, and an airlock for cosmonaut spacewalks to perform outside maintenance work
4/24/90	*HST: Hubble Space Telescope*	U.S.	Deployed by the Space Shuttle; largest and most powerful observatory placed in Earth's orbit
4/96	*Priroda to Mir*	Russia	Sent to study Earth's environmental health and ecology
12/4/96	*Mars Pathfinder*	U.S.	Landed on Mars and collected surface data

© NASA. "Space Program History," www.hq.nasa.gov/office/pao/History Encyclopaedia Britannica. "Space Exploration," www.britannica.com/bcom/eb/article/6/0,5716,120716+1+110126,00.html

Space Flight: Moon Walkers

Astronaut	Mission	Moon Landing Date
Neil A. Armstrong	Apollo 11	July 20, 1969
Edwin E. Aldrin	Apollo 11	July 20, 1969
Charles P. Conrad, Jr.	Apollo 12	Nov. 19, 1969
Alan L. Bean	Apollo 12	Nov. 19, 1969
Alan B. Shepard, Jr.	Apollo 14	Feb. 5, 1971
Edgar D. Mitchell	Apollo 14	Feb. 5, 1971
David R. Scott	Apollo 15	July 30, 1971
James B. Irwin	Apollo 15	July 30, 1971
John W. Young	Apollo 16	Apr. 21, 1972
Charles M. Duke, Jr.	Apollo 16	Apr. 21, 1972
Eugene A. Cernan	Apollo 17	Dec. 11, 1972
Harrison Schmitt	Apollo 17	Dec. 11, 1972

⊙ NASA. "The Apollo Missions," www.hq.nasa.gov/office/pao/History/apollo/welcome.html#chart

Railroads: Chronology

100 BC	Roads paved with stone blocks that had grooves cut in them built in Greece; wagons with wheels the width of the grooves were pulled over the roads by horses
1500s	Tramroads with wooden rails built in Europe to facilitate hauling of coal, ore, or stone from mines
early 1700s	Iron replaces wood on tramroads, spreads from Europe to Northern America
1705	Steam-powered pump invented to remove water from mines
1767	First cast-iron rails, produced in England
1803	First steam-pumping engine mounted on a car with wheels set to operate on rails of cast-iron tramroad at Pen-y-Darren, Wales
1804	First steam locomotive hauls freight and passengers over Pen-y-Darren tram line
1820	First wrought-iron rails introduced in England
1825	First railroad line, the Stockton & Darlington, travels 9 miles; designed to carry goods and passengers on regular schedules (England)
1828	First cornerstone on the Baltimore & Ohio Railroad laid (U.S.)
1846	Pennsylvania Railroad incorporated (U.S.)
1853	New York Central Railroad organized (U.S.)
1859	First Pullman sleeping car (U.S.)
1864	U.S. Post Office first tests a railway mail car
1869	Union Pacific and Central Pacific meet at Promitory, Utah; becomes first transcontinental route in U.S.
1889	Great Northern Railway Company organized (U.S.)
1895	Electric traction introduced on short sections of U.S. railroads

1917	One million miles of rail routes worldwide, about one-quarter of them in the U.S.
1918	U.S. government takes over railroads for purpose of increasing wartime efficiency
1925	Installation of centralized traffic control (CTC) increases track capacity
1935	First diesel-powered train in U.S.
1950–90	Soviet Union Railway adds a second Trans-Siberian line, the Baikal-Amur Magistral
1950–90	China doubles route length of its national system to 33,500 miles
1959–64	Tokyo-Osaka railway expands with the Shinkansen electric line (320 miles of track, 130 mph) (Japan)
1970	Great Northern, Northern Pacific, and the Chicago, Burlington & Quincy merge to form the Burlington Northern (U.S.)
1975	Japanese Shinkansen line extends to Kyushu island via underwater tunnel; 664 mile route; 171 mph max. speed
1983	France's first high-speed Train a Grande Vitesse (TGV) completed; 168 mph
1990s	High speed railways built extensively in France, Gremany, Italy, Spain
1990s	High speed railways planned in South Korea, Taiwan, China, Canada, U.S.
1990s	India continues new trunk route construction
1991	World's last steam locomotive factory switches to electric locomotive manufacture (China)
1994	Trans-Channel Tunnel opens between France and Britain; 30 miles long
1996	Union Pacific and Southern Pacific merge

⊙ National Railroad Museum. "Railroad History," www.NationalRRMuseum.org/
Encyclopaedia Britannica. "Railroad," www.britannica.com
Microsoft® Encarta® Online Encyclopedia 2000. "Automobile,"
www.encarta.msn.com

Subways: Chronology

1860	Work begins on London's Metropolitan Railway, using the cut-and-cover construction method; this method involves digging a trench in the street above the railway, constructing a brick tunnel over the tracks, and then restoring the surface of the street.
1863	The world's first subway system, London's Metropolitan Railway, opens, carrying 9,500,000 passengers in its first year of service.
1866	Work begins on what will become London's "tube" line; to avoid causing disruption to the streets above, twin tunnels are excavated in a layer of clay approximately 60 feet below ground.
1870	In New York, in a 312-foot tunnel under Broadway, a subway car is operated by pneumatic pressure created by a giant fan; operation ceases in 1873.

1890	London's "tube" line opens; while earlier trains were steam-powered, all trains on the line now run on electric power.
1896	In Budapest, an electric subway begins operation.
1898	Boston's subway begins operation; it is the first subway system in the United States.
1898	Work begins on the Métro subway in Paris, using a variation of the cut-and-cover construction method that causes less disruption of street traffic.
1900	The Métro begins operation in Paris with 6.25 miles of track.
1902	Berlin's subway begins operation.
1904	The first section of the New York City subway opens.
1908	Philadelphia's subway begins operation.
1913	The Buenos Aires subway begins operation.
1919	Madrid's subway begins operation.
1927	Tokyo's subway begins operation.
1931	Kyoto's subway begins operation.
1933	Osaka's subway begins operation.
1935	Moscow's subway begins operation.
1943	Chicago's subway begins operation.
1954	Toronto's subway begins operation; it is the first subway system in Canada.
1955	Cleveland's subway begins operation.
1966	Montreal's subway begins operation.
1969	Mexico City's subway begins operation; this system is modeled after the Métro in Paris.
1971	The Victoria Line of the London Underground is completed; it is the first line to use automatic trains.
1976	San Francisco's BART (Bay Area Rapid Transit) system, the first completely automatic subway system, is completed.
1976	The Washington, D.C., Metro begins operation.
1979	Atlanta's subway begins operation.
1983	Baltimore's subway begins operation.
1984	Miami's subway begins operation.
1993	The Los Angeles subway begins operation.
2000	Moscow's subway system has the largest ridership, approximately 3.2 billion annually.
2000	With 256 miles of track, the London Underground has more track than any other subway system in the world.
2000	New York's subway system has more cars (6,273) and more stations (463) than any other system in the world.

⊙ Encyclopedia Britannica. "Subway," www.britannica.com

London Transport. "The Early Years," www.londontransport.co.uk/tube/ ciu_about.html

New York City Transit. "About New York City Transit," www.mta.nyc.ny.us/nyct/ facts/ffist.htm

Bridges: Major Types of Spans

Span Type	Function	Name	Location	Length
Beam	Most common bridge form. Carries vertical loads by bending. As the beam bridge bends, it undergoes horizontal compression on the top. At the same time, the bottom of the beam is subjected to horizontal tension. The supports carry the loads from the beam by compression vertically to the foundations.	Lake Ponchartrain Causeway (#2)	Metairie-Lewisburg, La., U.S.	23.9 mi. (38,462 m.)
Arch	Carries loads primarily by compression, which exerts both vertical and horizontal forces on the foundation. Arch foundations must therefore prevent both vertical settling and horizontal sliding.	New River Gorge	Fayette County, West Virginia, U.S.	0.32 mi. (518 m.)
Suspension	Carries vertical loads through curved cables in tension. These loads are transferred both to the towers, which carry them by vertical compression to the ground, and to the anchorages, which must resist the inward and sometimes vertical pull of the cables. The suspension bridge can be viewed as an upside-down arch in tension, with only the towers in compression.	Akashi-Kaikyo	Kobe, Akashi-Awaji Island, Japan	1.28 mi. (1,991 m.)
Cantilever	A beam is said to be cantilevered when it projects outward, supported only at one end. A cantilevered bridge is generally made with three spans, of which the outer spans are both anchored down at the shore and cantilever out over the channel to be crossed. The central span rests on the cantilevered arms extending from the outer spans. Towers carry the tension and compressions forces of the spans to central or far foundations.	Quebec	Quebec City, Quebec, Canada	0.34 mi. (549 m.)
Cable-stay	Carries the vertical main-span loads by nearly straight diagonal cables in tension. The towers transfer the cable forces to the foundations through vertical compression. The tensile forces in the cables also put the deck into horizontal compression.	Tatara Ohashi	Shikoku-Honshu, Japan	0.55 mi. (890 m.)

◉ Nova Online. "Super Bridge," www.pbs.org/wgbh/nova/bridge/build.html
Encyclopaedia Britannica. "The Elements of Bridge Design," www.britannica.com/bcom/eb/article/3/0,5716,127643+2+117290,00.html

THE SCIENCES: *Inventors and Discoverers*

Inventor/ Discoverer	Dates	Nationality	Major Invention/ Discovery
Acheson, Edward Goodrich	1856–1931	American	carborundum (1891)
Alexanderson, Ernst F. W.	1878–1975	American	high-frequency alternator (1906)
Alvarez, Luis Walter	1911–1988	American	radio distance & direction finder (1945)
Ampère, André-Marie	1775–1836	French	discovered electrodynamics
Appleton, Edward Victor	1892–1965	English	discovered ionospheric reflection of radio waves (1924)
Archimedes	c.287–c.212 BC	Greek	Archimedes screw
Aristarchus	c.310–230 BC	Greek	theory that Earth moves around Sun
Arkwright, Richard	1732–1792	English	water frame for spinning cotton (1769)
Armstrong, Edwin Howard	1890–1954	American	radio frequency-modulation system (1933)
Aspdin, Joseph	1779–1855	English	Portland cement (1824)
Babbage, Charles	1791–1871	English	laid groundwork for computer
Babcock, George Herman	1832–1893	American	co-invented water tube steam boiler (1867) [see Wilcox]
Bacon, Roger	c.1220–c.1292	British	spectacles with corrective lenses
Baekeland, Leo Hendrik	1863–1944	American	plastic Bakelite (1909)
Baird, John Logie	1888–1946	Scottish	first TV picture of moving objects (1926)
Bardeen, John	1908–1991	American	co-invented transistor (1947) [see Brattain; Shockley]
Beckman, Arnold O.	1900–	American	pH meter (1935)
Becquerel, Antoine-Henri	1852–1908	French	radioactivity (1896)
Begun, S. Joseph	1905–1995	American	magnetic recording (1934)
Bell, Alexander Graham	1847–1922	American	telephone (1876)
Bennett, Willard Harrison	1903–1987	American	radio frequency mass spectrometer (1950)
Benz, Carl Friedrich	1844–1929	German	first gas-powered automobile (1885)
Berliner, Emile	1851–1929	American	phonograph record disc (1887)
Bernoulli, Daniel	1700–1782	Swiss	related fluid flow to pressure (1738)
Berthollet, Claude-Louis	1748–1822	French	chlorine bleach (1785)
Bessemer, Henry	1813–1898	British	steel manufacturing (1856)
Binnig, Gerd Karl	1947–	German	co-invented scanning tunneling microscope (1981) [see Rohrer]
Bird, Forrest M.	1921–	American	respirator (1958) & pediatric ventilator (1970)
Birdseye, Clarence	1886–1956	American	frozen foods (1924)
Black, Harold Stephen	1898–1983	American	negative feedback principle
Black, Joseph	1728–1799	Scottish	discovered carbon dioxide (1756)
Blumberg, Baruch Samuel	1925–	American	co-invented vaccine for viral hepatitis (1971) [see Millman]
Boyle, Robert	1627–1691	English-born Irish	formulated Boyle's law (1662)
Brandt, George	1694–1768	Swedish	discovered cobalt (1730)
Brattain, Walter H.	1902–1987	American	co-invented transistor (1947) [see Bardeen; Shockley]

Brown, Rachel Fuller	1898–1980	American	co-invented antifungal antibiotic (1954) [see Hazen]
Brown, Robert	1773–1858	Scottish	discovered Brownian motion (1827) and nucleus of living cell (1831)
Burbank, Luther	1849–1926	American	developed types of potatoes and peaches and many other crops
Burroughs, William Seward	1855–1898	American	adding machine (1885)
Burton, William Meriam	1865–1954	American	efficient manufacture of gasoline (1913)
Bushnell, David	1742–1824	American	submarine (hand-powered) (1775)
Campbell, Donald L.	1904–	American	co-invented fluid catalytic cracking (1942) [see Martin]
Carlson, Chester F.	1906–1968	American	xerography (1938)
Carothers, Wallace Hume	1896–1937	American	nylon (1934)
Carrel, Alexis	1873–1944	French	method of suturing blood vessels
Carrier, Willis Haviland	1876–1950	American	air conditioning (1911)
Cartwright, Edmund	1743–1823	English	power loom (1785)
Carver, George Washington	c.1861–1943	American	developed peanut, sweet potato, and soybean products
Cavendish, Henry	1731–1810	English	discovered hydrogen (1766)
Celsius, Anders	1701–1744	Swedish	Celsius temperature scale (1742)
Colt, Samuel	1814–1862	American	revolver (1835)
Colton, Frank B.	1923–	American	Enovid—first oral contraceptive (1960)
Coolidge, William D.	1873–1975	American	X-ray tube (1916)
Copernicus, Nicolas	1473–1543	Polish	Sun-centered solar system theory
Cottrell, Frederick G.	1877–1948	American	electrostatic precipitator (1906)
Cray, Seymour R.	1925–1996	American	supercomputer (1976)
Crompton, Samuel	1753–1827	English	spinning mule (1779)
Curie, Marie	1867–1934	French	discovered polonium and radium (1898)
Curie, Pierre	1859–1906	French	discovered piezoelectricity (1880)
da Vinci, Leonardo	1452–1519	Italian	theories about anatomy, mechanics, flying, others
Daimler, Gottlieb	1834–1900	German	gasoline engine (1885)
Damadian, Raymond V.	1936–	American	magnetic resonance imaging scanner (MRI) (1977)
Darby, Abraham	c.1678–1717	English	high-quality iron (1709)
Davy, Humphry	1778–1829	English	discovered potassium and sodium (1806–7), miner's safety lamp (1825)
Dean, Mark	1957–	American	co-inventor of improved computer architecture (1984) [see Moeller]
Deere, John	1804–1886	American	better plow (1838)
Deforest, Lee	1873–1961	American	vacuum tube amplifier (1906)
Dennard, Robert	1932–	American	random access memory (RAM) (1968)
Diesel, Rudolf	1858–1913	German	internal combustion diesel engine (1896)
Djerassi, Carl	1923–	American	oral contraceptives
Dow, Herbert Henry	1866–1930	American	bromine extraction from brine (1889)
Draper, Charles Stark	1901–1987	American	gyroscopic gunsight
Drew, Richard	1886–1956	American	transparent adhesive tape (1930)
Dunlop, John Boyd	1840–1921	English	pneumatic tire (1888)

Inventor/ Discoverer	Dates	Nation- ality	Major Invention/ Discovery
Eastman, George	1854–1932	American	Kodak camera (1888), transparent film (1889)
Edgerton, Harold E.	1903–1990	American	flash tube (1931), stroboscopic photography
Edison, Thomas Alva	1847–1931	American	electric light bulb (1879); phonograph (1877), 1,091 other patents
Einstein, Albert	1879–1955	German/ American	theories of relativity (special, 1905; general, 1916)
Einthoven, Willem	1860–1927	Dutch	electrocardiograph (1903)
Elion, Gertrude Belle	1918–1999	American	drugs to fight various cancers
Engelbart, Douglas	1925–	American	computer mouse (1963–64)
Ericsson, John	1803–1889	Swedish/ American	screw propeller for ships (1836)
Faggin, Federico	1941–	American	co-invented computer microprocessor (1969) [see Hoff; Mazor]
Fahrenheit, Daniel Gabriel	1686–1736	German	mercury thermometer (1714), Fahrenheit temperature scale
Faraday, Michael	1791–1867	English	electromagnetic induction (1831)
Farnsworth, Philo Taylor	1906–1971	American	electronic television (1927)
Fergason, James	1934–	American	liquid-crystal display (1969)
Fermi, Enrico	1901–1954	American	nuclear reactor (1942)
Fitch, John	1743–1798	American	first American steamboat (1787)
Fleming, Alexander	1881–1955	Scottish	penicillin (1928)
Fleming, John Ambrose	1849–1945	English	two-electrode radio rectifier (1904)
Flemming, Walther	1843–1905	German	discovered mitotic cell division (1879)
Ford, Henry	1863–1947	American	assembly line (1913)
Forrester, Jay Wright	1918–	American	random-access magnetic core memory (1949)
Franklin, Benjamin	1706–1790	American	Franklin stove (1740)
Fulton, Robert	1765–1815	American	first steamboat to carry people and freight (1807)
Galileo	1564–1642	Italian	experimental scientific method
Galle, Johann Gottfried	1812–1910	German	discovered planet Neptune (1846)
Galvani, Luigi	1737–1798	Italian	discovered bioelectric forces in animal tissues
Geiger, Johannes	1882–1945	German	Geiger counter (1928)
Gerbert of Aurillac	c.945–1003	French	mechanical clock
Germer, Edmund	1901–	German/ American	fluorescent lamp, mercury-vapor lamp
Ginsburg, Charles P.	1920–1992	American	videotape recorder (1956)
Glauber, Johann Rudolf	1604–1668	German/ Dutch	many chemical compounds
Goddard, Robert Hutchings	1882–1945	American	liquid-propelled rocket engine (1926)
Goodyear, Charles	1800–1860	American	vulcanization of rubber (1839)
Graham, Thomas	1805–1869	Scottish	described colloids (1860s) and osmosis
Greatbatch, Wilson	1919–	American	cardiac pacemaker
Guericke, Otto von	1602–1686	German	air pump (1650)
Gutenberg, Johannes	c.1400–68	German	printing—developed movable type

Hadley, John	1682–1744	English	reflecting quadrant (1730)
Hall, Charles Martin	1863–1914	American	electrolytic aluminum manufacture (1886)
Hall, Robert N.	1919–	American	magnetron for microwave oven; CD-player laser (1962)
Halley, Edmond	1656–1742	English	theory that comets orbit the Sun
Hargreaves, James	c.1702–1778	English	spinning jenny (1764)
Harrison, John	1693–1776	English	accurate chronometer (1730–63)
Harvey, William	1578–1657	English	blood circulation (1628)
Hazen, Elizabeth Lee	1885–1975	American	co-invented antifungal antibiotic (1954) [see Brown]
Herschel, William	1738–1822	English	discovered planet Uranus (1781)
Hertz, Heinrich	1857–1894	German	discovered radio waves
Hewlett, William R.	1913–	American	audio oscillator
Higonnet, René Alphonse	1902–1983	French	co-invented Lithomat phototypesetter (1949) [see Moyroud]
Hillier, James	1915–	American	electron microscope (1937)
Hipparchus	c.190– after 127 BC	Greek	first star catalog
Hoe, Richard March	1812–1886	American	rotary printing press (1847)
Hoff, Marcian	1937–	American	co-invented computer microprocessor (1969) [see Faggin; Mazor]
Hollerith, Herman	1860–1929	American	statistics-tabulating machine (1884)
Hopper, Grace	1906–1992	American	improved data processing, computer languages
Houdry, Eugene	1892–1962	French	catalytic converter (1962)
Howe, Elias	1819–1867	American	sewing machine (1846)
Hubble, Edwin Powell	1889–1953	American	discovered external spiral galaxies (1923)
Hunt, Walter	1796–1859	American	safety pin (1849)
Huygens, Christiaan	1629–1695	Dutch	pendulum clock (1656)
Jacquard, Joseph Marie	1752–1834	French	automated loom (1801)
Jarvik, Robert K.	1946–	American	artificial heart
Jenner, Edward	1749–1823	English	smallpox vaccination (1796)
Julian, Percy Lavon	1899–1975	American	cortisone synthesis
Kay, John	1704–1764	English	flying shuttle for weaving (1733)
Keck, Donald B.	1941–	American	co-invented optical fiber (1970) [see Maurer; Schultz]
Kekule von Stradonitz, Friedrich	1829–1896	German	principles of molecular structure
Kettering, Charles Franklin	1876–1958	American	electrical ignition
Kilby, Jack S.	1923–	American	miniaturized integrated circuits (1958)
Koch, Robert	1843–1910	German	discovered several disease-causing bacteria
Kolff, Willem J.	1911–	Dutch	artificial kidney dialysis
Kwolek, Stephanie Louise	1923–	American	para-aramid fibers, Kevlar
Laënnec, René T. H.	1781–1826	French	stethoscope
Land, Edwin Herbert	1909–1991	American	Polaroid camera (1947)
Langmuir, Irving	1881–1957	American	long-life incandescent electric light
Lawrence, Ernest Orlando	1901–1958	American	cyclotron (1930)
Lear, William Powell	1902–1978	American	car radio, car eight-track tape player, aircraft autopilot
Leeuwenhoek, Antonie van	1632–1723	Dutch	discovered protozoa and bacteria (1674)

Inventor/ Discoverer	Dates	Nation- ality	Major Invention/ Discovery
Leibniz, Gottfried Wilhelm	1646–1716	German	integral and differential calculus (c. 1675)
Lilienthal, Otto	1848–1896	German	glider
Lippershey, Hans	c.1570–1619	Dutch	telescope (1608)
Lumière, Auguste	1862–1954	French	co-invented cinématograph (1895) [see Lumière]
Lumière, Louis	1864–1948	French	co-invented cinématograph (1895) [see Lumière]
Maiman, Theodore Harold	1927–	American	first laser (1960)
Malpighi, Marcello	1628–1694	Italian	capillary blood vessels (1661)
Marconi, Guglielmo	1874–1937	Italian	wireless telegraph/radio (1896)
Martin, Homer Z.	1910–1993	American	co-invented fluid catalytic cracking (1942) [see Campbell]
Maurer, Robert D.	1924–	American	co-invented optical fiber (1970) [see Keck; Schultz]
Maxim, Hiram Stevens	1840–1916	American/ English	Maxim machine gun (1884)
Mazor, Stanley	1941–	American	co-invented computer microprocessor (1969) [see Faggin; Hoff]
McCormick, Cyrus Hall	1809–1884	American	mechanical reaper (1831)
Meikle, Andrew	1719–1811	Scottish	threshing machine (1788)
Mercator, Gerardus	1512–1594	Flemish	Mercator projection in map-making (1569)
Mergenthaler, Ottmar	1854–1899	American	Linotype typesetter (1886)
Mestral, George de	1907–1990	Swiss	Velcro (1955)
Millman, Irving	1923–	American	co-invented vaccine for viral hepatitis (1971) [see Blumberg]
Moeller, Dennis	1950–	American	co-inventor of improved computer architecture (1984) [see Dean]
Monier, Joseph	1823–1906	French	reinforced concrete (1867)
Morse, Samuel F. B.	1791–1872	American	electric telegraph (1832–35), Morse Code (1838)
Moyer, Andrew J.	1899–1959	American	mass production of penicillin
Moyroud, Louis Marius	1914–	French	co-invented Lithomat phototypesetter (1949) [see Higonnet]
Mullis, Kary B.	1944–	American	polymerase chain reaction (1983)
Murphree, Eger V.	1891–1962	American	co-invented fluid catalytic cracking (1942) [see Tyson]
Newcomen, Thomas	1663–1729	English	atmospheric steam engine (1705)
Newton, Isaac	1642–1727	British	laws of motion and gravity, infinitesimal calculus
Nieuwland, Julius Arthur	1878–1936	American	first synthetic rubber—neoprene (1931)
Nobel, Alfred Bernhard	1833–1896	Swedish	dynamite (1867)
Noyce, Robert N.	1927–1990	American	integrated circuit (1959)
Oersted (or Ørsted), Hans	1777–1851	Danish	discovered electromagnetism (1820)
Ohm, Georg Simon	1789–1854	German	related current voltage and resistance (1827)

Olsen, Kenneth H.	1926–	American	magnetic core memory
Otis, Elisha Graves	1811–1861	American	safety elevator (1852)
Otto, Nikolaus August	1832–1891	German	four-stroke internal combustion engine (1861)
Oughtred, William	1574–1660	English	slide rule (c.1632)
Papin, Denis	1647–1712	French/English	pressure cooker (1679)
Parker, Louis W.	1906–1993	American	television receiver
Parkes, Alexander	1813–1890	English	synthetic plastic (1855), cold vulcanization (1841)
Parsons, Charles Algernon	1854–1931	English	steam turbine (1884)
Parsons, John T.	1913–	American	numerical control of machines
Pascal, Blaise	1623–1662	French	mechanical calculating machine (1642–44), law of pressure, syringe
Pasteur, Louis	1822–1895	French	pasteurization
Plunkett, Roy J.	1910–1994	American	Teflon (1949)
Poulsen, Valdemar	1869–1942	Danish	magnetic recording (1898), generation of radio waves (1903)
Priestley, Joseph	1733–1804	English	independently discovered oxygen (1774)
Ptolemy	fl. 127–145	Greek	theory that Earth is center of universe
Pythagoras	c.580–c.500 BC	Greek	theory of numbers
Raman, Chandrasekhara V.	1888–1970	Indian	discovered Raman effect—light diffusion (1928)
Ritter, Johann Wilhelm	1776–1810	German	ultraviolet light (1801)
Roebuck, John	1718–1794	British	manufactured sulfuric acid (1746)
Roemer (or Rømer), Ole	1644–1710	Danish	calculated speed of light (1676)
Roentgen, Wilhelm Conrad	1845–1923	German	X-ray tube (1895)
Rohrer, Heinrich	1933–	Swiss	co-invented scanning tunneling microscope (1981) [see Binnig]
Rubin, Benjamin A.	1917–	American	vaccination needle (1965)
Rutherford, Daniel	1749–1819	Scottish	discovered nitrogen (1772)
Rutherford, Ernest	1871–1937	English	discovered alpha and beta rays in radioactivity
Sarett, Lewis Hastings	1917–1999	American	cortisone (1944)
Savery, Thomas	1650–1715	English	first practical steam engine (1698)
Schawlow, Arthur L.	1921–1999	American	co-invented laser (1958) [see Townes]
Scheele, Carl Wilhelm	1742–1786	Swedish	discovered oxygen (1772)
Schick, Jacob	1877–1937	American	electric razor (1928)
Schultz, Peter C.	1942–	American	co-invented optical fiber (1970) [see Keck; Maurer]
Semon, Waldo Lonsbury	1898–1999	American	vinyl (1926)
Sheehan, John C.	1915–1992	American	synthetic penicillin (1957)
Shockley, William Bradford	1910–1989	American	co-invented transistor (1947) [see Bardeen; Brattain]
Sholes, Christopher L.	1819–1890	American	typewriter (1868)

Inventor/ Discoverer	Dates	Nationality	Major Invention/ Discovery
Siemens, Charles William	1823–1883	German/ English	regenerative open-hearth steel furnace (1861)
Sikorsky, Igor	1889–1972	American	helicopter (1909/1939)
Singer, Isaac Merrit	1811–1875	American	domestic sewing machine (1851)
Sobrero, Ascanio	1812–1888	Italian	discovered nitroglycerine (1846)
Spencer, Percy LeBaron	1894–1970	American	microwave oven (1945)
Sperry, Elmer Ambrose	1860–1930	American	gyroscopic compass (1908) and stabilizers
Stanley, William, Jr.	1858–1916	American	transformer (1885)
Steinmetz, Charles Proteus	1865–1923	American	theory of alternating current
Stibitz, George Robert	1904–1995	American	digital computer (1940)
Sturgeon, William	1783–1850	English	first useful electromagnet (1825)
Szilard, Leo	1898–1964	American	nuclear reactor (1942)
Taylor, Frederick Winslow	1856–1915	American	time and motion studies for industrial management (1881)
Tesla, Nikola	1856–1943	Serbian/ American	induction motor (1883), Tesla coil (1891)
Theiler, Max	1899–1972	American	yellow fever vaccine (1937)
Thompson, John Taliaferro	1860–1940	American	Thompson submachine gun (1920)
Thomson, Joseph John	1856–1940	English	discovered electron (1897)
Timken, Henry	1831–1909	American	tapered roller bearing (1898)
Torricelli, Evangelista	1608–1647	Italian	barometer (1643)
Townes, Charles Hard	1915–	American	co-invented laser (1958) [see Schawlow]
Trevithick, Richard	1771–1833	British	first railroad locomotive (1801)
Tull, Jethro	1674–1741	English	drill for sowing seeds (1701)
Tyson, Charles W.	1914–1978	American	co-invented fluid catalytic cracking (1942) [see Murphree]
Villard, Paul	1860–1934	French	discovered gamma rays in radioactivity (1900)
Volta, Alessandro	1745–1827	Italian	electric battery (1800)
Wang, An	1920–1990	American	magnetic memory core (1948)
Watt, James	1736–1819	Scottish	steam engine separate condenser (1765)
Westinghouse, George	1846–1914	American	air brakes (1869)
Whitney, Eli	1765–1825	American	cotton gin (1793)
Wilcox, Stephen	1830–1893	American	co-invented water tube steam boiler (1867) [see Babcock]
Wright, Orville	1871–1948	American	airplane (1903)
Wright, Wilbur	1867–1912	American	airplane (1903)
Zeppelin, Ferdinand Graf von	1838–1917	German	dirigible airships
Zworykin, Vladimir Kosma	1889–1982	American	cathode ray tube (1929)

⊙ National Inventors Hall of Fame. "Inventure Place," www.invent.org/

Novelists and Short-Story Writers

The following list spans time periods and nationalities. In addition to works whose literary merit has been recognized by scholars, the list highlights best-selling authors and writers who have influenced the development of specific genres.

Name	Dates	Nationality	Selected Works
Abe, Kobo	1924–1993	Japanese	*The Woman in the Dunes* (1962); *The Box Man* (1973)
Achebe, Chinua	1930–	Nigerian	*Things Fall Apart* (1958)
Agee, James	1909–1955	American	*A Death in the Family* (1957)
Amis, Kingsley	1922–1995	English	*Lucky Jim* (1954)
Anderson, Sherwood	1876–1941	American	Stories: *Winesburg, Ohio* (1919)
Asimov, Isaac	1920–1992	Russian-born American	*Foundation and Empire* (1952); Stories: *I, Robot* (1950)
Atwood, Margaret	1939–	Canadian	*The Circle Game* (1966); *The Handmaid's Tale* (1985); *The Blind Assassin* (2000)
Austen, Jane	1775–1817	English	*Sense and Sensibility* (1811); *Pride and Prejudice* (1813); *Emma* (1816); *Persuasion* (1818)
Baldwin, James	1924–1987	American	*Another Country* (1962)
Balzac, Honoré de	1799–1850	French	*The Human Comedy* (1842–53); *Cousin Bette* (1846)
Barth, John	1930–	American	*The Floating Opera* (1956); *The Sot-Weed Factor* (1960); *Giles Goat-Boy* (1966)
Bellow, Saul	1915–	American	*The Adventures of Augie March* (1953); *Seize the Day* (1956); *Herzog* (1964)
Benét, Stephen Vincent	1898–1943	American	Stories: "The King of the Cats" (1929); "The Devil and Daniel Webster" (1937)
Bierce, Ambrose	1842–1914	American	Stories: *An Occurrence at Owl Creek Bridge* (1891); *The Eyes of the Panther* (1891)
Blackwood, Algernon Henry	1869–1951	English	Stories: *The Willows* (1907); *The Wendigo* (1910)
Böll, Heinrich	1917–1985	German	*Group Portrait with Lady* (1971); *The Lost Honor of Katharina Blum* (1974)
Borges, Jorge Luis	1899–1986	Argentine	Stories: *Fictions* (1944); *The Aleph* (1949); *The Maker* (1960)
Bowles, Paul	1910–	American	*The Sheltering Sky* (1948). Stories: "A Distant Episode" (1945); "Pages from Cold Point" (1947)
Bradbury, Ray	1920–	American	*The Martian Chronicles* (1950); *Fahrenheit 451* (1953)
Breton, André	1896–1966	French	*The Communicating Vessels* (1932); *Mad Love* (1937)
Brontë, Charlotte	1816–1855	English	*Jane Eyre* (1847)
Brontë, Emily	1818–1848	English	*Wuthering Heights* (1847)

Novelists and Short-Story Writers *(cont.)*

Name	Dates	Nationality	Selected Works
Bukowski, Charles	1920–1994	American	*Post Office* (1971); *Factotum* (1975); *Hollywood* (1989)
Burgess, Anthony	1917–1993	English	*A Clockwork Orange* (1962)
Burroughs, William S.	1914–1997	American	*Naked Lunch* (1962); *The Soft Machine* (1961)
Cain, James M.	1892–1977	American	*The Postman Always Rings Twice* (1934); *Double Indemnity* (1936)
Caldwell, Erskine	1903–1987	American	*Tobacco Road* (1932); *God's Little Acre* (1933)
Camus, Albert	1913–1960	French	*The Stranger* (1942); *The Plague* (1947)
Capote, Truman	1924–1984	American	*The Grass Harp* (1951); *Breakfast at Tiffany's* (1958). Non-fiction: *In Cold Blood* (1965)
Cather, Willa	1873–1947	American	*O Pioneers!* (1913); *My Ántonia* (1918)
Cervantes Saavedra, Miguel de	1547–1616	Spanish	*Don Quixote* (1605–15)
Chandler, Raymond	1888–1959	American	*The Big Sleep* (1939); *The Lady in the Lake* (1943)
Cheever, John	1912–1982	American	*The Wapshot Chronicle* (1957); *Falconer* (1977)
Christie, Agatha	1891–1976	English	*Murder on the Orient Express* (1934); *And Then There Were None* (1940)
Clarke, Arthur C.	1917–	English	*2001: A Space Odyssey* (1968)
Clavell, James	1924–1994	Australian-born American	*Tai-Pan* (1966); *Shogun* (1975)
Cocteau, Jean	1889–1963	French	*Thomas the Imposter* (1923); *Les Enfants terribles* (1929)
Colette [Sidonie-Gabrielle Colette]	1873–1954	French	*Gigi* (1944)
Conrad, Joseph	1857–1924	English	*Lord Jim* (1900); *Heart of Darkness* (1902)
Cooper, James Fenimore	1789–1851	American	*The Last of the Mohicans* (1826); *The Deerslayer* (1841)
Crane, Stephen	1871–1900	American	*The Red Badge of Courage* (1895)
Crichton, [John] Michael	1942–	American	*The Andromeda Strain* (1969); *Jurassic Park* (1990)
Davies, Robertson	1913–1995	Canadian	*What's Bred in the Bone* (1985)
Defoe, Daniel	1660–1731	English	*Robinson Crusoe* (1719); *Moll Flanders* (1722)
Dickens, Charles	1812–1870	English	*The Pickwick Papers* (1836–37); *A Christmas Carol* (1843); *A Tale of Two Cities* (1859); *Great Expectations* (1861)
Dinesen, Isak [Karen Blixen]	1885–1962	Danish	Stories: *Seven Gothic Tales* (1934); *Winter's Tales* (1942); Memoir: *Out of Africa* (1937)
Doctorow, E. L.	1931–	American	*Ragtime* (1975); *Billy Bathgate* (1989)
Dos Passos, John	1896–1970	American	*U.S.A.* (trilogy; 1930–36)

Dostoyevsky, Fyodor Mikhaylovich	1821–1881	Russian	*Crime and Punishment* (1866); *The Idiot* (1869); *The Brothers Karamazov* (1880)
Doyle, Sir Arthur Conan	1859–1930	English	*A Study in Scarlet* (1887); *The Adventures of Sherlock Holmes* (1892)
Dreiser, Theodore	1871–1945	American	*Sister Carrie* (1900); *An American Tragedy* (1925)
Du Maurier, Daphne	1907–1989	English	*Rebecca* (1938)
Dumas, Alexandre père	1802–1870	French	*The Count of Monte Cristo* (1844–45); *The Three Musketeers* (1844)
Eco, Umberto	1932–	Italian	*The Name of the Rose* (1980); *Foucault's Pendulum* (1989)
Eliot, George [Mary Ann Evans]	1819–1880	English	*Silas Marner* (1861); *Middlemarch* (1871–72)
Ellison, Harlan	1934–	American	Stories: "Repent, Harlequin!" Said the Ticktockman (1965); *A Boy and His Dog* (1969)
Ellison, Ralph	1914–1994	American	*Invisible Man* (1952)
Faulkner, William	1897–1962	American	*As I Lay Dying* (1930); *Sanctuary* (1931); *Light in August* (1932); *Absalom, Absalom!* (1936)
Fielding, Henry	1707–1754	English	*Tom Jones* (1749)
Finney, Jack	1911–1995	American	*Invasion of the Body Snatchers* (1955)
Fitzgerald, F. Scott	1896–1940	American	*The Great Gatsby* (1925); *Tender Is the Night* (1934)
Flaubert, Gustave	1821–1880	French	*Madame Bovary* (1857); *A Sentimental Education* (1869)
Ford, Ford Madox	1873–1939	English	*The Good Soldier* (1915)
Forster, E. M.	1879–1970	English	*Howard's End* (1910); *A Passage to India* (1924)
Fowles, John	1926–	English	*The Collector* (1963); *The French Lieutenant's Woman* (1969)
Fuentes, Carlos	1928–	Mexican	*The Old Gringo* (1986)
Galsworthy, John	1867–1933	English	*The Forsyte Saga* (1922)
García Márquez, Gabriel	1928–	Colombian	*One Hundred Years of Solitude* (1967); *Love in the Time of Cholera* (1988)
Gide, André	1868–1951	French	*The Immoralist* (1902); *The Counterfeiters* (1926)
Gogol, Nikolai	1809–1852	Russian	*Dead Souls* (1842). Stories: "Diary of a Madman" (1935); "The Overcoat" (1842)
Golding, William	1911–1993	English	*Lord of the Flies* (1954)
Goldsmith, Oliver	1730–1774	English	*The Vicar of Wakefield* (1766)
Gordimer, Nadine	1923–	South African	*The Lying Days* (1953); *The Conversationist* (1974); *The House Gun* (1998)
Gorky, Maxim	1868–1936	Russian	*Mother* (1906); Stories: "Chelkash" (1895); "Twenty-Six Men and a Girl" (1899)
Grass, Günther	1927–	German	*The Tin Drum* (1959)
Graves, Robert	1895–1985	English	*I, Claudius* (1934)
Greene, Graham	1904–1991	English	*The End of the Affair* (1951); *The Quiet American* (1957); *Our Man in Havana* (1958)

Novelists and Short-Story Writers *(cont.)*

Name	Dates	Nation-ality	Selected Works
Grisham, John	1955–	American	*The Firm* (1991); *The Client* (1993)
Hammett, [Samuel] Dashiell	1894–1961	American	*The Maltese Falcon* (1930); *The Glass Key* (1931); *The Thin Man* (1934)
Hardy, Thomas	1840–1928	English	*Far from the Madding Crowd* (1874); *The Return of the Native* (1878); *Tess of the D'Urbervilles* (1891); *Jude the Obscure* (1896)
Hawthorne, Nathaniel	1804–1864	American	*The Scarlet Letter* (1850); *The House of the Seven Gables* (1851); *The Blithedale Romance* (1852)
Heller, Joseph	1923–2000	American	*Catch-22* (1961)
Hemingway, Ernest	1899–1961	American	*The Sun Also Rises* (1926); *A Farewell to Arms* (1929); *For Whom the Bell Tolls* (1940); *The Old Man and the Sea* (1952).
Henry, O.	1862–1910	American	Stories: "The Gift of the Magi" (1905); "The Ransom of Red Chief" (1910)
Hesse, Hermann	1877–1962	German	*Siddhartha* (1922); *Steppenwolf* (1927)
Highsmith, Patricia	1921–1995	American	*Strangers on a Train* (1949); *The Talented Mr. Ripley* (1955)
Hilton, James	1900–1954	English-born American	*Goodbye, Mr. Chips* (1934)
Himes, Chester	1909–1984	American	*If He Hollers Let Him Go* (1945); *Cotton Comes to Harlem* (1965)
Howells, William Dean	1837–1920	American	*The Rise of Silas Lapham* (1885)
Hugo, Victor Marie	1802–1885	French	*The Hunchback of Notre Dame* (1831); *Les Misérables* (1862)
Hurston, Zora Neale	1903–1960	American	*Their Eyes Were Watching God* (1937)
Huxley, Aldous	1894–1963	English	*Crome Yellow* (1921); *Antic Hay* (1923); *Brave New World* (1932)
Irving, John	1942–	American	*The World According to Garp* (1978); *A Prayer for Owen Meany* (1989)
Irving, Washington	1783–1859	American	Stories: *The Sketch Book* (1819–20)
James, Henry	1843–1916	American	*The American* (1877); *Portrait of a Lady* (1881); *The Ambassadors* (1903)
Jong, Erica	1942–	American	*Fear of Flying* (1973)
Joyce, James	1882–1941	Irish	*Portrait of the Artist as a Young Man* (1916); *Ulysses* (1922); Stories: *Dubliners* (1914)
Kafka, Franz	1883–1924	German	*Metamorphosis* (1915); *Amerika* (1927)
Keneally, Thomas	1935–	Australian	*The Chant of Jimmie Blacksmith* (1972); *Schindler's List* (1982)
Kerouac, Jack	1922–1969	American	*On the Road* (1957)

Kesey, Ken	1935–	American	*One Flew Over the Cuckoo's Nest* (1962)
King, Stephen	1947–	American	*Carrie* (1974); *The Shining* (1977); *The Tommyknockers* (1987)
Knowles, John	1926–	American	*A Separate Peace* (1959)
Krantz, Judith	1927–	American	*Scruples* (1978); *Princess Daisy* (1980); *I'll Take Manhattan* (1986)
L'Amour, Louis	1908–1988	American	*How the West Was Won* (1963)
Laclos, Pierre Choderlos de	1741–1803	French	*Les Liaisons dangereuses* (1782)
Lampedusa, Tomasi di	1896–1957	Italian	*The Leopard* (1958)
Lawrence, D. H.	1885–1930	English	*Sons and Lovers* (1913); *Lady Chatterly's Lover* (1928)
Le Carré, John	1931–	English	*The Spy Who Came in from the Cold* (1963); *Tinker, Tailor, Soldier, Spy* (1974)
Le Guin, Ursula K.	1929–	American	*The Left Hand of Darkness* (1969); *The Dispossessed* (1974)
Lee, Harper	1926–	American	*To Kill a Mockingbird* (1960)
Lessing, Doris	1919–	English	*Children of Violence* (5 vols.; 1952–69); *The Golden Notebook* (1962)
Levin, Ira	1929–	American	*A Kiss Before Dying* (1953); *Rosemary's Baby* (1967)
Lewis, [Harry] Sinclair Lewis	1885–1951	American	*Babbitt* (1922); *Arrowsmith* (1925); *Elmer Gantry* (1927)
London, Jack	1876–1916	American	*The Call of the Wild* (1903); *White Fang* (1906)
Mahfouz, Naguib	1911–	Egyptian	*New Cairo* (1946); *The Palace of Desire* (1957); *Wedding Song* (1987)
Mailer, Norman	1923–	American	*The Naked and the Dead* (1948); *The Executioner's Song* (1979)
Malamud, Bernard	1914–1986	American	*The Natural* (1952); *The Assistant* (1957)
Mann, Thomas	1875–1955	German	*Buddenbrooks* (1900); *The Magic Mountain* (1924); *Doctor Faustus* (1947)
Mansfield, Katherine	1888–1923	New Zealander	Stories: "Prelude" (1918); "The Garden Party" (1922)
Maugham, William Somerset	1874–1965	English	*The Moon and Sixpence* (1916); *The Razor's Edge* (1944)
Maupin, Armistead	1944–	American	*Tales of the City* (1978)
McCarthy, Mary	1912–1989	American	*The Group* (1963); Autobiography: *Memories of a Catholic Girlhood* (1957)
McCullers, Carson	1917–1967	American	*The Heart is a Lonely Hunter* (1940); *The Ballad of the Sad Café* (1951)
McCullough, Colleen	1937–	Australian	*The Thorn Birds* (1977)
Melville, Herman	1819–1891	American	*Typee* (1846); *Moby Dick* (1851); Stories: "Bartleby the Scrivener" (1853)
Michener, James	1907–1997	American	*Hawaii* (1959); *Cheskapeake* (1978)

Novelists and Short-Story Writers *(cont.)*

Name	Dates	Nation-ality	Selected Works
Miller, Henry	1891–1980	American	*Tropic of Cancer* (1934); *Tropic of Capricorn* (1939)
Mishima, Yukio	1925–1970	Japanese	*The Sailor Who Fell From Grace with the Sea* (1963)
Mitchell, Joseph	1908–1996	American	Stories: *Up in the Old Hotel* (1992)
Mitchell, Margaret	1900–1949	American	*Gone with the Wind* (1936)
Morrison, Toni	1931–	American	*Song of Solomon* (1977); *Beloved* (1987); *Jazz* (1992)
Murasaki, Lady Shikibu	c.978–c.1014	Japanese	*The Tale of Genji* (c.1010)
Murdoch, Iris	1919–1999	English	*A Severed Head* (1961); *The Good Apprentice* (1985)
Nabokov, Vladimir Vladimirovich	1889–1977	Russian-born American	*Lolita* (1955); *Pnin* (1957); *Pale Fire* (1962)
Naipaul, V. S.	1932–	Trinidadian	*A Bend in the River* (1979); *Way in the World* (1994)
Natsume, Soseki	1867–1916	Japanese	*I Am a Cat* (1905–6); *The Wayfayer* (1912-13)
Nin, Anaïs	1903–1977	French-born American	*Cities of the Interior* (5 vols.; 1959); *Seduction of the Minotaur* (1961)
Noma, Hiroshi	1915–1991	Japanese	*Zone of Emptiness* (1952)
O'Connor, [Mary] Flannery	1925–1964	American	*Wise Blood* (1949); *The Violent Bear It Away* (1955)
O'Hara, John	1905–1970	American	*Appointment in Samarra* (1934); *Butterfield 8* (1935)
Oates, Joyce Carol	1938–	American	*Do With Me What You Will* (1973); *Bellefleur* (1980)
Orwell, George	1903–1950	English	*Animal Farm* (1945); *1984* (1949)
Page, Thomas Nelson	1853–1922	American	Stories: *In Ole Virgina, Marse Chan, and Other Stories* (1887)
Parker, Dorothy	1893–1967	American	"Lady with a Lamp" (1932); "The Waltz" (1933)
Pasternak, Boris Leonidovich	1890–1960	Russian	*Doctor Zhivago* (1957)
Paton, Alan Stewart	1903–1988	South African	*Cry the Beloved Country* (1948)
Petronius, Gaius	d. AD 66	Roman	*The Satyricon* (c.50)
Poe, Edgar Allan	1809–1849	American	Stories: "The Fall of the House of Usher" (1839); "The Tell-Tale Heart" (1843); "The Pit and the Pendulum" (1843); "The Cask of Amontillado" (1846)
Porter, Katherine Anne	1890–1980	American	*Ship of Fools* (1962). Stories: "Pale Horse, Pale Rider" (1939); "Noon Wine" (1939)
Potok, Chaim	1929–	American	*The Chosen* (1967); *The Promise* (1969)
Proust, Marcel	1871–1922	French	*Remembrance of Things Past* (7 vols.; 1913–27)

Puig, Manuel	1932–1990	Argentinian	*The Kiss of the Spider Woman* (1976)
Pushkin, Alexander Sergeevich	1789–1837	Russian	*Eugene Onegin* (1831); *The Captain's Daughter* (1836)
Rabelais, François	c.1494–1553	French	*Gargantua and Pantagruel* (1532–64)
Rand, Ayn	1905–1982	Russian-born American	*The Fountainhead* (1943); *Atlas Shrugged* (1957)
Réage, Pauline	1908–1998	French	*The Story of O* (1955)
Remarque, Erich Maria	1898–1970	German	*All Quiet on the Western Front* (1929)
Rice, Anne	1941–	American	*Interview with the Vampire* (1976); *Cry to Heaven* (1982); *The Vampire Lestat* (1985)
Robbins, Tom	1936–	American	*Another Roadside Attraction* (1971); *Even Cowgirls Get the Blues* (1976)
Roth, Philip	1933–	American	*Goodbye, Columbus* (1959); *Portnoy's Complaint* (1969); *The Human Stain* (2000)
Rushdie, Salman	1947–	Indian	*Midnight's Children* (1980); *The Satanic Verses* (1989)
Sagan, Francoise	1935–	French	*Bonjour tristesse* (1954)
Saki [Hector Hugh Munro]	1870–1916	Scottish	*The Unbearable Bassington* (1912); Stories: "Tobermory" (1911); "The Open Window" (1914)
Salinger, J. D.	1919–	American	*The Catcher in the Rye* (1951); *Franny and Zooey* (1961)
Sand, George [Amandine Lucie Aurore Dupin]	1804–1876	French	*The Devil's Pool* (1846); *The Country Waif* (1848)
Sandburg, Carl	1878–1967	American	*Remembrance Rock* (1948); Stories: *Rootabaga Stories* (1922)
Saroyan, William	1908–1981	American	*The Human Comedy* (1943); Stories: *The Daring Young Man on the Flying Trapeze* (1934)
Sartre, Jean-Paul	1905–1980	French	*Nausea* (1938)
Scott, Sir Walter	1771–1832	Scottish	*Rob Roy* (1817); *Ivanhoe* (1819)
Shelley, Mary Wollstonecraft	1791–1851	English	*Frankenstein* (1818)
Shute, Nevil	1899–1960	Australian	*A Town Like Alice* (1950); *On the Beach* (1957)
Sinclair, Upton	1878–1968	American	*The Jungle* (1906)
Singer, Isaac Bashevis	1904–1991	Polish-born American	*The Magician of Lublin* (1960); *Enemies, a Love Story* (1972); Stories: "The Spinoza of Market Street" (1944); "Gimpel the Fool" (1945)
Smiley, Jane	1949–	American	*A Thousand Acres* (1991); *Horse Heaven* (2000)
Solzhenitsyn, Aleksandr I.	1918–	Russian	*One Day in the Life of Ivan Denisovich* (1962); *The Cancer Ward* (1968)
Southern, Terry	1926–1995	American	*Candy* (1958); *Blue Movie* (1970)
Spark, Muriel	1918–	Scottish-born English	*Memento Mori* (1959); *The Girls of Slender Means* (1963)

Novelists and Short-Story Writers (cont.)

Name	Dates	Nationality	Selected Works
Stein, Gertrude	1874–1946	American	*The Making of Americans* (1906–11); Autobiography: *The Autobiography of Alice B. Toklas* (1933)
Steinbeck, John Ernst	1902–1968	American	*The Grapes of Wrath* (1939); *Of Mice and Men* (1937); *Cannery Row* (1945)
Stendhal [Marie-Henri Beyle]	1788–1842	French	*The Charterhouse of Parma* (1839)
Sterne, Laurence	1713–1768	Irish-born English	*Tristam Shandy* (1759-67)
Stevenson, Robert Louis	1850–1894	Scottish	*Treasure Island* (1883); *The Strange Case of Dr. Jekyll and Mr. Hyde* (1886)
Stoker, Bram	1847–1912	Irish	*Dracula* (1897)
Stowe, Harriet Beecher	1811–1896	American	*Uncle Tom's Cabin* (1852)
Styron, William	1925–	American	*The Confessions of Nat Turner* (1967); *Sophie's Choice* (1979)
Swift, Jonathan	1667–1745	Irish	*Gulliver's Travels* (1726)
Tanizaki, Jun'ichiro	1886–1965	Japanese	*The Secret History of the Lord Musashi* (1935); *Seven Japanese Tales* (1963)
Thackeray, William Makepeace	1811–1863	English	*Barry Lyndon* (1844); *Vanity Fair* (1847–48)
Theroux, Paul	1941–	American	*The Family Arsenal* (1976); *The Mosquito Coast* (1981)
Thurber, James	1894–1961	American	Story: "The Secret Life of Walter Mitty" (1939)
Tolstoy, Leo	1828–1910	Russian	*War and Peace* (1863–69); *Anna Karenina* (1875–77); Play: *Redemption* (1911)
Trollope, Anthony	1815–1882	English	*Barchester Towers* (1857); *He Knew He Was Right* (1869)
Ts'ao Hsueh-ch'in	c.1715–1763	Chinese	*Dream of the Red Chamber* (c.1763)
Turgenev, Ivan	1818–1883	Russian	*Fathers and Sons* (1862); Stories: "The Diary of a Superfluous Man" (1850)
Twain, Mark [Samuel Clemens]	1835–1910	American	*Tom Sawyer* (1876); *Huckleberry Finn* (1884)
Updike, John	1932–	American	*Rabbit, Run* (1960); *Gertrude and Claudius* (2000)
Vidal, Gore	1925–	American	*The City and the Pillar* (1948); *Burr* (1974)
Voltaire [Francois-Marie Arouet]	1694–1778	French	*Candide* (1759)
Vonnegut, Kurt, Jr.	1922–	American	*Player Piano* (1952); *Slaughterhouse Five* (1969)
Walker, Alice	1944–	American	*The Color Purple* (1982)
Warren, Robert Penn	1905–1989	American	*All the King's Men* (1946); *World Enough and Time* (1950)

Waugh, Evelyn	1903–1966	English	*Decline and Fall* (1928); *A Handful of Dust* (1934); *Brideshead Revisited* (1945)
Weldon, Faye	1933–	English	*The Life and Loves of a She-Devil* (1983)
Wells, H. G.	1866–1946	English	*The Invisible Man* (1897); *The War of the Worlds* (1898)
Welty, Eudora	1909–	American	*Delta Wedding* (1946); *The Optimist's Daughter* (1972)
West, Nathaniel	1903–1940	American	*Miss Lonelyhearts* (1933); *The Day of the Locust* (1939)
Wharton, Edith	1862–1937	American	*Ethan Frome* (1911); *The Age of Innocence* (1920)
Wodehouse, P. G.	1881–1975	English-born American	*My Man Jeeves* (1919)
Wolfe, Thomas	1900–1938	American	*Look Homeward, Angel* (1929)
Wolfe, Tom	1930–	American	*The Bonfire of the Vanities* (1987)
Woolf, Virginia	1882–1941	English	*Mrs. Dalloway* (1925); *To the Lighthouse* (1927)
Wouk, Herman	1915–	American	*The Caine Mutiny* (1951)
Wright, Richard	1908–1960	American	*Native Son* (1940)
Yourcenar, Marguerite	1903–1987	French-born American	*The Memoirs of Hadrian* (1951)

⊙ Brown, Susan Windisch, ed. *Contemporary Novelists*, 6th ed. Detroit: St. James, 1996.
   Goring, Rosemary, ed. *Larousse Dictionary of Writers*. Edinburgh: Larousse, 1994.
   Riggs, Thomas, ed. *Reference Guide to Short Fiction*, 2nd. ed. Detroit: St. James, 1999.
   Vinson, James, and Daniel Kirkpatrick, eds. *Great Foreign Language Writers*. New York: St. Martin's, 1984.

British Poets Laureate

The first English poet laureate, Ben Jonson, was appointed in 1616, but the royal office did not become official until 1668. English poet laureates are appointed for life.

Laureate-ship	Poet	Dates	Major Works
1668	John Dryden	1631–1700	"Absalom and Achitophel" (1681); "Mac Flecknoe" (1682)
1689	Thomas Shadwell	1643?–1692	*The Virtuoso* (1676); *The Squire of Alsatia* (1688)
1692	Nahum Tate	1652–1715	"Absalom and Achitophel" (2nd part 1681); "Dido and Aeneas" (1689)
1715	Nicholas Rowe	1674–1718	*Tamberlane* (1701); *The Fair Penitent* (1703)
1718	Laurence Eusden	1688–1730	[unknown]
1730	Colley Cibber	1671–1757	*She Would and She Would Not* (1702); *The Careless Husband* (1704)
1757	William Whitehead	1715–1785	"The Danger of Writing Verse" (1741); "A Charge to the Poets" (1762)
1785	Thomas Warton	1728–1790	[unknown]
1790	Henry James Pye	1745–1813	[unknown]
1813	Robert Southey	1774–1843	"The Curse of Kehama" (1810); "Roderick: The Last of the Goths" (1814)

British Poets Laureate *(cont.)*

Laureate-ship	Poet	Dates	Major Works
1843	William Wordsworth	1770–1850	"Tintern Abbey" (1798); "Ode: Intimations of Immortality" (1807)
1850	Alfred, Lord Tennyson	1809–1892	*Maud and Other Poems* (1855); *Idylls of the King* (1859–85)
1896	Alfred Austin	1835–1913	[unknown]
1913	Robert Bridges	1844–1930	*The Growth of Love* (1890); *Poetical Works* (1898–1905)
1930	John Masefield	1878–1967	*Salt-Water Ballads* (1902); *Collected Poems* (1923)
1968	Cecil Day-Lewis	1904–1972	*The Magnetic Mountain* (1933); *Poems in Wartime* (1940)
1972	Sir John Betjeman	1906–1984	*Collected Poems* (1962); *A Nip in the Air* (1972)
1984	Ted Hughes	1930–1998	*Crow* (1970); *River* (1983)
1998	Andrew Motion	1952–	*The Pleasure Steamers* (1978); *Dangerous Play* (1984)

American Poets Laureate

The official title of this honor is Poet Laureate Consultant in Poetry to the Library of Congress. The Consultant position has been awarded since 1937, but the title of Poet Laureate was not created until 1986. The position is awarded annually by the Library of Congress.

Laureate-ship	Poet	Dates	Major Works
1986–87	Robert Penn Warren	1905–1989	*Promises: Poems, 1954–56*; *Now and Then: Poems, 1976–1978*
1987–88	Richard Wilbur	1921–	*Poems* (1957); *New and Collected Poems* (1988)
1988–90	Howard Nemerov	1920–1991	*Guide to the Ruins* (1950); *Collected Poems* (1977)
1990–91	Mark Strand	1934–	*Selected Poems* (1980); *Blizzard of One* (1998)
1991–92	Joseph Brodsky	1940–1996	*A Part of Speech* (1980); *Watermark* (1993)
1992–93	Mona Van Duyn	1921–	*To See, To Take* (1970); *Near Changes* (1990)
1993–95	Rita Dove	1952–	*The Yellow House on the Corner* (1980); *Museum* (1983)
1995–97	Robert Haas	1941–	*Praise* (1980); *Human Wishes* (1990)
1997–2000	Robert Pinsky	1940–	*Sadness and Happiness* (1975); *An Explanation of America* (1979)
2000–2001	Stanley Kunitz	1905–	*Selected Poems* (1958); *The Poems of Stanley Kunitz, 1928–1978*

Playwrights

The following list spans time periods and nationalities. In addition to recognized masters, the list features important theatrical innovators and the authors of popular plays.

Name	Dates	Nationality	Major Works
Aeschylus	525–456 BC	Greek	*The Oresteia* (458 BC)
Albee, Edward	1928–	American	*The Zoo Story* (1959); *Who's Afraid of Virginia Woolf?* (1962)
Aristophanes	c.448–c.380 BC	Greek	*The Birds* (414 BC); *Lysistrata* (411 BC); *The Frogs* (405 BC)
Beckett, Samuel	1906–1989	Irish-born French	*Waiting for Godot* (1953); *Endgame* (1957); *Happy Days* (1961)
Brecht, Bertolt	1898–1956	German	*Mother Courage* (1938–39); *The Good Woman of Setzuan* (1938–41); *The Caucasian Chalk Circle* (1943–45); *The Threepenny Opera* (1928); *The Rise and Fall of the City of Mahagonny* (1930)
Büchner, Georg	1813–1837	German	*Danton's Death* (1835); *Wozzeck* (1837)
Calderón de la Barca, Pedro	1600–1681	Spanish	*Life is a Dream* (1635)
Chekhov, Anton Pavlovich	1860–1904	Russian	*The Seagull* (1896); *Three Sisters* (1900); *The Cherry Orchard* (1904); Stories: "The Steppe" (1888); "Ward No. 6" (1892); "The Lady with the Dog" (1899)
Corneille, Pierre	1606–1684	French	*Médée* (1635); *Le Cid* (1637)
Coward, Sir Noel	1899–1973	English	*Private Lives* (1930); *Blithe Spirit* (1941); *Present Laughter* (1942)
Dryden, John	1631–1700	English	*All for Love* (1678); *Marriage à la Mode* (1672)
Euripides	484–406 BC	Greek	*Medea* (431 BC); *Hippolytus* (428 BC); *Electra* (413 BC); *The Bacchae* (posthumous)
Fugard, Athol	1932–	South African	*The Blood Knot* (1963); *"Master Harold" and the Boys* (1982)
García Lorca, Federico	1898–1936	Spanish	*Blood Wedding* (1933); *Yerma* (1934) *The House of Bernarda Alba* (posthumous; 1945)
Giraudoux, Jean	1882–1944	French	*Amphitryon '38* (1939); *Ondine* (1939); *The Madwoman of Chaillot* (1945)
Hellman, Lillian	1905–1984	American	*The Children's Hour* (1934); *The Little Foxes* (1939); *Watch on the Rhine* (1941)
Henley, Beth	1952–	American	*Crimes of the Heart* (1982)
Ibsen, Henrik	1828–1906	Norwegian	*Peer Gynt* (1867); *A Doll's House* (1878–79); *Ghosts* (1881); *The Wild Duck* (1884); *Hedda Gabler* (1890)
Inge, William	1913–1973	American	*Come Back, Little Sheba* (1950); *Picnic* (1953); *The Dark at the Top of the Stairs* (1957)
Ionesco, Eugène	1912–1994	Romanian-born French	*The Bald Soprano* (1948); *The Lesson* (1951); *Rhinoceros* (1958)

Playwrights *(cont.)*

Name	Dates	Nationality	Major Works
Jonson, Ben	1572–1637	English	*Volpone* (1605–06); *The Alchemist* (1610); *Bartholomew Fair* (1614)
Kaiser, Georg	1878–1945	German	*The Burghers of Calais* (1914)
Kaufman, George S.	1889–1961	American	*Dinner at Eight* (1932); *Stage Door* (1936); *You Can't Take it With You* (1936)
Kushner, Tony	1957–	American	*Angels in America, Parts One and Two* (1992, 1993)
Mamet, David	1947–	American	*American Buffalo* (1977); *Speed-the-Plow* (1987)
Marlowe, Christopher	1564–1593	English	*The Tragical History of Doctor Faustus* (1604); *The Jew of Malta* (1633)
McNally, Terrence	1939–	American	*And Things That Go Bump in the Night* (1965); *Love! Valour! Compassion!* (1994); *Master Class* (1996)
Miller, Arthur	1915–	American	*Death of a Salesman* (1949); *The Crucible* (1953)
Molière [Jean Baptiste Poquelin]	1622–1673	French	*The School for Wives* (1662); *Tartuffe* (1664); *Le Misanthrope* (1666)
Molnár, Ferenc	1878–1952	Hungarian	*Liliom* (1909); *The Guardsman* (1910); *The Swan* (1920)
O'Casey, Sean	1880–1964	Irish	*Juno and the Paycock* (1924); *The Plough and the Stars* (1926)
O'Neill, Eugene	1888–1953	American	*Anna Christie* (1921); *Mourning Becomes Electra* (1931); *The Iceman Cometh* (1946); *Long Day's Journey into Night* (1956)
Odets, Clifford	1906–1963	American	*Waiting for Lefty* (1935); *Awake and Sing!* (1935)
Osborne, John	1929–1994	English	*The Entertainer* (1957); *Luther* (1961)
Pinter, Harold	1930–	English	*The Birthday Party* (1958); *The Caretaker* (1960); *The Homecoming* (1965)
Pirandello, Luigi	1867–1936	Italian	*Six Characters in Search of an Author* (1921); *Henry IV* (1922)
Plautus	c.251 BC–c.184 BC	Roman	*Pseudolus* (192 BC); *The Menaechmi* (?); *Miles Gloriosus* (?)
Rabe, David	1940–	American	*The Basic Training of Pavlo Hummel* (1969); *Streamers* (1975)
Racine, Jean	1639–1699	French	*Andromaque* (1667); *Bérénice* (1671); *Phèdre* (1677)
Rostand, Edmond	1868–1918	French	*Cyrano de Bergerac* (1898)
Seneca, Lucius Annaeus	c.4 BC–AD 65	Roman	*Medea; Phaedra; Agamemnon* (all undated)

Shakespeare, William	1564–1616	English	*Romeo and Juliet* (1594–95); *A Midsummer's Night Dream* (1595–96); *Hamlet* (1600–1); *Othello* (1604–5); *King Lear* (1605–6); *Macbeth* (1605–6)
Shaw, George Bernard	1856–1950	English	*Arms and the Man* (1894); *Mrs. Warren's Profession* (1893); *Candida* (1895); *Caesar and Cleopatra* (1898); *Man and Superman* (1901–3); *Major Barbara* (1905); *Pygmalion* (1913); *Saint Joan* (1923)
Sheridan, Richard Brinsley	1751–1816	Anglo-Irish	*The Rivals* (1775); *The School for Scandal* (1777); *The Critic* (1779)
Simon, Neil	1927–	American	*Barefoot in the Park* (1963); *The Odd Couple* (1965); *Brighton Beach Memoirs* (1983); *Lost in Yonkers* (1991)
Sophocles	496–406 BC	Greek	*Antigone* (c. 442 BC); *Oedipus Rex* (c. 425 BC); *Oedipus at Colonus* (406 BC)
Soyinka, Wole	1934–	Nigerian	*Three Plays* (1963); *The Road* (1965); *The Forest of a Thousand Daemons* (1968); *Ake* (1981)
Stoppard, Tom	1932–	English	*Rosencrantz and Guildenstern are Dead* (1967); *The Real Inspector Hound* (1968)
Strindberg, August	1849–1912	Swedish	*The Father* (1887); *Miss Julie* (1888); *A Dream Play* (1902)
Synge, J. M.	1871–1909	Irish	*Riders to the Sea* (1904); *The Playboy of the Western World* (1908)
Vega, Lope de	1562–1635	Spanish	*The Peasant in His Nook* (1611–15); *The King's Best Magistrate* (1620–23)
Wasserstein, Wendy	1950–	American	*The Heidi Chronicles* (1989); *The Sisters Rosenzweig* (1993)
Wilde, Oscar	1854–1900	Irish	*Salome* (1892); *An Ideal Husband* (1895); *The Importance of Being Earnest* (1895)
Wilder, Thornton	1897–1975	American	*Our Town* (1938); *The Skin of Our Teeth* (1942); *The Matchmaker* (1954)
Williams, Tennessee	1911–1983	American	*The Glass Menagerie* (1945); *A Streetcar Named Desire* (1947); *Cat on a Hot Tin Roof* (1955)
Wilson, August	1945–	American	*Ma Rainey's Black Bottom* (1985); *Fences* (1986); *The Piano Lesson* (1990)
Wilson, Lanford	1937–	American	*The Hot L Baltimore* (1973); *Talley's Folly* (1980)

⊙ Billington, Michael, ed. *Contemporary Dramatists*, 5th ed. Detroit: Gale Research, 1993.
 Hartnoll, Phyllis, ed. *The Oxford Companion to the Theatre*, 4th ed. Oxford: Oxford University Press, 1993.
 Hawkins, Mark-Dady, ed. *International Dictionary of Theatre*, 3 vols. Chicago: St. James, 1992.

Children's and Young Adult Authors

With the exception of several foreign language classics, this list emphasizes writers in English and includes award-quality children's and young adult works as well as popular favorites.

Name	Dates	Nation-ality	Major Works
Alcott, Louisa May	1832–1888	American	*Little Women* (1868–69)
Anderson, Hans Christian	1805–1875	Danish	*Fairy Tales* (1858–72)
Atwater, Richard and Florence	1892–1948; 1896–1979	Both American	*Mr. Popper's Penguins* (1938)
Bagnold, Enid	1889–1981	English	*National Velvet* (1935)
Baum, Frank [Lyman [Baum]	1856–1919	American	*The Wonderful Wizard of Oz* (1900)
Bemelmans, Ludwig	1898–1962	Austrian-born American	*Madeleine* (1939)
Blume, Judy	1938–	American	*Are You There God? It's Me, Margaret* (1970); *Super Fudge* (1980)
Bond, Michael	1926–	English	*A Bear Called Paddington* (1958)
Brown, Margaret Wise	1910–1952	American	*Goodnight, Moon* (1947)
Burnett, Frances (Eliza) Hodgson	1849–1924	American	*The Secret Garden* (1911)
Burnford, Sheila	1918–1984	Scottish-born Canadian	*The Incredible Journey* (1961)
Burton, Virginia Lee	1909–1968	American	*Mike Mulligan and His Steam Shovel* (1939)
Carle, Eric	1929–	American	*The Very Hungry Caterpillar* (1969)
Cleary, Beverly	1916–	American	*Henry Huggins* (1950); *Ramona the Pest* (1968)
Dahl, Roald	1916–1990	English	*James and the Giant Peach* (1961); *Charlie and the Chocolate Factory* (1964)
De Brunhoff, Jean	1899–1937	French	*The Story of Babar* (1937)
Dixon, Franklin W. [see Stratemeyer, Edward L.]			
Dodge, Mary Mapes	1831–1905	American	*Hans Brinker and the Silver Skates* (1865)
Eastman, P. D. [Philip Dey]	1909–1986	American	*Are You My Mother?* (1960)
Fitzhugh, Louise	1928–1974	American	*Harriet the Spy* (1964)
Gág, Wanda	1893–1946	American	*Millions of Cats* (1928)
Garis, Howard	1873–1962	American	Creator of the Uncle Wiggily stories, beginning in 1910
Gipson, Fred	1908–1973	American	*Old Yeller* (1956)
Grahame, Kenneth	1859–1932	English	*The Wind in the Willows* (1908)
Gramatky, Hardie	1907–1979	American	*Little Toot* (1939)
Grimm, Wilhem and Jakob	1786–1859; 1785–1863	Both German	Stories: *Grimms' Fairy Tales* (1812–15)
Hamilton, Virginia	1936–	American	*Zeely* (1967); *The House of Dies Drear* (1968)

Harris, Joel Chandler	1848–1908	American	*Uncle Remus: His Songs and Sayings* (1880)
Hinton, S. E.	1950–	American	*The Outsiders* (1967); *That Was Then, This Is Now* (1970); *Rumblefish* (1975)
Hoban, Russell	1925–	American	*Bedtime for Frances* (1960)
Hope, Laura Lee [see Stratemeyer, Edward L.]			
John, Crockett	1906–1975	American	*Harold and the Purple Crayon* (1955)
Juster, Norton	1929–	American	*The Phantom Toll Booth* (1961)
Keats, Ezra Jack	1916–1983	American	*The Snowy Day* (1963); *Whistle for Willie* (1964)
Keene, Carolyn [see Stratemeyer, Edward L.]			
Konigsburg, E. L. (Elaine Loeb)	1930–	American	*From the Mixed-Up Files of Mrs. Basil E. Frankweiler* (1967)
L'Engle, Madeline	1918–	American	*A Wrinkle in Time* (1962)
Lewis, C. S. (Clive Staples)	1898–1963	English	Creator of the *Chronicles of Narnia* series (1950–56)
Lindgren, Astrid	1907–	Swedish	*Pippi Longstocking* (1945)
Lobel, Arnold	1933–1987	American	*Frog and Toad are Friends* (1970)
Lowry, Lois	1937–	American	*A Summer to Die* (1977); *Anastasia at Your Service* (1984)
MacLachlan, Patricia	1938–	American	*Sarah, Plain and Tall* (1985)
Martin, Ann M.	1955–	American	Creator of the *Baby-Sitters Club* series beginning 1986
McCloskey, Robert	1914–	American	*Make Way for Ducklings* (1941)
Milne, A. A. (Alan Alexander)	1882–1956	English	*Winnie the Pooh* (1926); *The House at Pooh Corner* (1928)
Montgomery, L. M. (Lucy Maud)	1874–1942	Canadian	*Anne of Green Gables* (1908)
Norton, Mary	1903–1992	English	*The Borrowers* (1953); *Bed-Knob and Broomstick* (1957)
O'Hara, Mary [Mary O'Hara Alsop]	1885–1980	American	*My Friend Flicka* (1941)
Patterson, Katherine	1932–	American	*Bridge to Terabithia* (1977)
Perrault, Charles	1628–1703	French	*Stories: Tales of Mother Goose* (1697)
Piper, Watty [Mabel Caroline Bragg]	1870–1945	American	*The Little Engine That Could* (1930)
Porter, Eleanor Hodgman	1868–1920	American	*Pollyanna* (1913)
Potter, Beatrix [Helen Beatrix Potter]	1866–1943	English	*The Tale of Peter Rabbit* (1902)
Pyle, Howard	1853–1911	American	*The Merry Adventures of Robin Hood* (1883)
Rawlings, Marjorie Kinnan	1896–1953	American	*The Yearling* (1938)
Rey, H. A. (Hans Augusto)	1898–1977	American	*Curious George* (1941)
Rowling, J. K.	1966–	English	The *Harry Potter* series, beginning with *Harry Potter and the Sorcerer's Stone* (1998)

Name	Dates	Nationality	Major Works
Scarry, Richard	1919–1994	American	*Richard Scarry's Best Word Book Ever* (1963); *Cars and Trucks and Things That Go* (1974)
Sendak, Maurice	1928–	American	*Where the Wild Things Are* (1963)
Seuss, Dr. [Theodore Seuss Geisel]	1904–1991	American	*Horton Hatches the Egg* (1940); *The Cat in the Hat* (1957)
Sewell, Anna	1820–1878	English	*Black Beauty* (1877)
Silverstein, Shel [Shelby]	1932–	American	*The Giving Tree* (1964); *Where the Sidewalk Ends* (1974); *A Light in the Attic* (1981)
Smith, Betty	1904–1972	American	*A Tree Grows in Brooklyn* (1943)
Stine, R. L. (Robert Lawrence)	1943–	American	The *Goosebumps* series, starting with *Welcome to Dead House* (1992)
Stratemeyer, Edward L.	1862–1930	American	The *Bobbsey Twins* series (under the pseudonym Laura Lee Hope) (beg. 1904); the *Hardy Boys* series (under the pseudonym Franklin W. Dixon) (beg. 1927); and *Nancy Drew* series (under the pseudonym Carolyn Keene) (beg. 1930)
Thompson, Kay	1912–1998	American	*Eloise* (1955)
Tolkien, J. R. R.	1892–1973	English	*The Hobbit* (1937); *The Lord of the Ring* (3 vols., 1954–56)
Travers, P. L. (Pamela Lyndon)	1906–1996	Australian-born English	*Mary Poppins* (1934)
Van Allsburg, Chris	1949–	American	*Jumanji* (1981); *The Polar Express* (1985)
Verne, Jules	1828–1905	French	*A Voyage to the Center of the Earth* (1864); *Twenty Thousand Leagues Under the Sea* (1870); *Around the World in Eighty Days* (1873)
White, E. B. (Elwyn Brooks)	1899–1985	American	*Stuart Little* (1945); *Charlotte's Web* (1952)
White, T. H. (Terence Hanbury)		Indian-born English	*The Sword in the Stone* (1938); *The Once and Future King* (1958)
Wilder, Laura Ingalls	1867–1957	American	*Little House on the Prairie* (1935)
Williams, Margery (Winifred)	1888–1944	English-born American	*The Velveteen Rabbit* (1922)
Wyss, J. D. (Johann David)	1743–1818	Swiss	*The Swiss Family Robinson* (1812–13)
Zindel, Paul	1936–	American	*The Pigman* (1968); *My Darling, My Hamburger* (1969)

⊙ Carpenter, Humphrey, and Mari Pritchard, eds. *The Oxford Companion to Children's Literature.* New York: Oxford University Press, 1991.

Pendergast, Sara and Tom, eds. *St. James Guide to Children's Writers,* 5th ed. Detroit: St. James, 1999.

Silvey, Anita, ed. *Children's Books and Their Creators.* Boston: Houghton Mifflin, 1995.

Top 20 U.S. Newspapers (in Circulation)

Rank	Newspaper	Daily Circulation (as of 9/30/99)	Website
1	Wall Street Journal	1,752,693	www.wsj.com
2	USA Today	1,671,539	www.usatoday.com
3	New York Times	1,086,293	www.nytimes.com
4	Los Angeles Times	1,078,186	www.latimes.com
5	Washington Post	763,305	www.washingtonpost.com
6	New York Daily News	701,831	www.mostnewyork.com
7	Chicago Tribune	657,690	www.chicago.tribune.com
8	Newsday	574,941	www.newsday.com
9	Houston Chronicle	542,414	www.chron.com
10	Dallas Morning News	490,249	www.dallasnews.com
11	Chicago Sun-Times	468,170	www.suntimes.com
12	Boston Globe	462,850	www.boston.com/globe/
13	San Francisco Chronicle	456,742	www.sfgate.com
14	New York Post	438,158	www.nypostonline.com
15	Arizona Republic	433,296	www.azcentral.com
16	Newark Star-Ledger	407,129	www.nj.com
17	Philadelphia Inquirer	399,339	www.phillynews.com
18	Rocky Mountain News	396,114	www.rockymountainnews.com
19	Cleveland Plain Dealer	386,312	www.cleveland.com
20	San Diego Union-Tribune	376,604	www.uniontrib.com

⊙ Editor & Publisher Online. "Top Newspapers by ABC Circulation Audit,"
  www.mediainfo.com/ephome/research/researchhtm/usdaily.htm
  Detroit Free Press. "100 Largest Newspapers," www.freep.com/jobspage/
  links/top100.htm

ARTS AND LEISURE: *Art*

Major Painters and Sculptors

The following charts display a selection of 150 of Western civilization's most renowned painters and 50 of its best-known sculptors, each identified by two or three notable works. Reference sources for both tables are provided at the end of the section.

Painters

Artist	Dates	Nationality	Notable Works
Angelico, Fra (Guido di Pietro)	c.1400–1455	Florentine	*Madonna of the Star* (c.1428–33); *The Deposition* (c.1440); *The Annunciation* (c.1451–55)
Bacon, Francis	1909–1992	Irish-born English	*Three Studies for Figures at the Base of a Crucifixion* (1944); *Pope Innocent X* (1953)
Beardsley, Aubrey Vincent	1872–1898	English	Illustrations for *Morte D'Arthur* (1893); *Salomé* (1894); *Lysistrata* (1896)

Major Painters and Sculptors (cont.)

Artist	Dates	Nationality	Notable Works
Bellini, Giovanni	c.1430–1516	Venetian	*The Agony in the Garden* (1459); *The Feast of the Gods* (1514)
Bellows, George Wesley	1882–1925	American	*Stag at Sharkey's* (1907); *Cliff Dwellers* (1913); *Love of Winter* (1914)
Benton, Thomas Hart	1889–1975	American	*Cotton Pickers* (1928–29); *The Jealous Lover of Lone Green Valley* (1930); *Persephone* (1939)
Bingham, George Caleb	1811–1879	American	*Fur Traders Going Down the Missouri* (1845); *Raftsmen Playing Cards* (1847)
Boccioni, Umberto	1882–1916	Italian	*States of Mind: The Farewells* (1911); *Dynamism of a Soccer Player* (1913)
Bonnard, Pierre	1867–1947	French	*The Circus Rider* (1897); *Nude with a Lamp* (c.1912); *The Rape of Europa* (1919)
Bosch, Hieronymus	c.1450–1516	Dutch	*The Ship of Fools* (1500); *The Temptation of St. Anthony* (c.1506); *The Garden of Earthly Delights* (c.1505–10)
Botticelli, Sandro (Alessandro di Mariano Filipepi)	1445–1510	Florentine	*Adoration of the Magi* (c.1475); *Primavera* (c.1475–78); *The Birth of Venus* (c.1483)
Boucher, François	1703–1770	French	*Miss O'Murphy* (1732); *The Triumph of Venus* (1740); *La Toilette* (1742)
Braque, Georges	1882–1963	French	*Man with a Guitar* (1911); *Clarinet* (1913); *Woman with a Mandolin* (1937)
Bronzino (Agnolo di Cosimo)	1503–1572	Florentine	*Portrait of a Young Man* (1535); *Venus, Cupid, Folly and Time* (1545); *Andrea Doria as Neptune* (c.1550–55)
Bruegel, Pieter, the Elder	c.1525–1569	Flemish	*The Triumph of Death* (1562); *The Tower of Babel* (1563); *The Peasant Wedding* (c.1567)
Burchfield, Charles Ephraim	1893–1967	American	*February Thaw* (1920); *Six O'Clock* (1936); *Over the Dam* (1936)
Caravaggio (Michelangelo Merisi)	c.1573–1610	Italian	*A Basket of Fruit* (1596); *Amore Vincitore* (1598–99); *The Calling of St. Matthew* (1599–1600)
Cassatt, Mary Stevenson	1844–1926	American	*Alexander Cassatt and His Son Robert* (1884–85); *La Toilette* (c.1891); *The Bath* (1892)
Cézanne, Paul	1839–1906	French	*The Card Players* (1890–92); *Still Life With Apples and Oranges* (1895–1900)
Chagall, Marc	1887–1985	Russian-born French	*The Wedding* (1910); *I and the Village* (1911); *Birthday* (1915)

Chardin, Jean-Baptiste Siméon	1699–1779	French	*The Skate (The Ray)* (1729); *Boy Playing With Cards* (1740); *Girl with Racket and Shuttlecock* (1740)
Copley, John Singleton	1738–1815	American	*Henry Pelham (Boy with a Squirrel)* (1765); *Paul Revere* (1768–70); *Watson and the Shark* (1778)
Corot, Jean-Baptiste Camille	1796–1875	French	*View of the Forest of Fontainebleau* (1831); *Morning, the Dance of the Nymphs* (c.1850); *The Letter* (1865)
Courbet, Jean Désiré Gustave	1819–1877	French	*The Meeting* (1854); *The Painter's Studio* (1855); *The Sleepers* (1862)
Cranach, Lucas	1472–1553	German	*Crucifixion* (1503); *Venus and Cupid* (1509); *Nymph of Spring* (1518)
Curry, John Steuart	1897–1946	American	*Baptism in Kansas* (1928); *Tornado Over Kansas* (1929); *Circus Elephants* (1932)
Dali, Salvador	1904–1989	Spanish	*The Persistence of Memory* (1931); *Sleep* (1937); *Crucifixion* (1951)
Daumier, Honoré	1808–1879	French	*The Legislative Paunch* (1833–34); *The Print Collector* (1857–63); *Advice to a Young Artist* (c.1865)
David, Jacques-Louis	1748–1825	French	*The Death of Socrates* (1787); *Marat Assassinated* (1793); *Intervention of the Sabine Women* (1799)
De Chirico, Giorgio	1888–1978	Italian	*The Song of Love* (1914); *The Mystery and Melancholy of a Street* (1914); *Grand Metaphysical Interior* (1917)
Degas, Edgar	1834–1917	French	*The Orchestra of the Opera* (1870); *The Rape* (1868–69); *Dance Class* (1871)
de Kooning, Willem	1904–1997	Dutch-born American	*Woman* (1943); *Woman I* (1950–52); *Woman on the Dune* (1967)
Delacroix, Eugène	1798–1863	French	*The Death of Sardanapalus* (1827); *Liberty Leading the People* (1830)
Derain, André	1880–1954	French	*Henri Matisse* (1905); *Houses of Parliament at Night* (1905–6)
Dix, Otto	1891–1969	German	*Sunrise* (1913); *Sylvia von Harden* (1926); *Metropolis* (1927–28)
Dubuffet, Jean	1901–1985	French	*Corps de Dame: La Juive* (1950); *The Cow with the Subtile Nose* (1954); *Texturology* (1958)
Duchamp, Marcel	1887–1968	French-born American	*Nude Descending a Staircase No. 2* (1912); *Mona Lisa (with mustache)* (1919)
Dufy, Raoul	1877–1953	French	*The Three Umbrellas* (1906); *Open Window at Nice* (1928); *Regatta at Crowes* (1934)
Durand, Asher Brown	1796–1886	American	*The Beeches* (1845); *Kindred Spirits* (1849); *Progress (The Advance of Civilization)* (1853)
Dürer, Albrecht	1471–1528	German	*The Young Hare* (1502); *Adam and Eve* (1507); *Study of Praying Hands* (1508)

Major Painters and Sculptors *(cont.)*

Artist	Dates	Nationality	Notable Works
Eakins, Thomas	1844–1916	American	*Max Schmitt in a Single Scull* (1871); *The Gross Clinic* (1875); *The Swimming Hole* (1883)
Ensor, James Sydney	1860–1949	Belgian	*Red Apples and White Bowl* (1883); *The Entry of Christ into Brussels* (1889); *The Intrigue* (1890)
Ernst, Max	1891–1976	German-born French	*Oedipus Rex* (1922); *Two Children are Threatened by a Nightingale* (1924); *Napoleon in the Desert* (1941)
Eyck, Jan van	c.1390–1441	Flemish	*Adam and Eve* (c.1432); *The Arnolfini Marriage* (1434); *Madonna with Canon van der Paele* (1436)
Fragonard, Jean-Honoré	1732–1806	French	*The Swing* (1769); *Progress of Love* (1771–73); *The Bolt* (1778)
Friedrich, Caspar David	1774–1840	German	*Moonrise Over the Sea* (1822); *Man and Woman Gazing at the Moon* (c.1830–35); *The Stages of Life* (c.1835)
Gainsborough, Thomas	1727–1788	English	*Mr. and Mrs. Robert Andrews* (1748–49); *The Blue Boy* (1770); *Mrs. Sarah Siddons* (1785)
Gauguin, Paul	1848–1903	French	*Four Breton Women* (1886); *By the Sea* (1892); *Tahitian Women with Mango Blossoms* (1899)
Gérard, François	1770–1837	French	*Cupid and Psyche* (1796); *Caroline Murat and her Children* (1808)
Géricault, Théodore	1791–1824	French	*The Charging Chasseur* (1812); *The Raft of the Medusa* (1819); *Madwoman* (1822)
Ghirlandaio, Domenico (Domenico di Tommaso Bigordi)	1449–1494	Florentine	*Old Man with His Grandson* (1480); *Scenes from the Life of St. Francis* (1485); *Adoration of the Magi* (1487)
Giotto (Giotto di Bondone)	c.1266–1337	Florentine	*The Mourning of Christ* (c.1305); *The Presentation of the Virgin* (1305–13); *Madonna in Glory* (1310)
Gogh, Vincent van	1853–1890	Dutch	*Self-Portrait* (1887); *Sunflowers* (1888); *Starry Night* (1889)
Goya y Lucientes, Francisco José de	1746–1828	Spanish	*Don Manuel Osorio de Zúñiga* (1788); *The Naked Maja* (1800–5); *The Shootings of the Third of May* (1814)
Greco, El (Doménikos Theotokópoulos)	1541–1614	Cretan-born Spanish	*Christ Driving the Traders from the Temple* (1600–5); *Vision of St. John the Divine* (1608–14)
Gris, Juan (José Victoriano González)	1887–1927	Spanish	*Pablo Picasso* (1912); *Guitar and Flowers* (1912); *Fruit Dish and Bottle* (1917)
Grosz, George	1893–1959	German-born American	*To Oskar Panizza* (1917–18); *Ecce Homo* (1921); *Twilight* (1922)

Hals, Frans	1580–1666	Dutch	*The Laughing Cavalier* (1624); *The Gypsy Girl* (1628–30); *Regentesses of the Old Men's Almshouse* (1664)
Henri, Robert	1865–1929	American	*Figures on a Boardwalk* (1892); *Blue-Eyed Man* (1910); *Catharine* (1913)
Hicks, Edward	1780–1849	American	*The Peaceable Kingdom* (1840–45); *The Grave of William Penn* (c.1847); *The Cornell Farm* (1848)
Hockney, David	1937–	English	*A Bigger Splash* (1967); *Nichols Canyon* (1980)
Hogarth, William	1697–1764	English	*The Rake's Progress* (1733–35); *Marriage à la Mode* (1743–45)
Holbein, Hans, the Elder	c.1465–1524	German	*Study of a Bearded Man* (c.1508); *The Martyrdom of Saint Sebastian* (1515–17)
Holbein, Hans, the Younger	c.1497–1543	German	*Body of the Dead Christ in the Tomb* (1521–22); *Erasmus of Rotterdam* (1523); *The Ambassadors* (1533)
Homer, Winslow	1836–1910	American	*Snap the Whip* (1872); *Breezing Up* (1876); *Right and Left* (1909)
Hopper, Edward	1882–1967	American	*Lighthouse at Two Lights* (1929); *Early Sunday Morning* (1930); *Nighthawks* (1942)
Ingres, Jean-Auguste Dominique	1780–1867	French	*Male Torso* (1800); *La Grande Odalisque* (1814); *Ulysses* (1827)
Johns, Jasper	1930–	American	*Flag* (1954–55); *Dancers on a Plane* (1979); *Perilous Night* (1982)
Kandinsky, Wassily	1866–1944	Russian	*The Summer Landscape* (1909); *Improvisation 31 (Sea Battle)* (1913); *Yellow-Red-Blue* (1925)
Kirchner, Ernst Ludwig	1880–1938	German	*Five Women in the Street* (1913); *Friedrichstrasse, Berlin* (1914)
Klee, Paul	1879–1940	Swiss	*Twittering Machine* (1922); *The Goldfish* (1925); *Cat and Bird* (1928)
Klimt, Gustav	1862–1918	Austrian	*Adele Bloch-Bauer I* (1907); *Danae* (1907–8); *The Kiss* (1907–8)
Kline, Franz Joseph	1910–1962	American	*Chinatown* (1948); *New York, NY* (1953); *Painting No. 2* (1954)
Kokoschka, Oskar	1886–1980	Austrian	*Knight Errant* (1915); *That For Which We Fight* (1943); *Golda Meir, Prime Minister* (1973)
Kollwitz, Käthe Schmidt	1867–1945	German	*Peasants' War* (1902–8); *The War* (1923); *Death* (1934–35)
Leonardo da Vinci	1452–1519	Florentine	*The Annunciation* (c.1472–73); *The Last Supper* (c.1495–97); *Mona Lisa* (c.1503–7)
Leutze, Emanuel Gottlieb	1816–1868	German-born American	*Washington Crossing the Delaware* (1851); *Westward the Course of Empire Takes Its Way* (1860)

Major Painters and Sculptors (cont.)

Artist	Dates	Nationality	Notable Works
Lichtenstein, Roy	1923–1997	American	*Drowning Girl* (1962); *George Washington* (1962); *Statue of Liberty* (1982)
Lippi, Fra Filippo	c.1406–1469	Florentine	*The Annunciation* (1440); *The Nativity* (c.1445); *Madonna and Child with Two Angels* (1464)
Magritte, René	1898–1967	Belgian	*The Human Condition* (1934); *Tomb of the Wrestlers* (1960); *The Blank Signature* (1965)
Manet, Édouard	1832–1883	French	*Luncheon on the Grass* (1862–63); *The Fifer* (1866); *A Bar at the Folies Bergère* (1881–82)
Mantegna, Andrea	1431–1506	Italian	*The Death of the Virgin* (1461); *The Dead Christ* (1490); *Parnassus* (1497)
Marc, Franz	1880–1916	German	*Siberian Dogs in the Snow* (1909–10); *Blue Horses* (1911); *Stables* (1914)
Marsh, Reginald	1898–1954	American	*Pip and Flip* (1932); *High Yaller* (1934); *Twenty Cent Movie* (1936)
Matisse, Henri	1869–1954	French	*Dance* (1909); *The Red Studio* (1911); *Large Composition with Masks* (1953)
Michelangelo Buonarroti	1475–1564	Florentine	Sistine Chapel frescos: *Book of Genesis* (1508–12); *The Last Judgment* (1534–41)
Millet, Jean-François	1814–1875	French	*The Sower* (1850); *The Gleaners* (1857); *The Man with a Hoe* (1863)
Miró, Joan	1893–1983	Spanish	*The Harlequin's Carnival* (1924–25); *The Poetess* (1940); *Woman* (1976)
Modigliani, Amedeo	1884–1920	Italian	*Lunja Czechowska* (1917); *Madame Amédée (Woman with Cigarette)* (1918); *Reclining Nude* (1916)
Monet, Claude	1840–1926	French	*Impression: Sunrise* (1872); *Two Haystacks* (1891); *Waterlilies* (c.1900)
Moreau, Gustave	1826–1898	French	*Orpheus* (1865); *Diomedes Devoured by His Horses* (1865); *Salome* (1876)
Moses, Grandma (Anna Mary Robertson Moses)	1860–1961	American	*Out for the Christmas Tree* (1946); *A Country Wedding* (1951); *Bennington* (1953)
Motherwell, Robert	1915–1991	American	*Personnage* (1945); *Elegy to the Spanish Republic #34* (1953–54); *Reconciliation Elegy* (1978)
Munch, Edvard	1863–1944	Norwegian	*The Scream* (1893); *Vampire* (1895); *The Dance of Life* (1900)
O'Keeffe, Georgia	1887–1986	American	*Red Poppy* (1927); *Summer Days* (1936); *Sky Above White Clouds I* (1962)
Parrish, Maxfield	1870–1966	American	*The Dinky Bird* (1904); *Daybreak* (1922); *Stars* (1926)

Peale, Charles Willson	1741–1827	American	*The Staircase Group* (1795); *The Artist in His Museum* (1822)
Peale, Raphaelle	1774–1825	American	*A Dessert* (1814); *Still Life with Cake* (1822); *After the Bath* (1823)
Peale, Rembrandt	1778–1860	American	*George Washington* (1795); *Thomas Jefferson* (1804); *Napoléon Bonaparte* (1810)
Picasso, Pablo	1881–1973	Spanish	*Les Demoiselles d'Avignon* (1907); *Guernica* (1937); *The Charnel House* (1945)
Piero della Francesca	c.1420–1492	Italian	*The Baptism of Christ* (1442); *The Flagellation of Christ* (c.1456)
Pissarro, Camille	1830–1903	French	*The Road to Versailles* (1870); *The Oise Near Pontoise* (1873); *The Pork Butcher* (1883)
Pollock, Jackson (Paul Jackson Pollock)	1912–1956	American	*Blue (Moby Dick)* (1943); *Galaxy* (1947); *Blue Poles No. 11* (1952)
Poussin, Nicolas	1594–1665	French	*The Rape of the Sabine Women* (1636–37); *The Dance to the Music of Time* (c.1640)
Raphael (Raffaello Sanzio)	1483–1520	Italian	*The Three Graces* (1504–5); *The School of Athens* (1509–11); *The Transfiguration* (1518–20)
Rembrandt Harmenszoon van Rijn	1606–1669	Dutch	*The Anatomy Lesson of Dr. Nicholaes Tulp* (1632); *The Night Watch* (1642); *The Staalmeesters* (1662)
Remington, Frederic	1861–1909	American	*The Scout: Friends or Foes?* (1890); *Old Stage Coach of the Plains* (1901); *The Fight for the Waterhole* (1903)
Renoir, Pierre Auguste	1841–1919	French	*A Girl with a Watering Can* (1876); *The Luncheon of the Boating Party* (1881); *The Bathers* (1884–87)
Repin, Ilya Yefimovich	1844–1930	Russian	*Volga Boatmen* (1873); *Modest Mussorgsky* (1881); *Ivan Grozny and His Son Ivan* (1885)
Rivera, Diego	1886–1957	Mexican	murals: National Palace, Mexico City (*History of Mexico*) (1929–36); Detroit Institute of Arts (1932–33)
Rockwell, Norman	1894–1978	American	*Rosie the Riveter* (1943); *Freedom of Speech* (1943); *Freedom from Want* (1943)
Rossetti, Dante Gabriel	1828–1882	English	*Sir Tristram and La Belle Yseult Drinking the Love Potion* (1867); *Astarte Syriaca* (1875–77)
Rothko, Mark (Marcus Rothkowitz)	1903–1970	Russian-born American	*Magenta, Black, Green on Orange* (1949); *Orange and Yellow* (1956); *Black on Grey* (1970)
Rousseau, Henri	1844–1910	French	*Sleeping Gypsy* (1897); *The Ball Players* (1908); *The Dream* (1910)
Rubens, Peter Paul	1577–1640	Flemish	*St. Sebastian* (c.1615); *The Rape of the Daughters of Leucippus* (c.1618); *The Three Graces* (c.1635)

Major Painters and Sculptors (cont.)

Artist	Dates	Nationality	Notable Works
Ryder, Albert Pinkham	1847–1917	American	*The Flying Dutchman* (1887); *Siegfried and the Rhine Maidens* (1888–91); *Death on a Pale Horse* (c.1910)
Sargent, John Singer	1856–1925	American	*El Jaleo* (1882); *The Daughters of Edward Darley Boit* (1888); *Lord Ribblesdale* (1902)
Schiele, Egon	1890–1918	Austrian	*Self Portrait* (1910); *The Embrace* (1917); *Family* (1918)
Seurat, Georges	1859–1891	French	*Bathing at Asnières* (1883–84); *A Sunday Afternoon on the Island of La Grande Jatte* (1884–86)
Sloan, John French	1871–1951	American	*Easter Eve* (1907); *Haymarket* (1907); *Backyards, Greenwich Village* (1914)
Steen, Jan	c.1626–1679	Dutch	*Skittle Players Outside an Inn* (1652); *The Cat Family* (1660); *The Feast of St. Nicholas* (c.1667)
Stella, Joseph	1877–1946	American	*Battle of Lights, Coney Island* (1913); *The Gas Tank* (1918); *Brooklyn Bridge* (1920)
Still, Clyfford	1904–1980	American	*1946-H (Indian Red and Black)* (1946); *Painting* (1951); *1953* (1953)
Stuart, Gilbert Charles	1755–1828	American	*The Skater* (1782); *George Washington* (the "Athenaeum Head") (1796); *James Monroe* (1817)
Sully, Thomas	1783–1872	American	*The Torn Hat* (1820); *Queen Victoria* (1838); *Andrew Jackson* (1845)
Tanguy, Yves	1900–1955	American	*Mama, Papa is Wounded!* (1927); *Indefinite Divisibility* (1942); *Rose of the Four Winds* (1950)
Tiepolo, Giovanni Battista	1696–1770	Italian	*The Martyrdom of St. Bartholomew* (1722); *The Adoration of the Magi* (1753); *Crucifixion* (1755–60)
Tintoretto (Jacobo Robusti)	c.1518–1594	Italian	*Susannah and the Elders* (c.1550); *Crucifixion* (1564–87); *The Last Supper* (1592–94)
Titian (Tiziano Vecelli)	c.1490–1576	Italian	*Sacred and Profane Love* (1512–15); *Bacchus and Ariadne* (1522–23); *Triple Portrait Mask* (c.1570)
Toulouse-Lautrec, Henri de	1864–1901	French	*At the Moulin Rouge* (1892); *Jane Avril at the Jardin de Paris* (1893); *The Salon in the Rue Des Moulins* (1894)
Trumbell, John	1765–1843	American	*Declaration of Independence* (1786–94); *The Resignation of General Washington* (1824)
Turner, Joseph Mallord William	1775–1851	English	*The Grand Canal, Venice* (1835); *Norham Castle: Sunrise* (c.1835–40); *Dawn After the Wreck* (c.1840)
van der Weyden, Rogier	1400–1464	Flemish	*The Annunciation* (1435); *The Descent from the Cross* (c.1438)

Van Dyck, Sir Anthony	1599–1641	Flemish	*Frans Snyder* (1620); *The Lamentation* (1634); *Charles I of England* (c.1635)
Velázquez, Diego Rodríguez de Silva y	1599–1660	Spanish	*Los Borrachos (The Triumph of Bacchus)* (c.1628–29); *Las Meninas (The Maids of Honor)* (1656)
Vermeer, Jan	1632–1675	Dutch	*A View of Delft* (c.1660); *A Maidservant Pouring Milk* (c.1660); *The Lace Maker* (c.1665)
Veronese, Paolo (Paolo Caliari)	1528–1588	Italian	*Marriage at Cana* (1562–63); *Feast in the House of Levy* (1573); *The Find of Moses* (1570–75)
Warhol, Andy	1928?–1987	American	*Campbell Soup Cans* (1961–62); *Marilyn* (1964); *Flowers* (1964)
Watteau, Jean-Antoine	1684–1721	French	*The Embarkation for Cythera* (1717); *Le Mezzetin* (1718); *Gersaint's Shopsign* (1720)
West, Benjamin	1738–1820	American	*The Death of General Wolf* (1770); *King Lear* (1788); *Death on a Pale Horse* (1788)
Whistler, James Abbott McNeill	1834–1903	American	*Wapping* (1860–64); *Arrangement in Grey and Black* ("Whistler's Mother") (1871)
Wood, Grant	1891–1942	American	*Woman with Plants* (1929); *American Gothic* (1930); *Daughters of Revolution* (1932)
Wyeth, Andrew Newell	1917–	American	*Christina's World* (1948); *The Trodden Weed* (1951); *The Helga Pictures* (1971–85)

Sculptors

Artist	Dates	Nationality	Notable Works
Archipenko, Aleksandr Porfiryevich	1887–1964	Ukrainian-born American	*Médrano II* (1915); *Woman Combing Her Hair* (1915)
Barlach, Ernst	1870–1939	German	*Shepherd in a Storm* (1908); *The Warrior of the Spirit* (1928)
Bernini, Gianlorenzo	1598–1680	Italian	*The Goat Amalthea Nursing the Infant Zeus and a Young Satyr* (1609); *Abduction of Proserpina* (1621–22)
Boccioni, Umberto	1882–1916	Italian	*Antigraceful* (1913); *Unique Forms of Continuity in Space* (1913)
Borglum, Gutzon	1871–1941	American	*The Aviator* (1919); *Mount Rushmore Memorial* (1927–41)
Botero, Fernando	1932–	Colombian	*Reclining Nude* (1984); *Ballerina* (1989)
Bourgeois, Louise	1911–	American	*Mortise* (1950); *Spider* (1996–97)
Brancusi, Constantin	1876–1957	Romanian-born French	*Sleeping Muse* (1906); *Bird in Space* (1919)
Calder, Alexander	1898–1976	American	*Cow* (1929); *Black Camel with Blue Head and Red Tongue* (1971)
Cellini, Benvenuto	1500–1571	Florentine	*Salt Cellar of Francis I* (1539–43); *Perseus and Medusa* (1545–54)
Degas, Edgar	1834–1917	French	*The Little Fourteen-Year-Old Dancer* (1880–81); *Woman Washing Her Left Leg* (c.1890)

Major Painters and Sculptors *(cont.)*

Artist	Dates	Nationality	Notable Works
Donatello (Donato di Niccolo de Betto Bardi)	1386–1466	Italian	*David* (c.1430–35); *St. Jerome* (c.1450)
Dubuffet, Jean	1901–1985	French	*Shadow Knight* (1954); *The Amphigoric One* (1954)
Duchamp, Marcel	1887–1968	French-born American	*Bicycle Wheel* (1913); *Boite-en-Valise* (1961)
Epstein, Jacob	1880–1959	American-born English	*An American Soldier* (1917); *Princess Menen* (1949)
Ernst, Max	1891–1976	German-born French	*Head "H"* (1948); *Capricorn* (1948–75)
Flannagan, John Bernard	1895–1942	American	*Christ* (1925); *Gorilla* (1938)
Ghiberti, Lorenzo	1378–1455	Florentine	*Sacrifice of Abraham* (1401); *St. John the Baptist* (1412–16)
Giacometti, Alberto	1901–1966	Swiss	*The Palace at 4 AM* (1932–33); *Walking Man II* (1960)
Girardon, François	1628–1715	French	*Pluto and Persephone (Allegory of Fire)* (1677–99); *Louis XIV (equestrian)* (1683–92)
Greenough, Horatio	1805–1852	American	*George Washington* (1832–41); *The Rescue* (1837–51)
Hoffman, Malvina	1885–1966	American	*Egyptian Dancer, Nyota Inyoka* (1932); *Swami Vivekananda* (1950)
Hosmer, Harriet Goodhue	1830–1908	American	*Puck* (1856); *Zenobia, Queen of Palmyra* (c.1857)
Hyatt, Anna Vaughn (Anna Huntington)	1876–1973	American	*Lion* (1908); *Zebra and Foal* (1939); *Sybil Ludington's Ride* (1960)
Lachaise, Gaston	1882–1935	French-born American	*Floating Woman* (1927); *Standing Woman* (1930–33)
Lewis, Edmonia (Wildfire)	c.1845–19??	American	*Forever Free* (1867); *The Death of Cleopatra* (1876)
Lipchitz, Jacques (Chaim Jacob Lipchitz)	1891–1973	French	*Bas-Relief I* (1918); *Death Mask of Amedeo Modigliani* (1920)
Maillol, Aristide	1861–1944	French	*Modesty* (c.1900); *Torso of a Young Woman* (c.1930); *The Three Nymphs* (1930–38)
Manship, Paul	1885–1966	American	*Dancer and Gazelles* (1916); *Diana and a Hound* (1925)
Marini, Marino	1901–1980	Italian	*Horseman* (1947); *L'Idea del Cavaliere (The Concept of the Rider)* (1952–54)
Mears, Helen Farnsworth	1876–1916	American	*Augustus Saint-Gaudens* (1898); *Aphrodite* (1912)
Michelangelo Buonarroti	1475–1564	Florentine	*Bacchus* (1496–98); *Pietà* (1498–1500); *David* (1501–4)
Moore, Sir Henry	1898–1986	British	*Three Motives Against Wall, No. 1* (1958–59); *Knife Edge Mirror Two Piece* (1977–78)
Nevelson, Louise	1900–1988	Russian-born American	*Mountain Figure* (1946–48); *Gate of Eternity* (1958); *Sky Gate—New York* (1978)

Noguchi, Isamu	1904–1988	American	*Giacometti's Shadow* (1982–83); *Cloud Mountain* (1983)
Oldenburg, Claes	1929–	American	*Glass Case with Pies (Assorted Pies in a Case)* (1962); *Clarinet Bridge* (1992)
Picasso, Pablo	1881–1973	Spanish	*Gorilla* (1926); *Dove* (1954); *Steel Sculpture* (1967)
Remington, Frederic	1861–1909	American	*Bronco Buster* (1895); *Comin' Through the Rye* (1902); *The Mountain Man* (1903)
Rodin, Auguste	1840–1917	French	*The Kiss* (1889); *The Thinker* (1904); *Gustav Mahler* (1909)
Rosso, Medardo	1858–1928	Italian	*Impression of an Omnibus* (1883–84); *Sick Child* (1895); *Boulevard Impression, Paris at Night* (1895)
Saint-Gaudens, Augustus	1848–1907	American	*Charles Stewart Butler and Lawrence Smith Butler* (1880–81); *Diana of the Tower* (1892–99)
Sansovino, Andrea (Andrea Contucci)	c.1467–1529	Italian	*Baptism of Christ* (1502); tombs of Cardinals Ascanio Sforza and Girolamo Basso della Rovere* (1509)
Sansovino, Jacopo	1486–1570	Italian	*Doorknocker with Nereid, Triton, and Putti* (c.1550); *Madonna and Child* (c.1550)
Sluter, Claus	c.1340–1406	Dutch	*Memorial to Philip the Bold* (1389–1406); *The Moses Well* (1395–1405)
Smith, David	1906–1965	American	*Sentinel I* (1956); *Cubi XXVI* (1965)
Tatlin, Vladimir	1885–1953	Russian	*Corner Counter-relief* (1914–15); *Model of the Monument to the Third International* (1920)
Verrocchio, Andrea del	1435–1488	Florentine	*Giuliano de' Medici* (c.1475–78); *Putto Poised on a Globe* (c.1480)
Watts, George Frederic	1817–1904	English	*Hugh Lupus* (1876–83); *Physical Energy* (1904)
Whitney, Anne	1821–1915	American	*Africa* (1864); *Roma* (1869); *Harriet Beecher Stowe* (1892)
Whitney, Gertrude	1875–1942	American	*Titanic Memorial* (1914); *WashingtonHeights War Memorial* (1922); *Peter Stuyvesant* (1939)

⊙ Chilvers, Ian. *The Concise Oxford Dictionary of Art and Artists*, 2d ed. New York: Oxford University Press, 1996.

Curtis, Penelope. *Sculpture 1900–1945*. New York: Oxford University Press, 1999.

Metropolitan Museum of Art, New York. "The Collection," www.metmuseum.org/collections/search.asp

Museum of Modern Art, New York. "Index of Artists," www.moma.org/docs/indexofartists/

Vaughan, William, ed. *Encyclopedia of Artists*. New York: Oxford University Press, 2000.

Tate Gallery/Tate Britain, London. "Tate Collections," www.tate.org.uk/collections/

ARTS AND LEISURE: *Photography*

Photographers

Name	Dates	Nationality	Major Works
Abbott, Berenice	1898–1991	American	Portraiture, documentary photography
Adams, Ansel	1902–1984	American	Landscape photography
Arbus, Diane	1923–1971	American	Portraiture, fashion photography
Atget, Eugène	1857–1927	French	Social documentary
Atkins, Anna	1799–1871	English	Scientific illustration
Avedon, Richard	1923–	American	Portraiture, fashion photography
Beaton, Sir Cecil	1904–1980	English	Portraiture, fashion photography
Bellocq, E. J.	1873–1949	American	Portraiture, social documentary
Bing, Ilse	1899–1998	German-born American	Abstract and surrealist photography
Bourke-White, Margaret	1904–1971	American	Photojournalism
Brady, Matthew	1823–1896	American	Daguerreotype portraiture, documentary photography
Brandt, Bill	1904–1983	German-born English	Photojournalism, social documentary
Brassaï (Gyula Halász)	1899–1984	French	Documentary photography
Cameron, Julia Margaret	1815–1879	English	Portraiture, costume photography
Capa, Robert	1913–1954	Hungarian-born American	Photojournalism
Cartier-Bresson, Henri	1908–	French	Photojournalism
Coburn, Alvin Langdon	1882–1966	American-born English	Portraiture, abstract photography
Cunningham, Imogen	1883–1976	American	Portraiture, botanical photography
Curtis, Edward Sheriff	1868–1952	American	Portraiture, documentary photography
Daguerre, Louis-Jacques-Mandé	1787–1851	French	Invention of the daguerreotype process
Doisneau, Robert	1912–1994	French	Photojournalism, fashion photography
Eisenstaedt, Alfred	1898–1995	German-born American	Photojournalism
Emerson, Peter Henry	1856–1936	English	Documentary photography, naturalist photography
Evans, Walker	1903–1975	American	Documentary photography
Feininger, Andreas	1906–1999	French-born American	Architectural and industrial photography, photojournalism, technique innovation
Fenton, Roger	1819–1869	English	Documentary photography, landscape and still-life photography
Frank, Robert	1924–	Swiss-born American	Industrial photography, fashion photography, cinematography
Friedlander, Lee	1934–	American	Portraiture, social documentary

Gilpin, Laura	1891–1979	American	Landscape photography, documentary photography
Hausmann, Raoul	1886–1971	Austrian	Photomontage, abstract photography
Hawes, Josiah Johnson	1808–1901	American	Daguerreotype portraiture and documentary photography
Henri, Florence	1893–1982	Swiss	Abstract photography
Hine, Lewis Wickes	1874–1940	American	Social documentary
Jackson, William Henry	1843–1942	American	Landscape photography
Käsebier, Gertrude	1852–1934	American	Portraiture
Kertész, André	1894–1985	Hungarian-born American	Photojournalism
Lange, Dorothea	1895–1965	American	Social documentary
Lartigue, Jacques-Henri	1894–1986	French	Documentary photography
Leibovitz, Annie	1949–	American	Celebrity portraiture, advertising photography
Levitt, Helen	1913–	American	Social documentary
Man Ray (Emmanuel Rudnitsky)	1890–1976	American	Surrealist photography
Mapplethorpe, Robert	1946–1989	American	Photomontage, still-life photography, erotic photography
Miller, Lee	1907–1977	American	Surrealist photography, portraiture, documentary photography
Model, Lisette	1901/06–1983	Austrian-born American	Documentary photography
Modotti, Tina	1896–1942	Italian-born American	Social documentary, still-life photography
Moholy-Nagy, László	1895–1946	Hungarian-born American	Abstract photography, art instruction
Morgan, Barbara	1900–1992	American	Dance photography, portraiture, still-life photography
Muybridge, Eadweard	1830–1904	English	Documentary photography, motion studies
Nadar (Gaspard Félix Tournachon)	1820–1910	French	Portraiture, aerial photography
Newton, Helmut	1920–	German-born American	Fashion photography, celebrity photography
O'Sullivan, Timothy H.	1840–1882	American	Documentary photography
Orkin, Ruth	1921–1985	American	Photojournalism, cinematography
Parks, Gordon	1912–	American	Photojournalism, social documentary
Ritts, Herb	1952–	American	Fashion photography, celebrity photography
Salomon, Erich	1886–1944	German	Photojournalism
Sander, August	1876–1964	German	Documentary photography
Seymour, David	1911–1956	Polish-born American	Photojournalism
Sherman, Cindy	1954–	American	Art photography
Siskind, Aaron	1903–1991	American	Social documentary, abstract photography
Smith, W. Eugene	1918–1978	American	Photojournalism
Southworth, Albert Sands	1811–1894	American	Daguerreotype portraiture and documentary photography

Photographers *(cont.)*

Name	Dates	Nationality	Major Works
Steichen, Edward	1879–1973	American	Art photography, portraiture
Stieglitz, Alfred	1864–1946	American	Art photography
Strand, Paul	1890–1976	American	Art photography, documentary photography
Sudek, Josef	1896–1976	Czech	Still-life photography, impressionist photography
Talbot, William Henry Fox	1800–1877	English	Calotype innovation, photographic illustration
Ulmann, Doris	1884–1934	American	Social documentary
Van Der Zee, James	1886–1983	American	Documentary photography, portraiture
Vishniac, Roman	1897–1990	Russian-born American	Microphotography, documentary photography
Weegee (Arthur Fellig)	1899–1968	Austrian-born American	Crime photography, documentary photography
Wegman, William	1942/44–	American	Art photography
Weston, Edward	1886–1958	American	Abstract photography
White, Clarence H.	1871–1925	American	Art photography, landscape photography
White, Minor	1908–1976	American	Art photography, abstract photography
Winogrand, Garry	1928–1984	American	Photojournalism

⊙ Capa, Cornell, ed. *The International Center of Photography Encyclopedia of Photography.* New York: Crown, 1986.
Masters of Photography. www.masters-of-photography.com
Artnet.com. "Research Library: Artist Biographies," www.artnet.com/library/bios

ARTS AND LEISURE: *Museums*

50 Great Art Museums

Name	Location	Telephone/Website
Ashmolean Museum of Art	Oxford, England	011-44-1865-27-80-00 www.ashmol.ox.ac.uk
Art Gallery of Ontario	Ontario, Canada	(416) 979-6648 www.ago.on.ca
Art Institute of Chicago	Chicago, IL	(312) 443-3600 www.artic.edu
British Museum	London, England	011-44-207-636-1555 www.thebritishmuseum.ac.uk
Carnegie Museum of Art	Pittsburgh, PA	(412) 622-3131 www.cmoa.org
Capitoline Museum	Rome, Italy	011-39-6-39-96-78-00 www.comune.roma.it/museicapitolini/pinacoteca
Centre Pompidou	Paris, France	011-33-1-44-78-12-33 www.centrepompidou.fr
Corcoran Gallery of Art	Washington, D.C.	888-CORCORAN www.corcoran.edu
Courtauld Institute Galleries	London, England	011-44-207-848-2526 www.courtauld.edu
Dallas Museum of Art	Dallas, TX	(214) 922-1200 www.dm-art.org

Fine Arts Museum, San Francisco	San Francisco, CA	(415) 863-3300 www.famsf.org
Frick Collection	New York, NY	(212) 288-0070 www.frick.org
Galleria dell'Accademia	Florence, Italy	011-39-55-23-885 www.sbas.firenze.it/accademia
Guggenheim Museum	New York, NY	(212) 423-3500 www.guggenheim.org
Guggenheim Museum, Bilbao	Bilbao, Spain	011-34-9-44-35-90-80 www.guggenheim-bilbao.es/ idioma.htm
Hamburger Kunsthalle	Hamburg, Germany	011-49-40-42-85-26-12 www.hamburger-kunsthalle.de
J. Paul Getty Museum	Los Angeles, CA	(310) 440-7300 www.getty.edu/museum
Library of Congress	Washington, D.C.	(202) 707-5000 www.loc.gov
Louvre (Musée de Louvre)	Paris, France	011-33-1-40-20-51-51 www.louvre.fr
Metropolitan Museum of Art	New York, NY	(212) 535-7710 www.metmuseum.org
Musée d' Orsay	Paris, France	011-33-1-40-49-48-14 www.musee-orsay.fr
Museo del Prado	Madrid, Spain	011-34-9-13-30-28-00 www.mcu.es/prado
Museum of Contemporary Art	Los Angeles, CA	(213) 621-2766 www.moca-la.org
Museum of Fine Arts, Boston	Boston, MA	(617) 267-9300 www.mfa.org
Museum of Modern Art	New York, NY	(212) 708-9400 www.moma.org
National Archaeological Museum	Athens, Greece	011-30-1-821-7717, 821-7724 www.culture.gr/2/21/214/21405m/ e21405m1.html
National Building Museum	Washington, D.C.	(202) 272-2448 www.nbm.org
National Gallery, London	London, England	011-44-207-747-2885 www.nationalgallery.org.uk
National Gallery of Art	Washington, D.C.	(202) 737-4215 www.nga.gov
National Museum of American Art	Washington, D.C.	(202) 357-2531 www.nmaa.si.edu
National Museum of Scotland	Edinburgh, Scotland	011-44-31-12-25-75-34 www.museum.scotland.net
National Portrait Gallery	Washington, D.C.	(202) 357-2866 www.npg.si.edu
Norton Simon Museum	Pasadena, CA	(626) 449-6840 www.nortonsimon.org
Peggy Guggenheim Collection	Venice, Italy	011-39-41-240-5411 www.guggenheim.org/venice
Picasso Museum	Paris, France	011-33-1-42-71-25-21 www.musexpo.com/english/ picasso/index.html
Philadelphia Museum of Art	Philadelphia, PA	(215) 736-8100 www.philamuseum.org
Pushkin State Museum of Fine Arts	Moscow, Russia	011-7-09-52-03-95-78 www.museum.ru/gmii
Rijksmuseum	Amsterdam, the Netherlands	011-31-20-674-7047 www.rijksmuseum.nl
Rodin Museum	Paris, France	011-33-1-44-18-61-10 www.musee-rodin.fr
Royal Academy of Art	London, England	011-44-207-300-8000 www.royalacademy.org.uk
San Francisco Museum of Modern Art	San Francisco, CA	(415) 357-4000 www.sfmoma.org/index-r.html

50 Great Art Museums *(cont.)*

Name	Location	Telephone/Website
St. Louis Art Museum	Saint Louis, MO	(314) 721-0072 www.slam.org
State Hermitage Museum	Saint Petersburg, Russia	011-7-81-21-10-90-79 www.hermitagemuseum.org
Stedelijk Museum of Modern Art	Amsterdam, the Netherlands	011-31-20-573-2911 www.stedelijk.nl
Tate Gallery	London, England	011-44-207-887-8008 www.tate.org.uk
Uffizi Gallery	Florence, Italy	011-39-55-23-88-65-16-52 www.uffizi.firenze.it/ welcomeE.html
Van Gogh Museum	Amsterdam, the Netherlands	011-31-20-570-5200 www.vangoghmuseum.nl
Vatican Museums	Vatican City	011-39-6-69-88-49-47 www.christusrex.org/www1/ vaticano/0-Musei.html
Victoria and Albert Museum	London, England	011-44-207-942-2000 www.vam.ac.uk
Whitney Museum of American Art	New York, NY	(212) 570-3676 www.whitney.org

⊙ International Council of Museums (ICOM). www.icom.org
  MuseumSpot. www.museumspot.com
  Roberts, Fletcher, et.al., eds. *Traveler's Guide to Art Museum Exhibitions 2000*, New
    York: Abrams, 1999.
  Smithsonian Museums and Research Centers. www.si.edu/info/
    museums_research.htm

Other Notable Museums

American Museum of the Moving Image
Long Island City, NY
(718) 784-0077   www.ammi.org
Known For: motion picture and television history

American Museum of Natural History
New York, NY
(212) 769-5100   www.anmh.org
Known For: paleontology, zoology

Bronx Zoo
Bronx, NY
(718) 367-1010
   http://wcs.org/home/zoos/
   bronxzoo
Known For: zoology

Children's Museum of Boston
Boston, MA
(617) 426-8855   www.tcmboston.org
Known For: discovery for children

Colonial Williamsburg
Williamsburg, VA
800-HISTORY   www.history.org
Known For: colonial American history

Ellis Island and the Statue of Liberty
New York, NY
(212) 883-1986   www.ellisisland.org
Known For: American immigration museum

Gettysburg
Gettysburg, PA
(717) 334-6274   www.gettysburg.com
Known For: American Civil War battleground

Graceland
Memphis, TN
800-238-2000
   www.elvis-presley.com
Known For: Elvis Presley memorabilia

Henry Ford Museum
Dearborn, MI
(313) 271-2455   www.hfmgv.org
Known For: U.S. automotive history

International Football Hall of Fame
Manchester, England
www.int-foot-fame.com
Known For: soccer hall of fame, open in 2001

Kennedy Space Center
Cape Canaveral, FL
(321) 452-8612
www.kennedyspacecenter.com
Known For: space exploration

Monticello
Charlottesville, VA
(804) 984-9822
www.monticello.org
Known For: Thomas Jefferson home

Mount Vernon
Mount Vernon, VA
(703) 780-2000
www.mountvernon.org
Known For: George Washington home

National Air and Space Museum
Washington, D.C.
(202) 357-2700   www.nasm.si.edu
Known For: historic air- and space-craft

National Archives
Washington, D.C.
(202) 501-5205   www.nara.gov
Known For: American historical documents

National Baseball Hall of Fame
Cooperstown, NY
(607) 547-7299
www.baseballhalloffame.org
Known For: baseball memorabilia

National Football Hall of Fame
Canton, OH
(330) 456-8270
www.profootballhof.com
Known For: pro football memorabilia

National Museum of the American Indian
New York, NY
(212) 514-3700   www.si.edu/nmai
Known For: American Indian history, culture

Palace of Versailles
Versailles, France
011 33 1 39 51 23 66
www.chateauversailles.org
Known For: French royal history

Rock and Roll Hall of Fame
Cleveland, OH
888-764-ROCK   www.rockhall.com
Known For: rock-and-roll memorabilia

San Diego Zoo
San Diego, CA
(619) 234-3153
www.sandiegozoo.com
Known For: zoology

Theatre Museum
London, England
011 44 207 943 4700
http://theatremuseum.vam.ac.uk
Known For: British theatre history

Tower of London
London, England
011 44 207 709 0765
www.armouries.org.uk
Known For: British history, arms and armor

U.S. Holocaust Memorial Museum
Washington, D.C.
(202) 488-0400   www.ushmm.org

Holocaust/WWII history
The White House, Washington, D.C.
(202) 456-7041 www.whitehouse.gov
Known For: home of the president, museum

⊙ International Council of Museums (ICOM). www.icom.org
   MuseumSpot. www.museumspot.com
   Smithsonian Museums and Research Centers. www.si.edu/info/
   museums_research.htm

100 Notable Architects

These architects are among the best known in history. Dates given for major works are completion dates. Architects have been chosen for their influence on the history of architecture, as well as for the fame and importance of their works.

Name	Dates	Nationality	Major Works
Aalto, Alvar	1898–1976	Finnish	Finlandia Conference Center, Helsinki (1975); Baker Dormitory, Massachusetts Institute of Technology, Cambridge (1949)
Adam, Robert	1728–1792	English	Theatre Royal, Drury Lane, London (1776); Apsley House, London (1778)
Alberti, Leone Battista	1404–1472	Italian	Sant' Andra, Mantua (1472); façade of Santa Maria Novella, Florence (1471)
Andrews, John	1933–	Australian	American Express Tower, Sydney (1970); School of Art, Kent State University (1970)
Apollodorus of Damascus	2nd century AD	Roman	Trajan's Baths, Rome (109); Trajan's Forum, Rome (112)
Ashbee, C. R.	1863–1942	English	The Wodehouse, Staffordshire (1901)
Asplund, Erik Gunner	1885–1943	Swedish	Bredenburg Department Store, Stockholm (1935); Goteburg Law Courts Annex (1937)
Barragán, Luis	1902–1987	Mexican	Hotel Pierre Marquez Gardens, Acapulco (1955); Eggerstrom House, Mexico City (1968)
Barry, Charles	1795–1860	English	Houses of Parliament, London (1860)
Bentley, John Francis	1830–1902	English	Westminster Cathedral, London (1903)
Berlage, Hendrick Petrus	1856–1934	Dutch	Municipal Museum, The Hague (1935); Stock Exchange, Amsterdam (1903)
Bernini, Gioanlorezo	1598–1680	Italian	St. Peter's, Rome (1626 renovation); Piazza di San Pietro, Rome (1667)
Borromini, Francesco	1599–1667	Italian	Lateran Tombs, Rome (1655); Villa Falconieri, Frascati (1667)
Bramante, Donate	1444–1514	Italian	S. Maria Presso San Satiro, Milan (1478 renovation); Belvedere Court (1504)
Brunelleschi, Filippo	1377–1446	Italian	Cathedral of Santa Maria del Fiore, Florence (cupola, lantern & tribune morte) (1446)
Burlington, Richard Boyle, 3rd Earl of	1664–1753	English	Wade House, London (1723); Assembly Rooms, York (1732)
Burton, Decimus	1800–1881	English	Cornwall Terrace, London (nd); Hyde Park Screen, London (1835)
Butterfield, William	1814–1900	English	Keble College, Oxford (1883); All Saints, (London) 1859
Chambers, William	1732–1790	English	Trent Palace, Middlesex (1777); Theatre Royal, Liverpool (1772)
Cortona, Pietro	1596–1669	Italian	Santi Luci et Marchina, Rome (1650)
Deane, Thomas	1792–1871	Irish	Museum of Natural History, Oxford (1861); Trinity College Library, Dublin (1862)

Fischer von Erlach, Johann	1656–1723	Austrian	Holy Trinity Plague Column, Vienna (1689); Imperial Library, Vienna (1730)
Gandon, James	1743–1823	Irish	County Hall, Nottingham (1772); Emsworth, Dublin (1794)
Gaudi, Antonio	1852–1926	Spanish	Casa Vicens, Barcelona (1880); Casa Mila, Barcelona (1910)
Gibbs, James	1682–1754	Scottish	Alexander Pope Villa, Middlesex (1720); Radcliffe Library, Oxford (1754)
Gehry, Frank	1929–	American	California Aerospace Museum, Santa Monica (1984); Guggenheim Museum, Bilbao (1997)
Goff, Bruce	1904–1982	American	Hopewell Baptist Church, Oklahoma (1950); Nicol House, Kansas City (1967)
Gomez de Mora, Juan	1580–1648	Spanish	Encarnación Church, Madrid (1611–16)
Gropius, Walter	1883–1969	German	Chicago Tribune Building, Chicago (1922); Pan Am Building, New York (1957)
Guimard, Hector	1867–1942	French	Humbert De Romans Auditorium, Paris (1901)
Hansen, Christian	1803–1883	Danish	Mint, Athens (1836); Observatory, Copenhagen (1861)
Hildebrandt, Johann	1668–1745	Austrian	Garden House, Siebenbrunn Palace (1730); Parish Church, Asperdorf (1733)
Hittorff, Jacques	1792–1867	German	Church of St. Vincent De Paul, Paris (1848)
Horta, Victor	1861–1947	Belgian	Horta House, Belgium (1089); Hallet House, Brussels (1903)
Iktinos	c.450–400 BC	Greek	The Parthenon, Athens (437 BC)
Jefferson, Thomas	1742–1826	American	Monticello, Virginia (1782)
Jones, Inigo	1573–1652	English	Whitehall Palace, London (1622); Somerset House, London (1635)
Kahn, Albert	1869–1942	American	General Motors Building, Detroit (1925); Fisher Building, Detroit (1929)
Keyser, Hendrick de	1565–1621	Dutch	Zuiderkerk, Amsterdam, Netherlands (1614)
Krier, Rob	1938–	Austrian	Façade for Hotel, Salzburg Germany (1988); Apartment Building, Bilbao Spain (1992)
Kroll, Lucien	1927–	Belgian	Medical Facility Buildings Complex, Belgium (1977)
Latrobe, Benjamin	1764–1820	American	Roman Catholic Cathedral, Baltimore (1818); Capitol Building, Washington DC (1817)
Le Brun, Charles	1619–1690	French	Palais de Versailles (1678)
Le Corbusier	1887–1965	French	Villa Planiex, Paris (1927); Musuem, Ahmedabad India (1957)
Loos, Adolf	1870–1933	Czechoslovakian	American bar, Vienna (1907); Muller House, Prague (1930)
Lutyens, Edwin Landeer	1869–1944	English	Munstead Wood, Surrey (1896); Tigbourne Court, Surrey (1899)
Mackintosh, Charles Rennie	1868–1928	Scottish	Glasgow School of Art, Glasgow (1909)
Maki, Fumihiko	1928–	Japanese	Toyota Memorial Hall, Nagoya (1960); National Museum of Modern Art, Kyoto (1986)

Name	Dates	Nationality	Major Works
Mansart, Francois	1598–1666	French	Chateau of Berry (1623); Hotel du Jars, Paris (1645)
Meier, Richard	1934–	American	High Museum of Art, Atlanta (1983); Getty Center, Los Angeles (1997)
Mendelson, Erich	1887–1953	German-born American	Atomic Energy Commission Labratories, Berkeley (1953)
Michelangelo Buonarrati	1475–1564	Italian	San Lorenzo façade, Florence (1517); St. Peter's, Rome (1564)
Mies Van der Rohe, Ludwig	1886–1969	German-born American	Wolf House, Germany (1926); Toronto Dominion Center, Canada (1969)
Moore, Charles W.	1925–1993	American	Hood Museum of Art, Hanover NH (1985)
Morgan, Julia	1872–1957	American	Elliott House, Berkeley CA (1920); Hearst Estate, California (1941)
Nash, John	1752–1835	English	Terraces and façades, Regents Park, London (1827)
Neumann, Johann	1687–1753	German	High Altar, Cathedral of Worms (1749); Schloss Augustusburg (1748)
Neutra, Richard	1892–1970	Austrian-born American	Lincoln Memorial Museum, Gettysburg PA (1959): Hall of Records, Los Angeles (1961)
Niemeyer, Oscar	1907–	Brazilian	City of Brasília (1964); Mondadori Headquarters, Milan (1975)
O'Gorman, Juan	1905–1982	Mexican	Diego Rivera House, Mexico City (1930); Juan O'Gorman House II (1956)
Olmstead, Frederick Law	1822–1903	American	Park System, Rochester NY (1888); United States Capitol Grounds (1874)
Palladio, Andrew	1508–1580	Italian	Villa of Leonardo Emo, Vincenza, Italy (1567)
Pei, I. M.	1917–	American	Le Grand Louvre, Paris (1983)
Perrault, Claude	1613–1688	French	East Façade of the Louvre, Paris (1670)
Piano, Renzo	1937–	Italian	Centre Pompidou, Paris (1977 with Richard Rogers)
Playfair, William	1790–1857	English	Donaldson Hospital, Edinburgh (1842–54): National Gallery of Scotland (1850–57)
Plečnik, Jože	1872–1957	Yugoslav	Market, Ljubljana (1942); Monastery of the German Knights, Ljubljana (1953)
Pugin, Augustus	1812–1852	English	Manor House, Wiburton (1848); St. Augustine's Church, Kent (1850)
Rastrelli, Bartolomeo	1700–1771	Russian	Fourth Winter Palace, Petrograd (1762)
Renwick, James	1818–1895	American	Smithsonian Institution, Washington DC (1855)
Richardson, Henry Hobson	1838–1886	American	Grace Church, Massachusetts (1869); City Hall, Albany NY (1882)
Riefeld, Gerrit T.	1888–1964	Dutch	Juliana Hall and Entrance, Utrecht (1936); Van Sloobe House, Heerlen (1964)
Roebling, John	1806–1859	American	Brooklyn Bridge, New York City (1883)

Roebling, Washington Augustus	1837–1926	American	Brooklyn Bridge, New York City (1883; with father, John)
Saarien, Eliel	1910–1961	Finnish	Railway station, Viborg (1904); City Hall, Lahti (1912)
Sansovino, Jacopo	1486–1570	Italian	Piazza San Marco, Venice (1540)
Schindler, Rudolph	1887–1953	American	Buena Shore Club, Chicago (1918); Tucker House, Hollywood (1950)
Schinkel, Karl Friedrich	1791–1841	German	Schauspielhaus, Berlin (1821)
Scott, H. M. Baillie	1865–1945	English	The Garth, Cobham, Surrey (1900); Oakhams, Kent (1921)
Scott, George Gilbert	1811–1878	English	Exeter College Chapel, Oxford (1860); St. Mary Abbots Church, London (1872)
Shaw, Richard Norman	1831–1913	English	New Scotland Yard, London (1907)
Soane, John	1753–1857	English	St. Peter's Church, Walworth (1824); Holy Trinity Marylebone, London (1827)
Soleri, Paolo	1919–	Italian	Cosanti Foundaion, Scottsdale AZ (1976); Dome House, Arizona (1949)
Stirling, Sir James	1926–1992	English	House, Isle of Wight (1956); Biennale Bookshop, Venice (1989)
Street, George Edmund	1824–1881	English	Law Courts, London (1882)
Stuart, James	1713–1788	English	Infirmary, Greenwich Hospital (1764); Chapel, Greenwich Hospital (1788)
Sullivan, Louis	1856–1924	American	Guaranty Building, Buffalo (1896); Stock Exchange, Chicago (1894)
Thomson, Alexander	1817–1875	Scottish	New Campus, University of Glasgow (1850); Egyptian Halls, Glasgow (1871)
Vasari, Giogorio	1511–1574	Italian	Uffizi Palace, Florence (1580)
Voysey, Charles F.	1857–1941	English	Memorial Manor House, Tonbridge (1920)
Wagner, Otto	1841–1918	Austrian	Synagogue, Budapest (1871); Lupus Sanatorium, Vienna (1913)
Warschavick, Gregori	1896–1972	Brazilian	First Modern House Exhibition, São Paulo (1930); Raul Crespi Beach House (1943)
Webb, Aston	1879–1930	English	Victoria Azzize Courts, Birmingham (1891); Victoria & Albert Museum London (1909)
Webb, Philip	1831–1915	English	Standen, Sussex (1892); 19 Lincoln's Inn Fields, London (1869)
White, Stanford	1853–1906	American	Boston Public Library (1888); J. Pierpont Morgan Library, New York (1907 with McKim, Mead and White)
Wren, Sir Christopher	1632–1723	English	Royal Hospital, Greenwich (1691); St. Paul's Cathedral. London (1710)
Wright, Frank Lloyd	1867–1959	American	Robie House, Chicago (1909); Falling Water, Bear Run PA (1936)
Wyatt, James	1764–1813	English	Lee Priory, Kent (1790); Ashbridge Park, Hertfordshire (1813)

Ⓒ University of Buffalo. "Cyburia-Famous Architects resources page." http://cyburbia.ap.buffalo.edu/cgi-bin/pairc/archtcts
Van Vynckt, Randall J., ed. *International Dictionary of Architects and Architecture.* London: St James, 1993.

Classical Orders of Architecture

ELEMENTS OF CLASSICAL ORDERS

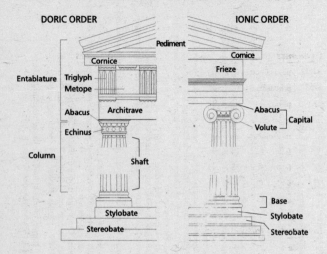

DORIC ORDER

- Pediment
- Cornice
- Entablature
  - Triglyph
  - Metope
  - Abacus — Architrave
  - Echinus
- Column
  - Shaft
- Stylobate
- Stereobate

IONIC ORDER

- Cornice
- Frieze
- Abacus — Capital
- Volute — Capital
- Base
- Stylobate
- Stereobate

TYPES OF COLUMNS

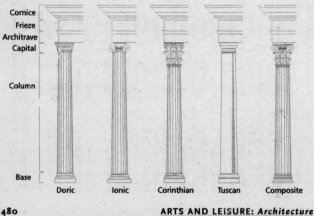

- Cornice
- Frieze
- Architrave
- Capital
- Column
- Base

Doric   Ionic   Corinthian   Tuscan   Composite

Common Music Notation

Treble (G) clef   Alto (C) clef   Bass (F) clef

Flat ♭ Sharp ♯

Dynamics

ppp	pianississimo	very, very quiet
pp	pianissimo	very quiet
p	piano	quiet
	mezzopiano	moderately quiet
	mezzoforte	moderately loud
f	forte	loud
ff	fortissimo	very loud
fff	fortississimo	very, very loud
	sforzando	suddenly very loud

Interpretive Indicators

cantabile	singing style
dolce	soft and sweet
expressivo	expressively
legato	smooth
staccato	detached

Crescendo and Diminuendo

<

>

Tempo Indicators

adagio	slow
largo	slow and dignified
andante	flowing, at a walking pace
allegro	quick and bright
allegretto	not as quick as allegro
vivace	fast and lively
presto	very quick
accelerando	getting faster
ritardando (rit.)	holding back
rallentando (rall.)	getting slower
rubato	flexible tempo

Notes   Rests

o	Whole note (semibreve)	—
♩	Half note (minim)	—
♩	Quarter note (crotchet)	
♪	Eighth note (quaver)	
♪	Sixteenth note (semiquaver)	
♪	Thirty-second note (demisemiquaver)	

Staff Line

⊙ Sacher, Jack, ed. *Music A to Z.* New York: Grosset & Dunlap, 1963.
Randel, Don Michael, ed. *The New Harvard Dictionary of Music.* Cambridge, Mass.: Belknap, 1986.

45 Major Orchestras

Orchestra	Year Established	Orchestra	Year Established
Academy of St. Martin in the Fields (London)	1958	Mariinsky Theater (Kirov) Orchestra	1860
Atlanta Symphony Orchestra	1947	Metropolitan Operas Orchestra	1883
Baltimore Symphony Orchestra	1916	Minnesota Orchestra	1903
Bamberg Symphony Orchestra	1946	National Symphony Orchestra (Washington, D.C.)	1931
Basle Chamber Orchestra	1926		
Bavarian Radio Symphony Orchestra	1960	New York Philharmonic	1842
Berlin Philharmonic Orchestra	1882	Orchestre de la Suisse Romande	1918
Boston Symphony Orchestra	1881	Orchestre de Paris	1967
Chicago Symphony Orchestra	1890	Orchestre symphonique de Montréal	1934
Cincinnati Symphony Orchestra	1895		
City of Birmingham Symphony Orchestra	1920	Orpheus Chamber Orchestra	1972
		Philadelphia Orchestra	1900
Cleveland Orchestra	1918	Prague Symphony Orchestra	1934
Czech Philharmonic Orchestra	1896	RAI National Symphony Orchestra	1994
Dallas Symphony Orchestra	1900		
Detroit Symphony Orchestra	1900	Royal Concertgebouw Orchestra	1888
Dresden Sächsische Staatskapelle	1548	Royal Opera House Covent Garden Orchestra	1945
English Chamber Orchestra	1948	Royal Philharmonic Orchestra	1946
English National Opera Orchestra	1931	Royal Scottish National Orchestra	1894
Houston Symphony Orchestra	1913	Saint Louis Symphony Orchestra	1880
Israel Philharmonic Orchestra	1936		
Leipzig Gewandhaus Orchestra	1781	San Francisco Symphony Orchestra	1911
London Philharmonic Orchestra	1932		
		Seattle Philharmonic Orchestra	1944
London Symphony Orchestra	1904	Vienna Philharmonic	1842
Los Angeles Philharmonic Orchestra	1919	Warsaw Philharmonic Orchestra	1946

⊙ Cummings, David, ed. *Random House Encyclopedic Dictionary of Classical Music*. New York: Random House, 1997.

"Orchestral News," ourworld.compuserve.com/homepages/John_Woolard

Sadie, Stanley, ed. *The Norton/Grove Concise Encyclopedia of Music*. New York: Norton, 1994.

125 Major Composers

This section contains composers from different historical eras, countries, and musical genres, both popular and classical. The list includes men and women known for innovation and mastery within their particular musical periods, composers who have experimented with those conventions, and composers whose acclaim comes from the enduring popularity of their work.

Name	Dates	Nationality	Major Works
Adams, John	1947–	American	*Harmonium*; Opera: *Nixon in China*
Adès, Thomas	1971–	English	*Toys for Orchestra*; Opera: *Powder Her Face*

Albeniz, Isaac	1860–1909	Spanish	Rapsodia espanola Op. 70 for Piano and Orchestra; Suite espanola Op. 47 for Piano
Arne, Thomas Augustine	1710–1778	English	Various symphonies; Songs: "Rule Britannia"; Blow, "Blow, Thou Winter Wind"
Auber, Daniel-Francois	1782–1871	French	Operas: *Fra Diavolo*; *Manon Lescaut*
Bach, Johann Sebastian	1685–1750	German	*Art of the Fugue*; *Brandenberg Concertos*; *St. Matthew Passion*
Barber, Samuel	1910–1981	American	Adagio for Strings; Song Cycle: *Knoxville: Summer of 1915*; Opera: *Antony and Cleopatra*
Bartók, Béla	1881–1945	Hungarian	Concerto for Orchestra; Ballet: *Miraculous Mandarin*; Opera: *Bluebeard's Castle*
Beethoven, Ludwig van	1770–1827	German	Sonatas for Piano; Various symphonies; Opera: *Fidelio*
Bellini, Vincenzo	1801–1835	Italian	Operas: *Norma*; *I Puritani*; *La Sonnambula*
Berg, Alban	1885–1935	Austrian	Concerto for Violin; Operas: *Wozzeck*; *Lulu*
Berio, Luciano	1925–	Italian	*Sequences*; *Sinfonia*; Opera: *La vera storia*
Berlin, Irving	1888–1989	Russian-born American	Musicals: *As Thousands Cheer*; *Annie Get Your Gun*; *Call Me Madam*
Berlioz, Hector	1803–1869	French	*Damnation of Faust*; *Symphonie fantastique*; Opera: *Les Troyens*
Bernstein, Leonard	1918–1990	American	*Mass*; Musicals: *On the Town*; *West Side Story*
Bizet, Georges	1838–1875	French	*L'Arlesienne Suites*; Operas: *Carmen*; *The Pearl Fishers*
Blitzstein, Marc	1905–1964	American	Operas: *The Cradle Will Rock*, *Regina*
Borodin, Alexander	1833–1887	Russian	*Polovtsian Dances*; Opera: *Prince Igor*; Various quartets
Boulez, Pierre	1925–	French	*Le Marteau sans maître*; Sonatas for Piano; *Pli selon pli*
Brahms, Johannes	1833–1897	German	Chamber music; symphonies; Concerto for Violin and Cello; *Variations on a Theme by Haydn*
Britten, Benjamin	1913–1976	English	*Young Person's Guide to the Orchestra*; Operas: *Peter Grimes*; *Billy Budd*
Bruzdowicz, Joanna	1943–	Polish	Operas: *The Penal Colony*; *The Gates of Paradise*; *Tides and Waves*
Byrd, William	1543–1623	English	Consort music; Various music for keyboard; Various sacred choral music
Cage, John	1912–1992	American	Music for String Quartet; Sonatas and Interludes for Prepared Piano
Chopin, Frédéric	1810–1849	Polish	Concertos for Piano; Various music for piano (Ballades; Etudes; Nocturnes)
Copland, Aaron	1900–1990	American	*Fanfare for the Common Man*; Ballets: *Appalachian Spring*; *Rodeo*
Corelli, Arcangelo	1653–1713	Italian	Various concerti grossi

Name	Dates	Nation-ality	Major Works
Davies, Peter Maxwell	1934–	English	Strathclyde Concertos; Opera: The Lighthouse
Debussy, Claude	1862–1918	French	Chamber music; Prelude a l'après-midi d'un faune; Opera: Pelleas et Melisande
Donizetti, Gaetano	1797–1848	Italian	Operas: Don Pasquale; La Fille du Regiment; Lucia di Lammermoor
Dukas, Paul	1865–1935	French	The Sorcerer's Apprentice
Dvořák, Antonin	1841–1904	Bohemian	Concerto for Violin; Various symphonies; Opera: Rusalka
Edgar, Edward	1857–1934	English	Concerto for Cello; Enigma Variations; Pomp and Circumstance marches
Fauré, Gabriel	1845–1924	French	Chamber music; Pavane for Orchestra; Various songs
Franck, César	1822–1890	French	Organ music; Chamber music; Symphony in D Minor
Gershwin, George	1898–1937	American	American in Paris; Rhapsody in Blue; Opera: Porgy and Bess
Glass, Philip	1937–	American	Operas: Einstein on the Beach; The Voyage; Soundtrack: Mishima
Glinka, Mikhail	1804–1857	Russian	Operas: A Life for the Tsar; Russlan and Ludmilla
Gluck, Christoph Willibald	1714–1787	German	Operas: Orfeo ed Euridice; Iphigénie en Tauride
Gounod, Charles	1818–1893	French	Operas: Faust; Roméo et Juliette
Grieg, Edvard	1843–1907	Norwegian	Concerto for Piano; Peer Gynt Suites
Handel, George Frideric	1685–1759	German	Royal Fireworks Music; Water Music; Oratorio: Messiah
Haydn, Franz Joseph	1732–1809	Austrian	Sacred choral music; Various symphonies; Oratorio: The Creation
Henze, Hans Werner	1926–	German	Various symphonies; Operas: The Young Lord; The English Cat
Hindemith, Paul	1895–1963	German	Symphonic Metamorphosis of Themes by Weber; Opera: Mathis der Maler
Holst, Gustav	1874–1937	English	The Planets
Humperdinck, Engelbert	1854–1921	German	Opera: Hansel und Gretel
Ives, Charles	1874–1954	American	Sonatas for piano; Various symphonies; Three Places in New England
Janácek, Leos	1854–1928	Czech	Music for piano; Operas: Jenufa; The Cunning Little Vixen
Josquin des Prez	c.1450–1521	French	Various masses, motets, chansons
Khachaturian, Aram	1903–1978	Armenian	Ballet: Gayne; Soundtracks: The Battle of Stalingrad; Othello
Kodály, Zóltan	1882–1967	Hungarian	Peacock Variations; Opera: Háry János
Lalo, Édouard	1823–1892	French	Concerto in D Minor for Cello; Symphony in G Minor; Symphony espagnole for Violin and Orchestra
Lasso, Orlando di	1532–1594	Franco-Flemish	Various madrigals and motets; Requiem

Leoncavallo, Ruggero	1858–1919	Italian	Opera: *I Pagliacci*
Ligeti, György	1923–	Hungarian	*Atmosphères*; Opera: *Le grand macabre*
Liszt, Franz	1811–1886	Hungarian	Annees de Pelerinage for Piano; Les Preludes for Orchestra; Totentanz for Piano and Orchestra
Lloyd Webber, Andrew	1948–	English	Musicals: *Jesus Christ, Superstar*; *Evita*; *Cats*
Lully, Jean Baptiste	1632–1687	French	Opera: *Atys*; Ballet: *Le Bougeois Gentilhomme*
Machaut, Guillaume de	c.1300–1377	French	*Notre Dame Mass*; Various chansons
Mahler, Gustav	1860–1911	Austrian	Various symphonies; *Das Lied von der Erde*; Song Cycle: *Kindertotenlieder*
Marenzio, Luca	?1553–1599	Italian	Madrigals
Massenet, Jules	1842–1912	French	Ballet: *Le Cid*; Operas: *Manon*; *Thaïs*
Mendelssohn, Felix	1809–1847	German	Music for piano; Incidental music for *Midsummer Night's Dream*; Oratorio: *Elijah*
Menotti, Gian Carlo	1911–	American (b. Italy)	Operas: *Amahl and the Night Visitors*; *The Medium*
Messiaen, Olivier	1908–1992	French	Music for Organ; Music for Piano; *Quatuor pour la fin du temps*
Meyerbeer, Giacomo	1791–1864	German	Operas: *L'Africaine*; *Les Huguenots*
Monteverdi, Claudio	1567–1643	Italian	Various masses; Operas: *La Favola d'Orfeo*; *L'Incoronazione di Poppea*
Mozart, Wolfgang Amadeus	1756–1791	Austrian	Chamber Music; Mass in C Minor ("The Great"); Opera: *Die Zauberflote*
Mussorgsky, Modest	1839–1881	Russian	*Night on Bald Mountain*; *Pictures at an Exhibition*; Opera: *Boris Godounov*
Nielsen, Carl	1865–1931	Danish	Various symphonies
Offenbach, Jacques	1819–1880	French	*Gaite Parisienne*; Opera: *Les Contes d'Hoffmann*
Orff, Carl	1895–1982	German	Oratorio: *Carmina Burana*
Paganini, Niccoló	1782–1840	Italian	Various caprices; Concerto for Violin
Palestrina, Giovanni Pierluigi da	c.1525–1594	Italian	Various masses and motets
Penderecki, Krzystof	1933–	Polish	Various concertos; *Threnody for the Victims of Hiroshima*
Pergolesi, Giovanni Battista	1710–1736	Italian	*Stabat Mater*; Opera: *La Serva padrona*
Ponchielli, Amilcare	1834–1886	Italian	Ballet: *Dance of the Hours*; Opera: *La Gioconda*
Poulenc, Francis	1899–1963	French	Ballet: *Les Biches*; Operas: *Dialogue of the Carmelites*; *Les Mamelles de Tirésias*
Prokofiev, Sergei	1891–1953	Russian	*Peter and the Wolf*; Ballet: *Cinderella*; Opera: *The Love of Three Oranges*
Puccini, Giacomo	1858–1924	Operas	Operas: *La Boheme*; *Madama Butterfly*; *Tosca*
Purcell, Henry	1659–1695	English	*Music for the Funeral of Queen Mary*; Opera: *Dido and Aeneas*
Rachmaninov, Sergei	1873–1943	Russian	Concertos for Piano; Chamber Music; *Rhapsody on a Theme of Paganini*

Name	Dates	Nationality	Major Works
Ravel, Maurice	1875–1937	French	*Bolero; Rhapsodie espagnole;* Ballet: *Daphnis et Chloé*
Reich, Steve	1936–	American	*Desert Music; Music for 18 Musicians*
Respighi, Ottorino	1879–1936	Italian	*Fountains of Rome; Pines of Rome*
Rimsky-Korsakov, Nikolai	1844–1908	Russian	*Russian Easter Overture; Schherazade;* Ballet: *Coq d'Or*
Rodgers, Richard	1902–1979	American	Musicals: *Pal Joey; Oklahoma!; South Pacific*
Rossini, Gioacchino	1792–1868	Italian	*Stabat Mater;* Operas: *Barber of Seville; La Cenerentola*
Saint-Saëns, Camille	1835–1921	French	*Carnival of the Animals;* Symphony No. 3 ("Organ"); Opera: *Samson et Dalila*
Satie, Erik	1866–1925	French	Music for piano
Scarlatti, Domenico	1685–1757	Italian	Sonatas for keyboard
Schoenberg, Arnold	1874–1951	German	Music for piano; *Verklarte Nacht;* Song Cycle: *Pierrot Lunaire*
Schubert, Franz	1797–1828	Austrian	*Rosamunde;* Song Cycle: *Die Schone Mullerin;* Various symphonies
Schumann, Robert	1810–1856	German	Music for piano; Concerto for Cello; Song Cycle: *Dichterliebe*
Schütz, Heinrich	1585–1672	German	*Symphoniæ sacræ;* three Passions
Scriabin, Alexander	1872–1915	Russian	Music for piano
Sessions, Roger	1896–1985	American	Concerto for Orchestra; Various symphonies
Shostakovich, Dmitri	1906–1975	Russian	Various concertos and symphonies; Music for piano
Sibelius, Jean	1865–1957	Finnish	Concerto for Violin; *Finlandia;* Various symphonies
Smetena, Bedrich	1824–1884	Czech	*Ma Vlast* (including "The Moldau"); Opera: *The Bartered Bride;* Various quartets
Sondheim, Stephen	1930–	American	Musicals: *Company; Sweeney Todd; Passion*
Stockhausen, Karlheinz	1928–	German	*Klavierstucke; Kontakte*
Strauss, Johann, II	1825–1899	Austrian	Various waltzes; Opera: *Die Fledermaus*
Strauss, Richard	1864–1949	German	*Also Sprach Zarathustra; Don Juan;* Opera: *Der Rosenkavalier*
Stravinsky, Igor	1882–1971	Russian-born American	Ballets: *The Firebird; The Rite of Spring;* Opera: *The Rake's Progress*
Sullivan, Arthur	1842–1900	English	Operas (collab. W. S. Gilbert): *H.M.S. Pinafore; The Pirates of Penzance; The Mikado*
Szymanowski, Karol	1882–1937	Polish	Concertos for Violin; Various string quartets
Takemitsu, Toru	1930–1996	Japanese	*November Steps; River Run*
Tallis, Thomas	c.1505–1585	English	Sacred choral music
Taverner, John	c.1490–1545	English	Festal masses
Tchaikovsky, Pyotr Ilyich	1840–1893	Russian	*Overture for 1812;* Ballets: *The Nutcracker; Swan Lake*

Telemann, Georg Philipp	1681–1767	German	Various concertos and oratorios; Chamber Music
Thomson, Virgil	1896–1989	American	Operas: (collab. Gertrude Stein) *Four Saints in Three Acts*; *The Mother of Us All*
Varèse, Edgard	1883–1965	French-born American	*Deserts; Ionisation*
Vaughan Williams, Ralph	1872–1958	English	*Fantasia on a theme by Thomas Tallis; Fantasia on Greensleeves*
Verdi, Giuseppe	1813–1901	Italian	*Requiem Mass*; Operas: *La Traviata; Aida*
Victoria, Tomás Luis de	c.1548–1611	Spanish	Various masses and motets
Vivaldi, Antonio	1678–1741	Italian	*Four Seasons; Gloria*; Various concertos
Wagner, Richard	1813–1883	German	Operas: *Tristan und Isolde*; *Der Ring des Nibelungen; Parsifal*
Walton, William	1902–1993	English	Soundtracks: *Henry V*; Operas: *Troilus and Cressida; The Bear*
Weber, Carl Maria von	1786–1826	German	*Invitation to the Dance*; Operas: *Der Freischütz; Oberon*
Webern, Anton	1918–1945	Austrian	*Five Orchestral Pieces*; *Music for String Quartet*
Weill, Kurt	1900–1950	German-born American	Operas: *The Threepenny Opera*; *The Rise and Fall of the City of Mahagonny*; Musicals: *One Touch of Venus*
Zwilich, Ellen Taaffe	1939–	American	*Concerto Grosso*; *Three Movements for Orchestra*

⊙ Maxwell Macmillan International. *Baker's Biographical Dictionary of Musicians.* New York: Schirmer, 1992.

Morta, Brian, and Paula Collins, eds. *Contemporary Composers.* Chicago and London: St. James, 1992.

Sadie, Julie Anne, and Rhian Samuel, eds. *The Norton/Grove Dictionary of Women Composers.* New York: Norton, 1995.

50 Notable Conductors

This list includes conductors of classical and popular orchestral music. It represents a wide range of temperament and style, differing approaches to musical interpretation, and general historical importance to the development of the field.

Name	Dates	Nationality
Abbado, Claudio	1933–	Italian
Ashkenazy, Vladimir	1937–	Russian
Barenboim, Daniel	1942–	Argentine-born Israeli
Beecham, Sir Thomas	1879–1961	British
Bernstein, Leonard	1918–1990	American
Böhm, Karl	1894–1981	Austrian
Caldwell, Sarah	1924–	American
Chailly, Riccardo	1953–	Italian
Chung, Myung-Wha	1953–	Korean-born American
Davies, Dennis Russell	1944–	American
De Sabata, Victor	1892–1967	Italian

50 Notable Conductors *(cont.)*

Name	Dates	Nationality
Dorati, Antal	1906–1988	Hungarian-born American
Dutoit, Charles	1936–	Swiss
Fiedler, Arthur	1894–1979	American
Foss [Fuchs], Lukas	1922–	German-born American
Fricsay, Ferenc	1914–1963	Hungarian-born Austrian
Furtwängler, Wilhelm	1886–1954	German
Gergiev, Valery	1953–	Russian
Groves, Sir Charles	1915–1992	British
Järvi, Neeme	1937–	Estonian
Karajan, Herbert von	1908–1989	German
Kleiber, Carlos	1930–	German-born Austrian
Kleiber, Erich	1890–1956	Austrian
Klemperer, Otto	1885–1973	German
Koussevitzky, Serge	1874–1951	Russian
Kubelik, Rafael	1914–1996	Czech-born Swiss
Leppard, Raymond	1927–	British
Levine, James (Lawrence)	1943–	American
Mahler, Gustav	1860–1911	Austrian
Markevitch, Igor	1912–1983	Russian-born French
Masur, Kurt	1927–	German
Mata, Eduardo	1942–1995	Mexican
Mehta, Zubin	1936–	Indian
Mitropoulos, Dimitri	1896–1960	Greek-born American
Muti, Riccardo	1941–	Italian
Ormandy, Eugene (Blau)	1899–1985	Hungarian-born American
Ozawa, Seiji	1935–	Chinese-born Japanese
Previn, André	1929–	German-born American
Queler, Eve	1936–	American
Rattle, Simon	1955–	British
Salonen, Esa-Pekka	1958–	Finnish
Sargent, Sir (Harold) Malcolm (Watts)	1895–1967	British
Schippers, Thomas	1930–1977	American
Solti, Sir Georg (György)	1912–1997	Hungarian-born British
Stokowski, Leopold	1882–1977	British-born American
Szell, George	1897–1970	Hungarian-born American
Tilson Thomas, Michael	1944–	American
Toscanini, Arturo	1867–1957	Italian-born American
Walter, Bruno [B. W. Schlesinger]	1876–1962	German-born American
Zukerman, Pinchas	1948–	Israeli

⊙ Musiker, Ruben, and Naomi Musiker. *Conductors and Composers of Popular Orchestral Music*. Westport, Conn.: Greenwood, 1998.

Slominsky, Nicolas, and Laura Kuhn, eds. *Baker's Biographical Dictionary of 20th Century Classical Musicians*. New York: Schirmer, 1997.

100 Noted Classical Instrumentalists

The following instrumentalists are listed by instrument, in score order.

Name	Dates	Nationality	Instrument
Argerich, Martha	Argentinian	1941–	piano
Arrau, Claudio	Chilean	1903–1991	piano
Ashkenazy, Vladimir	Russian	1937–	piano
Ax, Emmanuel	American	1949–	piano
Backhaus, Wilhelm	German	1884–1969	piano
Barenboim, Daniel	Argentinian	1942–	piano
Bauer, Harold	British	1873–1951	piano
Brendel, Alfred	Austrian	1931–	piano
Casadesus, Robert	French	1899–1972	piano
Cliburn, Van	American	1934–	piano
Cortot, Alfred	French	1877–1962	piano
Firkusny, Rudolf	Czech	1912–1994	piano
Fischer, Edwin	Swiss	1886–1960	piano
Friedman, Ignaz	Polish	1882–1948	piano
Gieseking, Walter	German	1895–1956	piano
Gilels, Emil	Russian	1916–1985	piano
Godowsky, Leopold	Polish	1870–1938	piano
Gould, Glenn	Canadian	1932–1982	piano
Hess, Myra	British	1890–1965	piano
Hofmann, Josef	Polish	1876–1957	piano
Horowitz, Vladimir	Russian	1903–1989	piano
Johannesen, Grant	American	1921–	piano
Kempff, Wilhelm	German	1895–1991	piano
Kissin, Yevgeny	Russian	1971–	piano
Larrocha, Alicia de	Spanish	1923–	piano
Lhevinne, Joseph	Russian	1874–1944	piano
Lipatti, Dinu	Romanian	1917–1950	piano
Liszt, Franz	Hungarian	1811–1886	piano
Michelangeli, Arturo Benedetti	Italian	1920–1995	piano
Oborin, Lev	Russian	1907–1974	piano
Ohlsson, Garrick	American	1948–	piano
Paderewski, Ignacy Jan	Polish	1860–1941	piano
Rachmaninoff, Serge	Russian	1873–1943	piano
Richter, Sviatoslav	Russian	1915–1997	piano
Rubinstein, Artur	Polish	1887–1982	piano
Schnabel, Arthur	Austrian	1882–1951	piano
Serkin, Rudolf	Austrian	1903–1991	piano
Tureck, Roslyn	American	1914–	piano
Watts, André	American	1946–	piano
Kirkpatrick, Ralph	American	1911–1984	harpsichord

100 Noted Classical Instrumentalists *(cont.)*

Name	Dates	Nationality	Instrument
Landowska, Wanda	Polish	1879–1959	harpsichord
Valenti, Fernando	American	1926–1990	harpsichord
Grandjany, Marcel	American	1891–1975	harp
Salzedo, Carlos	American	1885–1961	harp
Biggs, E. Power	American	1906–1977	organ
Dupré, Marcel	French	1886–1971	organ
Schweitzer, Albert	Swiss	1875–1965	organ
Auer, Leopold	Russian	1845–1930	violin
Bull, Ole	Norwegian	1810–1880	violin
Chang, Sarah	American	1980–	violin
Elman, Mischa	Russian	1891–1967	violin
Francescatti, Zino	French	1902–1991	violin
Grumiaux, Arthur	Belgian	1921–1986	violin
Heifetz, Jascha	American	1901–1987	violin
Joachim, Joseph	German	1831–1907	violin
Kreisler, Fritz	Austrian	1875–1962	violin
Menuhin, Yehudi	American	1916–1999	violin
Midori	Japanese	1971–	violin
Milstein, Nathan	Russian	1904–1992	violin
Mozart, Leopold	Austrian	1719–1787	violin
Mutter, Anne-Sophie	German	1963–	violin
Oistrakh, David	Russian	1908–1974	violin
Paganini, Niccoló	Italian	1782–1840	violin
Perlman, Itzhak	Israeli	1945–	violin
Ricci, Ruggiero	American	1918–	violin
Salerno-Sonnenberg, Nadja	Italian	19??–	violin
Stern, Isaac	American	1920–	violin
Szigeti, Joseph	Hungarian	1892–1973	violin
Ysaye, Eugene	Belgian	1858–1931	violin
Zimbalist, Efrem	Russian	1890–1985	violin
Aronowitz, Cecil	British	1916–1978	viola
Primrose, William	British	1903–1982	viola
Casals, Pablo	Spanish	1876–1973	violoncello
Du Pré, Jacqueline	British	1945–1987	violoncello
Feuermann, Emmanuel	German	1902–1942	violoncello
Harrell, Lynn	American	1944–	violoncello
Ma, Yo-Yo	American	1955–	violoncello
Piatigorsky, Gregor	Russian	1903–1976	violoncello
Popper, David	Czech	1843–1913	violoncello
Rostropovich, Mstislav	Russian	1927–	violoncello
Starker, Janos	Hungarian	1924–	violoncello

Koussevitzky, Serge	Russian	1874–1951	double bass
Giuliani, Mauro	Italian	1781–1829	guitar
Segovia, Andrés	Spanish	1893–1987	guitar
Williams, John	Australian	1941–	guitar
Galway, James	Irish	1939–	flute
Rampal, Jean-Pierre	French	1922–2000	flute
Goossens, Leon	British	1897–1988	oboe
Holliger, Heinz	Swiss	1939–	oboe
Kell, Reginald	British	1906–1981	clarinet
Stoltzman, Richard	American	1942–	clarinet
Camden, Archie	British	1888–1979	bassoon
Weisberg, Arthur	American	19??–	bassoon
Brain, Dennis	British	1921–1957	horn
Tuckwell, Barry	Australian	1931–	horn
André, Maurice	French	1933–	trumpet
Marsalis, Wynton	American	1961–	trumpet
Pryor, Arthur	American	1870–1942	trombone
Phillips, Harvey	American	1929–	tuba

⊙ Cummings, David, ed. *Random House Encyclopedic Dictionary of Classical Music*. New York: Random House, 1997.

Kennedy, Michael, ed. *The Concise Oxford Dictionary of Music*. Oxford and New York: Oxford University Press, 1996.

International Directory of Musicians. "Instrumental soloists, groups and conductors," www.musicbase.org/instrumental.html.

50 Major Classical Singers

Singers on this list represent a broad range of vocal styles and approaches to classical repertory. They range from performers whose popularity has endured for decades to singers whose technical mastery has set the standard for vocal performance.

Name	Dates	Nationality	Range
Angeles, Victoria de los	1923–	Spanish	soprano
Bartoli, Cecilia	1966–	Italian	mezzo-soprano
Battle, Kathleen	1948–	American	soprano
Bergonzi, Carlo	1924–	Italian	tenor
Bocelli, Andrea	1958–	Italian	tenor
Caballé, Montserrat	1933–	Spanish	soprano
Callas, Maria	1923–1977	American	soprano
Calvé, Emma	1858–1942	French	soprano
Carreras, José	1946–	Spanish	tenor
Caruso, Enrico	1873–1921	Italian	tenor
Crespin, Régine	1927–	French	soprano
Domingo, Placido	1941–	Spanish	tenor
Fischer-Dieskau, Dietrich	1925–	German	baritone
Fleming, Renee	1959–	American	soprano
Freni, Mirella	1935–	Italian	soprano

50 Major Classical Singers *(cont.)*

Name	Dates	Nationality	Range
Garden, Mary	1874–1967	Scottish	soprano
Hampson, Thomas	1955–	American	baritone
Hempel, Frieda	1885–1955	German	soprano
Horne, Marilyn	1934–	American	mezzo-soprano
Jurinac, Sena	1921–	Yugoslav	soprano
Lehmann, Lilli	1848–1929	German	soprano
Ludwig, Christa	1928–	German	mezzo-soprano
McCormack, John	1884–1945	Irish	tenor
Melba, Nellie	1861–1931	Australian	soprano
Melchior, Lauritz	1890–1973	Danish	tenor
Milanov, Zinka	1906–1989	Yugoslavian	soprano
Nilsson, Birgit	1918–	Swedish	soprano
Norman, Jessye	1945–	American	soprano
Pavarotti, Luciano	1935–	Italian	tenor
Pears, Peter	1910–1986	English	tenor
Pons, Lily	1898–1976	French	soprano
Ponselle, Rosa	1897–1981	American	soprano
Price, Leontyne	1927–	American	soprano
Ramey, Samuel	1942–	American	bass
Schipa, Tito	1888–1965	Italian	tenor
Schwarzkopf, Elisabeth	1915–	German	soprano
Scotto, Renata	1934–	Italian	soprano
Sembrich, Marcella	1858–1935	Polish	soprano
Sills, Beverly	1929–	American	soprano
Souzay, Gérard	1918–	French	baritone
Stevens, Rise	1913–	American	mezzo-soprano
Stratas, Teresa	1938–	Canadian	soprano
Sutherland, Joan	1926–	Australian	soprano
Te Kanawa, Kiri	1944–	New Zealand	soprano
Tebaldi, Renata	1922–	Italian	soprano
Terfel, Bryn	1965–	Welsh	baritone
Tetrazzini, Luisa	1871–1940	Italian	soprano
Turner, Eva	1892–1990	English	soprano
Vickers, Jon	1926–	Canadian	tenor
Von Stade, Frederica	1945–	American	mezzo-soprano

⊙ Warrack, John, and Ewan West, eds. *Concise Oxford Dictionary of Opera.* New York: Oxford University Press, 1996.

Anderson, James. *The Harper Dictionary of Opera and Operetta.* New York: HarperCollins, 1989.

Kutsch, K. J., and Leo Rieners. *A Concise Biographical Dictionary of Singers.* New York: Chilton, 1969.

These singers and groups represent a range of music styles and periods. "Popular" refers to musicians who redefined the limits of public taste or captured the spirit of the time, as well as those who had high record sales. The songs following each artist are indicative of the vocal and stylistic range of that singer or group.

[Note: Although line-ups often change, each group listing includes the members most commonly associated with that band. Unless otherwise noted, all singers and groups are from the United States.]

Abba [Anni-Fri "Frida" Lyngstad; Agnetha Fältskog; Bjorn Ulvaeus; Benny Andersson], b. Sweden. *Songs:* "Mamma Mia" (1976); "Take A Chance on Me" (1978)

Andrews Sisters, The [Patti, Maxine, and LaVerne Andrews]. *Songs:* "Boogie Woogie Bugle Boy" (1940); "Don't Sit Under the Apple Tree (With Anyone Else But Me)" (1942)

Armstrong, Louis "Satchmo" (1901–1971). *Songs:* "Ain't Misbehavin'" (1929); "Hello, Dolly" (1964)

Autry, Gene (1907–1998). *Songs:* "Here Comes Santa Claus" (1947); "Rudolph the Red-Nosed Reindeer" (1949)

Baez, Joan [Joan Chandos Baez] (1941–). *Songs:* "The Night They Drove Old Dixie Down" (1971); "Diamonds and Rust" (1975)

Beach Boys, The [original singers: Brian Wilson; Carl Wilson; Dennis Wilson; Mike Love; Al Jardine]. *Songs:* "California Girls" (1965); "Good Vibrations" (1966)

Beatles, The [John Lennon; Paul McCartney; George Harrison; Ringo Starr], b. England. *Songs:* "I Want to Hold Your Hand" (1964); "Hey Jude" (1968)

Bee Gees [Barry Gibb; Maurice Gibb; Robin Gibb], b. England. *Songs:* "Stayin' Alive" (1977); "Night Fever" (1978)

Bennett, Tony [Anthony Dominick Benedetto] (1926–). *Songs:* "Stranger in Paradise" (1953); "I Left My Heart in San Francisco" (1962)

Blondie [Debbie Harry; Chris Stein; Frank Infante; Jimmy Destri; Nigel Harrison; Clem Burke]. *Songs:* "Heart of Glass" (1979); "Call Me" (1980)

Bowie, David [David Robert Jones] (1947–), b. England. *Songs:* "Space Oddity" (1973); "Let's Dance" (1983)

Brown, James (1928–). *Songs:* "I Got You (I Feel Good)" (1965); "Get Up (I Feel Like Being a Sex Machine)" (1970)

Calloway, Cab [Cabell Calloway] (1907–1997). *Songs:* "Minnie the Moocher" (1931); "Jumpin' Jive" (1939)

Campbell, Glen (1936–). *Songs:* "Wichita Lineman" (1968); "Rhinestone Cowboy" (1975)

Cantor, Eddie [Isadore Itzkowitz] (1892–1964). *Songs:* "Yes, We Have No Bananas" (1923); "Makin' Whoopee" (1928)

Carey, Mariah (1970–). *Songs:* "Dreamlover" (1993); "Endless Love" (1994; with Luther Vandross)

Cher [Cherilyn LaPierre] (1946–) *Songs:* "If I Could Turn Back Time" (1989); "Believe" (1998)

Chicago [Peter Cetera; Robert Lamm; James Pankow; Lee Loughnane; Terry Kath; Walt Parazaider; Danny Seraphine]. *Songs:* "Does Anybody Really Know What Time It Is?" (1970); "Hard To Say I'm Sorry" (1982)

Cline, Patsy [Virginia Paterson Hensley] (1932–1963). *Songs:* "Walkin' After Midnight" (1957); "Crazy" (1961)

Cole, Nat "King" (1917–1965). *Songs:* "Mona Lisa" (1949); "Unforgettable" (1952)

Collins, Phil (1951–), b. England. *Songs:* "Against All Odds (Take a Look at Me Now)" (1984); "You'll Be in My Heart" (1999)

Como, Perry (1912–). *Songs:* "Papa Loves Mambo" (1954); "Hot Diggity (Dog Ziggity Boom)" (1956)

Credence Clearwater Revival [John Fogerty; Tom Fogerty; Stu Cook; Doug Clifford]. *Songs:* "Proud Mary" (1969); "Have Your Ever Seen the Rain?" (1971)

Crosby, Bing [Harry Ellis] (1903–1977). *Songs:* "White Christmas" (1942); "Singing on a Star" (1944)

Darin, Bobby (1936–1973). *Songs:* "Splish Splash" (1958); "Mack the Knife" (1959)

Denver, John (1943–1997). *Songs:* "Take Me Home, Country Roads" (1971); "Sunshine on My Shoulders" (1974)

Diamond, Neil (1941–). *Songs:* "Sweet Caroline (Good Times Never Seemed So Good)" (1969); "Cracklin' Rosie" (1970)

Dion, Celine (1968–), b. Canada. *Songs:* "Beauty and the Beast" (1992; with Peabo Bryson); "My Heart Will Go On" (1997)

Doors, The [Jim Morrison; Ray Manzarek; Robby Krieger; John Densmore]. *Songs:* "Light My Fire" (1967); "Riders on the Storm" (1971)

Drifters, The [lead singers: Clyde McPhatter; Ben E. King; Rudy Lewis; Johnny Moore]. *Songs:* "There Goes My Baby" (1959); "Under the Boardwalk" (1964)

Dylan, Bob [Robert Zimmerman] (1941–). *Songs:* "Blowin' in the Wind" (1963); "Like a Rolling Stone" (1965)

Eagles, The [Glenn Frey; Don Henley; Randy Meisner; Bernie Leadon]. *Songs:* "Take It to the Limit" (1976); "Hotel California" (1977)

Estefan, Gloria [Gloria Fajardo] (1957–). *Songs:* [with Miami Sound Machine:] "Rhythm is Gonna Get You" (1987); [solo:] "Turn the Beat Around" (1994)

Eurythmics [Annie Lennox; Dave Stewart], b. England. *Songs:* "Sweet Dreams (Are Made of This)" (1983); "Sisters Are Doing It For Themselves" (1985; with Aretha Franklin)

Fitzgerald, Ella (1918–1996). *Songs:* "A-Tisket, A-Tasket" (1938); Various composers' songbooks

Franklin, Aretha (1942–). *Songs:* "Respect" (1967); "(You Make Me Feel Like) A Natural Woman" (1967)

Garland, Judy [Frances Gumm] (1922–1969). *Songs:* "Over the Rainbow" (1939); "Get Happy" (1951)

Gaye, Marvin [Marvin Pentz Gay, Jr.] (1939–1984). *Songs:* "Ain't No Mountain High Enough" (1967; with Tammi Terrell); "What's Going On" (1971)

Guns N' Roses [W. Axl Rose; Michael "Duff" McKagan; Izzy Stradlin'; Slash; Steven Adler]. *Songs:* "Sweet Child O' Mine" (1988); "Welcome to the Jungle" (1988)

Haley, Bill (1925–1981) **and His Comets.** *Songs:* "(We're Gonna) Rock Around the Clock" (1955); "See You Later, Alligator" (1956)

Hall, Daryl [Daryl Franklin Hohl] (1948–) **and John Oates** (1949–). *Songs:* "Kiss On My List" (1981); "I Can't Go For That (No Can Do)" (1981)

Holiday, Billie [Eleanor Gough McKay] (1915–1959). *Songs:* "Strange Fruit" (1939); "God Bless the Child" (1940)

Holly, Buddy (1936–1959) **and the Crickets.** *Songs:* "Peggy Sue" (1957); "Maybe Baby" (1958)

Horne, Lena (1917–). *Songs:* "Stormy Weather" (1943); "If You Can Dream" (1956)

Houston, Whitney (1963–). *Songs:* "Greatest Love of All" (1986); "It's Not Right But It's Okay" (1999)

Jackson, Janet (1966–). *Songs:* "What Have You Done For Me Lately" (1986); "Rhythm Nation" (1989)

Jackson, Michael (1958–). *Songs:* "Beat It" (1983); "Black or White" (1991)

Joel, Billy (1949–). *Songs:* "Piano Man" (1974); "Only the Good Die Young" (1978)

John, Elton [Reginald Kenneth Dwight] (1947–), b. England. *Songs:* "Rocket Man" (1972); "Candle in the Wind" (1997)

Jones, Tom [Tom Jones Woodward] (1940–), b. South Wales. *Songs:* "It's Not Unusual" (1965); "She's a Lady" (1972)

Knight, Gladys (1944–) **and the Pips** [Merald "Bubba" Knight; Edward Patten; Langston George]. *Songs:* "Midnight Train to Georgia" (1973); "That's What Friends Are For" (1985; with Dionne Warwick, Elton John, and Stevie Wonder)

Lee, Peggy [Norma Egstrom] (1920–). *Songs:* "I Got It Bad And That Ain't Good" (1942); "Fever" (1958)

Lennon, John (1940–1980), b. England. *Songs:* "Give Peace a Chance" (1969); "Imagine" (1971)

Lewis, Jerry Lee (1935–). *Songs:* "Great Balls of Fire" (1957); "Breathless" (1958)

Lynn, Loretta (1935–). *Songs:* "Blue Kentucky Girl" (1965); "Coal Miner's Daughter" (1969)

Madonna [Madonna Louise Ciccone] (1958–). *Songs:* "Material Girl" (1985); "Ray of Light" (1998)

Manilow, Barry [Barry Alan Pincus] (1946–). *Songs:* "I Write the Songs" (1975); "Copacabana (At the Copa)" (1978)

Mathis, Johnny (1935–). *Songs:* "Chances Are" (1957); "Misty" (1959)

Midler, Bette (1945–). *Songs:* "The Rose" (1980); "Wind Beneath My Wings" (1989)

Miracles, The [William "Smokey" Robinson; Emerson Rogers; Bobby Rogers; Ronnie White; Warren "Pete" Moore]. *Songs:* "The Tracks of My Tears" (1965); "I Second That Emotion" (1967)

Moody Blues, The [Justin Hayward; John Lodge; Ray Thomas; Mike Pinder; Graeme Edge], b. England. *Songs:* "Nights in White Satin" (1967); "I'm Just a Singer (In a Rock and Roll Band)" (1973)

Murray, Anne [Morna Anne Murray] (1945–), b. Canada. *Songs:* "Danny's Song" (1973); "You Needed Me" (1978)

Newton-John, Olivia (1948–), b. Australia. *Songs:* "I Honestly Love You" (1974); "Physical" (1981)

Nirvana [Kurt Cobain; Krist Novoselic; Dave Grohl]. *Songs:* "Smells Like Teen Spirit" (1991); "All Apologies" (1993)

Orbison, Roy (1936–1988). *Songs:* "In Dreams" (1963); "Oh, Pretty Woman" (1964)

Parton, Dolly (1946–). *Songs:* "Heartbreaker" (1978); "Islands in the Stream" (1983, with Kenny Rogers)

Peter, Paul and Mary [Peter Yarrow; Paul Stookey; Mary Travers]. *Songs:* "If I Had a Hammer (The Hammer Song)" (1962); "Blowin' in the Wind" (1963)

Pink Floyd [Roger Waters; Syd Barrett; Nick Mason; Rick Wright; Dave Gilmor], b. England. *Songs:* "Money" (1973); "Comfortably Numb" (1979)

Presley, Elvis (1935–1977). *Songs:* "Heartbreak Hotel" (1956); "Burning Love" (1972)

Prince [Prince Roger Nelson; also "The Artist Formerly Known As Prince"] (1958–). *Songs:* "Little Red Corvette" (1982); "Cream" (1991)

Queen [Freddie Mercury (b. Zanzibar); Brian May; John Deacon; Roger Taylor], b. England. *Songs:* "Bohemian Rhapsody" (1976); "Another One Bites the Dust" (1980)

Reddy, Helen (1941–), b. Australia. *Songs:* "I Am Woman" (1972); "Delta Dawn" (1973)

Richie, Lionel (1949–). *Songs:* "All Night Long (All Night)" (1983); "Hello" (1984)

Righteous Brothers, The [Bill Medley; Bobby Hatfield]. *Songs:* "You've Lost That Lovin' Feelin'" (1964); "(You're My) Soul and Inspiration" (1966)

Rogers, Kenny [Kenneth Donald Rogers] (1938–). *Songs:* "The Gambler" (1978); "Coward of the County" (1980)

Rolling Stones, The [Mick Jagger; Keith Richards; Brian Jones; Bill Wyman; Charlie Watts], b. England. *Songs:* "(I Can't Get No) Satisfaction" (1965); "Start Me Up" (1981)

Ronstadt, Linda (1946–). *Songs:* "You're No Good" (1975); "Hurt So Bad" (1980)

Ross, Diana [Diane Earle] (1944–). *Songs:* "Theme From *Mahogany* (Do You Know Where You're Going To?)" (1975); "I'm Coming Out" (1980)

Simon and Garfunkel [Paul Simon; Art Garfunkel]. *Songs:* "The Sounds of Silence" (1965); "Mrs. Robinson" (1968)

Simon, Carly (1945–). *Songs:* "You're So Vain" (1972); "Nobody Does It Better" (1977)

Simon, Paul (1941–). *Songs:* "50 Ways to Leave Your Lover" (1976); "You Can Call Me Al" (1986)

Sinatra, Frank [Francis Albert Sinatra] (1915–1998). *Songs:* "Young at Heart" (1953); "My Way" (1969)

Sly and the Family Stone [Sylvester "Sly Stone" Stewart; Freddie Stone; Cynthia Robinson; Jerry Martini; Rosie Stone; Larry Graham; Gregg Errico]. *Songs:* "Dance to the Music" (1968); "Everyday People" (1969)

Smith, Bessie (1894–1937). *Songs:* "'Taint Nobody's Bizness If I Do" (1923); "St. Louis Blues" (1925)

Springfield, Dusty [Mary O'Brien] (1939–1999), b. England. *Songs:* "Son of a Preacher Man" (1969); "The Windmills of Your Mind" (1969)

Springsteen, Bruce (1949–). *Songs:* "Born to Run" (1975); "Born in the USA" (1984)

Stewart, Rod [Roderick Stewart] (1945–), b. England. *Songs:* "Tonight's the Night (Gonna Be Alright)" (1976); "Have I Told You Lately" (1993)

Streisand, Barbra [Barbara Joan Streisand] (1942–). *Songs:* "The Way We Were" (1973); "Love Theme from 'A Star is Born' (Evergreen)" (1977)

Summer, Donna [Adrian Donna Gaines] (1948–). *Songs:* "Last Dance" (1978); "Bad Girls" (1979)

Supremes, The [Diana Ross; Mary Wilson; Florence Ballard; Cindy Birdsong]. *Songs:* "Stop! In the Name of Love" (1965); "You Keep Me Hangin' On" (1966)

Taylor, James (1948–). *Songs:* "Fire and Rain" (1970); "How Sweet It Is (To Be Loved by You)" (1975)

Tormé, Mel [Melvin Howard Tormé] (1925–). *Songs:* "The Christmas Song (Chestnuts Roasting on an Open Fire)" (1946); "Careless Hands" (1949)

Turner, Tina (1938–). *Songs:* "What's Love Got to Do With It" (1984); "Typical Male" (1986)

Vallee, Rudy (1901–1986). *Songs:* "My Time is Your Time" (1929); "I'm Just a Vagabond Lover" (1930)

Waller, Thomas "Fats" (1904–1943). *Songs:* "Ain't Misbehavin'" (1929); "Honeysuckle Rose" (1929)

Warwick(e), Dionne [Marie Dionne Warwick] (1940–). *Songs:* "Don't Make Me Over" (1963); "(Theme From) Valley of the Dolls" (1968)

Waters, Ethel (1896–1977). *Songs:* "Heat Wave" (1933); "Cabin in the Sky" (1940)

Who, The [Roger Daltrey, John Entwhistle, Keith Moon, Pete Townsend], b. England. *Songs:* "I Can't Explain" (1965); "Pinball Wizard" (1969)

Wonder, Stevie [Steveland Morris] (1950–). *Songs:* "My Cherie Amour" (1969); "I Just Called to Say I Love You" (1984)

Wynette, Tammy (1942–1998). *Songs:* "Stand By Your Man" (1968); "D-I-V-O-R-C-E" (1968)

⊙ Buckley, Jonathan, and Mark Ellington, eds. *The Rough Guide to Rock.* London: Rough Guides, 1996.

Hardy, Phil, and Dave Laing, eds. *The Faber Companion to 20th-Century Popular Music.* Boston: Faber and Faber, 1990.

Romanowski, Patricia, and Holly George-Warren, eds. *The New Rolling Stone Encyclopedia of Rock & Roll.* New York: Fireside, 1995.

75 Major Jazz Musicians

This section lists jazz musicians of a variety of styles and periods, included here because of their significance to the development of jazz and their mastery of their chosen instrument (many are also composers). They are American unless otherwise noted.
Instruments are listed in order of prominence in each musician's work. For selected jazz vocalists, see 100 Popular Singers and Music Groups.

Name	Dates	Instrument(s)
Adderly, Cannonball	1928–1975	alto/soprano sax
Allen, Red	1908–1967	trumpet
Ammons, Gene	1925–1974	tenor sax
Armstrong, Louis	1901–1971	trumpet, vocals
Bailey, Buster	1902–1967	clarinet
Baker, Chet	1929–1988	trumpet, vocals
Basie, Count	1904–1984	piano, organ
Bechet, Sidney	1897–1959	soprano sax, clarinet
Biederbecke, Bix	1903–1931	cornet, piano
Blakey, Art	1919–1990	drums
Blanton, Jimmy	1918–1942	bass
Brown, Clifford	1930–1956	trumpet
Brubeck, Dave	1920–	piano
Carter, Benny	1907–	alto sax, trumpet
Charles, Ray	1930–	piano, alto sax, vocals
Cheatham, Doc	1905–1997	trumpet, vocals
Christian, Charlie	1916–1942	guitar
Clarke, Kenny	1914–1985	drums
Cole, Nat "King"	1917–1965	piano, vocals
Coleman, Ornette	1930–	alto/tenor sax, trumpet, violin
Coltrane, John	1926–1967	tenor/soprano sax
Corea, Chick	1941–	piano, keyboards

75 Major Jazz Musicians *(cont.)*

Name	Dates	Instrument(s)
Davis, Miles	1926–1991	trumpet, flugelhorn
Desmond, Paul	1924–1977	alto sax
Dolphy, Eric	1928–1964	alto sax, clarinet/bass clarinet, flute
Dorham, Kenny	1924–1972	trumpet
Dorsey, Tommy	1905–1956	trombone
Eldridge, Roy	1911–1989	trumpet, flute, covals, drums
Ellington, Duke	1899–1974	piano
Evans, Bill	1929–1980	piano
Farmer, Art	1928–	trumpet, flugelhorn, flumpet
Getz, Stan	1927–1991	tenor sax
Gillespie, Dizzy	1917–1993	trumpet, vocals, piano
Goodman, Benny	1909–1986	clarinet
Gordon, Dexter	1923–1990	tenor/soprano sax
Grappelli, Stephane French,	1908–1997	violin, piano
Hampton, Lionel	1908–	vibraphone, drums, piano, vocals
Hancock, Herbie	1940–	piano, keyboards
Hawkins, Coleman	1904–1969	tenor sax
Henderson, Joe	1937–	tenor/soprano sax, flute
Hines, Earl	1903–1983	piano
Hinton, Milt	1910–	bass
Hodges, Johnny	1906–1970	alto/soprano sax
Hutcherson, Bobby	1941–	vibraphone, marimba
Jackson, Milt	1923–	vibraphone, piano, vocals, guitar
Jacquet, Illinois	1922–	tenor/alto sax, bassoon
Johnson, J. J. (James Louis)	1924–	trombone
Jones, Philly Joe	1923–1985	drums
Kirk, Rahsaan Roland stritch, clarinet, trumpet	1936–1977	flugelhorn, tenor sax, manzello,
Marsalis, Wynton	1961–	trumpet
Mingus, Charles Jr.	1922–1979	bass, piano
Mobley, Hank	1930–1986	tenor sax
Monk, Thelonious Sphere	1917–1982	piano
Montgomery, Wes	1925–1968	guitar
Morgan, Lee	1938–1972	trumpet
Navarro, Fats	1923–1950	trumpet
Oliver, King (Joe)	1885–1938	coronet
Parker, Charlie "Bird"	1920–1955	tenor/alto sax
Peterson, Oscar Canadian,	1925–	piano
Powell, Bud	1924–1966	piano
Redman, Don	1900–1964	sax, vocals
Reinhardt, Django Belgian,	1910–1953	guitar
Roach, Max	1924–	drums

Rollins, Sonny	1930–	tenor sax
Silver, Horace	1928–	piano
Sims, Zoot	1925–1985	tenor/alto/soprano sax, clarinet
Smith, Jimmy	1925–	organ
Smith, Stuff	1909–1967	violin, vocals
Stewart, Slam (Leroy)	1914–1987	bass
Tatum, Art	1909–1956	piano
Tyner, McCoy	1938–	piano
Waller, Fats (Thomas)	1904–1943	piano, organ, vocals
Webster, Ben	1909–1973	tenor sax
Williams, Tony	1945–1997	drums
Young, Lester	1909–1959	tenor sax, clarinet

⊙ Feather, Leonard, and Ira Gitler. *The Biographical Encyclopedia of Jazz.* New York: Oxford University Press, 1999.

ARTS AND LEISURE: *Opera*

100 Major Operas

This list contains operas from a variety of historical periods and spans compositional styles from classical to modern to experimental. The choices often represent the stylistic pinnacles of their composers' musical idioms. Also included are operas whose enduring popularity has ensured them a place in the standard repertory, as well as works of critical importance in the evolution of the art form.

Opera*	Composer	Premiere
Africaine, L'	Giacomo Meyerbeer	1865
Aïda	Giuseppe Verdi	1871
Amahl and the Night Visitors	Gian Carlo Menotti	1951
Antony and Cleopatra	Samuel Barber	1966
Aoki okami (The Dark Blue Wolf)	Saburo Takata	1972
Ariadne auf Naxos	Richard Strauss	1916
Armida	Joseph Hayden	1784
Aufstieg und Fall der Stadt Mahagonny	Kurt Weill	1930
Ballad of Baby Doe, The	Douglas Moore	1956
Barbiere di Siviglia, Il	Gioacchino Rossini	1816
Bartered Bride, The	Bedrich Smetana	1866
Béatrice et Bénédict	Hector Berlioz	1862
Beggar's Opera, The	John Gay	1728
Billy Budd	Benjamin Britten	1951
Bluebeard's Castle	Béla Bartók	1918
Bohème, La	Giacomo Puccini	1896
Carmen	Georges Bizet	1875
Cavalleria Rusticana	Pietro Mascagni	1890
Contes d'Hoffmann, Les	Jacques Offenbach	1881
Così fan tutte	Wolfgang Amadeus Mozart	1790
Death in Venice	Benjamin Britten	1973
Devil and Daniel Webster, The	Douglas Moore	1939
Dialogues des Carmélites, Les	Francis Poulenc	1931

100 Major Operas *(cont.)*

Opera*	Composer	Premiere
Dido and Aeneas	Henry Purcell	1689
Don Giovanni	Wolfgang Amadeus Mozart	1787
Don Pasquale	Gaetano Donizetti	1843
Einstein on the Beach	Philip Glass	1976
Elektra	Richard Strauss	1909
Eugene Onegin	Pyotr Ilyich Tchaikovsky	1879
Fairy Queen, The	Henry Purcell	1692
Faust	Charles Gounod	1859
Favola d'Orfeo, La	Claudio Monteverdi	1607
Fidelio	Ludwig van Beethoven	1814
Fledermaus, Die	Johann Strauss	1874
Fliegende Holländer, Der	Richard Wagner	1843
Four Saints in Three Acts	Virgil Thomson	1934
Giocanda, La	Amilcare Ponchielli	1876
Giulio Cesare in Egitto	George Frideric Handel	1724
Götterdämmerung	Richard Wagner	1876
Guillaume Tell	Gioacchino Rossini	1829
Hamlet	Ambrose Thomas	1868
Hänsel und Gretel	Englebert Humperdinck	1893
Háry János	Zoltán Kodály	1926
Iphigénie en Aulide	Christoph Willibald Gluck	1774
Iphigénie en Tauride	Christoph Willibald Gluck	1779
King Priam	Michael Tippett	1962
Lady Macbeth of Mtsensk	Dmitri Shostakovich	1934
Lakmé	Léo Delibes	1883
Le Nozze di Figaro, Le	Wolfgang Amadeus Mozart	1786
Lohengrin	Richard Wagner	1850
Love of Three Oranges, The	Sergei Prokofiev	1921
Lucia di Lammermoor	Gaetano Donizetti	1835
Madama Butterfly	Giacomo Puccini	1904
Maid of Orleans, The	Pyotr Ilyich Tchaikovsky	1887
Makropulos Affair, The	Leos Janácek	1926
Mamelles de Tirésias, Les	Francis Poulenc	1947
Manon	Jules Massenet	1884
Manon Lescaut	Giacomo Puccini	1893
Midsummer's Night Dream, A	Benjamin Britten	1961
Mikado, The	Arthur Sullivan (collab. W. S. Gilbert)	1885
Moses und Aron	Arnold Schoenberg	1954
Oberon	Carl Maria von Weber	1826
Orfeo ed Euridice	Christoph Willibald Gluck	1762
Orphée aux Enfers	Jacques Offenbach	1858
Otello	Giuseppe Verdi	1887
Pagliacci, I	Ruggiero Leoncavallo	1892
Parsifal	Richard Wagner	1882
Pêcheurs de Perles, Les	Georges Bizet	1863
Pélleas et Mélisande	Claude Debussy	1902
Peter Grimes	Benjamin Britten	1945
Pilgrim's Progress, The	Ralph Vaughan Williams	1951

ARTS AND LEISURE: *Opera*

Pirates of Penzance, The	Arthur Sullivan (collab. W. S. Gilbert)	1879
Prince Igor	Alexander Borodin	1890
Rake's Progress, The	Igor Stravinsky	1951
Rheingold, Das	Richard Wagner	1869
Rigoletto	Giuseppe Verdi	1851
Ritorno d'Ulisse in Patria, Il	Claudio Monteverdi	1640
Roméo et Juliette	Charles Gounod	1867
Rosenkavalier, Der	Richard Strauss	1911
Rusalka	Antonín Dvorak	1901
Salome	Richard Strauss	1905
Samson et Dalila	Camille Saint-Saëns	1877
Serse	George Frideric Handel	1738
Serva padrona, La	Giovanni Battista Pergolesi	1733
Siegfried	Richard Wagner	1876
Snow Maiden, The	Nikolai Rimsky-Korsakov	1882
Sonnambula, La	Vincenzo Bellini	1835
Tosca	Giacomo Puccini	1900
Traviata, La	Giuseppe Verdi	1853
Tristan und Isolde	Richard Wagner	1865
Troilus and Cressida	William Walton	1954
Trovatore, Il	Giuseppe Verdi	1853
Troyens, Les	Hector Berlioz	1890
Turandot	Giacomo Puccini	1926
Walküre, Die	Richard Wagner	1870
War and Peace	Sergei Prokofiev	1945
Werther	Jules Massenet	1892
Wozzeck	Alban Berg	1925
Yuzuru (The Twilight Heron)	Ikuma Dan	1952
Zauberflöte, Die	Wolfgang Amadeus Mozart	1791

*Most German, French, and Italian titles have been left in the original language. Most Russian, eastern European, and Japanese titles have been translated.

⊙ Boyden, Matthew. *Opera: The Rough Guide*. London: Rough Guides, 1999.
   Larue, C. Steven, ed. *The International Dictionary of Opera*. Detroit & London: St. James, 1993.
   Mondadori, Arnoldo, ed. *The Simon and Schuster Book of the Opera*. New York: Simon & Schuster, 1977.

25 Major Opera-Producing Organizations

Opera Company/House	Location	Year Established
Bayerische Staatsoper	Munich, Germany	1818
Bayreuth Festspiele	Bayreuth, Germany	1876
Bolshoi Theatre	Moscow, Russia	1825
Boston Lyric Opera	Boston, Massachusetts	1976
English National Opera	London, England	1974
Glyndebourne Festival Opera	Glyndebourne, England	1994
Houston Grand Opera	Houston, Texas	1955
Lyric Opera of Chicago	Chicago, Illinois	1954
Metropolitan Opera Association	New York, New York	1883

25 Major Opera Producing Organizations *(cont.)*

Opera Company/House	Location	Year Established
New National Theatre	Tokyo, Japan	1997
New York City Opera	New York, New York	1944
Opera Australia, Sydney	Sydney, Australia	1996
Opera National de Paris	Paris, France	1875
Opera-Comique	Paris, France	1714
Royal Opera House	London, England	1858
Royal Swedish Opera	Stockholm, Sweden	1773
Salzburger Festspiele	Salzburg, Germany	1927
San Francisco Opera	San Francisco, California	1923
Santa Fe Opera	Santa Fe, New Mexico	1957
Seattle Opera Association	Seattle, Washington	1964
Spoleto Festival USA	Charleston, South Carolina	1977
Teatro alla Scala	Milan, Italy	1778
Teatro Colon	Buenos Aires, Argentina	1908
Teatro dell'Opera	Rome, Italy	1946
Wiener Staatsoper	Vienna, Austria	1869

⊙ Kuhn, Laura. *Baker's Dictionary of Opera*. New York: Schirmer, 2000.

Orrey, Leslie, ed. *The Encyclopedia of Opera*. New York: Scribner's, 1976.

Warrack, John, and Ewan West. *The Oxford Dictionary of Opera*. New York: Oxford University Press, 1992.

ARTS AND LEISURE: *Dance*
25 Major Ballets

The following ballets are drawn from a range of historical periods, musical styles, and choreographic idioms. Selections include classical works, groundbreaking modernist experiments, and Broadway musicals.

Ballet	Choreographer	Composer	Premiere
Afternoon of a Faun	Vaslav Nijinsky	Claude Debussy	1912
Apollo (Apollon Musagete)	George Balanchine	Igor Stravinsky	1928
Appalachian Spring	Martha Graham	Aaron Copland	1944
Billy the Kid	Eugene Loring	Aaron Copland	1938
Coppelia	Arthur Saint-Léon	Léo Delibes	1870
Daphnis et Chloe	Michel Fokine	Maurice Ravel	1912
Don Quixote	Marius Petipa and Aleksandr Gorsky	Ludwig Minkus	1869
Fall River Legend	Agnes de Mille	Morton Gould	1948
Fancy Free	Jerome Robbins	Leonard Bernstein	1944
Firebird	Michel Fokine	Igor Stravinsky	1911
Giselle	Jean Corralli; Jules Perrot; Marius Petipa	Adolphe Adam	1841
La Bayadere	Marius Petipa	Ludwig Minkus	1877
La Valse	George Balanchine	*Valses Nobles et Sentimentales* (1911, orchestrated 1912); *La Valse* (1920), by Maurice Ravel	1951
Le Cigne (The Dying Swan)	Michel Fokine	Camille Saint-Saëns (from *Carnival of the Animals*)	1905
Le Sacre du Printemps/ The Rite of Spring	Vaslav Nijinsky	Igor Stravinsky	1913

Le Spectre de la Rose	Michel Fokine	Carl-Maria von Weber (from *Invitation to the Dance*)	1911
Les Sylphides	Michel Fokine	Frederic Chopin	1909
Nutcracker, The	Marius Petipa	Peter Ilyich Tchaikovsky	1892
Petrouchka	Michel Fokine	Igor Stravinsky	1911
Rodeo	Agnes de Mille	Aaron Copeland	1942
Romeo and Juliet	Leonid Lavrovsky	Sergei Prokofiev	1940
Slaughter on Tenth Avenue	George Balanchine	Richard Rodgers	1936
Sleeping Beauty, The	Marius Petipa	Peter Ilyich Tchaikovsky	1890
Swan Lake	Marius Petipa; Lev Ivanov	Peter Ilyich Tchaikovsky	1895
Sylvia où la Nymphe de Diane	Louis Merante	Léo Delibes	1876

⊙ Clarke, Mary, and Clement Crisp. *The Ballet Goer's Guide*. New York: Knopf, 1981.
Reynolds, Nancy, and Susan Reiner-Torn. *Dance Classics: A Viewer's Guide to the Best-Loved Ballets and Modern Dances*. Pennington, N.J.: a capella books, 1991.

25 Major Dance Companies

Company	Location	Established*
Adventures in Motion Pictures Company	London, England	1987
Alvin Ailey American Dance Theater	New York, New York	1958
American Ballet Theatre	New York, New York	1939
Ballett Frankfurt	Frankfurt, Germany	1984
Béjart Ballet Lausanne	Lausanne, Switzerland	1987
Bill T. Jones/Arnie Zane Dance Company	New York, New York	1982
Bolshoi Theatre	Moscow, Russia	1776
Dance Theatre of Harlem	New York, New York	1969
Feld Ballet/NY	New York, New York	1990
Garth Fagan Dance	Rochester, New York	1991
The Joffrey Ballet	Chicago, Illinois	1956
José Limón Dance Foundation	New York, New York	1945
Kirov Ballet	St. Petersburg, Russia	1935
Mark Morris Dance Group	New York, New York	1980
Martha Graham Dance Company	New York, New York	1926
Merce Cunningham Dance	New York, New York	1953
New York City Ballet	New York, New York	1948
Paris Opera Ballet	Paris, France	1671
Paul Taylor Dance Company	New York, New York	1954
Pilobolus Dance Theatre	Washington Depot, Connecticut	1971
Royal Ballet	London, England	1956
Royal Winnipeg Ballet	Winnipeg, Canada	1939
Streb/Ringside	New York, New York	1985
Tanztheater Wuppertal	Wuppertal, Germany	1978
White Oak Dance Project	White Oak, Georgia	1990

*This list is composed of currently active companies. Because some companies have changed their names since being founded, "Established" refers to the year of the first appearance of the most current name.

⊙ Gaynor Minden, Inc. "Dance Links," www.dancer.com/dance-links/
Reynolds, Nancy, ed. *The Dance Catalog*. New York: Harmony Books, 1979.

75 Noted Dancers and Choreographers

This section features popular, classical, and experimental dancers, dance teams, and choreographers. The list includes popular performers noted for their consummate skill and technique, as well as artists whose work challenges traditional definitions of dance.

Name	Dates	Nation-ality	Genre*, Choreographic Achievements
Ailey, Alvin	1931–1990	American	MD/Ch; *Revelations* (1960), *Cry* (1971)
Ashton, Sir Frederick	1906–1988	British	BD/Ch; *Symphonic Variations* (1947), *Ondine* (1958)
Astaire, Adele	1898–1981	American	SD
Astaire, Fred	1899–1987	American	SD/FD
Balanchine, George	1904–1983	Russian-born American	BD/Ch; *Serenade* (1934), *Agon* (1957)
Baryshnikov, Mikhail	1948–	Russian-born American	BD/SD/FD
Bausch, Pina	1940–	German	PMD/Ch/Filmmaker; *Actions for Dancers* (1971), *Palermo, Palermo* (1990)
Béjart, Maurice	1927–	French	BCh; *Najinski, Clown of God* (1971), *Ring Around the Ring* (1991)
Bennett, Michael	1943–1987	American	SD/Ch/Director; *Company* (1970), *A Chorus Line* (1975)
Beriosova, Svetlana	1932–1998	Russian	BD
Bourne, Matthew	1961–	British	BD/Ch; *Highland Fling* (1994), *Swan Lake* (1995)
Caccialanza, Gisella	1915–1998	American	BD
Castle, Vernon	1887–1918	American	Ballroom dance
Castle, Irene	1893–1969	American	Ballroom dance
Charisse, Cyd	1921–	American	FD
Childs, Lucinda	1940–	American	PMD/Ch; *Museum Piece* (1965), *Einstein on the Beach* (1976)
Coles, Charles (Honi)	1911–1992	American	TD
Cunningham, Merce	1919–	American	MD/Ch; *Summerspace* (1958), *CRWDSPCR* (1993)
de Mille, Agnes	1905–1993	American	BD/Ch; *Oklahoma!* (1943), *Fall River Legend* (1948)
Duncan, Isadora	1878–1927	American	MD/Ch; *Dance Idylles* (1901–1904), *Marche Slave* (1917)
Dunham, Katherine	1910–	American	MD/Ch/Ethnographer; *Cabin in the Sky* (1940), *Rites de Passage* (1941)
Fagan, Garth	1940–	Jamaican-born American	MD/Ch; *From Before* (1978), *The Lion King* (1997)
Farrell, Suzanne	1945–	American	BD
Feld, Eliot	1943–	American	BD/Ch; *At Midnight* (1967)
Fokine, Michel	1880–1942	Russian	BCh; *The Firebird* (1910), *Petrouchka* (1911)
Fonteyn, Margot	1919–1991	British	BD
Fosse, Bob	1927–1987	American	SD/FD/Ch; *Pippin* (1972), *Dancin'* (1978)
Glover, Savion	1973–	American	TD/Ch; *Bring in Da Noise, Bring in Da Funk* (1995)

ARTS AND LEISURE: Dance

Godunov, Alexander	1950–1995	Russian	BD
Goslar, Lotte	1907–1997	German	MD/Mime
Graham, Martha	1893–1991	American	MD/Ch; *Appalachian Spring* (1944), *Clytemnestra* (1958)
Grisi, Carlotta	1819–1899	Italian	BD
Hawkins, Erick	1909–1994	American	BD
Hines, Gregory	1946–	American	TD
Holm, Hanya	1893–1992	German-born American	MD/Ch; *Trend* (1937), *Kiss Me, Kate* (1948)
Horton, Lester	1906–1953	American	MD/Ch/Teacher; *Aztec Ballet* (1934), *Liberian Suite* (1952)
Humphrey, Doris	1895–1958	American	MD/Ch; *The Shakers* (1930), *With My Red Fires* (1936)
Jamison, Judith	1944–	American	MD
Joffrey, Robert	1930–1988	American	BD/Ch; *Pas de Déesses* (1954), *Astarte* (1967)
Jones, Bill T.	1952–	American	MD/Ch; *Last Summer at Uncle Tom's Cabin/The Promised Land* (1990), *Still/Here* (1994)
Kelly, Gene	1912–1996	American	SD/FD/Ch; *On the Town* (1949), *An American in Paris* (1952)
Kirkland, Gelsey	1952–	American	BD
Limón, José	1908–1972	American	MD/Ch; *The Moor's Pavane* (1949), *A Choreographic Offering* (1962)
Lubovitch, Lar	1943–	American	BD/MD/Ch; *Cavalcade* (1980), *The Red Shoes* (1993)
Makarova, Natalia	1940–	Russian	BD
Markova, Alicia	1910–	British	BD
Massine, Léonide	1895–1979	Russian	BD/Ch; *Parade* (1917), *Gaîté Parisienne* (1938)
Mitchell, Arthur	1934–	American	BD/Ch; *Convergences* (1968), *Tones* (1974)
Monk, Meredith	1943–	American	PD/Ch/Composer/Filmmaker; *Quarry* (1976), *American Archaeology #1: Roosevelt Island* (1994)
Morris, Mark	1956–	American	PD/Ch; *Gloria* (1981), *Nixon in China* (1989)
Nicholas, Fayard & Harold (The Nicholas Brothers)	1917– , 1924–2000	American	TD
Nijinsky, Vaslav	1890–1950	Russian	BD/Ch; *L'Aprés-midi d'un faune* (1912), *Le Sacre du printemps* (1913)
Nureyev, Rudolf	1938–1993	Russian	BD
Otake, Eiko and Koma	1952– , 1948–	Japanese	PD/Ch; *New Moon Stories* (1986), *River* (1995)
Pavlova, Anna	1882–1931	Russian	BD
Perrot, Jules	1810–1892	French	BD/Ch; *Giselle* (1841)
Petipa, Marius	1818–1910	French	BD/Ch; *The Sleeping Beauty* (1890)
Plisetskaya, Maya	1925–	Russian	BD
Primus, Pearl	1920–1994	American	MD/Ch; *Strange Fruit* (1945), *Michael, Row Your Boat Ashore* (1979)
Rainer, Yvonne	1934–	American	PD/Ch/Filmmaker; *The Mind is a Muscle* (1966), *This Is the Story of a Woman Who . . .* (1973)
Rivera, Chita	1933–	American	SD

Name	Dates	Nation-ality	Genre*, Choreographic Achievements
Robbins, Jerome	1918–1998	American	BD/SD/Ch; *Fancy Free* (1944), *West Side Story* (1957)
Robinson, Bill Bojangles	1878–1949	American	TD
Rogers, Ginger	1911–1995	American	SD/FD
Shawn, Ted	1891–1972	American	MD/Ch; *Grecian Suite* (1914), *The Kinetic Molpai* (1935)
Spessivtzeva, Olga	1905–1991	Russian	BD
Stroman, Susan	c.1955–	American	SD/Ch; *Crazy for You* (1992), *Contact* (1999)
St. Denis, Ruth	1879–1968	American	MD/Ch/Teacher; *Radha* (1904), *Death and After-Life in India, Greece, and Egypt* (1916, with Ted Shawn)
Taylor, Paul	1930–	American	MD/Ch; *Diggity* (1978), *Musical Offering* (1986)
Tharp, Twyla	1941–	American	MD/Ch; *Push Comes to Shove* (1976), *Jump Start* (1995)
Toumanova, Tamara	1919–1996	Russian	BD
Tudor, Anthony	1908–1987	British	BD/Ch; *Lilac Garden* (1936), *Pillar of Fire* (1942)
Tune, Tommy	1939–	American	SD/Ch/Director; *The Best Little Whorehouse in Texas* (1978), *Grand Hotel* (1989)
Weidman, Charles	1901–1975	American	MD/Ch; *Flickers* (1940), *... And Daddy Was a Fireman* (1941)
Wigman, Mary	1886–1973	German	MD/Ch; *Vision IV: Witch Dance* (1926), *Totenmal* (1930)
Youskevitch, Igor	1912–1994	Russian	BD

* Key to genres:

BD = Ballet dancer	SD = Stage dancer
TD = Tap dancer	FD = Film dancer
MD = Modern dancer	Ch = Choreographer
PMD = Postmodern dancer	BCh = Ballet Choreographer

⊙ Brenser, Martha, ed. *Fifty Contemporary Choreographers*. London and New York: Routledge, 1999.

Cohen-Stratyner, Barbara Naomi. *Biographical Dictionary of Dance*. New York: Schirmer, 1982.

ARTS AND LEISURE: *Theater*

125 Significant American Plays and Musicals

The following plays and musicals cover the wide range of popular American theatre for the past two centuries. The shows on this list include long-running favorites, commercial blockbusters, and critically regarded works. Although not every show had its world premiere in the United States, this list charts the evolving theatrical tastes of the nation and pushes the boundaries of those sensibilities.

Title	Author(s)	Premiere	Performances*	Major Awards**
Abie's Irish Rose	Anne Nichols	1922	2,327	PP
Alison's House	Susan Glaspell	1930	41	
Angels in America:				
Millennium Approaches	Tony Kushner	1993	367	PP; NYDC; TA
Perestroika	Tony Kushner	1993	216	TA
Annie	Book: Thomas Meehan	1977	2,377	NYDC; TA
	Lyrics: Martin Charnin			
	Music: Charles Strouse			
Anything Goes	Book: Guy Bolton, P.G. Wodehouse,	1934	420	
	Howard Lindsay, Russel Crouse			
	Music/Lyrics: Cole Porter			
Arsenic and Old Lace	Joseph Kesselring	1941	1,444	
Bat, The	Mary Robert Rinehart / Avery Hopwood	1920	867	
Black Crook, The	Book: Charles M. Barras	1866	475	
	Music/Lyrics: Various			
Boys in the Band, The	Mart Crowley	1968	1,000	
Brighton Beach Memoirs	Neil Simon	1983	1,299	NYDC
Bring in Da Noise, Bring in Da Funk	Created by Savion Glover / Reg E. Gaine / George C. Wolfe	1996	1,135	
	Music: Anne Duquesnay / Zane Mark / Darryl Waters			
Buried Child	Sam Shepherd	1978	152	PP
Cabaret	Book: Joe Masteroff	1966	1,165	NYDC; TA
	Lyrics: Fred Ebb			
	Music: John Kander			
Cabin in the Sky	Book: John Root	1940	156	
	Lyrics: John Latouche			
	Music: Vernon Duke			
Camelot	Book/Lyrics: Alan Jay Lerner	1960	873	
	Music: Frederick Loewe			
Carousel	Book/Lyrics: Oscar Hammerstein II	1945	890	NYDC
	Music: Richard Rodgers			

Title	Author(s)	Premiere	Performances*	Major Awards**
Cat on a Hot Tin Roof	Tennessee Williams	1955	694	PP; NYDC
Cats	Book/Lyrics: T. S. Eliot	1982	7,485	TA
	Music: Andrew Lloyd Webber			
Children's Hour, The	Lillian Hellman	1934	691	
Chorus Line, A	Book: James Kirkwood / Nicholas Dante	1975	6,137	PP; NYDC; TA
	Lyrics: Edward Kleban			
	Music: Marvin Hamlisch			
Company	Book: George Furth	1970	706	NYDC; TA
	Music/Lyrics: Stephen Sondheim			
Contrast, The	Royall Tyler	1787	[in repertory]	
Cradle Will Rock, The	Book/Music/Lyrics: Marc Blitzstein	1938	108	
Craig's Wife	George Kelly	1925	360	PP
Crimes of the Heart	Beth Henley	1981	535	PP; NYDC
Damn Yankees	Book: George Abbott / Douglass Wallop	1955	1,019	TA
	Music/Lyrics: Richard Adler / Jerry Ross			
Dancin'	Conceived by Bob Fosse	1978	1,774	
Death of a Salesman	Arthur Miller	1949	742	PP; NYDC; TA
Deathtrap	Ira Levin	1978	1,809	
Diary of Anne Frank, The	Frances Goodrich/Albert Hackett	1955	717	PP; NYCDDA; TA
Effect of Gamma Rays on Man-in-the-Moon Marigolds, The	Paul Zindel	1970	819	PP; NYDC
Emperor Jones, The	Eugene O'Neill	1920	204	
Fantasticks, The	Book/Lyrics: Tom Jones	1960	[still running]	
	Music: Harvey Schmidt			
Fashion, or Life in New York	Anna Cora Mowatt	1845	20	
Fences	August Wilson	1987	526	PP; NYDC; TA
Fiddler on the Roof	Book: Joseph Stein	1964	3,242	NYDC; TA
	Lyrics: Sheldon Harnick			
	Music: Jerry Bock			

Title	Credits	Year	Perfs	Awards
Finian's Rainbow	Book: E. Y. Harburg / Fred Saidy Lyrics: E. Y. Harburg Music: Burton Lane	1947	725	
For Colored Girls Who Have Considered Suicide/When the Rainbow Is Enuf	Ntozake Shange	1976	742	
Gin Game, The	D. L. Coburn	1977	517	PP
Glass Menagerie, The	Tennessee Williams	1945	561	NYDC
Glengarry Glen Ross	David Mamet	1984	378	PP; NYDC
Godspell	Conceived by John-Michael Tebelak Music/Lyrics: Stephen Schwartz	1971	2,124	
Grease	Book/Music/Lyrics: Jim Jacobs / Warren Casey	1972	3,388	
Great White Hope, The	Howard Sackler	1968	556	PP; NYDC; TA
Guys And Dolls	Book: Jo Swerling / Abe Burrows Music/Lyrics: Frank Loesser	1950	1,200	NYDC; TA
Gypsy	Book: Arthur Laurents Lyrics: Stephen Sondheim Music: Jules Styne	1959	702	
Hair	Book/Lyrics: Gerome Ragni / James Rado Music: Galt MacDermott	1967	1,836	
Harvey	Mary Chase	1944	1,775	PP
Heidi Chronicles, The	Wendy Wasserstein	1989	621	PP; NYDC; TA
Hello, Dolly!	Book: Michael Stewart Music/Lyrics: Jerry Herman	1964	2,844	NYDC; TA
Hot L Baltimore, The	Lanford Wilson	1973	1,116	NYDC
House of Blue Leaves, The	John Guare	1971	337	NYDC
How I Learned to Drive	Paula Vogel	1997	400	PP; NYDDCA
How to Succeed in Business Without Really Trying	Book: Abe Burrows / Jack Weinstock / Willie Gilbert Music/Lyrics: Frank Loesser	1961	1,417	PP; NYDC; TA

Title	Author(s)	Premiere	Performances*	Major Awards**
Iceman Cometh, The	Eugene O'Neill	1946	136	
Inherit the Wind	Jerome Lawrence / Robert E. Lee	1955	806	
J.B.	Archibald MacLeish	1958	364	PP; TA
King and I, The	*Book/Lyrics:* Oscar Hammerstein II	1951	1,246	TA
	Music: Richard Rodgers			
Kiss Me, Kate	*Book:* Sam and Bella Spewack	1948	1,077	TA
	Music/Lyrics: Cole Porter			
Kiss of the Spider Woman	*Book:* Terrence McNally	1993	906	NYDC; TA
	Lyrics: Fred Ebb			
	Music: John Kander			
Les Misérables	*Book:* Alain Boubil / Claude-Michael Schönberg	1987	[still running]	TA
	Music: Claude-Michael Schönberg			
	Lyrics: Herbert Kretzmer / James Fenton			
Life with Father	*Book:* Howard Lindsay / Russel Crouse	1939	3,224	
Lion King, The	*Music:* Elton John / Hans Zimmer / Lebo M /	1997	[still running]	TA
	Mark Mancina / Jay Rifkin			
	Lyrics: Tim Rice			
Little Foxes, The	Lillian Hellman	1939	410	
Little Mary Sunshine	*Book/Music/Lyrics:* Rick Besoyan	1959	1,143	
Little Shop of Horrors	*Book/Lyrics:* Howard Ashman	1982	2,209	NYDC
	Music: Alan Menken			
Long Day's Journey into Night	Eugene O'Neill	1956	390	PP; NYDC; TA
Lost in Yonkers	Neil Simon	1991	780	PP; TA
Love! Valour! Compassion!	Terrence McNally	1995	249	NYDC; TA
Man of La Mancha	*Book:* Dale Wasserman	1965	2,328	NYDC; TA
	Lyrics: Joe Darion			
	Music: Mitch Leigh			
Man Who Came to Dinner, The	George Kaufmann / Moss Hart	1939	739	
M. Butterfly	David Henry Hwang	1988	777	

Title	Credits	Year	Performances	Awards
Member of the Wedding, The	Carson McCullers	1950	501	NYDC
Mister Roberts	Thomas Heggen / Joshua Logan	1948	1,157	TA
Music Man, The	Book/Music/Lyrics: Meredith Willson	1957	1,375	NYDC; TA
My Fair Lady	Book/Lyrics: Alan Jay Lerner	1956	2,717	NYDC; TA
	Music: Frederick Loewe			
New York Idea, The	Langdon Mitchell	1906	66	
No Place to Be Somebody	Charles Gordone	1969	250	PP
Octoroon, The	Dion Boucicault	1859	48	
Odd Couple, The	Neil Simon	1965	964	
Of Thee I Sing	Book: George S. Kaufman / Morrie Ryskind	1931	444	PP
	Lyrics: Ira Gershwin			
	Music: George Gershwin			
Oh, Calcutta!	Various contributors	1969	1,314	
Oklahoma!	Book/Lyrics: Oscar Hammerstein II	1943	2,212	
	Music: Richard Rodgers			
On the Town	Book/Lyrics: Betty Comden / Adolph Green	1944	463	
	Music: Leonard Bernstein			
One Touch of Venus	Book: S. J. Perelman / Ogden Nash	1943	567	
	Lyrics: Ogden Nash			
	Music: Kurt Weill			
Our American Cousin	Tom Taylor	1858	[in repertory]	
Our Town	Thornton Wilder	1938	336	PP
Pal Joey	Book: John O'Hara	1940	374	
	Lyrics: Lorenz Hart			
	Music: Richard Rodgers			
Phantom of the Opera, The	Book: Richard Stilgoe / Andrew Lloyd Webber	1988	[still running]	TA
	Lyrics: Charles Hart / Richard Stilgoe			
	Music: Andrew Lloyd Webber			
Piano Lesson, The	August Wilson	1990	329	PP; NYDC
Picnic	William Inge	1953	477	PP; NYDC

Title	Author(s)	Premiere	Performances*	Major Awards**
Pippin	Book: Roger O. Hirson Music/Lyrics: Stephen Schwartz	1972	1,944	
Porgy and Bess	Book/Lyrics: Dubose Heyward / Ira Gershwin Music: George Gershwin	1935	124	
Raisin in the Sun, A	Lorraine Hansberry	1959	530	NYDC
Rent	Book/Music/Lyrics: Jonathan Larson	1996	[still running]	PP; TA
Sherlock Holmes	William Gillette	1899	256	
Show Boat	Book/Lyrics: Oscar Hammerstein II Music: Jerome Kern	1927	575	
Shuffle Along	Book: Flournoy Miller / Aubrey Lyles Lyrics: Noble Sissle Music: Eubie Blake	1921	504	
Skin of Our Teeth, The	Thornton Wilder	1942	359	PP
Soldier's Play, A	Charles Fuller	1981	468	PP; NYDC
Sound of Music, The	Book: Howard Lindsay / Russel Crouse Lyrics: Oscar Hammerstein II Music: Richard Rodgers	1959	1,443	TA
South Pacific	Book: Oscar Hammerstein II / Joshua Logan Lyrics: Oscar Hammerstein II Music: Richard Rodgers	1949	1,925	PP; NYDC; TA
Streamers	David Rabe	1976	478	NYDC
Street Scene	Elmer Rice	1929	601	PP
Streetcar Named Desire, A	Tennessee Williams	1947	855	PP; NYDC
Strike Up the Band	Book: Morrie Ryskind / George S. Kaufman Lyrics: Ira Gershwin Music: George Gershwin	1930	191	
Subject Was Roses, The	Frank D.Gilroy	1964	832	PP; NYDC; TA
Sunday in the Park with George	Book: James Lapine Music/Lyrics: Stephen Sondheim	1984	604	PP; NYDC

Sweeney Todd, The Demon Barber of Fleet Street	Book: Hugh Wheeler Music/Lyrics: Stephen Sondheim	1979	557	NYDC; TA
Tea and Sympathy	Robert Anderson	1953	712	
Teahouse of the August Moon, The	John Patrick	1953	1,027	PP; NYDC; TA
Ten Nights in a Barroom	William W. Pratt	1858	7	
That Championship Season	Jason Miller	1972	844	PP; NYDC; TA
Three Men on a Horse	John Cecil Holm / George Abbott	1935	835	
Three Tall Women	Edward Albee	1994	582	PP; NYDC
Time of Your Life, The	William Saroyan	1939	185	PP; NYDC
Tobacco Road	Jack Kirkland	1933	3,182	
Torch Song Trilogy	Harvey Fierstein	1982	1,222	TA
Uncle Tom's Cabin	George L. Aiken	1853	325	
Waiting For Lefty	Clifford Odets	1935	168	
West Side Story	Book: Arthur Laurents Lyrics: Stephen Sondheim Music: Leonard Bernstein	1957	734	
Who's Afraid of Virginia Woolf?	Edward Albee	1962	664	NYDC; TA
Women, The	Clare Boothe Luce	1936	657	
You Can't Take It With You	George S. Kaufman / Moss Hart	1936	837	PP
You're a Good Man, Charlie Brown	Book/Music/Lyrics: Clark Gesner	1967	1,597	

*As of October 15, 2000. Performances in the original New York City run (Broadway, Off-Broadway, etc.), where applicable. In instances where the production transferred from a non-profit theatre to a commercial run, the number of performances in the longer run is given.

**PP=Pulitzer Prize; NYDC=New York Drama Critics Circle Award; TA=Antoinette Perry (Tony) Award for Best Play or Best Musical

© Bordman, Gerald. *The Oxford Companion to American Theatre.* New York: Oxford University Press, 1992.
   Brown, Gene. *Show Time.* New York: Macmillan, 1997.
   Theatre.com. "Theatre.com New York Theatre Awards," www.theatre.com/awards/

Major Regional Theater Companies

A Contemporary Theatre
700 Union
Seattle, WA 98101-2330
(206) 292-7660

Actors Theatre of Louisville
316 West Main Street
Louisville, KY 40202-2916
(502) 584-1265

Alabama Shakespeare Festival
1 Festival Drive
Montgomery, AL 36117-4605
(334) 271-5300

Alley Theatre
615 Texas Avenue
Houston, TX 77002-2710
(713) 228-9341

Alliance Theatre Company
1280 Peachtree Street NE
Atlanta, GA 30309-3502
(404) 733-4650

American Conservatory Theater
30 Grant Street
San Francisco, CA 94108-3800
(415) 439-2400

The American Place Theatre
111 West 46th Street
New York, NY 10036-8502
(212) 840-2960

American Repertory Theatre
64 Brattle Street
Cambridge, MA 02138-3443
(617) 495-2668

Arena Stage
1101 6th Street NW
Washington, DC 20001-3628
(202) 554-9066

Atlantic Theatre Company
336 West 20th Street
New York, NY 10011-3302
(212) 645-8015

Cleveland Public Theatre
6415 Detroit Avenue
Cleveland, OH 44102-3011
(216) 631-2727

Crossroads Theatre Company
7 Livingston Avenue
New Brunswick, NJ 08901-1903
(732) 249-5581

Denver Center Theatre Company
1050 13th Street
Denver, CO 80204-2157
(303) 893-4000

Ensemble Studio Theatre
549 West 52nd Street
New York, NY 10019-5012
(212) 247-4982

George Street Playhouse
9 Livingston Avenue
New Brunswick, NJ 08901-1903
(732) 846-2895

Goodman Theatre
200 South Columbus Drive
Chicago, IL 60603-6402
(312) 443-3811

Goodspeed Opera House
Box A
East Haddam, CT 06423-0281
(860) 873-8664

The Guthrie Theatre
725 Vineland Place
Minneapolis, MN 55403-1139
(612) 347-1100

Hartford Stage Company
50 Church Street
Hartford, CT 06103-1201
(860) 525-5601

Huntington Theatre Company
264 Huntington Street
Boston, MA 02115-4606
(617) 266-7900

Indiana Repertory Theatre
140 West Washington Street
Indianapolis, IN 46204-3403
(317) 635-5277

Intiman Theatre
P.O. Box 19760
Seattle, WA 98109-6760
(206) 269-1928

La Jolla Playhouse
Box 12039
La Jolla, CA 92039-2039
(619) 550-1070

Lincoln Center Theater
150 West 65th Street
New York, NY 10023-6903
(212) 362-7600

Lond Wharf Theatre
222 Sargent Drive
New Haven, CT 06511-5919
(203) 787-4284

Manhattan Theatre Club
311 West 43rd Street, 8th Floor
New York, NY 10036-6413
(212) 399-3000

Mark Taper Forum
135 North Grand Avenue
Los Angeles, CA 90012-3013
(213) 972-7574

McCarter Theatre Center for the Performing Arts
91 University Place
Princeton, NJ 08540-5121
(609) 683-9100

National Theatre of the Deaf
Box 659
Chester, CT 06412-0659
(860) 526-4971 (voice), -4974 (TTY)

New York Shakespeare Festival
Joseph Papp Public Theatre
425 Lafayette Street
New York, NY 10003-7021
(212) 539-8530

New York Theatre Workshop
79 East 4th Street
New York, NY 10003-8904
(212) 780-9037

Old Globe Theatre
Box 2171
San Diego, CA 92112-2171
(619) 231-1941

Oregon Shakespeare Festival
Box 158
Ashland, OR 97520-0158
(541) 482-2111

Playwrights Horizons
416 West 42nd Street
New York, NY 10036-6809
(212) 564-1235

Roundabout Theatre Company
231 West 39th Street, Suite 1200
New York, NY 10018-3109
(212) 719-9393

Shakespeare & Company
The Mount
Box 865
Lenox, MA 01240-0865
(413) 637-1199

Seattle Repertory Theatre
155 Mercer Street
Seattle, WA 98109-4639
(206) 443-2210

South Coast Repertory
Box 2197
Costa Mesa, CA 92628-2197
(714) 708-5500

Steppenwolf Theatre Company
1650 North Halsted
Chicago, IL 60614-5518
(312) 335-1888

Trinity Repertory Company
201 Washington Street
Providence, RI 02903-3226
(401) 521-1100

Utah Shakespearean Festival
351 West Center Street
Cedar City, UT 84720-2470
(435) 586-7880

The Walnut Street Theatre Company
825 Walnut Street
Philadelphia, PA 19107-5107
(215) 574-3550

Williamstown Theatre Festival
Sep.–May:
100 East 17th Street, 3rd Floor
New York, NY 10003-2160
(212) 228-2286
June–Aug.:
Box 517
Williamstown, MA 01267-0517
(413) 458-3200

Yale Repertory Theatre
Box 208244, Yale Station
New Haven, CT 06520-8244
(203) 432-1560

⊙ Charles, Jill, ed. *Regional Theatre Directory 2000–2001.* Dorset, Vt.: Theatre Directories, 2000.

Theatre Communications Group. *Theatre Directory 2000–2001.* New York: Theatre Communications Group, 2000.

75 Noted Stage Actors

The following list includes performers of both plays and musicals. It contains not only actors noted for their excellence in creating roles, but also men and women whose colorful off-stage personalities distinguish(ed) their on-stage performances. Actors in this list span a range of historic periods, styles, and approaches to stagecraft.

Name	Dates	Nationality	Famous Roles Played in the U.S.
Adams, Maude	1872–1953	American	Peter Pan, *Peter Pan*; Lady Babble, *The Little Minister*
Anderson, Judith	1898–1992	Australian-born American	Medea, *Medea*; Lady Macbeth, *Macbeth*
Bancroft, Anne	1931–	American	Gittel Mosca, *Two for the Seesaw*; Annie Sullivan, *The Miracle Worker*
Bankhead, Tallulah	1903–1968	American	Regina, *The Little Foxes*; Sabina, *The Skin of Our Teeth*
Barrymore, Ethel	1879–1959	American	Mme. Trentoni, *Captain Jinks of the Horse Marines*; Miss Moffat, *The Corn is Green*
Barrymore, John	1882–1942	American	Hamlet, *Hamlet*; Richard III, *Richard III*
Barrymore, Lionel	1878–1954	American	Giuseppe, *The Mummy and the Humming Bird*; Colonel Ibbetson, *Peter Ibbetson*
Bernhardt, Sarah	1844–1923	French	Marguerite, *Camille*; Tosca, *Tosca* (non-operatic version)
Booth, Edwin	1833–1893	American	Hamlet, *Hamlet*; Richard III, *Richard III*
Booth, John Wilkes	1838–1865	American	Romeo, *Romeo and Juliet*; Pescara, *The Apostate*
Brynner, Yul	1915–1985	Russian-born American	The King, *The King and I*
Buckley, Betty	1947–	American	Grizabella, *Cats*; Margaret, *Carrie*
Campbell, Mrs. Patrick (Beatrice Stella Tanner)	1865–1940	English	Paula, *The Second Mrs. Tanqueray*; Eliza Doolittle, *Pygmalion*
Channing, Carol	1921–	American	Lorelei Lee, *Gentlemen Prefer Blondes*; Dolly Levi, *Hello, Dolly!*
Cobb, Lee J. (Leo Jacoby)	1911–1976	American	Mr. Carp, *Golden Boy*; Willy Loman, *Death of a Salesman*
Cook, Barbara	1927–	American	Cunegonde, *Candide*; Marion the Librarian, *The Music Man*
Cornell, Katherine	1893–1974	German-born American	Elizabeth Barrett, *The Barretts of Wimpole Street*; Juliet, *Romeo and Juliet*
Cronyn, Hume	1911–	Canadian-born American	Polonius, *Hamlet*; Tobias, *A Delicate Balance*

Davis, Ossie	1917–	American	Jeb, *Jeb*; Purlie, *Purlie Victorious*
Dee, Ruby	1923–	American	Ruth Younger, *A Raisin in the Sun*; Lena, *Boesman and Lena*
Dewhurst, Colleen	1926–1991	American	Mary Follet, *All the Way Home*; Josie Hogan, *A Moon for the Misbegotten*
Duse, Eleonora	1858–1924	Italian	Marguerite, *Camille*; Ellida Wangel, *The Lady from the Sea*
Ferrer, José	1912–1992	American	Cyrano, *Cyrano de Bergerac*; Jim Downs, *The Shrike*
Fiske, Minnie Maddern	1865–1932	American	Tess, *Tess of the D'Urbervilles*; Becky Sharp, *Becky Sharp*
Fontanne, Lynn	1887–1983	English-born American	Katherine, *The Taming of the Shrew*; Clair Zachanassian, *The Visit*
Forrest, Edwin	1806–1872	American	Metamora, *Metamora*; Spartacus, *The Gladiator*
Gielgud, John	1904–2000	English	Hamlet, *Hamlet*; Benedick, *Much Ado About Nothing*
Gillette, William H.	1855–1937	American	Lewis Dumont, *Secret Service*; Sherlock Holmes, *Sherlock Holmes*
Gilpin, Charles	1878–1930	American	William Custis, *Abraham Lincoln*; Brutus Jones, *The Emperor Jones*
Guinness, Alec	1914–2000	English	The Unidentified Guest, *The Cocktail Party*; Dylan Thomas, *Dylan*
Hagen, Uta	1919–	German-born American	Georgie, *The Country Girl*; Martha, *Who's Afraid of Virginia Woolf?*
Harris, Julie	1925–	American	Frankie, *The Member of the Wedding*; Sally Bowles, *I Am a Camera*
Harris, Rosemary	1930–	English	Eleanor of Aquitaine, *The Lion in Winter*; Lady Teazle, *The School for Scandal*
Harrison, Rex	1908–1990	English	Shepherd Henderson, *Bell, Book and Candle*; Henry Higgins, *My Fair Lady*
Hayes, Helen	1900–1993	American	Mary Stuart, *Mary of Scotland*; Queen Victoria, *Victoria Regina*
Holliday, Judy	1922–1965	American	Billie Dawn, *Born Yesterday*; Ella Peterson, *Bells are Ringing*
Jefferson, Joseph	1829–1905	American	Asa Trenchard, *Our American Cousin*; Rip Van Winkle, *Rip Van Winkle*
Jones, James Earl	1931–	American	Jack Jefferson, *The Great White Hope*; Troy, *Fences*
Lahr, Bert	1895–1967	American	Louis Blore, *DuBarry was a Lady*; Hyacinth Beddoes Laffoon, *The Beauty Part*

Name	Dates	Nationality	Famous Roles Played in the U.S.
Lane, Nathan	1956–	American	Buzz, *Love! Valour! Compassion!;* Pseudolus, *A Funny Thing Happened on the Way to the Forum;*
Langtry, Lillie (Emilie Charlotte Le Breton)	1852–1929	English	Galatea, *Pygmalion and Galatea;* Mrs. Trevelyan, *The Degenerates*
Lansbury, Angela	1925–	English	Mame, *Mame;* Mrs. Lovett, *Sweeney Todd*
Lawrence, Gertrude	1898–1952	English	Amanda Prynne, *Private Lives;* Anna, *The King and I*
Le Gallienne, Eva	1899–1991	English-born American	Masha, *The Three Sisters;* Hedda Gabler, *Hedda Gabler*
Lunt, Alfred	1893–1980	American	Petruchio, *The Taming of the Shrew;* Anton Schill, *The Visit*
LuPone, Patti	1949–	American	Eva Peron, *Evita;* Reno Sweeney, *Anything Goes*
Macready, William Charles	1793–1873	English	Macbeth, *Macbeth;* Rob Roy, *Rob Roy*
March, Frederic	1897–1975	American	Mr. Antrobus, *The Skin of Our Teeth;* James Tyrone, *Long Day's Journey into Night*
Martin, Mary	1913–1990	American	Nellie Forbush, *South Pacific;* Peter Pan, *Peter Pan*
McDonald, Audra	1971–	American	Sharon, *Master Class;* Sarah, *Ragtime*
Merman, Ethel	1908–1984	American	Reno Sweeney, *Anything Goes;* Mama Rose, *Gypsy*
Modjeska, Helena	1840–1909	Polish	Adrienne Lecouvreur (non-operatic version); Rosalind, *Twelfth Night*
Morse, Robert	1931–	American	J. Pierpont Finch, *How to Succeed in Business Without Really Trying;* Truman Capote, *Tru*
Mostel, Zero	1915–1977	American	John, *Rhinoceros;* Tevye, *Fiddler on the Roof*
Nazimova, Alla	1879–1945	Russian	Hedda, *Hedda Gabler;* Christine Mannon, *Mourning Becomes Electra*
Olivier, Laurence	1907–1989	English	Antony, *Antony and Cleopatra;* Archie Rice, *The Entertainer*
Page, Geraldine	1924–1987	American	Alma, *Summer and Smoke;* Princess Kosmonopolis, *Sweet Bird of Youth*

Patinkin, Mandy	1952–	American	Che, *Evita*; George Seurat, *Sunday in the Park with George*
Peters, Bernadette	1948–	American	Wicked Witch, *Into the Woods*; Annie Oakley, *Annie Get Your Gun*
Preston, Robert	1918–1987	American	Prof. Harold Hill, *The Music Man*; Henry II, *The Lion in Winter*
Richardson, Ralph	1902–1983	English	Falstaff, *Henry IV, Parts 1 and 2*; General St. Pé, *The Waltz of the Toreadors*
Rivera, Chita (Deolores Conchita Figueroa del Rivero)	1933–	American	Anita, *West Side Story*, The Spider Woman, *Kiss of the Spider Woman*
Robards, Jason, Jr.	1922–	American	Jamie Tyrone in both *Long Day's Journey into Night* and *A Moon for the Misbegotten*
Robeson, Paul	1898–1976	American	Joe, *Show Boat*; Othello, *Othello*
Schildkraut, Joseph	1896–1964	Austrian	Liliom, *Liliom*; Otto Frank, *The Diary of Anne Frank*
Stritch, Elaine	1925–	American	Performed in *Angel in the Wings*; Joanne, *Company*
Tandy, Jessica	1909–1994	English-born American	Blanche duBois, *A Streetcar Named Desire*; Agnes, *A Delicate Balance*
Taylor, Laurette	1884–1946	American	Peg, *Peg o' My Heart*; Amanda Wingfield, *The Glass Menagerie*
Tree, Herbert Beerbohm	1853–1917	English	Svengali, *Trilby*; Professor Higgins, *Pygmalion*
Verdon, Gwen	1926–2000	American	Lola, *Damn Yankees*; Charity, *Sweet Charity*
Vereen, Ben	1946–	American	Judas, *Jesus Christ, Superstar*; Leading Player, *Pippin*
Waters, Ethel	c.1900–1977	American	Petunia, *Cabin in the Sky*; Berenice, *The Member of the Wedding*
Welles, Orson	1915–1985	American	Dr. Faustus, *Dr. Faustus*; Lear, *King Lear*
Wong, B. D.	1962–	American	Song Liling, *M. Butterfly*; Ming, *A Language of Their Own*
Worth, Irene	1916–	American	Miss Alice, *Tiny Alice*; Princess Kosmonopolis, *Sweet Bird of Youth*

☉ Bordman, Gerald. *The Oxford Companion to American Theatre*. New York: Oxford University Press, 1992.
Brown, Dennis. *Actors Talk: Profiles and Stories from the Acting Trade*. New York: Limelight, 1999.

ARTS AND LEISURE: *Motion Pictures*

Treasures of American Film

The National Film Preservation Board, in consultation with the Librarian of Congress, chooses up to 25 films each year to be included in the National Film Registry. Congress charges the board with "maintaining and preserving films that are culturally, historically, or aesthetically significant" by publishing the list, obtaining copies of the films for the Library of Congress, and seeking ways to further the conservation of America's film heritage. The films in the National Film Registry, chosen from 1989 to 1999, are:

Adam's Rib (1949)
The Adventures of Robin Hood (1938)
The African Queen (1951)
All About Eve (1950)
All Quiet on the Western Front (1930)
All That Heaven Allows (1955)
American Graffiti (1973)
An American in Paris (1951)
Annie Hall (1977)
The Apartment (1960)
The Awful Truth (1937)
Badlands (1973)
The Band Wagon (1953)
The Bank Dick (1940)
The Battle of San Pietro (1945)
Ben-Hur (1926)
The Best Years of Our Lives (1946)
Big Business (1929)
The Big Parade (1925)
The Big Sleep (1946)
The Birth of a Nation (1915)
The Black Pirate (1926)
Blacksmith Scene (1893)
Blade Runner (1982)
The Blood of Jesus (1941)
Bonnie and Clyde (1967)
Bride of Frankenstein (1935)
The Bridge on the River Kwai (1957)
Bringing Up Baby (1938)
Broken Blossoms (1919)
Cabaret (1972)
Carmen Jones (1954)
Casablanca (1942)
Castro Street (1966)
Cat People (1942)
Chan Is Missing (1982)
The Cheat (1915)
Chinatown (1974)
Chulas Fronteras (1976)
Citizen Kane (1941)
The City (1939)
City Lights (1931)
Civilization (1916)
The Conversation (1974)
Cops (1922)

A Corner in Wheat (1909)
The Cool World (1963)
The Crowd (1928)
Czechoslovakia 1968 (1968)
David Holzman's Diary (1968)
The Day the Earth Stood Still (1951)
Dead Birds (1964)
The Deer Hunter (1978)
Destry Rides Again (1939)
Detour (1946)
Do the Right Thing (1989)
The Docks of New York (1928)
Dodsworth (1936)
Dog Star Man (1964)
Don't Look Back (1967)
Double Indemnity (1944)
Dr. Strangelove (Or, How I Learned to Stop
  Worrying and Love the Bomb) (1964)
Duck Amuck (1953)
Duck Soup (1933)
E.T. The Extra-Terrestrial (1982)
Easy Rider (1969)
Eaux d'Artifice (1953)
El Norte (1983)
The Emperor Jones (1933)
The Exploits of Elaine (1914)
Fantasia (1940)
Fatty's Tintype Tangle (1915)
Flash Gordon Serial (1936)
Footlight Parade (1933)
Force of Evil (1948)
The Forgotten Frontier (1931)
42nd Street (1933)
The Four Horsemen of the Apocalypse (1921)
Frank Film (1973)
Frankenstein (1931)
Freaks (1932)
The Freshman (1925)
From the Manger to the Cross (1912)
Fury (1936)
The General (1927)
Gerald McBoing Boing (1951)
Gertie the Dinosaur (1914)
Gigi (1958)
The Godfather (1972)

The Godfather, Part II (1974)
The Gold Rush (1925)
Gone With the Wind (1939)
The Graduate (1967)
The Grapes of Wrath (1940)
Grass (1925)
The Great Dictator (1940)
The Great Train Robbery (1903)
Greed (1924)
Gun Crazy (1949)
Gunga Din (1939)
Harlan County, U.S.A. (1976)
Harold and Maude (1972)
The Heiress (1949)
Hell's Hinges (1916)
Hindenburg Disaster Newsreel Footage (1937)
High School (1968)
High Noon (1952)
His Girl Friday (1940)
The Hitch-Hiker (1953)
Hospital (1970)
The Hospital (1971)
How Green Was My Valley (1941)
How the West Was Won (1962)
The Hustler (1961)
I Am a Fugitive From a Chain Gang (1932)
The Immigrant (1917)
In the Land of the Head Hunters (a.k.a. *In the Land of the War Canoes*, 1914)
Intolerance (1916)
Invasion of the Body Snatchers (1956)
It Happened One Night (1934)
It's a Wonderful Life (1946)
The Italian (1915)
Jammin' the Blues (1944)
Jazz on a Summer's Day (1959)
The Jazz Singer (1927)
Killer of Sheep (1977)
King: a Filmed Record . . . Montgomery to Memphis (1970)
King Kong (1933)
The Kiss (1896)
Kiss Me Deadly (1955)
Knute Rockne, All American (1940)
The Lady Eve (1941)
Lambchops (1929)
Lassie Come Home (1943)
The Last of the Mohicans (1920)
The Last Picture Show (1972)
Laura (1944)
Lawrence of Arabia (1962)
The Learning Tree (1969)
Letter From An Unknown Woman (1948)
The Life and Death of 9413-A Hollywood Extra (1927)

The Life and Times of Rosie the Riveter (1980)
The Little Fugitive (1953)
Little Miss Marker (1934)
The Lost World (1925)
Louisiana Story (1948)
Love Me Tonight (1932)
M*A*S*H (1970)
Magical Maestro (1952)
The Magnificent Ambersons (1942)
The Maltese Falcon (1941)
The Manchurian Candidate (1962)
Manhatta (1921)
March of Time: Inside Nazi Germany— 1938 (1938)
Marty (1955)
Master Hands (1936)
Mean Streets (1973)
Meet Me in St. Louis (1944)
Meshes of the Afternoon (1943)
Midnight Cowboy (1969)
Mildred Pierce (1945)
Modern Times (1936)
Modesta (1956)
Morocco (1930)
Motion Painting No. 1 (1947)
A Movie (1958)
Mr. Smith Goes to Washington (1939)
The Music Box (1932)
My Darling Clementine (1946)
My Man Godfrey (1936)
The Naked Spur (1953)
Nanook of the North (1922)
Nashville (1975)
A Night at the Opera (1935)
The Night of the Hunter (1955)
Night of the Living Dead (1968)
Ninotchka (1939)
North By Northwest (1959)
Nothing But a Man (1964)
On the Waterfront (1954)
One Flew Over the Cuckoo's Nest (1975)
Out of the Past (1947)
The Ox-Bow Incident (1943)
The Outlaw Josey Wales (1976)
Pass the Gravy (1928)
Paths of Glory (1957)
Phantom of the Opera (1925)
The Philadelphia Story (1940)
Pinocchio (1940)
A Place in the Sun (1951)
The Plow That Broke the Plains (1936)
Point of Order (1964)
The Poor Little Rich Girl (1917)
Powers of Ten (1978)
Primary (1960)

The Prisoner of Zenda (1937)
The Producers (1968)
Psycho (1960)
The Public Enemy (1931)
Pull My Daisy (1959)
Raging Bull (1980)
Raiders of the Lost Ark (1981)
Rear Window (1954)
Rebel Without a Cause (1955)
Red River (1948)
Republic Steel Strike Riot Newsreel Footage
    (1937)
Return of the Secaucus 7 (1980)
Ride the High Country (1962)
Rip Van Winkle (1896)
The River (1937)
Road to Morocco (1942)
Roman Holiday (1953)
Safety Last (1923)
Salesman (1969)
Salt of the Earth (1954)
Scarface (1932)
The Searchers (1956)
Seventh Heaven (1927)
Shadow of a Doubt (1943)
Shadows (1959)
Shane (1953)
She Done Him Wrong (1933)
Sherlock, Jr. (1924)
Shock Corridor (1963)
The Shop Around the Corner (1940)
Show Boat (1936)
Singin' in the Rain (1952)
Sky High (1922)
Snow White (1933)
Snow White and the Seven Dwarfs (1937)
Some Like It Hot (1959)
Stagecoach (1939)
Star Wars (1977)
Steamboat Willie (1928)
A Streetcar Named Desire (1951)

Sullivan's Travels (1941)
Sunrise (1927)
Sunset Boulevard (1950)
Sweet Smell of Success (1957)
Tabu (1931)
Tacoma Narrows Bridge Collapse (1940)
Taxi Driver (1976)
The Ten Commandments (1956
Tevye (1939)
The Thief of Baghdad (1924)
The Thin Man (1934)
To Be or Not To Be (1942)
To Fly (1976)
To Kill a Mockingbird (1962)
Tootsie (1982)
Top Hat (1935)
Topaz (1943–45)
Touch of Evil (1958)
Trance and Dance in Bali (1936–39)
The Treasure of The Sierra Madre
    (1948)
Trouble in Paradise (1932)
Tulips Shall Grow (1942)
Twelve O'Clock High (1949)
2001: A Space Odyssey (1968)
Verbena Tragica (1939)
Vertigo (1958)
West Side Story (1961)
Westinghouse Works, 1904 (1904)
What's Opera, Doc? (1957)
Where Are My Children? (1916)
The Wild Bunch (1969)
The Wind (1928)
Wings (1927)
Within Our Gates (1920)
The Wizard of Oz (1939)
Woman of the Year (1942)
A Woman under the Influence (1974)
Woodstock (1970)
Yankee Doodle Dandy (1942)
Zapruder Film (1963)

⊙ Library of Congress, National Film Preservation Board. www.loc.gov/film/
    U.S. Public Law 285. 104th Cong., 2d sess, 11 October 1996.

Classic Foreign-Language Films

The following films in languages other than English are notable for several reasons: they advanced the art of filmmaking, were milestones in the history of censorship, were major films in the directors' careers, or were extremely popular or influential in their day.

Abbreviations: AA = Best Foreign-Language Film Academy Award®; AAN = nomination.

À bout de souffle [Breathless] (France 1959). Director: Jean-Luc Godard
À nous la liberté [Freedom for Us] (France 1931). Director: René Clair

L'âge d'or [The Golden Age] (France 1930). Director: Luis Buñuel

Aguirre, der Zorn Gottes [Aguirre, the Wrath of God] (Peru/Germany/Mexico 1972). Director: Werner Herzog

Alexander Nevsky (USSR 1938). Director: Sergei Eisenstein

Alexis Zorbas [Zorba the Greek] (Greece 1964; Best Picture AAN). Director: Michael Cacoyannis

Amarcord (Italy 1974; AA). Director: Federico Fellini

L'année dernière à Marienbad [Last Year at Marienbad] (France/Italy 1961). Director: Alain Resnais

Apu Trilogy, The [Panther Panchali; Aparajito; The World of Apu] (India 1955–1959). Director: Satyajit Ray

Andrei Rublev (USSR 1966). Director: Andrei Tarkovsky

Au revoir les enfants [Goodbye, Children] (France 1987; AAN). Director: Louis Malle

L'Avventura [The Adventure] (Italy 1960). Director: Michelangelo Antonioni

Ba wang bie ji [Farewell My Concubine] (China/Hong Kong 1993; AAN). Director: Kaige Chen

Babettes gæstebud [Babette's Feast] (Denmark 1987; AA). Director: Gabriel Axel

Battleship Potemkin, The (USSR 1925). Director: Sergei Eisenstein

Blechtrommel, Die [The Tin Drum] (West Germany 1978; AA). Director: Volker Schlöndorff

Belle époque [The Age of Beauty] (Spain 1992; AA). Director: Fernando Trueba

Belle et la Bête, La [Beauty and the Beast] (France 1946). Director: Jean Cocteau

Blaue Engel, Der [The Blue Angel] (Germany 1930). Director: Josef von Sternberg

Büchse der Pandora, Die [Pandora's Box] (Germany 1928). Director: G. W. Pabst

Central do Brasil [Central Station] (Brazil 1998; AAN). Director: Walter Salles

Citta Aperta [Open City] (Italy 1945). Director: Roberto Rossellini

Cousin, Cousine (France 1976; AAN). Director: Jean-Charles Tacchella

Cyrano de Bergerac (France 1990; AAN). Director: Jean-Paul Rappeneau

Da hong deng long gao gao gua [Raise the Red Lantern] (China/Hong Kong/Taiwan 1992; AAN). Director: Yimou Zhang

Dolce Vita, La [The Sweet Life] *(Italy 1960).* Director: Federico Fellini

8 ½ (Italy 1963; AA). Director: Federico Fellini

Elvira Madigan (Sweden 1967). Director: Bo Widerberg

Enfants du Paradis, Les [Children of Paradise] (France 1944). Director: Marcel Carné

Extase [Ecstasy] (Czechoslovakia 1933). Director: Gustav Machaty

Fanny and Alexander (Sweden 1983; AA). Director: Ingmar Bergman

Giardino dei Finzi-Contini, Il [The Garden of the Finzi-Continis] (Italy/West Germany 1970; AA). Director: Vittorio de Sica

Grande Illusion, La (France 1937; Best Picture AAN). Director: Jean Renoir

Hsi yen [The Wedding Banquet] (Taiwan 1993; AAN). Director: Ang Lee

Indochine (France 1992; AA). Director: Régis Wargnier

Ivan the Terrible (I and II) *(USSR 1943–1946).* Director: Sergei Eisenstein

Ju Dou (China 1990; AAN). Director: Yang Fengliang

Kabinett des Doktor Caligari, Das [The Cabinet of Dr. Caligari] (Germany 1919). Directors: Carl Mayer and Hans Janowitz

Kolya (Czech Republic 1996; AA). Director: Jan Sverák

Ladri di biciclette [The Bicycle Thief] (Italy 1948). Director: Vittorio de Sica

Letzte Mann, Der [The Last Laugh] (Germany 1924). Director: F. W. Murnau

M (Germany 1931). Director: Fritz Lang

*Madame de . . . (France/*Italy *1953).* Director: Max Ophüls

Mediterraneo (Italy 1991; AA). Director: Gabriele Salvatores

Metropolis (Germany 1926). Director: Fritz Lang

Classic Foreign-Language Films *(cont.)*

Napoléon (France 1925). Director: Abel Gance

Nuovo Cinema Paradiso (Italy 1988; AA). Director: Giuseppe Tornatore

Orfeu Negro [Black Orpheus] (Brazil/France/Italy 1959; AA). Director: Marcel Camus

Ossessione (Italy 1942). Director: Luchino Visconti

Parapluies de Cherbourg, Les [The Umbrellas of Cherbourg] (France/West Germany 1963; AAN). Director: Jacques Demy

Passion de Jeanne d'Arc, La [The Passion of Joan of Arc] (France 1928). Director: Carl Dreyer

Pelle erobreren [Pelle the Conqueror] (Denmark 1987; AA). Director: Bille August

Popiól i diament [Ashes and Diamonds] *(Poland 1958)*. Director: Andrzej Wajda

Postino, Il [The Postman] (Italy 1994; Best Picture AAN). Director: Michael Radford

Potomok Chingis-Khana [Storm over Asia] (USSR 1928). Director: Vsevolod Pudovkin

Pred dozhdot [Before the Rain] (U.K./France/Macdeonia 1994; AAN). Director: Milcho Manchevski

Quatre cents coups, Les [The 400 Blows] (France 1958). Director: François Truffaut

Rashomon (Japan 1951). Director: Akira Kurosawa

Règle du jeu, La [The Rules of the Game] *(France 1939)*. Director: Jean Renoir

Reise der Hoffnung [Journey of Hope] (Switzerland 1990; AA). Director: Xavier Koller

Salaam Bombay! (India 1988; AAN). Director: Mira Nair

Sang d'un poète, Le [The Blood of a Poet] (France 1930). Director: Jean Cocteau

Shichinin no samurai [Seven Samurai] *(Japan 1954)*. Director: Akira Kurosawa

Sjunde inseglet, Det [The Seventh Seal] (Sweden 1957). Director: Ingmar Bergman

Strada, La (Italy 1954; [AA 1956]). Director: Federico Fellini

Todo sobre mi madre [All About My Mother] (Spain 1999; AA). Director: Pedro Almodóvar

Tokyo monogatari [Tokyo Story] (Japan 1953). Director: Yasujiro Ozu

Tristana *(Spain/France/Italy 1970; AA)*. Director: Luis Bunuel

Triumph des Willens [The Triumph of the Will] (Germany 1934). Director: Leni Riefenstahl

Ugetsu Monogatari [Tales of Ugetsu] (Japan 1952). Director: Kenji Mizoguchi

Viskningar och rop [Cries and Whispers] (Sweden 1972; Best Picture AAN). Director: Ingmar Bergman

Vita è bella, La [Life Is Beautiful] (Italy 1997; AA; Best Picture AAN). Director: Roberto Benigni

Z (Algeria/France 1969; AA; Best Picture AAN). Director: Costa-Gavras

Zéro de Conduite (France 1933). Director: Jean Vigo

⊙ Canby, Vincent, et al. *The New York Times Guide to the Best 1,000 Movies Ever Made.* New York: Times Books, 1999.

Internet Movie Database. www.imdb.com

Wiley, Mason, and Damien Bona. *Inside Oscar.* 10th ed. New York: Ballantine, 1996.

Wilmington, Michael. *Chicago Tribune.* "The Essentials: Foreign Movies," www.chicagotribune.com/ws/1997l2essentials/foreign/front3.htm

Included in this list are actors who are known primarily for their work in films. They are not merely popular actors, but respected by audiences, critics, and the film community. Many received multiple awards or nominations in long and distinguished careers, while others shone brightly for only a few years but left indelible impressions.

Name	Dates	Selected Films*
Andrews, Julie (Julia Wells)	1934–	Mary Poppins (1964; AA); The Sound of Music (1965; AAN)
Astaire, Fred (Frederick Austerlitz)	1899–1987	Top Hat (1935); Shall We Dance? (1937)
Bacall, Lauren (Betty Jean Perske)	1924–	To Have and Have Not (1944); The Mirror Has Two Faces (1996; SAAN)
Bancroft, Anne (Anna Maria Italiano)	1931–	The Miracle Worker (1962; AA); The Graduate (1968; AAN)
Bara, Theda (Theodosia Goodman)	1890–1955	A Fool There Was (1916); Cleopatra (1917)
Barrymore, Ethel (Edith Blythe)	1879–1959	None But the Lonely Heart (1944; SAA); The Spiral Staircase (1946; SAAN)
Barrymore, John (John Blythe)	1882–1942	Dr. Jekyll and Mr. Hyde (1920); Dinner at Eight (1933)
Beatty, Warren (Henry Warren Beaty)	1937–	Bonnie and Clyde (1967; AAN); Heaven Can Wait (1978; AAN)
Bergman, Ingrid	1915–1982	Gaslight (1943; AA); Joan of Arc (1948; AAN)
Bogart, Humphrey	1899–1957	Casablanca (1943; AAN); The African Queen (1951; AA)
Borgnine, Ernest (Ermes Effron Borgnino)	1917–	Marty (1955; AA); The Wild Bunch (1969)
Brando, Marlon	1924–	On the Waterfront (1954; AA); The Godfather (1972; AA)
Burstyn, Ellen (Edna Rae Gillooly)	1932–	The Exorcist (1973; AAN); Alice Doesn't Live Here Anymore (1974; AA)
Burton, Richard (Richard Walter Jenkins Jr.)	1925–1984	The Spy Who Came in from the Cold (1965; AAN); Who's Afraid of Virginia Woolf? (1966; AAN)
Cage, Nicolas (Nicholas Kim Coppola)	1964–	Raising Arizona (1987); Leaving Las Vegas (1995; AA)
Cagney, James	1899–1986	Angels with Dirty Faces (1938; AAN); Yankee Doodle Dandy (1942; AA)
Caine, Michael (Maurice Joseph Micklewhite)	1933–	Educating Rita (U.K. 1983; AAN); Hannah and Her Sisters (1986)
Chaney, Lon, Sr. (Leonidas F. Chaney)	1883–1930	The Hunchback of Notre Dame (1923); The Phantom of the Opera (1925)
Chaplin, Charles	1889–1977	The Tramp (1915); The Great Dictator (1940; AAN)
Charisse, Cyd (Tula Ellice Finklea)	1921–	Brigadoon (1954); Silk Stockings (1957)
Cher (Cherilyn Sarkisian LaPierre)	1946–	Mask (1985; AAN); Moonstruck (1987; AA)
Clift, Montgomery	1920–1966	From Here to Eternity (1953; AAN); Judgment at Nuremberg (1961; SAAN)
Close, Glenn	1947–	Fatal Attraction (1987; AAN); Dangerous Liaisons (1988; AAN)
Colbert, Claudette (Lily Claudette Chauchoin)	1903–1996	It Happened One Night (1934; AA); Since You Went Away (1944; AAN)
Connery, Sean (Frank J. Cooper)	1930–	Doctor No (1963); The Untouchables (1987; SAA)
Cooper, Gary	1901–1961	Sergeant York (1941; AA); High Noon (1952; AA)
Crawford, Joan (Lucille le Sueur)	1906–1977	Mildred Pierce (1945; AA); Sudden Fear (1952; AAN)
Crosby, Bing (Harry Lillis Crosby)	1905–1977	Going My Way (1944; AA); The Bells of St. Mary's (1945; AAN)
Curtis, Tony (Bernard Schwartz)	1925–	The Defiant Ones (1958; AAN); Spartacus (1960)
Davis, Bette (Ruth Elizabeth Davis)	1908–1989	Jezebel (1938; AA); All About Eve (1950; AAN)
Day-Lewis, Daniel	1957–	My Left Foot (U.K. 1989; AA); In the Name of the Father (Ireland/ U.K. 1993; AAN)
de Havilland, Olivia	1916–	To Each His Own (1946; AA); The Heiress (1949; AA)

Name	Dates	Selected Films
De Niro, Robert	1943–	Taxi Driver (1976; AAN); Raging Bull (1980; AA)
Dean, James	1931–1955	East of Eden (1955; AAN); Rebel Without a Cause (1955)
Dietrich, Marlene (Maria Magdalena von Losch)	1901–1992	Blonde Venus (1933); Touch of Evil (1958)
Douglas, Kirk (Issur Danielovitch Demsky)	1916–	Lust for Life (1956; AAN); Spartacus (1960)
Douglas, Michael	1944–	Fatal Attraction (1987); Wall Street (1987; AA)
Dunaway, Faye	1941–	Bonnie and Clyde (1967; AAN); Network (1976; AA)
Duvall, Robert	1931–	The Godfather (1972; SAAN); Tender Mercies (1983; AA)
Eastwood, Clint	1930–	A Fistful of Dollars (Italy 1964); Dirty Harry (1971)
Fairbanks, Douglas (Douglas Ullman)	1883–1939	The Mark of Zorro (1920); The Thief of Baghdad (1923)
Ferrer, José (José Vicente Ferrer y Cintrón)	1912–1992	Cyrano de Bergerac (1950; AA); Moulin Rouge (1952; AAN)
Field, Sally (Sally Mahoney)	1946–	Norma Rae (1979; AA); Places in the Heart (1984; AA)
Fields, W. C. (William Claude Dukinfield)	1879–1946	My Little Chickadee (1940); Never Give a Sucker an Even Break (1941)
Fonda, Henry	1905–1982	The Grapes of Wrath (1940; AAN); On Golden Pond (1981; AA)
Fonda, Jane	1937–	Coming Home (1978; AA); On Golden Pond (1981; SAAN)
Ford, Harrison	1942–	Star Wars (1977); Blade Runner (1982)
Foster, Jodie	1962–	The Accused (1988; AA); The Silence of the Lambs (1991; AA)
Freeman, Morgan	1937–	Driving Miss Daisy (1989; AAN); The Shawshank Redemption (1994; AAN)
Gable, Clark	1901–1960	It Happened One Night (1934; AA); Gone with the Wind (1939; AAN)
Garbo, Greta (Greta Gustafson)	1905–1990	Anna Christie (1930; AAN); Queen Christina (1933)
Gardner, Ava	1922–1990	The Killers (1946); Mogambo (1953; AAN)
Garland, Judy (Frances Gumm)	1922–1969	The Wizard of Oz (1939); A Star is Born (1954; AAN)
Gish, Lillian (Lillian de Guiche)	1893–1993	Birth of a Nation (1914); Duel in the Sun (1946; SAAN)
Goddard, Paulette (Marion Levy)	1911–1990	Modern Times (1936); The Diary of a Chambermaid (1946)
Goldberg, Whoopi (Caryn Johnson)	1949–	The Color Purple (1985; AAN); The Player (1992)
Grable, Betty	1916–1973	Moon over Miami (1941); How to Marry a Millionaire (1953)
Grant, Cary (Archibald Leach)	1904–1986	His Girl Friday (1940); None but the Lonely Heart (1944; AAN)
Guinness, Alec	1914–2000	The Lavender Hill Mob (U.K. 1951; AAN); The Bridge on the River Kwai (U.K. 1957; AA)
Hackman, Gene	1930–	The French Connection (1971; AA); Unforgiven (1992; SAA)
Hanks, Tom	1956–	Philadelphia (1993; AA); Saving Private Ryan (1998; AAN)
Harlow, Jean (Harlean Carpentier)	1911–1937	Public Enemy (1931); Dinner at Eight (1933)
Harrison, Rex	1908–1990	Cleopatra (1963; AAN); My Fair Lady (1964; AA)
Hayworth, Rita (Margarita Carmen Cansino)	1918–1987	Only Angels Have Wings (1939); The Lady from Shanghai (1948)
Hepburn, Audrey (Audrey Hepburn-Ruston)	1929–1993	Roman Holiday (1953; AA); Breakfast at Tiffany's (1961; AAN)

Hepburn, Katharine	1907–	Morning Glory (1933, AA); On Golden Pond (1981; AA)
Heston, Charlton (John Charlton Carter)	1924–	Ben-Hur (1959; AA); Planet of the Apes (1968)
Hoffmann, Dustin	1937–	Kramer vs. Kramer (1979; AA); Rain Man (1988; AA)
Holden, William (William Beedle)	1918–1981	Sunset Boulevard (1950: AAN); Stalag 17 (1953; AA)
Hopkins, Anthony	1937–	The Silence of the Lambs (1991; AA); The Remains of the Day (U.K./U.S. 1993; AAN)
Hunter, Holly	1958–	Broadcast News (1987; AAN); The Piano (1993; AA)
Huston, Anjelica	1952–	Prizzi's Honor (1985; SAA); The Grifters (1990; AAN)
Jackson, Glenda	1937–	Women in Love (U.K. 1970: AA); A Touch of Class (1973; AA)
Jackson, Samuel L.	1948–	Pulp Fiction (1994; SAAN); Shaft (2000)
Jones, Jennifer (Phyllis Isley)	1919–	The Song of Bernadette (1943; AA); Love is a Many-Splendored Thing (1955; AAN)
Jones, Tommy Lee	1946–	Coal Miner's Daughter (1980); The Fugitive (1993; SAA)
Karloff, Boris (William Pratt)	1887–1969	Frankenstein (1931); The Mummy (1932)
Keaton, Buster (Joseph Francis Keaton)	1895–1966	The Navigator (1924); The General (1927)
Keaton, Diane (Diane Hall)	1946–	Annie Hall (1977: AA); Reds (1981; AAN)
Keitel, Harvey	1939–	The Last Temptation of Christ (1988); Bugsy (1991; SAAN)
Kelly, Gene	1912–1996	Anchors Aweigh (1945; AAN); An American in Paris (1951)
Kelly, Grace	1928–1982	Rear Window (1954); The Country Girl (1954: AA)
Kidman, Nicole	1967–	Dead Calm (Australia/U.S. 1989); The Portrait of a Lady (1996)
Lancaster, Burt	1913–1994	Elmer Gantry (1960: AA); Atlantic City (1981; AAN)
Lange, Jessica	1949–	Tootsie (1982; SAA); Blue Sky (1994: AA)
Laughton, Charles	1899–1962	The Private Life of Henry VIII (U.K. 1933: AA); Witness for the Prosecution (1957: AAN)
Leigh, Vivien (Vivien Mary Hartley)	1913–1967	Gone with the Wind (1939; AA); A Streetcar Named Desire (1951: AA)
Lemmon, Jack (John Uhler Lemmon III)	1925–	The Apartment (1960; AAN); Save the Tiger (1973; AA)
Lombard, Carole (Jane Peters)	1908–1942	My Man Godfrey (1935; AAN); Nothing Sacred (1937)
Loren, Sophia (Sophia Scicoloni)	1934–	Two Women (Italy 1961; AA); Marriage, Italian Style (Italy 1964; AAN)
Lugosi, Bela (Bela Ferenc Blasko)	1882–1956	Dracula (1930); Son of Frankenstein (1939)
MacLaine, Shirley (Shirley Mclean Beaty)	1934–	The Turning Point (1977; AAN); Terms of Endearment (1983; AA)
Malkovich, John	1953–	Places in the Heart (1984; SAAN); In the Line of Fire (1993; SAAN)
March, Frederic (Frederick McIntyre Bickel)	1897–1975	Dr. Jekyll and Mr. Hyde (1932; AA); The Best Years of Our Lives (1946; AA)
Marx Brothers, The:		Animal Crackers (1930); Horse Feathers (1932)
Chico (Leonard)	1886–1961	
Harpo (Adolph)	1888–1964	
Groucho (Julius)	1890–1977	
Zeppo (Herbert)	1901–1979	

Name	Dates	Selected Films
Mason, James	1909–1984	A Star is Born (1954; AAN); The Verdict (1982; SAAN)
Matthau, Walter (Walter Matasschanskayasky)	1920–2000	The Fortune Cookie (1966; SAA); The Odd Couple (1968)
McDaniel, Hattie	1895–1952	Show Boat (1935); Gone with the Wind (1939; SAA)
Midler, Bette	1945–	Divine Madness (1980); For the Boys (1991; AAN)
Milland, Ray (Reginald Alfred Truscott-Jones)	1907–1986	Beau Geste (1939); The Lost Weekend (1945; AA)
Mitchum, Robert	1917–1997	Night of the Hunter (1955); Farewell, My Lovely (1975)
Monroe, Marilyn (Norma Jean Mortenson)	1926–1962	Gentlemen Prefer Blondes (1953); The Seven Year Itch (1955)
Montgomery, Robert (Henry Montgomery Jr.)	1904–1981	Night Must Fall (1937; AAN); The Lady in the Lake (1946)
Muni, Paul (Muni Weisenfreund)	1895–1967	The Story of Louis Pasteur (1936; AA); The Last Angry Man (1959: AAN)
Newman, Paul	1925–	Hud (1963; AAN); The Color of Money (1986; AA)
Nicholson, Jack	1937–	One Flew Over the Cuckoo's Nest (1975; AA); As Good as It Gets (1997; AA)
Nolte, Nick	1941–	The Prince of Tides (1991; AAN); Affliction (1997; AAN)
O'Toole, Peter	1932–	Lawrence of Arabia (U.K. 1962; AAN); Goodbye, Mr. Chips (1969; AAN)
Olivier, Laurence	1907–1989	Wuthering Heights (1939; AAN); Hamlet (U.K. 1948; AA)
Pacino, Al	1939–	The Godfather (1972; SAAN); Scent of a Woman (1992; AA)
Page, Geraldine	1924–1987	Sweet Bird of Youth (1962; AAN); The Trip to Bountiful (1985; AA)
Peck, Gregory	1916–	Gentleman's Agreement (1947; AAN); To Kill a Mockingbird (1962; AA)
Penn, Sean	1960–	Dead Man Walking (1995; AAN); Sweet and Lowdown (1999; AAN)
Perkins, Anthony	1932–1992	Fear Strikes Out (1957); Psycho (1960)
Pfeiffer, Michelle	1957–	Dangerous Liaisons (1988; SAAN); The Fabulous Baker Boys (1989; AAN)
Pickford, Mary (Gladys Louise Smith)	1892–1979	Polyanna (1919); Coquette (1929; AA)
Poitier, Sidney	1927–	The Blackboard Jungle (1955); Lilies of the Field (1963; AA)
Powell, William	1892–1984	The Thin Man (1934; AAN); Life With Father (1947; AAN)
Power, Tyrone	1913–1958	Jesse James (1939); The Mark of Zorro (1940
Redford, Robert	1936–	Butch Cassidy and the Sundance Kid (1969); The Sting (1973; AAN)
Redgrave, Vanessa	1937–	Julia (1977; SAA); The Bostonians (1984; AAN)
Reynolds, Burt	1936–	Deliverance (1972); Boogie Nights (1997; SAAN)
Robeson, Paul	1898–1976	Show Boat (1935); Song of Freedom (U.K. 1937)
Rogers, Ginger (Virginia McMath)	1911–1995	Top Hat (1935); Kitty Foyle (1940; AA)
Rooney, Mickey (Joe Yule Jr.)	1920–	The Human Comedy (1943; AAN); The Black Stallion (1979; SAAN)
Russell, Rosalind	1908–1976	Mourning Becomes Electra (1947; AAN); Auntie Mame (1958; AAN)

Name	Years	Films
Sarandon, Susan (Susan Tomaling)	1946–	Thelma and Louise (1991; AAN); Dead Man Walking (1995; AA)
Scott, George C.	1927–1999	Anatomy of a Murder (1959; SAAN); Patton (1970; AA)
Sellers, Peter	1925–1980	The Pink Panther (1964); Dr. Strangelove (1964; AAN)
Shearer, Norma	1904–1993	The Divorcee (1930; AA); The Barretts of Wimpole Street (1934; AAN)
Spacek, Sissy (Mary Elizabeth Spacek)	1949–	Coal Miner's Daughter (1980; AA); Crimes of the Heart (1986; AAN)
Spacey, Kevin (Kevin Spacey Fowler)	1959–	The Usual Suspects (1995; SAA); American Beauty (1999; AA)
Stanwyck, Barbara (Ruby Stevens)	1907–1990	Stella Dallas (1937; AAN); Double Indemnity (1944; AAN)
Stewart, James	1908–1997	The Philadelphia Story (1940; AA); It's a Wonderful Life (1946; AAN)
Streep, Meryl (Mary Louise Streep)	1949–	Sophie's Choice (1982; AA); The Bridges of Madison County (1995; AAN)
Taylor, Elizabeth	1932–	Cat on a Hot Tin Roof (1958; AAN); Butterfield 8 (1960; AA)
Temple, Shirley	1928–	Curly Top (1935); Heidi (1937)
Thompson, Emma	1959–	Howards End (U.K. 1992: AA); In the Name of the Father (Ireland/U.K. 1993: SAAN)
Tracy, Spencer	1900–1967	Boys' Town (1938: AA); Judgment at Nuremberg (1961; AAN)
Turner, Lana (Julia Jean Mildred Frances Turner)	1920–1995	The Bad and the Beautiful (1952); Peyton Place (1957: AAN)
Valentino, Rudolph (Rodolfo d'Antonguolla)	1895–1926	The Sheik (1921); Blood and Sand (1922)
Washington, Denzel	1954–	Glory (1989; SAA); Malcolm X (1992; AAN)
Wayne, John (Marion Michael Morrison)	1907–1979	Stagecoach (1939); True Grit (1966; AA)
Weaver, Sigourney (Susan Weaver)	1949–	Aliens (1979: AAN); Gorillas in the Mist (1988; AAN)
Welles, Orson	1915–1985	Citizen Kane (1941; AAN); Touch of Evil (1958)
West, Mae	1892–1980	I'm No Angel (1933); Myra Breckinridge (1970)
Williams, Robin	1952–	Good Morning, Vietnam (1987; AAN); Good Will Hunting (1997; SAA)
Winters, Shelley (Shirley Schrift)	1922–	A Place in the Sun (1951: AAN); The Diary of Anne Frank (1959; SAA)
Woodward, Joanne	1930–	The Three Faces of Eve (1957; AA); Mr. and Mrs. Bridge (1991; AAN)
Young, Loretta (Gretchen Michaela Young)	1913–2000	Ramona (1936); The Farmer's Daughter (1947: AA)

*Abbreviations: AA = Best Actor or Actress Academy Award®. AAN = nomination; SAA = Best Supporting Actor or Actress Academy Award®, SAAN = supporting nomination.

☉ Internet Movie Database. www.imdb.com
Internet Movie Database. "Academy Awards, USA," http://us.imdb.com/Sections/Awards/Academy_Awards_USA/
Walker, John, ed. Halliwell's Filmgoer's Companion. 12th ed. New York: Harper Perennial, 1997.

125 Favorite Television Series

The regularly scheduled, prime-time series included in this list are considered favorites for several reasons: they ran for more than five years, were among the top 20 shows in the Neilsen ratings for at least one season, or were pathbreaking shows that showed the direction of television's future.

Adam-12 (1968–75); police drama

Adventures of Ozzie and Harriet, The (1952–66); situation comedy

Alfred Hitchcock Presents (1955–65); suspense anthology

Alice (1976–85); situation comedy

All in the Family/Archie Bunker's Place (1971–83); situation comedy

Andy Griffith Show, The (1960–68); situation comedy

Baretta (1975–78); police drama

Barney Miller (1975–82); situation comedy

Benson (1979–86); situation comedy

Beverly Hillbillies, The (1962–71); situation comedy

Beverly Hills 90210 (1990–2000); drama

Bewitched (1964–72), situation comedy

Bob Newhart Show, The (1972–78); situation comedy

Bonanza (1959–73); western

Brady Bunch, The (1969–74); situation comedy

Cagney & Lacey (1982–88); police drama

Candid Camera (1948–50; 1953; 1960–67; 1990); humor

Carol Burnett Show, The (1967–79); comedy variety

Charlie's Angels (1976–81); detective drama

Cheers (1982–93); situation comedy

Columbo (1971–77; 1989–90; 1992–93); police drama

Cops (1989–); police documentary

Cosby Show, The (1984–92); situation comedy

Dallas (1978–91); drama

Dean Martin Show, The (1965–74); comedy variety

Death Valley Days (1952–72; 1975); western anthology

Dick Van Dyke Show, The (1961–66); situation comedy

Diff'rent Strokes (1978–86); situation comedy

Different World, A (1987–93); situation comedy

Doris Day Show, The (1968–73); situation comedy

Dragnet (1952–59; 1967–70); police drama

Dukes of Hazzard, The (1979–85); comedy adventure

Dynasty (1981–89); drama

Ed Sullivan Show, The (1948–71); variety

Eight Is Enough (1977–81); comedy/ drama

Ellen/These Friends of Mine (1994–98); situation comedy

Emergency (1972–77); medical drama

F.B.I., The (1965–74); police drama

Facts of Life, The (1979–88); situation comedy

Falcon Crest (1981–90); drama

Fall Guy, The (1981–86); adventure

Family Matters (1989–98); situation comedy

Fireside Theatre, The (1949–58; 1963); dramatic anthology

Ford Theater (1949–57); dramatic anthology

Friends (1994–); situation comedy

Fugitive, The (1963–67); adventure

Garry Moore Show, The (1950–51; 1958–67); variety

Gilligan's Island (1964–67); situation comedy

Gomer Pyle, U.S.M.C. (1964–70); situation comedy

Good Times (1974–79); situation comedy

Growing Pains (1985–92); situation comedy

Gunsmoke (1955–75); western

Happy Days (1974–84); situation comedy

Hawaii Five-O (1968–80); police drama

Hee Haw (1969–93); country variety

Hill Street Blues (1981–87); police drama

Hogan's Heroes (1965–71); situation comedy

Home Improvement (1991–99); situation comedy

Honeymooners, The (1952–59); situation comedy

I Dream of Jeannie (1965–70); situation comedy

I Love Lucy (1951–61); situation comedy

Incredible Hulk, The (1978–82); adventure/drama

I've Got a Secret (1952–76); quiz show/audience participation

Jack Benny Show, The (1950–65); comedy

Jackie Gleason Show, The (1962–70); comedy/variety

Jeffersons, The (1975–85); situation comedy

Kate & Allie (1984–89); situation comedy

Knots Landing (1979–93); drama

Kojak (1973–78; 1989–90); police drama

Kraft Television Theatre (1947–58); drama anthology

Lassie (1954–71); adventure

Laverne & Shirley (1976–83); situation comedy

Law & Order (1990–); police/legal drama

Lawrence Welk Show, The (1955–82); music

Leave It to Beaver (1957–63); situation comedy

Little House on the Prairie (1974–83); adventure/drama

Lone Ranger, The (1949–57); western

Love Boat, The (1977–86); situation comedy

M*A*S*H (1972–83); situation comedy

MacGyver (1985–92); adventure

Married ... with Children (1987–97); situation comedy

Mary Tyler Moore Show, The (1970–77); situation comedy

Miami Vice (1984–89); police drama

Milton Berle Show, The/Texaco Star Theater (1948–67); comedy/variety

Mission: Impossible (1966–73; 1988–90); adventure

Mork & Mindy (1978–82); situation comedy

Murphy Brown (1988–98); situation comedy

Newhart (1982–90); situation comedy

Night Court (1984–92); situation comedy

Northern Exposure (1990–95); drama

Odd Couple, The (1970–75; 1982–83); situation comedy

One Day at a Time (1974–84); situation comedy

Partridge Family, The (1970–74); situation comedy

Perry Como Show, The (1948–63); musical variety

Perry Mason (1957–66); legal drama

Price is Right, The (1957–86); quiz show/audience participation

Quantum Leap (1989–93); science fiction

Quincy, M.E. (1976–83); police drama

Rawhide (1959–66); western

Red Skelton Show, The/The Red Skelton Hour (1951–71); comedy/variety

Rescue 911 (1989–92); informational

Rockford Files, The (1974–80); detective drama

Roseanne (1988–97); situation comedy

Sanford and Son (1972–77); situation comedy

Seinfeld (1990–98); situation comedy

Simpsons, The (1989–); cartoon

60 Minutes (1968–); newsmagazine

$64,000 Question, The (1955–58); quiz show

Star Trek (1966–69); science fiction

Star Trek: The Next Generation (1987–94); science fiction

Three's Company (1977–84); situation comedy

Trapper John, M.D. (1979–86); medical drama

20/20 (1978–); newsmagazine

Twilight Zone, The (1959–65; 1985–88); science fiction anthology

Twin Peaks (1990–91); drama

Unsolved Mysteries (1988–); mystery anthology

Untouchables, The (1959–63; 1992–94); police drama

Walt Disney (1954–83; 1986–90; 1997–); anthology

Waltons, The (1972–81); drama

What's My Line? (1950–67); quiz show/panel show

Who Wants to Be a Millionaire? (1999–); quiz show

WKRP in Cincinnati (1978–82); situation comedy

X-Files, The (1993–); science fiction

You Bet Your Life/The Groucho Show (1950–61); quiz show

Your Hit Parade (1950–59; 1974); music

⊙ Classic TV Database. www.classic-tv.com/
  McNeil, Alex. *Total Television*. 4th ed. New York: Penguin, 1996.

ARTS AND LEISURE: *Radio*

75 Favorite Radio Programs

These regularly scheduled, nationally syndicated radio programs ran for at least 10 years in national broadcasts or were series noted for their quality or influence on future entertainment. The "golden age" of radio ended when television became the dominant household medium, but some long-running programs can be found on talk radio even today.

Adventures of Ozzie and Harriet, The (1944–54); situation comedy

Aldrich Family, The (1939–53); situation comedy

Amos 'n' Andy (1929–60); situation comedy

Baby Snooks Show (1944–51); situation comedy

Backstage Wife (1935–59); soap opera

Big Sister (1936–52); soap opera

Big Town (1937–52); crime

Blondie (1939–50); situation comedy

Bob Hope Show, The (1935–55); comedy

Breakfast Club, The (1933–68); variety show

Buck Rogers in the 25th Century (1932–36, 1939–47); science fiction

Camel Caravan, The (1933–54); comedy/variety

Charlie McCarthy Show, The (1937–56); comedy

Cities Service Concerts (1927–56); music show

Colgate Sports Newsreel, The (1939–56); talk show

Death Valley Days (1930–45); western anthology

Dr. Laura (1994–); advice

Eddie Cantor Show, The (1931–49); comedy/variety

Father Coughlin (1930–42); religious commentary

Fibber McGee and Molly (1935–57); comedy

Gang Busters (1935–57); crime anthology

Gene Autry's Melody Ranch (1940–56); music/variety/adventure

Goldbergs, The (1929–34, 1937–45, 1949–50); comedy/drama

Grand Central Station (1937–54); drama anthology

Grand Ole Opry (1925–57); country/variety

Green Hornet, The (1930–50); crime

House Party (1945–67); audience participation

Howard Stern Show, The (1991–); talk/comedy

Information, Please (1938–48); quiz show

Jack Armstrong, the All-American Boy (1933–51); adventure

Jack Benny Program, The (1932–58); comedy

Jimmy Fidler (1934–50); gossip

Just Plain Bill (1932–55); soap opera

Kate Smith Hour, The (1931–51); musical/variety

Let's Pretend (1939–54); children's fantasy

Little Orphan Annie (1931–43); adventure

Lone Ranger, The (1934–55); adventure

Lum and Abner (1931–53); comedy

Lux Radio Theatre, The (1934–55); drama anthology

Ma Perkins (1933–60); soap opera

Major Bowes' Original Amateur Hour (1935–46, 1948–52); talent contest

Manhattan Merry-Go-Round (1932–49); popular music

March of Time, The (1931–45); news documentary

Mr. District Attorney (1939–52); crime drama

Mr. Keen, Tracer of Lost Persons (1937–55); detective drama

One Man's Family (1933–59); drama

Our Gal Sunday (1937–59); soap opera

People Are Funny (1942–59); audience participation

People's Platform, The (1938–52); discussion show

Pepper Young's Family (1936–59); soap opera

Perry Mason (1943–55); crime drama

Prairie Home Companion, A (1989–); music/folklore

Queen for a Day (1945–57); audience participation

Quiz Kids, The (1940–53); quiz show

Radio Guild, The (1929–38, 1939–40); drama

Ripley's Believe It or Not (1930–48); "strange facts"

Red Skelton Show, The (1941–44, 1945–53); variety

Right to Happiness, The (1939–60); soap opera

Romance of Helen Trent, The (1933–60); soap opera

Roy Rogers Show, The (1944–55); western

Rush Limbaugh Show, The (1988–); talk/politics

Second Mrs. Burton, The (1946–60); soap opera

Shadow, The (1930–54); crime

Sherlock Holmes (1930–36, 1939–50, 1955); mystery

Singing Story Lady, The (1932–45); children's show

Stars Over Hollywood (1941–54); drama anthology

Stella Dallas (1938–55); soap opera

Story of Mary Marlin, The (1935–45, 1951–52); soap opera

Suspense (1942–62); dramatic anthology

Tom Mix Ralston Straight Shooters, The (1933–50); western

Truth or Consequences (1941–57); quiz show

Walter Winchell's Journal (1930–57); news/gossip

Young Dr. Malone (1939–60); soap opera

Your Hit Parade (1935–59); popular music

⊙ Buxton, Frank, and Bill Owen. *The Big Broadcast, 1920–1950.* New York: Viking, 1972.
Dunning, John. *Tune in Yesterday: The Ultimate Encyclopedia of Old-Time Radio, 1925–1976.* Englewood Cliffs, N.J.: Prentice-Hall, 1976.

ARTS AND LEISURE: *Travel*

World Travel Requirements for U.S. Citizens

Country	Travel Requirements
Afghanistan	Passport; visa; travel warning
Albania	Passport; visa; onward/return transportation ticket
Algeria	Passport; visa; proof of business, hotel reservation, and airline ticket
Andorra	Passport; visa not required for stay of up to 90 days
Angola	Passport; visa; onward/return transportation ticket; sufficient funds; yellow fever and cholera immunizations
Anguilla	Proof of U.S. citizenship; onward/return transportation ticket; sufficient funds
Antigua and Barbuda	Passport or proof of U.S. citizenship
Argentina	Passport; visa not required for stay of up to 90 days
Armenia	Passport; visa; official invitation required for stays longer than 21 days
Aruba	Passport or proof of U.S. citizenship; visa not required for stay of up to 90 days; onward/return transportation ticket; sufficient funds
Australia	Passport; Electronic Travel Authority (ETA)
Austria	Passport; visa not required for stay of up to 90 days
Azerbaijan	Passport; visa
Azores	Passport; visa not required for stay of up to 90 days
Bahamas	Proof of U.S. citizenship; onward/return transportation ticket
Bahrain	Passport; visa; onward/return transportation ticket; sufficient funds; yellow fever immunization if arriving from infected region
Bangladesh	Passport; visa; onward/return transportation ticket; yellow fever immunization if arriving from infected region
Barbados	Passport or proof of U.S. citizenship
Belarus	Passport; visa
Belgium	Passport; visa not required for stay of up to 90 days
Belize	Passport; visa not required for stay of up to 30 days; onward/return transportation ticket; sufficient funds
Benin	Passport; visa; onward/return transportation ticket; yellow fever and cholera immunization
Bermuda	Passport or proof of U.S. citizenship; onward/return transportation ticket
Bhutan	Passport; visa; onward/return transportation ticket; yellow fever immunization recommended
Bolivia	Passport; visa not required for stay of up to 30 days; tourist cards issued on arrival
Bosnia and Herzegovina	Passport; visa
Botswana	Passport; visa not required for stay of up to 90 days; onward/return transportation ticket; sufficient funds
Brazil	Passport; visa; onward/return transportation ticket; yellow fever immunization if arriving from infected region
Brunei	Passport; visa not required for stay of up to 90 days; onward/return transportation ticket; yellow fever immunization if arriving from infected region
Bulgaria	Passport; visa not required for stay of up to 30 days
Burkina Faso	Passport; visa; yellow fever immunization; cholera immunization recommended
Burma (Myanmar)	Passport; visa

Burundi	Passport; visa; onward/return transportation ticket; itinerary from airline or travel agent; yellow fever and cholera immunizations
Cambodia	Passport; visa
Cameroon	Passport; visa; onward/return transportation ticket; sufficient funds; yellow fever and cholera immunizations
Canada	Passport or proof of U.S. citizenship; visa not required for stay of up to 180 days
Cape Verde	Passport; visa; yellow fever immunization if arriving from an infected region
Cayman Islands	Proof of U.S. citizenship; onward/return transportation ticket; sufficient funds
Central African Republic	Passport; visa; onward/return transportation; yellow fever immunization
Chad	Passport; visa; yellow fever immunization
Chile	Passport; visa not required for stay of up to 90 days
China, People's Republic of	Passport; visa; letter of confirmation from Chinese tour agency or relative in China
Colombia	Passport; onward/return transportation ticket
Comoros Islands	Passport; visa; onward/return transportation ticket; anti-malarial suppressants recommended
Congo, Democratic Republic of the	Passport; visa; onward/return transportation ticket; yellow fever immunization
Congo, Republic of the	Passport; visa; onward/return transportation ticket; yellow fever and cholera immunizations
Cook Islands	Passport; visa not required for stay of up to 31 days; onward/return transportation ticket; sufficient funds
Costa Rica	Passport or original U.S. birth certificate; visa not required for stays of up to 90 days; onward/return transportation ticket
Côte d'Ivoire	Passport; visa not required for stay of up to 90 days; onward/return transportation; sufficient funds; yellow fever immunization
Croatia	Passport; visa not required for stay of up to 90 days
Cuba*	Passport; visa
Curaçao	Passport or proof of U.S. citizenship; visa not required for stay of up to 14 days; onward/return transportation ticket; sufficient funds
Cyprus	Passport; visa not required for stay of up to 90 days; onward/return transportation ticket; AIDS test may be required
Czech Republic	Passport; visa not required for stay of up to 30 days; sufficient funds
Denmark	Passport; visa not required for stay of up to 90 days
Djibouti	Passport; visa; onward/return transportation ticket and sufficient funds; yellow fever immunization
Dominica	Proof of U.S. citizenship; onward/return transportation ticket
Dominican Republic	Passport; tourist card
Ecuador	Passport; visa not required for stay of up to 90 days
Egypt	Passport; visa; yellow fever immunization required if arriving from an infected region;
El Salvador	Passport; visa
Equatorial Guinea	Passport; sufficient funds; smallpox, yellow fever, and cholera immunization
Eritrea	Passport; visa; onward/return transportation ticket; sufficient funds
Estonia	Passport; visa not required for stay of up to 90 days
Ethiopia	Passport; visa; yellow fever immunization
Fiji	Passport; visa not required for stay of up to 6 months; onward/return transportation ticket; sufficient funds
Finland	Passport; visa not required for stay of up to 90 days

Country	Travel Requirements
France	Passport; visa not required for stay of up to 90 days
French Guiana	Passport; visa not required for stay of up to 90 days
French Polynesia	Passport; visa not required for stay of up to 30 days
Gabon	Passport; visa; letter from sponsor or hotel; yellow fever immunization
Gambia	Passport; visa
Georgia	Passport; visa; letter of invitation
Germany	Passport; visa not required for stay of up to 90 days; sufficient funds; health insurance
Ghana	Passport; visa; onward/return transportation ticket; yellow fever immunization
Gibraltar	Passport; visa not required for stay of up to 90 days
Greece	Passport; visa not required for stay of up to 90 days; AIDS test may be required
Greenland	Passport; visa not required for stay of up to 90 days
Grenada	Passport recommended; birth certificate and photo ID accepted; visa not required for stay of up to 90 days
Guadeloupe	Passport; proof of U.S. citizenship and photo ID accepted; visa not required for stay of up to 90 days
Guatemala	Passport required for stay of up to 90 days
Guinea	Passport; visa; letter describing purpose; onward/return transportation ticket; yellow fever immunization
Guinea-Bissau	Passport; visa; letter describing purpose; onward/return transportation ticket; sufficient funds
Guyana	Passport; onward/return transportation ticket
Haiti	Passport; visa not required for stay of up to 90 days
Holy See (Vatican City)	Passport required for entry into Italy; visitors dealt with on a case-by-case basis
Honduras	Passport; visa not required for stay of up to 90 days; onward/return transportation ticket
Hong Kong	Passport; visa not required for stay of up to 90 days; onward/return transportation ticket
Hungary	Passport; visa not required for stay of up to 90 days; onward/return transportation sufficient funds
Iceland	Passport; visa not required for stay of up to 90 days
India	Passport; visa; onward/return transportation ticket; yellow fever immunization if arriving from an infected region
Indonesia	Passport; visa not required for stay of up to 60 days; onward/return transportation; sufficient funds
Iran	Passport; visa (diplomatic relations suspended; travel not recommended)
Iraq*	Passport; visa; AIDS test
Ireland	Passport; visa not required for stay of up to 90 days; onward/return transportation ticket
Israel	Passport; onward/return transportation; sufficient funds
Italy	Passport; visa not required for stay of up to 90 days
Jamaica	Passport or U.S. birth certificate and valid driver's license; onward/return transportation ticket; sufficient funds
Japan	Passport; visa not required for stay of up to 90 days; onward/return transportation ticket
Jordan	Passport; visa
Kazakhstan	Passport; visa; letter of invitation from tourist agency or local police

Kenya	Passport; visa not required for stay of up to 30 days; onward/return transportation ticket; yellow fever immunization recommended; anti-malarial pills recommended
Kiribati (Gilbert Islands)	Passport; visa; onward/return transportation ticket; sufficient funds
Korea, Democratic People's Republic of (North Korea)*	Passport; visa
Korea, Republic of (South Korea)	Passport; visa not required for stay of up to 30 days; onward/return transportation ticket; immunization certificate required if arriving from an infected region
Kuwait	Passport; visa; onward/return transportation ticket
Kyrgyz Republic (Kyrgyzstan)	Passport; visa
Laos	Passport; visa; onward/return transportation ticket; sufficient funds
Latvia	Passport; visa not required for stay of up to 90 days
Lebanon	Passport; visa
Lesotho	Passport; onward/return transportation ticket; sufficient funds
Liberia	Passport; visa; onward/return transportation ticket; sufficient funds; yellow fever, cholera, and tetanus immunizations and medical certificate verifying visitor's good health
Libya*	Passport; visa
Liechtenstein	Passport; visa not required for stay of up to 90 days
Lithuania	Passport; visa not required for stay of up to 90 days
Luxembourg	Passport; visa not required for stay of up to 90 days
Macau	Passport; visa not required for stay of up to 60 days
Macedonia, former Yugoslav Republic of	Passport; visa
Madagascar	Passport; visa; onward/return transportation ticket; sufficient funds; yellow fever and cholera immunizations required if arriving from infected region
Malawi	Passport; visa not required for stay of up to 6 months
Malaysia	Passport; visa not required for stay of up to 90 days; yellow fever and cholera immunizations required if arriving from infected region
Maldives	Passport; visa; onward/return transportation ticket, sufficient funds; hotel reservations; yellow fever and cholera immunizations required if arriving from infected region
Mali	Passport; visa; onward/return transportation ticket; yellow fever immunization; cholera immunization recommended
Malta	Passport; visa not required for stay of up to 90 days; onward/return transportation ticket; immunizations required if arriving from an infected region
Marshall Islands Republic of the	Passport; onward/return transportation ticket; sufficient funds; health certificate required if arriving from an infected area
Martinique	Passport; proof of U.S. citizenship and photo ID accepted; visa not required for stay of up to 90 days
Mauritania	Passport; visa; letter of invitation; onward/return transportation ticket; sufficient funds
Mauritius	Passport; visa not required for stay of up to 90 days; onward/return transportation ticket; sufficient funds; confirmation from hotel
Mexico	Proof of U.S. citizenship; visa not required for stay of up to 90 days; tourist card

Country	Travel Requirements
Micronesia, Federated States of	Proof of U.S. citizenship; onward/return transportation ticket; sufficient funds; health certificate may be required if arriving from an infected region; typhoid and tetanus immunizations recommended
Moldova	Passport; visa
Monaco	Passport; visa not required for stay of up to 90 days
Mongolia	Passport; visa; onward/return transportation ticket; must register with Civil Registration Information Center Police Department on arrival
Morocco	Passport; visa not required for stay of up to 90 days
Mozambique	Passport; visa; letter detailing itinerary and address in Mozambique; yellow fever and cholera immunizations
Namibia	Passport; visa not required for stay of up to 90 days; onward/return transportation ticket; sufficient funds
Nauru	Passport; visa; onward/return transportation ticket; sponsorship from a resident of Nauru
Nepal	Passport; visa
Netherlands	Passport; visa not required for stay of up to 90 days; onward/return transportation ticket; sufficient funds and health insurance may be required
Netherlands Antilles	Passport or proof of U.S. citizenship; visa not required for stay of up to 14 days; onward/return transportation; sufficient funds may be required
New Zealand	Passport and arrival card; visa not required for stay of up to 90 days; onward/return transportation ticket, visa for next destination, and sufficient funds may be required
Nicaragua	Passport; onward/return transportation ticket
Niger	Passport; visa; onward/return transportation ticket; sufficient funds; yellow fever immunization; cholera immunization recommended if arriving from infected region
Nigeria	Passport; visa; letter of invitation; onward/return transportation ticket; sufficient funds; hotel confirmation; yellow fever immunization
Norway	Passport; visa not required for stay of up to 90 days
Oman	Passport; visa
Pakistan	Passport; visa; onward/return transportation ticket
Palau, The Republic of	Passport or proof of U.S. citizenship; visa not required for stay of up to 30 days; onward/return transportation ticket
Panama	Passport or proof of U.S. citizenship and photo ID; visa or tourist card; onward/return transportation ticket; sufficient funds
Papua New Guinea	Passport; visa valid for up to 60 days; onward/return transportation ticket; sufficient funds
Paraguay	Passport; visa not required for stay of up to 90 days
Peru	Passport; visa not required for stay of up to 90 days; onward/return transportation ticket
Philippines	Passport; visa not required for stay of up to 21 days; onward/return transportation ticket
Poland	Passport; visa not required for stay of up to 90 days
Portugal	Passport; visa not required for stay of up to 90 days
Qatar	Passport; visa
Reunion	Passport; visa not required for stay of up to 90 days
Romania	Passport; visa not required for stay of up to 30 days
Russia	Passport; original U.S. birth certificate may be required; visa; confirmation from tourist agency in Russia
Rwanda	Passport; visa not required for stay of up to 30 days

Saint Kitts and Nevis	Passport or proof of U.S. citizenship and photo ID; onward/return transportation ticket
Saint Lucia	Passport or proof of U.S. citizenship and photo ID; onward/return transportation ticket
St. Martin	Passport; visa not required for stay of up to 90 days
St. Pierre	Passport or proof of U.S. citizenship and photo ID; visa not required for stay of up to 90 days
Saint Vincent and the Grenadines	Proof of U.S. citizenship and photo ID; onward/return transportation ticket; sufficient funds
Samoa	Passport; visa not required for stay of up to 30 days; onward/return transportation ticket
San Marino	Passport; visa not required for stay of up to 90 days
São Tomé and Príncipe	Passport; visa; letter stating purpose of travel; yellow fever immunization
Saudi Arabia	Passport; tourist visa not available; onward/return transportation ticket; meningitis and cholera immunization highly recommended
Senegal	Passport; visa not required for stay of up to 90 days; onward/return transportation ticket; yellow fever immunization
Serbia and Montenegro	Passport; visa (diplomatic relations suspended; travel not recommended)
Seychelles	Passport; visa issued on arrival for stay of up to 30 days; onward/return transportation ticket; sufficient funds
Sierra Leone	Passport; visa; onward/return transportation ticket; sufficient funds; yellow fever and cholera immunization; malarial suppressants recommended
Singapore	Passport; visa not required for stay of up to 30 days; onward/return transportation ticket; yellow fever and cholera immunizations recommended; AIDS test may be required
Slovak Republic	Passport; visa not required for stay of up to 30 days
Slovenia	Passport; visa not required for stay of up to 90 days
Solomon Islands	Passport; visitors permit; onward/return transportation ticket sufficient funds
Somalia	Passport
South Africa	Passport; visa not required for stay of up to 90 days; onward/return transportation ticket; sufficient funds; yellow fever immunization required if arriving from infected region; malarial suppressants recommended
Spain	Passport; visa not required for stay of up to 90 days
Sri Lanka	Passport; visa not required for stay of up to 30 days; onward/return transportation ticket; sufficient funds; yellow fever and cholera immunizations if arriving from infected area
Sudan	Passport; visa; onward/return transportation ticket; sufficient funds; yellow fever, cholera, and meningitis immunizations recommended; malarial suppressants recommended
Suriname	Passport; visa; onward/return transportation ticket
Swaziland	Passport; visa not required for stay of up to 60 days; yellow fever and cholera immunizations required if arriving from infected area; malarial suppressants recommended
Sweden	Passport; visa not required for stay of up to 90 days
Switzerland	Passport; visa not required for stay of up to 90 days
Syria	Passport; visa
Tahiti	Passport; visa not required for stay of up to 30 days
Taiwan	Passport; visa not required for stay of up to 14 days; onward/return transportation ticket
Tajikistan	Passport; visa

Country	Travel Requirements
Tanzania	Passport; visa; yellow fever and cholera immunizations recommended if arriving from infected region; malarial suppressants recommended
Thailand	Passport; visa not required for stays of up to 30 days
Togo	Passport; visa; sufficient funds; yellow fever immunization
Tonga	Passport; visa not required for stay of up to 30 days; onward/return transportation ticket
Trinidad and Tobago	Passport; visa not required for stay of up to 90 days
Tunisia	Passport; visa not required for stay of up to 120 days; onward/return transportation ticket
Turkey	Passport; visa
Turkmenistan	Passport; visa; letter of invitation
Turks and Caicos	Proof of U.S. citizenship and photo ID; onward/return transportation ticket; sufficient funds
Tuvalu	Passport; visitor permit; onward/return transportation ticket; sufficient funds
Uganda	Passport; visa; yellow fever immunization; typhoid and malarial suppressants recommended
Ukraine	Passport; visa; invitation and confirmation letter from receiving party
United Arab Emirates	Passport; visa; sufficient funds
United Kingdom (England, Scotland, Wales)	Passport; visa not required for stay of up to 6 months
Uruguay	Passport; visa not required for stay of up to 90 days
Uzbekistan	Passport, visa
Vanuatu	Passport; visa not required for stay of up to 30 days; onward/return transportation ticket
Venezuela	Passport; tourist card
Vietnam	Passport; visa
Virgin Islands, British	Proof of U.S. citizenship and photo ID; onward/return transportation ticket; sufficient funds
West Indies, British	Proof of U.S. citizenship and photo ID; onward/return transportation ticket; sufficient funds
West Indies, French	Passport or proof of U.S. citizenship and photo ID; visa not required for stay of up to 90 days
Yemen, Republic of	Passport; visa; onward/return transportation ticket; letter of invitation; yellow fever, cholera immunizations and malarial suppressants recommended
Zambia	Passport; visa; yellow fever immunization and malarial suppressants recommended
Zimbabwe	Passport; visa; onward/return transportation ticket; sufficient funds; malarial suppressants recommended

* Requires special authorization. Contact Licensing Division, Office of Foreign Assets Control, Department of the Treasury, 1500 Pennsylvania Avenue, NW, Treasury Annex, Washington, DC 20220; (202) 622-2480.

⊙ U.S. Department of State. "Foreign Entry Requirements Page," www.travel.state.gov/ foreignentryreqs.html

World Airports

City	Code	City	Code
Aberdeen, Scotland	ABZ	Dublin, Ireland	DUB
Abingdon, England	ABB	Dusseldorf, Germany	DUS
Abu Dhabi, United Arab Emirates	AUH	Edinburgh, Scotland	EDI
		Edmonton (Edmonton International), AB, Canada	YEG
Acapulco, Mexico	ACA		
Adelaide, Australia	ADL	Fairbanks, AK, USA	FAI
Albuquerque, NM, USA	ABQ	Frankfurt, Germany	FRA
Amman, Jordan	AMM	Ft. Lauderdale, FL	FLL
Amsterdam, Netherlands	AMS	Geneva, Switzerland	GVA
Anchorage, AK, USA	ANC	Glasgow, Scotland	GLA
Asunción, Paraguay	ASU	Gothenburg, Sweden	GOT
Athens, Greece	ATH	Governors Harbour, Bahamas	GHB
Atlanta, GA, USA	ATL	Greenland Kangerlussuaq	SFJ
Auckland, New Zealand	AKL	Guadalajara, Mexico	GDL
Austin, TX, USA	AUS	Guam	GUM
Baghdad, Iraq	BGT	Guangzhou, China	CAN
Baltimore, MD, USA	BWI	Guatemala City, Guatemala	GUA
Bangkok, Thailand	BKK	Guayaquil, Ecuador	GYE
Barbuda, Antigua and Barbuda	BBQ	Halifax, NS, Canada	YHZ
Barcelona, Spain	BCN	Hamburg, Germany	HAM
Basel, Switzerland	BSL	Hanoi, Vietnam	HAN
Beijing, China	PEK	Helsinki, Finland	HEL
Belfast, Northern Ireland	BFS	Hiroshima, Japan	HIW
Belgrade, Yugoslavia	BJY	Hong Kong, Hong Kong	HKG
Belize City, Belize	BZE	Honolulu, HI, USA	HNL
Berlin, Germany	BER	Houston (Intercontinental), TX, USA	IAH
Bogotá, Colombia	BOG		
Bombay, India	BOM	Indianapolis, IN, USA	IND
Boston, MA, USA	BOS	Istanbul, Turkey	IST
Bridgetown, Barbados	BGI	Jakarta, Indonesia	CGK
Brussels, Belgium	BRU	Jedda, Saudi Arabia	JED
Bucharest, Romania	OTOP	Jerusalem, Israel	JRS
Budapest, Hungary	BUD	Johannesburg, South Africa	JNB
Buenos Aires, Argentina	EZE	Kansas City, KS, USA	KCK
Cairo, Egypt	CAI	Kathmandu, Nepal	KTM
Calcutta, India	CCU	Kiev, Ukraine	KBP
Calgary, Canada	YYC	Kingston, Jamaica	KIN
Cancun, Mexico	CUN	Kuala Lumpur, Malaysia	KUL
Cape Town, South Africa	CPT	Larnaca, Cyprus	LCA
Caracas, Venezuela	CCS	Las Vegas, NV, USA	LAS
Charleston, SC, USA	CHS	Lima, Peru	LIM
Charlotte, NC, USA	CLT	Lisbon, Portugal	LIS
Chicago, IL, USA	CHI	Ljubljana, Slovenia	LJU
Cincinnati, OH, USA	CVG	London (Gatwick), England	LGW
Cleveland, OH, USA	CLE	London (Heathrow), England	LHR
Columbia, SC, USA	CAE	Los Angeles, CA, USA	QLA
Copenhagen, Denmark	CPH	Lyons, France	LYS
Dallas/Ft. Worth, TX, USA	DFW	Madrid, Spain	MAD
Dakar, Senegal	DKR	Managua, Nicaragua	MGA
Delhi, India	DEL	Manchester, England	MAN
Denver, CO, USA	QDV	Manila, Philippines	MNL
Detroit, MI, USA	DTT	Marseilles, France	MRS
Dominica, Dominica	DOM	Mazatlan, Mexico	MZT

World Airports (cont.)

City	Code	City	Code
Melbourne, Australia	MEL	Salt Lake City, UT, USA	SLC
Mexico City, Mexico	MEX	San Antonio, TX, USA	SAT
Miami, FL, USA	MIA	San Diego, CA, USA	SAN
Milan (Malpensa), Italy	MXP	San Francisco, CA, USA	QSF
Milwaukee, WI, USA	MKE	San Juan, Puerto Rico	SJU
Minneapolis, MN, USA	MSP	Santiago, Chile	SCL
Montreal, QC, Canada	YUL	Santo Domino, Dominican	SDQ
Moscow (Sheremetyevo), Russia	SVO	Republic	
Munich, Germany	MUC	São Paulo, Brazil	GRU
Nagoya, Japan	NGO	Sapporo, Japan	CTX
Nairobi, Kenya	NBO	Seattle, WA, USA	SEA
Naples, Italy	NAP	Seoul, Korea	SEL
Nassau, Bahamas	NAS	Shanghai, China	SHA
Newark, NJ USA	EWR	Shannon, Ireland	SNN
New Orleans, LA, USA	MSY	Singapore, Singapore	SIN
New York (Kennedy), NY, USA	JFK	Sofia, Bulgaria	SOF
New York (La Guardia), NY, USA	LGA	St. Croix, U.S. Virgin Islands	STX
Nice, France	NCE	St. Louis, MO, USA	STL
Oostende, Belgium	OST	St. Lucia, St. Lucia	SLU
Orlando, FL, USA	MCO	St. Maarten, Netherlands Antilles	SXM
Osaka, Japan	KIX	St. Petersburg, Russia	LED
Oslo, Norway	OSL	Stockholm, Sweden	ARN
Ottawa, Canada	YOW	Stuttgart, Germany	STR
Panama City, Panama	PTY	Sydney, Australia	SYD
Paradise City, Bahamas	PID	Taipei, Taiwan	TPE
Paris (Charles de Gaulle),	CDG	Tallinn, Estonia	TLL
France		Tampa, FL, USA	TPA
Paris (Orly), France	ORY	Tehran, Iran	THR
Perth, Australia	PER	Tel Aviv, Israel	TLV
Philadelphia, PA, USA	PHL	Tokyo (Narita), Japan	NRT
Pittsburgh, PA, USA	PIT	Toronto, ON, Canada	YYZ
Portland, OR, USA	PDX	Tortola, British Virgin Island	EIS
Prague, Czech Republic	PRG	Tulsa, OK, USA	TUL
Puerto Vallarta, Mexico	PVR	Vancouver, Canada	YVR
Raleigh-Durham, NC, USA	RDU	Vienna, Austria	VIE
Reno, NV, USA	RNO	Warsaw, Poland	WAW
Reykjavik, Iceland	RKV	Washington, D.C. (Dulles), USA	IAD
Rio de Janeiro, Brazil	GIG	Washington, D.C. (National), USA	DCA
Riyadh, Saudi Arabia	XWM	Xian Xianyang, China	XIY
Rome (Leonardo Da Vince/,	FCO	Zurich, Switzerland	ZRH
Fuimicino) Italy			

⊙ Airlines of the Web. "Cities with Airports Page," www.flyaow.com/citycode.htm
  Federal Aviation Administration. "Airport Codes Page," www.faa.gov/
  aircodeinfo.htm

Major Airlines

Airline	Code	Based In	Airline	Code	Based In
Aer Lingus	EI	Ireland	Aeromexico	AM	Mexico
Aeroflot	SU	Russian	Aeroperu	AP	Peru
		Federation	Air Afrique	RK	Côte
Aerolinean	AR	Argentina			d'Ivoire
Argentinas			Air Canada	AC	Canada

ARTS AND LEISURE: *Travel*

Air China International	CA	China	KLM (Royal Dutch Airlines)	KL	Netherlands
Air France	AF	France	Korean Air	KE	Korea
Air India	AI	India	Lacsa Airlines	LR	Costa Rica
Air Jamaica	JM	Jamaica	Lauda Air	NG	Austria
Air Lanka Limited	UL	Sri Lanka	LOT (Polish Airlines)	LO	Poland
Air New Zealand	NZ	New Zealand			
Air Pacific	FJ	Fiji	Lufthansa Airlines	LH	Germany
Alaska Airlines	AS	United States			
Alitalia	AZ	Italy	Malaysia Airlines	MH	Malaysia
All Nippon Airlines	NH	Japan	Malev (Hungarian Airlines)	MA	Hungary
Aloha Airlines	AQ	United States	MEA (Middle East Airlines)	ME	Lebanon
America West Airlines	HP	United States			
			Mexicana Airlines	MX	Mexico
American Airlines	AA	United States	Midwest Express Airlines	YX	United States
Ansett Australian Airlines	AN	Australia			
			Northwest Airlines	NW	United States
Asiana Airlines	OZ	South Korea	Philippine Airlines	PR	Philippines
Austrian Airlines	OS	Austria	PIA (Pakistan International Airlines)	PK	Pakistan
Avianca Airlines	AV	Colombia			
Aviateca	GU	Guatemala			
Balkan Bulgarian Airlines	LZ	Bulgaria	Qantas Airlines	QF	Australia
			Reno Air	QQ	United States
British Airways	BA	United Kingdom	Royal Air Maroc	AT	Morocco
British Midland	BD	United Kingdom	Royal Jordanian	RJ	Jordan
BWIA International	BW	Trinidad & Tobago	Sabena Airlines	SN	Belgium
			Saudi Arabian Airlines	SV	Saudi Arabia
Canadian Airlines	CP	Canada			
Cathay Pacific Airlines	CX	Hong Kong	Scandinavian Airlines	SK	Sweden and Denmark
China Airlines	CI	Taiwan	Singapore Airlines	SQ	Singapore
Continental Airlines	CO	United States	South African Airways	SA	South Africa
Copa Airlines	CM	Panama	Southwest Airlines	WN	United States
Czech Airlines (CSA)	OK	Czech Republic	Swiss Air	SR	Switzerland
			TACA International Airlines	TA	El Salvador and Honduras
Delta Air Lines	DL	United States			
Egypt Air	MS	Egypt			
El Al Israel Airlines	LY	Israel	TAP Air Portugal	TP	Portugal
			Thai Airways International	TG	Thailand
Emirates Air	EK	United Arab Emirates			
			Tower Air	FF	United States
Finnair	AY	Finland	Turkish Airlines	TK	Turkey
Garuda Indonesia Airlines	GA	Indonesia	TWA (Trans World Airlines)	TW	United States
Hawaiian Airlines	HA	United States (Hawaii)	United Airlines	UA	United States
			US Airways	US	United States
Iberia	IB	Spain	Varig Brazilian Airlines	RG	Brazil
Icelandair	FI	Iceland			
Japan Airlines	JL	Japan	Virgin Atlantic	VS	Great Britain

⊙ AirportsCheck. "Airline Codes Page," www.virtualsfo.com/yourTravelCenter/
   flightInformation/airlineCodes.htm

   National Association of Commissioned Travel Agents (NACTA). "International
   Airline Directory Page," www.nacta.com/intair.htm

   Travel-On, Ltd. "Travel Resources: Airline Codes Page," www.tvlon.com/
   Airlines.htm

Distances: World Cities (in Miles)

	Athens, Greece	Beijing, China	Berlin, Germany	Bombay, India	Brussels, Belgium	Cairo, Egypt	Hong Kong	Jerusalem, Israel	London, England
Athens, Greece	—	4,741	1,119	3,218	1,298	702	5,382	782	1,486
Beijing, China	4,741	—	4,585	2,956	4,656	4,696	1,254	4,433	5,071
Berlin, Germany	1,119	4,585	—	3,916	403	1,802	5,512	1,806	557
Bombay, India	3,218	2,956	3,916	—	4,281	2,709	2,734	2,496	4,477
Brussels, Belgium	1,298	4,656	403	4,281	—	2,000	5,909	2,052	199
Cairo, Egypt	702	4,696	1,802	2,709	2,000	—	5,131	264	2,187
Hong Kong	5,382	1,254	5,512	2,734	5,909	5,31	—	4,873	6,052
Jerusalem, Israel	782	4,433	1,806	2,496	2,052	264	4,873	—	2,246
London, England	1,486	5,071	557	4,477	199	2,187	6,052	2,246	—
Madrid, Spain	1,475	5,742	1,159	4,689	817	2,089	6,623	2,239	783
Manila, Philippines	5,993	1,764	6,141	3,195	6,537	5,709	629	5,455	6,679
Moscow, Russia	1,384	3,608	1,006	3,128	1,404	1,805	4,506	1,660	1,559
Nairobi, Kenya	2,831	5,725	3,948	2,815	4,067	2,182	5,498	2,275	4,228
Paris, France	1,303	5,119	545	4,365	165	2,001	6,057	2,074	213
Rio de Janeiro, Brazil	5,989	10,720	6,161	8,300	5,802	6,096	11,019	6,360	5,708
Rome, Italy	646	5,057	736	3,837	735	1,323	5,836	1,428	897
Seoul, Korea	5,304	598	5,067	3,491	5,424	5,286	1,307	5,024	5,519
Singapore	5,620	2,769	6,162	2,419	6,556	5,127	1,593	4,915	6,739
Sydney, Australia	9,528	5,547	10,005	6,310	10,407	8,959	4,512	8,782	10,562

Madrid, Spain	Manila, Phillippines	Moscow, Russia	Nairobi, Kenya	Paris, France	Rio de Janeiro, Brazil	Rome, Italy	Seoul, Korea	Singapore	Sydney, Australia
1,475	5,993	1,384	2,831	1,303	5,989	646	5,304	5,620	9,528
5,742	1,764	3,608	5,725	5,119	10,720	5,057	598	2,769	5,547
1,159	6,141	1,006	3,948	545	6,161	736	5,067	6,162	10,005
4,689	3,195	3,128	2,815	4,365	8,300	3,837	3,491	2,419	6,310
817	6,537	1,404	4,067	165	5,802	735	5,424	6,556	10,407
2,089	5,709	1,805	2,182	2,001	6,096	1,323	5,286	5,127	8,959
6,623	629	4,506	5,498	6,057	11,019	5,836	1,307	1,593	4,512
2,239	5,455	1,660	2,275	2,074	6,360	1,428	5,024	4,915	8,782
783	6,679	1,559	4,228	213	5,708	897	5,519	6,739	10,562
—	7,252	2,141	3,840	652	5,002	856	6,226	7,072	10,996
7,252	—	5,135	5,858	6,685	11,250	6,460	1,624	1,490	3,888
2,141	5,135	—	3,929	1,550	7,120	1,476	4,117	5,226	9,005
3,840	5,858	3,929	—	4,020	5,521	3,333	6,288	4,633	7,561
652	6,685	1,550	4,020	—	5,639	694	5,587	6,667	10,543
5,002	11,250	7,120	5,521	5,639	—	5,664	11,226	9,764	8,447
856	6,460	1,476	3,333	694	5,664	—	5,584	6,127	10,140
6,226	1,624	4,117	6,288	5,587	11,226	5,584	—	2,900	5,160
7,072	1,490	5,226	4,633	6,667	9,764	6,127	2,900	—	3,925
10,996	3,888	9,005	7,561	10,543	8,447	10,140	5,160	3,925	—

⊙ Indo.com. "How Far Is It?" www.indo.com/distance/

Distances: U.S. Cities (in Miles)

	Atlanta, GA	Baltimore, MD	Boston, MA	Chicago, IL	Cleveland, OH	Dallas, TX	Detroit, MI	Houston, TX	Indianapolis, IN
Atlanta, GA	—	578	938	585	553	717	599	701	426
Baltimore, MD	578	—	360	608	307	1,211	401	1,253	510
Boston, MA	938	360	—	856	552	1,551	618	1,607	809
Chicago, IL	585	608	856	—	312	798	238	937	163
Cleveland, OH	553	307	552	312	—	1,023	96	1,114	263
Dallas, TX	717	1,211	1,551	798	1,023	—	997	224	763
Detroit, MI	599	401	618	238	96	997	—	1,106	240
Houston, TX	701	1,253	1,607	937	1,114	224	1,106	—	866
Indianapolis, IN	426	510	809	163	263	763	240	866	—
Las Vegas, NV	1,748	2,109	2,380	1,525	1,834	1,077	1,762	1,232	1,599
Los Angeles, CA	1,944	2,327	2,606	1,749	2,057	1,251	1,987	1,382	1,818
Memphis, TN	332	793	1,137	481	630	419	625	484	386
Miami, FL	605	955	1,255	1,186	1,086	1,108	1,156	968	1,024
Minneapolis, MN	905	938	1,126	354	632	860	539	1,054	510
New York, NY	748	170	190	719	408	1,373	489	1,421	648
Pittsburgh, PA	522	195	483	413	114	1,069	211	1,139	330
San Francisco, CA	2,145	2,464	2,708	1,863	2,175	1,493	2,095	1,651	1,957
Seattle, WA	2,181	2,335	2,496	1,737	2,028	1,683	1,935	1,891	1,873
St. Louis, MO	467	735	1,042	259	494	544	456	678	234

Las Vegas, NV	Los Angeles, CA	Memphis, TN	Miami, FL	Minneapolis, MN	New York, NY	Pittsburgh, PA	San Francisco, CA	Seattle, WA	St. Louis, MO
1,748	1,944	332	605	905	748	522	2,145	2,181	467
2,109	2,327	793	955	938	170	195	2,464	2,335	735
2,380	2,606	1,137	1,255	1,126	190	483	2,708	2,496	1,042
1,525	1,749	481	1,186	354	719	413	1,863	1,737	259
1,834	2,057	630	1,086	632	408	114	2,175	2,028	494
1,077	1,251	419	1,108	860	1,373	1,069	1,493	1,683	544
1,762	1,987	625	1,156	539	489	211	2,095	1,935	456
1,232	1,382	484	968	1,054	1,421	1,139	1,651	1,891	678
1,599	1,818	386	1,024	510	648	330	1,957	1,873	234
—	231	1,417	2,185	1,298	2,240	1,924	420	868	1,380
231	—	1,615	2,348	1,528	2462	2,145	344	954	1,595
1,417	1,615	—	868	701	956	660	1,813	1,872	244
2,185	2,348	868	—	1,510	1,088	1,011	2,601	2,734	1,062
1,298	1,528	701	1,510	—	1,023	744	1,591	1,396	464
2,240	2,462	956	1,088	1,023	—	318	2,582	2,413	879
1,924	2,145	660	1,011	744	318	—	2,273	2,140	562
420	344	1,813	2,601	1,591	2,582	2,273	—	678	1,750
868	954	1,872	2,734	1,396	2,413	2,140	678	—	1,723
1,380	1,595	244	1,062	464	879	562	1,750	1,723	—

⊙ Indo.com. "How Far Is It?" www.indo.com/distance/

Tourism Departments
The United States and Major Foreign Destinations

State	Mailing Address	Phone/Fax/Website
Alabama	Alabama Bureau of Tourism and Travel 401 Adams Avenue, Suite 12 Montgomery, AL 36103-49	Phone: (334) 242-4159 or 800-ALABAMA Fax: (334) 242-4554 www.touralabama.org/
Alaska	Alaska Division of Tourism P.O. Box 110801 Juneau, AK 99811-0801	Phone: (907) 465-2012 Fax: (907) 465-3767 www.dced.state.ak.us/ tourism/
Arizona	Arizona Office of Tourism 2702 N. 3rd Street, Suite 4015 Phoenix, AZ 85004	Phone: (602) 248-1501 or 800-842-8257 Fax: (602) 240-5432 www.arizonaguide.com/
Arkansas	Arkansas Department of Parks & Tourism One Capitol Mall Little Rock, AR 72201	Phone: (501) 682-7777 or 800-628-8725 Fax: (501) 682-1364 www.arkansas.com/
California	California Division of Tourism 801 K Street, Suite 1600 Sacramento, CA 95814	Phone: (916) 322-2881 Fax: (916) 322-3402 gocalif.ca.gov/
Colorado	Colorado Travel and Tourism Authority 1672 Pennsylvania Street Denver, CO 80203	Phone: (303) 832-6171 or 800-265-6723 www.colorado.com/
Connecticut	Connecticut Office of Travel & Tourism 505 Hudson Street Hartford, CT 06106	Phone: (860) 270-8089 Fax: (860) 270-8077 www.ctbound.org/
Delaware	Delaware Economic Development Office 99 Kings Highway Dover, DE 19901	Phone: (302) 739-4271 Fax: (302) 739-5749 www.state.de.us/ tourism/
Florida	Florida Tourism 661 E. Jefferson Street, Suite 300 Tallahassee, FL 32301	Phone: (850) 488-5607 Fax: (850) 224-9783 www.flausa.com/
Georgia	Georgia Dept. of Industry, Trade & Tourism 285 Peachtree Center Avenue, NE Marquis Two Tower, Suite 1000 Atlanta, GA 30303-1230	Phone: (404) 656-3553 Fax: (404) 651-9462 www.georgia.org/
Hawaii	Hawaii Visitors and Convention Bureau 2270 Kalakaua Avenue, #801 Honolulu, HI 96815	Phone: (808) 923-1811 Fax: (808) 924-0290 www.gohawaii.com/

Idaho	Idaho Recreation and Tourism	Phone: (208) 334-2470
	P.O. Box 83720	or 800-242-5858
	Boise, ID 83720-0093	Fax: (208) 334-2631
		www.visitid.org/
Illinois	Illinois Bureau of Tourism and Film	Phone: (312)814-4734
	100 West Randolph, Suite 3-400	Fax: (312) 814-6175
	Chicago, IL 60601	www.enjoyillinois.com/
Indiana	Department of Commerce, Tourism	Phone: (317) 232-8860
	Development Division	or 888-ENJOY-IN
	1 North Capitol, Suite 700	(365-6946)
	Indianapolis, IN 46204-2288	Fax: (317) 233-6887
		www.enjoyindiana.com/
Iowa	Iowa Department of Economic	Phone: (515) 242-4700
	Development	Fax: (515) 242-4809
	Division of Tourism	www.traveliowa.com/
	200 E. Grand Avenue	
	Des Moines, IA 50309	
Kansas	Kansas Travel and Tourism	Phone: (785) 296-2009
	700 SW Harrison Street, Suite 1300	or 800-2KANSAS
	Topeka, KS 66603-3755	(252-6727)
		Fax: (785) 296-6988
		www.kansas
		commerce.com/
Kentucky	Kentucky Department of Travel	Phone: (502) 564-4930
	500 Mero Street, 22nd Floor	Fax: (502) 564-5695
	Frankfort, KY 40601-1968	www.kentucky
		tourism.com
Louisiana	Louisiana Office of Tourism	Phone: (225) 342-8100
	1051 N. 3rd Street	Fax: (225) 342-8390
	P.O. Box 94291	www.louisiana
	Baton Rouge, LA 70804	travel.com/
Maine	Maine Office of Tourism	Phone: (207) 287-5711
	59 State House Station,	or (207) 287-3180
	Augusta, ME 04333-0059	Fax: (207) 287-8070
		www.visitmaine.com/
Maryland	Maryland Office of Tourism	Phone: (410) 767-6294
	Development	or 800-719-5900
	217 East Redwood Street, 9th Floor	Fax: (410) 333-6643
	Baltimore, MD 21202	www.mdisfun.org
Massachusetts	Massachusetts Office of Travel &	Phone: (617)973-8500
	Tourism	or 800-447-6277
	10 Park Plaza, Suite 4510	Fax: (617) 973-8555
	Boston, MA 02116	www.mass-vacation
		.com/

Tourism Departments *(cont.)*

State	Mailing Address	Phone/Fax/Website
Michigan	Travel Michigan Michigan Economic Development Corporation Victor Office Center, 2nd Floor 201 N. Washington Square Lansing, MI 48913	Phone: (517) 373-0670 or 800-78-GREAT (784-7328) Fax: (517) 373-0059 www.michigan.org/
Minnesota	Minnesota Office of Tourism 500 Metro Square 121 7th Place East St. Paul, MN 55101	Phone: (651) 296-2755 Fax: (651) 296-7095 www.explore minnesota.com/
Mississippi	Mississippi Department of Economic and Community Development Division of Tourism Development P.O. Box 849 Jackson, MS 39205	Phone: (601) 359-3297 or 800-WARMEST (927-6378) Fax: (601) 359-5757 www.visit mississippi.org/
Missouri	Missouri Division of Tourism P.O. Box 1055 Jefferson City, MO 65102	Phone: (573) 751-4133 Fax: (573) 751-5160 www.missouri tourism.org/
Montana	Montana Travel Promotion 1424 Ninth Avenue Helena, MT 59620	Phone: (406) 444-2654 Fax: (406) 444-1800 www.visitmt.com/
Nebraska	Nebraska Division of Travel & Tourism P.O. Box 98907 Lincoln, NE 68509-8907	Phone: (402) 471-3796 Fax: (402) 471-3026 www.visitnebraska.org
Nevada	Nevada Commission on Tourism 401 North Carson Street Carson City, NV 89701	Phone: (775) 687-4322 or 800-237-0774 Fax: (775) 687-6779 www.travelnevada.com/
New Hampshire	New Hampshire Office of Travel & Tourism Development P.O. Box 1856 Concord, NH 03302-1856	Phone: (603) 271-2665 Fax: (603) 271-6784 www.visitnh.gov/
New Jersey	New Jersey Commerce & Economic Growth Commission Office of Travel & Tourism 20 West State Street, P.O. Box 826 Trenton, NJ 08625-0826	Phone: (609) 633-2377 or (609) 292-2470 Fax: (609) 633-7418 www.state.nj.us/travel/
New Mexico	New Mexico Department of Tourism P.O. Box 20002 Santa Fe, NM 87503	Phone: (505) 827-7400 or 800-545-2040 Fax: (505) 827-7402 www.newmexico.org/
New York	New York State Division of Tourism P.O. Box 2603 Albany, NY 12220-0603	Phone: (518) 474-4116 Fax: (518) 486-6416 www.iloveny.state.ny.us/

North Carolina	North Carolina Travel & Tourism 301 N. Wilmington Street Raleigh, NC 27601	Phone: (919) 733-4171 Fax: (919) 733-8582 www.visitnc.com/
North Dakota	North Dakota Tourism 604 E. Boulevard Avenue Liberty Memorial Building Bismarck, ND 58505-0825	Phone: (701) 328-2525 or 800-HELLOND (435-5663) Fax: (701) 328-4878 www.ndtourism.com/
Ohio	Ohio Division of Travel & Tourism P.O. Box 1001 Columbus, OH 43216-1001	Phone: (614) 466-8844 Fax: (614) 466-6744 www.ohiotourism.com/
Oklahoma	Oklahoma Travel & Tourism Division P.O. Box 52002 Oklahoma City, OK 73152	Phone: (405) 521-4554 or 1-800-652-6552 Fax: (405) 521-3992 www.travelok.com/
Oregon	Oregon Tourism Commission 775 Summer NE Salem, OR 97310	Phone: (503) 986-0000 Fax: (503) 986-0001 www.traveloregon.com/
Pennsylvania	Pennsylvania Tourism Forum Building, Room 404 Harrisburg, PA 17120	Phone: (717) 232-8880 or 800-VISITPA (847-4872) Fax: (717) 787-0687 www.state.pa.us/visit
Rhode Island	Rhode Island Tourism Division One West Exchange Street Providence, RI 02903	Phone: (401) 222-2601 Fax: (401) 222-2102 or (401) 273-8370 www.visitrhode island.com
South Carolina	South Carolina Tourism 1205 Pendleton Street, Suite 112 Columbia, SC 29201	Phone: (803) 734-0128 Fax: (803) 734-1163 www.travelsc.com/
South Dakota	South Dakota Department of Tourism 711 East Wells Avenue Pierre, SD 57501-3369	Phone: (605) 773-3301 Fax: (605) 773-3256 www.travelsd.com/
Tennessee	Tennessee Department of Tourist Development 320 Sixth Avenue, North, 5th Floor Nashville, TN 37243	Phone: (615) 741-2159 or 800-836-6200 Fax: (615) 741-7225 www.tourism.state.tn. us/index.html
Texas	Texas Tourism Division 1700 N. Congress Avenue, Suite 200 Austin, TX 78711-2728	Phone: (512) 462-9191 Fax: (512) 936-0450 www.traveltex.com/
Utah	The Utah Travel Council Council Hall/Capitol Hill Salt Lake City, UT 84114-1396	Phone: (801) 538-1900 or 800-200-1160 Fax: (801) 538-1399 www.utah.com/

Tourism Departments *(cont.)*

State	Mailing Address	Phone/Fax/Website
Vermont	State of Vermont, Dept. of Tourism & Marketing 6 Baldwin Street, 4th Floor Drawer 33 Montpelier, VT 05633-1301	Phone: (802) 828-3516 Fax: (802) 828-3233 www.travel-vermont.com/
Virginia	Virginia Tourism Corporation 901 East Byrd Street Richmond, VA 23219	Phone: (804) 371-8145 Fax: (804) 786-1919 www.virginia.org/
Washington	Washington State Tourism 210 11th Avenue, Suite 101 P.O. Box 42500 Olympia, WA 98504-2500	Phone: (360) 586-2102 Fax: (360) 753-4470 www.tourism.wa.gov/
Washington, D.C.	Washington, D.C. Convention & Visitors Association 212 New York Avenue, N.W., Suite 600 Washington, DC 20005	Phone: (202) 789-7000 Fax: (202) 789-7037 www.washington.org/
West Virginia	West Virginia Division of Tourism 2101 Washington St., E. Charleston, WV 25305	Phone: (304) 558-2288 ext. #343 or 800-CALL WVA (225-5982) Fax: (304) 558-0108 www.state.wv.us/tourism/
Wisconsin	Wisconsin Department of Tourism 201 W. Washington Avenue P.O. Box 7976 Madison, WI 53707-7976	Phone: (608) 266-7621 Fax: (608) 266-3403 or (608) 261-8213 www.travelwisconsin.com/
Wyoming	Wyoming Tourism I-25 at College Drive Cheyenne, WY 82002	Phone: (307) 777-7777 Fax: (307) 777-2878 www.wyomingtourism.org/

Country	Mailing Address	Phone/Fax/Website
Australia	Australian Tourism Industry Association P.O. Box E328 Canberra, ACT 2600	Phone: 011-61-2-6273-1000 Fax: 011-61-2-6273-4999 www.australia.com/
Brazil	Embratur Office (Rio de Janeiro) Rua Uruguaiana, 174 8ffl Andar - Centro Rio de Janeiro / RJ CEP: 20050-092	Phone: 011-55-21-509-6017 (tourist information) or 011-55-21-509-6720 (administration) Fax: 011-55-21-509-7381 or -7429 www.embratur.gov.br/

Canada	Canadian Tourism Commission 8th Floor West, 235 Queen Street Ottawa, ON K1A 0H6	Phone: (613) 946-1000 www.travelcanada.ca/
Egypt	Egyptian Tourist Authority Misr Travel Tower Abbassia Square, Cairo	Phone: 011-20-2-285- 4509 or 284-1970 Fax: 011-20-2-285-4363 www.touregypt.net/
England	British Tourist Authority (USA:New York office) 551 Fifth Avenue, Suite 701 New York, NY 10176-0799	Phone: (212) 986-2200 or 800-462-2748 Fax: (212) 986-1188 www.travelbritain.org/
France	French Government Tourist Office (USA: California office) 9454 Wilshire Blvd, Suite 715 Beverly Hills, CA 90212-2967	Phone: (310) 271-6665 Fax: (310) 276-2835 www.francetourism.com/
India	Government of India Tourist Office (India office) KFC Building, 48 Church Street Bangalore-560 001 Karnataka	Phone: 011-91-80-558-5417 www.tourism inindia.com/
Ireland	Irish Tourist Board (Ireland office) Information Service P.O. Box 273 Dublin 8	Phone: 011-353-1-602-4000 Fax: 011-353-1-602-4100 www.ireland.travel.ie/
Italy	Ente nazionale italiano per il turismo (Italy office) via Marghera no. 2 00185 ROMA	Phone: 011-39-6-49-711 Fax: 011-39-6-446-3379 www.init.it/
Japan	Japan National Tourist Organization (USA:New York office) One Rockefeller Plaza, Suite 1250 New York, NY 10020	Phone: (212) 757-5640 Fax: (212) 307-6754 www.jnto.go.jp/
South Africa	South African Tourism (USA: New York office) 500 Fifth Avenue, Suite 2040 New York, NY 10110	Phone: (212) 730-2929 or 800-822-5368 Fax: (212) 764-1980 www.satour.org
Thailand	Tourism Authority of Thailand (Thailand office) Le Concorde Building 202 Ratchadaphisek Road Huai Khwang Bangkok 10310	Phone: 011-66-2-694-1222 Fax: 011-66-2-694-1372 www.tourism thailand.org/

⊙ Embassy of the United States in Switzerland. "U.S. Tourist Offices Page,"
   www.usembassy.ch/usa/tourist.html
   Tourism Offices Worldwide Directory. www.towd.com

Visitors' and Convention Bureaus in Major World Tourist Destinations

City	Mailing Address	Phone/Fax
Amsterdam	Amsterdam RAI Europaplein 22-30 Postbus 77777 Amsterdam, 1078 GZ Netherlands	Phone: 011-31-20-549-1212 Fax: 011-31-20-646-3042
Bangkok	Tourism Authority of Thailand 372 Bamrung Muang Road Bangkok, 10100 Thailand	Phone: 011-66-2-223-7850 Fax: 011-66-2-226-0303
Barcelona	Barcelona Convention Bureau Tarragona 149-157 Barcelona, 08015 Spain	Phone: 011-34-93-423-1800 Fax: 011-34-93-423-2649
Beijing	Beijing International Convention Center No 8 Beichendong Road Chauyang District Beijing, 100101 China	Phone: 011-86-10-649-10-248 Fax: 011-86-10-649-10-256
Berlin	Berlin Tourismus Marketing AM Karlsbad 11 Berlin, 99 10785 Germany	Phone: 011-30-26-47-48-52 Fax: 011-30-26-47-48-99
Bordeaux	Bordeaux Lac Bordeaux, 33300 France	Phone: 011-33 56 508449 Fax: 011-33 56 431776
Brussels	Belgium Convention and Incentive Bureau Grasmarkt 61 rue du Marche aux Herbes Brussels, B1000 Belgium	Phone: 011-32-2-513-2721 Fax: 011-32-2-513-8803
Budapest	Budapest Convention Centre 1123 Budapest Jagello ut 1-3 Budapest, H-1444 Hungary	Phone: 011-361-166-6756 Fax: 011-361-185-2127
Buenos Aires	Centro Argentino Para La Difusion Y El Formento De Eventos Florida 253 Piso 7 Of. J Buenos Aires, 1349 Argentina	Phone: 011-54-1-394-5496 Fax: 011-54-1-256-22 PIASA AR

Cancun	Cancun Convention and Visitors Bureau Av. Nader Esq Coba S/N Sm.5 Cancun Q.Roo, 77500 Mexico	Phone: 011-52-98-84-65-31 Fax: 011-52-98-87-66-48
Cape Town	Cape Tourism Authority Tourist Information Center Adderley Street Cape Town, 8000 South Africa	Phone: 011-27-21-418-5202 Fax: 011-21-418-5227
Copenhagen	Wonderful Copenhagen Convention and Visitors Bureau Gammel Kongevej 1 Copenhagen V, DK-1610 Denmark	Phone: 011-45-3-325-7400 Fax: 011-45-3-325-7410
Curaçao	Curaçao Convention Bureau Division of Curaçao Tourism Board P.O. Box 3266 Curaçao, Netherlands Antilles	Phone: 011-599-961-6000 Fax: 011-599-961-2305
Florence	Tuscany Convention Bureau Via Borgognissanti #8 Florence, 50123 Italy	Phone: 011-39-55-521-2774 Fax: 011-39-55-528-7263
Frankfurt	Frankfurt Tourist Board Kaiserstrasse 52 Frankfort, D-60329 Germany	Phone: 011-49-69-21-23-03-96 Fax: 011-49-69-21-23-07-76
Hong Kong	Hong Kong Tourist Association 9-11/F Citicorp Centre 18 Whitfield Road North Point Hong Kong, Hong Kong	Phone: 011-852-801-7111 Fax: 011-852-807-6589
Istanbul	Pamfilya Tourism Incorporated Destination Management Ysb Kaya Aldogan Sok 7/1 Zincirlikuyo Istanbul, 80300 Turkey	Phone: 011-212-274-3840 Fax: 011-212-274-3844
Jakarta	Jakarta Convention Bureau Gedung Dinas Pariwisata DKI Jakarta Jalan Kuningan Barat No. 2 Jakarta, 12710 Indonesia	Phone: 011-62-21-520-9691 Fax: 011-62-21-522-9136
Kuala Lumpur	Malaysia Tourism Promotion Board P.O. Box 10328 Kuala Lumpur, 50480 Malaysia	Phone: 011-6-03-293-5188 Fax: 011-6-03-293-5884

Visitors' and Convention Bureaus in Major World Tourist Destinations (cont.)

City	Mailing Address	Phone/Fax
London	London Tourist Board and Convention Bureau Glen House Stag Place London, SW1E 5LT England	Phone: 011-44-207-932-2007 Fax: 011-44-207-932-2068
Madrid	Madrid Department of Tourism Mayor 69 Madrid, 28013 Spain	Phone: 011-34-1-588-0002 Fax: 011-34-1-588-2930
Melbourne	Melbourne Convention and Marketing Bureau 114 Flinders Street, Level 5 Melbourne, VIC 3000 Australia	Phone: 011-61-3-96-54-22-88 Fax: 011-61-3-96-54-81-95
Montreal	Greater Montreal Convention and Tourism Bureau 1555 Peel Street, #600 Montreal, PQ H3A 3L8 Canada	Phone: (514) 844-5400 Fax: (514) 844-5757
Nice	Nice Office of Tourism et des Congres BP 4079 Cedex 04 Nice, 06302 France	Phone: 011-33-04-93-92-82-82 Fax: 011-33-04-93-92-82-98
Paris	Paris Convention and Visitors Bureau 127 avenue des Champs Elysees Paris, 75008 France	Phone: 011-33-1-49-52-53-95 Fax: 011-33-1-49-52-53-90
Rio de Janeiro	Rio Convention and Visitors Bureau Rua Visconde de Piraja 547 GR 610/617 Rio de Janeiro, 22415-900 Brazil	Phone: 011-55-21-259-6165 Fax: 011-55-21-511-2592
Singapore	Singapore Convention Bureau #37-00 Raffles City Tower 250 North Bridge Road Singapore, 0617	Phone: 011-65-339-6622
Stockholm	Congrex BV Linnegatan 89A P.O. Box 5619 Stockholm, S-11486 Sweden	Phone: 011-46-8-459-6622 Fax: 011-46-8-662-6095

Tokyo	Tokyo Convention and Visitors Bureau Marunouchi Branch 9th Floor 8-1, Marunouchi 3-chome Chiyoda-ku Tokyo, 100-0005 Japan	Phone: 011-81-3-3212-8728 Fax: 011-81-3-3212-6732
Toronto	Tourism Toronto 207 Queen's Quay West Toronto, ON M5J 1A7 Canada	Phone: (416) 203-3830 Fax: (416) 203-2600
Zurich	Zurich Tourist Association and Convention Bureau Verkehrsverein Zurich Bahnhofbrucke #1 Zurich, CH8023 Switzerland	Phone: 011-41-1-211-4086 Fax: 011-41-1-211-3981

⊙ American Society of Association Executives. "Search the CVB Directory Page,"
http://info.asaenet.org/convctrs/cvbdir_SQL.cfm
  International Association of Convention & Visitor Bureaus. "Official Tourism
  Organization Around the World Page," www.officialtravelinfo.com/

U.S. Campground Associations

Association	Address/Phone/Fax/Website
American Camping Association	5000 State Road 67 North Martinsville, IN 46151-7902 Phone: (765) 342-8456 Fax: (765) 342-2065 www.acacamps.org
Kampgrounds of America, Inc. (KOA)	P.O. Box 30558 Billings, MT 59114 Phone: (406) 248-7444 Fax: (406) 248-7414 www.koakampgrounds.com
National Association of RV Parks and Campgrounds (ARVC)	113 Park Avenue Falls Church, VA 22046 Phone: (703) 241-8808 Fax: (703) 241-1004 www.gocampingamerica.com
National Recreation Reservation Service (Forest Service and Army Corps of Engineers campgrounds)	Phone: (877) 444-6777 www.reserveusa.com
Northeast Campground Association	P.O. Box 146 Stafford, CT 06075 Phone/Fax: (860) 684-6389 www.campnca.org

U.S. Campground Associations (cont.)

Tentings Plus of the Northwest

P.O. Box 91
St. Ignatius, MT 59865
Phone: (410) 489-7604
www.tenting-hostels.com

Yogi Bear's Jellystone Park
   Camp Resorts

Phone: 800-558-2954
www.campjellystone.com

⊙ CampNet America. www.kiz.com/campnet/html/campnet.htm
   Go Camping America! "Camping Directory Page," www.gocampingamerica.com/
   main.html

U.S. RV Organizations

Association	*Address/Phone/Fax/Website*
The Escapees RV Club	100 Rainbow Drive Livingston, TX 77351 Phone: 888-757-2582 or (936) 327-8873 Fax: (936) 327-4388 www.escapees.com
Family Motor Coach Association	8291 Clough Pike Cincinnati, OH 45244 Phone: 800-543-3622 or (513) 474-3622 www.fmca.com
The Good Sam Club	P.O. Box 6888 Englewood, CO 80155-6888 Phone: 800-234-3450 www.goodsamclub.com
Life On Wheels Association	P.O. Box 9755 Moscow, ID 83843 www.lifeonwheels.com
Loners of America	P.O. Box 3314 IN Napa, CA 94558-0331 www.napanet.net/~mbost/
Passport America	18315B Landon Road Gulfport, MS 39503 Phone: 800-681-6810 Fax: (228) 831-4616 www.passportamerica.com
United RV Campers Club	6245 Rufe Snow Drive, Suite 280 Fort Worth, TX 76148 Phone: 800-521-6978 www.unitedrvcampers.com

⊙ RV Links. www.rvlinks.org/
   The RV Mall. "RV Organizations Page," www.thervmall.com/rvorg.htm

U.S. National Parks

Park	*Location*
Acadia National Park	Maine
Adams National Historical Park	Massachusetts
Appomattox Court House National Historical Park	Virginia
Arches National Park	Utah
Badlands National Park	South Dakota
Big Bend National Park	Texas
Biscayne National Park	Florida
Black Canyon of the Gunnison National Park	Colorado
Boston National Historical Park	Massachusetts
Bryce Canyon National Park	Utah
Canyonlands National Park	Utah
Capitol Reef National Park	Utah
Carlsbad Caverns National Park	New Mexico
Chaco Culture National Historical Park	New Mexico
Channel Islands National Park	California
Chesapeake & Ohio Canal National Historical Park	Washington, D.C., Maryland, West Virginia
Colonial National Historical Park	Virginia
Crater Lake National Park	Oregon
Cumberland Gap National Historical Park	Kentucky
Dayton Aviation Heritage National Historical Park	Ohio
Death Valley National Park	California, Nevada
Denali National Park & Preserve	Alaska
Dry Tortugas National Park	Florida
Everglades National Park	Florida
Gates of the Arctic National Park & Preserve	Alaska
Glacier Bay National Park & Preserve	Alaska
Glacier National Park	Montana
Grand Canyon National Park	Arizona
Grand Teton National Park	Wyoming
Great Basin National Park	Nevada
Great Smoky Mountain National Park	North Carolina, Tennessee
Guadalupe Mountains National Park	Texas
Haleakala National Park	Hawaii
Harpers Ferry National Historical Park	West Virginia
Hawaii Volcanoes National Park	Hawaii
Hopewell Culture National Historical Park	Ohio
Hot Springs National Park	Arkansas
Independence National Historical Park	Pennsylvania
Inupiat Heritage Center National Historical Park	Alaska
Isle Royale National Park	Michigan

U.S. National Parks *(cont.)*

Park	Location
Jean Lafitte National Historic Park & Preserve	Louisiana
Joshua Tree National Park	California
Kalaupapa National Historical Park	Hawaii
Kaloko-Honokohau National Historical Park	Hawaii
Katmai National Park & Preserve	Alaska
Kenai Fjords National Park	Alaska
Keweenaw National Historical Park	Michigan
Klondike Gold Rush National Historical Park	Alaska
Klondike Gold Rush—Seattle Unit National Historical Park	Washington
Kobuk Valley National Park	Alaska
Lake Clark National Park & Preserve	Alaska
Lassen Volcanic National Park	California
Lowell National Historical Park	Massachusetts
Lyndon B. Johnson National Historical Park	Texas
Mammoth Cave National Park	Kentucky
Marsh-Billings-Rockefeller National Historical Park	Vermont
Mesa Verde National Park	Colorado
Minute Man National Historical Park	Massachusetts
Mojave National Preserve	California
Morristown National Historical Park	New Jersey
Mount Rainier National Park	Washington
Natchez National Historical Park	Mississippi
National Park of American Samoa	American Samoa
New Bedford Whaling National Historical Park	Massachusetts
New Orleans Jazz National Historical Park	Louisiana
Nez Perce National Historical Park	Idaho
North Cascades National Park	Washington
Olympic National Park	Washington
Pecos National Historical Park	New Mexico
Petrified Forest National Park	Arizona
Pu`uhonua O Honaunau National Historical Park	Hawaii
Redwood National Park	California
Rocky Mountain National Park	Colorado
Saguaro National Park	Arizona
Salt River Bay National Historic Park & Ecological Preserve	Virgin Islands
San Antonio Missions National Historical Park	Texas
San Francisco Maritime National Historical Park	California
San Juan Island National Historical Park	Washington
Saratoga National Historical Park	New York
Sequoia and Kings Canyon National Park	California
Shenandoah National Park	Virginia
Sitka National Historical Park	Alaska

Theodore Roosevelt National Park	North Dakota		
Tumacácori National Historical Park	Arizona		
Valley Forge National Historical Park	Pennsylvania		
Virgin Islands National Park	Virgin Islands		
Voyageurs National Park	Minnesota		
Wind Cave National Park	South Dakota		
Women's Rights National Historical Park	New York		
Wrangell-St. Elias National Park & Preserve	Alaska		
Yellowstone National Park	Idaho, Montana, Wyoming		
Yosemite National Park	California		
Zion National Park	Utah		

⊙ Multicom Publishing, Inc. "Exploring America's National Parks Page,"
   www.americanparks.com
   National Park Services. "Visit Your Parks Park Guide," www.nps.gov/parks.html

U.S. National Forests

Forest	Location	Forest	Location
Allegheny	Pennsylvania	Coconino	Arizona
Angeles	California	Coeur d'Alene	Idaho
Angelina	Texas	Colville	Washington
Apache-Sitgreaves	Arizona	Conecuh	Alabama
Apalachicola	Florida	Coronado	Arizona
Arapaho	Colorado	Croatan	North Carolina
Ashley	Utah	Custer	Montana
Beaverhead	Montana	Daniel Boone	Kentucky
Bienville	Mississippi	Davy Crockett	Texas
Bighorn	Wyoming	Deerlodge	Montana
Bitterroot	Montana	Delta	Mississippi
Black Hills	South Dakota	Deschutes	Oregon
Boise	Idaho	Desoto	Mississippi
Bridger-Teton	Wyoming	Dixie	Utah
Caribbean	Puerto Rico	El Dorado	California
Caribou	Idaho	Finger Lakes	New York
Carson	New Mexico	Fishlake	Utah
Challis	Idaho	Flathead	Montana
Chattahoochee	Georgia	Francis Marion	South Carolina
Chequamegon	Wisconsin	Fremont	Oregon
Cherokee	Tennessee	Gallatin	Montana
Chippewa	Minnesota	George Washington	Virginia
Chugach	Alaska	Gifford Pinchot	Washington
Cibola	New Mexico	Gila	New Mexico
Clearwater	Idaho	Grand Mesa	Colorado
Cleveland	California	Green Mountain	Vermont

Forest	Location	Forest	Location
Gunnison	Colorado	Ouachita	Arkansas
Helena	Montana	Ozark-St. Francis	Arkansas
Hiawatha	Michigan	Pawnee	Colorado
Holly Springs	Mississippi	Payette	Idaho
Homochitto	Mississippi	Pike	Colorado
Hoosier	Indiana	Pisgah	North Carolina
Humboldt	Nevada	Plumas	California
Huron-Manistee	Michigan	Prescott	Arizona
Inyo	California	Rio Grande	Colorado
Jefferson	Virginia	Rogue River	Oregon
Kaibab	Arizona	Roosevelt	Colorado
Kaniksu	Idaho	Routt	Colorado
Kisatchie	Louisiana	Sabine	Texas
Klamath	California	Salmon	Idaho
Kootenai	Montana	Sam Houston	Texas
Lake Tahoe Basin	California	San Bernardino	California
Management Area		San Isabel	Colorado
Lassen	California	San Juan	Colorado
Lewis and Clark	Montana	Santa Fe	New Mexico
Lincoln	New Mexico	Sawtooth	Idaho
Lolo	Montana	Sequoia	California
Los Padres	California	Shasta-Trinity	California
Malheur	Oregon	Shawnee	Illinois
Manti-LaSal	Utah	Shoshone	Wyoming
Mark Twain	Missouri	Sierra	California
Medicine Box	Wyoming	Siskiyou	Oregon
Mendocino	California	Siuslaw	Oregon
Modoc	California	Six Rivers	California
Monongahela	West Virginia	Snoqualmie	Washington
Mount Baker	Washington	St. Joe	Idaho
Mount Hood	Oregon	Stanislaus	California
Nantahala	North Carolina	Sumter	South Carolina
Nebraska	Nebraska	Superior	Minnesota
Nez Perce	Idaho	Tahoe	California
Nicolet	Wisconsin	Talladega	Alabama
Ocala	Florida	Targhee	Idaho
Ochoco	Oregon	Thunder Basin	Wyoming
Oconee	Georgia	Toiyabe	Nevada
Okanogan	Washington	Tombigee	Mississippi
Olympic	Washington	Tongass	Alaska
Osceola	Florida	Tonto	Arizona
Ottawa	Michigan	Tuskegg	Alabama

Uinta	Utah	Wenatchee	Washington
Umatilla	Oregon	White Mountain	Maine
Umpqua	Oregon	White Mountain	New Hampshire
Uncompahgre	Colorado	White River	Colorado
Uwharrie	North Carolina	Willamette	Oregon
Wallowa-Whitman	Oregon	William B.	Alabama
Wasatch-Cache	Utah	Bankhead	
Wayne	Ohio	Winema	Oregon

⊙ National Park Services. "Visit Your Parks Park Guide," www.nps.gov/parks.html

U.S. National Monuments and Memorials

Monument/Memorial   *Location*

Agate Fossil Beds National Monument	Nebraska
Alibates Flint Quarries National Monument	Texas
Aniakchak National Monument & Preserve	Alaska
Arkansas Post National Memorial	Arkansas
Arlington House, The Robert E. Lee Memorial	Virginia
Aztec Ruins National Monument	New Mexico
Bandelier National Monument	New Mexico
Black Canyon of the Gunnison National Monument	Colorado
Booker T. Washington National Monument	Virginia
Buck Island Reef National Monument	Virgin Islands
Cabrillo National Monument	California
Canyon De Chelly National Monument	Arizona
Cape Krusenstern National Monument	Alaska
Capulin Volcano National Monument	New Mexico
Casa Grande Ruins National Monument	Arizona
Castillo de San Marcos National Monument	Florida
Castle Clinton National Monument	New York
Cedar Breaks National Monument	Utah
Chamizal National Memorial	Texas
Chiricahua National Monument	Arizona
Colorado National Monument	Colorado
Congaree Swamp National Monument	South Carolina
Coronado National Memorial	Arizona
Craters of the Moon National Monument	Idaho
Desoto National Memorial	Florida
Devils Postpile National Monument	California
Devils Tower National Monument	Wyoming
Dinosaur National Monument	Colorado
Effigy Mounds National Monument	Iowa
Ellis Island National Monument	New York
El Malpais National Monument	New Mexico

Monument/Memorial	Location
El Morro National Monument	New Mexico
Father Marquette National Memorial	Michigan
Federal Hall National Monument	New York
Florissant Fossil Beds National Monument	Colorado
Fort Caroline National Memorial	Florida
Fort Clatsop National Monument	Oregon
Fort Frederica National Monument	Georgia
Fort Matanzas National Monument	Florida
Fort McHenry National Monument	Maryland
Fort Moultrie National Monument	South Carolina
Fort Pulaski National Monument	Georgia
Fort Stanwix National Monument	New York
Fort Sumter National Monument	South Carolina
Fort Union National Monument	New Mexico
Fossil Butte National Monument	Wyoming
Franklin Delano Roosevelt Memorial	Washington, D.C.
General Grant National Monument	New York
George Washington Birthplace National Monument	Virginia
George Washington Carver National Monument	Missouri
Gila Cliff Dwellings National Monument	New Mexico
Grand Portage National Monument	Minnesota
Great Sand Dunes National Monument	Colorado
Hagerman Fossil Beds National Monument	Idaho
Hamilton Grange National Memorial	New York
Hohokam Pima National Monument	Arizona
Home of Franklin D. Roosevelt National Monument	New York
Homestead National Monument of America	Nebraska
Hovenweep National Monument	Utah
Jefferson National Expansion Memorial	Missouri
Jewel Cave National Monument	South Dakota
John Day Fossil Beds National Monument	Oregon
John D. Rockefeller Jr. Memorial Parkway	Wyoming
Johnstown Flood National Memorial	Pennsylvania
Korean War Veterans Memorial	Washington, D.C.
Lava Beds National Monument	California
Lincoln Boyhood National Memorial	Indiana
Lincoln Memorial	Washington, D.C.
Little Bighorn Battlefield National Monument	Montana

Lyndon Baines Johnson Memorial Grove on the Potomac	Virginia
Montezuma Castle National Monument	Arizona
Mount Rushmore National Monument	South Dakota
Muir Woods National Monument	California
Natural Bridges National Monument	Utah
Navajo National Monument	Arizona
Ocmulgee National Monument	Georgia
Oklahoma City National Memorial	Oklahoma
Oregon Caves National Monument	Oregon
Organ Pipe Cactus National Monument	Arizona
Perry's Victory & International Peace Memorial	Ohio
Petroglyph National Monument	New Mexico
Pinnacles National Monument	California
Pipe Spring National Monument	Arizona
Pipestone National Monument	Minnesota
Port Chicago Naval Magazine National Memorial	California
Poverty Point National Monument	Louisiana
Rainbow Bridge National Monument	Utah
Roger Williams National Memorial	Rhode Island
Russell Cave National Monument	Alabama
Salinas Pueblo Missions National Monument	New Mexico
Scotts Bluff National Monument	Nebraska
Statue of Liberty National Monument	New York
Sunset Crater Volcano National Monument	Arizona
Thaddeus Kosciuszko National Memorial	Pennsylvania
Thomas Jefferson Memorial	Washington, D.C.
Timpanogos Cave National Monument	Utah
Tonto National Monument	Arizona
Tumacacori National Monument	Arizona
Tuzigoot National Monument	Arizona
U.S.S. *Arizona* Memorial	Hawaii
Vietnam Veterans Memorial	Washington, D.C.
Walnut Canyon National Monument	Arizona
Washington Monument	Washington, D.C.
White Sands National Monument	New Mexico
Wright Brothers National Memorial	North Carolina
Wupatki National Monument	Arizona
Yucca House National Monument	Colorado

⊙ National Park Services. "Visit Your Parks Park Guide," www.nps.gov/parks.html

U.S. National Military Sites

Monument/Memorial	Location
Chickamauga & Chattanooga National Military Park	Georgia
Fredericksburg & Spotsylvania County Battlefields National Military Park	Virginia
Gettysburg National Military Park	Pennsylvania
Guilford Courthouse National Military Park	North Carolina
Horseshoe Bend National Military Park	Alabama
Kings Mountain National Military Park	North Carolina
Pea Ridge National Military Park	Arkansas
Shiloh National Military Park	Tennessee
Vicksburg National Military Park	Mississippi

National Battlefields/Parks/Sites

Battlefield/Park/Site	Location
Antietam National Battlefield	Maryland
Big Hole National Battlefield	Montana
Brices Cross Roads National Battlefield Site	Mississippi
Cowpens National Battlefield	South Carolina
Fort Donelson National Battlefield	Tennessee
Fort Necessity National Battlefield	Pennsylvania
Kennesaw Mountain National Battlefield Park	Georgia
Manassas National Battlefield Park	Virginia
Monocacy National Battlefield	Maryland
Moores Creek National Battlefield	North Carolina
Petersburg National Battlefield	Virginia
Richmond National Battlefield Park	Virginia
Stones River National Battlefield	Tennessee
Tupelo National Battlefield	Mississippi
Wilson's Creek National Battlefield	Missouri

U.S. National Cemeteries

Cemetery	Location
Antietam National Cemetery	Maryland
Battleground National Cemetery	Washington, D.C.
Fort Donelson National Cemetery	Tennessee
Fredericksburg National Cemetery	Virginia
Gettysburg National Cemetery	Pennsylvania
Poplar Grove National Cemetery	Virginia
Shiloh National Cemetery	Tennessee
Stones River National Cemetery	Tennessee
Vicksburg National Cemetery	Mississippi
Yorktown National Cemetery	Virginia

⊙ National Park Services. "Visit Your Parks Park Guide," www.nps.gov/parks.html

U.S. National Seashores, Lakeshores, and Recreation Areas

Seashore/Recreation Area	Location
Amistad National Recreation Area	Texas
Apostle Islands National Lakeshore	Wisconsin
Assateague Island National Seashore	Maryland, Virginia
Big South Fork National River & Recreation Area	Tennessee
Bighorn Canyon National Recreation Area	Montana
Boston Harbor Islands National Recreation Area	Massachusetts
Canaveral National Seashore	Florida
Cape Cod National Seashore	Massachusetts
Cape Hatteras National Seashore	North Carolina
Cape Lookout National Seashore	North Carolina
Chattahoochee River National Recreation Area	Georgia
Chickasaw National Recreation Area	Oklahoma
Cumberland Island National Seashore	Georgia
Curecanti National Recreation Area	Colorado
Cuyahoga Valley National Recreation Area	Ohio
Delaware Water Gap National Recreation Area	New Jersey, Pennsylvania
Fire Island National Seashore	New York
Gateway National Recreation Area	New Jersey, New York
Gauley River National Recreation Area	West Virginia
Glen Canyon National Recreation Area	Arizona, Utah
Golden Gate National Recreation Area	California
Gulf Islands National Seashore	Florida, Mississippi
Indiana Dunes National Lakeshore	Indiana
Lake Chelan National Recreation Area	Washington
Lake Mead National Recreation Area	Arizona
Lake Meredith National Recreation Area	Texas
Lake Roosevelt (formerly Coolee Dam) National Recreation Area	Washington
Mississippi National River & National Recreation Area	Minnesota
Missouri National Recreation River	Nebraska
Padre Island National Seashore	Texas
Pictured Rocks National Lakeshore	Michigan
Point Reyes National Seashore	California
Ross Lake National Recreation Area	Washington
Santa Monica Mountains National Recreation Area	California
Sleeping Bear Dunes National Lakeshore	Michigan
Whiskeytown-Shasta-Trinity National Recreation Area	California

⊙ National Park Services. "Visit Your Parks Park Guide," www.nps.gov/parks.html

U.S. National Preserves, Reserves, Rivers, Islands, and Trails

National Geographical Feature	Location
Alagnak Wild River	Alaska
Alcatraz Island	California
Aniakchak National Preserve	Alaska
Appalachian National Scenic Trail	Connecticut, Georgia, Maine, Maryland, Massachusetts, New Hampshire, New Jersey, New York, North Carolina, Pennsylvania, Tennessee, Vermont, Virginia, West Virginia
Bering Land Bridge National Preserve	Alaska
Big Cypress National Preserve	Florida
Big South Fork National River & Recreation Area	Tennessee
Big Thicket National Preserve	Texas
Blackstone River Valley National Heritage Corridor	Massachusetts, Rhode Island
Bluestone National Scenic River	West Virginia
Buffalo National River	Arizona
California National Historic Trail	California, Colorado, Kansas, Missouri, Nebraska, Nevada, Oregon, Utah, Wyoming
Cane River Creole National Historic Park and Heritage Area	Louisiana
Chattahoochee National Scenic River	Georgia
City of Rocks National Reserve	Idaho
Delaware and Lehigh National Heritage Corridor	Pennsylvania
Delaware National Scenic River	New Jersey, Pennsylvania
Denali National Park & Preserve	Alaska
Ebey's Landing National Historical Reserve	Washington
Ellis Island	New York
Gates of the Arctic National Park & Preserve	Alaska
Glacier Bay National Park & Preserve	Alaska
Great Egg Harbor National Scenic River	New Jersey
Ice Age National Scenic Trail	Wisconsin
Illinois & Michigan Canal National Heritage Corridor	Illinois
Jean Lafitte National Historic Park & Preserve	Louisiana
Juan Bautista de Anza National Historic Trail	California
Katmai National Park & Preserve	Alaska
Lake Clark National Preserve	Alaska

Lewis & Clark National Trail	Idaho, Illinois, Iowa, Kansas, Missouri, Montana, Nebraska, North Dakota, Oregon, South Dakota, Washington
Little River Canyon National Preserve	Alabama
Lower Saint Croix National Scenic Riverway	Wisconsin
Mississippi National River & Recreation Area	Minnesota
Mojave National Preserve	California
Mormon Pioneer National Historic Trail	Illinois, Iowa, Nebraska, Utah, Wyoming
Natchez Trace National Scenic Trail	Mississippi, Tennessee
New Jersey Coastal Heritage Trail Route	New Jersey
New Jersey Pinelands National Reserve	New Jersey
New River Gorge National River	West Virginia
Niobrara National Scenic River	Nebraska
Noatak National Preserve	Alaska
North Country National Scenic Trail	Michigan, Montana, New York, North Dakota, Ohio, Pennsylvania, Wisconsin
Obed Wild and Scenic River	Tennessee
Oregon National Historic Trail	Idaho, Kansas, Missouri, Nebraska, Oregon, Wyoming
Overmountain Victory National Historic Trail	Georgia, North Carolina, South Carolina, Tennessee, Virginia
Ozark National Scenic River	Missouri
Pony Express National Historic Trail	California, Colorado, Kansas, Missouri, Nevada, Utah, Wyoming
Potomac Heritage National Scenic Trail	Maryland, Pennsylvania, Virginia, Washington, D.C.
Quinebaug and Shetucket Rivers Valley National Heritage Corridor	Connecticut
Rio Grande Wild and Scenic River	Texas
Saint Croix National Scenic River	Wisconsin
Salt River Bay & Ecological Preserve	Virgin Islands
Santa Fe National Historic Trail	New Mexico
Selma To Montgomery National Historic Trail	Alabama
Tallgrass Prairie National Preserve	Kansas
Theodore Roosevelt Island	Virginia
Timucuan Ecological & Historic Preserve	Florida
Upper Delaware Scenic & Recreational River	Pennsylvania
Wrangell–St. Elias National Park & Preserve	Alaska
Yukon Charley Rivers National Preserve	Alaska

⊙ National Park Services. "Visit Your Parks Park Guide," www.nps.gov/parks.html

ARTS AND LEISURE: *Sports and Games*

Major League Baseball Teams
American League

Division	Team	Stadium & Address	Phone/Website
East	Baltimore Orioles	Oriole Park at Camden Yards 333 West Camden Street Baltimore, MD 21201	(410) 685-9800 www.theorioles.com
	Boston Red Sox	Fenway Park 4 Yawkey Way Boston, MA 02215	(617) 267-1700 www.redsox.com
	New York Yankees	Yankee Stadium East 161st Street & River Avenue Bronx, NY 10451	(718) 293-6000 www.yankees.com
	Tampa Bay Devil Rays	Tropicana Field One Tropicana Drive St. Petersburg, FL 33705	(727) 825-3137 www.devilray.com
	Toronto Blue Jays	SkyDome 1 Blue Jays Way Toronto, Ontario M5V1J1	(416) 341-1000 www.bluejays.ca
Central	Chicago White Sox	Comiskey Park 333 West 35th Street Chicago, IL 60616	(312) 674-1000 www.chisox.com
	Cleveland Indians	Jacobs Field 2401 Ontario Street Cleveland, OH 44115	(216) 420-4200 www.indians.com
	Detroit Tigers	Comerica Park 2100 Woodward Avenue Detroit, MI 48201	(313) 962-4000 www.detroittigers.com
	Kansas City Royals	Kauffman Stadium 1 Royal Way Kansas City, MO 64129	(816) 921-8000 www.kcroyals.com
	Minnesota Twins	Hubert H. Humphrey Metrodome 34 Kirby Puckett Place Minneapolis, MN 55415	(612) 375-1366 www.mntwins.com
West	Anaheim Angels	Edison Field 2000 Gene Autry Way Anaheim, CA 92806	(714) 634-2000 www.angelsbaseball.com
	Oakland Athletics	Oakland Coliseum 7677 Oakport Street Oakland, CA 94621	(510) 638-4900 www.oaklandathletics.com
	Seattle Mariners	Safeco Field P.O. Box 4100 Seattle, WA 98134	(206) 346-4000 www.mariners.org
	Texas Rangers	The Ballpark in Arlington 1000 Ballpark Way Arlington, TX 76011	(817) 273-5222 www.texasrangers.com

National League

Division	Team	Stadium & Address	Phone/Website
East	Atlanta Braves	Turner Field 755 Hank Aaron Drive Atlanta, GA 30315	(404) 522-7630 www.atlantabraves.com
	Florida Marlins	Pro Player Stadium 2269 NW 199th Street Miami, FL 33056	(305) 626-7400 www.floridamarlins.com
	Montreal Expos	Olympic Stadium 4549 Avenue Pierre de Coubertin Montreal, Quebec H1V3N7	800-463-9767 www.montrealexpos.com
	New York Mets	Shea Stadium 123-01 Roosevelt Avenue Flushing, NY 11368	(718) 507-6387 www.mets.com
	Philadelphia Phillies	Veterans Stadium 3501 South Broad Street Philadelphia, PA 19148	(215) 463-5000 www.phillies.com
Central	Chicago Cubs	Wrigley Field 1060 West Addison Chicago, IL 60613	(773) 404-2827 www.cubs.com
	Cincinnati Reds	Cinergy Field 100 Cinergy Field Cincinnati, OH 45202	(513) 421-4510 www.cincinnatireds.com
	Houston Astros	Enron Field 501 Crawford Street Houston, TX 77002	(713) 259-8500 www.astros.com
	Milwaukee Brewers	Miller Park Brewers Way Milwaukee, WI 53214	(414) 933-4114 www.milwaukeebrewers.com
	Pittsburgh Pirates	PNC Park P.O. Box 7000 Pittsburgh, PA 15212	(412) 323-5000 www.pirateball.com
	St. Louis Cardinals	Busch Stadium 250 Stadium Plaza St. Louis, MO 63102	(314) 421-3060 www.stlcardinals.com
West	Arizona Diamondbacks	Bank One Ballpark 401 East Jefferson Street Phoenix, AZ 85004	(602) 462-6000 www.azdiamondbacks.com
	Colorado Rockies	Coors Field 2001 Blake Street Denver, CO 802050	(303) 292-020 www.coloradorockies.com
	Los Angeles Dodgers	Dodger Stadium 1000 Elysian Park Avenue Los Angeles, CA 90012	(323) 224-1500 www.dodgers.com
	San Diego Padres	Qualcomm Stadium 9449 Friars Road San Diego, CA 92108	(619) 881-6500 www.padres.com
	San Francisco Giants	Pacific Bell Park 24 Willie Mays Plaza San Francisco, CA 94107	(415) 972-2000 www.sfgiants.com

⊙ ESPN. "Baseball," espn.go.com/mlb/index.html
  Major League Baseball. "Franchise Information," www.majorleaguebaseball.com/u/
  baseball/mlbcom/history/franc_teamcontactinfo.html

Major League Baseball: World Series Championships

The World Series has been an annual event since 1903, with the exception of two years: 1904, when the New York Giants refused to play the Boston Pilgrims, and 1994, when a players' strike cut short the regular season. The best-of-seven-games format has been followed throughout the World Series' history, with the exception of four years (1904, 1919, 1920, 1921), when the champion team had to win five games out of nine.

Note: AL = American League; NL = National League; "Score" shows number of games won; MVP = Most Valuable Player

Year	Winning Team	Losing Team	Score	Series MVP
1903	Boston Pilgrims (AL)	Pittsburgh Pirates (NL)	5–3	—
1905	New York Giants (NL)	Philadelphia Athletics (AL)	4–1	—
1906	Chicago White Sox (AL)	Chicago Cubs (NL)	4–2	—
1907	Chicago Cubs (NL)	Detroit Tigers (AL)	4–0 (1 tie)	—
1908	Chicago Cubs (NL)	Detroit Tigers (AL)	4–1	—
1909	Pittsburgh Pirates (NL)	Detroit Tigers (AL)	4–3	—
1910	Philadelphia Athletics (AL)	Chicago Cubs (NL)	4–1	—
1911	Philadelphia Athletics (AL)	New York Giants (NL)	4–2	—
1912	Boston Red Sox (AL)	New York Giants (NL)	4–3 (1 tie)	—
1913	Philadelphia Athletics (AL)	New York Giants (NL)	4–1	—
1914	Boston Braves (NL)	Philadelphia Athletics (AL)	4–0	—
1915	Boston Red Sox (AL)	Philadelphia Phillies (NL)	4–1	—
1916	Boston Red Sox (AL)	Brooklyn Robins (NL)	4–1	—
1917	Chicago White Sox (AL)	New York Giants (NL)	4–2	—
1918	Boston Red Sox (AL)	Chicago Cubs (NL)	4–2	—
1919	Cincinnati Reds (NL)	Chicago White Sox (AL)	5–3	—
1920	Cleveland Indians (AL)	Brooklyn Robins (NL)	5–2	—
1921	New York Giants (NL)	New York Yankees (AL)	5–3	—
1922	New York Giants (NL)	New York Yankees (AL)	4–0 (1 tie)	—
1923	New York Yankees (AL)	New York Giants (NL)	4–2	—
1924	Washington Senators (AL)	New York Giants (NL)	4–3	—
1925	Pittsburgh Pirates (NL)	Washington Senators (AL)	4–3	—
1926	St. Louis Cardinals (NL)	New York Yankees (AL)	4–3	—
1927	New York Yankees (AL)	Pittsburgh Pirates (NL)	4–0	—
1928	New York Yankees (AL)	St. Louis Cardinals (NL)	4–0	—
1929	Philadelphia Athletics (AL)	Chicago Cubs (NL)	4–1	—
1930	Philadelphia Athletics (AL)	St. Louis Cardinals (NL)	4–2	—
1931	St. Louis Cardinals (NL)	Philadelphia Athletics (AL)	4–3	—
1932	New York Yankees (AL)	Chicago Cubs (NL)	4–0	—
1933	New York Giants (NL)	Washington Senators (AL)	4–1	—
1934	St. Louis Cardinals (NL)	Detroit Tigers (AL)	4–3	—
1935	Detroit Tigers (AL)	Chicago Cubs (NL)	4–2	—
1936	New York Yankees (AL)	New York Giants (NL)	4–2	—
1937	New York Yankees (AL)	New York Giants (NL)	4–1	—
1938	New York Yankees (AL)	Chicago Cubs (NL)	4–0	—
1939	New York Yankees (AL)	Cincinnati Reds (NL)	4–0	—
1940	Cincinnati Reds (NL)	Detroit Tigers (AL)	4–3	—
1941	New York Yankees (AL)	Brooklyn Dodgers (NL)	4–1	—

1942	St. Louis Cardinals (NL)	New York Yankees (AL)	4-1	—
1943	New York Yankees (AL)	St. Louis Cardinals (NL)	4-1	—
1944	St. Louis Cardinals (NL)	St. Louis Browns (AL)	4-2	—
1945	Detroit Tigers (AL)	Chicago Cubs (NL)	4-3	—
1946	St. Louis Cardinals (NL)	Boston Red Sox (AL)	4-3	—
1947	New York Yankees (AL)	Brooklyn Dodgers (NL)	4-3	—
1948	Cleveland Indians (AL)	Boston Braves (NL)	4-2	—
1949	New York Yankees (AL)	Brooklyn Dodgers (NL)	4-1	—
1950	New York Yankees (AL)	Philadelphia Phillies (NL)	4-0	—
1951	New York Yankees (AL)	New York Giants (NL)	4-2	—
1952	New York Yankees (AL)	Brooklyn Dodgers (NL)	4-3	—
1953	New York Yankees (AL)	Brooklyn Dodgers (NL)	4-2	—
1954	New York Giants (NL)	Cleveland Indians (AL)	4-0	—
1955	Brooklyn Dodgers (NL)	New York Yankees (AL)	4-3	Johnny Podres
1956	New York Yankees (AL)	Brooklyn Dodgers (NL)	4-3	Don Larsen
1957	Milwaukee Braves (NL)	New York Yankees (AL)	4-3	Lew Burdette
1958	New York Yankees (AL)	Milwaukee Braves (NL)	4-3	Bob Turley
1959	Los Angeles Dodgers (NL)	Chicago White Sox (AL)	4-2	Larry Sherry
1960	Pittsburgh Pirates (NL)	New York Yankees (AL)	4-3	Bobby Richardson
1961	New York Yankees (AL)	Cincinnati Reds (NL)	4-1	Whitey Ford
1962	New York Yankees (AL)	San Francisco Giants (NL)	4-3	Ralph Terry
1963	Los Angeles Dodgers (NL)	New York Yankees (AL)	4-0	Sandy Koufax
1964	St. Louis Cardinals (NL)	New York Yankees (AL)	4-3	Bob Gibson
1965	Los Angeles Dodgers (NL)	Minnesota Twins (AL)	4-3	Sandy Koufax
1966	Baltimore Orioles (AL)	Los Angeles Dodgers (NL)	4-0	Frank Robinson
1967	St. Louis Cardinals (NL)	Boston Red Sox (AL)	4-3	Bob Gibson
1968	Detroit Tigers (AL)	St. Louis Cardinals (NL)	4-3	Mickey Lolich
1969	New York Mets (NL)	Baltimore Orioles (AL)	4-1	Donn Clendenon
1970	Baltimore Orioles (AL)	Cincinnati Reds (NL)	4-1	Brooks Robinson
1971	Pittsburgh Pirates (NL)	Baltimore Orioles (AL)	4-3	Roberto Clemente
1972	Oakland Athletics (AL)	Cincinnati Reds (NL)	4-3	Gene Tenace
1973	Oakland Athletics (AL)	New York Mets (NL)	4-3	Reggie Jackson
1974	Oakland Athletics (AL)	Los Angeles Dodgers (NL)	4-1	Rollie Fingers
1975	Cincinnati Reds (NL)	Boston Red Sox (AL)	4-3	Pete Rose
1976	Cincinnati Reds (NL)	New York Yankees (AL)	4-0	Johnny Bench
1977	New York Yankees (AL)	Los Angeles Dodgers (NL)	4-2	Reggie Jackson
1978	New York Yankees (AL)	Los Angeles Dodgers (NL)	4-2	Bucky Dent
1979	Pittsburgh Pirates (NL)	Baltimore Orioles (AL)	4-3	Willie Stargell
1980	Philadelphia Phillies (NL)	Kansas City Royals (AL)	4-2	Mike Schmidt
1981	Los Angeles Dodgers (NL)	New York Yankees (AL)	4-2	Ron Cey/ Pedro Guerrero/ Steve Yeager
1982	St. Louis Cardinals (NL)	Milwaukee Brewers (AL)	4-3	Darrell Porter
1983	Baltimore Orioles (AL)	Philadelphia Phillies (NL)	4-1	Rick Dempsey
1984	Detroit Tigers (AL)	San Diego Padres (NL)	4-1	Alan Trammell
1985	Kansas City Royals (AL)	St. Louis Cardinals (NL)	4-3	Bret Saberhagen
1986	New York Mets (NL)	Boston Red Sox (AL)	4-3	Ray Knight

Year	Winning Team	Losing Team	Score	Series MVP
1987	Minnesota Twins (AL)	St. Louis Cardinals (NL)	4–3	Frank Viola
1988	Los Angeles Dodgers (NL)	Oakland Athletics (AL)	4–1	Orel Hershiser
1989	Oakland Athletics (AL)	San Francisco Giants (NL)	4–0	Dave Stewart
1990	Cincinnati Reds (NL)	Oakland Athletics (AL)	4–0	Jose Rijo
1991	Minnesota Twins (AL)	Atlanta Braves (NL)	4–3	Jack Morris
1992	Toronto Blue Jays (AL)	Atlanta Braves (NL)	4–2	Pat Borders
1993	Toronto Blue Jays (AL)	Philadelphia Phillies (NL)	4–1	Paul Molitor
1995	Atlanta Braves (NL) 5	Cleveland Indians (AL)	4–2	Tom Glavine
1996	New York Yankees (AL)	Atlanta Braves (NL)	4–2	John Wetteland
1997	Florida Marlins (NL)	Cleveland Indians (AL)	4–2	Livan Hernandez
1998	New York Yankees (AL)	San Diego Padres (NL)	4–0	Scott Brosius
1999	New York Yankees (AL)	Atlanta Braves (NL)	4–0	Mariano Rivera

⊙ Major League Baseball. "History: World Series," www.majorleaguebaseball.com/u/
baseball/mlbcom/2000/postseason/history.

National Baseball Hall Of Fame

Year	*Inductees*	*Year*	*Inductees*	*Year*	*Inductees*
1936	Ty Cobb		George Sisler		Rube Waddell
	Walter Johnson		Al Spalding		Ed Walsh
	Christy Mathewson		Lou Gehrig	1947	Mickey Cochrane
	Babe Ruth	1942	Rogers Hornsby		Frankie Frisch
	Honus Wagner	1944	Kenesaw Mountain Landis		Lefty Grove
1937	Morgan Bulkeley				Carl Hubbell
	Ban Johnson	1945	Roger Bresnahan	1948	Herb Pennock
	Nap Lajoie		Dan Brouthers		Pie Traynor
	Connie Mack		Fred Clarke	1949	Mordecai Brown
	John McGraw		Jimmy Collins		Charlie Gehringer
	Tris Speaker		Ed Delahanty		Kid Nichols
	George Wright		Hugh Duffy	1951	Jimmie Foxx
	Cy Young		Hugh Jennings		Mel Ott
1938	Pete Alexander		King Kelly	1952	Harry Heilmann
	Alexander Cartwright		Jim O'Rourke		Paul Waner
	Henry Chadwick		Wilbert Robinson	1953	Ed Barrow
1939	Cap Anson	1946	Jesse Burkett		Chief Bender
	Eddie Collins		Frank Chance		Tom Connolly
	Charlie Comiskey		Jack Chesbro		Dizzy Dean
	Candy Cummings		Johnny Evers		Bill Klem
	Buck Ewing		Clark Griffith		Al Simmons
	Willie Keeler		Tommy McCarthy		Bobby Wallace
	Charley Radbourn		Joe McGinnity		Harry Wright
			Eddie Plank	1954	Bill Dickey
			Joe Tinker		Rabbit Maranville
					Bill Terry
				1955	Home Run Baker

	Joe DiMaggio		Rube Marquard		Duke Snider
	Gabby Hartnett		Satchel Paige		Tom Yawkey
	Ted Lyons		George Weiss	1981	Rube Foster
	Ray Schalk	1972	Yogi Berra		Bob Gibson
	Dazzy Vance		Josh Gibson		Johnny Mize
1956	Joe Cronin		Lefty Gómez	1982	Hank Aaron
	Hank Greenberg		Will Harridge		Happy Chandler
1957	Sam Crawford		Sandy Koufax		Travis Jackson
	Joe McCarthy		Buck Leonard		Frank Robinson
1959	Zack Wheat		Early Wynn	1983	Walter Alston
1961	Max Carey		Ross Youngs		George Kell
	Billy Hamilton	1973	Roberto		Juan Marichal
1962	Bob Feller		Clemente		Brooks Robinson
	Bill McKechnie		Billy Evans	1984	Luis Aparicio
	Jackie Robinson		Monte Irvin		Don Drysdale
	Edd Roush		George Kelly		Rick Ferrell
1963	John Clarkson		Warren Spahn		Harmon
	Elmer Flick		Mickey Welch		Killebrew
	Sam Rice	1974	Cool Papa Bell		Pee Wee Reese
	Eppa Rixey		Jim Bottomley	1985	Lou Brock
1964	Luke Appling		Jocko Conlan		Enos Slaughter
	Red Faber		Whitey Ford		Arky Vaughan
	Burleigh Grimes		Mickey Mantle		Hoyt Wilhelm
	Miller Huggins		Sam Thompson	1986	Bobby Doerr
	Tim Keefe	1975	Earl Averill		Ernie Lombardi
	Heinie Manush		Bucky Harris		Willie McCovey
	John Ward		Billy Herman	1987	Ray Dandridge
1965	Pud Galvin		Judy Johnson		Catfish Hunter
1966	Casey Stengel		Ralph Kiner		Billy Williams
	Ted Williams	1976	Oscar Charleston	1988	Willie Stargell
1967	Branch Rickey		Roger Connor	1989	Al Barlick
	Red Ruffing		Cal Hubbard		Johnny Bench
	Lloyd Waner		Bob Lemon		Red Schoendienst
1968	Kiki Cuyler		Fred Lindstrom		Carl Yastrzemski
	Goose Goslin		Robin Roberts	1990	Joe Morgan
	Joe Medwick	1977	Ernie Banks		Jim Palmer
1969	Roy Campanella		Martín Dihigo	1991	Rod Carew
	Stan Coveleski		Pop Lloyd		Fergie Jenkins
	Waite Hoyt		Al López		Tony Lazzeri
	Stan Musial		Amos Rusie		Gaylord Perry
1970	Lou Boudreau		Joe Sewell		Bill Veeck
	Earle Combs	1978	Addie Joss	1992	Rollie Fingers
	Ford Frick		Larry MacPhail		Bill McGowan
	Jesse Haines		Eddie Mathews		Hal Newhouser
1971	Dave Bancroft	1979	Warren Giles		Tom Seaver
	Jake Beckley		Willie Mays	1993	Reggie Jackson
	Chick Hafey		Hack Wilson	1994	Steve Carlton
	Harry Hooper	1980	Al Kaline		Leo Durocher
	Joe Kelley		Chuck Klein		Phil Rizzuto

National Baseball Hall Of Fame *(cont.)*

Year	Inductees	Year	Inductees	Year	Inductees
1995	Richie Ashburn		Tommy Lasorda		Nestor Chylak
	Leon Day		Phil Niekro		Nolan Ryan
	William Hulbert		Willie Wells		Frank Selee
	Mike Schmidt	1998	George Davis		Joe Williams
	Vic Willis		Larry Doby		Robin Yount
1996	Jim Bunning		Lee MacPhail	2000	Sparky Anderson
	Bill Foster		Bullet Rogan		Carlton Fisk
	Ned Hanlon		Don Sutton		Bid McPhee
	Earl Weaver	1999	George Brett		Tony Pérez
1997	Nellie Fox		Orlando Cepeda		Turkey Stearnes

⊙ National Baseball Hall of Fame. "Hall of Famers Listed by Induction Year," baseball-halloffame.org/hofers_and_honorees/lists/induction_year.htm

National Basketball Association Teams

Division	Team	Stadium & Address	Phone/Website
Atlantic	Boston Celtics	FleetCenter One FleetCenter Boston, MA 02114	(617) 931-2222 www.nba.com/celtics
	Miami Heat	AmericanAirlines Arena 601 Biscayne Boulevard Miami, FL 33132	(786) 777-4328 www.nba.com/heat
Atlantic	New Jersey Nets	Continental Airlines Arena 50 Route 120 North East Rutherford, NJ 07073	800-765-6387 www.nba.com/nets
	New York Knicks	Madison Square Garden Two Pennsylvania Plaza New York, NY 10121	(212) 465-5867 www.nba.com/knicks
	Orlando Magic	TD Waterhouse Centre One Magic Place, 600 West Amelia Street Orlando, FL 32801	(407) 896-2442 www.nba.com/magic
	Philadelphia 76ers	First Union Center 3601 South Broad Street Philadelphia, PA 19148	(215) 339-7676 www.nba.com/sixers
	Washington Wizards	MCI Center 601 F Street NW Washington, DC 20004	(202) 661-5050 www.nba.com/wizards
Midwest	Dallas Mavericks	Reunion Arena 777 Sports Street Dallas, Texas 75207	(972) 988-3865 www.nba.com/mavericks
	Denver Nuggets	Pepsi Center 1000 Chopper Circle Denver, CO 80204	(303) 405-1212 www.nba.com/nuggets

	Houston Rockets	The Compaq Center 10 Greenway Plaza East Houston, TX 77046	(713) 627-3865 www.nba.com/rockets
	Minnesota Timberwolves	Target Center 600 First Avenue North Minneapolis, MN 55403	(612) 337-3865 www.nba.com/timberwolves
	San Antonio Spurs	Alamodome 100 Montana Street San Antonio, TX 78203	(210) 554-7700 www.nba.com/spurs
	Utah Jazz	Delta Center 301 West South Temple Salt Lake City, UT 84101	(801) 355-3865 www.nba.com/jazz
	Vancouver Grizzlies	General Motors Place 800 Griffiths Way Vancouver, British Columbia V6B 6G1	(604) 899-4667 www.nba.com/grizzlies
Central	Atlanta Hawks	Philips Arena One CNN Center, South Tower Atlanta, GA 30303	(404) 827-3865 www.nba.com/hawks
	Charlotte Hornets	Charlotte Coliseum 100 Paul Buck Boulevard Charlotte, NC 28217	(704) 357-4700 www.nba.com/hornets
	Chicago Bulls	United Center 1901 West Madison Street Chicago, IL 60612	(312) 455-4000 www.nba.com/bulls
	Cleveland Cavaliers	Gund Arena One Center Court Cleveland, OH 44115	(216) 420-2287 800-332-2287 www.nba.com/cavs
	Detroit Pistons	The Palace of Auburn Hills Two Championship Drive Auburn Hills, MI 48326	(248) 377-0100 www.nba.com/pistons
	Indiana Pacers	Conseco Fieldhouse 125 South Pennsylvania Street Indianapolis, IN 46204	(317) 917-2500 www.nba.com/pacers
	Milwaukee Bucks	Bradley Center 1001 North Fourth Street Milwaukee, WI 53203	(414) 227-0500 www.nba.com/bucks
	Toronto Raptors	Air Canada Centre 40 Bay Street Toronto, Ontario M5J 2X2	(416) 366-3865 www.nba.com/raptors
Pacific	Golden State Warriors	Arena in Oakland 7000 Coliseum Way Oakland, CA 94621	(510) 569-2121 www.nba.com/warriors
	Los Angeles Clippers	Staples Center 1111 South Figueroa Street Los Angeles, CA 90015	(213) 742-7555 www.nba.com/clippers
	Los Angeles Lakers	Staples Center 1111 South Figueroa Street Los Angeles, CA 90015	(310) 673-1300 www.nba.com/lakers

National Basketball Association Teams *(cont.)*

Division	Team	Stadium & Address	Phone/Website
Pacific	Phoenix Suns	America West Arena 201 East Jefferson Street Phoenix, AZ 85004	(602) 379-7867 www.nba.com/suns
	Portland Trail Blazers	The Rose Garden One Center Court Portland, OR 97227	(503) 224-4400 www.nba.com/blazers
	Sacramento Kings	ARCO Arena One Sports Parkway Sacramento, CA 95834	(916) 928-6900 www.nba.com/kings
	Seattle SuperSonics	Key Arena 351 Elliott Avenue Seattle, WA 98119	(206) 283-3865 www.nba.com/sonics

⊙ ESPN. "NBA Clubhouses," espn.go.com/nba/clubhouses/index.html
National Basketball Association. "Teams," www.nba.com/teamindex.html

Women's National Basketball Association Teams

Division	Team	Stadium & Address	Phone/Website
Eastern	Charlotte Sting	Charlotte Coliseum 100 Paul Buck Boulevard Charlotte, NC 28217	(704) 424-9622 www.wnba.com/sting
	Cleveland Rockers	Gund Arena One Center Court Cleveland, OH 44115	(216) 263-7625 www.wnba.com/rockers
	Detroit Shock	The Palace of Auburn Hills Two Championship Drive Auburn Hills, MI 48326	(248) 377-0100 www.wnba.com/shock
	Indiana Fever	Conseco Fieldhouse 125 South Pennsylvania Street Indianapolis, IN 46204	(317) 917-2500 www.wnba.com/fever
	Miami Sol	AmericanAirlines Arena 601 Biscayne Boulevard Miami, FL 33132	(786) 777-4765 www.wnba.com/sol
	New York Liberty	Madison Square Garden Two Pennsylvania Plaza New York, NY 10121	(212) 564-9622 www.wnba.com/liberty
	Orlando Miracle	TD Waterhouse Centre One Magic Place, 600 West Amelia Street Orlando, FL 32801	(407) 916-9622 www.wnba.com/miracle
	Washington Mystics	MCI Center 601 F Street NW Washington, DC 20004	(202) 661-5050 www.wnba.com/mystics
Western	Houston Comets	The Compaq Center 10 Greenway Plaza East Houston, TX 77046	(713) 627-9622 www.wnba.com/comets

Los Angeles Sparks	The Great Western Forum 3900 West Manchester Blvd. Inglewood, CA 90385	(310) 426-6031 www.wnba.com/sparks
Minnesota Lynx	Target Center 600 First Avenue North Minneapolis, MN 55403	(612) 673-8400 www.wnba.com/lynx
Phoenix Mercury	America West Arena 201 East Jefferson Street Phoenix, AZ 85004	(602) 252-9622 www.wnba.com/mercury
Portland Fire	The Rose Garden One Center Court Portland, OR 97227	(503) 797-9622 www.wnba.com/fire
Sacramento Monarchs	ARCO Arena One Sports Parkway Sacramento, CA 95834	(916) 419-9622 www.wnba.com/monarchs
Seattle Storm	Key Arena 351 Elliott Avenue Seattle, WA 98119	(206) 374-9622 www.wnba.com/storm
Utah Starzz	Delta Center 301 West South Temple Salt Lake City, UT 84101	(801) 355-3865 www.wnba.com/starzz

⊙ ESPN. "WNBA," espn.go.com/wnba/index.html
  Women's National Basketball Association. "Teams," www.wnba.com/
  teamindex.html

National Basketball Association Championships

The NBA Championship is a best-of-seven-games series.

Note: "Score" shows number of games won; MVP = Most Valuable Player

Year	Winning Team	Losing Team	Score	Series MVP
1947	Philadelphia Warriors	Chicago Stags	4–1	—
1948	Baltimore Bullets	Philadelphia Warriors	4–2	—
1949	Minneapolis Lakers	Washington Capitols	4–2	—
1950	Minneapolis Lakers	Syracuse Nationals	4–2	—
1951	Rochester Royals	New York Knicks	4–3	—
1952	Minneapolis Lakers	New York Knicks	4–3	—
1953	Minneapolis Lakers	New York Knicks	4–1	—
1954	Minneapolis Lakers	Syracuse Nationals	4–3	—
1955	Syracuse Nationals	Fort Wayne Pistons	4–3	—
1956	Philadelphia Warriors	Fort Wayne Pistons	4–1	—
1957	Boston Celtics	St. Louis Hawks	4–3	—
1958	St. Louis Hawks	Boston Celtics	4–2	—
1959	Boston Celtics	Minneapolis Lakers	4–0	—
1960	Boston Celtics	St. Louis Hawks	4–3	—
1961	Boston Celtics	St. Louis Hawks	4–1	—
1962	Boston Celtics	Los Angeles Lakers	4–3	—

National Basketball Association Championships *(cont.)*

Year	Winning Team	Losing Team	Score	Series MVP
1963	Boston Celtics	Los Angeles Lakers	4–2	—
1964	Boston Celtics	San Francisco Warriors	4–1	—
1965	Boston Celtics	Los Angeles Lakers	4–1	—
1966	Boston Celtics	Los Angeles Lakers	4–3	—
1967	Philadelphia 76ers	San Francisco Warriors	4–2	—
1968	Boston Celtics	Los Angeles Lakers	4–2	—
1969	Boston Celtics	Los Angeles Lakers	4–3	Jerry West
1970	New York Knicks	Los Angeles Lakers	4–3	Willis Reed
1971	Milwaukee Bucks	Baltimore Bullets	4–0	Kareem Abdul-Jabbar
1972	Los Angeles Lakers	New York Knicks	4–1	Wilt Chamberlain
1973	New York Knicks	Los Angeles Lakers	4–1	Willis Reed
1974	Boston Celtics	Milwaukee Bucks	4–3	John Havlicek
1975	Golden State Warriors	Washington Bullets	4–0	Rick Barry
1976	Boston Celtics	Phoenix Suns	4–2	Jo Jo White
1977	Portland Trail Blazers	Philadelphia 76ers	4–2	Bill Walton
1978	Washington Bullets	Seattle SuperSonics	4–3	Wes Unseld
1979	Seattle SuperSonics	Washington Bullets	4–1	Dennis Johnson
1980	Los Angeles Lakers	Philadelphia 76ers	4–2	Magic Johnson
1981	Boston Celtics	Houston Rockets	4–2	Cedric Maxwell
1982	Los Angeles Lakers	Philadelphia 76ers	4–2	Magic Johnson
1983	Philadelphia 76ers	Los Angeles Lakers	4–0	Moses Malone
1984	Boston Celtics	Los Angeles Lakers	4–3	Larry Bird
1985	Los Angeles Lakers	Boston Celtics	4–2	Kareem Abdul-Jabbar
1986	Boston Celtics	Houston Rockets	4–2	Larry Bird
1987	Los Angeles Lakers	Boston Celtics	4–2	Magic Johnson
1988	Los Angeles Lakers	Detroit Pistons	4–3	James Worthy
1989	Detroit Pistons	Los Angeles Lakers	4–0	Joe Dumars
1990	Detroit Pistons	Portland Trail Blazers	4–1	Isiah Thomas
1991	Chicago Bulls	Los Angeles Lakers	4–1	Michael Jordan
1992	Chicago Bulls	Portland Trail Blazers	4–2	Michael Jordan
1993	Chicago Bulls	Phoenix Suns	4–2	Michael Jordan
1994	Houston Rockets	New York Knicks	4–3	Hakeem Olajuwon
1995	Houston Rockets	Orlando Magic	4–0	Hakeem Olajuwon
1996	Chicago Bulls	Seattle SuperSonics	4–2	Michael Jordan
1997	Chicago Bulls	Utah Jazz	4–2	Michael Jordan
1998	Chicago Bulls	Utah Jazz	4–2	Michael Jordan
1999	San Antonio Spurs	New York Knicks	4–1	Tim Duncan
2000	Los Angeles Lakers	Indiana Pacers	4–2	Shaquille O'Neal

⊙ National Basketball Association. "Year-by-Year Finals Champions and MVPs," www.nba.com/history/awards_finalschampsmvp.html

Women's National Basketball Association Championships

In 1997, the inaugural season for the Women's National Basketbal Association (WNBA) ended with a one-game championship. The championship format since then has been a best-of-three-game series.

Note: "Score" shows number of games won; MVP = Most Valuable Player

Year	Winning Team	Losing Team	Score	Series MVP
1997	Houston Comets	New York Liberty	1–0	Cynthia Cooper
1998	Houston Comets	Phoenix Mercury	2–1	Cynthia Cooper
1999	Houston Comets	New York Liberty	2–1	Cynthia Cooper
2000	Houston Comets	New York Liberty	2–0	Cynthia Cooper

⊙ Women's National Basketball Association. "WNBA Championship 2000," www.wnba.com/championship2000/index.html

Basketball Hall Of Fame

Year	Inductees	Year	Inductees
1959	Forrest "Phog" Allen		Bob Kurland
	Henry Clifford Carlson		John J. O'Brien
	Luther Gulick		Andy Phillip
	Edward J. Hickcox		Ernest C. Quigley
	Chuck Hyatt		John S. Roosma
	Matthew "Pat" Kennedy		Leonard D. Sachs
	Angelo "Hank" Luisetti		Arthur A. Schabinger
	Walter E. Meanwell		Christian Steinmetz
	George L. Mikan		David Tobey
	Ralph Morgan		Arthur L. Trester
	James Naismith		Edward A. Wachter
	Harold G. Olsen		David H. Walsh
	John J. Schommer	1962	Jack McCracken
	Amos Alonzo Stagg		Frank Morgenweck
	Oswald Tower		Harlan "Pat" Page
1960	Ernest A. Blood		Barney Sedran
	Victor A. Hanson		Lynn W. St. John
	George T. Hepbron		John "Cat" Thompson
	Frank W. Keaney	1963	Robert F. Gruenig
	Ward L. Lambert		William A. Reid
	Ed Macauley	1964	John W. Bunn
	Branch McCracken		Harold "Bud" Foster
	Charles "Stretch" Murphy		Nat Holman
	Henry V. Porter		Ned Irish
	John R. Wooden		R. William Jones
1961	Bernhard "Bennie" Borgmann		Ken Loeffler
			John "Honey" Russell
	Forrest S. DeBernardi	1965	Walter A. Brown
	George H. Hoyt		Paul "Tony" Hinkle
	George E. Keogan		Howard A. Hobson
			William G. Mokray

Year	Inductees	Year	Inductees
1966	Everett S. Dean		Eddie Hickey
	Joe Lapchick		John B. McLendon, Jr.
1967	Clair F. Bee		Ray Meyer
	Howard G. Cann		Pete Newell
	Amory T. Gill	1979	Lester Harrison
	Alvin "Doggie" Julian		Jerry R. Lucas
1968	Arnold "Red" Auerbach		Oscar P. Robertson
	Henry "Dutch" Denhart		Everett F. Shelton
	Henry "Hank" Iba		J. Dallas Shirley
	Adolph F. Rupp		Jerry A. West
	Chuck Taylor	1980	Thomas B. Barlow
1969	Ben Carnevale		Ferenc Hepp
	Robert E. Davies		J. Walter Kennedy
1970	Bob Cousy		Arad A. McCutchan
	Bob Pettit	1981	Everett N. Case
	Abe Saperstein		Al Duer
1971	Edgar A. Diddle		Clarence "Big House" Gaines
	Robert L. Douglas		Hal Greer
	Paul Endacott		Slater N. Martin
	Max Friedman		Frank V. Ramsey, Jr.
	Edward Gottlieb		Willis Reed, Jr.
	W. R. Clifford Wells	1982	Bill Bradley
1972	John Beckman		Dave DeBusschere
	Bruce Drake		Lloyd R. Leith
	Arthur C. Lonborg		Dean E. Smith
	Elmer H. Ripley		Jack Twyman
	Adolph Schayes		Louis G. Wilke
	John R. Wooden	1983	John Havlicek
1973	Harry A. Fisher		Sam Jones
	Maurice Podoloff		Jack Gardner
	Ernest J. Schmidt		Cliff Fagan
1974	Joe Brennan		Ed Steitz
	Emil S. Liston	1984	Senda Berenson Abbott
	Bill Russell		W. Harold Anderson
	Robert "Fuzzy" Vandivier		Al Cervi
1975	Thomas J. Gola		Marv K. Harshman
	Edward "Moose" Krause		Bertha F. Teague
	Harry Litwack		Nate Thurmond
	Bill Sharman		L. Margaret Wade
1976	Elgin Baylor	1986	Billy Cunningham
	Charles T. Cooper		Tom Heinsohn
	Lauren "Laddie" Gale		William "Red" Holzman
	William "Skinny" Johnson		Zigmund "Red" Mihalik
	Frank J. McGuire		Fred R. Taylor
1977	Paul J. Arizin		Stanley H. Watts
	Joe Fulks	1987	Rick Barry
	Clifford O. Hagan		Walter Frazier
	John P. Nucatola		Bob Houbregs
	Jim Pollard		Pete Maravich
1978	Justin "Sam" Barry		Robert Wanzer
	Wilt Chamberlain	1988	Clyde E. Lovellette
	James E. Enright		Bobby McDermott

	Ralph H. Miller	1995	Kareem Abdul-Jabbar
	Wes Unseld		Anne Donovan
1989	William "Pop" Gates		Aleksandr Gomelsky
	K. C. Jones		John Kundla
	Lenny Wilkens		Vern Mikkelsen
1990	David Bing		Player Cheryl Miller
	Elvin E. Hayes		Earl Strom
	Donald Neil Johnston	1996	Kresimir Cosic
	Vernon "Earl the Pearl"		George Gervin
	Monroe		Gail Goodrich
1991	Nate Archibald		Nancy Lieberman-Cline
	Dave Cowens		David Thompson
	Harry J. Gallatin		George Yardley
	Bob Knight	1997	Alex English
	Larry Fleisher		Pete Carril
	Larry O'Brien		Joan Crawford
	Borislav Stankovic		Denise Curry
1992	Sergei Belov		Antonio Diaz-Miguel
	Lou Carnesecca		Don Haskins
	Lusia Harris-Stewart		Bailey Howell
	Connie Hawkins	1998	Larry Bird
	Bob Lanier		Jody Conradt
	Al McGuire		Alex Hannum
	Jack Ramsay		Marques Haynes
	Nera D. White		Aleksandar Nikolic
	Phil Woolpert		Arnie Risen
1993	Walt Bellamy		Lenny Wilkens
	Julius "Dr. J" Erving	1999	Wayne Embry
	Dan Issel		Billie Moore
	Ann E. Meyers		Kevin McHale
	Dick McGuire		John Thompson
	Calvin J. Murphy		Fred Zollner
	Uljana Semjonova	2000	Danny Biasone
	Bill Walton		Bob McAdoo
1994	Carol Blazejowski		C. M. Newton
	Denny Crum		Pat Summitt
	Chuck Daly		Isiah Thomas
	Harry "Buddy" Jeannette		Morgan Wootten
	Cesare Rubini		

◉ MassLive-Online. "Basketball Hall of Fame: Inductees," www.masslive.com/bball-hof/inductees.html

NCAA: Men's Basketball Championships

Note: OT = overtime; 3OT = triple overtime

Year	Winning Team (School)	Losing Team (School)	Score
1939	University of Oregon	Ohio State University	46–33
1940	Indiana University	Villanova University	60–42
1941	University of Wisconsin	Washington State University	39–34
1942	Stanford University	Dartmouth College	53–38
1943	University of Wyoming	Georgetown University	46–34
1944	University of Utah	Dartmouth College	42–40 (OT)
1945	Oklahoma State University	New York University	49–45

NCAA: Men's Basketball Championships *(cont.)*

Year	Winning Team (School)	Losing Team (School)	Score
1946	Oklahoma State University	University of North Carolina	43–40
1947	College of the Holy Cross	University of Oklahoma	58–47
1948	University of Kentucky	Baylor University	58–42
1949	University of Kentucky	Oklahoma State University	46–36
1950	City College of New York	Bradley University	71–68
1951	University of Kentucky	Kansas State University	68–58
1952	University of Kansas	St. John's University (New York)	80–63
1953	Indiana University	University of Kansas	69–68
1954	La Salle University	Bradley University	92–76
1955	University of San Francisco	La Salle University	77–63
1956	University of San Francisco	University of Iowa	83–71
1957	North Carolina	University of Kansas	54–53 (3OT)
1958	University of Kentucky	Seattle University	84–72
1959	University of California	West Virginia University	71–70
1960	Ohio State University	University of California	75–55
1961	University of Cincinnati	Ohio State University	70–75 (OT)
1962	University of Cincinnati	Ohio State University	71–59
1963	Loyola University (Illinois)	University of Cincinnati	60–58 (OT)
1964	University of California at Los Angeles	Duke University	98–83
1965	University of California at Los Angeles	University of Michigan	91–80
1966	University of Texas at El Paso	Kentucky	72–65
1967	University of California at Los Angeles	University of Dayton	79–64
1968	University of California at Los Angeles	University of North Carolina	78–55
1969	University of California at Los Angeles	Purdue University	92–72
1970	University of California at Los Angeles	Jacksonville University	80–69
1971	University of California at Los Angeles	*Vacated** (Villanova University)	68–62
1972	University of California at Los Angeles	Florida State University	81–76
1973	University of California at Los Angeles	Memphis State University	87–66
1974	North Carolina State University	Marquette University	76–64
1975	University of California at Los Angeles	University of Kentucky	92–85

1976	Indiana University	University of Michigan	86–68
1977	Marquette University	University of California at Los Angeles	67–59
1978	University of Kentucky	Duke University	94–88
1979	Michigan State University	Indiana State University	75–64
1980	University of Louisville	*Vacated** (UCLA)	59–54
1981	Indiana University	University of North Carolina	63–50
1982	University of North Carolina	Georgetown University	63–62
1983	North Carolina State University	University of Houston	54–52
1984	Georgetown University	University of Houston	84–75
1985	Villanova University	Georgetown University	66–64
1986	University of Louisville	Duke University	72–69
1987	Indiana University	Syracuse University	74–73
1988	University of Kansas	University of Oklahoma	83–79
1989	University of Michigan	Seton Hall University	80–79 (OT)
1990	University of Nevada at Las Vegas	Duke University	103–73
1991	Duke University	University of Kansas	72–65
1992	Duke University	University of Michigan	71–51
1993	University of North Carolina	University of Michigan	77–71
1994	University of Arkansas	Duke University	76–72
1995	University of California at Los Angeles	University of Arkansas	89–78
1996	University of Kentucky	Syracuse University	76–67
1997	University of Arizona	University of Kentucky	84–79 (OT)
1998	University of Kentucky	University of Utah	78–69
1999	University of Connecticut	Duke University	77–74
2000	Michigan State University	University of Florida	89–76

* Student-athletes representing Villanova in 1971 and UCLA in 1980 were declared ineligible subsequent to the tournament. By NCAA rules, the teams' and ineligible student-athletes' records were deleted, and the teams' places in the standings were vacated.

⊙ FinalFour.net. "NCAA Division I Men's Final Four Participants," www.finalfour.net/2000/history/pastff.html

NCAA: Women's Basketball Championships

Note: OT = overtime

Year	Winning Team (School)	Losing Team (School)	Score
1982	Louisiana Tech University	Cheyney State College	76–62
1983	University of Southern California	Louisiana Tech University	69–67
1984	University of Southern California	University of Tennessee	72–61
1985	Old Dominion University	University of Tennessee	70–65

NCAA: Women's Basketball Championships *(cont.)*

Year	Winning Team (School)	Losing Team (School)	Score
1986	University of Texas	University of Southern California	97–81
1987	University of Tennessee	Louisiana Tech University	67–44
1988	Louisiana Tech University	Auburn University	56–54
1989	University of Tennessee	Auburn University	76–60
1990	Stanford University	Auburn University	88–81
1991	University of Tennessee	University of Virginia	70–67 (OT)
1992	Stanford University	Western Kentucky University	78–62
1993	Texas Tech University	Ohio State University	84–82
1994	University of North Carolina	Louisiana Tech University	60–59
1995	University of Connecticut	University of Tennessee	70–64
1996	University of Tennessee	University of Tennessee	83–65
1997	University of Tennessee	Old Dominion University	68–59
1998	University of Tennessee	Louisiana Tech University	93–75
1999	Purdue University	Duke University	62–45
2000	University of Connecticut	University of Tennessee	71–52

Ⓒ FinalFour.net. "Women's Final Four Year-by-Year Results," www.finalfour.net/
2000/history/wff-results.html

National Football League Teams
American Football Conference

Division	Team	Stadium & Address	Phone/Website
East	Buffalo Bills	Ralph Wilson Stadium One Bills Drive Orchard Park, NY 14127	(716) 648-1800 www.buffalobills.com
	Indianapolis Colts	RCA Dome 100 South Capital Avenue Indianapolis, IN 46225	(317) 297-2658 www.colts.com
	Miami Dolphins	Pro Player Stadium 2269 NW 199th Street Miami, FL 33056	(305) 620-2578 www.miamidolphins.com
	New England Patriots	Foxboro Stadium 60 Washington Street (Route 1) Foxbora, MA 02035	800-828-7080 www.patriots.com
	New York Jets	Giants Stadium 50 Route 120 East Rutherford, NJ 07073	(201) 560-8200 www.newyorkjets.com
Central	Baltimore Ravens	PSINet Stadium 1101 Russell Street Baltimore, MD 21230	(410) 230-8000 www.ravenszone.net

	Cincinnati Bengals	Paul Brown Stadium One Paul Brown Stadium Cincinnati, OH 45202	(513) 621-3550 www.cincinnatibengals.com
	Cleveland Browns	Cleveland Browns Stadium 1085 West 3rd Street Cleveland, OH 44114	(440) 891-5001 www.clevelandbrowns.com
	Jacksonville Jaguars	ALLTEL Stadium 1 ALLTEL Stadium Place Jacksonville, FL 32202	(904) 633-2000 www.jaguars.com
	Pittsburgh Steelers	Three Rivers Stadium 300 Stadium Circle Pittsburgh, PA 15212	(412) 432-7800 www.steelers.com
	Tennessee Titans	Adelphia Coliseum 460 Great Circle Road Nashville, TN 37228	(615) 565-4000 www.titansonline.com
West	Denver Broncos	Mile High Stadium 1900 Eliot Street Denver, CO 80204	(303) 433-7466 www.denverbroncos.com
	Kansas City Chiefs	Arrowhead Stadium One Arrowhead Drive Kansas City, MO 64129	(816) 920-9300 www.kcchiefs.com
	Oakland Raiders	Network Associates Coliseum 7000 Coliseum Way Oakland, CA 94621	800-949-2626 www.raiders.com
	San Diego Chargers	Qualcomm Stadium 9449 Friars Road San Diego, CA 92108	(619) 525-8266 www. chargers.org
	Seattle Seahawks	Husky Stadium 201 South King Street Seattle, WA 98104	(206) 543-2200 www.seahawks.com

National Football Conference

Division	Team	Stadium & Address	Phone/Website
East	Arizona Cardinals	Sun Devil Stadium Fifth Street Tempe, AZ 85287	(480) 965-8777 www.azcardinals.com
	Dallas Cowboys	Texas Stadium 2401 East Airport Freeway Irving, TX 75062	(214) 953-1500 www.dallascowboys.com
	New York Giants	Giants Stadium 50 Route 120 East Rutherford, NJ 07073	(201) 935-8111 www.giants.com
	Philadelphia Eagles	Veterans Stadium 3501 South Broad Street Philadelphia, PA 19148	(215) 463-5500 www.eaglesnet.com

National Football League Teams *(cont.)*
National Football Conference

Division	Team	Stadium & Address	Phone/Website
	Washington Redskins	FedEx Field 1600 Raljon Road Landover, MD 20785	(410) 481-7328 (202) 432-7328 www.redskins.com
Central	Chicago Bears	Soldier Field 425 McFetridge Place Chicago, IL 60605	(847) 295-6600 www.chicagobears.com
	Detroit Lions	Pontiac Silverdome 1200 Featherstone Road Pontiac, MI 48342	800-616-7627 www.detroitlions.com
	Green Bay Packers	Lambeau Field 1265 Lombardi Avenue Green Bay, WI 54304	(920) 496-5700 www.packers.com
	Minnesota Vikings	Hubert H. Humphrey Metrodome 500 11th Avenue South Minneappolis, MN 55415	(612) 828-6500 www.vikings.com
	Tampa Bay Buccaneers	Raymond James Stadium Tampa Bay Road & Dale Mabry Highway Tampa, FL 33607	(813) 879-2827 800-282-0683 www.buccaneers.com
West	Atlanta Falcons	Georgia Dome 2695 East Katella Avenue Atlanta, GA 30313	(770) 965-3115 www.atlantafalcons.com
	Carolina Panthers	Ericsson Stadium 800 South Mint Street Charlotte, NC 28202	(704) 358-7621 www.panthers.com
	New Orleans Saints	Louisiana Superdome Sugar Bowl Drive New Orleans, LA 70112	(504) 731-1700 www.neworleanssaints.com
	St. Louis Rams	Trans World Dome 100 North Broadway St. Louis, MO 63102	(314) 342-5000 www.stlouisrams.com
	San Francisco 49ers	3Com Park Giants Drive & Gilman Avenue San Francisco, CA 94124	(415) 656-4900 www.sf49ers.com

◉ ESPN. "Football," football.espn.go.com/nfl/index
National Football League. "NFL Teams," www.nfl.com/teams

Football: Super Bowl Championships

Note: MVP = Most Valuable Player

Year	Winning Team	Losing Team	Score	Series MVP
1967 (I)	Green Bay Packers	Kansas City Chiefs	35–10	Bart Starr
1968 (II)	Green Bay Packers	Oakland Raiders	33–14	Bart Starr
1969 (III)	New York Jets	Baltimore Colts	16–7	Joe Namath
1970 (IV)	Kansas City Chiefs	Minnesota Vikings	23–7	Len Dawson
1971 (V)	Baltimore Colts	Dallas Cowboys	16–13	Chuck Howley
1972 (VI)	Dallas Cowboys	Miami Dolphins	24–3	Roger Staubach
1973 (VII)	Miami Dolphins	Washington Redskins	14–7	Jake Scott
1974 (VIII)	Miami Dolphins	Minnesota Vikings	24–7	Larry Csonka
1975 (IX)	Pittsburgh Steelers	Minnesota Vikings	16–6	Franco Harris
1976 (X)	Pittsburgh Steelers	Dallas Cowboys	21–17	Lynn Swann
1977 (XI)	Oakland Raiders	Minnesota Vikings	32–14	Fred Biletnikoff
1978 (XII)	Dallas Cowboys	Denver Broncos	27–10	Harvey Martin, Randy White
1979 (XIII)	Pittsburgh Steelers	Dallas Cowboys	35–31	Terry Bradshaw
1980 (XIV)	Pittsburgh Steelers	Los Angeles Rams	31–19	Terry Bradshaw
1981 (XV)	Oakland Raiders	Philadelphia Eagles	27–10	Jim Plunkett
1982 (XVI)	San Francisco 49ers	Cincinnati Bengals	26–21	Joe Montana
1983 (XVII)	Washington Redskins	Miami Dolphins	27–17	John Riggins
1984 (XVIII)	Los Angeles Raiders	Washington Redskins	38–9	Marcus Allen
1985 (XIX)	San Francisco 49ers	Miami Dolphins	38–16	Joe Montana
1986 (XX)	Chicago Bears	New England Patriots	46–10	Richard Dent
1987 (XXI)	New York Giants	Denver Broncos	39–20	Phil Simms
1988 (XXII)	Washington Redskins	Denver Broncos	42–10	Doug Williams
1989 (XXIII)	San Francisco 49ers	Cincinnati Bengals	20–16	Jerry Rice
1990 (XXIV)	San Francisco 49ers	Denver Broncos	55–10	Joe Montana
1991 (XXV)	New York Giants	Buffalo Bills	20–19	Ottis Anderson
1992 (XXVI)	Washington Redskins	Buffalo Bills	37–24	Mark Rypien
1993 (XXVII)	Dallas Cowboys	Buffalo Bills	52–17	Troy Aikman
1994 (XXVIII)	Dallas Cowboys	Buffalo Bills	30–13	Emmitt Smith
1995 (XXIX)	San Francisco 49ers	San Diego Chargers	49–26	Steve Young
1996 (XXX)	Dallas Cowboys	Pittsburgh Steelers	27–17	Larry Brown
1997 (XXXI)	Green Bay Packers	New England Patriots	35–21	Desmond Howard
1998 (XXXII)	Denver Broncos	Green Bay Packers	31–24	Terrell Davis
1999 (XXXIII)	Denver Broncos	Atlanta Falcons	34–19	John Elway
2000 (XXXIV)	St. Louis Rams	Tennessee Titans	23–16	Kurt Warner

⊙ FOXSports. "Super Bowl Most Valuable Players," foxsports.com/superbowl34/almanac/mvps.sml

SuperBowl.com. "Super Bowl Recaps," www.superbowl.com/u/xxxv/history

Pro Football Hall Of Fame

Year	Inductees	Year	Inductees
1963	Sammy Baugh		Dan Reeves
	Bert Bell		Ken Strong
	Joe Carr		Joe Stydahar
	Dutch Clark		Emlen Tunnell
	Harold "Red" Grange	1968	Cliff Battles
	George Halas		Art Donovan
	Mel Hein		Elroy Hirsch
	Wilbur "Pete" Henry		Wayne Millner
	Cal Hubbard		Marion Motley
	Don Hutson		Charley Trippi
	Curly Lambeau		Alex Wojciechowicz
	Tim Mara	1969	Albert Glen "Turk" Edwards
	George Preston Marshall		
	John "Blood" McNally		Earle "Greasy" Neale
	Bronko Nagurski		Leo Nomellini
	Ernie Nevers		Joe Perry
	Jim Thorpe		Ernie Stautner
1964	Jimmy Conzelman	1970	Jack Christiansen
	Ed Healey		Tom Fears
	Clarke Hinkle		Hugh McElhenny
	Link Lyman		Pete Pihos
	Mike Michalske	1971	Jim Brown
	Art Rooney		Bill Hewitt
	George Trafton		Frank "Bruiser" Kinard
1965	Guy Chamberlin		Vince Lombardi
	Paddy Driscoll		Andy Robustelli
	Dan Fortmann		Y. A. Tittle
	Otto Graham		Norm Van Brocklin
	Sid Luckman	1972	Lamar Hunt
	Steve Van Buren		Gino Marchetti
	Bob Waterfield		Ollie Matson
1966	Bill Dudley		Clarence "Ace" Parker
	Joe Guyon	1973	Raymond Berry
	Arnie Herber		Jim Parker
	Walt Kiesling		Joe Schmidt
	George McAfee	1974	Tony Canadeo
	Steve Owen		Bill George
	Hugh "Shorty" Ray		Lou Groza
	Clyde "Bulldog" Turner		Dick "Night Train" Lane
1967	Chuck Bednarik	1975	Roosevelt Brown
	Charles Bidwill		George Connor
	Paul Brown		Dante Lavelli
	Bobby Layne		Lenny Moore

1976	Ray Flaherty		Fran Tarkenton
	Len Ford		Doak Walker
	Jim Taylor	1987	Larry Csonka
1977	Frank Gifford		Len Dawson
	Forrest Gregg		Joe Greene
	Gale Sayers		John Henry Johnson
	Bart Starr		Jim Langer
	Bill Willis		Don Maynard
1978	Lance Alworth		Gene Upshaw
	Weeb Ewbank	1988	Fred Biletnikoff
	Alphonse "Tuffy" Leemans		Mike Ditka
			Jack Ham
	Ray Nitschke		Alan Page
	Larry Wilson	1989	Mel Blount
1979	Dick Butkus		Terry Bradshaw
	Yale Lary		Art Shell
	Ron Mix		Willie Wood
	Johnny Unitas	1990	Buck Buchanan
1980	Herb Adderley		Bob Griese
	David "Deacon" Jones		Franco Harris
	Bob Lilly		Ted Hendricks
	Jim Otto		Jack Lambert
1981	Morris "Red" Badgro		Tom Landry
	George Blanda		Bob St. Clair
	Willie Davis	1991	Earl Campbell
	Jim Ringo		John Hannah
1982	Doug Atkins		Stan Jones
	Sam Huff		Tex Schramm
	George Musso		Jan Stenerud
	Merlin Olsen	1992	Lem Barney
1983	Bobby Bell		Al Davis
	Sid Gillman		John Mackey
	Sonny Jurgensen		John Riggins
	Bobby Mitchell	1993	Dan Fouts
	Paul Warfield		Larry Little
1984	Willie Brown		Chuck Noll
	Mike McCormack		Walter Payton
	Charley Taylor		Bill Walsh
	Arnie Weinmeister	1994	Tony Dorsett
1985	Frank Gatski		Bud Grant
	Joe Namath		Jimmy Johnson
	Pete Rozelle		Leroy Kelly
	O. J. Simpson		Jackie Smith
	Roger Staubach		Randy White
1986	Paul Hornung	1995	Jim Finks
	Ken Houston		Henry Jordan
	Willie Lanier		Steve Largent

Pro Football Hall of Fame *(cont.)*

Year	Inductees	Year	Inductees
	Lee Roy Selmon		Anthony Muñoz
	Kellen Winslow		Mike Singletary
1996	Lou Creekmur		Dwight Stephenson
	Dan Dierdorf	1999	Eric Dickerson
	Joe Gibbs		Tom Mack
	Charlie Joiner		Ozzie Newsome
	Mel Renfro		Billy Shaw
1997	Mike Haynes		Lawrence Taylor
	Wellington Mara	2000	Howie Long
	Don Shula		Ronnie Lott
	Mike Webster		Joe Montana
1998	Paul Krause		Dan Rooney
	Tommy McDonald		Dave Wilcox

⊙ Pro Football Hall of Fame. "Hall of Famers by Class of Induction,"
www.profootballhof.com/players/mainpage.cfm?cont_id=22818

NCAA: Division I-A Football Champions

NCAA Division I-A football teams did not compete in national championship football tournaments until 1998. Prior to that, since 1869, the title of "Champion" was bestowed on teams exclusively by an annual selection process.

Retroactive Poll Champions

Champion teams were selected through a process of polling, historical research, and mathematical ratings.

Year	Teams (Schools)	Year	Teams (Schools)
1869	Princeton University	1885	Princeton University
1870	Princeton University	1886	Yale University
1871	*no team selected*	1887	Yale University
1872	Princeton University	1888	Yale University
1873	Princeton University	1889	Princeton University
1874	Yale University	1890	Harvard University
1875	Harvard University	1891	Yale University
1876	Yale University	1892	Yale University
1877	Yale University	1893	Princeton University
1878	Princeton University	1894	Yale University
1879	Princeton University	1895	University of Pennsylvania
1880	Princeton University; Yale University	1896	Lafayette College; Princeton University
1881	Yale University	1897	University of Pennsylvania
1882	Yale University		
1883	Yale University		
1884	Yale University		

1898	Harvard University	1918	University of Michigan; University of Pittsburgh
1899	Harvard University		
1900	Yale University	1919	Harvard University; University of Illinois; Notre Dame University; Texas A&M University
1901	University of Michigan		
1902	University of Michigan		
1903	University of Michigan; Princeton University	1920	University of California
1904	University of Michigan; University of Pennsylvania	1921	University of California; Cornell University
1905	University of Chicago	1922	University of California; Cornell University; Princeton University
1906	Princeton University		
1907	Yale University	1923	University of Illinois; University of Michigan
1908	Louisiana State University; University of Pennsylvania	1924	Notre Dame University
		1925	University of Alabama
1909	Yale University	1926	University of Alabama; Stanford University
1910	Harvard University; University of Pittsburgh	1927	University of Illinois; Yale University
1911	Pennsylvania State University; Princeton University	1928	Georgia Tech University
		1929	Notre Dame University
1912	Harvard University; Pennsylvania State University	1930	University of Alabama; Notre Dame University
1913	Harvard University	1931	University of Southern California
	Army (U.S. Military Academy at West Point) Cornell University	1932	University of Southern California
		1933	University of Michigan
1916	University of Pittsburgh	1934	University of Minnesota
1917	Georgia Tech University	1935	University of Minnesota

Associated Press Poll Champions

This selection process conducted by the Associated Press initiated a widely circulated poll of sportswriters and broadcasters.

Year	Teams (Schools)	Year	Teams (Schools)
1936	University of Minnesota	1944	Army (U.S. Military Academy at West Point)
1937	University of Pittsburgh		
1938	Texas Christian University	1945	Army (U.S. Military Academy at West Point)
1939	Texas A&M University		
1940	University of Minnesota	1946	Notre Dame University
1941	University of Minnesota	1947	Notre Dame University
1942	Ohio State University	1948	University of Michigan
1943	Notre Dame University	1949	Notre Dame University

Consensus Poll National Champions

Involving numerous jounalistic agencies, this selection process increased the poll's circulation.

Year	Teams (Schools)	Year	Teams (Schools)
1950	University of Oklahoma	1972	University of Southern California
1951	University of Tennessee		
1952	Michigan State University	1973	Notre Dame University;
1953	University of Maryland		University of Alabama
1954	University of California at Los Angeles; Ohio State University	1974	University of Southern California; University of Oklahoma
1955	University of Oklahoma	1975	University of Oklahoma
1956	University of Oklahoma	1976	University of Pittsburgh
1957	Ohio State University; Auburn University	1977	Notre Dame University
		1978	University of Alabama; University of Southern California
1958	Louisiana State University; University of Iowa		
1959	Syracuse University	1979	University of Alabama
1960	University of Minnesota; University of Mississippi	1980	University of Georgia
		1981	Clemson University
1961	University of Alabama; Ohio State University	1982	Pennsylvania State University
1962	University of Southern California	1983	University of Miami
		1984	Brigham Young University
1963	University of Texas	1985	University of Oklahoma
1964	University of Alabama; University of Arkansas; Notre Dame University	1986	Pennsylvania State University
		1987	University of Miami
1965	Michigan State University; University of Alabama	1988	Notre Dame University
		1989	University of Miami
1966	Notre Dame University; Michigan State University	1990	University of Colorado; Georgia Tech University
1967	University of Southern California	1991	University of Washington; University of Miami
1968	Ohio State University	1992	University of Alabama
1969	University of Texas	1993	Florida State University
1970	University of Nebraska; University of Texas; Ohio State University	1994	University of Nebraska
		1995	University of Nebraska
		1996	University of Florida
		1997	University of Michigan; University of Nebraska
1971	University of Nebraska		

Bowl Championship Series

Created in 1998, the Bowl Championship Series (BCS) Committee selects two teams to play a national championship game. This selection process is based on four principal criteria: subjective polls of sportswriters and coaches, computer rankings, schedule strength, and number of losses. The two teams with the lowest point total in these four categories play in the championship game.

Year	Teams (Schools)
1998*	University of Tennessee
1999*	Florida State University

* championship game played in January the following year

⊙ National Collegiate Athletic Association Football. "NCAA Division I-A Past Champions," www.ncaafootball.net/d1_past_champs.html

Heisman Memorial Trophy Winners

The Heisman Memorial Trophy is awarded annually to the outstanding college football player in the United States. In 1935, awarded by the Downtown Athletic Club (DAC) of New York City, it was known as the DAC Trophy. In 1936, the trophy was renamed to honor DAC Athletics Director John W. Heisman, who died that October.

DB = Defensive Back; FB = FB; HB = HB; QB = QB; RB = RB; TB = Tailback; WR = WR

Year	Winner	School	Position
1935	Jay Berwanger	University of Chicago	HB
1936	Larry Kelley	Yale University	End
1937	Clint Frank	Yale University	HB
1938	Davey O'Brien	Texas Christian University	QB
1939	Nile Kinnick	University of Iowa	HB
1940	Tom Harmon	University of Michigan	HB
1941	Bruce Smith	University of Minnesota	HB
1942	Frank Sinkwich	University of Georgia	HB
1943	Angelo Bertelli	Notre Dame University	QB
1944	Les Horvath	Ohio State University	QB/HB
1945	Doc Blanchard	Army	FB
1946	Glenn Davis	Army	HB
1947	Johnny Lujack	Notre Dame University	QB
1948	Doak Walker	Southern Methodist University	HB
1949	Leon Hart	Notre Dame University	End
1950	Vic Janowicz	Ohio State University	HB
1951	Dick Kazmaier	Princeton University	HB
1952	Billy Vessels	University of Oklahoma	HB
1953	Johnny Lattner	Notre Dame University	HB
1954	Alan Ameche	University of Wisconsin	FB
1955	Howard Cassady	Ohio State University	HB
1956	Paul Hornung	Notre Dame University	QB
1957	John David Crow	Texas A&M University	HB
1958	Pete Dawkins	Army	HB
1959	Billy Cannon	Louisiana State University	HB

Year	Winner	School	Position
1960	Joe Bellino	Navy	HB
1961	Ernie Davis	Syracuse University	HB
1962	Terry Baker	Oregon State University	QB
1963	Roger Staubach	Navy	QB
1964	John Huarte	Notre Dame University	QB
1965	Mike Garrett	University of Southern California	HB
1966	Steve Spurrier	University of Florida	QB
1967	Gary Beban	UCLA	QB
1968	O.J. Simpson	University of Southern California	HB
1969	Steve Owens	University of Oklahoma	HB
1970	Jim Plunkett	Stanford University	QB
1971	Pat Sullivan	Auburn University	QB
1972	Johnny Rodgers	University of Nebraska	WR
1973	John Cappelletti	Penn State University	RB
1974	Archie Griffin	Ohio State University	RB
1975	Archie Griffin	Ohio State University	RB
1976	Tony Dorsett	University of Pittsburgh	RB
1977	Earl Campbell	University of Texas	RB
1978	Billy Sims	University of Oklahoma	RB
1979	Charles White	University of Southern California	RB
1980	George Rogers	University of South Carolina	RB
1981	Marcus Allen	University of Southern California	RB
1982	Herschel Walker	University of Georgia	RB
1983	Mike Rozier	University of Nebraska	RB
1984	Doug Flutie	Boston College	QB
1985	Bo Jackson	Auburn University	RB
1986	Vinny Testaverde	University of Miami	QB
1987	Tim Brown	Notre Dame University	WR
1988	Barry Sanders	Oklahoma State University	RB
1989	Andre Ware	University of Houston	QB
1990	Ty Detmer	Brigham Young University	QB
1991	Desmond Howard	University of Michigan	WR
1992	Gino Torretta	University of Miami	QB
1993	Charlie Ward	Florida State University	QB
1994	Rashaan Salaam	University of Colorado	RB
1995	Eddie George	Ohio State University	RB
1996	Danny Wuerffel	University of Florida	QB
1997	Charles Woodson	University of Michigan	DB/Receiver
1998	Ricky Williams	University of Texas	TB
1999	Ron Dayne	University of Wisconsin	TB
2000	Chris Weinke	Florida State University	QB

⊙ College Football Hall of Fame. "Heisman Memorial Trophy,"
www.collegefootball.org/heisman
Heisman Memorial Trophy Trust. "Winners," www.heisman.com/winners.html

National Hockey League Teams

Eastern Conference

Division	Team	Stadium & Address	Phone/Website
Atlantic	New Jersey Devils	Continental Airlines Arena 50 Route 120 North East Rutherford, NJ 07073	(201) 935-3900 www.newjerseydevils.com
	New York Islanders	Nassau Veterans Memorial Coliseum 1255 Hempstead Turnpike Uniondale, NY 11553	(516) 542-9276 www.newyorkislanders.com
	New York Rangers	Madison Square Garden Two Pennsylvania Plaza New York, NY 10121	(212) 465-6741 www.newyorkrangers.com
	Philadelphia Flyers	First Union Center One CoreStates Complex Philadelphia, PA 19148	(215) 336-2000 www.philadelphiaflyers.com
	Pittsburgh Penguins	Civic Arena 66 Mario Lemieux Place Pittsburgh, PA 15219	(412) 323-1919 www.pittsburgh penguins.com
Northeast	Boston Bruins	FleetCenter One FleetCenter Boston, MA 02114	(617) 624-1750 www.bostonbruins.com
	Buffalo Sabres	Marine Midland Arena One Seymour H. Knox III Plaza Buffalo, NY 14203	(716) 855-4444 www.sabres.com
	Montréal Canadiens	Le Centre Molson 1260 de La Gauchetiére Street W Montréal, Québec H3B 5E8	(440) 891-5001 www.canadiens.com
	Ottawa Senators	Corel Centre 1000 Palladium Drive Kanata, Ontario K2V 1A5	800-444-7367 www.ottawasenators.com
	Toronto Maple Leafs	Air Canada Centre 40 Bay Street Toronto, Ontario M5J 2X2	(416) 815-5700 www.toronto mapleleafs.com
Southeast	Atlanta Thrashers	Philips Arena One Philips Drive Atlanta, GA	(404) 584-7825 www.atlantathrashers.com
	Carolina Hurricanes	Raleigh Entertainment & Sports Arena 5000 Aerial Center Morrisville, NC 27560	888-645-8491 www.caneshockey.com
	Florida Panthers	National Car Rental Center 2555 Panther Parkway Sunrise, FL 33323	(954) 835-8000 www.floridapanthers.com
	Tampa Bay Lightning	Ice Palace 401 Channelside Drive Tampa, FL 33602	(813) 301-2500 www.tampabay lightning.com

National Hockey League Teams *(cont.)*

Division	Team	Stadium & Address	Phone/Website
Southeast	Washington Capitals	MCI Center 601 F Street NW Washington, DC 20004	(202) 432-7328 www.washingtoncaps.com

Western Conference

Division	Team	Stadium & Address	Phone/Website
Central	Chicago Blackhawks	United Center 1901 West Madison Street Chicago, IL 60612	(312) 455-4500 www.chicago blackhawks.com
	Columbus Blue Jackets	Nationwide Arena 150 East Wilson Bridge Road Worthington, OH 43085	800-645-2657 www.columbus bluejackets.com
	Detroit Red Wings	Joe Louis Arena 600 Civic Center Drive Detroit, MI 48226	(810) 645-6666 www.detroitredwings.com
	Nashville Predators	Nashville Arena 501 Broadway Nashville, TN 37203	(615) 770-7825 www.nashville predators.com
	St. Louis Blues	Kiel Center 1401 Clark Avenue St. Louis, MO 63103	(314) 241-1888 www.stlouisblues.com
Northwest	Calgary Flames	Pengrowth Saddledome at Stampede Park 555 Saddledome Rise SE Calgary, Alberta T2G 2W1	(403) 777-4630 www.calgaryflames.com
	Colorado Avalanche	Pepsi Center 100 Chopper Place Denver, CO 80204	(303) 405-1100 www.colorado avalanche.com
	Edmonton Oilers	Skyreach Centre 7424-118 Avenue Edmonton, AB T5G 3G8	(403) 414 4000 www.edmontonoilers.com
	Minnesota Wild	Xcel Energy Center 199 West Kellogg Boulevard St. Paul, MN 55102	(651) 222-9453 www.wild.com
	Vancouver Canucks	General Motors Place 800 Griffiths Way0 Vancouver, British Columbia V6B 6G1	(604) 280-4400 www.orcabay.com/ canucks
Pacific	Anaheim Mighty Ducks	Arrowhead Pond of Anaheim 2695 East Katella Avenue Anaheim, CA 92806	(714) 704-2500 www.mightyducks.com
	Dallas Stars	Dr. Pepper Star Center 211 Cowboy Parkway Irving, TX 75063	(214) 467-8277 www.dallasstars.com

Los Angeles Kings	Staples Center 1111 South Figueroa Street Los Angeles, CA 90015	888-546-4752 www.lakings.com
Phoenix Coyotes	Cellular One Ice Den 9375 East Bell Road Scottsdale, AZ 85260	(602) 503-5555 www.nhlcoyotes.com
San Jose Sharks	San Jose Arena 525 West Santa Clara Street San Jose, CA 95113	(408) 287-9200 800-225-2277 www.sj-sharks.com

⊙ ESPN. "Hockey," sports.espn.go.com/nhl/index
National Hockey League. "Teams," www.nhl.com/lineups/team/index.html

National Hockey League: Stanley Cup Championships

The Stanley Cup is the oldest trophy awarded to professional athletes in North America. Originally presented to amateur Canadian hockey teams (from 1893), it became the property of the National Hockey Association in 1910. In 1926, the Stanley Cup playoffs became an event exclusively for National Hockey League (NHL) teams. Since 1939, the competition has been a best-of-seven-games series. Listed here are the results of the Stanley Cup finals since the 1926–27 season.

Note: "Score" shows number of games won; MVP = Most Valuable Player (awarded the Conn Smythe Trophy)

Year	Winning Team	Losing Team	Score	Series MVP
1927	Ottawa Senators	Boston Bruins	2–0	—
1928	New York Rangers	Montreal Maroons	3–2	—
1929	Boston Bruins	New York Rangers	2–0	—
1930	Montreal Canadiens	Boston Bruins	2–0	—
1931	Montreal Canadiens	Chicago Blackhawks	3–2	—
1932	Toronto Maple Leafs	New York Rangers	3–0	—
1933	New York Rangers	Toronto Maple Leafs	3–1	—
1934	Chicago Blackhawks	Detroit Red Wings	3–1	—
1935	Montreal Maroons	Toronto Maple Leafs	3–0	—
1936	Detroit Red Wings	Toronto Maple Leafs	3–1	—
1937	Detroit Red Wings	New York Rangers	3–2	—
1938	Chicago Blackhawks	Toronto Maple Leafs	3–1	—
1939	Boston Bruins	Toronto Maple Leafs	4–1	—
1940	New York Rangers	Toronto Maple Leafs	4–2	—
1941	Boston Bruins	Detroit Red Wings	4–0	—
1942	Toronto Maple Leafs	Detroit Red Wings	4–3	—
1943	Detroit Red Wings	Boston Bruins	4–0	—
1944	Montreal Canadiens	Chicago Blackhawks	4–0	—
1945	Toronto Maple Leafs	Detroit Red Wings	4–3	—
1946	Montreal Canadiens	Boston Bruins	4–1	—
1947	Toronto Maple Leafs	Montreal Canadiens	4–2	—
1948	Toronto Maple Leafs	Detroit Red Wings	4–0	—
1949	Toronto Maple Leafs	Detroit Red Wings	4–0	—

National Hockey League:
Stanley Cup Championships *(cont.)*

Year	Winning Team	Losing Team	Score	Series MVP
1950	Detroit Red Wings	New York Rangers	4–3	—
1951	Toronto Maple Leafs	Montreal Canadiens	4–1	—
1952	Detroit Red Wings	Montreal Canadiens	4–0	—
1953	Montreal Canadiens	Boston Bruins	4–1	—
1954	Detroit Red Wings	Montreal Canadiens	4–3	—
1955	Detroit Red Wings	Montreal Canadiens	4–3	—
1956	Montreal Canadiens	Detroit Red Wings	4–1	—
1957	Montreal Canadiens	Boston Bruins	4–1	—
1958	Montreal Canadiens	Boston Bruins	4–2	—
1959	Montreal Canadiens	Toronto Maple Leafs	4–1	—
1960	Montreal Canadiens	Toronto Maple Leafs	4–0	—
1961	Chicago Blackhawks	Detroit Red Wings	4–2	—
1962	Toronto Maple Leafs	Chicago Blackhawks	4–2	—
1963	Toronto Maple Leafs	Detroit Red Wings	4–1	—
1964	Toronto Maple Leafs	Detroit Red Wings	4–3	—
1965	Montreal Canadiens	Chicago Blackhawks	4–3	Jean Beliveau
1966	Montreal Canadiens	Detroit Red Wings	4–2	Roger Crozier
1967	Toronto Maple Leafs	Montreal Canadiens	4–2	Dave Keon
1968	Montreal Canadiens	St. Louis Blues	4–0	Glenn Hall
1969	Montreal Canadiens	St. Louis Blues	4–0	Serge Savard
1970	Boston Bruins	St. Louis Blues	4–0	Bobby Orr
1971	Montreal Canadiens	Chicago Blackhawks	4–3	Ken Dryden
1972	Boston Bruins	New York Rangers	4–2	Bobby Orr
1973	Montreal Canadiens	Chicago Blackhawks	4–2	Yvon Cournoyer
1974	Philadelphia Flyers	Boston Bruins	4–2	Bernie Parent
1975	Philadelphia Flyers	Buffalo Sabres	4–2	Bernie Parent
1976	Montreal Canadiens	Philadelphia Flyers	4–0	Reggie Leach
1977	Montreal Canadiens	Boston Bruins	4–0	Guy Lafleur
1978	Montreal Canadiens	Boston Bruins	4–2	Larry Robinson
1979	Montreal Canadiens	New York Rangers	4–1	Bob Gainey
1980	New York Islanders	Philadelphia Flyers	4–2	Bryan Trottier
1981	New York Islanders	Minnesota North Stars	4–1	Butch Goring
1982	New York Islanders	Vancouver Canucks	4–0	Mike Bossy
1983	New York Islanders	Edmonton Oilers	4–0	Bill Smith
1984	Edmonton Oilers	New York Islanders	4–1	Mark Messier
1985	Edmonton Oilers	Philadelphia Flyers	4–1	Wayne Gretzky
1986	Montreal Canadiens	Calgary Flames	4–1	Patrick Roy
1987	Edmonton Oilers	Philadelphia Flyers	4–3	Ron Hextall
1988	Edmonton Oilers	Boston Bruins	4–0	Wayne Gretzky
1989	Calgary Flames	Montreal Canadiens	4–2	Al MacInnis
1990	Edmonton Oilers	Boston Bruins	4–1	Bill Ranford

Year	Winner	Finalist		Series MVP
1991	Pittsburgh Penguins	Minnesota North Stars	4–2	Mario Lemieux
1992	Pittsburgh Penguins	Chicago Blackhawks	4–0	Mario Lemieux
1993	Montreal Canadiens	Los Angeles Kings	4–1	Patrick Roy
1994	New York Rangers	Vancouver Canucks	4–3	Brian Leetch
1995	New Jersey Devils	Detroit Red Wings	4–0	Claude Lemieux
1996	Colorado Avalanche	Florida Panthers	4–0	Joe Sakic
1997	Detroit Red Wings	Philadelphia Flyers	4–0	Mike Vernon
1998	Detroit Red Wings	Washington Capitals	4–0	Steve Yzerman
1999	Dallas Stars	Buffalo Sabres	4–2	Joe Nieuwendyk
2000	New Jersey Devils	Dallas Stars	4-2	Scott Stevens

☉ ESPN. "Stanley Cup Finals: Playoff History," espn.go.com/nhl/playoffs00/s/history/index.html

National Hockey League. "Stanley Cup Champions and Finalists," www.nhl.com/hockeyu/history/cup/champs.html

Hockey Hall Of Fame

Year	Inductees	Year	Inductees
1945	Dan Bain		Bill Cook
	Hobey Baker		Moose Goheen
	Dubbie Bowie		Ernie Johnson
	Chuck Gardiner		Mickey MacKay
	Eddie Gerard	1958	Frank Boucher
	Frank McGee		King Clancy
	Howie Morenz		Sprague Cleghorn
	Tom Phillips		Alex Connell
	Harvey Pulford		Red Dutton
	Art Ross		Frank Foyston
	Hod Stuart		Frank Fredrickson
	Georges Vezina		Herb Gardiner
1947	Dit Clapper		George Hay
	Aurel Joliat		Dick Irvin
	Frank Nighbor		Ching Johnson
	Lester Patrick		Duke Keats
	Eddie Shore		Hughie Lehman
	Cyclone Taylor		George McNamara
1950	Scotty Davidson		Paddy Moran
	Graham Drinkwater	1959	Jack Adams
	Mike Grant		Cy Denneny
	Si Griffis		Tiny Thompson
	Newsy Lalonde	1960	George Boucher
	Joe Malone		Sylvio Mantha
	George Richardson		Jack Walker
	Harry Trihey	1961	Syl Apps
1952	Dickie Boon		Charlie Conacher

Year	Inductees	Year	Inductees
	George Hainsworth		Babe Siebert
	Hap Day		Jack Stewart
	Joe Hall	1965	Marty Barry
	Percy LeSueur		Clint Benedict
	Frank Rankin		Arthur Farrel
	Maurice Richard		Red Horner
	Milt Schmidt		Syd Howe
	Oliver Seibert		Jack Marshall
	Bruce Stuart		Bill Mosienko
1962	Punch Broadbent		Ernie Russell
	Harry Cameron		Blair Russel
	Rusty Crawford		Fred Scanlan
	Jack Darragh		Frank Brimsek
	Jimmy Gardner		Ted Kennedy
	Billy Gilmour		Elmer Lach
	Shorty Green		Ted Lindsay
	Riley Hern		Babe Pratt
	Tom Hooper		Kenny Reardon
	Bouse Hutton	1967	Turk Broda
	Harry Hyland		Neil Colville
	Jack Laviolette		Harry Oliver
	Fred Maxwell	1968	Bill Cowley
	Billy McGimsie	1969	Sid Abel
	Reg Noble		Bryan Hextall
	Didier Pitre		Red Kelly
	Jack Ruttan		Roy Worters
	Sweeney Schriner	1970	Babe Dye
	Joe Simpson		Bill Gadsby
	Alf Smith		Tom Johnson
	Barney Stanley	1971	Busher Jackson
	Nels Stewart		Gordie Roberts
	Marty Walsh		Terry Sawchuk
	Harry "Moose" Watson		Cooney Weiland
	Harry Westwick	1972	Jean Beliveau
	Fred Whitcroft		Bernie Geoffrion
	Phat Wilson		Hap Holmes
1963	Ebbie Goodfellow		Gordie Howe
	Joe Primeau		Hooley Smith
	Earl Seibert	1973	Doug Harvey
1964	Doug Bentley		Chuck Rayner
	Bill Durnan		Tommy Smith

1974	Billy Burch	1987	Bobby Clarke
	Art Coulter		Eddie Giacomin
	Tommy Dunderdale		Jacques Laperriere
	Dickie Moore	1988	Tony Esposito
1975	George Armstrong		Guy Lafleur
	Ace Bailey		Buddy O'Connor
	Gordie Drillon		Brad Park
	Glenn Hall	1989	Herbie Lewis
	Pierre Pilote		Darryl Sittler
1976	Johnny Bower		Vladislav Tretiak
	Bill Quackenbush	1990	Bill Barber
1977	Alex Delvecchio		Fernie Flaman
	Tim Horton		Gilbert Perreault
1978	Andy Bathgate	1991	Mike Bossy
	Jacques Plante		Denis Potvin
	Marcel Pronovost		Bob Pulford
1979	Harry Howell		Clint Smith
	Bobby Orr	1992	Marcel Dionne
	Henri Richard		Woody Dumart
1980	Harry Lumley		Bob Gainey
	Lynn Patrick		Lanny McDonald
	Gump Worsley	1993	Guy Lapointe
1981	John Bucyk		Edgar Laprade
	Frank Mahovlich		Steve Shutt
	Allan Stanley		Billy Smith
1982	Yvan Cournoyer	1994	Lionel Conacher
	Rod Gilbert		Harry Percival Watson
	Norm Ullman	1995	Bun Cook
1983	Ken Dryden		Larry Robinson
	Bobby Hull	1996	Bobby Bauer
	Stan Mikita		Borje Salming
1984	Phil Esposito	1997	Mario Lemieux
	Jacques Lemaire		Bryan Trottier
	Bernie Parent	1998	Roy Gordon Conacher
1985	Gerry Cheevers		Michel Goulet
	Bert Olmstead		Peter Stastny
	Jean Ratelle	1999	Wayne Gretzky
1986	Leo Boivin	2000	Walter Bush, Jr.
	Dave Keon		Joe Mullen
	Serge Savard		Denis Savard

⊙ Hockey Hall of Fame. "Honoured Players," www.hhof.com/html/hmi11500.htm

Tennis: Championships

Although tennis championship games were played from the late 1800s, the tournaments were not officially designated "opens" (open to both professional and amateur tennis players) until 1968 in England, the United States, and France, and until 1969 in Australia.

U.S. Open Singles Champions

Year	Men	Women
1881	Richard Sears	
1882	Richard Sears	
1883	Richard Sears	
1884	Richard Sears	
1885	Richard Sears	
1886	Richard Sears	
1887	Richard Sears	Ellen Hansell
1888	Henry Slocum	Bertha Townsend
1889	Henry Slocum	Bertha Townsend
1890	Oliver Campbell	Ellen Roosevelt
1891	Oliver Campbell	Mabel Cahill
1892	Oliver Campbell	Mabel Cahill
1893	Robert Wrenn	Aline Terry
1894	Robert Wrenn	Helen Helwig
1895	Fred Hovey	Juliette Atkinson
1896	Robert Wrenn	Elisabeth Moore
1897	Robert Wrenn	Juliette Atkinson
1898	Malcolm Whitman	Juliette Atkinson
1899	Malcolm Whitman	Marion Jones
1900	Malcolm Whitman	Myrtle McAteer
1901	William Larned	Elisabeth Moore
1902	William Larned	Marion Jones
1903	Hugh Doherty	Elisabeth Moore
1904	Holcombe Ward	May Sutton
1905	Beals Wright	Elisabeth Moore
1906	William Clothier	Helen Homans
1907	William Larned	Evelyn Sears
1908	William Larned	Maud Barger-Wallach
1909	William Larned	Hazel Hotchkiss
1910	William Larned	Hazel Hotchkiss
1911	William Larned	Hazel Hotchkiss
1912	Maurice McLoughlin	Mary Browne
1913	Maurice McLoughlin	Mary Browne
1914	Richard William	Mary Browne
1915	William Johnston	Molla Bjurstedt
1916	Richard William	Molla Bjurstedt
1917	R. L. Murray	Molla Bjurstedt
1918	R. L. Murray	Molla Bjurstedt
1919	William Johnston	Hazel Hotchkiss Wrightman

1920	Bill Tilden	Molla Bjurstedt Mallory
1921	Bill Tilden	Molla Bjurstedt Mallory
1922	Bill Tilden	Molla Bjurstedt Mallory
1923	Bill Tilden	Helen Wills
1924	Bill Tilden	Helen Wills
1925	Bill Tilden	Helen Wills
1926	Rene Lacoste	Molla Bjurstedt Mallory
1927	Rene Lacoste	Helen Wills
1928	Henri Cochet	Helen Wills
1929	Bill Tilden	Helen Wills
1930	John Doeg	Betty Nuthall
1931	H. Ellsworth Vines	Helen Wills Moody
1932	H. Ellsworth Vines	Helen Jacobs
1933	Fred Perry	Helen Jacobs
1934	Fred Perry	Helen Jacobs
1935	Wilmer Alison	Helen Jacobs
1936	Fred Perry	Alice Marble
1937	Don Budge	Anita Lizana
1938	Don Budge	Alice Marble
1939	Bobby Riggs	Alice Marble
1940	Don McNeill	Alice Marble
1941	Bobby Riggs	Sarah Palfrey Cooke
1942	F. R. Schroeder, Jr.	Pauline Betz
1943	Joseph Hunt	Pauline Betz
1944	Frank Parker	Pauline Betz
1945	Frank Parker	Sarah Palfrey Cooke
1946	Jack Kramer	Pauline Betz
1947	Jack Kramer	Louise Brough
1948	Pancho Gonzales	Margaret Osborne duPont
1949	Pancho Gonzales	Margaret Osborne duPont
1950	Arthur Larsen	Margaret Osborne duPont
1951	Frank Sedgman	Maureen Connolly
1952	Frank Sedgman	Maureen Connolly
1953	Tony Trabert	Maureen Connolly
1954	Vic Seixas	Doris Hart
1955	Tony Trabert	Doris Hart
1956	Ken Rosewall	Shirley Fry
1957	Malcolm Anderson	Althea Gibson
1958	Ashley Cooper	Althea Gibson
1959	Neale A. Fraser	Maria Bueno
1960	Neale A. Fraser	Darlene Hard
1961	Roy Emerson	Darlene Hard
1962	Rod Laver	Margaret Smith
1963	Rafael Osuna	Maria Bueno
1964	Roy Emerson	Maria Bueno
1965	Manual Santana	Margaret Smith
1966	Fred Stolle	Maria Bueno

Tennis Championships *(cont.)*

U.S. Open Singles Champions

Year	Men	Women
1967	John Newcombe	Billie Jean King
1968	Arthur Ashe	Virginia Wade
1969	Rod Laver	Margaret Smith Court
1970	Ken Rosewall	Margaret Smith Court
1971	Stan Smith	Billie Jean King
1972	Ilie Nastase	Billie Jean King
1973	John Newcombe	Margaret Smith Court
1974	Jimmy Connors	Billie Jean King
1975	Manual Orantes	Chris Evert
1976	Jimmy Connors	Chris Evert
1977	Guillermo Vilas	Chris Evert
1978	Jimmy Connors	Chris Evert
1979	John McEnroe	Tracy Austin
1980	John McEnroe	Chris Evert Lloyd
1981	John McEnroe	Tracy Austin
1982	Jimmy Connors	Chris Evert Lloyd
1983	Jimmy Connors	Martina Navratilova
1984	John McEnroe	Martina Navratilova
1985	Ivan Lendl	Hana Mandlikova
1986	Ivan Lendl	Martina Navratilova
1987	Ivan Lendl	Martina Navratilova
1988	Mats Wilander	Steffi Graf
1989	Boris Becker	Steffi Graf
1990	Pete Sampras	Gabriela Sabatini
1991	Stefan Edberg	Monica Seles
1992	Stefan Edberg	Monica Seles
1993	Pete Sampras	Steffi Graf
1994	Andre Agassi	Arantxa Sanchez Vicario
1995	Pete Sampras	Steffi Graf
1996	Pete Sampras	Steffi Graf
1997	Patrick Rafter	Martina Hingis
1998	Patrick Rafter	Lindsay Davenport
1999	Andre Agassi	Serena Williams
2000	Marat Safin	Venus Williams

Wimbledon Singles Champions

Year	Men	Women
1877	Spencer Gore	
1878	P. Frank Hadow	
1879	J. T. Hartley	
1880	J. T. Hartley	
1881	William Renshaw	
1882	William Renshaw	

1883	William Renshaw	
1884	William Renshaw	Maud Watson
1885	William Renshaw	Maud Watson
1886	William Renshaw	Blanche Bingley
1887	Herbert Lawford	Lottie Dod
1888	Ernest Renshaw	Lottie Dod
1889	William Renshaw	Blanche Bingley Hillyard
1890	Willoughby J. Hamilton	Helena Rice
1891	Wilfred Baddeley	Lottie Dod
1892	Wilfred Baddeley	Lottie Dod
1893	Joshua Pim	
1894	Joshua Pim	Blanche Bingley Hillyard
1895	Wilfred Baddeley	Charlotte Cooper
1896	Harold Mahony	Charlotte Cooper
1897	Reginald Doherty	Blanche Bingley Hillyard
1898	Reginald Doherty	Charlotte Cooper
1899	Reginald Doherty	Blanche Bingley Hillyard
1900	Reginald Doherty	Blanche Bingley Hillyard
1901	Arthur Gore	Charlotte Cooper Sterry
1902	Hugh Doherty	Muriel Robb
1903	Hugh Doherty	Dorothea Douglass
1904	Hugh Doherty	Dorothea Douglass
1905	Hugh Doherty	May Sutton
1906	Hugh Doherty	Dorothea Douglass
1907	Norman Brookes	May Sutton
1908	Arthur Gore	Charlotte Cooper Sterry
1909	Arthur Gore	Dora Boothby
1910	Tony Wilding	Dorothea Douglass Lambert-Chambers
1911	Tony Wilding	Dorothea Douglass Lambert-Chambers
1912	Tony Wilding	Ethel W. Larcombe
1913	Tony Wilding	Dorothea Douglass Lambert-Chambers
1914	Norman Brookes	Dorothea Douglass Lambert-Chambers
1915–18	*tournament not played due to World War I*	
1919	Gerald Patterson	Suzanne Lenglen
1920	Bill Tilden	Suzanne Lenglen
1921	Bill Tilden	Suzanne Lenglen
1922	Gerald Patterson	Suzanne Lenglen
1923	William Johnston	Suzanne Lenglen
1924	Jean Borotra	Kathleen McKane
1925	Rene Lacoste	Suzanne Lenglen
1926	Jean Borotra	Kathleen McKane
1927	Henri Cochet	Helen Wills
1928	Rene Lacoste	Helen Wills
1929	Henri Cochet	Helen Wills
1930	Bill Tilden	Helen Wills Moody
1931	Sidney Wood	Cilly Aussem

Tennis Championships *(cont.)*

Wimbledon Singles Champions

Year	Men	Women
1932	H. Ellsworth Vines	Helen Wills Moody
1933	Jack Crawford	Helen Wills Moody
1934	Fred Perry	Dorothy Round
1935	Fred Perry	Helen Wills Moody
1936	Fred Perry	Helen Jacobs
1937	Don Budge	Dorothy Round
1938	Don Budge	Helen Wills Moody
1939	Bobby Riggs	Alice Marble
1940–45	*tournament not played due to World War II*	
1946	Yvon Petra	Pauline Betz
1947	Jack Kramer	Margaret Osborne
1948	Bob Falkenburg	Louise Brough
1949	Ted Schroeder	Louise Brough
1950	Budge Patty	Louise Brough
1951	Dick Savitt	Doris Hart
1952	Frank Sedgman	Maureen Connolly
1953	Vic Seizas	Maureen Connolly
1954	Jaroslav Drobny	Maureen Connolly
1955	Tony Trabert	Louise Brough
1956	Lew Hoad	Shirley Fry
1957	Lew Hoad	Althea Gibson
1958	Ashley Cooper	Althea Gibson
1959	Alex Olmedo	Maria Bueno
1960	Neale Fraser	Maria Bueno
1961	Rod Laver	Angela Mortimer
1962	Rod Laver	Karen Hantze-Susman
1963	Chuck McKinley	Margaret Smith
1964	Roy Emerson	Maria Bueno
1965	Roy Emerson	Margaret Smith
1966	Manuel Santana	Billie Jean King
1967	John Newcombe	Billie Jean King
1968	Rod Laver	Billie Jean King
1969	Rod Laver	Ann Haydon-Jones
1970	John Newcombe	Margaret Smith Court
1971	John Newcombe	Evonne Goolagong
1972	Stan Smith	Billie Jean King
1973	Jan Kodes	Billie Jean King
1974	Jimmy Connors	Chris Evert
1975	Arthur Ashe	Billie Jean King
1976	Bjorn Borg	Chris Evert
1977	Bjorn Borg	Virginia Wade
1978	Bjorn Borg	Martina Navratilova

1979	Bjorn Borg	Martina Navratilova
1980	Bjorn Borg	Evonne Goolagong
1981	John McEnroe	Chris Evert Lloyd
1982	Jimmy Connors	Martina Navratilova
1983	John McEnroe	Martina Navratilova
1984	John McEnroe	Martina Navratilova
1985	Boris Becker	Martina Navratilova
1986	Boris Becker	Martina Navratilova
1987	Pat Cash	Martina Navratilova
1988	Stefan Edberg	Steefi Graf
1989	Boris Becker	Steffi Graf
1990	Stefan Edberg	Martina Navratilova
1991	Michael Stich	Steffi Graf
1992	Andre Agassi	Steffi Graf
1993	Pete Sampras	Steffi Graf
1994	Pete Sampras	Conchita Martinez
1995	Pete Sampras	Steffi Graf
1996	Richard Kralicek	Steffi Graf
1997	Pete Sampras	Martina Hingis
1998	Pete Sampras	Jana Novotna
1999	Pete Sampras	Lindsay Davenport
2000	Pete Sampras	Venus Williams

French Open Singles Champions

Year	Men	Women
1891	J. Briggs	
1892	J. Schoepfer	
1893	L. Riboulet	
1894	Andre Vacherot	
1895	Andre Vacherot	
1896	Andre Vacherot	
1897	Paul Ayme	Cecilia Masson
1898	Paul Ayme	Cecilia Masson
1899	Paul Ayme	Cecilia Masson
1900	Paul Ayme	Cecilia Prevost
1901	Andre Vacherot	P. Girod
1902	Marcel Vacherot	Cecilia Masson
1903	Max Decugis	Cecilia Masson
1904	Max Decugis	Katie Gillou
1905	Maurice Germot	Katie Gillou
1906	Maurice Germot	Katie Fenwick
1907	Max Decugis	C. de Kermel
1908	Max Decugis	Katie Fenwick
1909	Max Decugis	Jeanne Matthey
1910	Maurice Germot	Jeanne Matthey
1911	Andre Gobert	Jeanne Matthey
1912	Max Decugis	Jeanne Matthey

Tennis Championships *(cont.)*

French Open Singles Champions

Year	Men	Women
1913	Max Decugis	Marguerite Broquedis
1914	Max Decugis	Marguerite Broquedis
1915–19	*tournament not played due to World War I*	
1920	Andre Gobert	Suzanne Lenglen
1921	Jean Samzaeuilh	Suzanne Lenglen
1922	Henri Cochet	Suzanne Lenglen
1923	Pierre Blancy	Suzanne Lenglen
1924	Jean Borotra	Didi Vlasto
1925	Rene Lacoste	Suzanne Lenglen
1926	Henri Cochet	Suzanne Lenglen
1927	Rene Lacoste	Kea Bouman
1928	Henri Cochet	Helen Wills
1929	Rene Lacoste	Helen Wills
1930	Henri Cochet	Helen Wills Moody
1931	Jean Borotra	Cilly Aussem
1932	Henri Cochet	Helen Wills Moody
1933	Jack Crawford	Margaret Scriven
1934	Gottfried von Cramm	Margaret Scriven
1935	Fred Perry	Hilda Sperling
1936	Gottfried von Cramm	Hilda Sperling
1937	Henner Henkel	Hilda Sperling
1938	Don Budge	Simone Mathieu
1939	Don McNeill	Simone Mathieu
1940–45	*tournament not played due to World War II*	
1946	Marcel Bernard	Margaret Osborne
1947	Joseph Asboth	Pat Canning Todd
1948	Frank Parker	Nelly Landry
1949	Frank Parker	Margaret Osborne duPont
1950	Budge Patty	Doris Hart
1951	Jaroslav Drobny	Shirley Fry
1952	Jaroslav Drobny	Doris Hart
1953	Ken Rosewall	Maureen Connolly
1954	Tony Trabert	Maureen Connolly
1955	Tony Trabert	Angela Mortimer
1956	Lew Hoad	Althea Gibson
1957	Sven Davidson	Shirley Bloomer
1958	Merv Rose	Susi Koermoczi
1959	Nicola Pietrangeli	Christine Truman
1960	Nicola Pietrangeli	Darlene Hard
1961	Manuel Santana	Ann Haydon
1962	Rod Laver	Margaret Smith

1963	Roy Emerson	Lesley Turner
1964	Manuel Santana	Margaret Smith
1965	Fred Stolle	Lesley Turner
1966	Tony Roche	Ann Haydon
1967	Roy Emerson	Francoise Durr
1968	Ken Rosewall	Nancy Richey
1969	Rod Laver	Margaret Smith Court
1970	Jan Kodes	Margaret Smith Court
1971	Jan Kodes	Evonne Goolagong
1972	Andres Gimano	Billie Jean King
1973	Ilie Nastase	Margaret Smith Court
1974	Bjorn Borg	Chris Evert
1975	Bjorn Borg	Chris Evert
1976	Adriano Panatta	Sue Barker
1977	Guillermo Vilas	Mima Jausovec
1978	Bjorn Borg	Virginia Ruzici
1979	Bjorn Borg	Chris Evert Lloyd
1980	Bjorn Borg	Chris Evert Lloyd
1981	Bjorn Borg	Hana Mandlikova
1982	Mats Wilander	Martina Navratilova
1983	Yannick Noah	Chris Evert Lloyd
1984	Ivan Lendl	Martina Navratilova
1985	Mats Wilander	Chris Evert Lloyd
1986	Ivan Lendl	Chris Evert Lloyd
1987	Ivan Lendl	Steffi Graf
1988	Mats Wilander	Steffi Graf
1989	Michael Chang	Arantxa Sanchez Vicario
1990	Andres Gomez	Monica Seles
1991	Jim Courier	Monica Seles
1992	Jim Courier	Monica Seles
1993	Sergi Bruguera	Steffi Graf
1994	Sergi Bruguera	Arantxa Sanchez Vicario
1995	Thomas Muster	Steffi Graf
1996	Yevgeny Kafelnikov	Steffi Graf
1997	Gustavo Kuerten	Iva Majolif
1998	Carlos Moya	Arantxa Sanchez Vicario
1999	Andre Agassi	Steffi Graf
2000	Gustavo Kuerten	Mary Pierce

Australian Open Singles Champions

Year	Men	Women
1905	Rodney Heath	
1906	Tony Wilding	
1907	Horace Rice	
1908	Fred Alexander	
1909	Tony Wilding	
1910	Rodney Heath	

Australian Open Singles Champions

Year	Men	Women
1911	Norman Brookes	
1912	Cecil Parke	
1913	Ernie Parker	
1914	Arthur O'Hara Wood	
1915	Gordon Lowe	
1916–18	*tournament not played due to World War I*	
1919	A. R. F. Kingscote	
1920	Arthur O'Hara Wood	
1921	Rhys Gemmell	
1922	James Anderson	Mall Molesworth
1923	Arthur O'Hara Wood	Mall Molesworth
1924	James Anderson	Sylvia Lance
1925	James Anderson	Daphne Akhurst
1926	John Hawkes	Daphne Akhurst
1927	Gerald Patterson	Esna Boyd
1928	Jean Borotra	Daphne Akhurst
1929	John Gregory	Daphne Akhurst
1930	Gar Moon	Daphne Akhurst
1931	Jack Crawford	Coral Buttsworth
1932	Jack Crawford	Coral Buttsworth
1933	Jack Crawford	Joan Hartigan
1934	Fred Perry	Joan Hartigan
1935	Jack Crawford	Dorothy Round
1936	Adroam Qiost	Joan Hartigan
1937	Viv McGrath	Nancye Wynne
1938	Don Budge	Dorothy Bundy
1939	John Bromwich	Emily Westacott
1940	Adrian Quist	Nancye Wynne
1941–45	*tournament not played due to World War II*	
1946	John Bromwich	Nancye Wynne Bolton
1947	Dinny Pails	Nancye Wynne Bolton
1948	Adrian Quist	Nancye Wynne Bolton
1949	Frank Sedgman	Doris Hart
1950	Frank Sedgman	Louise Brough
1951	Dick Savitt	Nancye Wynne Bolton
1952	Ken McGregor	Thelma Coyne Long
1953	Ken Rosewall	Maureen Connolly
1954	Merv Rose	Thelma Coyne Long
1955	Ken Rosewall	Beryl Pemrose
1956	Lew Hoad	Mary Carter
1957	Ashley Cooper	Shirley Fry
1958	Ashley Cooper	Angela Mortimer
1959	Alex Olmedo	Mary Carter Reitano

1960	Rod Laver	Margaret Smith
1961	Roy Emerson	Margaret Smith
1962	Rod Laver	Margaret Smith
1963	Roy Emerson	Margaret Smith
1964	Roy Emerson	Margaret Smith
1965	Roy Emerson	Margaret Smith
1966	Roy Emerson	Margaret Smith
1967	Roy Emerson	Nancy Richey
1968	Bill Bowrey	Billie Jean King
1969	Rod Laver	Margaret Smith Court
1970	Arthur Ashe	Margaret Smith Court
1971	Ken Rosewall	Margaret Smith Court
1972	Ken Rosewall	Virginia Wade
1973	John Newcombe	Margaret Smith Court
1974	Jimmy Connors	Evonne Goolagong
1975	John Newcombe	Evonne Goolagong
1976	Mark Edmondson	Evonne Goolagong
1977*	Roscoe Tanner	Kerry Reid
1977**	Vitas Gerulaitis	Evonne Goolagong
1978	Guillermo Vilas	Chris O'Neill
1979	Guillermo Vilas	Barbara Jordan
1980	Brian Teacher	Hana Mandlikova
1981	Johan Kriek	Martina Navratukiva
1982	Johan Kriek	Chris Evert Lloyd
1983	Mats Wilander	Martina Navratilova
1984	Mats Wilander	Chris Evert Lloyd
1985	Stefan Edberg	Martina Navratilova
1986	*tournament not played*	
1987	Stefan Edberg	Hana Mandlikova
1988	Mats Wilander	Steffi Graf
1989	Ivan Lendl	Steffi Graf
1990	Ivan Lendl	Steffi Graf
1991	Boris Becker	Monica Seles
1992	Jim Courier	Monica Seles
1993	Jim Courier	Monica Seles
1994	Pete Sampras	Steffi Graf
1995	Andre Agassi	Mary Pierce
1996	Boris Becker	Monica Seles
1997	Pete Sampras	Martina Hingis
1998	Petr Korda	Martina Hingis
1999	Yevgeny Kafelnikov	Martina Hingis
2000	Andre Agassi	Lindsay Davenport

*January 1977
**December 1977

⊙ CNN/Sports Illustrated. "Tennis," sportsillustrated.cnn.com/tennis/index.html
  ESPN. "Tennis," espn.go.com/tennis/index.html

International Tennis Hall Of Fame

Year	Inductees	Year	Inductees
1955	Oliver Campbell		Theodore Pell
	Joseph Clark		Ted Schroeder
	James Dwight	1967	Louise Brough Clapp
	Malcolm Whitman		Margaret Osbourne du Pont
	Richard Sears		Bobby Riggs
	Henry Slocum		Bill Talbert
	Robert Wrenn	1968	Maureen Connolly Brinker
1956	May Sutton Bundy		Allison Danzig
	William Clothier		Pancho Gonzales
	Dwight Davis		Jack Kramer
	William Larned		Eleonora Sears
	Holcombe Ward	1969	Karl Behr
	Beals Wright		Charles Garland
1957	Mary K. Browne		Doris Hart
	Maurice McLoughlin	1970	Shirley Fry-Irvin
	Hazel Hotchkiss Wightman		Clarence Griffin
	Richard N. Williams II		Perry Jones
1958	Bill Johnson		Tony Trabert
	Molla Bjurstedt Mallory	1971	Althea Gibson
	R. Lindley Murray		Elisabeth Moore
	Maud Barger-Wallach		Arthur Nielsen
1959	Bill Tilden		Vic Seixas
	Helen Wills (Moody Roark)	1972	Bryan Grant
1961	Fred Alexander		Gardnar Mulloy
	Malcolm Chace		Elizabeth Ryan
	Harold Hackett	1973	Darlene Hard
	Frank Hunter		Alastair Martin
	Vincent Richards		Gene Mako
1962	John Doeg	1974	Juliette Atkinson
	Helen Hull Jacobs		Bob Falkenburg
	Ellsworth Vines		Fred Hovey
1963	Wilmer Allison		Bertha Townsend Toulmin
	Sarah Palfrey Danzig	1975	Lawrence Baker, Sr.
	Julian Myrick		Fred Perry
	John Van Ryne		Ellen Roosevelt
1964	George Adee	1976	Jean Borotra
	Don Budge		Jacques Brugnon
	George Lott		Mabel Cahill
	Alice Marble		Henri Cochet
	Frank Shields		Rene Lacoste
	Sidney Wood		Dick Savitt
1965	Pauline Betz Addie	1977	Manuel Alonso
	James Van Alen		Norman Brookes
	Ellen Hansell		Budge Patty
	Don McNeill		Betty Nuthall Shoemaker
	Watson Washburn		Gottfried von Cramm
1966	Joe Hunt	1978	Maria Bueno
	Frank Parker		Pierre Etchebaster

	Kathleen McKane Godfree	John Newcombe
	Harry Hopman	Nicola Pietrangeli
	Suzanne Lenglen	Tony Roche
	Anthony Wilding	Ted Tinling
1979	Margaret Smith Court	1987 Bjorn Borg
	Jack Crawford	Billie Jean Moffitt King
	Gladys Heldman	Alex Olmedo
	Al Laney	Dennis Ralston
	Rafael Osuna	Stan Smith
	Frank Sedgman	1988 Evonne Goolagong Cawley
1980	Lawrence Doherty	1989 Gerald Patterson
	Reginald Doherty	Virginia Wade
	King Gustav V of Sweden	1990 Joseph F. Cullman III
	Lew Hoad	Jan Kodes
	Ken Rosewall	1991 Ashley Cooper
1981	Dorothea Douglass	Ilie Nastase
	Chambers	Guillermo Vilas
	W. E. "Slew" Hester	1992 Tracy Austin
	Rod Laver	Philippe Chatrier
	Mary Outerbridge	Bob Hewitt
1982	Roy Emerson	Frew McMillan
	William McChesney Martin	1993 Angela Mortimer Barrett
1983	Clarence Clark	Lamar Hunt
	Lottie Dod	1994 Arthur "Bud" Collins, Jr.
	Jaroslav Drobny	Hana Mandlikova
	Ernest Renshaw	1995 Chris Evert
	William Renshaw	1996 Rosemary "Rosie" Casals
1984	John Bromwich	Dan Maskell
	Neale Fraser	1997 H. W. "Bunny" Austin
	Adrian Quist	Lesley Turner Bowrey
	Manuel Santana	Walter Clopton Wingfield
	Pancho Segura	1998 Jimmy Connors
1985	Arthur Ashe	Herman David
	David Gray	1999 John McEnroe
	Ann Haydon Jones	Ken McGregor
	Fred Stolle	2000 Malcolm Anderson
1986	Dorothy Round Little	Robert Kelleher
	Chuck McKinley	Martina Navratilova

◉ International Tennis Hall of Fame. "Hall of Fame Enshrinees,"
www.tennisfame.org/enshrinees_chrono.html

Men's Professional Golf Association: Championships

The four major championship tournaments of the PGA Tour are listed here.

Masters Tournament

Year	Winner	Year	Winner	Year	Winner
1934	Horton Smith	1939	Ralph Guldahl	1943–45	*no tournament played*
1935	Gene Sarazen	1940	Jimmy Demaret		
1936	Horton Smith	1941	Craig Wood	1946	Herman Keiser
1937	Byron Nelson	1942	Byron Nelson	1947	Jimmy Demaret
1938	Henry Picard				

Men's Professional Golf Association: Championships *(cont.)*

Masters Tournament

Year	Winner	Year	Winner	Year	Winner
1948	Claude Harmon	1966	Jack Nicklaus	1984	Ben Crenshaw
1949	Sam Snead	1967	Gay Brewer, Jr.	1985	Bernhard Langer
1950	Jimmy Demaret	1968	Bob Goalby	1986	Jack Nicklaus
1951	Ben Hogan	1969	George Archer	1987	Larry Mize
1952	Sam Snead	1970	Billy Casper	1988	Sandy Lyle
1953	Ben Hogan	1971	Charles Coody	1989	Nick Faldo
1954	Sam Snead	1972	Jack Nicklaus	1990	Nick Faldo
1955	Cary Middlecoff	1973	Tommy Aaron	1991	Ian Woosnam
1956	Jack Burke, Jr.	1974	Gary Player	1992	Fred Couples
1957	Doug Ford	1975	Jack Nicklaus	1993	Bernhard Langer
1958	Arnold Palmer	1976	Ray Floyd	1994	Jose Maria Olazabal
1959	Art Wall, Jr.	1977	Tom Watson		
1960	Arnold Palmer	1978	Gary Player	1995	Ben Crenshaw
1961	Gary Player	1979	Fuzzy Zoeller	1996	Nick Faldo
1962	Arnold Palmer	1980	Seve Ballesteros	1997	Tiger Woods
1963	Jack Nicklaus	1981	Tom Watson	1998	Mark O'Meara
1964	Arnold Palmer	1982	Craig Stadler	1999	Jose Maria Olazabal
1965	Jack Nicklaus	1983	Seve Ballesteros		
				2000	Vijay Singh

PGA Championship

Year	Winner	Year	Winner	Year	Winner
1916	James M. Barnes	1937	Denny Shute	1956	Jack Burke
1917–18	*no tournament played*	1938	Paul Runyan	1957	Lionel Hebert
		1939	Henry Picard	1958	Dow Finsterwald
1919	James M. Barnes	1940	Byron Nelson	1959	Bob Rosburg
1920	Jock Hutchison	1941	Vic Ghezzi	1960	Jay Hebert
1921	Walter Hagen	1942	Sam Snead	1961	Jerry Barber
1922	Gene Sarazen	1943	*no tournament played*	1962	Gary Player
1923	Gene Sarazen			1963	Jack Nicklaus
1924	Walter Hagen	1944	Bob Hamilton	1964	Bobby Nichols
1925	Walter Hagen	1945	Byron Nelson	1965	Dave Marr
1926	Walter Hagen	1946	Ben Hogan	1966	Al Geiberger
1927	Walter Hagen	1947	Jim Ferrier	1967	Don January
1928	Leo Diegel	1948	Ben Hogan	1968	Julius Boros
1929	Leo Diegel	1949	Sam Snead	1969	Ray Floyd
1930	Tommy Armour	1950	Chandler Harper	1970	Dave Stockton
1931	Tom Creavy			1971	Jack Nicklaus
1932	Olin Dutra	1951	Sam Snead	1972	Gary Player
1933	Gene Sarazen	1952	Jim Turnesa	1973	Jack Nicklaus
1934	Paul Runyan	1953	Walter Burkemo	1974	Lee Trevino
1935	Johnny Revolta	1954	Chick Harbert	1975	Jack Nicklaus
1936	Denny Shute	1955	Doug Ford	1976	Dave Stockton

Year	Winner	Year	Winner	Year	Winner
1977	Lanny Wadkins	1985	Hubert Green	1993	Paul Azinger
1978	John Mahaffey	1986	Bob Tway	1994	Nick Price
1979	David Graham	1987	Larry Nelson	1995	Steve Elkington
1980	Jack Nicklaus	1988	Jeff Sluman	1996	Mark Brooks
1981	Larry Nelson	1989	Payne Stewart	1997	Davis Love III
1982	Raymond Floyd	1990	Wayne Grady	1998	Vijay Singh
1983	Hal Sutton	1991	John Daly	1999	Tiger Woods
1984	Lee Trevino	1992	Nick Price	2000	Tiger Woods

U.S. Open Championship

Year	Winner	Year	Winner	Year	Winner
1895	Horace Rawlins	1929	Bobby Jones	1966	Billy Casper
1896	James Foulis	1930	Bobby Jones	1967	Jack Nicklaus
1897	Joe Lloyd	1931	Billy Burke	1968	Lee Trevino
1898	Fred Herd	1932	Gene Sarazen	1969	Orville Moody
1899	Willie Smith	1933	Johnny Goodman	1970	Tony Jacklin
1900	Harry Vardon	1934	Olin Dutra	1971	Lee Trevino
1901	Willie Anderson	1935	Sam Parks Jr	1972	Jack Nicklaus
1902	Laurie Auchterlonie	1936	Tony Manero	1973	Johnny Miller
		1937	Ralph Guldahl	1974	Hale Irwin
1903	Willie Anderson	1938	Ralph Guldahl	1975	Lou Graham
1904	Willie Anderson	1939	Byron Nelson	1976	Jerry Pate
1905	Willie Anderson	1940	Lawson Little	1977	Hubert Green
1906	Alex Smith	1941	Craig Wood	1978	Andy North
1907	Alex Ross	1942–45	no tournament played	1979	Hale Irwin
1908	Fred McLeod			1980	Jack Nicklaus
1909	George Sargent	1946	Lloyd Mangrum	1981	David Graham
1910	Alex Smith	1947	Lew Worsham	1982	Tom Watson
1911	John McDermott	1948	Ben Hogan	1983	Larry Nelson
1912	John McDermott	1949	Cary Middlecoff	1984	Fuzzy Zoeller
1913	Francis Ouimet	1950	Ben Hogan	1985	Andy North
1914	Walter Hagen	1951	Ben Hogan	1986	Ray Floyd
1915	Jerome Travers	1952	Julius Boros	1987	Scott Simpson
1916	Charles Evans Jr.	1953	Ben Hogan	1988	Curtis Strange
1917–18	no tournament played	1954	Ed Furgol	1989	Curtis Strange
		1955	Jack Fleck	1990	Hale Irwin
1919	Walter Hagen	1956	Cary Middlecoff	1991	Payne Stewart
1920	Edward Ray	1957	Dick Mayer	1992	Tom Kite
1921	James Barnes	1958	Tommy Bolt	1993	Lee Janzen
1922	Gene Sarazen	1959	Billy Casper	1994	Ernie Els
1923	Bobby Jones	1960	Arnold Palmer	1995	Corey Pavin
1924	Cyril Walker	1961	Gene Littler	1996	Steve Jones
1925	Willie MacFarlane	1962	Jack Nicklaus	1997	Ernie Els
		1963	Julius Boros	1998	Lee Janzen
1926	Bobby Jones	1964	Ken Venturi	1999	Payne Stewart
1927	Tommy Armour	1965	Gary Player	2000	Tiger Woods
1928	Johnny Farrell				

Men's Professional Golf Association: Championships *(cont.)*

British Open Championship

Year	Winner	Year	Winner	Year	Winner
1860	Willie Park	1899	Harry Vardon	1946	Sam Snead
1861	Tom Morris, Sr.	1900	J. H. Taylor	1947	Fred Daly
1862	Tom Morris, Sr.	1901	James Braid	1948	Henry Cotton
1863	Willie Park	1902	Alexander Herd	1949	Bobby Locke
1864	Tom Morris, Sr.	1903	Harry Vardon	1950	Bobby Locke
1865	Andrew Strath	1904	Jack White	1951	Max Faulkner
1866	Willie Park	1905	James Braid	1952	Bobby Locke
1867	Tom Morris, Sr.	1906	James Braid	1953	Ben Hogan
1868	Tom Morris, Jr.	1907	Arnaud Massy	1954	Peter Thomson
1869	Tom Morris, Jr.	1908	James Braid	1955	Peter Thomson
1870	Tom Morris, Jr.	1909	J. H. Taylor	1956	Peter Thomson
1871	*no tournament played*	1910	James Braid	1957	Bobby Locke
		1911	Harry Vardon	1958	Peter Thomson
1872	Tom Morris, Jr.	1912	Edward Ray	1959	Gary Player
1873	Tom Kidd	1913	J. H. Taylor	1960	Kel Nagle
1874	Mungo Park	1914	Harry Vardon	1961	Arnold Palmer
1875	Willie Park	1915–19	*no tournament played*	1962	Arnold Palmer
1876	Robert Martin			1963	Bob Charles
1877	Jamie Anderson	1920	George Duncan	1964	Tony Lema
1878	Jamie Anderson	1921	Jock Hitchison	1965	Peter Thomson
1879	Jamie Anderson	1922	Walter Hagen	1966	Jack Nicklaus
1880	Robert Ferguson	1923	Arthur Havers	1967	Roberto Devicenzo
1881	Robert Ferguson	1924	Walter Hagen		
1882	Robert Ferguson	1925	James Barnes	1968	Gary Player
1883	Willie Fernie	*1926	Robert Jones, Jr.	1969	Tony Jacklin
1884	Jack Simpson	1927	Robert Jones, Jr.	1970	Jack Nicklaus
1885	Bob Martin	1928	Walter Hagen	1971	Lee Trevino
1886	David Brown	1929	Walter Hagen	1972	Lee Trevino
1887	Willie Park, Jr.	1930	Robert Jones Jr	1973	Tom Weiskopf
1888	Jack Burns	1931	Tommy Armour	1974	Gary Player
1889	Willie Park, Jr.	1932	Gene Sarazen	1975	Tom Watson
1890	John Ball	1933	Denny Shute	1976	Johnny Miller
1891	Hugh Kirkaldy	1934	Henry Cotton	1977	Tom Watson
1892	Harold Hilton	1935	Alfred Perry	1978	Jack Nicklaus
1893	William Auchterlonie	1936	Alfred Padgham	1979	Seve Ballesteros
		1937	Henry Cotton	1980	Tom Watson
1894	J. H. Taylor	1938	R. A. Whitcombe	1981	Bill Rogers
1895	J. H. Taylor	1939	Richard Burton	1982	Tom Watson
1896	Harry Vardon	1940–45	*no tournament played*	1983	Tom Watson
1897	Harold Hilton			1984	Seve Ballesteros
1898	Harry Vardon			1985	Sandy Lyle

Year		Year		Year	
1986	Greg Norman	1991	Ian Baker-Finch	1997	Justin Leonard
1987	Nick Faldo	1992	Nick Faldo	1998	Mark O'Meara
1988	Seve Ballesteros	1993	Greg Norman	1999	Paul Lawrie
1989	Mark Calcavecchia	1994	Nick Price	2000	Tiger Woods
		1995	John Daly		
1990	Nick Faldo	1996	Tom Lehman		

◉ Professional Golf Association. "PGA Tournaments," www.pgatour.com/tournaments/index.html

Ladies' Professional Golf Association: Championships

The four major championship tournaments of the LPGA Tour are listed here.

Nabisco Championship

Formerly Colgate Dinah Shore (1972–81) and Nabisco Dinah Shore (1982–99)

Year	Winner	Year	Winner	Year	Winner
1972	Jane Blalock	1982	Sally Little	1992	Dottie Pepper
1973	Mickey Wright	1983	Amy Alcott	1993	Helen Alfredsson
1974	JoAnn Prentice	1984	Juli Inkster	1994	Donna Andrews
1975	Sandra Palmer	1985	Alice Miller	1995	Nanci Bowen
1976	Judy Rankin	1986	Pat Bradley	1996	Patty Sheehan
1977	Kathy Whitworth	1987	Betsy King	1997	Betsy King
1978	Sandra Post	1988	Amy Alcott	1998	Pat Hurst
1979	Sandra Post	1989	Juli Inkster	1999	Dottie Pepper
1980	Donna Caponi	1990	Betsy King	2000	Karrie Webb
1981	Nancy Lopez	1991	Amy Alcott		

McDonald's LPGA Championship

Formerly LPGA Championship (1955–87) and Mazda LPGA (1987–93)

Year	Winner	Year	Winner	Year	Winner
1955	Beverly Hanson	1971	Kathy Whitworth	1987	Jane Geddes
1956	Marlene Hagge	1972	Kathy Ahern	1988	Sherri Turner
1957	Louise Suggs	1973	Mary Mills	1989	Nancy Lopez
1958	Mickey Wright	1974	Sandra Haynie	1990	Beth Daniel
1959	Betsy Rawls	1975	Kathy Whitworth	1991	Meg Mallon
1960	Mickey Wright	1976	Betty Burfeindt	1992	Betsy King
1961	Mickey Wright	1977	Chako Higuchi	1993	Patty Sheehan
1962	Judy Kimball	1978	Nancy Lopez	1994	Laura Davies
1963	Mickey Wright	1979	Donna Caponi	1995	Kelly Robbins
1964	Mary Mills	1980	Sally Little	1996	Laura Davies
1965	Sandra Haynie	1981	Donna Caponi	1997	Chris Johnson
1966	Gloria Ehret	1982	Jan Stephenson	1998	Se Ri Pak
1967	Kathy Whitworth	1983	Patty Sheehan	1999	Juli Inkster
1968	Sandra Post	1984	Patty Sheehan	2000	Juli Inkster
1969	Betsy Rawls	1985	Nancy Lopez		
1970	Shirley Englehorn	1986	Pat Bradley		

Ladies' Professional Golf Association: Championships (cont.)

U.S. Women's Open Championship

Year	Winner	Year	Winner	Year	Winner
1946	Patty Berg	1966	Sandra Spuzich	1985	Kathy Baker
1947	Betty Jameson	1967	Catherine LaCoste	1986	Jane Geddes
1948	Babe Zaharias			1987	Laura Davies
1949	Louise Suggs	1968	Susie Berning	1988	Liselotte Neumann
1950	Babe Zaharias	1969	Donna Caponi		
1951	Betsy Rawls	1970	Donna Caponi	1989	Betsy King
1952	Louise Suggs	1971	JoAnne Carner	1990	Betsy King
1953	Betsy Rawls	1972	Susie Berning	1991	Meg Mallon
1954	Babe Zaharias	1973	Susie Berning	1992	Patty Sheehan
1955	Fay Crocker	1974	Sandra Haynie	1993	Lauri Merten
1956	Kathy Cornelius	1975	Sandra Palmer	1994	Patty Sheehan
1957	Betsy Rawls	1976	JoAnne Carner	1995	Annika Sörenstam
1958	Mickey Wright	1977	Hollis Stacy		
1959	Mickey Wright	1978	Hollis Stacy	1996	Annika Sörenstam
1960	Betsy Rawls	1979	Jerilyn Britz		
1961	Mickey Wright	1980	Amy Alcott	1997	Alison Nicholas
1962	Murle Breer	1981	Pat Bradley	1998	Se Ri Pak
1963	Mary Mills	1982	Janet Anderson	1999	Juli Inkster
1964	Mickey Wright	1983	Jan Stephenson	2000	Karrie Webb
1965	Carol Mann	1984	Hollis Stacy		

Du Maurier Classic

Formerly La Canadienne (1973) and Peter Jackson Classic (1974–82)

Year	Winner	Year	Winner	Year	Winner
1973	Jocelyne Bourassa	1981	Jan Stephenson	1991	Nancy Scranton
		1982	Sandra Haynie	1992	Sherri Steinhauer
1974	Carole Jo Callison	1983	Hollis Stacy	1993	Brandie Burton
		1984	Juli Inkster	1994	Matha Nause
1975	JoAnne Carner	1985	Pat Bradley	1995	Jenny Lidback
1976	Donna Caponi	1986	Pat Bradley	1996	Laura Davies
1977	Judy Rankin	1987	Jody Rosenthal	1997	Colleen Walker
1978	JoAnne Carner	1988	Sally Little	1998	Brandie Burton
1979	Amy Alcott	1989	Tammie Green	1999	Karrie Webb
1980	Pat Bradley	1990	Cathy Johnston	2000	Meg Mallon

⊙ Ladies Professional Golf Association. "LPGA Tour: The Majors,"
www.lpga.com/tour/comptour/majors/majors.html

World Golf Hall Of Fame

Year	Inductees	Year	Inductees
1951	Betty Jameson (via LPGA Hall of Fame)	1979	Louise Suggs
			Walter Travis
1974	Patty Berg	1980	Lawson Little
	Walter Hagen		Henry Cotton
	Ben Hogan	1981	Lee Trevino
	Robert T. Jones, Jr.		Ralph Guldahl
	Byron Nelson	1982	Julius Boros
	Jack Nicklaus		Kathy Whitworth
	Arnold Palmer	1983	Bob Hope
	Gary Player		Jimmy Demaret
	Francis Quimet	1985	JoAnne Carner
	Gene Sarazen	1986	Cary Middlecoff
	Sam Snead	1987	Robert Trent Jones, Sr.
	Harry Vardon		Betsy Rawls
	Babe Didriksen Zaharias	1988	Tom Watson
			Peter Thomson
1975	Willie Anderson		Bob Harlow
	Fred Corcoran	1989	Raymond Floyd
	Joseph C. Dey		Nancy Lopez
	Chick Evans		Roberto De Vicenzo
	Tom Morris Jr.		Jim Barnes
	John H. Taylor	1990	William C. Campbell
	Glenna C. Vare		Paul Runyan
	Joyce Wethered		Gene Littler
1976	Tommy Armour		Horton Smith
	James Braid	1991	Pat Bradley (via LPGA Hall of Fame)
	Tom Morris, Sr.		
	Jerome Travers	1992	Hale Irwin
	Mickey Wright		Chi Chi Rodriguez
1977	John Ball		Richard Tufts
	Herb Graffis		Harry Cooper
	Sandra Haynie (via LPGA Hall of Fame)	1993	Patty Sheehan (via LPGA Hall of Fame)
	Bobby Locke	1994	Dinah Shore (via LPGA Hall of Fame)
	Carol Mann (via LPGA Hall of Fame)	1995	Betsy King (via LPGA Hall of Fame)
	Donald Ross		
1978	Billy Casper	1998	Johnny Miller (via PGA Hall of Fame)
	Harold Hilton	1999	Amy Alcott (via LPGA Hall of Fame)
	Dorothy Campbell		
	Hurd Howe		Seve Ballesteros
	Bing Crosby		Nick Faldo
	Clifford Roberts		Lloyd Mangrum (via PGA Hall of Fame)

World Golf Hall of Fame *(cont.)*

Year	Inductees	Year	Inductees
2000	Deane Beman	(2000)	Juli Inkster
	Sir Michael Bonallack		(via LPGA Hall of Fame)
	Jack Burke		John Jacob
	Neil Coles		Judy Rankin
	Beth Daniel		(via LPGA Hall of Fame)
	(via LPGA Hall of Fame)		

⊙ World Golf Village. "World Golf Hall of Fame: Inductees," www.wgv.com/
wgvf_HallOfFameInductees1.html

Men's Soccer: World Cup Finals

Held every four years since 1930 (except during World War II), the men's World Cup brings soccer teams from all over the globe to compete for the highest title in the world's most popular sport.

Year	Winning Team	Losing Team	Score	Host Nation
1930	Uruguay	Argentina	4–2	Uruguay
1934	Italy	Czechoslovakia	2–1	Italy
1938	Italy	Hungary	4–2	France
1950	Uruguay	Brazil	2–1	Brazil
1954	West Germany	Hungary	3–2	Switzerland
1958	Brazil	Sweden	5–2	Sweden
1962	Brazil	Czechoslovakia	3–1	Chile
1966	England	West Germany	4–2	England
1970	Brazil	Italy	4–1	Mexico
1974	West Germany	Holland	2–1	West Germany
1978	Argentina	Holland	3–1	Argentina
1982	Italy	West Germany	3–1	Spain
1986	Argentina	West Germany	3–2	Mexico
1990	West Germany	Argentina	1–0	Italy
1994	Brazil	Italy	1–0	United States
1998	France	Brazil	3–0	France

Women's Soccer: World Cup Finals

Women's soccer joined the World Cup competition in 1991.

Year	Winning Team	Losing Team	Score	Host Nation
1991	United States	Norway	2–1	China
1995	Norway	Germany	2–0	Sweden
1999	United States	China	5–4	United States

⊙ Fédération Internationale de Football Association (FIFA). "Women's World Cup
History," wwc99.fifa.com
Washington Post. "World Cup History," washingtonpost.com/wp-
srv/sports/soccer/longterm/worldcup98/history.htm

Olympic Games: Host Cities

Inspired by the Olympic Games of ancient Greece, the modern Olympic Games were established in 1896, when fewer than 250 athletes (all male) competed in 43 athletic events. Featured at the 2000 Summer Olympics in Sydney were some 300 events, in which more than 10,000 athletes (male and female) participated.

Summer Games

Year	Host City	Year	Host City
1896 (I)	Athens, Greece	1948 (XIV)	London, England
1900 (II)	Paris, France	1952 (XV)	Helsinki, Finland
1904 (III)	St. Louis, Missouri, USA	1956 (XVI)	Melbourne, Australia
		1960 (XVII)	Rome, Italy
1908 (IV)	London, England	1964 (XVIII)	Tokyo, Japan
1912 (V)	Stockholm, Sweden	1968 (XIX)	Mexico City, Mexico
1916 (VI)	*Games canceled due to World War I*	1972 (XX)	Munich, Germany
1920 (VII)	Antwerp, Belgium	1976 (XXI)	Montreal, Quebec, Canada
1924 (VIII)	Paris, France	1980 (XXII)	Moscow, Russia, USSR
1928 (IX)	Amsterdam, The Netherlands		
1932 (X)	Los Angeles, California, USA	1984 (XXIII)	Los Angeles, California, USA
1936 (XI)	Berlin, Germany	1988 (XXIV)	Seoul, South Korea
1940 (XII)	*Games canceled due to World War II*	1992 (XXV)	Barcelona, Spain
		1996 (XXVI)	Atlanta, Georgia, USA
1944 (XIII)	*Games canceled due to World War II*	2000 (XXVII)	Sydney, Australia
		2004 (XXVIII)	Athens, Greece

Winter Games

Year	Host City	Year	Host City
1924 (I)	Chamonix, France	1964 (IX)	Innsbruck, Austria
1928 (II)	St. Moritz, Switzerland	1968 (X)	Grenoble, France
1932 (II)	Lake Placid, New York, USA	1972 (XI)	Sapporo, Japan
		1976 (XII)	Innsbruck, Austria
1936 (IV)	Garmisch-Partenkirchen, Germany	1980 (XIII)	Lake Placid, New York, USA
1940 (—)	*Games canceled due to World War II*	1984 (XIV)	Sarajevo, Yugoslavia
		1988 (XV)	Calgary, Alberta, Canada
1944 (—)	*Games canceled due to World War I*	1992 (XVI)	Albertville, France
		1994 (XVII)	Lillehammer, Norway
1948 (V)	St. Moritz, Switzerland	1998 (XVIII)	Nagano, Japan
1952 (VI)	Oslo, Norway	2002 (XIX)	Salt Lake City, Utah, USA
1956 (VII)	Cortina D'Ampezzo, Italy		
1960 (VIII)	Squaw Valley, California, USA	2006 (XX)	Turin, Italy

◉ Amateur Athletic Association of Los Angeles. "Olympics Primer," www.aafla.org/OlympicInformationCenter/OlympicPrimer/OlympicPrimer.htm
International Olympics Committee. "History of the Games," www.museum.olympic.org/e/news/news_e.html

PRIZES AND AWARDS

Nobel Prize (1901–2000)

The Nobel Prizes were established by the will of Alfred Bernhard Nobel, Swedish manufacturer, inventor, and philanthropist (1833–1896). They are given annually to those persons who have made the most outstanding contributions in the fields of physics, chemistry, physiology or medicine, and economic sciences, as well as to those who have produced the most distinguished literary work of an idealist tendency, and to those who have contributed most toward world peace. Independent award committees select each year's laureates; a committee may bestow joint awards or no award at all, if it so chooses.

Category: Peace

Year	Name/Organization (Country of Origin)	Year	Name/Organization (Country of Origin)
1901	Henri Dunant (Switzerland); Frederick Passy (France)	1926	Aristide Briand (France) and Gustav Stresemann (Germany)
1902	Elie Ducommun and Albert Gobat (Switzerland)	1927	Ferdinand Buisson (France) and Ludwig Quidde (Germany)
1903	Sir William R. Cremer (U.K.)	1928	[no award]
1904	Institut de Droit International (Belgium)	1929	Frank B. Kellogg (U.S.)
		1930	Lars O. J. Söderblom (Sweden)
1905	Bertha von Suttner (Austria)	1931	Jane Addams and Nicholas M. Butler (U.S.)
1906	Theodore Roosevelt (U.S.)		
1907	Ernesto T. Moneta (Italy) and Louis Renault (France)	1932	[no award]
		1933	Sir Norman Angell (U.K.)
1908	Klas P. Arnoldson (Sweden) and Frederik Bajer (Denmark)	1934	Arthur Henderson (U.K.)
		1935	Karl von Ossietzky (Germany)
1909	Auguste M. F. Beernaert (Belgium) and Baron Paul H. B. B. d'Estournelles de Constant de Rebecque (France)	1936	Carlos de S. Lamas (Argentina)
		1937	Lord Cecil of Chelwood (U.K.)
		1938	Office International Nansen pour les Réfugiés (Switzerland)
1910	Bureau International Permanent de la Paix (Switzerland)	1939	[no award]
		1940	[no award]
		1941	[no award]
1911	Tobias M. C. Asser (Holland) and Alfred H. Fried (Austria)	1942	[no award]
		1943	[no award]
1912	Elihu Root (U.S.)	1944	International Red Cross
1913	Henri La Fontaine (Belgium)	1945	Cordell Hull (U.S.)
1914	[no award]	1946	Emily G. Balch and John R. Mott (U.S.)
1915	[no award]		
1916	[no award]	1947	American Friends Service Committee (U.S.) and British Society of Friends' Service Council (U.K.)
1917	International Red Cross		
1918	[no award]		
1919	Woodrow Wilson (U.S.)		
1920	Léon Bourgeois (France)	1948	[no award]
1921	Karl H. Branting (Sweden) and Christian L. Lange (Norway)	1949	Lord John Boyd Orr (Scotland)
		1950	Ralph J. Bunche (U.S.)
1922	Fridtjof Nansen (Norway)	1951	Léon Jouhaux (France)
1923	[no award]	1952	Albert Schweitzer (French Equatorial Africa)
1924	[no award]		
1925	Sir Austen Chamberlain (U.K.) and Charles G. Dawes (U.S.)	1953	George C. Marshall (U.S.)

1954	Office of U.N. High Commissioner for Refugees	1980	Adolfo Pérez Esquivel (Argentina)
1955	[no award]	1981	Office of the United Nations High Commissioner for Refugees
1956	[no award]		
1957	Lester B. Pearson (Canada)		
1958	Rev. Dominique Georges Henri Pire (Belgium)	1982	Alva Myrdal (Sweden) and Alfonso García Roble (Mexico)
1959	Philip John Noel-Baker (U.K.)		
1960	Albert John Luthuli (South Africa)	1983	Lech Walesa (Poland)
		1984	Bishop Desmond Tutu (South Africa)
1961	Dag Hammarskjöld (Sweden)		
1962	Linus Pauling (U.S.)	1985	International Physicians for the Prevention of Nuclear War
1963	Intl. Comm. of Red Cross; League of Red Cross Societies (both Geneva)		
		1986	Elie Wiesel (U.S.)
		1987	Oscar Arias Sánchez (Costa Rica)
1964	Rev. Dr. Martin Luther King, Jr. (U.S.)		
		1988	U.N. Peacekeeping Forces
1965	UNICEF (United Nations Children's Fund)	1989	Dalai Lama (Tibet)
		1990	Mikhail S. Gorbachev (USSR)
1966	[no award]		
1967	[no award]	1991	Daw Aung San Suu Kyi (Burma)
1968	René Cassin (France)		
1969	International Labour Organization	1992	Rigoberta Menchú (Guatemala)
		1993	F. W. de Klerk and Nelson Mandela (both South Africa)
1970	Norman E. Borlaug (U.S.)		
1971	Willy Brandt (West Germany)	1994	Yasir Arafat (Palestine) and Yitzhak Rabin (Israel)
1972	[no award]		
1973	Henry A. Kissinger (U.S.); Le Duc Tho (North Vietnam)	1995	Joseph Rotblat and Pugwash Conference on Science and World Affairs (U.K.)
1974	Eisaku Sato (Japan); Sean MacBride (Ireland)		
		1996	Carlos Filipe Ximenes Belo and José Ramos-Horta (East Timor)
1975	Andrei D. Sakharov (USSR)		
1976	Mairead Corrigan and Betty Williams (both Northern Ireland)		
		1997	International Campaign to Ban Landmines and Jody Williams (U.S.)
1977	Amnesty International		
1978	Menachem Begin (Israel) and Anwar el-Sadat (Egypt)	1998	John Hume and David Trimble (both Northern Ireland)
1979	Mother Teresa of Calcutta (India)	1999	Medecins Sans Frontières
		2000	Kim Dae Jung (South Korea)

Category: Literature

Year	Name (Country of Origin)	Year	Name (Country of Origin)
1901	René F. A. Sully Prudhomme (France)	1908	Rudolf Eucken (Germany)
		1909	Selma Lagerlöf (Sweden)
1902	Theodor Mommsen (Germany)	1910	Paul von Heyse (Germany)
1903	Björnstjerne Björnson (Norway)	1911	Maurice Maeterlinck (Belgium)
1904	Frédéric Mistral (France) and José Echegaray (Spain)	1912	Gerhart Hauptmann (Germany)
		1913	Rabindranath Tagore (India)
1905	Henryk Sienkiewicz (Poland)	1914	[no award]
1906	Giosuè Carducci (Italy)	1915	Romain Rolland (France)
1907	Rudyard Kipling (U.K.)		

Nobel Prize (1901–2000) *(cont.)*

Category: Literature

Year	Name (Country of Origin)	Year	Name (Country of Origin)
1916	Verner von Heidenstam (Sweden)	1961	Ivo Andric (Yugoslavia)
1917	Karl Gjellerup (Denmark) and Henrik Pontoppidan (Denmark)	1962	John Steinbeck (U.S.)
		1963	Giorgios Seferis (Seferiades) (Greece)
1918	[no award]	1964	Jean-Paul Sartre (France) (declined)
1919	Carl Spitteler (Switzerland)		
1920	Knut Hamsun (Norway)	1965	Mikhail Sholokhov (USSR)
1921	Anatole France (France)	1966	Shmuel Yosef Agnon (Israel) and Nelly Sachs (Sweden)
1922	Jacinto Benavente (Spain)		
1923	William B. Yeats (Ireland)	1967	Miguel Angel Asturias (Guatemala)
1924	Wladyslaw Reymont (Poland)		
1925	George Bernard Shaw (Ireland)	1968	Yasunari Kawabata (Japan)
1926	Grazia Deledda (Italy)	1969	Samuel Beckett (Ireland)
1927	Henri Bergson (France)	1970	Aleksandr Solzhenitsyn (USSR)
1928	Sigrid Undset (Norway)		
1929	Thomas Mann (Germany)	1971	Pablo Neruda (Chile)
1930	Sinclair Lewis (U.S.)	1972	Heinrich Böll (Germany)
1931	Erik A. Karlfeldt (Sweden)	1973	Patrick White (Australia)
1932	John Galsworthy (U.K.)	1974	Eyvind Johnson and Harry Martinson (both Sweden)
1933	Ivan G. Bunin (Russia)		
1934	Luigi Pirandello (Italy)	1975	Eugenio Montale (Italy)
1935	[no award]	1976	Saul Bellow (U.S.)
1936	Eugene O'Neill (U.S.)	1977	Vicente Aleixandre (Spain)
1937	Roger Martin du Gard (France)	1978	Isaac Bashevis Singer (U.S.)
1938	Pearl S. Buck (U.S.)	1979	Odysseus Elytis (Greece)
1939	Frans Eemil Sillanpää (Finland)	1980	Czeslaw Milosz (U.S.)
1940	[no award]	1981	Elias Canetti (Bulgaria)
1941	[no award]	1982	Gabriel García Márquez (Colombia)
1942	[no award]		
1943	[no award]	1983	William Golding (U.K.)
1944	Johannes V. Jensen (Denmark)	1984	Jaroslav Seifert (Czechoslovakia)
1945	Gabriela Mistral (Chile)		
1946	Hermann Hesse (Switzerland)	1985	Claude Simon (France)
1947	André Gide (France)	1986	Wole Soyinka (Nigeria)
1948	Thomas Stearns Eliot (U.K.)	1987	Joseph Brodsky (U.S.)
1949	William Faulkner (U.S.)	1988	Naguib Mahfouz (Egypt)
1950	Bertrand Russell (U.K.)	1989	Camilo José Cela (Spain)
1951	Pär Lagerkvist (Sweden)	1990	Octavio Paz (Mexico)
1952	François Mauriac (France)	1991	Nadine Gordimer (South Africa)
1953	Sir Winston Churchill (U.K.)		
1954	Ernest Hemingway (U.S.)	1992	Derek Walcott (Trinidad)
1955	Halldór Kiljan Laxness (Iceland)	1993	Toni Morrison (U.S.)
		1994	Kenzaburo Oe (Japan)
1956	Juan Ramón Jiménez (Spain)	1995	Seamus Heaney (Ireland)
1957	Albert Camus (France)	1996	Wislawa Szymborska (Poland)
1958	Boris Pasternak (USSR) (declined)		
		1997	Dario Fo (Italy)
1959	Salvatore Quasimodo (Italy)	1998	José Saramago (Portugal)
1960	St. John Perse (Alexis St.-Léger Léger) (France)	1999	Gunter Grass (Germany)
		2000	Gao Xingjian (China)

Category: Physics

Year	Name (Country of Origin)
1901	Wilhelm K. Roentgen (Germany)
1902	Hendrik A. Lorentz and Pieter Zeeman (Netherlands)
1903	A. Henri Becquerel (France)
1904	John Strutt (Lord Rayleigh) (U.K.)
1905	Philipp Lenard (Germany)
1906	Sir Joseph Thomson (U.K.)
1907	Albert A. Michelson (U.S.)
1908	Gabriel Lippmann (France)
1909	Guglielmo Marconi (Italy) and Ferdinand Braun (Germany)
1910	Johannes D. van der Waals (Netherlands)
1911	Wilhelm Wien (Germany)
1912	Gustaf Dalén (Sweden)
1913	Heike Kamerlingh-Onnes (Netherlands)
1914	Max von Laue (Germany)
1915	Sir William Bragg and William L. Bragg (U.K.)
1916	[no award]
1917	Charles G. Barkla (U.K.)
1918	Max Planck (Germany)
1919	Johannes Stark (Germany)
1920	Charles E. Guillaume (Switzerland)
1921	Albert Einstein (Germany)
1922	Niels Bohr (Denmark)
1923	Robert A. Millikan (U.S.)
1924	Karl M. G. Siegbahn (Sweden)
1925	James Franck and Gustav Hertz (Germany)
1926	Jean B. Perrin (France)
1927	Arthur H. Compton (U.S.)
1928	Sir Owen Richardson (U.K.)
1929	Prince Louis Victor de Broglie (France)
1930	Sir Chandrasekhara Raman (India)
1931	[no award]
1932	Werner Heisenberg (Germany)
1933	Erwin Schrödinger (Austria) and Paul A. M. Dirac (U.K.)
1934	[no award]
1935	James Chadwick (U.K.)
1936	Victor F. Hess (Austria)
1937	Clinton J. Davisson (U.S.) and George P. Thomson (U.K.)
1938	Enrico Fermi (Italy)

Year	Name (Country of Origin)
1939	Ernest Orlando Lawrence (U.S.)
1940	[no award]
1941	[no award]
1942	[no award]
1943	Otto Stern (U.S.)
1944	Isidor Isaac Rabi (U.S.)
1945	Wolfgang Pauli (Austria)
1946	Percy Williams Bridgman (U.S.)
1947	Sir Edward Appleton (U.K.)
1948	Patrick M. S. Blackett (U.K.)
1949	Hideki Yukawa (Japan)
1950	Cecil Frank Powell (U.K.)
1951	Sir John Douglas Cockcroft (U.K.) and Ernest T. S. Walton (Ireland)
1952	Edward Mills Purcell and Felix Bloch (U.S.)
1953	Fritz Zernike (Netherlands)
1954	Max Born (U.K.)
1955	Polykarp Kusch and Willis E. Lamb, Jr. (U.S.)
1956	William Shockley, Walter H. Brattain, and John Bardeen (all U.S.)
1957	Tsung Dao Lee and Chen Ning Yang (China)
1958	Pavel A. Cherenkov, Ilya M. Frank, and Igor E. Tamm (all USSR)
1959	Emilio Segre and Owen Chamberlain (both U.S.)
1960	Donald A. Glaser (U.S.)
1961	Robert Hofstadter (U.S.)
1962	Lev D. Landau (USSR)
1963	Eugene Paul Wigner, Maria Goeppert Mayer (both U.S.), and J. Hans D. Jensen (Germany)
1964	Charles Hard Townes (U.S.), Nikolai G. Basov, and Aleksandr M. Prochorov (both USSR)
1965	Richard P. Feynman, Julian S. Schwinger (both U.S.), and Shinichiro Tomonaga (Japan)
1966	Alfred Kastler (France)
1967	Hans A. Bethe (U.S.)
1968	Luis Walter Alvarez (U.S.)
1969	Murray Gell-Mann (U.S.)

Category: Physics

Year	Name (Country of Origin)
1970	Hannes Alfvén (Sweden) and Louis Néel (France)
1971	Dennis Gabor (U.K.)
1972	John Bardeen, Leon N. Cooper, and John Robert Schrieffer (all U.S.)
1973	Ivar Giaever (U.S.), Leo Esaki (Japan), and Brian D. Josephson (U.K.)
1974	Antony Hewish (U.K.) and Martin Ryle (U.K.)
1975	James Rainwater (U.S.), Ben Mottelson, and Aage N. Bohr (both Denmark)
1976	Burton Richter and Samuel C. C. Ting (both U.S.)
1977	Philip W. Anderson, John H. Van Vleck (both U.S.), and Nevill F. Mott (U.K.)
1978	Arno A. Penzias and Robert W. Wilson (both U.S.), Piotr L. Kapitsa (USSR)
1979	Steven Weinberg, Sheldon L. Glashow (both U.S.), and Abdus Salam (Pakistan)
1980	James W. Cronin and Val L. Fitch (both U.S.)
1981	Nicolaas Bloembergen, Arthur L. Schawlow (both U.S.), and Kai M. Siegbahn (Sweden)
1982	Kenneth G. Wilson (U.S.)
1983	Subrahmanyam Chandrasekhar and William A. Fowler (both U.S.)
1984	Carlo Rubbia (Italy) and Simon van der Meer (Netherlands)
1985	Klaus von Klitzing (Germany)
1986	Ernst Ruska, Gerd Binnig (both Germany), and Heinrich Rohrer (Switzerland)

Year	Name (Country of Origin)
1987	K. Alex Müller (Switzerland) and J. Georg Bednorz (Germany)
1988	Leon M. Lederman, Melvin Schwartz, and Jack Steinberger (all U.S.)
1989	Norman F. Ramsey (U.S.), Hans G. Dehmelt (U.S.) and Wolfgang Paul (Germany)
1990	Richard E. Taylor (Canada), Jerome I. Friedman, and Dr. Henry W. Kendall (both U.S.)
1991	Pierre-Gilles de Gennes (France)
1992	George Charpak (France)
1993	Joseph H. Taylor and Russell A. Hulse (both U.S.)
1994	Clifford G. Shull (U.S.) and Bertram N. Brockhouse (Canada)
1995	Martin L. Perl and Frederick Reines (both U.S.)
1996	David M. Lee, Robert C. Richardson, and Douglas D. Osheroff (all U.S.)
1997	Steven Chu, William D. Phillips (both U.S.), and Claude Cohen-Tannoudji (France)
1998	Robert B. Laughlin (U.S.), Horst L. Störmer (Germany), and Daniel C. Tsui (U.S.)
1999	Gerardus 't Hooft, Martinus J.G. Veltman (both Netherlands)
2000	Zhores I. Alferov (Russia) and Herbert Kroemer (U.S.); Jack S. Kilby (U.S.)

Category: Chemistry

Year	Name (Country of Origin)
1901	Jacobus H. van't Hoff (Netherlands)
1902	Emil Fischer (Germany)
1903	Svante A. Arrhenius (Sweden)
1904	Sir William Ramsay (U.K.)
1905	Adolf von Baeyer (Germany)

Year	Name (Country of Origin)
1906	Henri Moissan (France)
1907	Eduard Buchner (Germany)
1908	Sir Ernest Rutherford (U.K.)
1909	Wilhelm Ostwald (Germany)
1910	Otto Wallach (Germany)
1911	Marie Curie (France)

1912	Victor Grignard (France)
1913	Alfred Werner (Switzerland)
1914	Theodore W. Richards (U.S.)
1915	Richard Willstätter (Germany)
1916	[no award]
1917	[no award]
1918	Fritz Haber (Germany)
1919	[no award]
1920	Walther Nernst (Germany)
1921	Frederick Soddy (U.K.)
1922	Francis W. Aston (U.K.)
1923	Fritz Pregl (Austria)
1924	[no award]
1925	Richard Zsigmondy (Germany)
1926	Theodor Svedberg (Sweden)
1927	Heinrich Wieland (Germany)
1928	Adolf Windaus (Germany)
1929	Sir Arthur Harden (U.K.) and Hans K. A. S. von Euler-Chelpin (Sweden)
1930	Hans Fischer (Germany)
1931	Karl Bosch and Friedrich Bergius (both Germany)
1932	Irving Langmuir (U.S.)
1933	[no award]
1934	Harold C. Urey (U.S.)
1935	Frédéric and Irène Joliot-Curie (both France)
1936	Peter J. W. Debye (Netherlands)
1937	Walter N. Haworth (U.K.); and Paul Karrer (Switzerland)
1938	Richard Kuhn (Germany)
1939	Adolf Butenandt (Germany) and Leopold Ruzicka (Switzerland)
1940	[no award]
1941	[no award]
1942	[no award]
1943	Georg Hevesy De Heves (Hungary)
1944	Otto Hahn (Germany)
1945	Artturi Illmari Virtanen (Finland)
1946	James B. Sumner (U.S.), John H. Northrop and Wendell M. Stanley (all U.S.)
1947	Sir Robert Robinson (U.K.)
1948	Arne Tiselius (Sweden)
1949	William Francis Giauque (U.S.)
1950	Otto Diels and Kurt Alder (both Germany)
1951	Glenn T. Seaborg and Edwin H. McMillan (both U.S.)

1952	Archer John Porter Martin and Richard Laurence Millington Synge (both U.K.)
1953	Hermann Staudinger (Germany)
1954	Linus C. Pauling (U.S.)
1955	Vincent du Vigneaud (U.S.)
1956	Sir Cyril Hinshelwood (U.K.) and Nikolai N. Semenov (USSR)
1957	Sir Alexander Todd (U.K.)
1958	Frederick Sanger (U.K.)
1959	Jaroslav Heyrovsky (Czechoslovakia)
1960	Willard F. Libby (U.S.)
1961	Melvin Calvin (U.S.)
1962	Max F. Perutz and John C. Kendrew (U.K.)
1963	Carl Ziegler (Germany) and Giulio Natta (Italy)
1964	Dorothy Mary Crowfoot Hodgkin (U.K.)
1965	Robert B. Woodward (U.S.)
1966	Robert Sanderson Mulliken (U.S.)
1967	Manfred Eigen (Germany), Ronald G. W. Norrish, and George Porter (both U.K.)
1968	Lars Onsager (U.S.)
1969	Derek H. R. Barton (U.K.) and Odd Hassel (Norway)
1970	Luis F. Leloir (Argentina)
1971	Gerhard Herzberg (Canada)
1972	Christian Boehmer Anfinsen, Stanford Moore, and William Howard Stein (all U.S.)
1973	Ernst Otto Fischer (West Germany) and Geoffrey Wilkinson (U.K.)
1974	Paul J. Flory (U.S.)
1975	John W. Cornforth (Australia) and Vladimir Prelog (Switzerland)
1976	William N. Lipscomb, Jr. (U.S.)
1977	Ilya Prigogine (Belgium)
1978	Peter Mitchell (U.K.)
1979	Herbert C. Brown (U.S.) and Georg Wittig (West Germany)
1980	Paul Berg, Walter Gilbert (both U.S.), and Frederick Sanger (U.K.)
1981	Roald Hoffmann (U.S.) and Kenichi Fukui (Japan)
1982	Aaron Klug (U.K.)

Nobel Prize (1901–2000) *(cont.)*

Category: Chemistry

Year	Name (Country of Origin)
1983	Henry Taube (U.S.)
1984	R. Bruce Merrifield (U.S.)
1985	Herbert A. Hauptman and Jerome Karle (both U.S.)
1986	Dudley R. Herschback, Yuan T. Lee (both U.S.), and John C. Polanyi (Canada)
1987	Donald J. Cram, Charles J. Pedersen (both U.S.), and Jean-Marie Lehn (France)
1988	Johann Deisenhofer, Robert Huber, and Hartmut Michel (all West Germany)
1989	Thomas R. Cech and Sidney Altman (both U.S.)
1990	Elias James Corey (U.S.)
1991	Richard R. Ernst (Switzerland)
1992	Rudolph A. Marcus (U.S.)

Year	Name (Country of Origin)
1993	Kary B. Mullis (U.S.) and Michael Smith (Canada)
1994	George A. Olah (U.S.)
1995	F. Sherwood Rowland, Mario Molina (both U.S.), and Paul Crutzen (Netherlands)
1996	Richard E. Smalley, Robert F. Curl, Jr. (both U.S.), and Harold W. Kroto (U.K.)
1997	Paul D. Boyer (U.S.), Jens C. Skou (Denmark), and John E. Walker (U.K.)
1998	Walter Kohn (U.S.) and John A. Pople (U.K.)
1999	Ahmed H. Zewail (Egypt and U.S.)
2000	Alan J. Heeger (U.S.), Alan G. McDiarmid (U.S.), and Hideki Shirakawa (Japan)

Category: Physiology or Medicine

Year	Name (Country of Origin)
1901	Emil A. von Behring (Germany)
1902	Sir Ronald Ross (U.K.)
1903	Niels R. Finsen (Denmark)
1904	Ivan P. Pavlov (USSR)
1905	Robert Koch (Germany)
1906	Camillo Golgi (Italy) and Santiago Ramón y Cajal (Spain)
1907	Charles L. A. Laveran (France)
1908	Paul Ehrlich (Germany) and Elie Metchnikoff (USSR)
1909	Theodor Kocher (Switzerland)
1910	Albrecht Kossel (Germany)
1911	Allvar Gullstrand (Sweden)
1912	Alexis Carrel (France)
1913	Charles Richet (France)
1914	Robert Bárány (Austria)
1915	[no award]
1916	[no award]
1917	[no award]
1918	[no award]
1919	Jules Bordet (Belgium)
1920	August Krogh (Denmark)
1921	[no award]
1922	Archibald V. Hill (U.K.) and Otto Meyerhof (Germany)
1923	Sir Frederick Banting (Canada) and John J. R. Macleod (Scotland)

Year	Name (Country of Origin)
1924	Willem Einthoven (Netherlands)
1925	[no award]
1926	Johannes Fibiger (Denmark)
1927	Julius Wagner-Jauregg (Austria)
1928	Charles Nicolle (France)
1929	Christiaan Eijkman (Netherlands) and Sir Frederick Hopkins (U.K.)
1930	Karl Landsteiner (U.S.)
1931	Otto H. Warburg (Germany)
1932	Sir Charles Sherrington (U.K.) and Edgar D. Adrian (U.S.)
1933	Thomas H. Morgan (U.S.)
1934	George H. Whipple, George R. Minot, and William P. Murphy (U.S.)
1935	Hans Spemann (Germany)
1936	Sir Henry Dale (U.K.) and Otto Loewi (Germany)
1937	Albert Szent-Györgyi von Nagyrapolt (Hungary)
1938	Corneille Heymans (Belgium)
1939	Gerhard Domagk (Germany)
1940	[no award]
1941	[no award]

1942 [no award]
1943 Henrik Dam (Denmark) and Edward A. Doisy (U.S.)
1944 Joseph Erlanger and Herbert Spencer Gasser (both U.S.)
1945 Sir Alexander Fleming, Ernst Boris Chain, and Sir Howard Florey (all U.K.)
1946 Herman J. Muller (U.S.)
1947 Carl F. and Gerty T. Cori (U.S.) and Bernardo A. Houssay (Argentina)
1948 Paul Mueller (Switzerland)
1949 Walter Rudolf Hess (Switzerland) and Antonio Caetano de Abreu Freire Egas Moniz (Portugal)
1950 Philip S. Hench, Edward C. Kendall (both U.S.), and Tadeus Reichstein (Switzerland)
1951 Max Theiler (South Africa)
1952 Selman A. Waksman (U.S.)
1953 Fritz A. Lipmann (Germany-U.S.) and Hans Adolph Krebs (Germany-U.K.)
1954 John F. Enders, Thomas H. Weller, and Frederick C. Robbins (all U.S.)
1955 Hugo Theorell (Sweden)
1956 Dickinson W. Richards, Jr., André F. Cournand (both U.S.), and Werner Forssmann (Germany)
1957 Daniel Bovet (Italy)
1958 Joshua Lederberg, George W. Beadie and Edward L. Tatum (all U.S.)
1959 Severo Ochoa and Arthur Kornberg (both U.S.)
1960 Sir Macfarlane Burnet (Australia) and Peter Brian Medawar (U.K.)
1961 Georg von Bekesy (U.S.)
1962 James D. Watson (U.S.), Maurice H. F. Wilkins, and Francis H. C. Crick (both U.K.)
1963 Alan Lloyd Hodgkin, Andrew Fielding Huxley (both U.K.), and Sir John Carew Eccles (Australia)
1964 Konrad E. Bloch (U.S.) and Feodor Lynen (Germany)
1965 François Jacob, André Lwolff, and Jacques Monod (all France)

1966 Charles Brenton Huggins (U.S.) and Francis Peyton Rous (U.S.)
1967 Haldan K. Hartline, George Wald, and Ragnar Granit (all U.S.)
1968 Robert W. Holley, Har Gobind Khorana, and Marshall W. Nirenberg (all U.S.)
1969 Max Delbruck, Alfred D. Hershey, and Salvador E. Luria (all U.S.)
1970 Julius Axelrod (U.S.), Ulf S. von Euler (Sweden), and Sir Bernard Katz (U.K.)
1971 Earl W. Sutherland, Jr. (U.S.)
1972 Gerald M. Edelman (U.S.), and Rodney R. Porter (U.K.)
1973 Karl von Frisch, Konrad Lorenz (both Austria), and Nikolaas Tinbergen (Netherlands)
1974 George E. Palade, Christian de Duve (both U.S.), and Albert Claude (Belgium)
1975 David Baltimore, Howard M. Temin, and Renato Dulbecco (all U.S.)
1976 Baruch S. Blumberg and D. Carleton Gajdusek (both U.S.)
1977 Rosalyn S. Yalow, Roger C. L. Guillemin, and Andrew V. Schally (all U.S.)
1978 Daniel Nathans, Hamilton Smith (both U.S.), and Werner Arber (Switzerland)
1979 Allan McLeod Cormack (U.S.) and Godfrey Newbold Hounsfield (U.K.)
1980 Baruj Benacerraf, George D. Snell (both U.S.), and Jean Dausset (France)
1981 Roger W. Sperry, David H. Hubel (both U.S.), and Torsten N. Wiesel (Sweden)
1982 Sune Bergstrom, Bengt Samuelsson (both Sweden), and John R. Vane (U.K.)
1983 Barbara McClintock (U.S.)
1984 Cesar Milstein (U.K./ Argentina), Georges J. F. Kohler (West Germany), and Niels K. Jerne (U.K./ Denmark)
1985 Michael S. Brown and Joseph L. Goldstein (both U.S.)

Nobel Prize (1901–2000) *(cont.)*

Category: Physiology or Medicine

Year	Name (Country of Origin)
1986	Rita Levi-Montalcini (dual U.S./Italy) and Stanley Cohen (U.S.)
1987	Susumu Tonegawa (Japan)
1988	Gertrude B. Elion, George H. Hitchings (both U.S.), and Sir James Black (U.K.)
1989	J. Michael Bishop and Harold E. Varmus (both U.S.)
1990	Joseph E. Murray and E. Donnall Thomas (both U.S.)
1991	Erwin Neher and Bert Sakmann (both Germany)
1992	Edmond H. Fischer and Edwin G. Krebs (both U.S.)
1993	Phillip A. Sharp (U.S.) and Richard J. Roberts (U.K.)

Year	Name (Country of Origin)
1994	Alfred G. Gilman and Martin Rodbell (both U.S.)
1995	Edward B. Lewis, Eric F. Wieschaus (both U.S.), and Christiane Nüsslein-Volhard (Germany)
1996	Peter C. Doherty (Australia) and Rolf M. Zinkernagel (Switzerland)
1997	Stanley B. Prusiner (U.S.)
1998	Robert F. Furchgott, Louis J. Ignarro, and Ferid Murad (all U.S.)
1999	Günter Blobel (U.S.)
2000	Arvid Carlsson (Sweden), Paul Greengard (U.S.), and Eric R. Kandel (U.S.)

Category: Economic Science

Year	Name (Country of Origin)
1969	Ragnar Frisch (Norway) and Jan Tinbergen (Netherlands)
1970	Paul A. Samuelson (U.S.)
1971	Simon Kuznets (U.S.)
1972	Kenneth J. Arrow (U.S.) and Sir John R. Hicks (U.K.)
1973	Wassily Leontief (U.S.)
1974	Gunnar Myrdal (Sweden) and Friedrich A. von Hayek (U.K.)
1975	Leonid V. Kantorovich (USSR) and Tjalling C. Koopmans (U.S.)
1976	Milton Friedman (U.S.)
1977	Bertil Ohlin (Sweden) and James E. Meade (U.K.)
1978	Herbert A. Simon (U.S.)
1979	Sir Arthur Lewis (U.K.) and Theodore Schultz (U.S.)
1980	Lawrence R. Klein (U.S.)
1981	James Tobin (U.S.)
1982	George J. Stigler (U.S.)
1983	Gerard Debreu (U.S.)
1984	Sir Richard Stone (U.K.)

Year	Name (Country of Origin)
1985	Franco Modigliani (U.S.)
1986	James M. Buchanan (U.S.)
1987	Robert M. Solow (U.S.)
1988	Maurice Allais (France)
1989	Trygve Haavelmo (Norway)
1990	Harry M. Markowitz, William F. Sharpe, and Merton H. Miller (all U.S.)
1991	Ronald Coase (U.S.)
1992	Gary S. Becker (U.S.)
1993	Robert W. Fogel and Douglass C. North (both U.S.)
1994	John F. Nash, John C. Harsanyi (both U.S.), and Reinhard Selten (Germany)
1995	Robert E. Lucas, Jr. (U.S.)
1996	James A. Mirrlees (U.K.) and William Vickrey (U.S.)
1997	Robert C. Merton and Myron S. Scholes (both U.S.)
1998	Amartya Sen (India)
1999	Robert A. Mundell (Canada)
2000	James J. Heckman and Daniel L. McFadden (both U.S.)

⊙ The Nobel Foundation. "The Nobel Foundation," www.nobel.se/nobel-foundation/index.html

The Nobel Foundation. *Les Prix Nobel.* Stockholm: The Nobel Foundation, 1991.

Schlessinger, Bernard S., and June H. Schlessinger, eds. *The Who's Who of Nobel Prize Winners 1901–1995.* Phoenix: Oryx, 1996.

Academy Awards (1927–99)

The Academy Awards (the Oscars) are presented annually by the American Academy of Motion Pictures Arts and Sciences for artistic achievement in motion pictures. There are various explanations for the nickname Oscar, the most popular being that in 1935 it was named after an uncle of Margaret Herrick, the Academy's librarian and future executive director. Winners in each category are listed below by year.

1927–28
Picture: *Wings*
Actor: Emil Jannings, *The Last Command*
Actress: Jaynor Gaynor, *Seventh Heaven, Street Angel,* and *Sunrise*
Supporting Actor: [no award]
Supporting Actress: [no award]
Director: Frank Borzage, *Seventh Heaven*

1928–29
Picture: *Broadway Melody*
Actor: Warner Baxter, *In Old Arizona*
Actress: Mary Pickford, *Coquette*
Supporting Actor: [no award]
Supporting Actress: [no award]
Director: Frank Loyd, *The Divine Lady*

1929–30
Picture: *All Quiet on the Western Front*
Actor: George Arliss, *Disraeli*
Actress: Norma Shearer, *The Divorcée*
Supporting Actor: [no award]
Supporting Actress: [no award]
Director: Lewis Milestone, *All Quiet on the Western Front*

1930–31
Picture: *Cimarron*
Actor: Lionel Barrymore, *A Free Soul*
Actress: Louise Dressler, *Min and Bill*
Supporting Actor: [no award]
Supporting Actress: [no award]
Director: Norman Taurog, *Skippy*

1931–32
Picture: *Grand Hotel*
Actor (tie): Wallace Beery, *The Champ*; Frederic March, *Dr. Jekyll and Mr. Hyde*
Actress: Helen Hayes, *The Sins of Madelon Claudet*
Supporting Actor: [no award]
Supporting Actress: [no award]
Director: Frank Borzage, *Bad Girl*

1932–33
Picture: *Cavalcade*
Actor: Charles Laughton, *The Private Life of Henry VIII*
Actress: Katharine Hepburn, *Morning Glory*
Supporting Actor: [no award]
Supporting Actress: [no award]
Director: Frank Lloyd, *Cavalcade*

1934
Picture: *It Happened One Night*
Actor: Clark Gable, *It Happened One Night*
Actress: Claudette Colbert, *It Happened One Night*
Supporting Actor: [no award]
Supporting Actress: [no award]
Director: Frank Capra, *It Happened One Night*

1935
Picture: *Mutiny on the Bounty*
Actor: Victor McLaglen, *The Informer*
Actress: Bette Davis, *Dangerous*
Supporting Actor: [no award]
Supporting Actress: [no award]
Director: John Ford, *The Informer*

1936
Picture: *The Great Ziegfeld*
Actor: Paul Muni, *The Story of Louis Pasteur*
Actress: Luise Rainer, *The Great Ziegfeld*
Supporting Actor: Walter Brennan, *Come and Get It*
Supporting Actress: Gale Sondergaard, *Antony Adverse*
Director: Frank Capra, *Mr. Deeds Goes to Town*

1937
Picture: *The Life of Emile Zola*
Actor: Spencer Tracy, *Captains Courageous*
Actress: Luise Rainer, *The Good Earth*
Supporting Actor: Joseph Schildkraut, *The Life of Emile Zola*
Supporting Actress: Alice Brady, *In Old Chicago*
Director: Leo McCarey, *The Awful Truth*

1938
Picture: *You Can't Take It With You*
Actor: Spency Tracy, *Boy's Town*
Actress: Bette Davis, *Jezebel*
Supporting Actor: Walter Brennan, *Kentucky*
Supporting Actress: Fay Bainter, *Jezebel*
Director: Frank Capra, *You Can't Take It With You*

1939

Picture: Gone With the Wind
Actor: Robert Donat, Goodbye, Mr. Chips
Actress: Vivien Leigh, Gone With the Wind
Supporting Actor: Thomas Mitchell, Stagecoach
Supporting Actress: Hattie McDaniel, Gone With the Wind
Director: Victor Fleming, Gone With the Wind

1940

Picture: Rebecca
Actor: James Stewart, The Philadelphia Story
Actress: Ginger Rogers, Kitty Foyle
Supporting Actor: Walter Brennan, The Westerner
Supporting Actress: Jane Darwell, The Grapes of Wrath
Director: John Ford, The Grapes of Wrath

1941

Picture: How Green Was My Valley
Actor: Gary Cooper, Sergeant York
Actress: Joan Fontaine, Suspicion
Supporting Actor: Donald Crisp, How Green Was My Valley
Supporting Actress: Mary Astor, The Great Lie
Director: John Ford, How Green Was My Valley

1942

Picture: Mrs. Miniver
Actor: James Cagney, Yankee Doodle Dandy
Actress: Greer Garson, Mrs. Miniver
Supporting Actor: Van Heflin, Johnny Eager
Supporting Actress: Teresa Wright, Mrs. Miniver
Director: William Wyler, Mrs. Miniver

1943

Picture: Casablanca
Actor: Paul Lukas, Watch on the Rhine
Actress: Jennifer Jones, The Song of Bernadette
Supporting Actor: Charles Coburn, The More the Merrier
Supporting Actress: Katina Paxinou, For Whom the Bell Tolls
Director: Michael Curtiz, Casablanca

1944

Picture: Going My Way
Actor: Bing Crosby, Going My Way
Actress: Ingrid Bergman, Gaslight
Supporting Actor: Barry Fitzgerald, Going My Way
Supporting Actress: Ethel Barrymore, None but the Lonely Heart
Director: Leo McCarey, Going My Way

1945

Picture: The Lost Weekend
Actor: Ray Milland, The Lost Weekend
Actress: Joan Crawford, Mildred Pierce
Supporting Actor: James Dunn, A Tree Grows in Brooklyn
Supporting Actress: Anne Revere, National Velvet
Director: Billy Wilder, The Lost Weekend

1946

Picture: The Best Years of Our Lives
Actor: Frederic March, The Best Years of Our Lives
Actress: Olivia de Havilland, To Each His Own
Supporting Actor: Harold Russell, The Best Years of Our Lives
Supporting Actress: Anne Baxter, The Razor's Edge
Director: William Wyler, The Best Years of Our Lives

1947

Picture: Gentleman's Agreement
Actor: Ronald Coleman, A Double Life
Actress: Loretta Young, The Farmer's Daughter
Supporting Actor: Edmund Gwenn, Miracle on 34th Street
Supporting Actress: Celeste Holm, Gentleman's Agreement
Director: Elia Kazan, Gentleman's Agreement

1948

Picture: Hamlet
Actor: Laurence Olivier, Hamlet
Actress: Jane Wyman, Johnny Belinda
Supporting Actor: Walter Huston, The Treasure of the Sierra Madre
Supporting Actress: Claire Trevor, Key Largo
Director: John Huston, The Treasure of the Sierra Madre

1949

Picture: All the King's Men
Actor: Broderick Crawford, All the King's Men
Actress: Olivia de Havilland, The Heiress
Supporting Actor: Dean Jagger, Twelve O'Clock High

Supporting Actress: Mercedes
  McCambridge, *All the King's Men*
Director: Joseph L. Mankiewicz, *A
  Letter to Three Wives*

1950

Picture: *All About Eve*
Actor: José Ferrer, *Cyrano de Bergerac*
Actress: Judy Holliday, *Born Yesterday*
Supporting Actor: George Sanders, *All
  About Eve*
Supporting Actress: Josephine Hull,
  Harvey
Director: Joseph L. Mankiewicz, *All
  About Eve*

1951

Picture: *An American in Paris*
Actor: Humphrey Bogart, *The African
  Queen*
Actress: Vivien Leigh, *A Streetcar
  Named Desire*
Supporting Actor: Karl Malden, *A
  Streetcar Named Desire*
Supporting Actress: Kim Hunter, *A
  Streetcar Named Desire*
Director: George Stevens, *A Place in the
  Sun*

1952

Picture: *The Greatest Show on Earth*
Actor: Gary Cooper, *High Noon*
Actress: Shirley Booth, *Come Back, Little
  Sheba*
Supporting Actor: Anthony Quinn, *Viva
  Zapata!*
Supporting Actress: Gloria Grahame,
  The Bad and the Beautiful
Director: John Ford, *The Quiet Man*

1953

Picture: *From Here to Eternity*
Actor: William Holden, *Stalag 17*
Actress: Audrey Hepburn, *Roman
  Holiday*
Supporting Actor: Frank Sinatra, *From
  Here to Eternity*
Supporting Actress: Donna Reed, *From
  Here to Eternity*
Director: Fred Zinnemann, *From Here
  to Eternity*

1954

Picture: *On the Waterfront*
Actor: Marlon Brando, *On the
  Waterfront*
Actress: Grace Kelly, *The Country Girl*
Supporting Actor: Edmond O'Brien, *The
  Barefoot Contessa*
Supporting Actress: Eva Marie Saint, *On
  the Waterfront*
Director: Elia Kazan, *On the Waterfront*

1955

Picture: *Marty*
Actor: Ernest Borgnine, *Marty*
Actress: Anna Magnani, *The Rose Tattoo*
Supporting Actor: Jack Lemmon, *Mr.
  Roberts*
Supporting Actress: Jo Van Fleet, *East of
  Eden*
Director: Delbert Mann, *Marty*

1956

Picture: *Around the World in 80 Days*
Actor: Yul Brynner, *The King and I*
Actress: Ingrid Bergman, *Anastasia*
Supporting Actor: Anthony Quinn, *Lust
  for Life*
Supporting Actress: Dorothy Malone,
  Written on the Wind
Director: George Stevens, *Giant*

1957

Picture: *The Bridge on the River Kwai*
Actor: Alec Guiness, *The Bridge on the
  River Kwai*
Actress: Joanne Woodward, *The Three
  Faces of Eve*
Supporting Actor: Red Buttons,
  Sayonara
Supporting Actress: Miyoshi Umeki,
  Sayonara
Director: David Lean, *The Bridge on the
  River Kwai*

1958

Picture: *Gigi*
Actor: David Niven, *Separate Tables*
Actress: Susan Hayward, *I Want to Live!*
Supporting Actor: Burl Ives, *The Big
  Country*
Supporting Actress: Wendy Hiller,
  Separate Tables
Director: Vincente Minelli, *Gigi*

1959

Picture: *Ben-Hur*
Actor: Charlton Heston, *Ben-Hur*
Actress: Simone Signoret, *Room at the
  Top*
Supporting Actor: Hugh Griffith, *Ben-
  Hur*
Supporting Actress: Shelley Winters, *The
  Diary of Anne Frank*
Director: William Wyler, *Ben-Hur*

1960

Picture: *The Apartment*
Actor: Burt Lancaster, *Elmer Gantry*
Actress: Elizabeth Taylor, *Butterfield 8*
Supporting Actor: Peter Ustinov,
  Spartacus
Supporting Actress: Shirley Jones, *Elmer
  Gantry*
Director: Billy Wilder, *The Apartment*

1961

Picture: West Side Story
Actor: Maximilian Schell, *Judgment at Nuremberg*
Actress: Sophia Loren, *Two Women*
Supporting Actor: George Chakiris, *West Side Story*
Supporting Actress: Rita Moreno, *West Side Story*
Director: Robert Wise and Jerome Robbins, *West Side Story*

1962

Picture: Lawrence of Arabia
Actor: Gregory Peck, *To Kill a Mockingbird*
Actress: Anne Bancroft, *The Miracle Worker*
Supporting Actor: Ed Begley, *Sweet Bird of Youth*
Supporting Actress: Patty Duke, *The Miracle Worker*
Director: David Lean, *Lawrence of Arabia*

1963

Picture: Tom Jones
Actor: Sidney Poitier, *Lilies of the Field*
Actress: Patricia Neal, *Hud*
Supporting Actor: Melvyn Douglas, *Hud*
Supporting Actress: Margaret Rutherford, *The V.I.P.'s*
Director: Tony Richardson, *Tom Jones*

1964

Picture: My Fair Lady
Actor: Rex Harrison, *My Fair Lady*
Actress: Julie Andrews, *Mary Poppins*
Supporting Actor: Peter Ustinov, *Topkapi*
Supporting Actress: Lila Kedrova, *Zorba the Greek*
Director: George Cukor, *My Fair Lady*

1965

Picture: The Sound of Music
Actor: Lee Marvin, *Cat Ballou*
Actress: Julie Christie, *Darling*
Supporting Actor: Martin Balsam, *A Thousand Clowns*
Supporting Actress: Shelley Winters, *A Patch of Blue*
Director: Robert Wise, *The Sound of Music*

1966

Picture: A Man for All Seasons
Actor: Paul Scofield, *A Man for All Seasons*
Actress: Elizabeth Taylor, *Who's Afraid of Virginia Woolf?*
Supporting Actor: Walter Matthau, *The Fortune Cookie*
Supporting Actress: Sandy Dennis, *Who's Afraid of Virginia Woolf?*
Director: Fred Zinnemann, *A Man for All Seasons*

1967

Picture: In the Heat of the Night
Actor: Rod Steiger, *In the Heat of the Night*
Actress: Katharine Hepburn, *Guess Who's Coming to Dinner?*
Supporting Actor: George Kennedy, *Cool Hand Luke*
Supporting Actress: Estelle Parsons, *Bonnie and Clyde*
Director: Mike Nichols, *The Graduate*

1968

Picture: Oliver!
Actor: Cliff Robertson, *Charly*
Actress (tie): Katharine Hepburn, *The Lion in Winter*, Barbra Streisand, *Funny Girl*
Supporting Actor: Jack Albertson, *The Subject Was Roses*
Supporting Actress: Ruth Gordon, *Rosemary's Baby*
Director: Carol Reed, *Oliver!*

1969

Picture: Midnight Cowboy
Actor: John Wayne, *True Grit*
Actress: Maggie Smith, *The Prime of Miss Jean Brodie*
Supporting Actor: Gig Young, *They Shoot Horses, Don't They?*
Supporting Actress: Goldie Hawn, *Cactus Flower*
Director: John Schlesinger, *Midnight Cowboy*

1970

Picture: Patton
Actor (declined): George C. Scott, *Patton*
Actress: Glenda Jackson, *Women in Love*
Supporting Actor: John Mills, *Ryan's Daughter*
Supporting Actress: Helen Hayes, *Airplane*
Director: Franklin J. Schaffner, *Patton*

1971

Picture: The French Connection
Actor: Gene Hackman, *The French Connection*

Actress: Jane Fonda, *Klute*
Supporting Actor: Ben Johnson, *The Last Picture Show*
Supporting Actress: Cloris Leachman, *The Last Picture Show*
Director: William Friedkin, *The French Connection*

1972
Picture: *The Godfather*
Actor: Marlon Brando, *The Godfather*
Actress: Liza Minnelli, *Cabaret*
Supporting Actor: Joel Grey, *Cabaret*
Supporting Actress: Eileen Heckart, *Butterflies Are Free*
Director: Bob Fosse, *Cabaret*

1973
Picture: *The Sting*
Actor: Jack Lemmon, *Save the Tiger*
Actress: Glenda Jackson, *A Touch of Class*
Supporting Actor: John Houseman, *The Paper Chase*
Supporting Actress: Tatum O'Neal, *Paper Moon*
Director: George Roy Hill, *The Sting*

1974
Picture: *The Godfather, Part II*
Actor: Art Carney, *Harry and Tonto*
Actress: Ellen Burstyn, *Alice Doesn't Live Here Anymore*
Supporting Actor: Robert De Niro, *The Godfather, Part II*
Supporting Actress: Ingrid Bergman, *Murder on the Orient Express*
Director: Francis Ford Coppola, *The Godfather, Part II*

1975
Picture: *One Flew Over the Cuckoo's Nest*
Actor: Jack Nicholson, *One Flew Over the Cuckoo's Nest*
Actress: Louise Fletcher, *One Flew Over the Cuckoo's Nest*
Supporting Actor: George Burns, *The Sunshine Boys*
Supporting Actress: Lee Grant, *Shampoo*
Director: Milos Foreman, *One Flew Over the Cuckoo's Nest*

1976
Picture: *Rocky*
Actor: Peter Finch, *Network*
Actress: Faye Dunaway, *Network*
Supporting Actor: Jason Robards, *All the President's Men*
Supporting Actress: Beatrice Straight, *Network*
Director: John G. Avildsen, *Rocky*

1977
Picture: *Annie Hall*

Actor: Richard Dreyfuss, *The Goodbye Girl*
Actress: Diane Keaton, *Annie Hall*
Supporting Actor: Jason Robards, *Julia*
Supporting Actress: Vanessa Redgrave, *Julia*
Director: Woody Allen, *Annie Hall*

1978
Picture: *The Deer Hunter*
Actor: Jon Voight, *Coming Home*
Actress: Jane Fonda, *Coming Home*
Supporting Actor: Christopher Walken, *The Deer Hunter*
Supporting Actress: Maggie Smith, *California Suite*
Director: Michael Cimino, *The Deer Hunter*

1979
Picture: *Kramer vs. Kramer*
Actor: Dustin Hoffman, *Kramer vs. Kramer*
Actress: Sally Field, *Norma Rae*
Supporting Actor: Melvyn Douglas, *Being There*
Supporting Actress: Meryl Streep, *Kramer vs. Kramer*
Director: Robert Benton, *Kramer vs. Kramer*

1980
Picture: *Ordinary People*
Actor: Robert De Niro, *Raging Bull*
Actress: Sissy Spacek, *Coal Miner's Daughter*
Supporting Actor: Timothy Hutton, *Ordinary People*
Supporting Actress: Mary Steenburgen, *Melvin and Howard*
Director: Robert Redford, *Ordinary People*

1981
Picture: *Chariots of Fire*
Actor: Henry Fonda, *On Golden Pond*
Actress: Katharine Hepburn, *On Golden Pond*
Supporting Actor: John Gielgud, *Arthur*
Supporting Actress: Maureen Stapleton, *Reds*
Director: Warren Beatty, *Reds*

1982
Picture: *Gandhi*
Actor: Ben Kingsley, *Gandhi*
Actress: Meryl Streep, *Sophie's Choice*
Supporting Actor: Louis Gossett, Jr., *An Officer and a Gentleman*
Supporting Actress: Jessica Lange, *Tootsie*
Director: Richard Attenborough, *Gandhi*

1983

Picture: Terms of Endearment

Actor: Robert Duvall, Tender Mercies

Actress: Shirley MacLaine, Terms of Endearment

Supporting Actor: Jack Nicholson, Terms of Endearment

Supporting Actress: Linda Hunt, The Year of Living Dangerously

Director: James L. Brooks, Terms of Endearment

1984

Picture: Amadeus

Actor: F. Murray Abraham, Amadeus

Actress: Sally Field, Places in the Heart

Supporting Actor: Haing S. Ngor, The Killing Fields

Supporting Actress: Peggy Ashcroft, A Passage to India

Director: Milos Foreman, Amadeus

1985

Picture: Out of Africa

Actor: William Hurt, Kiss of the Spider Woman

Actress: Geraldine Page, The Trip to Bountiful

Supporting Actor: Don Ameche, Cocoon

Supporting Actress: Anjelica Huston, Prizzi's Honor

Director: Sydney Pollack, Out of Africa

1986

Picture: Platoon

Actor: Paul Newman, The Color of Money

Actress: Marlee Matlin, Children of a Lesser God

Supporting Actor: Michael Caine, Hannah and Her Sisters

Supporting Actress: Dianne Wiest, Hannah and Her Sisters

Director: Oliver Stone, Platoon

1987

Picture: The Last Emperor

Actor: Michael Douglas, Wall Street

Actress: Cher, Moonstruck

Supporting Actor: Sean Connery, The Untouchables

Supporting Actress: Olympia Dukakis, Moonstruck

Director: Bernardo Bertolucci, The Last Emperor

1988

Picture: Rain Man

Actor: Dustin Hoffman, Rain Man

Actress: Jodie Foster, The Accused

Supporting Actor: Kevin Kline, A Fish Called Wanda

Supporting Actress: Geena Davis, The Accidental Tourist

Director: Barry Levinson, Rain Man

1989

Picture: Driving Miss Daisy

Actor: Daniel Day-Lewis, My Left Foot

Actress: Jessica Tandy, Driving Miss Daisy

Supporting Actor: Denzel Washington, Glory

Supporting Actress: Brenda Fricker, My Left Foot

Director: Oliver Stone, Born on the Fourth of July

1990

Picture: Dances With Wolves

Actor: Jeremy Irons, Reversal of Fortune

Actress: Kathy Bates, Misery

Supporting Actor: Joe Pesci, GoodFellas

Supporting Actress: Whoopi Goldberg, Ghost

Director: Kevin Costner, Dances With Wolves

1991

Picture: The Silence of the Lambs

Actor: Anthony Hopkins, The Silence of the Lambs

Actress: Jodie Foster, The Silence of the Lambs

Supporting Actor: Jack Palance, City Slickers

Supporting Actress: Mercedes Ruehl, The Fisher King

Director: Jonathan Demme, The Silence of the Lambs

1992

Picture: Unforgiven

Actor: Al Pacino, Scent of a Woman

Actress: Emma Thompson, Howard's End

Supporting Actor: Gene Hackman, Unforgiven

Supporting Actress: Marisa Tomei, My Cousin Vinny

Director: Clint Eastwood, Unforgiven

1993

Picture: Schindler's List

Actor: Tom Hanks, Philadelphia

Actress: Holly Hunter, The Piano

Supporting Actor: Tommy Lee Jones, The Fugitive

Supporting Actress: Anna Paquin, The Piano

Director: Steven Spielberg, Schindler's List

1994
  Picture: *Forrest Gump*
  Actor: Tom Hanks, *Forrest Gump*
  Actress: Jessica Lange, *Blue Sky*
  Supporting Actor: Martin Landau, *Ed Wood*
  Supporting Actress: Dianne Wiest, *Bullets Over Broadway*
  Director: Robert Zemeckis, *Forrest Gump*

1995
  Picture: *Braveheart*
  Actor: Nicolas Cage, *Leaving Las Vegas*
  Actress: Susan Sarandon, *Dead Man Walking*
  Supporting Actor: Kevin Spacey, *The Usual Suspects*
  Supporting Actress: Mira Sorvino, *Mighty Aphrodite*
  Director: Mel Gibson, *Braveheart*

1996
  Picture: *The English Patient*
  Actor: Geoffrey Rush, *Shine*
  Actress: Frances McDormand, *Fargo*
  Supporting Actor: Cuba Gooding, Jr., *Jerry Maguire*
  Supporting Actress: Juliette Binoche, *The English Patient*
  Director: Anthony Minghella, *The English Patient*

1997
  Picture: *Titanic*
  Actor: Jack Nicholson, *As Good As It Gets*
  Actress: Helen Hunt, *As Good As It Gets*
  Supporting Actor: Robin Williams, *Good Will Hunting*
  Supporting Actress: Kim Basinger, *L. A. Confidential*
  Director: James Cameron, *Titanic*

1998
  Picture: *Shakespeare in Love*
  Actor: Roberto Benigni, *Life Is Beautiful*
  Actress: Gwyneth Paltrow, *Shakespeare in Love*
  Supporting Actor: James Coburn, *Affliction*
  Supporting Actress: Judi Dench, *Shakespeare in Love*
  Director: Steven Spielberg, *Saving Private Ryan*

1999
  Picture: *American Beauty*
  Actor: Kevin Spacey, *American Beauty*
  Actress: Hilary Swank, *Boys Don't Cry*
  Supporting Actor: Michael Caine, *Cider House Rules*
  Supporting Actress: Angelina Jolie, *Girl, Interrupted*
  Director: Sam Mendes, *American Beauty*

⊙ Harkness, John. *The 1999 Academy Awards Handbook.* New York: Pinnacle, 1999.
  Osborne, Robert. *70 Years of the Oscar: The Official History of the Academy Awards* New York: Abbeville, 1999.
  Oscar.com. "History-Past Winners," www.oscar.com/history/pastwinners/pas-index.html

Pulitzer Prizes (1917–2000)

The Pulitzer Prizes were established in 1917 by the will of Joseph Pulitzer (1847–1911), publisher of the New York World, for outstanding achievements in American journalism, letters, music (beginning in 1943), and drama. The prizes are bestowed by an advisory board that has exercised its broad powers to create new award categories and to withhold any award where entries fall below its standards of excellence. Winners in each major category are listed below by year

1917
  Editorial Writing: No author named, *New York Tribune*
  Novel: [no award]
  Drama: [no award]
  History: J. J. Jusserand, *With Americans of Past and Present Days*

  Biography or Autobiography: Laura E. Richards and Maude Howe Elliott (asst. by Florence Howe Hall), *Julia Ward Howe*
  Poetry: [no award]

1918
  Editorial Writing: No author named, *Louisville Courier Journal*

1918

Novel: Ernest Poole, *His Family*
Drama: Jesse Lynch Williams, *Why Marry?*
History: James Ford Rhodes, *A History of the Civil War, 1861-1865*
Biography or Autobiography: William Cabell Bruce, *Benjamin Franklin, Self-Revealed*
Poetry: [no award]

1919

Editorial Writing: [no award]
Novel: Booth Tarkington, *The Magnificent Ambersons*
Drama: [no award]
History: [no award]
Biography or Autobiography: Henry Adams, *The Education of Henry Adams*
Poetry: [no award]

1920

Editorial Writing: Harvey E. Newbranch, *Evening World Herald*, Omaha, Nebraska
Novel: [no award]
Drama: Eugene O'Neill, *Beyond the Horizon*
History: Justin H. Smith, *The War with Mexico*
Biography or Autobiography: Albert J. Beveridge, *The Life of John Marshall*
Poetry: [no award]

1921

Editorial Writing: [no award]
Novel: Edith Wharton, *The Age of Innocence*
Drama: Zona Gale, *Miss Lulu Bett*
History: William Sowden Sims and Burton J. Hendrick, *The Victory at Sea*
Biography or Autobiography: Edward Bok, *The Americanization of Edward Bok*
Poetry: [no award]

1922

Editorial Writing: Frank M. O'Brien, *New York Herald*
Novel: Booth Tarkington, *Alice Adams*
Drama: Eugene O'Neill, *Anna Christie*
History: James Truslow Adams, *The Founding of New England*
Biography or Autobiography: Hamlin Garland, *A Daughter of the Middle Border*

Poetry: Edwin Arlington Robinson, *Collected Poems*

1923

Editorial Writing: William Allen White, Emporia (Kansas) *Gazette*
Novel: Willa Cather, *One of Ours*
Drama: Owen Davis, *Icebound*
History: Charles Warren, *The Supreme Court in United States History*
Biography or Autobiography: Burton J. Hendrick, *The Life and Letters of Walter H. Page*
Poetry: Edna St. Vincent Millay, *The Ballad of the Harp-Weaver: A Few Figs from Thistles: Eight Sonnets in American Poetry*

1924

Editorial Writing: No author named, *Boston Herald*
Novel: Margaret Wilson, *The Able McLaughlins*
Drama: Hatcher Hughes, *Hell-Bent fer Heaven*
History: Charles Howard McIlwain, *The American Revolution—A Constitutional Interpretation*
Biography or Autobiography: Michael Idvorsky Pupin, *From Immigrant to Inventor*
Poetry: Robert Frost, *New Hampshire: A Poem with Notes and Grace Notes*

1925

Editorial Writing: No author named, *Charleston (South Carolina) News and Courier*
Novel: Edna Ferber, *So Big*
Drama: Sidney Howard, *They Knew What They Wanted*
History: Frederic L. Paxson, *History of the American Frontier*
Biography or Autobiography: M. A. Dewolfe Howe, *Barrett Wendell and His Letters*
Poetry: Edwin Arlington Robinson, *The Man Who Died Twice*

1926

Editorial Writing: Edward M. Kingsbury, *New York Times*
Novel: Sinclair Lewis, *Arrowsmith*
Drama: George Kelly, *Craig's Wife*
History: Edward Channing, *A History of the United States*

Biography or Autobiography: Harvey
Cushing, *The Life of Sir William Osler*
Poetry: Amy Lowell, *What's O'Clock*

1927

Editorial Writing: F. Lauriston Bullard,
Boston Herald
Novel: Louis Bromfield, *Early Autumn*
Drama: Paul Green, *In Abraham's
Bosom*
History: Samuel Flagg Bemis,
Pinckney's Treaty
Biography or Autobiography: Emory
Holloway, *Whitman*
Poetry: Leonora Speyer, *Fiddler's
Farewell*

1928

Editorial Writing: Grover Cleveland
Hall, *Montgomery (Alabama)
Advertiser*
Novel: Thornton Wilder, *The Bridge of
San Luis Rey*
Drama: Eugene O'Neill, *Strange
Interlude*
History: Vernon Louis Parrington,
Main Currents in American Thought
Biography or Autobiography: Charles
Edward Russell, *The American
Orchestra and Theodore Thomas*
Poetry: Arlington Robinson, *Tristram*

1929

Editorial Writing: Louis Isaac Jaffe,
Norfolk Virginian-Pilot
Novel: Julia Peterkin, *Scarlet Sister Mary*
Drama: Elmer L. Rice, *Street Scene*
History: Fred Albert Shannon, *The
Organization and Administration of
the Union Army, 1861-1865*
Biography or Autobiography: Burton J.
Hendrick, *The Training of an
American. The Earlier Life of Walter
H. Page*
Poetry: Stephen Vincent Benét, *John
Brown's Body*

1930

Editorial Writing: [no award]
Novel: Oliver Lafarge, *Laughing Boy*
Drama: Marc Connelly, *The Green
Pastures*
History: Claude H. Van Tyne, *The War
of Independence*
Biography or Autobiography: Marquis
James, *The Raven*
Poetry: Conrad Aiken, *Selected Poems*

1931

Editorial Writing: Charles S. Ryckman,
Fremont (Nebraska) Tribune
Novel: Margaret Ayer Barnes, *Years of
Grace*
Drama: Susan Glaspell, *Alison's House*
History: Bernadotte E. Schmitt, *The
Coming of the War: 1914*
Biography or Autobiography: Henry
James, *Charles W. Eliot*
Poetry: Robert Frost, *Collected Poems*

1932

Editorial Writing: [no award]
Novel: Pearl S. Buck, *The Good Earth*
Drama: George S. Kaufman, Morrie
Ryskind, George and Ira Gershwin,
Of Thee I Sing
History: John J. Pershing, *My
Experiences in the World War*
Biography or Autobiography: Henry F.
Pringle, *Theodore Roosevelt*
Poetry: George Dillon, *The Flowering
Stone*

1933

Editorial Writing: No author named,
Kansas City (Missouri) Star
Novel: T. S. Stribling, *The Store*
Drama: Maxwell Anderson, *Both Your
Houses*
History: Frederick J. Turner, *The
Significance of Sections in American
History*
Biography or Autobiography: Allan
Nevins, *Grover Cleveland*
Poetry: Archibald MacLeish,
Conquistador

1934

Editorial Writing: E. P. Chase, *Atlantic
(Iowa) News-Telegraph*
Novel: Caroline Miller, *Lamb in His
Bosom*
Drama: Sidney Kingsley, *Men in White*
History: Herbert Agar, *The People's
Choice*
Biography or Autobiography: Tyler
Dennett, *John Hay*
Poetry: Robert Hillyer, *Collected Verse*

1935

Editorial Writing: [no award]
Novel: Josephine Winslow Johnson,
Now in November
Drama: Zoë Akins, *The Old Maid*
History: Charles McLean Andrews, *The
Colonial Period of American History*

1935 (cont.)

Biography or Autobiography: Douglas S. Freeman, *R. E. Lee*

Poetry: Audrey Wurdemann, *Bright Ambush*

1936

Editorial Writing: Felix Morley, *Washington Post*; and George B. Parker, *Scripps-Howard Newspaper*

Novel: Harold L. Davis, *Honey in the Horn*

Drama: Robert E. Sherwood, *Idiot's Delight*

History: Andrew C. McLaughlin, *A Constitutional History of the United States*

Biography or Autobiography: Ralph Barton Perry, *The Thought and Character of William James*

Poetry: Robert P. Tristram Coffin, *Strange Holiness*

1937

Editorial Writing: John W. Owens, *The Baltimore Sun*

Novel: Margaret Mitchell, *Gone With the Wind*

Drama: Moss Hart and George S. Kaufman, *You Can't Take It With You*

History: Van Wyck Brooks, *The Flowering of New England: 1815–1865*

Biography or Autobiography: Allan Nevins, *Hamilton Fish*

Poetry: Robert Frost, *A Further Range*

1938

Editorial Writing: William Wesley Waymack, *The Register and Tribune, Des Moines, Iowa*

Novel: John Phillips Marquand, *The Late George Apley*

Drama: Thornton Wilder, *Our Town*

History: Paul Herman Buck, *The Road to Reunion 1865–1900*

Biography or Autobiography: Marquis James, *Andrew Jackson*

Poetry: Marya Zaturenska, *Cold Morning Sky*

1939

Editorial Writing: Ronald G. Callert, *The Oregonian*, Portland, Oregon

Novel: Marjorie Kinnan Rawlings, *The Yearling*

Drama: Robert E. Sherwood, *Abe Lincoln in Illinois*

History: Frank Luther Mott, *A History of American Magazines*

Biography or Autobiography: Carl van Doren, *Benjamin Franklin*

Poetry: John Gould Fletcher, *Selected Poems*

1940

Editorial Writing: Bart Howard, *St. Louis Post-Dispatch*

Novel: John Steinbeck, *The Grapes of Wrath*

Drama: William Saroyan, *The Time of Your Life*

History: Carl Sandburg, *Abraham Lincoln: The War Years*

Biography or Autobiography: Ray Stannard Baker, *Woodrow Wilson, Life and Letters*

Poetry: Mark Van Doren, *Collected Poems*

1941

Editorial Writing: Reuben Maury, *New York Daily News*

Novel: [no award]

Drama: Robert E. Sherwood, *There Shall Be No Night*

History: Marcus Lee Hansen, *The Atlantic Migration, 1607–1860*

Biography or Autobiography: Ola Elizabeth Winslow, *Jonathan Edward*

Poetry: Leonard Bacon, *Sunderland Capture*

1942

Editorial Writing: Geoffrey Parsons, *New York Herald Tribune*

Novel: Ellen Glasgow, *In This Our Life*

Drama: [no award]

History: Margaret Leech, *Reveille in Washington, 1860–1865*

Biography or Autobiography: Forrest Wilson, *Crusader in Crinoline*

Poetry: William Rose Benét, *The Dust Which is God*

1943

Editorial Writing: Forrest W. Seymour, *Register and Tribune*, Des Moines, Iowa

Novel: Upton Sinclair, *Dragon's Teeth*

Drama: Thornton Wilder, *The Skin of Our Teeth*

History: Esther Forbes, *Paul Revere and the World He Lived In*

Biography or Autobiography: Samuel Eliot Morison, *Admiral of the Ocean Sea*

Poetry: Robert Frost, *A Witness Tree*

Music: William Schuman, *Secular Cantata No. 2. A Free Song*

1944

Editorial Writing: Henry J. Haskell, *Kansas City* (Missouri) *Star*

Novel: Martin Flavin, *Journey in the Dark*

Drama: [no award]

History: Merle Curti, *The Growth of American Thought*

Biography or Autobiography: Carleton Mabee, *The American Leonardo: The Life of Samuel F. B. Morse*

Poetry: Stephen Vincent Benét, *Western Star*

Music: Howard Hanson, *Symphony No. 4, Opus 34*

1945

Editorial Writing: George W. Potter, *Providence Journal-Bulletin*

Novel: John Hersey, *A Bell for Adano*

Drama: Mary Chase, *Harvey*

History: Stephen Bonsal, *Unfinished Business*

Biography or Autobiography: Russell Blaine Nye, *George Bancroft: Brahmin Rebel*

Poetry: Karl Shapiro, *V-Letter and Other Poems*

Music: Aaron Copeland, *Appalachian Spring*

1946

Editorial Writing: Hodding Carter, *Delta Democrat-Times*, Greenville, Mississippi

Novel: [no award]

Drama: Howard Lindsay and Russel Crouse, *State of the Union*

History: Arthur Meier Schlesinger, Jr., *The Age of Jackson*

Biography or Autobiography: Linnie Marsh Wolfe, *Son of the Wilderness*

Poetry: [no award]

Music: Leo Sowerby, *The Canticle of the Sun*

1947

Editorial Writing: William H. Grimes, *The Wall Street Journal*

Novel: Robert Penn Warren, *All the King's Men*

Drama: [no award]

History: James Phinney Baxter 3rd, *Scientists Against Time*

Biography or Autobiography: William Allen White, *The Autobiography of William Allen White*

Poetry: Robert Lowell, *Lord Weary's Castle*

Music: Charles Ives, *Symphony No. 3*

1948

Editorial Writing: Virginius Dabney, *Richmond Times-Dispatch*

Novel: James Michener, *Tales of the South Pacific*

Drama: Tennessee Williams, *A Streetcar Named Desire*

History: Bernard Devoto, *Across the Wide Missouri*

Biography or Autobiography: Margaret Clapp, *Forgotten First Citizen: John Bigelow*

Poetry: W. H. Auden, *The Age of Anxiety*

Music: Walter Piston, *Symphony No. 3*

1949

Editorial Writing: Herbert Elliston, *Washington Post*; John H. Crider, *Boston Herald*

Novel: James Gould Cozzens, *Guard of Honor*

Drama: Arthur Miller, *Death of a Salesman*

History: Roy Franklin Nichols, *The Disruption of American Democracy*

Biography or Autobiography: Robert E. Sherwood, *Roosevelt and Hopkins*

Poetry: Peter Viereck, *Terror and Decorum*

Music: Virgil Thompson, *Louisiana Story* (soundtrack)

1950

Editorial Writing: Carl M. Saunders, *Jackson* (Mississippi) *Citizen Patriot*

Novel: A. B. Guthrie, Jr., *The Way West*

Drama: *South Pacific*, by Richard Rodgers, Oscar Hammerstein II, and Joshua Logan

History: Oliver W. Larkin, *Art and Life in America*

Biography or Autobiography: Samuel Flagg Bemis, *John Quincy Adams and the Foundations of American Foreign Policy*

Poetry: Gwendolyn Brooks, *Annie Allen*

Music: Gian-Carlo Menotti, *The Consul*

1951

Editorial Writing: William Harry Fitzpatrick, *New Orleans States*

Novel: Conrad Richter, *The Town*

Drama: [no award]

History: R. Carlyle Buley, *The Old Northwest, Pioneer Period 1815–1840*

Biography or Autobiography: Margaret Louise Colt, *John C. Calhoun: American Portrait*

Poetry: Carl Sandburg, *Complete Poems*

Music: Douglas S. Moore, *Giants in the Earth*

1952

Editorial Writing: Louis Lacoss, *St. Louis Globe Democrat*

Novel: Herman Wouk, *The Caine Mutiny*

Drama: Joseph Kramm, *The Shrike*

History: Oscar Handlin, *The Uprooted*

Biography or Autobiography: Merlo J. Pusey, *Charles Evans Hughes*

Poetry: Marianne Moore, *Collected Poems*

Music: Gail Kubik, *Symphony Concertante*

1953

Editorial Writing: Vermont Connecticut Royster, *Wall Street Journal*

Novel: Ernest Hemingway, *The Old Man and the Sea*

Drama: William Inge, *Picnic*

History: George Dangerfield, *The Era of Good Feelings*

Biography or Autobiography: David J. Mays, *Edmund Pendleton 1721–1803*

Poetry: Archibald MacLeish, *Collected Poems 1917–1952*

Music: [no award]

1954

Editorial Writing: Don Murray, *Boston Herald*

Novel: [no award]

Drama: John Patrick, *The Teahouse of the August Moon*

History: Bruce Catton, *A Stillness at Appomattox*

Biography or Autobiography: Charles A. Lindbergh, *The Spirit of St. Louis*

Poetry: Theodore Roethke, *The Waking*

Music: Quincy Porter, *Concerto for Two Pianos and Orchestra*

1955

Editorial Writing: Royce Howes, *Detroit Free Press*

Novel: William Faulkner, *A Fable*

Drama: Tennessee Williams, *Cat on a Hot Tin Roof*

History: Paul Horgan, *Great River: The Rio Grande in North American History*

Biography or Autobiography: William S. White, *The Taft Story*

Poetry: Wallace Stevens, *Collected Poems*

Music: Gian-Carlo Menotti, *The Saint of Bleecker Street*

1956

Editorial Writing: Lauren K. Soth, *Register and Tribune, Des Moines, Iowa*

Novel: Mackinlay Kantor, *Andersonville*

Drama: Albert Hackett and Frances Goodrich, *The Diary of Anne Frank*

History: Richard Hofstadter, *The Age of Reform*

Biography or Autobiography: Talbot Faulkner Hamlin, *Benjamin Henry Latrobe*

Poetry: Elizabeth Bishop, *Poems – North and South*

Music: Ernst Toch, *Symphony No. 3*

1957

Editorial Writing: Buford Boone, *Tuscaloosa (Alabama) News*

Novel: [no award]

Drama: Eugene O'Neill, *Long Day's Journey Into Night*

History: George F. Kennan, *Russia Leaves the War: Soviet-American Relations, 1917–1920*

Biography or Autobiography: John F. Kennedy, *Profiles in Courage*

Poetry: Richard Wilbur, *Things of This World*

Music: Norman Dello Joio, *Meditation on Ecclesiastics*

1958

Editorial Writing: Harry S. Ashmore, *Arkansas Gazette*

Novel: James Agee, *A Death in the Family*

Drama: Ketti Frings, *Look Homeward, Angel*

History: Bray Hammond, *Banks and Politics*

Biography or Autobiography: Douglas Southall Freeman, *George Washington* (Volumes I - VI); John Alexander Carroll and Mary Wells Ashworth, *George Washington* (Volume VIII)

Poetry: Robert Penn Warren, *Promises: Poems 1954-1956*

Music: Samuel Barner, *Vanessa*

1959

Editorial Writing: Ralph McGill, *Atlanta* (Georgia) *Constitution*

Novel: Robert Lewis Taylor, *The Travels of Jaimie McPheeters*

Drama: Archibald MacLeish, *J. B.*

History: Leonard D. White and Jean Schneider, *The Republican Era: 1869-1901*

Biography or Autobiography: Arthur Walworth, *Woodrow Wilson, American Prophet*

Poetry: Stanley Kunitz, *Selected Poems 1928-1958*

Music: John LaMontaine, *Concerto for Piano and Orchestra*

1960

Editorial Writing: Lenoir Chambers, *Norfolk Virginian-Pilot*

Novel: Allen Drury, *Advise and Consent*

Drama: Jerome Weidman, George Abbott, Jerry Bock and Sheldon Harnick, *Fiorello!*

History: Margaret Leech, *In the Days of McKinley*

Biography or Autobiography: Samuel Eliot Morison, *John Paul Jones*

Poetry: W. D. Snodgrass, *Heart's Needle*

Music: Elliot Carter, *Second String Quartet*

1961

Editorial Writing: William J. Dorvillier, San Juan (Puerto Rico) *Star*

Novel: Harper Lee, *To Kill a Mockingbird*

Drama: Tad Mosel, *All the Way Home*

History: Herbert Feis, *Between War and Peace: The Postdam Conference*

Biography or Autobiography: David Donald, *Charles Sumner and the Coming of the Civil War*

Poetry: Phyllis McGinley, *Times Three: Selected Verse From Three Decades*

Music: Walter Piston, *Symphony No. 7*

1962

Editorial Writing: Thomas M. Storke, Santa Barbara (California) *News-Press*

Novel: Edwin O'Connor, *The Edge of Sadness*

Drama: Frank Loesser and Abe Burrows, *How to Succeed in Business Without Really Trying*

History: Lawrence H. Gipson, *The Triumphant Empire: Thunder-Clouds Gather in the West 1763-1766*

Biography or Autobiography: [no award]

Poetry: Alan Dugan, *Poems*

Music: Robert Ward, *The Crucible*

1963

Editorial Writing: Ira B. Harkley, Jr., Pascagoula (Mississippi) *Chronicle*

Novel: William Faulkner, *The Reivers*

Drama: [no award]

History: Constance McLaughlin Green, *Washington, Village and Capital. 1800-1878*

Biography or Autobiography: Leon Edel, *Henry James*

Poetry: William Carlos Williams, *Pictures from Breughel*

Music: Samuel Barber, *Piano Concerto No. 1*

1964

Editorial Writing: Hazel Brannon Smith, *Lexington (Mississippi) Advertiser*

Novel: [no award]

Drama: [no award]

History: Sumner Chilton Powell, *Puritan Village: The Formation of a New England Town*

Biography or Autobiography: Walter Jackson Bate, *John Keats*

Poetry: Louis Simpson, *At the End of the Open Road*

Music: [no award]

1965

Editorial Writing: John R. Harrison, *Gainesville (Florida) Sun*

Novel: Shirley Ann Grau, *The Keepers of the House*

Drama: Frank D. Gilroy, *The Subject Was Roses*

History: Irwin Unger, *The Greenback Era*

Biography or Autobiography: Ernest Samuels, *Henry Adams*

Poetry: John Berryman, *77 Dream Songs*

Music: [no award]

1966

Editorial Writing: Robert Lasch, *St. Louis Post-Dispatch*

Novel: Katherine Anne Porter, *Collected Stories*

Drama: [no award]

History: Perry Miller, *The Life of the Mind in America*

Biography or Autobiography: Arthur M. Schlesinger, Jr., *A Thousand Days*

Poetry: Richard Eberhart, *Selected Poems*

Music: Leslie Bassett, *Variations for Orchestra*

1967

Editorial Writing: Eugene Patterson, *Atlanta Constitution*

Novel: Bernard Malamud, *The Fixer*

Drama: Edward Albee, *A Delicate Balance*

History: William H. Goetzmann, *Exploration and Empire: The Explorer and the Scientist in the Winning of the American West*

Biography or Autobiography: Justin Kaplan, *Mr. Clemens and Mark Twain*

Poetry: Anne Sexton, *Live or Die*

Music: Leon Kirchner, *Quarter No. 3*

1968

Editorial Writing: John S. Knight, *Knight Newspapers*

Novel: William Styron, *The Confessions of Nat Turner*

Drama: [no award]

History: Bernard Bailyn, *The Ideological Origins of the American Revolution*

Biography or Autobiography: George E. Kennan, *Memoirs*

Poetry: Anthony Hecht, *The Hard Hours*

Music: George Crumb, *Echoes of Time and the River*

1969

Editorial Writing: Paul Greenberg, *Pine Bluff* (Arkansas) *Commercial*

Novel: N. Scott Momaday, *House Made of Dawn*

Drama: Howard Sackler, *The Great White Hope*

History: Leonard W. Levy, *Origins of the Fifth Amendment*

Biography or Autobiography: Benjamin Lawrence Reid, *The Man from New York: John Quinn and His Friends*

Poetry: George Oppen, *Of Being Numerous*

Music: Karel Husa, *String Quartet No. 3*

1970

Editorial Writing: Philip L. Geyelin, *Washington Post*

Novel: Jean Stafford, *Collected Stories*

Drama: Charles Gordone, *No Place To Be Somebody*

History: Dean Acheson, *Present at the Creation: My Years in the State Department*

Biography or Autobiography: T. Harry Williams, *Huey Long*

Poetry: Richard Howard, *Untitled Subjects*

Music: Charles Wuorinen, *Time's Encomium*

1971

Editorial Writing: Horance G. Davis, Jr., *Gainesville* (Florida) *Sun*

Novel: [no award]

Drama: Paul Zindel, *The Effect of Gamma Rays on Man-in-the-Moon Marigolds*

History: Macgregor Burns, *Roosevelt: The Soldier of Freedom*

Biography or Autobiography: Lawrance Thompson, *Robert Frost: The Years of Triumph, 1915–1938*

Poetry: William S. Merwin, *The Carrier of Ladders*

Music: Mario Davidovsky, *Synchronisms No. 6 for Piano and Electronic Sound*

1972

Editorial Writing: John Strohmeyer, *Bethlehem* (Pennsylvania) *Globe-Times*

Novel: Wallace Stegner, *Angle of Repose*

Drama: [no award]

History: Carl N. Degler, *Neither Black Nor White*

Biography or Autobiography: Joseph P. Lash, *Eleanor and Franklin*

Poetry: James Wright, *Collected Poems*

Music: Jacob Druckman, *Windows*

1973

Editorial Writing: Roger B. Linscott, *Berkshire Eagle*, Pittsfield, Massachusetts

Novel: Eudora Welty, *The Optimist's Daughter*

Drama: Jason Miller, *That Championship Season*

History: Michael Kammen, *People in Paradox: An Inquiry Concerning the Origins of American Civilization*

Biography or Autobiography: W. A. Swanberg, *Luce and His Empire*

Poetry: Maxine Kumin, *Up Country*
Music: Elliot Carter, *String Quartet No. 3*

1974
Editorial Writing: F. Gilman Spencer, *The Trentonian*, Trenton, New Jersey
Novel: [no award]
Drama: [no award]
History: Daniel J. Boorstein, *The Americans: The Democratic Experience*
Biography or Autobiography: Louis Sheaffer, *O'Neill, Son and Artist*
Poetry: Robert Lowell, *The Dolphin*
Music: Donald Martino, *Notturno*

1975
Editorial Writing: John Daniell Maurice, *Charleston (West Virginia) Daily Mail*
Novel: Michael Shaara, *The Killer Angels*
Drama: Edward Albee, *Seascape*
History: Dumas Malone, *Jefferson and His Time, Vols. I–V*
Biography or Autobiography: Robert Caro, *The Power Broker: Robert Moses and the Fall of New York*
Poetry: Gary Snyder, *Turtle Island*
Music: Dominick Argento, *From the Diary of Virginia Woolf*

1976
Editorial Writing: Philip P. Kerby, *Los Angeles Times*
Novel: Saul Bellow, *Humboldt's Gift*
Drama: James Kirkwood, Nicholas Dante, Edward Kleban, and Marvin Hamlisch, *A Chorus Line*
History: Paul Horgan, *Lamy of Santa Fe*
Biography or Autobiography: R. W. B. Lewis, *Edith Wharton: A Biography*
Poetry: John Ashbery, *Self-Portrait in a Convex Mirror*
Music: Ned Rorem, *Air Music*

1977
Editorial Writing: Warren L. Lerude, Foster Church, and Norman F. Cardoza, (Nevada) *Evening Gazette* and *Nevada State Journal*
Novel: [no award]
Drama: Michael Cristofer, *The Shadow Box*
History: David M. Potter, *The Impending Crisis, 1841–1867*
Biography or Autobiography: John E. Mack, *A Prince of Our Disorder: The Life of T. E. Lawrence*
Poetry: James Merrill, *Divine Comedies*
Music: Richard Wernick, *Visions of Terror and Wonder*

1978
Editorial Writing: Meg Greenfield, *The Washington Post*
Novel: James Alan McPherson, *Elbow Room*
Drama: Donald L. Coburn, *The Gin Game*
History: Alfred D. Chandler, Jr., *The Visible Hand: The Managerial Revolution in American Business*
Biography or Autobiography: Walter Jackson Bate, *Samuel Johnson*
Poetry: Howard Nemerov, *Collected Poems*
Music: Michael Colgrass, *Deja Vu for Percussion Quartet and Orchestra*

1979
Editorial Writing: Edwin M. Yoder, Jr., *The Washington Star*
Novel: John Cheever, *The Stories of John Cheever*
Drama: Sam Shepherd, *Buried Child*
History: Don E. Fehrenbacher, *The Dred Scott Case*
Biography or Autobiography: Leonard Baker, *Days of Sorrow and Pain: Leo Baeck and the Berlin Jews*
Poetry: Robert Penn Warren, *Now and Then*
Music: Joseph Schwantner, *Aftertones of Infinity*

1980
Editorial Writing: Robert L. Bartley, *The Wall Street Journal*
Novel: Norman Mailer, *The Executioner's Song*
Drama: Lanford Wilson, *Talley's Folly*
History: Leon F. Litwack, *Been in the Storm So Long*
Biography or Autobiography: Edmund Morris, *Theodore Roosevelt*
Poetry: Donald Justice, *Selected Poems*
Music: David Del Tredici, *In Memory of a Summer Day*

1981
Editorial Writing: [no award]
Novel: John Kennedy Toole, *A Confederacy of Dunces*
Drama: Beth Henley, *Crimes of the Heart*
History: Lawrence A. Cremin, *American Education: The National Experience, 1783–1876*
Biography or Autobiography: Robert K. Massie, *Peter the Great: His Life and World*

1981 (cont.)

 Poetry: James Schuyler, *The Morning of the Poem*
 Music: [no award]

1982

 Editorial Writing: Jack Rosenthal, *The New York Times*
 Novel: John Updike, *Rabbit is Rich*
 Drama: Charles Fuller, *A Soldier's Play*
 History: C. Vann Woodward (ed.), *Mary Chesnut's Civil War*
 Biography or Autobiography: William McFeely, *Grant: A Biography*
 Poetry: Sylvia Plath, *The Collected Poems*
 Music: Roger Sessions, *Concerto for Orchestra*

1983

 Editorial Writing: No authors named, *The Miami Herald* Editorial Board
 Novel: Alice Walker, *The Color Purple*
 Drama: Marsha Norman, *'Night, Mother*
 History: Rhys L. Isaac, *The Transformation of Virginia, 1740–1790*
 Biography or Autobiography: Russell Baker, *Growing Up*
 Poetry: Galway Kinnell, *Selected Poems*
 Music: Ellen Taaffe Zwilich, *Symphony No. 1 (Three Movements for Orchestra)*

1984

 Editorial Writing: Albert Scardino, *The George Gazette*, Savannah
 Novel: William Kennedy, *Ironweed*
 Drama: David Mamet, *Glengarry Glen Ross*
 History: [no award]
 Biography or Autobiography: Louis R. Harlan, *Booker T. Washington*
 Poetry: Mary Oliver, *American Primitive*
 Music: Bernard Rands, *"Canti del Sole"* for Tenor and Orchestra

1985

 Editorial Writing: Richard Aregood, *The Philadelphia Daily News*
 Novel: Alison Lurie, *Foreign Affairs*
 Drama: James Lapine, Stephen Sondheim, *Sunday in the Park With George*
 History: Thomas K. McCraw, *Prophets of Regulation*
 Biography or Autobiography: Kenneth Silverman, *The Life and Times of Cotton Mather*
 Poetry: Carolyn Kizer, *Yin*

 Music: Stephen Albert, *Symphony, River Run*

1986

 Editorial Writing: Jack Fuller, *Chicago Tribune*
 Novel: Larry McMurtry, *Lonesome Dove*
 Drama: [no award]
 History: Walter A. McDougall, *The Heavens and the Earth*
 Biography or Autobiography: Elizabeth Frank, *Louise Bogan: A Portrait*
 Poetry: Henry Taylor, *The Flying Change*
 Music: George Perle, *Wind Quintet IV*

1987

 Editorial Writing: Jonathan Freedman, *The Tribune*, San Diego, California
 Novel: Peter Taylor, *A Summons to Memphis*
 Drama: August Wilson, *Fences*
 History: Bernard Bailyn, *Voyagers to the West*
 Biography or Autobiography: David J. Garrow, *Bearing the Cross*
 Poetry: Rita Dove, *Thomas and Beulah*
 Music: John Harbison, *The Flight into Egypt*

1988

 Editorial Writing: Jane Healy, *The Orlando Sentinel*
 Novel: Toni Morrison, *Beloved*
 Drama: Alfred Uhry, *Driving Miss Daisy*
 History: Robert V. Bruce, *The Launching of Modern American Science 1846–1876*
 Biography or Autobiography: David Herbert Donald, *Look Homeward: A Life of Thomas Wolfe*
 Poetry: William Meredith, *Partial Accounts*
 Music: William Bolcom, *12 New Etudes for Piano*

1989

 Editorial Writing: Louis Wille, *The Chicago Tribune*
 Novel: Anne Tyler, *Breathing Lessons*
 Drama: Wendy Wasserstein, *The Heidi Chronicles*
 History: James M. McPherson, *Battle Cry of Freedom*
 Biography or Autobiography: Richard Ellmann, *Oscar Wilde*

Poetry: Richard Wilbur, *New and Collected Poems*
Music: Roger Reynolds, *Whispers Out of Time*

1990

Editorial Writing: Thomas J. Hylton, *The Pottstown (Pennsylvania) Mercury*
Novel: Oscar Hijuelos, *The Mambo Kings Play Songs of Love*
Drama: August Wilson, *The Piano Lesson*
History: Stanley Karnow, *In Our Image*
Biography or Autobiography: Sebastian De Grazia, *Machiavelli in Hell*
Poetry: Charles Simic, *The World Doesn't End*
Music: Mel Powell, *"Duplicates": A Concerto for Two Pianos and Orchestra*

1991

Editorial Writing: Ron Casey, Harold Jackson and Joey Kennedy, *The Birmingham (Alabama) News*
Novel: John Updike, *Rabbit at Rest*
Drama: Neil Simon, *Lost in Yonkers*
History: Laurel Thatcher Ulrich, *A Midwife's Tale*
Biography or Autobiography: Steven Naifeh and Gregory White Smith, *Jackson Pollack*
Poetry: Mona Van Duyn, *Near Changes*
Music: Shulamit Ran, *Symphony*

1992

Editorial Writing: Maria Henson, *Lexington (Kentucky) Herald-Leader*
Novel: Jane Smiley, *A Thousand Acres*
Drama: Robert Schenkkan, *The Kentucky Cycle*
History: Mark E. Neely, Jr., *The Fate of Liberty: Abraham Lincoln and Civil Liberties*
Biography or Autobiography: Lewis B. Puller, Jr., *Fortunate Son: The Healing of a Vietnam Vet*
Poetry: James Tate, *Selected Poems*
Music: Wayne Peterson, *The Face of the Night, The Heart of the Dark*

1993

Editorial Writing: [no award]
Novel: Robert Olen Butler, *A Good Scent from a Strange Mountain*
Drama: Tony Kushner, *Angels in America: Millennium Approaches*
History: Gordon S. Wood, *The Radicalism of the American Revolution*
Biography or Autobiography: David McCullough, *Truman*

Poetry: Louise Gluck, *The Wild Iris*
Music: Christopher Rouse, *Trombone Concerto*

1994

Editorial Writing: R. Bruce Dold, *Chicago Tribune*
Novel: E. Annie Proulx, *The Shipping News*
Drama: Edward Albee, *Three Tall Women*
History: [no award]
Biography or Autobiography: David Levering Lewis, *W. E. B. Du Bois: Biography of a Race 1868–1919*
Poetry: Yusef Komunyakaa, *Neon Vernacular: New and Selected Poems*
Music: Gunther Schuller, *Of Reminiscences and Reflections*

1995

Editorial Writing: Jeffrey Good, *St. Petersburg (Florida) Times*
Novel: Carol Shields, *The Stone Diaries*
Drama: Horton Foote, *The Young Man From Atlanta*
History: Doris Kearns Goodwin, *No Ordinary Time: Franklin and Eleanor Roosevelt: The Home Front in World War II*
Biography or Autobiography: Joan D. Hedrick, *Harriet Beecher Stowe: A Life*
Poetry: Philip Levine, *The Simple Truth*
Music: Morton Gould, *Stringmusic*

1996

Editorial Writing: Robert B. Semple, Jr., *The New York Times*
Novel: Richard Ford, *Independence Day*
Drama: Jonathan Larson, *Rent*
History: Alan Taylor, *William Cooper's Town: Power and Persuasion on the Frontier of the Early American Republic*
Biography or Autobiography: Jack Miles, *God: A Biography*
Poetry: Jorie Graham, *The Dream of the Unified Field*
Music: George Walker, *Lilacs, for voice and orchestra*

1997

Editorial Writing: Michael Gartner, *The Daily Tribune, Ames, Iowa*
Novel: Steven Millhauser, *Martin Dressler: The Tale of an American Dreamer*
Drama: [no award]

1997 (cont.)

History: Jack N. Rakove, *Original Meanings: Politics and Ideas in the Making of the Constitution*

Biography or Autobiography: Frank McCourt, *Angela's Ashes*

Poetry: Lisel Mueller, *Alive Together: New and Selected Poems*

Music: Wynton Marsalis, *Blood on the Fields*

1998

Editorial Writing: Bernard L. Stein, *The Riverdale* (New York) *Press*

Novel: Philip Roth, *American Pastoral*

Drama: Paula Vogel, *How I Learned to Drive*

History: Edward J. Larson, *Summer for the Gods: The Scopes Trial and America's Continuing Debate Over Science and Religion*

Biography or Autobiography: Katharine Graham, *Personal History*

Poetry: Charles Wright, *Black Zodiac*

Music: Aaron Jay Kernis, *String Quartet No. 2, Musica Instrumentalis*

1999

Editorial Writing: New York Daily News Editorial Board

Novel: Michael Cunningham, *The Hours*

Drama: Margaret Edson, *Wit*

History: Edwin G. Burrows and Mike Wallace, *Gotham: A History of New York City to 1898*

Biography or Autobiography: A. Scott Berg, *Lindbergh*

Poetry: Mark Strand, *Blizzard of One*

Music: Melinda Wagner, *Concert for Flute, Strings and Percussion*

2000

Editorial Writing: John C. Bersia, *The Orlando Sentinel*

Novel: Jhumpa Lahiri, *Interpreter of Maladies*

Drama: Donald Margulies, *Dinner with Friends*

History: David M. Kennedy, *Freedom from Fear: The American People in Depression and War 1929–1945*

Biography or Autobiography: Stacy Schiff, *Vera (Mrs. Vladimir Nabokov)*

Poetry: C. K. Williams, *Repair*

⊙ Bates, J. Douglas. *The Pulitzer Prize: The Inside Story of America's Most Prestigious Award.* New York: Carol Publishing, 1991.

Brennan, Elizabeth A., and Elizabeth C. Clarage. *Who's Who of Pulitzer Prize Winners.* Phoenix: Oryx, 1999.

The Pulitzer Prize Organization. "Pulitzer Prize Archive," www.pulitzer.org/Archive/archive.html

Booker Prize (1969–2000)

The Booker Prize was established in 1968 by Booker McConnell, a multinational company, for achievement in an English-language novel. Contestants are authors from the United Kingdom, the Commonwealth countries, the Republic of Ireland, and South Africa. Authors and titles are listed below by year.

1969

P. H. Newby, *Something to Answer For*

1970

Bernice Rubens, *The Elected Member*

1971

V. S. Naipaul, *In a Free State*

1972

John Berger, *G*

1973

J. G. Farrell, *The Siege of Krishnapur;* Stanley Middleton, *Holiday*

1974

Nadine Gordimer, *The Conservationist*

1975

Ruth Prawer Jhabvala, *Heat and Dust*

1976

David Storey, *Saville*

1977

Paul Scott, *Staying On*

1978

Iris Murdoch, *The Sea, The Sea*

1979

Penelope Fitzgerald, *Offshore*

1980
 William Golding, *Rites of Passage*
1981
 Salman Rushdie, *Midnight's Children*
1982
 Thomas Keneally, *Schindler's Ark*
1983
 J. M. Coetzee, *The Life and Times of Michael K.*
1984
 Anita Brookner, *Hotel Du Lac*
1985
 Keri Hulme, *The Bone People*
1986
 Kingsley Amis, *The Old Devils*
1987
 Penelope Lively, *Moon Tiger*

1988
 Peter Carey, *Oscar and Lucinda*
1989
 Kazuo Ishiguro, *The Remains of the Day*
1990
 A. S. Byatt, *Possession*

1991
 Ben Okri, *The Famished Road*
1992
 Michael Ondaatje, *The English Patient;* Barry Unsworth, *Sacred Hunger*
1993
 Roddy Doyle, *Paddy Clarke Ha Ha Ha*
1994
 James Kelman, *How Late It Was, How Late*
1995
 Pat Barker, *The Ghost Road*
1996
 Graham Swift, *Last Orders*
1997
 Arundhati Roy, *The God of Small Things*
1998
 Ian McEwan, *Amsterdam*
1999
 J. M. Coetzee, *Disgrace*
2000
 Margaret Atwood, *The Blind Assassin*

⊙ The Booker Prize. "Previous Winners," www.bookerprize.co.uk/site/fiction/previous/previousfset.html
  Booker McConnell Prize Pages. "Winning and Shortlisted Titles by Year," www.utc.edu/~engldept/booker/booker.htm

Templeton Award for Progress in Religion (1973–2000)

The Templeton Award for Progress in Religion was established in 1972 by financier John Marks Templeton (1912–) on the grounds that the Nobel Prizes exclude recognition for advances in spirituality. The Templeton Award is currently the world's largest annual monetary award of $945,000.

Year	Recipient	Year	Recipient
1973	Mother Teresa	1983	Aleksandr Solzhenitsyn
1974	Brother Roger	1984	The Rev. Michael Bourdeaux
1975	Sir Sarvepalli Radhakrishnan	1985	Sir Alister Hardy
1976	Leon Joseph Cardinal Suenens	1986	Rev. Dr. James McCord
		1987	Rev. Professor Stanley L. Jaki
1977	Chiara Lubich	1988	Dr. Inamullah Khan
1978	Professor Thomas F. Torrance	1989	awarded jointly to The Very
1979	Rev. Nikkyo Niwano		Reverend Lord MacLeod and
1980	Professor Ralph Wendell Burhoe		Professor Carl Friedrich von Weizsacker
1981	Dame Cecily Saunders	1990	awarded jointly to Baba Amte
1982	Rev. Dr. Billy Graham		and Professor L. Charles Birch

Templeton Award for Progress in Religion
(1973–2000) *(cont.)*

Year	Recipient	Year	Recipient
1991	The Rt. Hon. Lord Jakobovits	1996	William R. "Bill" Bright
1992	Rev. Dr. Kyung-Chik Han	1997	Pandurang Shastri Athavale
1993	Charles W. Colson	1998	Sir Sigmund Sternberg
1994	Michael Novak	1999	Ian G. Barbour
1995	Paul Charles William Davies	2000	Freeman Dyson

⊙ Forker, Wilbert, ed. *The Templeton Foundation Prize for Progress in Religion.* Edinburgh: Scottish Academic Press, 1989.
John Templeton Foundation. "The Templeton Prize for Progress in Religion," www.templetonprize.org

The Emmy Awards (1950–2000)

The Emmy Awards were established in 1948 by the National Academy of Television Arts and Sciences for excellence in television performance and production. The award's name is a variation of Immy, a term for an early image orthicon camera tube. While the categories' names have changed with time, they have always included awards for acting achievement and for outstanding programs. Once awarded to programs broadcast within a calendar year, the Emmys are now awarded on the basis of the September-to-August television season. Winners in each major category are listed below by year.

1950
Best Drama: Pulitzer Prize Playhouse
Best Actor: Alan Young
Best Actress: Gertude Berg

1951
Best Comedy: The Red Skelton Show
Best Drama: Studio One
Best Actor: Sid Caesar
Best Actress: Imogene Coca

1952
Best Comedy: I Love Lucy
Best Drama: Robert Montgomery Presents
Best Comedy Actor: Jimmy Durante
Best Comedy Actress: Lucille Ball
Best Drama Actor: Thomas Mitchell
Best Drama Actress: Helen Hayes

1953
Best Comedy: I Love Lucy
Best Drama: The U.S. Steel Hour
Best Actor: Donald O'Connor, *Colgate Comedy Hour*
Best Actress: Eve Arden, *Our Miss Brooks*

1954
Best Comedy: I Love Lucy
Best Drama: The U.S. Steel Hour
Best Actor: Danny Thomas, *Make Room for Daddy*

Best Actress: Loretta Young, *The Loretta Young Show*

1955
Best Comedy: The Phil Silvers Show
Best Drama: Producers' Showcase
Best Actor: Phil Silvers, *The Phil Silvers Show*
Best Actress: Lucille Ball, *I Love Lucy*

1956
Best Comedy: The Phil Silvers Show
Best Drama: Producer's Showcase
Best Comedy Actor: Sid Caesar, *Caesar's Hour*
Best Comedy Actress: Nanette Fabray, *Caesar's Hour*
Best Drama Actor: Robert Young, *Father Knows Best*
Best Drama Actress: Loretta Young, *The Loretta Young Show*

1957
Best Comedy: The Phil Silvers Show
Best Drama: Gunsmoke
Best Actor: Robert Young, *Father Knows Best*
Best Actress: Jane Wyatt, *Father Knows Best*

1958–1959
Best Comedy: The Jack Benny Show

Best Drama: Playhouse 90, Alcoa-
  Goodyear Theatre
Best Comedy Actor: Jack Benny,
  The Jack Benny Show
Best Comedy Actress: Jane Wyatt, Father
  Knows Best
Best Drama Actor: Raymond Burr, Perry
  Mason
Best Drama Actress: Loretta Young,
  The Loretta Young Show

1959–60

Best Comedy: The Art Carney Special
Best Drama: Playhouse 90
Best Actor: Robert Stack,
  The Untouchables
Best Actress: Jane Wyatt, Father Knows
  Best

1960–61

Best Comedy: The Jack Benny Show
Best Drama: Macbeth, [Hallmark Hall
  of Fame]
Best Actor: Raymond Burr, Perry
  Mason
Best Actress: Barbara Stanwyck,
  The Barbara Stanwyck Show

1961–62

Best Comedy: The Bob Newhart Show
Best Drama: The Defenders
Best Actor: E. G. Marshall, The
  Defenders
Best Actress: Shirley Booth, Hazel

1962–63

Best Comedy: The Dick Van Dyke Show
Best Drama: The Defenders
Best Actor: E. G. Marshall,
  The Defenders
Best Actress: Shirley Booth, Hazel

1963–64

Best Comedy: The Dick Van Dyke Show
Best Drama: The Defenders
Best Actor: Dick Van Dyke, The Dick
  Van Dyke Show
Best Actress: Mary Tyler Moore,
  The Dick Van Dyke Show

1964–65

Best Comedy: The Dick Van Dyke
  Show
Best Drama: The Magnificent Yankee,
  (Hallmark Hall of Fame)
Best Comedy Actor: Dick Van Dyke,
  The Dick Van Dyke Show
Best Comedy Actress: Barbara Streisand,
  My Name is Barbara

Best Drama Actor: Alfred Lunt,
  The Magnificent Yankee, Hallmark
  Hall of Fame;;
Best Drama Actress: Lynne Fontanne,
  The Magnificent Yankee (Hallmark
  Hall of Fame)

1965–66

Best Comedy: The Dick Van Dyke Show
Best Drama: The Fugitive
Best Comedy Actor: Dick Van Dyke,
  The Dick Van Dyke Show
Best Comedy Actress: Mary Tyler Moore,
  The Dick Van Dyke Show
Best Drama Actor: Bill Cosby, I Spy
Best Drama Actress: Barbara Stanwyck,
  The Big Valley

1966–67

Best Comedy: The Monkees
Best Drama: Mission: Impossible
Best Comedy Actor: Don Adams, Get
  Smart
Best Comedy Actress: Lucille Ball,
  The Lucy Show
Best Drama Actor: Bill Cosby, I Spy
Best Drama Actress: Barbara Bain,
  Mission: Impossible

1967–68

Best Comedy: Get Smart
Best Drama: Mission: Impossible
Best Comedy Actor: Don Adams, Get
  Smart
Best Comedy Actress: Lucille Ball,
  The Lucy Show
Best Drama Actor: Milburn Stone,
  Gunsmoke
Best Drama Actress: Barbara Bain,
  Mission: Impossible

1968–69

Best Comedy: Get Smart
Best Drama: NET Playhouse
Best Comedy Actor: Don Adams, Get
  Smart
Best Comedy Actress: Hope Lange,
  The Ghost and Mrs. Muir
Best Drama Actor: Carl Betz, Judd, For
  the Defense
Best Drama Actress: Barbara Bain,
  Mission: Impossible

1969–70

Best Comedy: My World And Welcome
  To It
Best Drama: Marcus Welby, M.D.
Best Comedy Actor: William Windom,
  My World and Welcome to It

1969–70 (cont.)

Best Comedy Actress: Hope Lange,
The Ghost and Mrs Muir

Best Drama Actor: Robert Young,
Marcus Welby, M.D.

Best Drama Actress: Susan Hampshire,
The Forsythe Saga

1970–71

Best Comedy: *All in the Family*

Best Drama: *The Senator: The Bold Ones*

Best Comedy Actor: Jack Klugman,
The Odd Couple

Best Comedy Actress: Jean Stapleton, *All in the Family*

Best Drama Actor: Hal Holbrook,
The Senator: The Bold Ones

Best Drama Actress: Susan Hampshire,
The First Churchills (Masterpiece Theatre)

1971–72

Best Comedy: *All in the Family*

Best Drama: *Elizabeth R* (Masterpiece Theatre)

Best Comedy Actor: Carroll O'Connor,
All in the Family

Best Comedy Actress: Jean Stapleton, *All in the Family*

Best Drama Actor: Peter Falk, *Columbo*

Best Drama Actress: Glenda Jackson,
Elizabeth R (Masterpiece Theatre)

1972–73

Best Comedy: *All in the Family*

Best Drama: *The Waltons*

Best Comedy Actor: Jack Klugman,
The Odd Couple

Best Comedy Actress: Mary Tyler Moore,
The Mary Tyler Moore Show

Best Drama Actor: Richard Thomas,
The Waltons

Best Drama Actress: Michael Learned,
The Waltons

1973–74

Best Comedy: *M*A*S*H*

Best Drama: *Upstairs, Downstairs* (Masterpiece Theatre)

Best Comedy Actor: Alan Alda,
M*A*S*H

Best Comedy Actress: Mary Tyler Moore,
The Mary Tyler Moore Show

Best Drama Actor: Telly Savalas, *Kojak*

Best Drama Actress: Michael Learned,
The Waltons

1974–75

Best Comedy: *The Mary Tyler Moore Show*

Best Drama: *Upstairs, Downstairs* (Masterpiece Theatre)

Best Comedy Actor: Tony Randall,
The Odd Couple

Best Comedy Actress: Valerie Harper,
Rhoda

Best Drama Actor: Robert Blake,
Baretta

Best Drama Actress: Jean Marsh,
Upstairs, Downstairs (Masterpiece Theatre)

1975–76

Best Comedy: *The Mary Tyler Moore Show*

Best Drama: *Police Story*

Best Comedy Actor: Jack Albertson,
Chico And The Man

Best Comedy Actress: Mary Tyler Moore,
The Mary Tyler Moore Show

Best Drama Actor: Peter Falk,
Columbo

Best Drama Actress: Michael Learned,
The Waltons

1976–77

Best Comedy: *The Mary Tyler Moore Show*

Best Drama: *Upstairs, Downstairs* [Masterpiece Theatre]

Best Comedy Actor: Carroll O'Connor,
All in the Family

Best Comedy Actress: Beatrice Arthur,
Maude

Best Drama Actor: James Garner,
The Rockford Files

Best Drama Actress: Lindsay Wagner,
The Bionic Woman

1977–78

Best Comedy: *All in the Family*

Best Drama: *The Rockford Files*

Best Comedy Actor: Carroll O'Connor,
All in the Family

Best Comedy Actress: Jean Stapleton, *All in the Family*

Best Drama Actor: Ed Asner, *Lou Grant*

Best Drama Actress: Sada Thompson,
Family

1978–79

Best Comedy: *Taxi*

Best Drama: *Lou Grant*

Best Comedy Actor: Carroll O'Connor,
All in the Family
Best Comedy Actress: Ruth Gordon,
Taxi
Best Drama Actor: Ron Leibman, Kaz
Best Drama Actress: Mariette Hartley,
The Incredible Hulk

1979–80
Best Comedy: Taxi
Best Drama: Lou Grant
Best Comedy Actor: Richard Mulligan,
Soap
Best Comedy Actress: Cathryn Damon,
Soap
Best Drama Actor: Ed Asner, Lou
Grant
Best Drama Actress: Barbara Bel
Geddes, Dallas

1980–81
Best Comedy: Taxi
Best Drama: Hill Street Blues
Best Comedy Actor: Judd Hirsh, Taxi
Best Comedy Actress: Isabel Sanford,
The Jeffersons
Best Drama Actor: Daniel J. Travanti,
Hill Street Blues
Best Drama Actress: Barbara Babcock,
Hill Street Blues

1981–82
Best Comedy: Barney Miller
Best Drama: Hill Street Blues
Best Comedy Actor: Alan Alda,
M*A*S*H
Best Comedy Actress: Carol Kane, Taxi
Best Drama Actor: Daniel J. Travanti,
Hill Street Blues
Best Drama Actress: Michael Learned,
Nurse

1982–83
Best Comedy: Cheers
Best Drama: Hill Street Blues
Best Comedy Actor: Judd Hirsh, Taxi
Best Comedy Actress: Shelley Long,
Cheers
Best Drama Actor: Ed Flanders, St.
Elsewhere
Best Drama Actress: Tyne Daly, Cagney
and Lacey

1983–84
Best Comedy: Cheers
Best Drama: Hill Street Blues
Best Comedy Actor: John Ritter, Three's
Company
Best Comedy Actress: Jane Curtin, Kate
and Allie

Best Drama Actor: Tom Selleck,
Magnum, P.I.
Best Drama Actress: Tyne Daly, Cagney
and Lacey

1984–85
Best Comedy: The Cosby Show
Best Drama: Cagney and Lacey
Best Comedy Actor: Robert Guillaume,
Benson
Best Comedy Actress: Jane Curtin, Kate
and Allie
Best Drama Actor: William Daniels, St.
Elsewhere
Best Drama Actress: Tyne Daly, Cagney
and Lacey

1985–86
Best Comedy: The Golden Girls
Best Drama: Cagney and Lacey
Best Comedy Actor: Michael J. Fox,
Family Ties
Best Comedy Actress: Betty White,
The Golden Girls
Best Drama Actor: William Daniels, St.
Elsewhere
Best Drama Actress: Sharon Gless,
Cagney and Lacey

1986–87
Best Comedy: The Golden Girls
Best Drama: L.A. Law
Best Comedy Actor: Michael J. Fox,
Family Ties
Best Comedy Actress: Rue McClanahan,
The Golden Girls
Best Drama Actor: Bruce Willis,
Moonlighting
Best Drama Actress: Sharon Gless,
Cagney and Lacey

1987–88
Best Comedy: The Wonder Years
Best Drama: thirtysomething
Best Comedy Actor: Michael J. Fox,
Family Ties
Best Comedy Actress: Beatrice Arthur,
The Golden Girls
Best Drama Actor: Richard Kiley,
A Year in the Life
Best Drama Actress: Tyne Daly, Cagney
and Lacey

1988–89
Best Comedy: Cheers
Best Drama: L.A. Law
Best Comedy Actor: Richard Mulligan,
Empty Nest
Best Comedy Actress: Candice Bergen,
Murphy Brown

1988–89 (cont.)

Best Drama Actor: Carroll O'Connor, *In the Heat of the Night*
Best Drama Actress: Dana Delany, *China Beach*

1989–90

Best Comedy: Murphy Brown
Best Drama: L.A. Law
Best Comedy Actor: Ted Danson, *Cheers*
Best Comedy Actress: Candice Bergen, *Murphy Brown*
Best Drama Actor: Peter Falk, *Columbo*
Best Drama Actress: Patricia Wettig, *thirtysomething*

1990–91

Best Comedy: Cheers
Best Drama: L.A. Law
Best Comedy Actor: Burt Reynolds, *Evening Shade*
Best Comedy Actress: Kirstie Alley, *Cheers*
Best Drama Actor: James Earl Jones, *Gabriel's Fire*
Best Drama Actor: Patricia Wettig, *thirtysomething*

1991–92

Best Comedy: Murphy Brown
Best Drama: Northern Exposure
Best Comedy Actor: Craig T. Nelson, *Coach*
Best Comedy Actress: Candice Bergen, *Murphy Brown*
Best Drama Actor: Christopher Lloyd, *Avonlea*
Best Drama Actress: Dana Delany, *China Beach*

1992–93

Best Comedy: Seinfeld
Best Drama: Picket Fences
Best Comedy Actor: Ted Danson, *Cheers*
Best Comedy Actress: Roseanne Barr, *Roseanne*
Best Drama Actor: Tom Skerritt, *Picket Fences*
Best Drama Actress: Kathy Baker, *Picket Fences*

1993–94

Best Comedy: Frasier
Best Drama: Picket Fences
Best Comedy Actor: Kelsey Grammer, *Frasier*

Best Comedy Actress: Candice Bergen, *Murphy Brown*
Best Drama Actor: Dennis Franz, *NYPD Blue*
Best Drama Actress: Sela Ward, *Sisters*

1994–95

Best Comedy: Frasier
Best Drama: NYPD Blue
Best Comedy Actor: Kelsey Grammer, *Frasier*
Best Comedy Actress: Candice Bergen, *Murphy Brown*
Best Drama Actor: Mandy Patinkin, *Chicago Hope*
Best Drama Actress: Kathy Baker, *Picket Fences*

1995–96

Best Comedy: Frasier
Best Drama: ER
Best Comedy Actress: John Lithgow, *3rd Rock From the Sun*
Best Comedy Actor: Helen Hunt, *Mad About You*
Best Drama Actor: Dennis Franz, *NYPD Blue*
Best Drama Actress: Kathy Baker, *Picket Fences*

1996–97

Best Comedy: Frasier
Best Drama: Law and Order
Best Comedy Actor: John Lithgow, *3rd Rock From the Sun*
Best Comedy Actress: Helen Hunt, *Mad About You*
Best Drama Actor: Dennis Franz, *NYPD Blue*
Best Drama Actress: Gillian Anderson, *The X-Files*

1997–98

Best Comedy: Frasier
Best Drama: The Practice
Best Comedy Actor: Kelsey Grammer, *Frasier*
Best Comedy Actress: Helen Hunt, *Mad About You*
Best Drama Actor: Andre Braugher, *Homicide: Life on the Street*
Best Drama Actress: Christine Lahti, *Chicago Hope*

1998–99

Best Comedy: Ally McBeal
Best Drama: The Practice

Best Comedy Actor: John Lithgow, *3rd
Rock from the Sun*
Best Comedy Actress: Helen Hunt, *Mad
About You*
Best Drama Actor: Dennis Franz,
NYPD Blue
Best Drama Actress: Edie Falco, *The
Sopranos*
1999–2000
Best Comedy: *Will & Grace*

Best Drama: *The West Wing*
Best Comedy Actor: Michael J. Fox, *Spin
City*
Best Comedy Actress: Patricia Heaton,
Everybody Loves Raymond
Best Drama Actor: James Gandolfini,
The Sopranos
Best Drama Actress: Sela Ward, *Once
and Again*

⊙ Academy of Television Arts and Sciences. "Emmy Awards Index,"
www.emmys.tv/awards/index.htm

O'Neil, Thomas. *The Emmys: Star Wars, Showdowns, and the Supreme Test of TV's
Best.* New York: Penguin, 1992.

Antoinette Perry Awards (1947–2000)

*The Antoinette Perry Awards (the Tonys) were established by the American Theatre
Wing in 1947 for distinguished achievement in American theater produced on
Broadway. The award is named after Antoinette Perry (1888–1946), chairman of the
board and secretary of the American Theatre Wing. The categories have evolved greatly
over time, and categories are opened only if the Nomination Board considers there to be
sufficiently excellent nominees in a particular year; the following list of winners reflects
such anomalies.*

1947
Play: [no award]
Actor: (tie) José Ferrer, *Cyrano de
Bergerac*; Frederic March, *Years Ago*
Actress: (tie) Ingrid Bergman, *Joan of
Lorraine*; Helen Hayes, *Happy
Birthday*
Director: Eliza Kazan, *All My Sons*
Musical: [no award]
Actor: [no award]
Actress: [no award]
Director: [no award]
1948
Play: *Mister Roberts* (Thomas Heggen/
Joshua Logan)
Actor: (triple) Henry Fonda, *Mister
Roberts*; Paul Kelly, *Command
Decision*; Basil Rathbone, *The Heiress*
Actress: (triple) Judith Anderson,
Medea; Katharine Cornell, *Antony
and Cleopatra*; Jessica Tandy,
A Streetcar Named Desire
Director: [no award]
Musical: [no award]
Actor: Paul Hartman, *Angel in
the Wings*
Actress: Grace Hartman, *Angel in
the Wings*
Director: [no award]

1949
Play: *Death of a Salesman* (Arthur
Miller)
Actor: Rex Harrison, *Anne of
the Thousand Days*
Actress: Martita Hunt, *The Madwoman
of Chaillot*
Director: Elia Kazan, *Death of
a Salesman*
Musical: *Kiss Me, Kate* (Bella and
Samuel Spewack/Cole Porter)
Actor: Ray Bolger, *Where's Charley?*
Actress: Nanette Fabray, *Love Life*
Director: [no award]
1950
Play: *The Cocktail Party* (T. S. Eliot)
Actor: Sidney Blackmer, *Come Back,
Little Sheba*
Actress: Shirley Booth, *Come Back, Little
Sheba*
Featured/Supporting Actor: [no award]
Featured/Supporting Actress:
[no award]
Director: [no award]
Musical: *South Pacific* (Joshua Logan,
Oscar Hammerstein II, Richard
Rodgers)
Actor: Ezio Pinza, *South Pacific*

1950 (cont.)

Actress: Mary Martin, *South Pacific*

Director: Joshua Logan, *South Pacific*

1951

Play: The Rose Tattoo (Tennessee Williams)

Actor: Claude Rains, *Darkness at Noon*

Actress: Uta Hagen, *The Country Girl*

Director: [no award]

Musical: Guys and Dolls (Jo Swerling/ Abe Burrows/Frank Loesser)

Actor: Robert Alda, *Guys and Dolls*

Actress: Ethel Merman, *Call Me Madam*

Director: George S. Kaufman, *Guys and Dolls*

1952

Play: The Fourposter (Jan de Hartog)

Actor: José Ferrer, *The Shrike*

Actress: Julie Harris, *I Am a Camera*

Director: [triple] José Ferrer, *The Shrike/ The Fourposter/Stalag 17*

Musical: The King and I (Oscar Hammerstein II/Richard Rodgers)

Actor: Phil Silvers, *Top Banana*

Actress: Gertrude Lawrence, *The King and I*

Director: [no award]

1953

Play: The Crucible (Arthur Miller)

Actor: Tom Ewell, *The Seven Year Itch*

Actress: Shirley Booth, *The Time of the Cuckoo*

Director: Joshua Logan, *Picnic*

Musical: Wonderful Town (Joseph Fields/Jerome Chodorov/Betty Comden/Adolph Green/Leonard Bernstein)

Actor: Thomas Mitchell, *Hazel Flagg*

Actress: Rosalind Russell, *Wonderful Town*

Director: [no award]

1954

Play: The Teahouse of the August Moon (John Patrick)

Actor: David Wayne, *The Teahouse of the August Moon*

Actress: Audrey Hepburn, *Ondine*

Director: Alfred Lunt, *Ondine*

Musical: Kismet (Charles Lederer/ Luther Davis/Robert Wright/ George Forrest/Alexander Borodin)

Actor: Alfred Drake, *Kismet*

Actress: Dolores Gray, *Carnival in Flanders*

Director: [no award]

1955

Play: The Desperate Hours (Joseph Hayes)

Actor: Alfred Lunt, *Quadrille*

Actress: Nancy Kelly, *The Bad Seed*

Director: Robert Montgomery, *The Desperate Hours*

Musical: The Pajama Game (George Abbott/Richard Bissell/Richard Adler/Jerry Ross)

Actor: Walter Slezak, *Fanny*

Actress: Mary Martin, *Peter Pan*

Director: [no award]

1956

Play: The Diary of Anne Frank (Frances Goodrich/Albert Hackett)

Actor: Paul Muni, *Inherit the Wind*

Actress: Julie Harris, *The Lark*

Director: Tyrone Guthrie, *The Matchmaker*

Musical: Damn Yankees (George Abbott/Douglass Wallop/ Richard Adler/Jerry Ross)

Actor: Ray Walston, *Damn Yankees*

Actress: Gwen Verdon, *Damn Yankees*

Director: [no award]

1957

Play: Long Day's Journey into Night (Eugene O'Neill)

Actor: Frederic March, *Long Day's Journey into Night*

Actress: Margaret Leighton, *Separate Tables*

Director: [no award]

Musical: My Fair Lady (Alan Jay Lerner/Frederick Loewe)

Actor: Rex Harrison, *My Fair Lady*

Actress: Judy Holliday, *Bells Are Ringing*

Director: Moss Hart, *My Fair Lady*

1958

Play: Sunrise At Campobello (Dore Schary)

Actor: Ralph Bellamy, *Sunrise At Campobello*

Actress: Helen Hayes, *Time Remembered*

Director: Vincent J. Donehue, *Sunrise At Campobello*

Musical: The Music Man (Meredith Wilson)

Actor: Robert Preston, *The Music Man*
Actress: (tie) Thelma Ritter, *New Girl in Town*; Gwen Verdon, *New Girl in Town*
Director: [no award]

1959

Play: J.B. (Archibald MacLeish)
Actor: Jason Robards, Jr., *The Disenchanted*
Actress: Gertrude Berg, *A Majority of One*
Director: Elia Kazan, *J.B.*
Musical: Redhead (Herbert and Dorothy Fields/Sidney Sheldon/David Shaw/Albert Hague)
Actor: Richard Kiley, *Redhead*
Actress: Gwen Verdon, *Redhead*
Director: [no award]

1960

Play: The Miracle Worker (William Gibson)
Actor: Melvyn Douglas, *The Best Man*
Actress: Anne Bancroft, *The Miracle Worker*
Director: Arthur Penn, *The Miracle Worker*
Musical: (tie) Fiorello! (Jerome Weidman/George Abbott/Sheldon Harnick/Jerry Bock); *The Sound of Music* (Howard Lindsay/Russel Crouse/Oscar Hammerstein II/Richard Rodgers)
Actor: Jackie Gleason, *Take Me Along*
Actress: Mary Martin, *The Sound of Music*
Director: George Abbott, *Fiorello!*

1961

Play: Becket (Jean Anouilh)
Actor: Zero Mostel, *Rhinoceros*
Actress: Joan Plowright, *A Taste of Honey*
Director: Sir John Gielgud, *Big Fish, Little Fish*
Musical: Bye, Bye Birdie (Michael Stewart/Lee Adams/Charles Strouse)
Actor: Richard Burton, *Camelot*
Actress: Elizabeth Seal, *Irma La Douce*
Director: Gower Champion, *Bye, Bye Birdie*

1962

Play: A Man for All Seasons (Robert Bolt)
Actor: Paul Scofield, *A Man for All Seasons*

Actress: Margaret Leighton, *The Night of the Iguana*
Director: Noel Williams, *A Man for All Seasons*
Musical: How to Succeed in Business Without Really Trying (Abe Burrows/Jack Weinstock/Willie Gilbert/Frank Loesser)
Actor: Robert Morse, *How to Succeed in Business Without Really Trying*
Actress: (tie) Anna Maria Alberghetti, *Carnival*; Diahann Carroll, *No Strings*
Director: Abe Burrows, *How to Succeed in Business Without Really Trying*

1963

Play: Who's Afraid of Virginia Woolf? (Edward Albee)
Actor: Arthur Hill, *Who's Afraid of Virginia Woolf?*
Actress: Uta Hagen, *Who's Afraid of Virginia Woolf?*
Director: Alan Schneider, *Who's Afraid of Virginia Woolf?*
Musical: A Funny Thing Happened on the Way to the Forum (Burt Shevelove/Larry Gelbart/Stephen Sondheim)
Actor: Zero Mostel, *A Funny Thing Happened on the Way to the Forum*
Actress: Vivien Leigh, *Tovarich*
Director: George Abbott, *A Funny Thing Happened on the Way to the Forum*

1964

Play: Luther (John Osborne)
Actor: Alec Guiness, *Dylan*
Actress: Sandy Dennis, *Any Wednesday*
Director: Mike Nichols, *Barefoot in the Park*
Musical: Hello, Dolly! (Michael Stewart/Jerry Herman)
Actor: Bert Lahr, *Foxy*
Actress: Carol Channing, *Hello, Dolly!*
Director: Gower Champion, *Hello, Dolly!*

1965

Play: The Subject Was Roses (Frank Gilroy)
Actor: Walter Matthau, *The Odd Couple*
Actress: Irene Worth, *Tiny Alice*
Director: Mike Nichols, *Luv and The Odd Couple*

1965 (cont.)

Musical: Fiddler on the Roof (Joseph Stein/Sheldon Harnick/Jerry Bock)

Actor: Zero Mostel, *Fiddler on the Roof*

Actress: Liza Minnelli, *Flora, the Red Menace*

Director: Jerome Robbins, *Fiddler on the Roof*

1966

Play: Marat/Sade (Peter Weiss)

Actor: Hal Holbrook, *Mark Twain Tonight!*

Actress: Rosemary Harris, *The Lion in Winter*

Director: Peter Brook, *Marat/Sade*

Musical: Man of LaMancha (Dale Wasserman/Joe Darion/Mitch Leigh)

Actor: Richard Kiley, *Man of LaMancha*

Actress: Angela Lansbury, *Mame*

Director: Albert Marre, *Man of LaMancha*

1967

Play: The Homecoming (Harold Pinter)

Actor: Paul Rogers, *The Homecoming*

Actress: Beryl Reid, *The Killing of Sister George*

Director: Peter Hall, *The Homecoming*

Musical: Cabaret (Joe Masteroff/Fred Ebb/John Kander)

Actor: Robert Preston, *I Do! I Do!*

Actress: Barbara Harris, *The Apple Tree*

Director: Harold Prince, *Cabaret*

1968

Play: Rosencrantz and Guildenstern Are Dead (Tom Stoppard)

Actor: Martin Balsam, *You Know I Can't Hear You When the Water's Running*

Actress: Zoe Caldwell, *The Prime of Miss Jean Brodie*

Director: Mike Nichols, *Plaza Suite*

Musical: Hallelujah, Baby! (Arthur Laurents, Betty Comden/Adolph Green/Jule Styne)

Actor: Robert Goulet, *The Happy Time*

Actress: (tie) Patricia Routledge, *Darling of the Day*; Leslie Uggams, *Hallelujah, Baby!*

Director: Gower Champion, *The Happy Time*

1969

Play: The Great White Hope (Howard Sackler)

Actor: James Earl Jones, *The Great White Hope*

Actress: Julie Harris, *Forty Carats*

Director: Peter Dews, *Hadrian VII*

Musical: 1776 (Peter Stone/Sherman Edwards)

Actor: Jerry Orbach, *Promises, Promises*

Actress: Angela Lansbury, *Dear World*

Director: Peter Hunt, *1776*

1970

Play: Borstal Boy (Frank McMahon)

Actor: Fritz Weaver, *Child's Play*

Actress: Tammy Grimes, *Private Lives*

Director: Joseph Hardy, *Child's Play*

Musical: Applause (Betty Comden/Adolph Green/Lee Adams/Charles Strouse)

Actor: Cleavon Little, *Purlie*

Actress: Lauren Bacall, *Applause*

Director: Ron Field, *Applause*

1971

Play: Sleuth (Anthony Shaffer)

Actor: Brian Bedford, *The School for Wives*

Actress: Maureen Stapleton, *The Gingerbread Lady*

Director: Peter Brook, *A Midsummer's Night Dream*

Musical: Company (George Furth/Stephen Sondheim)

Actor: Hal Linden, *The Rothschilds*

Actress: Helen Gallagher, *No, No, Nanette* [revival]

Director: Harold Prince, *Company*

1972

Play: Sticks and Bones (David Rabe)

Actor: Cliff Gorman, *Lenny*

Actress: Sada Thompson, *Twigs*

Director: Mike Nichols, *The Prisoner of Second Avenue*

Musical: Two Gentlemen of Verona (John Guare/Mel Shapiro/Galt MacDermot)

Actor: Phil Silvers, *A Funny Thing Happened on the Way to the Forum*

Actress: Alexis Smith, *Follies*
Director: Harold Prince and Michael
Bennett, *Follies*

1973

Play: That Championship Season (Jason
Miller)
Actor: Alan Bates, *Butley*
Actress: Julie Harris, *The Last of Mrs.
Lincoln*
Director: A. J. Antoon, *That
Championship Season*
Musical: A Little Night Music (Hugh
Wheeler/Stephen Sondheim)
Actor: Ben Vereen, *Pippin*
Actress: Glynis Johns, *A Little Night
Music*
Director: Bob Fosse, *Pippin*

1974

Play: The River Niger (Joseph A. Walker)
Actor: Michael Moriarty, *Find Your
Way Home*
Actress: Colleen Dewhurst, *A Moon for
the Misbegotten*
Director: José Quintero, *A Moon for
the Misbegotten*
Musical: Raisin (Robert Nemiroff/
Charlotte Zaltzberg/Robert Brittan/
Judd Woldin)
Actor: Christopher Plummer, *Cyrano*
Actress: Virgina Capers, *Raisin*
Director: Harold Prince, *Candide*

1975

Play: Equus (Peter Shaffer)
Actor: John Kani and Winston
Ntshona, *Sizwe Banzi is Dead* and
The Island
Actress: Ellen Burstyn, *Same Time, Next
Year*
Director: John Dexter, *Equus*
Musical: The Wiz (William F. Brown/
Charlie Smalls)
Actor: John Cullum, *Shenandoah*
Actress: Angela Lansbury, *Gypsy*
Director: Geoffrey Holder, *The Wiz*

1976

Play: Travesties (Tom Stoppard)
Actor: John Wood, *Travesties*
Actress: Irene Worth, *Sweet Bird of
Youth*
Director: Ellis Rabb, *The Royal Family*
Musical: A Chorus Line (James
Kirkwood/Nicholas Dante/Edward
Kleban/Marvin Hamlisch)

Actor: George Rose, *My Fair Lady*
Actress: Donna McKechnie, *A Chorus
Line*
Director: Michael Bennett, *A Chorus
Line*

1977

Play: The Shadow Box (Michael
Cristofer)
Actor: Al Pacino, *The Basic Training of
Pavlo Hummel*
Actress: Julie Harris, *The Belle of
Amherst*
Director: Gordon Davidson,
The Shadow Box
Musical: Annie (Thomas Meehan/
Martin Charnin/Charles Strouse)
Actor: Barry Bostwick, *The Robber
Bridegroom*
Actress: Dorothy Loudon, *Annie*
Director: Gene Saks, *I Love My Wife*

1978

Play: Da (Hugh Leonard)
Actor: Barnard Hughes, *Da*
Actress: Jessica Tandy, *The Gin Game*
Director: Melvin Bernhardt, *Da*
Musical: Ain't Misbehavin' (Songs by
"Fats" Waller)
Actor: John Cullum, *On the Twentieth
Century*
Actress: Liza Minnelli, *The Act*
Director: Richard Maltby, Jr., *Ain't
Misbehavin'*

1979

Play: The Elephant Man (Bernard
Pomerance)
Actor: Tom Conti, *Whose Life Is It
Anyway?*
Actress: (tie) Constance Cummings,
Wings; Carole Shelley, *The Elephant
Man*
Director: Jack Hofsiss, *The Elephant
Man*
*Musical: Sweeney Todd, The Demon
Barber of Fleet Street* (Hugh
Wheeler/Stephen Sondheim)
Actor: Len Cariou, *Sweeney Todd,
The Demon Barber of Fleet Street*
Actress: Angela Lansbury, *Sweeney
Todd, The Demon Barber of Fleet
Street*
Director: Harold Prince, *Sweeney Todd,
The Demon Barber of Fleet Street*

Antoinette Perry Awards (1947–2000) *(cont.)*

1970

Play: Children of a Lesser God (Mark Medoff)

Actor: John Rubinstein, *Children of a Lesser God*

Actress: Phyllis Frelich, *Children of a Lesser God*

Director: Vivian Matalon, *Morning's at Seven*

Musical: Evita (Tim Rice/Andrew Lloyd Webber)

Actor: Jim Dale, *Barnum*

Actress: Patti LuPone, *Evita*

Director: Harold Prince, *Evita*

1981

Play: Amadeus (Peter Shaffer)

Actor: Ian McKellen, *Amadeus*

Actress: Jane Lapotaire, *Piaf*

Director: Peter Hall, *Amadeus*

Musical: 42nd Street (Michael Stewart/Mark Bramble/Harry Warren/Al Dubin)

Actor: Kevin Kline, *The Pirates of Penzance*

Actress: Lauren Bacall, *Woman of the Year*

Director: Wilford Leach, *The Pirates of Penzance*

1982

Play: The Life and Adventures of Nicholas Nickleby (David Edgar)

Actor: Roger Rees, *The Life and Adventures of Nicholas Nickleby*

Actress: Zoe Caldwell, *Medea*

Director: Trevor Nunn and John Caird, *The Life and Adventures of Nicholas Nickleby*

Musical: Nine (Arthur Kopit/Maury Yeston)

Actor: Ben Harney, *Dreamgirls*

Actress: Jennifer Holliday, *Dreamgirls*

Director: Tommy Tune, *Nine*

1983

Play: Torch Song Trilogy (Harvey Fierstein)

Actor: Harvey Fierstein, *Torch Song Trilogy*

Actress: Jessica Tandy, *Foxfire*

Director: Gene Saks, *Brighton Beach Memoirs*

Musical: Cats (T. S. Eliot/Andrew Lloyd Webber)

Actor: Tommy Tune, *My One and Only*

Actress: Natalia Makarova, *On Your Toes*

Director: Trevor Nunn, *Cats*

1984

Play: The Real Thing (Tom Stoppard)

Actor: Jeremy Irons, *The Real Thing*

Actress: Glenn Close, *The Real Thing*

Musical: La Cage aux Folles (Harvey Fierstein/Jerry Herman)

Actor: George Hearn, *La Cage aux Folles*

Actress: Chita Rivera, *The Rink*

Director: Arthur Laurents, *La Cage aux Folles*

1985

Play: Biloxi Blues (Neil Simon)

Actor: Derek Jacobi, *Much Ado About Nothing*

Actress: Stockard Channing, *Joe Egg*

Director: Gene Saks, *Biloxi Blues*

Musical: Big River (William Hauptman/Roger Miller)

Actor: [no award]

Actress: [no award]

Director: Des McAnuff, *Big River*

1986

Play: I'm Not Rappaport (Herb Gardner)

Actor: Judd Hirsch, *I'm Not Rappaport*

Actress: Lily Tomlin, *The Search for Signs of Intelligent Life in the Universe*

Director: Jerry Zaks, *The House of Blue Leaves* [revival]

Musical: The Mystery of Edwin Drood (Rupert Holmes)

Actor: George Rose, *The Mystery of Edwin Drood*

Actress: Bernadette Peters, *Song & Dance*

Director: Wilford Leach, *The Mystery of Edwin Drood*

1987

Play: Fences (August Wilson)

Actor: James Earl Jones, *Fences*

Actress: Linda Lavin, *Broadway Bound*

Director: Lloyd Richards, *Fences*

Musical: *Les Misérables* (Alain
Boublil/Herbert Kretzmer/Claude-
Michel Schönberg)
Actor: Robert Lindsay, *Me and My Girl*
Actress: Maryann Plunkett, *Me and My Girl*
Director: Trevor Howard and John
Caird, *Les Misérables*

1988

Play: *M. Butterfly* (David Henry
Hwang)
Actor: Ron Silver, *Speed the Plow*
Actress: Joan Allen, *Burn This*
Director: John Dexter, *M. Butterfly*
Musical: *The Phantom of the Opera*
(Richard Stigloe/Charles Hart/
Andrew Lloyd Webber)
Actor: Michael Crawford, *The Phantom
of the Opera*
Actress: Joanna Gleason, *Into the
Woods*
Director: Harold Prince, *The Phantom
of the Opera*

1989

Play: *The Heidi Chronicles* (Wendy
Wasserstein)
Actor: Philip Bosco, *Lend Me a Tenor*
Actress: Pauline Collins, *Shirley
Valentine*
Director: Jerry Zaks, *Lend Me a Tenor*
Musical: *Jerome Robbins' Broadway*
Actor: Jason Alexander, *Jerome Robbins'
Broadway*
Actress: Ruth Brown, *Black and White*
Director: Jerome Robbins, *Jerome
Robbins' Broadway*

1990

Play: *The Grapes of Wrath* (Frank
Galati)
Actor: Robert Morse, *Tru*
Actress: Maggie Smith, *Lettice and
Lovage*
Director: Frank Galati, *The Grapes of
Wrath*
Musical: *City of Angels*, (Larry Gelbart/
David Zippel/Cy Coleman)
Actor: James Naughton, *City of
Angels*
Actress: Tyne Daly, *Gypsy*
Director: Tommy Tune, *Grand Hotel*

1991

Play: *Lost in Yonkers* (Neil Simon)

Actor: Nigel Hawthorne, *Shadowlands*
Actress: Mercedes Ruehl, *Lost in
Yonkers*
Director: Jerry Zaks, *Six Degrees of
Separation*
Musical: *The Will Rogers Follies* (Peter
Stone/Betty Comden/Adolph Green/
Cy Coleman)
Actor: Jonathan Pryce, *Miss Saigon*
Actress: Lea Salonga, *Miss Saigon*
Director: Tommy Tune, *The Will Rogers
Follies*

1992

Play: *Dancing at Lughnasa* (Brian
Friel)
Actor: Judd Hirsch, *Conversations with
My Father*
Actress: Glenn Close, *Death and
the Maiden*
Director: Patrick Mason, *Dancing at
Lughnasa*
Musical: *Crazy for You* (Ken Ludwig/
Ira and George Gershwin)
Actor: Gregory Hines, *Jelly's Last Jam*
Actress: Faith Prince, *Guys and Dolls*
Director: Jerry Zaks, *Guys and Dolls*

1993

Play: *Angels in America - Millennium
Approaches* (Tony Kushner)
Actor: Ron Liebman, *Angels in America
- Millennium Approaches*
Actress: Madeline Kahn, *The Sisters
Rosensweig*
Director: George C. Wolfe, *Angels in
America - Millennium Approaches*
Musical: *Kiss of the Spider Woman*
(Terrence McNally/Fred Ebb/John
Kander)
Actor: Brent Carver, *Kiss of the Spider
Woman*
Actress: Chita Rivera, *Kiss of the Spider
Woman*
Director: Des McAnuff, *The Who's
Tommy*

1994

Play: *Angels in America - Perestroika*
(Tony Kushner)
Actor: Stephen Spinella, *Angels in
America - Perestroika*
Actress: Diana Rigg, *Medea*
Director: Stephen Daldry, *An Inspector
Calls*

1994 (cont.)

Musical: Passion (James Lapine/
Stephen Sondheim)
Actor: Boyd Gaines, *She Loves Me*
Actress: Donna Murphy, *Passion*
Director: Nicholas Hytner, *Carousel*

1995

Play: Love! Valour! Compassion!
(Terrence McNally)
Actor: Ralph Fiennes, *Hamlet*
Actress: Cherry Jones, *The Heiress*
Director: Gerald Gutierrez, *The Heiress*
Musical: Sunset Boulevard (Christopher
Hampton/Don Black/Andrew Lloyd
Webber)
Actor: Matthew Broderick, *How to
Succeed in Business Without Really
Trying*
Actress: Glenn Close, *Sunset Boulevard*
Director: Harold Prince, *Show Boat*

1996

Play: Master Class (Terrence McNally)
Actor: George Grizzard, *A Delicate
Balance*
Actress: Zoe Caldwell, *Master Class*
Director: Gerald Gutierrez, *A Delicate
Balance*
Musical: Rent (Jonathan Larson)
Actor: Nathan Lane, *A Funny Thing
Happened on the Way to the Forum*
Actress: Donna Murphy, *The King
and I*
Director: George C. Wolfe, *Bring in Da
Noise, Bring in Da Funk*

1997

Play: The Last Night of Ballyhoo (Alfred
Uhry)
Actor: Christopher Plummer,
Barrymore
Actress: Janet McTeer, *A Doll's House*
Director: Anthony Page, *A Doll's
House*

Musical: Titanic (Peter Stone/Maury
Yeston)
Actor: James Naughton, *Chicago*
Actress: Bebe Neuwirth, *Chicago*
Director: Walter Bobbie, *Chicago*

1998

Play: Art (Yasmina Reza/trans.
Christopher Hampton)
Actor: Anthony LaPaglia, *A View from
the Bridge*
Actress: Marie Mullen, *The Beauty
Queen of Leenane*
Director: Garry Hynes, *The Beauty
Queen of Leenane*
Musical: The Lion King (Roger
Allers/Irene Mecchi/Tim Rice/Elton
John/Hans Zimmer)
Actor: Alan Cumming, *Cabaret*
Actress: Natasha Richardson, *Cabaret*
Director: Julie Taymor, *The Lion King*

1999

Play: Side Man
Actor: Brian Dennehey, *Death of a
Salesman*
Actress: Judi Dench, *Amy's View*
Director: Robert Falls, *Death of a
Salesman*
Musical: Fosse
Actor: Martin Short, *Little Me*
Actress: Bernadette Peters, *Annie Get
Your Gun*
Director: Matthew Bourne, *Swan Lake*

2000

Play: Copenhagen
Actor: Stephen Dillane, *The Real
Thing*
Actress: Jennifer Ehle, *The Real Thing*
Director: Michael Blakemore,
Copenhagen
Musical: Contact
Actor: Brian S. Mitchell, *Kiss Me, Kate*
Actress: Heather Headley, *Aida*
Director: Michael Blakemore, *Kiss Me,
Kate*

⊙ The American Theatre Wing's Tony Awards. "Official Website of the American
Theatre Wing's Tony Awards," www.tonys.org
Stevenson, Isabelle. *The Tony Award: A Complete Listing with a History of the
American Theatre Wing.* New York: Heinemann, 1994.

National Book Awards (1950–99)

The National Book Award is administered by the National Book Foundation and is considered one of the most prestigious American literary honors, rivaled only by the Pulitzer Prize. The prize was called the American Book Award from 1980 to 1986, then reverted back to its original name in 1987. Winners in each major category are listed below by year

1950

Fiction: *The Man With The Golden Arm*, by Nelson Algren

Nonfiction: *Ralph Waldo Emerson*, by Ralph L. Rusk

Poetry: *Paterson: Book III and Selected Poems*, by William Carlos Williams

1951

Fiction: *The Collected Stories of William Faulkner*, by William Faulkner

Nonfiction: *Herman Melville*, by Newton Arvin

Poetry: *The Auroras of Autumn*, by Wallace Stevens

1952

Fiction: *From Here to Eternity*, by James Jones

Nonfiction: *The Sea Around Us*, by Rachel Carson

Poetry: *Collected Poems*, by Marianne Moore

1953

Fiction: *Invisible Man*, by Ralph Ellison

Nonfiction: *The Course of an Empire*, by Bernard A. De Voto

Poetry: *Collected Poems, 1917–1952*, by Archibald MacLeish

1954

Fiction: *The Adventures of Augie March*, by Saul Bellow

Nonfiction: *The Stillness at Appomattox*, by Bruce Catton

Poetry: *Collected Poems*, by Conrad Aitken

1955

Fiction: *A Fable*, by William Faulkner

Nonfiction: *The Measure of Man*, by Joseph Wood Krutch

Poetry: *The Collected Poems of Wallace Stevens*, by Wallace Stevens

1956

Fiction: *Ten North Frederick*, by John O'Hara

Nonfiction: *An American in Italy*, by Herbert Kubly

Poetry: *The Shield of Achilles*, by W. H. Auden

1957

Fiction: *The Field of Vision*, by Wright Morris

Nonfiction: *Russia Leaves the War*, by George F. Kennan

Poetry: *Things of the World*, by Richard Wilbur

1958

Fiction: *The Wapshot Chronicle*, by John Cheever

Nonfiction: *The Lion and the Throne*, by Catherine Drinker Bowen

Poetry: *Promises: Poems, 1954–1956*, by Robert Penn Warren

1959

Fiction: *The Magic Barrel*, by Bernard Malamud

Nonfiction: *Mistress to an Age: A Life of Madame De Stael*, by J. Christopher Herold

Poetry: *Words for the Wind*, by Theodore Roethke

1960

Fiction: *Goodbye, Columbus*, by Philip Roth

Nonfiction: *James Joyce*, by Richard Ellmann

Poetry: *Life Studies*, by Robert Lowell

1961

Fiction: *The Waters of Kronos*, by Conrad Richter

Nonfiction: *The Rise and Fall of the Third Reich*, by William L. Shirer

Poetry: *The Woman at the Washington Zoo*, by Randall Jarrell

1962

Fiction: *The Moviegoer*, by Walker Percy

Nonfiction: *The City in History: Its Origins, its Transformations and its Prospects*, by Lewis Mumford

Poetry: *Poems*, by Alan Dugan

1963

Fiction: *Morte D'Urban*, by J. F. Powers

Nonfiction: *Henry James, Vol. II: The Conquest of London, Henry James, Vol. III: The Middle Years*, by Leon Edel

1963 (cont.)

Poetry: *Traveling Through the Dark*, by William Stafford

1964

Fiction: *The Centaur*, by John Updike

History and Biography: *The Rise of the West: A History of the Human Community*, by William H. McNeill

Poetry: *Selected Poems*, by John Crowe Ransom

1965

Fiction: *Herzog*, by Saul Bellow

History and Biography: *The Life of Lenin*, by Louis Fischer

Poetry: *The Far Field*, by Theodore Roethke

1966

Fiction: *The Collected Stories of Katherine Anne Porter*, by Katherine Anne Porter

History and Biography: *A Thousand Days*, by Arthur M. Schlesinger, Jr.

Poetry: *Buckdancer's Choice: Poems*, by James Dickey

1967

Fiction: *The Fixer*, by Bernard Malamud

History and Biography: *The Enlightenment, Vol. I: An Interpretation the Rise of Modern Paganism*, by Peter Gay

Poetry: *Nights and Days*, by James Merrill

1968

Fiction: *The Eighth Day*, by Thornton Wilder

History and Biography: *Memoirs: 1925–1950*, by George F. Kennan

Poetry: *The Light Around the Body*, by Robert Bly

1969

Fiction: *Steps*, by Jerzy Konsinski

History and Biography: *White over Black: American Attitudes Toward the Negro, 1550–1812*, Winthrop D. Jordan

Poetry: *His Toy, His Dream, His Rest*, by John Berryman

1970

Fiction: *Them*, by Joyce Carol Oates

History and Biography: *Huey Long*, by T. Harry Williams

Poetry: *The Complete Poems*, by Elizabeth Bishop

1971

Fiction: *Mr. Sammler's Planet*, by Saul Bellow

History and Biography: *Roosevelt: The Soldier of Freedom*, by James MacGregor Burns

Poetry: *To See, To Take*, by Mona Van Duyn

1972

Biography: *Eleanor and Franklin: The Story of Their Relationship, Based on Eleanor Roosevelt's Private Papers*, by Joseph P. Lash

Fiction: *The Complete Stories of Flannery O'Connor*, by Flannery O'Connor

History: *Ordeal of the Union, Vols. VII & VIII: The Organized War, 1863–1864 and The Organized War to Victory*, by Allan Nevins

Poetry: *Selected Poems Frank O'Hara— The Collected Poems of Frank O'Hara*, by Howard Moss

1973

Biography: *George Washington, Vol. IV: Anguish and Farewell, 1793–1799*, by James Thomas Flexner

Fiction: *Augustus*, by John Barth; *Chimera*, by John Williams

History: *The Children of Pride Isaiah Trunk—Judenrat*, by Robert Manson Myers

Poetry: *Collected Poems, 1951–1971*, by A. R. Ammons

1974

Biography: *Macaulay: The Shaping of the Historian* (also won History award), by John Clive; *Malcolm Lowry: A Biography*, by Douglas Day

Fiction: *Gravity's Rainbow*, by Thomas Pynchon; *A Crown of Feathers and Other Stories*, by Isaac Bashevis Singer

History: *The Shaping of the Historian*, by John Clive

Poetry: *The Fall of America: Poems of these States*, by Allen Ginsberg; *Driving into the Wreck: Poems 1971–1972*, by Adrienne Rich

1975
Biography: *The Life of Emily Dickinson*, by Richard B. Sewall
Fiction: *Dog Soldiers*, by Robert Stone; *The Hair of Harold Roux*, by Thomas Williams
History: *The Ordeal of Thomas Hutchinson*, by Bernard Bailyn
Poetry: *Presentation Piece*, by Marilyn Hacker

1976
Fiction: *Jr*, by William Gaddis
History and Biography: *The Problem of Slavery in the Age of Revolution, 1770–1823*, by David Brion Davis
Poetry: *Self-portrait in a Convex Mirror*, by John Ashbery

1977
Biography/Autobiography: *Norman Thomas: The Last Idealist*, by W. A. Swanberg
Fiction: *The Spectator Bird*, by Wallace Stegner
History: *World of Our Fathers*, by Irving Howe
Poetry: *Collected Poems, 1930–1976*, by Richard Eberhart

1978
Biography/Autobiography: *Samuel Johnson*, by W. Jackson Bate
Fiction: *Blood Ties*, by Mary Lee Settle
History: *The Path Between the Seas: The Creation of the Panama Canal 1870–1914*, by David McCullough
Poetry: *The Collected Poems of Howard Nemerov*, by Howard Nemerov

1979
Biography/Autobiography: *Robert Kennedy and His Times*, by Arthur M. Schlesinger, Jr.
Fiction: *Going After Cacciato*, by Tim O'Brien
History: *Intellectual Life in the Colonial South, 1585–1763*, by Richard Beale Davis
Poetry: *Mirabell: Book of Numbers*, by James Merrill

1980
Autobiography: *Lauren Bacall by Myself*, by Lauren Bacall

Biography: *The Rise of Theodore Roosevelt*, by Edmund Morris
Fiction: *Sophie's Choice*, by William Styron
History: *The White House Years*, by Henry A. Kissinger
Poetry: *Ashes*, by Philip Levine

1981
Autobiography/Biography: *Walt Whitman*, by Justin Kaplan
Fiction: *Plains Song*, by Wright Morris
History: *Christianity, Social Tolerance and Homosexuality*, by John Boswell
Poetry: *The Need to Hold Still*, by Lisel Mueller

1982
Autobiography/Biography: *Mornings on Horseback*, by David McCullough
Fiction: *Rabbit is Rich*, by John Updike
History: *People of the Sacred Mountain: A History of the Northern Cheyenne Chiefs and Warrior Societies, 1830–1879*, by Father Peter John Powell
Poetry: *Life Supports: New and Collected Poems*, by William Bronk

1983
Autobiography/Biography: *Isak Dinesen: The Life of a Storyteller*, by Judith Thurman
Fiction: *The Color Purple*, by Alice Walker
History: *Voices of Protest: Huey Long, Father Coughlin and the Great Depression*, by Alan Brinkley
Poetry: *Selected Poems*, by Galway Kinnell

1984
Fiction: *Victory over Japan: A Book of Stories*, by Ellen Gilchrist
Nonfiction: *Andrew Jackson & the Course of American Democracy, 1833–1845*, by Robert V. Remini
Poetry: [no award]

1985
Fiction: *White Noise*, by Don DeLillo
Nonfiction: *Common Ground: A Turbulent Decade in the Lives of Three American Families*, by J. Anthony Lukas
Poetry: [no award]

1986

Fiction: World's Fair, by E. L. Doctorow

Nonfiction: Arctic Dreams, by Barry Lopez

Poetry: [no award]

1987

Fiction: Paco's Story, by Larry Heinemann

Nonfiction: The Making of the Atom Bomb, by Richard Rhodes

Poetry: [no award]

1988

Fiction: Paris Trout, by Pete Dexter

Nonfiction: A Bright Shining Lie: John Paul Vann and America in Vietnam, by Neil Sheehan

Poetry: [no award]

1989

Fiction: Spartina, by John Casey

Nonfiction: From Beirut to Jerusalem, by Thomas L. Friedman

Poetry: [no award]

1990

Fiction: Middle Passage, by Charles Johnson

Nonfiction: The House of Morgan: An American Banking Dynasty and the Rise of Modern Finance, by Ron Chernow

Poetry: [no award]

1991

Fiction: Mating, by Norman Rush

Nonfiction: Freedom, by Orlando Patterson

Poetry: What Work Is, by Philip Levine

1992

Fiction: All the Pretty Horses, by Cormac McCarthy

Nonfiction: Becoming a Man: Half a Life Story, by Paul Monette

Poetry: New & Selected Poems, by Mary Oliver

1993

Fiction: The Shipping News, by E. Annie Proulx

NON-Fiction: United States: Essays 1952–1992, by Gore Vidal

Poetry: Garbage, by A. R. Ammons

1994

Fiction: A Frolic of His Own, by William Gaddis

Nonfiction: How We Die: Reflections on Life's Final Chapter, by Sherwin B. Nuland

Poetry: A Worshipful Company of Fletchers, by James Tate

1995

Fiction: Sabbath's Theater, by Philip Roth

Nonfiction: The Haunted Land: Facing Europe's Ghosts After Communism, by Tina Rosenberg

Poetry: Passing Through: The Later Poems, by Stanley Kunitz

1996

Fiction: Ship Fever and Other Stories, by Andrea Barrett

Nonfiction: An American Requiem: God, My Father, and the War that Came Between Us, by James Carroll

Poetry: Scrambled Eggs & Whiskey, by Hayden Carruth

1997

Fiction: Cold Mountain, by Charles Frazier

Nonfiction: American Sphinx: The Character of Thomas Jefferson, by Joseph J. Ellis

Poetry: Effort at Speech: New & Selected Poems, by William Meredith

1998

Fiction: Charming Billy, by Alice McDermott

Nonfiction: Slaves in the Family, by Edward Ball

Poetry: This Time: New and Selected Poems, by Gerald Stern

1999

Fiction: Waiting, by Ha Jin

Nonfiction: Embracing Defeat: Japan in the Wake of WWII, by John W. Dower

Poetry: Vice: New and Selected Poems, by Ai (née Florence Anthony)

⊙ National Book Foundation. *The National Book Awards: 48 Years of Literary Excellence, Winners and Finalists, 1950–1997.* New York: National Book Foundation, 1998. National Book Foundation. "The National Book Foundation Homepage," www.publishersweekly.com/NBF/docs/nbf.html

PRIZES AND AWARDS

Newbery Medal (1922–2000)

The Newbery Medal was established in 1922 for excellence in American children's books. The award is named after English publisher John Newbery (1713–1767), a pioneer in the field of children's books.

Year	Author/Title
1922	Hendrik Willem van Loon, *The Story of Mankind*
1923	Hugh Lofting, *The Voyages of Doctor Dolittle*
1924	Charles Hawes, *The Dark Frigate*
1925	Charles Finger, *Tales from Silver Lands*
1926	Arthur Bowie Chrisman, *Shen of the Sea*
1927	Will James, *Smoky, the Cowhorse*
1928	Dhan Gopal Mukerji, *Gay Neck, the Story of a Pigeon*
1929	Eric P. Kelly, *The Trumpeter of Krakow*
1930	Rachel Field, *Hitty, Her First Hundred Years*
1931	Elizabeth Coatsworth, *The Cat Who Went to Heaven*
1932	Laura Adams Armer, *Waterless Mountain*
1933	Elizabeth Lewis, *Young Fu of the Upper Yangtze*
1934	Cornelia Meigs, *Invincible Louisa: The Story of the Author of Little Women*
1935	Monica Shannon, *Dobry*
1936	Carol Ryrie Brink, *Caddie Woodlawn*
1937	Ruth Sawyer, *Roller Skates*
1938	Kate Seredy, *The White Stag*
1939	Elizabeth Enright, *Thimble Summer*
1940	James Daughtery, *Daniel Boone*
1941	Armstrong Sperry, *Call It Courage*
1942	Walter Edmonds, *The Matchlock Gun*
1943	Elizabeth Janet Gray, *Adam of the Road*
1944	Esther Forbes, *Johnny Tremaine*
1945	Robert Lawson, *Rabbit Hill*
1946	Lois Lenski, *Strawberry Girl*
1947	Carolyn Sherwin Bailey, *Miss Hickory*
1948	William Pène de Bois, *The Twenty-One Balloons*
1949	Marguerite Henry, *King of the Wind*
1950	Marguerite de Angeli, *The Door in the Wall*
1951	Elizabeth Yates, *Amos Fortune, Free Man*
1952	Eleanor Estes, *Ginger Pye*
1953	Ann Nolan Clark, *Secret of the Andes*
1954	Joseph Krumgold, *And Now Miguel*
1955	Meindert DeJong, *The Wheel on the School*
1956	Jean Lee Latham, *Carry On, Mr. Bowditch*
1957	Virginia Sorenson, *Miracles on Maple Hill*
1958	Harold Keith, *Rifles for Watie*
1959	Elizabeth George Speare, *The Witch of Blackbird Pond*
1960	Joseph Krumgold, *Onion John*
1961	Scott O'Dell, *Island of the Blue Dolphins*
1962	Elizabeth George Speare, *The Bronze Bow*
1963	Madeleine L'Engle, *A Wrinkle in Time*
1964	Emily Neville, *It's Like This, Cat*
1965	Maia Wojciechowska, *Shadow of a Bull*
1966	Elizabeth Borton de Trevino, *I, Juan de Pareja*
1967	Irene Hunt, *Up a Road Slowly*
1968	E. L. Konigsburg, *From the Mixed-Up Files of Mrs. Basil E. Frankweiler*
1969	Lloyd Alexander, *The High King*
1970	William H. Armstrong, *Sounder*

Year	Author/Title
1971	Betsy Byars, *Summer of the Swans*
1972	Robert C. O'Brien, *Mrs. Frisby and the Rats of NIMH*
1973	Jean Craighead George, *Julie of the Wolves*,
1974	Paula Fox, *The Slave Dancer*
1975	Virginia Hamilton, *M. C. Higgins, the Great*
1976	Susan Cooper, *The Grey King*
1977	Mildred D. Taylor, *Roll of Thunder, Hear My Cry*
1978	Katherine Paterson, *Bridge to Terabithia*
1979	Ellen Raskin, *The Westing Game*
1980	Joan W. Blos, *A Gathering of Days: A New England Girl's Journal, 1830–1832*
1981	Katherine Paterson, *Jacob I Have Loved*
1982	Nancy Willard, *A Visit to Blake's Inn: Poems for Innocent and Experienced Travelers*
1983	Cynthia Voigt, *Dicey's Song*
1984	Beverly Cleary, *Dear Mr. Henshaw*
1985	Robin McKinley, *The Hero and the Crown*
1986	Patricia MacLachlan, *Sarah, Plain and Tall*
1987	Sid Fleischman, *The Whipping Boy*
1988	Russell Freedman, *Lincoln: A Photobiography*
1989	Paul Fleischman, *Joyful Noise: Poems for Two Voices*
1990	Lois Lowry, *Number the Stars*
1991	Jerry Spinelli, *Maniac Magee*
1992	Phyllis Reynolds Naylor, *Shiloh*
1993	Cynthia Rylant, *Missing May*
1994	Lois Lowry, *The Giver*
1995	Sharon Creech, *Walk Two Moons*
1996	Karen Cushman, *The Midwife's Apprentice*
1997	E. L. Konigsburg, *The View from Saturday*
1998	Karen Hesse, *Out of the Dust*
1999	Louis Sachar, *Holes*
2000	Christopher Paul Curtis, *Bud, Not Buddy*

⊙ American Library Association. "The Newbery Medal Homepage," www.ala.org/alsc/newbery.html

American Library Association. *The Newbery and Caldecott Awards: A Guide to the Medal and Honor Books.* Chicago: American Library Association, 1999.

Caldecott Medal (1938–2000)

The Caldecott Medal was established in 1938 by Frederic G. Melcher, chairman of the R. R. Bowker Publishing Company, for excellence in children's picture book illustrations. The medal is named after British illustrator Raymond Caldecott (1846–1886).

Year	Author/Title
1938	Helen Dean Fish (text); Dorothy P. Lathrop (illustrations), *Animals of the Bible, a Picture Book*
1939	Thomas Handforth, *Mei Li*
1940	Ingri and Edgar Parin d'Aulaire, *Abraham Lincoln*
1941	Robert Lawson, *They Were Strong and Good*
1942	Robert McCloskey, *Make Way for Ducklings*
1943	Virginia Lee Burton, *The Little House*
1944	James Thurber (text); Louis Slobodkin (illustrations), *Many Moons*

1945	Rachel Field (text); Elizabeth Orton Jones (illustrations), *Prayer for a Child*
1946	Maude and Miska Petersham, *The Rooster Crows*
1947	Golden MacDonald, pseud. [Margaret Wise Brown] (text); Leonard Weisgard (illustrations), *The Little Island*
1948	Alvin Tresselt (text); Roger Duvoisin (illustrations), *White Snow, Bright Snow*
1949	Berta and Elmer Hader, *The Big Snow*
1950	Leo Politi, *Song of the Swallows*
1951	Katherine Milhous, *The Egg Tree*
1952	Will, pseud. [William Lipkind] (text); Nicolas, pseud. [Nicholas Mordvinoff] (illustrations), *Finders Keepers*
1953	Lynd Ward, *The Biggest Bear*
1954	Ludwig Bemelmans, *Madeline's Rescue*
1955	Marcia Brown, *Cinderella, or the Little Glass Slipper*
1956	John Langstaff (text); Feodor Rojankovsky (illustrations), *Frog Went A-Courtin'*
1957	Janice Udry (text); Marc Simont (illustrations), *A Tree is Nice*
1958	Robert McCloskey, *Time of Wonder*
1959	Barbara Cooney, *Chanticleer and the Fox*
1960	Marie Hall Ets and Aurora Labastida (text); Marie Hall Ets (illustrations), *Nine Days to Christmas*
1961	Ruth Robbins (text); Nicholas Sidjakov (illustrations), *Baboushka and the Three Kings*
1962	Marcia Brown, *Once a Mouse*
1963	Ezra Jack Keats, *The Snowy Day*
1964	Maurice Sendak, *Where the Wild Things Are*
1965	Beatrice Schenk de Regniers (text); Beni Montresor (illustrations), *May I Bring a Friend?*
1966	Sorche Nic Leodhas, pseud. [Leclair Alger] (text); Nonny Hogrogian (illustrations), *Always Room for One More*
1967	Evaline Ness, *Sam, Bangs & Moonshine*
1968	Barbara Emberley (text); Ed Emberley (illustrations), *Drummer Hoff*
1969	Arthur Ransome (text); Uri Shulevitz (illustrations), *The Fool of the World and the Flying Ship*
1970	William Steig, *Sylvester and the Magic Pebble*
1971	Gail E. Haley, *a Story a Story*
1972	Nonny Hogrogian, *One Fine Day*
1973	Arlene Mosel (text); Blair Lent (illustrations), *The Funny Little Woman*
1974	Harve Zemach (text); Margot Zemach (illustrations), *Duffy and the Devil*
1975	Gerald McDermott, *Arrow to the Sun*
1976	Verna Aardema (text); Leo and Diane Dillon (illustrations), *Why Mosquitoes Buzz in People's Ears*
1977	Margaret Musgrove (text); Leo and Diane Dillon (illustrations), *Ashanti to Zulu: African Traditions*
1978	Peter Spier, *Noah's Ark*
1979	Paul Goble, *The Girl Who Loved Wild Horses*
1980	Donald Hall (text); Barbara Cooney (illustrations), *Ox-Cart Man*
1981	Arnold Lobel, *Fables*
1982	Chris van Allsburg, *Jumanji*
1983	Blaise Cendrars (text); Marcia Brown (translation and illustrations), *Shadow*
1984	Alice and Martin Provensen, *The Glorious Flight: Across the Channel with Louis Bleriot*
1985	Margaret Hodges (text); Trina Schart Hyman (illustrations), *Saint George and the Dragon*
1986	Chris Van Allsburg, *The Polar Express*

Caldecott Medal (1938–2000) *(cont.)*

Year   Author/Title

1987	Arthur Yorinks (text); Richard Egielski (illustrations), *Hey, Al*
1988	Jane Yolen (text); John Schoenherr (illustrations), *Owl Moon*
1989	Karen Ackerman (text); Stephen Gammell (illustrations), *Song and Dance Man*
1990	Ed Young, *Lon Po Po: a Red-Riding Hood Story from China*
1991	David Macaulay, *Black and White*
1992	David Wiesner, *Tuesday*
1993	Emily Arnold McCully, *Mirette on the High Wire*
1994	Allen Say, *Grandfather's Journey*
1995	Eve Bunting (text); David Diaz (illustrations), *Smoky Night*
1996	Peggy Rathmann, *Officer Buckle and Gloria*
1997	David Wisniewski, *Golem*
1998	Paul O. Zelinsky, *Rapunzel*
1999	Jacqueline Briggs (text); Mary Azarian (illustrations), *Snowflake Bentley*
2000	Simms Tarback, *Joseph Had a Little Overcoat*

⊙ American Library Association. "The Caldecott Medal
   Homepage,"http://ala.org/alsc/caldecott.html
   American Library Association. *The Newbery and Caldecott Awards: A Guide to the Medal and Honor Books.* Chicago: American Library Association, 1999.

Spingarn Medal (1915–99)

The Spingarn Medal was established in 1914 by the National Association for the Advancement of Colored People (NAACP). The award was named for Joel Elias Spingarn (1875–1939), who was then chairman of the NAACP's board of directors. Gold medals are given each year to the African American who reaches the highest achievement in his or her field in the previous year or over a period of time.

Year   Recipient

1915	Ernest E. Just (1883–1941), cell biologist
1916	Charles Young (1864–1922), army officer
1917	Harry T. Burleigh (1866–1949), singer and composer
1918	William Stanley Braithwaite (1878–1962), writer and editor
1919	Archibald H. Grimké (1849–1930), activist and writer
1920	W. E. B. Du Bois (1868–1963), educator and writer
1921	Charles S. Gilpin (1878–1930), actor
1922	Mary B. Talbert (1886–1923), civil rights activist
1923	George Washington Carver (c.1864–1943), botanist
1924	Roland Hayes (1887–1977), singer
1925	James Weldon Johnson (1871–1938), writer and U.S. consul
1926	Carter G. Woodson (1875–1950), historian
1927	Anthony Overton (1865–1946), businessman, judge and newspaper publisher
1928	Charles W. Chesnutt (1858–1932), writer
1929	Mordecai Wyatt Johnson (1890–1976), educator
1930	Henry A. Hunt (1866–1938), educator
1931	Richard Berry Harrison (1864–1935), actor
1932	Robert Russa Moton (1867–1940), educator
1933	Max Yergan (1892–1975), activist and YMCA promoter
1934	William Taylor Burwell Williams (1869–1941), educator
1935	Mary McLeod Bethune (1875–1955), educator
1936	John Hope (1868–1936), educator

1937	Walter White (1893–1955), writer
1938	[no award]
1939	Marian Anderson (1902–1993), singer
1940	Louis T. Wright (1891–1952), civil rights administrator and physician
1941	Richard Wright (1908–1960), writer
1942	A. Philip Randolph (1889–1979), labor leader
1943	William H. Hastie (1904–1976), judge
1944	Charles Drew (1904–1950), physician
1945	Paul Robeson (1898–1976), singer and actor
1946	Thurgood Marshall (1908–1993), Supreme Court Justice
1947	Percy Julian (1899–1975), chemist
1948	Channing H. Tobias (1882–1961), civil rights activist and diplomat
1949	Ralph J. Bunche (1904–1971), diplomat
1950	Charles Hamilton Houston (1895–1950), lawyer
1951	Mabel Keaton Staupers (1890–1989), nurse
1952	Harry T. Moore (1905–1951), civil rights leader
1953	Paul R. Williams (1894–1980), architect
1954	Theodore K. Lawless (1892–1971), physician
1955	Carl Murphy (1889–1967), newspaper editor and publisher
1956	Jackie Robinson (1919–1972), baseball player
1957	Martin Luther King, Jr. (1929–1968), clergyman and reformer
1958	Daisy Bates (1922–), civil rights activist, and the Little Rock Nine (nine students)
1959	Duke Ellington (1899–1974), bandleader and composer
1960	Langston Hughes (1902–1967), writer
1961	Kenneth B. Clark (1914–), psychologist
1962	Robert C. Weaver (1907–), housing administrator and cabinet member
1963	Medgar Wiley Evers (1925–1963), civil rights leader
1964	Roy Wilkins (1901–1981), civil rights leader
1965	Leontyne Price (1927–), singer
1966	John H. Johnson (1918–), publisher
1967	Edward W. Brooke III (1919–), politician
1968	Sammy Davis, Jr. (1925–1990), entertainer
1969	Clarence M. Mitchell, Jr. (1911–1984), civil rights activist and labor secretary of the NAACP
1970	Jacob Lawrence (1917–), painter
1971	Leon Howard Sullivan (1922–), civil rights activist and clergyman
1972	Gordon Parks (1912–), writer and photographer
1973	Wilson C. Riles (1917–), administrator and educator
1974	Damon Keith (1922–), administrator, judge, and lawyer
1975	Hank Aaron (1934–), baseball player
1976	Alvin Ailey (1931–1989), dancer and choreographer
1977	Alexander Haley (1924–1992), writer
1978	Andrew Young, Jr. (1932–), civil rights activist, minister and public official
1979	Rosa L. Parks (1913–), civil rights activist
1980	Rayford W. Logan (1897–1982), historian
1981	Coleman Young (1918–), politician
1982	Benjamin Elijah Mays (1895–1984), clergyman and educator
1983	Lena Horne (1917–), singer
1984	Tom Bradley (1917–1998), politician
1985	Bill Cosby (1937–), actor
1986	Benjamin Hooks (1925–), judge, public official and civil rights reformer
1987	Percy Ellis Sutton (1920–), activist, lawyer and politician
1988	Frederick Douglass Patterson (1901–1988); educator and founder of the United Negro College Fund

Spingarn Medal (1915–99) *(cont.)*

Year	Recipient
1989	Jesse Jackson (1941–), clergyman, civil rights leader, and politician
1990	L. Douglas Wilder (1931–), lawyer and politician
1991	Colin Powell (1937–), general and politician
1992	Barbara Jordan (1936–1996), U.S. representative
1993	Dorothy L. Height (1912–), civil rights activist
1994	Maya Angelou (1928–), poet
1995	John Hope Franklin (1915–) historian
1996	A. Leon Higginbotham (1928–), judge
1997	Carl T. Rowan (1925–), journalist
1998	Myrlie Evers-Williams (1933–), civil rights activist, chairwoman of NAACP, 1995–1998
1999	Earl G. Graves, Sr. (1935–), Chairman and CEO of *Black Enterprise Magazine*

⊙ Douglass, Melvin I. *Black Winners: A History of Spingarn Medalists, 1915–1983.* New York: T. Gaus, 1984.
  Louisville Free Public Library. "The Spingarn Medal," www.lfpl.org/reference/rflksgarn.htm

Pritzker Architecture Prize (1979–2000)

The Pritzker Prize, an annual international award honoring architects whose work offers significant contributions to humanity and the built environment, is considered to be the most prestigious in architecture. It is sponsored by the Hyatt Foundation.

Year	Recipient
1979	Philip Johnson, U.S.
1980	Luis Barragán, Mexico
1981	James Stirling, U.K.
1982	Kevin Roche, U.S.
1983	Ieoh Ming (I. M.) Pei, U.S.
1984	Richard Meier, U.S.
1985	Hans Hollein, Austria
1986	Gottfried Boehm, Germany
1987	Kenzo Tange, Japan
1988	Gordon Bunshaft, U.S., and Oscar Neimeyer, Brazil
1989	Frank O. Gehry, U.S.
1990	Aldo Rossi, Italy
1991	Robert Venturi, U.S.
1992	Alvaro Siza, Portugal
1993	Fumihiko Maki, Japan
1994	Christian de Portzamparc, France
1995	Tadao Ando, Japan
1996	Rafael Moneo, Spain
1997	Sverre Fehn, Norway
1998	Renzo Piano, Italy
1999	Sir Norman Foster, U.K
2000	Rem Koolhaas, Netherlands

⊙ "The Pritzker Architecture Prize," www.pritzkerprize.com

WORK AND HOME: *Business and Labor*

Labor Unions: Ten Largest AFL-CIO Affiliates

The American Federation of Labor - Committee for Industrial Organization is the biggest labor organization in the United States. Formed in 1955 by the merger of the country's two largest groups of trade unions, it combines the resources of 68 specialized labor groups into a single lobbying force. The table below lists its largest constitutent members.

Name	Primary Membership	Members
International Brotherhood of Teamsters (IBT)	Freight, trucking, airline, and other workers	1.5 million
Service Employees International Union (SEIU)	Hospital, home care, nursing home, and public service workers	1.4 million
United Food and Commercial Workers International Union (UFCW)	Retail food, meatpacking, poultry, and food processing workers	1.4 million
American Federation of State, County, and Municipal Employees (AFSCME)	Health care and public employees	1.3 million
American Federation of Teachers (AFT)	Public elementary and high school teachers, other public employees	1 million
United Automobile, Aerospace and Agricultural Implement Workers of America (UAW)	Factory employees of car, plane, and equipment manufacturers	750,000
International Brotherhood of Electrical Workers (IBEW)	Electricians, utility workers, electric-sign makers, broadcast employees	750,000
Communications Workers of America (CWA)	Media and telecommunications workers	740,000
International Association of Machinists and Aerospace Workers (IAM)	Railroad, auto, airplane, and aerospace mechanics	450,000
United Steelworkers of America (USWA)	Steel-manufacturing employees	400,000

⊙ AFL-CIO. "Unions Affiliated with the AFL-CIO," www.aflcio.org/unionand/unions.htm

Mooney, Green, Gleason, Baker, Gibson & Saindon, P.C. "MGGBGS Labor Union Page," www.mggbgs.com/labor.html

U.S. Stock Markets

Exchange	Founded	Description
American Stock Exchange	1920	This is the world's second largest floor-based exchange. Its 661 regular members that may buy and sell on the floor.

U.S. Stock Markets *(cont.)*

Exchange	Founded	Description
Chicago Mercantile Exchange	1874	Futures and option contracts are traded. These include currencies, interest rates, stock indices, and agricultural futures.
National Association of Securities Dealers Automated Quotation (NASDAQ)	1971	The world's first electronic stock exchange, it was started as a U.S. government project to create the first truly global securities market. It deals mainly in technology and development.
New York Stock Exchange (NYSE)	1790	A not-for-profit organization run by a 25-member board. 1,366 seats are available to member firms for the privilege of buying and selling on the floor.

⊙ NYSE: New York Stock Exchange. www.nyse.com
  Chicago Mercantile Exchange. www.cme.com
  NASDAQ. www.nasdaq.com
  American Stock Exchange. www.amex.com

Consumer Advocacy Organizations

Name	Mission	Phone/Website	Founded
Foundation for Taxpayer and Consumer Rights	Alerts taxpayers to fraud and waste in government	www.consumerwatch dog.org/ftcr	1985
Alliance against Fraud in Marketing	Organization of many groups that research and report about fraud in telemarketing and on the Internet	(202) 835-3323	1988
National Consumer Law Center	Researches and advocates on the needs of low-income consumers	www.consumerlaw.org	1984
American Council on Science and Health	Studies and reports on issues related to food, nutrition, biotechnology, pesticides, and food safety	www.asch.org/about/ index.html	1978
Hudson Center for Global Food Issues	Researches and analyzes agricultural and environmental concerns and reports to the public; known for skepticism of conventional wisdom	www.hcgf/	1961
National Community Reinvestment Coalition	Works to end discriminatory banking practices and increase flow of private capital and credit to underserved communities	(202) 628-9800 www.youthlink.net/ nrc.org	1990

Quackwatch	Combats health-related frauds, myths, fads, and fallacies	www.quackwatch.com	1969
Consumer Reports	Tests products and informs consumers	www.consumer reports.org	1936
Center for Science in the Public Interest	Researches and advocates on issues of food, nutrition, food safety, and related issues	(202) 332-9110 www.cspinet.org/ more/cspi.htm	1971
Consumer Federation of America	Develops and distributes studies of various consumer issues	(202) 387-6121	1968
Citizen Action	Advocate for programs to enable consumers to enjoy a diet that is adequate, safe, and healthy	(202) 776-0595	1975

⊙ Federal Trade Commission. "Consumer Protection," www.ftc.gov/ftc/consumer.htm

WORK AND HOME: *Personal Finance*
Household Budgeting

Making and keeping a household budget is the first step toward financial security. By adhering to spending guidelines, an individual, couple, or family can realize financial goals and plan for retirement. The fundamental principle is simple: expenditures should not exceed income. The only way to maintain this ratio is to set income and spending parameters and stick to them.

Record keeping is the foundation upon which a budget is built. Learning to keep financial records in order will allow you to find the information you need to plan your finances. A file cabinet, envelopes, and some folders are all you need to get started. Make a separate file for each category of bills, for each bank account, and for tax-related receipts. Once the bills are sorted you will be able to figure out the average monthly cost of your utilities, telephone, insurance, etc.

If you are not currently using a budget, chances are you have only a vague idea how much you spend on day-to-day living: groceries, lunches out, movies, and morning coffee. Some people find it helpful to spend a few weeks tracking their cash expenditures in order to have a basis for building a budget. Although it can be tedious, this exercise will enable you to decide if the money that seems to disappear mysteriously from your wallet can be put to better use in another area of your life.

Monthly Income and Expense Worksheet

Type	Amount	Type	Amount
Income		**Fixed Expenses**	
Monthly Income 1		Rent / Mortgage	
Monthly Income 2		Insurance	
Interest/Investment Income		Automobile Loan	
Other (rental, additional job)		Student Loan	
		Daily Childcare	
Total Income		Cable TV / Internet Access	
		Debt Repayment (credit cards)	
		Other	
		Other	
		Total Fixed Expenses	

Household Budgeting *(cont.)*

Type	Amount	Type	Amount
Flexible Expenses		Clothing	
Groceries		Household/Home Repair	
Telephone		Savings	
Utilities		Vacations	
Gasoline		Other	
Entertainment		Other	
Additional Childcare		Other	
Medical / Dental		**Total Flexible Expenses**	
Health / Beauty		**Total Income/Expenses**	

⊙ Blue, Ron. *Master Your Money*. Nashville, Tenn.: Thomas Nelson, 1993.
  Burket, Larry. *The Financial Planning Workbook*. Chicago: Moody, 1991.

Personal Savings

Banks

A bank acts as a middleman between you and the institutions with which you exchange money: employers, service providers, and creditors. It also offers a safe place for storing your money and may let you use that money to earn interest. For basic banking services, however, expect to pay some fees.

Before walking into your local branch and handing over your money, it is a good idea to shop around for a bank that offers accounts tailored to your needs with the lowest fees possible. Unlimited checking is great for people who write a lot of checks, but there is no need to pay extra for a service you are not going to use. Many banks require a minimum balance in order to waive basic fees, but if you have a limited cash flow it is possible to find a bank without such a requirement.

Types of Bank Accounts
Checking accounts

Basic checking	No-frills account with minimal check writing privileges
Unlimited checking	Usually requires a minimum balance for fee waiver
Interest-bearing	With a high balance, interest is earned
Joint checking	Shared between more than one person
ATM / Express	Fees charged for using teller windows to encourage ATM usage
Student / Senior	Special accounts with discounted rates for students and seniors
Money Market	Interest-bearing account with high minimum balance and limited check writing privileges

Savings accounts

Passbook	Interest-bearing account that requires account holder to present a ledger for each transaction
Statement	Interest-bearing account that uses a regular statement, not a passbook, to record transactions
Certificate of Deposit (CD)	Account requiring a minimum amount of time deposited, usually a period of three or six months or more than one year

Stocks

A stock is a small portion of a company that can be bought and sold at a profit or loss. Stocks are publicly traded through an organization called an exchange; various exchanges specialize in specific groupings or types of companies. The exchange determines the value of each stock and rates each company according to its own criteria. Most financial exchanges can be found at InvestorLinks: www.investorlinks.com/exch.html.

Stocks earn money in two ways: through dividends and through capital gains. Dividends are a company's means of distributing profits to its stockholders. Capital gains are profits made when the stock is sold at a higher price than the price at which it was bought.

Stocks are bought and sold through brokers, who charge a fee for their service. Brokers are available through traditional brokerage houses, although a growing number of people are finding brokers online. Online brokers often charge lower fees and require smaller initial investments.

EDGAR, the Securities and Exchange Commission database, is an invaluable resource if you wish to find information on any public company in the U.S. To search the database, register for free as a visitor at www.edgar-online.com.

Types of stock

Income	Regular dividends provide income for shareholders
Growth	Profits are reinvested in the company and the stock experiences long-term growth in value
Cyclical	Prices rise and fall depending upon economic conditions
Defensive	Based in industries that produce necessities of daily life
Penny	Inexpensive shares from small companies
Blue chip	Stable shares from older, more established companies
Value	Low-priced stocks that are expected to rise

To track the performance of stock you have bought, you can read the stock tables in a financial newspaper. Here's what the abbreviations mean:

Stock Table Listings

52 Weeks Hi/Lo	Highest and lowest prices for the past 52 weeks measure volatility and risk
Stock	Name of company, abbreviated
Sym	Trading symbol assigned by the exchange
Div	Dividend anticipated per share
Yld %	Percentage of stock's price paid as dividend
PE	Ration of stock's price to annual earnings of company
Vol 100s	Volume of shares traded the day before, shown in hundreds
Hi-Lo-Close	Previous day's high, low, and closing price
Net Chg	Comparison between the day's closing price and that of the day before

Bonds

Bonds provide a means for a corporation or a government to raise money from the public. Buying bonds makes an individual a lender rather than a part owner. The value of a bond is not tied to the value of the company and the amount of profit is generally a fixed interest rate. For these reasons, bonds usually considered safer than stocks; however, high-risk bonds do exist and care should be taken when evaluating a given bond.

Personal Savings *(cont.)*

Types of bonds

U.S. Treasury Bonds

Treasury bills (T-bills)	Mature after 13, 26, or 52 weeks
Treasury notes (T-notes)	Mature after 2, 5, or 10 years
Treasury bonds (T-bonds)	Mature after 30 years

U.S. Savings Bonds

Series EE	Bought at half of face value; reach full value as interest is added to principal
Series I	Bought at face value; indexed for inflation
Series HH	Issued only in exchange for other bonds; interest is paid semiannually
Corporate Bonds	Higher-risk than government bonds because of potential default by company
Municipal Bonds	Issued by local government to pay for capital projects

Credit rating agencies evaluate the potential creditworthiness of bond issues. Standard & Poor's (212-438-2400 or www.standardandpoors.com/ratings/index.htm) and Moody's (212-552-1658 or www.moodys.com/ratings/ratdefs.htm#1ttaxable) are two of the best-known agencies. Bonds in the AAA, AA, or A categories are considered to be the safest investments. A rating of BB or lower carries a higher risk.

Mutual Funds

A mutual fund is a diversified investment group run by an investment company. The group pools resources and spreads risks, making it generally safer than individual stock trading. Like all kinds of investments, mutual funds carry some risk; a portfolio may not perform as well as predicted and individual members of the group can lose some of their money.

There are two different types of mutual fund. A *closed-end fund* performs more like a stock and is traded on an exchange. An *open-end fund* is the kind most often entered into by average investors.

Mutual funds usually require a smaller initial investment than an individual stock purchase. The earnings structure is similar to that of stocks; namely money is earned both through dividends and through capital gains as the fund sells its stock. In addition, if the securities within a mutual fund increase in value and you sell your shares, you will also realize a capital gain.

To obtain information on mutual funds, you can research them at your public library. Some reports are available online: Morningstar Mutual Funds (www.morningstar.com), Value Line Mutual Fund Survey (www.valueline.com), and Standard & Poor's (www.standardpoor.com). To evaluate the overall cost of investing in a particular mutual fund, the SEC offers an online Mutual Fund Cost Calculator: www.sec.gov/mfcc/mfcc-int.htm.

Before investing in a mutual fund, review the prospectus carefully. A prospectus will disclose the fund's objectives, policies, management team, costs, and performance. Some funds carry sales charges, or loads, and others are no-load funds. Once you invest in a fund, you can track its performance in a newspaper such as the *Wall Street Journal* according to the table below:

Mutual Fund Listings

Fund name	Company name first, followed by its funds
NAV	Net asset value (dollar value per share)
Net chg.	Change in NAV from previous day

Total return	Percentage of gain or loss on the fund, year to date
Inv Obj.	Investment objective of the fund
Max. Init chrg.	Sales charge fee (load)

Real Estate

An investment in real estate can earn you money in two ways: rental income and capital gains. See "Home Buying" for more information.

Insurance

Some forms of insurance are considered an investment in a family's future. Whole life insurance, in particular, can function in this way. In fact, whole life insurance is considered a "security" subject to federal securities laws and protections, and is sold by prospectus. See "Insurance" for more information.

Education IRAs

An education IRA allows you to contribute up to $500 each year for a child under age 18. Anyone (including the child) can make contributions to the account but these contributions are not tax deductible. Money taken out of the account, including any interest, is tax free as long as it is used to cover educational expenses: books, tuition, fees, supplies, and equipment for college. Room and board are also valid uses if the student is enrolled at least half-time.

The U.S. Department of Education offers online resources to help you plan for sending your children to college: www.ed.gov/thinkcollege/early/tce_home.htm.

⊙ Bryan, Mark, and Julia Cameron. *Money Drunk, Money Sober: 90 Days to Financial Freedom*. New York: Ballantine, 1999.

Morris, Kenneth M., and Virginia B. Morris. *The Wall Street Journal Guide to Understanding Money & Investing*. New York: Simon & Schuster, 1999.

Retirement Planning

IRA

The Individual Retirement Arrangement (IRA) is a special, tax deductible account designed to help individuals save for retirement. These accounts are available through banks, mutual funds, life insurance companies, and brokerage houses. The funds deposited can be invested in numerous ways in order to earn dividends. These earnings are not taxed until they are distributed; if this falls after retirement, your tax bracket is likely to be lower.

The maximum contribution allowed by law is $2,000 per year. Withdrawals are permitted after the age of 59 1/2 and are required by April 1 of the year after you reach age 70 1/2. Early withdrawals are subject to a penalty of 10% in addition to any regular income tax. Certain types of withdrawals are exempt from this penalty, including those made for higher education, unreimbursed medical expenses in excess of 7.5% of your adjusted gross income, in case of disability, or towards the purchase of a first home.

A special type of IRA, called a Roth IRA, allows for contributions to continue after the age of 70 1/2 and funds can be left in the account indefinitely. Individuals with an income of less than $95,000 and couples with an income of less than $150,000 are eligible.

Employers can set up an IRA for you in the form of a Simplified Employee Pension (SEP). An employer is not limited by the $2,000 annual limit; the maximum allowed is up to 15% of the employee's income up to $30,000.

Retirement Planning (cont.)

401(k), 403 (b)

A 401(k) plan allows an employee to contribute a percentage of gross income to an individual retirement account. This money is deducted before any taxes are paid, reducing your taxable income by up to 15%. Some employers match your contributions, in effect increasing your income while reducing your tax burden.

The plan is managed by the company and usually includes a variety of investment options from which you can choose. Whether you wish to invest in stocks, bonds, or a mutual fund is up to you and you can change the plan to suit your changing needs. Costs of managing the plan, including your own investments, are usually absorbed by the company.

If you leave a company before retirement, you will be able to keep some or all of the matching funds, depending upon the company's policy. To avoid penalties, you will have to roll the money over into an individual or company-sponsored IRA. Some companies will allow you to maintain your original investment account but you will not be able to contribute any additional funds. Upon retirement you can cash in the account without penalty.

A 403(b) plan is similar to a 401(k) plan, but it is offered by nonprofit organizations such as hospitals, schools, or social service agencies. In either type of plan, the maximum annual contribution is $9,500 or up to 15% of your income, whichever is less.

Social Security

Social Security is a government-sponsored retirement plan; contributions to Social Security are automatically deducted from the paychecks of every worker in the United States and deposited into a special fund.

Each year that you work, you earn credits toward your retirement based upon your income up to a maximum of 4 credits per year. To be eligible to receive benefits, you must be over the age of 65 and have earned more than 40 credits. If you continue working past age 65, you can still collect benefits, but only within certain income limits. After the age of 70 you can collect benefits with no income limits.

Keep in mind that the average monthly Social Security payment was $500 for an individual in 1999; while these benefits are helpful to retirees, they do not constitute a living wage. Other retirement plans are essential in order to live comfortably after the age of 65.

For more information about Social Security, contact the Social Security Administration: 800-772-1213 or www.ssa.gov.

⊙ Arnone, William J. *Ernst & Young's Retirement Planning Guide.* New York: Wiley, 2000.

    Holzer, Bambi, with Elaine Floyd. *Retire Rich: The Baby Boomer's Guide to a Secure Future.* New York: Wiley, 1998.

    Howells, John. *Retirement on a Shoestring.* Guilford, Conn: Globe Pequot, 2000.

    Rye, David E. *1,001 Ways to Save, Grow, and Invest Your Money.* Franklin Lakes, N.J.: Career Press, 1999.

Insurance

People buy insurance for a variety of reasons, but the most basic reason is protection against future crises. Health insurance can bring an added benefit of facilitating preventive health care. Some types of life insurance also function as a long-term investment. Insurance plans vary significantly, which means that you will need to do some research in order to determine the plan that will suit your needs while giving you the most value for your money.

Health Insurance

Of all kinds of insurance available, health insurance is the most fundamental to everyday life. Without health insurance, routine visits to the doctor are unaffordable for most Americans, let alone the cost of medications, x-rays, lab tests, and so on. Even if you are in good health, it pays to have at least some kind of catastrophic coverage in the event of an accident or sudden illness; one hospital stay can wipe out any assets you have and land you in serious debt.

If you are employed full-time, chances are your employer will offer some type of health insurance and will subsidize the cost. You may be offered several options, or you may have a more limited selection. Generally, employers offer a choice between two basic plan types: fee-for-service or managed care.

Under a *fee-for-service* plan you can go to any doctor you wish, but you will need to pay more out-of-pocket costs. *Managed care* requires you to choose a participating physician from a Health Maintenance Organization (HMO), at a significantly reduced cost. Covered benefits vary greatly from plan to plan and it is essential to review your membership packet carefully. Some services are covered only partially and require that you pay the first portion of expenses (called a deductible).

If you are self-employed you are still eligible for health insurance, but the cost to you is likely to be much greater than if you were under group coverage. In certain fields, professional associations offer group insurance rates to self-employed members.

Life Insurance

The primary reason to buy life insurance is to compensate for lost income to your dependents in the event of your death. There is no benefit to buying life insurance if you are single and have no children or other dependents. The best way to gauge the amount of insurance you need is to multiply your annual income by 10. Proceeds from the policy could be invested at a 10 percent return rate, effectively replacing your income.

Types of Life Insurance

Term	Covers only a specific period of time; usually has lower initial premiums; renewal often brings an increase in premium price
Whole life	More of a long-term investment; premiums are usually level and increase only incrementally
Universal life	Offers the most flexibility; after initial payment you can reduce or increase the amount of death benefit

Companies offering life insurance are rated by numerous organizations: A.M. Best (908-439-2200 or www.ambest.com, Durr & Phelps (312-368-3157 or www.dcro.com), Moody's Investors Service (212-553-0377 or www.moodys.com), and Standard & Poor's (212-438-2000 or www.standardandpoors.com/ratings).

Property Insurance

Anything you own can be insured, but the type of insurance you buy depends upon whether or not you own your home. *Homeowner's insurance* covers both the value of your home and your possessions in case of fire or natural disaster. The insurance should cover the cost of rebuilding your home, not just the value of your home on the real estate market (which might be significantly lower). Your personal belongings can be covered either at their actual cash value or at full replacement value. *Renter's insurance* covers personal belongings only (usually the landlord's insurance will cover the building itself) either for actual cash value or full replacement value.

⊙ Baldwin, Ben G. *The New Life Insurance Investment Advisor: Achieving Financial Security for You and Your Family Through Today's Insurance Product.* New York: McGraw-Hill, 1994.

Bruel, Brian. *The Complete Idiot's Guide to Buying Insurance and Annuities.* New York: Alpha Books, 1996.

Nader, Ralph, and Wesley J. Smith. *Winning the Insurance Game: The Complete Consumer's Guide to Saving Money.* New York: Doubleday, 1993.

Home Buying

Process

The first element to buying a home is figuring out what you can afford. Generally, the monthly cost of buying and maintaining your home should not exceed 28% of your gross monthly income. Once you calculate your maximum monthly payment, a loan officer or mortgage broker can help you figure out your target price range.

After you've found a home you wish to buy and have agreed upon a price you are willing to pay, you will need to make a written offer to the seller. The offer should be contingent upon a satisfactory inspection (see below) to safeguard against any hidden problems or costs. If the seller agrees, you automatically go into the contract phase of the process and your offer becomes legally binding. Do not make an offer to which you are not willing to commit.

While you should take some time to personally inspect the house, a professional inspector's services are well worth the $300–500 cost. The inspector should be able to detect any major repair work that will need to be done in the foreseeable future, which you may wish to include in the contract as part of your negotiating strategy.

The sales contract is a legally binding agreement between buyer and seller. It will include all pertinent information about the property (i.e., the address, inclusions and exclusions, selling price, mortgage and inspection contingencies, septic system, closing and possession dates).

When setting up your title, you will need to choose the title type that best suits your needs.

Title Types

Joint tenancy	Equal ownership of property; automatic right of succession should the co-owner die
Tenancy-in-common	Equal ownership of property; each party chooses own successor to inherit his/her portion
Community property	Equal right of possession for husband and wife; upon death of one, the other receives half and the rest passes to any other successors
Sole and separate property	No one else has any interest in property; if married, will need additional document to rule out community property interest

Bank Guidelines

Banks and other mortgage lenders will ask you for a great deal of financial information, including your

- Past two years' earned income
- Past two years' dividend / interest income

- Income from other sources (i.e. alimony, child support)
- Current balances and recent statements from checking and savings accounts
- Current market value of all investments, such as stocks, bonds, or mutual funds
- Investments in IRÁs or other retirement funds
- Face amount and cash value of life insurance policies
- Value of major property, including automobiles
- Current debt carried, including car loans, credit card balances, or student loans
- Obstacles to mortgage approval include an inadequate down payment; low appraisal value of the property; insufficient income; too many prior debts; and an unsatisfactory credit history. If any of these areas might cause you a problem, speak with your loan officer about them in advance.

Mortgage Types

Mortgages fall into two main categories: fixed-rate and variable-rate. A fixed-rate mortgage is designed for long-term ownership; if you plan to move in and stay there for most of the next 30 years, this is your best option. If you anticipate selling the house within a few years and are hoping to realize a capital gain, you may be able to obtain a variable-rate mortgage at a lower interest rate.

Comparison shopping for the best rate is definitely in order. Many banks advertise their rates in the newspaper and online, but be sure to read the fine print in order to gauge overall costs and fees. A mortgage broker can do some of this legwork for you at additional cost. However, the time you save may well be worth it.

Some government resources for home buyers include Fannie Mae (www.fanniemae.com), Freddie Mac (www.freddiemac.com) and Ginnie Mae (www.ginniemae.com). First-timers might also benefit from consulting with the Mortgage Bankers Association of America (MBA 202-861-6500), an association that will help put you in touch with a real estate loan officer as well as answer any questions you may have.

Online mortgages are available through numerous sites:www.eloan.com; www.homeadvisor.msn.com; www.hsh.com; www.keystroke.com; www.iown.com; www.mortgagelocator.com; www.quickenmortgage.com. If online is your preferred way of doing business, many of these resources will prove invaluable.

Amortization Tables

Amortization is a repayment method in which the amount you borrow is repaid gradually though regular monthly payments of principal and interest. During the first few years, most of each payment is applied toward the interest owed. During the final years of the loan, payment amounts are applied almost exclusively to the remaining principal. The longer the term of your loan, the more interest you will ultimately pay.

Several factors are involved in calculating your schedule of monthly payments, known as an amortization table: amount of loan, interest rate, length of loan, amount of taxes due, and insurance. The final results will show the breakdown of each payment: how much is put towards interest and how much towards the principal.

While your loan officer will calculate your final table, you can obtain reasonably accurate estimates with an online calculator. Go to http://www.getreal-estate.net/javascrp/mamortiz.htm, http://www.commercial-link.com/amortiza.htm, or http://www.aahomeloans.com/amort/ to get started.

◉ Eilers, Terry. *How to Buy the Home You Want, for the Best Price, in Any Market*. New York: Hyperion, 1997.

Johnson, Randy. *How to Save Thousands of Dollars on Your Home Mortgage*. New York: Wiley, 1998.

Kibbey, H. L. *First Home Buying Guide: How to Do It Right the First Time!* Lake Oswego, Ore.: Panopoly, 1996.

Loans

Home Equity

A home equity loan is commonly referred to as a *second mortgage*. The difference between the amount you owe on your mortgage and the market value of your home is known as equity. Because real estate usually increases in value, after several years you may have more equity in your home than you might think.

Major expenses, especially those that will increase the value of your home such as major renovations, roofing, or adding rooms, can be financed through a home equity loan. However, a common pitfall is to use the equity in your home to pay off other debt, including credit cards. At face value it might seem wise to replace high-interest credit card debt with a lower-interest home equity loan. But if you find yourself unable to make those payments you risk losing your home.

Mortgage brokers and real estate loan officers can help you find a home equity loan (see *Real Estate* for more information).

Automobile

An auto loan can make it possible to drive a new car without having to come up with thousands of dollars in cash. Many loans require only a low down payment, and some require none at all. The lower the down payment the higher a price you will likely pay in the long run, as the interest rates can be quite excessive.

As with mortgages and other forms of major debt, it pays to shop around for the best deal. Setting your sights on a less expensive car might be prudent if you have limited cash available for a down payment. If you take on a heavy auto loan burden and are unable to make the payments, your car is subject to repossession.

Before you even go to look for a car, determine how much you can afford in monthly payments. Many car dealers offer in-house loans and they will have already calculated payments in advance. Unless you know what you can afford, you may wind up with a loan that looks like a good deal but does not really fit your budget.

For basic auto loan information, go to www.carfinance.com or www.1stopauto.com.

Personal

A personal loan, also known as an unsecured loan, should be considered a last resort if you are in need of funds. Because the risk to the lender is high, you will pay around 15% to 18% interest. Many banks offer personal lines of credit to their customers worth $1,000 or more.

Credit Cards

Rare is the person who never uses credit cards, and rarer still is the person who uses credit cards but does not carry long-term debt. Banks and credit companies continuously solicit people who might be suffering from cash-flow crunches, especially college students and recent graduates, with *special low introductory rates* that make the offers nearly impossible to refuse.

Breaking the cycle of credit card debt is essential to long-term financial security. Investments almost never pay more than credit cards cost, so to invest in mutual funds, stocks, or even an IRA before paying off your cards is a losing proposition. In the short-term, try to shop around for the lowest rate and transfer any outstanding balances to low-rate cards. Bankcard Holders of America (BH) is a nonprofit consumer organization that will send you a list of low-rate cards for $4. Write to them at 524 Branch Drive, Salem, VA 24153 or call (540) 389-5445.

A refusal to use credit cards can backfire, however, as it is essential to establish a credit rating in order to obtain a mortgage or other loan later in life. A credit card can also provide an easy way to track your spending and document tax-related expenses.

To obtain your credit report, contact one of the three credit bureaus below. Reports are free if you have been denied credit within the past 60 days and cost $8 at all other times:

Equifax	Experian (formerly TRW) TransUnion
P.O. Box 105873	P.O. Box 390
Atlanta, GA 30348	Springfield, PA 19064-0390
www.equifax.com	www.experian.com
800-682-7654	800-888-4213
	800-685-1111

If you have trouble managing your credit card debt, you can seek assistance from a number of agencies, including Consumer Credit Counseling Services (800-388-2227) and American Consumer Credit Counseling Service (24 Crescent Street, Waltham, MA, 02453; 800-769-3571; www.consumercredit.com)

⊙ Hammond, Bob. *Life After Debt: Free Yourself from the Burden of Money Worries Once and for All*. Franklin, N.J.: Career Press, 2000.

Mellan, Olivia, with Sherry Christie. *Overcoming Overspending: A Winning Plan for Spenders and Their Partners*. New York: Walker, 1995.

Taxes

Federal Income Taxes

If you are employed full-time, estimated federal taxes are withheld from your paycheck and sent to the Internal Revenue Service (IRS) on your behalf. Self-employed individuals must make quarterly estimated payments to the IRS or face penalties. At the end of the year, you must file a tax return (Form 1040 or 1040EZ) to reconcile the total amount of estimated taxes paid with the actual amount owed.

Income tax is known as a graduated tax, which means that people with higher incomes are taxed at a higher percentage rate than people with lower incomes. The rate at which you are taxed is known as a tax bracket.

You can reduce your tax burden by taking advantages of various deductions offered by the IRS. Some deductions are available to all taxpayers. The standard deduction is taken for each person who files taxes and varies depending upon family status. Dependent deductions are taken for each child supported by the taxpayer. In lieu of the standard deduction, you may choose to itemize certain expenses as permitted by law. These include state and local income taxes; property taxes; housing costs; donations to charities; business-related expenses; medical expenses; and tax-preparation fees. Itemized deductions must be listed on a separate form, known as Schedule A.

State Income Tax Rates

Not all states impose income taxes. Those that do use a system of graduated tax rates based on income levels, similar to that of the federal government. In this table, "Low Income" refers to the lowest annual income required for taxes to be charged; these earners are charged the rate in the "Low Rate" column. "High Income" earners are charged the highest tax rate, as seen in the "High Rate" column.

State	Low Rate (%)	High Rate (%)	Low Income	High Income	Exemption Single	Exemption Married	Exemption per Child
Alabama	2.0	5.0	500	3,000	1,500	3,000	300
Alaska	0	0	0	0			
Arizona	2.87	5.04	10,000	150,000	2,100	4,200	2,300
Arkansas	1.0	7.0	2,999	25,000	20***	40***	20***
California	1.0	9.3	5,264	34,548	72***	142***	227***
Colorado	4.75	4.75	Flat rate	Flat rate	0	0	0
Connecticut	3.0	4.5	10,000*	10,000*	12,000	24,000	0
Delaware	2.2	5.95	5,000	60,000	110***	220***	110***
District of Columbia	5.0	9.5	10,000	20,000	1,370	2,740	1,370
Florida	0	0	0	0	0	0	0
Georgia	1.0	6.0	750**	7,000**	2,700	5,400	2,700
Hawaii	1.6	8.75	2,000*	40,000*	1,040	2,080	1,040
Idaho	2.0	8.2	1,000*	20,000*	2,750	5,500	2,750
Illinois	3.0	3.0	Flat rate	Flat rate	2,000	4,000	2,000
Indiana	3.4	3.4	Flat rate	Flat rate	1,000	2,000	1,000
Iowa	0.36	8.98	1,162	52,290	40***	80***	40***
Kansas	3.5	6.45	15,000*	30,000*	2,250	4,500	2,250
Kentucky	2.0	6.0	3,000	8,000	20***	40***	20***
Louisiana	2.0	6.0	10,000*	50,000*	4,500	9,000	1,000
Maine	2.0	8.5	4,150*	16,500*	2,850	5,600	2,850
Maryland	2.0	4.85	1,000	3,000	1,850	3,700	1,850
Massachusetts	5.95	5.95	Flat rate	Flat rate	4,400	8,800	1,000
Michigan	4.3	4.3	Flat rate	Flat rate	2,800	5,600	2,800
Minnesota	5.5	8.0	17,250**	56,680**	2,750	5,500	2,750
Mississippi	3.0	5.0	5,000	10,000	6,000	9,500	1,500
Missouri	1.5	6.0	1,000	9,000	1,200	2,400	1,200
Montana	2.0	11.0	2,000	70,400	1,610	3,220	1,610
Nebraska	2.51	6.68	2,400*	26,500**	91***	182***	91***

State				State income tax limited to dividends and interest income	Single	Married	Dependents
Nevada	0	0	0	0	0	0	0
New Hampshire	State income tax limited to dividends and interest income				0	0	0
New Jersey	1.4	6.37	20,000*	*75,000**	1,000	2,000	1,500
New Mexico	1.7	8.2	5,500**	65,000**	2,750	5,500	2,750
New York	4.0	6.85	8,000*	20,000**	0	0	1,000
North Carolina	6.0	7.75	12,750*	60,000**	2,750	5,500	2,750
North Dakota	2.67	12.0	3,000	50,000	2,750	5,500	2,750
Ohio	0.716	7.228	5,000	200,000	1,050	1,050	1,050
Oklahoma	0.5	6.75	1,000	10,000	1,000	2,000	1,000
Oregon	5.0	9.0	2,350*	5,800*	132***	264***	132***
Pennsylvania	2.8	2.8	Flat rate	Flat rate	0	0	0
Rhode Island	26.0%	of	federal tax	liability	0	0	0
South Carolina	2.5	7.0	2,310	11,550	2,750	5,500	2,750
South Dakota	0	0	0	0	0	0	0
Tennessee	State income tax limited to dividends and interest income				0	0	0
Texas	0	0	0	0	0	0	0
Utah	2.30	7.0	750*	3,750*	2,063	4,125	2,063
Vermont	24.0% of	federal tax	liability		0	0	0
Virginia	2.0	5.75	3,000	17,000	800	1600	800
Washington	0	0	0	0	0	0	0
West Virginia	3.0	6.5	10,000*	60,000*	2,000	4,000	2,000
Wisconsin	4.73	6.75	7,500	15,001	0	0	50***
Wyoming	0	0	0	0	0	0	0

* For joint returns, the taxes are twice the tax imposed on half the income
** For single individual
*** Tax credits

© Federation of Tax Administrators. www.taxadmin.org

Taxes
State Sales Tax Rates

State	Sales Tax (%)	on Food	on Prescription Drugs	on Non-Prescription Drugs
Alabama	4.0	yes	no	yes
Alaska	0			
Arizona	5.0	no	no	yes
Arkansas	4.625	yes	no	yes
California	6.0	no	no	yes
Colorado	3.0	no	no	yes
Connecticut	6.0	no	no	yes
Delaware	0			
District of Columbia	5.75	no	no	no
Florida	6.0	no	no	no
Georgia	4.0	no	no	yes
Hawaii	4.0	yes	no	yes
Idaho	5.0	yes	no	yes
Illinois	6.25	1.0	1.0	1.0
Indiana	5.0	no	no	yes
Iowa	5.0	no	no	yes
Kansas	4.9	yes	no	yes
Kentucky	6.0	no	no	yes
Louisiana	4.0	3.0	no	yes
Maine	5.5	no	no	yes
Maryland	5.0	no	no	no
Massachusetts	5.0	no	no	yes
Michigan	6.0	no	no	yes
Minnesota	6.5	no	no	no
Mississippi	7.0	yes	no	yes
Missouri	4.225	yes	no	yes
Montana	0			
Nebraska	5.0	no	no	yes
Nevada	6.5	no	no	yes
New Hampshire	0			
New Jersey	6.0	no	no	no
New Mexico	5.0	yes	no	yes
New York	4.0	no	no	no
North Carolina	4.0	yes	no	yes
North Dakota	5.0	no	no	yes
Ohio	5.0	no	no	yes
Oklahoma	4.5	yes	no	yes
Oregon	0			
Pennsylvania	6.0	no	no	no
Rhode Island	7.0	no	no	no
South Carolina	5.0	yes	no	yes
South Dakota	4.0	yes	no	yes
Tennessee	6.0	yes	no	yes
Texas	6.25	no	no	yes

Utah	4.75	yes	no	yes
Vermont	5.0	no	no	no
Virginia	3.5	3.0	no	no
Washington	6.5	no	no	yes
West Virginia	6.0	yes	no	yes
Wisconsin	5.0	no	no	yes
Wyoming	4.0	yes	no	yes

Estate and Gift Taxes

Money that is inherited or received as a gift is subject to federal and state taxes. However, any number of individual gifts of up to $10,000 may be given annually without being subject to federal taxation. In addition, there is a federal tax-free amount of $675,000 in lifetime accumulation gift/estate value. In other words, if when you die your estate assets (after deduction of tax-exempt gifts) are less than $675,000, there should be no federal tax on your estate. This tax-free amount will rise to $1 million by 2006.

Some categories of giving are automatically tax-exempt: gifts to a spouse, to a political organization, to a charity, and gifts that are used to pay tuition or medical expenses.

Federal Estate Taxes as of 2001

Estate Value	Tax Rate	Estate Value	Tax Rate
$675,001–$750,000	37%	$2,000,001–$2,500,000	49%
$750,001–$1,000,000	39%	$2,500,001–$3,000,000	53%
$1,000,001–$1,250,000	41%	$3,000,001–$10,000,000	55%
$1,250,001–$1,500,000	43%	$10,000,001–$17,184,000	60%
$1,500,001–$2,000,000	45%	More than $17,184,000	55%

⊙ Internal Revenue Service. www.irs.gov
  Federation of Tax Administrators. www.taxadmin.org
  Tyson, Eric, and David J. Silverman. *Taxes for Dummies*. Foster City, Calif.: IDG, 2001.

WORK AND HOME: *In the Home*

Home Safety: Fire Safety Tips

Prevention

- Keep portable space heaters at least three feet from flammable items. Never leave a heater on unattended.
- Never smoke in bed or when sleepy.
- Keep matches and lighters out of the reach of children.
- Teach your children the importance of fire safety.
- Regularly monitor your house for electrical safety. If an appliance ever smokes or sparks, unplug it immediately and have it serviced. Do not overload extension cords.
- Store flammable liquids in metal cabinets. Storage areas should be cool, with adequate airflow.

Home Safety: Fire Safety Tips *(cont.)*

Readiness

- Smoke detectors cut the risk of death from fire in half. Install at least one on each floor, including the basement. Test detectors once a month and change batteries once a year. Replace detectors after 10 years, even if they appear to be working. Be sure to purchase smoke detectors certified by Underwriters Laboratories (UL) or Factory Mutual (FM). They should operate on lithium batteries, and should have a hush button.

- Install fire extinguishers on each floor and in the kitchen. Fire extinguishers should be UL or FM listed, and should be of the ABC type (A = wood and paper; B = flammable liquids; C = electrical).

- Post emergency numbers near telephones, but if a fire threatens your home, don't risk your life—evacuate first, and call the authorities from a safe location.

- Make an escape plan: draw a floor plan and identify two routes of escape for each room. Set a meeting place in front of your house.

- Consider installing fire escape ladders on upper floors.

- Test windows and doors for ease of use.

- Keep a bell and a flashlight in each room. Practice ringing the bells and yelling "Fire!"

- Twice a year, have the whole family practice evacuating your home. Learn to stay low to the ground—smoke and gases may be toxic. Practice evacuating while blindfolded—in a real fire, smoke will make it difficult to see. In house fires, people usually have about two minutes to escape.

- Always sleep with the bedroom doors closed. This retards entry of heat and smoke, increasing your escape time.

In the Event of a Fire

- Feel all doors before opening them. If a door is hot, use another route.
- If clothes catch fire, immediately "stop, drop, and roll."
- Do not attempt to save belongings. Remember, you have only about two minutes.
- After evacuating, give first aid as needed. Minor burns should be placed under cool running water. If the burn blisters or chars, see a doctor at once.
- Do not re-enter your house until fire authorities tell you it is safe to do so.

⊙ The Fire Escape Systems Store. "Fire Safety and Protection Tips," www.firesafetytips.com
  U.S. Fire Administration. "Fire Safety and Education," www.usfa.fema.gov/safety/sheets.htm

Home Safety: Electrical Safety Tips

Item	Precautions
Wiring	Have house wiring inspected about once every 10 years.
Fuses	Always use the correct fuse. The wrong fuse can allow circuits to overload and cause fires.

Circuits	Do not overload circuits. Most houses are wired at 15 amps, which means each circuit can safely carry about 1,500 watts.
Outlets	Cap unused outlets. Consider installing Ground Fault Circuit Interruptors in kitchens, bathrooms, and other areas with high risk of electric shock exposure. If installed, test them monthly.
Cords	Do not run cords under rugs or blankets, or rest furniture on them. Do not expose them to heat or wetness. Keep cords out of reach of children.
Extension cords	Do not use indoor cords outdoors. Store all cords indoors when not in use, to prevent weather damage.
Appliances	Follow instructions. Watch for overheating, sparking, malfunctioning, etc. Never use any appliance near water or wet surfaces. Buy appliances certified by Underwriters Laboratories or similar reputable third-party agency.

⊙ Mendelson, Cheryl. *Home Comforts*. New York: Scribner, 1999.
  National Electrical Safety Foundation. www.electricnet.com/orgs/nesf.htm
  National Safety Council. www.nsc.org
  Underwriters Laboratories. www.ul.com

Home Safety: Drinking Water

The Centers for Disease Control estimates that each year about 900,000 people fall sick from consuming contaminated water, and up to 900 die. Contaminants include lead, bacteria, arsenic, pesticides, radiation, volatile organic chemicals (VOCs), and trihalomethanes (THMs).

When water stands in pipes, contaminants can become concentrated. Never drink water from a tap until you have let it run for one to two minutes. If you have a well, make sure it uses a lead-free pump.

You may request water analysis results from your water supplier, or hire a private laboratory to test your water supply (at a cost of $50–200). In requests to water suppliers, be sure to list all contaminants that concern you to ensure a complete response. The best water filtration systems combine several filtration methods, such as activated carbon, depth or screen filters, and reverse osmosis or distillation.

Contaminant	Best Filtration Method
bacteria	ultraviolet, screen
lead	distillation, reverse osmosis
nuclear fission products	reverse osmosis, water softeners
particulates	depth filter
pesticides	activated carbon, reverse osmosis
radium	reverse osmosis
radon	activated carbon
uranium	reverse osmosis
volatile organic chemicals	activated carbon, reverse osmosis

⊙ Gabler, Raymond. *Is your water safe to drink?* Mt. Vernon, N.Y.: Consumers Union, 1988.
  Steinman, David, and Samuel Epstein. *The Safe Shopper's Bible*. New York: Macmillan, 1995.

Home Safety: Environmental Hazards

Substance	Description	Risk	Sources	Testing	Safety Guidelines	Reduction Methods
Asbestos	Mineral fiber	Lung cancer, mesothelioma, other cancers. Asbestos is only dangerous when its fibers are released into the air and inhaled.	Asbestos is a common building material that was once (pre-1975) widely used in insulation, sound-proofing, fireproofing, and texturizing.	Asbestos problems are determined by visual inspection or by air monitoring. Air monitoring technologies are not completely reliable.	There is no safe level for asbestos.	Removal, enclosure, or encapsulation. Asbestos abatement should always be done by professionals.
Carbon Monoxide	Colorless, odorless gas	Fatigue, shortness of breath, dizziness, nausea, heart and brain disorders; asphyxiation and death	Incomplete combustion from improperly ventilated heaters, furnaces, wood-burning stoves and fireplaces; car exhaust; tobacco smoke.	Carbon monoxide sensors sound an alarm when hazardous levels are detected.	More than 5 ppm is considered dangerous.	Make sure heaters are used and ventilated correctly. Inspect furnaces, stoves, and fireplaces and perform proper maintenance. Never idle a car in a garage.
Formaldehyde	Colorless water-soluble gas	Eye and lung irritation, neurological disorders	Urea formaldehyde foam (UFF) insulation, formaldehyde-treated wallboard, plywood. Contamination is especially common in mobile homes.	A PF-1 device is placed in the house for a week, then sent to a lab for analysis.	Limit exposure to 0.1 ppm	Improve ventilation, seal or remove the material, or treat it with ammonia (for professionals only).

Lead	Heavy, soft, bluish-gray metal	Lead poisoning has been linked to mental retardation, learning disabilities, kidney and blood ailments, and other health problems.	Lead-based paints, lead pipes, leaded gasoline, industrial pollution.	Annual blood tests for children. Portable X-ray fluorescence test for paint. Professional labs can test drinking water.	A blood lead level of over 15 ug/dl is dangerous for children and pregnant women. Safe levels in paint: 7 mg per square cm; in water: 5 ppb.	aint should be stripped by a professional. Lead painted doors and windows can be replaced. Encapsulation may be a viable option.
Radon	Radioactive gas	Lung cancer.	Water supply, soil, basement cracks. Products of radon decay attach to airborne dust particles, which are inhaled.	Test devices are exposed to air, then sent to lab for analysis.	Levels at or above 1 Working Load (WL) or 200 picocuries per liter (pCi/l) are considered dangerous.	Ventilation, crack sealing, covering exposed earth, suction, altering house air pressure, air cleaning.

◉ Altman, Roberta. *The Complete Book of Home Environmental Hazards.* New York: Facts on File, 1990.
Centers for Disease Control. www.cdc.gov
Lowe's Home Improvement. "Lowe's - Hidden Home Hazards." www.lowes.com/lowes/safety/safehome/safhomio.asp

Common Home Heating Systems

System	Fuel	Description	Comments
Active solar	Solar power	Large panels collect solar energy.	Systems are expensive; practical only in the sunniest, warmest areas.
Electric	Electricity	Electrical resistance units heat the rooms like a toaster.	Clean, efficient; inexpensive to install, no fumes. Produces comfortable, even heat. Utility bills are two to three times more expensive than gas or oil on average.
Electric heat pump	Electricity	A compressor extracts heat from external air and pumps it inside.	Easily overtaxed in cold climates; only suitable for areas with mild winters.
Forced Air	Gas or oil	A blower forces cool air across the hot surface of a heat exchanger. Air then travels through ducts into rooms. Return ducts collect cool air to be reheated.	By far the most common modern heating system. Efficient. Can be adapted for air conditioning. Can be drafty or uneven.
Hot water	Gas or oil	Water is heated in a boiler, then circulated through pipes to radiators.	Common through the 1940s.
Passive solar	Solar power	Newer homes often have more south-facing windows. If these are uncovered during the day and covered at night, some heat is retained.	Not a heating system, and not a stand-alone energy solution, but can considerably reduce conventional heating costs.

⊙ Johnson, Duane. *How a House Works.* The Family Handyman Series. Pleasantville, N.Y.: Readers Digest, 1994.

Calculating Heating and Cooling Needs

Winter Heating Zones

To find base BTU/hour for home heating, multiply your zone number (below) by floor space in square feet. For a well-insulated house, multiply total by 0.7; for a poorly insulated house, multiply by 1.5. Adjust capacity further if using a gas or oil furnace: multiply by 1.25 for gas, 1.3 for oil. If the heating system also heats the water supply, multiply by 1.2. Thus, for a well-insulated 2,500 square foot home in northern Virginia heated by a gas system that also heats the water supply:

$$2{,}500 \times 40 \text{ (zone)} \times 0.7 \text{ (insulation)} \times 1.25 \text{ (gas)} \times 1.2 \text{ (water heater)}$$
$$= 105{,}000 \text{ BTU/hr.}$$

Zone Heat Factor	Zone Description
90	Alaskan Coast
80	—
70	northern Maine, northern Minnesota, northern North Dakota, High Rockies
60	northern New England, Great Lakes states, northern plains states, Rockies
50	Washington State, eastern Oregon, central Nevada, central Midwest, mid-Atlantic, the Salt Lake basin
40	western Oregon, eastern California through central New Mexico through southern Missouri to northern Kentucky and Virginia
30	California wine country, California Central Valley through northern Texas to Kentucky and Tennessee, inland North Carolina
20	central Texas, the South to the Carolina coast
10	deep Texas, the Gulf Coast
5	southern Florida
0	Hawaii

Summer Cooling Zones

Divide number of square feet by your zone number, then multiply by 12,000. For a well-insulated house, multiply again by 0.85; for a poorly insulated house, multiply by 1.3. Thus, for the same 2,500 square foot well-insulated house in northern Virginia:

$$2,500 \text{ / } 600 \text{ (zone)} \times 12,000 \times 0.85 \text{ (insulation)}$$
$$= 42,500 \text{ BTU/hr.}$$

Zone Cooling Factor	Zone Description
700	Hawaii, New England, Great Lakes, northern plains states, Pacific Northwest
600	mid-Atlantic including Virginia and Kentucky, Midwest, mountain states, California coast
500	The South through the Southwest, central and eastern California
400	Gulf Coast
300	southern Texas, southern Florida

◉ HearthNet. "BTU Calculator," www.hearth.com/calc/btucalc.html
  Spel Group. "Heat Load Calculator," www.spelgroup.com/HLC.hlc.htm

Recycling: Common Recyclable Materials

Always contact your local recycling center for the latest information regarding accepted materials, preparation guidelines, and advice.

Material	Recyclable	Non-recyclable	To Prepare
Paper			
Newsprint	all		Tie with string, then bag or box. Keep stored paper away from damp and sun. Contact recycling center regarding whether to separate slick paper.

Material	Recyclable	Non-recyclable	To Prepare
Mixed Paper	Junk mail, slick paper, paper-board, wrapping paper, stationery, paper bags, phone books	Tissue, paper plates, fax or thermal paper, chemically treated paper, bubble envelopes, foil paper, plastic-coated paper-board	Remove staples, backing, and glue. Tie, bag, or box. Flatten boxes. (Phone books are often disposed of by the phone company.)
Glass and Plastic*			
Glass	Glass bottles	Window glass, glassware, light bulbs, or ceramics	Separate colored from clear glass. Rinse thoroughly and remove caps and neck rings. Contact recycling center regarding whether to remove labels. Do not include broken glass.
1 PETE	All		Rinse lightly and remove caps and collars.
2 HDPE	All		Rinse, remove caps and collars, and flatten. Recycling center may ask you to separate clear and colored.
3 V	All		Rinse, remove caps, collars, and labels, then flatten.
4 LDPE	Shrink wrap, cellophane		Shrink wrap and cellophane use chemicals which are unsuitable for recycling.
5 PP	Varies	Varies	Often not accepted. Contact your local recycling center.
6 PS	Varies	Varies	Often not accepted, but some centers accept polystyrene for conversion to building insulation. Contact the Association of Foam Packaging Recyclers at 800-944-8448.
7 Other		All	Not readily recyclable.
Metal			
Aluminum	Cans		Rinse, remove labels, and crush. Some recycling centers accept foil, TV dinner trays, and other aluminum products. For further information contact the Reynolds Aluminum Recycling Hotline: 800-228-2525.

Steel	Cans	Aerosol cans, some mixed-material cans	Rinse, remove labels, and crush. Rusty cans are acceptable. Some recycling centers will accept aerosol cans. Contact the Steel Can Recycling Hotline 800-937-1226.

*Refer to "Recycling: Codes" below for types of plastics associated with codes.

◉ McVicker, Dee. *Easy Recycling Handbook*. Gilbert, Ariz.: Grassroots Books, 1994.

Recycling: Codes

The symbol [insert symbol] on plastics, metals, and other materials indicates that the material is recyclable. On plastics, the symbol will contain one of the following numbers, indicating the type of plastic.

No.	Abbr.	Material	Description	Examples
1	PETE	polyethylene terephthalate	a clear plastic, denser than water	two-liter carbonated beverage bottles
2	HDPE	high density polyethylene	clear or translucent plastic with a dull finish, floats in water	detergent bottles, dairy bottles
3	V	vinyl		some shampoo bottles
4	LDPE	low density polyethylene		food wrap
5	PP	polypropylene	a hard, durable plastic	food containers and lids
6	PS	polystyrene	a foamed plastic, trade name Styrofoam™	food containers and foam boxes, hot drink cups
7		Other		

◉ Gall, Timothy L., and Susan B. Gall. *Consumers' Guide to Product Grades and Terms*. Detroit: Gale Research, 1993.
  SPI's Voluntary Plastic Container Coding System. Washington, D.C.: Society of the Plastics Industry, 1992.

Recycling: Preferred Packaging Materials

The following materials are ranked in order of preference for use in commerical packaging in terms of their reusability.

Rank	Material	Explanation
1	Glass	Inexpensive to produce, reusable
2	Aluminum	Expensive to produce from scratch, but efficient to recycle
3	Paper	The least harmful paper has high post-consumer recycled content and is unbleached.
4	Plastic	Non-biodegradable. Recycling is vital to limit the disposal of plastic in landfills.
5	Multimaterial	Cost-prohibitive to recycle; avoid as much as possible

◉ Carliss, Jennifer. *Taking out the Trash*. Washington, D.C.: Island, 1992.

Automobile Safety: Air Bags

Air bags reduce the risk of dying in a direct frontal crash by about 30 percent. Almost all adults are safer riding or driving with an airbag than without one. However, airbags can be a source of injury for children and some adults.

The main source of risk is proximity. For maximum safety, a driver's chest should be at least 10 inches from the center of the steering wheel, and a passenger's chest should be at least 10 inches from the dashboard. These margins can almost always be achieved by moving the seats and/or tilting their backs. Seatbelts should be worn, and should fit snugly. Children 12 and under should always ride in the back seat. Under no circumstances should you *ever* place a rear-facing child safety seat in front of an air bag.

If you are unable to seat yourself as recommended, or you have been advised by a doctor that you are at special risk from an air bag, you may apply to the National Highway Traffic Safety Administration (NHTSA) for an air bag on-off switch. You may also apply for a switch if you must accommodate a child 12 or under in your front seat.

⊙ U.S. National Highway Traffic Safety Administration (NHTSA). "Air Bag On-Off Switches: Questions and Answers," www.nhtsa.dot.gov/people/injury/airbags/

Automobile Safety: Child Safety Seats

Age Guidelines

- Children up to one year old should ride in a rear-facing infant's safety seat or convertible seat. The seat *must* be installed in the rear seat. Never place a rear-facing safety seat in front of an air bag.
- Children over one year old who weigh at least 20 pounds should sit facing forward in a convertible child safety seat.
- Children between 40 and 80 pounds (about 4 to 8 years old) should ride in a booster seat.
- All children aged 12 and under should sit in the back seat, properly restrained.
- A seat that has been in a crash should be replaced immediately. The seat may have sustained damage that is not visible.

Buying Tips

- When buying any safety seat or booster seat, make sure it bears a label reading, "This child restraint system conforms to all applicable U.S. Federal Motor Vehicle Safety Standards."
- High-backed booster seats provide head and neck protection. Five-point harnesses or shields provide full body protection for children up to about 40 pounds. Children 40 to 80 pounds may ride in the seats using the vehicle's lap and shoulder belts.
- Check the seat for ease of installation and use. Try adjusting the harness straps. Make sure the seat can be installed properly in your make and model of car.
- Read the instruction booklet thoroughly and follow all guidelines properly.

⊙ National Highway Traffic Safety Administration. "Child Transportation Safety Tips," www.nhtsa.dot.gov/people/injury/childps/
National Highway Traffic Safety Administration. "A Parent's Guide to Booster Seats," www.nhtsa.dot.gov/people/injury/childps/

WORK AND HOME: Pets

Dog Breeds (as recognized by the American Kennel Club)

Herding Dogs

Australian Cattle Dog
Australian Shepherd
Bearded Collie
Belgian Malinois
Belgian Sheepdog
Belgian Tervuren
Border Collie
Bouvier des Flandres
Briard
Canaan Dog
Collie
German Shepherd Dog
Old English Sheepdog
Puli
Shetland Sheepdog
Welsh Corgi (Cardigan)
Welsh Corgi
(Pembroke)

Hounds

Afghan Hound
Basenji
Basset Hound
Beagle
Black and Tan
Coonhound
Bloodhound
Borzoi
Dachshund
Foxhound (American)
Foxhound (English)
Greyhound
Harrier
Ibizan Hound
Irish Wolfhound
Norwegian Elkhound
Otterhound
Petit Basset Griffon
Vendeen
Pharaoh Hound
Rhodesian Ridgeback
Saluki
Scottish Deerhound
Whippet

Non-Sporting Dogs

American Eskimo Dog
Bichon Frise
Boston Terrier
Bulldog
Chinese Shar-pei
Chow Chow
Dalmatian
Finnish Spitz
French Bulldog
Keeshond
Lhasa Apso
Löwchen
Poodle (Standard &
Miniature)
Schipperke
Shiba Inu
Tibetan Spaniel
Tibetan Terrier

Sporting Dogs

American Water Spaniel
Brittany
Chesapeake Bay
Retriever
Clumber Spaniel
Cocker Spaniel
Curly-Coated Retriever
English Cocker Spaniel
English Setter
English Springer
Spaniel
Field Spaniel
Flat-Coated Retriever
German Shorthaired
Pointer
German Wirehaired
Pointer
Golden Retriever
Gordon Setter
Irish Setter
Irish Water Spaniel
Labrador Retriever
Pointer
Sussex Spaniel
Vizsla
Weimaraner
Welsh Springer Spaniel
Wirehaired Pointing
Griffon

Terriers

Airedale Terrier
American Staffordshire
Terrier
Australian Terrier
Bedlington Terrier
Border Terrier
Bull Terrier
Cairn Terrier
Dandie Dinmont
Terrier
Fox Terrier (Smooth)
Fox Terrier (Wire)
Irish Terrier
Jack Russell Terrier
Kerry Blue Terrier
Lakeland Terrier
Manchester Terrier
(Standard)
Miniature Bull
Terrier
Miniature Schnauzer
Norfolk Terrier
Norwich Terrier
Scottish Terrier
Sealyham Terrier
Skye Terrier
Soft Coated Wheaten
Terrier
Staffordshire Bull
Terrier
Welsh Terrier
West Highland White
Terrier

Dog Breeds *(cont.)*

Toy Dogs

Affenpinscher
Brussels Griffon
Cavalier King Charles
  Spaniel
Chihuahua
Chinese Crested
English Toy Spaniel

Havanese
Italian Greyhound
Japanese Chin
Maltese
Manchester Terrier (Toy)
Miniature Pinscher
Papillon

Pekingese
Pomeranian
Poodle (Toy)
Pug
Shih Tzu
Silky Terrier
Yorkshire Terrier

Working Dogs

Akita
Alaskan Malamute
Anatolian Shepherd
Bernese Mountain Dog
Boxer
Bullmastiff
Doberman Pinscher
Giant Schnauzer

Great Dane
Great Pyrenees
Greater Swiss Mountain
  Dog
Komondor
Kuvasz
Mastiff
Newfoundland

Portuguese Water
  Dog
Rottweiler
Saint Bernard
Samoyed
Siberian Husky
Standard Schnauzer

Miscellaneous

Plott Hound

Polish Lowland
  Sheepdog

Spinone Italiano

⊙ American Kennel Club. "List of Breeds," www.akc.org/breeds/recbreeds/list.cfm
  American Kennel Club Staff. *The Complete Dog Book, 19th Edition.* Foster City, Calif.:
  IDG, 1997.

Cat Breeds *(as recognized by the Cat Fanciers' Association)*

Championship Class

Abyssinian
American Curl
American Shorthair
American Wirehair
Balinese
Birman
Bombay
British Shorthair
Burmese
Chartreux
Colorpoint Shorthair
Cornish Rex

Devon Rex
Egyptian Mau
Exotic
Havana Brown
Javanese
Japanese Bobtail
Korat
Maine Coon
Manx
Norwegian Forest Cat
Ocicat
Oriental

Persian
Ragdoll
Russian Blue
Scottish Fold
Selkirk Rex
Siamese
Singapura
Somali
Tonkinese
Turkish Angora
Turkish Van

Provisional Class

European Burmese *(if shown in International Division, may compete with
                Championship Class)*

Miscellaneous Class

American Bobtail

LaPerm
Siberian

Sphynx

⊙ Cat Fanciers' Association. "CFA Breeds," www.cfainc.org/breeds.html
  Helgren, J. Anne. *Barron's Encyclopedia of Cat Breeds: A Complete Guide to the
  Domestic Cats of North America.* Hauppauge, N.Y.: Barron's, 1997.

WORK AND HOME: *Communications*

Internet

How to Use

The Internet (a.k.a. the World Wide Web or the Web) is rapidly becoming a major means of communication in the United States. According to AC Nielsen, 64% of Americans age 12 or older used the Internet in the year 2000. Using the Internet requires three components: hardware, software, and a data connection.

Hardware: A personal computer, as well as a modem or networking card. All new personal computers on the market today are technologically capable of accessing the Internet.

Software: A browser program such as Microsoft Internet Explorer or Netscape Communicator. These programs can also be used for basic electronic mail (e-mail), although more sophisticated e-mail programs such as Eudora or Microsoft Outlook allow the user to save and organize messages.

Data connection: Dialup connections, using a modem and an ordinary telephone line, have been the standard until recently. Users contract with an Internet Service Provider (ISP), which provides a telephone number for establishing a connection. Some ISPs offer free access but require that you use an advertising-supported browser program. As new technology develops, faster connections are becoming available in many locations: a cable modem uses the cable television network to access the Internet, and a DSL connection provides high-speed access via telephone lines. Contact your cable and telephone companies to see if this service is available in your area.

Search Engines

Information on the Internet is composed of individual units called Web pages. Many of these pages are linked together into thematically based networks. Because of the decentralized nature of the Internet, no single directory exists for all of these pages. Search engines are programs that can comb through these pages and find information based on keywords.

Portals

Some companies have developed Internet directories based on specific categories of information. Users can follow a series of links to find Web pages that fit into these categories. A portal also contains a search engine to look for information both within the portal and throughout the Internet.

E-mail

Most ISPs include an e-mail account as a basic feature. The ISP provides instructions on how to use e-mail software to send and receive messages. In addition, many Web sites and portals provide free e-mail accounts to users. Web-based e-mail, however, is not as flexible or sophisticated as e-mail software, and these accounts have limited storage space for archiving messages.

⊙ "CNET's Ultimate Guide to Search," www.cnet.com/internet/0-3817-7-1922932.html
   "CNET Web Services," http://webservices.cnet.com

Telephone: United States and Canada Area Codes

Code	State/Province	Code	State/Province	Code	State/Province
201	New Jersey	318	Louisiana	510	California
202	District of	319	Iowa	512	Texas
	Columbia	320	Minnesota	513	Ohio
203	Connecticut	321	Florida	514	Quebec
204	Manitoba	323	California	515	Iowa
205	Alabama	330	Ohio	516	New York
206	Washington	334	Alabama	517	Michigan
207	Maine	336	North Carolina	518	New York
208	Idaho	337	Louisiana	519	Ontario
209	California	347	New York	520	Arizona
210	Texas	352	Florida	530	California
212	New York	360	Washington	540	Virginia
213	California	361	Texas	541	Oregon
214	Texas	401	Rhode Island	559	California
215	Pennsylvania	402	Nebraska	561	Florida
216	Ohio	403	Alberta	562	California
217	Illinois	404	Georgia	570	Pennsylvania
218	Minnesota	405	Oklahoma	573	Missouri
219	Indiana	406	Montana	580	Oklahoma
225	Louisiana	407	Florida	601	Mississippi
228	Mississippi	408	California	602	Arizona
229	Georgia	409	Texas	603	New Hampshire
231	Michigan	410	Maryland	604	British Columbia
240	Maryland	412	Pennsylvania	605	South Dakota
248	Michigan	413	Massachusetts	606	Kentucky
250	British Columbia	414	Wisconsin	607	New York
252	North Carolina	415	California	608	Wisconsin
253	Washington	416	Ontario	609	New Jersey
254	Texas	417	Missouri	610	Pennsylvania
256	Alabama	418	Quebec	612	Minnesota
262	Wisconsin	419	Ohio	613	Ontario
267	Pennsylvania	423	Tennessee	614	Ohio
270	Kentucky	425	Washington	615	Tennessee
281	Texas	435	Utah	616	Michigan
301	Maryland	440	Ohio	617	Massachusetts
302	Delaware	443	Maryland	618	Illinois
303	Colorado	450	Quebec	619	California
304	West Virginia	469	Texas	623	Arizona
305	Florida	478	Georgia	626	California
306	Saskatchewan	480	Arizona	630	Illinois
307	Wyoming	484	Pennsylvania	631	New York
308	Nebraska	501	Arkansas	650	California
309	Illinois	502	Kentucky	651	Minnesota
310	California	503	Oregon	660	Missouri
312	Illinois	504	Louisiana	661	California
313	Michigan	505	New Mexico	662	Mississippi
314	Missouri	506	New Brunswick	678	Georgia
315	New York	507	Minnesota	701	North Dakota
316	Kansas	508	Massachusetts	702	Nevada
317	Indiana	509	Washington	703	Virginia

704	North Carolina	801	Utah	902	Nova Scotia
705	Ontario	802	Vermont	903	Texas
706	Georgia	803	South Carolina	904	Florida
707	California	804	Virginia	905	Ontario
708	Illinois	805	California	906	Michigan
709	Newfoundland	806	Texas	907	Alaska
712	Iowa	807	Ontario	908	New Jersey
713	Texas	808	Hawaii	909	California
714	California	810	Michigan	910	North Carolina
715	Wisconsin	812	Indiana	912	Georgia
716	New York	813	Florida	913	Kansas
717	Pennsylvania	814	Pennsylvania	914	New York
718	New York	815	Illinois	915	Texas
719	Colorado	816	Missouri	916	California
720	Colorado	817	Texas	917	New York
724	Pennsylvania	818	California	918	Oklahoma
727	Florida	819	Quebec	919	North Carolina
732	New Jersey	828	North Carolina	920	Wisconsin
734	Michigan	830	Texas	925	California
740	Ohio	831	California	931	Tennessee
757	Virginia	832	Texas	937	Ohio
760	California	843	South Carolina	940	Texas
763	Minnesota	847	Illinois	941	Florida
765	Indiana	850	Florida	949	California
770	Georgia	856	New Jersey	954	Florida
773	Illinois	860	Connecticut	956	Texas
775	Nevada	864	South Carolina	970	Colorado
780	Alberta	865	Tennessee	972	Texas
781	Massachusetts	867	Northwest Territories	973	New Jersey
785	Kansas			978	Massachusetts
786	Florida	870	Arkansas	979	Texas
787	Puerto Rico	901	Tennessee		

⊙ North American Numbering Plan Administration. "Geographic NPAs in Service Sorted by Number," www.nanpa.com/area_codes/geographic_number.html

North American Numbering Plan Administration. "Area Code Maps," www.nanpa.com/number_resource_info/area_code_maps.html

North American Numbering Plan Administration. "Planned NPAs Not Yet in Service," www.nanpa.com/area_codes/npa_planned.html

Telephone: International Dialing Codes and City Codes

To call from the United States, dial 011, the international dialing code, the city code, and the telephone number.

International Dialing Code	City Code	International Dialing Code	City Code
Afghanistan 93		American Samoa 684	
Albania 355	Durres 52, Elbassan 545, Tirana 42	Andorra 376	
		Angola 244	Luanda 2, Huambo 416
Algeria 213	Algiers 2	Anguilla 264	

International Dialing Code	City Code	International Dialing Code	City Code
Antarctica 672		Burkina Faso 226	
Antigua and Barbuda 1-268 *		Burundi 257	
		Cambodia 855	Phnom Penh 23 or 22
Argentina 54	Buenos Aires 1, Cordoba 51, Santa Fe 42	Cameroon 237	
Armenia 374	Aparan 520, Kotaik 61, Talin 490	Canada 1	Ontario (Ottawa) 613, Ontario (Toronto Vicinity) 905,
Aruba 297			Ontario (Toronto Metro) 416, Prince
Ascension 247			Edward Island 902,
Australia 61	Canberra 262, Melbourne 39, Sydney 2		Quebec (Montreal) 514, Quebec (Quebec City) 418, Quebec
Austria 43	Linz 70, Linz Donau 732, Salzburg 662, Vienna 1		(Sherbrooke) 819, Vancouver 604
		Cape Verde Islands 238	
Azerbaijan 994	Baku 12	Cayman Islands 1-345 *	
Bahamas 1-242 *		Central African Republic 236	
Bahrain 973		Chad 235	
Bangladesh 880	Dhaka 2, Rangpur 521	Chatham Island 64	
Barbados 1-246 *		Chile 56	Concepción 41, Santiago 2, Valparaiso 32
Belarus 375	Loev 2347, Minsk 172, Mogilev 222	China 86	Beijing (Peking) 10, Hangzhou 571,
Belgium 32	Antwerp 3, Brussels 2, Ghent 9		Fuzhou (Fujian) 591, Ghuangzhou (Canton) 20,
Belize 501	Belize City 2, Belmopan 8, Orange Walk 3		Shanghai 21
		Christmas and Cocos Islands 672	
Benin 229		Colombia 57	Barranquila 53, Bogotá 1, Cali 2,
Bermuda 1-441 *			Cartagena 59, Medellín 4
Bhutan 975			
Bolivia 591	Cochabamba 42, La Paz 2, Santa Cruz 3	Comoros 269	
		Congo 242	
Bosnia-Herzegovina 387	Mostar 88, Sarajevo 71, Zenica 72	Congo, Democratic Republic of 243	Kinshasa 12
Botswana 267		Cook Islands 682	
Brazil 55	Brasilia 61, Rio de Janeiro 21, Salvador 71, São Paulo 11	Costa Rica 506	
		Croatia 385	Dubrovnik 20, Rijeka 51, Split 21, Zagreb 1
British Virgin Islands 1-284 *		Cuba 53	Havana 7
Brunei 673	Behawan 2, Kuala Belait 3, Tutong 4	Cyprus, Northern 90392	
Bulgaria 359	Plovdiv 32, Sofia 2, Varna 52	Cyprus, Republic of 357	Larnaca 4, Limassol 5, Nicosia 2

Czech Republic 420	Brno 5, Ostrava 69, Prague 2	Greece 30	Athens 1, Iraklion (Crete) 81, Thessaloniki 31
Denmark 45			
Diego Garcia 246		Greenland 299	
Djibouti 253		Grenada and Carriacuou 1-473 *	
Dominica 1-767 *		Grenadine Islands 784	
Dominican Republic 1-809 *		Guadeloupe 590	
Ecuador 593	Easter Island 56, Guayaquil 4, Quito 2	Guam 671	
		Guantanamo Bay 5399	
Egypt 20	Alexandria 3, Asyut 88, Cairo 2	Guatemala 502	Guatemala City 2
		Guinea 224	
El Salvador 503	La Fontera 503, Los Lagartos 503, Olomega 503,	Guinea-Bissau 245	
		Guyana 592	Georgetown 2, Linden 4, New Amsterdam 3
Equatorial Guinea 240			
Eritrea 291	Asmara 1, Makale 1, Massawa 1	Haiti 509	
		Honduras 504	
Estonia 372	Rakvere 32, Tallinn 2 or 372, Tartu 7	Hong Kong 852	
		Hungary 36	Budapest 1, Szolnok 56, Veszprem 88
Ethiopia 251	Addis Ababa 1, Debre Zeit 1, Dire Dawa 5	Iceland 354	
		India 91	Bombay (Mumbai) 22, Calcutta 33, New Delhi 11
Falkland Islands 500			
Faroe Islands 298			
Fiji Islands 679		Indonesia 62	Bandung 22, Jakarta 21, Medan 61
Finland 358	Helsinki 9, Turku 2, Vaasa 6	Iran 98	Tehran 21
France 33	Bordeaux 556, Marseille 491, Nice 493, Paris 1	Iraq 964	Baghdad 1
		Ireland 353	Cork 21, Donegal 77, Dublin 1
French Antilles 596	Basse Pointe 78, Grand Bourg 76, Pointe A Pitre 8 or 9	Israel 972	Haifa 4, Jerusalem 2, Nazareth 6, Tel Aviv 3
French Guiana 594		Italy 39	Bologna 51, Florence 55, Genoa 10, Milan 2, Naples 81, Rome/Vatican City 6, Venice 41
French Polynesia 689			
Gabon 241			
Gambia 220			
Georgia 995	Suhumi 881, Tbilisi 32	Ivory Coast 225	
Germany 49	Berlin 30, Bonn 228, Bremen 421, Cologne (Koln) 221, Dresden 351, Dussledorf 211, Essen 201, Frankfurt 69, Hamburg 40, Munich 89	Jamaica 876	
		Japan 81	Hiroshima 82, Kyoto 75, Nagasaki 958, Tokyo 3, Yokohama 45
		Jordan 962	Amman 6, Rbid 2, Zarqa 9
		Kazakhstan 7	Alma Ata 327, Chimkent 325, Guryev 312
Ghana 233	Accra 21, Kumasi 51, Takoradi 31	Kenya 254	Mombasa 11, Nairobi 2
Gibraltar 350		Kiribati 686	

International Dialing Code	City Code
Korea, North 850	
Korea, South 82	Inchon 32, Pusan (Busan) 51, Seoul 2, Taegu (Daegu) 53
Kuwait 965	
Kyrgyzstan 7	Bishkek 2, Osh 332
Laos 856	
Latvia 371	Daugavpils 54, Liepaia 34, Riga 34
Lebanon 961	Beirut 1, Tripoli 6
Lesotho 266	
Liberia 231	
Libya 218	Benghazi 61, Tripoli 21
Liechtenstein 423	
Lithuania 370	Kaunas 7, Klaipeda 6, Vilnius 2
Luxembourg 352	
Macedonia, Federal Republic of 389	Bitola 97, Lozovo 92, Skopje 91
Madagascar 261	
Malawi 265	
Malaysia 60	Ipoh 5, Johor Bahru 7, Kuala Lumpur 3
Maldives 960	
Mali 223	
Malta 356	
Mariana Islands 1-670 *	
Marshall Islands 692	Ebeye 329
Martinique 596	
Mauritania 222	
Mauritius 230	
Mayotte 269	
Mexico 52	Acapulco 74, Cancun 98, Guadalajara 3, Merida 99, Mexico City 5, Monterrey 8
Micronesia, Federated States of 691	Kosrae 370, Pohnpei 320, Truk 330, Yap 350

International Dialing Code	City Code
Midway Islands 808 *	
Miquelon 508	
Moldova 373	Benderi 32
Monaco 33 or 377	
Mongolia 976	Ulan Batar 1
Montenegro 3818	
Montserrat 664	
Morocco 212	Casablanca 2, Fes 5, Rabat (5 digits) 77, Rabat (6 digits) 7, Tangiers 99
Mozambique 258	
Myanmar (Burma) 95	Rangoon 1
Namibia 264	
Nauru 674	
Nepal 977	
Netherlands 31	Amsterdam 20, Rotterdam 10, The Hague 70
Netherlands Antilles 599	Bonaire 7, Curacao 9, Saba 46, St. Eustatius 38, St. Maarten 5
Nevis 809	
New Caledonia 687	
New Zealand 64	Auckland 9, Christchurch 3, Hamilton 7
Nicaragua 505	Chinandega 341, Leon 311, Managua 2
Niger 227	
Nigeria 234	Kaduna 62, Lagos 1, Port Hartcourt 84
Niue 683	
Norfolk Island 672	
North Korea 850	
Norway 47	Bergen 5, Oslo 22
Oman 968	
Pakistan 92	Islamabad 51, Karachi 21, Lahore 42
Palau 680	
Panama 507	
Papua New Guinea 675	

Paraguay 595	Asunción 21, Concepción 31, Villarrica 541
Peru 51	Arequipa 54, Lima 1
Philippines 63	Cebu City 32, Luzon 455, Manila 2, Subic 47
Poland 48	Bialystok 85, Gdansk 58, Katowice 32, Warsaw 22
Portugal 351	Coimbra 39, Lisbon 1, Setubal 65
Príncipe 239	
Puerto Rico 1-787 *	
Qatar 974	
Reunion Island 262	
Romania 40	Bacau 34, Bucharest 1, Constanta 41, Iasi 32
Russia 7	Magadan 413, Moscow 095, St. Petersburg 812
Rwanda 250	
St. Helena 290	
St. Kitts 1-869 *	
St. Lucia 1-758 *	
St Pierre Et Miquelon 508	
St. Vincent 1-784 *	
Saipan 670	
San Marino 378	
São Tomé 239	
Saudi Arabia 966	Jeddah 2, Mecca 2, Medina 4, Riyadh 1
Senegal Republic 221	Dakar 8, all others 9
Serbia, Republic Of 381	
Seychelles 248	
Sierra Leone 232	Freetown 22
Singapore 65	East 394, Jurong East 665, Orchard 834 or 835
Slovakia 421	Bratislava 7, Presov 91
Slovenia 386	
Solomon Islands 677	
Somalia 252	
South Africa 27	Cape Town 21, Johannesburg 11, Pietermaritzburg 331, Pretoria 12

Spain 34	Barcelona 3, Madrid 1, Malaga 5
Sri Lanka 94	Colombo Central 1, Kandy 8, Kotte 1
Sudan 249	Atbarah 21, Khartoum 11, Port Sudan 31, Wad Medani 51
Suriname 597	
Swaziland 268	
Sweden 46	Gothenburg 31, Malmo 40, Stockholm 8
Switzerland 41	Berne 31, Geneva 22, Lucerne 41, Zurich 1
Syria 963	Aleppo 21, Damascus 11, Homs 31
Taiwan 886	Changhua 4, Kaohsiung 7, Taipei 2
Tajikistan 7	
Tanzania 255	
Thailand 66	Bangkok 2, Chiang Mai 53, Nakhonsawan 56
Togo 228	
Tonga Islands 676	
Trinidad and Tobago 868	
Tunisia 216	Tunis 1
Turkey 90	Ankara 312, Istanbul Asya 216, Istanbul Avrupa 212, Izmir 232
Turkmenistan 993	
Turks and Caicos Islands 1-649 *	
Tuvalu 688	
Uganda 256	Entebbe 42, Jinja 43, Kampala 41
Ukraine 380	Kharkov 57, Kiev 44, Lviv 322
United Arab Emirates 971	Abu Dhabi 2, Dubai 4, Sharjah 6
United Kingdom 44	Birmingham 121, Edinburgh 131, Liverpool 151, London (Inner) 171, London (Outer) 181, Manchester 161, Nottingham 115
United States 1	

International Dialing Code	City Code
Uruguay 598	Mercedes 532, Montevideo 2, San Jose 342
U.S. Virgin Islands 340	
Uzbekistan 7	Karshi 375, Samarkand 3662, Tashkent 71 or 712
Vanuatu 678	
Vatican City 39	
Venezuela 58	Caracas 2, Maracaibo 61, Maracay 43, Valencia 4
Vietnam 84	Da Nang City 518, Hanoi 4, Ho Chi Minh City 8

International Dialing Code	City Code
Wake Island 1-808 *	
Wallis and Futuna Islands 681	
Western Samoa 685	
Yemen 967	Aden 2, Sanaa 1, Taiz 4
Yugoslavia 381	Belgrade 11
Zaire (Congo, Democratic Republic of) 243	Kinshasa 12
Zambia 260	Lusaka 1
Zanzibar 259	
Zimbabwe 263	Harare 4

*Country code can be dialed direct from U.S. without dialing 011.

◉ AT&T. "City and Country Codes," www.att.com/traveler/tools/codes.html
American Computer Resources. "International Calling Code Directory," www.the-acr.com/codes/cntrycd.htm
Steve Kropla. "International Dialing Codes," www.kropla.com/dialcode.htm

Postal Rates (as of January 2001 increase)

First Class Letters or Letter Packages	Sent within U.S.	Sent to Canada	Sent to Mexico	Sent to other countries
.5 oz.	$0.34	$0.60	$0.60	$0.80
1.0 oz.	$0.34	$0.60	$0.60	$0.80
1.5 oz.	$0.55	$0.85	$0.85	$1.60
2.0 oz.	$0.55	$0.85	$0.85	$1.60
2.5 oz.	$0.76	$1.10	$1.25	$2.40
3.0 oz.	$0.76	$1.10	$1.25	$2.40
3.5 oz.	$0.97	$1.35	$1.65	$3.20
4.0 oz.	$0.97	$1.35	$1.65	$3.20
4.5 oz.	$1.18	$1.60	$2.05	$4.00
5.0 oz.	$1.18	$1.60	$2.05	$4.00
5.5 oz.	$1.39	$1.85	$2.45	$4.80
6.0 oz.	$1.39	$1.85	$2.45	$4.80
6.5 oz.	$1.60	$2.10	$2.85	$5.60
7.0 oz.	$1.60	$2.10	$2.85	$5.60
7.5 oz.	$1.81	$2.35	$3.25	$6.40
8.0 oz.	$1.81	$2.35	$3.25	$6.40
8.5 oz.	$2.02	$3.10	$4.00	$7.55
9.0 oz.	$2.02	$3.10	$4.00	$7.55
9.5 oz.	$2.23	$3.10	$4.00	$7.55
10.0 oz.	$2.23	$3.10	$4.00	$7.55

10.5 oz.	$2.44	$3.10	$4.00	$7.55
11.0 oz.	$2.44	$3.10	$4.00	$7.55
11.5 oz.	$2.65	$3.10	$4.00	$7.55
12.0 oz.	$2.65	$3.10	$4.00	$7.55
12.5 oz.	$2.86	$3.75	$5.15	$8.70
13.0 oz.	$2.86	$3.75	$5.15	$8.70
Postcard	$0.20	$0.50	$0.50	$0.70

Domestic

Priority Mail (70 lbs. or less, 108 in. or less in combined length and girth)
2–3 Days Delivery:

up to 1 lb.	$3.50	up to 5 lbs.	$7.55
up to 2 lbs.	$3.95	over 5 lbs.	rate figured by weight and zone
up to 3 lbs.	$5.15		
up to 4 lbs.	$6.35		

Express Mail (70 lbs. or less, 108 in. or less in combined length and girth)
Next Day Delivery:

up to 8 oz.	$12.25	up to 4 lbs.	$21.70
over 8 oz to 2 lbs.	$16.00	up to 5 lbs.	$24.50
up to 3 lbs.	$18.85	over 5 lbs.	rate figured by weight and zone

Bound Printed Matter (advertising, promotional, directory, or editorial material bound by permanent fastenings): rate dependent on weight and zone.

Special Standard Mail (Book Rate; also used for film; printed music, test materials, and educational charts; sound recordings; play scripts; loose-leaf pages and binders consisting of medical information; and computer-readable media): rate dependent on weight

Other Services

Certificate of Mailing (evidence of mailing)	$0.75
Certified Mail (record of delivery kept at post office)	$1.90
Delivery Confirmation (date and time of delivery) Priority Mail	$0.40
Delivery Confirmation (date and time of delivery) Other Mail	$0.50
Signature Confirmation	$1.75
Insured Mail	rate according to value
Money Order (up to $700)	$0.75
Registered Mail	rate according to value
Return Receipt (Express Mail, certified, COD, registered, or mail insured for over $50)	$1.50
Return Receipt for Merchandise	$2.35
Collect on Delivery (COD): rate dependent on amount to be collected	maximum amount $600

Postal Rates *(cont.)*

International

Global Priority Mail (Expedited airmail in partnership with postal service of destination country)
Rates vary according to country. Maximum weight: 4 lbs.

Priority Mail Global Guaranteed (Expedited delivery in partnership with DSL Worldwide Express)
Rates vary according to country. Maximum weight: 70 lbs.

Express Mail International Service (Delivery available to more than 170 countries)
Rates and weight limits vary according to country.

⊙ U.S. Postal Service. www.usps.gov
U.S. Postal Service. "International Rate Calculator," http://ircalc.usps.gov
U.S. Postal Service. "Domestic Rate Calculator," http://postcalc.usps.gov

Postal Abbreviations by State

Alabama	AL	Missouri	MO
Alaska	AK	Montana	MT
Arizona	AZ	Nebraska	NE
Arkansas	AR	Nevada	NV
California	CA	New Hampshire	NH
Colorado	CO	New Jersey	NJ
Connecticut	CT	New Mexico	NM
Delaware	DE	New York	NY
District of		North Carolina	NC
Columbia	DC	North Dakota	ND
Florida	FL	Ohio	OH
Georgia	GA	Oklahoma	OK
Hawaii	HI	Oregon	OR
Idaho	ID	Pennsylvania	PA
Illinois	IL	Rhode Island	RI
Indiana	IN	South Carolina	SC
Iowa	IA	South Dakota	SD
Kansas	KS	Tennessee	TN
Kentucky	KY	Texas	TX
Louisiana	LA	Utah	UT
Maine	ME	Vermont	VT
Maryland	MD	Virginia	VA
Massachusetts	MA	Washington	WA
Michigan	MI	West Virginia	WV
Minnesota	MN	Wisconsin	WI
Mississippi	MS	Wyoming	WY

⊙ Hornor, Edith R., ed. *Almanac of the 50 States: Basic Data Profiles with Comparative Tables 2000.* Palo Alto, Calif.: Information Publications, 2000.
Kane, Joseph Nathan and Gerald. L. Alexander. *Nicknames and Sobriquets of U.S. Cities, States, and Counties,* 3rd ed. Lanham, Md.: Scarecrow Press, 1979.

Other Modes of Communication

Radio: Ham and CB

Ham radio operators are licensed by the government and are prohibited from any commercial activity. Each operator acts as a mini radio station and can broadcast around the world. Legend has it that the term "Ham" comes from the call letters of the first amateur radio broadcasters. Ham radio clubs exist worldwide, and the international amateur broadcast community is full of "Elmers," expert operators who enjoy passing on their skills to newcomers. To get a license you will need to take an inexpensive, volunteer-administered test; once you are licensed you can set up a radio with a simple antenna and start talking.

CB stands for "citizens band," and the CB is the easiest way to get on the radio. Although CB frequencies are regulated by the federal government, a license is not required for operation. Radio types vary from a simple, handheld walkie-talkie to a full "base station" radio system.

Telegraph

The telegraph uses a series of electric signals, organized in code, to send messages. Samuel Morse, inventor of the telegraph, first came up with the idea in the early 1830s, and the first telegraph line was built in 1843. The introduction of the telegraph brought high-speed communication to the United States for the first time and caused the federal government to cease operation of its Pony Express. The end product of a telegraph communication usually came in the form of a telegram, which was then delivered to the recipient. Radio telegraph for communicating with ships at sea was introduced in 1904. Today, communication via telegraph is more or less obsolete except among a select few radio hobbyists.

Telex

For international business communication with countries where telephone and internet communications are unreliable, telex service is available through companies like AT&T (http://www.att.net.au/products/telex.html). Telex provides a secure means of sending and receiving messages nearly everywhere in the world.

Fax

A fax, or facsimile, is a means of sending an image-based copy over a telephone line. A page can be scanned into a fax machine or sent directly from a computer using a modem.

Courier Services

Special delivery of packages and important documents can require the use of a custom service. Packages sent via courier can be easily tracked and delivery is usually guaranteed by the company. Federal Express (1-800-GO-FEDEX or www.fedex.com), Airborne Express (1-800-AIRBORNE or www.airborne.com), and UPS (1-800-PICK-UPS or www.ups.com) are the three best-known services. However, hundreds of companies offer specialized delivery in local areas, nationally, or internationally.

⊙ American Radio Relay League. www.arrl.org
   Crenshaw, Gerry. "New Ham Partner," http://web2airmail.net/gerryc/newham.html
   Federal Communications Commission. "Amateur Radio Service," www.fcc.gov/wtb/amateur/
   Cody, Andrew. "How to Buy a CB Radio," www.iserv.net/~codyspc/cbindex.htm
   Deliver-It! Worldwide Transportation Yellow Pages. www.deliver-it.com/

Alphabets

Arabic

ا ا	'alif	'
ب ب ب ب	bā	b
ت ت ت ت	tā'	t
ث ث ث ث	thā'	th
ج ج ج ج	jīm	j
ح ح ح ح	ḥā'	ḥ
خ خ خ خ	khā'	kh
د د	dāl	d
ذ ذ	dhāl	dh
ر ر	rā'	r
ز ز	zay	z
س س س س	sīn	s
ش ش ش ش	shīn	sh
ص ص ص ص	ṣād	ṣ
ض ض ض ض	ḍād	ḍ
ط ط ط ط	ṭā'	ṭ
ظ ظ ظ ظ	ẓā'	ẓ
ع ع ع ع	'ayn	'
غ غ غ غ	ghayn	gh
ف ف ف ف	fā'	f
ق ق ق ق	qāf	q
ك ك ك ك	kāf	k
ل ل ل ل	lām	l
م م م م	mīm	m
ن ن ن ن	nūn	n
ه ه ه ه	hā'	h
و و	wāw	w
ي ي ي ي	yā'	y

Hebrew

א	aleph	'
ב	beth	b, bh
ג	gimmel	g, gh
ד	daleth	d, dh
ה	he	h
ו	waw	w
ז	zayin	z
ח	heth	ḥ
ט	teth	ṭ
י	yodh	y
כ ך	kaph	k, kh
ל	lamed	l
מ ם	mem	m
נ ן	nun	n
ס	samekh	s
ע	'ayin	'
פ ף	pe	p, ph
צ ץ	sadhe	ṣ
ק	qoph	q
ר	resh	r
שׂ	śin	ś
שׁ	shin	s
ת	taw	t, th

Greek

Α α	alpha	a
Β β	beta	b
Γ γ	gamma	g
Δ δ	delta	d
Ε ε	epsilon	e
Ζ ζ	zeta	z
Η η	eta	ē
Θ θ	theta	th
Ι ι	iota	i
Κ κ	kappa	k
Λ λ	lambda	l
Μ μ	mu	m
Ν ν	nu	n
Ξ ξ	xi	x
Ο ο	omicron	o
Π π	pi	p
Ρ ρ	rho	r, rh
Σ σ	sigma	s
Τ τ	tau	t
Υ υ	upsilon	u
Φ φ	phi	ph
Χ χ	chi	kh
Ψ ψ	psi	ps
Ω ω	omega	ō

Russian

А а		a
Б б		b
В в		v
Г г		g
Д д		d
Е е		e
Ё ё		yo
Ж ж		zh
З з		z
И и		i
Й й		ĭ
К к		k
Л л		l
М м		m
Н н		n
О о		o
П п		p
Р р		r
С с		s
Т т		t
У у		u
Ф ф		f
Х х		kh
Ц ц		ts
Ч ч		ch
Ш ш		sh
Щ щ		shch
Ъ ъ		(hard sign)
Ы ы		y
Ь ь		(soft sign)
Э э		é
Ю ю		yu
Я я		ya

Morse Code and Signaling

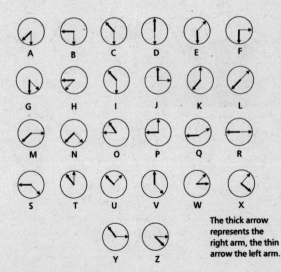

●▬	▬●●●	▬●▬●	▬●●	●	●●▬●
A	B	C	D	E	F
▬▬●	●●●●	●●	●▬▬▬	▬●▬	●▬●●
G	H	I	J	K	L
▬▬	▬●	▬▬▬	●▬▬●	▬▬●▬	●▬●
M	N	O	P	Q	R
●●●	▬	●●▬	●●●▬	●▬▬	▬●●▬
S	T	U	V	W	X
▬●▬▬	▬▬●●				
Y	Z				

●▬▬▬▬	●●▬▬▬	●●●▬▬	●●●●▬	●●●●●
1	2	3	4	5
▬●●●●	▬▬●●●	▬▬▬●●	▬▬▬▬●	▬▬▬▬▬
6	7	8	9	0

▬▬●●▬▬	●▬●▬●▬	●●▬▬●●	▬●▬●▬●
comma	full stop	question mark	semicolon
▬▬▬●●●	▬●●●●▬	●▬▬▬▬●	▬●▬▬●▬
colon	hyphen	apostrophe	parenthesis

The thick arrow represents the right arm, the thin arrow the left arm.

American Sign Language (ASL)

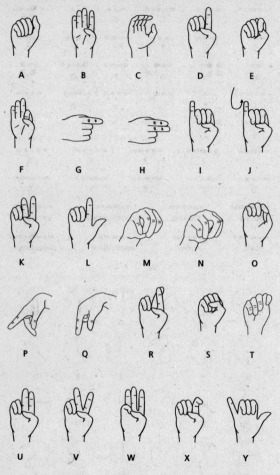

A   B   C   D   E

F   G   H   I   J

K   L   M   N   O

P   Q   R   S   T

U   V   W   X   Y

Z

Braille

A	B	C	D	E
F	G	H	I	J
K	L	M	N	O
P	R	Q	S	T
U	V	W	X	Y
Z	and	for	of	the

NATO Alphabet

A	Alpha	N	November
B	Bravo	O	Oscar
C	Charlie	P	Papa
D	Delta	Q	Quebec
E	Echo	R	Romeo
F	Foxtrot	S	Sierra
G	Golf	T	Tango
H	Hotel	U	Uniform
I	India	V	Victor
J	Juliet	W	Whiskey
K	Kilo	X	X-ray
L	Lima	Y	Yankee
M	Mike	Z	Zulu

WORK AND HOME: *Style and Usage*

Usage

Even the best writers are sometimes troubled by questions of correct usage. A guide to some of the most common questions is provided here, with discussion of the following topics:

singular or plural	*we* (with phrase following)
-s plural or singular	*I who, you who,* etc.
comparison of adjectives and adverbs	*you and I* or *you and me*
nouns ending in *-ics*	collective nouns
group possessive	*none* (pronoun)
may or *might*	*as* (followed by a pronoun)
I or *me, we* or *us*	

singular or plural

1. When subject and complement are different in number (i.e., one is singular, the other plural), the verb normally agrees with the subject, e.g.,

> (Plural subject)
> *Their wages were a mere pittance.*
> *Liqueur chocolates are our specialty.*

(The Biblical *The wages of sin is death* reflects an obsolete idiom in which *wages* took a singular verb.)

> (Singular subject)
> *What we need is customers.*
> *Our specialty is liqueur chocolates.*

2. A plural word or phrase used as a name, title, or quotation counts as singular, e.g.,

> *Sons and Lovers* has always been one of Lawrence's most popular novels.

3. A singular phrase (such as a prepositional phrase following the subject) that happens to end with a plural word should nevertheless be followed by a singular verb, e.g.,

> *Everyone except the French* has (not *want*) *Britain to join.*
> *One in six* has (not *have*)*his problem* .

See also *-s* plural or singular; nouns ending in *–ics*.

-s plural or singular

Some nouns, though they have the plural ending *-s*, are nevertheless usually treated as singular, taking singular verbs and pronouns referring back to them.

1. *News*
2. Diseases:
   measles
   mumps
   rickets
   shingles
   Measles and *rickets* can also be treated as ordinary plural nouns.
3. Games:
   billiards
   dominoes
   checkers
   craps
   quoits
   darts
4. Countries:
   the Bahamas
   the Philippines
   the Netherlands
   the United States

These are treated as singular when considered as a unit, which they commonly are in a political context, or when the complement is singular, e.g.,

> *The Philippines* is *a predominantly agricultural country.*
> *The United States* has withdrawn its ambassador.

The Bahamas and *the Philippines* are also the geographical names of the groups of islands that the two nations comprise, and in this use can be treated as plurals, e.g.,

> *The Bahamas* were *settled by British subjects.*

See also nouns ending in -ics.

comparison of adjectives and adverbs

The two ways of forming the comparative and superlative of adjectives and adverbs are:

1. Addition of suffixes *-er* and *-est*. Monosyllabic adjectives and adverbs almost always require these suffixes, e.g., *big* (bigger, biggest), *soon* (*sooner, soonest*), and normally so do many adjectives of two syllables, e.g., *narrow* (*narrower, narrowest*), *silly* (*sillier, silliest*).

2. Use of adverbs *more* and *most*. These are used with adjectives of three syllables or more (e.g., *difficult, memorable*), participles (e.g., *bored, boring*), many adjectives of two syllables (e.g., *afraid, awful, childish, harmless, static*), and adverbs ending in *-ly* (e.g., *highly, slowly*).

Adjectives with two syllables sometimes use suffixes and sometimes use adverbs.

There are many that never take the suffixes, e.g.,

antique	*bizarre*
breathless	*constant*
futile	*steadfast*

There is also a large class that is acceptable with either, e.g.,

clever	*pleasant*
handsome	*tranquil*
solemn	*cruel*
common	*polite*

The choice is largely a matter of preference.

nouns ending in -ics

Nouns ending in *-ics* denoting subjects or disciplines are sometimes treated as singular and sometimes as plural. Examples are:

apologetics	*mechanics*
genetics	*politics*
optics	*economics*
classics (as a study)	*metaphysics*
phonetics	*statistics*
linguistics	*electronics*
mathematics	*obstetrics*
physics	*tactics*
dynamics	*ethics*

When used strictly as the name of a discipline they are treated as singular:

Psychometrics is unable to investigate the nature of intelligence.

So also when the complement is singular:

Mathematics is his strong point.

When used more loosely, to denote a manifestation of qualities, often accompanied by a possessive, they are treated as plural:

His politics were a mixture of fear, greed, and envy.
I don't understand the mathematics of it, which are complicated.
The acoustics in this hall are dreadful.

So also when they denote a set of activities or pattern of behavior, as with words like:

acrobatics	athletics
dramatics	gymnastics
heroics	hysterics

E.g., The mental gymnastics required to believe this are beyond me.

group possessive

The group possessive is the construction by which the ending -'s of the possessive case can be added to the last word of a noun phrase, which is regarded as a single unit, e.g.,

The king of Spain's daughter
John and Mary's baby
Somebody else's umbrella
A quarter of an hour's drive

Expressions like these are natural and acceptable.

I or me, we or us, etc.

There is often confusion about which case of a personal pronoun to use when the pronoun stands alone or follows the verb to be.

1. When the personal pronoun stands alone, as when it forms the answer to a question, strictly formal usage requires it to have the case it would have if the verb were supplied:

"Who called him?" "I" (in full, I called him or I did).
"Which of you did he approach?" "Me" (in full, he approached me).

Informal usage permits the objective case in both kinds of sentence, but this is not acceptable in formal style. However, the nominative case often sounds stilted. One can avoid the problem by providing a verb, e.g.,

"Who likes cooking?" "I do."
"Who can cook?" "I can."
"Who is here?" "I am."

2. When a personal pronoun follows it is, it was, it may be, it could have been, etc., formal usage requires the nominative case:

Nobody could suspect that it was she.
We are given no clues as to what it must have felt like to be he.

Informal usage favors the objective case (not acceptable in formal style):

> *I thought it might have been* him *at the door.*
> *Don't tell me it's* them *again!*

When *who* or *whom* follows, the nominative case is obligatory in formal usage and quite usual informally:

> *It was* I *who painted that sign.*

The informal use of the objective case often sounds incorrect:

> *It was* her *who would get into trouble.*

In constructions that have the form *I am* + noun or noun phrase + *who*, the verb following *who* agrees with the noun (the antecedent of *who*) in number (singular or plural):

> *I am the sort of person who likes peace and quiet.*
> *You are the fourth of my colleagues who has told me that.*

may or might

There is sometimes confusion about whether to use *may* or *might* with the perfect tense when referring to a past event, e.g., *He may have done* or *He might have done.*

1. If uncertainty about the action or state denoted by the perfect remains – that is, if the truth of the event is still unknown at the time of speaking or writing— then either *may* or *might* is acceptable:

> *As they all wore so many different clothes of identically the same kind,*
> *there* may *have been several more or several less.*
> *For all we knew our complaint went unanswered, although of course they*
> might *have tried to call us while we were out of town.*

2. If there is no longer uncertainty about the event, or the matter was never put to the test, and therefore the event did not in fact occur, use *might*:

> *If that had come ten days ago my whole life* might *have been different .*
> *You should not have let him come home alone; he* might *have gotten lost.*

It is a common error to use *may* instead of *might* in the following circumstances:

> *If they had not invaded, then eventually we* may *have agreed to give them aid.*
> *I am grateful for his intervention, without which they* may *have remained in*
> *the refugee camp indefinitely.*
> *Schoenberg* may *never have gone atonal but for the breakup of his marriage.*

In each of these sentences "might" should be substituted for "may."

we (with phrase following)

Expressions consisting of *we* or *us* followed by a qualifying word or phrase, e.g., *we Americans* or *us Americans*, are often misused with the wrong case of the first person plural pronoun. In fact the rules are exactly the same as for *we* or *us* standing alone.

If the expression is the subject, *we* should be used:

> (Correct) *We were not always laughing as heartily as we Americans are sup-*
> *posed to do.*
> (Incorrect) *We all make mistakes, even* us *judges.*

Usage *(cont.)*

If the expression is the object or the complement of a preposition, *us* should be used:

> (Correct) To us *Americans, personal liberty is a vital principle.*
> (Incorrect)*The president said some nice things about* we *reporters in the press corps.*

I who, you who, etc.

The verb following a personal pronoun (*I, you, he,* etc.) + *who* should be the same as what would be used with the pronoun as a subject:

> *I, who* have *no savings to speak of, had to pay for the work.*
> *They made me, who* have *no savings at all, pay for the work* (not "who has").

When it is (*it was,* etc.) precedes *I who,* etc., the same rule applies: the verb agrees with the personal pronoun:

> *It's I who* have *done it.*
> *It could have been we who* were *mistaken.*

you and I or you and me

When a personal pronoun is linked by *and* or *or* to a noun or another pronoun, there is often confusion about which case to put the pronoun in. In fact the rule is exactly as it would be for the pronoun standing alone.

1. If the two words linked by *and* or *or* constitute the subject, the pronoun should be in the nominative case, e.g.,

> *Only she and her mother cared for the old house.*
> *That's what we would do, that is, John and I would.*
> *"Who could go?" "Either you or he."*

The use of the objective case is quite common in informal speech, but it is nonstandard, e.g.,

> *Perhaps only her and Mrs. Natwick had stuck to the christened name.*
> *That's how we look at it, me and Martha.*
> *Either Mary had to leave or me.*

2. If the two words linked by *and* or *or* constitute the object of the verb, or the complement of a preposition, the objective case should be used:

> *The afternoon would suit her and John better.*
> *It was time for Kenneth and me to go down to the living room.*

The use of the nominative case is very common informally. It probably arises from an exaggerated fear of the error indicated under 1 above. It remains, however, nonstandard, e.g.,

> *It was this that set Charles and I talking of old times .*
> *Why is it that people like you and I are so unpopular?*
> *Between you and I . . .*

This last expression is very commonly heard. *Between you and me* should always be substituted.

collective nouns

Collective nouns are singular words that denote many individuals, e.g., *audience, government, orchestra, the clergy, the public.*

It is normal for collective nouns, being singular, to be followed by singular verbs and pronouns (*is, has, consists,* and *it* in the examples below):

> *The government is determined to beat inflation, as it has promised.*
> *Their family is huge: it consists of five boys and three girls.*
> *The bourgeoisie is despised for not being proletarian.*

The singular verb and pronouns are preferable unless the collective is clearly and unmistakably used to refer to separate individuals rather than to a united body, e.g.,

> *The cabinet has made its decision.*

but

> *The cabinet are sitting at their places around the table with the president.*

The singular should always be used if the collective noun is qualified by a singular word like this, that, every, etc.:

> *This family is divided.*
> *Every team has its chance to win.*

none (pronoun)

The pronoun *none* can be followed either by singular verb and singular pronouns, or by plural ones. Either is acceptable, although the plural tends to be more common.

> Singular: *None of them was allowed to forget for a moment.*
> Plural: *None of the orchestras ever play there.*
> *None of the authors expected their books to become best-sellers.*

as (followed by a pronoun)

In the following sentences, formal usage requires the nominative case (*I, he, she, we, they*) on the assumption that the pronoun would be the subject if a verb were supplied:

> *You are just as intelligent as he* (in full, "as he is").
> *He might not have heard the song so often as I* (in full, "as I had").

Informal usage permits such constructions as

> *You are just as intelligent as him.*

Formal English uses the objective case (*me, him, her, us, them*) only when the pronoun would be the object if a verb were supplied:

> *I thought you preferred John to Mary, but I see that you like her just as much as him* (meaning "just as much as you like him").

⊙ Kirkpatrick, E.M. *The Oxford Essential Thesaurus.* New York: Berkeley, 1998.

Punctuation

Punctuation is an essential element of good writing because it makes the author's meaning clear to the reader. Although precise punctuation styles may vary somewhat among published sources, there are a number of fundamental principles worthy of consideration. Discussed below are the punctuation marks used in English:

comma	apostrophe
semicolon	quotation marks
colon	parentheses
period	dash
question mark	hyphen
exclamation point	

Comma

The comma is the most frequently used mark of punctuation in the English language. It signals to the reader a pause, which generally clarifies the author's meaning, and establishes a sensible order to the elements of written language. Among the most typical functions of the comma are the following:

1. It can separate the clauses of a compound sentence when there are two independent clauses joined by a conjunction, especially when the clauses are not very short:

> *It never occurred to me to look in the attic, and I'm sure it didn't occur to Rachel either.*
> *The Nelsons wanted to see the Grand Canyon at sunrise, but they overslept that morning.*

2. It can separate the clauses of a compound sentence when there is a series of independent clauses, the last two of which are joined by a conjunction:

> *The bus ride to the campsite was very uncomfortable, the cabins were not ready for us when we got there, the cook had forgotten to start dinner, and the rain was torrential.*

3. It is used to precede or set off, and therefore indicate, a nonrestrictive dependent clause (a clause that could be omitted without changing the meaning of the main clause):

> *I read her autobiography, which was published last July.*
> *They showed up at midnight, after most of the guests had gone home.*
> *The coffee, which is freshly brewed, is in the kitchen.*

4. It can follow an introductory phrase:

> *Having enjoyed the movie so much, he agreed to see it again.*
> *Born and raised in Paris, she had never lost her French accent.*
> *In the beginning, they had very little money to invest.*

5. It can set off words used in direct address:

> *Listen, people, you have no choice in the matter.*
> *Yes, Mrs. Greene, I will be happy to feed your cat.*

6. The comma can separate two or more coordinate adjectives (adjectives that could otherwise be joined with *and*) that modify one noun:

> *The cruise turned out to be the most entertaining, fun, and relaxing vacation I've ever had.*
> *The horse was tall, lean, and sleek.*

Note that cumulative adjectives (those not able to be joined with *and*) are not separated by a comma:

> *She wore bright yellow rubber boots.*

7. Use a comma to separate three or more items in a series or list:

> *Charlie, Melissa, Stan, and Mark will be this year's soloists in the spring concert.*
> *We need furniture, toys, clothes, books, tools, housewares, and other useful merchandise for the benefit auction.*

Note that the comma between the last two items in a series is sometimes omitted in less precise style:

> *The most popular foods served in the cafeteria are pizza, hamburgers and nachos.*

8. Use a comma to separate and set off the elements in an address or other geographical designation:

> *My new house is at 1657 Nighthawk Circle, South Kingsbury, Michigan.*
> *We arrived in Pamplona, Spain, on Thursday.*

9. Use a comma to set off direct quotations (note the placement or absence of commas with other punctuation):

> *"Kim forgot her gloves," he said, "but we have a pair she can borrow."*
> *There was a long silence before Jack blurted out, "This must be the world's ugliest painting."*
> *"What are you talking about?" she asked in a puzzled manner.*
> *"Happy New Year!" everyone shouted.*

10. A comma is used to set off titles after a person's name:

> *Katherine Bentley, M.D.*
> *Steven Wells, Esq.*

Semicolon

The semicolon has two basic functions:

1. It can separate two main clauses, particularly when these clauses are of equal importance:

> *The crowds gathered outside the museum hours before the doors were opened; this was one exhibit no one wanted to miss.*
> *She always complained when her relatives stayed for the weekend; even so, she usually was a little sad when they left.*

2. It can be used as a comma is used to separate such elements as clauses or items in a series or list, particularly when one or more of the elements already includes a comma:

> *The path took us through the deep, dark woods; across a small meadow; into a cold, wet cave; and up a hillside overlooking the lake.*
> *Listed for sale in the ad were two bicycles; a battery-powered, leaf-mulching lawn mower; and a maple bookcase.*

Colon

The colon has five basic functions:

1. It can introduce something, especially a list of items:

Punctuation *(cont.)*

> *In the basket were three pieces of mail: a postcard, a catalog, and a wedding invitation.*
> *Students should have the following items: backpack, loose-leaf notebook, pens and pencils, pencil sharpener, and ruler.*

2. It can separate two clauses in a sentence when the second clause is being used to explain or illustrate the first clause:

> *We finally understood why she would never go sailing with us: she had a deep fear of the water.*
> *Most of the dogs in our neighborhood are quite large: two of them are St. Bernards.*

3. It can introduce a statement or a quotation:

> *His parents say the most important rule is this: Always tell the truth.*
> *We repeated the final words of his poem: "And such is the plight of fools like me."*

4. It can be used to follow the greeting in a formal or business letter:

> *Dear Ms. Daniels:*
> *Dear Sir or Madam:*

5. In the U.S., the colon separates minutes from hours, and seconds from minutes, in showing time of day and measured lengths of time:

> *Please be at the restaurant before 6:45.*
> *Her best running time so far has been 00:12:35.*

Period

The period has two basic functions:

1. It is used to mark the end of a sentence:

> *It was reported that there is a shortage of nurses at the hospital. Several of the patients have expressed concern about this problem.*

2. It is often used at the end of an abbreviation:

> *On Fri., Sept. 12, Dr. Brophy noted that the patient's weight was 168 lbs. and that his height was 6 ft. 2 in.*

(Note that another period is not added to the end of the sentence when the last word is an abbreviation.)

Question Mark and Exclamation Point

The only sentences that do not end in a period are those that end in either a question mark or an exclamation point.

Question marks are used to mark the end of a sentence that asks a direct question (generally, a question that expects an answer):

> *Is there any reason for us to bring more than a few dollars?*
> *Who is your science teacher?*

Exclamation points are used to mark the end of a sentence that expresses a strong feeling, typically surprise, joy, or anger:

> *I want you to leave and never come back!*
> *What a beautiful view this is!*

Apostrophe

The apostrophe has two basic functions:

1. It is used to show where a letter or letters are missing in a contraction:

> *The directions are cont'd* [continued] *on the next page.*
> *We've* [we have] *decided that if she can't* [cannot] *go, then we aren't* [are not] *going either.*

2. It can be used to show possession:

   a. The possessive of a singular noun or an irregular plural noun is created by adding an apostrophe and an s:

   > *the pilot's uniform*
   > *Mrs. Mendoza's house*
   > *a tomato's bright red color*
   > *the oxen's yoke*

   b. The possessive of a regular plural noun is created by adding just an apostrophe:

   > *the pilots' uniforms* [referring to more than one pilot]
   > *the Mendozas' house* [referring to the Mendoza family]
   > *the tomatoes' bright red color* [referring to more than one tomato]

Quotation Marks

Quotation marks have two basic functions:

1. They are used to set off direct quotations (an exact rendering of someone's spoken or written words):

> *"I think the new library is wonderful," she remarked to David.*
> *We were somewhat lost, so we asked, "Are we anywhere near the art gallery?"*
> *In his letter he had written, "The nights here are quiet and starry. It seems like a hundred years since I've been wakened by the noise of city traffic and squabbling neighbors."*

Note that indirect quotes (which often are preceded by that, if, or whether) are not set off by quotation marks:

> *He told me that he went to school in Boston.*
> *We asked if we could still get tickets to the game.*

2. They can be used to set off words or phrases that have specific technical usage, or to set off meanings of words, or to indicate words that are being used in a special way in a sentence:

> *The part of the flower that bears the pollen is the "stamen."*
> *When I said "plain," I meant "flat land," not "ordinary."*
> *Oddly enough, in the theater, the statement "break a leg" is meant as an expression of good luck.*
> *What you call "hoagies," we call "grinders" or "submarine sandwiches."*
> *He will never be a responsible adult until he outgrows his "Peter Pan" behavior.*

Note that sometimes single quotation marks (the 'stamen.'), rather than double quotation marks as above (the "stamen."), may be used to set off words or phrases. What is most important is to be consistent in such usage.

Punctuation *(cont.)*

Parentheses

Parentheses are used, in pairs, to enclose information that gives extra detail or explanation to the regular text. Parentheses are used in two basic ways:

1. They can separate a word or words in a sentence from the rest of the sentence:

> *On our way to school, we walk past the Turner Farm (the oldest dairy farm in town) and watch the cows being fed.*
> *The stores were filled with holiday shoppers (even more so than last year).*

(Note that the period goes outside the parentheses, because the words in the parentheses are only part of the sentence.)

2. They can form a separate complete sentence:

> *Please bring a dessert to the dinner party. (It can be something very simple.) I look forward to seeing you there.*

(Note that the period goes inside the parentheses, because the words in the parentheses are a complete and independent sentence.)

Dash

A dash is used most commonly to replace the usage of parentheses within sentences. If the information being set off is in the middle of the sentence, a pair of dashes is used; if it is at the end of the sentence, just one dash is used:

> *On our way to school, we walk past the Turner Farm—the oldest dairy farm in town—and watch the cows being fed.*
> *The stores were filled with holiday shoppers—even more so than last year.*

Hyphen

A hyphen has three basic functions:

1. It can join two or more words to make a compound, especially when so doing makes the meaning more clear to the reader:

> *We met to discuss long-range planning.*
> *There were six four-month-old piglets at the fair.*
> *That old stove was quite a coal-burner.*

2. It can replace the word "to" when a span or range of data is given:

> *John Adams was president of the United States 1797-1801.*
> *Today we will look for proper nouns in the L-N section of the dictionary.*
> *The ideal weight for that breed of dog would be 75-85 pounds.*

3. It can indicate a word break at the end of a line. The break must always be between syllables:

> *It is important for any writer to know that there are numerous punctuation principles that are considered standard and proper, but there is also flexibility regarding acceptable punctuation. Having learned the basic "rules" of good punctuation, the writer will be able to adopt a specific and consistent style of punctuation that best suits the material he or she is writing.*

⊙ Garner, Bryan A. *A Dictionary of Modern American Usage.* New York: Oxford University Press, 1998.

Confused and Misused Words

adverse/averse Adverse means "unfavorable, opposed," and is usually applied to situations and events, not people, e.g., *The new drug has adverse side effects*. Averse is related in origin and also has the sense of "opposition," but its use is best restricted to describing a person's attitude, e.g., *I would not be averse to the prospect of traveling with you*.

affect/effect Both these words are both verbs and nouns, but only effect is common as a noun, usually meaning "a result, consequence, impression, etc.," e.g., *My father's strictness had no effect on my desire to learn*. As verbs they are used differently. Affect means "to produce an effect upon," e.g., *Smoking during pregnancy can affect a baby's development*. Effect means "to bring about," e.g., *Alterations were effected with some sympathy for the existing fabric*.

aggravate This word is commonly used in informal contexts to mean "to annoy or exasperate," rather than "to make worse or more serious"; this is considered incorrect by many people. An example of correct usage is *The psychological stress aggravates the horse's physical stress*.

all right/alright Although found widely, alright remains nonstandard, even where standard spelling is somewhat cumbersome, e.g., *I wanted to make sure it was all all right*.

all together/altogether These variants are used in different contexts. All together means "all at once" or "all in one place or in one group," e.g., *They came all together* or *We managed to get three bedrooms all together* (i.e., near each other). Altogether means "in total," e.g., *The hotel has twenty rooms altogether*.

amend/emend Amend, meaning "to make improvements or corrections in," is often confused with emend, a more technical word used in the context of textual correction. Examples of each are: *The Constitution was amended to limit presidential terms of office*; *The poems have been collected, arranged, and emended*.

anticipate Anticipate in the sense "expect, foresee" is well-established in informal use (e.g., *He anticipated a restless night*), but is regarded as incorrect by some people. The formal sense, "deal with or use before the proper time," is illustrated by the sentence *The specialist would find that the thesis he had been planning had already been anticipated*.

anyone/any one Anyone is written as two words only to emphasize a numerical sense, e.g., *Any one of us can do it*. Otherwise it is written as one word (e.g., *Anyone who wants to can come*).

averse See adverse.

born/borne Born is used with reference to birth (e.g., *was born in Detroit*). Borne, meaning "carried," is used in the expression *borne by* followed by the name of the mother (e.g., *was borne by Mary*), as well as in other senses (e.g., *a litter borne by four slaves*).

censor/censure Both these words are both verbs and nouns, but censor is used to mean "to cut unacceptable parts out of a book, movie, etc." or "a person who does this," while censure means "to criticize harshly" or "harsh criticism."

Confused and Misused Words *(cont.)*

compose/comprise Both these words can be used to mean "to constitute or make up," but compose is preferred in this sense, e.g., *Citizens act as witnesses in the courts and finally may compose the jury.* Comprise is correctly used to mean "to be composed of, consist of," e.g., *Each crew comprises a commander, a gunner, and a driver.*

continual/continuous Continual is used of something that happens very frequently, e.g., *There were continual interruptions,* whereas continuous is used of something that happens without pause, e.g., *There was a dull, continuous background noise.*

deprecate/depreciate Deprecate means "to express disapproval of, to deplore," e.g., *The establishment magazines began by deprecating the film's attitude towards terrorism,* while depreciate (apart from its financial senses) means "to disparage or belittle," e.g., *He was depreciating his own skills out of a strong sense of humility.*

disinterested/uninterested Disinterested is sometimes used in informal contexts to mean "not interested or uninterested," but this is widely regarded as incorrect. The proper meaning is "impartial," e.g., *I for one am making a disinterested search for information.* The use of the noun disinterest to mean "a lack of interest" is also objected to, but it is rarely used in any other sense.

effect See affect.

emend See amend.

enormity The original and preferred meaning is "extreme wickedness," as in *the enormity of the crime.* Enormity is commonly used to mean "enormousness; great size," e.g., *wilting under the enormity of the work,* but this is regarded as incorrect by many. Use the more precise enormousness for this sense.

exceptionable/exceptional Exceptionable means "open to objection," e.g., *There was nothing exceptionable in her behavior,* and is usually found in negative contexts. It is sometimes confused with the much more common word exceptional meaning "unusual, outstanding."

flammable See inflammable.

flaunt/flout These words are often confused because both suggest an element of arrogance or showing off. However, flaunt means "to display ostentatiously," e.g., *He liked to flaunt his wealth,* while flout means "to express contempt for or disobey (laws, convention, etc.)," e.g., *The fine is too low for those who flout the law continuously.*

-fuls/-s full The combining form -ful is used to form nouns meaning "the amount needed to fill," e.g., *cupful, spoonful.* The plural form of such words employs a final -s (*cupfuls, spoonfuls,* etc.). *Three cups full* would denote the individual cups rather than a quantity regarded in terms of a cup used as a measure, and would be used in such contexts as *They brought us three cups full of water.*

fulsome This word means "excessive, cloying, or insincere," but is often imprecisely used to mean "generous," as in the phrase *fulsome praise.*

hoi polloi This phrase, meaning "the common people, the masses," is usually preceded by the word *the*, e.g., *The hoi polloi grew weary and sat on the floor.* Strictly speaking, the *the* is unnecessary because *hoi* means "the" in Greek. Never use hoi polloi to mean "the elite," a disturbingly common error.

imply See infer.

incredible/incredulous The adjective incredible means "unbelievable" or "not convincing" and can be applied to a situation, statement, policy, or threat to a person, e.g., *I find this testimony incredible.* Incredulous means "disinclined to believe; skeptical" and is usually applied to a person's attitude, e.g., *You shouldn't wonder that I'm incredulous after all your lies.*

infer/imply Infer should be used to mean "to deduce or conclude," as in *We can infer from these studies that....* Its use to mean "to imply or suggest" is widely considered incorrect.

inflammable/flammable/nonflammable Both inflammable and flammable mean "easily set on fire or excited." The opposite is nonflammable. Where there is a danger of inflammable being understood to mean the opposite, i.e., "not easily set on fire," flammable should be used to avoid confusion.

ingenious/ingenuous Ingenious means "clever, skillful, or resourceful," e.g., *an ingenious device*, while ingenuous means "artless" or "frank," e.g., *We were charmed by the ingenuous honesty of the child.*

interment/internment Interment means "the burial of a corpse," while internment means "the confining of a prisoner."

irregardless See regardless.

inveigh/inveigle Inveigh (usually inveigh against) means "to speak or write about (something) with great hostility," while inveigle means "to persuade (someone) to do something by means of deception or flattery."

jibe/jive Jibe has several meanings; one is "to be in accord; to agree." A common error is to use jive for this sense, but as a verb jive really means "to taunt or sneer at," "to talk nonsense," or "to dance, especially to swing, jazz, or rock and roll music."

laudable/laudatory These words are sometimes confused. Laudable is the more common and means "commendable" or "praiseworthy," e.g., *The foundation pursued a laudable program of aid to schools and hospitals.* Laudatory means "expressing praise," e.g., *The proposed legislation enjoyed a laudatory editorial from the local newspaper.*

lay/lie In standard English lay is a transitive verb and lie intransitive. The intransitive use of lay, as in *The park ranger job gave him the opportunity of laying on the grass at lunchtime*, is best avoided. Similarly, the transitive use of lie, as in *Lie it on the table*, is also avoided by careful speakers and writers. In the first example, *laying* should be *lying*; in the second, *lie<* should be *lay*. These two verbs are often confused owing to their close similarity in form, including the fact that the past tense of *lie* is *lay*. A mnemonic using the traditional child's prayer *Now I lay me down to sleep ...* serves as a reminder that *lay* is transitive (with direct object *me*).

Confused and Misused Words *(cont.)*

like The use of like as a conjunction meaning "as" or "as if" (e.g., *I don't have a wealthy set of in-laws like you do* or *They sit up like they're begging for food*) should be avoided in formal writing or speech.

luxuriant/luxurious These words are sometimes confused. Luxuriant means "lush, profuse, or prolific," e.g., *forests of dark luxuriant foliage* or *luxuriant black eyelashes.* Luxurious, a much more common word, means "supplied with luxuries, extremely comfortable," e.g., *a luxurious hotel.*

masterful/masterly These words overlap in meaning and are sometimes confused. Apart from meaning "domineering," masterful also means "masterly" or "very skillful." However, it is generally used in this sense to describe a person, e.g., *He has only a marginal talent that he's masterful at exploiting*, while masterly usually describes an achievement or action, e.g., *This was a masterly use of the backhand volley.*

mutual This word is most properly defined as "reciprocal" (as in *mutual admiration*), but it frequently used to mean "common to two or more people," as in *a mutual friend* or *a mutual interest.* For clarity, use common or joint for this latter sense.

nonflammable See inflammable.

perquisite/prerequisite These words are sometimes confused. Perquisite usually means "an extra benefit or privilege," e.g., *There were no perquisites that came with the job, apart from one or two special privileges.* Prerequisite means "something required as a precondition," e.g., *A general education in the sciences is a prerequisite of professional medical training.*

prescribe/proscribe These words are sometimes confused, but they are nearly opposite in meaning. Prescribe means "to advise the use of" or "impose authoritatively," as in *The teachers would prescribe topics for the students to debate.* Proscribe means "to reject, denounce, or ban": *The superintendent proscribed tabloid newspapers from all school libraries.* (And a dictatorial regime might both prescribe and proscribe literature.)

protagonist The correct meaning of this word is "chief or leading character," e.g., *The choreographer creates movement that displays the protagonist's particular behavior and reactions.* Avoid using it loosely to mean "proponent; advocate or champion of a cause."

refute Strictly speaking, refute means "to prove (a person or statement) to be wrong," e.g., *No amount of empirical research can either confirm or refute the existence of God.* However, it is also sometimes used to mean "to deny or rebut." This usage is incorrect and should be avoided.

regardless/irregardless The latter word, with its illogical negative prefix, is widely heard, perhaps arising under the influence of such perfectly correct terms as "irrespective." It is to be avoided.

Scotch/Scots/Scottish In Scotland the terms Scots and Scottish are preferred to Scotch and they mean the same (e.g., *a Scots/Scottish accent*). Scotch is used in certain compound nouns, such as *Scotch broth*, *Scotch terrier*, and *Scotch whiskey*. Scotsman and Scotswoman are acceptable terms for persons from Scotland, never "Scotchman" or "Scotchwoman."

seasonable/seasonal Seasonable means "usual or suitable for the season" or "opportune," e.g., *Although seasonable, the weather was not suitable for picnics.* Seasonal means "of, depending on, or varying with the season," e.g., *Seasonal changes posed problems for mills situated on larger rivers.*

'til/till See until.

tortuous/torturous Tortuous means "full of twists and turns" or "devious; circuitous," e.g., *Both paths have proved tortuous and are strewn with awkward boulders.* Torturous, an adjective derived from "torture," means "involving torture; excruciating," e.g., *I found the concert a torturous experience because of the loudness of the music.*

triumphal/triumphant The more common of these triumphant, means "victorious" or "exultant," e.g., *Rosie returned triumphant with the file that had been missing.* Triumphal means "used in or celebrating a triumph," e.g., *The last element to be added was the magnificent triumphal arch.*

turbid/turgid Turbid is used of a liquid or color to mean "muddy; not clear," or of literary style, etc., to mean "confused," e.g., *the turbid utterances and twisted language of Carlyle.* Turgid means "swollen, inflated, or enlarged," but is also often used to describe literary style that is pompous or bombastic, e.g., *Communications from corporate headquarters were largely turgid memos filled with bureaucratic lingo.*

until/till/'til Until is more formal than till, and is more usual at the beginning of a sentence, e.g., *Until the 1920s it was quite unusual for women to wear short hair.* 'Til is considered incorrect in standard English and should be avoided.

venal/venial Venal means "corrupt, able to be bribed, or involving bribery," e.g., *Their venal court system can take decades to decide a case.* Venial means "slight, pardonable, excusable," or, of sins, "not mortal": *He forgave his wife's flirtations as merely venial offenses.*

worth while/worthwhile Worth while is used only predicatively, e.g., *Nobody had thought it worth while to call the police,* and means "worth the time or effort spent." Worthwhile also has this meaning but can be used both predicatively and attributively, e.g., *Only in unusual circumstances would investment be worthwhile* (predicative), or *He was a worthwhile subject for the experiment* (attributive). In addition, worthwhile has the sense "of value or importance," e.g., *It's great to be doing such a worthwhile job.*

⊙ Garner, Bryan A. *A Dictionary of Modern American Usage.* New York: Oxford University Press, 1998.

Proofreader's Marks

℘	delete	⁶⁶ ⁹⁹	quotation marks
⊘	delete and close up	( )	parentheses
⅄#	delete and leave space	[ ]	square brackets
∧	insert	=	hyphen
#	space	⅟M	em-dash
⊙	period	⅟N	en-dash
∧	comma	¶	new paragraph
∧	semicolon	diction/ary	break line or word
⁏ or ⊙	colon	∨	set as superscript
∨	apostrophe	∧	set as subscript

dictionary (transpose)	transpose
(tr)	transpose (note in margin)
(3)	spell out
(SP)	spell out (note in margin)
dictionary	capitalize
(cap)	set as capitals (note in margin)
Þictionary	make lower case
(lc)	set in lower case (note in margin)
dictionary	make boldface
(bf)	set in boldface (note in margin)
dictionary	make italic
(ital)	set in italic (note in margin)
dictionary	small caps
(sc)	set in small caps (note in margin)
(lf)	lightface (note in margin)
(rom)	set in roman (note in margin)

⊙ University of Chicago Press. *The Chicago Manual of Style*. 14th ed. Chicago: University of Chicago Press, 1993.

WORK AND HOME: *Measurement*

Common English Measures

Length

12 inches	= 1 foot	
3 feet	= 36 inches	= 1 yard
5,280 feet	= 1,760 yards	= 1 mile

Area

144 square inches	= 1 square foot	
9 square feet	= 1,296 square inches	= 1 square yard
4,840 square yards	= 43,560 square feet	= 1 acre
640 acres	= 1 square mile	

Volume

3 teaspoons	= 1 tablespoon		4 quarts	= 1 gallon
16 tablespoons	= 1 cup		2 gallons	= 1 peck
2 cups	= 1 pint		4 pecks	= 1 bushel
2 pints	= 1 quart			

Weight

437 1/2 grains	= 1 ounce
16 ounces	= 1 pound
2,000 pounds	= 1 ton

⊙ English Weights and Measures. http://home.clara.net/brianp/index.html.

Metric Measures

The metric system, a decimal (based on powers of 10) system of measurement, uses the same prefixes for each kind of measure. The root of the word indicates the measure in question:

-meter is for length
-liter is for volume
-gram is for weight

The chart below uses meter as an example. The root *meter* and symbol *m* can be changed to *liter (l)* or *gram (g)* as needed.

Symbol	Prefix	Value
Km	kilometer	1,000 meters
Hm	hectometer	100 meters
Dm	decameter	10 meters
m	meter	1 meter
dm	decimeter	.1 meter
cm	centimeter	.01 meter
mm	millimeter	.001 meter

Multiplying or dividing by factors of 10 reveals equivalent metric measures. Thus, 27 kilometers = (27 x 1,000) = 27,000 meters; 5 meters = (5 /.01) = 500 centimeters, and so on.

⊙ The World of Chemistry. "Metric System and Unit Conversion,"
http://edie.cprost.sfu.ca/~rhlogan/metric.html

English–Metric Conversions

Common Metric-to-English Conversions

Length

1 centimeter	≈ .3937 inch	≈ .0328 foot	≈ .0109 yard
1 meter	≈ 39.37 inches	≈ 3.28 feet	≈ 1.09 yards
1 kilometer	≈ .62 mile		

Weight

1 gram	≈ .035 ounce	≈ .0022 pound
1 kilogram	≈ 2.2 pounds	

Volume

1 liter	≈ 1.057 quarts	≈ .264 gallon

Common English-to-Metric Conversions

Length

1 inch	≈ 2.54 centimeters	≈ .0254 meter
1 foot	≈ 30.48 centimeters	≈ .3048 meter
1 yard	≈ 91.44 centimeters	≈ .9144 meter
1 mile	≈ 1,609 meters	≈ 1.609 kilometers

Weight

1 ounce	≈ 28.35 grams	≈ .02835 kilogram
1 pound	≈ 453.6 grams	≈ .4536 kilograms

Volume

1 quart	≈ .946 liter
1 gallon	≈ 3.785 liters

⊙ Heddens, James W. and William R. Speer. *Today's Mathematics*, 7th edition. New York: Macmillan, 1992.

Common Cooking Measures

Volume

3 teaspoons	= 1 tablespoon	16 tablespoons	= 1 cup	
4 tablespoons	= (cup	2 cups	= 1 pint	
5 1/2 tablespoons	= (cup	4 cups	= 2 pints	= 1 quart
8 tablespoons	= (cup	4 quarts	= 1 gallon	

Liquid weight

8 ounces	= 1 cup	64 ounces	= 1/2 gallon
16 ounces	= 1 pint	128 ounces	= 1 gallon
32 ounces	= 1 quart		

Dry Weight

8 ounces	= 1/2 pound	16 ounces	= 1 pound

⊙ English Weights and Measures. http://home.clara.net/brianp/index.html

Temperature Conversions

Celsius to Fahrenheit: $[(C \times 9) / 5] + 32 = F$
Fahrenheit to Celsius: $[(F - 32) \times 5] / 9 = C$
Celsius to Kelvin: $C + 273.15 = K$
Kelvin to Celsius: $K - 273.15 = C$
Fahrenheit / Kelvin: convert Fahrenheit or Kelvin figure to Celsius, then calculate

Degrees Fahrenheit	Degrees Celsius	Degrees Kelvin		Degrees Fahrenheit	Degrees Celsius	Degrees Kelvin
−25	−31.67	241.48		49	9.44	282.59
−20	−28.89	244.26		50	10.00	283.15
−15	−26.11	247.04		51	10.56	283.71
−10	−23.33	249.82		52	11.11	284.26
−5	−20.56	252.59		53	11.67	284.82
−4	−20.00	253.15		54	12.22	285.37
−3	−19.44	253.71		55	12.78	285.93
−2	−18.89	254.26		56	13.33	286.48
−1	−18.33	254.82		57	13.89	287.04
0	−17.78	255.37		58	14.44	287.59
1	−17.22	255.93		59	15.00	288.15
2	−16.67	256.48		60	15.56	288.71
3	−16.11	257.04		61	16.11	289.26
4	−15.56	257.59		62	16.67	289.82
5	−15.00	258.15		63	17.22	290.37
6	−14.44	258.71		64	17.78	290.93
7	−13.89	259.26		65	18.33	291.48
8	−13.33	259.82		66	18.89	292.04
9	−12.78	260.37		67	19.44	292.59
10	−12.22	260.93		68	20.00	293.15
11	−11.67	261.48		69	20.56	293.71
12	−11.11	262.04		70	21.11	294.26
13	−10.56	262.59		71	21.67	294.82
14	−10.00	263.15		72	22.22	295.37
15	−9.44	263.71		73	22.78	295.93
16	−8.89	264.26		74	23.33	296.48
17	−8.33	264.82		75	23.89	297.04
18	−7.78	265.37		76	24.44	297.59
19	−7.22	265.93		77	25.00	298.15
20	−6.67	266.48		78	25.56	298.71
21	−6.11	267.04		79	26.11	299.26
22	−5.56	267.59		80	26.67	299.82
23	−5.00	268.15		81	27.22	300.37
24	−4.44	268.71		82	27.78	300.93
25	−3.89	269.26		83	28.33	301.48
26	−3.33	269.82		84	28.89	302.04
27	−2.78	270.37		85	29.44	302.59
28	−2.22	270.93		86	30.00	303.15
29	−1.67	271.48		87	30.56	303.71
30	−1.11	272.04		88	31.11	304.26
31	−0.56	272.59		89	31.67	304.82
32	0.00	273.15		90	32.22	305.37
33	0.56	273.71		91	32.78	305.93
34	1.11	274.26		92	33.33	306.48
35	1.67	274.82		93	33.89	307.04
36	2.22	275.37		94	34.44	307.59
37	2.78	275.93		95	35.00	308.15
38	3.33	276.48		96	35.56	308.71
39	3.89	277.04		97	36.11	309.26
40	4.44	277.59		98	36.67	309.82
41	5.00	278.15		99	37.22	310.37
42	5.56	278.71		100	37.78	310.93
43	6.11	279.26		105	40.56	313.71
44	6.67	279.82		110	43.33	316.48
45	7.22	280.37		115	46.11	319.26
46	7.78	280.93		120	48.89	322.04
47	8.33	281.48		125	51.67	324.82
48	8.89	282.04		212	100	373.15

⊙ Perfectly Useless Software. "Handy-Dandy Super-Nifty Temperature Conversion Table," http://students.washington.edu/kyle/temptable.jpg
Also see: www.nws.mbay.net

WORK AND HOME: *Education and Learning*

College: Information Sources

With a high school diploma or equivalent, a student may pursue undergraduate studies toward an associate's degree (typically requiring two years of full-time coursework) or a bachelor's degree (typically requiring four years of full-time coursework). Most students earn undergraduate degrees while attending school full-time, while others take night or weekend classes while working. Financial assistance is available through loans, grants, and work-study programs.

Online Sources	Website/Phone
The Center for All Collegiate Information *a Web-only source*	www.collegiate.net/
Back to College c/o WD Communications P.O. Box 2001 Fullerton, CA 92837	www.back2college.com/ (714) 447-0734
CollegeDegree.com *a Web-only source*	www.collegedegree.com/
U.S.News Online: .edu *a Web-only source* *a service of:* U.S. News & World Report, Inc. 1050 Thomas Jefferson Street, NW Washington, D.C. 20007	www.usnews.com/usnews/edu/ college/cohome.htm (202) 955-2000
CollegeView *a Web-only source* *created by:* Hobsons 10200 Alliance Road Cincinnati, OH 45242	www.collegeview.com/ 800-927-8439
Overview *a Web-only source*	www.overview.com/
Universities.com *a Web-only source*	www.universities.com/

⊙ Aviezar, K. Patricia. *Peterson's Game Plan for Getting into College, First Edition.* Lawrenceville, N.J.: Peterson's, 2000.

Barron's. *Barron's Compact Guide to Colleges, 12th Edition.* Hauppauge, N.Y.: Barron's Educational Series, 2000.

Fiske, Edward B. *The Fiske Guide to Colleges 2001.* New York: Time Books, 2000.

Princeton Review. *Pocket Guide to Colleges.* New York: Random House, 2000.

Yale Daily News. *The Insider's Guide to the Colleges 2001.* New York: Griffin Trade Paperback, 2000.

Graduate School: Information Sources

With a four-year college degree or equivalent, a student may pursue graduate studies toward a masters, doctorate, or other higher degree. Most require at least two years of full-time coursework. Many students earn graduate degrees while attending school full-time, while many others take night or weekend classes while working. Financial assistance is available through loans, grants, and work-study programs.

Online Sources	Website/Phone
Council of Graduate Schools	www.cgsnet.org/ResoucesForStudents/ index.htm
One Dupont Circle NW, Suite 430	Phone: (202) 223-3791
Washington, D.C. 20036-1173	Fax: (202) 331-7157
GradView a Web-only source	www.gradview.com/
Gradschools.com *a Web-only source* *a service of:*	www.gradschools.com/linkus.html
Educational Directories Unlimited, Inc.	Phone: (610) 499-9200
University Technology Park	Fax: (610) 499-9205
1450 Edgmont Avenue, Suite 140	E-mail: info@edudirectories.com
Chester, PA 19013	
Peterson's: The Grad Channel *a Web-only source*	iiswinprd01.petersons.com/ GradChannel/
U.S.News Online: .edu beyond/bchome.htm *a Web-only source* *a service of:*	www.usnews.com/usnews/edu/
U.S. News & World Report, Inc.	Phone: (202) 955-2000
1050 Thomas Jefferson Street, NW	
Washington, D.C. 20007	
Graduate Record Examinations (Educational Testing Service) *a Web-only source* *General inquiries:*	www.gre.org/
GRE-ETS	Phone: (609) 771-7670
P.O. Box 6000	Fax: (609) 771-7906
Princeton, NJ 08541-6000	E-mail: gre-info@ets.org
All About Grad School *a Web-only source*	www.allaboutgradschool.com/ usgradschools/

⊙ Barron's. *Barron's Profiles of American Colleges, 23rd Edition.* Hauppauge, N.Y.: Barron's Educational Series, 1998.

Bloom, Dale F., Jonathan D. Karp, and Nicholas Cohen. *The Ph.D. Process: A Student's Guide to Graduate School in the Sciences.* New York: Oxford University Press, 1999.

Doughty, Harold R. *Guide to American Graduate Schools, Eighth Edition.* New York: Penguin, 1997.

Gourman, Jack. *The Gourman Report: A Rating of Graduate and Professional Programs in American and International Universities, Eighth Edition* (revised). New York: Random House, 1997.

International Universities: Information Sources

The opportunity to study abroad for a four-year or post-graduate degree is available in nearly every country, in every language, including English.

Online Sources	Website/Phone
International Association of Universities IAU/UNESCO Information Centre on Higher Education UNESCO House 1, rue Miollis 75732 PARIS Cedex 15 France	www.unesco.org/iau Phone: 011-33-1-45.68.26.12 Fax: 011-33-1-47.34.76.05 E-mail: centre.iau@unesco.org
EI Education International, Ltd. 205-5325 Cordova Bay Road Victoria, British Columbia V8Y 283 Canada	www.eiworldwide.com Phone: (250) 658-6283 Fax: (250) 658-6285 E-mail: info@educationinternational.com
The Internationalist "International Business Schools" *a Web-only source*	www.internationalist.com/ COMPANIES/Schools.html
Studyabroad.com *a Web-only source a service of:* Educational Directories Unlimited, Inc. University Technology Park 1450 Edgmont Avenue, Suite 140 Chester, PA 19013	www.studyabroad.com Phone: (610) 499-9200 Fax: (610) 499-9205 E-mail: info@edudirectories.com
World Universities *a Web-only source a service of:* Bauhinia World Connection Kee Wah Industrial Building 666 Castle Peak Road Kowloon, Hong Kong	www.bauhinia.com/university Phone: (852) 2785-6081 Fax: (852) 2785-1401 E-mail: info@bauhinia.com
Central and Eastern European Directory On-Line *a Web-only source*	www.ceebd.co.uk/ceeed/educatio.htm

⊙ Education International. *The Guide to Universities and Colleges in Canada.* Brussels, Belgium: Education International, 1999.

Gourman, Jack. *The Gourman Report: A Rating of Undergraduate Programs in American and International Universities, Tenth Edition.* New York: Random House, 1997.

International Association of Universities. *World List of Universities, 21st Edition.* New York: Grove's Dictionaries, 2000.

Student Financial Aid: Information Sources

Financial assistance for post-secondary education in the United States is available in the form of grants, loans, and work-study programs. The primary criteria for funding are financial need and merit.

Online Sources	Website/Phone
U.S. Department of Education	www.ed.gov/prog_info/SFA/ StudentGuide/
400 Maryland Avenue, SW Washington, D.C. 20202-0498	www.ed.gov/finaid.html www.ed.gov/offices/OSFAP/Students/ www.fafsa.ed.gov/ Phone: 800-433-3243 800-730-8913 (for TTY users) (319) 337-5665 (if no 800 access)
National Association of Student Financial Aid Administrators 1129 20th Street NW, Suite 400 Washington, D.C. 20036-3489	www.nasfaa.org/nasfaa/ Phone: (202) 785-0453
Nellie Mae 50 Braintree Hill Office Park, Suite 300 Braintree, MA 02184	www.nelliemae.com/ Phone: 800-367-8848 Fax: 800-931-2200
Sallie Mae 11600 Sallie Mae Drive Reston, VA 20193	www.salliemae.com/ 800-239-4269 (info about financing a college education) 800-891-1410 (info about PLUS*) *Parent Loans for Undergraduate Students
FinAid! ("The SmartStudent™ Guide to Financial Aid") *a Web-only source*	www.finaid.org/
Student Loan Funding Resources, LLC One West Fourth Street, Suite 200 Cincinnati, OH 45202	www.studentloanfunding.com Phone: 877-477-7537 (toll-free) Fax: 513-763-4340

⊙ Cassidy, Daniel J. *The Scholarship Book 2001: The Complete Guide to Private-Sector Scholarships, Fellowships, Grants, and Loans for the Undergraduate.* Upper Saddle River, N.J.: Prentice Hall, 2000.

College Board. *College Cost & Financial Aid Handbook 2001.* New York: Henry Holt, 2000.

Davis, Herm, and Joyce Lain Kennedy. *College Financial Aid for Dummies.* Foster City, CA: IDG, 1999.

Standard Admission Tests

For students entering undergraduate and graduate schools, standardized entrance examinations are typical requirements. For the schools' admissions officers, the scores on these tests provide a basis on which to judge students from varying educational backgrounds with a common yardstick. Different admissions tests are designed to satisfy different academic criteria, so it is important that prospective students familiarize themselves with the examination requirements of their chosen schools. Twelve of the standard admissions tests administered in the United States are discussed here.

Pronunciation note: These tests are best known by their abbreviated names, which are not pronounced as words, but as initials, letter by letter. For example, the ACT is not pronounced like the word "act"; rather, each letter is spoken: "A-C-T."

Standard Admission Tests *(cont.)*

ACT (or ACT Assessment) (American College Testing)
¥ Administered by ACT (a nonprofit organization that, until 1996, went by the name American College Testing Program), for college-bound students (typically high school juniors and seniors).
¥ Measures proficiency in English, mathematics, reading, and science.
¥ Many schools that require the taking of SAT II tests will accept the ACT in lieu of the SAT IIs.

AP (Advanced Placement)
¥ Sponsored by the College Examination Board and administered in high schools, for college-bound students.
¥ AP exams are available for more than 30 subjects.
¥ A passing score on an AP exam in any given subject typically earns either college credit or advanced placement in that subject.

DAT (Dental Admissions Test)
¥ Administered by the American Dental Association (ADA), as required for admittance into dental school.
¥ Measures academic aptitude, scientific comprehension, and perceptual ability.

GMAT (Graduate Management Admissions Test)
¥ Administered by the Educational Testing Service (ETS), for prospective business-school graduate students.
¥ Measures verbal, mathematical, and analytical writing skills.

GRE (Graduate Record Examination)
¥ Administered by the Educational Testing Service (ETS), for prospective graduate students.
¥ Measures verbal, quantitative, and analytical reasoning skills.
¥ Many graduate schools base the student s eligibility for merit-based grants, fellowships, and assistantships partly or largely on GRE scores.

LSAT (Law School Admissions Test)
¥ Administered by Law School Admission Services (LSAS), as required for admittance into law school.
¥ Measures critical reading, logical reasoning, analytical reasoning, and strategic thinking skills.

MCAT (Medical College Admissions Test)
¥ Administered by the Association of American Medical Colleges (AAMC), as required for admittance into medical school.
¥ Measures proficiency in the basic sciences, general problem-solving, critical thinking, and communication.
¥ The MCAT is often considered the most intensive of the admissions examinations.

OAT (Optometry Admission Test)
¥ Administered by the Association of Schools and Colleges of Optometry (ASCO), as required for admittance into optometry school.
¥ Measures proficiency in physics, chemistry, biology, reading comprehension, and quantitative reasoning.

PCAT (Pharmacy College Admissions Test)
¥ Administered by the Psychological Corporation, for prospective pharmacy-school graduate students.
¥ Measures scientific, mathematical, and verbal skills.

PSAT (Preliminiary Scholastic Assessment Test)

- Administered by the Educational Testing Service (ETS), for college-bound students (typically high school sophomores and juniors).
- Shorter than (but very similar in content to) the SAT, the PSAT is often taken as practice, in preparation for the SAT.
- PSAT scores are commonly considered by scholarship committees.

SAT (or SAT I) (Scholastic Assessment Test)

- Administered by the Educational Testing Service (ETS), for college-bound students (typically high school juniors and seniors).
- Measures proficiency in mathematics, vocabulary and reading.
- The SAT is the most widely distributed college admissions test in the United States.

SAT II (Scholastic Assessment Test II)

- Administered by the Educational Testing Service (ETS), for college-bound students (typically high school juniors and seniors).
- SAT II exams are available for more than 20 subjects.
- Unlike the SAT I, which measures general math and verbal skills, each SAT II exam measures the student's knowledge of a specific discipline.

⊙ Kaplan. "Test Prep Info Center," www.kaptest.com/

Paul, William Henry. *Getting In: Inside the College Admissions Process.* Cambridge, Mass.: Perseus, 1997.

TurboGrad. "SAT Prep & More," www.turbograd.com/default.asp

Libraries: Dewey Decimal System

The Dewey Decimal System (or "Dewey Decimal Classification") is based on a library classification system formulated in 1873 by American librarian Melvil Dewey (1851–1931). First published in 1876, the Dewey Decimal System uses numerical categorization for organizing, as well as locating, the contents of a library and has been adopted by more than 200,000 libraries in nearly 140 countries. In simplest terms, the system divides all subject matter into ten main classes, which are then divided and subdivided, making the classification progressively more specific. The listing that follows gives the main classes and their primary divisions.

000	Generalities	120	Epistemology
000	Generalities & Computer Science	130	Paranormal Phenomena & Occult
010	Bibliographies	140	Specific Schools of Philosophy
020	Library & Information Sciences	150	Psychology
030	General Encyclopedias	160	Logic
040	*Unassigned*	170	Ethics
050	General Periodicals	180	Ancient, Medieval, & Oriental Philosophy
060	General Organizations and Museums	190	Modern Western Philosophy
070	Journalism & Publishing	200	Religion
080	General Collections	200	General Religion
090	Manuscripts & Rare Books	210	Natural Theology
100	Philosophy & Psychology	220	Bible
100	Philosophy	230	Christian Theology
110	Metaphysics	240	Christian Moral & Devotional Theology

250	Christian Religious Orders & Local Church	580	Botanical Sciences
260	Christian Social and Ecclesiastical Theology	590	Zoological Sciences
		600	Applied Sciences & Technology
270	Christian Church History & Geography	600	General Technology
		610	Medical Sciences
280	Christian Denominations & Sects	620	Engineering
		630	Agriculture
290	Non-Christian and Comparative Religion	640	Home Economics & Family Living
300	Social Sciences	650	Management
300	Sociology, Anthropology, & Culture	660	Chemical Technologies
		670	Manufacturing
310	General Statistics	680	Application-specific Manufacturing
320	Political Science		
330	Economics	690	Building
340	Law	700	Arts
350	Public Administration	700	Art Theory, History, & Education
360	Social Concerns & Services		
370	Education	710	Civic & Landscape Art
380	Trade, Commerce, & Communications	720	Architecture
		730	Sculpture
390	Customs, Etiquette, & Folklore	740	Drawing & Decorative Arts
		750	Painting
400	Languages	760	Graphic and Printed Arts
400	Language	770	Photography
410	Linguistics	780	Music
420	English (& Old English) Language	790	Sports, Recreation, & Performing Arts
430	Germanic & Scandinavian Languages	800	Literature
		800	General Literature & Rhetoric
440	French Language		
450	Italian, Romanian, & Rhaeto-Romantic Languages	810	American Literature
		820	English (& Old English) Literature
460	Spanish & Portuguese Languages		
		830	Germanic Literature
470	Latin Language	840	French Literature
480	Classical Greek Language	850	Italian, Romanian, & Rhaeto-Romantic Literature
490	Other Languages		
500	Natural Sciences & Mathematics	860	Spanish & Portuguese Literature
500	General Science & Mathematics	870	Latin Literature
		880	Classical Greek Literature
510	Mathematics	890	Literature of Other Languages
520	Astronomy & Allied Sciences		
		900	History & Geography
530	Physics	900	General History
540	Chemistry & Allied Sciences	910	Geography & Travel
550	Earth Sciences	920	Biography, Geneaology, & Insignia
560	Paleontology		
570	Life Sciences	930	Ancient World History

940	European History	970	North American History
950	Asian History	980	South American History
960	African History	990	History of Other Areas

⊙ Fowler, Allen. *The Dewey Decimal System.* Danbury, Conn.: Grolier, 1997.

Mortimer, Mary. *Learn Dewey Decimal System, 21st Edition.* Lanham, Md.: Scarecrow, 1999.

Online Computer Library Center, Inc. "Dewey Decimal Classification," www.oclc.org/oclc.fp/

Library of Congress Classification System

The Library of Congress Classification System (also known as the LCC) is the library classification system that was designed and developed for the U.S. Library of Congress in Washington, D.C. Much of the groundwork for the current system was laid by Librarian of Congress Herbert Putnam (1861–1955) a hundred years ago. Used in many academic libraries, the LCC is an alpha-numeric system, in which each book (or magazine, etc.) is assigned a "call number" comprised of letters and numerals. The first level of classification is identified by one letter (using all letters of the alphabet except I, O, W, X, and Y). The second, more specific level uses two or three letters, and the next level introduces numerals, making the classification progressively more specific. The listing that follows gives the main classes and their primary alphabetic divisions.

A	General Works	BP	Islam; Bahaism; Theosophy, etc.
AC	Collections; Series; Collected works	BQ	Buddhism
AE	Encyclopedias	BR	Christianity
AG	Dictionaries; Other General Reference Works	BS	The Bible
		BT	Doctrinal Theology
AI	Indexes	BV	Practical Theology
AM	Museums; Collectors & Collecting	BX	Christian Denominations
		C	Auxiliary Sciences of History
AN	Newspapers	CB	History of Civilization
AP	Periodicals	CC	Archaeology
AS	Academies & Learned Societies	CD	Diplomatics, Archives, Seals
		CE	Technical Chronology, Calendar
AY	Yearbooks; Almanacs; Directories	CJ	Numismatics
AZ	History of Scholarship & Learning; The Humanities	CN	Inscriptions, Epigraphy
		CR	Heraldry
B	Philosophy; Psychology; Religion	CS	Genealogy
		CT	Biography
B	Philosophy (General)	D	History: General & Old World
BC	Logic	D	History (General)
BD	Speculative Philosophy	DA	Great Britain
BF	Psychology	DAW	Central Europe
BH	Aesthetics	DB	Austria; Liechtenstein; Hungary; Czechoslovakia
BJ	Ethics; Social Usages; Etiquette	DC	France
BL	Religion; Mythology; Rationalism	DD	Germany
		DE	Mediterranean Region; Greco-Roman World
BM	Judaism		

Library of Congress Classification System (cont.)

DF	Greece	HQ	The Family; Marriage; Women
DG	Italy		
DH	Belgium; Luxemburg	HS	Societies: Secret, Benevolent, etc.; Clubs
DJ	Holland		
DJK	Eastern Europe	HT	Communities; Classes; Races
DK	Russia (& former Soviet Union); Poland	HV	Social Pathology; Social & Public Welfare; Criminology
DL	Northern Europe; Scandinavia	HX	Socialism Communism; Anarchism
DP	Spain; Portugal		
DQ	Switzerland	J	Political Science
DR	Balkan Peninsula	J	General Legislative & Executive Papers
DS	Asia		
DT	Africa	JA	Collections & General Works
DU	Oceania (South Seas)	JC	Political Theory; Theory of the State
DX	Gypsies		
E	History (General): North America; United States	JF	Constitutional History & Administration (General)
F	History: United States Local History; Latin America; South America	JK	Constitutional History & Administration: United States
		JL	Constitutional History & Administration: British America; Latin America
G	Geography; Maps; Anthropology; Recreation		
		JN	Constitutional History & Administration: Europe
G	Geography (General); Atlases; Maps	JQ	Constitutional History & Administration: Asia; Africa; Australia; Oceania
GA	Mathematical Geography; Cartography		
		JS	Local Government; Municipal Government
GB	Physical Geography		
GC	Oceanography	JV	Colonies and Colonization; Emigration & Immigration; International Migration
GE	Environmental Sciences		
GF	Human Ecology; Anthropogeography		
		JX	International Law
GN	Anthropology	JZ	International Relations
GR	Folklore	K	Law
GT	Manners & Customs	K	Law (General)
GV	Recreation & Leisure	KD	United Kingdom; Ireland
H	Social Sciences	KDZ	America; North America
HA	Statistics	KE	Canada
HB	Economic Theory; Demography	KF	United States
		KG	Latin America (General)
HC	Economic History & Conditions (by region)	KH	South America (General)
		KJ-KK	Europe
HD	Economic History & Conditions	KL	History of Law: The Ancient Orient
HE	Transportation & Communications	KM	General
		KN-KP	South Asia; Southeast Asia; East Asia
HF	Commerce		
HG	Finance	KQ-KT	Africa
HJ	Public Finance	KU	Australia
HM	Sociology	KV-KW	Pacific Area Jurisdictions
HN	Social History & Conditions; Social Problems		

KZ	Law of Nations	PJ	Oriental Languages and
L	Education		Literature (General); Semitic
L	Education (General)		Languages & Literature
LA	History of Education	PK	Indo-Iranian Languages &
LB	Theory & Practice of		Literature
	Education	PL	Languages & Literature of
LC	Special Aspects of Education		Eastern Asia, Africa, &
LD	Educational Institutions:		Oceania
	United States	PM	Hyperborean, Indian, &
LE	Educational Institutions:		Artificial Languages
	America (outside of United	PN	Literature (General)
	States)	PQ	Romance Literature
LF	Educational Institutions:	PR	English Literature
	Europe	PS	American Literature
LG	Educational Institutions:	PT	Germanic Literature
	Asia; Africa; Australia;	PZ	Juvenile Belles Lettres
	Oceania	Q	Science
LH	School Magazines & Papers	Q	Science (General)
LJ	Student Fraternities &	QA	Mathematics
	Societies in United States	QB	Astronomy
LT	Textbooks	QC	Physics
M	Music (and Books on Music)	QD	Chemistry
M	Music (General);	QE	Geology
	Instrumental Music; Vocal	QH	Natural History (General);
	Music		Biology (General)
ML	Literature of Music	QK	Botany
MT	Musical Instruction and	QL	Zoology
	Study	QM	Human Anatomy
N	Fine Arts	QP	Physiology
N	Visual Arts (General) [for	QR	Microbiology
	Photography, see TR]	R	Medicine
NA	Architecture	R	Medicine (General)
NB	Sculpture	RA	Public Aspects of Medicine
NC	Drawing; Design; Illustration	RB	Pathology
ND	Painting	RC	Internal Medicine; Practice of
NE	Print Media		Medicine
NK	Decorative Arts; Applied Arts;	RD	Surgery
	Decoration & Ornament	RE	Ophthalmology
NX	Arts in General	RF	Otorhinolaryngology
P	Language & Literature	RG	Gynecology & Obstetrics
P	Philology & Linguistics	RJ	Pediatrics
	(General)	RK	Dentistry
PA	Classical Languages &	RL	Dermatology
	Literature	RM	Therapeutics; Pharmacology
PB	Celtic Languages & Literature	RS	Pharmacy; Materia Medica
PC	Romance Languages	RT	Nursing
PD	Germanic Languages	RV	Botanic, Thomsonian, &
PE	English		Eclectic Medicine
PF	West Germanic	RX	Homeopathy
PG	Slazvic, Baltic, & Albanian	RZ	Other Systems of Medicine
	Languages & Literature	S	Agriculture
PH	Finno-Ugrian & Basque	S	Agriculture (General)
	Languages & Literature	SB	Plant Culture

SD	Forestry
SF	Animal Culture
SH	Aquaculture; Fisheries; Angling
SK	Hunting
T	Technology
T	Technology (General)
TA	Engineering (General); Civil Engineering (General)
TC	Hydraulic Engineering; Ocean Engineering
TD	Environmental Technology; Sanitary Engineering
TE	Highway Engineering; Roads & Pavements
TF	Railroad Engineering & Operation
TG	Bridge Engineering
TH	Building Construction
TJ	Mechanical Engineering; Machinery
TK	Electrical Engineering; Electronics; Nuclear Engineering
TL	Motor Vehicles; Aeronautics; Astronautics
TN	Mining Engineering; Metallurgy
TP	Chemical Technology
TR	Photography
TS	Manufactures
TT	Handicrafts; Arts & Crafts
TX	Home Economics
U	Military Science

U	Military Science (General)
UA	Armies: Organization, Description, Facilities, etc.
UB	Military Administration
UC	Maintenance & Transportation
UD	Infantry
UE	Cavalry; Armored & Mechanized Cavalry
UF	Artillery
UG	Military Engineering; Air Forces; Air Warfare
UH	Other Services
V	Naval Science
V	Naval Science (General)
VA	Navies: Organization, Description, Facilities, etc.
VB	Naval Administration
VC	Naval Maintenance
VD	Naval Seamen
VE	Marines
VF	Naval Ordnance
VG	Minor Services of Navies
VK	Navigation, Merchant Marine
VM	Naval Architecture; Shipbuilding; Marine Engineering
Z	Library Science
Z	Books in General; Book Industries and Trade; Libraries & Library Science; Bibliography
ZA	Information Resources (General)

⊙ The Library Corporation (TLC). "LC Classification Outline, 6th Edition: Contents," www.tlcdelivers.com/tlc/crs/lcs00001.htm

U.S. Library of Congress. "The Library of Congress Cataloging," lcweb.loc.gov/catdir/catdir.html

U.S. Library of Congress (Office for Subject Cataloging Policy, Collection Services). *LC Classification Outline, Sixth Edition.* Washington, D.C.: Library of Congress, 1990.

Index

Barbados
    foreign embassy in the U.S., 204
    general information, 33
    population of, 157
    telephone dialing codes, 706
    travel requirements for, 534
    UN membership, 1
Barber, Samuel, 483
Barbour, Philip P., 221, 265
Barbuda and Antigua
    foreign embassy in the U.S., 204
    general information, 28
    population of, 158
    telephone dialing codes, 706
    travel requirements for, 534
    UN membership, 1
Barcelona, Spain, 159, 554
Bardeen, John, 436
barium (element), 396
Barkley, Alben W., 193, 230
Barlach, Ernst, 467
Barron v. Baltimore (1833), 268
Barrymore, John, 516, 525
Barrymore, Lionel, 516
Barth, John, 443
Bartók, Béla, 483
baryons, 399
baseball, major league, 570–576
bases and acids, 394
BASIC (Beginner's All-Purpose
        Instruction Code), 420
basketball, 576–586
Basketball Hall of Fame, 581–583
Basse-Terre, Guadeloupe, 69
Basseterre, Saint Kitts and Nevis, 122
Baton Rouge, Louisiana, 309
Baum, Frank (Lyman Baum), 456
Bausch, Pina, 504
beam bridges, 435
Bean, Alan L., 432
Beardsley, Aubrey Vincent, 459
Beatty, Warren, 525
Beaufort Wind Scale, 366–367
Becharof (lake), 287
Beckett, Samuel, 453
Beckman, Arnold O., 436
Becquerel, Antoine-Henri, 436
Beethoven, Ludwig van, 483
Beginner's All-Purpose Instruction Code
        (BASIC), 420
Begun, S. Joseph, 436
Beijing, China, 47, 158, 554

Beirut, Lebanon, 88
Béjart, Maurice, 504
Belarus
    foreign embassy in the U.S., 205
    general information, 33–34
    population of, 156
    telephone dialing codes, 706
    travel requirements for, 534
    UN membership, 1
Belgium
    foreign embassy in the U.S., 205
    general information, 34–35
    population of, 156
    telephone dialing codes, 706
    travel requirements for, 534
    UN membership, 1
    visitors' and convention bureau, 554
Belgrade, Serbia, 127
Belize
    foreign embassy in the U.S., 205
    general information, 35
    population of, 157
    telephone dialing codes, 706
    travel requirements for, 534
    UN membership, 1
Bell, Alexander Graham, 436
Bell, John, 221
Bellini, Giovanni, 460
Bellini, Vincenzo, 483
Bellona (Roman deity), 189
Bellow, Saul, 443
Bellows, George Wesley, v
Belmopan, Belize, 35
Belo Horizonte, Brazil, 159
Bemelmans, Ludwig, 456
Benét, Stephen Vincent, 443
Benin
    foreign embassy in the U.S., 205
    general information, 35–36
    population of, 157
    telephone dialing codes, 706
    travel requirements for, 534
    UN membership, 1
Bennett, Michael, 504
Bennett, Willard Harrison, 436
Bentley, Helen Delich, 226
Benton, Thomas Hart, 460
Benz, Carl Friedrich, 436
Bergman, Ingrid, 525
Beriosova, Svetlana, 504
berkelium (element), 396
Berlin, Germany, 66, 159, 554

cerium (element), 396
Cernan, Eugene A., 432
Cervantes Saavedra, Miguel de, 444
cervical cancer, 321
cesium (element), 396
Cézanne, Paul, 460
Chad
    foreign embassy in the U.S., 206
    general information, 45–46
    population of, 156
    telephone dialing codes, 706
    travel requirements for, 535
    UN membership, 1
Chad (lake), 15
Chagall, Marc, 460
championship cat breeds, 702
championships
    Australian Open (tennis), 611–613
    Du Maurier Classic (golf), 620
    French Open (tennis), 609–611
    LPGA Championship (golf), 619
    Masters Tournament (golf), 616
    Nabisco Championship (golf), 619
    NBA (basketball), 579–580
    NCAA (basketball), 583–586
    NCAA (football), 592–595
    Stanley Cup (hockey), 599–601
    Super Bowl (football), 589
    U.S. Open (golf), 617–619
    U.S. Open (tennis), 604–606
    Wimbledon (tennis), 606–609
    WNBA (basketball), 581
    World Series (baseball), 572–574
Champlain (lake), 287
Chandler, Raymond, 444
Chaney, Lon, Sr., 525
Changchun, China, 159
Channing, Carol, 516
Chaos (Greek deity), 187
Chaplin, Charles, 525
Chardin, Jean-Baptiste, 461
Charisse, Cyd, 504, 525
Charities (Greek deities), 188
Charles River Bridge v. *Warren Bridge*
    (1837), 268
Charlotte, North Carolina, 308
Charlotte Amalie, Virgin Islands, 152,
    307
Chase, Salmon Portland, 265
Chase, Samuel, 266
Chase-Smith, Margaret, 231
Chatham Island, 706

Cheever, John, 444
Chekhov, Anton Pavlovich, 453
chemistry, 393–399, 628–630
Chengdu, China, 159
Chenoweth, Helen, 227
Cher, 525
Cherokee Nation v. *Georgia* (1831), 269
Chesapeake, Virginia, 309
Cheves, Langdon, 221
Chicago, Illinois, 159, 308
Chichagof Island, 283
chickenpox (varicella), 324
chief justices (Supreme Court), 265
Chihuahuan Desert, 284
children
    Children's Museum of Boston, 474
    child safety seats, 700
    literature for, 456–458, 669–672
    recommended diet, 336
Childs, Lucinda, 504
Chile
    foreign embassy in the U.S., 206
    general information, 46
    population of, 156
    telephone dialing codes, 706
    travel requirements for, 535
    UN membership, 1
China
    dynasties of, 167
    foreign embassy in the U.S., 206
    general information, 46–47
    population of, 156
    telephone dialing codes, 706
    travel requirements for, 535
    UN membership, 1
    visitors' and convention bureau, 554
Chisholm, Shirley Anita, 226
Chisinau, Moldova, 101
Chittagong, Bangladesh, 159
chlorine (element), 396
Chloris (Greek deity), 187
choking, first aid for, 327–328
cholesterol test, 318
choline, 337
Chongqing, China, 159
Chopin, Frédéric, 483
choreographers, 504–506
Christian Coalition, 202
Christian-Green, Donna M., 228
Christianity, holidays and festivals,
    173–175
Christie, Agatha, 444

Delaware *(cont.)*
    racial makeup of, 313
    sales tax rates, 690
    state flowers, birds, and trees, 291
    time zone, 349
    tourism department, 548
Delhi, India, 158
Demeter (Greek deity), 187
de Mille, Agnes, 504
Democratic Party, 236
De Niro, Robert, 526
Denmark
    foreign embassy in the U.S., 207
    general information, 54
    population of, 157
    telephone dialing codes, 707
    travel requirements for, 535
    UN membership, 1
    visitors' and convention bureau, 555
Dennard, Robert, 437
Dennis v. *U.S.* (1951), 269
dental exam, 319
Denver, Colorado, 308
Denver Center Theatre Company, 514
Department of Agriculture (USDA),
    194
Department of Commerce (DOC), 194
Department of Defense (DOD), 195
Department of Education, 195
Department of Energy (DOE), 195
Department of Health and Human
    Services (HHS), 195
Department of Housing and Urban
    Development (HUD), 195
Department of Justice (DOJ), 196
Department of Labor (DOL), 196
Department of State, 196
Department of the Interior (DOI), 196
Department of the Treasury, 197
Department of Transportation (DOT),
    196
Department of Veterans Affairs, 197
depression, 324
Derain, André, 461
deserts, 11, 284
Des Moines, Iowa, 309
Detroit, Michigan, 159, 308
Dewey, Thomas E., 234
Dewey Decimal System, 743–745
Dewhurst, Colleen, 517
Dhaka, Bangladesh, 33, 158

diabetes, 319, 325, 339
diameter measurement, 380
diameter of earth, 8
diamond, 408
Diana (Roman deity), 189
Dickens, Charles, 444
Diego Garcia, 707
Diesel, Rudolph, 437
diet
    additives, 340–341
    food guide pyramid, 334–335
    labeling, 341–342
    recommended daily, 335–336
    serving size, 335
    types, 339–340
    vitamins and minerals, 337–339
Dietrich, Marlene, 526
digital rectal exam, 318
Dinesen, Isak, 444
Diocletian and the Tetrarchy, 171
Dionysus (Greek deity), 187
Dirksen, Everett, 230
Disabled American Veterans, 281
Discordia (Roman deity), 189
diseases, common, 323–326
distances between major cities,
    544–547
District of Columbia
    area codes, 704
    area of, 290
    House of Representatives and, 224
    population of, 312
    postal abbreviation, 712
Dix, Otto, 461
Dixiecrats, 237
Dixon, Franklin W. *See* Stratemeyer,
    Edward L.
Djerassi, Carl, 437
Djibouti
    foreign embassy in the U.S., 207
    general information, 54–55
    population of, 157
    telephone dialing codes, 707
    travel requirements for, 535
    UN membership, 1
DNA, 400
Doctorow, E. L., 444
Dodge, Mary Mapes, 456
dog breeds, 701–702
Doha, Qatar, 119
Dole, Bob, 230, 231

Indonesia
    foreign embassy in the U.S., 210
    general information, 76–77
    population of, 156
    telephone dialing codes, 707
    travel requirements for, 536
    UN membership, 1
    visitors' and convention bureau,
        555
influenza, 325
Inge, William, 453
Ingres, Jean-Auguste Dominique, 463
inositol, 337
In re Debs (1895), 269
In re Gault (1967), 269
Institute of Museum and Library
    Services, 198
instrumentalists, classical, 489–491
insurance, 681, 682–684
integers, 380
International Association of Univer-
    sities, 740
International Atomic Energy Agency, 6
International Bank for Reconstruction
    and Development (World Bank),
    6
International Committee of the Red
    Cross (ICRC), 6
International Court of Justice, 3, 6
International Football Hall Of Fame,
    475
The Internationalist, 740
International Labor Organization
    (ILO), 6
International Monetary Fund (IMF),
    6
International Organization for
    Standardization (ISO), 6
international organizations, 1–7
International Relations Committee,
    220
International Tennis Hall of Fame,
    614–615
internet, 703
interpretive indicators, musical, 481
Intiman Theatre, 514
Inuus (Roman deity), 189
inventors and discoverers, 436–442
iodine (dietary), 338
iodine (element), 396, 408
Ionesco, Eugène, 453

ionic order, 480
ionosphere, 412
Iowa
    area codes, 704–705
    area of, 290
    capital, 290
    date of admittance, 289
    electoral votes, 235
    features and attractions, 296
    income tax rates, 688
    membership in Congress, 224
    motto and nickname, 292
    poison control center, 344
    population of, 312
    postal abbreviation, 712
    racial makeup of, 313
    sales tax rates, 690
    state flowers, birds, and trees, 291
    time zone, 349
    tourism department, 549
Iran, Islamic Republic of
    foreign embassy in the U.S., 210
    general information, 77–78
    Iranian hostage rescue mission,
        279
    population of, 156
    telephone dialing codes, 707
    travel requirements for, 536
    UN membership, 1
Iraq
    foreign embassy in the U.S., 210
    general information, 78
    Gulf War, 280
    population of, 156
    telephone dialing codes, 707
    travel requirements for, 536
    UN membership, 1
IRAs (Individual Retirement Accounts),
    681
Iredell, James, 267
Ireland
    foreign embassy in the U.S., 210
    general information, 78–79
    population of, 157
    size of, 11
    telephone dialing codes, 707
    tourism department, 553
    travel requirements for, 536
    UN membership, 1
Irene (Greek deity), 188
iridium (element), 396

Madison, Wisconsin, 309
Madras, India, 159
Madrid, Spain, 133, 159, 556
magnesium (dietary), 338
magnesium (element), 397, 408
Magritte, René, 464
Mahfouz, Naguib, 447
Mahler, Gustav, 485
Mailer, Norman, 447
mailing rates, 710–712
Maillol, Aristide, 468
Maiman, Theodore Harold, 440
Maine
    area codes, 704–705
    area of, 290
    capital, 290
    date of admittance, 289
    electoral votes, 235
    features and attractions, 297
    income tax rates, 688
    membership in Congress, 224
    motto and nickname, 292
    poison control center, 344
    population of, 312
    postal abbreviation, 712
    racial makeup of, 313
    sales tax rates, 690
    state flowers, birds, and trees, 291
    time zone, 349
    tourism department, 549
major league baseball, 570–576
Majuro, Marshall Islands, 97
Makarova, Natalia, 505
Malabo, Equatorial Guinea, 58
Malamud, Bernard, 447
Malawi
    foreign embassy in the U.S., 212
    general information, 93
    population of, 156
    telephone dialing codes, 708
    travel requirements for, 537
    UN membership, 2
Malaysia
    foreign embassy in the U.S., 212
    general information, 94
    population of, 156
    telephone dialing codes, 708
    travel requirements for, 537
    UN membership, 2
    visitors' and convention bureau, 555

Maldives
    foreign embassy in the U.S., 212
    general information, 94–95
    population of, 157
    telephone dialing codes, 708
    travel requirements for, 537
    UN membership, 2
Male (Maale), Maldives, 95
Mali
    foreign embassy in the U.S., 212
    general information, 95
    population of, 156
    telephone dialing codes, 708
    travel requirements for, 537
    UN membership, 2
Malkovich, John, 527
Maloney, Carolyn B., 227
Malpighi, Marcello, 440
Malta
    foreign embassy in the U.S., 212
    general information, 95–96
    population of, 157
    telephone dialing codes, 708
    travel requirements for, 537
    UN membership, 2
Mamet, David, 454
mammals, endangered, 374–375
Mamoutzou, Mayotte, 99
Managua, Nicaragua, 108
Manama, Bahrain, 32
Manchester, England, 159
Manet, Édouard, 464
manganese (dietary), 338
manganese (element), 397, 408
Manhattan Island, 283
Manhattan Theatre Club, 515
Manila, Philippines, 116
Manitoba, 704
Manitoba (lake), 15
Mankin, Helen Douglas, 225
Mann, Thomas, 447
manned space missions, 427–429
Mansfield, Katherine, 447
Mansfield, Mike, 230
Manship, Paul, 468
Mantegna, Andrea, 464
Mapp v. *Ohio* (1961), 270
Maputo, Mozambique, 103, 159
Maracaibo (lake), 15
Marbury v. *Madison* (1803), 270
Marc, Franz, 464

Mauritius
    foreign embassy in the U.S., 213
    general information, 98–99
    population of, 157
    telephone dialing codes, 708
    travel requirements for, 537
    UN membership, 2
Maxim, Hiram Stevens, 440
May, Catherine Dean, 225
Mayotte
    general information, 99
    population of, 158
    telephone dialing codes, 708
Mazor, Stanley, 440
Mbabane, Swaziland, 136
McCarter Theatre Center for the
        Performing Arts, 515
McCarthy, Carolyn, 228
McCarthy, Karen, 227
McCarthy, Mary, 447
McClellan, George B., 233
McCloskey, Robert, 457
McCormack, Cyrus Hall, 440
McCormack, John W., 223
McCormick, Ruth Hanna, 224
McCullers, Carson, 447
McCulloch v. Maryland (1819), 270
McDaniel, Hattie, 528
McDonald, Audra, 518
McDonald's LPGA Championship
        (golf), 619
McElroy, Mary Arthur, 192
McFarland, E. W., 230
McGovern, George, 234
McKenna, Joseph, 267
McKinley, Ida Saxton, 192
McKinley, John, 267
McKinley, William, 190, 233
McKinney, Cynthia, 227
McLean, John, 267
McMillan, Clara Gooding, 225
McNally, Terrence, 454
McNary, Charles L., 230
McReynolds, James Clark, 267
Mead (lake), 287
mean (mathematical), 380
Mears, Helen Farnsworth, 468
measurements, 735–737
mechanics, physical laws regarding,
        414
Medellin, Columbia, 159

median (mathematical), 380
medicine and drugs, 317–332,
        630–632
Meek, Carry P., 227
Meikle, Andrew, 440
meitnerium (element), 397
Melbourne, Australia, 159, 556
Melpomene (Greek deity), 188
Melville, Herman, 447
Memphis, Tennessee, 308
mendelevium (element), 397
Mendelssohn, Felix, 485
menopause, exam for, 320
Menotti, Gian Carlo, 485
Mercator, Gerardus, 440
merchant Marine, global, 8
mercury (element), 397, 408
Mercury (planet), 384
Mercury (Roman deity), 189
Mergenthaler, Ottmar, 440
Merman, Ethel, 518
Mesa, Arizona, 308
mesons, 399
mesosphere, 412
Messiaen, Oliver, 485
Mestral, George de, 440
metals, recycling, 698–699
meteorology symbols, 360–361
Metis (Greek deity), 188
metric measurements, 735–736
Metro Manila, Philippines, 158
metropolitan areas (U.S.), 310–311
Mexican War, 278
Mexico
    foreign embassy in the U.S., 213
    general information, 99–100
    population of, 156
    telephone dialing codes, 708
    travel requirements for, 537
    UN membership, 2
    visitors' and convention bureau,
        555
Mexico City, Mexico, 100, 158
Meyerbeer, Giacomo, 485
Meyers, Jan, 227
Meyner, Helen Stevenson, 226
Miami, Florida, 160, 308
Michelangelo Buonarroti, 464, 468
Michener, James, 447
Michigan
    area codes, 704–705

Newman, Paul, 528
New Mexico
  area codes, 704–705
  area of, 290
  capital, 290
  date of admittance, 289
  electoral votes, 235
  features and attractions, 300
  income tax rates, 689
  membership in Congress, 224
  motto and nickname, 293
  poison control center, 345
  population of, 313
  postal abbreviation, 712
  racial makeup of, 314
  sales tax rates, 690
  state flowers, birds, and trees, 291
  time zone, 349
  tourism department, 550
New Orleans, Louisiana, 308
newspapers, 459
New Testament, books of, 177
Newton, Isaac, 440
Newton's laws, 413
New York, New York, 158, 308
New York Shakespeare Festival, 515
New York (state)
  area codes, 704–705
  area of, 290
  capital, 290
  date of admittance, 289
  electoral votes, 235
  features and attractions, 300
  income tax rates, 689
  membership in Congress, 224
  motto and nickname, 293
  poison control center, 345
  population of, 313
  postal abbreviation, 712
  racial makeup of, 314
  sales tax rates, 690
  state flowers, birds, and trees, 291
  time zone, 349
  tourism department, 550
New York Theatre Workshop, 515
New York Times v. *Sullivan* (1964),
    271
New Zealand
  foreign embassy in the U.S., 214
  general information, 107–108
  population of, 157

telephone dialing codes, 708
travel requirements for, 538
UN membership, 2
Niamey, Niger, 108
Nicaragua
  foreign embassy in the U.S., 214
  general information, 108
  population of, 157
  telephone dialing codes, 708
  travel requirements for, 538
  UN membership, 2
Nicaragua (lake), 15
Nice, France, 556
Nicholas, Fayard & Harold, 505
Nicholson, Jack, 528
nickel (element), 397, 409
Nicosia, Cyprus, 53
Nielsen, Carl, 485
Nieuwland, Julius Arthur, 440
Niger
  foreign embassy in the U.S., 214
  general information, 108–109
  population of, 156
  telephone dialing codes, 708
  travel requirements for, 538
  UN membership, 2
Nigeria
  foreign embassy in the U.S., 214
  general information, 109
  telephone dialing codes, 708
  travel requirements for, 538
  UN membership, 2
Niihau, Hawaii, 283
Nijinsky, Vaslav, 505
Nike (Greek deity), 188
nimbostratus clouds, 364
Nin, Anaïs, 448
niobium (element), 397
Nipigon (lake), 15
nitrogen (element), 397, 409
Niue, 109–110, 708
Nixon, Richard Milhous, 191, 194,
    234
Nixon, Thelma Catherine Ryan, 192
Nobel, Alfred Bernhard, 440
nobelium (element), 397
Nobel Prize, 624–632
Noguchi, Isamu, 469
Nolan, Mae Ella, 224
Nolte, Nick, 528
Noma, Hiroshi, 448

Peale, Charles Willson, 465
Peale, Raphaelle, 465
Peale, Rembrandt, 465
Peck, Gregory, 528
Peckham, Rufus Wheeler, Jr., 267
Pelosi, Nancy, 227
Penderecki, Krzystof, 485
Penn, Sean, 528
Pennington, William, 222
Pennsylvania
    area codes, 704–705
    area of, 290
    capital, 290
    date of admittance, 289
    electoral votes, 235
    features and attractions, 302
    income tax rates, 689
    membership in Congress, 224
    motto and nickname, 293
    poison control center, 346
    population of, 313
    postal abbreviation, 712
    racial makeup of, 314
    sales tax rates, 690
    state flowers, birds, and trees, 291
    time zone, 349
    tourism department, 551
Perez de Cuellar, Javier, 4
performers. See film; theater
Pergolesi, Giovanni Battista, 485
perimeter, 380
periodic table of the elements, 395
Perkins, Anthony, 528
Permanent Select Committee on
    Intelligence, 220
Perot, Ross, 234
perpetual calendar, 350–355
Perrault, Charles, 457
Perrot, Jules, 505
Persephone (Greek deity), 188
Persian Gulf War, 280
Persipina (Roman deity), 189
personal finance, 677–691
Peru
    foreign embassy in the U.S., 214
    general information, 115–116
    population of, 156
    telephone dialing codes, 709
    travel requirements for, 538
    UN membership, 2
Peters, Bernadette, 519

Petipa, Marius, 505
petition, freedom to, 249
Petronius, Gaius, 448
pets, 701–702
Pettis, Shirley Neil, 226
Pfeiffer, Michelle, 528
Pfost, Gracie Bowers, 225
pharmaceuticals, 328–331
Philadelphia, Pennsylvania, 159, 308
Philippines
    foreign embassy in the U.S.,
        214–215
    general information, 116
    population of, 156
    telephone dialing codes, 709
    travel requirements for, 538
    UN membership, 2
Phnom Penh, Cambodia, 42
Phoenix, Arizona, 159, 308
pH of common substances, 394
phosphorus (dietary), 339
phosphorus (element), 397
photography, 470–472
physics, 413–415, 627–628
Picasso, Pablo, 465, 469
Pickford, Mary, 528
Picus (Roman deity), 189
Pierce, Franklin, 190, 233
Pierce, Jane Appleton, 191
Piero della Francesca, 465
Pinckney, Charles Cotesworth, 232
Pinsky, Robert, 452
Pinter, Harold, 454
pi (π), 380
Piper, Watty, 457
Pirandello, Luigi, 454
Pisces (zodiac sign), 359
Pissarro, Camille, 465
Pitcairn Islands, 116–117
Pitney, Mahlon, 267
Pittsburgh, Pennsylvania, 308
planets, 384–387
Plano, Texas, 309
Plantagenet (Anjou), house of,
    167–168
plastic, recycling, 698–699
plate tectonics, 411
platinum (element), 397, 409
Plautus, 454
plays and musicals, 506–513
playwrights, 453–455

Saroyan, William, 449
Sartre, Jean-Paul, 449
Saskatchewan, 704
satellites of the planets, 384–387
Satie, Erik, 486
Saturn (planet), 384, 385–386
Saturn (Roman deity), 189
Satyrs (Greek deities), 188
Saudi Arabia
    foreign embassy in the U.S., 216
    general information, 125–126
    Gulf War, 280
    population of, 156
    telephone dialing codes, 709
    travel requirements for, 539
    UN membership, 2
Savery, Thomas, 441
Savoy, house of, 173
Saxe-Coburg-Gotha, house of, 168
Saxony, house of, 170
Scalia, Antonin, 267
scandium (element), 397
Scarlatti, Domenico, 486
Scarry, Richard, 458
Schakowsky, Janice, 228
Schawlow, Arthur L., 441
Scheele, Carl Wilhelm, 441
Schenck v. *U.S.* (1919), 271
Schenk, Lynn, 227
Schick, Jacob, 441
Schiele, Egon, 466
Schildkraut, Joseph, 519
Schmitt, Harrison, 432
Schneider, Claudene, 226
Schoenberg, Arnold, 486
Schroeder, Patricia Scott, 226
Schubert, Franz, 486
Schultz, Peter C., 441
Schumann, Robert, 486
Schütze, Heinrich, 486
Science Committee (House), 220
Scorpio (zodiac sign), 358
Scotland, embassy in U.S., 216
Scott, David R., 432
Scott, George C., 529
Scott, Hugh D., Jr., 230
Scott, Sir Walter, 449
Scott, Winfield, 233
Scottsdale, Arizona, 309
Scriabin, Alexander, 486
sculptors, 467–469

seaborgium (element), 397
search engines (internet), 703
seas, general statistics on, 17
Seastrand, Andrea, 227
Seattle, Washington, 160, 308
Seattle Repertory Theatre, 515
Second Republic of France, 169, 173
Secretariat (United Nations), 4
Securities and Exchange Commission
    (SEC), 200
Security Council (United Nations), 3
Sedgwick, Theodore, 221
select committees, 220, 229
Selective Service System, 200
Selene (Greek deity), 188
selenium (dietary), 339
selenium (element), 397
Sellers, Peter, 529
Semon, Waldo Lonsbury, 441
Senate. *See* United States Senate
Sendak, Maurice, 458
Seneca, Lucius Annaeus, 454
Senegal
    foreign embassy in the U.S., 216
    general information, 126–127
    population of, 156
    telephone dialing codes, 709
    travel requirements for, 539
    UN membership, 2
Seoul, South Korea, 85, 158
Serbia and Montenegro
    foreign embassy in the U.S., 216
    general information, 127–128
    population of, 156, 157
    telephone dialing codes, 708, 709
    travel requirements for, 539
service academies, 282
serving sizes, 335
Sessions, Roger, 486
The Settlement, Christmas Island,
    47
Seurat, Georges, 466
Seuss, Dr. (Theodore Seuss Geisel),
    458
Severi dynasty, 171
Sewell, Anna, 458
Seychelles
    foreign embassy in the U.S., 216
    general information, 128
    population of, 158
    telephone dialing codes, 709

Woodbury, Levi, 268
Woodhouse, Chase Going, 225
Woods, William Burnham, 268
Woodward, Joanne, 529
Woolf, Virginia, 451
Woolsey, Lynn, 227
Wordsworth, William, 452
working dogs, 702
World Bank, 6
World Cup (soccer), 622
World Golf Hall of Fame, 621–622
World Health Organization (WHO), 7
world history summarized, 160–166
World Series, 572–574
World Trade Organization (WTrO), 7
World Universities, 740
World War I, 278
World War II, 279
World War II (museum), 475
Worth, Irene, 519
Wouk, Herman, 451
Wrangell Island, 283
Wright, James C., Jr., 223
Wright, Orville, 442
Wright, Richard, 451
Wright, Wilbur, 442
writers. *See* literature
Wuhan, China, 159
Wyeth, Andrew Newell, 467
Wyoming
    area codes, 704–705
    area of, 290
    capital, 290
    date of admittance, 289
    electoral votes, 235
    features and attractions, 304
    income tax rates, 689
    membership in Congress, 224
    motto and nickname, 293
    poison control center, 347
    population of, 313
    postal abbreviation, 314
    racial makeup of, 314
    sales tax rates, 691
    state flowers, birds, and trees, 292
    time zone, 349
    tourism department, 552
Wyss, J. D., 458

X
xenon (element), 398
Xian, China, 159

Y
Yale Repertory Theatre, 515
Yamoussoukro, Côte d'Ivoire, 51
Yangon, Myanmar, 159
Yaounde, Cameroon, 43
Yellowstone (lake), 287
Yemen
    foreign embassy in the U.S., 218
    general information, 153–154
    population of, 156
    telephone dialing codes, 710
    travel requirements for, 540
    UN membership, 2
Yerevan, Armenia, 29
Yogi Bear's Jellystone Park Camp Resorts, 558
Yonkers, New York, 309
York, house of, 168
Yoruban holidays and festivals, 176
Young, John W., 432
Young, Loretta, 529
Youngstown Sheet & Tube Co. Sawyer (1952), 271
Yourcenar, Marguerite, 451
Youskevitch, Igor, 506
ytterbium (element), 398
yttrium (element), 398, 410
Yugoslavia, 2, 710. *See also* Macedonia, former Yugoslav Republic of

Z
Zagreb, Croatia, 52
Zaire, 710
Zambia
    foreign embassy in the U.S., 218
    general information, 154–155
    population of, 156
    telephone dialing codes, 710
    travel requirements for, 540
    UN membership, 2
Zanzibar, 710
Zarembo Island, 283
Zeppelin, Ferdinand Graf von, 442
Zeus (Greek deity), 188
Zimbabwe
    foreign embassy in the U.S., 218
    general information, 155

O**X**FORD
BERKLEY

No matter what your question, Oxford has the answer:

☐ **THE OXFORD ESSENTIAL DICTIONARY**
0-425-16420-9/$6.99

☐ **THE OXFORD ESSENTIAL THESAURUS**
0-425-16421-7/$6.99

☐ **THE OXFORD ESSENTIAL SPELLING DICTIONARY**
0-425-16388-1/$5.99

☐ **THE OXFORD ESSENTIAL QUOTATIONS DICTIONARY**
0-425-16387-3/$5.99

☐ **THE OXFORD PORTUGUESE DICTIONARY**
0-425-16389-X/$4.99